$(x^2 + 2x - 3)(x + 2)$

$x^3 + 2x^2 + 2x^2$

WITHDRAWN

assistant

WITHDRAWN

$3 \quad \frac{-1}{2} \quad \frac{+1}{0} \quad \frac{-1}{-1}$

2

$\frac{3}{2}$

THE WATERGATE HEARINGS

The Watergate Hearings

BREAK-IN AND COVER-UP

Proceedings of the Senate Select Committee
on Presidential Campaign Activities
as edited by the staff of

The New York Times

Narrative by R. W. Apple, Jr.
Chronology by Linda Amster
General Editor: Gerald Gold

THE VIKING PRESS   NEW YORK

The New York Times
Staff for
The Watergate Hearings: Break-in and Cover-up

EDITORS: John Lubell, Robert Sheridan, Robert Slosser

RESEARCH ASSISTANT: Dana Little

PICTURES: Renato E. Perez

Copyright © 1973 by The New York Times Company
All rights reserved
No copyright is claimed in official government
documents contained in this volume.

Published in 1973 by The Viking Press, Inc.
625 Madison Avenue, New York, N.Y. 10022

Published simultaneously in Canada by
The Macmillan Company of Canada Limited

SBN 670-75152-9

Library of Congress catalog card number: 73-14191
Printed in U.S.A.

*This hardbound edition published by arrangement
with Bantam Books, Inc.*

Contents

Illustrations follow page 438.

Acknowledgments

No matter how brief, tentative and close-to-the-news his manuscript, every author owes thanks to large numbers of people. In my case, the first acknowledgment must be to the gifted Washington staff of The New York Times, whose reports formed the basis of my narrative—James M. Naughton, Walter Rugaber, John Herbers, Seymour Hersh, Christopher Lydon, John Crewdson, Anthony Ripley, David E. Rosenbaum and so many others. The work of Gerald Gold, Linda Amster and their colleagues on the New York editorial staff is evident in the chronology, transcript and other sections of this book; that of Al Marlens, the imaginative editor of The Times's News of the Week in Review section, who commissioned the valuable week-by-week summaries of Watergate developments, is less obvious but equally important. My wife, who beat me consistently at tennis to drive me back to the typewriter; our dogs, who paid my feverish efforts no attention whatsoever, and my parents, who spent hours in museums during one of their infrequent visits to Washington because I had to type instead of talking to them —all contributed to the product. Finally, I express my gratitude to Jean Highland, my editor, who managed simultaneously to sympathize with my problems and to demand that I get on with it; she must have had an ancestor who first spoke of the carrot and the stick. Whatever errors of omission or commission may be found herein are my own, the result, in large measure, of a desire to put into the hands of the reader a timely account of the first phase of the Watergate hearings while the Senate—and the American public —were still deciding.

R. W. Apple Jr.

Washington, September, 1973

THE WATERGATE HEARINGS

"THERE WAS A CANCER GROWING
ON THE PRESIDENCY . . ."

Prologue

This is the story of the first phase of the historic Watergate hearings, which lasted from May 17 until August 7, 1973, and dealt with the break-in at the Watergate complex, its origins and consequences, and the attempt to conceal from the courts and the public its true character. The hearings also dealt with "Watergate" in its broader sense—the whole spectrum of covert and often illegal activities carried out by the Nixon White House, which John Mitchell was to call "the White House horrors"— though not in as much detail. But much of the Watergate story unfolded outside the rococo hearing room on Capitol Hill; indeed, much of it had taken place before the committee assembled.

By mid-May of 1973, the Watergate scandal, with all of its subplots and ancillary horrors, was already a long-running show. The break-in at the Democratic National Committee's headquarters in the Watergate complex on the Potomac—a series of modern buildings with balconies like filed-down shark's teeth—had taken place almost a year before, on June 17, 1972, and seven operatives of the Nixon campaign had been convicted for their part in the bugging scheme. But the web of evidence had been spun slowly around the higher-ups, while the nation was distracted by the Presidential election and high prices and the negotiation of semipeace with semihonor in Indochina. The full import of the case had not yet been driven home to the American people, particularly that vast segment of the population with the good sense to occupy itself, most of the time, with things more edifying than the latest hijinks in Washington. But that was about to change, with the opening of the nationally televised hearings of the Senate Select Committee on Presidential Campaign Activities, popularly known as the Watergate committee or (after its chairman, Senator Sam J. Ervin Jr.) as the Ervin committee. Beginning on May 17, exactly 11 months after the break-in, it took 37 days of testimony from witnesses great and small, repentant and obdurate, in the first phase of its proceedings. By the time the committee paused for a summer recess, the nation had devoured the details of this, the greatest scandal in American public life since the unfondly remembered days of President Ulysses S. Grant.

In the weeks leading up to May 17, Richard Milhous Nixon, the archetypal loser of American politics, transformed by the bizarre events of the 1972 campaign into the biggest winner in history, had been backed into a corner. The sweetness of his diplomatic triumphs in Peking and Moscow and his electoral triumph at home had vanished in the bitterness of Watergate almost as soon as he descended from the stand outside the Capitol where he took the oath of office for his second term on January 20, 1973. With newspaper headlines suggesting almost daily the involvement of high-level members of his staff, the President dug in. At two impromptu news conferences in March, he reiterated his 1972 claim that thorough investigation had shown that no one on the White House staff was involved, and he definitely told the nascent Watergate committee that executive privilege—the murky doctrine designed to protect the confidentiality of Presidential deliberations—would make it impossible for his aides to testify.

It looked for a brief moment as if Nixon might be able to stonewall the committee; there had not yet been a single break in the Administration's ranks. Then, in the third week of March, there were two, and that was enough. On March 19, James W. McCord, one of the convicted Watergate conspirators, wrote to the judge who had presided over the trial, John J. Sirica, charging that ranking White House officials had been involved in covering up the true dimensions of the scandal and that he and his co-defendants had been under pressure to remain silent. And on March 22, L. Patrick Gray 3d, the acting

Director of the Federal Bureau of Investigation, told the Senate committee considering his nomination as permanent Director that John W. Dean 3d, the White House counsel, had "probably lied" during the agency's Watergate investigation. Four days later, the Watergate grand jury reconvened, and the Senate's investigators began probing more deeply.

Out of the grand jury room and the committee offices there now tumbled story after story: Dean had promised to tell all . . . Jeb Stuart Magruder, the number two man at the Committee for the Re-election of the President (C.R.P.), had confessed that he lied to the grand jury . . . John N. Mitchell, the former Attorney General and campaign manager, had been fingered as the master plotter . . . Dean had implicated "the Prussians," the two ranking members of the White House staff, H. R. Haldeman and John D. Ehrlichman.

Suddenly, on April 17, the White House wall of silence cracked. Nixon himself appeared in the press room—a rare event—to announce that "serious charges" had been brought to his attention on March 21, months after they had come to the attention of almost everyone else in Washington. As a result, the President said, he had ordered a major new investigation. Later, the White House press secretary, Ronald L. Ziegler, who had been the mouthpiece for so many sneering denials of Watergate stories in the newspapers, described his past statements as "inoperative"—a word, with its overtones of newspeak, that was to be thrown back at the Administration repeatedly in the weeks that followed. This was the first of Nixon's attempts to clear the air, but it failed, like the later ones, because the President answered none of the questions surrounding the case. Implicit in what he said was the theme "Trust me—I'll get to the bottom of this." But by remaining silent so long, he had already squandered much of the trust reposed in Presidents by most ordinary Americans—even in Richard Nixon, who had won their votes but never their affection.

The next fortnight was a tunnel of horrors for Nixon and his men. Every event seemed to put the Administration more on the defensive. Richard Kleindienst, the old Goldwaterite who had replaced John Mitchell as Attorney

General, disqualified himself from the case because some of his best friends were under investigation; clearly, that meant Mitchell, Dean—and who knew whom else? Ziegler admitted that the Dean "investigation"—on which Nixon had based his denials up until April 17—had produced no written report. Dean issued a cryptic, but nonetheless clearly threatening, statement vowing that no one would make a "scapegoat" of him. Magruder quit as Assistant Secretary of Commerce, an action that was widely (and correctly) interpreted as an admission of complicity. Gray quit as acting Director of the F.B.I., which was taken (again correctly) as the same thing. Day by day, the headlines and the admissions mounted, and with them the pressure on the President. It seemed as if there could be no more, that the flow of surprises had to wane. Instead, it waxed.

On April 30, Nixon made another attempt to restore confidence. The White House announced the resignations of Haldeman, Ehrlichman and Kleindienst and the scarcely concealed firing of Dean. But the President took some of the edge off what might have seemed a bold stroke; he brought in no outsiders, as so many members of his own party, among others, had suggested. Instead, in a game of bureaucratic musical chairs, he shifted Elliot L. Richardson from Defense to Justice, and named Leonard Garment, already a White House staff member, to succeed Dean. For Haldeman and Ehrlichman, who had antagonized the Congress, the press and the bureaucracy with a fine evenhandedness during four years in their seats just outside the throne room, no replacements were named. In a television speech that night, Nixon praised them as two of the finest public servants he had ever known, even though he conceded for the first time that "there has been an effort to conceal the facts" in the case. Few who had known the Nixon White House in its first incarnation were prepared to believe that such an effort could have taken place with Nixon, Haldeman *and* Ehrlichman in the dark. Fewer still could discern in Nixon's statements any sign that he realized that he had erred (if only in choosing ill-qualified counselors), or that he meant to change his mode of operation.

Despite the President's acceptance of "responsibility"

(not blame) for whatever had gone wrong, he again failed in his avowed determination to put the scandal behind him. It was not only the Democratic professionals who were sniping at the man in the White House; the Republicans, and especially the Republican conservatives who had always considered Nixon one of their own, grumped audibly through late March and April. There was an appeal from Barry Goldwater, the blunt-spoken Arizonan, for frank discussion of the facts, and there was this indictment from James Jackson Kilpatrick, perhaps the White House's favorite columnist: "The White House record by and large has been a record of evasion, dissembling expostulation and silence. What in the world is wrong with Richard Nixon?" On the streets of Washington, bumper stickers that said "Honk if you think he's guilty" began to show up in increasing numbers.

Still the scandal spread, like some awful political malignancy; still the President seemed able only to rail at those who made that diagnosis, not to agree to radical surgery. The day after the speech, he displayed his fury at a Cabinet meeting, vowing that he would do everything in his power to frustrate the Presidential ambitions of Senator Charles Percy, Republican of Illinois, who had had the temerity to push for the appointment of a special Watergate prosecutor. At the trial of Daniel Ellsberg for allegedly stealing the Pentagon Papers, the judge, W. Matthew Byrne Jr., disclosed that Ehrlichman had offered him the directorship of the F.B.I., which seemed to many lawyers a clear breach of ethics. But that was as nothing compared to the revelation that undercover agents working for one of Ehrlichman's assistants had tried to steal files from the office of Ellsberg's psychiatrist. Wiretaps were messy enough, and so was bugging the offices of the political opposition; but an attempt to pry into a man's psyche seemed positively monstrous. Then Dean, increasingly the President's most important accuser, told investigators that Nixon had congratulated him in September, 1972, for his part in the cover-up.

With the Gallup poll showing that fully half of the American people disbelieved his disclaimers, Nixon made two important concessions. He tacitly agreed to allow Richardson to appoint a truly independent special prosecutor (after several refusals, Richardson chose Archibald Cox of the Harvard Law School) and he sent to the Ervin committee a new set of guidelines, indicating that there would be relatively little invocation of executive privilege. By doing so, he guaranteed a free-wheeling investigation, and the federal city settled back to wait for it to begin. But there were still more stunning developments before Senator Ervin could gavel the hearings to order. On May 10, Mitchell and Maurice Stans, a former Commerce Secretary who headed the Finance Committee to Re-elect the President, were indicted in New York for conspiracy to obstruct justice and for perjury in connection with campaign contributions by a discredited financier, Robert L. Vesco. The next day, the Pentagon Papers trial was thrown out of court following the disclosure that Ellsberg had been overheard on an apparently illegal wiretap. One by one, governmental agencies of the utmost sensitivity had been cast into ill repute by the spreading scandal: the F.B.I., the C.I.A. (which had provided tools and disguises used in the raid on Ellsberg's psychiatrist's office), the judiciary. The first murmurs about impeachment began to be heard. And the slippage of White House influence became starkly visible on Capitol Hill, where, for the first time, the House of Representatives rebelled against Nixon's Indochina policies, voting to cut off funds for the bombing of Cambodia.

As the hearings began, then, the Government of the United States was gripped by crisis—true crisis, not the ersatz product of editorialists. In an age when public trust in institutions had already been badly eroded, the astonishing revelations of the Watergate scandal had worsened matters. The President and his key associates, their working hours occupied with the scandal, had little time for the pressing problems of the economy; foreign leaders wondered privately whether Nixon would ever be able to resume the confident foreign-policy leadership he had provided during his first term. Would the President be able to survive, or would he be forced to resign? If he survived, would he survive only as a political cripple? Would public confidence, which is even more important to a President than an electoral mandate, be re-established?

Those were the overriding questions that lay behind the polite opening inquiries of the Senators.

The Committee

In theory, the Watergate committee's job was recommending legislation designed to prevent a recurrence of Watergate. In fact, as Sam Ervin so often said, it saw its job in far broader terms—namely, ferreting out all that it could about not only illegal but also unethical and improper actions during the 1972 campaign and exposing its findings to as broad an audience as possible. In other words, the committee's role was more investigative and educational than legislative. If its proceedings overlapped and occasionally interfered with those of the courts, said Ervin, a former justice of the North Carolina Supreme Court, that was too bad; it was "more important that the American people get the truth than that a few people go to jail."

The Senators who gathered on May 17 in the marble-pillared Senate Caucus Room, the venue of the Teapot Dome investigation and the Army-McCarthy hearings, had been chosen by the Senate leadership of the two parties. They by no means constituted an elite; many Senators had been unwilling to serve, and many others had been eliminated for other reasons. For example, the leadership had decided that no past or potential Presidential candidates should be included on the panel for fear that its proceedings would become too partisan. Thus, no Muskie, no McGovern, no Humphrey, no Goldwater, no Kennedy. The seven men finally chosen were the following:

Ervin: The grandfatherly North Carolinian had built up during his years in the Senate broad bipartisan respect for his fairness and his knowledge of the Constitution. But he was also a leader in the struggle between a Congress that believed recent Presidents had usurped much of its power and a White House determined to yield nothing to Capitol Hill. With his gnarled syntax and his eyebrows sweeping nervously up and down, like an eagle's wings, as someone said, Sam Ervin sometimes seemed slightly befuddled. But he was to prove a resolute questioner and a potent leader.

Herman E. Talmadge, 59, Democrat of Georgia. Talmadge's cigar, his quiet voice and his corn-pone accent concealed one of the best minds in the Senate, at least in the judgment of his peers. But he had to be prodded into serving on the committee, and some members of the staff considered him rather lazy.

Daniel K. Inouye, 48, Democrat of Hawaii. A Nisei who lost his right arm in World War II, Inuoye tried hard to keep the hearings fair. Although moderate by political instinct, he was often outraged by what he heard from the witness stand and showed it.

Joseph M. Montoya, 57, Democrat of New Mexico. Montoya was placed on the committee, at a time when it seemed that the role of the Cuban-American Watergate burglars was more important than it turned out to be, because he was the only Senator with a Spanish surname. He was the weakest questioner on the panel; according to the stock joke in Washington, Montoya listened only to his own questions, never to the witnesses' answers.

Howard H. Baker Jr., 47, Republican of Tennessee. A son-in-law of the late Everett M. Dirksen, Baker was in the toughest spot politically. As ranking Republican, he wanted to do what he could to protect a Republican Administration, but he also had political ambitions that would be ill-served by his playing the patsy. He walked the narrow line so skillfully, and television projected his easy articulateness and boyish good looks so effectively, that he was soon under discussion as a Presidential possibility. More than any other Senator, he sought to depict the moral climate in the White House that spawned Watergate.

Edward J. Gurney, 59, Republican of Florida. A Nixonite from the beginning, he was identified by the White House before the hearings as the Administration's best hope, and he did not disappoint. Frequently at odds with his colleagues over procedural questions, he also threw fat pitches to many of the witnesses.

Lowell P. Weicker Jr., 42, Republican of Connecticut. Young, tall, rich and sometimes short of temper, Weicker was the only member of the committee not from the South or West. He ran his own investigation to provide him with material for questions, earning the enmity of some of his fellow members. His questioning, though disorganized, was more pointed than anyone else's. Some thought him a showboat; some thought his work valuable.

There were two other key participants: Samuel Dash, an owlish Georgetown University law professor who had written a book on electronic surveillance, the chief counsel and supervisor of a staff of 40; and Fred D. Thompson, the chief minority counsel, an experienced Federal prosecutor from Tennessee who knew relatively little of Washington. Both interrogated key witnesses, as did a number of their assistants.

The First Week (May 17–20, 1973)

It began precisely at 10 A.M. With more than 300 spectators packed into the caucus room, with Ellsberg watching intently from the fifth row, with 11 klieg lights blazing and four television cameras focused on the committee, Senator Ervin rapped his new, hand-carved gavel on the green table and launched into his opening statement. If the allegations about the Watergate burglars were true, he said, "what they were seeking to steal was not the jewels, money or other property of American citizens, but something much more valuable—their most precious heritage, the right to vote in a free election." Because of the "black cloud of distrust" cast by Watergate, said the Senator, his glasses perched on the end of his nose, "our citizens do not know whom to believe." The committee, he added, would "spare no one, whatever his station in life may be"; it would "provide full and open public testimony in order that the nation can proceed toward the healing of the wounds that now afflict the body politic."

Ervin's statement was a declaration of faith in the system, of his conviction that the best possible remedy for Watergate was an informed public. Much the same theme ran through Baker's remarks, which followed. "It is the American people who must decide," he said, "based on the evidence spread before them, what Watergate means about how we all should conduct our public business in the future." He was carefully nonpartisan, praising the "unanimity of purpose" that he said had developed in the weeks preceding the hearings. It was all very low-key —purposely so, it seemed to many in the room. None of the Senators wanted to be accused of having helped to run an inquisitorial circus. The calm continued as the committee interrogated the first witness in its effort to understand what Weicker called "the acts of men who almost stole America."

The first man to sit down at the witness table, which was draped in brown felt, had figured little in the mountains of words written about Watergate. His name was Robert C. Odle Jr., and he had served as the director of administration at the Nixon re-election committee. He was a perfect example of the young men who had worked for Nixon but might just as well have worked for I.B.M. —conservative, cautious, unquestioning, buttoned-down, hair carefully barbered, polite. With a pointer in his hand, Odle peered through his steel-rimmed glasses at the committee as he explained organization charts. Most of his testimony was devoted to laying the groundwork for later witnesses, but two things Odle said seemed to pique the Senators' interest. First, he testified that, only hours after the Watergate burglary, he removed from the files of Jeb Stuart Magruder, the deputy campaign director, a folder containing "things which have no place in a political campaign." That seemed to suggest that the cover-up had got under way almost at once. Second, he said that John Mitchell had played a central part in campaign planning as early as the fall of 1971. That conflicted directly with Mitchell's testimony before another Senate committee in March, 1972, when he said: "I do not have and did not have any responsibilities, and I have no party responsibilities now." Odle, who had begun by saying that he still believed in "President Nixon and his hopes and dreams for America," finished by mid-afternoon. The two other witnesses, Bruce Kehrli, a young special assistant to the President, and Sergeant Paul W. Leeper of the

Washington police, who had helped to apprehend the Watergate burglars, answered a few relatively perfunctory questions, and the first day was over. At the White House, it was announced that Nixon had not watched and would not watch the hearings on television.

James W. McCord Jr., the man whose letter to Judge Sirica had helped to unravel the cover-up, brought melodrama into the hearing room the next morning. A former C.I.A. agent, he had worked at the re-election committee as security director and had placed the bugs at the Watergate. He felt he had been abandoned by his committee superiors, and he had no qualms about implicating them, up to and including the President of the United States. A dry man, who talked in a small, grainy voice with something of the manner of a accountant, he seemed ill-suited to his role. Yet much of what James McCord had to say was explosive indeed. So explosive that the Senators, still on their good behavior, kept pointing out that much of his testimony was hearsay. "I am not trying to exclude it," Baker said of one piece of testimony. "I wish simply to identify it [as hearsay] as we go along."

McCord told a tale of phone calls taken in highway booths, of meetings in a car at an overlook along the Potomac River, of messages delivered third-hand—all allegedly part of an elaborate effort to buy his silence, directed by the White House. Specifically, McCord testified that John J. Caulfield, a former White House official then working in the Treasury Department, had promised him at a clandestine meeting on January 12, 1973, that he would be given executive clemency, financial aid and eventually a job if he would remain silent. Calmly and precisely, McCord read from his prepared statement three sentences that more directly implicated Nixon than anything said before: "Caulfield stated that he was carrying the message of executive clemency to me 'from the very highest levels of the White House.' He stated that the President of the United States was in Key Biscayne, Fla., that weekend, had been told of the forthcoming meeting with me and would be immediately told of the results of the meeting. He further stated that 'I may have a message

to you at our next meeting from the President himself.' "
And that was not all; McCord described another meeting
with Caulfield, a former New York City policeman who
had worked for Dean at the White House, in which Caulfield said: "The President's ability to govern is at stake.
Another Teapot Dome scandal is possible, and the
Government may fall. Everybody else is on track but
you. You are not following the game plan." Much of
what was said during the hearings had been expected
by those following the case, because it had leaked out of
closed, preliminary examinations. But McCord's dramatic
implication of the President stunned everyone but the
Senators and a few staff members. If true, if corroborated
by other witnesses, his testimony meant that Nixon had
been hip-deep in the cover-up. But for the moment, it was
his word against that of the White House.

Ziegler, meeting with reporters who had been watching
the hearings on television in the press room, flatly denied
McCord's account. But it had an immediate impact: for
the first time in memory, a White House press secretary
was forced to entertain not one but more than a dozen
questions about a President's ability to continue in office.
Bombarded with inquiries about impeachment and resignation, Ziegler said that "the President of the United States
has a lot to do and a lot to accomplish in the second term,
and he fully intends to do that."

The President was not the only villain in McCord's
testimony. For the first time in public, McCord reported
that he had been told by G. Gordon Liddy, another of the
Watergate conspirators, that Mitchell, Dean and Magruder
had approved the Watergate plot in early 1972. And, in a
comment almost lost in the hubbub, he said he had been
given almost daily access, while at the re-election committee, to the highly sensitive files of the Justice Department's Internal Security Division—files dealing with
organizations believed to be planning anti-Republican
demonstrations. Such material is normally available only
to the highest officials of the government, and only in
cases where the national security is threatened. Could all
of this possibly be true? No one knew for sure, but Baker,
at least, was impressed, and he praised McCord for his
precision.

The Wiretaps

James McCord had something in common with many other men in Washington that week of May 13; he, like the others, seemed enmeshed in tragedy. Outside the hearing room, the most startling development moved Henry Kissinger's name from the diplomatic file to the Watergate file. The intellectual, highly disciplined Harvard don had seemed the Nixon man least likely to be dragged into the Watergate muck; in many ways, he was not even a "Nixon man." He was accessible; he conducted cogent, mutually useful background talks with the press; he had wit; his power seemed earned by hard and productive work. His staff worked as hard as he did, and with unusual loyalty.

But while the Senators were doing their work on the Hill, Henry Kissinger's carefully insulated White House status was fraying a bit. The Federal Bureau of Investigation and sources in the Justice Department disclosed that in 1969 Kissinger had asked for—and, with the President's approval, had been given—wiretaps on his associates, other White House aides and newsmen. The phones of 17 persons were wiretapped. Two weeks earlier, in the kind of tergiversation he had often been accused of, Kissinger had conceded having read the logs of some tapped conversations, but had sanctimoniously denied having authorized them. The explanation given after the fact for the taps, to no one's surprise, was "national security," which the Administration said was endangered by the publication of a New York Times story reporting, for the first time, American bombing in Cambodia. Among those reportedly bugged were key Kissinger associates, including Helmut Sonnenfeld, Winston Lord and Anthony Lake, as well as correspondents of The New York Times and the Columbia Broadcasting System. (Much later, it emerged that William Safire, a Presidential speechwriter hired by The Times as a balancing conservative voice for its editorial page, had also been on the list while in Government.) The taps, according to White House spokesmen, were meant to cut off leaks as well as to protect the innocent from suspicion.

That somewhat spavined excuse did nothing to put to rest the disturbing questions about Kissinger's conduct— questions that could only pain him and his admirers. For one thing, it was not clear that the taps were even legal, let alone proper; the Supreme Court decisions on the subject are murky. And it was hard for many to understand why they were necessary as a result of the Cambodia story: Surely the Cambodians, friendly and unfriendly, with bombs bursting in their villages, knew they were being attacked. The ultimate question that Kissinger never answered about the taps on his staff was this: Why didn't he talk to his aides instead of bugging them—and then either accept their explanations or fire them? As far as the newsmen were concerned, did anyone really believe that the Government had the right to listen to reporters' private conversations, as well as those of their wives and children, simply because they had printed something that the Government did not like? It was a measure of the prestige that Henry Kissinger had built in Washington—the result of his intellect, his diligence, his social grace, and above all his flashes of color in a gray sea of Administration mediocrity—that he was never questioned closely on these issues, not even months later, when he came before the Senate Foreign Relations Committee for confirmation as Secretary of State.

Elliot Richardson emerged better from a week of travail. Derided as the Movable Brahmin, the Attorney-General-designate struggled through *his* Senate hearings as the latest symbol of Administration half-measures. He had already served Nixon as Deputy Secretary of State, as Secretary of Health, Education, and Welfare and as Secretary of Defense; what worse token of new departures could the President have seized upon for the crucial position at Justice? But after an embarrassing number of refusals from other candidates, Richardson prevailed upon Archibald Cox, who had been Solicitor General in the Kennedy Administration, to accept the job of special prosecutor. Crew-cut, aristocratic and sometimes autocratic, Cox lacked prosecutorial experience but enjoyed a reputation for stubborn independence, which in the context of the moment was priceless. Richardson retained the right to fire him, if need be, but ceded to Cox full authority for the investigation "for all practical day-to-day purposes." Most of those who had doubted that every lead would be exhaustively pursued seemed satisfied that under Cox even Nixon would not be sheltered. In the event, both Cox and Richardson proved to be so independent that the White House felt that neither could be fired without creating the public impression of another cover-up. They became hostages for probity.

The Second Week (May 21–27, 1973)

McCord was back at the little brown-covered table when the hearings went into their second week on Tuesday, May 22. During the intervening weekend, there had been the usual complement of disclosures: Caulfield had told the Senate committee's staff that he was operating on Dean's instructions when he offered clemency to McCord; Mitchell had told Helen Thomas of United Press International, the interlocutor of the Mitchell family for months, that someone was trying to make him "the fall guy" in the Watergate case; Haldeman was reported to have told the C.I.A. that it was "the President's wish" that it go slow during its 1972 Watergate investigation.

Among other things, McCord gave the committee and the television audience a lesson in how to tap a phone, holding aloft a disassembled mechanism and demonstrating how the transmitter should be "interconnected on series with the wiring within the phone itself." On a more substantive level, he testified that Liddy and E. Howard Hunt, another of the convicted conspirators, had hatched an unsuccessful plot to break into the office of a flamboyant Las Vegas newspaper publisher, Hank Greenspun, to steal documents damaging to an unnamed Democratic Presidential candidate, and then to escape in a plane belonging to reclusive billionaire Howard Hughes. (Greenspun told reporters who tracked him down that what was really in his office safe was a set of documents relating to Hughes's dealings with the Justice Department, which could well have given rise to influence-peddling charges against Nixon.) McCord also described his state of mind early in 1972 when he agreed to participate in the Watergate operation. He provided the Senators—especially

Baker, who had shown a special interest in motivation—with two explanations: First, he said, he considered any operation "sanctioned" by Dean and Mitchell to be not only legal but clearly in the national interest; "left alone," he added, "I would not have undertaken the operation." Second, McCord told the committee, he had become perturbed, not by the Democratic candidates themselves, but by the "realistic threat" of anti-Nixon demonstrations from such "violence-oriented" groups as the Vietnam Veterans Against the War. His comments provided one of the earliest and best descriptions of the twisted thinking of men in responsible positions at the Nixon headquarters. By his own admission, McCord had only the word of Liddy, a known hothead who had once threatened to kill Magruder, that the Watergate operation had high-level approval. But zealots were apparently taken seriously at 1701 Pennsylvania Avenue, where the committee was quartered; so pervasive was the mistrust of the press and of ordinary political intelligence that a Liddy could be viewed as an oracle, and the entirely peaceful Vietnam Veterans could be transformed into anarchists. Paranoia toward outsiders, absolute faith in insiders—result, disaster. It was a pattern that ran through much that the committee uncovered.

Jack Caulfield, a fleshy, red-faced ex-cop, followed McCord on the stand. He confirmed that Dean had authorized his offer of clemency to McCord, then cut the ground from under his friend's testimony by declaring that he had "no knowledge of my own" that Nixon had approved the offer. Still, the grim-faced Caulfield said that Dean had cited authority for the offer from "way up at the top"—a phrase that he said he took to mean that the offer came from a level no lower than Ehrlichman's. (The only people above that level were Nixon and his alter ego, Haldeman.) Under subsequent questioning, he went further conceding that Dean's remark indicated to him that the counsel "was talking about the President." Caulfield also confirmed that he had transmitted to McCord, through telephone calls by a former colleague on the New York City police force, Anthony Ulasewicz, a message from John Dean. "A year is a long time," the message allegedly began, apparently a suggestion that clemency could be granted after that period without arousing public indignation. "Your wife will be taken care of; you will be rehabilitated with employment when this is all over." It was left to Dean to clarify the pivotal question of whether or not Nixon had been the instigator of the effort to shut McCord up—an effort, according to both McCord and Caulfield, that had consumed a considerable amount of Republican money. McCord said that he had been paid more than $100,000—"lawyers' fees" to the true believers, hush money to nearly everyone else—including $46,000 in crisp new $100 bills delivered by Hunt's wife. Caulfield testified that Ulasewicz had been paid from the start of his career as a special White House undercover agent in July, 1969, not from government funds but from a special account maintained by Herbert W. Kalmbach, a California lawyer who represented Nixon. (Kalmbach had also helped to raise the money paid to McCord and his fellow burglars, but the full scope of his activities didn't become known until later in the hearings.)

On Wednesday, with McCord sitting immediately behind him, McCord's former lawyer, Gerald Alch of Boston, a slick and curly-haired associate of F. Lee Bailey, sought to destroy McCord's credibility. McCord had implicated Alch in the White House cover-up, together with other lawyers representing Watergate defendants. Alch not only denied any such involvement; he accused McCord's new lawyer, Bernard Fensterwald, of having said, "We're going after the President of the United States." It was a sensational counterstroke to McCord's sensational accusations, an assertion, however indirect, that all that McCord had said grew out of a vendetta against Nixon for having allowed McCord to suffer while the big boys went free.

The first comic relief of the hearings came that same day, from Tony Ulasewicz, the ex-cop with the basset-hound face. He told the committee that the people he had known during his days on the force in New York would never have bungled a job the way McCord and his associates did, and he said the easiest way to obtain information about an opposition political party was "to write a postal card asking them to mail you all their leaflets. They will put you on their mailing list and you will have everything." He did not say whether he had proffered these insights to his Republican confreres during 1972.

If Odle had brought into the hearing room a suggestion of the Nixon style, if McCord had brought the electricity of accusation, Bernard L. Barker brought on Thursday a note of pathos. There he sat, an earnest, round faced man, a veteran of the searing Bay of Pigs debacle, looking and talking more like the real estate man he usually was than the undercover operative he had occasionally become. He testified in his muddled way that he had joined the Watergate operation because he thought he could get help later from Hunt, who had led the Bay of Pigs invasion, and from "others in high places" in a new attempt to overthrow Fidel Castro. Inouye of Hawaii sought to appeal to Barker's vanity, prefacing a question with the comment, "You are a wise man." Barker, a melancholy look on his face, interrupted. "If I was a wise man," he said, "I would not probably be sitting right here." Then Weicker: "Do you still feel that national security is a proper justification for Watergate?" The answer, more than anything said in all the weeks of testimony, constituted an epitaph to the confused ethics of the Nixon Administration and its agents—the improvisation of threats to security, the exaltation of ends and denigration of means. "I feel it was a justification for Watergate," said Bernard Barker, shortly before he returned to his jail cell, there to shed his seersucker suit. "But, quite frankly, I am just a human being. I get confused about all these things. Sometimes I do not know the answers to these questions."

The Counterattack

At the White House, the man who had weathered with pride Six Crises and more was still trapped beneath what one of his remaining lieutenants called a Niagara of accusations. Once again, while the Senate committee's proceedings spun out across the television networks to an audience that sometimes reached as many as 25 million, Richard Nixon fought back.

First, he issued what amounted to a legal brief, a 4,000-word document that was both a reaffirmation of his innocence and a confession. After almost a year of declaring his desire for a full, unimpeded inquiry, Nixon conceded that immediately after the Watergate break-in he had ordered that the investigation be carefully limited in the interests of "national security." As the President anticipated, there were many who read his words as an admission that he had ordered a cover-up at the earliest opportunity. Second, he launched a long-expected counteroffensive, in sharp contrast to his curiously passive posture of the previous weeks. Before a friendly audience of 600 former prisoners of war at a rain-plagued gala in a tent on the south lawn of the White House, Nixon lashed out at persons who steal government secrets and endanger the nation. It was another attempt to portray himself as the sole, incorruptible, unchallengeable guardian of the public weal.

The statement, like others before it, seemed largely designed to answer the latest charges while offering no clues to the overall question of what had gone wrong in the White House in 1972. The President said that from the time he entered office in 1969, he and his associates had worried about leaks of national security matters and about domestic violence and unrest. Accordingly, he said, the White House set up special investigative units—not American gestapos, perhaps, but certainly far beyond the American libertarian tradition—to get to the bottom of it all. Against that background, Nixon made the following admissions:

On the 1971 burglary of the Ellsberg's psychiatrist's office by the White House "plumbers": "Because of the emphasis I put on the crucial importance of protecting the national security, I can understand how highly motivated individuals could have felt justified in engaging in specific activities that I would have disapproved had they been brought to my attention." On attempts in 1972 to use the

C.I.A. as a cover for the Watergate burglary: "I wanted justice done with regard to Watergate, but in the scale of national priorities with which I had to deal . . . I also had to be deeply concerned with insuring that neither the covert operations of the C.I.A. nor the operations of the special investigations unit should be compromised. [A critical translation: I had to act illegally to cover other illegal acts.] Therefore, I instructed Mr. Haldeman and Mr. Ehrlichman to insure that the investigations of the break-in not expose either an unrelated covert operation of the C.I.A. or the activities of the White House investigative unit . . . It now seems that later, through whatever complex of individual motives and possible misunderstandings, there were apparently wide-ranging efforts to limit the investigation or to conceal the involvement of members of the Administration." On his own responsibility: "With hindsight, it is apparent that I should have given more heed to the warning signals I received along the way about Watergate and less to the reassurances . . . None of these [acts] took place with my specific approval or knowledge. To the extent that I may in any way have contributed to the climate in which they took place, I did not intend to; to the extent that I failed to prevent them, I should have been more vigilant."

The President had gone much further than ever before; he had acknowledged his obvious responsibility, even if he was ignorant of "specific acts," in managing a White House where the violation of law and of simple ethical standards became a commonplace. Yet his statement did not stem the flow of criticisms and suspicions; it was a styptic pencil applied to a hemorrhage. The reaction was much the same as that to his statement of August 29, 1972, that no one then employed in the White House had been involved in Watergate; to his April 17 statement acknowledging the possibility of White House involvement; and to his April 30 television appearance implying that Haldeman and Ehrlichman had been unjustly hounded from office. One Republican Senator, a strong Nixon ally, described the President's statement as "sickeningly, transparently inadequate."

Why? For one thing, by the President's account, he

based his directive to limit the Watergate probe on his fears that the F.B.I. would compromise C.I.A. secrets. Yet C.I.A. officials said that the Administration had discussed political considerations, not security problems, with them. For another, though Nixon now admitted that he tried to limit the investigation, he had said on April 17: "Throughout this entire matter, all Government employes and especially White House staff members are expected fully to cooperate." But much more damning than specific discrepancies was the President's concession that he had set up an unprecedented snooping operation in the White House and then allowed it to get out of hand. Nixon suggested that "it went beyond its charter . . . totally without my knowledge or authority." That took him off the hook of having urged or condoned illegal acts, but left him trapped in an equally painful snare: if he hadn't known, he had been a fool or an incompetent or both.

None of this was lost on the public, the same public that had given him, only six months before, majorities in every state of the union save hopelessly permissive Massachusetts. A new Gallup Poll showed that Nixon's popularity had dropped to its lowest point since he entered the White House—45 per cent, down 24 per cent since the announcement of an end of American involvement in Vietnam. But there was no disposition to impeach in the House of Representatives; the dominant Democrats had a whole portfolio of reasons for hesitation. Impeachment would (1) polarize the nation; (2) depict the Democrats as sore losers trying to undo the results of the November, 1972, balloting; (3) promote Vice President Agnew into the Presidency, thereby rendering him all but unbeatable in November, 1976; (4) exceed the evidence adduced so far. "There is tremendous uneasiness, having to face what nobody wants to face," said one Capitol Hill sage. "People are walking around here with their fingers in their ears." Unfortunately, the Constitution provides no remedy against a miscreant President other than impeachment. So the Senate committee plowed on, trying the case in what the movies on the late-late show always call "the court of public opinion." Things were getting less tidy every day.

The Third Week (June 4–10, 1973)

The committee's first order of business when it reassembled was a request from Cox that the hearings be postponed for one to three months. Otherwise, he said, there was a "grave danger" that the guilty would go unpunished and the full facts be hidden forever if the public hearings continued. Sam Ervin clung to his view that public knowledge took priority over punishment. "The people of this land," he said, "are entitled to know the truth without further delay and are entitled to have their government resume its operations in a manner to promote their interest." The committee unanimously supported the chairman's view, then turned its attention to Mrs. Sally J. Harmony, a 45-year-old woman who had worked for Liddy at the re-election committee. Her importance as a witness lay in the fact that Liddy alone among the conspirators had clung to the undercover man's code and refused to talk either to the Senators or the grand jury. But the committee interrogated her with extraordinary gentleness, perhaps out of chivalry, perhaps because Cox had put it on the defensive. She testified that she had typed telephone logs and intelligence memorandums for Liddy on special forms headed "Gemstone"—the code name for data from Watergate taps installed late in May, before the June 17 break-in. She said that she had forged a pass to McGovern headquarters. But no one bothered to ask her about depositions from co-workers quoting her as having told them that she perjured herself "for Gordon" before the grand jury.

Robert A. F. Reisner, the baby-faced, 26-year-old former administrative assistant to Magruder, was a more productive witness. He told of placing, at Magruder's direction, two Gemstone reports in a file that Magruder took to a meeting with Mitchell. Prodded by Ervin, he also said that duplicate copies of the documents were sent to Haldeman's office. Reisner's was the first sworn testimony suggesting that Mitchell and Magruder had known of the taps before June 17—something both of them had repeatedly denied. It was not a good day for Mitchell, the gruff former Attorney General. Already under indictment in New York, he was now linked to the Gemstone papers by Reisner, and on the same day he was accused of having personally chosen three sites, including the Watergate complex, for wiretapping during the 1972 campaign. That accusation came in a deposition given by Ehrlichman in a civil suit brought by the Democrats. Citing Magruder and Dean as his sources, Ehrlichman testified that Mitchell had personally circled or checked off three targets on a list handed to him at a meeting in Florida in March, 1972 —Watergate, McGovern's headquarters in Washington, and the Democrats' national convention headquarters in Miami Beach. Mitchell, in the picture sketched by Ehrlichman in a 242-page deposition, was one of the prime movers in the operation, together with Magruder and Dean. The allegations against Mitchell were particularly damaging because he had already admitted having attended three meetings at which bugging plans were discussed, including the one in Florida in March, 1972. But he had insisted that he always rejected the proposals.

Next was Hugh W. Sloan Jr., an intense young man with a finely chiseled nose and deep shadows around his eyes, who had served as treasurer of the Finance Committee to Re-elect the President soon after the break-in. More sensitive than most of the Nixonites to what he saw going on around him, he was one of the first to begin cooperating with investigators, and Sam Ervin liked what he heard from Sloan on the stand. "I think you have strengthened my faith in the old adage that 'an honest man is the noblest work of God,'" the 76-year-old Senator said at one point. Out of his background as campaign treasurer, he told the Senators strange tales of tens of thousands of dollars in cash being collected and disbursed, often without explanation. One of the disbursements was a payment of $83,000 to Liddy—the first installment in a budget of $250,000. He checked with Magruder, Sloan said, and was told to go ahead. Then he checked with Stans, the head of the finance committee, who told him the same thing, adding, when asked what the money was for, "I do not want to know and you don't want to know." Shortly after the break-in, Sloan went on, he met with Magruder, who urged him to understate the amount given to Liddy when discussing the matter with the authorities, presumably to help sustain a cover story. Sloan recalled telling Magruder, "I have no intention of perjuring myself," and Magruder replying, "You may have to." Then Sloan went to see Mitchell, he said, "essentially asking for guidance. The campaign literally at this point was falling apart before your eyes." Mitchell's response, according to Sloan: "When the going gets tough, the tough get going." In other words, stick to your story, brazen it through. That night, bewildered, he attended an office cocktail party and told friends from the White House that "there was something very wrong at the campaign committee." The next day he went to see Dwight Chapin, the President's appointments secretary. As Sloan drily described that meeting: "Mr. Chapin evaluated my condition at that point as being somewhat overwrought and suggested a vacation. . . . He suggested that the important thing is that the President be protected." Wandering through the White House corridors like Diogenes, Sloan stopped next at Ehrlichman's office. No passion for truth burned there; Ehrlichman, Sloan told the Senators, offered to help get him a lawyer but added: "Do not tell me any details; I do not want to know." A lawyer, one of the three closest associates of the President of the United States, with potential felonies popping all around him, didn't want to know. As Sloan told the story, it had a devastating impact in the hearing room and on television. Ehrlichman had trouble convincing anyone that he was ignorant of the cover-up, at least of the broad strategy, after that. Eventually, Sloan said, he decided that he would tell the United States attorney bits of the truth or the whole truth, depending on how the questions were framed; as it turned out, he got by without either lying or revealing the true scope of the Liddy payments because of inept interrogation.

Herbert L. Porter, the former scheduling director for the re-election committee, who followed Sloan to the stand on Friday, was another of the young Nixon pros. But whereas Sloan was dark, Porter was fair; and, more important, whereas Sloan had balked at perjury when it was

urged on him by Magruder, Porter, under the same kind
of pressure, had chosen to go along. Naturally, the Senators wondered why. Natty in a glen plaid suit and his
mod aviator glasses, Porter attempted to explain. Magruder had come to him on June 28 or 29, Porter said, following a meeting with Mitchell and others, and had said
substantially the following: "Now, Gordon [Liddy] was
authorized some money for dirty tricks, nothing illegal,
but nonetheless, things that could be very embarrassing to
the President of the United States and to Mr. Mitchell
and Mr. Haldeman and others. Now, your name was
brought up as someone who we can count on to help
in this situation. Would you corroborate a story that the
money was authorized for something a little bit more
legitimate-sounding than dirty tricks? Even though the
dirty tricks were legal, it still would be very embarrassing."
Between them they invented a story about spending $100,-
000 for student agents to infiltrate radical groups, and both
told it to the F.B.I. and to the grand jury. They thus played
a central role in confining the initial prosecution to the
seven men who played an active role in the break-in, denying to the prosecution the data that would have enabled
it to trace the Liddy money to higher-ups in the campaign. Porter stuck to his story, he said, until Magruder
advised him on April 11, 1973, to make a clean breast
of things. He also said that Magruder told him after a
meeting at the White House on the 14th that "it is all
over, the President has directed everybody to tell the
truth." And he said that Kenneth W. Parkinson, the chief
attorney for the re-election committee, had told him as
late as March 28 not to worry about his perjury because
"all you have done, you have just embellished a little,
that is all, you have not got a problem."

After hearing out Porter's tale, Baker, still searching
for motivation, was dissatisfied. He wanted to know why
Porter chose to "abdicate your own conscience." "I kind
of drifted along," the witness said uncomfortably. Then
at another point: "In all honesty [I said nothing] probably
because of the fear of group pressure that would ensue,
of not being a team player." Then: "I first met Mr. Nixon
when I was eight years old in 1946, when he ran for
Congress in my home district . . . I felt as if I had known

this man all my life—not personally, perhaps, but in spirit. I felt a deep sense of loyalty to him. I was appealed to on this basis." And finally, after a few more thrusts from an uncharacteristically glowering Baker: "I had been told by others in the campaign that this kind of thing was a normal activity in a campaign . . . I had never been involved in a political campaign before . . . These things were all new to me and I accepted them for what they were." It was, as Howard Baker commented, "a terrible indictment of politics." But it was more than that: it was a picture, applicable to others besides the shaken Porter, of naiveté, the elevation of loyalty into the highest of virtues, an utter lack of independent values, a siege mentality.

The Fourth Week (June 11–17, 1973)

Now the tempo began to accelerate, with the appearances of men who had stood at or near the center of the Nixon re-election operation, the first pounding interrogation by the Senators and the first sign of a partisan division on the committee. The week began with two days of testimony by Maurice H. Stans, the Nixon finance chairman—the man who raised more than $50 million for the most lavish campaign in American Presidential history. Stans, already under indictment in New York in the Vesco case, did not want to testify; his lawyer argued that it might prejudice a fair trial. But Sam Ervin —he was emerging as a kind of folk hero, with Mr. Sam T-shirts sweeping the nation—rejected Stans's plea. The chairman said Stans had the choice of pleading the Fifth Amendment, risking a contempt of Congress citation or testifying. He chose the latter course, then proceeded to enter a general denial of any "intentional violations" of campaign financing laws and any knowledge of the Watergate burglary, of "any sabotage program" or of any attempted cover-up. He said he was in charge of collecting money, others were in charge of spending it and the two operations were enclosed in "watertight compartments." Stans has been around Washington for so long that some people refer to him as Uncle Maury. He was President Eisenhower's budget director and President Nixon's Commerce Secretary. He is smart, he is rich and he knows where to mine the political money. But he also has a reputation for unscrupulousness and for uncritically accepting the laissez-faire attitudes of the big contributors. That reputation was intensified by the stories of hundreds of thousands of dollars, some of it laundered in Mexico or raised from dubious sources, flowing in and out of his office safe. But he was his usual confident, distinguished-looking self on the stand, and he yielded not an inch under questioning. Most of the Senators found it impossible to swallow his assertions that he had given Kalmbach $75,000 in cash (later used as hush money) without receiving an explanation of the purpose, and that he had approved an even larger disbursement to Liddy without a proper accounting.

With Talmadge and Ervin in the van, the Senators hammered away at the witness. Talmadge ridiculed Stans's claim that he had not bothered much with details by producing a document that Stans had written about a control system for the purchase of bumper strips. "You are considered to be one of the most able certified accountants in America," he taunted. "Why did you worry about bumper strips instead of those funds?" Stans replied lamely that the law required him to account for the proceeds of sales of such articles.

Ervin was even rougher; he was clearly nettled by Stans's bland denials. First, he zeroed in on Stans's insistence that the destruction of some of the committee's cash account books, through which the funds that paid for Watergate had passed, was unrelated to a cover-up. He called it "quite a queer coincidence" and "rather a suspicious coincidence." Stans rejected the adjectives, but Ervin pressed on. Stans insisted, over and over again, that the records had been destroyed, within the provisions of the law in force at the time, to protect the confidentiality of contributors. Finally, Ervin asked sarcastically: "Mr. Stans, do you not think that men who have been honored by the American people as you have ought to have their course of action guided by ethical principles which are superior to the minimum requirements of the criminal laws?" Then the North Carolinian delved into a $50,000 cash contribution to a group of Maryland fat cats who were holding a banquet honoring Vice President Agnew. Stans admitted that it had been sent in cash so that it could be mixed with other receipts.

This exchange, the sharpest of the hearings up until then ensued:

ERVIN: In other words, they were holding a fund-raising dinner in the Vice President's honor and they wanted to make it appear that they took in $50,000 more than they actually took in, didn't they?

STANS: They wanted to make it look more successful than it apparently was.

ERVIN: Yes, in other words, they wanted to practice a deception on the general public, as to the amount of honor that was paid to the Vice President.

STANS: Mr. Chairman, I am not sure this is the first time that has happened in American politics.

ERVIN: You know, there has been murder and larceny in every generation, but that hasn't made murder meritorious or larceny legal.

After several more exchanges of similar heat, Gurney of Florida, the sole Administration loyalist on the panel, broke in to say: "I for one have not appreciated the harassment of this witness by the chairman." Ervin, suddenly all courtliness, drawled his best: "Well, I am sorry that my distinguished friend from Florida does not approve of my method of examining the witness. I am an old country lawyer and I don't know the finer ways of doing it. I just have to do it my way." The audience exploded in laughter and applause. After a moment or two, Sam Ervin, the old country lawyer who went to the Harvard Law School, gaveled for silence. Stans's anticlimactic closing statement included a maudlin passage praising the selflessness of millionaires. Clement Stone of Chicago, he told the committee, had given $2 million, but "has never asked for anything from his Government or the Administration in return." In fact, Stone had told half of Chicago and a quarter of Washington just how hard he was lobbying for the job of Ambassador to London (he never got it). Stans could not resist a final sanctimonious touch. He ended with this: "All I ask, Mr. Chairman and members of the committee, is that when you write your report you give me back my good name."

Much of what Jeb Stuart Magruder now began to tell the committee had been forecast for several months. The witness was boyishly handsome, and, except for a controlled nervousness manifested in his constant repositioning of the ashtray on the table before him, his manner bespoke nothing dramatic. Yet the impact of his testimony was devastating. For the first time, one of the key participants was describing in detail how Watergate came about and how it was covered up. In the process, Magruder confessed his own guilt, said that he, Mitchell and Dean, among others, had approved the break-in, and identified five other men, including Haldeman, who, he said, took part in or knew about the conspiracy to obstruct justice. Just as McCord had decided to talk, in part, because he saw a photograph of a smiling Magruder at a time when he, McCord, was faced with years in jail, Magruder said he had decided to tell the truth only after some of the others in the cover-up began to have trouble with their memories. According to Magruder, one of those with a faulty memory was Stans; Magruder said that he and Mitchell had told Stans on June 24, 1972, that the burglary operation had been paid for with money that Stans had raised. Stans had been unable, in response to a direct question two days before, to recall anything about such a meeting.

Earnest and handsome in his tennis tan and his subdued businessman's clothes, Magruder looked to James M. Naughton of The Times like "Machiavelli in pinstripes." He seemed the very prototype of young men who graduated from the best colleges in the 1950's and later attached themselves to Richard Nixon in pursuit of their vision of the American Dream. Explaining his motives, Magruder described himself as a man in the grip of mindless pragmatism. At Williams College, he had studied ethics with William Sloan Coffin Jr., whom he admired greatly, and later saw him deliberately violate the law in the antiwar movement. Mr. Coffin, on a public platform, advised young men to burn their draft cards as a Vietnam protest. Never pausing to consider the differences between overt civil disobedience and clandestine crime conducted under the cloak of governmental protection, Magruder remarked, "When these subjects came up, although I was aware they were illegal and I am sure others did, we had become somewhat inured to using some activities that would help us accomplish a cause, what we thought was a legitimate cause." He now saw that his was "an absolutely incorrect decision" and "that two wrongs do not make a right."

By Magruder's account, the Watergate burglary was only the partial fulfillment of a grandiose scheme by Liddy, which was originally presented to Magruder, Mitchell and Dean in the office of the Attorney General on January 27, 1972. The plan included wiretapping, surveillance, photographing of documents, abduction of radical demonstrators who might disrupt the Republican convention —they were to be "detained in a place like Mexico and returned at the end of the convention"—and the employment of call girls at the Democratic convention "aboard a yacht in Miami set up for sound and photographs." The men who heard the plan were "appalled," Magruder said, not by its character but by its cost, $1 million.

Liddy packed up his charts, restrained his fevered imagination and finally scaled the plan down to $250,000 with only the wiretapping and photography plans remaining. Magruder said Mitchell had approved the final version, unenthusiastically but unequivocally, at a meeting March 30, 1972, at Key Biscayne, Fla. His comment, as quoted by Magruder: "O.K., let's give him a quarter of a million dollars and see what he can come up with." For the first time, a direct contradiction of Mitchell's frequent and fervent denials had been spread on the public record. Magruder's version acquired a kind of instant credibility (though it was challenged later) because most politicians, most reporters and most members of the general public found it hard to believe that Magruder or Dean or Liddy could have carried out such an enterprise without Mitchell's help—or, at the very least, approval.

Magruder testified that one of the primary goals of the bugging scheme was to find evidence that would be damaging to Lawrence F. O'Brien, the Democratic national chairman, who people in the President's camp thought "could be very difficult in the coming campaign." No such evidence was ever found, and the burglars, of course, were caught red-handed. Magruder was in Los Angeles when McCord and his team were apprehended, and, by his account, he and his colleagues began almost at once and almost by instinct to destroy documents and concoct a cover story. Under questioning by Baker, Magruder said: "I think there was no question that the cover-up began that Saturday when we realized there was a break-in. I do not think there was ever any discussion that there would not be a cover-up." Baker pressed on: the decision to authorize the break-in, he said, "a decision really that is going to affect history, was made in an almost casual way." "Yes, sir," answered Magruder. "An historic decision to go forward with this plan was followed with another decision to cover it up without any great debate or discussion of the matter," Baker said. "That is correct, sir," replied Magruder; ". . . if it had gotten out that people like Mr. Mitchell and others had been involved at that point in time, I honestly thought that his [Nixon's] re-election would probably be negated." That was it, with the bark off.

In his 5½ hours of testimony, Magruder discussed the Watergate roles of more than a dozen of the top figures at the White House and the re-election committee. Aside from his accusations against Mitchell, and his admissions about his own complicity, he sowed a mine field of names and dates for future witnesses. He gave the following picture, man by man: Haldeman—his office received documents about the burglary plan, through Gordon C. Strachan, a Haldeman aide, but Magruder did not know whether Haldeman actually read them. Haldeman knew by mid-January, 1973, that Magruder had lied to the grand jury and planned to commit perjury at the Watergate trial. Ehrlichman—Magruder had no direct evidence, but assumed that Dean was working on Ehrlichman's orders. Dean—he participated in the planning of the burglary and played the central role in developing and maintaining the cover-up; he never conducted an investigation for the President. Charles W. Colson, another ranking Nixon adviser—he urged early in 1972 that espionage plans be expedited and spoke of the need to gather derogatory material about Larry O'Brien, but Magruder was vague regarding Colson's knowledge of the actual burglary. Strachan—he received daily summaries from Magruder, and therefore knew all the details of the burglary and cover-up; he also read the transcript of the initial, unsuccessful taps at the Watergate complex. Stans—he was told the basic facts of the situation on June 24, 1972, by Mitchell and Magruder. Sloan—because he had paid large sums of money to Liddy, he knew that something was being covered up, but not what. Kalmbach—he raised the hush money. Robert C. Mardian, political coordinator— he sat in on meetings at which the cover-up was planned. Frederick C. LaRue, an assistant to Mitchell—he attended the Key Biscayne meeting. It was an awesome list, a list that would form the basis of much future questioning. And not a man on it had spoken up before McCord started to sing.

The Fifth Week (June 25–July 1, 1973)

Magruder had implicated everyone of consequence in the campaign, both at the White House and at the re-election committee, except for one man—the President of the United States. That role fell to John Wesley Dean 3d, the ousted White House counsel, the man who had vowed not to be a scapegoat and was now about to make good on that vow. His testimony had been delayed by weeks of bargaining for immunity and then by the visit to the United States of Soviet leader Leonid I. Brezhnev. By the time he sat down at the witness table on June 25, Arrow-shirt handsome, with his stunning blonde wife behind him, his appearance had been as relentlessly ballyhooed as Clark Gable's return from the wars or Hank Aaron's 714th home run. John Dean disappointed no one.

Speaking in a husky but well-modulated baritone, Dean accused Nixon of participating actively in the cover-up of the bugging and burglary at the Watergate; of asserting that $1 million for hush money for the arrested underlings would not be too much; of offering executive clemency to McCord in return for his silence, and, as a last resort, of trying to find others, including the former Attorney General, to take the rap. Everyone in the hearing room and most in the television audience realized that the accusations, if sustained, would constitute the "high crimes and misdemeanors" set out in the Constitution as one basis for the impeachment of a President. Dean spoke from his experience at the center of the conspiracy he described and from which, by his own account, he defected when he concluded that he was being set up as its principal victim. Hunched over the witness stand, his boyish face accented by horn-rimmed glasses, the 34-year-old lawyer delivered his momentous testimony without once becoming ruffled. When Talmadge asked how he could maintain such charges against the Chief Executive, Dean replied quietly and coolly: "Well Senator, I have been asked to tell the truth, and I have told it exactly the way I know it." Others would come forward with their own versions of the truth, including the President, although he would not speak out for many weeks yet, and then only through a television speech and news conferences, not to the committee but directly to the American public. Dean provided no documentation for his allegations against the President, and he knew as he spoke that it was unlikely that Mitchell or Haldeman—the only men in a position to do so, other than the President—would corroborate his story. It is likely, he said, that "it is going to be my word against one man's word, it is going to be my word against two men's, it is going to be my word against three men's, and, probably, in some cases, it is going to be my word against four men." But the President and those who still sought to protect him, for all their power, had to contend with the fact that Dean had been a compelling witness and that five days' grilling had not forced him to retreat from his story in any significant way.

Dean told his story on the first day of the week in a detailed, chronological statement of 245 pages. He had been largely a functionary, he said, despite the splendiferous title. The men who ran things were Haldeman and Ehrlichman—the two whom outsiders sometimes referred to as "the Berlin Wall"—and everyone below them did what they were told. Dean rarely saw the President until his last few weeks in the White House, he said, and it never occurred to him to try. He simply reported to Haldeman and Ehrlichman, and on Watergate matters he took orders from them and from officials of the re-election committee. But, even in his early days, he got a good look at what he called "a climate of excessive concern over the political impact of demonstrators, excessive concern over leaks, and insatiable appetite for all political intelligence, all coupled with a do-it-yourself White House staff, regardless of the law." Watergate, he asserted, was "an inevitable outgrowth" of this mood—a mood that once reached such proportions that Nixon himself, looking out an upstairs window at a lone picket with a 10-foot antiwar banner in Lafayette Park, far across Pennsylvania Avenue, reacted sufficiently strongly to prompt one aide to look for "thugs" to remove the dissenter.

Watergate was not the only consequence. Dean disclosed, in the most startling piece of testimony he gave all week, that the White House had compiled lists of political enemies that it hoped to punish, especially after Nixon's re-election, by manipulating the potent Federal bureaucracy. It was already known that the Administration had turned the F.B.I. and the C.I.A. to its political purposes. Dean's testimony, and a document he had written, made clear a readiness to use the Internal Revenue Service, the dispensation of Federal grants and contracts and, as the Dean memorandum said, "litigation, prosecution, etc." The memorandum, which Dean said he had drafted in August, 1971, bore the heading, "Dealing with Our Political Enemies." In it, he wrote: "This memorandum addresses the matter of how we can maximize the fact of our incumbency in dealing with persons known to be active in their opposition to our Administration. Stated a bit more bluntly—how we can use the available Federal machinery to screw our political enemies." The two enemies lists showed the siege mentality at work. On them were not just "radic-libs" such as Paul Newman, the McGovernite actor; not just liberal establishment newspapers such as The New York Times, The Washington Post and The St. Louis Post-Dispatch, with their fierce opposition to the Vietnam war; not just the 12 black Representatives in Congress at the time (a nice comment on the Administration's racial attitudes, that); not just the Presidents of Harvard, Yale and the Massachusetts Institute of Technology; but also executives at the companies that make Otis elevators, IBM computers, Van Heusen shirts and Volkswagen advertisements; and Joe Namath, missassigned by the football freaks in the White House to the New York Giants; and Arnold Picker, a relatively conservative Democrat who raised money for Lyndon Johnson and Edmund Muskie; and Samuel M. Lambert, formerly head of the National Education Association, who had voted for Nixon.

Ervin was so outraged that he accused the President of seeking to undermine the constitutional rights of free speech, peaceful assembly and the redress of grievances. Weicker, for his part, disclosed that Administration officials, in an effort to intimidate him, had been trying to plant false stories about him, including one that he planned to switch to the Democratic party.

None of this was directly traceable to the President, at least not through the testimony of Dean. But the former counsel thought that it, too, grew out of what he almost, but not quite, called the President's paranoia, particularly about demonstrations. "We never found a scintilla of evidence that these demonstrators were part of a master plan," he said, "nor that they were funded by the Democratic political funds; nor that they had any direct connection with the McGovern campaign. This was explained to Mr. Haldeman, but the President believed that the opposite was, in fact, true." Dean also carefully avoided accusing the President of having had advance knowledge of the Watergate break-in. Instead, he focused on a series of four meetings that he had had with the President —the sinew of his case against Nixon.

On September 15, 1972, he said, he received a call asking him to go to the Oval Office. There "the President told me that Bob [Haldeman] had kept him posted on my handling of the Watergate case, told me I had done a good job and he appreciated how difficult a task it had been and the President was pleased that the case had stopped with Liddy." Dean also testified that in accepting the compliment he cautioned Nixon that he, Dean, did not know how long the investigation could be contained at a sub-White House level. This was the first sworn public testi-

mony implicating the President in the cover-up. Dean said
it was clear to him that Nixon was aware of all that he,
Haldeman and Ehrlichman had done to keep the stain
from spreading. But it was a flawed piece of evidence;
a reasonable man *could* have concluded from what Dean
quoted Nixon as having said that Nixon was pleased with
Dean's craftsmanship on the White House position papers
then being formulated, and that he was expressing the
relief any politician would have felt when he was reassured
that his staff was indeed clean. Not likely, but possible.

It was not until early in 1973 that Dean began seeing
the President on a regular basis, when a congressional
investigation was in the offing. In a meeting he had with
Haldeman and the President on March 13, the subject
turned to Watergate: "I told the President about the fact
that there were money demands being made by the seven
convicted defendants, and that the sentencing of these individuals was not far off. . . . I told the President about the
fact that there was no money to pay these individuals to
meet their demands. He asked me how much it would cost.
I told him I could only make an estimate and that it might
be as high as a million dollars or more. He told me that
was no problem and he also looked over at Haldeman
and then repeated the same statement. . . . The President
referred to the fact that Hunt had been promised clemency
. . . the conversation then turned back to a question regarding the money that was paid to the defendants. He
asked me how this was done. I told him I didn't know
much about it other than the fact that the money was
laundered so it could not be traced and then there were
secret deliveries."

Meeting number three on Dean's list of four came only
eight days later, on March 21, as the White House was
being battered with daily revelations about Watergate;
he said that he decided then that the time had come for
everyone to 'fess up. "I began," said Dean, "by telling
the President that there was a cancer growing on the
Presidency and that if the cancer was not removed that
the President himself would be killed by it." He then
recited to Nixon the basic data about the cover-up, including names and what seemed to him to be specific
crimes. Despite his efforts, Dean told the Senators, whose

attention never wandered, he realized when he had finished that "I had not really made the President understand." The meeting was later referred to by Nixon in his April 17 statement, in which he announced that serious new charges had come to his attention on March 21 and that, as a result, he had begun "an intensive new inquiry into this whole matter." Dean challenged that assertion, arguing that in fact, "the President commenced no investigation at all. Rather, the President, Haldeman and Ehrlichman commenced to protect themselves against the unraveling of the cover-up." Dean decided to hire a lawyer and to go to the Federal prosecutors. But Nixon called him to his hideaway in the Executive Office Building, across the street from the White House, at 9 A.M. on April 15. The President was cordial, Dean testified, but began "asking me a number of leading questions which made me think that the conversation was being taped and that a record was being made to protect himself"—a prescient comment. Dean went on: "The President told me I could not talk about national security areas and I should not talk about conversations I had with him because they were privileged conversations. Toward the end of the conversation, the President recalled the fact that at one point we had discussed the difficulty in raising money and that he had said that $1 million was nothing to raise to pay to maintain the silence of the defendants. He said that he had of course been only joking when he made that comment." It certainly sounded, as Dean told it, like the conversation of a man preparing his defense. On April 30, Dean was fired after having refused to sign either of two letters of resignation, both admitting his guilt, that the President handed him.

From Tuesday through Friday, John Dean expertly fielded all the questions the committee could throw at him, including some propounded, in absentia, by the White House. The White House questions, accusatory in nature and accompanied by a statement that amounted to a White House defense, were asked by Inouye, who said he was acting out of a sense of fairness to the President. Many of the questions were phrased as countercharges; one of them said, "Dean's activity in the cover-up also made him, perhaps unwittingly, the principal author of the political and constitutional crisis" of Watergate. Dean stood fast, supplying a few additional details but nothing that altered the outlines of his main charges. Then, incredibly, the word came from the Western White House, 3,000 miles away, that the questions, prepared by a Presidential counsel, J. Fred Buzhardt, constituted nothing more than "a hypothesis." The President had not seen them, said Gerald Warren, the deputy press secretary; the list supplied to Inouye "is not the President's position, it is not the White House position." The President, he added, stood on his May 22 statement acknowledging the existence of a cover-up but proclaiming his total innocence of involvement. But Warren, like everyone else, knew that Nixon could not stand on it for long; Dean had seen to that.

The Sixth Week (July 9–15, 1973)

Now came the defense. First, there was John Mitchell, the former Attorney General—a shaken man, according to those who had talked with him, who seldom left his Manhattan apartment, who was dipping more and more frequently into the oversized bottle of Dewar's he kept there, who felt nothing but scorn for the young men who had been parading through the hearing room, proclaiming their newfound understanding of what they had done wrong. Alternately scornful, impatient and exasperated, Mitchell clung steadfastly through 2½ days of testimony to his insistence that he had never authorized the Watergate break-in; he conceded that he had attended the March 30 meeting in Florida, where Magruder said Mitchell had "signed off" on the wiretapping scheme, but he said he had reacted with some such language as "We don't need this. I'm tired of hearing it. Out." With equal determination, he maintained that he had deliberately withheld information from President Nixon about the burglary and cover-up in order to guarantee the President's re-election. The President, he said, never asked for information. Whatever his obligations as an attorney, a former Attorney General and a trusted confidant of the President to report the facts and to uphold the law, Mitchell said, "four more years" was more important. Talmadge asked whether he was not putting "the expediency of the election" above principle. Mitchell replied: "In my mind, the re-election of Richard Nixon, compared to what was available on the other side, was so much more important that, yes, I would put it just that way."

In contrast to the effusive Dean, Mitchell's testimony was terse and carefully limited, the performance of a cautious lawyer. At one point, he recalled that he had not told lawyers in a civil suit the facts because they had failed to ask precisely the right questions; he seemed perfectly willing to do the same thing with the Senators. In many ways, furthermore, the dour old Wall Street lawyer seemed to be constructing his testimony so as to limit his legal liability. Certainly, said Mitchell, he had taken part in the cover-up, but the perpetrators of the "design not to have the stories come out"—including Haldeman and Ehrlichman—had acted independently of each other. Lawyers read that as a denial of any conspiracy. Yes, he had heard Jeb Magruder outlining his planned perjury, but he had not ordered it. Lawyers read that as a denial of subornation of perjury.

By the second day, the gentleness with which the Senators and staff members had treated Mitchell (as well as most earlier witnesses) began to evaporate. Inouye asked, for instance: "To what length are you now willing to go to deceive in an effort to avoid further implication of the President in the activities under investigation by this panel? More specifically, are you willing to lie to protect the President?" Mitchell, his familiar, football-shaped face slightly flushed, ended the day by muttering into the microphone, "It's a great trial being conducted up here, isn't it?" Things only got worse on Thursday. Sam Dash, the usually mild chief counsel, who had been handling more of the questioning than anyone else, all but accused Mitchell of lying in an earlier deposition, then told him bluntly that in order to believe his testimony the committee would have to disbelieve six previous witnesses. Mitchell said that he disagreed violently with Dash's reading of the transcript. He left the committee with the impression that he would play his role much the same way if given another chance—"I still believe," he said, "that the most important thing to this country was the

re-election of Richard Nixon"—and he did all he could
to shoot down Magruder's and Dean's testimony. Of Magruder's assertion that Mitchell had seen the results of
the first, faulty Watergate taps on June 9, and, indeed,
had reacted angrily enough to prompt the June 17 re-
entry to place more effective bugs, Mitchell declared: "It
happens to be a palpable, damnable lie."

Mitchell was followed by Richard A. Moore, a White
House special counsel on whom Mr. Nixon's defenders
had counted to refute much of Dean's testimony about
cover-up planning from February, 1973, on. A white-
haired, somewhat rumpled, bulky and courtly man wholly
unlike most of the White House staff members in style
and appearance, he had been a confidant—a "father
figure," as Dean described him—to many of the younger
aides. Moore set out at once to disprove Dean's assertion
that Nixon had known of the cover-up as early as Sept.
15, 1972, the date of the first key Nixon-Dean meeting. He said that, in fact, Dean had told him on March
20 that to his knowledge no one had yet informed the
President of the cover-up. "Nothing said in my meetings
with Dean or my meetings with the President," Moore continued, "suggests in any way that before March 21 the
President had known, or that Dean believed he had known,
of any involvement of White House personnel in the
bugging or cover-up."
But Moore faltered badly under the aggressive—some
thought cruel—cross-examination of Terry Lenzner, a
deputy counsel who had once been one of the stars of the
antipoverty program. Moore mumbled, became confused,
contradicted himself, forgot details. It was not an im-
pressive performance from a man who had always been
admired for his candor, even by those who liked very
few people at the White House. At one point, Moore
even blurted out, under close questioning about a previous
response, "I'll let the answer stand, whatever it is."
Ultimately, he admitted, like so many other witnesses,
that his judgment had probably been bad, that he should
have warned the President earlier, but his interrogators
were unable to resolve the basic contradictions between
his story and Dean's. And at least some of those watch-

ing in the caucus room thought that Moore and Mitchell had slightly strengthened the President's case with their testimony—if only because they showed that the Administration and its friends had not been so rattled as to preclude a coherent defense. Moore also provided one other thing—one of the few first-hand accounts of Nixon's state of mind vis-à-vis Watergate, while the bombs of accusation were falling about him. "I racked my brain, I have searched my mind," the President was quoted as having said at a private meeting with Moore. "Were there any clues I should have seen that should have tipped me off?" Maybe there were such indications, he added, and maybe he should have noticed them and paid them heed.

But the attention of the nation was beginning to swing away from what was said in the hearing room. Mitchell's rebuttal, the rebuttals of Haldeman and Ehrlichman still to come, suddenly looked less important. It was Dean vs. Nixon in the main event, and the White House was fighting with all the weapons it had. The Administration and the Watergate committee slowly, almost ritualistically, moved toward a constitutional confrontation. In a statement from San Clemente, the White House announced that Nixon would not testify, directly or indirectly, before the committee, and that the committee would be given no documents that related to the President's performance of official duties. For him to act otherwise, Nixon said, would be to abuse the doctrine of separation of powers as conceived by the founding fathers. The committee, increasingly frustrated by its inability to resolve contradictions on the question of Presidential involvement in the testimony it had taken and expected to take from the remaining witnesses on its list, conceded at once that it had no means of compelling Nixon to testify. But it chose to fight on the question of the papers, not only because its lawyers considered their constitutional position stronger, but also because they thought access to the documents essential to effective cross-examination of future witnesses. The committee's position was surprisingly unanimous; even Gurney said on a television broadcast that "we ought to be able to get any documents that have a direct bearing on this Watergate affair." To that end,

Baker, ever the compromiser, drafted a letter to the President, asking for a meeting with Nixon to search for ways to avoid "the very grave possibility of a fundamental constitutional confrontation." Nixon agreed, in a telephone conversation with Ervin, to meet with the chairman, but Warren described the President's concession as no more than an act of "simple courtesy." He insisted that "there will be no change" in policy—a comment which Ervin, choosing to read the auguries favorably, dismissed as the utterance of "a press agent." Ervin used a stick as well as a carrot, predicting that the committee would subpoena the documents if Nixon indeed proved obdurate. He had a legal maxim, as usual, to express the belief of many politicians, Republican and Democratic, that if Nixon continued to hold out he would seem to be guilty even if he were not. "Every man," said the chairman, "is presumed to intend the natural consequences of his acts." If Nixon refused to release the papers, in other words, the committee's search for the truth would be hampered, and rational men would assume that that was what he intended all along. With the struggle at this peak of intensity, there was an abrupt pause, a haphazard stroke of melodrama: Nixon was taken to the Bethesda Naval Hospital with viral pneumonia, there to remain for a week until he recovered.

The Tapes

It came out by accident. Donald Sanders, the deputy minority counsel for the Watergate committee, was quizzing Alexander P. Butterfield, a former White House operations man, in a private session. Recalling reports that some Presidential aides had taped conversations, and Dean's suspicions that Nixon had done likewise, Sanders routinely asked Butterfield whether he had reason to believe that recordings of White House Watergate discussions had been made. Out tumbled a tale, not of amateurish, occasional tapings, but of a highly sophisticated, highly secret electronic system that permitted substantially all of the meetings and telephone conversations of the President himself to be recorded, from the spring of 1971 on. On Monday, July 16, Butterfield repeated the story in public.

The existence of the tapes made inevitable the test of wills and constitutional interpretation that had already seemed probable, and the epic battle was joined during the next two weeks.

It could not have been otherwise. The tapes may be the only tool available to the Senators in attempting to determine the crucial point: Was Dean telling the truth about his series of meetings with the President? No other direct testimony implicated Nixon, and none that was still to come would do so. "We now know there were tape recordings of those meetings," said Sam Dash. "I don't have to draw the line underneath and add it up." No, he didn't. Clearly, the tapes had the potential either to clear the President, or, if they proved that Dean was telling the truth, to impeach him.

So the committee listened with more than usual attentiveness as Butterfield, a lean, 47-year-old former fighter pilot who now heads the Federal Aviation Administration, told about the taping system. According to his account, the President ordered the installation of listening devices to record either meetings or phone conversations or both at the White House, the Executive Office Building and the Presidential retreat at Camp David, Md. Did the President ever ask that the system be turned off, lest he be distracted? "No, sir," said Butterfield, "as a matter of fact, the President seemed to be totally, really oblivious." As for himself, he hoped that he had not "given away something that the President planned to use at a later date in support of his position." The White House quickly confirmed the outlines of Butterfield's testimony, adding that the system was "similar to that employed by the last Administration." That brought superheated denials from old Kennedy and Johnson hands—Joseph A. Califano Jr. called it "a damned outrageous smear on a dead President"—but later, it developed that there had indeed been some taping in the preceding years, though apparently not on so systematic a basis or so large a scale.

Butterfield said the tapes were made "to preserve the history of the Presidency," but there were troublesome questions about their usefulness for that purpose or for the Senate's purposes. For one: How could any person act or speak spontaneously if he could always see, in his mind's eye, the historian of the 22d century poring over every supposedly private word? Moreover, by careful splicing, dubbing and re-recording, experts said, material could be added in such a way that detection of additions would be difficult. The committee was well aware of these problems, but it had no alternative; so it sent to the White House a formal request for the tapes. One from Cox followed shortly. Nixon was in no mood for compromise. Leaving Bethesda on Friday, the 20th, still weak but recovered from pneumonia, the President went to the White House to tell his staff that suggestions that he resign were "poppycock." "Let others wallow in Watergate," he snapped, "we are going to do our job." Those of his aides with good political antennae, such as Melvin R. Laird, pressed Nixon to give up the tapes. Unless he did, they argued, he would drive the public to the conclusion that he had something to hide—a conclusion that 71 per cent of them, according to George Gallup, had already reached. But the President felt surrounded; he told friends that the committee was out to get him.

Four forces collided the next week, when Nixon returned from two days of brooding at Camp David in the Catoctin Mountains: the President, unwilling to release, even under subpoena, the crucial tapes and certain documents as well; the Watergate committee; the special prosecutor, Archibald Cox (both of these wanted the documents for the light they might shed on malfeasance within the Administration); and finally the courts, which must adjudicate the claims and privileges put forward by the parties. It was a momentous battle. However complex and submerged in legal jargon, what was unfolding in Washington would be remembered by future generations as the current one remembers Dred Scott and Marbury v. Madison.

The President took his stand behind the doctrine of "the separation of powers"—that American inheritance from Locke and Montesquieu—and delivered a hard "no," not only to Sam Ervin but to Cox as well. The tapes "are entirely consistent with what I know to be the truth and what I have stated to be the truth," he argued, adding a curious postscript: "However, as in any verbatim recordings of informal conversations, they contain comments that persons with different perspective and motivations would inevitably interpret in different ways." For that, Ervin supplied a blunt translation: the President was saying that the tapes "sustain his position" of noninvolvement, but "he's not going to let anybody else hear them for fear they might draw a different conclusion." The committee unanimously voted two subpoenas—one seeking the Dean tapes; the other, documents.

The Ervin committee's request raised obvious seperation-of-powers questions, but Cox served at the President's pleasure, as a member of the same governmental branch. Not relevant, replied Nixon, rejecting Cox's request in a letter written by Charles Alan Wright, the lanky, brilliant constitutional conservative from the University of Texas who had been hired to represent the President. The materials requested would eventually be used in the courts, the judicial branch, and *that* raised separation-of-powers problems. It was "for the President, and only for the President" to decide whether the tapes should be released, wrote Wright; he had decided no, so they would be kept confidential. The letter was written almost in the tone of a law professor lecturing a slow-witted student, which Cox, a professor at Harvard and a former Solicitor General, decidedly is not. To some, it seemed like an invitation to resign. Cox did not resign; instead, he issued a subpoena and asserted that Nixon's position was "without legal foundation."

Nixon was running the risk of a total collapse in public support. He was running the larger risk that the Congress, if ultimately frustrated in its effort to get the tapes, would turn to impeachment as the only means of obtaining them. And he was running the risk of letting some or all of the probable defendants in the next round of Watergate trials go free; under the rule enunciated in the Brady case (1963), the Government must allow defendants access to all the evidence in its possession that might tend to exonerate them. But Nixon decided that he must fight the subpoenas.

The President's case was set out in letters delivered on Thursday, July 29, to Judge Sirica, who had presided over the first Watergate trial, and to Ervin. Ervin read the letter out in the hearing room. Nixon would not supply Presidential papers, a category which he applied to all the tapes and some of the documents. The President offered, however, to make public non-Presidential documents that were specifically requested. Nonsense, replied Ervin; how could the committee ask for what it couldn't identify? (The witnesses had not been able to make even the briefest notes from their files, because of White House restrictions, so they had been unable to steer the committee toward documentary evidence.) The President could have complied with the subpoenas, said Ervin, his voice edged with irony, "and the Constitution would not collapse, and the heavens would not fall, but the committee might be aided by the President in determining the truth of his involvement." Then, still in public, with John Ehrlichman waiting on the witness stand, the committee voted unanimously to go to court—in the simplest terms, to sue the President. No congressional committee had ever done that before.

Six blocks to the west, Judge Sirica mounted to the bench, grave as ever, to read the letter to *him*. Citing an obscure advisory opinion by Attorney General James Speed in 1865, Nixon in effect argued that the Cox subpoena was null and void because the President could not be required to act by another branch of government. (That seemed to suggest that even the Supreme Court could not force Nixon to surrender the tapes, but at the White House, Gerry Warren later said that "the President, just as in any other matter, would abide be a definitive decision of the Supreme Court." But what did "definitive" mean? And would the President defy an undefinitive order? No comment.) Cox argued that he had "an enforceable right to access to the documents and objects sought," and Sirica signed an order requiring Richard M. Nixon to show cause by August 7 why the tapes "should not be produced."

And so the case began its journey through the courts— through the welter of appearances and hearings and decisions and appeals to Judge Sirica (who ordered Nixon to allow him to listen to the tapes and *then* decide whether they should be released) and then to the Court of Appeals (which tried vainly to promote a compromise) and finally, almost certainly to the Supreme Court.

The Seventh Week (July 16–22, 1973)

While the controversy swirled about the tapes, the committee pressed on with a series of witnesses whose testimony was minor only because of its timing, coming as it did in the same week as the Butterfield disclosure and between the dramatic charges of Dean and the appearances of Haldeman and Ehrlichman, the closest things to Presidential spokesmen that the committee would hear. Nonetheless, the committee and the television audience were provided with crucial testimony about the cornerstone of the Watergate cover-up, the enormous cash payments to the Watergate defendants. The four men who testified agreed that they did not know who ordered the cover-up, but, for one reason or another, they all participated actively.

Herbert W. Kalmbach, who had been Nixon's personal attorney and had profited enormously from that connection, gaining such clients for his California law firm as United Airlines and Atlantic Richfield, was also an expert in handling covert campaign funds. Tall, athletic-looking, a perfect central-casting vision of a member of the Newport Beach or Palm Beach crowd, he testified that, as early as 1970, he had assembled $400,000 in cash contributions and delivered it in clandestine meetings with men he had never seen before and whose names he still did not know. He now suspected, he told the committee, that the money was used in a vain attempt to defeat Governor George C. Wallace in the 1970 Alabama gubernatorial primary, thereby trying to insure that he would not be a Presidential candidate in 1972. Kalmbach, then, was another of the no-questions-asked Nixon men, men who got the job done, men who could be counted on. It was not a pretty picture that Kalmbach helped to complete—that of a President surrounded by an Attorney General, a White House counsel and a personal attorney, all of whom were quite ready to act unethically and even illegally.

When money was needed for the seven Watergate defendants, Kalmbach was called upon again, this time by Dean, using the editorial we—"We would like to have you raise funds for the defense . . ." By September of 1972, Kalmbach testified, he raised nearly a quarter of a million dollars. He assumed, he said, that the money was simply for legal fees and family support for the men facing trial as a result of the Watergate break-in. He thought that the payments were necessary "to discharge what I assumed to be a moral obligation"; to him, that seemed "a very human thing to do." Kalmbach never learned exactly who incurred that moral obligation, or in exactly what circumstances, since he never asked. But, concerned about the "covert nature of this activity," he went to see Ehrlichman, seeking reassurances as to "the propriety of this assignment." Under questioning by Sam Dash, he described their meeting of July 26, 1972:

KALMBACH: I said, John, I am looking right into your eyes. I said, I know you know that my family and my reputation mean everything to me, and it is just absolutely necessary, John, that you tell me, first, that John Dean has the authority to direct me in this assignment, that it is a proper assignment, and that I am to go forward with it.

DASH: And did he look at you in the eyes?

KALMBACH: Yes, he did.

DASH: What did he say to you?

KALMBACH: He said, Herb, John Dean does have the authority. It is proper, and you are to go forward.

Now, Kalmbach testified, he realized that the money was used to buy the silence of the Watergate defendants and that he had committed "an improper, illegal act." Asked how he felt, Kalmbach replied, "As if I had been kicked in the stomach." More in sorrow than in anger, Sam Ervin told him: "Some people, unfortunately, are lightning bugs; they carry their illumination behind them."

While Kalmbach had been crisscrossing the country, meeting secretly in public parks, automobiles and hotel rooms, talking in code words over pay telephones in a frenzy of money-raising, the stuff had been delivered by Tony Ulasewicz, his bagman—the wise-cracking ex-cop who had convulsed the committee back in May. Ulasewicz, who bears a striking resemblance in profile to Alfred

Hitchcock, outlined in details befitting a mystery movie the procedures by which he channeled $220,000 to the Watergate conspirators or their lawyers between June and September, 1972. He said that he carried sums as large as $75,000 in paper sacks because they were less conspicuous and therefore more secure than briefcases, that he always used public telephones to get or give instructions and that he became so burdened with coins for the calls that he wore a bus driver's coin changer. Most of the time, he said, he left his "cookies"—the payoffs—in packets of $100 bills in public lockers or on ledges in hotel lobbies where he could observe the pickups. But in August, Ulasewicz told the committee, he concluded that "something here is not kosher" and "retired" from the case.

But the Watergate defendants were seeking more and more money, so Ulasewicz's chores fell to Fredrick C. LaRue, a Mississippian who had worked for his close friend, Mitchell, at the re-election committee. LaRue, who wears thick glasses and conventional suits, was a low-key witness, in sharp contrast to the flamboyant Tony U. But he told a similar story: how he had assembled from campaign funds and a secret White House kitty of $350,000 left over from the 1968 campaign, $230,000 that he then dispatched to the defendants by a messenger service. More important, LaRue testified on the role of Mitchell in planning and then covering up the break-in itself. On the much-disputed March 30 meeting at Key Biscayne, he took the middle ground. Magruder had said that Mitchell "signed off" (approved) the eavesdropping plan at the meeting, albeit reluctantly. Mitchell had insisted that he rejected it out of hand. To the best of *his* recollection, said LaRue, who was at the meeting, Mitchell said something to the effect that "well, this is not something that will have to be decided at this meeting." But LaRue, who had pleaded guilty several days before to a one-count charge of conspiracy to obstruct justice, also said that Mitchell had told Magruder, at a meeting in Mitchell's apartment two days after the break-in, that "it might be a good idea if Mr. Magruder had a fire." What Mitchell was telling Magruder to destroy were the transcripts of the early Watergate taps, a significant point because Mitchell had claimed never to have seen them. Clearly, LaRue was not the kind of witness that John Mitchell had desperately hoped that he would turn out to be.

Robert C. Mardian, a former Assistant Attorney General and a former official at the re-election committee, was the last of the quartet to testify. He, too, had some bad news for Mitchell. Testifying without apparent emotion, the trim, bald Goldwater conservative said that he had once related to Mitchell Liddy's statement that the electronic eavesdropping scheme had Mitchell's advance approval, and that "Mitchell didn't deny it." Mardian had interviewed Liddy at length only three days after the Watergate break-in and said he had a "pretty vivid" recollection of the conversation. There was one other bombshell in his account of that meeting: Mardian said Liddy gave him the clear impression that Nixon had authorized the burglary of Ellsberg's psychiatrist's office with the help of the C.I.A. Both the President and the C.I.A. had denied any involvement in that episode, which was carried out by Liddy and other White House agents.

The Eighth Week (July 23–29, 1973)

The committee, still preoccupied with the question of the tapes but determined to conclude as quickly as possible so that its members could return to their homes for the annual summer recess, resumed on July 24 with Gordon Strachan, who had given a few hints the preceding Friday about how much Haldeman had known about the break-in. Strachan, yet another of the earnest and faceless young Nixon men, but one of the brightest, had served as Haldeman's liaison man with the re-election committee; he had been the conduit between Mitchell/Magruder on the one hand and Haldeman/Nixon on the other. A strategic position indeed. He said that he never been given anything more than "very general, carefully hedged, characteristically vague" reports by Magruder on the Liddy project, and he contradicted Magruder's report of having shown Strachan the Gemstone report. But he acknowledged that Magruder had called him after the Key Biscayne meeting to report that "a sophisticated political intelligence system

has been approved with a budget of 300 [i.e., $300,000]"
—a vital corroboration of Magruder's testimony. He relayed that report to Haldeman, Strachan said, and was
sure Haldeman had read it because of an internal control
system they had. Strachan had other valuable tidbits: he
said that he had shredded incriminating papers after Haldeman had told him to "make sure our files are clean";
said that he had "confidence in John Dean's ability to state
the facts as he recalls them," and told a piquant little story
about delivering hush money to LaRue, at which time
LaRue donned a pair of gloves before picking up the
money and saying "I never saw you." (This last in December, 1972, while the White House was piously denying
all.) But Strachan's most memorable phrase came in response to a question about what advice he would give to
young people interested in politics. "My advice," he said,
"would be to stay away."

John Ehrlichman had been under attack for weeks when
the moment finally came for him to tell his story; accused
not only by the press but also by many of his former
colleagues in the Nixon Administration, he had been
hounded from office. But there was no sign of despondency
about him as he took the witness stand to follow Strachan,
no sign of the contrition showed by so many of the young
men who had worked for and with him; John Ehrlichman
fought back. Scowling, snapping, pointing his finger at his
interrogators, administering karate chops to the witness
table, he admitted neither illegal acts nor errors of judgment. "I am here to refute very charge of illegal conduct,"
he said, and he was nothing if not combative in his attempt
to do so. A teetotaling Christian Scientist himself, he closed
out the week Friday afternoon by attacking Senators'
drinking habits. Their critics had called Haldeman and
Ehrlichman arrogant in their days of power, and Ehrlichman almost seemed to be making an effort to live up to
the adjective in his eclipse.

Ehrlichman took what had become the standard White
House line in recent weeks: John Dean, he suggested on
almost every page of testimony, had been the sun and the
moon of the Watergate operation and especially of the
cover-up. It was as if Ehrlichman's testimony had been

carefully coordinated with what the President's current aides were saying, and also with what Haldeman was planning to say the following week. Perhaps it had, although there were the usual denials; John J. Wilson, a crusty, reactionary Washington lawyer, was simultaneously Haldeman's lawyer, Ehrlichman's lawyer and an unofficial consultant to Nixon. His limousine, license plate JJW-2, had been spotted outside the White House frequently. At any rate, Ehrlichman asserted that Dean had repeatedly misled him and the President and had frustrated all their efforts to find out the truth. Quite an accomplishment, it seemed to some of the Senators, for a relatively junior staff member. But they could not shake the husky, bushy-browed lawyer, even though they pummeled him with skeptical questions and reminded him that his responses contradicted the sworn testimony of many of the other witnesses.

Ehrlichman said that Dean had lied when he testified that Ehrlichman asked him to "deep six"—throw into the Potomac River—sensitive documents from a White House safe. He said that Dean had lied when he said Ehrlichman had asked Nixon to provide executive clemency for E. Howard Hunt. He denied that he had briefed Mitchell, as Mitchell had testified, on the activities of the plumbers. He swore that the meeting with Kalmbach, where Kalmbach had told of looking him in the eye and seeking assurances about the hush money, had never happened. He insisted that Pat Gray had misunderstood his instructions about another key set of documents; Gray had said that he burned the papers because Ehrlichman had told him that they "should never see the light of day," but Ehrlichman said he had merely given them to Gray for safe-keeping. It was either one of the great examples of stonewalling in the 20th century, or a demonstration of a faulty memory, or an astonishing testament to the mendacity of a lot of other witnesses. Daniel Inouye, the usually circumspect Senator from Hawaii, had no doubt about which of the three explanations was true. After one exchange on Wednesday, he leaned back in his chair and muttered, "What a liar!" To his embarrassment, the remark was picked up by his microphone and broadcast coast to coast.

Then there was the matter of the plumbers, the White House investigative unit formed in 1971 to plug leaks of classified documents. Why, the Senators wanted to know, couldn't the F.B.I have handled the matter? Well, said Ehrlichman, people in the White House had become convinced that J. Edgar Hoover, an admittedly aged and idiosyncratic figure by that time, was not pursuing the F.B.I. investigation of Ellsberg with sufficient vigor. For example, Ehrlichman testified, Hoover would not even permit his agents to interview Ellsberg's father-in-law, Louis Marx, a New York toy manufacturer, because he was an old friend of Hoover's. Like so many of Ehrlichman's assertions, that did not fit with other information. The hard-digging Weicker called Marx and discovered that (1) Hoover and Marx were not friends, having met only once almost 30 years before, and (2) he had, in fact, been interviewed. Unshaken, Ehrlichman replied coolly that that had not been his understanding. So, when Egil Krogh Jr., Ehrlichman's assistant and leader of the plumbers, asked for approval of a covert operation against Ellsberg's psychiatrist, Dr. Lewis Fielding, Ehrlichman initialed his approval and scribbled a note on the margin, "if done under assurances that it is not traceable." A burglary was certainly not what he had in mind, Ehrlichman insisted; despite the fact that he had ordered that this operation be clandestine, he now said he thought the Ellsberg psychiatric files could be obtained by conventional means, such as bribing a nurse.

But even if he had approved the burglary, said the one-time Seattle zoning lawyer, so what? He argued, with the support of his feisty counsel, Wilson, who insisted on joining the discussion, that the burglary—the attempt to pry into Ellsberg's innermost thoughts and secrets—fell "well within the constitutional duty and obligation of the President." Frustrated liberals had often and ill-advisedly accused the Nixon Administration of fascist tactics; now, even to the more moderate, Ehrlichman seemed to be insisting that the welfare of the state overrode very nearly all other considerations, and that the President alone could decide what was necessary for the welfare of the state. It had the sound of 1939 about it.

Talmadge, no liberal, followed up. "If you had thought

that the psychiatrist's profile had been in a lock box in a bank in Washington you would not authorize the entry, would you?" No, said Ehrlichman, but the President could authorize it if, say, there were documents in the bank outlining a nuclear attack against the United States. That was too much for Ervin, who lectured the witness, quoting William Pitt the elder ("The poorest man may in his cottage bid defiance to all the forces of the Crown. It may be frail—its roof may shake—the wind may blow through it—the storm may enter—the rain may enter, but the king of England cannot enter . . ."), a Supreme Court case from the Lincoln era and the Bible to demonstrate his displeasure with the witness. Ehrlichman never budged. He closed with a warning against truth-seekers "whose eyes are clouded by preconception or partisanship"—fairly obviously, a verdict on the committee's performance—and a response to Strachan's advice to young people to stay away from politics. He urged them to come to Washington, but to remain on their guard. "You will encounter a local culture which scoffs at patriotism and family life and morality just as it adulates the opposite. . . . But you will also find in politics and government many great people who know that a pearl of great price is not to be had for the asking and who feel that this country and its heritage are worth the work, the abuse, the struggle and the sacrifices."

The Ninth Week (July 30–Aug. 5, 1973)

The week belonged to Bob Haldeman, the powerful, hard-nosed, exacting number two man of the Nixon Administration. His testimony had long been awaited, because he was closer to the President than any other aide: the first man to see him in the morning, the last man to see him at night, as the saying around Washington had it. But the public he also presumably served saw little of him, and, not surprisingly, came to think of him as a kind of Mephistopheles in a crew cut. After Ehrlichman had had his final moments before the committee, Haldeman took the stand and surprised everyone with his demeanor.

Haldeman was different—from his own reputation as well as from his old colleague. From the moment he began reading his opening statement, it was clear that Haldeman had no intention of emulating Ehrlichman's behavior. His voice was mellow and calm, his style deferential; indeed, it seemed to many that he and Ehrlichman had exchanged personalities for the nonce. Nonetheless, arguing that he and Nixon had been "badly misled" by Dean and others, he identified himself totally with the President. He sounded his tonic note early: "I have full confidence that when the entire truth is known, it will be clear to the American people that President Nixon had no knowledge of or involvement in either the Watergate affair itself or the subsequent effort of a 'cover-up' of the Watergate." But as the questioning unfolded, Haldeman was unable to recall the important details about a large number of key events described by other witnesses. He had no clear memory, for example, of when he first learned of the Watergate burglary (he admitted that that was "incredible"); or of Dean's alleged warning that Liddy was dangerous; or of Strachan's relayed report of the approval of the Liddy bugging scheme ("a three-line item in a rather thick political matters memorandum would not strike my attention"). Perhaps most significant for the Cox and Ervin investigations of the cover-up, Haldeman also professed surprising ignorance of two other matters: the ultimate disposition of a $350,000 cash fund he controlled in the White House, which was in fact used for Watergate payoffs (was he so casual about money when he ran the Los Angeles office of J. Walter Thompson?); and an order to Strachan to make sure their files were "clean." Strachan a minor White House functionary, shredded documents that would otherwise have provided important evidence for the prosecution, and said Haldeman told him to do it.

In his opening statement, Haldeman almost off-handedly pictured the Democrats as having been involved in far more serious political sabotage than the Republicans in 1972, including burning of Republican offices and harassment of candidates' families. Weicker, the Connecticut Republican, who had come to detest the Nixon White House as a betrayal of his party's values, challenged him. He produced a Haldeman memorandum to Dean which appeared to constitute an order that Dean spread a dubious story linking Communists to demonstrations in which Mc-

Govern supporters also participated. The memo seemed to corroborate Dean's comments about the paranoia in the White House and, specifically, in Nixon's and Haldeman's minds.

But nothing Haldeman had to say so astounded the Senators as what he had to say about the Nixon tapes. As the days passed, the members of the committee had come to view the tapes as well-nigh indispensable in their effort to extricate themselves from the Sargasso Sea of contradictions left behind by their witnesses, and when Haldeman said on Monday that he had listened to some of the tapes—in one case long after leaving the White House—they were dumfounded. Although Nixon had insisted that the tapes were being kept under his "sole personal control," Haldeman told of keeping several of them at his house for 48 hours in July while listening to one key recording at the President's request. Haldeman's lawyer, John J. Wilson, read a White House letter asking Haldeman not to discuss what he had heard, but Haldeman seemed suspiciously ready not to comply, and he testified freely on the tapes' contents when the committee instructed him to. He said, among other things, that the tapes of meetings between the President and Dean in September, 1972, and March, 1973, disproved Dean's contentions—central to his argument—that Nixon had had substantial early knowledge of the cover-up. Ervin was openly skeptical; he suspected, he said, that there had been a little "canoodling together" by the White House and Haldeman to leak a laundered version of the tapes while keeping the originals from the committee. Weicker wondered how, in all fairness, the White House could permit Haldeman to hear the tapes while denying that privilege to Dean and other suspects in the case. Inouye wondered how anyone could be sure that the tapes had not been tampered with while in Haldeman's possession, unguarded. And Dash wondered how Nixon could continue to claim that the tapes were confidential when he had permitted Haldeman, a private citizen, to keep some of them in a box on his closet shelf. No real answers were forthcoming from the President's spokesman. Nixon himself had only one oblique comment, astonishing the guests at a gala state dinner by breaking into his toast to deride those who were preoccupied with "murky, small, unimportant, vicious little things." Translation, supplied for the few who needed it by his elder daughter Tricia: Watergate.

With the last superstar having been questioned there was a race for adjournment. Both the Senators and the staff were feeling not only the pressure of Nixon's comments but also the strain of weeks of investigation and interrogation. The weariness showed on Monday when Dash and Thompson, normally the politest of men, wrangled over a line of questioning. On Tuesday, the 72-year-old Wilson, talking to reporters before the television cameras, scornfully described Inouye as "that little Jap"; he later apologized, citing his own weariness. So the questioning was tauter, less rambling than usual when Richard Helms, former Director of the C.I.A., Ambassador to Iran, rival to such as John J. McCloy for the title of Mr. Establishment, appeared on Thursday.

Chain-smoking on the witness stand, Helms told of White House pressure to involve the C.I.A. in the cover-up, sharply contradicting what Haldeman and Ehrlichman had just finished telling the committee. It was a potent rebuttal; it would not be easy in Washington to find anyone who knew Dick Helms and ever doubted his word. Perhaps most significantly, Helms gave testimony indicating the birth of a cover-up only a week after the break-in. Haldeman had testified that at a June 23, 1972, meeting Helms had been unable to assure him that a thorough investigation of the Watergate burglary would not compromise C.I.A. operations in Mexico (some of the money that paid for the burglary, it will be recalled, came from checks laundered in that country). On that basis, Haldeman had said, the investigation was somewhat truncated. The question was never asked, said Helms in reply; Haldeman had made only "an incoherent reference" to a Mexican problem. And Helms swore that the meeting had been opened with a statement that the Watergate scandal threatened serious political problems in the campaign—thus putting all the discussion that followed into a framework of political expediency, not national security. Helms and the two witnesses who briefly followed him— General Robert E. Cushman Jr. and Lieutenant General

Vernon A. Walters, former and current Deputy C.I.A. Director respectively—conceded that the C.I.A. had assisted the White House in ways it probably should not have—supplying spy gear (including a red wig) to E. Howard Hunt; intervening with the F.B.I. to limit the investigation at the behest of Haldeman, and rewriting a memorandum that would have linked Hunt to the White House at an early date. But Helms insisted, banging his hand on the table, that he had ultimately drawn the line, and he intimated that he had been forced out of the C.I.A. precisely because he had done so.

Walters also implicated Dean in the C.I.A. aspect of the case. Twice, said the general, a noted linguist who had once worked personally for Nixon, Dean had tried to involve the agency in the early stages of the cover-up. On June 26, 1972, Walters testified, Dean had suggested that the C.I.A. take the blame for the break-in. Walters said that he had replied: "Mr. Dean, any attempt to involve the agency in the stifling of this affair would be a disaster. It would destroy the credibility of the agency with the Congress, with the nation . . . I am quite prepared to resign before I do anything that will implicate the agency in this matter." But the next day Dean was back, vainly asking Walters whether the C.I.A. could "go bail or pay the salaries of these defendants while they are in jail."

The Tenth Week (Aug. 6–7, 1973)

Pat Gray, who led off the final week of testimony in the first phase of the hearings, was in a way that is difficult to analyze the saddest and one of the most likable men in the whole parade of accused evil-doers. He had resigned in disgrace as Acting Director of the F.B.I. in April, and now he looked markedly older than he had six months before. He had soldiered along with the others, but somehow he was different; perhaps it was his essential humility, perhaps his contrition seemed less fabricated for the cameras, perhaps the fact that he was older and therefore virtually precluded from a fresh start.

He had conceded in his opening statement on Friday of the preceding week that he had burned documents relating to the investigation because Dean and Ehrlichman

had given them to him with "the clear implication" that
they should be destroyed. He had said that before; but
this time, he admitted that he had read some of them
before throwing them onto a post-Christmas bonfire. He
described this action as a "grievous misjudgment," spoke
of his "shame" at having carried out "a mere political
chore," and said that he would "carry the burden of that
act with me always." And he confirmed that he had told
the President on July 6, 1972, that "people on your staff
are trying to mortally wound you by using the F.B.I. and
the C.I.A."—a clear warning, from a man Nixon professed
to admire, almost nine months before the President concluded, by his own subsequent account, that something
was amiss. Talmadge asked: "Do you think a reasonable
and prudent man, on the basis of the warning you gave
him at that time, would have been alerted to the fact that
his staff was engaged in something improper, unlawful and
illegal?" Gray: "I do, because, frankly, I expected the
President to ask me some questions." No questions were
ever asked, Gray testified, and in keeping with his 26
years in the Navy—with its tradition of "aye, aye, sir"—
he pressed no further. Ervin, his fertile brain still ticking
over despite his admitted weariness, recalled "the old
ancient adages which say there is none so blind as he who
will not see and none so deaf as him who will not hear."
There was one other fascinating item, which seemed to
hark back to Dean's feeling that, as the cover-up came
unraveled, the President was talking not to him but to the
public record—that he was, in effect, documenting his
defense. On March 23, 1973, Gray said, Nixon told him,
"Pat remember, I told you to conduct a thorough investigation." He said it gave him "an eerie feeling." Gray
added, under questioning by Inouye: "I thought he was
trying to put that on the record, so to speak . . . [although]
I didn't know that these conversations were being taped."

The concluding witnesses were the two men who had
been charged with the prosecution—Richard G. Kleindienst, the former Attorney General, and Henry E. Petersen,
the Assistant Attorney General in charge of the Criminal
Division. They told the committee that they had obtained
the first "credible" evidence implicating senior White

House and re-election committee officials (but not the President) at a pre-dawn meeting on April 15 at Klein-dienst's home. They said that they had briefed Nixon that same Sunday afternoon, Kleindienst reciting emotionally from notes scribbled on his wife's stationery and Petersen self-conscious in sneakers and a dirty T-shirt. The two men testified that they had told the President—based on private allegations by Magruder and Dean—that Magruder, Dean, Haldeman, Ehrlichman, Mitchell, LaRue and Mardian had taken part either in planning or covering up the Watergate operation. Kleindienst recalled Nixon as having been "dumfounded"; Petersen remarked upon the President's calm.

Petersen, while accepting the broad White House thesis that the truth had been kept from Nixon until March or April, stated bluntly that it had taken "longer than I would've liked" for Nixon to drop the suspects from his staff. At one point, the raspy-voiced, crusty prosecutor declared, he warned Nixon that even Petersen's wife—"no left-wing kook"—wondered whether the President was not involved and that if he, Petersen ever obtained any evidence of involvement he would "waltz it over to the House of Representatives" as a basis for impeachment. On April 30, the day Dean, Haldeman and Ehrlichman "resigned," Nixon called Petersen to say, "You can tell your wife that the President has done what needed to be done."

Both men tried hard to convince the committee that they had done their jobs well. Kleindienst commented that "you have to have evidence to indict somebody. We do not put people on the rack and extract the truth out of them. We do not crush their fingernails or beat them over the head." Kleindienst, ruddy, relaxed, a leg draped nonchalantly over the arm of the witness chair, also defended himself for not having reported vague conversations about lenient sentences with Dean and Ehrlichman to Nixon: "It was not my habit to interrogate the President of the United States," he said in another context. For his part Petersen—an extremely engaging witness who reminded at least one observer of Will Rogers—conceded that he had had early suspicions, which he described as "visceral," and attributable to a sensation that "nobody acts innocent" in the Watergate case. For one thing,

Ehrlichman had upbraided him for the conduct of Earl J. Silbert, the chief assistant United States attorney on the case, asserting that Silbert was acting "like a local prosecutor," which was precisely what Silbert was. Nonetheless, Petersen insisted that he had seen nothing hard until April, and he expressed bitterness that the prosecution had been taken from his hands and placed in those of Cox. "We would have broken that case wide open," he said. Some of the Senators, and most of the reporters in the room, were skeptical; what would have been so remarkable about breaking the case open nine months after the fact? Where were the investigators when Carl Bernstein and Robert Woodward, the two young reporters for The Washington Post, were camping on doorsteps in late 1972 and early 1973, thereby producing major breaks in the case? No one asked. Phase one of the hearings was over, unpunctuated by speeches or summaries or the appeals for a finer tomorrow that Senators love so well. After 181 hours of testimony, everyone was confused and worn out.

Afterword

If the hearings had produced a flood of contradictions, they had also produced insights and generated conclusions of considerable value. Among them were the following:

• The root causes of Watergate lay in an abnormal sensitivity to criticism, a morbid fear of dissent and, simultaneously, a passion for political intelligence and an insensitivity to the legal and constitutional restraints on the Presidency on the part of the White House staff, from top to bottom, and on the part of Nixon himself.

• Officials who were presenting themselves to the nation as the apostles of law and order were either consenting to or attempting to cover up, or both, a whole series of illegal and unethical acts. Some (Haldeman, Ehrlichman, Stans) still denied it, but an astonishing number had broken down in the months after McCord became the first to talk (Mitchell, Magruder, Dean, Sloan, Porter, LaRue, Mardian, Strachan, Gray, Kalmbach).

• The President's involvement remained, as Attorney General Richardson put it, an "unsettled question." But at a minimum, Nixon had been shown as a man whose staff lay beyond his control, as a man willing to contort the concept of national security to meet his own narrow political ends and as a man dangerously reluctant to listen to the warnings of friends.

Except for his occasional jibes at the wallowers in Watergate, Nixon remained silent about the charges developed by the committee through the summer. He was damaged by Dean's and Gray's testimony, he was damaged by the controversy over the tapes, he was damaged by what many Americans saw as the inconsistency of his own past explanations. There were other problems: the economy was in bad shape (inflation, dollar crises abroad), and Nixon's remedies did not seem to work; the endless modifications in the explanation of the funding of his San Clemente and Key Biscayne houses bespoke the same instinct to conceal as Watergate (it was finally revealed after months of backing and filling that the Government had spent $10 million in improvements and security on the two properties, and that Nixon had bought the San Clemente estate with loans from his friend Robert H. Abplanalp, the aerosol tycoon). In mid-August, Gallup reported that only 31 per cent of the country's adult population approved of the President's handling of his job—a stunning decline from the total of 68 per cent only seven months before. Few wanted him impeached, the polls indicated; fewer still believed him. He and the nation were on dead center.

The counterattack began on the night of Wednesday, Aug. 15, when the President sat down before the television cameras to explain himself to the American people. It was his major effort to win back enough confidence to enable him to govern—and it was a disaster. His 30-minute speech, and an accompanying White Paper, answered none of the questions that had accumulated over the summer; instead, they constituted yet another general denial of wrongdoing, yet another plea to be believed on faith, yet another attack on those who persisted in believing that Watergate must be thoroughly aired before the country could move on. "We have reached a point at which a continued, backward-looking obsession with Watergate is causing this nation to neglect matters of far greater importance to all of the American people," he said.

By Nixon standards, the speech was relatively free of emotionalism and self-pity, but its central theme was a charade: he kept appealing to the nation to let the courts handle things, yet he himself was grossly handicapping the legal system by withholding key evidence. The professionals immediately concluded that the speech had been a flop—like all Nixon's others on the subject—and the public agreed, if a series of special polls were to be believed. Nixon's mood darkened, and he seemed to lose control. Stopping off in New Orleans en route to California, he brusquely grabbed Press Secretary Ziegler and shoved him at a group of trailing reporters, while the cameras rolled. Moments later, he gave a speech to a veterans' group that seemed to suggest that he was on the verge of a breakdown—not the substance of the speech, but his manner of delivering it. He paced about, gesturing broadly and woodenly; he stumbled; he grinned strangely. He looked, as someone said, like Ed Sullivan on speed.

But when he appeared on the lawn at San Clemente two days later for his first news conference in five months, he had reasserted control, even if there was a nervous flutter in his voice. In the face of some of the most aggressive questioning ever inflicted on a President (had he not violated his oath of office, and should he not therefore be impeached?), Nixon stood his ground. "I shall not resign," he said; and he showed that he was still the same old Nixon of the enemies list, blaming "people who do not accept the mandate of 1972, who do not want the foreign-policy leadership that I want to give, who do not want to cut down the size of government bureaucracy that burdens us so greatly" for keeping Watergate alive. (That wasn't much of a description of Sam Ervin, or of Barry Goldwater, either.) Most important, he finally dealt with some specifics. Yes, he said, he had told Dean that $1 million *could* be raised for the Watergate defendants, but he said that he had added that the defendants would want executive clemency and that could not be granted, so the plan wouldn't work. Yes, Pat Gray had called and warned him (he was not clear whether Gray had used the words "mortally wound"), but he had told Gray to press on with the investigation, and he meant it. His answers needed following up, cross-checking and elaboration, but at least they were something, and there seemed a mood of relief in the country and in the press corps when the news conference was over. Why in the world, people wondered, hadn't he done it weeks before?

In one sense, Nixon's words fell onto fertile ground. The long first phase of the hearings had seemed like enough to many Americans, although they applauded what Ervin and his colleagues had been able to bring out. Or at least that was the report brought back by the members of Congress returning from their holidays across the nation, and it had an immediate effect. The Senators on the committee were reluctant to risk a backlash, they had developed real confidence in Cox's ability to pursue the case to its conclusion and their own investigators had turned up relatively little new material in the areas of the next two phases of the hearings—financing and "dirty tricks." So the committee voted, in mid-September, to allot only 18 days to the two final phases, less than half what they had given to phase one. Ervin said that he and his colleagues would hear only "very highly revelant witnesses" and would attempt only to sketch a "broad outline" of the situation before retiring to write their report.

All hands denied, of course, that the committee was responding to Nixon's pressure. But there was no denying that there had been a subtle shift in the political landscape. Despite the new problems posed by a kickback investigation of Vice President Agnew, the seemingly indestructible Nixon was staging what must have been the 3,242d rally of his long political career. Watergate did not go away; indeed, there were continuing sensations, including the indictment of Ehrlichman and three of the plumbers by a Los Angeles grand jury in the burglary of Ellsberg's psychiatrist's office. Yet the White House was beginning to function again—and to function, at least for the moment, in a spirit of greater openness that was startling. A bit ineptly at first, but with evident determination, Nixon began seeking a new working relationship with Congress. He even felt steady enough to concede that confidence in his leadership had been badly shaken. His prescription: maintaining his own poise and "doing something." He looked, as the committee prepared to resume its deliberations, as if he were going to survive, albeit in a weakened condition, until the end of his second term. He wouldn't resign, the nation and the Congress were unwilling to impeach him and public attention was coming to focus on other matters, particularly the economy. The tapes remained the one bomb with a burning fuse. Impeachment would again be a possibility if Nixon refused a Supreme Court order to hand them over to Ervin and Cox. And impeachment might be a possibility if he turned them over and they bore out the charges of John W. Dean. For all their complexity, the hearings had left behind that one searing question: Who's telling the truth—Nixon or Dean?

CHRONOLOGY OF WATERGATE-RELATED EVENTS

By Linda Amster

This chronology, based on news reports and testimony given in Watergate-related congressional and judicial proceedings, reconstructs major incidents leading to the June 17, 1972 break-in at the Democratic National Committee headquarters and the cover-up that subsequently evolved. Inconsistencies within the chronology result from the various participants' conflicting versions of events that occurred. In keeping with the policy of the Senate Select Committee on Presidential Campaign Activities, this chronology is concerned only with those incidents of 1972 campaign sabotage and financing which relate directly to the Watergate affair as they were discussed in the first phase of the hearings.

1969

Jan. 20. Richard M. Nixon is inaugurated as the 37th President of the United States.

June 13. Mitchell claims that Presidential powers permit wiretapping, without court supervision or regard to the Fourth Amendment, of any domestic group "which seeks to attack and subvert the Government by unlawful means."

1970

June 5. At a meeting in the Oval Office of the White House attended by Hoover (F.B.I.), Helms (C.I.A.), Bennett (D.I.A.) and Gayler (N.S.A.), President Nixon establishes an interagency committee to formulate plans for strengthened domestic intelligence operations. Hoover is appointed head of the committee.

June 25. Interagency committee submits a 43-page report (Huston plan) to President Nixon, recommending surreptitious entry, covert mail coverage and other activities it warns are "clearly illegal."

July 23. President Nixon approves the recommendations of the interagency committee.

July 28. After Hoover protests the July 23 decision, President Nixon retracts his authorization of interagency committee recommendations. Huston later states that the authorization was never formally rescinded.

1971

April 16. In Miami for a reunion of Bay of Pigs veterans, Hunt renews his acquaintanceship with Barker by leaving a note, "If you are the same Barker I once knew, contact me."

June 13. The New York Times begins publishing the Pentagon Papers, an event which causes a "quantum jump" in White House anxiety about leaks of classified information. Within a week President Nixon authorizes a White House secret special investigations unit to "stop security leaks and to investigate other sensitive security matters." Known as the plumbers unit, the team is supervised by Ehrlichman, headed by Krogh, and includes Liddy, Hunt and Young.

June 28. Ellsberg is indicted on two counts: theft of Government property and unauthorized possession of "documents and writings related to the national defense," in connection with the release of the Pentagon Papers.

July 1. Young leaves the National Security Council to join the White House staff.

July 1. A transcript of a Colson-Hunt telephone call on this day reveals that Hunt replied affirmatively when Colson asked whether "we should go down the line to nail the guy [Dr. Ellsberg] cold."

July 2. Colson sends Haldeman a transcript of his July 1 phone call with Hunt. A covering memo says, "I think it would be worth your time to meet him. . . . Needless to say, I did not even approach what we had been talking about, but merely sounded out his ideas." Colson later asserts that, on the basis of the transcript, Haldeman directed him to put Hunt in touch with Ehrlichman, and "if Ehrlichman likes him, go ahead and hire him."

July 6. Hunt is hired as a $100-a-day consultant assigned to Colson's staff in the White House.

July 7. At Colson's request, Ehrlichman sets up liaison between Hunt and Cushman, the Deputy Director of the C.I.A. Ehrlichman later denies this, but Cushman produces a C.I.A. memo corroborating his version.

July 19. Krogh recommends, and Ehrlichman hires, Liddy for the staff of the Domestic Council.

July 20. Two F.B.I. agents visit Dr. Fielding, Ellsberg's psychiatrist. He refuses to discuss his patient.

July 22. Hunt visits Cushman at C.I.A. headquarters and the next day is provided with a wig, glasses, a speech-alteration device and identification in the name of Edward Joseph Warren.

July 26. Dr. Fielding again tells the F.B.I. he will not discuss Ellsberg.

August. Hunt shifts to plumbers unit, although still on Colson's staff.

Aug. 3. Hoover writes Krogh of the F.B.I.'s efforts and willingness to investigate the Pentagon Papers. Ehrlichman later testifies that this was only a "bureaucratic device," intended to give the appearance of action by the F.B.I.

Aug. 11. Ehrlichman approves a memo sent him by Krogh and Young, recommending "a covert operation" to obtain Ellsberg's psychiatric files, "if done under your assurance that it is not traceable."

Aug. 15. A telephone with a White House number is installed in Hunt's office in the Executive Office Building of the White House complex.

Aug. 25. Hunt and Liddy, authorized by Krogh, fly to Los Angeles and perform surveillance on Dr. Fielding's office. They conclude that a burglary can be accomplished.

Aug. 26. Young writes Ehrlichman that covert operations against Ellsberg will be part of a larger scheme to "slowly develop a very negative picture around the whole Pentagon study affair . . . and then to identify Ellsberg's associates and supporters on the New Left with this negative image. . . . If the present Hunt/Liddy project No. 1 is successful, it will be absolutely essential to have an overall game plan developed for its use in conjunction with the congressional investigation."

Aug. 27. At 6 A.M. at Dulles Airport, Hunt gives to his C.I.A. contact film he wants processed immediately. The C.I.A. later maintains that aid to Hunt was terminated at this time because his requests seemed to involve clandestine domestic operations and to supersede their original agreement, notification being made by phone from Cushman to Ehrlichman.

Aug. 27. Ehrlichman sends Colson a memo about the "Hunt/Liddy Special Project No. 1," which says, "On the assumption that the proposed undertaking by Hunt and Liddy would be carried out and would be successful, I would appreciate receiving from you by next Wednesday a game plan as to how you believe the material should be used."

Sept. 3-4. A successful break-in is effected at Dr. Fielding's office by Hunt, Liddy, De Diego, Martinez and Barker. De Diego later asserts that they found and filmed the Ellsberg file. Barker says they did not.

Sept. 9. Colson sends Dean the "Priority List" of 20 "political enemies."

Sept. 16. At a news conference, President Nixon says, "I would remind all concerned that the way we got into Vietnam was through . . . the complicity in the murder of Diem." A week later, at Colson's suggestion that Hunt "improve on the record," Hunt begins to splice together fake diplomatic cables implicating officials of the Kennedy Administration in Diem's assassination.

Oct. 1. McCord begins part-time work at the Committee for the Re-election of the President (C.R.P.).

Dec. 1. Liddy leaves the Domestic Council, becomes counsel of C.R.P.

Dec. 12. Magruder later testifies that he and Liddy met for the first time today and that Liddy said he had been promised $1-million for a "broad-gauged intelligence plan"; Magruder replied that if Liddy could document and justify such a budget he would be given a chance to present it to Mitchell.

Dec. 30. The Government indictment against Ellsberg is expanded to 12 criminal charges, including conspiracy and the violation of espionage statutes. Russo is also indicted in connection with the release of the Pentagon Papers.

1972

Jan. 9. McCord becomes full-time security coordinator for C.R.P. and for the Republican National Committee (R.N.C.).

Jan. 27. At a 4 P.M. meeting of Mitchell, Magruder, Liddy and Dean in Mitchell's office, Liddy displays six charts detailing his $1-million plan for what Mitchell later describes as "mugging squads, kidnapping teams, prostitutes to compromise the opposition and electronic surveillance." Mitchell tells Liddy to come up with a more "realistic" plan.

Feb. 4. Mitchell, Dean, Liddy and Magruder meet in Mitchell's office to discuss Liddy's revised espionage proposal, a $500,000 plan focusing on wiretapping and photography. Mitchell puts off final decision. Magruder later says that Mitchell chose the Democratic National Committee (D.N.C.) headquarters at Watergate and other top priority targets for surveillance; Mitchell denies this.

Feb. 4. Mitchell later testifies that from this day until June 15, 1972, he did not see or speak to Liddy (thus disclaiming that he berated Liddy for the results of the May break-in).

Feb. 15. Stans becomes chairman of the Finance Committee to Re-elect the President (F.C.R.P.) and Sloan its treasurer. LaRue joins the C.R.P. staff as chief deputy to Mitchell.

Feb. 21. Gregory, a college student, flies from Utah to Washington, D. C., and meets Hunt, who is using the alias "Ed Warren." Gregory agrees to infiltrate Democratic campaigns for $175 a week.

March 1. Mitchell becomes director of C.R.P.

March 15. Telephone with White House number is removed from Hunt's office in the Executive Office Building.

March 27. Liddy becomes counsel to F.C.R.P. Sedam succeeds him as counsel to C.R.P.

March 29. The White House later states that Hunt's employment was terminated on this date. Clawson states Hunt was fired on June 19.

March 30. At a meeting in Key Biscayne, Fla., Mitchell, LaRue and Magruder discuss Liddy's third espionage proposal. Magruder later says that Mitchell approved the plan and authorized $250,000 for it; Mitchell denies this; LaRue says the decision was tabled.

April 3. Gulf Resources and Chemical Corporation of Houston makes a $100,000 contribution to C.R.P., in violation of Federal laws which prohibit corporations from making political contributions. To safeguard its origin, the money is transferred to the corporate account of a Mexican subsidiary, Compania de Asufre Veracruz SA, which then gives a $100,000 "legal fee" to Manuel Ogarrio, an attorney representing Gulf Resources in Mexico City.

April 4. Ogarrio converts $89,000 of the $100,000 into four checks, all payable to himself and drawn on his account at the Banco Internacional in Mexico City. The checks are for $15,000, $18,000, $24,000 and $32,000.

April 5. Andreas tells Dahlberg (both are Minnesota businessmen) he will contribute $25,000 to the Nixon campaign if the transaction can be conducted through a third party. Dahlberg confers with Stans and agrees to pick the money up in Florida.

April 5. A courier delivers the four Ogarrio checks and $11,000 in cash to the office of W. Liedtke, president of the Pennzoil Corporation in Houston, and head of an ad hoc group of Texas fund raisers for C.R.P. The $100,000 is put in a suitcase containing an additional $600,000 in cash and negotiable securities, flown in a Pennzoil plane to Washington and brought to Sloan's office.

April 7. Sloan later says that on or about this date Liddy told him he would soon want $83,000, the first payment in a $250,000 budget authorized for him, and that Sloan checked with Magruder, who confirmed that Sloan should give Liddy the money; Sloan then checked with Stans, who a few days later reported back that Mitchell said Sloan should follow Magruder's instructions.

April 7. New Federal election campaign law becomes effective, requiring full disclosure of all campaign contributions.

April 9. Dahlberg picks up Andreas's $25,000 contribution at the Indian Creek Country Club in Miami. The General Accounting Office (G.A.O.) later considers that the contribution was "completed" on this day and therefore was subject to post-April 7 campaign finance reporting regulations.

April 10. Dahlberg converts the $25,000 contribution into a cashier's check issued in his name.

April 10. Vesco, under investigation by the S.E.C. for an alleged $224-million mutual fund swindle, gives Stans a $200,-000 campaign contribution.

April 11. Dahlberg gives the $25,000 check to Stans, who gives it to Sloan, who gives it to Liddy.

April 12. According to McCord, Liddy today gave him $65,000 in $100 bills from the $83,000 that Sloan had given him. Liddy tells McCord that Mitchell has approved the operation and wants it to go into effect within 30 days. By June 17, Liddy has given McCord a total of $76,000, of which McCord spends $58,000 on tape recorders, transmitters, antennas, walkie-talkies and other Watergate-related equipment.

April 14. Incorporation papers for McCord Associates are filed with the clerk in Montgomery County, Md.

April 19. Barker deposits the checks totaling $89,000 in his corporate account at the Republic National Bank in Miami, but the teller refuses to accept the unnotarized $25,000 Dahlberg check.

April 20. Barker deposits the $25,000 check in his firm's account after presenting the teller with a falsely notarized statement, signed by himself, certifying that the check has been endorsed in Barker's presence.

May 1. McCord contacts Baldwin, a former F.B.I. agent, and offers him a job as a security guard for C.R.P.

May 2. Hoover, Director of the F.B.I., dies.

May 5. McCord rents room 419 in the name of McCord Associates at the Howard Johnson's Motor Lodge across from the Watergate complex.

May 7. F.C.C. grants McCord temporary licenses for radio transmitters. Walkie-talkies confiscated after the break-in are tuned to frequencies assigned McCord by the F.C.C.

May 15. McCord and Gregory walk briefly through Mc-Govern headquarters in Washington, D. C. McCord wants to plant a bug in Mankiewicz's office, but there is not enough time.

May 22. Barker, Martinez, Gonzalez, De Diego, Pico and Sturgis come to Washington from Miami and register in the Manger Hamilton Hotel. During the next few days they meet with Hunt, Liddy, McCord and Gregory to finalize plans for break-ins at the D.N.C. and at McGovern headquarters. Liddy shoots out a light in an alley near McGovern headquarters.

May 26. Barker's team checks into the Watergate Hotel and is joined by Liddy and Hunt. McCord assigns Baldwin to monitor the D.N.C. from Howard Johnson's, stating that he will plant electronic devices there that night.

May 26. The first D.N.C. break-in attempt fails. Hunt and Gonzalez spend the night hiding from security guards in the Watergate complex, unable to open a door to a staircase leading to D.N.C. offices.

May 26-27. Overnight attempt to break into McGovern headquarters is foiled because a man is standing in front of the door.

May 27. A second break-in attempt at the D.N.C. offices fails. At 11:30 P.M. the six Miamians and McCord successfully carry two suitcases with bugging and photographic material into the Watergate office building, but Gonzalez is unable to pick the lock on the door to the D.N.C. offices.

May 28. In the morning, Gonzalez flies to Miami for new, better lock picks and returns to Washington in the evening.

May 28. Late at night, the third break-in attempt at D.N.C. offices is successfully executed. McCord, Barker, Martinez, Gonzalez and Sturgis enter the premises, while De Diego and Pico stand guard outside. Martinez photographs documents, and McCord plants wiretaps on phones of Oliver and Lawrence O'Brien. Hunt and Liddy direct the operation. They adjourn to Hunt's and Liddy's hotel room for a victory celebration.

May 28. Second attempt to break into McGovern's headquarters fails when Gregory is discovered there late at night.

May 29 or 30. Baldwin begins monitoring the D.N.C. after a two-day delay in picking up the radio band. (McCord finally uses a visual scope and successfully locates Oliver's band; he is unable to pick up Lawrence O'Brien's.) Baldwin begins making transcripts of the conversations and gives daily logs to McCord, who passes them on to Liddy. Mrs. Harmony, Liddy's secretary, transcribes the conversations.

May 29. Barker and his men return to Miami.

June 5. A regular Federal grand jury is empaneled in the District of Columbia. After June 17, it will undertake the investigation of the Watergate break-in.

June 8. Liddy gives Magruder the "Gemstone" transcripts of wiretapped D.N.C. conversations and photographs of D.N.C. documents taken during the break-in.

June 9. Magruder later testifies that on this day he gave Mitchell the Gemstone transcripts and D.N.C. photographs; Mitchell complained there was "no substance to them" and then directed Liddy to correct the faulty tap and get better information. Mitchell calls this allegation a "palpable, damnable lie."

June 10. Barker and Sturgis bring two rolls of 35-mm film to Rich Photos, Inc., in Miami for quick processing. The owner later says each roll showed Lawrence O'Brien's correspondence, held by gloved fingers.

June 12. Baldwin poses as the nephew of a former Democratic National Committee chairman and is given a tour of D.N.C. premises.

June 15. Gregory tells Hunt he is quitting as an undercover agent.

June 16. Barker, Martinez, Sturgis and Gonzalez fly to Washington from Miami and register at the Watergate Hotel, where they are joined by McCord, Liddy and Hunt.

June 17. Second break-in at D.N.C. headquarters is interrupted at 2:30 A.M. McCord, Barker, Sturgis, Gonzalez and Martinez are captured by Washington police and charged with second-degree burglary. Police confiscate their cameras and electronic surveillance equipment and sequenced $100 bills, part of Barker's $89,000 withdrawals from his April deposits.

June 17. Hunt engages attorneys Caddy and Rafferty, who confer with the defendants at the police station at about 10 A.M.

June 17. Baldwin says that at Hunt's direction, Baldwin removes his monitoring equipment from the motel and brings it to McCord's home in Rockville, Md. Hunt testifies he told Baldwin to "take it anywhere but Mr. McCord's home."

June 17. At 8:30 A.M. Liddy calls Magruder in California and reports that McCord and others have been arrested in the D.N.C. break-in. Magruder tells Mitchell, LaRue and Mardian, while Porter stands guard. Magruder testifies that Mitchell ordered Mardian to have Liddy contact Kleindienst about the release of the men. Mardian says this is untrue.

June 17. Liddy and Moore locate Attorney General Kleindienst on the Burning Tree golf course. Liddy asks Kleindienst to effect release of the five suspects. Kleindienst refuses. Liddy goes to C.R.P. headquarters and shreds some files.

June 17. Magruder phones Reisner and instructs him and Odle to collect and remove incriminating files from his office.

June 18. Barker is identified as a wealthy real-estate man with important G.O.P. links in Florida. McCord's association with C.R.P. and the R.N.C. is disclosed. Mitchell issues a statement without mentioning McCord by name: "This man and the other people involved were not operating either on our behalf or with our consent."

June 18. Haldeman, in Key Biscayne, Fla., calls Magruder and directs him to return to Washington to take care of any problems relating to the break-in.

June 19. Hunt's name is found in address books of Barker and Martinez. The White House first identifies him as a consultant to Colson but later disclaims that he is on Colson's staff. Clawson later states that Hunt's employment was terminated on this day; White House states it was on March 29.

June 19. From Key Biscayne, Ziegler says he will not comment on a "third-rate burglary attempt" and predicts that "certain elements may try to stretch this beyond what it is."

June 19. It is disclosed that McCord has been fired. Mitchell terms his "apparent actions . . . wholly inconsistent with the principles upon which we are conducting our campaign."

June 19. Dean orders Kehrli, a staff secretary to the President, to retrieve documents from Hunt's White House office. Items are removed, in the presence of the Secret Service, to Kehrli's office.

June 19. Odle sends Magruder a memo marked "Confidential Eyes Only," which lists 14 checks made out to McCord or his company from November to June.

June 19. A meeting is held in Mitchell's Watergate apartment, with Mitchell, Dean, Magruder, Mardian and LaRue in attendance. Magruder and LaRue later testify that Mitchell suggested the destruction of incriminating files at this meeting; Mitchell, Dean and Mardian deny that such destruction was ordered.

June 19. Odle and Reisner return the incriminating files to Magruder. Reisner later testifies that about this time he saw files resembling these in an out-box marked "Destroy" in Magruder's office.

June 19. Justice Department announces it has begun a "full investigation" of the Watergate break-in.

June 19. Dean later testifies that on this day Liddy briefed Ehrlichman on the Watergate break-in; later he, Colson and Ehrlichman decided that Dean should take custody of Hunt's belongings, and Ehrlichman instructed Dean to tell Hunt to leave the country; Dean relayed the message but later rescinded it.

June 19. Rejecting Mitchell's June, 1969, wiretap doctrine, the Supreme Court rules that no domestic group or person can be tapped without a warrant.

June 19. Strachan later says that today Haldeman told him to "make sure our files are clean"; Strachan then destroyed his "political matters" files. Haldeman later denies ordering documents destroyed.

June 19. Dean later testifies that on this or the following day he told Kleindienst of his concern that "this matter could lead directly to the White House"; Petersen was called in and also informed and Dean got the impression that Petersen "realized the problems a wide-open investigation of the White House might create in an election year."

June 19. Gray vetoes giving the F.B.I. summary report of the Watergate investigation to Haldeman and Kleindienst.

June 20. Lawrence O'Brien reveals a D.N.C. $1-million civil suit against C.P.R. and those arrested, charging invasion of privacy and violation of the civil rights of Democrats.

June 20. President Nixon later says that within a few days of the break-in he instructed Ehrlichman and Haldeman "to insure that the investigation . . . not expose either an unrelated covert operation of the C.I.A. or the activities of the White House investigations unit—and to see that this was personally coordinated" between Walters and Gray.

June 20. Ehrlichman later testifies that today he and President Nixon discussed welfare reform and busing, but not the break-in. Under questioning by Dash, Ehrlichman revises this, saying that their discussion also dealt with Government wiretapping and might have touched on Watergate.

June 20. Mitchell later says that today he apologized to President Nixon "for not knowing what the hell had happened and I should have kept a stronger hand on what the people in the committee were doing."

June 20. Dean receives the contents of Hunt's safe and discovers the forged diplomatic cable and files on the Pentagon Papers and Ellsberg. He later testifies that Ehrlichman told him today to shred the documents and "deep six" a briefcase containing electronic equipment.

June 20. On this or the following day, Dean puts in his safe $15,200 from Haldeman's office which apparently had originally been authorized for Colson. He removes part of the money in October for honeymoon expenses, replacing it with a personal check.

June 20. LaRue testifies that at a meeting in his apartment today, Liddy told him and Mardian about the entire Watergate scheme, the burglary of Ellsberg's psychiatrist's office and other activities in which he had been engaged. Mardian says this meeting occurred on June 21.

June 21. Mitchell says that he has undertaken a "precautionary check" of the Watergate break-in, using employes of C.R.P. and private investigators, and is satisfied that there is no connection to C.R.P. or White House officials.

June 21. Mitchell later states that on this or the following day Mardian briefed him on Liddy's role in Watergate and other espionage activities.

June 21. Ehrlichman later testifies that today he called Gray and instructed him to deal directly with Dean on the Watergate investigation.

June 21. According to later testimony, on this or the following day, Helms denied C.I.A. involvement in the Watergate break-in to Gray. At an evening meeting, Gray and Dean discuss scheduling of F.B.I. interviews and arrange for them to be conducted through the Washington field office rather than F.B.I. headquarters. Gray raises the theory of C.I.A. complicity in the break-in, and also informs Dean of the discovery of the Dahlberg and Ogarrio checks.

June 21. Sloan later testifies that about this time Magruder told him he (Sloan) might have to perjure himself about the amount of money disbursed to Liddy, suggesting a range of $75,000–$80,000. Later, before seeing F.B.I. agents, Sloan is given some advice by Mitchell: "When the going gets tough, the tough get going."

June 22. In an impromptu news conference, his first in three months, President Nixon denies any White House involvement in the break-in and says attempted surveillance "has no place whatever in our electoral process or in our governmental process."

June 22. Gray testifies that today Dean informed him that Dean will sit in on F.B.I. interviews of the White House staff. Gray tells Dean there was evidence linking the break-in to C.R.P. At a later meeting, Gray discusses the theory that the break-in might be a C.I.A. operation because of all the former C.I.A. men involved. Gary later testifies to telling

Dean of Helms's denial of C.I.A. involvement and Gray's intention of "pursuing all leads" unless instructed otherwise by the C.I.A.

June 22. The F.B.I. informs Federal prosecutor Silbert that money in Barker's bank account can be traced to C.R.P. checks.

June 22. Gray later testifies before the Senate Judiciary Committee that on this day Dean "probably lied" to F.B.I. agents, saying he did not know if Hunt had an office in the White House complex and would have to check. Dean states he said he would check not on the existence of Hunt's office, but on whether F.B.I. agents could see it.

June 22. In a call to Helen Thomas of U.P.I., Martha Mitchell says she has given her husband an ultimatum to get out of politics. The call is interrupted when the phone is ripped out of the wall by an R.N.C. security guard.

June 23. At the President's request, at 1 P.M. Haldeman and Ehrlichman meet with Walters and Helms. Helms asserts that no C.I.A. operations in Mexico would be jeopardized by an F.B.I. probe, but Haldeman instructs Walters to ask Gray to keep the F.B.I. investigation away from C.I.A.-related matters in Mexico. Walters later says that, from the conversation, he believes it was "implicit" that President Nixon wanted this done.

June 23. Dean later testifies that today he called Gray and told him to see Walters, who would call for an appointment: "He has something to tell you."

June 23. At 2:30 P.M. Walters asks Gray not to press his investigation into Mexico since it might jeopardize C.I.A. activities. Gray says he will "see what he [can] do."

June 23. Gray testifies that he told Dean he would hold off temporarily an F.B.I. interview with Ogarrio, at Dean's request that Gray not expose C.I.A. sources in connection with the $114,000. Gray asserts that the F.B.I. slowed its Mexican inquiry until July 6.

June 23. Silbert discloses Barker's withdrawal of $89,000, deposited in his corporate account in April in the form of four checks drawn on the Banco Internacional in Mexico City.

Barker claims that the checks were part of a real-estate venture that fell through.

June 23. Stans testifies that today he learned for the first time that F.C.R.P. might be linked to the break-in, when La-Rue told him that Dahlberg's campaign contribution was discovered in Barker's bank account.

June 24. Magruder testifies that today he and Mitchell discussed with Stans problems concerning the amount of money that had been disbursed to Liddy. They asked Stans to "try to work with Mr. Sloan to see if Mr. Sloan could be more cooperative." Stans denies this.

June 25. Martha Mitchell phones Helen Thomas and says she is a "political prisoner," and that she is leaving her husband because of "all those dirty things that go on" in the campaign.

June 25. Baldwin agrees to cooperate with the Government in the Watergate break-in case.

June 26. Walters later says that on this day he told Dean that the C.I.A. was not involved in the break-in and refused to give C.I.A. assistance for defendants' bail and salaries.

June 27. Dean gives the F.B.I. the "routine" contents of Hunt's office.

June 27. Gray later states that Dean asked Gray not to interview Dahlberg because of C.I.A. interest in him.

June 27. Gray calls Helms and asks whether Ogarrio or Dahlberg are C.I.A.-connected; Gray requests a meeting for the following day. Helms calls back later to confirm that the C.I.A. has no interest in Dahlberg or Ogarrio. Gray says he will therefore proceed with F.B.I. interviews.

June 28. Gray informs Dean of this afternoon's scheduled meeting with Helms. Gray later testifies that Ehrlichman then called Gray and told him to cancel the meeting because "it isn't necessary." Gray complied.

June 28. Mitchell fires Liddy for refusing to cooperate with the F.B.I.

June 28. Gray meets with Dean and Ehrlichman in Ehrlichmans' office, and Dean gives Gray two incriminating files from Hunt's safe. Dean says they are "political dynamite" and "should never see the light of day." Ehrlichman later says he had no knowledge of the files' contents. Gray first states he had no knowledge of the files' contents and that he destroyed them in an office "burn bag" on July 3, 1972, but then testifies to taking the files home and reading one document—the forged cable—before destroying the files

June 28. A Walters memorandum indicates that today Dean asked Walters's assistance in restricting the F.B.I. probe to the five defendants and away from the names on the $114,000 in checks. When Walters replied that, as Deputy Director of the C.I.A., he had no authority to act independently, Dean then said that Gray's cancellation of today's appointment with Helms might "well be reversed."

June 28. Dean later testifies that he, Mitchell, LaRue and Mardian met in Mitchell's office to discuss "the need for support money in exchange for the silence of the men in jail"; Mitchell later referred Dean to Ehrlichman and Haldeman for arrangements to have Kalmbach raise the money. Mitchell says he was in New York, did not attend this meeting and acquiesced only to support payments, not to hush money.

June 28. Magruder asks Porter to perjure himself by corroborating that $100,000 was issued to Liddy for something "more legitimate-sounding than dirty tricks"—a program to infiltrate radical groups. Porter agrees.

June 28. Mrs. Harmony, at Liddy's request, puts nine stenographic notebooks containing his dictation through a paper shredder.

June 29. Gray later testifies that today, at Dean's request, he gave instructions cancelling an F.B.I. interview with Ogarrio and attempts to interview Dahlberg.

June 29. Stans gives Kalmbach $75,000 after Kalmbach says, "I am here on a special mission on a White House project and I need all the cash I can get." This is the first of approximately $500,000 which ended in the hands of the defendants and their lawyers.

June 29. Kalmbach and Dean meet in Lafayette Park and discuss money for the defendants. Kalmbach says he suggests the establishment of a public committee, but Dean says the funds must be raised in "absolute secrecy." Kalmbach agrees to raise money. The G.A.O. later estimates that during the summer Kalmbach raised $210,000–$230,000.

June 30. Ulasewicz agrees to deliver money to the defendants and their lawyers. Kalmbach gives him the first money, $75,000. Eventually, Ulasewicz clandestinely distributes a total of $219,000.

June 30. Ziegler says there is "no White House involvement in the Watergate incident."

July 1. The F.B.I. begins a nationwide search for Hunt. It is called off on July 7 after Hunt's attorney says he will appear voluntarily.

July 1. Mitchell quits as President Nixon's campaign manager, citing "the one obligation which must come first: the happiness and welfare of my wife and daughter." The President names MacGregor to fill the post, with Malek and Magruder as deputy directors.

July 5. Gray tells Walters that Gray will need written C.I.A. authorization before restricting the F.B.I.'s investigation.

July 5. Sloan agrees to Magruder's request that he corroborate falsified figures on the amount of money Liddy was given.

July 6. Sloan reverses his July 5 decision and tells Magruder that he (Sloan) will not perjure himself about the money given to Liddy.

July 6. At a morning meeting, Walters tells Gray that he cannot put in writing a claim that the F.B.I. Watergate probe will jeopardize C.I.A. operations in Mexico. After receiving Walters's assurance, Gray orders F.B.I. interviews of Ogarrio and Dahlberg. Later, Gray speaks to President Nixon; Gray later testifies he said: "People on your staff are trying to mortally wound you by using the C.I.A. and F.B.I.." President Nixon says that Gray warned, "The matter of Watergate might lead higher," but did not specify possible involvement of White House aides or interference with the C.I.A. or F.B.I.

July 7. Mitchell says he is "baffled" by the motives behind the break-in. "If my own investigation had turned up a link between this committee [C.R.P.] or the White House and the raid, I would have been less inclined to leave. I would have wanted to stick around and clear it up."

July 7. Ulasewicz makes the first in a series of payments to the defendants and their attorneys. His last is Sept. 19.

July 12. Gray tells Walters he has recommended dismissing all those involved in the Watergate break-in; that there has been pressure to prevent the subpoenaing of C.R.P. financial records; that he is prepared to resign over apparent White House attempts to implicate the F.B.I. and C.I.A. in a cover-up. Walters tells Gray of the C.I.A.'s assistance to Hunt in 1971 and assures him that such aid ended by Aug. 31.

July 13. At a private meeting Gray tells Walters of his July 6 conversation with President Nixon. He says he urged the President to "get rid of whoever is involved no matter how high."

July 13. Sloan later says that on this day, after Sloan refused to perjure himself or take the Fifth Amendment, LaRue suggested that he resign.

July 14. Sloan resigns as treasurer of F.C.R.P.

July 20. Dalbey, Gray's chief legal adviser in the F.B.I., sends Gray a memo informing him that all F.B.I. records are "in the custody of the Attorney General and technically may not be released from the department without his consent. . . . The authority and obligation of the F.B.I. are to keep the Attorney General fully informed and to leave the rest to him."

July 21. Gray sends an F.B.I. report to Dean without channeling it through the Attorney General. The report indicates that C.R.P. officials tried to impede the F.B.I. investigation.

July 22. Liddy's name is made public for the first time, when Shumway discloses Liddy's dismissal on June 28.

July 26. Dean requests, and eventually receives from Gray, F.B.I. interview reports of the Watergate break-in investigation.

July 26. Kalmbach later says that on this day Ehrlichman assured him that Dean had authority to instruct Kalmbach to raise funds for the defendants and that it was legal and proper for Kalmbach to do so. Ehrlichman denies this.

July 28. Baldwin appears before the Watergate break-in grand jury.

July 28. Dean goes to Gray's office to pick up copies of F.B.I. agents' interviews related to the Watergate investigation.

July 29. Justice Douglas stays the opening of the Ellsberg-Russo trial in order to allow defense attorneys time to appeal to the Supreme Court their contention that the Government should be required to divulge details of wiretapped conversation.

Aug. 1. The Washington Post reveals that a $25,000 check, given to Stans for the re-election campaign, has been deposited in Barker's bank account.

Aug. 8. Kleindienst later says that on this or the following day Ehrlichman called him to complain that Petersen was harassing Stans; Kleindienst replied that Ehrlichman's actions could leave him open to a charge of obstruction of justice.

Aug. 9. The Washington Post reports Stans's denial that a $25,000 campaign contribution helped to finance the Watergate break-in.

Aug. 10. MacGregor names Liddy as the person who gave Barker Dahlberg's $25,000 check for conversion to cash, but says he does not know why it was done. This is the first public admission that campaign contributions were involved in the Watergate break-in.

Aug. 11. Judge Richey of the U. S. District Court, Washington, denies a C.R.P. request to postpone the Democratic National Committee civil suit until after the election.

Aug. 16. After being coached by Dean, Magruder perjures himself before the grand jury.

Aug. 19. Representative Patman, chairman of the House Banking and Currency Committee, orders a staff investigation of the Watergate break-in and laundered money.

Aug. 22. President Nixon is renominated 1,347 to 1 at the Republican National Convention.

Aug. 23. Democrats begin taking depositions in their civil suit against C.R.P.

Aug. 23. Dahlberg says, in testimony relating to Barker's inpending Florida trial, that he personally gave the $25,000 check to Stans.

Aug. 24. Stans testifies to Florida prosecutors that he does not know how Barker got $114,000 in campaign contributions.

Aug. 25. Representative Patman threatens use of congressional subpoena to obtain an overdue G.A.O. report on campaign financing.

Aug. 26. The G.A.O. releases its report, citing 11 "apparent and possible violations" by F.C.R.P. of the new Federal Election Campaign Act, involving up to $350,000 and including the transfer of $114,000 to Barker's bank account. The G.A.O. refers these matters to the Justice Department and asks it to investigate a possible secret fund.

Aug. 28. Kleindienst promises that the Justice Department will undertake "the most extensive, thorough and comprehensive investigation since the assassination of President Kennedy."

Aug. 29. At a news conference President Nixon says "both sides" apparently made "technical violations" of the new campaign finance reporting law, but refuses to specify Democratic violations. He says Dean has conducted a complete Watergate investigation and "I can state categorically that his investigation indicates that no one in the White House staff, no one in this Administration, presently employed was involved in this very bizarre incident. . . . What really hurts is if you try to cover it [wrongdoing] up." Dean later testifies that this is the first time he heard about his report.

Aug. 30. Stans tells House Banking and Currency Committee investigators that he has no knowledge of any routing of campaign funds through Mexico.

Sept. 1. Republicans file a motion seeking dismissal of the D.N.C. civil suit, alleging that publicity on the Watergate break-in makes a fair trial impossible.

Sept. 2. Judge Richey rules that Mitchell and MacGregor can be called for questioning in the D.N.C. suit, but that the five Watergate break-in defendants cannot, pending the out-come of the criminal investigation. He stays depositions from the five men.

Sept. 2. After testifying in the D.N.C. suit, Mitchell tells reporters he was "in no way involved" in the break-in and "can swear now that [he] had no advance knowledge."

Sept. 5. Stans admits to Patman committee having ap-proved the Mexican transfer of four checks totaling $89,000 on April 3.

Sept. 7. Lawrence O'Brien says he has "unimpeachable evidence" that his personal office phone was tapped for several weeks before the June 17 break-in. He reveals the May break-in and says he is a "clear victim" of a "Republican-sponsored invasion."

Sept. 8. Ziegler says that Dean's report on his Watergate investigation will not be released to the press.

Sept. 9. The Washington Post reveals that the Justice De-partment has concluded its Watergate investigation without implicating any present White House or C.R.P. staff.

Sept. 11. Democrats file an amended complaint in their Watergate break-in civil suit, adding the names of Stans, Liddy, Sloan and Hunt to the original five defendants and increasing damages from $1-million to $3.2-million.

Sept. 12. In an interview published in The New York Times, Barker admits his role in the break-in, but refuses to implicate others.

Sept. 13. Stans calls the Patman committee's report that he approved the routing of a $100,000 campaign contribu-tion through Mexico "rubbish" and "transparently political."

Sept. 13. C.R.P. files at $2.5-million countersuit against the Democrats, charging them with abusing the court.

Sept. 14. Stans files a $5-million libel suit against Lawrence O'Brien, charging that he has been "falsely" and "maliciously" accused of "a number of criminal acts" in the Democrats' amended suit of Sept. 11.

Sept. 15. Barker pleads guilty in Watergate break-in case.

Sept. 15. A Federal grand jury in Washington returns an eight-count indictment against the five men arrested in the break-in, and Liddy and Hunt. The charges include tapping telephones, planting electronic eavesdropping devices and stealing documents. John W. Hushen, director of public information at the Justice Department, says indictments have ended the investigation. "We have absolutely no evidence to indicate that any others should be charged."

Sept. 15. Dean later testifies that today he spoke to President Nixon for the first time about Watergate; in Haldeman's presence Nixon said he was "pleased that the case had stopped with Liddy"; Dean replied that he tried to "contain the case" and keep it "out of the White House," but that it might still "unravel." President Nixon and Haldeman both deny that Dean suggested others were involved in the break-in, and that there was a cover-up.

Sept. 16. Kleindienst says the investigation by the F.B.I. and the United States attorney's office was "one of the most intensive, objective and thorough" in many years.

Sept. 16. Petersen denies a "whitewash," asserting that the F.B.I. investigation was carried out by 333 agents from 51 field offices, who developed 1,897 leads, conducted 1,551 interviews and expanded 14,098 man-hours. He adds that the grand jury met for 125 hours and examined 50 witnesses.

Sept. 19. Seven men indicted by Watergate break-in grand jury plead not guilty and are released on bonds ranging from $10,000 to $50,000. Kleindienst says they were acting without orders from their superiors.

Sept. 19. Ulasewicz makes his last payoff "drop," deciding no longer to make such deliveries.

Sept. 20. Opening his formal campaign, Agnew says, ". . . someone set up these people and encouraged them to undertake this caper to embarrass them and to embarrass the Republican party."

Sept. 20. Judge Richey rules that Sloan, Liddy, Stans and Hunt can be named as defendants in the Democrats' civil suit, but dismisses on technical grounds the original action against the five men arrested in the break-in, leaving the Sept. 11 amended complaint as the only civil action remaining.

Sept. 21. Saying it will be impossible to bring the D.N.C. suit to trial before the election, Judge Richey orders a stay of all proceedings, including the taking of depositions, until the Watergate break-in criminal trial is over.

Sept. 21. LaRue begins making the payoff deliveries, which will total about $230,000, $210,000 of it given to Hunt's attorney.

Sept. 29. The Washington Post reports that while he was Attorney General, Mitchell controlled a secret fund that was used to gather information about the Democrats. Mitchell denies this.

Oct. 2. Gray says no pressure has been put on him or any of his special agents in their investigation and that it "strains the credulity" that President Nixon could have done a "con job" on the whole American people.

Oct. 2. Petersen writes the House Banking and Currency Committee asking them to delay their investigation into possible banking law violations connected to Watergate on the grounds that it might jeopardize a fair criminal trial.

Oct. 3. By a vote of 20–15, the Patman committee decides it will not hold hearings, virtually eliminating any chance of public disclosure of possible Watergate-related banking law violations until after the election.

Oct. 4. Judge Sirica issues an order enjoining all those connected with the Watergate break-in case from commenting publicly on it.

Oct. 5. At an impromptu news conference, President Nixon says that the F.B.I. Watergate probe makes the 1948 investigation of Alger Hiss seem like a "Sunday school exercise." He says he will comment no further because of pending Federal criminal proceedings.

Oct. 5. The Los Angeles Times discloses that Baldwin monitored D.N.C. conversations and delivered sets of eavesdropping logs to the re-election committee in the weeks preceding the June 17 break-in.

Oct. 6. Judge Sirica modifies his ban on "extrajudicial" statements, deleting the phrase "all witnesses and potential witnesses including complaining witnesses and alleged victims."

Oct. 6. The first formal complaint of the 1972 Presidential campaign is filed with the Fair Campaign Practices Committee in the 1972 Presidential election. Representative Jerome Waldie (Dem., Calif.) charges that Republicans involved in the Watergate case "violated the level of political ethics."

Oct. 10. The Washington Post reports that the Watergate break-in was a result of a massive campaign of sabotage, directed by White House and C.R.P. officials and financed by a secret fund controlled by Mitchell and others. Ziegler later suspends rules imposed last summer by the White House, barring any criticism of the press, by asserting that the article is based on "hearsay, innuendo and guilt by association."

Oct. 10. Representative Patman announces that his committee will convene in two days in another attempt to investigate the Watergate break-in. He issues letters to Dean, Mitchell, MacGregor and Stans asking them to appear.

Oct. 10. McCord phones Chilean Embassy, identifying himself as a Watergate defendant and requesting a visa. Assuming that the embassy's phones are tapped, McCord then files a motion for Government disclosure of any wiretaps on his line, hoping that, in the interest of national security, the Government will drop its case against him rather than reveal taps on embassy phones.

Oct. 11. Dean, MacGregor, Mitchell and Stans decline to appear before the Patman committee, Dean on plea of executive privilege and the others on advice of counsel.

Oct. 12. Representative Patman fails to reconvene the House Banking and Currency Committee.

Oct. 12. Senator Kennedy, as chairman of the Judiciary Subcommittee on Administrative Practices and Procedures, orders a "preliminary inquiry" into the Watergate incident. This is the first time the idea of a Senate Watergate probe is raised.

Oct. 17. Judge Sirica sets Nov. 15 for start of criminal trial, despite pleas from prosecution and defense attorneys for more time.

Oct. 18. Ziegler says that "no one here at the White House directed activities involving sabotage, spying and espionage."

Oct. 20. Senator Jackson calls for creation of a bipartisan 12-man commission to investigate Watergate after the election.

Oct. 25. Sloan discloses that he told Florida prosecutors in pretrial hearings a week earlier that because he questioned the legality of the $114,000 campaign contributions he did not deposit them in the C.R.P account and instead gave them to the Finance Committee counsel, Liddy. This is the first time any C.R.P. official publicly acknowledges concern that the contributions might have been illegal.

Oct. 25. The Government offers McCord to accept a plea of guilty to one substantive count and, in return for his testimony as a Government witness, recommend leniency. (The Government says it will not recommend a disposition allowing McCord to remain at liberty.) McCord rejects the offer.

Oct. 25. In a television address, Senator McGovern warns that the nation faces a "moral and a constitutional crisis of unprecedented dimensions" because of President Nixon's "widespread abuse of power."

Oct. 25. Judge Sirica agrees to subpoena tapes and documents of interviews by The Los Angeles Times with Baldwin.

Oct. 26. MacGregor, acknowledging that C.R.P. officials controlled a special cash fund, is the first C.R.P. official to do so. He denies the fund has been used to sabotage the Democrats' campaign. He names Magruder, Stans, Liddy and Porter as men who controlled the fund and insists that Haldeman had nothing to do with it.

Oct. 26. Baldwin is named by U.S. attorney's office as a co-conspirator in the Watergate break-in.

Oct. 27. Judge Sirica postpones the Watergate trial until Jan. 8, 1973, on the advice of his physician.

Oct. 29. An Administration "White Paper" on Watergate is discussed at a high-level White House campaign strategy meeting.

Nov. 1. At the Barker trial in Miami, Sloan reveals that he passed the Dahlberg check to Liddy. He is not allowed to answer questions on how the check was transmitted to

Barker, because Judge Paul Baker had limited testimony to the charge of false notarization.

Nov. 1. At a two and a half hour trial Barker is found guilty of falsely notarizing Dahlberg's signature on a $25,000 campaign check traced to C.R.P.

Nov. 7. Nixon and Agnew are re-elected in a landslide, capturing 60.8 per cent of the popular vote and 97 per cent of the electoral vote.

Nov. 8. MacGregor resigns as director of C.R.P. Mardian resigns as political coordinator.

Nov. 16. White House denies the existence of a "White Paper" on Watergate.

Nov. 30. McCord later says that today Dorothy Hunt told him that no money would be forthcoming "unless you fellows agree to plead guilty and take executive clemency . . . and keep your mouths shut"; she told him Hunt's lawyer (Bittman) read the C.R.P. lawyer (Parkinson) a letter from Hunt which threatened "to blow the White House out of the water," and she asserted her husband had information that could cause President Nixon to be impeached.

Dec. 1. LaRue later says that today he received $280,000 in cash to be used for payoffs.

Dec. 6. The Washington Post reports McCord recruited Cubans for the break-in. McCord later says he thinks this was planted by the Administration in an effort to make him seem the "ringleader" and to draw attention away from Hunt, Liddy and the White House.

Dec. 7. Kathleen Chenow, a White House secretary, is first to confirm the existence of the "plumbers unit," naming its members as Young, Liddy, Hunt and Krogh. She says reports on the team's investigations into leaks to the news media were regularly sent to Ehrlichman, and that telephone bills in their office in the Executive Office Building were sent to her private home and then forwarded to the White House.

Dec. 8. Judge Byrne declares a mistrial in the Pentagon Papers trial, citing the four-month lapse between the seating of the jury and the actual opening of the trial.

Dec. 8. A United Airlines jet crashes in Chicago, killing Dorothy Hunt. Her pocketbook, containing $10,000 in $100 bills, is recovered.

Dec. 8. The Washington Post quotes Chenow as saying that the telephone in the "plumbers" office was used almost exclusively by Hunt in conversations with Barker and that she forwarded bills to an aide in Ehrlichman's office.

Dec. 12. The White House confirms the existence of the plumbers unit but denies that Liddy or Hunt were members of it or that Barker was called on the plumbers phone.

Dec. 19. Judge Sirica orders John F. Lawrence, Washington bureau chief of The Los Angeles Times, jailed for contempt of court in refusing to yield Baldwin tapes of interview by reporters Jack Nelson and Ronald J. Strow, contending that, unlike other First Amendment cases, identity of sources is not being sought (Baldwin was named in The Los Angeles Times articles).

Dec. 21. After Baldwin releases it from its pledge of confidentiality, The Los Angeles Times turns over the tapes of its interviews to Judge Sirica, ending contempt-of-court proceedings. Lawrence is released after spending a few hours in jail.

Dec. 21. McCord and his attorneys, Alch and Shankman, meet in a Washington, D. C., restaurant. McCord later testifies that Alch suggested that McCord should claim the break-in was a C.I.A. operation and stated that the C.I.A. would cooperate in this defense. Alch denies having made such a proposal.

Dec. 25. Sometime in the next few days Gray burns the incriminating Hunt documents with the Christmas trash.

Dec. 26. McCord and Alch meet in Boston. Alch shows him testimony by a Washington policeman stating that McCord claimed the break-in was C.I.A.-inspired. McCord insists the policeman has perjured himself, and he refuses the C.I.A. defense.

Dec. 26. Sloan gives testimony behind closed doors in connection with the D.N.C. suit, naming Kalmbach as C.R.P.'s "chief fund raiser" before Stans. This is made public on Feb. 10, 1973.

Dec. 31. McCord sends an anonymous letter to Caulfield: "If the Watergate operation is laid at the C.I.A.'s feet where it does not belong, every tree in the forest will fall. . . . If they want it to blow, they are on the right course."

1973

Jan. 3. Dean later testifies that on this day Hunt repeated his demands for more money and executive clemency. Hunt says that he never sought a promise of clemency and that payments of more than $156,000 had been for his legal defense and not for his silence.

Jan. 4. Dean later says that today Ehrlichman confided that he gave Colson approval of Presidential clemency for Hunt.

Jan. 5. Dean later testifies that today Ehrlichman told him he had discussed clemency for Hunt with President Nixon. Ehrlichman denies saying this.

Jan. 8. Watergate break-in criminal trial opens, Judge Sirica presiding. Screening of jurors begins.

Jan. 8. McCord, Barker and Alch share a cab to Bittman's office building; Alch and Bittman confer. McCord later testifies that Alch told him to expect contact from someone at "the White House." Alch says he told McCord that "a friend" would call.

Jan. 9. At 12:30 A.M. McCord receives an anonymous call at a pay phone near his home: "A year is a long time. Your wife and family will be taken care of. You will be rehabilitated with employment when this is over." Dean has instructed Caulfield to see that this message is delivered; Caulfield passed the assignment on to Ulasewicz.

Jan. 10. Hunt offers to plead guilt to charges of conspiracy, second-degree burglary and wiretapping. He asks that three other counts also charging burglary and eavesdropping be withdrawn.

Jan. 10. Dean later testifies that today Mitchell and C.R.P. attorney Paul O'Brien told him that "since Hunt had been given assurance of clemency, Caulfield should give the same assurance to McCord." Mitchell calls this a "complete fabrication."

Jan. 11. Senator Sam J. Ervin agrees to head a Senate investigation of Watergate.

Jan. 11. At the criminal trial, Hunt says he has no knowledge of any political espionage other than the Watergate break-in and that to his "personal knowledge" no "higher-ups" were involved.

Jan. 11. The Justice Department files a suit against the C.R.P. in the U.S. District Court, charging it with eight campaign violations, among which is the failure to report disbursements to Liddy by Sloan.

Jan. 11. In a letter to Representative Patman, Petersen says that no Federal laws were violated when Barker deposited $114,000 in G.O.P. campaign funds in his bank account or when campaign contributions were routed through Mexican banks.

Jan. 12. McCord and Caulfield hold their first meeting at night at an overlook of the George Washington Parkway. Caulfield offers executive clemency "from the highest level of the White House" and McCord says he will continue his independent course. McCord tells Caulfield of his calls to embassies. McCord later testifies that Caulfield said the President knew of the meeting and would be told of its results. Caulfield denies saying this.

Jan. 13. The New York Times reveals that at least four of the five men arrested in the June break-in are still being paid by persons unnamed, and that C.R.P. officials cannot account for $900,000 in cash contributions.

Jan. 14. C.R.P. public relations man Shumway labels The New York Times allegations "a serious act of journalistic recklessness and irresponsibility."

Jan. 14. McCord and Caulfield meet a second time at the overlook on the George Washington Parkway. Caulfield says, "The President's ability to govern is at stake. Another Teapot Dome scandal is possible. . . . Everybody else is on track but you." McCord again rejects offer of executive clemency.

Jan. 15. Barker, Gonzalez, Martinez and Sturgis plead guilty to all seven counts of the Watergate break-in indictment. They deny being threatened or coerced into such a plea.

Jan. 16. The four Watergate defendants who have pleaded guilty all deny that they have been "paid by anybody for anything."

Jan. 17. Alch submits a memorandum to Judge Sirica contending that McCord acted under duress, "breaking a law to avoid a greater harm," namely, violence against President Nixon and high-level Republicans.

Jan. 17. The Watergate trial goes into secret session when Baldwin is asked to name people he overheard on the tapped D.N.C. lines. Baldwin asserts that he monitored about 200 conversations and gave daily logs to McCord.

Jan. 18. The second Ellsberg-Russo Pentagon Papers trial opens in Los Angeles.

Jan. 18. Kleindienst asserts that the White House has not interfered in the Justice Department Watergate investigation, and that there is no need for a special prosecutor.

Jan. 19. Kalmbach later says that today Mitchell, Dean and LaRue asked him to raise more hush money and he refused.

Jan. 20. President Nixon is inaugurated for a second term. The sequestered Watergate jury watches the Inaugural parade on television.

Jan. 23. Sloan testifies that at Magruder's direction he gave Liddy $199,000, but does not know what the money was for. Judge Sirica elicits that Mitchell and Stans approved the payments to Sloan.

Jan. 23. Magruder testifies that Liddy was provided with about $235,000 for intelligence operations. He also establishes for the first time that Liddy was hired by C.R.P. on Dean's recommendation.

Jan. 24. Judge Sirica denounces the argument that McCord acted under duress as "ridiculous," and refuses to let Alch present it to the jury.

Jan. 25. In their third meeting, Caulfield and McCord take a two-hour drive to Virginia. McCord again refuses executive clemency and is told he is "fouling up the game plan." Caulfield reports back to Dean on the meeting.

Jan. 26. F.C.R.P. pleads no contest in the U.S. District Court and is fined the maximum $8,000 for eight campaign violations among which is failure to report the money given to Liddy by Sloan.

Jan. 26–28. A Gallup poll taken this weekend, following the announcement of the peace settlement in Vietnam, puts the President's popularity at a high of 68 per cent, matching his previous high point in November, 1969, when his plan for the "Vietnamization" of the war was announced.

Jan. 27. At the Ellsberg-Russo trial, Judge Byrne orders the Government prosecutor to give defense attorneys copies of secret analyses of the impact of the release of the Pentagon Papers on the grounds that they might contain evidence of an exculpatory nature.

Jan. 30. After deliberating only 90 minutes, the Watergate jury finds Liddy guilty on all six counts and McCord on all eight counts. They are jailed, with Judge Sirica postponing decisions on bond pending sentence. The trial lasted 16 days, and 62 witnesses were heard.

Jan. 31. In a news conference, President Nixon indicates that a policy statement on executive privilege will be forthcoming.

Feb. 2. Judge Sirica says he is "not satisfied" that the full Watergate story was disclosed at the trial and suggests the names of "several persons" who ought to be questioned. He hopes the Senate committee will be "granted power by Congress by a broad enough resolution to get to the bottom of what happened in this case."

Feb. 2. Representative Patman writes Kleindienst denouncing the prosecution in the Watergate trial and suggesting that Kleindienst resign if he cannot effectively investigate members of his own party.

Feb. 6. Judge Richey releases the depositions he sealed on Sept. 21 of pretrial depositions in the D.N.C. civil suit. They suggest that Mitchell had prior knowledge of intelligence gathering activities.

Feb. 7. The Senate votes 70–0 to establish a Select Committee of four Democrats and three Republicans to conduct a full-scale investigation of the Watergate break-in and related sabotage efforts against the Democrats in the 1972 campaign. The resolution stipulates that the investigation and written report be completed by February 28, 1974.

Feb. 7. The New York Times reports that Strachan, a Haldeman aide, knew of the Liddy-Hunt political intelligence operations as early as February, 1972. This is the first charge linking a White House official to such operations. Ziegler refuses to comment on the allegations concerning Strachan, but denies any involvement by Haldeman.

Feb. 7. Ziegler says the Administration will cooperate with the Senate investigation if it is handled "in a nonpartisan way." He declines to say if White House staff members will be permitted to testify or provide information.

Feb. 9. A Schlesinger letter indicates that today Dean phoned him and requested that the C.I.A. ask the Justice Deparment to return a "packet of material" sent to them in connection with the break-in. Schlesinger replied that he would discuss this matter with Walters. (Dean was probably referring to documents that included a photograph of Liddy, taken by Hunt, standing in front of the office of Ellsberg's psychiatrist, which Dean also mentioned to Krogh on March 28, 1973.)

Feb. 10-11. Dean, Ehrlichman, Haldeman and Moore meet at the La Costa Resort Hotel near San Clemente, Calif., for two days of discussion on strategy to be adopted before the Ervin committee. Dean later says they decided to "take a posture of full cooperation but privately . . . attempt to restrain the investigation and make it as difficult as possible to get information and witnesses. . . . The ultimate goal would be to discredit the hearings." Moore denies this was their decision.

Feb. 14. Colson later says that today he urged President Nixon to make Mitchell admit his involvement in the break-in, and the President refused.

Feb. 15. Moore later says that today Mitchell refused his request for help in raising money for the Watergate defendants.

Feb. 17. Gray is nominated as permanent Director of the F.B.I.

Feb. 21. At Schlesinger's request, Walters says that today he told Dean he could not comply with Dean's Feb. 9 request for C.I.A. assistance in retrieving a package of Watergate-related materials from the Justice Department.

Feb. 21. Senator Ervin is named chairman, Senator Baker vice chairman and Dash chief counsel of the Senate Watergate committee.

Feb. 26. C.R.P. obtains subpoenas ordering 12 reporters and news executives to relinquish their notes, tapes and other private material relating to articles on the D.N.C. bugging.

Feb. 27. Dean later testifies that today he had his first meeting with President Nixon regarding Watergate since Sept. 15; the President instructed Dean to report directly to him on all Watergate matters, since Haldeman and Ehrlichman were "principals" in the case, and Dean could "be more objective than they"; Dean warned the President that the cover-up might not be contained indefinitely. The White House denies that Dean said any White House aides were implicated in Watergate.

Feb. 27. Ehrlichman later says that today President Nixon instructed him and Haldeman to "press on" certain matters, while Dean was to concentrate on such issues as executive privilege, the grand jury and the Ervin committee.

Feb. 28. Dean later testifies that today he told President Nixon of his own involvement in the cover-up and was told "not to worry."

Feb. 28. The Democratic National Committee again amends its civil suit, adding the names of Magruder and Porter and doubling the amount of damages to $6.4-million. A memo filed with the suit suggests "possible involvement" of Ehrlichman, Haldeman, Colson, Chapin, Kalmbach, LaRue, Mardian, Odle, Segretti and others.

Feb. 28. Confirmation hearings open on Gray's nomination to be permanent F.B.I. Director. Gray acknowledges having shown F.B.I. Watergate files to Dean and offers to open them to any Senator who wants to see them.

Feb. 28. Porter and Magruder assert: "Neither of us had advance knowledge of the Watergate incident."

March 1. Dean later testifies that today President Nixon tells him that Gray must not hand over any further F.B.I. reports to the Senate Judiciary Committee; the President added that Dean, as Counsel to the President, could justify his own receipt of F.B.I. reports as "perfectly proper."

March 2. At an impromptu news conference, President Nixon claims executive privilege for Dean and reiterates: "No one on the White House staff at the time he [Dean] conducted the investigation—that was last July and August— was involved or had knowledge of the Watergate matter."

March 6. At his confirmation hearings, Gray asserts that the F.B.I.'s Watergate probe was "as aggressive and as exhaustive an investigation as the F.B.I. has ever conducted or is capable of conducting within the four walls of its jurisdiction." Ehrlichman later says that today the White House "abandoned" the Gray nomination.

March 7. At his confirmation hearings, Gray discloses having given Dean 82 F.B.I. reports and asserts he is "unalterably convinced" that Dean has concealed nothing about the contents of Hunt's safe. He also gives the first official confirmation of links between Chapin, Kalmbach and G.O.P. espionage activities.

March 7. Dean later testifies that today President Nixon told him to have Kleindienst forbid Gray to hand over any more F.B.I. files to the Senate Judiciary Committee.

March 7. The White House says Dean turned over everything taken from Hunt's office safe to the F.B.I.

March 12. President Nixon issues a policy statement, citing executive privilege as the reason that members and former members of his staff "normally shall . . . decline a request for a formal appearance before a committee of the Congress." He pledges: "Executive privilege will not be used as a shield to prevent embarrassing information from being made available but will be exercised only in those particular instances in which disclosure would harm the public interest."

March 13. Gray supplies the Senate Judiciary Committee with a list showing that he met or talked with Dean 33 times between June and September, 1972. The committee, in a direct challenge to President Nixon's policy statement, votes unanimously to "invite" Dean to testify.

March 13. Dean later testifies that today, in Haldeman's presence, he discussed executive clemency for Hunt and Hunt's demands for as much as $1-million in hush money with President Nixon, who replied that raising such a sum would be "no problem." The President and Haldeman say this conversation occurred on March 21 and that President Nixon neither offered executive clemency nor approved raising hush money.

March 14. Dean volunteers to President Nixon to be a test case for executive privilege. He points out that no aides can testify before the Senate committee until the matter of executive privilege has been resolved through litigation.

March 14. Dean declines the Senate Judiciary Committee's invitation to appear, citing the President's statement on executive privilege, but agrees to answer written questions that relate directly to the Gray nomination.

March 15. In an impromptu news conference, President Nixon calls the break-in "espionage by one political organization against another," a change from previous White House characterizations of it as men acting independently. Nixon claims that Dean has a "double privilege" in refusing to appear before the Senate Judiciary Committee—Presidential privilege and the lawyer-client relationship—and suggests the issue be resolved by the courts.

March 15. Dean testifies that today he, President Nixon and Moore had a routine discussion of today's Presidential news conference, the legal issues involved in requests for Dean's appearance before the Senate Judiciary Committee, and the President's reminiscences of his role in the Alger Hiss investigation. (On June 4, President Nixon will request a summary of this meeting.)

March 16. Hunt leaves the last of at least five messages to the White House requesting more money.

March 16. The Administration rescinds Gray's offer to open F.B.I. Watergate files to all Senate members. At a meeting of Kleindienst, Ervin and Baker a decision is reached to limit access to Ervin, Baker and their respective committee counsels.

March 17. According to his statement of Aug. 15, 1973, President Nixon learned of the Ellsberg psychiatrist burglary today. (In his May 22, 1973 speech, he says he learned of it on March 21.)

March 18. Senator Ervin says on C.B.S. "Face the Nation" that White House aides who invoke executive privilege to keep from testifying before his committee should be found in contempt of Congress. He affirms the March 16 decision to restrict F.B.I. Watergate files.

March 19. McCord writes Judge Sirica charging that he and other Watergate break-in defendants were under "political pressure" to plead guilty and remain silent, that perjury was committed at the trial, and that higher-ups were involved in the break-in.

March 19. Dean later states that today, after hearing of Hunt's latest demand for money, Dean had "about reached the end of the line" and decided to end his role in the cover-up.

March 19. Kleindienst instructs Gray to revoke his Feb. 28 offer, which allowed any Senator access to the F.B.I. Watergate files. He also tells Gray not to answer any further substantive questions about the Watergate or any other F.B.I. investigation.

March 20. Gray tells the Judiciary committee of his new orders from Kleindienst and pleads with them to vote his nomination "up or down" so he can get out of the "mine field" he is walking between the executive and legislative branches.

March 20. Moore later testifies that today, at a meeting with Dean and President Nixon, he got the impression that the President had no knowledge of the Watergate cover-up.

March 21. In his April 17 statement and April 30 speech, President Nixon says that today, after new charges were brought to his attention, he began "intensive new inquiries" into Watergate, "personally" ordering "all those conducting the investigations to get all the facts and to report them directly to me." Gray, Petersen and Kleindienst deny ever receiving such a directive from the President, although Kleindienst was contacted indirectly on March 28. In his Aug. 15 supplementary statement, the President says that after March 21 he "immediately began new inquiries." Pressed on this

point during his Aug. 22 news conference, he refers to his
March 27 conversation with Ehrlichman.

March 21. Dean later testifies that today, in a morning
meeting, he told President Nixon, "there [is] a cancer growing
on the Presidency," and disclosed the involvement of
Mitchell, Haldeman, Strachan, Kalmbach, Magruder and
himself in the Watergate break-in and cover-up. Ehrlichman
says that, judging from the President's reactions, he has
"great difficulty believing" that Dean gave the President such
a report. Haldeman says such a conversation is not on tape.

March 21. Ehrlichman later testifies that today the only
topic at his afternoon meeting with Dean was executive
privilege; Dean recommended blanket immunity for the White
House staff, and Ehrlichman disagreed.

March 21. Magruder says that today Mitchell said he
would help him get executive clemency if Magruder told
the truth to U.S. prosecutors. Mitchell later says that he
made Magruder an offer of assistance, but not of executive
clemency.

March 21. Judge Richey cites the First Amendment and
quashes C.R.P. subpoenas which would have required newsmen to reveal their unpublished material on the Watergate
incident.

March 21. A letter by Dean on executive clemency is disclosed. Written in April, 1972, to the Federation of American
Scientists, it said: "Precedents indicate that no recent President has ever claimed a blanket immunity that would prevent
his assistants from testifying before Congress on any subject."

March 22. Caulfield tells McCord the Administration will
provide $100,000 in cash for his bail, and to contact him
if he needs it. This is the last conversation between the two
men.

March 22. Mitchell, Dean, Ehrlichman, Haldeman and
President Nixon discuss White House strategy vis-à-vis the
Ervin committee.

March 22. Gray, under questioning by Senator Robert C.
Byrd, says that Dean "probably lied" to F.B.I. agents investigating the Watergate incident when he said on June 22,
1972, that he did not know if Hunt had an office in the

White House. The White House issues a statement in Dean's defense; Dean demands a "correction" from Gray.

March 23. Judge Sirica discloses the contents of McCord's March 19 letter and postpones sentencing him. Later, McCord meets with Dash and Lipset.

March 23. Judge Sirica gives five Watergate conspirators provisional maximum sentences, urging them to cooperate with the grand jury and the Senate committee. The sentences are: 35 years for Hunt, 40 years each for Barker, Gonzalez, Martinez and Sturgis. He sentences Liddy to from 6 years, 8 months to 20 years.

March 23. Dean later says that today President Nixon told him to go to Camp David and "analyze the situation." When Dean arrived, Haldeman phoned, instructing him to write a report on everything he knew about Watergate.

March 23. Judge Richey gives the D.N.C. permission to add the names of Magruder, Porter, McCord, Barker, Sturgis, Gonzalez and Martinez to its civil suit.

March 24. At a second meeting with Dash and Lipset, McCord says that Dean and Magruder had prior knowledge of the Watergate break-in.

March 26. Kleindienst says McCord's allegations contain "nothing new so far that was not covered by our investigation. I'm just as certain as I can be that Magruder and Dean didn't know anything about it."

March 26. The Los Angeles Times reports McCord's allegations against Dean and Magruder and reveals that he has named Hunt as the person who offered him executive clemency in return for silence.

March 26. Magruder's resignation as an assistant commerce secretary is announced.

March 26. Ziegler says, "I should tell you that the President has talked to John Dean this morning . . . and following that conversation, and based on that conversation, I would again flatly deny any prior knowledge on the part of Mr. Dean regarding the Watergate matter." In June Ziegler says that today President Nixon spoke not with Dean, but with Haldeman.

March 26. The Federal grand jury reconvenes to hear new Watergate charges.

March 26. Silbert discloses that McCord twice refused Government offers of reduced charges in exchange for information.

March 27. President Nixon later says that today he "had a contact made with the Attorney General himself and . . . told him . . . to report to me directly anything he found." Kleindienst testifies that he received no directive from the President.

March 27. Before the Federal grand jury, Hunt denies knowledge of higher-ups in the break-in and invokes the Fifth Amendment.

March 27. In a telephone call to The New York Times, Martha Mitchell says someone is trying to make her husband "the goat" for the Watergate incident.

March 27. Magruder later says that today Mitchell advised him that he would take care of everything.

March 28. Ehrlichman phones Kleindienst, recording the conversation. He says President Nixon wants Kleindienst to know that there is no information that anybody "in the White House had any prior knowledge of this burglary," and that if any information to the contrary "ever turns up" regarding White House or C.R.P. personnel, Kleindienst should "just contact him."

March 28. Hunt is granted immunity by Judge Sirica; spends almost four hours in closed session before the grand jury.

March 28. Dean later testifies that today he returned from six days at Camp David and gave an evasive answer when Mitchell and Magruder asked how he would testify at the hearings.

March 28. McCord tells the Ervin committee during four hours of closed-door testimony, later leaked, that Mitchell had prior knowledge of the Watergate plot.

March 28. Dean later testifies that on this or the following day he told Krogh that the Justice Department had a photograph of Liddy, taken by Hunt, standing in front of the office of Ellsberg's psychiatrist. When asked if Ehrlichman ordered the break-in, Krogh replied that his orders came from the "Oval Office" and that Ehrlichman did not know of the break-in until after it had occurred.

March 29. Mitchell terms McCord's allegations of March 28 "slanderous." Colson denies any prior knowledge of the Watergate break-in. The White House reiterates that no one on its staff had knowledge or was involved in the break-in.

March 30. President Nixon directs Ehrlichman to conduct an independent inquiry without informing the Justice Department. Gray later testifies to the Ervin committee that he never received any requests for information from Ehrlichman; Ehrlichman says he questioned about ten people and considers it an "inquiry" rather than an "investigation."

March 30. In an attempt to compromise with the Ervin committee, the White House says its staff will testify in closed sessions before the committee or the grand jury.

March 30. Judge Sirica gives Liddy immunity before the grand jury and postpones McCord's sentence until June so that McCord can testify further.

March 30. Magruder telephones Reisner several times, hoping to arrange a meeting with him before Reisner's appearance before the Ervin committee. Reisner declines. After Reisner's appearance, Magruder calls and cautions him to be careful because people's lives and futures are at stake.

March 31. Ziegler says, "Any member of the White House staff called by the grand jury will be required by the President to testify. That is a restatement of the policy in effect."

April 2. Ervin labels the Administration's offer of closed-door testimony "executive poppycock," and says the White House staff are not "nobility and royalty" and will be arrested if they refuse to appear before his committee to give sworn, public testimony.

April 2. Ziegler scores the Ervin committee as "plagued by irresponsible leaks of tidal wave proportions."

April 2. Dean's lawyers tell the United States attorneys he will talk freely.

April 3. Judge Sirica sentences Liddy to 8–18 months for contempt of court for refusing to answer grand jury questions despite promise of immunity from further prosecution. Liddy's original sentence will be interrupted while he serves the contempt term and then resume.

April 3. Senator Ervin announces that, in order to stop leaks, there will be no more secret testimony.

April 5. In San Clemente, Ehrlichman and Judge Bryne discuss the directorship of the F.B.I. and Byrne briefly meets President Nixon. Byrne, who is still trying the Ellsberg-Russo case, says he "could not consider such a proposal, but would reflect" on it.

April 5. Gray's nomination as Director of the F.B.I. is withdrawn.

April 5. McCord appears before the grand jury with immunity.

April 5. Ehrlichman confers with Paul O'Brien and later says this is the first time he learned of Liddy's activities against the Democrats.

April 7. In Santa Monica, at a second meeting with Ehrlichman, Judge Byrne rejects the directorship of the F.B.I.

April 9. The New York Times reports that McCord has told the grand jury that Dorothy Hunt was the conduit for cash payments made to Watergate defendants for their silence and guilty pleas. McCord alleges that she named Parkinson as the person responsible for the pressure and the channeling of payments. Parkinson denies the allegations.

April 9-14. Dean later says that in these days he, Haldeman and Ehrlichman on several occasions discussed pinning the blame for Watergate on Mitchell.

April 11. Porter later testifies that today Magruder told him to confess his perjury to the United States attorneys.

April 12. Magruder confesses his perjury to the United States attorneys.

April 12. News reports allege that in his grand jury testimony McCord has claimed that Mitchell ordered a priority list of electronic eavesdropping targets and received transcripts of wiretapped D.N.C. conversations. Mitchell denies both charges.

April 12. Judge Richey rejects a request by Senate investigators to keep further pretrial testimony by McCord secret.

April 13. Fensterwald discloses that McCord, his client, has led F.B.I. agents to four Maryland sites to recover electronic equipment that he "stashed away."

April 14. Emerging from the White House, Mitchell says he has conferred with President Nixon and expects Presidential aides to testify before the Select Committee. The meeting is not announced by the White House. Ziegler later says that Mitchell met not with President Nixon but with Ehrlichman.

April 14. Ehrlichman later says that today President Nixon received his first detailed report on Watergate, based on Ehrlichman's inquiry and implicating Mitchell, Dean and Magruder; he was directed to relay this to Kleindienst. At night, Ehrlichman phoned Kleindienst, who told him to turn over this information to the Justice Department in order to avoid obstruction of justice charges. Kleindienst testifies that Ehrlichman replied: "It really doesn't make any difference anymore," because Magruder had started talking to the United States attorneys.

April 14. In a secret meeting with Government prosecutors, Magruder implicates Dean, Liddy and Mitchell in prior knowledge and cover-up of the Watergate break-in.

April 14. Magruder later testifies he told Porter today that at a White House meeting President Nixon directed everyone to tell the truth.

April 14. Dean turns over documents to Silbert and implicates Haldeman, Ehrlichman, Mitchell and Magruder. Judge Sirica refuses his request for immunity.

April 15. President Nixon later says that today he met with Kleindienst and Petersen to review "facts which had come to my attention."

April 15. In an early morning session, Government prosecutors give Kleindienst and Petersen a report based on recent interviews with Dean and Magruder which implicate Ehrlichman, Haldeman, Mitchell, Mardian and others in the Watergate break-in and cover-up. Kleindienst and Petersen inform President Nixon. Petersen suggests the President fire Ehrlichman and Haldeman, but not Dean, who is cooperating in the investigation. Kleindienst later describes the President's reaction as "dumfounded" and "upset"; Petersen says he was "calm."

April 15. President Nixon and Kleindienst agree that Kleindienst will disqualify himself from all future aspects of the Watergate investigation.

April 15. Dean later says that today he told President Nixon he had spoken to Federal prosecutors, and the President asked "leading questions, which made me think that the conversation was being taped"; Nixon remarked that his March 13 comment about raising $1-million in hush money was a joke.

April 15. Ehrlichman later testifies that today Gray told him he would deny having received Hunt's files and wanted Ehrlichman to corroborate this; Ehrlichman refused. Gray denies this.

April 15. Silbert confers with Dean.

April 15. The Justice Department later states that today it learned of White House involvement in the burglary of Ellsberg's psychiatrist's office. Ehrlichman says they knew of it almost a year earlier.

April 16. In a morning meeting, President Nixon presents for Dean's signature two letters, either of resignation or, alternatively, of indefinite absence. Dean refuses. At a second meeting, Dean later says he told President Nixon he would not be a scapegoat and would only resign with the two Presidential advisers.

April 16. Petersen informs Gray that Dean has confessed to giving him Hunt's sensitive files. Gray denies having received them.

April 17. Gray admits to Petersen that he took Hunt's files from Dean, but maintains that he destroyed them without reading them.

April 17. Dean later says that today President Nixon informed him that he was issuing a statement on Watergate;

Dean felt he was being set up and decided to issue a "scape-goat" statement.

April 17. President Nixon announces that, after "serious charges" were brought to his attention on March 21, he ordered a new, "intensive" investigation that has produced "major developments" and "real progress . . . in finding the truth" about the Watergate break-in.

April 17. Ziegler says that all previous White House statements on Watergate are "inoperative," since they were based on "investigations prior to the developments announced today."

April 18. Petersen tells President Nixon that the Watergate prosecution team has learned of the burglary of Dr. Fielding's office, and that Judge Byrne does not yet know of it. Nixon replies that "this is a national security matter," and instructs Petersen to "stay out of that."

April 18. Senator Ervin issues guidelines on the Watergate investigation, asserting that the committee alone will be the final judge of whether a witness can refuse to answer its questions. Sworn testimony will be required by all witnesses in open session.

April 19. Kleindienst announces that he has disqualified himself from the Watergate investigation because of his "close personal and professional relationship" with some of those being linked to the break-in.

April 19. Ziegler confirms that Dean did not submit a written report to President Nixon on his alleged Watergate probe.

April 19. Dean announces he will not be made a "scape-goat." Hunt testifies before the grand jury; Liddy, Dean and Magruder refuse to do so.

April 19. Ehrlichman records a phone conversation with Kalmbach, in which Ehrlichman asserts that Dean is out to "get" him and Haldeman and requests that Kalmbach not incriminate him before the grand jury the following day. Kalmbach assents. Ehrlichman later denies that he meant for Kalmbach to commit perjury.

April 20. Mitchell testifies before the grand jury on his presence at three meetings where wiretapping was discussed, asserting that he gave "an absolute, final disapproval" to such an operation.

April 20. McCord files a $1.5-million suit against C.R.P. and Magruder, Liddy and Hunt, claiming they had entrapped him in activities that led to his conviction.

April 22. Dean gets a "stroking call" from President Nixon, who wishes him a happy Easter and assures him he is still the Presidential counsel.

April 23. The White House again denies prior Presidential knowledge of the break-in and denies the involvement of key aides. It discloses that President Nixon met with John J. Wilson on April 19. They confer again on April 25.

April 24. The White House denies that an offer of executive clemency was made to the Watergate defendants in exchange for silence and guilty pleas.

April 25. Petersen tells Kleindienst of President Nixon's April 18 order and threatens to resign if Judge Byrne is not told of the Dr. Fielding break-in. They meet with the President, who "without hesitation" rescinds his order. Nixon later says that today Kleindienst told him of Hunt's involvement in the Dr. Fielding break-in and he directed it to be disclosed "immediately" to Judge Byrne.

April 26. The New York Daily News reports that Gray burned documents belonging to Hunt at Dean's request.

April 26. Magruder's resignation as assistant secretary of commerce is announced. He is the first high Nixon aide to leave the Administration since the recent Watergate disclosures.

April 26. Petersen tells Gray they are both "expendable" and advises him to get a lawyer.

April 27. Gray resigns as acting Director of the F.B.I. after disclosure that he destroyed Hunt's files.

April 27. The President agrees with Ehrlichman and Haldeman that they should take an indefinite leave of absence.

April 27. Ehrlichman admits to the F.B.I. that at President Nixon's request he ordered a secret White House investigation of the Pentagon Papers by Krogh and Young, but he denies prior knowledge of the burglary of Dr. Fielding's office.

April 27. Judge Byrne discloses a Justice Department memorandum which reveals the burglary of Ellsberg's psychiatrist's office, committed by Liddy and Hunt.

April 29. Haldeman and Ehrlichman submit their resignations, effective April 30.

April 30. The White House announces the resignations of Ehrlichman, Haldeman, Kleindienst and Dean. Richardson is named to replace Kleindienst and to direct the Watergate investigation; Garment is named to temporarily replace Dean.

April 30. In a televised address, President Nixon accepts responsibility for the Watergate incident, but denies any personal involvement in the break-in or cover-up. He concedes for the first time that "there had been an effort to conceal the facts," and discloses the new probe of March 21. Nixon says Richardson will have license to appoint a special prosecutor.

April 30. In meeting with reporters and photographers after his speech, President Nixon asks them to give him "hell every time you think I'm wrong."

April 30. Judge Byrne discloses his two meetings with Ehrlichman but refuses to reveal what position he was offered.

May 1. F.B.I. agents are stationed outside the offices of Ehrlichman and Haldeman, nine hours after the President makes their resignations public.

May 1. Ziegler apologizes to The Washington Post and its reporters Woodward and Bernstein for his criticisms of their Watergate articles.

May 1. With only five Senators present, a resolution drafted by Senator Percy, urging the appointment of a special prosecutor from outside the executive branch, is passed. A similar resolution is introduced in the House.

May 2. The White House announces Young's resignation from the National Security Council staff and Krogh's leave of absence from the Department of Transportation.

May 2. Judge Byrne reveals the details of his April 5 and 7 meetings with Ehrlichman and asks for a dismissal and mistrial motion in the Pentagon Papers case.

May 2. Hoping to change its March 16 agreement with Kleindienst, the Ervin committee votes to request that Richardson make F.B.I. Watergate files available to all its members.

May 2. Connally announces his switch to the Republican party, and dismisses Watergate as a "silly, stupid, illegal act."

May 2. Hunt testifies before the Federal Watergate grand jury that Young and Krogh personally directed the break-in at the office of Ellsberg's psychiatrist and that the C.I.A. supplied materials for the job.

May 3. White House delivers a memo to John J. Wilson, attorney for Ehrlichman and Haldeman, outlining the President's position on executive privilege. Haldeman and Ehrlichman appear before the Federal grand jury investigating Watergate.

May 4. Dean discloses that he removed Watergate-related documents from the White House to protect them from "illegitimate destruction." He asks the U.S. District Court to take charge of them.

May 4. Haig is appointed on an interim basis as a Presidential assistant, replacing Haldeman.

May 4. Judge Bryne releases Hunt's May 2 testimony before the Federal Watergate grand jury.

May 5. Julie Nixon Eisenhower later says that today President Nixon suggested to his family that he should perhaps resign over Watergate as an act of patriotism.

May 6. Senator Ervin asserts he would call the President before his committee if he felt it necessary. "I know of no law that says that the President is exempt from the duties which devolve on other citizens."

May 7. Richardson pledges to appoint a special prosecutor who will report exclusively to him and have "all the independence, authority and staff support" he needs.

May 7. Judge Sirica grants Hunt immunity from further prosecution.

May 7. Senator McClellan announces that his appropriations subcommittee on intelligence operations will probe C.I.A. involvement in the Watergate incident.

May 8. In a reversal of previous policy, the White House sends new guidelines to the Ervin committee indicating that use of executive privilege will be held to a minimum and that there will be no objection to granting immunity to past or present Administration aides.

May 8. The Select Committee announces that its public hearings will begin on May 17 and that it will seek immunity for Dean. Dean is served with a subpoena for his appearance.

May 8. The New York Times reports that Nixon resisted disclosure of White House involvement in the burglary of Ellsberg's psychiatrist's office on at least two occasions in recent weeks. Ziegler later denies this.

May 9. Richardson's confirmation hearings as Attorney General open.

May 9. The Justice Department says it will invoke a 30-day delay in Dean's immunity. Eight previous requests for immunity were processed with no delay.

May 9. Krogh resigns as under secretary of transportation, claiming "full responsibility" for the break-in at the office of Ellsberg's psychiatrist, which was done "without the knowledge or permission of any superior. . . ."

May 10. Mitchell and Stans are indicted by a Federal grand jury in New York on three counts of conspiracy to obstruct justice and six counts of perjury relating to Vesco's $200,000 campaign contribution. They deny all charges.

May 10. President Nixon appoints Buzhardt a special counsel on Watergate, reporting directly to him. Connally is named a special adviser to the President on domestic and foreign affairs.

May 10. Acting F.B.I. Director Ruckelshaus sends Judge Byrne a memo disclosing a wiretap on Ellsberg's phone in 1969 or 1970. Judge Byrne requests the logs of the tapes, but the records are missing.

May 11. The Pentagon Papers case is dismissed on grounds of Government misconduct. The dismissal is worded so as to preclude a retrial.

May 11. Judge Sirica grants immunity to Barker, Gonzalez, Martinez and Sturgis.

May 14. Judge Sirica takes possession of Hunt's papers that Dean placed in his safe-deposit box. He orders them made available to the Ervin committee and Federal prosecutors.

May 14. Richardson discloses that Garment and Haig have suggested candidates for the position of special prosecutor, but that he has rejected them because they "didn't satisfy the kinds of criteria I'm using." Senator Hart says such recommendations show a "singular lack of sensitivity."

May 15. Ervin committee votes unanimously to apply for limited immunity for Dean.

May 16. Ziegler concedes that President Nixon did not directly order Dean to investigate the Watergate break-in. He confirms a New York Times article which said that Ehrlichman was the intermediary between the President and Dean, and that Nixon received only one informal oral report from Ehrlichman.

May 16. President Nixon sends Congress a special message proposing a bipartisan 17-member committee on election reforms, to report its recommendations by December 1.

May 17. Televised Senate Watergate inquiry opens. Ervin says the "aim of the committee is to provide full and open public testimony in order that the nation can proceed toward the healing of the wounds that now afflict the body politic."

May 17. At confirmation hearings, Richardson releases guidelines for a special prosecutor, pledging that the prosecutor will have "the greatest degree of independence" that the Attorney General can provide. Ziegler asserts that Richardson is "free to grant total independence . . . if he choses."

May 17. Walters takes memorandums he wrote to himself in June and July, 1972, from Buzhardt at the White House, who has had them for about a week, and gives them to Senator Symington, of the Armed Services Committee's subcommittee on central intelligence.

May 18. Cox is named special prosecutor. He says his main task will be to "restore confidence in the honor, integrity and decency of government."

May 18. Mitchell phones U.P.I. and says, "Somebody has tried to make me the fall guy, but it isn't going to work. . . . The only thing I did was to try to get the President re-elected. I never did anything mentally or morally wrong."

May 18. Senator Symington discloses that he has turned over to the Ervin committee and the Senate Armed Services Committee memorandums given him the previous day by Walters, of conversations Walters had with Haldeman, Ehrlichman, Dean and Gray in June and July, 1972. They indicate that political implications, not national security, were the major concern of White House aides who tried to restrict the F.B.I. probe, and are printed by The New York Times on June 3.

May 19. The G.A.O. reveals Kalmbach's admission that he solicited $230,000 in the summer of 1972 for payments to the Watergate defendants.

May 21. Cox says that, if necessary, he will follow the Watergate investigation into the "Oval Office."

May 21. Stans and Mitchell plead not guilty in the Vesco trial.

May 22. In a statement, while again denying prior knowledge of the Watergate burglary or cover-up, President Nixon admits ordering some aides to restrict the Watergate probe on grounds of national security. He maintains that shortly after the break-in he was "advised that there was a possibility of C.I.A. involvement in some way." Walters later says that the President never asked him about possible C.I.A. involvement.

May 22. The Government informs Dean by letter that his request for immunity will not be granted, but offers to let him plead guilty to one count of obstructing justice.

May 24. In remarks before returned prisoners of war, President Nixon defends Government secrecy as vital to the national security and condemns "making heroes out of those who steal secrets and publish them in the newspaper."

May 24. Caulfield's resignation is accepted by the Bureau of Alcohol, Tobacco and Firearms.

May 25. Cox and Richardson are sworn in.

May 29. Ziegler rules out as "constitutionally inappropriate" any oral or written testimony by President Nixon to the Ervin committee, saying such testimony "would do violence to the separation of powers."

May 30. Ehrlichman tells the Senate appropriations subcommittee on intelligence operations investigating C.I.A. involvement in Watergate and the Pentagon Papers that President Nixon was aware of the F.B.I. investigation into Mexican aspects of the break-in within six days after it occurred and had instructed him and Haldeman to have the C.I.A. curb the F.B.I. probe.

May 30. Judge Sirica delays immunity for Dean and Magruder for 20 days and asks the Justice Department for opinions on whether he can legally deny their immunity requests.

May 30. Judge Richey delays for 90 days the $6.4-million D.N.C. Watergate civil suit trial against the Republicans at the request of D.N.C. attorneys who want additional time to seek new evidence.

May 31. Senator Ervin says he has read the documents Dean took for safekeeping, and they reveal a "Gestapo mentality" in the Administration.

June 3. Senator Ervin reveals that he has rejected Cox's request for a postponement of his committee's proceedings until indictments have been returned. "The American people are entitled to find out what actually happened without having to wait while justice travels on leaden feet."

June 3. The New York Times and The Washington Post report that Dean met with Nixon 35 or 40 times between late January and April to discuss Watergate. The White House says the reports are part of a "careful, coordinated strategy . . . to prosecute a case against the President in the press, using innuendo, distortion of fact, and outright falsehood. . . . We categorically deny the assertions and implications of this story."

June 4. The White House acknowledges that several times earlier in the year Dean and Nixon met to discuss Watergate. Warren says logs of times and places of their conversations will not be released.

June 4. In his Sept. 5, 1973, news conference, President Nixon said that today was the only time he listened to two tapes and that "there is nothing whatever in the tapes that is inconsistent with the statement that I made on May 22 . . . or that I made on the 15th of August." On Sept. 9, 1973, the New York Times reports that Bull privately told the Ervin committee in August that on June 4, at President Nixon's request, he listened to the tape of the March 15 Nixon-Dean-Moore meeting and read his summary of the conversation first to President Nixon and then, at the President's request, to Ziegler. Ziegler confirmed this to the Watergate committee.

June 4. Cox writes the Ervin committee requesting a suspension of its hearings for one to three months.

June 5. The Select Committee unanimously rejects Cox's request to suspend its hearings. It also rejects a request from Talmadge and Gurney to immediately call high-level witnesses in order to determine Nixon's role as quickly as possible.

June 5. A Los Angeles County grand jury begins hearings on the break-in at Ellsberg's psychiatrist's office.

June 6. Nixon announces that Haig will replace Haldeman, Laird will replace Ehrlichman, Wright will be White House counsel on a consultant basis, and Ziegler will continue as press secretary.

June 6. Reversing its June 4 position, the White House agrees to give the Select Committee the logs of the Nixon-Dean conversations.

June 7. The New York Times reveals that President Nixon approved the interagency committee's illegal recommendations in 1970. It publishes three memos by Huston which Dean had relinquished to Judge Sirica.

June 8. McCord asks Judge Sirica for a new trial on grounds that the Government withheld evidence and perjury was committed in the January trial. Sirica postpones sentencing McCord for an indefinite period.

June 8. Judge Gagliardi dismisses Stans's objections that his right to a fair trial in the Vesco case would be jeopardized by testifying before the Ervin committee.

June 9. The New York Times quotes Senator Ervin as saying that the Senate investigation will be expanded to include the 1971 Ellsberg break-in, the I.T.T. case, and the Administration's 1970 domestic intelligence plan.

June 11. Agnew denounces the "swelling flood of prejudicial publicity" and the "Perry Masonish impact" of the televised hearings, declaring that they "can hardly hope to find the truth and can hardly fail to muddy the waters of justice beyond repair."

June 12. The Federal district court in Washington, D. C., rejects Cox's plea to halt broadcasts of the Ervin proceedings.

June 12. Judge Sirica grants Dean and Magruder immunity before the Ervin committee. He denies Dean immunity before the grand jury. Dean pleads the Fifth Amendment before the grand jury.

June 13. The Washington Post reports that Federal prosecutors have a memo from Young to Krogh and Ehrlichman giving detailed plans for the impending break-in at Dr. Fielding's office. Ehrlichman reverses his earlier denials and acknowledges that he approved "some sort of proposal" involving an investigation of Ellsberg and Los Angeles.

June 15. Ervin committee grants Strachan immunity, but the Justice Department invokes a 30-day delay in granting it.

June 15. Oliver, whose D.N.C. phone was tapped, files a $5.5-million damage suit against C.R.P. and individuals including Mitchell and Dean.

June 16. The New York Times reports that the House Judiciary Committee is planning an investigation into Justice Department-F.B.I. operations. Open hearings will be scheduled for late 1973 or early 1974.

June 18. At the request of the Senate, the Ervin proceedings are postponed for the week of Soviet party leader Leonid I. Brezhnev's visit.

June 18. Garment tells Dash that the White House will waive all claims to executive privilege and attorney-client privilege in connection with Dean's testimony.

June 25. Ziegler says the White House will not comment on this week's Watergate hearings (Dean's testimony).

June 26. Reversing its position of June 25, the White House comments on Watergate and asserts that President Nixon stands by his May 22 statement, disclaiming all knowledge of the cover-up until March 21.

June 27. The "enemies list" is released.

June 27. Senator Inouye reads a White House rebuttal of Dean's testimony. Prepared by Buzhardt, it charges that Dean was the "mastermind" of the cover-up and Mitchell his "patron."

June 27. Bull later tells the Ervin committee that at 9 P.M. tonight, Haig informed him that President Nixon wanted the tape of his April 15 conversation with Dean flown immediately from Washington to San Clemente. Bull replied that no convenient courier flight was available at this hour and was then instructed to arrange for the Secret Service to play the tape for Buzhardt. Later, Buzhardt briefed President Nixon by phone on the contents of the tapes.

June 27. LaRue pleads guilty to one count of conspiracy to obstruct justice, agreeing to testify as a Government witness. He reveals that he committed perjury before the grand jury in August. Judge Sirica postpones sentencing until he can evaluate how cooperative LaRue has been with Government attorneys.

June 28. White House disavows that Buzhardt's statement represents an official Administration position.

June 28. The White House again affirms that it would be "constitutionally inappropriate" for President Nixon to testify before the Ervin committee.

June 28. Senator Weicker announces that he has asked Cox to investigate a smear campaign against him by the Administration, as an attempt to influence his work on the Ervin committee.

June 29. Silbert, Glanzer and Campbell, the original Justice Department Watergate prosecutors, withdraw from the case, defending their investigation as forthright, vigorous and professional.

June 29. Haldeman discusses his forthcoming testimony regarding Presidential tapes with White House attorneys.

June 29. Colson acknowledges before the House armed services subcommittee on intelligence operations that he arranged through Ehrlichman to obtain C.I.A. help for Hunt. He denies knowing what it would be used for or discussing executive clemency for Hunt.

July 2. Ziegler says President Nixon will answer charges against him after the Senate Watergate committee completes the first part of its hearings.

July 7. President Nixon writes Senator Ervin that he will neither appear before nor open his files to the Select Committee, on grounds of the doctrine of the separation of powers. Senator Ervin replies that the committee probably has the power to subpoena the President, but that he opposes this measure. "If the President wants to withhold information from the committee and the American people, I would just let him take the consequences of that."

July 8. Ehrlichman testifies before the Los Angeles grand jury that he had no prior knowledge of the break-in at the office of Ellsberg's psychiatrist or that "consideration was given to obtaining information from Dr. Ellsberg's psychiatric file."

July 9. Haldeman testifies that today, at President Nixon's request, Bull delivered the tape of the September 15, 1972 Nixon-Dean meeting to him at a guest office he was using in the Executive Office Building. He took it home, listened to it and returned it two days later, after reporting on its contents to President Nixon via Buzhardt. Haldeman's attorneys later amended this, saying that Bull delivered the tape "plus phone call tapes for that day" to Haldeman at the home of Higby, one of his former aides at the White House.

July 9. Huston says that Nixon never formally rescinded the 1970 intelligence gathering plan.

July 12. In a closed morning session, the Ervin committee discusses possible subpoena of White House files. Senator Baker proposes that one last attempt be made to have President Nixon relinquish them voluntarily. A letter is sent to the White House, asking for a meeting. During the lunch recess, Ervin gets a call from President Nixon, who agrees to meet privately as a "courtesy." Shortly thereafter, the President enters Bethesda (Md.) Naval Hospital with viral pneumonia.

July 13. Senator Ervin suggests that representatives of the White House and his committee pick out the pertinent documents from the Presidential files and submit them to the committee. "I see no great difficulty with a little cooperation."

July 16. Butterfield reveals that since 1970 President Nixon has taped all conversations and phone calls in his offices, in the Lincoln room and at Camp David. Buzhardt confirms the existence of the recording equipment, alleging that similar systems were used by previous Administrations; the Secret Service says this is the only Administration to request installation of such a system.

July 17. After President Nixon forbids the Secret Service to testify before the Select Committee about his recording system, Ervin sends him a letter, asking for cooperation in making relevant tapes available.

July 18. Cox writes President Nixon requesting the tapes. He argues that since he is part of the executive branch, the doctrine of separation of powers does not apply to him.

July 19. Judge Sirica grants Cox's request for a second grand jury to investigate campaign irregularities apart from those related to Watergate. Its hearings will begin on Aug. 13.

July 19. Someone claiming to be Treasury Secretary Schultz phones Senator Ervin at the lunch recess and says that President Nixon will make the tapes available to the committee. A few minutes after so announcing publicly, Senator Ervin learns the phone call was a hoax.

July 20. Leaving the hospital, President Nixon labels rumors that he is planning to resign as "just plain poppycock." He adds, "Let others wallow in Watergate; we are going to do our job."

July 23. President Nixon rejects the Ervin committee's request for tapes on the grounds of Presidential privilege. He also refuses to yield to Cox requested tapes of eight specific conversations. The committee and Cox issue subpoenas, which are accepted by Garment and Buzhardt.

July 24. Warren confirms that President Nixon has discontinued the practice of taping his conversations.

July 25. President Nixon informs Judge Sirica that he will not release the tapes Cox has requested because to do so would jeopardize the "independence of the three branches of Government."

July 25. President Nixon announces the resignation of John Connally as an unpaid, part-time Presidential adviser.

July 25. After finishing his questioning of Ehrlichman, Senator Inouye says to himself, "What a liar." But his microphone is still turned on. He first denies, then admits saying it.

July 26. After President Nixon "respectfully refuses" to release tapes subpoenaed by the Ervin committee, the committee Senators vote unanimously to take the matter before the courts. Cox obtains a show-cause order from Judge Sirica directing President Nixon to explain by Aug. 7 why he should not be compelled to release the tapes. Warren says the President "would abide by a definitive decision of the highest court" regarding the tapes.

July 27. Cox states that any Supreme Court ruling is "definitive." Warren maintains that some Supreme Court rulings are "less than definitive."

July 29. Senators Ervin and Baker propose, in a television interview, that they privately hear President Nixon's tapes and omit irrelevant portions.

July 30. Warren says that President Nixon will not compromise his position on the tapes.

July 30. Haldeman reveals listening to the Sept. 15 tape earlier this month and to a March 21 tape in April.

July 31. Dash suggests that by allowing Haldeman to listen to tapes after he left the White House employ, President Nixon may have undermined his claim of confidentiality.

July 31. Representative Robert F. Drinan (Mass., Dem.) becomes the first member of Congress to introduce an impeachment resolution against the President for "high crimes and misdemeanors."

July 31. The House Armed Services Committee unanimously votes to cite Liddy for contempt of Congress for his refusal to answer questions on July 20.

Aug. 1. The Ervin committee releases a Colson memo of March 30, 1972, which details other internal memos that link President Nixon and Mitchell to a favorable I.T.T. settlement and Mitchell to perjury in the Kleindienst confirmation hearings.

Aug. 1. The California Bar Association discloses that in May it began an inquiry into the conduct of six of its members tied to Watergate: President Nixon, Ehrlichman, Kalmbach, Mardian, Strachan and Segretti.

Aug. 1. Toasting visiting Japanese Premier Kakevi Tanaka, Nixon says that a nation should not "be remembered only for the petty, little, indecent things that seem to obsess us. . . . Let others spend their time dealing with the murky, small, unimportant, vicious little things. We . . . will spend our time building a better world."

Aug. 1. Wilson, Haldeman's attorney, calls Senator Inouye "that little Jap." He later refuses to apologize, saying, "I wouldn't mind being called a little American."

Aug. 2. Judge Sirica hints that he may postpone the D.N.C. suit if more indictments are forthcoming in the Watergate investigation.

Aug. 2. McCord reveals in the Armed Forces Journal that if the F.B.I. had searched his car after his arrest, they would have discovered $18,000 and enough evidence to break the Watergate case.

Aug. 7. Select Committee hearings recess until September. In 37 daily sessions, it had taken sworn testimony from 33 witnesses and compiled 7,537 pages of testimony.

Aug. 7. In a 34-page brief to Judge Sirica, White House attorneys say that "the President is answerable to the Nation but not the courts" in his exercise of executive privilege.

Aug. 9. The Ervin committee files suit in Federal District Court, Washington, D. C., seeking an order to force President Nixon to relinquish tapes.

Aug. 13. Cox files a rebuttal to the White House brief, declining to release Presidential tapes, stating that President Nixon has "no constitutional power" to withhold evidence.

Aug. 13. A second Watergate grand jury is empaneled in Washington, D. C., to investigate illegal campaign financing, the I.T.T. settlement and other obstructions of justice.

Aug. 14. Judge Sirica grants immunity to Hunt in his forthcoming appearance before the new Federal grand jury.

Aug. 14. The Gallup Poll reveals that, at 31 per cent, President Nixon's popularity is the lowest of any President's in 20 years. It has dropped 37 points in seven months.

Aug. 15. In a televised address, President Nixon denies any guilt, charging that Dean's accusations are uncorroborated. He offers no rebuttal to specific questions, and defends his refusal to yield the tapes.

Aug. 16. Magruder pleads guilty to a one-count indictment for conspiracy to obstruct justice, defraud the United States and unlawfully intercept wire and oral communications by eavesdropping at D.N.C. headquarters. Judge Sirica postpones sentencing until he can evaluate how cooperative Magruder has been with Government attorneys.

Aug. 17. White House lawyers file a response to Cox's Aug. 13 brief, stating that the President has "absolute power" to withhold the tapes on grounds of confidentiality.

Aug. 22. Cox and Wright present their arguments on the Presidential tapes in United States District Court. Judge Sirica says he will rule on the case within a week.

Aug. 22. In his first news conference in five months, the President says he has turned from Watergate, which is "water under the bridge," to the "people's business." He accepts "all" the blame for the climate that produced the break-in and cover-up, and reiterates his position on the Presidential tapes.

Aug. 29. White House attorneys file papers rejecting the Ervin committee's demand for Presidential tapes and charging that the committee conducted a "criminal investigation and trial" that exceeded the authority granted to Congress by the Constitution. They assert that, as President or as an individual, Nixon "owes no duty" to the committee to yield the tapes. In response, the committee files a motion for summary judgment that the two subpoenas issued on its behalf be enforced with a minimum of further court proceedings.

Aug. 29. Judge Sirica orders President Nixon to make the tapes available to him for a decision on their use by the grand jury. The White House issues a statement that Nixon "will not comply with the order," and that his attorneys are considering appeal or "how otherwise to sustain" the President's legal position.

Aug. 30. After President Nixon confers with Wright, Buzhardt and Haig, the White House announces that he will appeal Judge Sirica's ruling that he must yield tapes of his conversations.

Aug. 30. Judge Sirica refuses to consolidate the suits brought against the President by Cox and the Select Committee.

Sept. 4. The United States Court of Appeals for the District of Columbia, acting before any appeal is filed with it, orders that all court proceedings at the intermediate Federal level be completed by the end of next week, in order to clear the way for a decision by the appellate court before the end of September and for an appeal to the Supreme Court immediately after it reconvenes on Oct. 1.

Sept. 4. A Los Angeles County grand jury returns secret indictments in Los Angeles Superior Court against Ehrlichman, Liddy, Krogh and Young on charges of burglary and conspiracy to commit burglary in connection with the Dr. Fielding break-in. In addition, Ehrlichman is charged with perjury before the grand jury on July 8, and Krogh is charged with solicitation to commit burglary.

Sept. 4. Krogh hands over to California prosecutors a 53-point memorandum in which he admits he approved the "mission" that resulted in the break-in at the office of Ellsburg's psychiatrist and says that "general authorization" for the "covert activity" was given by Ehrlichman.

Sept. 5. At his second news conference in two weeks, when pressed about the investigation ordered personally by him on March 21, President Nixon says that when Dean "was unable to write a report, I turned to Mr. Ehrlichman," who "did talk to the Attorney General . . . I think it was the 27th of March." He says the investigation was "conducted in the most thorough way." The President also defends executive privilege regarding the tapes: "Confidentiality once destroyed cannot . . . be restored." He says his lawyers will discuss what constitutes a "definitive" Supreme Court ruling, but declines to say whether he will voluntarily relinquish the tapes should the Supreme Court rule in his favor. The President concedes that in the past four months his confidence has been "worn away" "by innuendo, by leak, by, frankly, leers and sneers of commentators."

Sept. 6. Judge Sirica grants President Nixon's attorney a two-week delay in filing a response to the Ervin committee's latest motion, making it virtually impossible that a final ruling on the tapes will be reached before Congress adjourns its 1973 session.

Sept. 6. Attorneys for President Nixon appeal Judge Sirica's Aug. 29 decision, contending that the judge has no power to compel the President to make his private records available.

Sept. 6. Krogh pleads not guilty to charges of burglary, conspiracy and solicitation of burglary in connection with the break-in at the office of Ellsberg's psychiatrist. He tells reporters his defense will be based on his belief that "what I undertook was fully authorized and lawful" as a matter of "extraordinary national importance."

Sept. 7. Replying to the May 2 request, Attorney General Richardson assures the Ervin committee that it will have access, wherever possible, to F.B.I. Watergate reports, with the understanding that there will probably be some instances where access will have to be deferred or denied. Access will be allowed to such members of the staff as Ervin and Baker jointly designate.

Sept. 7. Cox files a petition in the U.S. Court of Appeals for the District of Columbia, asking that President Nixon be ordered to deliver tapes of his conversations directly to the grand jury, without the prior judicial screening requested by Judge Sirica in his Aug. 29 ruling. If such judicial review is not eliminated, Cox requests that it be regulated by court-established guidelines for Sirica to use in screening the tapes.

Sept. 7. Ehrlichman and Young plead not guilty to indictments brought against them by the California grand jury.

Sept. 10. White House attorneys file a 95-page brief in the U.S. Court of Appeals, requesting a nullification of Judge

Sirica's Aug. 29 ruling, on grounds that any discussions of Watergate that President Nixon might have had with his aides were in line with "his constitutional duty to see that the laws are faithfully executed," and thus are exempt from any grand jury scrutiny. They charge that Judge Sirica's decision "was reached by casting the Constitution in the mold of Watergate rather than by applying constitutional practices and restraints to the facts of Watergate," and assert that "it is more important that the privacy of the Presidency be preserved than that every possible bit of evidence that might assist in criminal prosecutions be produced." The judicial branch is "absolutely without power to reweigh that choice or to make a different resolution of it."

Sept. 10. Cox files a 46-page brief with the U.S. Court of Appeals, requesting that the Presidential tapes either be delivered directly to the grand jury without judicial inspection or that Judge Sirica be provided with specific guidelines as to what he can properly delete as privileged information. Cox labels executive privilege with regard to the tapes "intolerable," on the grounds that "the predominant public interest" makes law enforcement more important than Presidential privacy.

Sept. 10. Judge Sirica files papers with the U.S. Court of Appeals in reply to the two briefs submitted today by the White House and Cox. He defends his Aug. 29 ruling, but indicates no objection to court-provided guidelines for his screening of the Presidential tapes.

Sept. 11. Judges Roger Robb and Edward Allen Tamm of the U.S. Court of Appeals for the District of Columbia disqualify themselves from judicial proceedings on the Presidential tapes. Judge Robb reportedly withdraws because a former law partner had worked for C.R.P.; no reason is given for Judge Tamm's action.

Sept. 11. For more than three hours, the U.S. Court of Appeals hears arguments by Wright and Cox over tape recordings of nine Presidential conversations. Pressed under cross-examination, Wright says, "It is clear beyond peradventure that if the President had engaged in a conspiracy, he would be wholly beyond the jurisdiction of the grand jury or this court. That no President can be indicted before he is impeached is as clear as anything can be."

Sept. 12. In their first meeting since August 7, in a 75-minute closed-door session, the Ervin committee votes to resume its hearings on Sept. 24 and end them by November 1, holding three sessions a week. This will give them only 18 days to finish the break-in phase of their hearings and to examine the two broader phases of their investigation: Presidential campaign sabotage and financing. Denying suggestions that the committee is responding to White House and G.O.P. pressure, Ervin says the hearings will focus on "key witnesses" and "salient points" without going into "such detail that we won't be able to see the forest for the bushes and the trees."

Sept. 12. Judge Gagliardi of the Federal District Court in New York City grants a postponement in the Mitchell-Stans trial, at the urging of the U.S. Court of Appeals for the Second Circuit. Defense attorneys had argued that such a delay was necessary because demands on their clients' time by the Ervin committee, D.N.C. attorneys, the special prosecutors and others, had left them insufficient time to prepare their own cases.

Sept. 13. The seven judges of U.S. Court of Appeals for the District of Columbia unanimously adopt a 600-word memorandum urging an out-of-court compromise to the dispute over the Presidential tapes. They recommend that portions of the recordings be examined by Cox, Wright and the President or his delegate, who would then decide which parts could properly be released to the grand jury. Cox indicates his willingness to comply; the White House says it is studying the proposal.

Sept. 13. Attorneys for Mitchell issue a subpoena for a wide range of unspecified White House tapes and documents, covering a 15-month period beginning November 1, 1971, which might be related even indirectly to the obstruction-of-justice charges that Mitchell faces. This appears to be the first defense effort to imply a possible link between the Mitchell-Stans case and President Nixon. The Government moves to quash the subpoena, calling it "a broad-ranging blunderbuss fishing expedition."

Sept. 14. Barker, Sturgis, Gonzales and Martinez file a petition in U.S. District Court that their Jan. 15, 1973 guilty plea be changed to not guilty for conspiracy, burglary and wiretapping in connection with the D.N.C. break-in. They contend they were victims of a "cruel fraud," originally pleading guilty to keep from exposing secret national security operations.

Sept. 17. Hunt petitions the U.S. District Court to withdraw his plea of guilty and to dismiss the burglary, wiretapping and conspiracy charges against him, stemming from the D.N.C. break-in. Claiming that he thought he had acted lawfully to protect the national security, Hunt's petition says, "Whether or not the evidence, unexposed because of now known notorious corruption by Government officials would have established the defendant's innocence, such misconduct so gravely violated his constitutional rights as to require dismissal of the proceedings."

Sept. 19. In a brief filed with the U.S. Court of Appeals for the District of Columbia, President Nixon's lawyers state that, "To tear down the office of the American Presidency is too high a price to pay, even for Watergate."

Sept. 20. In similar letters filed with the U.S. Court of Appeals, Cox and White House attorneys say that in meetings on Sept. 17, 19 and 20, they had failed to agree reach an out-of-court settlement on access to the Presidential tapes.

Sept. 20. Cox files a brief in U.S. District Court challenging five of the original bugging conspirators to substantiate their charges that they were lured into their crime by "high government officials," by submitting "detailed, factual statements under oath."

Sept. 20. Liddy pleads not guilty to charges relating to the break-in at the office of Ellsberg's psychiatrist.

RULES OF PROCEDURE FOR THE SELECT COMMITTEE ON PRESIDENTIAL CAMPAIGN ACTIVITIES

With Guidelines, and
S. Res. 60 (93d Cong.)
S. Res. 278 (91st Cong.)
United States Senate

Senate Select Committee on Presidential Campaign Activities

SAM J. ERVIN, JR., North Carolina, *Chairman*
HOWARD H. BAKER, JR., Tennessee, *Vice Chairman*

HERMAN E. TALMADGE, Georgia   EDWARD J. GURNEY, Florida
DANIEL K. INOUYE, Hawaii   LOWELL P. WEICKER, JR.,
JOSEPH M. MONTOYA, New Mexico   Connecticut

SAMUEL DASH, *Chief Counsel and Staff Director*
FRED D. THOMPSON, *Minority Counsel*
RUFUS L. EDMISTEN, *Deputy Chief Counsel*

DAVID M. DORSEN, *Assistant Chief Counsel*
TERRY F. LENZNER, *Assistant Chief Counsel*
JAMES HAMILTON, *Assistant Chief Counsel*
CARMINE S. BELLINO, *Chief Investigator*
WAYNE H. BISHOP, *Chief Field Investigator*
EUGENE BOYCE, *Hearings Record Counsel*
R. PHILLIP HAIRE, *Assistant Counsel*
MARC LACKRITZ, *Assistant Counsel*
WILLIAM T. MAYTON, *Assistant Counsel*
RONALD D. ROTUNDA, *Assistant Counsel*
DONALD G. SANDERS, *Deputy Minority Counsel*
HOWARD S. LIEBENGOOD, *Assistant Minority Counsel*
H. WILLIAM SHURE, *Assistant Minority Counsel*
ROBERT SILVERSTEIN, *Assistant Minority Counsel*
LAURA MATZ, *Administrative Assistant*
CAROLYN ANDRADE, *Office Manager*
JOAN C. COLE, *Secretary to the Minority*

S. Res. 60

93D CONGRESS, 1ST SESSION

IN THE SENATE OF THE UNITED STATES

FEBRUARY 5, 1973

MR. ERVIN (for himself and MR. MANSFIELD) submitted the following resolution; which was ordered to be placed on the calendar.

FEBRUARY 7, 1973

Considered, amended, and agreed to

RESOLUTION

To establish a select committee of the Senate to conduct an investigation and study of the extent, if any, to which illegal, improper, or unethical activities were engaged in by any persons, acting individually or in combination with others, in the presidential election of 1972, or any campaign, canvass, or other activity related to it.

Resolved, SECTION 1. (a) That there is hereby established a select committee of the Senate, which may be called, for convenience of expression, the Select Committee on Presidential Campaign Activities, to conduct an investigation and study of the extent, if any, to which illegal, improper, or unethical activities were engaged in by any persons, acting either individually or in combination with others, in the presidential election of 1972, or in any related campaign or canvass conducted by or in behalf of any person seeking nomination or election as the candidate of any political party for the office of President of the United States in such election, and to determine whether in its judgment any occurrences which may be revealed by the investigation and study indicate the necessity or desirability of the enactment of new congressional legislation to safeguard the electoral process by which the President of the United States is chosen.

(b) The select committee created by this resolution shall consist of seven Members of the Senate, four of whom shall be appointed by the President of the Senate from the majority Members of the Senate upon the recommendation of the majority leader of the Senate, and three of whom shall be appointed by the President of the Senate from the minority Members of the

Senate upon the recommendation of the minority leader of the Senate. For the purposes of paragraph 6 of rule XXV of the Standing Rules of the Senate, service of a Senator as a member, chairman, or vice chairman of the select committee shall not be taken into account.

(c) The select committee shall select a chairman and vice chairman from among its members, and adopt rules of procedure to govern its proceedings. The vice chairman shall preside over meetings of the select committee during the absence of the chairman, and discharge such other responsibilities as may be assigned to him by the select committee or the chairman. Vacancies in the membership of the select committee shall not affect the authority of the remaining members to execute the functions of the select committee and shall be filled in the same manner as original appointments to it are made.

(d) A majority of the members of the select committee shall constitute a quorum for the transaction of business, but the select committee may fix a lesser number as a quorum for the purpose of taking testimony or depositions.

SEC. 2. That the select committee is authorized and directed to do everything necessary or appropriate to make the investigation and study specified in section 1(a). Without abridging or limiting in any way the authority conferred upon the select committee by the preceding sentence, the Senate further expressly authorizes and directs the select committee to make a complete investigation and study of the activities of any and all persons or groups of persons or organizations of any kind which have any tendency to reveal the full facts in respect to the following matters or questions:

(1) The breaking, entering, and bugging of the headquarters or offices of the Democratic National Committee in the Watergate Building in Washington, District of Columbia;

(2) The monitoring by bugging, eavesdropping, wiretapping, or other surreptitious means of conversations or communications occurring in whole or in part in the headquarters or offices of the Democratic National Committee in the Watergate Building in Washington, District of Columbia;

(3) Whether or not any printed or typed or written document or paper or other material was surreptitiously removed from the headquarters or offices of the Democratic National Committee in the Watergate Building in Washington, District of Columbia, and thereafter copied or reproduced by photography or any other means for the information of any person or political committee or organization:

(4) The preparing, transmitting, or receiving by any person for himself or any political committee or any organization of any report or information concerning the activities mentioned in subdivision (1), (2), or (3) of this section, and the information contained in any such report;

(5) Whether any persons, acting individually or in combination with others, planned the activities mentioned in subdivision (1), (2), (3), or (4) of this section, or employed any of the participants in such activities to participate in them, or made any payments or promises of payments of money or other things of value to the participants in such activities or their families for their activities, or for concealing the truth in respect to them or any of the persons having any connection with them or their activities, and, if so, the source of the moneys used in such payments, and the identities and motives of the persons planning such activities or employing the participants in them;

(6) Whether any persons participating in any of the activities mentioned in subdivision (1), (2), (3), (4), or (5) of this section have been induced by bribery, coercion, threats, or any other means whatsoever to plead guilty to the charges preferred against them in the District Court of the District of Columbia or to conceal or fail to reveal any knowledge of any of the activities mentioned in subdivision (1), (2), (3), (4), or (5) of this section, and, if so, the identities of the persons inducing them to do such things, and the identities of any other persons or any committees or organizations for whom they acted;

(7) Any efforts to disrupt, hinder, impede, or sabotage in any way any campaign, canvass, or activity conducted by or in behalf of any person seeking nomination or election as the candidate of any political party for the office of President of the United States in 1972 by infiltrating any political committee or organization or headquarters or offices or home or whereabouts of the person seeking such nomination or election or of any person aiding him in so doing, or by bugging or eavesdropping or wiretapping the conversations, communications, plans, headquarters, offices, home, or whereabouts of the person seeking such nomination or election or of any other person assisting him in so doing, or by exercising surveillance over the person seeking such nomination or election or of any person assisting him in so doing, or by reporting to any other person or to any political committee or organization any information obtained by such infiltration, eavesdropping, bugging, wiretapping, or surveillance;

(8) Whether any person, acting individually or in combination with others, or political committee or organization induced any of the activities mentioned in subdivision (7) of this section or paid any of the participants in any such activities for their services, and, if so, the identities of such persons, or committee, or organization, and the source of the funds used by them to procure or finance such activities;

(9) Any fabrication, dissemination, or publication of any false charges or other false information having the purpose of

discrediting any person seeking nomination or electing as candidate of any political party to the office of President of the United States in 1972;

(10) The planning of any of the activities mentioned in subdivision (7), (8), or (9) of this section, the employing of the participants in such activities, and the source of any moneys or things of value which may have been given or promised to the participants in such activities for their services, and the identities of any persons or committees or organizations which may have been involved in any way in the planning, procuring, and financing of such activities.

(11) Any transactions or circumstances relating to the source, the control, the transmission, the transfer, the deposit, the storage, the concealment, the expenditure, or use in the United States or in any other country, of any moneys or other things of value collected or received for actual or pretended use in the presidential election of 1972 or in any related campaign or canvass or activities preceding or accompanying such election by any person, group of persons, committee, or organization of any kind acting or professing to act in behalf of any national political party or in support of or in opposition to any person seeking nomination or election to the office of President of the United States in 1972;

(12) Compliance or noncompliance with any act of Congress requiring the reporting of the receipt or disbursement or use of any moneys or other things of value mentioned in subdivision (11) of this section;

(13) Whether any of the moneys or things of value mentioned in subdivision (11) of this section were placed in any secret fund or place of storage for use in financing any activity which was sought to be concealed from the public, and, if so, what disbursement or expenditure was made of such secret fund, and the identities of any person or group of persons or committee or organization having any control over such secret fund or the disbursement or expenditure of the same;

(14) Whether any books, checks, canceled checks, communications, correspondence, documents, papers, physical evidence, records, recordings, tapes, or materials relating to any of the matters or questions the select committee is authorized and directed to investigate and study have been concealed, suppressed, or destroyed by any persons acting individually or in combination with others, and, if so, the identities and motives of any such persons or groups of persons;

(15) Any other activities, circumstances, materials, or transactions having a tendency to prove or disprove that persons acting either individually or in combination with others, engaged in any illegal, improper, or unethical activities in connection with the presidential election of 1972 or any campaign, canvass, or activity related to such election;

(16) Whether any of the existing laws of the United States are inadequate, either in their provisions or manner of enforcement to safeguard the integrity or purity of the process by which Presidents are chosen.

SEC. 3. (a) To enable the select committee to make the investigation and study authorized and directed by this resolution, the Senate hereby empowers the select committee as an agency of the Senate

(1) to employ and fix the compensation of such clerical, investigatory, legal, technical, and other assistants as it deems necessary or appropriate;

(2) to sit and act at any time or place during sessions, recesses, and adjournment periods of the Senate;

(3) to hold hearings for taking testimony on oath or to receive documentary or physical evidence relating to the matters and questions it is authorized to investigate or study;

(4) to require by subpena or otherwise the attendance as witnesses of any persons who the select committee believes have knowledge or information concerning any of the matters or questions it is authorized to investigate and study;

(5) to require by subpena or order any department, agency, officer, or employee of the executive branch of the United States Government, or any private person, firm, or corporation, or any officer or former officer or employee of any political committee or organization to produce for its consideration or for use as evidence in its investigation and study any books, checks, canceled checks, correspondence, communications, document, papers, physical evidence, records, recordings, tapes, or materials relating to any of the matters or questions it is authorized to investigate and study which they or any of them may have in their custody or under their control;

(6) to make to the Senate any recommendations it deems appropriate in respect to the willful failure or refusal of any person to appear before it in obedience to a subpena or order, or in respect to the willful failure or refusal of any person to answer questions or give testimony in his character as a witness during his appearance before, it, or in respect to the willful failure or refusal of any officer or employee of the executive branch of the United States Government or any person, firm, or corporation, or any officer or former officer or employee of any political committee or organization, to produce before the committee any books, checks, canceled checks, correspondence, communications, document, financial records, papers, physical evidence, records, recordings, tapes, or materials in obedience to any subpena or order;

(7) to take depositions and other testimony on oath anywhere within the United States or in any other country;

(8) to procure the temporary or intermittent services of individual consultants, or organizations thereof, in the same

manner and under the same conditions as a standing committee of the Senate may procure such services under section 202(i) of the Legislative Reorganization Act of 1946;

(9) to use on a reimbursable basis, with the prior consent of the Government department or agency concerned and the Committee on Rules and Administration, the services of personnel of any such department or agency;

(10) to use on a reimbursable basis or otherwise with the prior consent of the chairman of any other of the Senate committees or the chairman of any subcommittee of any committee of the Senate the facilities or services of any members of the staffs of such other Senate committees or any subcommittees of such other Senate committees whenever the select committee or its chairman deems that such action is necessary or appropirate to enable the select committee to make the investigation and study authorized and directed by this resolution;

(11) to have access through the agency of any members of the select committee, chief majority counsel, minority counsel, or any of its investigatory assistants jointly designated by the chairman and the ranking minority member to any data, evidence, information, report, analysis, or document or papers relating to any of the mattters or questions which it is authorized and directed to investigate and study in the custody or under the control of any department, agency, officer, or employee of the executive branch of the United States Government having the power under the laws of the United States to investigate any alleged criminal activities or to prosecute persons charged with crimes against the United States which will aid the select committee to prepare for or conduct the investigation and study authorized and directed by this resolution; and

(12) to expend to the extent it determines necessary or appropriate any moneys made available to it by the Senate to perform the duties and exercise the powers conferred upon it by this resolution and to make the investigation and study it is authorized by this resolution to make.

(b) Subpenas may be issued by the select committee acting through the chairman or any other member designated by him, and may be served by any person designated by such chairman or other member anywhere within the borders of the United States. The chairman of the select committee, or any other member thereof is hereby authorized to administer oaths to any witnesses appearing before the committee.

(c) In preparing for or conducting the investigation and study authorized and directed by this resolution, the select committee shall be empowered to exercise the powers conferred upon committees of the Senate by section 6002 of title 18 of the United States Code or any other Act of Congress regulating the granting of immunity to witnesses.

SEC. 4. The select committee shall have authority to recommend the enactment of any new congressional legislation which its investigation considers it is necessary or desirable to safeguard the electoral process by which the President of the United States is chosen.

SEC. 5. The select committee shall make a final report of the results of the investigation and study conducted by it pursuant to this resolution, together with its findings and its recommendations as to new congressional legislation it deems necessary or desirable, to the Senate at the earliest practicable date, but no later than February 28, 1974. The select committee may also submit to the Senate such interim reports as it considers appropriate. After submission of its final report, the select committee shall have three calendar months to close its affairs, and on the expiration of such three calendar months shall cease to exist.

SEC. 6. The expenses of the select committee through February 28, 1974, under this resolution shall not exceed $500,000, of which amount not to exceed $25,000 shall be available for the procurement of the services of individual consultants or organizations thereof. Such expenses shall be paid from the contingent fund of the Senate upon vouchers approved by the chairman of the select committee. The minority members of the select committee shall have one-third of the professional staff of the select committee (including a minority counsel) and such part of the clerical staff as may be adequate.

S. Res. 278

91ST CONGRESS, 1ST SESSION
(Report No. 91–515)

IN THE SENATE OF THE UNITED STATES

NOVEMBER 5, 1969

MR. CANNON, from the Committee on Rules and Administration, reported the following resolution; which was ordered to be placed on the calendar

NOVEMBER 11, 1969
Considered and agreed to

RESOLUTION

Relating to fees of witnesses appearing before Senate committees.
Resolved, That witnesses summoned to appear before the

Senate or any of its committees shall be entitled to a witness fee rated at not to exceed $25 for each full day spent in traveling to and from the place of examination and for each full day in attendance. A witness shall also be entitled to reimbursement of the actual and necessary transportation expenses incurred by him in traveling to and from the place of examination, in no case to exceed 20 cents a mile for the distance actually traveled by him for the purpose of appearing as a witness if such distance is not more than six hundred miles or 12 cents a mile if such distance is more than six hundred miles.

EXCERPTS FROM TESTIMONY BEFORE THE SENATE SELECT COMMITTEE ON PRESIDENTIAL CAMPAIGN ACTIVITIES

Opening Statements by Senators Sam J. Ervin Jr. and Howard H. Baker Jr.

May 17, 1973

SENATOR ERVIN: We are beginning these hearings today in an atmosphere of the utmost gravity. The questions that have been raised in the wake of the June 17 break-in strike at the very undergirding of our democracy. If the many allegations made to this date are true, then the burglars who broke into the headquarters of the Democratic National Committee at the Watergate were in effect breaking into the home of every citizen of the United States. And if these allegations prove to be true, what they were seeking to steal was not the jewels, money or other property of American citizens, but something much more valuable —their most precious heritage, the right to vote in a free election.

Since that day, a mood of incredulity has prevailed among our populace, and it is the constitutional duty of this committee to act expeditiously to allay the fears being expressed by the citizenry, and to establish the factual bases upon which these fears have been founded.

The first phase of the committee's investigation will probe the planning and execution of the wiretapping and break-in of the Democratic National Committee's headquarters at the Watergate complex, and the alleged cover-up that followed. Subsequent phases will focus on allegations of campaign espionage and subversion and allegations of extensive violations of campaign financing laws. The clear mandate of the unanimous Senate resolution provides for a bipartisan investigation of every phase of political espionage and illegal fund raising. Thus it is clear that we have the full responsibility to recommend any remedial legislation necessary.

In pursuing its task, it is clear that the committee will be dealing with the workings of the democratic process under which we operate in a nation that still is the last, best hope of mankind in his eternal struggle to govern himself decently and effectively.

We will be concerned with the integrity of a governmental system designed by men who understood the lessons of the past and who, accordingly, established a framework of separated governmental powers in order to prevent any one branch of the government from becoming dominant over the others.

The founding fathers, having participated in the struggle against arbitrary power, comprehended some eternal truths respecting men and government. They knew that those who are entrusted with power are susceptible to the disease of tyrants, which George Washington rightly described as "love of power and the proneness to abuse it." For that reason, they realized that the power of public officers should be defined by laws which they, as well as the people, are obligated to obey, a truth enunciated by Daniel Webster when he said that "whatever government is not a government of laws is a despotism, let it be called what it may."

To the end of ensuring a society governed by laws, these men embodied in our Constitution the enduring principles in which they so firmly believed, establishing a legislature to make all laws, an executive to carry them out, and a judicial system to interpret them.

Recently, we have been faced with massive challenges to the historical framework created in 1787, with the most recent fears having been focused upon assertions by Administrations of both parties of executive power over the Congress—for example, in the impoundment of appropriated funds and the abuse of executive privilege. Those challenges, however, can and are being dealt with by the working of the system itself—that is, through the enactment of powerful statutes by the Congress, and the rendering of decisions by the courts upholding the law-making power of the Congress.

In dealing with the challenges posed by the multitudinous allegations arising out of the Watergate affair, however, the select committee has a task much more difficult and complex than dealing with intrusions of one branch of the government upon the power of the others. It must probe into assertions that the very system itself has been subverted and its foundations shaken.

To safeguard the structural scheme of our governmental system, the founding fathers provided for an electoral process by which the elected officials of this nation should be chosen. The Constitution, later adopted amendments, and more specifically, statutory law, provide that the electoral processes shall be conducted by the people, outside the confines of the formal branches of the government, and through a political process that must operate under the strictures of law and ethical guidelines, but independent of the overwhelming power of the government itself. Only then can we be sure that each electoral process cannot be made to serve as the mere handmaiden of a particular Administration in power.

If the allegations that have been made in the wake of the Watergate affair are substantiated, there has been a very serious subversion of the integrity of the electoral process, and the committee will be obliged to consider the manner in which such a subversion affects the continued existence of this nation as a representative democracy, and how, if we are to survive, such subversions may be prevented in the future.

It has been asserted that the 1972 campaign was influenced by a wide variety of illegal or unethical activities, including the widespread wiretapping of the telephones, political headquarters, and even the residences of candidates and their campaign staffs and of members of the press; by the publication of forged documents designed to defame certain candidates or enhance others through fraudulent means; the infiltration and disruption of opponents' political organizations and gatherings; the raising and handling of campaign contributions through means designed to circumvent, either in letter or in spirit, the provisions of campaign disclosure acts; and even the acceptance of campaign contributions based upon promises of illegal interference in governmental processes on behalf of the contributors.

Finally, and perhaps most disturbingly, it has been alleged that, following the Watergate break-in, there has been a massive attempt to cover up all the improper activities, extending even so far as to pay off potential witnesses and, in particular, the seven defendants in the Watergate trial in exchange for their promise to remain silent—activities which, if true, represent interference in the integrity of the prosecutorial and judicial processes of this nation. Moreover, there has been evidence of the use of governmental instrumentalities in efforts to exercise political surveillance over candidates in the 1972 campaign.

Let me emphasize at the outset that our judicial process thus far has convicted only the seven persons accused of burglarizing and wiretapping in the Democratic National Committee headquarters at the Watergate complex on June 17. The hearings which we initiate today are not designed to intensify or reiterate unfounded accusations or to poison further the political climate of our nation. On the contrary, it is my conviction and that of the other committee members that the accusations that have been leveled and the evidence of wrongdoing that has surfaced has cast a black cloud of distrust over our entire society. Our citizens do not know whom to believe, and many of them have concluded that all the processes of government have become so compromised that honest governance has been rendered impossible.

We believe that the health, if not the survival of our social structure and of our form of government requires the most candid and public investigation of all the evidence and of all the accusations that have been leveled at any persons, at whatever level, who were engaged in the 1972 campaign. My colleagues on the committee and I are determined to uncover all the relevant facts surrounding these matters, and to spare no one, whatever his station in life may be, in our efforts to accomplish that goal. At the same time, I want to emphasize that the purpose of these hearings is not prosecutorial or judicial, but rather investigative and informative.

No one is more cognizant than I of the separation of powers issues that hover over these hearings. The committee is fully aware of the ongoing grand jury proceedings that are taking place in several areas of the country, and of the fact that criminal indictments have been returned already by one of these grand juries. Like all Americans, the members of this committee are vitally interested in seeing that the judicial processes operate effectively and fairly, and without interference from any other branch of government.

The investigation of this select committee was born of crisis, unabated as of this very time, the crisis of a mounting loss of confidence of American citizens in the integrity of our electoral process which is the bedrock of our democracy. The American people are looking to this committee, as the representative of all the Congress, for enlightenment and guidance regarding the details of the allegations regarding the subversion of our electoral and political processes.

As the elected representatives of the people, we would be derelict in our duty to them if we failed to pursue our mission expeditiously, fully, and with the utmost fairness. The aim of the committee is to provide full and open public testimony in order that the nation can proceed toward the healing of the wounds that now afflict the body politic. It is that aim that we are here to pursue today, within the terms of the mandate imposed upon us by our colleagues and in full compliance with all applicable rules of law. The nation and history itself are watching us. We cannot fail our mission.

SENATOR BAKER: I believe there is no need for me to further emphasize the gravity of the matters that we begin to explore publicly here this morning. Suffice it to say there are most serious charges and allegations made against individuals, and against institutions. The very integrity of our political process itself has been called into question.

Commensurate with the gravity of the subject matter under review and the responsibilities of this committee and the witnesses who come before it, we have a great burden to discharge and carry. This committee is not a court, nor is it a jury. We do not sit to pass judgment on the guilt or innocence of anyone.

The greatest service that this committee can perform for the Senate, the Congress, and for the people of this nation is to achieve a full discovery of all of the facts that bear on the subject of this inquiry. This committee was created by the Senate to do exactly that. To find as many of the facts, the circumstances and the relationships as we could, to assemble those facts into a coherent and intelligible presentation and to make recommendations to the Congress for any changes in statute law or the basic charter document of the United States that may seem indicated.

But this committee can serve another quite important function that neither a grand jury investigation nor a jury proceeding is equipped to serve, and that is to develop the facts in full view of all of the people of America. Although juries will eventually determine the guilt or the innocence of persons who have been and may be indicted for specific violations of the law, it is the American people who must be the final judge of Watergate. It is the American people who must decide, based on the evidence spread before them, what Watergate means about how we all should conduct our public business in the future.

When the resolution which created this committee was being debated on the floor of the Senate in February of this year, I and other Republican Senators expressed concern that the inquiry might become a partisan effort by one party to exploit the temporary vulnerability of another. Other Congressional inquiries in the past had been conducted by committees made up of equal numbers of members from each party. I offered an amendment to the resolution which would have given the Republican members equal representation on this committee. That amendment did not pass.

But any doubts that I might have had about the fairness and impartiality of this investigation have been swept away during the last few weeks. Virtually every action taken by this committee since its inception has been taken with complete unanimity of purpose and procedure. The integrity and fairness of each member of this committee and of its fine professional staff have been made manifest to me, and I know they will be made manifest to the American people during the course of this proceeding. This is not in any way a partisan undertaking, but, rather it is a bipartisan search for the unvarnished truth.

I would like to close, Mr. Chairman, with a few thoughts on the political process in this country. There has been a great deal of discussion across the country in recent weeks about the impact that Watergate might have on the President, the office of the Presidency, the Congress, on our ability to carry on relations with other countries, and so on.

The constitutional institutions of this Republic are so strong and so resilient that I have never doubted for a moment their ability to function without interruption. On the contrary, it seems clear to me the very fact that we are now involved in the public process of cleaning our own house, before the eyes of the world, is a mark of the greatest strength. I do not believe that any other political system could endure the thoroughness and the ferocity of the various inquiries now under way within the branch of government and in our courageous, tenacious free press.

No mention is made in our Constitution of political parties. But the two-party system, in my judgment, is as integral and as important to our form of government as the three formal branches of the central government themselves. Millions of Americans participated actively, on one level or another, and with great enthusiasm, in the Presidential election of 1972.

This involvement in the political process by citizens across the land is essential to participatory democracy. If one of the effects of Watergate is public disillusionment with partisan politics, if people are turned off and drop out of the political system, this will be the greatest Watergate casualty of all.

If, on the other hand, this national catharsis in which we are now engaged should result in a new and better way of doing political business, if Watergate produces changes in laws and campaign procedures, then Watergate may prove to be a great national opportunity to revitalize the political process and to involve even more Americans in the day-to-day work of our two great political parties.

I am deeply encouraged by the fact that I find no evidence at this point in time to indicate that either the Democratic National Committee or the Republican National Committee played any role in whatever may have gone wrong in 1972. The hundreds of seasoned political professionals across this country, and the millions of people who devoted their time and energies to the campaigns, should not feel implicated or let down by what has taken place.

With these thoughts in mind, I intend to pursue, as I know each member of this committee intends to pursue, an objective and even-handed but thorough, complete, and energetic inquiry into the facts. We will inquire into every fact and follow every lead, unrestrained by any fear of where that lead might ultimately take us.

Testimony by Robert C. Odle Jr.

May 17, 1973

Says Magruder had file removed from his desk soon after Watergate break-in.

MR. ODLE: I would like to use this opportunity to make just one brief point. I joined the staff of the Committee for the Re-election of the President more than two years ago because I believed in President Nixon and in his hopes and dreams for America. I still do.

During my association with the committee, I came into contact with more than 400 members of its national staff, salaried and volunteer. It now appears tragically that some of those people have acted unethically.

The point I want to make is this, that when we discuss the committee, we should remember that in addition to those who did wrong and who did act unethically, there were a million volunteers across the nation and 400 people at national headquarters who did nothing unethical or illegal.

MR. DASH: Now, Mr. Odle, who were the initial persons who came over and formed the Committee to Re-elect the President or gave it its start?

A. There was Mr. Jeb Magruder, Mr. Harry S. Fleming, Mr. Hugh W. Sloan Jr., myself, Dr. Robert Merrick, Mr. Herbert Porter, and a number of secretaries who went there to assist us.

SENATOR WEICKER: Did you participate in the emptying of Mr. Magruder's desk with Robert Reisner on June 17?

A. Yes, sir, Mr. Magruder asked Mr. Reisner and myself to take certain things home over the weekend, because at the time it appeared that he was concerned for the security of them. My best recollection is that I took home a file folder and he took home some other file folders and brought them back the following Monday or sometime.

Q. Now, who made the suggestion that Mr. Magruder's desk be emptied?

A. Well, I don't—first of all, I am not exactly sure of the chronology of events. I don't believe that anybody made the suggestion that the desk be emptied, although he expressed concern over the telephone from California—

Q. Will you give the committee your best recollection of that conversation?

A. My best recollection is that he was extremely concerned that we might be subject to similar activities, that there might be retaliation, that he was concerned for the security of the office building and the files and the papers, and he wanted certain things to be taken home over the weekend.

As I remember it, Mr. Reisner took home a lot of advertising matters, I believe.

All I know is the way it ended up is that I had a file and Mr. Reisner had some files and we brought them back the next week.

Q. Then what did you do with that file?

A. I put it in my briefcase.

Q. Then what happened to the file?

A. Then on Monday I returned it.

Q. Did Mr. Strachan participate rather actively in matters over at the Committee to Re-elect the President? A. Yes, sir.

Q. Can you tell me why, what his specific mission was?

A. Mr. Haleman obviously was worried a lot with a lot of other things besides the campaign. He was the chief of staff at the White House and a very busy man working on Government substantive policies and he was assisting the President. Mr. Strachan was there to devote himself more to what was going on politically so if Mr. Haldeman wanted to be aware of what was going on politically and simply asked Mr. Strachan, Mr. Strachan was simply the eyes and ears, you might say.

Testimony by James W. McCord Jr.

May 18   *Says Caulfield offered executive clemency
in the name of the President and asked for
silence.*

May 22   *Says Hunt and Liddy made plans for burglary at Las Vegas newspaper.*

May 18, 1973

MR. DASH: Could you briefly state for the committee, Mr.
McCord, what that was that Mr. Liddy wanted you to do?

MR. McCORD: Gradually, the discussion in December, January, February of 1972 with Mr. Liddy, gradually developed into
more and more conversation on his part with me in the offices of
the Committee for the Re-election of the President regarding the
technical devices and political matters pertaining to the forthcoming convention, and that became apparent that he had an interest
in several areas of intelligence gathering pertaining to the Democratic party and the Democratic convention, and in which it was
contemplated or planned by him and by others whom he referred
to in these conversations as John Mitchell; John Dean, counsel
to the President; Jeb Magruder, then in January the interim director of the Committee to Re-elect the President; in which it appeared
that those men, the four of them, were in the—by late January—
the planning stage in which political intelligence was to be discussed at meetings at the Attorney General's office, Mr. Mitchell's
office, and in which Mr. Liddy was seeking from me certain information regarding the costs and the types of electronic devices
that could be used in bugging.

That the part of the budget proposal which he was working,
working on, the second part dealt with photography operations,
clandestine photography operations, and a third part dealt with
the broad area of political espionage, political intelligence.

The topic of photography, clandestine photography, in which
he was preparing the budget and preparing to meet with the
gentlemen I have referred to before, in planning sessions, dealt
with photographic equipment and the cost of photographic equipment and specific items of equipment that would be used against
the Democratic party, the Democratic hierarchy in Washington
primarily, but also in Miami, Fla. The electronic devices which
he referred to specifically were of a variety of types.

Q. I am not asking specifically what the types were, but how
were they to be used, where were they to be placed from your
understanding?

A. The initial interests specified by Mr. Liddy in this regard were, number one, against Mr. Larry O'Brien, then chairman of the Democratic National Committee in Washington, D. C., at his residence and subsequently at his office in the Watergate office building. Perhaps other officers of the Democratic National Committee. The McGovern headquarters in Washington, D. C., were mentioned quite early in 1972. And there was some general reference to the Democratic National Convention facility or site wherever it might be located at this convention in the summer of 1972.

Q. All right now, Mr. McCord, in connection with this assignment in which you were having these discussions with Mr. Liddy, did you come to associate yourself with Mr. E. Howard Hunt, Bernard Barker, Eugenio Martinez, Frank Sturgis and Virgilio Gonzalez? A. Yes, I did.

Q. And as a result of that association and your agreement with Mr. Liddy, did you with Mr. Barker, Sturgis, Martinez and Gonzalez illegally enter the Democratic National Committee headquarters on two occasions, one on or about May 30, 1972, and the other in the early morning hours of June 17, 1972? A. I did.

Q. On the first occasion on or about May 30, 1972, you installed two telephone interception devices or wiretaps on two office telephones, one on the telephone of Spencer Oliver and the other on the telephone of Lawrence O'Brien? A. I did.

Q. Will you tell the committee, Mr. McCord, why, after a lifetime of work as a law enforcement officer without, as you have testified, any blemish on your career, did you agree with Mr. Liddy to engage in his program of burglaries and illegal wiretapping and specifically the two break-ins on May 30 and June 17 of the National Democratic Committee headquarters at the Watergate?

A. There were a number of reasons associated with the ultimate decision of mine to do so. One of the reasons, and a very important reason to me, was the fact that the Attorney General himself, Mr. John Mitchell, had his, at his office, had considered and approved the operation, according to Mr. Liddy.

Secondly, that the counsel for the President, Mr. John Dean, had participated in those decisions with him. That one was the top legal officer for the United States at the Department of Justice, and the second gentleman the top legal officer in the White House, and it was a matter that had currently been given—

Q. Did you have any knowledge, directly or indirectly, that would lead you to believe or have information that the C.I.A. was involved in this plan?

A. I had just the contrary, that there was no indication, no intelligence, no statements to me that this was a C.I.A. operation; that, quite the contrary, that it was an operation which involved the Attorney General of the United States at that point in time— subsequently, he became the director of the Committee to Re-elect the President—involved the counsel to the White House; involved

Mr. Jeb Magruder and Mr. Liddy, who was then general counsel, at that point in time, of the Committee to Re-elect the President and, subsequently, was the finance committee general counsel. Therefore, in my mind there was an absolute certainty that the C.I.A. was not involved, neither did I ever receive any statement from any of the other codefendants, at any point in time up to June 17 or subsequently, that this was a C.I.A. operation.

Q. For the record, your restatement of your belief that the Attorney General, Mr. Magruder, other than Mr. Liddy, was hearsay based on what Mr. Liddy told you and Mr. Hunt? A. That is correct.

Q. Now, Mr. McCord, did you engage in any other break-ins or wiretaps on your own or with Mr. Hunt, Mr. Liddy, or others such as the break-in in Mr. Ellsberg's psychiatrist's office? A. I did not.

Q. Now, after your arrest, which you testified to, did you receive any money? A. Yes, I did.

Q. From whom did you receive that money?

A. From the wife of E. Howard Hunt, Mrs. Hunt.

Q. Can you tell us how much money you did receive?

A. Yes, I received legal fees of $25,000 for the payment of lawyers. I received a continuation of salary from July through January at the rate of $3,000 a month, which the others were receiving as well.

Q. Did you have knowledge, information, and belief as to where this money came from?

A. I was told that it came from the Committee to Re-elect the President by Mrs. Hunt.

Q. Now, after your arrest and at the time of the indictment, after the trial or during the trial, did you receive any pressure, suggestions from any persons concerning what you should do about that trial with regard to your plea, behavior, or conduct?

A. Yes, I did.

Q. Would you now please state to the committee from whom you received such directions or pressures, and what it was?

A. Yes, it extended over a period of time beginning, to the best of my recollection, in late September or early October, 1972, and it continued through the night before my conviction on Jan. 29, 1973. The persons who communicated information to me, which I construed as political pressure, included Mr. E. Howard Hunt; Mrs. Hunt speaking for Mr. Hunt, she stated; my attorney, Mr. Gerald Alch; John P. Caulfield.

Conversations with Mr. Hunt began, to the best of my recollection, in late September or early October, 1972, when I was seeing him at the courthouse on various pretrial exercises or events, motions, that were transpiring, in which we would talk about various matters, including the situation that we were in, what the trial appeared to be at that point in time—that is, what the future looked like for us; and in telephone conversations, with him to me.

In other words, both in person and by telephone, Mr. Hunt

stated that the defendants were going to be provided with, given executive clemency after a period of time in prison, if interested, if they pled guilty, and were sentenced in a plea of not guilty, that they were going to be given financial support while they were in prison; that is, their families would be; and that rehabilitation, not specified but rehabilitation, perhaps a job, would be provided for the men after the release from prison.

Q. All right. Let us leave out for the moment Mrs. Hunt. Would you now proceed to any conversations you had leading up to contacts with Mr. Caulfield and what Mr. Caulfield did state to you?

A. I have a statement sir, in this regard.

The subject is political pressure on the writer to accept executive clemency and remain silent.

Political pressure from the White House was conveyed to me in January, 1973, by John Caulfield to remain silent, take executive clemency by going off to prison quietly, and I was told that while there, I would receive financial aid and later rehabilitation and a job. I was told in a January meeting in 1973 with Caulfield that the President of the United States was aware of our meeting, that the results of the meeting would be conveyed to the President, and that at a future meeting there would likely be a personal message from the President himself.

On the afternoon of Jan. 8, 1973, the first day of the Watergate trial, Gerald Alch, my attorney, told me that William O. Bittman, attorney for E. Howard Hunt, wanted to meet with me at Bittman's office that afternoon. When I asked why, Alch said that Bittman wanted to talk with me about "whose word I would trust regarding a White House offer of executive clemency." Alch added that Bittman wanted to talk with both Bernard Barker and me that afternoon.

I had no intention of accepting executive clemency, but I did want to find out what was going on, and by whom, and exactly what the White House was doing now. A few days before, the White House had tried to lay the Watergate operation off on C.I.A., and now it was closer that I was going to have to find out what was up now. To do so involved some risks. To fail to do so was, in my opinion, to work in a vacuum regarding White House intentions and plans, which involved even greater risks, I felt.

Around 4:30 P.M. that afternoon, Jan. 8, while waiting for a taxi after the court session, Bernard Barker asked my attorneys and me if he could ride in the cab with us to Bittman's office, which we agreed to. There he got out of the cab and went up towards Bittman's office. I had been under the impression during the cab ride that Bittman was going to talk to Barker and me jointly, and became angered at what seemed to me to be the arrogance and audacity of another man's lawyer calling in two other lawyers' clients and pitching them for the White House.

Alch saw my anger and took me aside for about a half-hour

after the cab arrived in front of Bittman's office, and let Barker go up alone. About 5 P.M. we went up to Bittman's office. There Alch disappeared with Bittman, and I sat alone in Bittman's office for a period of time, became irritated, and went next door, where Bernard Shankman and Austin Mittler, attorneys for me and Hunt respectively, were talking about legitimate legal matters.

I might add at this point, parenthetically, no knowledge whatever that either Bernard Shankman or Austin Mittler had any knowledge whatever of the events which I am discussing in this memorandum.

Alch finally came back, took me aside and said that Bittman told him I would be called that same night by a friend I had known from the White House.

I assumed this would be John Caulfield, who had originally recruited me for the Committee for the Re-election of the President position.

About 12:30 P.M. that same evening I received a call from an unidentified individual who said that Caulfield was out of town and asked me to go to a pay phone booth near the Blue Fountain Inn on Route 355 near my residence, where he had a message for me from Caulfield. There the same individual called and read the following message:

"Plead guilty.

"One year is a long time. You will get executive clemency. Your family will be taken care of and when you get out you will be rehabilitated and a job will be found for you.

"Don't take immunity when called before the grand jury."

Q. Now, Mr. McCord, did you recognize that voice at all? Do you know who was speaking to you on the telephone?

A. I do not know who the man was—the voice I heard over the telephone before in previous calls.

SENATOR GURNEY: Would you proceed.

A. I would be glad to. Sometime in July, 1972, shortly after I got out of jail, which was in June, 1972, about midday there was a note in my mailbox at my residence and when I opened the letter, which had not been stamped nor sent through the mails, it was a note from Jack Caulfield signed "Jack" which said, "Go to the phone booth on Route 355 near your home," and he gave three alternate times at which I could appear at the phone booth for a telephone call from him.

To the best of my recollection, one of those times was very shortly thereafter, an hour or two later, and another time was the next day, and it seems to me that the third time was the following evening.

I went to the telephone, to that telephone booth on Route 355, that afternoon, the same afternoon, as I best recall, and I heard the voice that I have referred to in this memorandum of today. I do not know the individual's identity; he had an accent that I would refer to as a New York accent. He said that he had formerly worked for Jack Caulfield. He said, "I am a friend of Jack's, I formerly worked with him. Jack will want to talk with you shortly. He will be in touch with you soon."

I received a call subsequently from Mr. Caulfield. To the best of my recollection it came to my home first and it said, "Go to the same phone booth on Route 355," which I did, and there Mr. Caulfield told me that he was going overseas in a few days. He said, "If you have any problems—if you have any problems —call my home and leave word and I will call you back from overseas to your residence."

He said, "When you call my home ask for Mr. Watson."

Q. Mr. Watson?

A.—Watson, he said. Also, "After my return if you ever need to call me at my office," he gave a number, the office number and he said: "Simply leave word that Mr. Watson is calling."

So it was a name that both of us were to use, my name and his name. I did not contact him during the next 30 days and I next heard from him, to the best of my recollection, sometime in September, 1972, on a Sunday afternoon.

I can't recall the exact date but I do recall that Mr. Clark MacGregor, then the head of the Committee for the Re-election of the President, had just finished a television appearance on one of the talk programs such as "Meet the Press," and Mr. Caulfield called me at home and again asked that I go to the telephone booth on Route 355, which I did. He stated that he had trouble getting my home phone number because it was an unlisted number, and he stated: "We are worried about you"—this is Mr. Caulfield's statement—and he went on then to read briefly the words of a deposition which he planned to give to the Democratic National Committee—I had read in the papers a few days before that he had been scheduled as a witness before the Democratic National Committee—and he read the deposition to me indicating that this was, in effect, what he planned to say in the deposition.

There was some reference during the conversation to something with a double agent, in quotes; Mr. Clark MacGregor, as I recall, in his television appearance had referred to the possibility of there being a double agent in the Watergate operation and the inference was that it was Mr. Baldwin, and I told Mr. Caulfield that, so far as I was concerned, whoever had drawn that conclusion had drawn absolutely an erroneous conclusion, that I had seen absolutely nothing that would indicate such, and I simply wanted to go on the record with Mr. Caulfield to that effect.

I told the caller I would not discuss such matters over the phone. He said that Caulfield was out of town.

On Wednesday evening, Jan. 10, the same party, to the best of my recollection, called and told me by phone that Jack would want to talk with me by phone on Thursday night, the following night, Jan. 11, when he got back into town and requested that I go to the same phone booth on Route 355 near the Blue

Fountain Inn. He also conveyed instructions regarding a personal meeting with Mr. Caulfield on Friday night, Jan. 12.

On Friday night, Jan. 12, from about 7 P.M. to 7:30 P.M., I met with Caulfield at the second overlook—that is, overlooking the Potomac at the parking area, for looking at the Potomac area on George Washington Parkway in Virginia.

MR. DASH: Mr. McCord, how did you know to go there? How was it arranged?

A. I met with Caulfield at the second overlook on George Washington Parkway—that is, the second one leaving Washington and going out to Virginia—and talked with him in his car, in his automobile. Caulfield advised that he had been attending a law enforcement meeting in San Clemente, Calif., and had just returned. I advised him that I had no objection to meeting with him to tell him my frame of mind but that I had no intention of taking executive clemency or pleading guilty; that I had come to the meeting at his request and not of my own, and was glad to tell him my views.

He said that the offer of executive clemency which he was passing along, and of support while in prison and rehabilitation and help toward a job later, "was a sincere offer." He explained that he had been asked to convey this message to me and he was only doing what he was told to do. He repeated this last statement several times during the course of the meeting we had then, and I might add during subsequent meetings which he and I had.

My response was that I would not even discuss executive clemency or pleading guilty and remaining silent, but I was glad to talk with him, so that there was no misunderstanding on anyone's part about it.

I might explain that the trial was going on during this period. This was the first week of the trial which began on Jan. 8.

Caulfield stated that he was carrying the message of executive clemency to me "from the very highest levels of the White House." He stated that the President of the United States was in Key Biscayne, Fla., that weekend, had been told of the forthcoming meeting with me, and would be immediately told of the results of the meeting.

SENATOR ERVIN: Now the same rule previously announced. This evidence is competent to show what, if anything, John Caulfield did to induce Mr. McCord to plead guilty and keep silent. It is not any evidence at the present state of the hearing that connects, that makes any indication whatever and has any relevancy as to the President.

A. He further states that "I may have a message to you at our next meeting from the President himself."

I advised Caulfield that I had seen the list of witnesses for the trial and had seen Jeb Magruder's name, appearing as a Government witness. I advised him that it was clear then that

Magruder was going to perjure himself and that we were not going to get a fair trial. Further, I told him that it was clear that some of those involved in the Watergate case were going to trial and others were going to be covered for [I was referring to John Mitchell, John Dean and Magruder] and I so named those individuals, incidentally, in the conversation, and I said that this was not my idea of American justice.

The executive clemency offer was made two or three times during this meeting, as I recall, and I repeated each time that I would not even discuss it, nor discuss pleading guilty, which I had been asked to do in the first telephone call received on the night of Jan. 8, from Caulfield's friend, whose identity I do not know. I told him, referring to Mr. Caulfield, that I was going to renew the motion on disclosure of Government wiretapping of our telephones.

I did not hear from Caulfield on Saturday, but on Sunday afternoon he called and asked to meet me that afternoon about an hour later at the same location on George Washington Parkway. He stated that there was no objection to renewing the motion on discovery of Government wiretapping, and that if that failed, that I would receive executive clemency after 10 to 11 months. I told him I had not asked anyone's permission to file the motion.

He went on to say that, "The President's ability to govern is at stake. Another Teapot Dome scandal is possible, and the Government may fall. Everybody else is on track but you. You are not following the game plan. Get closer to your attorney. You seem to be pursuing your own course of action. Do not talk if called before the grand jury, keep silent and do the same if called before a Congressional committee."

He—talking about Caulfield—asked for a commitment that I would remain silent and I responded that I would make none. I gave him a memorandum on the dates of the two calls of mine in September, 1972, and October, 1972, that I was sure had been intercepted, and said that I believed the Government had lied about them. He said that he would check and see if in fact the Government had done so.

On Monday night, Jan. 15, 1973, Caulfield called me again at the phone booth on Route 355 near my residence. I informed him that I had no desire to talk further, that if the White House had any intention of playing the games straight and giving us the semblance of a fair trial they would check into the perjury charge of mine against Magruder, and into the existence of the two intercepted calls previously referred to, and hung up.

On Tuesday evening, Caulfield called and asked me again to meet him and I responded not until they had something to talk about on the perjured testimony and the intercepted calls. He said words to the effect "give us a week," and a meeting was subsequently arranged on Jan. 25, 1973, when he said he would have something to talk about.

About 10 A.M., on Thursday, Jan. 25, 1973, in a meeting lasting until about 12:30 A.M.—correction, 12:30 P.M.—we drove in his car toward Warrenton, Va., and returned—that is, we drove there and returned—and a conversation ensued which repeated the offers of executive clemency and financial support while in prison, and rehabilitation later. I refused to discuss it.

He stated that I was "fouling up the game plan." I made a few comments about the "game plan." He said that "they" had found no record of the interception of the two calls I referred to, and said that perhaps I'll wait until the appeals. He asked what my plans were regarding talking publicly, and I said that I planned to do so when I was ready; that I had discussed it with my wife and she said that I should do what I felt I must and not to worry about the family. I advised Jack that my children were now grown and could understand what I had to do, when the disclosures came out.

He responded by saying that "you know that if the Administration gets its back to the wall, it will have to take steps to defend itself." I took that as a personal threat and I told him in response that I had had a good life, that my will was made out and that I had thought through the risks and would take them when I was ready. He said that if I had to go off to jail that the Administration would help with the bail premiums.

I advised him that it was not a bail premium, but $100,000 straight cash and that that was a problem I would have to worry about, through family and friends. On the night before sentencing, Jack called me and said that the Administration would provide the $100,000 in cash if I could tell him how to get it funded through an intermediary. I said that if we ever needed it I would let him know. I never contacted him thereafter; neither have I heard from him.

That completes the statement.

MR. THOMPSON: Mr. McCord, I would like to limit my questions to one area. That is what you know about the planning of the Watergate break-in. First of all, I would like to separate what Mr. Hunt told you someone said about it from what Mr. Liddy told you someone said about it. Did Mr. Hunt indicate to you that he knew anything about these meetings that Mr. Liddy referred to with Mitchell, Magruder and Dean?

A. The question is, did Mr. Hunt indicate—

Q. Yes, sir.

A. That he knew anything about the meetings?

Q. Yes, sir.

A. Yes, he did.

Q. What did he say about those meetings? Did he indicate he was present at any of those meetings?

A. The meetings, as best I recall, in which these references by Mr. Hunt took place, took place in Mr. Hunt's office, in the Robert F. Mullen Company offices at 1700 Pennsylvania Avenue. They took place in April and May of 1972. To the best of my recollection, Mr. Liddy was present in all of the discussions.

Mr. Liddy, during those discussions, as best I recall, would raise the topic that the planning and the progress of the operation itself was going forward, comments about what Mr. Mitchell was saying to him about what could be done in terms of the priorities of the operation; that is, which ones were to be done first and second.

Mr. Hunt's comments, his exact words I cannot recall, but his comments made to me—and not to me, made in three-way discussions that were taking place during that period of time—indicated to me that he had separate, independent knowledge, perhaps from Mr. Liddy, perhaps from other sources, of his own that Mr. Mitchell and Mr. Dean and Mr. Magruder had planned operations in the Attorney General's office to begin with and that at least Mr. Mitchell and Mr. Magruder had had subsequent discussions after the first meeting in the Attorney General's office, and that Mr. Magruder and Mr. Mitchell had had discussion with Mr. Liddy in Mr. Mitchell's offices at the Committee to Re-elect the President regarding the on-going plans to carry out the operations.

Does this answer your question somewhat?

Q. Well, I think it naturally raises several other questions. What did he say, as best you can recall, to indicate to you that he had any independent knowledge other than what Mr. Liddy might have told him?

A. It would fall into two separate categories. I said, one, what Mr. Liddy had told him before and, secondly, what he had learned from others. I mentioned to this committee the name of another individual, but I will not mention it at this point, that Mr. Hunt referred to in conversations, in which they were talking about the Watergate operations and the planning for the operations and so on. The statement—

Q. I think you should refer to the name.

A. He referred to the name of Mr. Colson. That was interjected into the conversation by Mr. Hunt in the meetings with Mr. Liddy and me in his office, Hunt's offices, at 1700 Pennsylvania Avenue, and, specifically, when Mr. Hunt had a plan, a typed plan, operational plan, for the entry of the Democratic National Committee headquarters.

Q. Do you recall anything that Mr. Hunt said to you, about Mr. Colson's involvement, or did you just get the general impression that Mr. Colson was involved in some way from what Mr. Hunt told you?

A. I believe my previous testimony, which I will restate before this committee, was to the effect that, when I had met Mr. Hunt in his offices at 1700 Pennsylvania Avenue with Mr. Liddy, that he had referred to his previous work at the White House for Mr. Colson, referring to him as his superior; that during the session that Mr. Hunt, Mr. Liddy, and I had in Mr. Hunt's offices, Mr. Hunt had a typed plan that he had typed himself, step-by-step, for the entry of the Democratic National Committee headquarters; that at one point, he held this plan in his hands, and his words were, he interjected the name of Mr. Colson into the conversation at that point, words to the effect, "I will see Colson." And he held the paper in his hand in this sense.

From that statement, I drew the conclusion that he was going to see Mr. Colson and discuss our giving him the operational plan. That is a conclusion, but this is also the words as best I recall, with which Mr. Hunt raised the name of Mr. Colson.

Q. I am sure that will need to be pursued. But getting back to my original point, is that innocent of knowledge Mr. Hunt had of these meetings we referred to, he did not bring Mr. Colson into the conversation with regard to these particular meetings that you previously referred to, did he?

A. I believe you asked me if he appeared to have knowledge. I said he appeared to have knowledge of the previous meetings of the Attorney General, in the Attorney General's office, of Mr. Liddy, Mr. Magruder and Mr. Dean and my response was to the effect that he had it from Mr. Liddy from what he told me, and I believed also that he had this information from others.

Q. You say that you think he had independent knowledge, and, of course, this is a serious matter. I think we have to determine whether or not we are relying on Mr. Liddy or Mr. Hunt and Mr. Liddy for this information, which, of course, is extremely important information. Anything you can state that Mr. Hunt told you to indicate that he had any independent knowledge of these meetings, I think would be very relevant. You can do it now or supply—you have supplied several memorandums that are very helpful in that regard. If you want to do that at a subsequent time, I think that would be appropriate.

A. I would be glad to submit the committee a memorandum if that would be helpful to you, and set it forth in exactly the detail as best I recall.

Q. Now, let us get back to the meetings in a little bit more detail, Mr. McCord. How many meetings did Mr. Liddy say there were when the over-all surveillance operations were discussed?

A. At what point in time?

Q. Well, how many meetings, over all, up until June 17, did Mr. Liddy indicate that he, Mitchell, Magruder and Dean, or any combination of these people, had to discuss generally?

A. He did not say the number. It was stated to me in various and sundry meetings with Mr. Liddy between January and June 17 by Mr. Liddy that he had had several meetings with Mr. Mitchell; that there appeared to be ongoing meetings with Mr. Mitchell from the planning stage until the completion of the plans for the second entry operation on June 17; that there appeared to be continuous discussions between at least Mr. Liddy and Mr. Magruder, according to statements which Mr. Liddy made to me, and they began with the planning and they continued through the ongoing operation itself. The monitoring and the planning for the second operation and discussions at various stages, according to Mr. Liddy, of the various priorities of the bugging and photography operations, what was to come first, what was to come second.

Q. Did Mr. Liddy come to you after each important meeting, or after each meeting where these plans were discussed, and give you a summary of the meetings, what was discussed and what the conclusions were?

A. Not after each meeting at all, but we would see each other regularly during the week. I would say not once a day but every other day, most weeks between January and June 17. Sometimes he would tell me, I am getting ready to go up to see the Attorney General to discuss this operation, referring to the Watergate operation, to discuss the operations that he had planned.

Sometimes he would tell me, I have just come back from that operation, concluding what we are going to do now.

Q. Were some of these meetings, according to what he told you, while Mr. Mitchell was still Attorney General. A. Yes.

Q. And some after he came to the Committee to Re-elect? A. Yes.

Q. Were money figures discussed? A. Oh, yes.

Q. According to what he said—according to Mr. Liddy, what was the original proposed budget for the over-all surveillance operation? I assume we are talking about the over-all operation, not just the Watergate break-in, is that correct?

A. We are taking about three categories—political espionage, photography operations, and electronic operations, and the original figure in February that Mr. Liddy proposed, as I saw it in writing, in a draft on his desk on one occasion and in a typed memorandum on a second occasion, was approximately $450,000.

Q. All right, according to him, was that budget approved?

A. The sequence of the events were that there were planning meetings in January or February or both in the Attorney General's offices, in which Mr. Dean and Mr. Magruder, Mr. Liddy and Mr. Mitchell and sometimes Mitchell discussed the original amount, the $450,000 amount, and subsequently, approximately 30 days after the first formal meetings and I heard referred to by Mr. Liddy, there was a figure of approximately $250,000, which he said had been approved for the operation. And he referred also to some additional funds which he had in the order of approximately $100,000, but that figure is not absolutely certain in my mind, with a total of something around $300,000 or $350,000.

Q. According to him, was this money problem the need for subsequent meetings? Was that a concern of the people involved? Was there quite a bit of discussion as to exactly how much money should be spent on this project?

A. Money was a topic that he said was discussed. He said the individual operations were discussed—that is, specifically the three parts of his budget which he had prepared on charts, which he had taken to at least one of the meetings. That is the three parts of political espionage and photography and so on. It was not limited, the discussion was not limited to the matter of funding. My understanding was all aspects of the operation were discussed in those meetings by the four individuals.

Q. Let me just ask you this: Did he tell you that John Mitchell ever told him that this budget is just too high and you will have to do it for less or something to that extent? A. No, he did not.

Q. Did he ever tell you that they specifically discussed the Watergate operation in any of these meetings? A. Oh, yes, sure.

Q. That the Watergate break-in specifically was discussed? A. Very definitely.

Q. What did he say about that particular discussion?

A. It was a contiguous discussion. He sat in with Mr. Magruder from the earliest planning session in January through the first entry operation, Memorial Day weekend and then even to the second operation in June, and he talked to me at various times and it was clear from what he said that their committee—that Mr. Liddy was having such meetings—he stated they were having such meetings in which the Watergate operation was a part, of Watergate, referring to the Democratic National Committee headquarters himself.

So I would say there were many such discussions by Mr. Liddy with me in which he stated that meetings had occurred with Mr. Mitchell and Magruder specifically on this after February.

Q. You mentioned, you mentioned I believe, that you had frequent contact with Liddy. Did you have frequent contact with Mr. Magruder at the Committee to Re-elect? A. Yes, I did.

Q. Would you see him on a daily basis?

A. We would see each other on a daily basis. We would speak hello, exchange greetings. My point of contact at the committee was his deputy, Mr. Odle. My business was transacted primarily with Mr. Odle, their offices were adjoining.

Q. Their offices were close together?

A. So we would see each other frequently in that sense.

Q. Just to speak, or did you ever discuss any substantive matters concerning the re-election of the President or the operation of the Committee to Re-elect the President?

A. We had some meetings, one particular meeting with the Attorney General and Mr. Magruder lasting over an hour in which we discussed over-all security of the committee and the security of the Mitchell family.

Q. At that time in March you had pretty much made up your mind, I assume, you would, if the thing was funded, that you would participate for the reasons that you have given?

A. The decision process, I think, on my part took place after the 30-day delay that I referred to here in which it appeared that this whole matter was being considered, reconsidered, discussed and so on by Mr. Mitchell. It was also very material to me that he had considered it while in the Attorney General's office, that the discussion had taken place there and he apparently had approved it and so on, but I had some reasons for considering the 30-day delay important, and this was part of my motivation.

Q. You say you saw Mr. Liddy often and you saw Mr. Magruder often and you had this one meeting with the two of them. Did anything they said to you or did anything that you overheard them say to other people, any telephone conversations that you might have accidentally heard indicate to you that what Liddy was telling you was in fact true, or did any of these things in your mind corroborate what Mr. Liddy was telling you?

A. About what, the meetings with the Attorney General in his office? Mr. Liddy had some charts which I have described to this committee before, which he said cost some $7,000 to prepare, in which he set forth the plans, as I understood it, the cost of the operation. The fact that he would go to so much trouble and to so much expense, it was obvious to me this was officially approved by somebody in the operation within the committee itself and the Attorney General in order for that amount of money to be spent for material of this sort, to go to that much trouble.

Q. Pardon me, did you ever see the charts themselves?

A. Yes, I saw the charts when he brought them in the day before he said a meeting was scheduled with the Attorney General. He pointed to the chart and said, "These are for the briefing with the Attorney General tomorrow. These are connected with the papers which I have shown to you—the draft and the type of budget draft that he had and showed to me on a day or two before. He did not unwrap the charts themselves. They were in brown wrapping paper. He said they had been prepared commercially, locally—not locally, he said they had been prepared commercially and he subsequently told me that he had been told by John Dean to destroy the charts, and because they cost so much he did not plan to do so.

Q. He told you he was using these charts in discussion with the Attorney General and others? A. Correct.

Q. So far as conversations by these gentlemen concerning their participation, were there any conversations or anything that they said that you heard which indicated that what Mr. Liddy said about the meeting discussing these things was true?

A. By these gentlemen you are referring to?

Q. I am talking about Mr. Mitchell, Mr. Magruder or Mr. Dean.

A. That is correct. They did not discuss it with me.

SENATOR ERVIN: You say that from after the return of the bills, every indictment, in September down to the day, last day of the trial, that you were urged to plead guilty and remain silent by a number of people. Did Mr. Hunt ever urge you to plead guilty and remain silent? That is, E. Howard Hunt?

A. The words most frequently used by Mr. Hunt with me was that executive clemency would be available to me.

Q. Yes. How many times did he urge you to plead guilty? That is, Hunt?

A. I mean to correct that statement. I do not recall Mr. Hunt using those words with me to plead guilty.

Q. Did he urge you to or not to remain silent?

A. Not in the exact words, no, sir.

Q. What words did he use as far as you remember?

A. He used words to the effect that—he used words stating that "executive clemency is going to be made available to us," and he spoke in terms as though it already had been committed—I say already, already as of the time that he first mentioned it to me.

Q. Now, you stated that you were paid some money through the instrumentality of Mrs. Hunt, and also that your lawyer fees were taken care of, as I understood you? Do you know who paid your lawyer fees?

A. I was told that both monies came from the Committee to Re-elect the President.

Q. Now, did your lawyer urge you to enter a plea of guilty? I am talking about Mr. Gerald Alch. A. I do not recall that, no, sir.

Q. But he did go with you to Mr. Bittman's office? A. Yes, sir.

Q. And Mr. Bittman was the lawyer for Mr. Hunt, was he not? A. Yes, sir.

Q. And then after that, you did not talk to Mr. Bittman yourself? A. No, sir.

Q. But Mr. Alch did? A. Yes, sir.

Q. And after his conversation with Mr. Bittman he told you that Mr. Bittman urged you to plead guilty and remain silent and said you would get executive clemency?

A. I will correct that, sir, if I left that impression. I believe the words were that in the afternoon of Jan. 8, Mr. Alch said that Mr. Bittman wanted to talk with me about "whose word I would trust regarding a White House offer of executive clemency," and then at the meeting at his office Mr. Alch came back to me after a meeting with Mr. Bittman and told me that I would be contacted by "a friend I have formerly known in the White House," and contacted that evening. I believe that was the substance of the conversation.

Q. How long had you known—when did you first know John or Jack Caulfield?

A. I first met him in early 19—early September, 1971. I had heard of him before.

Q. Where was he working at the time you first met him?

A. At the White House.

Q. Did Mr. Caulfield later have any association with the committee? A. Yes, sir.

Q. And after that association did he go to one of the executive departments? Do you know which department?

A. I believe it was the Treasury Department.

Q. Did you ever discuss with Mr. Liddy the exercising of electronic surveillance over the offices of Senator Muskie? A. Yes, sir.

Q. And——
A. I will correct that, sir. We discussed the lease of a building. I don't recall electronic surveillance except in some broad general terms this might be a future target. There was nothing beyond that and this was stated in February, 1972.

Q. Now, Senator Muskie was one of the candidates for the Democratic nomination for President at that time? A. Yes, sir.

Q. Did you rent any office near the Muskie headquarters? A. I did.

Q. Where was this office located with reference to the headquarters of Senator Muskie?
A. It was the next building to Senator Muskie's office.

Q. And I believe the lease was taken in your name and that of John B. Hayes? A. Yes, sir.

Q. Who was John B. Hayes?
A. That was another name for Mr. Liddy.

Q. And later, Mr. McGovern took over these headquarters from Senator Muskie, did not he?
A. I think after June 17, yes, sir.

Q. Was there ever any discussion between you and Mr. Liddy about exercising any kind of surveillance over Senator McGovern's headquarters?
A. There were, sir. They were in the context of the location of First Street primarily.

Q. And this room was rented for possible use of that commission, was not it?
A. 1908 K Street was, yes sir.

Q. Did you ever make any effort to bug Senator Muskie's or Senator McGovern's headquarters?
A. Never Senator Muskie's. Senator McGovern's, there was a visit to the office by me, I believe on two, or three occasions in toto, on one of which I had some electronic equipment with me but it was never installed because there were other people working there at the time.

Q. In other words, you never found any time that the office was empty? A. That is correct.

Q. You know who paid the rent on this office?
A. Which one, sir?

Q. Up there by the Muskie and McGovern headquarters?
A. The one at the Muskie office, Mr. Liddy furnished the funds for that and furnished a cashier's check to pay for it.

SENATOR BAKER: What was the electronic assignment that you had?
A. Installation of the technical bugging devices in the Democratic National Committee that were previously authorized by the Attorney General.

Q. Did you have instructions as to where they should be placed?
A. Yes.

Q. Where?

A. In the office themselves in connection with senior personnel officers of the Democratic National Committee and, specifically, Mr. O'Brien's telephone extension.

Q. How many bugs did you plant?

A. Two.

Q. One of them was on Mr. O'Brien's telephone?

A. That was an extension of a call director that was identified as Mr. O'Brien's. The second was Mr. Oliver's.

Q. The second one was where?

A. In a telephone that belonged to Mr. Spencer Oliver, who is an executive director of the Democratic state chairmen of the organization.

Q. Were you specifically instructed by someone to plant those two bugs or just the O'Brien bug? Would you give us some detail on that?

A. Sure. Mr. Liddy had passed along instructions from Mr. John Mitchell. He set the priorities. Mr. Mitchell had stated priorities of the installation were, first of all, Mr. O'Brien's offices and such other installations as that might provide information of interest to Mr. Mitchell and to whoever else the monitoring was to go to beyond Mr. Mitchell.

Q. So the Oliver phone was bugged more or less by your choice, then, as distinguished from the O'Brien phone?

A. No, I think the basic choice was this: The wording from Mr. Liddy was that Mr. Mitchell wanted it placed in a senior official's office, if not Mr. O'Brien's office, some other; in other words, two such installations.

Q. Now, you weren't apprehended on this first occasion, Memorial weekend. What was the purpose of the second entry into the Democratic National Headquarters?

A. Mr. Liddy had told me that Mr. Mitchell, John Mitchell, liked the "takes"; that is, the documents that had been photographed on the first entry into the Democratic National Committee headquarters, and that he wanted a second photographic operation to take place, and that in addition, as long as that team was going in, that Mr. Mitchell wanted, had passed instructions to Mr. Liddy, to check to see what the malfunctioning of the second device that was put in besides Mr. Oliver's, and see what the problem was because it was one of the two things— either a malfunction of the equipment or the fact that the installation of the device was in a room which was surrounded by four walls. In other words, it was shielded, and he wanted this corrected and another device installed.

He also said Mr. Mitchell wanted a room bug as opposed to a device on a telephone installed in Mr. O'Brien's office itself in order to transmit not only telephone conversations but conversations out of the room itself, beyond whatever might be spoken on the telephone.

Q. Did you ever conduct electronic surveillance or clandestine activities against anyone other than the D.N.C., the Democratic National Committee, at the Watergate complex, and the McGovern headquarters which you have already described? A. No.

Q. Mr. McCord, please tell me whether or not you knew that this sort of activity was illegal?

A. I knew certain things that came to me at the beginning of the operation and early in the operation which indicated that it might be legal, may well be legal, and I was so advised.

Q. By whom?

A. First of all, if I may explain, coming through Mr. Liddy and coming through my knowledge of the Attorney General, who was then Attorney General, and that was that the Attorney General, first of all, had the authority on his own signature to approve wiretapping within the United States for either national security reasons or for domestic security reasons.

Q. What was your motivation? Why did you do this?

A. There were several motivations, but one of the basic motivations was the fact that this man, the Attorney General, had approved it in his offices over a series of meetings in which he had obviously given careful consideration to it, while he was the top legal officer of the United States Government, and that the counsel to the President had sat in with him during such discussions; the fact that I was advised that it was within the Attorney General's purview and authority to authorize such operations if it were in the national interest to do so.

Q. Did you believe that?

A. I believed that he had the authority to do it. I believed that several things—not only was I told certain things pertaining to some matters I previously testified to this committee regarding Las Vegas and an incident out there, but I was also aware that many things came over the Attorney General's desk that I was not privy to, that Mr. Liddy was not privy to, but which the Attorney General was privy to, matters which might come to him through highly sensitive sources, wiretap information, which might provide a justification for such an operation, a justification beyond what was known to me.

I can put it conversely as well. I knew that, I felt that the Attorney General in his position as the top legal officer, if this operation were clearly illegal, would turn it down out of hand, that he would have no trouble making a decision on the matter immediately. I knew from previous contact with him that he was a very decisive man, that he did not agonize over decisions, and yet apparently, he took this one under careful consideration and considered it for some 30 days in making the decision, and frankly, I had it, my conclusion was that he took it as well to higher authority and got a final approval from his superior before embarking upon this task.

Quite candidly and quite frankly, this is exactly my motivation, my reason, the basic motivation of mine for being involved.

SENATOR TALMADGE: Did you yourself ever attend a meeting in Mr. Mitchell's office?

A. No, sir.

Q. On any matter?

A. I attended meetings, yes, in his office at the Committee to Re-elect the President when he subsequently came over and I visited at his offices at the Attorney General's office at the Department of Justice in December on another matter but not to discuss these particular operations.

Q. How many different visits or conversations did you ever have with Mr. Mitchell?

A. Numerous, sir.

Q. A dozen, 15, 20, more?

A. I would guess 15.

Q. Does he know you by your name? A. Yes, sir.

Q. You know him? A. Yes, sir.

Q. You called him Mr. Attorney General, I presume? A. Yes, sir.

Q. What did he call you? [Laughter.]

A. Before June 17? [Laughter.]

Q. Before and after.

A. I haven't seen him since June 17. He called me Jim, I believe.

Q. He called you Jim, so you were on a first-name basis with him. And that is the only evidence that you have that would involve either the President of the United States or the Attorney General? A. I am sorry, sir, I missed the question.

Q. The evidence that you have just reported, including the individuals that you have named, based on what they heard others say, which is hearsay, is the only evidence that you had involving either the President or the former Attorney General, is that correct?

A. No, sir. The charts, for example, that I have described here earlier.

Q. I am sorry, I can't hear you—the what?

A. The charts of Mr. Liddy which Mr. Liddy——

Q. Targets?

A. The charts.

Q. The charts?

A. Yes, sir, the cardboard charts, were one other evidence of his meetings with Mr. Mitchell, and subsequently the money which Mr. Liddy transmitted to me for use in the operation he stated came through the duties to the organization of Mr. Mitchell.

Q. Those charts you are also relying on is hearsay testimony on that. A. That is correct, sir. That is correct, sir.

Q. Now, what made you think that either Mr. Caulfield or Mr. Hunt had authority to offer executive clemency to you?

A. Mr. Caulfield because he told me that he was conveying a message from the very top level of the White House.

Q. You assumed when he said top level that meant the President of the United States?

A. I assumed it meant one of three people, sir.

Q. All right, name them.

A. Mr. Haldeman, Mr. Ehrlichman or the President.

Q. And what made you think Mr. Hunt had authority to offer executive clemency?

A. I did not believe that he had the authority but I believe that the message he was conveying probably—that the message did originate with the White House because of several things: one, that I knew from conversations with him and with his wife that he was in touch with the attorneys for the Committee for the Re-election of the President, for one thing.

Q. Who was Mr. Hunt's immediate superior?

A. His immediate superior at the White House, as I understood it from him, was Mr. Charles Colson, if that is your question, sir.

SENATOR WEICKER: Did you or the Committee to Re-elect the President receive reports from the Internal Security Division of the Justice Department? A. Yes, sir, I did.

Q. Was Mr. Mardian head of that division?

A. He had been, sir.

Q. Did you receive copies of F.B.I. reports?

A. I can explain a partial answer to that, sir, if you want me to, an answer that involves F.B.I. reports.

I have raised with, I believe, Mr. Odle the problem of receiving adequate information concerning violence in demonstrations that might affect the committee headquarters in Washington and subsequently, the committee headquarters in Miami, and I asked if there were any way in which there could be some type of liaison to receive information from the F.B.I. specifically, because I knew that they would have information that was not available to us and we knew that such information was being made available to other parties for the convention itself if it directly affected those parties.

As I recall, he sent a memorandum to Mr. Mitchell asking for approval of my contact with that organization.

The next that I heard was a call from Mr. Mardian in which he referred to that memorandum and he stated that Mr. Mitchell had given approval to my contact to acquire that type of information and that I should go to the Internal Security Division of the Department of Justice where such information as did affect, might affect, the security of the committee would be made available to me, some of which was as I have described in those reports, yes, sir.

Q. So you received data from the Internal Security Division of the Justice Department? A. I did.

Q. And you received data from the F.B.I.?

A. Not from the F.B.I. directly, no, sir.

Q. From whom did you receive such data?

A. From the Internal Security Division. I do not believe the F.B.I. was ever aware of that.

Q. You say there was a subsequent memorandum?

A. The memorandum which Mr. Odle wrote on this subject I subsequently received, which had Mr. Mitchell's initials on it.

Q. Do you feel or do you know whether or not similar information, similar access to this information was given to the Democratic party?

A. I understood that they did have through some channels some access to information of this type; whether it came from that office, I do not know.

Q. Now I would like you to describe for me as best you can types of information, further detail, that you received from the Internal Security Division. Did you receive from the Internal Security Division, for example, or from the F.B.I. any information as it related to the candidates or their staffs?

A. Yes, sir, there was one such report that I do recall specifically.

Q. Can you give me details on that report?

A. One such report dealt with, as I recall, a funding operation that was reported in which the McGovern committee purportedly funded a so-called barnstorming tour of several members of the Vietnam Veterans Against the War on the West Coast, as I recall, starting from Los Angeles, Calif., and going up the Coast.

It came concurrently with some other information that that same group was planning violence at the Republican National Convention involving danger to, threats to life of individuals. I think that was succeeded very shortly, in a matter of days, by the indictment of members of the Vietnam Veterans Against the War at Tallahassee because of the violence that they did plan, including a number of things that would endanger the lives of the people at the Republican National Convention.

Q. Now, can you tell me precisely as to what the dates were in which this type of activity took place?

A. My best recollection would have been within the last two weeks of May, 1972.

Q. On how many different occasions did you receive this material?

A. Almost daily, sir.

May 22, 1973

MR. McCORD: One of the statements that we did not get into on the last meeting, I think primarily because of the factor of time, was a memorandum which I had written to the committee dated May 4, 1973, the subject of pressure on the defendants to blame the Watergate operation on C.I.A. and other matters.

I am prepared to go into that statement at this time. If it has your approval.

I have a further addition relevant to that in the statement which I could read at this time.

The topic of it is the December, 1972, letter to John Caulfield. This letter is relevant to the May 4, 1973, memo submitted to Senate Watergate committee and the Federal grand jury, on the subject of pressure to place the blame on C.I.A. for the Watergate operation.

A letter was written to John Caulfield during the week of Dec. 25, 1972. Reference to this letter appeared in the press last weekend. And geared—speaking of my own feelings and at the time the letter was written—and geared because of what appeared to me to be a ruthless attempt by the White House to put the blame for the Watergate operation on C.I.A., where it did not belong, I sought to head it off by sending a letter to Caulfield.

This letter was couched in strong language because it seemed to me at the time that this was the only language that the White House understood. The letter read in substance as follows, to the best of my memory:

"Dear Jack: I am sorry to have to write you this letter. If Helms goes and the Watergate operation is laid at C.I.A.'s feet, where it does not belong, every tree in the forest will fall. It will be a scorched desert. The whole matter is at the precipice right now. Pass the message that if they want it to blow, they are on exactly the right course. I am sorry that you will get hurt in the fallout."

The letter was unsigned.

Now, the above letter to Caulfield brings to mind another set of communications of mine on Dec. 6, 1972. On Dec. 4, 1972, Judge Sirica had stated in open court that the jury in January, 1973, would want to know who had hired the men for the Watergate operation and why.

On December 6, 1972, The Washington Star carried an article which appeared to me to be an Administration-planted story answering Judge Sirica's query stating that "reliable sources state that McCord recruited the four Cubans and that they believed that they were working for the President on an extremely sensitive mission." This was untrue.

This appeared to me to be laying the groundwork for a false claim at the trial that I was the "ringleader" of the Watergate plot. This would draw attention away from Hunt and Liddy, and I believe possibly away from the White House, since both of them had formerly worked at the White House and I had not.

That same evening Dec. 6, 1972, I sent telegrams to William O. Bittman, attorney for Hunt, and Bernard Barker's residence in Miami, Fla., stating that the story was untrue as they both knew, and I asked for comments by return mail from Barker. I also wrote Hunt a letter on the matter stating that, as he also knew, the story was untrue and he could either correct it or I would do so.

With the letter to Caulfield in late December, 1972, I was trying to head off an effort to falsely lay the Watergate operation off on C.I.A. In the telegrams and letter to Hunt and the others in December, 1972, that I have just referred to, I was trying to head off an effort to falsely lay the recruitment of the Cubans off on the writer which would, in turn, shift the focus of the trial off of those formerly connected with the White House, namely, Liddy and Hunt, than from those who in effect had actually recruited them, namely Mr. Hunt.

Newspapers over the weekend have also referred to some calls to some local embassies. I will try to explain those in the statement that I will read at this time.

In July, 1972, Mrs. Hunt had told me that Paul O'Brien, attorney for C.R.P., had told her husband that when the Watergate case broke in June, the Committee for the Re-election of the President told O'Brien that the Watergate operation was a C.I.A. operation. I believe I referred to this in the earlier statement. She said that Howard Hunt had exploded at this and told O'Brien that this was not true; that it was not a C.I.A. operation.

A few days later Mrs. Hunt told me that the C.R.P. lawyers were now reporting that the Administration was going to allege at the trial that Liddy had stolen $16,000 and had bribed Hunt and McCord to perform the operation. I told her that it looked like they were now changing their cover stories, referring to the Administration, and I would not sit still for either false story, and I shortly wrote my attorney, Gerald Alch, repeating this information and setting forth these same views of mine.

In September, 1972, the indictments came out and no one was being indicted among the higher-ups, so there looked like a further cover-up to me.

Also in September and October, 1972, there began to be a series of telephone anomalies on my phone that indicated to me that the phone had been tapped.

In an effort to test the truthfulness of the Government on a forthcoming motion for disclosure of wiretapping of the defendants' phones in the Watergate case, including my own, I made two calls in September and October, 1972, to two local embassies. On Oct. 10, 1972, I asked for the filing of a motion for Government disclosure of any interceptions and two weeks later the Government came back with a denial of any, saying a search of Government records had been made. I knew that two weeks was too short a time to search 12 different Government agencies for such records, and believed the Government was not telling the truth.

There is an attachment to this, The New York Times of to-day's date. The title of the article "Warning Against Blaming of C.I.A. Laid to McCord."

Continuing on a separate subject in a statement. The topic of this memorandum is sanction of the Watergate operation.

John Mitchell, by virtue of his position as Attorney General of the United States, and John Dean, by virtue of his position as counsel to the President, by their consideration and approval of the Watergate operation, in my opinion, gave sanction to the Watergate operation by both the White House and the Attorney General's offices.

I had been accustomed to working in an atmosphere where such sanction by the White House and the Attorney General, was more than enough. As with White House staffers, it was not my habit to question when two such high offices sanctioned an activity—it carried the full force and effect of Presidential sanction.

For the preceding 30 years I had been working in an environment where, if there were ever any question of the legality of a matter or an activity, it would always be sent to high legal officials for a legal decision on the matter; where, if they sanctioned it, that was sufficient.

I can elaborate on this another way. Left alone, I would not have undertaken the operation. I had plenty of other things to do in connection with my security work at the Committee to Reelect the President.

Liddy wanted help. He came to me seeking that help with the word that it had the approval of the Attorney General and the counsel to the President. He said that it was part of the C.R.P. mission, in order to obtain the information regarding not only political intelligence but also regarding violence-oriented groups who would be planning violence against the committee in Washington, and later at the August convention site, thereby endangering the lives and property of the committee and its personnel. My mission was protection of such lives and property.

Uppermost in everyone's minds at that point in time, and certainly in mine, was the bloodshed which had occurred at the 1968 Democratic convention in Chicago, and I constantly sought intelligence from any source which might help forewarn us and help us avoid in 1972 that danger to the lives of our people.

The Vietnam Veterans Against the War was one violence-oriented group that was already saying in the spring of 1972 that they were going to cause destruction to life and property at the August Republican convention, using, in their own words, their own bodies and weapons as the spearhead of the attack there—these are their exact words, and some of them have since been indicted in Tallahassee, Fla., with additional plans to damage the life and property in the convention.

Later in the summer of 1972 the V.V.A.W. did, in fact have offices in the D.N.C. in Washington, as I understand. I had also received information from the Internal Security Division in May, 1972, that some individuals in Florida planned to forge college press credentials to get into both the Democratic and Republican convention sites, and blow up the communication centers of both parties there and cause havoc on the convention floor.

Now, we also had word from C.R.P. sources alleging that the McGovern committees had "a pipeline" directly into the offices of the Committee to Re-elect the President in Washington; allegedly, they were feeding out, on a regular basis, policy position papers, i.e., plans and strategy, which were rather important to the success of a candidate's campaign. If the other side is reading your poker hand, he can negate your plans.

We had word that one of the volunteers at the Committee to Re-elect the President had, in fact, prior to coming aboard the committee, threatened the life of John Mitchell and of other persons. This was at about the same time Governor Wallace was almost killed in an assassination attempt. There were numerous threats in writing and by phone against John Mitchell and his wife. One such call came to the unlisted telephone of Mrs. Mitchell at their apartment and got her greatly upset, as it would any woman, because it appeared that even the unlisted telephone number appeared then no longer safe.

We certainly had sufficient indications that violence-oriented groups were out to endanger both life and property. With some 250,000 demonstrators planning to go to the convention in early 1972 and there were statements that some would be out to commit violence, the questions were, who are such people, who is funding them, encouraging them, who is in collusion with them, what are they planning next and where? Are any of them being supported and encouraged by any staff members of the McGovern committee or D.N.C.?

I had no indication whatever that Larry O'Brien or Senator McGovern had either any knowledge of or part in such—just the contrary, I was completely convinced that they did not. But I was not so sure that, without their knowledge, other staff members might not be working behind their backs to quietly encourage groups such as V.V.A.W. McGovern's early political base was with some of the radical groups.

My questions were, what was the extent of such encouragement, if any, and how far did it go? Did they let such groups use their telephones and work in their offices? There were indications in the summer of 1972 that such groups actually did just that in California and in D.N.C. headquarters, in Washington.

My next statement has to do with the intelligence advisory committee I previously referred to in the C.I.A. memorandum, which I referred to Mr. Robert Mardian.

In May, 1972, Robert Mardian had told me that he, John Mitchell, Robert Haldeman and John Ehrlichman were key members of an "intelligence advisory committee." I now assume that this was the Intelligence Evaluation Committee, referred to, I believe in The New York Times of May 21, 1973.

I have previously submitted a tape to the Senate Watergate committee which I believe contains material which was the product of that committee, and which I obtained from the evaluation section of the Internal Security Division of the Department of Justice, a contact established through Mr. Robert Mardian, in May, 1972.

I have no knowledge of the sources of that committee.

Robert Mardian, during a brief conversation in June, 1972, stated that he was going to be "in charge of intelligence operations at Miami during the convention." He did not elaborate further.

The next item is headed "Las Vegas Matter," which was referred to in the previous testimony on Friday.

In January or February, 1972, Gordon Liddy told me that he was going out to Las Vegas, Nev., in connection with casing the office of Hank Greenspun, editor of The Las Vegas Sun.

Liddy said that Attorney General John Mitchell has told him that Greenspun had in his possession blackmail type information involving a Democratic candidate for President, that Mitchell wanted that material, and Liddy said that this information was in some way racketeer-related, indicating that if this candidate became President, the racketeers or national crime syndicate could have a control or influence over him as President. My inclination at this point in time, speaking of today, is to disbelieve the allegation against the Democratic candidate referred to above and to believe that there was in reality some other motive for wanting to get into Greenspun's safe.

Liddy told me one day in February, 1972, that he was going out to Las Vegas, and might need my help if there was an alarm system in the offices, when an entry operation was mounted to enter a safe in Greenspun's offices to get the information. A few days later Liddy told me that he had been to Las Vegas and looked over the offices and that there was no such alarm system, and my services were not needed.

Subsequently in about April or May, 1971, Liddy told me that he had again been to Las Vegas for another casing of Greenspun's offices. Liddy said that there were then plans for an entry operation to get into Greenspun's safe. He went on to say that, after the entry team finishes its work, they would go directly to an airport near Las Vegas where a Howard Hughes plane would be standing by to fly the team directly into a Central-American country so that the team would be out of the country before the break-in was discovered.

Around the same time Liddy made this last statement to me about the Howard Hughes plane, Hunt told me in his office one day that he was in touch with the Howard Hughes company and that they might be needing my security services after the election.

He said that they had quite a wide investigative and security operation and asked me for my business card and asked if I would be interested. I said I would like to know more about what was involved, gave him a card, but never heard from him again on this subject. However, I did read in the newspapers after July 1, 1972, that Hunt had apparently handled a Howard Hughes campaign donation to the Committee to Re-elect the President sometime in 1972. Gordon Liddy told me in February, 1972, that he, too, had handled a Howard Hughes campaign check, a donation to the 1972 campaign. This is the extent of my knowledge on this matter.

That completes my prepared statement and I will be glad to answer any questions.

SENATOR BAKER: Mr. McCord, speaking of electronic surveillance, do you know of or did you ever investigate the bugging of Republican headquarters of the Committee for the Re-election of the President headquarters—here, New York, or elsewhere?

A. Yes, sir.

Q. Would you describe that for the committee?

A. It was a regular ongoing activity at the offices in Washington and at the New York arm of the Committee for the Re-election of the President, which was referred to as the November Group. They had offices, I believe, on Park Avenue in New York.

Q. Did you discover any incident of that sort?

A. There was one incident on June 16 of some concern at the New York office of the Committee for the Re-election of the President. There had been earlier signs of possibly some illegal activity at those offices prior to June 16 which I could describe, if you would like.

Q. I would like.

A. On the afternoon of June 16, 1972, about midafternoon, I received a call from the head of the office of the November Group in New York City, who stated that he and his entire office staff were quite concerned about an incident that had just occurred. He went ahead to relate that one of the secretaries at the office had received a call from a male individual in Los Angeles, Calif., and that she had immediately told that party that she would call him back on the WATS line, which is a leased line, call him back on that line and immediately did so.

And during the conversation that the two of them had, about a few minutes into the conversation there was a click over the phone which was heard by her and by the male on the other end of the line, and what appeared to be a tape recording was played over the telephone line which was, as she described it when I talked with her, an anti-Nixon and antiwar harangue.

Q. Were there other incidents of telephone tapping against the Republican National Committee or the C.R.P. or any other Republican-affiliated groups brought to your attention or which you investigated?

A. There were two earlier occasions at the November Group offices when I was called to the November Group offices from Washington in which they had highly suspicious telephone anomalies, as it is known. Telephone conversations within the office itself when another person picking up a telephone extension on a different line, for example, not connected with the one in which the call was being made, could overhear the conversation that was going on. Other strange anomalies, clicks and so on, of a wide variety that indicated some problems in the telephone area.

Q. Mr. McCord, I am not trying to create the impression that, because there were apparently taps in the Republican phones, that that justifies taps on the Democratic phones. I do not believe that but I am anxious to know your state of mind and the reason and rationale for your security operations, including the break-in into the Watergate.

Now, my final question in that respect is, did you ever discover the source or responsibility for any of these efforts at electronic interception on the Republican operations? A. No, sir.

Q. You recognize the term Gemstone? A. Yes, sir.

Q. Can you describe for us what it means?

A. That term I first heard, first read about in the newspaper itself referring to, according to the newspaper accounts, referring to—it as a code name for the monitoring, the typing of final monitoring logs of report or logs coming out of the National Democratic Committee. I did not as such know it during the operation but I know something about the nature of the paper that it was on. I think that code name had some reference to that.

Q. Where is the information that you gained? Is it in the Gemstone file? Does the U.S. Attorney's office have it? Where is it?

A. The material which I had received from—Mr. Baldwin was doing the monitoring, Alfred Baldwin—was turned over, all of it, to Mr. Liddy, Gordon Liddy.

SENATOR TALMADGE: Mr. McCord, among other things in your testimony this morning, you stated that many efforts were made to persuade you or to coerce you to state that the bugging operation on the Democratic National Committee was a C.I.A. operation. Will you state the individuals who urged you to do that? One you stated was Mr. Hunt. Am I correct?

A. Sir, I believe I will correct that impression if I left it. I had heard from Mr. Bernard Barker specifically that Mr. Hunt had brought pressure to bear upon Mr. Barker and the Cubans to use as their defense that this was a C.I.A. operation. Mr. Hunt did not directly put that pressure upon me. Others did.

Q. Now, who else besides Barker was involved in urging you to blame this on the C.I.A.? You stated two other names. I think one of them was Bittman and the other one was named Alch?

A. Yes, sir, I referred to conversations with Mr. Gerald Alch and Mrs. Hunt.

Q. Now, who is Mr. Alch?

A. He was my defense attorney through the trial in January, 1973, whose services I had engaged at that time.

Q. All right, now. Mr. Alch and who else urged you to do that?

A. I believe I have stated in my testimony that stories were circulating earlier stemming out of the Committee for the Re-election of the President that the committee lawyers themselves had been told that early in July . . .

Q. Let's get specific now. I don't want stories circulating. I want to name the days, names, and places. That is evidence. Rumors are not. A. Yes, sir.

Q. And I believe in your own testimony in chief, the memorandum you read, you also referred to a man by the name of Bittman, did you not? A. Yes, sir.

Q. Now, who is Mr. Bittman?

A. Bittman is the attorney, William O. Bittman, the attorney for E. Howard Hunt, one of the other defendants.

Q. All right, did he have any connection with the Government in any way or any connection with the Republican National Committee or the Committee to Re-elect the President? What I am trying to get at is the source of this pressure that you have contended was brought upon you to blame this on the C.I.A. Thus far, you have not connected that either with the Committee to Re-elect the President or the White House or any other individuals, to my knowledge. One was your own lawyer, one was engaged in the crime with you, and the third one was the lawyer for Mr. Liddy, was it—Bittman?

A. Mr. Hunt.

Q. He was Mr. Hunt's lawyer. And those three individuals are the only ones that urged you to blame this on the C.I.A. Is that a fair statement? A. Yes, sir, that is essentially correct.

Q. So no one else anywhere whatever urged you to blame it on the C.I.A. except these three individuals, is that correct? A. None that I can recall at this time, no, sir.

Q. Now, did Mr. Barker or the other of the so-called Cuban Americans ever come to you during the trial and tell you that they had been offered executive clemency by Mr. Hunt? A. Yes, sir.

Q. Will you describe the attitude and demeanor at that time?

A. Yes, sir, Mr. Barker specifically—I can recall specifically during the first week of the trial and beginning on the first day, on Jan. 8, Mr. Barker came to me in the corridor outside, I believe, the courtroom of the U.S. District Court building in Washington during breaks in the court proceedings and proceeded to relate to me the pressure which he said was being imposed upon him and upon the other men who were defendants—Mr. Sturgis, Mr. Gonzalez, Mr. Martinez—pressure that he stated was stemming from Mr. Hunt and other unnamed individuals, to plead guilty and to go off to jail or prison and ultimately to receive executive clemency and to receive financial support for their families while they were in prison and promises—and he stated promises were made that they would be given help in obtaining a job or "rehabilitation" at the prison. Mr. Barker spoke to me several times during that week regarding that particular pressure upon him which he described as intense.

He stated first that he was planning not to plead guilty and then subsequently, as the days progressed during the week itself, he began to tell me that he was thinking more and more seriously about it, and as I recall, about Wednesday of that week, roughly, in that week sometime, he seemed to have his mind made up that he would go ahead and accede to the pressure and plead guilty, and he put it in just about those words, and to accept the executive clemency.

He was not the only one. His family, his wife and his daughter, related the same pressure to me, sometimes in his presence.

Q. Did any of the other so-called Cuban Americans besides Mr. Barker relate similar pressure? A. Yes, sir, all of them.

Q. Every one of them? A. Yes, sir.

Q. Now, did Mr. Hunt or Mrs. Hunt ever give you any information that they were sent to you by the Committee to Re-elect the President or the White House or anybody to do this?

A. Executive clemency?

Q. Yes. A. Yes, sir.

Q. Will you relate that?

A. Yes, sir, during the meetings, personal meetings and telephone meetings, beginning in July, 1972, concerning money beginning in October, 1972, concerning executive clemency—the term "executive clemency" I first heard, I believe, from Mr. Hunt in early October—late September or early October—when I would see him at the courthouse or when he would call me by telephone.

Thereafter, he subsequently mentioned it in almost every call. His wife referred to it. In substance, what they were saying was that the defendants were being promised executive clemency if they went off to prison and had to serve time. Sometimes the word "executive clemency" would be followed or accompanied by other statements about financial support and rehabilitation.

Q. Did Mrs. Hunt state who gave her authority to make such a promise?

A. My recollection of her conversations were that she was saying that she was transmitting this word to me from her husband. She did not specifically mention that I can recall now who gave it to him. I can draw only one conclusion as to where it came from, because—

Q. She did not state the source of her authority to make that promise, though?

A. I can't recall such statements on her part.

Q. Who did she say she was in communication with?

A. With the attorneys for the Committee to Re-elect the President, the attorneys for the committee.

Q. Who specifically? More than one individual is involved with the committee. I want you to name specific names if you know.

A. She stated that she herself was in communication with Mr. Kenneth Parkinson, one of the attorneys for the Committee to Re-elect the President. She stated that her husband, Mr. Hunt, had been in touch in July with Mr. Paul O'Brien, also an attorney with Mr. Parkinson for the Committee to Re-elect the President.

SENATOR GURNEY: Did they [the other defendants] ever tell you who was applying pressure to them?

A. My recollection is that they stated Mr. Hunt. There was some, I have a vague recollection that the names of, it was put in the same context that Mr. Barker did that others were doing so. That is a very vague recollection. I can be sure only about the name of Mr. Hunt.

Q. You mentioned in the statement about the C.I.A.—at least the statements were certainly very shocking. They involve a new man coming on board the C.I.A., a change from Mr. Helms to another man and the fact that the new man could be, could work with and dealt with, and your records might have been able to have been doctored, all in this so-called C.I.A. cover-up. Would you go into that at more length? Where did you get this information?

A. What I transmitted to you, sir, and this is the source of it, were the words as I best recall it transmitted to me, communicated to me, by Mr. Alch in the two meetings that I referred to, one at the Monocle Restaurant here in Washington, near a couple of blocks from here about, on Dec. 21, and the second—

Q. Who is us? Did he have someone else with him?

A. Well, he had Mr. Bernard Shankman, my local attorney. He did not meet with us.

Q. Now, would you recall again what he said specifically about the C.I.A.?

A. I stated as I best recall, that he had just come from a meeting with William O. Bittman, attorney for Mr. Howard Hunt. He stated that he had a suggestion concerning what I use as my defense during the trial, which was that I use as my defense that the Watergate operation was a C.I.A. operation. I do not recall exactly what I said in response except to say something to the effect that you are my attorney, what is your counsel on this, do you think I should?

And his response was, "Yes, I think so," and he proceeded to discuss, to ask some questions of me. He said—he asked me whether I could be ostensibly recalled from my retirement. That is, a person once retired, can he be recalled, and I said, yes, he can, and he said, "Well, you can ostensibly, we could use as our defense you could ostensibly have been recalled to the C.I.A. to undertake the Watergate operation, could you not," and I said it is technically possible or words to that effect. That he said if so, then, my personnel records at C.I.A. could be doctored to reflect such a recall, and this is my best recollection of the exact words.

Q. Well, now, who was going to do that?

A. He did not say.

Q. Did you ask him?

A. No. I was listening to the rest of the story. I wanted to hear the rest of the statement out. He said that Schlesinger, the new director of C.I.A., whose appointment had just been announced, could be subpoenaed and would go along with it, that was his quote.

Q. Did he offer any evidence as to how he knew that Mr. Schlesinger would "go along with it"? A. No, sir.

Q. Go on.

A. He went on to mention some testimony. He did not have any paper with him but he went on to mention some testimony by Mr. Gary Bittenbender, and he recited testimony that he said Bittenbender had given in which Bittenbender purportedly claimed that I told him the day of the arrest that the Watergate operation was a C.I.A. operation. My response was that, if such a statement had been made, it was perjured testimony or a false statement.

Q. Why did he bring that up, do you know?

A. I can give you an impression if you want an impression.

Q. Yes.

A. Which was that, and that impression stems from what I later saw in his office, which was a written statement—my impression was that he had received access to some type of interview with Mr. Bittenbender in which such a statement was obtained, perhaps by the Federal authorities in some case.

Q. Go on.

A. He said he could be interviewed—correction. He went on to mention the name of Mr. Victor Marchetti, who he referred to as writing a book about C.I.A., and he said we could subpoena Marchetti and have him testify about customs and traditions of C.I.A. agents in case they are arrested, or caught, wherein they are trained to deny any connection with C.I.A.

SENATOR WEICKER: Mr. McCord, did you actually receive any F.B.I. reports while at the Internal Security Division?

A. I saw some material that was attributed to the F.B.I. I did not take any with me, I made extracts of some of the material that was shown to me.

Q. You have indicated recently that the Vietnam Veterans Against the War had an office in the Democratic National Committee or McGovern headquarters. Where did you receive that information?

A. I do not recall the source of it now, except that it came to me some time during the summer of 1972.

Q. When you say in the summer of 1972, was it before June 17? A. No, sir.

Q. After June 17? A. Yes, sir.

Q. How many times were you personally in contact with Robert Mardian?

A. I can recall two or three times.

Q. Was this at the time that the Internal Security Division or at the time he had left that division and was working for the Committee to Re-elect the President?

A. Only after he had come to the Committee to Re-elect the President.

MR. DASH: I think that one of the areas that has not been covered is the role of the person who was on the other side of the wiretap which you installed in May, the end of May, 1972. Now, did you employ Mr. Baldwin, Mr. Alfred Baldwin, for that purpose? A. Yes, I did.

Q. What was his particular assignment with regard to monitoring the wiretap?

A. His assignment was to listen on a radio receiver that received the transmissions from the Democratic National Committee telephones in which the electronic devices had been installed in connection with the two dates of Memorial Day weekend and June 17, 1972.

Q. In his monitoring, how was he recording what he was hearing?

A. He was listening with headphones to the conversations that were being transmitted and would take down the substance of the conversations, the time, the date, on the yellow legal-sized scratch pad, and then ultimately would type them up a summary of them by time, chronological summary, and turn that typed log in to me and I would deliver them to Mr. Liddy.

Q. Did you deliver them to Mr. Liddy directly? A. Yes.

Q. Now, did there come a time when you were delivering those logs that they were retyped?

A. I know of at least one instance in which that occurred because I saw them being retyped.

Q. What was the purpose of retyping the log? Did Mr. Liddy explain that to you?

A. I believe some general explanation, in substance, that he wanted them in a more final complete form for discussion with Mr. Mitchell and whoever else received them.

Q. Now, who did this retyping?

A. Sally Harmony, who was the secretary to Mr. Liddy at the Committee for the Re-election of the President.

Q. As a matter of fact, could you briefly describe, without going into any of the contents, what a log would be, what actually would be entered on the log which Mr. Baldwin would first type and then be retyped by Miss Harmony?

A. It would be similar to any other telephone conversation that one person might make to another beginning with a statement on the log of the time of the call, who was calling who; a summary of what was said during the conversation itself, including names of persons who were mentioned that Mr. Baldwin apparently believed were of sufficient significance to set forth in the log.

Q. [Would it] be true that anybody reading would have no difficulty knowing it [the log] came from a telephone conversation? A. That is correct.

Testimony by John J. Caulfield

May 22, 1973

MR. CAULFIELD: In July of 1972, after [McCord's] arrest, I had Mr. Ulasewicz call his home and tell him to go to a designated public telephone booth near his house where I would be calling him. I called him at that public telephone and simply asked him if there was anything I could do for him or his family at this time of personal difficulty.

I did not see or hear from Mr. McCord again until I received an anonymous letter at my home in December of 1972. It was typewritten, a note of approximately two paragraphs in length and, to the best of my knowledge said, "Dear Jack—I am sorry to have to tell you this but the White House is bent on having the C.I.A. take the blame for the Watergate. If they continue to pursue this course, every tree in the forest will fall and it will be a scorched earth. Jack, even you will be hurt in the fallout."

In early January of 1973, I was attending a drug conference in San Clemente, Calif., when I received a telephone call in my hotel room from John Dean. He asked that I go outside the hotel and call him back from a public telephone, which I did. He told me that he had a very important message which he wanted me to deliver to James McCord, that Mr. McCord was expecting to hear from me and McCord would understand what the message referred to. He said the message consisted of three things:

1. "A year is a long time";
2. "Your wife and family will be taken care of";
3. "You will be rehabilitated with employment when this is all over."

I immediately realized that I was being asked to do a very dangerous thing and I said to Mr. Dean that I did not think it was wise to send me on such a mission since Mr. McCord knew, as many others did, that I had worked closely with Mr. Dean and Mr. Ehrlichman at the White House and therefore it might be quickly guessed that any messages I was conveying were probably from one of the two.

The reason I raised this question with him was because, frankly, I did not wish to convey the message. Mr. Dean asked if I could think of any other way to do it and I suggested that perhaps I could get Mr. Ulasewicz to convey the message over the telephone anonymously, stating the message came from me. Mr. Dean felt this would be all right, so I hung up the telephone and called Mr. Ulasewicz in New York.

He did not wish to convey the message at first but I convinced him to do it merely as a matter of friendship to me. Mr. Ulasewicz called Mr. McCord's home and, presumably, delivered the same message which Mr. Dean had given to me. He then called me back, in California, and reported that he had delivered the message and Mr. McCord's attitude had been one of satisfaction.

I called Mr. Dean and told him that the message had been delivered by Mr. Ulasewicz and that Mr. McCord had seemed satisfied.

The next day I received another telephone call from Mr. Dean at my hotel in which he said that Mr. McCord wanted to see me as soon as I got back. I objected to seeing Mr. McCord, but finally Mr. Dean got my concurrence to do so. I was not instructed to say anything more than what had been in the message to him.

Mr. Ulasewicz had conveyed instructions to Mr. McCord for holding our meeting on Friday night, Jan. 12. At approximately 7 P.M. that evening I met with Mr. McCord at the second overlook on the George Washington Parkway.

I said, "I guess you received the message then?" Mr. McCord then said words to the effect, "Jack, I am different from all the others. Anybody who knew me at the C.I.A. knows that I always follow my own independent course. I have always followed the rule that if one goes (I took this to mean going to jail) all who are involved must go. People who I am sure are involved are sitting outside with their families. I saw a picture in the newspaper of some guy who I am sure was involved sitting with his family. I can take care of my family. I don't need any Joes, I want my freedom."

I stated that I was only delivering a message and had nothing to do with its formulation or had no control over what was being done.

I did say that the "people" who had asked me to convey the message had always been honorable toward me and that I thought it was a "sincere offer."

He asked me who I was speaking with at the White House and I said I could not reveal any names but that they were from the "highest level of the White House."

He continually said that all he was interested in was his freedom and that he was not pleased that others who he felt had been involved were not suffering the consequences that he was. In the context of demanding his immediate freedom, he said that he knew of a way in which his freedom could be obtained and asked me if I could convey his plan to the people at the White House with whom I was talking.

His plan, simply, was as follows: On two occasions, one in September, 1972, and the other in October, 1972, Mr. McCord told me that he had called telephone numbers at foreign embassies in Washington and he stated he was sure these embassies were subjects of national security wiretaps. On both occasions he had stated that he was a man involved in the Watergate scandal and, without giving his name, had inquired as to the possibility of acquiring visas and other traveling papers necessary to travel to these foreign countries.

It was Mr. McCord's theory that if the Government searched its wiretap records it would find records of these two calls. Meanwhile, Mr. McCord and his attorneys would make a motion in court, aimed at dismissing the case against Mr. McCord because of the use of wiretap evidence by the prosecution.

At no time in our first meeting do I recall saying anything about the President but I specifically renewed the offer of executive clemency, as indicated above and referred to it as coming from "the highest levels of the White House." At some point in the conversation Mr. McCord said to me, "Jack, I didn't ask to see you." This puzzled me since my clear understanding from Mr. Dean was that McCord had specifically asked to see me.

In any event, I called Mr. Dean on Friday night, Jan. 12, and reported that Mr. McCord did not seem interested in accepting the offer made in Mr. Dean's original message to him, that Mr. McCord wanted his immediate freedom and that he, Mr. McCord, felt that he had a way to obtain that freedom.

The following day I saw Mr. Dean in his office in the White House and explained to him Mr. McCord's suggestion for obtaining his freedom, as Mr. McCord had described it to me. Mr. Dean said, "Well, I'll check on that." He then turned the conversation back to the offer of executive clemency. To the best of my knowledge he said, "Jack, I want you to go back to him and tell him that we are checking on these wiretaps but this time impress upon him as fully as you can that this offer of executive clemency is a sincere offer which comes from the very highest levels of the White House."

I said, "I have not used anybody's name with him, do you want me to?"

He said, "No, I don't want you to do that but tell him that this message comes from the very highest levels."

I said, "Do you want me to tell him it comes from the President?"

He said words to the effect, "No, don't do that. Say that it comes from way up at the top."

At the meeting with Mr. Dean he also impressed upon me that this was a very grave situation which might someday threaten the President, that it had the potential of becoming a national scandal and that many people in the White House were quite concerned over it. Mr. Dean said that none of the other then defendants in the Watergate burglary "were any problem," and that Mr. Mc-Cord "was not cooperating with his attorney."

At no time, either before or after this meeting with Mr. Dean, did I ever speak to any other White House officials about this offer of executive clemency. I specifically never spoke to the President of the United States and have no knowledge of my own as to whether he personally had endorsed this offer or, indeed, whether anyone had ever discussed it with him.

Since I had worked extensively for Mr. Dean and Mr. Ehrlichman and had formed an impression that Mr. Dean rarely made decisions on matters of consequence without speaking to Mr. Ehrlichman, my guess was that when Mr. Dean referred to "high White House officials" he at least meant Mr. Ehrlichman. I know that he was in conversation with someone about my contacts with Mr. McCord since, when I was in his office on Jan. 13, he received a telephone call and I heard him say, "I'm receiving a report on that right now" to the party on the other end.

At any rate, I then called Mr. McCord and arranged a meeting with him, again at the second overlook of the George Washington Parkway early in the afternoon on Sunday, Jan. 14. On this occasion we both got out of our cars and walked down a path from the overlook toward the Potomac River.

This meeting lasted only 10 to 15 minutes. I did most of the talking. I told Mr. McCord that the White House was checking into the wiretapping situation and that I had been asked to impress upon him once again that the offer of executive clemency was a sincere and believable offer coming from the very highest levels of the White House.

I explained to him that among the reasons why I believed that such a commitment would be kept were that the White House officials with whom I was in contact were extremely concerned about the Watergate burglary developing into a major scandal affecting the President and therefore such a promise would not be given lightly. I told him that the White House officials with whom I was talking were complaining because they did not feel that Mr. McCord was the only one of the Watergate burglary defendants who was refusing to cooperate.

At no time on this occasion or on any other occasion do I recall telling Mr. McCord to keep silent if called before the grand jury or any Congressional committees.

Later on Sunday I telephoned Mr. Dean to report on my meeting with Mr. McCord. I told him that in my opinion McCord had absolutely no interest in the offer of executive clemency. I told Mr. Dean that Mr. McCord was still adamant in his belief that the White House had the power to have the charges against him dismissed if it would merely pursue the wiretaps which he had mentioned.

Mr. Dean said that I should tell him that there wasn't much

likelihood that anything would be done about the wiretap situation and, in response to my comments about McCord's refusal to consider executive clemency, he said something like, "Well, what the hell does he know, anyway."

On Tuesday, Jan. 16, I again called [McCord] an attempt to meet with him, and he again was highly irritated about the White House's failure to do something about the wiretap situation and again mentioned Mr. Magruder. I said I would inquire further about the wiretaps and I might have something for him "in a week or so."

Subsequently I called him and arranged to meet with him again, the exact date of this meeting being unsure in my mind. We again met at the overlook on the George Washington Parkway. He got into my car and we drove out the parkway, pursuing a course in the general direction of Warrenton, Va.

I gave him my private telephone number at the Treasury Department and told him that if he or his wife ever wanted me to do anything for them, they should feel free to call me. I told McCord that if he or his wife should decide to call me to simply use the name "Watson" and I would know who it was. Frankly, this was merely a device to save me from any possible embarrassment.

I do not have a specific recollection as to how it arose, but I believe he asked me if he was still the only one of the Watergate defendants that the White House was concerned about. I said that I thought he was, but that I had no knowledge of what relationship existed between the White House and the other Watergate defendants. He said the Cuban defendants were quite nervous and in his opinion might make a statement at any time and that I "could pass that along for whatever it was worth."

I again asked if there was anything I could do for him. He said one thing that I could do was to see whether bail money could be raised for him pending an appeal in his case. I said I would check into this.

Toward the end of our conversation, realizing that he definitely was going to make a statement on the Watergate burglary at a time of his choosing and that such a statement would in all probability involve allegations against people in the White House and other high Administration officials, I gave him what I considered to be a small piece of friendly advice.

I said, words to the effect that, "Jim, I have worked with these people and I know them to be as tough-minded as you and I. When you make your statement don't underestimate them. If I were in your shoes, I would probably be doing the same thing."

I later called Mr. Dean and advised him of Mr. McCord's request for bail funding and he said words to the effect that, "Maybe we can handle that through Alch."

Sometime later, Mr. Dean called me and asked me to tell McCord that the bail money presented too many problems and that maybe consideration could be given to paying premiums. I later called McCord and reported this. His reaction was, "I am negotiating with a new attorney and maybe he can get it handled."

This is the last conversation I have had to date with James McCord.

May 23, 1973

MR. DASH: Although you state that you made no mention of the President to Mr. McCord during the meeting, you do know, do you not, that the President is the only person in this country who can grant executive clemency in a Federal criminal matter? A. Yes, sir, I do.

Q. Did you understand when you were speaking with Mr. Dean that Mr. Dean wanted you to transmit the message to Mr. McCord that the offer of executive clemency was made with the proper authority? A. Yes, sir.

Q. Was it your intention during your meetings with Mr. McCord to leave him with the clear understanding that persons with authority to make such a representation as to executive clemency were in fact extending this offer to him?

A. Yes, sir. But, of course, I have not and did not at that time have any direct knowledge that the President had made such an offer, endorsed such an offer, or in any way was involved in that offer.

Q. And was it your understanding, especially with the discussions you had with Mr. Dean, that there was serious concern at the White House, at least Mr. Dean was conveying to you, involving a possible scandal—that there was a real effort to get Mr. McCord to accept this offer because of the concern or trouble that probably he might be able to raise in the Watergate case?

A. That was my clear impression, Mr. Dash, yes, sir.

MR. THOMPSON: Would you on some occasions act as an intermediary between Mr. Ehrlichman and Tony Ulasewicz, for jobs which Mr. Ulasewicz would do? A. Yes sir.

Q. Would you say that would be on frequent occasions?

A. That would be infrequent after July of 1970.

Q. Occasionally. A. Oh, yes; yes sir.

Q. Now, Mr. Caulfield, in your statement here, you state that you were guessing that Mr. Dean probably was referring to Mr. Ehrlichman when he referred to high White House sources? A. Yes, that was my guess.

Q. What would you say was the relationship between Mr. Dean and Mr. Ehrlichman during this period of time? Did Mr. Dean in many matters, in effect, report to Mr. Ehrlichman? A. Yes, sir.

Q. Or answer to Mr. Erlichman?

A. Yes, sir, on many matters having to do with Mr. Dean's work as well.

Q. Did you ever talk with Mr. Ehrlichman about this matter,

this business of possible executive clemency for Mr. McCord with anyone? A. No, sir.

Q. Did you ever talk to anyone there at the White House besides Mr. Dean?

A. Absolutely no one but Mr. John Dean.

SENATOR MONTOYA: Did you ever get paid from the President's attorney? A. No, sir.

Q. Were you working or being paid from the payroll attributable to the Department of the Treasury or to the White House?

A. The White House payroll, sir.

Q. Did Mr. Haldeman assign things to you?

A. On only one or two occasions that I could recall, Senator. Very rarely; in fact, almost never.

Q. Let me read an extended text. On page 9: "About 10 o'clock A.M. on Thursday, Jan. 25, 1973, in a meeting lasting until about 12:30 A.M., we drove in his car toward Warrenton, Va., and returned and a conversation ensued which repeated the offers of executive clemency and financial support while in prison and rehabilitation later. I refused to discuss it. He stated that I was fouling up the game plan. I made a few comments about the game plan." You recall that?

A. No sir, I do not. As I indicated in my statement, this trip here was one of friendly conversation between two friends. I have no recollection of offering him executive clemency on that occasion. I have no recollection about stating that he was fouling up the game plan.

Q. Now, you mentioned that Mr. Dean had instructed you to say that it comes from way up at the top. A. Yes, sir.

Q. What did you conceive that to be at the time?

A. Well, sir, in my mind I believed that he was talking about the President. Although—

Q. How would you have interpreted that without any further explanation? The same way? A. I do not understand, Senator.

Q. You mentioned that it was your impression that it must have come from the President. Now, did you, when you reached that impression, question Mr. Dean any further about it? A. No, sir.

SENATOR WEICKER: Mr. Chairman, I just have two or three brief questions; then I will yield.

Mr. Caulfield, turn to page 19 of your testimony. You state there, "I have been asked by the U.S. Attorney's office and by Senator investigators and am trying as best I can to recall what impressions I had at this particular point in time. As best as these impressions can be stated, I believed that I was going back to see Mr. McCord to again extend an offer of executive clemency and that by my doing so I was doing a great service for the President of the United States in a very sensitive matter."

My first question to you, very simply, is this: Using your

words, I would like you to comment and explain to me why it is—why it is—that you thought that you were doing a great service for the President of the United States?

A. Well, sir, to go back a little bit, it was a great honor for me to serve as a member of the President's staff. I had come from a rather humble background, a police officer. I did receive this great opportunity to serve on the President's staff. I felt very strongly about the President, extremely strongly about the President. I was very loyal to his people that I worked for, I place a high value upon loyalty.

Now, out of the blue, I am injected into this scandal. I am being asked by one of my former superiors to deliver a message that I know to be executive clemency. I tried to avoid it, as my statement indicates. I imposed upon my friend to do it, hoping that all parties would be satisfied. I was not successful.

I was brought back in again to it, now being asked to see Mr. McCord directly. I did go to see him.

Now I am becoming further implicated into this matter. I had this conversation with John Dean, who was the counsel to the President. I had been there three years. I know what the relations are and how they exist. I make certain judgments based upon those relationships. In my mind, I felt that the President probably did know about it.

Now, I am going out the door, to become more specific, and it crossed my mind that this conceivably was for the President. I believed it. I had to think about that. And based upon all of that background, I believed I was doing something for the President of the U.S., and I did it, sir.

SENATOR GURNEY: Referring to the previous testimony by Mr. McCord, at page 320 of the record, he had this to say about his conversations and meeting with you:

"Caulfield stated that he was carrying the message of executive clemency to me from the very highest levels of the White House. He stated that the President of the United States was in Key Biscayne, Fla., that weekend," referring to the weekend following Jan. 8, "following meetings that we were in then, and that the President had been told of the results of the meeting."

Did you ever learn that the President had learned of the results of any of your meetings with Mr. McCord? A. Absolutely not, sir.

Q. He also stated this further on in the testimony on the next page. Mr. McCord: "He," meaning you, "further stated 'I may have a message to you at our next meeting from the President.'" Did you ever tell him that? A. No, sir.

Q. Did you ever have any communication with the President of the United States with regard to this so-called executive clemency offer to Mr. McCord? A. None whatsoever, sir.

Q. Did you ever hear Mr. Dean in any of your conversations

with Mr. Dean ever refer to the fact that he had informed the President of these meetings? A. No, sir.

Q. Did Mr. Dean ever say to you: "The President has instructed me to make this offer of executive clemency to McCord through you," or through anybody else as far as that is concerned? A. Absolutely not, sir.

Q. Did you ever apply any pressure to Mr. McCord in any of these meetings for him to do anything in regard to this upcoming trial? A. No, sir.

Q. Did you ever urge him or advise him to plead guilty? A. Never.

SENATOR TALMADGE: Mr. Caulfield, are you still on the Federal payroll? A. Yes, sir.

Q. Did you call Mr. John Ehrlichman immediately after the break-in at the Watergate on June 17? A. Yes, sir.

Q. What did he say?

A. Well, I received a telephone call on the afternoon of June 17, about 3 or 4 P.M., as I recall, from a gentleman I worked with in the United States Secret Service, Mr. Patrick Boggs, and he called me and he said, "Do you know Jim McCord," and I said, "Yes, I know Jim McCord."

He said, "Well, we have received a report that there is a break-in at the Democratic National Committee. We are concerned because of our protective capabilities or responsibilities, rather in that area. We have some agents checking into it. Some of the people appear not to have given their correct names and we are getting a report that one of those not giving the correct name is Jim McCord."

He said, "Now, do you want to call John Ehrlichman or should I call him?"

After I had recovered from the shock I indicated, "Well, you go ahead and try and reach him and I will try to reach him as well."

And I called the White House board and I was told that he was en route to his residence. By the time that I did reach him Mr. Boggs had already contacted him. And I said to Mr. Ehrlichman, I said, "John, it sounds like there is a disaster of some type. Did you speak to Mr. Boggs?" He said, "Yes, what is this all about?" I said, "I haven't the foggiest notion what it is all about but they are saying they believed Jim McCord, who works for the committee, has been arrested in a burglary at the Democratic National Committee."

He said—I forget what he said exactly, I think it was a long silence, as I recall, and I said, "My God, you know, I cannot believe it." He said, "Well, I guess I had better place a call to John Mitchell." I said, "I think that would be very appropriate."

SENATOR ERVIN: Now, when you performed this mission for John Dean on these three occasions, what did you expect or, rather, what did you understand was expected of McCord in return for executive clemency? Did you infer from your conversation with Dean that under Dean's statements, McCord was expected to plead guilty, keep silent, receive a short sentence, and then receive clemency?

A. If he accepted the offer, that would be the way I would interpret it, yes, sir.

Testimony by Anthony T. Ulasewicz

May 23, 1973

Describes his duties as investigator.

SENATOR INOUYE: According to Mr. Caulfield's testimony you were a member of a "private security entity in Washington, D. C., providing investigative support for the White House." Is that correct?

MR. ULASEWICZ: That is correct.

Q. You worked under Mr. Caulfield but were on the payroll of Mr. Kalmbach? A. That is correct.

Q. Will you describe some of your duties. One of the newspapers described you as the super spy. Is that a correct statement?

A. The newspapers have painted quite a few pictures of me recently, but I was no spy, of course, of any kind. I did investigative work in support of whatever Mr. Caulfield related to me. I did no slanderous spying as the newspapers' allegations, etc. I would best put in its category is probably supporting anybody who is conducting legitimate investigations. I used no wiretaps, I never use any surveillance, etc.

SENATOR BAKER: You think your wiremen [in the New York Police Department] were better than McCord's wiremen?

A. I will tell you, any old retired man in the New York City Police Department who would become involved in a thing like that, he thought he had to for whatever reason it was, he would not have walked in with any army, that is for sure.

Q. How could you have gained the information that Mr. McCord obviously or apparently was seeking?

A. If it is a question of obtaining information from the Democratic party, Republican party or anybody else, the easiest way is to write a postal card asking them to mail you all their leaflets. They will put you on their mailing list and you will have everything. [Mr. Ulasewicz testified again on July 18, 1973. See p. 461.]

Testimony by Gerald Alch

May 23   *Disputes testimony of McCord, his former
client, and says McCord sought to "get" the
President.*

May 24   *Suggests lie-detector tests be taken.*

May 23, 1973

MR. ALCH: Mr. McCord has made allegations concerning my conduct in the defense of his liberty. These allegations are, in some instances, completely false and, in other instances, have been twisted out of context into untruths, presumably to serve his present purpose, whatever that may be, but which impugn my personal standards of ethical and legal behavior.

On a Saturday morning [in July] I met with him for the first time. He identified himself as one of those arrested in the Watergate building on June 17, 1972. He told me that he had taken a calculated risk in doing what he did and was prepared to face the consequences. Within that framework, however, he indicated he wanted the most effective legal representation possible.

I asked Mr. McCord to give me specific details attending the Watergate break-in, but he specifically declined so to do except to state his personal motivation, i.e., the protection of others. I explained to him that since he had been physically apprehended in the Watergate complex, he could obviously not deny that fact and inquired as to his motivation in so acting.

He told me that as chief of security for the Committee to Re-elect the President, he had received information to the effect that various antiwar demonstrations by groups which he described as "radical" were being planned for the upcoming Presidential election and that these demonstrations had, in the past and would invariably in the future, lead to violence or the threat thereof to various prominent Republican officials, including, but not limited to members of the Committee to Re-elect the President and included, but not limited to the President of the United States. I told him that I would explore whether or not this motivation could, in any way, be embraced by a recognized legal defense.

He would, almost daily, send to me clippings from various newspapers published throughout the country, reflecting reports of antiwar groups, activities which in some instances involved violence. In fact, at one point, he sent to me a typed memorandum reflecting this alleged motivation for his conduct which memorandum included various legal citations of law, which he believed to be in support of the defense he wished me to present. I have made available to this honorable committee copies of three such memorandums, accompanied by a hand-written note from Mr. McCord which reads as follows:

"Gerald, I well understand that it is your job and not mine to work up a defense. Nevertheless, I have been putting together some ideas and collecting every newspaper clipping I can find which may be of help later. I am strongly oriented toward the grounds of self-defense and defense of others and of property as my defense. I believe we can make the strongest defense on these grounds. We both of course have to talk this out at length and you have the final say in this matter. With best regards, Jim."

I do this to emphasize this fact: that Mr. McCord was from the beginning in complete agreement with the defense ultimately presented in his behalf. At no time did he ever state to me that he believed the Watergate "operation" to be legal as a result of the alleged involvement of the then Attorney General, the counsel to the President, or anyone else. Mr. McCord explained to me his belief of a direct relationship between these potentially violent antiwar groups and the Democratic party and that his participation in the Watergate burglary was accomplished in the hope of obtaining advance evidence of planned potentially violent demonstrations.

I advised that the law of "duress" allowed for the perpetrator to possess criminal intent, that is, to know that he was breaking the law and that therefore, based upon what he had told me with regard to his own motivation, this defense was not only compatible therewith, but in my opinion, constituted the only defense available. Mr. McCord wholeheartedly agreed. And I commenced to prepare the case on this basis.

I also received from Mr. McCord an outline of a proposed book he was in the process of writing entitled "Counter Espionage Agent for the Republicans—The True Story of the Watergate Case." Copies of this outline have also been provided to this honorable committee.

It was an outline listing such chapters [as] "The Beginnings," "The Committee to Re-elect the President," "Background to Violence and Political Espionage," "Jack Anderson, the Man Who Brought You the Eagleton Case," "The Political Opposition," "The Watergate Incident, the True Story," "The Defendants," "The Grand Jury," "The Lawyer," "The Investigators," "The Congressional Committees," "The October Phase," "The News Media," "The Final Story," with a prologue, as the book goes to print, "If the Democrats Had Had Alarms and Guards."

There were other memoranda that I received from time to time from Mr. McCord which suggested for consideration other potential defense material which I rejected. One such memorandum, copies of which have been provided to this honorable committee, listed and discussed such topics as "The Mafia and Democratic National Committee Funds and Personnel," "Flying Tigers and Anna Chennault," "Israel and the Mafia."

On several occasions, Mr. McCord told me that he was convinced there existed a concerted effort on the part of his co-defendants and their counsel to make him the "fall guy" of the Watergate operation. On one particular occasion, he mailed to me a memorandum, copies of which have been provided.

I advised Mr. McCord that I had kept abreast of newspaper coverage of the Watergate incident and that, in all honesty, could discern no effort on anyone's part to foist upon him prime responsibility for the offenses charged. He disagreed with me and I told him that I would subsequently discuss the matter with other defense counsel.

At another time prior to January, 1973, Mr. McCord advised that he had made telephone calls to the Israeli Embassy on Sept. 19, 1972, and to the Chilean Embassy on Oct. 10, 1972. He did not divulge the contents of these telephone conversations.

His theory was that the Government, rather than reveal such activity, would dismiss the cases against him.

I received a letter from him dated Aug. 23 reflecting these thoughts, copies of which I have made available to this honorable committee.

It is interesting to note the last paragraph of this memorandum which reads as follows:

"Enjoyed the visit with you and appreciated your advice. I have got a great lawyer and am well aware of that fact. With best regards, Jim."

In addition, I have provided this honorable committee with copies of undated memorandum from Mr. McCord, reflecting four telephone calls: one from Chile to McCord's office; another from Mr. McCord's office to the Chilean military attaché; a call to the Israeli Embassy from Mr. McCord's home and a similar call to the Chilean Embassy. As a result thereof, I made an appropriate motion for disclosure of any Government electronic surveillance in any way pertaining to Mr. McCord. Mr. Silbert's response was that he had no knowledge of any such surveillance. Again, at my client's insistence, I made a second similar motion at the bench during trial, explaining to Chief Judge Sirica that I was doing so at my client's insistence that such calls had, in fact, been made and had been electronically intercepted.

The Government again stated its total lack of knowledge of any. such activity and, accordingly, no action was taken on my motion.

With regard to the allegations of Mr. McCord to the effect that I suggested that the C.I.A. be brought into the case in a defense posture, I state the following:

As heretofore explained, I had decided to base Mr. McCord's defense on the theory of "duress" for two basic reasons. (1) It was the only legally recognized defense that I felt was supportable. (2) More importantly, it appeared to be the factual truth, based upon Mr. McCord's explanation of his own motive.

In December of 1972, I attended one of several meetings of

defense counsel, the purpose of which was to discuss various aspects of trial strategy. I proceeded to explain the defense that I was contemplating. A discussion ensued wherein some of the other defense attorneys reasoned that this "security motive" would be applicable only to McCord, in view of his position as chief of security for the Committee to Re-elect the President.

In the general discussion that followed, the question arose as to whether or not the C.I.A. could have been involved. It was pointed by others that all of the individuals apprehended in the Watergate complex had some prior connection with the C.I.A. and that one of the Cuban-Americans had been in possession of what appeared to be C.I.A.-forged documents.

Before the meeting went on to other topics, it was agreed that each lawyer would ask his respective client whether or not he had any knowledge of any C.I.A. involvement. When the meeting terminated, I telephoned Mr. McCord at his office and asked him to meet with me and local counsel, Mr. Shankman, at the Monocle Restaurant for lunch. During lunch, which lasted for approximately 45 minutes, I asked Mr. McCord whether, to his knowledge, the C.I.A. was in any way involved with the Watergate venture.

He did not directly respond to this specific question, but did become quite upset at what he believed to be the antagonism of the White House against the C.I.A. He cited the dismissal of Helms as C.I.A. director and the appointment of Schlesinger in his place, as an attempted "hatchet job" by the Administration against the C.I.A. He did venture his observation that if any C.I.A. officials were subpoenaed that they would not and could not comply with said subpoena.

Because of the brevity of the luncheon and because of the obvious need for more detailed pretrial preparation meetings, I asked Mr. McCord to come to Boston in a few days, which he agreed to do.

On or about Dec. 26, 1972, Mr. McCord came to Boston and initiated our conversation by stating that the C.I.A. was not involved and that he would have no part of any attempt to involve that agency. He asked that I relay this position to other defense counsel at our next meeting, which I agreed to do, and in fact did.

I did not, after advising other defense counsel of Mr. McCord's denial of C.I.A. involvement, engage with other counsel in any further conversation of any potential defense involving the C.I.A. At no time did I suggest to Mr. McCord that the so-called C.I.A. defense be utilized, for the defense of "duress" had already been agreed upon, but I merely asked him whether or not there was a factual basis for this contention.

Mr. McCord's allegation that I announced my ability to forge his C.I.A. personal records with the cooperation of then Acting C.I.A. Director Schlesinger is absurd and completely untrue. I have never had the privilege of meeting Mr. Schlesinger and no such statement was ever made. My local counsel, Bernard Shankman, who was present at the Monocle, can corroborate this.

Mr. Shankman, Mr. McCord, and I hailed a cab and at the last minute, co-defendant Barker asked if he could ride in the cab with us. Why Mr. Barker was going to Mr. Bittman's office, I do not know. There was no significant conversation with Mr. Barker in the cab.

Mr. McCord has alleged that I told him that the purpose of going to Bittman's office was that Mr. Bittman wanted to talk with him about "whose word he would trust regarding a White House offer of executive clemency" and that Mr. Bittman wanted to talk to Mr. Barker as well.

This is not true. I merely said to Mr. McCord that prior to the scheduled daily postcourt meeting between he, Mr. Shankman and myself, that we would stop at Mr. Bittman's office, for I wanted to discuss with him the ramifications and details of Mr. Hunt's proposed change of plea.

When we arrived at Mr. Bittman's office, Mr. McCord has alleged that I sensed his anger at Mr. Barker's presence, and therefore delayed going up to Mr. Bittman's office for approximately 30 minutes. The simple truth is that I suggested that we three have a cocktail and Mr. McCord, Mr. Shankman and I went into a restaurant directly across the street from Mr. Bittman's office for just that purpose.

When we arrived at Mr. Bittman's office, I went with Mr. McCord and Mr. Shankman to the firm's library and went back to Mr. Bittman's office to see if he was there. I had a discussion with him in which he confirmed the judge's refusal to entertain any change of plea by Mr. Hunt until after opening statements. At this point, I mentioned to Mr. Bittman that I felt my client was becoming a bit paranoid, that he felt he was being made the "patsy" or "fall guy."

I mentioned it at that time since in my mind, that allegation seemed inconsistent with Mr. Hunt's desire to plead guilty. After I mentioned Mr. McCord's apprehension, my recollection is that Mr. Bittman said in words or substance, "Tell McCord he will receive a call from a friend of his." Mr. Bittman did not mention the "White House" as alleged by Mr. McCord. The identity of this friend was not made known to me, nor did I make inquiry in this matter. I considered the possibility, without actually knowing, that the purpose of this call was to allay Mr. McCord's fears that his co-defendants were turning against him, and that the caller could very well be Mr. Bittman's client, Mr. Hunt.

I considered this possibility in view of the context of the conversation immediately preceding Mr. Bittman's remark, that is, my statement in accordance with Mr. McCord's request, of his apprehension with regard to his co-defendants. I subsequently told Mr. McCord just what Mr. Bittman had told me, that he would receive a call from a friend. I did not mention the words "the

White House" because Mr. Bittman did not mention those words to me. Mr. McCord nodded, said, "O.K.," and had no further response to my statement.

Some time later—the trial was in progress—Mr. McCord told me that he had been in contact with a man by the name of Caldwell. He specifically stated that he did not wish to tell me who this man was or the subject matter of his conversation with him. In response, I told Mr. McCord that that was his prerogative.

In this regard, I respectfully invite the attention of this honorable committee to Mr. McCord's letter to Chief Judge Sirica of March 19, 1973, of which I had no prior knowledge. I respectfully refer to the next to the last paragraph on page 2 of this letter in which Mr. McCord, after alleging such things as political pressure applied to the defendants to plead guilty and remain silent, stated, and I quote, "I have not discussed the above with my attorneys as a matter of protection for them."

Mr. McCord has alleged that the subject of executive clemency was discussed on this day, Jan. 8, 1973.

This is not true. In late 1972, during one of the pretrial meetings of defense lawyers in Washington, I had an occasion to say to Mr. Bittman, "Bill, what do you think our clients will receive as a sentence should they be convicted?"

Mr. Bittman responded in substance, as if theorizing, "You can never tell, Christmas time rolls around and there could be executive clemency."

I scoffed at this notion and told Mr. Bittman that in my opinion, the President would not touch this case with a 10-foot pole, let alone exercise executive clemency.

This subject had not been on any agenda, but arose in which I characterize as "lawyer's talk." Subsequently, but not on the same day, I mentioned this to Mr. McCord in a most skeptic manner, and said to him, "Jim, it can be Christmas, Easter and Thanksgiving all rolled up into one, but in my opinion, the President wouldn't touch this with a 10-foot pole." Mr. McCord laughed and agreed with me.

That was the only occasion that the words "executive clemency" were ever mentioned by me to my client. I have neither met John Dean nor spoken to him in my life. I have neither met John Caulfield nor spoken to him in my life.

As the trial approached the completion of the Government's case, I conferred with Mr. McCord at one of our daily post-trial meetings and told him that a decision would have to be made regarding whether or not he would take the stand. I explained to him that if he elected to testify, it would be his obligation to answer any and all relevant questions. It was at this time that Mr. McCord told me that he had evidence to the effect that the Watergate operation had been approved by John Mitchell.

I asked him the nature of the evidence and he told me he had been so advised by Mr. Liddy. I asked him if he had any other corroborative evidence and he told me he did not. I told him that although this was technically hearsay, it would be admissible as a declaration by one co-conspirator to another and told him to understand beyond any doubt that should he take the stand, that question would in my opinion be asked and an answer required.

I told him that if he elected to take the stand, full disclosure would be necessary; that I was with him all the way, but that this crucial decision of whether or not to testify could only be his. I did advise him, however, to resolve this question as soon as possible and not advise me of his decision at the last minute, thereby precluding adequate time for preparation of direct and cross-examination.

Mr. McCord was extremely upset over what he believed to be unfair newspaper coverage of his disclosures. He kept smashing his fist on my suitcase. At this point, Mr. Fensterwald said to Mr. McCord, "The reporters have been asking me whether or not you or I had ever had any past relationship. I told him that we had."

At this point, Mr. McCord looked up with a surprised expression. Mr. Fensterwald said, "Well, after all, you have in the past submitted to me checks which were donations to the Committee for the Investigation of the Assassination of the President." Mr. McCord smiled and said, "Oh, yeah, that's right."

[Next] morning, in court, I asked for and received a continuance of sentencing to June 15, 1973. I advised the court of Mr. McCord's desire to cooperate fully with both the grand jury and Senate committee and further advised of Mr. McCord's preference to first testifying before the Senate committee.

Subsequently, while I was still on trial in Chicago, I did receive several phone calls from Mr. Fensterwald and I recall that in one telephone conversation he said to me, "What do you think of all that is going on?" referring to the disclosures being made by Mr. McCord. To this I replied, "Whatever is right for Jim McCord is all right with me."

Mr. Fensterwald replied, "We're going after the President of the United States." I replied that I was not interested in any vendettas against the President but only in the best interest of my client, to which Mr. Fensterwald replied, "Well, you'll see, that's who we're going after, the President."

During another telephone conversation with Mr. Fensterwald, he stated that he was most displeased with the reaction of the Republican members of this honorable committee, to Mr. McCord's submitted memoranda and further stated that "I'll submit memoranda but I don't want the Republicans to see them."

Subsequently my contact with Mr. McCord and Mr. Fensterwald diminished. On May 8, 1973, my secretary gave me a message reflecting a call from The Los Angeles Times in regard to a four-page memorandum of Mr. McCord, involving the C.I.A., that was about to be published the following morning.

I called Mr. McCord that night, was told by his wife that he was not in, and I left a message for him to call me. He never did. The following day, The New York Times published a memorandum by Mr. McCord, alleging that I had stated that I could obtain forged C.I.A. documents with the cooperation of the director of the C.I.A.

At approximately 5:30 P.M. on May 8, 1973, I contacted Mr. Fensterwald by telephone and asked him to explain these false allegations made by Mr. McCord.

Mr. Fensterwald stated, "I can only hazard the guess that it is the result of Mr. McCord's faulty recollection." He added, "I can tell you one thing, it's a terrible cliché, but I think you will agree with it, that there is no zealot like a convert." I had had no further contact from Mr. McCord.

Mr. McCord has accused me of exerting pressure upon him, but I respectfully request this honorable committee to take note of the following facts:

1. Mr. McCord did not plead guilty.

2. He admitted, under oath, in response to a question put to him by Senator Ervin, that I never urged him to enter a plea of guilty.

3. In his letter of March 19, 1973, to Chief Judge Sirica, in referring to his allegations of improprieties, including but not limited to political pressure, stated, "I have not discussed the above with my attorneys as a matter of protection for them."

4. Mr. McCord proceeded to trial defense based upon what he told me to be the truth.

I have done nothing wrong and am, therefore, not afraid, but am upset as a practicing criminal trial lawyer.

How can a lawyer effectively represent his client when faced with the possibility that the man for whom he is working night and day is constantly making a record of privileged conversations with the intent of subsequently violating this privilege by making false accusations and by selectively extracting statements out of context and twisting them into untruths?

Mr. McCord has made accusations directed towards many men. I am in no position to judge his credibility in that regard. I do, however, have first-hand knowledge of his relationship with me, and in regard to his accusations against me, he is not telling the truth. As I watched Mr. McCord on national television on May 18, 1973, and listened to him falsely accuse me of professional misconduct, which accusations are false in every respect, I immediately and vividly recalled his praise for me throughout the trial, his confidence in me at the time professed of the guilty verdict and his further expression of gratitude during the period of his incarceration and I asked myself, "What kind of a man is this?"

May 24, 1973

MR. DASH: Now as to Mr. McCord's first complaint that you suggested he use C.I.A. involvement as a defense, it is true, is it not, that the question, at least of C.I.A. involvement, was the subject of discussion between you and Mr. McCord on two occasions in December, one at the Monocle Restaurant and another time in your office in Boston?

A. I specifically asked him whether or not there was any factual basis to the contention that the C.I.A. was involved.

Q. Did you on either occasion show Mr. McCord a statement from a D. C. Police officer, Gary Bittenbender, indicating that Mr. McCord told Bittenbender that Watergate was a C.I.A. operation?

A. Yes sir. That statement had been provided to me pursuant to my discovery motions filed in the case, by the Government. It was a report in which it quoted a District of Columbia policeman, Mr. Bittenbender, by name, as saying that at the time of Mr. McCord's arrest, I believe at the District of Columbia Jail, Mr. McCord said, referring to the other four men who had been arrested with him, "These are all good men, ex-C.I.A. men." I naturally called that to my client's attention because there loomed a distinct possibility that that statement might be introduced against him at trial. In fact it was not.

Q. All right. Now, Mr. Alch, in the statement that you submitted to the committee, as you read it, that was not included in that statement, is that true?

A. It was not, sir. I believe I mentioned it when I met with you the night before my testimony.

Q. Did you ever mention during either of the two meetings at the Monocle Restaurant and in your office in Boston when you asked Mr. McCord about the C.I.A. involvement—did you ever mention during either of these meetings the name Victor Marchetti who might be a witness on C.I.A. training?

A. I did mention the name Victor Marchetti, not in the context of his being a witness. It came up this way: In the course of discussing Mr. McCord's background with the C.I.A., I mentioned to him that I had recently heard that a man by that name had come out with a book about the C.I.A. I mentioned that to Mr. McCord. He said to me words to the effect that Mr. Marchetti was not in good grace with the C.I.A. or any ex-members of the C.I.A. He said he did not think highly of the man and that was the extent of the conversation.

Q. Now, after your meeting of December, 1972, at the Monocle Restaurant with Mr. McCord, did you call your partner, Mr. Bailey, and raise the question of the C.I.A. defense?

A. I would constantly keep Mr. Bailey advised of the development of all cases that I was working on.

Mr. Bailey told me that unless Mr. McCord or anyone else

could come up with any factual evidence of any C.I.A. involvement, that if Mr. McCord wished to pursue that defense without any such factual evidence, that I was to withdraw from the case and that I was to tell that to Mr. McCord.

When Mr. McCord met with me in Boston at our next meeting, he initiated the conversation by saying to me, there is no C.I.A. involvement and I will have no part of anything that is going to put the blame on the C.I.A. That rendered my withdrawal direction from Mr. Bailey moot.

Q. In your statement on page 10, you say during the meeting with defendants in December, and prior to your Monocle meeting with Mr. McCord, "the question arose as to whether the C.I.A. was involved." Would you tell us how the question arose, who raised it? Do you know how that was raised, this question? Who raised it?

A. I am not sure. It may have been Mr. Bittman. I cannot be positive.

Q. Are you aware Mr. McCord sent Mr. John Caulfield a note complaining of a White House effort to blame the C.I.A. for Watergate and threatening "that all the trees in the forest would fall if this effort continued." Were you aware of this? A. I was not.

Q. So it is no fiction, really, that Mr. McCord was deeply concerned over what he believed was a conspiracy to have him implicate the C.I.A. in the Watergate case?

A. I have no knowledge to contradict that statement by Mr. McCord.

Q. Actually according to your own statement, when you first raised the C.I.A. involvement with Mr. McCord in the Monocle Restaurant, you said he did not really respond to it, but launched into a complaint about how the White House was treating the C.I.A. I think that was your statement. A. That is correct.

Q. Therefore, Mr. Alch, when you raised the question of C.I.A. involvement with him for the very first time after the meeting with Mr. Bittman and the other lawyers, it is likely, is it not, taking into consideration the entire circumstances of Mr. McCord's concern, that Mr. McCord could have concluded that you had joined in the conspiracy he honestly believed existed to blame the C.I.A. in the Watergate case.

A. In my judgment, that would be giving him the benefit of a doubt to which I do not believe he is entitled, for this reason: I suppose, hypothetically speaking, that it is possible for a man to misinterpret a question put to him as to whether or not the C.I.A. was involved, on the one hand, and a suggestion that it was, on the other. That is a point of discrepancy, in answer to a hypothetical question—could possibly be the subject of a misinterpretation.

However, on his allegation that I said to him words to the effect that I could cause his personnel records to be doctored and that the director of the C.I.A. would go along with it, it escapes me how that type of allegation can be a misunderstanding. I did not say it.

Q. Now, Mr. Caulfield, in his testimony before this committee, stated that at one of the meetings that he had with Mr. Dean during the time he was making offers of executive clemency to Mr. McCord, that Mr. Dean told him, Mr. Caulfield, that Mr. McCord was "not cooperating with his attorney." Could Mr. Dean have referred to or been referring to anyone other than you?

A. Well, the fact is that I was Mr. McCord's attorney at that time, to my knowledge, and the only reason I add that caveat is this: I was informed that, when—I was not informed—when I read a transcript of, I believe, Mr. Caulfield's testimony, I believe he said that in one of his meetings with Mr. McCord prior to the completion of trial, that the subject of bail came up, and Mr. Caulfield stated, "Maybe your lawyer Alch can handle it," or words to that effect, to which, according to Mr. Caulfield, Mr. McCord replied, "Well, I am negotiating with another lawyer. Maybe he can handle it."

If that statement about "I am not cooperating with your attorney" or "get close to your attorney" was directed toward me, I can't explain it because, as I have explained to the committee yesterday, Mr. McCord was cooperating with me every day.

Q. And you have no other explanation of why Mr. Dean might have made that statement?

A. I do not. As I told the committee yesterday, I had never met the man nor spoken to him in my life.

SENATOR ERVIN: Yes. Now, there was a meeting of most of these lawyers and it had been pointed out in the press that Mr. Sturgis had apparently C.I.A. connections issued in the name of Mr. Martin, I believe. A. Yes, sir.

Q. It was also apparent that it came out in the press that other members of those of the group who broke into the Watergate had false credentials? A. That is correct, sir.

Q. And the press had suggested since McCord had been involved in the Watergate—I mean in the C.I.A.—and Hunt had worked for the C.I.A.—and Baker had been in the Bay of Pigs operations, C.I.A. and possibly others, that perhaps there was a C.I.A. involvement. Was that not speculated in the press? A. In the press, yes, sir.

Q. And at this meeting, of course, the first thing a lawyer tried to find out from his client is what kind of defense, if any, he has got, is that not true? A. Of course.

Q. So the lawyers would be discussing at that time what possible defense they had, and it was suggested by one of the other counsel that perhaps they could have—get evidence that would sustain a defense that would lay this break-in on the C.I.A., was it not, at the meeting with lawyers?

A. Yes, sir. But, Senator, I do not mean to split hairs but I do wish again to point out that it did not come out in the sense that "let us make this a C.I.A. defense." It did not come out that way. It was not presented that way. The way it was presented was, could this be a C.I.A. defense because of all of these things? Let us go back and ask our client. That is the way it happened.

Q. Well, the only way the lawyers can find out whether their clients have a defense is to discuss matters like this.

A. Ask them.

Q. And try to investigate it. A. Of course.

Q. And it was suggested in this meeting of lawyers by some attorney other than yourself? A. Yes, sir.

Q. That the lawyers involved should try to ascertain from their clients whether the C.I.A. was involved, whether they had any knowledge enough to implicate C.I.A., was it not? A. That is right.

Q. And immediately after that you went in and talked to Mr. McCord about it, did you not? A. Yes, sir.

Q. Did Mr. McCord ever mention the President to you at any time in any conversation he ever had with you? A. No, sir. No, sir.

Q. And Mr. McCord was not present, so far as you know, and did not overhear any of the phone conversations between you and Mr. Fensterwald on that point?

A. Not to my knowledge, but my record—

Q. So far as it appears down to this day, there is no evidence that Mr. McCord ever mentioned the President of the United States except he said that Mr. Caulfield mentioned the President of the United States in a conversation with him.

Now, Mr. McCord says, someone, I believe he said you, suggested that if they changed the record at the C.I.A. to show he had been called back to duty, there might be a chance to have a defense of that kind. You say you never said that?

A. Mr. McCord said much stronger words than that, Senator. He said I told him that I would effectuate the forgery of his C.I.A. records with the cooperation of the C.I.A. director. That is pretty strong talk.

Q. I do not believe that is the testimony Mr. McCord gave this committee. My recollection, and I do not guarantee—but my recollection is that he said you, or somebody, said that by letting the record of the C.I.A. show—wait a minute now, here is McCord's statement. He said "if so," that is you, "my personnel records at C.I.A. could be doctored to reflect such a recall." He stated Schlesinger, the new director of C.I.A., whose new appointment had just been announced, could be subpoenaed and would go along with it. . . .

He did not accuse you of anything except saying that the records, that you advocate that. You were just expressing a surmise?

A. Well, Senator, perhaps through a lawyer's, and an experienced lawyer's eyes, looking at it really close, dissecting it, that conclusion might be proper. But not to the average person who reads it on the street.

Q. And I would not criticize you a bit if you recommended a

plea of guilty because you had a client who was caught red-handed at the burglary and the defense was on very precarious grounds at best, and so if he did say that you urged him to plead guilty, I think it would be a compliment to your intelligence as a lawyer rather than a reflection on it.

A. With all due respect I reject the compliment, for this reason, Senator: First of all, because he specifically said to you I never suggested that he enter a plea of guilty. The reason when this proposition was put to me, or this offer was put to me by the Government—I practice this way. I do not—that is too important a decision for me to make, I simply take it back to the client and say, here it is, What do you say? He said, no.

Q. Let us go to executive clemency. You did attend a meeting with Mr. Bittman? A. Yes, sir.

Q. Now, Mr. Bittman was representing Hunt? A. Yes, sir.

Q. Hunt—you knew that Hunt had been a consultant in the White House or the Executive Office?

A. I honestly was not sure of what Mr. Hunt's position was.

Q. You knew he had been working for the Committee to Re-elect the President, didn't you? A. That I did.

Q. And you do not know what contacts were—had been—Mr. Hunt and any of his former associates in the Committee to Re-elect the President or between his counsel and any of those people? A. No sir.

Q. You participated in the trial and heard the evidence. A. Yes, sir.

Q. And you know that it was proved on trial, as shown on the trial, or at least evidence tended to show that the notebook of Mr. Hunt, which was introduced into evidence, had the White House phone number on it, didn't you?

A. If it was I certainly don't recall.

Q. You don't recall it?

A. Because Mr. Hunt's local counsel—I don't recall.

Q. You discussed the question of executive privilege with Mr. McCord, didn't you?

A. I didn't discuss the question, I relayed to him the conversation I had with Mr. Bittman.

Q. Yes, and you relayed the conversation in which Bittman had said, in effect, that you can never tell, Christmas time rolls around and there could be executive clemency.

A. I did with a singular addition of my own.

Q. Yes, and you said it was absurd to expect executive clemency, the President wouldn't touch it with a 10-foot pole or something like that.

A. That is what I said.

Q. And McCord agreed with you? A. He did.

Q. Now, you on one occasion you told Mr. McCord that Mr. Bittman—rather Mr. Bittman told you in one of these meetings of the lawyers, that Mr. McCord was going to receive a message, a telephone call. A. Yes, sir.

Q. And didn't you ask Mr. Bittman what business other people had—you had been talking about the case, hadn't you?

A. At that particular point we had been talking about my client's apprehension that his co-defendants were conspiring against him.

Q. Anyway, he told you your client—somebody else was going to communicate by telephone with your client? A. Yes, sir.

Q. And it was a short time after that, according to the evidence, your client did receive a telephone call and had three conferences with Mr. Caulfield. A. Not to my knowledge.

Q. Don't you think it is reasonable now, he got a call, and you told him in advance that he is going to get the call, and then you receive a call and had some negotiations or conversations at least about executive privilege—don't you think Mr. McCord is liable, because in his mind he associated those conversations he had pursuant to this telephone call with you—can't you see where he would reasonably draw a deduction that the telephone call which resulted in this indicated that you knew something about executive clemency?

A. No, for this reason. I again reiterate how close we were in our contact and I what we would tell each other. If he thought, and he has now labeled this as improper conduct on my part— the question I keep asking myself is, in that, if he did make the surmise and conclude that I was engaged in improper conduct— this was before the trial began, or was it before the trial began or whenever it happened—why wouldn't the man come up to me and confront me with it? That is what I don't understand.

Q. Well, you go and tell him that he is going to receive a phone call. A. Yes, sir.

Q. And he does receive a phone call. A. Yes, sir.

Q. And as a result of receiving a phone call he has an offer of executive clemency made to him. A. Yes, sir.

Q. And you say that it wasn't reasonable for him to infer from those facts that you knew about the offer of executive clemency?

A. I say it was not reasonable for him to infer or assume and later allege that that was in any way the basis of improper conduct on my part.

SENATOR BAKER: There is a conflict between your testimony and that of Mr. McCord. Do you have any suggestions as to how this committee can reconcile that apparently irreconcilable difference in proof and give us some indication of where the truth lies?

A. Two.

Q. Tell us.

A. One, speak to the third party who was there, Mr. Bernard Shankman.

I suggest that both Mr. McCord and I, if he is willing, submit to a polygraph test conducted by a competent examiner, accredited by the American Polygraph Association. I state my willingness to do.

Q. Moving then to another subject, it would appear to me a material conflict between your testimony and the statements of Mr. Fensterwald, given publicly after our hearings on yesterday, may produce for this committee a similar dilemma. Would you now tell us what method you could suggest to bring the testimony of other witnesses to bear or other circumstantial evidence or any evidence, to try to find who is telling the truth in that respect?

A. Polygraph.

SENATOR TALMADGE: Mr. Chairman, it is perfectly obvious, of course, to all members of the committee that the testimony of Mr. Alch varies significantly from that of Mr. McCord in any number of instances. I want all witnesses to be put on notice that at an appropriate time, wherever there is any evidence of perjury, I expect to ask the staff of this committee to submit a transcript of that possible perjury to the appropriate prosecuting attorney for action as the situation may arise.

Testimony by Bernard L. Barker

May 24, 1973

Says break-in sought proof of Cuban aid to Democrats.

MR. HAMILTON: Mr. Barker, who recruited you for these activities?

MR. BARKER: E. Howard Hunt.

Q. And was Mr. Hunt your supervisor in the Watergate operations? A. That is correct.

Q. And had Mr. Hunt also been your commanding officer in the Bay of Pigs operation?

A. I was Mr. Hunt's principal assistant in the Bay of Pigs operation.

Q. Mr. Barker, what was your motivation for participating in these operations.

A. The original operation was the Ellsberg operation. It was explained to me that this was a matter of national security. At no time was I told any different from the original motivation for which I had been recruited.

Q. Mr. Barker, is it correct that part of your motivation for participating in these operations was to gain later assistance from Mr. Hunt and others in high places for a Cuban liberation operation? It that correct?

A. Our team, which was composed of myself and Mr. Martinez,

Mr. Sturgis and Mr. Gonzalez—to us, this was our prime motivation.

Q. What sort of documents were you primarily looking for in the Democratic headquarters?

A. I was looking for documents that would involve contributions to a national and foreign agent—the Democratic campaign, especially to Senator McGovern, and possibly also to Senator Kennedy.

Q. From any particular foreign government?

A. The foreign government that existed on the island of Cuba.

Q. Were any documents of this particular type found during the first entry into the Watergate? A. No, sir.

Q. Mr. Barker, were any offers of executive clemency transmitted to you or threats communicated to you in order to induce you to remain silent? A. No.

Q. Would you tell this committee why you chose to plead guilty?

A. I was guilty. I was caught inside the national Democratic headquarters at 2:30 in the morning.

MR. THOMPSON: Was it your opinion at that time that it was a C.I.A. operation?

A. The only opinion that I can intelligently make is that it was a result of the operation in which I was involved. It was explained at that particular time and place that national security was above F.B.I. and C.I.A.

However, there was a doubt in my mind at that time to the effect of what did it mean, what did national security mean as above F.B.I. or C.I.A.? And that question has still not been solved in my mind.

Q. Let me ask you this: Do you recall a trip you took in a taxi to Mr. Bittman's office after a day of trial with Mr. McCord and Mr. Alch and Mr. Shankman? What is your recollection of that?

A. I went there to meet Mr. Rothblatt. And to the best of my recollection, nothing was discussed, nothing was told to me about the meetings that the attorneys had that I can remember at this time.

Q. Mr. McCord testified Tuesday morning to this effect in response to the following questions from Senator Talmadge "Did Mr. Barker or other Cuban-Americans come to you during the trial and tell you they had been offered executive clemency by Mr. Hunt?" Mr. McCord says, "Yes, sir." Is that true?

A. I do not know whether he was saying the truth or not, but I was never offered clemency by anyone.

Q. Mr. Hunt told you [the evidence was overwhelming]?

A. Mr. Hunt told me that he had been advised by his attorney that the evidence against us was overwhelming. Mr. Hunt had not been caught inside of the Watergate, I had. I considered him a very intelligent—and still do—capable man, and if Mr. Hunt at the time was going to plead guilty and I was caught inside, I think it would be ridiculous and it has been proven for me to plead anything but guilty.

SENATOR ERVIN: If Mr. E. Howard Hunt had pressured you into pleading guilty, you could not tell us that under your code of ethics?

A. I do not think that this applies to anything like that for this nature. It was my decision.

Q. He told you that he was going to plead guilty and the evidence against you was overwhelming? A. That is true.

Q. And then you decided to plead guilty?

A. Yes, but this is not pressure. This is my decision, not his decision.

SENATOR BAKER: You have a real estate business in Miami. You were previously involved in the Bay of Pigs operations for the C.I.A. You are a veteran of the U.S. Army in World War II where you were a captain in the Army Air Corps. You were a German prisoner of war for 17 months.

Mr. Barker, what on earth would motivate you at your station in life, at your age and with that background, to do something that surely you knew to be illegal?

A. Senator, E. Howard Hunt, under the name of Eduardo, represents to the Cuban people their liberation. I cannot deny my services in the way that it was proposed to me on a matter of national security, knowing that with my training I had personnel available for this type of operation. I could not deny this request at the time.

Q. Why were you concerned with infiltration of a group which was demonstrating either against the war or in presence of the last rites for J. Edgar Hoover? Why did you do that?

A. I was following Mr. Hunt's instructions.

Q. What was your motivation? What persuaded you to enter the Watergate complex?

A. Our mission at those times were only to obtain and to try to locate documents that would prove that the Democratic party and Senator McGovern were receiving contributions nationally and —national and foreign contributions from organizations that were leftist organizations and inclined to violence in the United States, and also from the Castro government.

Q. Did you ever find any such documentation?

A. No, we did not find these documents. No, sir.

SENATOR TALMADGE: How did you get involved in the Bay of Pigs operation?

A. The same way I got involved in the Ellsberg one. I considered it my duty to help my country.

Q. Mr. Hunt recruited you?

A. That is in Cuba. No. In Cuba.

Q. Who?

A. At the American Embassy.

Q. Who did you think your backers were?

A. Sir, I was not there to think. I was there to follow orders, not to think.

Q. Didn't you wonder who was giving you the orders?

A. No. I had absolute confidence in, as I do now, the people I was dealing with, sir.

Q. Who did you think you were working for?

A. I was working for Mr. Hunt and those things that Mr. Hunt represents.

Q. What did he represent?

A. Eduardo represents the liberation of Cuba, the anti-Communist symbol. It represents the Government of the United States in one form, in its covert form.

Q. How did you think you could liberate Cuba by participating in a burglary in Washington, D. C.?

A. If we helped Mr. Hunt and this Government in matters which I will further add I believe in, it would establish a situation in which, besides the right that the Cuban people have to be free and independent, it would establish us as having aided this Government in this mission. I view that in the same way where hundreds of Cubans have been helping in Africa, in Vietnam, and in other areas of the world, where the people in my particular association are extremely grateful to those sectors of this country who favor our liberation. Mr. Hunt represented this to the greatest degree.

SENATOR GURNEY: About the [Ellsberg] mission, be as brief as possible because I want to get to the Watergate.

A. Mr. Hunt gave me the address of the place where we were to make the entry. Then the general plan was given to us. We proceeded to the area, and eventually made the entry. I personally searched for those documents.

Q. What documents?

A. A file of Daniel Ellsberg at his psychiatrist's office. This file was not there. I searched his desk and the file cabinet. The men also helped me in the search. The only thing that I found in connection with him was an address book which had his name. This we photographed, and we also photographed the file cabinet to prove that we—we had forced them open, and then we left.

SENATOR INOUYE: You are a wise man. You know that if Mr. Hunt did in fact tell you to keep silent, he would be guilty of the crime of obstructing justice?

A. Pardon me if I smile, Senator. If I was a wise man, I would not probably be sitting right here.

SENATOR WEICKER: Now, Mr. Barker, it is 1973. Do you still feel that national security is a proper justification for Watergate?

A. I feel it was a proper justification for Ellsberg and, although not in the same degree, I feel it was a justification for Watergate. But, quite frankly, I am just a human being. I get confused about all these things. Sometimes I do not know the answers to these questions. I do not pretend to have all the answers, sir.

Testimony by Alfred C. Baldwin 3d

May 24, 1973

Recalls surveillance of Kennedy's office.

SENATOR WEICKER: Now, at any time, were you sent to the Capitol area to conduct surveillances?

MR. BALDWIN: I believe it was the day after Governor Wallace was shot that I was instructed to go to the Capitol Rotunda, where there were planned sit-ins.

Q. During this period of time, were you sent to areas outside the offices of various Senators and Congressmen to observe persons in those areas? A. That is correct.

Q. Now, Mr. Baldwin, would you try to the best of your ability to recall these areas or the specific offices to which you went in order to observe persons in those areas?

A. I am going to do some great injustice to some of the Representatives, I am sure, with their names. But I know I went to Senator Kennedy's office.

Q. Why did you go to Senator Kennedy's office?

A. On one particular day at the Capitol, a large number of demonstrators had been receiving Senate passes to the gallery area. This was also the day that the three astronauts appeared and the information circulating amongst the different security officers up there was that the passes were being issued by—I believe it was Senator Kennedy's office—and I am not sure he—it might have been Senator Gravel's office at that time.

On one of my phone calls to Mr. McCord, I advised him of this and he then advised me to go to the Senator's office to determine what groups were in the area, how the passes were being handed out and distributed, who was doing it; obtain any literature that was being handed out; basically try to determine what groups were in the area of the Senator's office. That is on that particular day.

Q. Now, you mentioned Senator Kennedy's office and possibly also Senator Gravel's office. Were there any other Representatives or Senators whose offices you recall going to in order to observe persons moving about on that day?

A. Representatives from New York. I believe it was Bella Abzug —I do not know if my pronunciation is correct on that—and Representative Chisholm. I believe—

Q. Senator Javits?

A. That is correct. Because it is Mr. Javits of New York.

Q. Senator Proxmire? A. That is correct.

Q. Congressman Koch?

A. If he is the gentleman from New York, I believe that possibly is one of the other gentlemen from New York.

Q. Now, there have been reports that in fact, you are not employed by the Committee to Re-elect the President, and you have stated here already that you believe you were employed by the Committee to Re-elect the President. Did any event during this period of time serve to confirm that belief in your mind?

A. Well, I was instructed that if at any time I was stopped by any Government agency or law enforcement body regarding the weapon or regarding my presence in a particular area, that I was to do two things: number one, advise them that I worked for the Committee to Re-elect the President; that I was in the security office of that department; and if that did not work, to go on and say that I was working for former Attorney General Mitchell. Then, as a last resort, I had Mr. McCord's business card that said, James McCord, director of security, Committee to Re-elect the President, and a telephone number. I was to give the person that card and they would call and verify it.

So, on at least three or four occasions, that procedure had to be followed, where I had to identify myself. I had no authority to carry the weapons, so when I flew home to Connecticut, I would declare the weapon and I was flying Allegheny Airlines. So every time I would fly, I would have to declare the weapon. They would verify the fact, they would call right in front of me—the ticket agent, and the manager would come out, usually from the office, and they would make a call. They would say, no problem and hand the gun back to me.

Another time I was questioned by the F.B.I. liaison officer on Capitol Hill. He verified it.

Then the day at Andrews Air Force Base, I was stopped by the air security police and they had to call down to committee headquarters and verify. On all occasions, I was told I was O.K., all my items of identity were returned to me and I was on my way.

Q. At any time, did you hand those logs [of wiretaps] to individuals other than Mr. McCord?

A. The one incident where I was telephoned from Miami and told to deliver the logs to the Republican headquarters, the Committee to Re-elect the President, on Pennsylvania Avenue, which I did.

Testimony by Sally H. Harmony

June 5, 1973

Says she typed memos on eavesdropping activities for Liddy.

MR. DASH: While you were working for Mr. Liddy, will you tell the committee what his duties were and something about his work hours?

MRS. HARMONY: Mr. Liddy, when he first began, was counsel for the Committee for the Re-election. I would say in about two weeks, he changed as counsel to the finance committee.

Q. Did he have any other assignment or responsibility, to your knowledge?

A. When I was employed by Mr. Liddy—I think it is in the early part of June—he mentioned the fact that he might be involved in clandestine activity.

Q. Did you ever type any general intelligence memo to Mr. Liddy?

A. Yes, sir, on a couple of occasions. Yes, I did.

Q. Could you now describe what those memos were, the format of those memos?

A. I typed two that I can recall the content of that did come from Senator McGovern's office, headquarters.

Q. Mrs. Harmony, don't give us the actual contents of the memo, but could you describe it or characterize what the memo referred to, whether they were telephone conversations or was it a—what was the form of the memo?

A. This was a question and answer. It was two people discussing something and it was put down—when I typed it, I typed it in a question and answer form. It dealt with goods and services for the Democratic National Convention.

Q. Now, you did refer to the fact that you did type telephone logs, telephone conversations. How often did that occur?

A. I think I may have done eight of them.

Q. In what form did you get them in the first place?

A. Mr. Liddy dictated them to me.

Q. Did you recognize any names, without giving us any content of those logs? Did you recognize any names that appeared in those telephone conversations?

A. Yes, there were two names.

Q. Could you just give the names to the committee that you did recognize?

A. The name of Spencer Oliver and another name given as Maxie.

Q. Did you type these telephone logs on any particular stationery?

A. Yes, Mr. Liddy had printed stationery with the name "Gemstone" across the top of it. I don't recall, sir, that all of these logs were typed on that particular stationery. I think probably.

Q. Now, after you typed either the telephone logs on such stationery or any of the memoranda, intelligence memoranda you have testified to, to whom did you give these memoranda or telephone logs?

A. I returned them to Mr. Liddy.

Q. Did you ever type any memorandum for either Mr. Magruder or Mr. Mitchell. A. No, sir.

Q. Did you ever deliver any of this for Mr. Magruder or Mr. Mitchell? A. No, sir.

Q. Did you ever see any photographs in Mr. Liddy's office of documents from the Democratic National Committee? A. Yes I did.

Q. Did they have a letterhead on them?

A. There were a stack of photographs I mentioned, the number of 20 or 25—I can't be definite how many were there. The only one that I recognize that I can put anything with was the one signed by Larry O'Brien. It was a typed letter.

Q. Did you ever prepare a pass for McGovern headquarters for Mr. Liddy?

A. The day of June 16, right in the afternoon, Mr. Liddy was looking for some stationery which he couldn't find. We Xeroxed and made a sample of McGovern letterhead which I dictated in a memo to be typed.

Q. And what was the nature of the message on it?

A. The nature of the message, it was to whom it may concern, and it was "this will authorize the bearer to enter premises" for some such reason.

Q. Did it have a signature attached to it?

A. I was asked to put the initials GH/W/JP as the secretary would type something.

Q. What about the signature to the pass?

A. The signature was signed Gary Hart with the initials like a secretary would sign it.

Q. Who signed that?

A. I did.

Q. What happened to that pass, do you know?

A. Yes, I was informed the following week that Mr. Hunt had it in his possession.

Q. During any conversation that you had with Mr. Magruder in March, 1973, did he ever talk to you about any conversation he had with Mr. Mitchell?

A. Yes, I think it was probably later than March, it was after Mr. Magruder went to the Commerce Department to work. I was called by Mr. Magruder or he had talked to his secretary, who was still there, who transferred the call. Mr. Magruder indicated to me he had talked with Mr. Mitchell and assured Mr. Mitchell. This was after he knew I was going to talk with the Hill people. He said, "I have indicated to Mr. Mitchell that he has no reason to be concerned about any of your testimony."

Testimony by Robert Reisner

June 5, 1973

Says reports on espionage were prepared for meeting with Mitchell.

MR. LENZNER: What was your position with the Committee [to Re-elect the President]?

MR. REISNER: I was administrative assistant to Mr. Jeb Magruder.

Q. Now, approximately when did you see these documents and describe the circumstances surrounding your observations?

A. During the week prior to June 17, and perhaps it was during the two weeks prior to June 17—I cannot be certain on exactly the time—I observed documents similar to this here.

Q. You are referring to the stationery?

A. I am referring to the stationery with "Gemstone" at the time. On that occasion, it was simply in Mr. Magruder's hands or lying on his desk. I am not certain. Subsequently, I was handed the document and I was handed it in such a way that it was indicated to me very clearly that it was not [for] me to observe, that it was not for my inspection. At that time, it was handed to me and I did—that was the second time that I saw it. It was during those two weeks prior to the 17th.

Q. That was Mr. Magruder who handed them to you in his office, is that correct? A. Yes, he did.

Q. What were his instructions? What were you supposed to do with these materials?

A. I was preparing Mr. Magruder's files for a meeting with Mr. Mitchell. Now, he was campaign director at this time and it was a daily activity. I was handed the documents and I was asked to put them in Mr. Mitchell's files. The nature of that is that things that Mr. Magruder might have wished to take up with Mr. Mitchell were put in the file marked "Mr. Mitchell's File," and that is all. That does not indicate any more than that.

MR. THOMPSON: How much cash was in the safe?

A. How much cash at that time? It seems to me it was in the neighborhood of several thousand dollars—perhaps as much as five or six.

Q. Do you recall any names, any amounts of individuals who were receiving money from Mr. Porter's safe?

A. Well, I can remember that there were, in addition to Mr. Liddy—now, Mr. Liddy was—it was Mr. Porter that indicated to me that Mr. Liddy was receiving money. There was an individual who was referred to by a code name and that code name was "Sedan Chair" and that that individual was—

Q. Sedan Chair? two words?

A. Yes. I believe it was actually "Sedan Chair 2."

Q. It was someone in the Humphrey committee, from what you can tell?

A. From what I can tell, I mean it purported to be.

SENATOR ERVIN: As I understand, you reported that your log shows prior to Feb. 4 that there was a meeting at the White House attended by Magruder, Liddy and Dean. A. Yes, sir.

Q. And then, your log shows that on Feb. 4 there was a meeting of Liddy, John Mitchell, Jeb Stuart Magruder and John W. Dean 3d? A. Yes, sir.

Q. You stated that in March that Mr. Magruder went to Key Biscayne in Florida for the purpose of meeting with Mr. Mitchell? A. Yes, sir.

Q. And it was after he came back from Key Biscayne that Mr. Magruder told you to call Liddy and tell Liddy that it was arranged?

A. Mr. Chairman, to be precise, my recollection is that on one occasion I was asked to call Mr. Liddy and to make such a statement. My recollection is that it was, could have occurred shortly after the trip because the time seems correct. I cannot be absolutely certain.

Q. And I understand from your testimony that Mr. Magruder had a file called the Mitchell file in which he placed documents which related to matters he wished to discuss with Mr. Mitchell? A. Yes, sir.

Q. According to your best recollection, the file contained some Gemstone reports for what was in those papers on one occasion? A. Yes, sir.

Q. Did anyone else receive copies of memos that Mr. Magruder sent to Mr. Mitchell?

A. Yes, sir, each document to Mr. Mitchell went through me— would have been a formal document to Mr. Mitchell. A duplicate copy was sent to Mr. Haldeman's office.

Q. Mr. Haldeman was chief of staff in the White House?

A. That is correct. In fairness to the nature of what we were doing there, we were working for the President who was the candidate and, therefore, we were providing him the opportunity, if he wished, or if Mr. Haldeman wished to see any documents that were taking place in his campaign.

Q. Now, did you receive a phone call or any communication from Mr. Magruder after you were subpoenaed to go before the grand jury or before our committee?

A. Yes, sir. On that Friday, which was, I believe, March 30.

Q. What did Mr. Magruder ask you to do?

A. He asked me to get together with him. He called me at

home and asked me to get together with him that morning. He asked me whether he could take me to work. I indicated that I didn't think that was appropriate, because I presumed that the reason I was being subpoenaed before this committee was to discuss Mr. Magruder; therefore, I didn't think it was appropriate for us to meet.

He then called me again that morning to urge a meeting. I suggested there should be a third person there. We set a meeting. Then I chose not to attend the meeting. I wanted to be firm about not meeting with him.

Q. What was Magruder's reaction when you told him that?

A. His response was extremely agitated. He felt he wanted to know what I thought I was doing.

He said, I can't understand this. He said, you know, are you not going to be cooperative? Are you not going—everyone else has been cooperative, or something to that effect.

Now, in fairness to Mr. Magruder here, because I think it is bordering on a very serious point that I have discussed with your staff, there was a fourth phone call on that day.

I think he said that he was upset, that he was sorry if he was overly anxious. He said he just wanted me to realize that there were some extremely serious matters concerned here and that I should treat them in that way.

Q. Did he tell you at that time that you should be careful about what you said because people's lives and futures were at stake?

A. Yes, he did. That was in the second phone call, and that was by way of explaining to me why he was so concerned.

SENATOR WEICKER: Do you know of any phone calls as between Mr. Magruder and Mr. Colson? A. Yes, sir.

Q. Concerning demonstration projects?

A. It is my impression that Mr. Colson was—let me go back. I think I have described earlier in testimony here that at the time of Mr. Hoover's death there was a demonstration. I think it was here on Capitol Hill. At that time, it seems to me Mr. Magruder received a phone call in which he was instructed to get counter-demonstrators. Now, I was not monitoring the phone call. I was sitting in front of him when he received the phone call, so I do not know exactly who it was. It was my impression that it was Mr. Colson that did that.

The reason that I say that is that I think I subsequently said— I expressed some surprise about the activity. And he indicated to me something along the lines of, "It is a throwaway, we have to do things like this, because that allows us to say no when it is important."

Q. Now, were there any other projects, aside from the conversations you have referred to, that were discussed as between Mr. Magruder and whom you thought to be Mr. Colson?

A. When I say thought to be, you know, it was my impres-

sion that it was from the circumstances, and if asked who I
thought it was, I thought it was Mr. Colson. But I cannot say that.

Testimony by Hugh W. Sloan Jr.

June 6, 1973

Tells of pressure not to testify in a related Florida case.

MR. DASH: With regard to cash contributions, could you give
us a general idea as to the total amount that you handled and
over what period this took place.

MR. SLOAN: Yes, sir. I would say in terms of the total
campaign effort up to the April 7 period, the receipts in behalf
of the President's re-election in total amounted to approximately
$20 million. Of that figure, my best recollection would be that $1.7
million or $1.8 million came in the form of currency.

Q. Going back to the balance of cash which was not deposited, could you give—and I refer to a chart which is just in
place up on the easel to my left—could you give us an accounting
of the individuals who received cash disbursements and, as you
do that, to the best of your knowledge tell the committee what
was the basis of that cash disbursement? Why was the money
given, if you know?

A. In the case of Mr. Kalmbach, he in a period from March,
'71, up until Secretary Stans came into the campaign, was
essentially my senior, from whom I took instructions. He was
the principal fund raiser for the President's re-election campaign, during that period. He, over this period, from March until
April 7, received, to the best of my recollection, approximately
$250,000 in cash.

Mr. Gordon Strachan, who was the political liaison between
Mr. Haldeman at the White House and the campaign committee—
this $350,000, Mr. Kalmbach, on a day just prior to April 7—and
I am not sure of the precise date but my best recollection would
be within 10 days prior to the effective date of the new law—
came to me and indicated that he had had a request from the
White House for $350,000 in cash, would I get that together for
him. In the conversation, he indicated that he had talked to Bob
Haldeman.

At some point in the same day, Mr. Strachan was present
in the committee. Mr. Kalmbach indicated to me that Mr. Strachan
would arrange to have this picked up.

Mr. Herbert Porter, who was a member of the staff of the
Committee for the Re-election of the President—he was in charge
of scheduling surrogates, speakers for the President, in place of
the President. This hundred thousand dollars covered a period
probably starting in either December of 1971 or January of '72.

He had a blanket authority to draw cash funds from Mr. Magruder.

Q. I think you have indicated that Mr. Porter had a blanket authority from Mr. Magruder and that later you checked or it was checked with Mr. Mitchell. Generally, who had the authority to approve your making cash payments to anybody?

A. In the earlier period, it would have been Mr. Kalmbach. He did not physically spend much time in Washington, D. C. He would be in and out every week or two. He would visit with Mr. Mitchell. At one point in time, fairly early, he indicated to me—and I believe that initially it was with regard to all funds—that I was not to disburse any money without Mr. Mitchell's approval.

Q. This is what period you are now talking about?

A. This would be prior to Mr. Mitchell leaving the Justice Department. It would be in probably the summer of '71. Mr. Liddy's situation is very similar to Mr. Porter's situation.

Q. I think the chart shows a total amount of $199,000.

A. Mr. Porter had blanket authority from Mr. Magruder to come to me and give me a figure of how much cash he would need. There came a time when—it came very close to the April 7 date and I am not positive whether it was before or after and my best recollection would be the chart—he came to me with a budget of $250,000. He did not release that from his hand; he merely showed me the figure. He said, I will be coming to you for substantial cash payment, the first item of which will be $83,000, and I would like to pick that up in a day or two.

He said, in the case of these additional expenditures, distributions beyond what I had given him previously—he indicated that the procedure had changed, that I was to clear each and every distribution from that point on with Mr. Magruder. I called Mr. Magruder with regard to this $250,000 budget. He indicated to me that what Mr. Liddy told me was correct, that I was to go ahead and pay the $83,000 on request, but that subsequent distributions were to be personally cleared with him by telephone prior to their being made and he wanted at that time to review both the timing and the amount.

Confronted with this, I at that point in time took up with Secretary Stans—I went to see him, I indicated to him that here was a situation where we had a budget running into the post-April 7 period out of pre-April 7 cash funds. I said, in my judgment, because I had been sitting on top of the total figures, that it seemed to me that the cash distributions were becoming massive and that this particular distribution of $83,000 was totally out of line with anything we had done before.

At that point in time, I requested that he reconfirm to me Mr. Magruder's authority to make these kinds of decisions and he indicated to me that he would take the matter up with Mr. Mitchell.

He returned from that meeting with Mr. Mitchell and he confirmed that Mr. Magruder continued to have this authority, that I should pay these funds, and with regard to my question of concern about purpose, he said, I do not want to know and you don't want to know.

Q. Now, what I would like to do, Mr. Sloan, is move ahead to the period of June 17, 1972, which was the date of the break-in of the Democratic national headquarters. Did anything occur on that date with regard to Mr. Liddy and you?

A. I ran into Mr. Liddy. I stopped him. He was obviously in a hurry. He was essentially heading down the hall. At that point in time he made the statement to me, to the best of my recollection, that: "My boys got caught last night. I made a mistake. I used somebody from here which I told them I would never do. I am afraid I am going to lose my job."

Q. On or about June 21 did you have a conversation with Mr. Magruder?

A. I believe he called me to his office. He indicated to me that we are going to have to—or suggested to me a figure of what I had given to Mr. Liddy in the range of somewhere $75,000 to $80,000. I did not know the precise amount of money that I had given to Mr. Liddy at that point. However, I did know that the sum was considerably larger than that because Mr. Magruder himself had authorized a payment for $83,000 in one simple installment.

I must have indicated to him, well, that just is not the right figure. I did not have the right figure, but that is too low. He must have been insistent because I remember making to him on that occasion a statement, "I have no intention of perjuring myself."

Q. What did he say to you when you said that?

A. He said, "You may have to."

Q. Did you have shortly after, either on that day or any day following, a conversation with Mr. Fred LaRue? A. Yes, sir.

Q. Who was Fred LaRue at that time?

A. He was a special assistant to Mr. Mitchell, who was the campaign director at that time. I believe by that point in time there was a general awareness within the campaign that an internal investigation was going on and that Mr. LaRue was conducting it in behalf of Mr. Mitchell.

I had a call from my own office from Jane Dannenhauer, my secretary, which indicated there were two agents from the F.B.I. in my office, who would appreciate the pleasure of seeing me at that point. Mr. LaRue indicated that I do not think he should go down there without seeing John Mitchell first. He said wait here, and he went down the hall to Mr. Mitchell's office. He came back and got me and I believe Mr. Mardian was in the room as well. I entered with Mr. LaRue in Mr. Mitchell's office.

Q. Did you have any discussion with Mr. Mitchell at that time?

A. I was essentially asking for guidance. The campaign literally at this point was falling apart before your eyes, nobody was coming up with any answers as to what was really going on. I had some very strong concerns about where all of this money had gone. I essentially asked for guidance, at which point he told me when the going gets tough the tough get going.

Q. Did you understand what he meant by that?

A. I am not sure I did but I understood that I was not getting any particular helpful guidance at that point.

Q. What did you do thereafter?

A. I believe some of these events I am describing today, or a moment ago, the Magruder-Mitchell-F.B.I. meetings probably happened on that Thursday, the 22d, because there was a party that evening on a boat on the Potomac.

I went to this cocktail party on this boat. I guess my mood would be essentially anger. I sought out at that party a number of people. I talked to Ken Cole, Mr. Ehrlichman's assistant on the Domestic Council; Mr. Chapin, the President's appointments secretary, and Mr. Pat Buchanan, who was a speech-writer for the President. I really do not remember the depth with which I expressed my concern with the problem, but I believe I was generally expressing a concern that there was something very wrong at the campaign committee.

Mr. Cole indicated to me that night that I was expressing to him and to Mr. Chapin that I felt that John Ehrlichman and Bob Haldeman should be aware that there was a problem. Mr. Chapin asked me to come see him the next day at noon.

Ken Cole, the next day, called me at some point—I do not know whether he called me himself or somebody in his office— but that John Ehrlichman would like to see me at 2 o'clock that afternoon.

I went to the Chapin meeting. I again—there has been a year here—I do not precisely know what degree of knowledge or what conclusions I had come to at this point. But I believe probably the tone of the conversation was that there is a tremendous problem there, something has to be done.

Mr. Chapin evaluated my condition at that point as being somewhat overwrought and suggested a vacation, which, in fact, I was planning to leave on the next week. It had been planned for a long time. He suggested that the important thing is that the President be protected.

In the Ehrlichman meeting—

Q. When did that occur?

A. That happened around—I believe it was a 12 o'clock meeting on the 23d. The Ehrlichman meeting—it would have been a Friday. In the Ehrlichman meeting at 2—I started into generally the same discussion of problems.

Q. Mr. Sloan, when you say problems, did that include any statements by you about cash disbursements that had been made to Mr. Liddy.

A. I do not believe I at that point in time was pointing fingers. I do not believe I mentioned the Magruder remark. I do

not believe I mentioned the money to Liddy or the Liddy remark.
I just said I believe somebody external to the campaign has to
look at this because it raised in my mind at that point possibility
of the entire campaign being involved and it—

Q. What was Mr. Ehrlichman's response?

A. I believe I expressed my concern, my personal concern with
regard to the money. I believe he interpreted my being there as
personal fear and he indicated to me that I had a special relationship with the White House, if I needed help getting a lawyer,
he would be glad to do that, but "do not tell me any details;
I do not want to know." My position would have to be until after
the election that I would have to take executive privilege.

Q. On Saturday, the 24th, did you receive a call from Mr.
Mardian?

A. He called and asked if I would come in to see him. I
believe I went down and found there was a meeting going on in
John Mitchell's office. Mr. Mardian and I went back to Mr. Mardian's office. He asked me, he said, we really have to get into this
money thing. He said, where did all the money go?

I started—I do not know if we we went through the entire
list. The focus was very much in the Liddy-Porter area. When
he got to Mr. Liddy, he blew up, staggered by the amount. He
said, "God damn, Magruder lied to John Mitchell. He told him it
was only $40,000."

We continued on beyond that point and covered the ground,
the information requested from me. I indicated to him, asked him
whether under these circumstances, with known investigations
under way, whether I should proceed with my plans to take a
vacation. He gave me a call later that evening, and said, why
don't you go ahead.

Q. On July 5, did Mr. Magruder get in touch with you again?

A. Yes sir. If I can go back for a minute to the earlier
Mardian meeting before I went to Bermuda, because it is pertinent to this particular item. I on that occasion had indicated to
Mr. Mardian that Mr. Magruder had made this suggestion to me
that it might be necessary to perjure myself, and I had indicated
to Mr. Mardian at that point in time—I understood Mr. Mardian
essentially to have taken over the investigation from Mr. LaRue
at this point. I said I just did not want to have any further dealings
with Mr. Magruder if things are going to be done that way.

I had a call from Mr. Magruder during the day, on the 5th
of July. He said he wanted to get together with me, would I like
to do it then, would I like to have a drink with him after work.
It was a very busy day, since I had just gotten back. I said, well,
let's do it after work.

We went to the Black Horse Tavern, I believe. He said, you
know, we have to resolve this Liddy matter. He said, what we
should do is you and I should go down to see the U.S. Attorney, Mr. Harold Titus. He said, I will tell Mr. Titus that I
authorized the payments to Mr. Liddy and you merely have to

confirm the fact that you did make those distributions under my instructions.

Then he said, but we have to agree on a figure. This time, the figure was even less than the time before; it was $40,000 or $45,000. No resolution was made on that occasion.

Q. What happened at that time?

A. I told Mr. Magruder when I saw him in his office—I believe I said I had absolutely no objection to going down to see the U.S. Attorney; however, you know, if I am asked point-blank, did Mr. Liddy ever receive $45,000, of course, I will say yes. But I said, I will not stop there. If I am asked more than that, I will also say yes. If he asks what the total figure is, I will tell him to the best of my knowledge.

Q. Did Mr. Magruder say anything when you told him that?

A. He just sort of said, fine, and dropped the subject. He never suggested going down to Mr. Titus again.

Q. Did Mr. LaRue meet with you shortly after that?

A. Yes, sir, I believe it was practically on the way out of Mr. Magruder's office. He took me by the arm and pulled me into an adjoining conference room and said, did you and Jeb get together?

I said, well, we had a discussion last night and one just now. He said, did you decide on the figure?

I told Mr. LaRue precisely what I told Mr. Magruder, and he dropped the subject.

Q. Now, the next day, on July 6, did you have a meeting with Mr. Parkinson and Mr. O'Brien, who were the attorneys for the Committee for the Re-election of the President?

A. I believe at the time I sought them out, they were essentially in a debriefing process of people who had been before the grand jury. Mr. Robert Odle was also there. I had asked everyone else to leave the room, I wanted to talk to the attorneys alone.

I recounted as fully as possible all the facts that I then had with regard to the money, also with regard to the Magruder continued suggestions of agreeing to a different figure.

Their reaction was incensed; they were angry.

They said, well, we have been lied to by the people here. We have not been able to see John Mitchell and we are a month into this thing. They seemed to have an extreme frustration about the information I had given them at that point. It was certainly my judgment that they, from their reactions, that they had not heard any of the critical information before from anybody and it had been told to other people within the campaign.

Q. Did they suggest you might take a little trip?

A. Yes, sir. They indicated that they felt under these circumstances, this new information that they had available to them, that they needed the time to confront the other officials of the political campaign with the information they then had.

Q. Now, later that evening, did you receive a telephone call?

A. Yes, sir, from Mr. LaRue. I don't recall precisely, but he impressed on me the urgency of departure, to the extent of suggesting that I had a reservation on, I believe, a 6 o'clock A.M. flight at Dulles. He urged me to take a room at the Dulles Marriott that evening and to leave my home immediately.

Q. Now, when you returned, did you have a meeting with Mr. LaRue again on July 13?

A. Yes, sir. I thought it was somewhat black humor, but he evidently resided in the Watergate himself.

I have really forgotten how we led in. We began to review the entire situation.

He, I think, impressed on me at that point that I might have some campaign problems; that I ought to think perhaps about taking the Fifth Amendment. I said—you know, it is obvious to me that there is a climate of suggestion and I cannot relate it to specific conversations of either—well, in the case of perjury, I can with Mr. Magruder, but with regard to taking the Fifth Amendment, I cannot. But it was obvious to me that I should take one of those two courses of action to essentially stay in the good graces of the campaign organization.

I indicated to him that I was prepared to do neither, that I felt I should tell the truth and if I have problems, I would have to face them.

Q. Did you shortly after your resignation, and could you give us the date, go to see the U.S. Attorneys, Assistant U.S. Attorneys, Mr. Silbert, Mr. Glanzer and Mr. Campbell? Did you report to them all that or generally all that you have been testifying to here in terms of activities, the cash transactions and the approaches that were made to you by Mr. Magruder? A. Yes, sir.

Q. And did you testify before the grand jury? A. Yes, sir.

MR. THOMPSON: Statements have been made to the effect, publicly to the effect Mr. Ehrlichman at one time told Mr. Dean to make a report about this matter. Did Mr. Dean ever contact you from June 17, 1972, up until the time he left the White House, about the Watergate matter?

A. I had numerous conversations with Mr. Dean over a period of time but with regard to your specific question in terms of an investigation, I would have to describe the transmittal of information essentially as my forcing it on him rather than him soliciting it from me.

Q. Another point. Did I understand your testimony correctly that you told three prosecutors in the criminal case on July 18 that Magruder had attempted to get you to perjure yourself? A. Yes, sir.

Q. The trial was the following January and you were a witness at that trial. A. Yes, sir.

Q. You told about the $199,000. A. Yes, sir.

SENATOR BAKER: I would like to know a little more about the extent and scope of the knowledge of Mr. Stans and Mr.

Mitchell. Did you ever talk with Mr. Stans or Mr. Mitchell about the Watergate situation?

A. Not to Mr. Mitchell. I met with Mr. Mitchell only on one occasion that has been referred to earlier. Mr. Stans was extremely defensive in all of the conversations I heard. He insisted from the end of the conversation I heard, he said, "Damn it, this is not a finance problem, you guys have to handle it and you have got to keep it away from Sloan and myself because we have nothing to do with it."

SENATOR ERVIN: Did you have a conversation with anyone concerning the trial in Miami, Fla.?

A. I did not. I had one conversation with John Dean myself not specifically with regard to the trial but in terms of the extradition proceedings in Virginia where he expressed a hope that my attorneys would oppose extradition. Following that one of my attorneys, Mr. Treese, received a direct phone call from Mr. Dean.

[Mr. Sloan testified again on June 7, 1973. See p. 222.]

Testimony by James T. Treese

June 6, 1973

Supports Sloan testimony on pressure from Dean.

SENATOR ERVIN: Mr. Treese, you were attorney for Mr. Hugh W. Sloan?

MR. TREESE: That is correct.

Q. And did you receive a call on or about Oct. 21, 1972, in which you received a suggestion about what Mr. Sloan should do about his testimony in Florida?

A. Senator, I received a call on Oct. 31 on that subject.

Q. Do you know who the call was from?

A. Yes, it was from John Dean. Mr. Dean called trying to locate Mr. Sloan. That happened to be the day that Mr. Sloan and Mr. Stoner departed for Florida in order to participate in the trial in Miami. He called to discuss the case very briefly with me and he said, are you prepared to advise your client to take the Fifth Amendment?

I laughed. To invoke the Fifth Amendment on that kind of case, knowing Hugh Sloan as I did and knowing about the case, what I did, was probably like swatting flies with sledgehammers. It was just so out of place and inappropriate that it did cause me to laugh. He pursued the matter and said Hugh could be a real hero around here if he took the Fifth. I did make a promise to him to try to get hold of Hugh and Jim Stoner at National Airport by having them paged at the Eastern Airline counter and I signed off with him at that point.

I tried to get them. It was about 15 minutes before their flight time and missed them. I called Mr. Dean back and said, you have absolutely nothing to worry about, Mr. Dean, Mr. Sloan is not going to take the Fifth Amendment. It is totally inappropriate in a case of this nature.

Testimony by Hugh W. Sloan Jr.

June 7, 1973

Says he believes Mitchell knew of payments to Liddy.

SENATOR WEICKER: In relation to, again, the Haldeman meeting, was there any discussion at all at that meeting of Mr. Magruder's perjury suggestion?

MR. SLOAN: I did not mention it by name, but in relating to why I had left—I was trying to give him an accounting of why I had made the personal decision I had. I said I have been asked to perjure myself on numerous occasions and in my judgment, there was pressure to take the Fifth Amendment, and I said, Bob, I am just not prepared to do that.

Q. What was his response?

A. I am not positive. I think I would be putting words in his mouth, but I think it was to the effect that, well, I realize there were mistakes made in the early period.

SENATOR MONTOYA: Doesn't it stand to reason that Mr. Mitchell was consulted on these expenditures by Mr. Magruder? Doesn't it stand to reason that he knew of the disbursements to Mr. Liddy and to Mr. Porter?

A. Senator, you know I would be making an assumption, obviously, with you. I think in an original sense it is inconceivable to me he would not be in a general sense, if his aides were doing their proper job, aware of this kind of situation. Certainly Mr. Stans indicated to me on two occasions that was the source of his confirmation, I should continue on making distributions. So Mr. Mitchell had some knowledge, yes, sir.

Testimony by Herbert L. Porter

June 7 *Says Magruder asked him to lie about payments to conspirators and he did.*

June 12 *Tells of seeing film strips of data from Muskie office.*

June 7, 1973

MR. DORSEN: Mr. Porter, while you were at the committee, did you know G. Gordon Liddy?

MR. PORTER: I did, sir.

Q. In connection with your duties at the committee, were you ever asked to give cash to Mr. Liddy?

A. Yes, sir, I was. Mr. Magruder told me that Mr. Liddy was going to be taking on dirty tricks and other special projects and that Mr. Liddy would be coming to me from time to time to request funds and that I was to, in turn, ask Mr. Sloan for the funds and turn them over to Mr. Liddy.

Q. Mr. Porter, prior to April 7, 1972, how much money did you receive from Hugh Sloan?

A. Approximately $52,000.

Q. After April 7, 1972, how much money did you receive from Hugh Sloan.

A. Approximately $17,000.

Q. And is it your best recollection and knowledge that you received from Mr. Sloan a total of approximately $69,000? A. Yes, sir, to the best of my knowledge.

Q. Following the break-in at the Watergate, did you have a conversation with Mr. Jeb Magruder concerning any statements you might make to the Federal Bureau of Investigation?

A. I am not sure of the exact date, whether it was June 28 or the 29th. Mr. Magruder asked me to come into his office, which I did. He shut the door and he told me that he had just come from a meeting with Mr. Mitchell, Mr. LaRue, himself, and fourth party whose name I cannot remember, where my name had been brought up as someone who could be—what was the term he used—counted on in a pinch or a team player or words to that effect.

He said that I believe at that time Mr. Liddy had been fired from the campaign. He said it was apparent, was the word he used, that Mr. Liddy and others had on their own illegally partici-pated in the break-in of the Watergate Democratic National Com-mittee, and Mr. Magruder swore to me that neither he nor any-body higher than Mr. Liddy in the campaign organization or at the White House had any involvement whatsoever in Watergate, at the Watergate break-in, and reinforced that by saying, "Doesn't that sound like something stupid that Gordon would do?" And you have to know Mr. Liddy. I agreed with that.

He said, "I want to assure you now that no one did." He said, however, he said, "There is a problem with some of the money." He said, "Now, Gordon was authorized money for some dirty tricks, nothing illegal," he said, but nonetheless, "things that could be very embarrassing to the President of the United States and to Mr. Mitchell and Mr. Haldeman and others. Now, your name was brought up as someone who we can count on to help in this situation." And I asked what is it you are asking me to do, and he said, "Would you corroborate a story that the money was authorized for something a little bit more legitimate-sounding than dirty tricks. Even though the dirty tricks were legal, it still would be very embarrassing."

He said, "You are aware that the Democrats have filed a civil suit against this committee." I said, yes, I have read that in the paper. He said, "Do you know what immediate discovery is?" I said I do not. They may get immediate discovery, which means they can come in at any moment and swoop in on our committee and take all of the files and subpoena all of the records and you know what would happen if they did that.

I conjured up in my mind that scene and became rather excitable and knew I didn't want to see that. So I said, well, be specific, and he said, well, you were in charge of the surrogate campaign, you were very concerned about radical elements disrupting rallies and so forth, and I said yes, and he said suppose that we had authorized Liddy, instead of the dirty tricks, we had authorized him to infiltrate some of these radical groups.

He said, how could such a program have cost a hundred thousand. And I thought very quickly of a conversation I had with a young man in California in December, as a matter of fact, and I said, Jeb, that is very easy. You could get 10 college-age students or 24- or 25-year-old students, people, over a period of 10 months. Mr. Magruder had prefaced his remark by saying from December on. And I said, you can pay them $1,000 a month, which they would take their expenses out of that, and I said that is $100,000. I said that is not very much for a $45 million campaign. And he said, now that is right.

He said, would you be willing, if I made that statement to the F.B.I., would you be willing to corroborate that when I came to you in December and asked you how much it would cost, that that is what you said? That was the net effect, the net of his question. I thought for a moment and I said, yes, I probably would do that. I don't remember saying yes, but I am sure I gave Mr. Magruder the impression I would probably do that and that was the end of the conversation.

Q. Later, did you tell the F.B.I. what Mr. Magruder asked you to tell them? A. Yes, sir, I did.

Q. What did you tell the Federal grand jury?

A. The same thing.

Q. Were you a witness at the trial of the seven defendants who were indicted in the Watergate case? A. Yes, sir.

Q. And did you give the same account? A. Yes, sir, I did.

MR. THOMPSON: What caused you to go to [the United States attorneys]?

A. Mr. Magruder called me in New York [on April 9], where I was employed, and stated that things were not looking too good for him. He said that things are getting a little hot down here. He said, well, I will keep you up to date, or keep you up to speed, or words to that effect.

He called me on Wednesday, on April 11, and said, Bart, if I were you, I would call Paul O'Brien, who was one of the lawyers for the committee, and tell him to call Earl Silbert and go down and tell Earl what you know.

I said, Jeb, you realize you are asking me to, in effect, put one of your feet in a six-feet-deep hole.

He said, yes, I know that, but, he said, I got you into this and, he said, the least I can do is help you get out of it.

So I called Mr. O'Brien on the telephone. This was on April 11. I told him I wanted him to call Mr. Silbert and that I wanted to go talk to Mr. Silbert.

Mr. O'Brien's response to me was, now, what do you want to do a stupid thing like that for?

I said, well, I just do.

He said, well, why don't you come in and see me on Friday, the 13th, and we will talk about it?

So I did and we—during the afternoon, Mr. O'Brien alternately said, gee, I don't know whether you have a problem here or not.

So, he said, well, I think maybe we ought to get another opinion here. So he called Mr. Parkinson on the telephone and there was a brief pause and he said, yes, I will tell him that. So he said, Parkinson thinks you should tell the truth.

I said, yes, that is what I called you about two days ago.

He then got a phone call from Mr. Magruder who was over at his attorney's office. They conversed briefly and I—he said, yes, I will tell Porter that; that is a good idea.

So he hung up and he said, you go over and talk to Magruder's lawyer. At this point, I did not have any counsel except Mr. Parkinson and Mr. O'Brien. He said, you go over and talk to Magruder's lawyer and see what he thinks you ought to do.

So I went over to the office of Mr. James Sharp and spoke briefly with him, I would say no more than 10 minutes.

I explained very quickly what I have just explained to you gentlemen here and he looked at me rather incredulously and he said, my God, you are an ant, he said, you are nothing. He said, do you realize the whole course of history is going to be changed?

I said, no, I didn't realize that, but I knew what my worries were.

He said, now, if Mr. Magruder is going to go down and talk to the Federal prosecutors, he said, we would certainly give you the courtesy of going down first.

I said, I would appreciate that very much.

The following Saturday afternoon, the next day, when I ran into Mr. Magruder across from St. John's Church at 5 o'clock in the afternoon, among other things, he told me that he had been to the U.S. attorney's office that morning, Saturday morning. I was rather stunned by that.

I said, how did that happen?

He said, well, Jim Sharp called me last night, said that he had set up an appointment with Earl Silbert for 8:30 this morning and instructed me absolutely not to call anybody or discuss it with anybody. I am sorry, he said.

Q. What did Mr. Magruder tell you on the 14th besides what you already related?

A. Mr. Magruder told me he had just come from a meeting at the White House and that it is all over, he said, and I said, what do you mean, it is all over? He said, it is all over, the President has directed everybody to tell the truth. Those were his exact words. He said I had a meeting with Mr. Ehrlichman and I told him the whole story and, boy, was he really shocked, words to that effect. He also told me that he had been to the Federal prosecutors that morning. He also told me that there were going to be several indictments and listed off a series of names, a number of names, people that he thought would be indicted.

Q. When is the first time you talked with Mr. O'Brien and Mr. Parkinson about this false story concerning the $100,000 to Mr. Liddy?

A. Mr. Parkinson [called] and we set up an appointment, I believe it was for 4 o'clock in the afternoon of March 28.

I had occasion to talk to Mr. O'Brien before I went to Mr. Parkinson's office. Mr. O'Brien said he did not think I had a problem. I think that was the way he put it. I went to see Mr. Parkinson.

I believe he had my trial testimony in front of him. I am not certain of that, however; I cannot be certain. But I do remember him sitting back and he said, well, all you have done, you have just embellished a little, that is all, you have not got a problem. He said, you have nothing to worry about.

Q. Did any of the prosecutors ever ask you if Magruder had tried to get you to perjure yourself? A. No, sir.

SENATOR ERVIN: Did [Mr. Magruder] say he had talked to Mitchell about the matter in addition to talking to Ehrlichman? A. Yes, sir, I think he did.

Q. And he told you that Mitchell had told him that he was going to deny complicity to the end? A. Yes, sir.

SENATOR BAKER: Did you ever have any qualms about what you were doing, about the propriety of hiring these people for the dirty tricks or whatever it was? I am probing into your state of mind, Mr. Porter.

A. I understand. I think the thought crossed my mind, Senator, in all honesty, that I really could not see what effect it had on re-electing a President of the United States. On the other hand, in all fairness, I was not the one to stand up in a meeting and say that this should be stopped, either, so I do not—I mean, there is space in between. I kind of drifted along.

Q. Now, you have reached now precisely that point that I would like to examine and I intend to examine it with other witnesses as this hearing proceeds. A. O.K.

Q. Where does the system break down when concern for what is right, as distinguished from what is legal, is never asserted or never thought about and you do not stand up and say so? At any time, did you ever think of saying, I do not think this is quite right, this is not quite the way it ought to be? Did you ever think of that? A. Yes, I did.

Q. What did you do about it?

A. I did not do anything.

Q. Why didn't you?

A. In all honesty, probably because of the fear of group pressure that would ensue, of not being a team player.

Q. What caused you to abdicate your own conscience and disapproval, if you did disapprove, of the practices or dirty tricks operation?

A. Well, Senator Baker, my loyalty to this man, Richard Nixon, goes back longer than any person that you will see sitting at this table throughout any of these hearings. I first met the President—

Q. I really very much doubt that, Mr. Porter. I have known Richard Nixon probably longer than you have been alive, and I really expect that the greatest disservice that a man could do to a President of the United States would be to abdicate his conscience.

A. I understand, Senator. I first met Mr. Nixon when I was 8 years old in 1946, when he ran for Congress in my home district. I wore Nixon buttons when I was 8 and when I was 10 and when I was 12 and when I was 16. My family worked for him; my father worked for him in campaigns, my mother worked for him in campaigns. I felt as if I had known this man all my life—not personally, perhaps, but in spirit. I felt a deep sense of loyalty to him. I was appealed to on this basis.

June 12, 1973

SENATOR WEICKER: Mr. Porter, in the disbursement of the monies, the list of which you gave to Senator Gurney, did you mention in that list the purchase of microfilm viewing equipment?

A. No sir, I did not. And that should be in there. I believe it was probably $68, $50 or $60, something like that. I would classify it as film strip viewing equipment, 35-millimeter film strip, not microfilm.

Q. And what was the nature of those film strips?

A. The nature of the film strips was that they were, appeared to be, 35-millimeter photographs or negatives of intra-office memos from Senator Muskie's campaign headquarters to his Senate offices and back again.

[Mr. Magruder] took them and said that he was going to show them to Mr. Mitchell. He came back and apparently, he did show them to Mr. Mitchell, because he was a little irate at me for not making sure that the batteries worked, and apparently, he got all the way to Mr. Mitchell's office and the batteries did not work, and he blamed it on me.

At a later date, Mr. Magruder said that Mr. Ken Rietz was going to be, was going to deliver these film strips to me and would I view them for him, for Mr. Magruder.

On one occasion, I think it was early December, there was a staff memo that I saw from one of the campaign officials to the Senator's role, I believe as chairman of a subcommittee on govermental operations, or something like that—

Q. Which Senator is this?

A. Senator Muskie—could be used as a great front to go to California and hold tax hearings that would be a great visual event for Senator Muskie and all at the taxpayers' expense and he could get a lot of value for his campaign.

We thought that was rather interesting, to say the least, and I told Mr. Magruder about it. He asked me to just copy the memo on a, I believe it was written on plain bond—and send it to Evans and Novak.

On one occasion, Senator Muskie's speech that he was going to deliver in the Senate against the nomination of William Rehnquist to the Supreme Court was on the film, and I specifically was—it was about 20 pages and I asked Mr. Magruder what he wanted me to do with it. He said, let me check, and he did check, and he got back to me and said, Mr. Mitchell would like to see it.

Testimony of Maurice H. Stans

June 12 *Denies any involvement in scandal and pleads ignorance about campaign activities.*

June 13 *Professes ignorance about many transactions and takes pounding from the Senators.*

June 12, 1973

MR. STANS: It is my understanding that the committee is probing three matters on which it might assume that I have some knowledge—the espionage charges, including the Watergate bugging, and the cover-up that allegedly followed; the sabotage charges, including the Segretti operation; and the handling of campaign finances. On these three matters I would like to state:

(1) I had no knowledge of the Watergate break-in or any other espionage efforts before I read about them in the press, or of the efforts to cover up after the event.

(2) I had no knowledge of any sabotage program to disrupt the campaign by Segretti or anyone else.

(3) To the best of my knowledge, there were no intentional violations of the laws relating to campaign financing by the finance committees for which I had responsibility. Because of the complexity of the new law that became effective in the course of the campaign, and the vast amount of work that had to be done, there may have been some unintended technical violations by the committee.

The finance committee paid any bill or made any payment which bore the approval of an appropriate official of the campaign committee.

The campaign committee was supposed to see that the amounts it O.K.'d were within the limits of an approved budget. It turned out that the controls did not work as they were intended, and spending overran the budget by more than $8 million.

In practical terms, the two committees operated in watertight compartments. They were physically separated on different floors. The campaign committee ran the campaign and created the debts; the finance committee raised the money and paid the bills.

There was only one forum for the exchange of opinions with respect to campaign spending, and that was the budget committee.

The meetings of the budget committee were not in my opinion very effective. Each one opened by me with a general statement of the current cash position and the expectations of future contributions, which until the last few days of the campaign never equaled the expected spending. I pressed continuously for reductions in overall spending, but the actual trend was constantly upward.

At times the meetings became bitter, and I walked out of one meeting at which I thought there was no understanding of the difficulties of fund-raising on the part of those who were doing the spending. The budget grew to $40 million, then $43 million, and ended up in excess of $48 million. A late surge of contributions, as a result of the effective organization we had built across the country, made it possible for us to end up with a surplus.

Our fund-raising operated under the old law until April 7, 1972. Under this law the fact that contributions need not be reported gave the committee and its contributors a right of confidentiality.

The issue of confidentiality versus disclosure of such information has never been fairly presented to the public. It has been made to appear that the committee engaged in secret, thereby concealed and suspect, transactions which would not have occurred had they been required to be disclosed. That is not true. The transactions were valid and proper and the question of whether they were to be reported was a question of law that involved important rights of individuals.

Much has also been made of the fact that a few records of the committee before April 7 were destroyed. The fact is that the very large part of such records has been preserved, and the committee believes that the others can be reconstructed if needed. But the important point is that there was no illegal act in throwing away any of these records, and even those that were retained could have been disposed of. There is no statutory requirement that records of transactions before April 7 be preserved.

When I joined the committee on Feb. 15, fund-raising and campaign activities had been engaged in for almost a year. Programs had been planned or committed by the campaign people, funds had been collected and disbursed, committees had been formed and terminated, and some well-publicized transactions had already occurred.

Patterns of payment to Herbert Porter and Gordon Liddy were a practice. Magruder had blanket authority to direct payments. Kalmbach had turned over to committee the funds in his possession. But no steps had been taken to comply with the new law, and the procedures generally were inadequate to cope with the volume of work sure to come.

MR. EDMISTEN: Now, Mr. Stans, I want to ask you if you identify or know anything about a document I have here. This is purportedly written by Mr. Jeb Magruder, a confidential memorandum for the Attorney General dated July 28, 1971.

A. I have never seen this memorandum before, to the best of my knowledge.

Q. With the indulgence of the committee, I will read it. This is a confidential memorandum to the Attorney General:

"Dick Whitney, who is Secretary Stans' political special assistant, spent some time with me discussing 1972. One idea which he brought up might be useful in other departments.

"The Secretary has built up a discretionary fund at Commerce that will total approximately $1,000,000. He is using this fund for conferences, hiring and other activities that will be beneficial to the President's re-election.

"If you feel it is appropriate, Secretary Stans might discuss this concept with other Cabinet officers to see if they can develop the same kind of fund within their own departments."

Now, down below on there there is a line for "Approve, Disapprove, Comment," and this, as I said, was signed by Mr. Jeb Magruder to the Attorney General dated July 28, 1971. What can you tell us about that?

A. I cannot tell you very much about it. I have no idea what the concept was. I think it must have been based on some misunderstanding or other. I had no fund in the Department of Commerce apart from an authorized budgeted fund of the department, and I think either Mr. Magruder or Mr. Whitney would be the ones to have to explain that memorandum.

Q. Well, somebody is a million dollars off there in some way, I would take it?

A. Well, if somebody is implying that we had a million dollars set aside in the Department of Commerce to help in the election campaign I would say they are off. I do not know what it means.

Q. Did you on May 10, 1972, write a memo to the Honorable John N. Mitchell in which you discussed a number of issues regarding the various open budget matters and may I show this memorandum to you?

A. I certainly did write it. I wrote it under the circumstance I described in my opening statement. I was frustrated, upset at the level of spending that was projected by the campaign people, and I proposed a number of reductions in the budget.

Q. Yes. Now, you pretty well covered the whole area of the campaign in this memo, did not you? You were rather familiar with the operation of the campaign committee if you were able to write this extensive a memo, I would take it?

A. Well, I do not think that is quite the right way to say it. I was not very familiar at all with the operation of the campaign committee. I was only familiar with their objectives as to how much they were going to spend and approximately a dozen categories in which they were going to spend it and I was objecting to the total amount that they were going to spend.

Q. I am sure, Mr. Stans, that you are familiar with Mr. Sloan's testimony before this committee that he discussed with you a payment of $83,000 to Mr. Liddy. Now, what is your testimony on that transaction?

A. Somewhere around the sixth of April, Mr. Sloan came to me and said that Gordon Liddy wanted a very substantial amount of money. I don't recall the amount he named. Mr. Sloan said,

"Liddy wants a substantial amount of money. Should I give it to him?"

And I said, "I don't know. I will find out from John Mitchell." I will quote my conversation with John Mitchell as best I can paraphrase it. It is not precise. But I saw John Mitchell a relatively short time after and said, "Sloan tells me that Gordon Liddy wants a substantial amount of money. What is it all about?"

And John Mitchell's reply was, "I don't know. He will have to ask Magruder because Magruder is in charge of the campaign and he directs the spending."

I said, "Do you mean, John, that if Magruder tells Sloan to pay these amounts or any amounts to Gordon Liddy that he should do so," and he said, "That is right."

Now, that is my recollection in a paraphrase of the discussion that took place. I went back to Sloan and reported it to him and found out that he had already talked to Magruder and had the same information.

Apparently Mr. Liddy showed Mr. Sloan a budget of $250,000 against which he intended to draw. To the best of my knowledge, Mr. Sloan did not tell me about that budget and I did not know that Mr. Liddy had authority to draw an amount of money of that size.

Q. Now, Mr. Stans, did you learn of the payment of cash of some $350,000 from the finance committee to Gordon Strachan when that payment was made?

A. Yes, I learned a little bit more about it, I think, than Mr. Sloan did, because back in February of last year, I heard from someone—I think it was Mr. Kalmbach, but I am not sure—that the White House would like to have some of the 1968 money that he had turned over to our committee to use for special polling purposes. No amount was mentioned at that time and I have no recollection of any other discussion about this subject until after the $350,000 was given by Mr. Sloan or Mr. Kalmbach to Gordon Strachan. I believe that Mr. Kalmbach takes full responsibility for that transaction. At a later date, I asked Mr. Sloan if the White House had ever gotten the money it wanted, and he said, yes, they got $350,000.

Q. Now, Mr. Stans, I do not want to drag this out, but I think the committee does want to know something about all of the allegations that have been made regarding four so-called Mexican checks, $89,000 drawn on a Mexican bank account.

A. On April 3 of last year, I received a telephone call from Bill Liedtke, who was then our finance chairman in the state of Texas. He said, "I have a U.S. citizen residing in Texas, a prospective contributor for $100,000, but he wants to give it in U.S. funds that are now in Mexico. Is this legal?"

I said, "I am quite sure it is, but let me check again and I will call you back."

I checked with our counsel, found out it was perfectly legal for a U.S. citizen to give any foreign funds he wanted, and called back to Liedtke and told him so.

Now, the next thing that I knew about the transaction was after April 22, when I came back from a vacation, and I learned from Mr. Sloan that on April 5, Mr. Liedtke's representative, Roy Winchester, had brought to Washington the committee $100,000 in the form of a contribution from an unnamed person, in the form of checks drawn on American banks by a Mexican bank.

At this point, I was of the understanding that the four checks totaled $100,000, and I did not know that the four checks totaled only $89,000 and that $11,000 of the $100,000 was in currency.

Q. Now, what did you have to do with the so-called Dahlberg check? You received checks, did you not, from Mr. Dahlberg?

A. Yes. Kenneth Dahlberg was a member of the early finance committee working in the state of Minnesota and Dwayne Andreas was a Minnesota resident who also has a place of living in Florida, in a hotel that he owned. As I understand it from Dahlberg, somewhere around, as early as January, Andreas said, I want to help the President's campaign and I will give you $25,000.

On 12 March, he instructed his secretary to get together $25,000 of money and put it in an envelope to be given to Mr. Dahlberg. Unfortunately, on the 14th, Dahlberg found suddenly that he had to go to Europe.

On the 5th of April, having in mind the change in the law that would take place in the next day or so, Andreas, in Florida, called Dahlberg in Minnesota and said, "I still have that money. I would like to give it to you before the change in the law; can you pick it up?"

And Dahlberg said, "I cannot get down there before the 7th."

Andreas said, "Well, I want the contribution to be made now, made effective now. So I will put it in an envelope in your name and put it in the safe deposit box in the hotel in your name. You can pick it up whenever it is ready, but I want the understanding between you and me that title has passed and it is your money and you accept it as of today."

Dahlberg said, "I do."

Q. Now, Mr. Stans, in late June or early July did you receive a call from Mr. Herbert Kalmbach requesting money from you?

A. On the 29th of June I received an urgent call from Mr. Kalmbach. He said he was in Washington at the Statler-Hilton Hotel. It was extremely vital that he see me right away, and he wanted me to come over there, and I did. I dropped everything and went over there to see him. He said, "I am here on a special mission on a White House project and I need all the cash I can get."

I said, "I don't have any cash to give to you. Will you take a check?"

He said, "No, I can't take a check, it must be in cash, and this has nothing to do with the campaign. But I am asking for it on high authority."

Q. What high authority did he say?

A. He did not say. "I am asking for it on high authority and you will have to trust me that I have cleared it properly."

As I said, I had no cash belonging to the committee at that time because we had closed it all out but I did have two parcels of money that were available, and I gave those to Mr. Kalmbach, they added up to $75,000 as funds outside the committee.

Q. Now, Mr. Stans, did you not ask him why he wanted this money? A. Yes, I did.

Q. What did he say?

A. He said, "This is for a White House project and that I have been asked to take care of and I cannot tell you. You will have to trust me."

He was personal counsel to the President. He was a man that I knew, was a man of highest integrity, trustworthiness and honesty, and I had no question to doubt, no reason to doubt anything he told me and I didn't.

It was a unique situation. I had no superior. I would have taken instruction from the President if he gave me any but he did not, and I would have been influenced by requests from certain people in the White House from time to time but I do not believe I had a superior in that sense.

Q. Well now, I just have one more question here, I want you to think carefully, Mr. Stans. Did you have a meeting on June 24 after the break-in with Mr. John Mitchell to find out from him what had happened?

A. I am not sure of the exact date. I had meetings from time to time with Mr. Mitchell.

Q. Do you recall at any time Mr. Mitchell telling you that there were others involved besides those who were apprehended? A. No, I do not.

MR. SANDERS: When did the budget committee actually begin to function? Do you recall?

A. I do not recall precisely but I think our first meetings were in April.

Q. Would you please state the membership of the budget committee at the time it was constituted?

A. There was John Mitchell, Jeb Magruder and, I believe, Bart Porter on the campaign committee side. There was myself, Hugh Sloan Jr. and Lee Nunn on the finance committee side. But in addition to the three from each side, meetings were attended by two or three other people from each committee so they were a little larger than six-man meetings.

Q. Did the budget committee ever take under consideration the allocation of any cash funds to Mr. Liddy or to Mr. Porter?

A. No. The budget committee did not specifically deal with

any allocation of cash funds to any individual, Porter, Liddy or anyone else.

Q. To your knowledge, did the budget committee ever take under consideration the allocation of funds to be expended for any intelligence-gathering operations?

A. I do not recall ever hearing any discussion of intelligence-gathering in the budget committee meetings.

Q. Prior to June 17, Mr. Stans, were you aware that an intelligence-gathering operation was under way? A. No, I was not.

Q. In fairness, Mr. Stans, let me cite to you what I am getting at here. In the Patrick Gray confirmation hearings it is stated by Mr. Gray that you were interviewed four times by the F.B.I. and that on the last date, which would have been July 28, you stated to this effect, and I presume he is paraphrasing you here, he says this:

"Stans became aware from general conversations that Liddy was assigned a 'security gathering' job and that certain cash disbursements would have to be made available to Liddy."

A. Well, I think we are talking about semantics here and I would like to correct the impression right away. I was told somewhere in May, I believe by Magruder, that Liddy had a responsibility for security at the San Diego convention.

SENATOR MONTOYA: What about the $75,000 contribution to Mr. Kalmbach about which he called you from the Statler-Hilton Hotel. Did you approve this?

A. Well, I gave him the money, as I said, from sources outside the committee, and relying on his good faith and on his assurances to me that it was an important transaction and that he had cleared it with high authorities and he was doing it at their request.

Q. When he mentioned that this request was coming from very high authority, what did go through your mind as to who that person might be?

A. I did not try to identify anyone as the party to that transaction. I did learn about six weeks ago from Mr. Kalmbach and his attorney who it was.

Q. Who was it?

A. He told me the request came, to raise the money came, from John Dean. That he asked Mr. Dean whether it was a legal transaction and Dean assured him it was. But being unwilling to proceed solely on that basis he went to Mr. Ehrlichman and asked Mr. Ehrlichman if it was something that should be done and whether it was legal and that Mr. Ehrlichman told him it was. Now that is hearsay but I got that as I said, about six or eight weeks ago from Mr. Kalmbach and his attorney.

Q. Did not Mr. Kalmbach tell you that this was not going to be used for the campaign, that it was going to be used for other purposes? A. Yes, he did.

Q. Did that arouse your curiosity?

A. No, not in the relationship that I had with Mr. Kalmbach, that he had with the White House. Don't forget Mr. Kalmbach had been entrusted with a very large sum of money that he had left over from the 1968 campaign, he had worked with the White House people in the handling of that sum of money, and I believed Mr. Kalmbach when he said it was important but he could not tell me what it was about, and I trusted him and I still do.

June 13, 1973

SENATOR GURNEY: Back to these Kalmbach monies again. In your initial discussion with Mr. Kalmbach about this money, did he say he was getting it to spend himself on a project for the White House, or did he say he was raising it to pass it on to somebody else to spend?

A. He did not say.

Q. You mentioned a later conversation, I think you said about six weeks ago, perhaps, with Mr. Kalmbach's attorney in which he told you that it was Mr. Dean who had requested Kalmbach to raise the money. What about this discussion? Did his attorney tell you whether Mr. Kalmbach raised the money to spend himself or whether he was raising it to pass on to someone else?

A. In that conversation, Mr. Kalmbach's attorney told me that Mr. Kalmbach had raised the money for the purpose of giving to a man named Tony. He did not give his last name or any other details, but he said it was for the purpose of paying legal fees for the lawyers representing the defendants in the Watergate case.

Q. Have you ever conferred with John Mitchell, Magruder, Haldeman, Ehrlichman, Dean or anybody else on the cover-up of Watergate?

A. I have no recollection of any discussion with anyone about the cover-up on the Watergate until after the disclosures that have occurred within the last two months.

Q. Have you ever discussed this Watergate affair or any aspect of it with the President of the United States?

A. Only in the sense that the President and I met once during the campaign and I had one telephone call from him, both in August.

Q. Both when?

A. In August of last year. In which he said that he was aware of the fact that I was receiving considerable punishment in the press for not answering their questions at the time. He said that he appreciated the sacrifice I was making in that respect as the matter would be over eventually, and he hoped that I could continue to take it. It was a pep talk, in other words, and that was the substance of the discussion over the telephone.

Now, in the subsequent meeting about 10 days later in his office in the Executive Office Building I talked about some of the problems of fund raising with him. The pending nationwide dinner which was going to take place in September at which he was going to participate, and matters of that type but there was no discussion of the Watergate, of cover-up or any subject of that type with the President.

SENATOR INOUYE: Mr. Secretary, last week one of your associates, Mr. Sloan, testified that he was quite apprehensive about an $81,000 cash disbursement to Mr. Liddy and he testified that he conferred with you on this matter and he wanted some indication from you that Mr. Magruder was authorized to make these cash payments, and so you indicated that you will look into this, and you had a meeting with Mr. Mitchell, the Attorney General.

Now, upon your return from the meeting this is what Mr. Sloan testified to, and I am quoting from the testimony:

By "he" he means you, sir. "He returned from that meeting with Mr. Mitchell and he confirmed that Mr. Magruder continued to have this authority that I should pay these funds and with regard to my question of concern about his purpose he said 'I do not want to know and you do not want to know.' "

Do you recall this, sir?

A. I recall the occasion but that was not the whole conversation, and I am not quite sure that it is entirely accurate but it is the substance of what was said. The context was one of total frustration that I had with the spending program of the campaign committee.

It was evident we were in a situation in which the campaign committee was calling all the signals, was making all the commitments. We really had nothing to say about it, and it was one, as I said, of total frustration with the whole situation. I threw up my hands, and I say that literally and I think Mr. Sloan quoted that yesterday, that we were just not going to have any influence in this situation.

The remark I made, and I cannot quote it precisely, was something to the effect that "I don't know what's going on in this campaign and I don't think you ought to try to know." We were the cashiers, we received the money, and we paid the bills. They had responsibility for everything they did. It did not seem that it was incumbent upon us to question the propriety of any payment, whether it was to Mr. Liddy or anybody else, and we did not.

Q. Wasn't this rather uncharacteristic of your background, sir, one who had received all of the honors that a certified public accountant can ever hope to get, one who has been described as having an accountant's mentality, one who is a stickler for details that you would put up your hand and say, "I do not want to know?"

A. It was uncharacteristic of my background as an accountant but it was not uncharacteristic of the responsibilities I had in this campaign which had absolutely nothing to do with accounting.

My job was to raise an unbelievable amount of money, $40 million or more.

Q. Mr. Secretary, you stated yesterday that Mr. Magruder told you sometime in May that Mr. Liddy was to provide security at the San Diego convention. Did I hear correctly, sir? A. Yes.

Q. So you provided funds to Mr. Liddy in May for security activity in San Diego?

A. I did not provide Mr. Liddy any funds. The funds came from the treasurer before the time of my conversation with Magruder, indicating that this was for convention security.

Q. When was the conversation with Mr. Magruder?

A. I have testified earlier that I think it was in the latter part of May. It may have been in the early part of June. But it had no relation to the timing of the Watergate developments.

Q. Mr. Secretary, are you aware that the transfer of the Republican convention from San Diego to Miami was made public on April 21?

A. I do not recall the exact date, but nevertheless, that was what Mr. Magruder told me as to what Liddy had been using the money for.

Q. Was there a mad rush to get as much money as you can before April 7?

A. Mad rush is not the correct word for it. It is a characterization that really is not very fair.

Q. Mr. Sloan has testified that in the last four or five days, they were just deluged, and I believe he used the word "avalanche."

A. There is no question about that. There was an avalanche of money in the last five days before April 7.

What I did when I took office on Feb. 15 was to plan an effort to reach as many people as possible among the larger contributors and give them the option they had of giving their contribution before April 7 and having the right of confidentiality or giving it later, and many people said, I do not care, I will give it later.

Now, there was an advantage in getting early money. Anyone who has ever run for office knows that the early money is the hardest to get. I took advantage of that opportunity to visit a number of cities in the country, met with a lot of people, urged those who were working with me in the states to make it clear that there was an option to the individual contributor.

Q. Why would a contributor desire, as you say, confidentiality or anonymity?

A. Oh, there are a number of reasons, Senator.

Q. Why don't we tell the people of the United States?

A. I would be very happy to tell the people of the United States, because I think contributors have been very badly maligned in their desire for confidentiality.

One is that sometimes it affects relationships with employers, with unions. Sometimes, and this is, I think, the most important point, it makes them a target. It makes them a target for a great many other political campaigns. It makes them a target for charitable drives of all types. And many people want to make their contribution and not be that kind of a target.

Now, there are some people, frankly, who give to both sides, both candidates. There are some like Mr. Dwayne Andreas, who is a close friend of Hubert Humphrey and contributed to his campaign, but was also a friend of the President and wanted to contribute to his campaign. So he wanted anonymity.

The greatest disservice that is done to people is to assume that because a man wants anonymity that he has a secret, sinister motive in doing so.

Contrary to what has been said on one or more occasions, we did not prefer getting cash. We did not ever solicit anyone to contribute in cash. It was the option of the contributors to give us money in cash. We had no need for it in substantial amounts, and as I said yesterday, we put in the bank about half of the money that we received in cash.

So the choice was that of the contributor and not of our committee to receive money in cash.

Q. I notice that other Presidential candidates voluntarily disclosed all of their contributions which were made prior to April 7. Was there any reason for refusing to do so on your part, sir?

A. I think, Senator, there were some of the other candidates for the Presidency who did not disclose the source of their contributions. I do not believe that Senator Jackson made that disclosure and I do not believe that Wilbur Mills made that disclosure and there may have been one or more others that did not disclose.

We viewed the disclosure of contributions by some of the candidates who had not received much money anyway as a political ploy in an effort to try to force us to disclosure.

Q. It is your testimony this morning that until March 23 of this year you had no reason to suspect that people like Mr. Kalmbach or Mr. Mitchell or Mr. Haldeman or Mr. Ehrlichman, were possibly involved in the Watergate and its ramifications? A. That is entirely correct, Senator.

SENATOR TALMADGE: Did you testify yesterday in effect that 'your whole purpose was raising money, that you did not take care of small detailed times?

A. That is pretty much true. I will not say that at times I did not get into detail.

Q. I will ask the staff to give the witness a copy of these documents. That is a document you wrote, both pages? A. Yes.

Q. I will read part of it. "It will be necessary for us to establish a system of control over the purchasing and distribution of all articles, such as bumper strips, banners, pins, jewelry and so forth," other details there. Page 2, "I think we need a lapel pin for our 1972 contributors," et cetera. Would that not indicate to you that you had more than a casual interest in the operations of the campaign?

A. Let us take them one by one, Senator. The question of accounting for the sale of articles like jewelry and pins and so forth was a new one. We never did that in previous elections, we did not do it in 1968.

The new law changed that. It required us to account for every dollar of receipts.

Now, I did not consider, I do not consider, this a detail.

Q. Now, that was dated Feb. 28, 1972, was it not? A. That is correct, sir.

Q. More than two months before the new accounting procedure contributions and disbursements went into effect April 7, 1972?

A. About five weeks, Senator, yes.

Q. While you were spending all your time worrying about bumper strips and you have got deposits of $750,000 and disbursements of $1.77 million? You are considered to be one of the most able certified accountants in America, why did you worry about bumper strips instead of those funds?

A. Well, Senator, the accounting for proceeds of sales of articles was an important responsibility under the statute.

Q. Tell us why you didn't report this Dahlberg check from Florida. I don't believe you got it until the 10th of April, did you?

A. This was a contribution which was promised by Mr. Dwayne Andreas in March.

Q. How do you consider that it could avoid being reported when the check didn't get to you until the 10th of April, do you take the position that it was constructively received before you got it?

A. No sir, I take the position that it qualified under the definition of the contribution of the Federal Corrupt Practices Act, and I would like to read the definition to you.

"The term 'contribution' includes a gift, subscription, loan, advance or deposit of money or anything of value and includes a contract promised or agreement to make a contribution whether or not legally enforceable."

Now, Mr. Andreas had made a promise, an agreement, to make a contribution well before April 7. He had not only done that, he had gone to the point of doing everything he could personally to make the money available as a contribution.

It was clear to me and it was clear to lawyers with whom I consulted that that contribution was received as a matter of law before April 7 even though it didn't come into our hands until the 11th and, Senator, the Department of Justice has agreed with us in a letter of Jan. 11, 1973, from Henry Petersen, the Assistant Attorney General, to Wright Patman. It says:

"The issue to be resolved is when the gifts became effective as a matter of law. From the evidence developed we are forced to conclude that for criminal purposes, at least, we cannot prove that this contribution had been made after the April 7 effective date of this act and, accordingly, have closed the matter."

Now, Senator, I fail to find any basis for criticism in the handling of that transaction. I acted on the basis of legal advice and it turns out that my legal advice was good.

As of April 7, we had millions of dollars of commitments from people to contribute. Many of these had been solicited by Mr. Kalmbach as early as 1971. I could have, under a literal construction of this law, concluded that every one of those did not need to be reported when the money came in, because it was a commitment before April 7. But I adopted a very much stricter standard for the purpose of accounting and it was that only in the case of a commitment where the individual contributor had done everything possible to hand it to us would I consider that a contribution under the second part of this definition.

SENATOR ERVIN: Since I am going to ask the witness questions about the exhibit testified to by the witness, Sloan, this shows the total cash receipts of approximately $1,777,000. Is that approximately correct? A. It is approximately correct.

Q. Are the records now in existence without having to have them reconstructed that would disclose the names and amounts of each contributor?

A. There are a considerable amount of records now in existence that would show that, yes.

Q. Why are there not complete records in existence that would show that?

A. Well, at one time, Mr. Chairman, some of the records were removed from the committee's files and destroyed.

Q. Why were they destroyed?

A. They were destroyed because there was no requirement that they be kept, and insofar as contributors were concerned we wanted to respect the anonymity that they had sought and that they were then entitled to under the law. We are talking now about contributions before April 7, 1972.

Q. Were they destroyed before or after the break-in?

A. They were destroyed after the break-in and I would insist, Mr. Chairman, that there is no relevance between the two.

Q. You swear, you are stating upon your oath that there is no connection between the destruction of these records and the break-in of the Watergate or any fear that the press or the public might find out from these records what the truth was about these matters?

A. Well, let me speak only with respect to myself. I will say to you that there was no connection between my destruction of the summary sheets given to me by Mr. Sloan and the Watergate affair.

Q. Well, it was quite a queer coincidence, was it not?

A. It would—

Q. Rather a suspicious coincidence that the records which showed these matters were destroyed six days after the break-in at the Watergate?

A. Mr. Chairman, the adjectives are yours.

Q. Sir?

A. The adjectives that you are using, queer coincidence and suspicion.

Q. Don't you think it is rather suspicious? A. No, I do not think so, Senator.

Q. Do you think it is kind of normal in the kind of things to expect people who had records concerning outlays of campaign funds to destroy those records after five men are caught in an act of burglary with money from the committee in their pockets?

A. On April 6 I asked Mr. Sloan to build up the records of all the contributors and he did so. I asked him on April 10 before I left on my vacation to balance out his cash account. He did both of those things pursuant to my requests.

Now, the fact that they came to me after the Watergate was pure and innocent coincidence.

Q. Well, why did you destroy the records?

A. For the reason I have already said, Mr. Chairman.

Q. Well, don't you think it was unwise on Mr. Sloan's part to destroy the original records, the only records, the original records they had of cash amounts received and expended?

A. There were reasons at the time. In retrospect we would have saved an awful lot of questions if we had kept them but we had reasons which we believed were valid and which were based on legal advice that we did not need to keep these records.

Q. Was Mr. Liddy the one who gave you the legal advice to destroy the records?

A. Mr. Liddy was one of those who gave us legal advice. I remind the chairman in all fairness that at the time Mr. Liddy gave us the legal advice he was in good standing as our counsel. There was no reason to suspect him in any way, and he was doing a good job as counsel. Now, I did get opinions from others.

Q. Why did you destroy the summary which Mr. Sloan gave you on the 3d of June?

A. The summary which Mr. Sloan gave me?

Q. Yes.

A. I have testified before that I had it on my desk for a few days, that I was interested in the names of the contributors because I wanted to be sure that we had a record of that. That I was interested in the balance he had on hand and that I was not interested, it was not my concern nor interest to know who the disbursements had gone to. Mr. Sloan had balanced that all out with the people who had gotten the money.

Q. What I am asking you is why were you interested in destroying the things you were interested in.

A. For two reasons, Mr. Chairman, which I will try to explain again: Number one, it was possible to determine at any time from remaining records and from the recollection of people who had given that money.

Number two, under the law, as we understood it, based upon advice of counsel there was no requirement that we keep these records and as I testified yesterday, the opinion of counsel, it was to the effect that we didn't have to keep any records before April 7 that we didn't want to. Now, we kept 99 per cent of our records.

Q. Except you kept no records of the cash receipts and expenditures.

A. That is not quite correct, Mr. Chairman. We have kept some records and we have been able from those records to reconstruct what has happened.

Q. Well, why destroy your previous records and why destroy your subsequent records and reduce yourself to the necessity of reconstructing something that you already had and destroyed?

A. Very simply, for the reason—

Q. It is too simple for me to understand, really.

A. Mr. Chairman, for the reason that we were seeking to protect the privacy, the confidentiality of the contributions on behalf of the contributors.

Q. In other words, you decided that the right of the contributors to have their contributions concealed was superior to the right of the American citizens to know who was making contributions to influence the election of the President of the United States.

Mr. Stans, do you not think that men who have been honored by the American people as you have ought to have their course of action guided by ethical principles which are superior to the minimum requirements of the criminal laws?

A. I do not have any quarrel with that, but there is an ethical question in whether or not I can take your money as a contributor with an understanding on your part that you are entitled to privacy in that contribution and then go around and release the figure to the public.

Q. Well, all the law said as you construe it, as your counsel construed it, was that you did not have to make a public reporting of these contributions. The law did not require you to destroy the records of those contributions, did it?

A. Mr. Chairman, the law did not even go that far. The law did not even require us to keep any records during that period of time, on the advice of my attorney.

Q. Will you please tell me why you disbursed $50,000 in cash to Mr. Lankler instead of by check?

A. It is my recollection that he asked for it in that form because he wanted to mix it into the receipts of the party that was being held in Maryland.

Q. In other words, they were holding a fund-raising dinner in the Vice President's honor and they wanted to make it appear that they took in $50,000 more than they actually took in, didn't they?

A. They wanted to make it look more successful than it apparently was.

Q. Yes. In other words, they wanted to practice a deception on the general public as to the amount of honor that was paid to the Vice President.

A. Mr. Chairman, I am not sure this is the first time that has happened in American politics.

Q. You know, there has been murder and larceny in every generation, but that hasn't made murder meritorious or larceny legal. Well, that was the objective, wasn't it? A. That was the objective, yes.

SENATOR GURNEY: Mr. Chairman, I would like to say some other things, too. I for one have not appreciated the harassment of this witness by the chairman in the questioning that was just finished. I think this Senate committee ought to act in fairness.

SENATOR ERVIN: Well, I have not questioned the veracity of the witness. I have asked the witness questions to find out what the truth is.

SENATOR GURNEY: I didn't use the word "veracity." I used the word "harassment."

SENATOR ERVIN: Well, I am sorry that my distinguished friend from Florida does not approve of my method of examining the witness. I am an old country lawyer and I don't know the finer ways to do it. I just have to do it my way.

SENATOR GURNEY: I didn't say that I do not approve; I just want to disassociate myself from—

SENATOR ERVIN: Now, within a few weeks after the break-in you knew that McCord, who had been employed as a security officer by the political committee, as I understand it, that is the Committee to Re-elect the President, had been arrested in the Watergate?

A. Yes, I knew that the day after.

Q. Then you found out from the press that four, Barker and Sturgis and Gonzalez and Martinez had money which had come from the proceeds of checks of the committee in their pockets at the time they were arrested and in their hotel rooms?

A. I knew that only from the press stories. I did not know it of myself.

Q. Then a short time later you knew that Magruder had paid substantially—or rather had directed Sloan and Sloan at Magruder's direction had paid substantial sums of money to Liddy. A. Yes.

Q. That you also knew that Liddy had been charged with complicity in the Watergate break-in?

A. Well, before that Mr. Liddy had refused to answer questions to the F.B.I. and on advice of counsel I fired him.

Q. And you knew that, in fact, Mr. Sloan told you that he had so much misgivings about the money that had been given to Liddy by him at Magruder's request that he was thinking about resigning.

A. Yes. That happened right around the 1st of July.

Q. Well, did not Mr. Sloan tell you that Mr. Magruder had sought to persuade him to commit perjury in respect to the amount of money that had been given to Mr. Liddy?

A. Yes, he did. He told me that after he had had the several conversations with Mr. Magruder and after he had told Mr. Magruder that he was going to tell the truth.

Q. Mr. Stans, did not all of these, this knowledge that you acquired one way or another about these matters that I have enumerated, engender in your mind a feeling that you ought to communicate, you ought to talk to the President about this matter? You knew all of this before you talked to the President in August, did you not?

A. Oh, yes. Mr. Chairman, the President had far more resources than I did, it was known that the White House was conscious of the problem. I had no knowledge that there was not common knowledge at the time, I had nothing to tell the President that would have been unusual.

Mr. Chairman, may I have the opportunity under the committee's rules of a closing statement.

Q. Yes sir.

A. Mr. Chairman, I want to thank the committee for your consideration and for the opportunity to me to present my story for the first time. First, I would like to talk about the people in the finance committee. I am confident that no one in the finance committee, except, of course, Gordon Liddy, had any knowledge of or participation in the Watergate affair or any other espionage or sabotage activities.

I want to say so particularly with respect to our two treasurers, Hugh Sloan and Paul Barry.

The second thing I would like to talk about briefly is about the contributors. It is true there were some large contributions, some very large contributions. But the idea is being purveyed in some circles that no one gives a substantial amount of money to a campaign without buying something in return, without the expectation of a favor.

That is a lie, and it is belittling to our self-respect as a people.

I would like to give a couple of examples. Clement Stone of Chicago, pretty well known now, gave $2 million to elect the President. He gave a lot in 1968. He is a very wealthy man and he can afford it. He believes in the President; he knows him as a friend. Clement Stone has never asked for anything from his Government or the Administration in return. He has done it because he believes it is a public service from a man of wealth.

I would like to give you another case: Ray Kroc is a man in Chicago who is responsible for the development of the McDonald hamburger chain. I visited with him in Chicago in September for about 45 minutes, I had never met him before. I talked about the campaign and we discussed his success story. Mr. Kroc said,

"On Oct. 3 I am going to have my 70th birthday, and in appreciation for what I have been able to achieve I am going to give millions of dollars of my money to charity."

I said, "Mr. Kroc, you are a beneficiary of the great American system and I am sure you believe in it. I have reason to believe that you think the President will help to preserve that system and I would like to make a suggestion. When you get to Oct. 3 and make those distributions to charity, why don't you at the same time give $250,000 to help re-elect the President." He did. There was no discussion in that meeting of anything else.

Now, what happened after his contribution became known. First the press accused him of making the contribution so that he can influence the Price Commission on matters affecting his company.

Secondly, he was accused of making the contribution so that he could get a lower minimum wage for the young people who work for his company. He was insulted by these insinuations and falsehoods, they were vicious and unfair, completely conjecture without any fact whatever.

I want to say one thing more about innocent people and I will be finished. In the course of all the things that have happened since June 17, a lot of innocent people have been drawn through the mire of unrelenting publicity, insinuations, accusations.

There have been very damaging effects on their business and on their personal lives. It is very unfair, somebody has got to speak up for those people. So when the committee concludes its work and writes its report, I hope it will make it clear that such people, and by name, are innocent victims of this tragedy.

I put myself in that category. I volunteered or was drafted, whatever the case may be, because I believed in my President. You know by now from what you have heard, but I know you cannot feel, the abuse to which I have been subjected because of the associations I fell into. All I ask, Mr. Chairman and members of the committee, is that when you write your report you give me back my good name.

Testimony by Jeb Stuart Magruder

June 14, 1973

Confesses own guilt and implicates Mitchell, Dean, Haldeman and others.

MR. MAGRUDER: I have a statement. I did help organize the Committee for the Re-election of the President beginning in May of 1971 and I remained there throughout the entire campaign. Unfortunately, we made some mistakes in the campaign which have led to a major national concern. For those errors in judgment that I made I take full responsibility. I am, after all, a mature man and I am willing to face the consequences of my own acts.

These mistakes were made by only a few participants in the campaign. Thousands of persons assisted in the campaign to re-elect the President and they did nothing illegal or unethical. As far as I know at no point during this entire period from the time of planning of the Watergate to the time of trying to keep it from the public view did the President have any knowledge of our errors in this matter. He had confidence in his aides and I must confess that some of us failed him.

I regret that I must today name others who participated with me in the Watergate affair. This is not through any desire to implicate others but simply to give you the facts to the best of my recollection. Thank you.

MR. DASH: Could you give us some of the context of the earlier plans on the intelligence operations that now Mr. Liddy was going to fill?

A. In September of 1971 we had a luncheon meeting, John Dean called and asked me to join him and Jack Caulfield for lunch. At that time they had envisioned a private investigating firm being formed by Mr. Caulfield, they called the project Sandwedge and the idea would be Mr. Caulfield would leave the White House for this private investigating firm and this firm would then be available then for the committees to re-elect the President.

In November of 1971 it was indicated to me that the project was not going to get off the ground and subsequently G. Gordon Liddy came into the picture after that.

Q. When Mr. Liddy did come into the picture were you aware of his prior relationships in the White House with the so-called plumbers group? A. No, I was not.

Q. Who finally approved Mr. Liddy's position at the committee? A. Mr. Mitchell.

Q. Did there come a time when Mr. Liddy did present his plan to the Attorney General, Mr. Mitchell?

A. The first meeting was Feb. 27. I am sorry, Jan. 27, 1971. And we had a meeting in Mr. Mitchell's office.

Q. Who attended that meeting in Mr. Mitchell's office on Jan. 27?

A. Mr. Mitchell, Mr. Dean, Mr. Liddy and myself.

Q. Prior to the meeting on Jan. 27, did you know any of the details of the plan that Mr. Liddy was going to present on that day? A. No, I did not.

Q. Could you describe in detail what occurred on Jan. 27 in Mr. Mitchell's office?

A. Mr. Liddy brought with him a series of charts, they were professionally done charts, and had color, some color, on each of the charts. As I recall there were approximately six charts.

Each chart contained a subject matter and was headed by a code word. I cannot recall many of the code words, the one I do recall is Gemstone. I think one was called Target but I cannot specifically recall the other code words. Each chart had a listing of certain types of activities with a budget and as I recall there was one chart that totaled up the activities and the budget totaled to the million figure that he had mentioned previously.

Q. Could you give us to your best recollection what some of these projects were?

A. They were, of course, the projects, including wire tapping, electronic surveillance, and photography. There were projects relating to the abduction of individuals, particularly members of radical groups that we were concerned about on the convention at San Diego. Mr. Liddy had a plan where the leaders would be abducted and detained in a place like Mexico and that they would then be returned to this country at the end of the convention.

He had another plan which would have used women as agents to work with members of the Democratic National Committee at their convention and here in Washington, and hopefully, through their efforts, they would obtain information from them.

Q. With regard to the use of these women as agents, did this involve the use of a yacht at Miami?

A. He envisoned renting a yacht in Miami and having it set up for sound and photographs.

Q. And what would the women be doing at that time?

A. Well, they would have been, I think you could consider them call girls.

Q. Now, what was the total budget that he presented at this meeting?

A. Approximately a million dollars.

Q. Mr. Magruder, what was Mr. Mitchell's reaction, Mr. Dean's reaction, your own reaction when you heard this presentation?

A. I think all three of us were appalled. The scope and size of the project was something that at least in my mind was not envisioned. I do not think it was in Mr. Mitchell's mind or Mr. Dean's, although I can't comment on their state of mind at that time.

Mr. Mitchell, in an understated way, which was his method of dealing with difficult problems like this, indicated that this was not an acceptable project.

Q. And did Mr. Mitchell give Mr. Liddy any instructions at the end of this meeting?

A. He indicated that he would go back to the drawing board and come up with a more realistic plan.

Q. So it would be true that Liddy, at least, left that meeting without being discouraged from continuing to plan an intelligence operation.

A. I would say he was discouraged, but he was given the right to come up with a more reasonable plan.

Q. Did you make any report of the meeting to anyone after the meeting?

A. Yes, I made a report to Mr. Strachan at the White House.

Q. Now, did you disclose everything concerning that meeting to Mr. Strachan?

A. I do not recall at that meeting whether Mr. Liddy had had these charts put into 8½ by 11 size to hand out. If he had, I would have sent those over to Mr. Strachan. I do remember discussing it. I do not recall in this meeting whether we had working papers and so I can't recall specifically; I think I just on the phone discussed the general nature of his proposal.

Q. Was this telephone conversation with Mr. Strachan in which you did report the general nature of the discussion consistent with your general reporting to Mr. Strachan as you did from time to time, matters that should get to the White House staff?

A. Yes, everything that I did at the committee everything that we did was staffed to Mr. Strachan so that he could alert other officials at the White House as to our activities.

Q. Was there a second meeting on the Liddy plan, Mr. Magruder?

A. Yes, the following week in February, Feb. 4, as I recall, we met at 11 A.M. in the morning.

Q. How did that meeting come about, who attended?

A. Mr. Liddy indicated that he was ready to discuss a reduced proposal. I alerted Mr. Dean and he set up an appointment with Mr. Mitchell and we reviewed a reduced proposal.

Q. Where was this meeting?

A. At the Justice Department.

Q. Was it in Mr. Mitchell's office? Were any targets specifically mentioned, either by Mr. Liddy or anybody?

A. We discussed the potential target of the Democratic National Committee headquarters, primarily because of information we had relating to Mr. O'Brien that we felt would be possibly damaging to the Democratic National Committee. We discussed the possibility of using electronic surveillance at the Fontainebleau Hotel, which was going to be the Democratic National Committee headquarters, and we discussed the potential of using the same method at the Presidential headquarters.

Also at that meeting, Mr. Mitchell brought up that he had information—it was either Mr. Mitchell or Mr. Dean—that they had information relating to Senator Muskie that was in Mr. Greenspun's office in Las Vegas. He was a publisher of the newspaper in Las Vegas.

Mr. Liddy was asked to review the situation in Las Vegas to see if there would be potential for any entry into Mr. Greenspun's.

Q. Do you know what was, what it was they were looking for in Mr. Greenspun's office? A. No, I do not.

Q. Do you know what the information was that Mr. Mitchell mentioned concerning Mr. O'Brien?

A. Yes. We had had information from reliable sources that at the Democratic National Convention, they had a business exposition. The business exposition was being put on by a separate business exposition company. It was our understanding that the fee the business concern paid to this business company was then kicked back or partially kicked back to the Democratic National Committee to assist them in the payment of their debts.

Q. What was the general kind of information that you would be looking for in these break-ins or electronic surveillance?

A. Well, I think at that time, we were particularly concerned about the I.T.T. situation. Mr. O'Brien has been a very effective spokesman against our position on the I.T.T. case and I think there was a general concern that if he was allowed to continue as Democratic National Chairman, because he was certainly their most professional political operator, that he could be very difficult in the coming campaign. So we had hoped that information might discredit him.

Q. What was Mr. Mitchell's reaction to this presentation at the second meeting?

A. We agreed that it would not be approved at that time, but we would take it up later; that he just didn't feel comfortable with it even at that level.

Q. But again, would it be true to say that at least Mr. Liddy was encouraged to continue in his planning? A. Yes, I think that is correct.

Q. Now, after this meeting, Mr. Magruder, did you report to anyone about the meeting?

A. Yes, I sent the documents that Mr. Liddy had given us at the meeting to Mr. Strachan.

Q. And did those documents contain all of what Mr. Liddy had presented at that meeting?

A. They did not contain, as an example, the discussion on targets because that was a discussion and that was not in the documents.

Q. Did you have a telephone conversation with Mr. Strachan concerning that meeting?

A. Yes, I indicated the general context of that meeting.

Q. And did that include Mr. Mitchell's suggestions concerning the Las Vegas mission?

A. I cannot recall specifically that point, but I would assume that I probably discussed the key targets that we had discussed.

Q. And that would include the Democratic National Committee headquarters and Mr. O'Brien? A. Yes.

Q. And thereafter, there was a meeting with Mr. Liddy and Mr. LaRue came?

A. Yes. We agreed, Mr. Liddy and I, that he would terminate from the committee all activities. Then we discussed the intelligence gathering and he indicated at one point that possibly, Mr. Hunt could become involved directly in this area.

Q. Did you know at that time that Mr. Hunt was working with Mr. Liddy?

A. I think by that time, I had been encouraged by certain staff members at the White House to be sure that Mr. Hunt was not employed by us directly, but employed by Mr. Liddy. So I think I was aware at that time that he was.

Q. What staff members at the White House made such encouragement?

A. Mr. Howard, Richard Howard.

Q. Who is Mr. Richard Howard?

A. He was Mr. Colson's assistant.

Q. After the Feb. 4 meeting in Mr. Mitchell's office, when the plan was not still approved, did there come a time when anyone else at the White House urged you to get the Liddy plan approved?

A. Yes. Mr. Charles Colson called me one evening and asked me in a sense would we get off the stick and get the budget approved for Mr. Liddy's plans, that we needed information, particularly on Mr. O'Brien. He did not mention, I want to make clear, anything relating to wiretapping or espionage at that time.

Q. In that discussion, did you get the impression that he knew what the Liddy plan was?

A. I want to be careful. I knew Mr. Hunt was a close friend of Mr. Colson's, he had been referred to me earlier by Mr. Colson. I did make the assumption that he did know but he did not say that he did.

Q. Now, did there come a time when you had a third and final meeting with Mr. Mitchell on the Liddy plan on or about March 30, 1972.

A. Yes. We had, there had been a delay in the decision-making process at the committee because of the I.T.T. hearings. Mr. Mitchell was on vacation at Key Biscayne. I went down to Key Biscayne, Mr. LaRue was there, and we met and went over approximately 30-some decision papers mainly relating to direct mail and advertising, the other parts of the campaign.

The last topic we discussed was the final proposal of Mr. Liddy's which was for approximately $250,000. We discussed it, brought up again the pros and cons, I think I can honestly say that no one was particularly overwhelmed with the project. But I think we felt that the information could be useful and Mr. Mitchell agreed to approve the project and I then notified the parties of Mr. Mitchell's approval.

Q. What was the form of the memorandum or decision paper that was presented to Mr. Mitchell at this meeting?

A. It was simply the same 8½ by 11 blank sheets typed up with the basics of the plan, the number of people he would have to hire, the number of electronic surveillance equipment and amounts he would have to purchase and so on.

Q. Now, prior to going down to Key Biscayne you would send over a copy to Mr. Strachan?

A. My formal position with Mr. Mitchell was we would send over key papers before we discussed it with Mr. Mitchell, so if there was any questions in those papers Mr. Haldeman or Mr. Strachan could get back to us their opinion on a subject.

Q. Now, this quarter million dollar project you say Mr. Mitchell approved in Key Biscayne, what was that project specifically?

A. It was specifically approval for initial entry into the Democratic National Committee headquarters in Washington, and that at a further date if the funds were available we would consider entry into the Presidential contenders' headquarters and also potentially at the Fontainebleau Hotel in Miami.

Q. Now, when you say that project was approved included the entry of the Democratic National Committee headquarters and perhaps other entries, did that also include the use of electronic surveillance or bugging?

A. It included electronic surveillance and photography of documents.

Q. Do you recall Mr. Sloan questioning an initial large sum of money, $83,000 which Mr. Liddy requested after the approval of the plan? A. Yes.

Q. Could you tell us what happened and how that was resolved?

A. Well, he had called me and said that Mr. Liddy wanted a substantial sum. I indicated that Mr. Liddy did have that approval. Mr. Sloan evidently then went to Mr. Stans. Mr. Stans went to Mr. Mitchell, Mr. Mitchell came back to me and said why did Gordon need this much money and I explained to him this was in effect front end money that he needed for the equipment, and the early costs of getting his kind of an operation together. Mr. Mitchell understood, evidently told Mr. Stans it had been approved and the approval was complete.

Q. Well, do you recall a discussion that you had with Mr. Liddy concerning an effort to enter the McGovern headquarters?

A. Yes. After the first entry of the D.N.C. headquarters, Mr. Strachan and I were in my office and Mr. Liddy came in and indicated that he had had trouble the night before, that they tried to do a survey of the McGovern headquarters and Mr. Liddy indicated that to assist this he had shot a light out. At that time both Mr. Strachan and I both became very concerned because we understood from Mr. Liddy that he would not participate himself nor would anyone participate in his activities that could be in any way connected with our committee.

Q. Now, there was this entry into the Democratic National Committee headquarters, which occurred May 27, Memorial Day weekend of 1972, did Mr. Liddy report that to you?

A. Yes. He simply indicated that he had made a successful entry and had placed wiretapping equipment in the Democratic National Committee.

Q. When did you get any of the fruits or the results of this bugging and photography operation?

A. Approximately a week and a half after the initial entry, I received the first reports. They were two forms, one, recapitulation of the telephone conversations. Not direct references to the phone conversations. And the second, photography, the pictures of documents that they had taken at the Democratic National Committee headquarters.

Q. Did you show these materials with the photographs to anybody?

A. Yes, I brought the materials into Mr. Mitchell in my 8:30 morning meeting I had each morning with him. He reviewed the documents, indicated that there was really no substance to these documents and he called Mr. Liddy up to his office and Mr. Mitchell indicated his dissatisfaction with the results of his work.

Q. Well, did he tell him anything more than he was dissatisfied? Did he ask for anything more?

A. He did not ask for anything more. He simply indicated that this was not satisfactory and it was worthless and not worth the money that he had been paid for it.

Q. Mr. Magruder, did he mention . . . he did not see any O'Brien telephone—

A. There was no information relating to any of the subjects he hoped to receive and Mr. Liddy indicated there was a problem with one wiretap and one was not placed in a proper phone and he would correct these matters and hopefully get the information that was requested.

Q. Did you show these documents to Mr. Strachan?

A. As I recall, because of the sensitive nature of these documents, I called Mr. Strachan and asked would he come over and look at them in my office. As I recall I only had one copy of these documents. As I recall, he did come over and look over the documents and indicate to me the lack of substance to the documents.

Q. What took place in Los Angeles when you first learned about the break-in?

A. Well, I was at breakfast at the Beverly Hills Hotel. I received a call from Mr. Liddy and he indicated there had been a problem the night before. I said well, what kind of a problem or something of that type and he indicated that our security chief had been arrested at the Watergate and I said you mean Mr. McCord and he said yes.

Q. Now, did you report that back to anybody?

A. Yes, I first talked with Mr. LaRue and indicated the problem, and Mr. LaRue then talked to Mr. Mitchell and then Mr. Mitchell and Mr. LaRue and I discussed it again together. Mr. Mitchell asked Mr. Mardian to call Mr. Liddy and ask him to see the Attorney General, the current Attorney General, Mr. Kleindienst, and see if there was any possibility that Mr. McCord could be released from jail.

Q. Did you call Mr. Strachan?

A. I told him—of course, he knew no more than we knew. He knew that they had been apprehended and we had a problem and just discussed in a sense that we had a problem and we did not quite know what to do about it. At that time, we had heard that there was some money at that time found on the individuals and we had hoped that it was money that had been found at the Democratic National Committee, but unfortunately it was our money.

Q. Did you receive a call from Mr. Haldeman?

A. Yes. The next morning, on Sunday, I received a call from Mr. Haldeman. He asked me what had happened. Again, I told him basically—

Q. From where was he calling?

A. Key Biscayne. He just asked me the basic background of the break-in and what had happened. I just told him what had happened. He indicated that I should get back to Washington immediately, since no one in any position of authority was at the committee and to talk with Mr. Dean and Mr. Strachan and Mr. Sloan and others on Monday to try to find out what actually had happened and whose money it was and so on.

Q. Now, you did return to Washington? A. Yes, I did.

Q. Did you have a meeting on that evening, the evening of June 19, when you came back to Washington, in Mr. Mitchell's apartment?

A. Yes, Mr. Mitchell flew back that Monday with Mr. LaRue and Mr. Mardian. We met in his apartment with Mr. Dean. That would have been Mr. Mitchell, Mr. LaRue, Mr. Dean, Mr. Mardian and myself.

One solution was recommended in which I was to, of course, destroy the Gemstone file. So I called my office and—

I asked Mr. Reisner to cull through my files, pull out any sensitive material that could be embarrassing to us. There was the suit that was placed against us by the Democratic National Committee that asked for immediate disclosure. As I recall, we all indicated that we should remove any documents that could be damaging, whether they related at all to the Watergate or not.

Q. Mr. Sloan has testified before the committee, Mr. Magruder, that shortly after your return and after the break-in, that you asked him to perjure himself concerning the amount of money that Mr. Sloan had given Mr. Liddy. Could you state your own recollection.

A. The first meeting was when I determined from him that the money was our money.

My understanding of the new election law indicated that he would be personally liable for cash funds that were not reported. These were not reported funds. So I indicated at that meeting that I thought he had a problem and might have to do something about it.

He said, you mean commit perjury? I said, you might have to do something like that to solve your problem and very honestly, was doing that in good faith to Mr. Sloan to assist him at that time.

Now, later we met three times. That was on the subject of

how much money had been allocated to Mr. Liddy. Mr. Sloan would not tell me what the figure was. He refused to tell me the figure. He said, I cannot tell you the figure.

I think the real problem was that he knew it was $199,000 and I was aghast at that figure, because there was no way Mr. Liddy should have received that much money in that short period of time.

Q. Now, Mr. Magruder, there came a time when you agreed to make up a story about how the break-in and the bugging took place and who was involved?

A. Yes. I want to state here, though, that there was never any feeling on my part, no one asked me to do anything. I personally felt that it was important to be sure that this story did not come out in its true form at that time, as I think did the other participants. So I want to make it clear that no one coerced me to do anything. I volunteered to work on the cover-up story.

Q. Who participated with you without coercing you in the working up of the fabricated story?

A. Well, there were a series of meetings. They were mainly held in Mr. Mitchell's office. The main participants typically were Mr. Mitchell, Mr. LaRue, Mr. Mardian, Mr. Dean. Much of the meetings would be on subjects that were perfectly, I think, acceptable to discuss.

You know it is very hard for me to pinpoint exactly when and how we came up with the cover-up story, but it became apparent when we found out the sums were in the $200,000 range that we had to come up with a very good story to justify why Mr. Liddy would have spent that amount of money on legal activities.

Q. Could you tell us why the story required that the break-in involvement be cut off at Mr. Liddy and not at you?

A. Well, there was some discussion about me and I volunteered at one point that maybe I was the guy who ought to take the heat, because it was going to get to me, and we knew that. And I think it was, there were some takers on that, but basically, the decision was that because I was in a position where they knew that I had no authority to either authorize funds or make policy in that committee, that if it got to me, it would go higher, whereas Mr. Liddy, because of his past background, it was felt that would be believable that Mr. Liddy was truly the one who did originate it.

Q. When you testified to the grand jury that time, did you testify to the false story? A. Yes, I did.

Q. What role did Mr. Dean play in preparing you for your grand jury appearance?

A. I was briefed by our lawyers and Mr. Mardian. Also, I was interrogated for approximately two hours by Mr. Dean and approximately a half hour in a general way by Mr. Mitchell.

Q. Now, after you appeared before the grand jury for the second time, did Mr. Dean give you any report?

A. Yes, the day after Mr. Dean indicated that I would not be indicted.

Q. During your appearances before the grand jury or preceding it what, if anything, was told to you concerning the question of executive clemency for yourself or for those who were going to accept the blame in the story?

A. They made assurances about income and being taken care of from the standpoint of my family and a job afterwards and also that there would be good opportunity for executive clemency. But having worked at the White House and being aware of our structure there, I did not take that as meaning that had a direct relationship to the President at all.

In fact, the use of his name was very common in many cases where it was inappropriate; in other words, where he had not had any dealings in the matter. So I knew that this did not necessarily mean it came from the President or anyone else higher than Mr. Dean or Mr. Mitchell.

Q. Did you have a meeting with Mr. Haldeman in January, 1973? A. Yes, I did.

Q. Could you briefly tell us what the nature of that meeting was and what was discussed?

A. It was to discuss future employment regarding myself and Mr. Porter's employment. Also I thought I had better see Mr. Haldeman and tell him what had actually happened. I thought probably that this maybe was becoming scapegoat time and maybe I was going to be the scapegoat, and so I went to Mr. Haldeman and I said I just want you to know that this whole Watergate situation and the other activities was a concerted effort by a number of people, and so I went through a literally monologue on what had occurred. That was my first discussion with Mr. Haldeman where I laid out the true facts.

Q. Do you know what day or date approximately in January that occurred?

A. It would have been before the Inaugural.

Q. All right. I want to go back. Putting you back to around June 24, do you recall having a meeting with Mr. Stans and with Mr. Mitchell? A. Yes, sir.

Q. At that time, do you recall whether Mr. Stans was informed as to what occurred, actually the true story?

A. Then, as I recall, we indicated to Mr. Stans the problem we had with the money, and would he try to work with Mr. Sloan to see if Mr. Sloan could be more cooperative.

In recollecting as best as I could that meeting, we did not get into great detail as to what had actually happened at the Watergate.

Q. Basically, you were telling Mr. Stans how this money was spent. A. Yes, that is correct.

SENATOR BAKER: On Jan. 27, Feb. 4 and March 30 you met to discuss the Liddy plan? A. Yes sir.

Q. Where was the third meeting?

A. In Key Biscayne.

Q. Who was present?

A. Mr. LaRue, Mr. Mitchell and myself.

Q. It is important for us to know, Mr. Magruder, what took place at that meeting. It is important for me to know exactly how the assent was given.

A. Well, as I recall, it was the last subject we brought up at our meeting. It had the figures and the amounts and it was quite obvious as to what they were for. There would be dollars next to equipment, as an example, and so on, and we discussed the pros and cons, Mr. LaRue and Mr. Mitchell and I, not any great feeling of acceptance to this plan, with the exception that supposedly these individuals were professional, the information could be valuable. Mr. Mitchell simply signed off on it in the sense of saying, "Okay, let's give him a quarter of a million dollars and let's see what he can come up with."

Q. You say Mr. Mitchell signed off on it. Do you mean physically initialed it or signed it?

A. No, sir, I mean said, we will give Mr. Liddy the $250,000.

Q. And he identified the targets? Did that include the Democratic National Committee headquarters at the Watergate? A. Yes, sir.

Q. Did he do that with a pencil?

A. He may have. He wrote some things on some documents. I cannot specifically recall what he wrote on the documents because I destroyed the documents.

Q. Was there any question in your mind that the plan was agreed to by Mr. Mitchell?

A. No, sir, there was no doubt. But it was a reluctant decision. I think that is important to note. It was not one that anyone was overwhelmed with at all. But it was made and he did make it.

Q. Tell me more about why it was a reluctant decision.

A. We knew it was illegal, probably inappropriate. We didn't think that much would come of it. We had at least 30 decisions we made that day about even greater sums of money than that $250,000.

Q. Did you have any decision to make that day that involved any illegal action? A. No, sir.

Q. Or any clandestine activity? A. No, sir.

Q. Did that stand out in your mind, why you made that decision reluctantly? A. Yes, sir, I think so.

Q. Did you ever express any reservations about it? A. Yes, sir.

Q. What did you say?

A. Well, that it was illegal and that it was inappropriate and that it may not work.

Q. To whom did you say that?

A. To Mr. Mitchell, Mr. LaRue, Mr. Strachan.

Q. What was Mr. Mitchell's reply?

A. I think he had similar reservations, sir.

Q. What did he say?

A. Well, by this time, we had some indications of lack of compatibility with Mr. Liddy's behavior and we knew that this was possibly an inappropriate program.

Q. What was Mr. LaRue's reaction?

A. Similar. He was not overwhelmed with the program.

Q. What was your reaction?

A. I was not overwhelmed with the program, but you must, I think, understand that I had personal feelings relating to Mr. Liddy and I was concerned about letting those personal feelings overcome a possible decision that might be made.

Q. What was Mr. Strachan's reaction?

A. I think he felt uncomfortable with Mr. Liddy. But again, I think we have to, in all honesty, say that we thought there may be some information that could be very helpful to us and because of a certain atmosphere that had developed in my working at the White House, I was not as concerned about its illegality as I should have been at that time.

Q. I still can't quite come to grips with why you all had an expressed reservation about this and you still went ahead with it.

A. I knew you would get to this line of questioning, so why don't I give you what I think is the appropriate response here.

I had worked for some two years, three years, really, in the White House and at that time, I was mainly engaged in the activities trying to generate some support for the President. During that time, we had worked primarily relating to the war situation and worked with antiwar groups.

Now, I had gone to college, as an example, under—and had a course in ethics as an example under William Sloane Coffin, whom I respect greatly. I have great regard for him. He was quoted the other day as saying, well, I guess Mr. Magruder failed my course in ethics. And I think he is correct.

During this whole time we were in the White House and during this time we were directly employed with trying to succeed with the President's policies we saw continuing violations of the law done by men like William Sloane Coffin. He tells me my ethics are bad. Yet he was indicted for criminal charges. He recommended on the Washington Monument grounds that students burn their draft cards and that we have mass demonstrations, shut down the city of Washington.

Now, here are ethical, legitimate people whom I respected. I respect Mr. Coffin tremendously. He was a very close friend of mine. I saw people I was very close to breaking the law without any regard for any other person's pattern of behavior or belief.

So consequently, when these subjects came up although I was aware they were illegal we had become somewhat inured to using some activities that would help us in accomplishing what we thought was a cause, a legitimate cause.

Now, that is absolutely incorrect; two wrongs do not make a right.

For the past year, I have obviously had to consider that and

I understand completely that that was an absolute, incorrect decision. But that is basically, I think, the reason why that decision was made, because of that atmosphere that had occurred and to all of us who had worked in the White House, there was that feeling of resentment and of frustration at being unable to deal with issues on a legal basis.

I fully accept the responsibility of having made an absolutely disastrous decision, or at least having participated. I didn't make the decision, but certainly participated in it.

Q. A decision really that is going to affect history that was made in almost a casual way. A. Yes, sir.

Q. When did you first begin planning the cover-up?

A. I think there was no question that the cover-up began that Saturday when we realized there was a break-in. I do not think there was ever any discussion that there would not be a cover-up. At least, I did not participate in any discussion that indicated anything else except at one point where we possibly thought that I might volunteer to become the key figure in the case.

Q. An historic decision to go forward with this plan was followed with another historic decision to cover it up without any great debate or discussion of the matter.

A. That is correct, sir. Now, I think to be fair, Senator, I think you have to realize that I felt, and I can't speak for the others, that the President had no knowledge of this plan and consequently if it had gotten out that people like Mr. Mitchell and others had been involved at that point in time, I honestly thought that his re-election would be probably negated.

Q. Did it ever occur to you that there might be other alternatives, that one of them might be to report this directly to the President or to the F.B.I. and make a clean breast of it at that moment, that that might have less effect on the election, rather than more effect—

A. As I said, we did indicate at one point that we might possibly do that up to a certain point. I think it was felt that if it ever reached Mr. Mitchell before the election, the President would lose the election. Since he was not involved, to my knowledge, I thought that was the best decision. I did not think it was a right decision, but I thought that was the best decision.

Q. Was there ever any consideration of presenting this material to the President for his information and knowledge and for his determination?

A. I would not have been in a position to do that. It would have been people at the other level. I do not know what occurred between Mr. Mitchell, Mr. Haldeman, Mr. Ehrlichman and the President.

SENATOR INOUYE: Learned commentators have suggested that we have at the present time in the White House two competing organizations, one headed by Mr. Mitchell and the other by Mr. Haldeman. Did you have two competing organizations?

A. No, I would disagree with that completely. To my knowledge, in every meeting I ever attended with Mr. Haldeman and Mr. Mitchell, they were on extremely good terms. I never saw any difficulty in Mr. Haldeman or Mr. Mitchell agreeing. In fact, I think that is one reason Mr. Mitchell agreed to run the campaign, because he knew Mr. Haldeman would be his chief day-to-day contact at the White House. I disagree with that statement. That has been bandied about, I know. I do not agree with that.

Q. We have received testimony that Mr. Strachan was a very important conduit, that he was the liaison between the committee and the White House; that on the other end was Mr. Haldeman. A. Yes, sir.

Q. Did you receive any indication that Mr. Strachan did in fact convey those memos and messages that you have been sending to him?

A. Well, Mr. Strachan had a method of working with Mr. Haldeman. And that was he would do a summary sheet capsulizing activities of the campaign. It was a straightforward memo that condensed much of the information that we would give Mr. Strachan. That was his typical method of dealing, I think, with Mr. Haldeman.

Q. Did you receive any feedback from Mr. Haldeman indicating that he had in fact received these memos? A. No, sir.

Q. Now, when you discussed this matter in January, I presume that you told Mr. Haldeman everything you knew about the cover-up?

A. I think my main purpose, Senator, was to just indicate that there were a number of people involved and that in case people's memory was growing short I hoped he realized it was not myself or any other single individual who was involved in this cover-up.

Q. This was in January? A. Yes, sir.

Q. Were you surprised when the President announced that he had decided to begin an investigation on March 21?

A. Was I surprised?

Q. Yes.

A. Well, knowing full well of Mr. Dean's role I could well imagine that the President possibly had been informed incorrectly, since he was investigating his own problem, I could see where he could very easily have misled individuals at the White House to protect himself.

Q. But you had notified Mr. Haldeman in January of the correct activities. A. Yes, sir.

Q. Mr. Magruder, in your testimony this morning, you have indicated that there were several who knew about the cover-up. I will list a few names. Mr. Dean knew about the cover-up? A. Yes, yes sir.

Q. Mr. Mitchell knew about the cover-up? A. Yes sir.

Q. Mr. Haldeman knew about the cover-up?

A. Directly from my knowledge only in January. I did not know directly before.

Q. Mr. Ehrlichman knew about the cover-up.

A. I did not ever know that Mr. Ehrlichman knew about the cover-up.

Q. Mr. Kalmbach?

A. I only knew in Mr. Kalmbach's case he was funding the cover-up.

Q. Mr. Mardian? A. Yes, sir.

Q. Mr. Kleindienst?

A. No, sir, I did not know of any involvement by Mr. Kleindienst.

Q. Mr. Gray?

A. No, sir, I had no direct knowledge of Mr. Gray's involvement.

Q. Mr. Strachan?

A. Yes, he was aware of the cover-up.

Q. Mr. LaRue?

A. Yes, he was aware.

Q. Mr. Krogh?

A. Mr. Egil Krogh? I cannot specifically recall any direct knowledge that I would have known that he knew about the cover-up.

Q. Mr. Colson?

A. I have no direct knowledge that Mr. Colson knew about the cover-up.

Q. Mr. Howard, Mr. Colson's aide?

A. I don't think he knew directly about the cover-up. I think he realized that we had some problems and we were taking care of.

Q. Mr. Stans?

A. Only the discussion I had in June with Mr. Stans which would indicate some knowledge after that point to some extent.

Q. Mr. Sloan?

A. Yes, I am sure he knew about the cover-up.

Q. Mr. Porter.

A. Only to the extent that he has testified that he assisted me for what he thought were legitimate reasons.

Q. Mr. Odle?

A. No, as far as I know he did not know.

Q. Finally, the President?

A. To my knowledge no, no direct knowledge.

SENATOR WEICKER: Would you tell the committee what Mr. Dean told you after your Aug. 16 grand jury appearance?

A. He simply notified me the next day that I would not be indicted.

Q. Do you have any indication as to the basis for that statement?

A. My understanding it was from official sources.

Q. Official sources being what?

A. Being the Justice Department.

Q. Did you know of any influence exerted by the White House over U.S. attorneys and/or the grand jury?

A. No, I do not. As a matter of fact, at least in relation to the U.S. attorneys, I got the opposite impression.

Q. You got the opposite impression from whom?

A. From Mr. Dean primarily.

Q. Well, if he gave you the opposite impression so far as the U.S. attorneys were concerned, who was he talking about when he indicated that you would not be indicted?

A. You were indicating whether there was any influence. My indication from Mr. Dean was that they had no influence over the U.S. attorney. But when evidently the U.S. attorneys had decided not to indict me after the Aug. 1 grand jury appearance and they transmitted that to the appropriate officials, Mr. Dean evidently was notified of that fact.

Q. On June 18, you received a call from Mr. Haldeman. Is that correct? A. Yes sir.

Q. You had given a complete description of the incident to Mr. Strachan. Did you make the assumption that all of this had been transmitted to Mr. Haldeman?

A. I didn't make that assumption. I did not know that background material. I think Mr. Haldeman called me because of the serious nature of the problem and to be sure that we were taking measures to handle the situation.

Q. Mr. Magruder, do you or did you operate from the presumption, when you were talking to Mr. Haldeman, that he knew what this break-in stemmed from?

A. Senator, that is a difficult question to answer. I had to assume that since I communicated completely with Mr. Strachan that these communications were known to Mr. Haldeman to some extent. But that is strictly an assumption on my part. And in fact, in the January meeting, Mr. Haldeman indicated to me that he did not have any knowledge of the break-in previous to that.

So, of course, I assumed it simply because I had been working with his assistant. But that is an assumption and purely that.

Q. But you did not feel that you had to give a backgrounder on the subject, did you?

A. He did not ask for a backgrounder, Senator, as I recall.

Q. Now we move to January, 1973, and the meeting with Mr. Haldeman. Was this conversation with Mr. Haldeman before or after the trial?

A. It was before the trial, before the Inauguration, sometime early in January, after the first of the year.

Q. Let us be very specific. The trial was not over, is that correct?

A. As I recall, the trial had just begun. I had not testified.

Q. And the story you told him, you told him before the trial was over? A. That is correct.

Q. So Mr. Haldeman knew that perjury was going to be committed? A. Yes, I think that would be correct.

SENATOR TALMADGE: You testified this morning that Mr. Dean was intimately involved in both the planning, the execution and the cover-up? A. Yes, sir.

Q. Now, to what extent was Mr. Colson involved?

A. To my direct knowledge only through the telephone conversations that he had with me and some references to that matter that his assistant Mr. Howard, had relating particularly to Howard Hunt. We did not discuss the specific Watergate wiretapping directly, I did not, with Mr. Colson, other than his admonition to me to in effect get on the stick and get the Liddy project approved so we can get the information on Mr. O'Brien, something to that effect.

Q. Now, to what extent was Mr. Stans involved?

A. To my knowledge, to no extent before June 17, other than as chairman of the finance committee being aware of the cash disbursements were being made to Mr. Liddy. Now, on June 24, I think it was, on a Saturday we did meet and discuss the Watergate problem with him and my best recollection is we didn't go into specifics.

Q. Is it your conclusion as a reasonable man in your position, that the Watergate affair could have been undertaken and completely isolated from the President by his closest aides and friends without his own personal knowledge?

A. Because I did work at the White House, Senator, and because I am very familiar with the staff system that did exist when Mr. Ehrlichman and Mr. Haldeman were his primary aides, it is very easy for me to see how he would not have been aware. Almost all of the work that was done by the key staff people and by our committee was capsulized and passed on to Mr. Haldeman and I am just positive that many things occurred in the White House that he did not or was not aware of. It was just the way that system worked. So I have no difficulty in believing that personally.

Q. What you are saying, as I understand it, is that his staff, was so completely remote, kept him so isolated, that this could have transpired without his knowledge, approval and consent. Is that your testimony?

A. Yes, sir, I can understand that very well.

SENATOR ERVIN: I was very much impressed with your testimony about the climate that prevailed in the White House and afterwards in the Committee to Re-elect the President. As a matter of fact, was there not a fear there of Americans that dissented from policies of Government? You spoke about your former professor—

A. The Reverend Coffin. Yes.

Q. He just came down and demonstrated. There were a great many demonstrations, weren't there?

A. He did quite a bit more than demonstrate.

Q. He was supposed to try to frustrate the draft.

A. He did, and he participated in many activities that were considered illegal.

Q. You were disturbed at the demonstrations, weren't you, the people at the White House? A. Yes, sir. We were.

Q. The reason I asked the question, I have had to spend my time fighting such laws and legislative proposals as no-knock laws, preventive detention laws, the claim that there was an inherent right of the President to bug anybody suspected of domestic subversion, and things of that kind. And I just could not understand why people got so fearful.

A. I would characterize that at least my reaction was stronger after three years of working in that atmosphere than it had been before.

Q. I am familiar with that kind of atmosphere. I came up here during Joe McCarthy days when Joe McCarthy saw a Communist hiding under every rose bush and I have been here fighting the no-knock laws and preventive detention laws and indiscriminate bugging by people who've found subversives hiding under every bed. In this nation, we have had a very unfortunate fear. And this fear went to the extent of deploring the exercise of personal rights for those who wanted to assemble and petition the Government for redress of grievances.

Some of it happened before you got into the White House and I am not blaming you, because even under a Democratic Administration, I had an investigation here where they became so afraid of people that they used military intelligence to spy on civilians whose only offense was that they were dissatisfied with the policies of the Government and assembled and petitioned for relief.

Now, I think that all grew out of this complement of fear, did not it, the whole Watergate incident?

A. I think from my own personal standpoint, I did lose some respect for the legal process simply because I did not see it working as I had hoped it would when I come here.

MR. THOMPSON: Since we are talking about your motivation and your frame of mind at that time, I feel like I should ask this question: Were you concerned about legitimate demonstrations, or were there more serious things going on in the country at that time? Up until that time had there been bombings of public buildings, for example?

A. Well I think it goes much deeper than that, not only were there bombings of public buildings, we had death threats against Mr. Mitchell's life. We had continuous demonstrations in front of our headquarters.

Q. Had there been a series of break-ins of F.B.I. offices, for example?

A. Yes, sir, many.

Q. Was it your opinion at the time there were plans afoot to make some attempt to overthrow the Government by illegal and improper means?

A. I would not go so far as to say overthrow the Government. I think we had some concern about them overthrowing our convention as they did the Democratic party convention in 1968.

Q. Let me ask you one question I think I should address myself to the question of Mr. Sloan, his statement to the prosecutors that you had tried to get him to perjure himself. Do you feel that you convinced them that this was not really a disparity or a difference or a direct conflict in testimony but a misunderstanding?

A. And it is a misunderstanding. Now, I fully admit that I tried, I had hoped and kept saying to him, isn't the figure a little lower, because I thought it was lower. I did not believe that that figure could be $199,000. To this day, I am positive that there is money that has not been expended from that $199,000.

MR. DASH: Mr. Magruder, I think the testimony seems to be that Mr. Dean introduced Mr. Liddy to you. A. Yes.

Q. But is it not true that you have also told us that Mr. Haldeman approved Mr. Liddy's appointment?

A. In the sense that no White House employe was allowed to move over to the Committee to Re-elect without his prior approval, which in a sense was a negative approval. We let Mr. Strachan know that we were contemplating hiring Mr. Liddy through Mr. Dean.

There were some salary discrepancies and discussions with another assistant of Mr. Haldeman's. That was straightened out in fact, that led to a memo which I sent to Mr. Haldeman explaining all the individuals who had been hired from the White House, at what salary, and so on. Mr. Liddy is included in that memo.

Q. So Mr. Haldeman was involved in solving the salary setup?

A. That is correct, yes.

Testimony by John W. Dean 3d

June 25 *Asserts Nixon took part in Watergate cover-up for eight months and says he warned him that Watergate was "a cancer growing on the Presidency."*

June 26 *Says Nixon misled the nation with Watergate denials, insists charges against the President are factual.*

June 27 *Details lists of White House political enemies and outlines purpose of lists.*

June 28 *Tells of White House concern over demonstrations and recalls plan for using I.R.S. audits as a political weapon.*

June 29 *Recounts his accusations against the President, saying he is prepared to stand on his word.*

June 25, 1973

MR. DEAN: To one who was in the White House and became somewhat familiar with its interworkings, the Watergate matter was an inevitable outgrowth of a climate of excessive concern over the political impact of demonstrators, excessive concern over leaks, an insatiable appetite for political intelligence, all coupled with a do-it-yourself White House staff, regardless of the law. However, the fact that many of the elements of this climate culminated with the creation of a covert intelligence operation as part of the President's re-election committee was not by conscious design, rather an accident of fate.

It was not until I joined the White House staff in July of 1970 that I fully realized the strong feelings that the President and his staff had toward antiwar demonstrators—and demonstrators in general.

The White House was continually seeking intelligence information about demonstration leaders and their supporters that would either discredit them personally or indicate that the demonstration was in fact sponsored by some foreign enemy. There were also White House requests for information regarding ties between major political figures (specifically members of the U.S. Senate) who opposed the President's war policies and the demonstration leaders.

I also recall that the information regarding demonstrators—or rather lack of information showing connections between the demonstration leaders and foreign governments or major political figures—was often reported to a disbelieving and complaining White House staff that felt the entire system for gathering such intelligence was worthless. I was hearing complaints from the President personally as late as March 12 of this year.

Approximately one month after I arrived at the White House I was informed about the project to restructure the Government's intelligence gathering capacities vis-à-vis demonstrators and domestic radicals.

After I was told of the Presidentially approved plan that called for bugging, burglarizing, mail covers and the like, I was instructed by Haldeman to see what I could do to get the plan implemented. I thought the plan was totally uncalled for and unjustified.

I talked with Mitchell about the plan, and he said he knew there was a great desire at the White House to see the plan implemented, but he agreed fully with F.B.I. Director Hoover, who opposed the plan, with one exception: Mitchell thought that an interagency evaluation committee might be useful, because it was not good to have the F.B.I. standing alone without the information of other intelligence agencies. After my conversation with Mitchell, I wrote a memorandum requesting that the evaluation committee be established, and the restraints could be removed later.

The interagency [Intelligence] Evaluation Committee was created, as I recall, in early 1971. I requested that Jack Caulfield, who had been assigned to my office, serve as the White House liaison to the I.E.C., and when Mr. Caulfield left the White House, Mr. David Wilson of my staff served as liaison. I am unaware of the I.E.C. ever having engaged in any illegal assignments, and certainly no such assignment was ever requested by my office. The reports from the I.E.C., or summaries of the reports, were forwarded to Haldeman and sometimes Ehrlichman.

In addition to the intelligence reports from the I.E.C., my office also received regular intelligence reports regarding demonstrators and radical groups from the F.B.I. and, on some occasions, from the C.I.A.

I became directly and personally aware of the President's own interest in my reports regarding demonstrations when he called me during a demonstration of the Vietnam Veterans Against the War on the Mall in front of the Capitol. This was the occasion in May, 1971, I believe that is the date, when the Government first sought to enjoin the demonstration and later backed down. The President called me for a first hand report during the demonstration and expressed his concern that I keep him abreast of what was occurring. Accordingly, we prepared hourly status reports and sent them to the President.

I was made aware of the President's strong feelings about even the smallest of demonstrations during the late winter of 1971, when the President happened to look out the windows of the residence of the White House and saw a lone man with a large 10-foot sign stretched out in front of Lafayette Park.

I ran in to Mr. Dwight Chapin who said that he was going to get some "thugs" to remove that man from Lafayette Park. He said it would take him a few hours to get them, but they could do the job. I told him I didn't believe that was necessary. I then called the Secret Service and within 30 minutes the man had been convinced that he should move to the back side of Lafayette Park. There the sign was out of sight from the White House. I told Mr. Chapin he could call off the troops.

I also recall that the first time I ever traveled with the President was on his trip in 1971 to the Football Hall of Fame.

When the President arrived at the motel where he was spending the night in Akron, across the street were chanting, Vietcong-flag-waving demonstrators. The President told the Secret Service agent beside him, in some rather blunt synonyms, to get the demonstrators out of there. The word was passed, but the demonstrators couldn't be moved.

In early February of 1972, I learned that any means—legal or illegal—were authorized by Mr. Haldeman to deal with demonstrators when the President was traveling or appearing someplace. I would like to add that when I learned of the illegal means that were being employed, I advised that such tactics not be employed in the future and if demonstrations occurred—they occurred.

We never found a scintilla of viable evidence indicating that these demonstrators were part of a master plan; nor that they were funded by the Democratic political funds; nor that they had any direct connection with the McGovern campaign. This was explained to Mr. Haldeman, but the President believed that the opposite was, in fact, true.

I believe that most anyone who worked at the White House during the past four years can attest to the concern that prevailed regarding leaks—any and all leaks. I would guess that I had been at the White House almost a year before Caulfield told me that he had been directed by Ehrlichman to wiretap a newsman's telephone in pursuit of a leak. He told me that he had been directed to perform the wiretap when Mr. Hoover was unwilling, but Mr. Ehrlichman wished to proceed.

I have no idea if the reason for the wiretap was related to national security and I believe Caulfield told me it was Joseph Kraft's telephone they tapped.

While there was an always present concern about leaks, that concern took a quantum jump when The New York Times began publishing the Pentagon Papers in June of 1971.

It was late June or early July that Jack Caulfield came to me to tell me that Colson had called him in, at Ehrlichman's direction, and instructed him to burglarize the Brookings Institute

[Institution] in an effort to determine if they had certain leaked documents. What prompted Mr. Caulfield to come to me was that he thought the matter was most unwise and that his instructions from Colson were insane.

Colson had instructed him to plant a fire bomb in the building and retrieve the documents during the commotion that would ensue. Mr. Caulfield said Colson's entire argument for burglarizing the Brookings was based on a publication he had obtained indicating that the Brookings was planning for the fall (1971) a study of Vietnam based on documents of a current nature, and a former consultant to the N.S.C. [National Security Council] worked there.

I arranged to see Ehrlichman and told him that the burglary of Brookings was insane and probably impossible. He said O.K. and he called Mr. Colson to call it off.

It was not until almost a year or more later that Mr. Mardian told me that he had gone to see the President to get instructions regarding the disposition of wiretap logs that related to newsmen and White House staffers who were suspected of leaking. These logs had been in possession of Mr. William Sullivan, an assistant director of the F.B.I.

The pre-re-election White House thrived on political gossip and political intelligence. I knew of the type of information they sought even before I joined the White House staff. During the summer of 1969, while I was working at the Justice Department, the then Deputy Attorney General, Richard Kleindienst, called me into his office and told me that the White House wanted some very important information. Mr. Kleindienst instructed me to call Mr. DeLoach, then deputy director of the F.B.I., and obtain from him information regarding the foreign travels of Mary Jo Kopechne.

It was not until I joined the White House staff that Caulfield was assigned to develop political intelligence on Senator Edward Kennedy. Mr. Caulfield told me that within some six hours of the accident at Chappaquiddick on July 18, 1969, he had a friend on the scene conducting a private investigation. Caulfield also informed me that his instructions were to continue surveillance of Senator Kennedy.

In the fall of 1971 I received a call from Larry Higby, who told 'me that Haldeman wanted 24-hour surveillance of Senator Kennedy.

Caulfield told me that he thought that this was most unwise because it could uncover his activities in that Senator Kennedy was bound to realize he was under surveillance and it could easily be misinterpreted as someone who was planning an attack on his life, and the police or the F.B.I. might be called in to investigate. I agreed fully with Caulfield. After some initial resistance, I convinced Higby that it was a bad idea and the day-in, day-out surveillance concept was called off. Instead, Caulfield was to keep a general overview of Senator Kennedy's activities and pursue specific investigations of activities that might be of interest.

Political intelligence often came from unexpected sources. For example, during the spring of 1972, a top man at the Secret Service brought me information regarding Senator McGovern. I asked Mr. Colson if he were interested. He was very interested and had the information published.

The persons on the White House staff who were most interested in political intelligence were Ehrlichman, Haldeman and Colson. Principally Colson and sometimes Haldeman.

In addition to the extensive efforts to obtain politically embarrassing information on Senator Kennedy, there were also frequent efforts to obtain politically embarrassing information on Mr. Lawrence O'Brien, the Democratic National Committee chairman, Senator Muskie and Senator McGovern.

It was the spring of 1971 that Mr. Haldeman discussed with me what my office should do during the forthcoming campaign year. He told me that we should take maximum advantage of the President's incumbency and the focus of everyone in the White House should be on the re-election of the President. It was decided that the principal area of concern for my office should be keeping the White House in compliance with the election laws and improving our intelligence regarding demonstrations.

Krogh suggested that Mr. Gordon Liddy might be available. Krogh spoke very highly of Liddy's ability as a lawyer and said that his F.B.I.-Treasury Department background in law enforcement would qualify him to handle a demonstration intelligence and security operation for the re-election committee. I did not know Mr. Liddy but I respected Krogh's judgment.

Several days later Mr. Krogh informed me that Liddy was interested. I told Liddy that among the responsibilities of the general counsel would be keeping abreast of the potential demonstrations that might affect the campaign. Liddy said he was interested. Krogh said that he first would have to clear it with Ehrlichman. I advised them that Mr. Mitchell and Mr. Magruder would be making the decision on filling the post.

When Krogh gave me the O.K. from Ehrlichman, I called Mr. Mitchell and arranged for Liddy to meet with Mitchell on Nov. 24, 1971. There was virtually no discussion of intelligence plans, other than that Liddy would draw up some sort of plans. Most of the conversation centered around title and compensation.

After this meeting, Mitchell called me to say that he wanted Magruder to interview Liddy because Magruder would be the man working with him most.

The next time I recall meeting with Mr. Liddy was at a meeting in Mitchell's office on Jan. 27, 1972. Liddy was going to present his intelligence plan. I met Magruder and Liddy at Mitchell's office. Liddy had a series of charts or diagrams which he placed on an easel and the presentation by Liddy began.

I did not fully understand everything Mr. Liddy was recommending at the time because some of the concepts were mind-boggling.

Plans called for mugging squads, kidnapping teams, prostitutes to compromise the opposition, and electronic surveillance. He explained that the mugging squad could, for example, rough up demonstrators that were causing problems. The kidnapping teams could remove demonstration leaders and take them below the Mexican border.

The prostitutes could be used at the Democratic convention to get information as well as compromise the person involved. I recall Liddy saying that the girls would be high class and the best in the business. When discussing the electronic surveillance he said that he had consulted with one of the best authorities in the country and his plan envisioned far more than bugging and tapping phones. He said that, under his plan, communication between ground facilities and aircraft could also be intercepted.

I recall Mitchell's reaction to the "Mission Impossible" plan. When the presentation was completed, he took a few long puffs on his pipe and told Liddy that the plan he had developed was not quite what he had in mind and the cost was out of the question.

He suggested he go back and revise his plan, keeping in mind that he was not interested in the demonstration problem.

At that point I thought the plan was dead, because I doubted if Mitchell would reconsider the matter.

On Feb. 4, 1972, Magruder scheduled another meeting in Mr. Mitchell's office on a revised intelligence plan. The only polite way I thought I could end the discussions was to inject that these discussions could not go on in the office of the Attorney General of the United States and that the meeting should terminate immediately.

After this second meeting in Mitchell's office, I told Haldeman what had been presented by Liddy and told him that I felt it was incredible, unnecessary and unwise. I told him that no one at the White House should have anything to do with this. I said that while the re-election committee needed an ability to deal with demonstrations it did not need bugging, mugging, prostitutes and kidnappers. Haldeman agreed and told me I should have no further dealings on the matter.

I returned from a four-day trip to the Far East on the morning of June 18. I called my assistant, Fred Fielding, it was at this time that I first learned from Mr. Fielding of the break-in at the D.N.C. headquarters. Mr. Fielding told me that he thought I should return home immediately as there might be a problem.

Accordingly, I flew back to Washington and arrived on Sunday evening. I had a brief conversation with Mr. Fielding and he informed me that he had learned from Jack Caulfield that Mr. McCord from the re-election committee was among those arrested in the D.N.C. on Saturday and also that one of the Cubans arrested had a check that was made out by Howard Hunt to some country club. I recall that my immediate reaction was that Chuck Colson was probably involved.

On Monday morning, June 19, I received a call from Jack Caulfield who repeated what Mr. Fielding had told me on Sunday evening. Mr. Caulfield informed me that he had received the information from Mr. Boggs of the Secret Service. I next received a call from Magruder and I told Magruder that I had just arrived back in the country and did not know any of the facts surrounding the incident, but I would look into it.

I next received a call from Ehrlichman, who instructed me to find out what I could and report back. I recall that Ehrlichman told me to find out what Colson's involvement was in the matter and he also suggested I speak with Mr. Kleindienst to see what the Justice Department knew about it.

I next received a call from Gordon Strachan who said he wanted to meet with me.

I next talked with Chuck Colson on the phone. I asked him what he knew about the incident and he vehemently proposed that he knew nothing and had no involvement in the matter whatsoever.

I recall asking Colson if Hunt still worked for him and again he became very defensive and stated that he was merely on his payroll because Ehrlichman had so requested.

Colson also expressed concern over the contents of Hunt's safe. Over the weekend of June 17-18, Hunt had told Colson to get the materials out of his—Hunt's—office safe.

I next contacted Liddy and asked to meet with him.

Mr. Liddy told me that the men who had been arrested in the D.N.C. were his men and he expressed concern about them. I asked him why he had men in the D.N.C. and he told me that Magruder had pushed him into doing it.

Liddy was very apologetic for the fact that they had been caught and that Mr. McCord was involved. He told me that he had used Mr. McCord only because Magruder had cut his budget so badly.

He also told me that he was a soldier and would never talk. He said that if anyone wished to shoot him on the street, he was ready. As we parted I said I would be unable to discuss this with him further. He said he understood.

After returning to my office Gordon Strachan told me that he had been instructed by Haldeman to go through all of Mr. Haldeman's files over the weekend and remove and destroy damaging materials. He told me that this material included such matters as memoranda from the re-election committee, documents relating to wiretap information from the D.N.C., notes of meetings with Haldeman, and a document which reflected that Haldeman had instructed Magruder to transfer his intelligence gathering from Senator Muskie to Senator McGovern. Strachan told me his files were completely clean.

That afternoon, Ehrlichman instructed me to call Liddy to have him tell Hunt to get out of the country. I did this without even thinking. Shortly after I made the call, however, I realized that no one in the White House should give such an instruction and raised the matter. Colson chimed in that he also thought it unwise and Ehrlichman agreed. I immediately called Liddy again to retract the request and he informed me that he had already passed the message and it might be too late to retract.

Colson raised the matter of Hunt's safe. Colson, without getting specific, said it was imperative that someone get the contents of Hunt's safe. Colson suggested, and Ehrlichman concurred, that I take custody of the contents of the safe.

It was on June 20 or 21 that Strachan and Mr. Richard Howard came to my office. Strachan informed me that Haldeman had authorized an expenditure by Colson of some funds, but the entire amount had not been expended and he was turning over the remainder to me to hold. I placed the cash, $15,200, in my safe. I informed Mr. Fielding of my office of the fact that the cash was in my safe and where it had come from.

The cash remained in my safe untouched until Oct. 12, 1972 when I removed a packet of bills amounting to $4,850 and placed my personal check for that amount with the remaining cash. I removed the $4,850 after I had failed to make arrangements to pay for the anticipated expenses of my wedding, and honeymoon.

At no time when I was making personal use of part of these funds did I plan—or believe—that I would not have to account for the entire amount at some point in time.

I have never sought to hide the fact that I made personal use of this money from anyone. I informed my lawyers, I informed the Government prosecutors in March, and I informed Mr. Dash at the outset of our discussions.

I met with Attorney General Kleindienst on either Monday, June 19, or Tuesday, June 20. I had been asked by Ehrlichman to talk with Kleindienst about the scope of the investigation.

I told Mr. Kleindienst that I did not have all the facts, but I was very concerned that this matter could lead directly to the President. I told him that I did not know if the President was involved, but I was concerned. I remember Kleindienst saying to me that he certainly hoped that the President was not involved or that I was not involved. I responded that I certainly had not been involved in any criminal activity.

Kleindienst called Henry Petersen and asked Petersen to come to his office. While we were waiting for Petersen, Kleindienst told me that my superiors at the White House never understood that once an investigation begins, it runs its full course. He said that he was always being asked to take care of this matter or that matter, as if by magic he could make something unpleasant go away.

When Petersen arrived at Kleindienst's office he gave a status report of the investigation. Kleindienst then related my concern to Petersen. Petersen was troubled by the case and the implications of it. Kleindienst had another meeting, so Petersen and I talked further. To the best of my recollection, we did not discuss specifics. I told him I had no idea where this thing might end, but I told him I didn't think the White House could withstand a wide open investigation.

Returning now to the contents of Mr. Hunt's safe, it was midmorning on Tuesday, June 20, when the G.S.A. men brought several cartons to my office, which contained the contents of Hunt's safe.

During the afternoon, Fielding and I began going through the cartons of Hunt's materials, [including a] briefcase, which contained electronic equipment.

Among the papers were numerous memoranda to Chuck Colson regarding Hunt's assessment of the plumbers unit, a number of materials relating to Mr. Daniel Ellsberg, a bogus cable, that is other cables spliced together into one cable, regarding the involvement of persons in the Kennedy Administration in the fall of the Diem regime in Vietnam, a memorandum regarding some discussion about the bogus cable with Colson and William Lambert, some materials relating to an investigation Hunt had conducted for Colson at Chappaquiddick, some materials relating to the Pentagon Papers.

[Meeting later with Ehrlichman], he told me to shred the documents and "deep six" the briefcase. I asked him what he meant by "deep six." He leaned back in his chair and said: "You drive across the river on your way home at night—don't you?" I said yes. He said, "Well, when you cross over the bridge on your way home, just toss the briefcase into the river."

After leaving Ehrlichman's office I thought about what he had told me to do and was very troubled. I raised it with Fielding and he shared my feelings that this would be an incredible action—to destroy potential evidence. I think Mr. Fielding appreciated my quandary—when Ehrlichman said something, he expected it to be done.

I believe that it was on June 21 that I first met with Gray in his office in the late morning regarding the F.B.I.'s investigation. At that meeting he told me he fully realized the sensitive nature of the investigation they were pursuing and that he had placed his most trusted senior people in charge.

He informed me that the F.B.I. had uncovered a number of major banking transactions that had transpired in the account of one of the arrested Cubans—Mr. Barker. He informed me that they had traced a $25,000 check to a Mr. Kenneth Dahlberg and four checks totaling $89,000 to a bank in Mexico City.

The fact that the F.B.I. was investigating these matters was of utmost concern to Mr. Stans when he learned of it.

In addition to the conversations that I was having with Gray regarding the status of the investigation, Mitchell, Ehrlichman and Haldeman thought that I should see the F.B.I. reports.

In early July I raised with him [Gray] my receiving some of the raw F.B.I. data regarding the investigation. Gray said that he would have to check but wanted an assurance from me that this information was being reported to the President and that was the principal purpose of the request. I assured him that it was being reported to the President. Even though I was not directly reporting to the President at that time, I was aware of the fact that Ehrlichman or Haldeman had daily discussions with the President, and I felt certain, because Haldeman often made notes, about the information I was bringing to their attention, that this information was being given to the President.

It was during the meeting in Mitchell's office on June 23 or 24 that Mardian first raised the proposition that the C.I.A. could take care of this entire matter if they wished. Mitchell suggested I explore with Ehrlichman and Haldeman having the White House contact the C.I.A. for assistance.

Ehrlichman thought it was a good idea. He told me to call General Walters because he was a good friend of the White House and the White House had put him in the deputy director position so they could have some influence over the agency.

When General Walters came to my office I asked him if there was any possible way the C.I.A. could be of assistance in providing support for the individuals involved. General Walters told me that while it could of course, be done, he told me that he knew the director's feelings about such a matter and the director would only do it on a direct order from the President. He then went on to say that to do anything to compound the situation would be most unwise and that to involve the C.I.A. would only compound the problem because it would require that the President become directly involved.

When I reported this to Ehrlichman, he very cynically said that General Walters seems to have forgotten how he got where he is today.

I would now like to explain the transmitting of the materials in Hunt's safe to the F.B.I.

I spoke with Ehrlichman on the 28th and informed him the material had been sent to the F.B.I. with the exception of the politically sensitive documents. He told me he was meeting later that day with Gray and I should bring them over at that time.

When Gray arrived Ehrlichman told him that we had some material for him that had come from Hunt's safe. Ehrlichman described it as politically sensitive, but not related to the Watergate per se. I said we did not believe they related to the Watergate in any way, but should they leak out they would be political dynamite in an election year. I believe at that point Gray placed the two envelopes in his briefcase. At no time while I was present with Gray and Ehrlichman was he instructed by myself or Ehrlichman to destroy the documents. Rather, he was merely told that they must never be leaked or made public. I departed and returned to my office.

On the afternoon of June 28, in a meeting in Mr. Mitchell's office there was a discussion of the need for support money in exchange for the silence for the men in jail. Mr. LaRue indicated that Mr. Stans had only a small amount of cash. I believe he said $70,000 or $80,000, but more would be needed. Mitchell asked me to get the approval of Haldeman and Ehrlichman to use Mr. Herb Kalmbach to raise the necessary money. Before I departed the meeting, Mr. Mitchell, in an aside for my ears only, told me that the White House, in particular Ehrlichman, should be very interested and anxious to accommodate the needs of these men. He was referring to activities that they had conducted in the past that related to the White House, such as the Ellsberg break-in.

I conveyed this request to Haldeman and Ehrlichman and they told me to proceed to contact Mr. Kalmbach.

It was while I was in San Clemente, at the end of August, that the President announced at a press conference the so called "Dean Report" which cleared everybody presently employed at the White House or in the Administration from any complicity in the Watergate matter. This statement was made on Aug. 29, 1972.

I had no advance knowledge that the President was going to indicated that I had investigated the matter and found no complicity on the part of anybody at the White House or anyone presently employed in the Administration. I first learned of the matter when I heard it on a television news broadcast.

Had I been consulted in advance by the President, I would have strongly opposed the issuing of such a statement. First, I was aware that Gordon Strachan had close, daily, liaison with Magruder and had carried information relating to wiretapped conversations into the White House and later destroyed incriminating documents at Haldeman's direction.

Secondly, I had never been able to determine whether Haldeman had advance knowledge or not, and in fact, had never asked him because I didn't feel I could.

Thirdly, I had always suspected, but never been able to completely substantiate my suspicion, that Colson was far more knowledgeable than he protested.

I don't know if the President's statement was meant to be a very literal play on carefully chosen words or whether he intended to give it the broad-brush interpretation that it later received.

The issuing of the so-called "Dean Report" was the first time I began to think about the fact that I might be being set up in case the whole thing crumbled at a later time.

On Sept. 15 the Justice Department announced the handing down of the seven indictments by the Federal grand jury. Late that afternoon I received a call requesting me to come to the President's Oval Office.

The President told me that Bob [Haldeman] had kept him posted on my handling of the Watergate case, told me I had done a good job and he appreciated how difficult a task it had been and the President was pleased that the case had stopped with Liddy. I told that I thought that there was a long way to go before this matter would end and that I certainly could make no assurances that the day would not come when the matter would start to unravel.

Early in our conversation the President said to me that former F.B.I. Director Hoover had told him shortly after he had assumed office in 1969 that his campaign had been bugged in 1968. The President said that at some point we should get the facts out on this and use this to counter the problems that we were encountering.

The President asked me when the criminal case would come to trial and would it start before the election. I told the President that I did not know. I said that the Justice Department had held off as long as possible the return of the indictments, but much would depend on which judge got the case. The President said that he certainly hoped that the case would not come to trial before the election.

The conversation then moved to the press coverage of the Watergate incident and how the press was really trying to make this into a major campaign issue. At one point in this conversation I recall the President telling me to keep a good list of the press people giving us trouble, because we will make life difficult for them after the election.

The conversation then turned to the use of the Internal Revenue Service to attack our enemies. I recall telling the President that we had not made much use of this because the White House didn't have the clout to have it done, that the Internal Revenue Service was a rather Democratically oriented bureaucracy and it would be very dangerous to try any such activities. The President seemed somewhat annoyed and said that the Democratic Administrations had used this tool well and after the election we would get people in these agencies who would be responsive to the White House requirements.

While the Segretti matter was not directly related to the Watergate, the cover-up of the facts surrounding Mr. Segretti's activities was consistent with other parts of the general White House cover-up which followed the Watergate incident.

I first heard of Mr. Segretti when Gordon Strachan called me in late June and told me that the F.B.I. had called a friend of his, by the name of Donald Segretti, and requested to interview him. Strachan gave me a very general description of Segretti's activities and said that he was a "dirty tricks" type operator who was being paid by Mr. Kalmbach. He also informed me that Mr. Chapin had been involved in hiring Segretti.

Several days after Segretti's F.B.I. interview, he called me and said he told the F.B.I. everything he knew about Mr. Hunt and the fact that he had no knowledge of the Watergate incident and that the agents had not pressed him in a manner that required him to reveal the names of Strachan, Chapin and Kalmbach.

I received a call from Mr. Chapin who indicated that Segretti was very concerned about the fact that he was being called before a Federal grand jury in Washington investigating the Watergate. And that he was concerned again that he might have to reveal the names of Strachan, Chapin and Kalmbach.

After my conversation with Chapin, I called Mr. Petersen at the Department of Justice and explained the problem. I told Petersen that to the best of my knowledge Segretti had no involvement in the Watergate incident but he had had dealing with Hunt in connection with some campaign activities he had been performing for the White House. I also informed him that he was being paid by the President's personal attorney, Mr. Kalmbach, and that he had been recruited by Chapin and Strachan. I said that these facts, if revealed, would be obviously quite embarrassing and could cause political problems during the waning weeks of the election. Mr. Petersen said that he understood the problem.

I later learned from Segretti that the names had come out during the grand jury appearance and I had a discussion later with Petersen also on the subject in which he told me that Mr. Silbert had tried to avoid getting into this area and in fact did not ask him the question which resulted in his giving the names, rather that a grand juror had asked the question despite the fact that the prosecutors had tried to gloss over it.

I had by this time learned the full story, that in fact Haldeman, in a meeting with Kalmbach, had approved Segretti's activities and authorized Kalmbach to make the payments to Segretti. In discussing this with Chapin and Strachan before their appearance, they both had great concern about revealing Haldeman's involvement. In fact, I recall that Strachan came into my office and said that he would, if necessary, perjure himself to prevent involving Haldeman in this matter.

On Oct. 10, 1972, an article based on leaked F.B.I. information reported the Segretti story for the first time publicly. Following the Oct. 10 story there commenced a series of stories involving Chapin, Strachan, Kalmbach and, later, Haldeman. These stories created a new frenzy in the White House press office. On Sunday, Oct. 15 I went to the White House where a meeting was in session in the Roosevelt room. In attendance at the meeting were Ehrlichman, Ziegler, Buchanan, Moore and Chapin. The purpose of this meeting was to prepare Ziegler for his press briefings on the Segretti-related stories.

I might also add that this session was not unlike many other sessions that had preceded it and that were to follow it in preparing Ziegler to meet with the White House press corps. It would, however, take me another 200 pages to give that story.

As the press accounts of Segretti's activities lingered on after the election as well as the continuing Watergate stories, there was serious discussion about putting the facts out. In late November, I recall a conversation with Haldeman in his office. I told him that I thought the then pending trial would be put back into a grand jury and it was very likely that any reconvened grand jury would get into questions of obstruction of justice which would lead right to us.

Haldeman said that the President wished, now that the election was over, to get rid of the Watergate and related matters by laying them open but based on what I had just told him he said it doesn't seem to be a very viable option.

It was the first week of December that Mitchell called me and said that we would have to use some of the $350,000 fund to take care of the demands that were being made by Hunt and the others for money. He indicated that the money that was taken out would be returned in order that the fund could be made whole again. He asked me to get Haldeman's approval.

I called Haldeman and described the situation in full to him and that I had told Mitchell that I was very reluctant to see White House money used. I told Haldeman that I didn't think this was a good idea to further involve the White House in raising money for these men but I frankly had no answer. Haldeman said he did not like it either, but since we had the assurance that the money would be returned, I should inform Strachan that he could make the delivery of the money to the committee.

I do not recall how much money was delivered by Strachan but I believe it was either $40,000 or $70,000.

It was sometime shortly before the trial when the demands reached the crescendo point once again. O'Brien and LaRue came to my office and told me the seriousness of the problem. Subsequently, Mitchell called me and told me that once again I should ask Haldeman to make available the necessary funds. I told him I thought it was time to get the entire money out of the White House rather than continue as we were with, every few weeks, further bites being taken out of the apple.

After we discussed the matter Haldeman said send the entire damn bundle to them but make sure that we get a receipt for $350,000. After receiving my instructions from Haldeman I called Strachan and told him that he was to deliver the remainder of the money to LaRue but that he was to make certain that he got a receipt for $350,000. Strachan later told me that LaRue refused to give him a receipt.

With each of these deliveries I am only aware of the fact that money was delivered to LaRue by Strachan and have no knowledge of how LaRue in turn delivered it to those who were making demands upon the committee, nor do I know how much, in fact, was paid.

O'Brien told me that Hunt was quite upset and wished to plead guilty but before he did so he wanted some assurances from the White House that he would receive executive clemency. O'Brien told me that Hunt would only take the assurances from Colson.

On the morning of Jan. 3, Colson called me. I told Mr. Colson that I was aware of the fact that Bittman wanted to discuss the matter of executive clemency for Hunt and that Hunt would only take assurance from him [Colson].

I next met with Ehrlichman, told him about the situation and he thought that Colson should meet with Bittman.

In trying to reconstruct as best as I can recall what occurred, there was a meeting in Ehrlichman's office on Jan. 3, after Mr. Colson had had a conversation with Bittman about Hunt's potential for executive clemency. I recall that when Colson came to the meeting with Ehrlichman he was extremely shaken, which was unlike Colson. He was not specific in his arguments to Ehrlichman but said that he felt it was imperative that Hunt be given some assurances of executive clemency. The meeting in Ehrlichman's office did not last long and Ehrlichman said that he would have to speak with the President. Ehrlichman told Colson that he should not talk with the President about this. On Jan. 4, I learned from Ehrlichman that he had given Colson an affirmative regarding clemency for Hunt.

After the meeting in Ehrlichman's office, Colson told me that although Ehrlichman had told him that he [Colson] should not discuss this matter with the President, that he, in fact, thought it was so important that he had taken it up with the President himself.

As I shall state later, the President himself raised this subject on two occasions with me, and told me that he had discussed the matter of executive clemency for Hunt with both Ehrlichman and Colson. The President raised this with me on March 13, 1973, and April 15, 1973.

Even before the Watergate criminal trial in January of this year, there had been press reports and rumors that the Senate was planning independent hearings on the Watergate and related matters. The White House Congressional relations staff reported that the subject of Watergate hearings was being discussed in the Senate Democratic Policy Committee, but they did not know the substance of those discussions. I was made aware of the interest of Ehrlichman and Haldeman in the prospects of such hearings because they had discussed it with me, and Bill Timmons told me they had discussed it with him.

Timmons continued to report to Haldeman and me that there were rumblings on the Hill that the Senate was going to proceed with hearings. Senator Kennedy's Subcommittee on Administrative Practices and Procedures had been conducting an investigation for several months, but it was uncertain as to whether they would proceed. It was learned in late December/early January that Senator Mansfield was pushing hard for Watergate hearings, but there was a debate as to who should handle the hearings. On Jan. 5 or 6, it was reported in the press that Senator Mansfield had sent letters to Senator Eastland and Senator Ervin regarding the holding of hearings.

The White House wanted Senator Eastland to hold such hearings because they felt that Senator Eastland would be friendly and that the White House had more friends on the Judiciary Committee than on Senator Ervin's Government Operations Committee. On Jan. 11 of this year, the Senate Democrats formally voted that Senator Ervin would head the inquiry into the Watergate incident and related matters, and I must add, much to the displeasure of the White House.

On Feb. 5, 1973, the chairman introduced his resolution to create this committee. An advance copy of the resolution was forwarded to me by Timmons and I was subsequently required to attend a luncheon meeting with Ehrlichman, Timmons and Johnson to discuss the resolution.

I was asked what I thought about the resolution and did I have any suggested amendments that the Republicans might offer. I had not had an opportunity to study the resolution closely so I reread it and offered a few suggestions off the top of my head: That it be broadened to cover other elections than the 1972 Presidential campaign: That the minority members have adequate staff: That it be bipartisan with equal representation of the Republicans and Democrats, and that the minority members have the power to call for an executive session when they believed it necessary. Wally Johnson indicated that he could get someone at the Justice Department to draft amendments and that he and Timmons would peddle them to friendly Republicans.

I later had discussions with Haldeman and Ehrlichman about the Senate hearings and they felt that it was time to develop a strategy for dealing with the Senate situation.

We had made it through the trial without any problems but the Senate hearings were a new and possibly larger problem. Accordingly, I suggested that there be a meeting called where these matters could be discussed. I also suggested that we might call on Mr. Bryce Harlow. Ehrlichman, Haldeman and Mitchell all agreed that Mr. Harlow's counsel would be most helpful. Accordingly, I had my secretary schedule a meeting in Ehrlichman's office on Feb. 6, 1973.

The meeting turned to a general discussion of the proposed amendments and Timmons was called for from the Congressional leadership meeting that was then in session in the Cabinet Room. Timmons reported that the Senate was going to begin debate on Senator Ervin's resolution that afternoon. Timmons was instructed to request Senator Hugh Scott to come to his office after the leadership meeting and I was instructed to go to Mr. Timmons's office to explain the amendments to the resolution to Senator

Scott. I was also told that I should tell the Senator to raise the 1968 bugging incident as a reason to expand the scope of the resolution to prior Presidential elections.

On Feb. 7, Timmons informed me that the White House amendments had been virtually rejected out of hand and the resolution adopted 77 to 0. Timmons told me he had discussed with Haldeman the possibilities of suggesting names for the Republican side of the select committee with Senator Scott and Scott seemed receptive. On Feb. 8, the members of this committee were named and I recall Timmons telling me that Haldeman had "chewed him out," but Timmons told me Scott had never given him a chance to make any recommendation. I received a call from Ehrlichman in San Clemente telling me that he wanted Mr. Moore and me to come to California that night so that he could discuss in full detail the problems of how to deal with the forthcoming Senate hearings.

Everyone was staying at the La Costa Resort Hotel, south of San Clemente. The meetings with Haldeman and Ehrlichman, Moore and myself ran for two days, and I would estimate they involved between 12 to 14 hours of discussion.

What had happened by this point in time was that the cover-up had become a way of life at the White House, and having made it to this point, those involved were becoming careless and more open about it. Also, the Senate was different than the courts, grand jury, F.B.I. and the like that had been dealt with earlier. It was realized that it was going to take an all-out effort by the White House to deal with the Senate inquiry, because of the scope of the resolution, the composition of the committee, the investigative powers of the committee, and the general feeling that the Senate was a hostile world for the White House.

It was during the morning meeting in Ehrlichman's office at San Clemente that there was a discussion of the members of this committee. Ehrlichman said that the White House could not look for any help from the Democrats. I recall that when we were discussing the Democratic members of the committee, and I read from the Congressional Directory the data on Senator Inouye, Ehrlichman said that his name is pronounced "ain't no way" and then said, indeed, there ain't-no-way he's going to give us anything but problems.

The Republican members of this committee were also discussed in that morning meeting. It was Ehrlichman who was doing most of the assessing. But occasionally, Haldeman would add a comment. Senator Weicker was an independent who could give the White House problems. Senator Gurney would help the White House and would not have to be told to do so.

Senator Baker was an unknown and neither Haldeman nor Ehrlichman knew which way he might go. I might add that in a subsequent discussion I had with the President he also reached a similar conclusion regarding the Republicans. He thought that Senator Baker might help, but was not sure. He was confident, however, that Senator Gurney would protect the White House and would do so out of political instinct and not have to be persuaded to do so.

Later, after the meeting had reconvened at La Costa, the discussion turned to a general approach of how to deal with the select committee.

After a general discussion, Ehrlichman and Haldeman concluded that the theory for dealing with this committee should be as follows: The White House will take a public posture of full cooperation, but privately will attempt to restrain the investigation and make it as difficult as possible to get information and witnesses. A behind-the-scenes media effort would be made to make the Senate inquiry appear very partisan. The ultimate goal would be to discredit the hearings and reduce their impact by attempting to show that the Democrats have engaged in the same type of activities.

During the meeting on Saturday afternoon [Feb. 11] Ehrlichman instructed me to call Wally Johnson and tell Johnson that he was to go visit with Senator Baker during the then Congressional recess to find out how Senator Baker planned to operate (that is—was he going to be friend or foe) and to ask Senator Baker how the White House could aid him, particularly regarding the selection of the minority counsel.

At one point in the meeting, Ehrlichman raised the question of whether or not the select committee was going to be able to obtain the grand jury minutes and other investigative records from the F.B.I. and the U.S. Attorney's office. I said I did not know and then a discussion of possible legal options ensued. No one really knew what the law might be regarding this matter, but Ehrlichman stated that the Attorney General will have to be told that the Justice Department should resist turning over such records, and that I should get word back to the attorney for the defendants that they should fight the release of these investigative records to the Senate.

When discussing how to handle the press coverage of the Senate hearings, Haldeman suggested that Pat Buchanan be used as a watchdog of the press. Mr. Buchanan could prepare speeches on the biased press coverage. He could write op-ed articles and actually attend the hearings and be a White House spokesman to take the pressure off Ziegler's daily briefings.

There was lengthy discussion of the importance of the minority counsel. Both Ehrlichman and Haldeman felt very strongly about having a man, as minority counsel, who would work with the White House. A number of suggestions were made and discussed. Ehrlichman thought that Mr. Fred Buzhardt would be an excellent choice. I was asked to come up with some names for consideration as soon as possible and report back.

It was toward the end of the meeting on Sunday afternoon, Feb. 11, that Ehrlichman raised the bottom line question: Would the seven Watergate defendants remain silent through the Senate hearings? I say this was a bottom line question because the entire strategy was based on this continued silence. I reported that I could not answer the question because I did not know. I said that I understood that they were still demanding more money, but as we had discussed previously, there was no more money available.

I told both Haldeman and Ehrlichman that I had carried their messages to Mitchell, that this is something he should take care of, but they were aware of Mitchell's feelings that the White House should be concerned about the matter. I said as far as I was concerned that they would have to take this up with Mitchell in that Mitchell felt it was a matter for the White House.

At this point, Ehrlichman told Mr. Moore—who was hearing all this for the first time—that he [Moore] should go to Mitchell and simply lay it out that it was Mitchell's responsibility to raise the necessary funds for these men. It had been decided at the outset of the first day of the meetings that Moore would go to New York and report to Mitchell on what had been resolved regarding dealing with the Senate hearings, and now Ehrlichman was telling Moore that an important element of his visit with Mitchell would be for him to raise the necessary future funds for the seven Watergate defendants.

On Feb. 13 I received a call from Johnson, who informed me that he had talked with Senator Baker by telephone. Johnson said that he had discussed the minority counsel position with Senator Baker, and the Senator did not want any official input from the White House and had already given some thought to the qualifications he was seeking in his minority counsel. Johnson told me that he didn't think Senator Baker had ruled out the White House's making some suggestions, but we would have to move quickly. Mr. Johnson also reported that Senator Baker had told him that the White House should be concerned with the President's posture vis-à-vis the Senate inquiry.

I returned to the office on Monday, Feb. 19, and spoke with Haldeman on either the 19th or 20th. He requested that I draw up an agenda for a meeting with the President regarding matters which the President should reflect on as a result of the La Costa meeting and subsequent matters which had come up. Mr. Haldeman and I went over the high points of what should be raised, including items that had not come up at La Costa, such as Magruder's desire to return to the White House and sending Mr. Stans for a confirmable post as a tactic to counter the Watergate hearings.

I prepared the agenda. I thought that I was going to attend the meeting with the President, but Haldeman called for the agenda, and not me. I have submitted to the committee a copy of the agenda. You will see that the agenda deals with five items to be discussed and resolved with the President. (1) Senator Baker's requested meeting with the President: (2) submitting Secretary Stans's name for a confirmable position: (3) what to do with

Mr. Magruder: (4) using Mr. Buchanan during the Senate hearings: and (5) getting the Attorney General back in touch with the White House.

Subsequent to Haldeman's meeting with the President, he informed me that (1) the President would meet with Senator Baker; (2) I should discuss with Mr. Stans his interest in a confirmable position; (3) Mr. Magruder could not return to the White House staff; (4) Mr. Buchanan could not be used at the Senate hearings; and (5) the President would meet with the Attorney General.

I have not explained at this point the details of this rather significant document, but I believe the document is rather self-explanatory of the continuing cover-up. I was not present when the President and Haldeman discussed these matters, but I had discussed them with Haldeman before he went to see the President and he informed me of the President's decisions after the meeting; thus, I assume that the agenda I had prepared was the basis of their discussions.

On Feb. 20 or 21, Timmons told he had arranged for the President to have an off-the-record, private meeting with Senator Baker.

After the President met with Senator Baker, I was informed by Haldeman that the Senator had appeared to be very interested in being cooperative and the President had the impression that he might be helpful. This, of course, was the White House hope, but nothing that was reported from the meeting made this anything more than a hope. Also, Senator Baker told the President that he wanted his contact point to be Mr. Kleindienst, rather than someone on the White House staff. Haldeman told me that Senator Baker had urged the President to waive executive privilege and send members of the White House staff to the hearings as quickly as possible, but the President had told Senator Baker that he was going to hold the line at written interrogatories. Finally, I was told that both the President and Senator Baker had discussed that there should be an effort to get the hearings over as quickly as possible.

This report of the meeting which Haldeman gave me was later confirmed in discussions I had with the President myself in early March of this year.

It was during this period of time, which I believe was mid-February, Magruder had a conversation with Mr. O'Brien in which he told O'Brien that he had received his final authorization for Liddy's activities from Gordon Strachan and that Strachan had reported that Haldeman had cleared the matter with the President. I reported this to Haldeman, who expressed concern over Magruder's statement. After I reported this information, the White House efforts to find a job for Magruder became intense.

I would now like to turn to my direct dealings with the President which began in late February of 1973 with regard to the

Watergate and related matters. I feel I can best set forth what
transpired at these meetings by discussing what occurred at each
meeting.

Meeting on Feb. 27: This was the first meeting I had had with
the President since my Sept. 15, 1972, meeting which related to
the Watergate. It was at this meeting that the President directed
that I report directly to him regarding all Watergate matters. He
told me that this matter was taking too much time from Haldeman's and Ehrlichman's normal duties and he also told me that
they were principals in the matter, and I, therefore, could be
more objective than they.

The President then told me of his meeting with Senator Baker
and the Attorney General. He told me that Senator Baker had
requested that the Attorney General be his contact point and
that I should keep in contact with the Attorney General to make
sure that the Attorney General and Senator Baker were working
together.

The President recounted that he had told Senator Baker that he
would not permit White House staff to appear before the Select
Committee, rather he would only permit the taking of written
interrogatories. He told me he would never let Haldeman and
Ehrlichman go to the Hill. He also told me that Senator Gurney
would be very friendly to the White House and that it would not
be necessary to contact him because the President said Senator
Gurney would know what to do on his own.

I had received word before I arrived at my office that the
President wanted to see me. He asked me if I had talked to the
Attorney General regarding Senator Baker. I told him that the
Attorney General was seeking to meet with both Senator Ervin
and Senator Baker, but that a meeting date had not yet been
firmed up.

He said that he had read in the morning paper about the
Vesco case and asked me what part if any his brother Ed had
had in the matter. I told him what I knew of his brother's involvement, which was that he was an innocent agent in the contribution transaction. We then discussed the leak to Time magazine
of the fact that the White House had placed wiretaps on newsmen
and White House staff people. The President asked me if I knew
how this had leaked. I told him that I did not. He asked me who
knew about it. I told him that Mr. Sullivan, Mr. Mark Felt and
Mr. Mardian were aware of it.

I told him that Sullivan had told me that he thought that Director Hoover had told somebody about it shortly after it happened
because Hoover was against it and that Sullivan said that he had
heard that this information had gone to Rockefeller and in turn
had come back from Governor Rockefeller to Dr. Kissinger. We
then talked about the executive privilege statement and the President expressed his desire to get the statement out well in advance
of the Watergate hearings so that it did not appear to be in response to the Watergate hearings.

Before departing his office, he again raised the matter that I should report to him directly and not through Haldeman and Ehrlichman. I told him that I thought he should know that I was also involved in the post-June 17 activities regarding Watergate. I briefly described to him why I thought I had legal problems, in that I had been a conduit for many of the decisions that were made and therefore could be involved in an obstruction of justice. He would not accept my analysis and did not want me to get into it in any detail other than what I had just related. He reassured me not to worry, that I had no legal problems. (I raised this on another occasion with the President, when Dick Moore was present.)

Meeting of March 1: The first meeting on this date and the afternoon meeting which occurred on March 1 related to preparing the President for his forthcoming press conference. The President asked me a number of questions about the Gray nomination hearings and facts that had come out during these hearings.

In particular I can recall him stating that there should be no problem with the fact that I had received the F.B.I. reports. He said that I was conducting an investigation for him and that it would be perfectly proper for the Counsel to the President to have looked at these reports. I did not tell the President that I had not conducted an investigation for him because I assumed he was well aware of this fact and that the so-called Dean investigation was a public relations matter, and that frequently the President made reference in press conferences to things that never had, in fact occurred. I was also aware that often in answering Watergate questions that he had made reference to my report and I did not feel that I could tell the President that he could not use my name. There had been considerable adverse publicity stemming from the Gray hearings and the fact that Gray was turning over F.B.I. information to the Senate Judiciary Committee.

He also told me the F.B.I. Watergate materials should not be turned over by Gray. I informed him that I had a meeting several days prior with Mr. Sullivan who had been at the F.B.I. for many years and Sullivan had alluded to the fact that the F.B.I. had been used for political purposes by past Administrations. I cited a few examples that Mr. Sullivan had given me. The President told me to get this information from Sullivan. He also told me that I should gather any material I could gather regarding the uses and abuses of the F.B.I. by past Administrations so that we could show that we had not abused the F.B.I. for political purposes. The President told me that he was convinced that he had been wiretapped in 1968 and the fact that DeLoach had not been forthcoming indicated to the President that DeLoach was probably lying. He told me that I should call Don Kendall, De Loach's employer, and tell him that DeLoach had better start telling the truth because "the boys are coming out of the woodwork." He said this ploy may smoke DeLoach out.

He also asked me who else might know about the bugging of

his 1968 campaign, and I suggested that Mr. Tolson, Hoover's former assistant, might have some knowledge of it. He told me that he probably ought to call Mr. Tolson and wish him happy birthday or good health and possibly get some information from him when he talked to him.

It was during the days after this March 1 meeting with the President that the name Dean began coming increasingly to the forefront in the Gray confirmation hearings, and the rumblings were that there was going to be a situation where Dean could be called to the committee to testify and a number of Senators were anxious to use me as a vehicle to test executive privilege. On March 4 or 5, I had a conversation with Ehrlichman in which I told him that I thought it would be very difficult to maintain a court test of executive privilege over me, when in fact I had only met with the President infrequently and had had very few conversations with him that would be protected. It was following this conversation with Ehrlichman that I began meeting and talking with the President, at his request, with ever increasing frequency.

The President instructed me to tell the Attorney General to cut off Gray from turning over any further Watergate reports to the Senate Judiciary Committee. He said this just had to cease.

Meeting of March 13: This was a rather lengthy meeting, the bulk of which was taken up by a discussion about the Gray hearings and the fact that the Senate Judiciary Committee had voted to invite me to appear in connection with Gray's nomination. It was at this time we discussed the potential of litigating the matter of executive privilege and thereby preventing anybody from going before any Senate committee until that matter was resolved. The President liked the idea very much, particularly when I mentioned to him that it might be possible that he could also claim attorney/client privilege on me so that the strongest potential case on executive privilege would probably rest on the Counsel to the President.

I told him that obviously, this area would have to be researched. He told me that he did not want Haldeman and Ehrlichman to go before the Ervin hearings and that if we were litigating the matter on Dean, that no one would have to appear. Toward the end of the conversation, we got into a discussion of Watergate matters specifically. I told the President about the fact that there were money demands being made by the seven convicted defendants. And that the sentencing of these individuals was not far off. It was during this conversation that Haldeman came into the office. After this brief interruption by Haldeman's coming in, but while he was still there, I told the President about the fact that there was no money to pay these individuals to meet their demands. He asked me how much it would cost. I told him that I could only make an estimate that it might be as high as a million dollars or more. He told me that that was no problem, and he also looked over at Haldeman and repeated the same statement.

He then asked me who was demanding this money and I told him it was principally coming from Hunt through his attorney. The President then referred to the fact that Hunt had been promised executive clemency. He said that he had discussed this matter with Ehrlichman and contrary to instructions that Ehrlichman had given Colson not to talk to the President about it, that Colson had also discussed it with him later. He expressed some annoyance at the fact that Colson had also discussed this matter with him.

The conversation then turned back to a question from the President regarding the money that was paid to the defendants. He asked me how this was done. I told him I didn't know much about it other than the fact that the money was laundered so it could not be traced and then there were secret deliveries. I told him I was learning about things I had never known before, but the next time I would certainly be more knowledgeable. This comment got a laugh out of Haldeman. The meeting ended on this note and there was no further discussion of the matter and it was left hanging just as I have described it.

Meeting on March 15: It was late in the afternoon after the President's press conference. The President was amazed and distressed that the press had paid so little attention to the fact that he made an historic announcement about Ambassador Bruce opening up the liaison office in Peking. He said he was amazed when the first question following that announcement was regarding whether or not Dean would appear before the Senate Judiciary Committee in connection with the Gray hearings. The conversation then rambled into a discussion of the Hiss case.

It was during the afternoon of March 20 that I talked again with Dick Moore about this entire cover-up matter. I told Moore that there were new and more threatening demands for support money. I told him that Hunt had sent a message to me—through Paul O'Brien—that he wanted $72,000 for living expenses and $50,000 for attorney's fees and if he did not receive it that week, he would reconsider his options and have a lot to say about the seamy things he had done for Ehrlichman while at the White House. I told Moore that I had about reached the end of the line, and was now in a position to deal with the President to end the cover-up.

Phone conversation of March 20: When the President called and we had a rather rambling discussion, I told him at the conclusion of the conversation that I wanted to talk with him as soon as possible about the Watergate matter because I did not think that he fully realized all the facts and the implication of those facts for people at the White House as well as himself. He said that I should meet with him the next morning about 10 o'clock.

Before going in to tell the President some of these things, I decided I should call Haldeman because I knew that his name would come up in the matter. I called Haldeman and told him what I was going to do and Haldeman agreed that I should proceed to so inform the President of the situation.

Meeting of March 21: As I have indicated, my purpose in requesting this meeting particularly with the President was that I felt it necessary that I give him a full report of all the facts that I knew and explain to him what I believed to be the implication of those facts. It was my particular concern with the fact that the President did not seem to understand the implications of what was going on.

For example, when I had earlier told him that I thought I was involved in an obstruction of justice situation he had argued with me to the contrary after I had explained it to him. Also, when the matter of money demands had come up previously he had very nonchalantly told me that that was no problem and I did not know if he realized that he himself could be getting involved in an obstruction of justice situation by having promised clemency to Hunt. What I had hoped to do in this conversation was to have the President tell me that we had to end the matter now.

I began by telling the President that there was a cancer growing on the Presidency and that if the cancer was not removed that the President himself would be killed by it. I also told him that it was important that this cancer be removed immediately because it was growing more deadly every day. I then gave him what I told him would be a broad overview of the situation.

I told him I did not know if Mitchell had approved the plans but I had been told that Mitchell had been a recipient of the wiretap information and that Haldeman had also received such information through Strachan. I then proceeded to tell him some of the highlights that had occurred during the cover-up. I told him that Kalmbach had been used to raise funds to pay these seven individuals for their silence at the instructions of Ehrlichman, Haldeman, and Mitchell and I had been the conveyor of this instruction to Kalmbach. I told him that after the decision had been made that Magruder was to remain at the re-election committee I had assisted Magruder in preparing his false story for presentation to the grand jury. I told him that cash that had been at the White House had been funneled back to the re-election committee for the purpose of paying the seven individuals to remain silent.

I then proceeded to tell him that perjury had been committed, and for this cover-up to continue it would require more paying and more money. I told him that the demands of the convicted individuals were constantly increasing. I then told the President how this was just typical of the type of blackmail that the White House would continue to be subjected to and that I didn't know how to deal with it.

I also told the President that I thought that I would, as a result of my name coming out during the Gray hearings, be called before the grand jury and that if I was called to testify before the grand jury or the Senate committee I would have to tell the facts the way I know them. I said I did not know if executive privilege would be applicable to any appearance I might have before the grand jury.

I concluded by saying that it was going to take continued perjury and continued support of these individuals to perpetuate the cover-up and that I did not believe it was possible to continue it; rather I thought it was time for surgery on the cancer itself and that all those involved must stand up and account for themselves and that the President himself get out in front of this matter. I told the President that I did not believe that all of the seven defendants would maintain their silence forever. In fact, I thought that one or more would very likely break rank.

After I finished, I realized that I had not really made the President understand because after he asked a few questions, he suggested that it would be an excellent idea if I gave some sort of briefing to the Cabinet and that he was very impressed with my knowledge of the circumstances but he did not seem particularly concerned with their implications.

It was after my presentation to the President and during our subsequent conversation the President called Haldeman into the office and the President suggested that we have a meeting with Mitchell, Haldeman and Ehrlichman to discuss how to deal with this situation. What emerged from that discussion after Haldeman came into the office was that John Mitchell should account for himself for the pre-June 17 activities and the President did not seem concerned about the activities which had occurred after June 17.

After I departed the President's office I subsequently went to a meeting with Haldeman and Ehrlichman to discuss the matter further. The sum and substance of that discussion was that the way to handle this now was for Mitchell to step forward and if Mitchell were to step forward we might not be confronted with the activities of those involved in the White House in the cover-up. Accordingly, Haldeman, as I recall, called Mitchell and asked him to come down the next day for a meeting with the President on the Watergate matter.

In the later afternoon of March 21 Haldeman and Ehrlichman and I had a second meeting with the President.

[It] was a tremendous disappointment to me because it was quite clear that the cover-up as far as the White House was going to continue. I recall that while Haldeman, Ehrlichman and I were sitting at a small table in front of the President in his Executive Office Building office that I for the first time said in front of the President that I thought that Haldeman, Ehrlichman and Dean were all indictable for obstruction of justice and that was the reason I disagreed with all that was being discussed at that point in time.

It had been my impression that Haldeman and Ehrlichman were going to try to get Mitchell to come forward and explain his involvement in the matter. This did not occur. Mitchell said that he thought that everything was going along very well with the exception of the posture of the President on executive privilege. He said that he felt that the President was going to have to come back down somewhat or it would appear he was preventing information from coming out of the White House.

The meeting with the President, Ehrlichman, Haldeman, Mitchell and me was again a general discussion of the Senate Watergate hearings situation and did not accomplish anything. Rather, it was a further indication that there would be no effort to stop the cover-up from continuing. I recall that Mitchell told the President that he felt that the only problem that he now had was the fact that he was asking for a public beating on his posture on executive privilege. Mitchell was not suggesting that members of the White House go to the Hill to testify, rather that some more cooperative position be developed to avoid the adverse publicity.

The meeting was almost exclusively on the subject of how the White House should posture itself vis-à-vis the Ervin committee hearings. There was absolutely no indication of any changed attitude and it was like one of many, many meetings I had been in before, in which the talk was of strategies for dealing with the hearings rather than any effort to get the truth out.

Following this meeting with the President, it was apparent to me that I had failed in turning the President around, but Ehrlichman and Haldeman began taking over with regard to dealing with a new problem, which had become John Dean, as they were aware that I was very unhappy about the situation.

On Friday, March 23, Paul O'Brien called to tell me about Judge Sirica's reading McCord's letter in open court. I then called Ehrlichman to tell him about it. He said he had a copy of the letter.

After my conversation with Ehrlichman, the President called. Referring to our meeting on March 21 and McCord's letter, he said: "Well, John, you were right in your prediction." He then suggested I go up to Camp David and analyze the situation. He did not instruct me to write a report, rather he said to go to Camp David, take your wife and get some relaxation. He then alluded to the fact that I'd been under some rather intense pressure lately. But he had been through this all his life and you can't let it get to you. He said that he was able to do his best thinking at Camp David, and I should get some rest and then assess where we are and where we go from here and report back to him. I told him I would go.

My wife and I arrived at Camp David in the midafternoon. As we entered the cabin in which we were staying the phone was ringing. The operator said it was the President calling but Haldeman came on the phone. Haldeman said that while I was there I should spend some time writing a report on everything I knew about the Watergate. I said I would do so. I asked him if it was for internal use or public use. He said that would be decided later.

I spent the rest of the day and the next day thinking about this entire matter. I reached the conclusion, based on earlier conversations I had with Ehrlichman, that he would never admit to his involvement in the cover-up. I didn't know about Haldeman, but I assumed that he would not because he would believe it a higher duty to protect the President. The more I thought about it the more I realized that I should step forward because there was no way the situation was going to get better—rather it would only get worse. My most difficult problem was how I could end this mess without mortally wounding the President.

I called Mr. Moore and talked with him about it. We talked about a Presidential speech, where the President would really lay the facts out, we talked about immunity for everyone involved; we talked about a special Warren type commission that would put the facts out; we talked about some half measures that might satisfy the public interest; but we both realized that nothing less than the truth would sell.

March 28, Haldeman called me at Camp David and requested that I return to Washington. He told me that he was meeting with Mitchell and Magruder and that they wished to meet with me about my knowledge of the meetings in Mitchell's office.

I went to meet with Mitchell and Magruder. They told me they wished to talk to me about how I would handle any testimonial appearances regarding the Jan. 27 and Feb. 4 meetings which had occurred in Mitchell's office.

Magruder said that it had been I who had suggested that the meetings be treated as dealing exclusively with the election law and that explained my presence. I told them that there was no certainty that I would be called before the grand jury or the Senate committee. That that if I were called, I might invoke executive privilege, so the question of my testimony was still moot. They were obviously both disappointed that I was being reluctant in agreeing to continue to perpetuate their earlier testimony.

On either March 28 or 29, Mr. Krogh came to my office. He said he had come to express sympathy for me as a result of the adverse publicity I had received during the Gray hearings. He then began telling me that he had not himself had a good day since his own confirmation hearings and that he had been haunted by his experiences at the White House.

I told Krogh that I thought that there was a very likely possibility that the Senate Watergate committee could stumble into the Ellsberg burglary. I told him that there were documents in the possession of the Justice Department which had been provided by the C.I.A. in connection with the Watergate investigation which contained pictures of Liddy standing in front of Mr. Ellsberg's doctor's office in California. I told him that I had learned from the C.I.A. that these pictures had been left in a camera returned by Hunt to the C.I.A. and the C.I.A. had developed the pictures. I said I did not believe that the Justice Department knew what the pictures were all about but that any investigator worth his salt would probably track down the incident as a result of the pictures. I told him that Ehrlichman had requested that I retrieve the documents from the Justice Department and get them back to the C.I.A. where they might be withheld from the committee investigations but the C.I.A. had been unwilling to do it.

Krogh was very distressed to hear this news but said that maybe it was for the best in that he had personally been haunted by this incident for so long that he would like to get it out in the open. I asked him if he had received his authorization to proceed with the burglary from Ehrlichman. Krogh responded that no, he did not believe that Ehrlichman had been aware of the incident until shortly after it had occurred: rather, he had received his orders right out of the "Oval Office." I was so surprised to hear this that I said, "You must be kidding." And he repeated again that he had received his instructions out of the Oval Office.

April 2 my attorneys went to the Government prosecutors and told them that I was willing to come forward with everything I knew about the case.

As I began explaining what I knew it was evident that the prosecutors had no conception of how extensive the cover-up was so I tried to provide them with all the details that I could remember. Also, as the conversations regarding the cover-up began to get into more and more specifics we moved into areas that came closer and closer to the President, but prior to April 15 I did not discuss any of the areas of Presidential involvement.

I felt that I should tell Haldeman that I was going to meet with the prosecutors so I called him. He said that I should not meet with the prosecutors because, as he said, "Once the toothpaste is out of the tube, it's going to be very hard to get it back in."

During the week of April 9 to April 14, I had several conversations with Ehrlichman and Haldeman. I recall some discussions, however, regarding getting Mitchell to step forward. The theory was—"if Mitchell takes the rap the public will have a high level person and be satisfied and the matter will end."

The more I told the prosecutors about the cover-up the more interested they became in it. At this time, Haldeman and Ehrlichman were still unaware of my direct dealings with the prosecutors.

I did not tell them at that point that I had had private meetings with the prosecutors or that I had told the prosecutors of the extent of involvement of Haldeman and Ehrlichman [but] I was quite confident that I had gotten the message through to Ehrlichman and Haldeman that they had a serious problem themselves and I had put them on final notice that I wasn't playing the cover-up game any longer.

I realized that indeed my message had gotten through, about one o'clock on Saturday night or Sunday morning, I received a call from Mr. Shaffer. He said that the prosecutor had called him and that the Attorney General had called Mr. Petersen and them and wanted a full report on everything that was going on before the grand jury and where the grand jury was headed. The meeting with the Attorney General was to occur about 2 A.M. at the Attorney General's home. The Attorney General was being summoned to the President's office the next morning to discuss the entire matter. I told Mr. Shaffer that I had hoped to tell the President personally that I had gone to the prosecutors several weeks ago.

I then wrote out a message for the President. In short, I told the President that I hoped he did not interpret my going to the prosecutors as an act of disloyalty, that I would meet with him if he wished to discuss the matter with me. Within 45 minutes of sending this message I had a call from the White House operator informing me that the President wished to meet me at 9 P.M.

Meeting with the President, April 15: The President was very cordial when we met. I told the President that I had gone to the prosecutors. And, that I did not believe that this was an act of disloyalty but, rather in the end it would be an act of loyalty. I informed the President that I told the prosecutors of my own involvement and the involvement of others. The President almost from the outset began asking me a number of leading questions, which made me think that the conversation was being taped and that a record was being made to protect himself.

I also recall that the conversation turned to the matter of Liddy not talking. He said something about Liddy was waiting for a signal and I told him that possibly he was waiting for a signal from the President.

It was during this part of the conversation that the President picked up the telephone and called Henry Petersen and pretended with Petersen that I was not in the room but that the matter of Liddy's coming forward and talking had arisen during our conversation. The President relayed to Petersen that if Liddy's lawyer wanted to see him to get a signal that the President was willing to do this. The President also asked me about Petersen and I told him if anyone could give him good advice Henry Petersen could.

Toward the end of the conversation the President recalled the fact that at one point we had discussed the difficulty in raising money and that he had said that one million dollars was nothing to raise to pay to maintain the silence of the defendants. He said that he had, of course, only been joking when he made that comment. As the conversation went on, and it is impossible for me to recall anything other than the high points of it, I became more convinced that the President was seeking to elicit testimony from me and put his perspective on the record and get me to agree to it. The most interesting thing that happened during the conversation was, very near the end, he got up out of his chair, went behind his chair to the corner of the Executive Office Building office and in a barely audible tone said to me, he was probably foolish to have discussed Hunt's clemency with Colson. I do not recall that I responded. The conversation ended shortly thereafter.

Meeting with the President, April 16: I received word on Monday morning, April 16, that the President had requested I come to the Oval Office. I went into Mr. Steve Bull's office.

Mr. Bull told be I would have to wait a few minutes because the President was in another meeting. A few minutes later Haldeman and Ehrlichman emerged laughing from the President's office and when they saw me in Mr. Bull's office their faces dropped. They said hello, put on a serious look and departed. I went into the President's office.

The President told me that he had been thinking about this entire matter and thought it might be a good idea if he had in his drawer a letter from me requesting that he accept my resignation or in the alternative an indefinite leave of absence. He said that he had prepared two letters for my signature and he would not do anything with them at this time but thought it would be good if he had them.

After reading the letters, I looked the President squarely in the eyes and told him that I could not sign the letters. He was annoyed with me, and somewhat at a loss for words. He said that maybe I would like to draft my own letter. I told him that the letters that he had asked me to sign were virtual confessions of anything regarding the Watergate. I also asked him if Ehrlichman and Haldeman had signed letters of resignations. I recall that he was somewhat surprised at my asking this and he said no they had not but they had given him a verbal assurance to the same effect. I then told him that he had my verbal assurance to the same effect.

It was a tense conversation. As I sat there talking with the President, I had very much on my mind the laughter in Ehrlichman's and Haldeman's voices when they walked out of the office. The President said that he would like me to draft my own letter and would also like a suggested draft letter for Haldeman and Ehrlichman or maybe a form letter that everyone could sign.

The President called me to come to his E.O.B. office about 4:00 that afternoon. He asked me if I had drafted a letter. I said that I had.

I then told him that I would not resign unless Haldeman and Ehrlichman resigned. I told him that I was not willing to be the White House scapegoat for the Watergate. He said that he understood my position and he wasn't asking me to be a scapegoat. The gist of the statement was twofold: First, the President had learned of new facts in the case over the weekend and as a result of this information had directed Henry Petersen to take charge and leave no stone unturned; secondly, that he had accepted requests from Haldeman, Ehrlichman and Dean to be placed on leave of absence. The President said virtually nothing about the statement and after reading it told me to talk with Len Garment, who he said was also preparing a draft.

After departing from the President's office, I called Mr. Garment and told him that the President had requested that I give him my input on the draft he was developing. Mr. Garment said he would come to my office, which he did. I gave him a copy of the draft statement, and he told me that he and I were thinking along similar lines, that is, that Haldeman, Ehrlichman and Dean had to resign. I told him I was ready and willing but only if Haldeman and Ehrlichman resigned as well.

April 17 call from the President: On April 17, the President called and informed me that he would issue a statement very shortly. That statement of April 17 is a matter of public record. I would only like to point out one or two items about the statement. The President said that on March 21, as a result of serious charges which came to his attention, some of which were publicly reported, began an intense new inquiry into the whole matter. I would merely refer the committee's attention back to my earlier testimony as to what the President did after my report to him on March 21 as to the White House's deep involvement in the cover-up. In short, the President, Haldeman and Ehrlichman commenced to protect themselves against the unraveling of the cover-up.

Secondly, I would also like to raise the paragraph that had been put in the statement that no one in a position of major importance in the Administration should be given immunity from prosecution. While this statement went virtually unnoticed by the public, it was very evident to me what the President was saying: Dean will not be a witness against anyone so the Government might as well stop dealing with him.

On Monday night, April 16, I had learned that the President had informed the Government that he allegedly had taped a conversation in which I had told him I was seeking immunity from the Government in exchange for testimony on Haldeman and Ehrlichman. I have no recollection of ever telling the President that I was so negotiating with the Government and the President told me very specifically that he did not want to do anything to interfere with any negotiations I was having with the Government.

When I learned this from my attorney I suggested that he request that the Government call for the tape and listen to the tape because I told him it must be a reference to the meeting I had with the President on April 15 and if that conversation were taped the Government would have a pretty good idea of the dimensions of the case they were dealing with. I was referring to the fact that the President had mentioned the million dollar conversation and the fact that he had talked to Colson about clemency for Hunt.

I do not in fact know if such a tape exists but if it does and has not been tampered with and is a complete transcript of the entire conversation that took place in the President's office, I think that this committee should have that tape because I believe that it would corroborate many of the things that this committee has asked me to testify about.

When the President issued his statement of April 17, I decided that indeed I was being set up and that it was time that I let the word out that I would not be a scapegoat. Accordingly, on April 19, I issued a statement to that effect.

On April 22, Easter Sunday, the President called me to wish me a happy Easter. It was what they refer to at the White House as a "stroking" call.

On April 30, while out of the city, I had a call from my secretary in which she informed me that the wire services were carrying a story that my resignation had been requested and accepted and that Haldeman and Ehrlichman were also resigning.

June 26, 1973

MR. DASH: Mr. Dean, you stated, did you not, that well before the so-called Liddy plan spelled out in meetings on Jan. 27 and Feb. 4, 1972, that there was an atmosphere in the White House conducive to the bugging and break-in of the Democratic National Commitee headquarters. Is that true?

A. That is correct.

Q. Is it not true that although you expressed amazement at the mind boggling, as you described it, Liddy plan in the Attorney General's office on Jan. 27, 1972, you, along with Mr. Mitchell, and Mr. Magruder did encourage Liddy to scale down this plan and budget and you didn't tell him to stop the activity?

A. That is correct. With hindsight, I probably should have been much more forceful in trying to stop the plan when I realized it was something that should not occur.

Q. Well, Mr. Dean, after the scaled down Liddy plan presented in Mitchell's office on Feb. 4, '72, which did not include the activity of mugging, kidnapping or prostitution, but primarily electronic surveillance or break-ins although you say you disassociated yourself from it, as the White House representative you did not, in fact, tell Liddy to stop it. A. That is correct.

Q. And although you say that you told Haldeman that the White House should not be involved with the plan you did not recommend that Haldeman put a stop to it, which you knew he could if he wanted to?

A. Given the circumstances that were existing at the time, I felt that someone wanted this. I knew I had put those on notice involved that I was going to have no part in it.

Q. Now, during January and June of 1972, did you, in fact, know that Mr. Magruder, who has testified before this committee, was giving Gordon Strachan full reports of the Liddy plan, including the break-in and the fruits of the break-in? A. No, I did not.

Q. Now, in fact, after the June 17 break-in and more specifically on June 19, I think your statement indicates that you were told by Mr. Strachan that he destroyed at the direction of Mr. Haldeman certain intelligence reports that came from the C.R.P., is that not true? A. That is correct.

Q. So that at that time you did have some knowledge of Mr. Strachan's knowledge? A. That is correct.

Q. Well, if Strachan did, in fact, receive reports from Magruder in the Liddy operation, do you have an opinion as to whether he would have forwarded these reports to Mr. Haldeman?

A. My opinion is that he would report everything he knew in some form to Mr. Haldeman.

Q. In your statement, you have described a number of meetings and activities occurring immediately after the arrest of the C.R.P. burglars in the Democratic National Committee headquarters in the Watergate on June 17, '72, and continuing for several months thereafter, involving such persons as Mr. Haldeman, Mr. Ehrlichman, Mr. Colson, Mr. Mardian, Mr. Mitchell, Mr. LaRue, Mr. Magruder, yourself and others.

Isn't it your testimony that this flurry of activity represented a massive cover-up operation to prevent the prosecutors, the F.B.I. and the public from learning of the involvement of high White House or C.R.P. officials, either in the Watergate break-in or embarrassing earlier illegal activities of a similar nature such as the Ellsberg break-in? A. That is correct, Mr. Dash.

Q. And did not this cover-up require a number of strategies such as perjury and subornation of perjury of Magruder, Porter and others, and the undermining of the judicial process, payoffs to indicted defendants to maintain their silence, limiting the F.B.I. inquiry so they would not stumble on other illegal intelligence activities of the White House? A. That is correct.

Q. And is it not true that you played a role in all of these cover-up activities? A. That is correct.

Q. Did you do these things on your own initiative, Mr. Dean, or at any direction of anybody else?

A. I would have to say that to describe it, I inherited a situation. The cover-up was in operation when I returned to my office on Monday, the 19th, and it just became the instant way of life at that point in time.

Q. From whom were you taking instructions?

A. I was taking instructions from Mr. Haldeman, Mr. Ehrlichman, I was taking instructions and suggestions from Mr. Mitchell and Mr. Mardian.

I was a conveyor of messages back and forth between each group and at times, I was making suggestions myself.

Q. Given such a massive cover-up operation that was under way with the approval and with the direction at times of Mr. Haldeman, Mr. Ehrlichman and Mr. Mitchell, do you have an opinion—and I am asking you at this point for just an opinion—

as to whether the President would have been informed of this cover-up operation from its inception?

A. Mr. Dash, I think it is unfair to ask me opinions. I can surmise from the way I know the White House operated. I had reached a conclusion in my own mind that this thing might well go right to the President.

Q. According to your own statement, in fact, you learned first-hand, did you not, that the President did know about the cover-up when you met with him on Sept. 15, 1972, the day the indictments came down cutting off at the involvement of Liddy. Is that so? A. That is correct.

Q. When the President told you on Sept. 15 that Bob Haldeman had kept him posted on your handling of the Watergate case, and complimented you on the good job you had done and on the difficulty of your tasks, did you have any doubt in your mind what the President was talking about? A. No, I did not.

Q. Indeed, Mr. Haldeman not only knew how you handled the Watergate case but, in effect, he had directed the operation, did he not, which included pay-offs to defendants, perjury and limiting the F.B.I. investigation?

A. The Kalmbach payments had been involved so I would say, yes, that he had, as well as being aware of the perjury.

Q. Now, if the President had been kept posted by Mr. Haldeman as to how you were handling the Watergate case he would have known of these illegal acts and according to your statement was, did in fact congratulate you for your successful performance of these acts, would that not be true from your point of view?

A. I think that is true.

Q. Therefore, Mr. Dean, whatever doubts you may have had prior to Sept. 15 about the President's involvement in the cover-up, did you have any doubts yourself about this after Sept. 15?

A. No, I did not.

Q. Mr. Dean, you opened up your statement when you first began to testify before this committee yesterday by purporting to soften the blow concerning the President by stating that you do not believe the President realized the full implications of his involvement. Now, if you have told the truth before this committee about what the President said to you on Sept. 15 and what you said to him, and as to the subsequent meetings you had with the President, can you honestly believe that the President, as a lawyer, and a sophisticated man in politics was not aware of the full implications of the cover-up activities?

A. Mr. Dash, I think my opening remarks were more directed at the human side of the situation than the legal side to the situation, that he had—he didn't realize the implications as far as what this would mean to people he had worked with for a number of years, people he was very fond of and I was not necessarily referring to the full legal implications of some of his activities.

Q. Well, do you have a belief as to whether or not he did have knowledge of the implications, the legal implications of this cover-up activity?

A. I would think the President would certainly have some appreciation of the legal problems involved, yes indeed.

MR. THOMPSON: I would like to ask you a few questions based upon some of your testimony yesterday concerning your contacts with Mr. Petersen.

A. The first time I had contact with Mr. Petersen is when the Attorney General called Mr. Petersen to his office and that was either on the 19th or the 20th.

Q. Do I recall your testimony correctly that you told him that you did not believe the White House could stand a wide open investigation?

A. I told him, we discussed the implications of a wide open investigation and how embarrassing that could be in an election year, that is correct.

Q. Well, did he indicate to you in any way that he would carry out anything less than a wide open investigation of this matter?

A. I left the meeting with an impression that Mr. Petersen would be fair in an investigation of the White House and that that interpretation of fairness would mean that we wouldn't have an investigation of everything that occurred in the White House for four years.

Q. Do I understand your testimony that you were only concerned that he not go back into the prior four years to bring up unrelated matters that had nothing to do with this particular incident?

A. The highlights of my recollection at that point are that we discussed what this would mean if this investigation led all the way to the President.

Q. As I understand your statement now, just based upon your knowledge, you know of no impropriety in conducting his part of the investigation on Mr. Petersen's part?

A. I know of no impropriety. I think he tried to be very fair with the White House in dealing with the White House and the fact that he had an investigation going on in a political year, that it could result in embarrassment.

Q. You mentioned also Mr. Ziegler, and of course, we all know the statements that he continuously made during this matter. Who was supplying Mr. Ziegler his information?

A. I would say that basically, I supplied a large amount of it. I think that Mr. Ziegler would check many times with Mr. Ehrlichman, sometimes with Mr. Haldeman, and often with the President himself, he would check out a given statement.

Q. Did Mr. Ziegler know the truth?

A. No, he did not. In fact, that was a very difficult situation. Mr. Ziegler, on countless occasions, asked me to brief him. I on several occasions asked Mr. Ehrlichman if I could brief Ziegler. I was given very specific instructions that I was not to brief Ziegler.

Q. Would it be fair to say, then, that on occasion, on numerous occasions, you misinformed Mr. Ziegler?

A. I would not say misinformed him as much as to tell him how to take the offensive so that he could save a given situation. I can think of one occasion where we talked about the secret fund that was at the White House and he said, how do I handle that? I said, well, that is a matter of interpretation. It is a secret to some people, but since we know of it, it obviously is not a secret, so you don't need to say it is a secret fund. So that is the way that was handled.

On, for example, the leaking to Time magazine of the story regarding surveillance of the White House staff and newsmen, that did present a real quandary to me, so I called Ehrlichman for guidance. I was aware what happened. I asked Ehrlichman for guidance on how to handle it. He said, just flat out deny it. Now, that was a flat out lie.

Q. After the break-in on the 15th I believe that you had a meeting in Mr. Mitchell's apartment with Mr. Mitchell, Mr. Mardian, Mr. Magruder, on the 19th after you returned to Washington.

In your listening between Mr. Mitchell and Mr. Magruder, did not your mind go back to those previous meetings? Did you not wonder whether or not in fact Mr. Liddy had been given the go-ahead?

A. That had already occurred to me. Magruder had told me this was all Liddy's fault. It was very clear to me then that Liddy had proceeded, either with or without authorization. It was after I talked with Liddy that I was very clear in my understanding that Liddy had been given authorization to proceed.

Q. You never talked to Mr. Mitchell about it. A. No sir.

Q. What had been your professional relationship with Mr. Mitchell while you were at the Justice Department? A. I would have to say it was sort of a father-son relationship in many ways.

Q. Were you concerned about his personal involvement after you heard about the break-in?

A. I indeed was but to this day there has been only one indication that he had any involvement in this thing at all and that was when I hypothesized to him what I thought had happened and he said something to the effect, "Well, yes, it was something like that but we thought it was going to be two or three times removed from the committee."

SENATOR TALMADGE: Mr. Dean, you realize, of course, that you have made very strong charges against the President of the United States that involves him in criminal offenses, do you not? A. Yes sir, I do.

Q. What makes you think that your credibility is greater than that of the President, who denies what you have said?

A. I have told it exactly the way I know it. I don't say that I— you are asking me a public relations question, really, in a sense, why I would have greater credibility than the President of the United States? I am telling you just as I know it.

Q. I believe you testified that you met with the President in March of this year and informed him fully about your participation and the participation of others in the cover-up of the Watergate incident. What was the President's reaction when you told him about the complicity of the individuals in the White House?

A. Well, I felt he had not gotten the message that I was trying to convey through to the President, and I think that the subsequent meeting that afternoon and the meeting the next day with the President indicated to me that there was more concern about this committee and its hearings than doing anything affirmative about what I told the President.

Q. What did the President say when you told him about you and Ehrlichman and Haldeman all being subject to indictment?

A. I don't recall the President's reaction as much as I recall Mr. Ehrlichman's reaction when he expressed displeasure. There was a general discussion, and I was just amazed at the discussion going on and I just kept shaking my head because the President would say to me, "Do you agree with this?" And I would say, "No, I don't," and finally I said, "The reason I don't agree with this is because I think that Mr. Haldeman, Mr. Ehrlichman and I are indictable for obstruction of justice."

Q. Did the President seem surprised when you gave him this information? A. No sir, he did not.

Q. Let us see if I have the sequence on the immediate aftermath of the break-in correct now. After the break-in in June, you saw Mr. Liddy.

A. Well, sir, I will give you the sequence. As I arrived back on Sunday night, the 18th, I was informed by my assistant that McCord had been one of the individuals arrested and that one of the Cubans had a check from Mr. Hunt. The next morning, I had a call from Mr. Magruder who told me that this whole thing is Liddy's fault. I then had a call from Mr. Ehrlichman who said, "I think you ought to meet with Liddy." I then met with Mr. Liddy about noon and he gave me his report. It was in that afternoon that Mr. Strachan came into my office and told me that he had been instructed by Mr. Haldeman to destroy documents.

Q. Mr. Strachan told you that Mr. Haldeman ordered him to go through Mr. Haldeman's files and destroy materials which included documents relating to wiretap information from the Democratic National Committee, is that correct? A. That is correct.

Q. Then shortly thereafter Mr. Ehrlichman told you to throw the contents of Hunt's safe in the river, is that correct?

A. Well, he told me I should throw the briefcase in the river and he told me to shred the documents.

Q. Now, after all of those facts occurred, were available to you why did you not, as Counsel of the President, go to him at that time and tell him what was happening?

A. Senator, I did not have access to the President. I never was presumptuous enough to try to pound on the door and get in because I knew that just did not work that way.

Q. You mean you were Counsel to the President of the United States, and you could not get access to him if you wanted to, is that your testimony?

A. No, sir, I thought it would be presumptuous of me to try, because I felt, I was told my reporting channel was Mr. Haldeman and Mr. Ehrlichman and I was reporting everything I knew to them.

Q. When you met with Attorney General Kleindienst on the 19th and 20th of June, did you tell him about the meetings of Jan. 27 and Feb. 4, 1972, with Mr. Liddy and Mr. Magruder and Mitchell during, when buggings were considered? A. No, sir, I did not.

Q. Why did you not tell him at that time?

A. Because I knew that would put him in a position that he would have to pursue his investigation, and Mr. Kleindienst had told me when we talked generally about the thing that he said he would never sit in the Attorney General's office and prosecute Mr. Mitchell and I did not want to put this on Mr. Kleindienst at this point in time.

SENATOR WEICKER: Now, Mr. Dean, would you be good enough then to read to the committee the memorandum from you to Mr. Mitchell dated September, 1970 [regarding the establishment of an interagency domestic intelligence unit].

[Mr. Dean reads the memorandum. See Documents.]

Q. So, after this memorandum was written, you then proceeded to set up the I.E.C. [Intelligence Evaluation Committee] insofar as the structure, the placing of it in the Internal Security Division [of the Justice Department], is that correct?

A. I believe that Mr. Mitchell did have a conversation with Mr. Hoover and reached some agreement as to their participation. I don't know how the decision was made to place it in the internal security unit, but I did learn about it at some point because they told me they had space set aside in the internal security unit's office.

There was a continual request for information regarding demonstrations and particularly information that would embarrass individuals in connection with their relationship with demonstrators or demonstration leaders.

Q. Outside of the area of demonstrations, did any information come to you from the Internal Security Division which could have a political value?

A. I am sure it could have, but without looking at my files, it is impossible for me to remember.

Q. All right. Let us move on to where you refer to your conversation with Mr. Mardian.

"It was not until almost a year or more later that I learned the reason for Mardian's trip to see the President. Mr. Mardian later told me, in a social conversation, that he had gone to see the President to get instructions regarding the disposition of wiretap logs that related to newsmen and White House staffers who were suspected of leaking."

Can you expand on your conversation with Robert Mardian?

A. He said, well, there were some wiretaps and I had gotten the logs from Sullivan and I had to get instructions on what to do with them and I was told to give them to Ehrlichman.

There had been on the rumor mill at the White House for sometime that the White House had instructed a surveillance of White House staff members and newsmen in dealing with leaks.

Q. Then comes Feb. 22 or 23 of this year, and to paraphrase your testimony I gather you were placed in position of trying to find out about the leaks with the F.B.I. relative to a potential *Time* magazine story?

A. That is right. I said that I had this inquiry from the press office regarding this and I had some information that in fact it had happened, and I wondered what the facts were. Mr. Sullivan told me that he had at one point gotten the most trusted people in the Washington field office to undertake the function.

Q. Mr. Dean, let me be very clear here so we try to put this story together. You were informed earlier in '72 by Mr. Mardian that he had in his possession the logs of the Kissinger taps, is that correct?

A. That is correct, that he had turned them over.

Q. And then in 1973 in an interview with Mr. Sullivan, Mr. Sullivan indicated to you that in fact the taps were accomplished by the Washington field office of the F.B.I. A. Yes.

Q. He indicated to you that Mr. Hoover disapproved of this particular set of taps, is that correct?

A. That is the impression I had. I had been told that something had to be done for Bill Sullivan. I was never clear on exactly what it was that Mr. Sullivan had done that the White House owed him some favor for.

Q. In your talk with Mr. Sullivan, or in your contacts with him, was he ever requested to prepare a memorandum relative to F.B.I. involvement with other Presidents in so far as the political aspects were concerned?

A. Yes, he was. The President was very interested and asked me to obtain the information from Mr. Sullivan. He himself typed out a memorandum that contained his best recollection of some of the political uses that have been made of the F.B.I. by preceding administrations.

Q. All right. Is there any other use that you made or the White House made of the F.B.I. on matters such as that?

A. I can recall again, after the fact, getting involved in a situation that involved an F.B.I. investigation that was made of Mr. Daniel Schorr. Mr. Higby, who was Mr. Haldeman's assistant, had received a request from Mr. Haldeman when he was traveling with the President, to direct the F.B.I. to do an investigation of Mr. Schorr. Mr. Hoover proceeded with the investigation but, to the dismay of the White House, he did a sort of a full field wide open investigation, and this became very apparent. So this put the White House in a rather scrambling position to explain what had happened. The long and short of the explanation was that Mr. Schorr was being considered for a post and that this was a part of a preliminary investigation.

Q. All right. Any other instances that you recollect as to the use of the F.B.I. by the White House that either involved the F.B.I. or the Internal Revenue Service, C.I.A., military intelligence, alcohol, tobacco and firearms, Secret Service.

A. At one point, one of the top officials at the Secret Service brought me a small intelligence print-out regarding Senator McGovern.

It had to do with Mr., with Senator McGovern attending a fund-raising function, I believe in Philadelphia, and apparently there were some references in the intelligence statement to the fact that either Communist, former Communist supporters were going to attend the fund-raiser.

I took the document to Mr. Colson and I said, "Are you interested in this? I assume it was given to me not to bury in my files."

He said, "I am very interested in it." He took it and later told me he had made arrangements to have it published.

I do not recall receiving anything that we might call politically embarrassing from the C.I.A. about any individual.

With regard to the I.R.S., after an article was published on Mr. Rebozo I got instructions that one of the authors of that article should have some problems. I did not know how to deal directly with the situation. I discussed it with Mr. Caulfield. I was reluctant to call Mr. Walters, who was the head of the Internal Revenue Service and suggest that he do anything about this. Mr. Caulfield apparently had friends in Internal Revenue Service and I believe he told me he was able to accomplish an audit on the individual. What the consequences of the audit was I do not know.

Q. Who is the individual?

A. I do not recall for certain. It was one of the, I think it was one of the Newsday persons who worked on a rather extensive article on Mr. Rebozo.

Q. I think it has become clear here this afternoon that another step has been taken, another step further along the road, the plan of 1970, which plan included bugging, breaking in, burglary and the like, that the first step was taken; and also, that even though that particular unit did not involve itself in any illegal activities, certainly the security arms of the United States Government were

in various instances which you have cited utilized for purposes
not intended.

A. I do, of course, know and as I have submitted in documents, other agencies were involved in seeking politically embarrassing information on individuals who were thought to be the
enemies of the White House.

There was also maintained what was called an "enemies list,"
which was rather extensive and continually being updated.

Q. I am not going to ask who was on it. I am afraid you
might answer. I wonder, are these documents that are in the
possession of the committee?

A. No, but I would be happy to submit them to the committee.

SENATOR MONTOYA: Now, let's go into the statements
made by the President. On Aug. 29, 1972, the President made
this statement:

"In addition to that, within our own staff, under my direction,
Counsel to the President, Mr. Dean, has conducted a complete
investigation of all leads which might involve any present members of the White House staff or anybody in the Government. I
can say categorically that his investigation indicates that no one
in the White House staff, no one in this Administration presently employed, was involved in this very bizarre incident."

Was the President telling the truth when he made that statement?

A. If that were to be a literal statement as to somebody being
involved in the very particular incident which occurred on June
17, that would have been a true statement.

I think it was a little broad.

Q. Mr. Dean, now I ask you about the press conference of
October, 1972, held by the President, and I quote from his press
conference:

"I conducted the investigation of the Hiss case. It was successful. The F.B.I. did a magnificent job, but that investigation involving the security of this country was basically a Sunday school
exercise compared to the amount of effort that was put into this"
—meaning the Watergate—"I agreed with the amount of effort
that was put into it. I wanted every lead carried out to the
end, because I wanted to be sure that no member of the White
House staff and no man or woman in a position of management
responsibility in the Committee for Re-election had anything to
do with this kind of reprehensible activity."

Now, would you say that the President was correct in making
those statements at that time?

A. I can say this, Senator. I certainly did not prepare anything
for the briefing book that would let him make that statement.

Q. Now, on April 17, 1973, the President said this: "I condemn
any attempts to cover up in this case, no matter who is involved."
Do you believe he was telling the truth on that date? A. No,
sir.

Q. Will you state why?

A. Well, because by that time, he knew the full implications of the case and Mr. Haldeman and Mr. Ehrlichman were certainly still on the staff and there was considerable resistance to their departure from the staff.

Q. Now, on May 22, 1973, the President made this statement: "With regard to the specific allegations that have been made I can and do state categorically.

"1. I had no prior knowledge of the Watergate operation.

"2. I took no part in nor was I aware of any subsequent efforts that may have been made to cover up Watergate.

"3. At no time did I authorize any offer of executive clemency for the Watergate defendants nor did I know of any such offer.

"4. I did not know until the time of my own investigation of any effort to provide the Watergate defendants with funds.

"5. At no time did I attempt nor did I authorize others to attempt to implicate the C.I.A. in the Watergate matter.

"6. It was not until the time of my own investigation that I learned of the break-in in the office of Mr. Ellsberg's psychiatrist, and I specifically authorized the furnishing of this information to Judge Byrne.

"7. I neither authorized nor encouraged subordinates to engage in illegal or improper campaign tactics."

Now, will you respond as to the correctness of this particular statement by the President?

A. Well, in totality, I think there are less than accurate statements in the statement. Let me take it point by point.

I do not know, with regard to point 1.

I believe the President was aware of an effort to cover up the Watergate, point 2.

On number 4, he indicated his own investigation started on the 21st. [Regarding point 3], a conversation with the President myself in which he mentioned the fact that he had talked to Colson and Ehrlichman regarding clemency for Mr. Hunt, and also prior to that I was aware of the fact that Mr. Colson told me in January that he had talked to the President, Ehrlichman told me he had talked to the President and that message was, in turn, relayed to Mr. Bittman and then relayed to Mr. Hunt.

Now, on point number 5, I have no first-hand knowledge on that.

Q. You didn't work on the arrangements to try to get C.I.A. to come into the picture and modify the impact?

A. On point number 6 I only have hearsay knowledge.

Q. What about number 7? Number 7 is as follows: "I neither authorized nor encouraged subordinates to engage in any illegal or improper campaign tactics."

A. I have no first-hand knowledge about that.

June 27, 1973

SENATOR GURNEY: We have had a great deal of testimony, 245 pages of your statement as well as the testimony yesterday, and I must say it is hard to know where to begin in all this. I think probably the best place to start always is at the beginning. Would you say that it is fair to say that Gordon Liddy's plan of bugging and electronic espionage really started out the whole Watergate affair?

A. Well, there was an atmosphere that might have been several precursors source to that plan. The plan was an accident of fate where they culminated into Mr. Liddy's specific proposal that was presented in the Attorney General's office in the two meetings which occurred in late January and early February.

Q. The Jan. 27 meeting occurred and as I recall, you testified that the original plan—and I do not know what the word was that you used to describe it, but—

A. I think I called it a "Mission Impossible" plan.

Q. Did you ever talk to Mr. Mitchell or Mr. Magruder after this horrendous plan?

A. As I recall, the only conversation I had was a very brief conversation. Mr. Liddy was taking the charts off the easel and they were preparing to leave the office when I paused in front of Mr. Mitchell's desk and he told me that this was certainly out of the question.

Q. Well, did it worry you that this man came up with kidnapping, prostitution, mugging, and all the rest of it? A. Yes, sir, it did.

Q. Why did you not go back to the President and tell him about this hair-raising scheme?

A. Well, I did go back, but I did not have access to the President, as I think I explained. I went to Mr. Haldeman.

Q. Did you try to gain access to the President?

A. Senator, I did not try.

I had never been into the President or called by the President before. My reporting channel was through Mr. Haldeman and I went back and told what I thought was the proper reporting channel. I told him what I had seen, told him my reaction to it, told him that I thought it was unwise, unnecessary, and Mr. Haldeman agreed with me.

Q. Now, then, you mentioned in your testimony yesterday in response to Mr. Dash that you inherited the cover-up. Would you tell how you inherited the cover-up?

A. When I came back to the office on the 18th and talked to Mr. Strachan, I realized that the cover-up was already in effect, in being, and I realized that when Mr. Strachan told me of the documents that he had destroyed and Mr. Haldeman's instruction, that there certainly wasn't going to be a revelation of the

White House involvement in the matter. I didn't at that point in time know the potentials of the White House involvement.

Q. Was not one of the first meetings of the cover-up held in John Mitchell's apartment on the 19th of June?

A. Senator, I would say that the day of, to my knowledge, the day of the 19th at the White House was a very busy day. That the calls I received from Mr. Ehrlichman, from Mr. Colson, the meetings I had with Mr. Ehrlichman and then again later with Mr. Colson about the safe were long before I went to the meeting at Mr. Mitchell's apartment, which I do not recall was on the 19th or 20th. I do recall a meeting in Mr. Mitchell's office but I do not recall specifically which day it was.

Q. Well, what you are saying is then that these several phone calls you had with all of these people really had to do with at least the beginnings of the cover-up, is that right? Well, you were in on it from the beginning, were you not? A. Yes, sir.

Q. You really did not inherit anything. You were in on the sort of hatching of it, were you not? Who set the policy on the cover-up?

A. I do not think it was a policy set. There was just no alternative at that point in time.

Q. Did you advise the President of what was going on?

A. Senator, the first time I ever talked to the President was one occasion that I recall before Sept. 15 which was in late August, to the best of my recollection, and that certainly was not an occasion to talk to the President about anything because his former law partners were in the office, Mrs. Nixon was in the office, there were several notaries or one notary there, some other members of the staff and it had to do with the signing of the President's testamentary papers and it was—just was not a very appropriate occasion to even give a whisper to the President that I would like to talk to him. So I must say that any time between June 19 and Sept. 15 I had no conversations with the President, and nor did I approach the President at any time other than through reporting to Mr. Haldeman and Mr. Ehrlichman.

Q. Do you not think as the President's attorney, you should have tried to go to him and warn him about what was being done?

A. I probably should have but I was assuming everything I reported to Mr. Haldeman and Ehrlichman was also being reported to the President.

Q. Turning to the offer of clemency to Mr. McCord, did you ever advise the President of the United States about that?

A. No, sir. I was proceeding on a conversation I had with Mr. Ehrlichman after Mr. Ehrlichman indicated and Mr. Colson also had indicated that they had talked directly with the President about the matter, something which was later confirmed by the President himself in conversations with him.

Q. Mr. Dean, finally, before wrapping up here, I would like to pin down the occasions this year prior to March 21, the meeting with the President, when you and he discussed the cover-up of Watergate.

A. All right. It was the meeting on the 27th [February] that I had with the President when he told me to report directly to him. Well, also, I might add at the conclusion of that meeting, as we were walking to the door to leave the office, he again complimented me on the fact that I had done a good job during the campaign, that this had been the only issue that they had had, that they had tried to make something of it but they had been unable to make anything of it and he was very complimentary of my handling of the job.

He then told me we have got, you know, you have got to fight back on situations like this. And I can recall something I cannot express in writing, a gesture when he sort of put his fist into his hand and said, you have just got to really keeping fighting back and I have got confidence in you that you can do that and this thing will not get out of hand.

I am now at the March 13 meeting, where the matter of executive clemency and the million dollars came up. That would be the next instance in the sequence. At March 13, there was a number of unspecified demands for money that had come to me through Mr. O'Brien. I had also been having conversations with Mr. Mitchell.

So there was this general problem that was existing before the 13th of March as to who was going to raise the support money and how it was going to get there. That is what prompted me to raise it with the President at the end of the meeting, because it was on my mind, and I told him that, you know, there were money problems, there was no money to pay these people and he said, "How much will it cost?"

I said, "My best estimate is a million dollars or more." He asked me who the demands were coming from. I told him principally from Mr. Hunt through his attorney. At that point in time, he said something to the effect that, well, Mr. Hunt has already been given an assurance of clemency.

He said, I talked to Mr. Ehrlichman about that and then Mr. Colson came and talked to me about it after he had been instructed not to talk to me about it.

Q. I am just trying to shorten it up. Did you discuss Watergate with him at all?

A. Not specifically, no.

Q. March 17. You had a meeting that day?

A. Yes, that was St. Patrick's Day, and I recall the President had a green tie on and sitting in the Oval Office. He was very relaxed and he had his feet up on the desk and was very—the thing that stuck in my mind from that particular conversation was that he wondered if the Senate would bite the bait that he had put out at his press conference on litigating over the question of Dean and executive privilege because he was convinced if they did you would never see any of the White House staff before the Senate.

Q. Then, I think it is also true, at least, according to my understanding, that during the rest of the year 1972 between the June 16 or was it the 17th, the 17th, the day of the break-in, except for a meeting on Sept. 15, even you have not testified to any discussions with the President about Watergate. Isn't that correct? A. That is correct.

Q. Now, then we come to the year 1973 and from what I have been able to gather in the questioning I have just finished your testimony is that on Feb. 28 you did discuss this matter of obstruction of justice and then you also testified to what you did here on March 13, and then, of course, we come to the meeting on March 21 when you told him most of what Watergate was all about. And the summary that I can see from the testimony, the President of the United States certainly didn't know anything about all this business, to this one Senator, until this thing on Feb. 28, according to your testimony, and on March 13 but especially, of course, the meeting on March 21 where you did discuss with him at great length the Watergate and he at a later press conference that he learned about it on that date.

SENATOR INOUYE: Mr. Chairman, the charges contained in Mr. Dean's testimony are extremely serious with potentially grave consequences. The President of the United States has been implicated, and because of the gravity of these charges, I believe that the witness, Mr. John Dean, should be subjected by this committee to the most intense interrogation to test his credibility.

It would appear to me that a most appropriate credibility test would be one prepared by the White House and as you, Mr. Chairman, know the White House has prepared a memorandum and a set of questions for use by this committee. These questions should serve as a substitute, admittedly not the very best, but a substitute for cross-examination of Mr. Dean by the President of the United States.

Accordingly, I believe that it would be most appropriate to use these questions and to use the memorandum, and I am certain that all of us here will agree that the President is entitled to his day in court.

I have here a letter dated June 27, 1973, from the White House, Washington. It reads as follows:

"Dear Senator Inouye: We have noted your public expression of your willingness to use questions and a memorandum, previously furnished to the committee staff, in questioning Mr. Dean. We have today forwarded more up-to-date questions to both the majority counsel and minority counsel for the committee.

"However, in view of your interest in this material, we thought it would be appropriate to send these questions directly to you. There is also enclosed herewith a slightly revised draft and updated version of the memorandum previously furnished to the committee staff. Sincerely, J. Fred Buzhardt, special counsel to the President."

Mr. Chairman, I will now proceed with the memo which was received this morning from the White House. It goes as follows:

"It is a matter of record that John Dean knew of and participated in the planning that went into the break-in at Watergate, though the extent of his knowledge of that specific operation or of his approval of the plan ultimately adopted have not yet been established. There is no reason to doubt, however, that John Dean was the principal actor in the Watergate cover-up, and that while other motivations may have played a part, he had a great interest in covering up for himself, pre-June 17.

"Dean came to the White House from Justice from a background of working on problems of demonstrations and intelligence. Among those working under him at the White House were Tom Huston and Caulfield. Dean was involved in discussions in 1971 about the Sandwedge plan Caulfield proposed. Ehrlichman was told that the original authors of the $1 million plan were Dean and Liddy."

If I may I would like to pause at this point. Would you like to, would you care to comment, sir?

A. Is that in question form?

Q. This is a quotation from Mr. Ehrlichman.

A. I have no recollection of advising Mr. Liddy of a $1 million plan. In fact to the contrary. When Operation Sandwedge was shelved, and I think I have in my testimony explained how that died a natural death, that the budget for that was set at a half million dollars, and all that were involved in reviewing that document thought that was an excessive amount of money.

Q. Well, I will continue to quote:

"Whatever the fact about this, it is clear that Dean attended the meetings that led up to adoption of the Watergate plan. Dean introduced Mitchell (who had sponsored Dean for his White House position) to Liddy in November, 1971."

A. Senator, may I comment right there.

Q. Please do so.

A. I do not believe Mr. Mitchell sponsored me, to my knowledge, to my White House position. I first heard of the White House interest in me when Mr. Krogh came to me and said would I be interested in going to the White House and would John Mitchell let me come to the White House? I said I did not know but I thought somebody else ought to take it up with Mr. Mitchell rather than myself. So to the contrary, I do not believe Mr. Mitchell sponsored me to the White House. In fact, I recall some conversations when he counseled me against going to the White House.

Q. I will continue.

"Dean introduced Magruder to Liddy in December, 1971, and suggested Liddy for the combined position of general counsel and chief of intelligence-gathering for C.R.P. He told Magruder that Mitchell had hired Liddy. Dean, Liddy, Mitchell and Magruder met to discuss intelligence plans of this kind on Jan. 27, 1972, and Feb. 4.

"Dean was not present at the final meeting on March 30 when the $250,000 plan was approved. It is not clear whether he was not there because he disapproved or simply because he was not in Key Biscayne or because he wanted to try to keep his own record clean."

A. I might comment there, Senator. First of all, after I returned from the second meeting in Mr. Mitchell's office, and reported to Mr. Haldeman what had occurred and told him of my feelings about what was occurring, and that I wanted to have no part in it and told him I thought no one in the White House should have any part in it. He agreed and told me to have no part in it and I have no knowledge that there was going to be a meeting in Key Biscayne and did not learn about that meeting until long after June 17 of 1972.

Q. "He is reported as having said that he did not think it was appropriate for him to be in on these conversations.

"He is also reported to have said at a meeting in Mitchell's office that 'we should not discuss this in front of Mitchell or in the Attorney General's office.'

"At some point during the spring, Magruder phoned Dean and asked him to talk to Liddy to try to calm him down. At another point, Dean, knowing that a bugging operation was under serious consideration, called Magruder and referred to the importance of Liddy's intelligence activities."

A. I would like to comment on that. I do not believe that is quite accurate, Senator. What happened is Mr. Strachan at the White House, called me, I believe I did receive a call from Mr. Magruder telling me that he had developed a very strained relationship with Mr. Liddy. Like when Strachan called me because I believe he told me he had been talking with Mr. Liddy he said, "What should I do?" I said it sounds like a personality and a personnel problem and I suggested that he not bother Mr. Mitchell with it but rather take it to Mr. Mardian and let Mr. Mardian resolve any problem because they do need a general counsel over there.

Q. "This arose after an argument between Magruder and Liddy. Dean urged Magruder not to let personal animosity 'get in the way of the project.' Also in March, 1973, Dean claimed to Haldeman that in the spring of 1972, he had told Haldeman that he had been to two meetings at which unacceptable and outlandish deals for intelligence-gathering had been rejected by himself and by Mitchell and that he, Dean, proposed not to attend any more such meetings. Haldeman has no personal recollection of Dean telling him about the meetings at the time but is 'willing to accept that as a possibility.'" Post-June 17.

A. If I might just comment there, following June 17 and the

break-in, the first time I had a discussion with Mr. Haldeman about these facts I had already reported them to Mr. Ehrlichman. He remembered perfectly well and very clearly the fact that I had come to him shortly after the second meeting.

Q. "Whatever the facts may be on the matters that are uncertain in the spring of 1972 about Dean's knowledge or specific approval of the break-in, it must have been clear to Dean as a lawyer when he heard on June 17 of Watergate that he was in personal difficulty. The Watergate affair was so clearly the outgrowth of the discussion and plans he had been in on that he might well be regarded a a conspirator with regard to them. He must immediately have realized that his patron, Mitchell, would also be involved.

"It appears that Ehrlichman called Dean on June 17 to advise him of the problem and to direct him to take charge of it for the White House. Even without an instruction this would have been his responsibility as Counsel for the President, from the time of the occurrence, and he was active in that role from the moment of his return to the city a day or two after the break-in. This is a statement from Mr. Ehrlichman's deposition.

"On June 19, Dean met with Liddy, Mitchell, Strachan and Magruder, and Sloan. Dean, Mitchell and Magruder also met with LaRue and Mardian that evening at Mitchell's apartment. At these meetings the cover-up plan was hatched. This is from the Magruder testimony. A series of meetings followed throughout the summer."

A. Senator, I just might footnote as you go along, I believe that the policy regarding the cover-up was set long before I returned from the Far East over the weekend of the break-in and when I came into the office and talked to Mr. Strachan I realized that the White House already decided initially that it was going to start destroying incriminating documents and certainly was not going to step forward as to what its knowledge of the matter was at that point in time.

Q. If I may ask at this point when you refer to the White House had decided, who do you mean by the White House?

A. I am sorry, I did not hear you.

Q. You have just testified that the White House had decided.

A. Well, I mean by that that certainly Mr. Haldeman and Mr. Ehrlichman, because Mr. Haldeman had given specific instructions to Mr. Strachan to destroy the incriminating documents that were in his possession.

Q. "At these meetings the cover-up plan was hatched. A series of meetings followed throughout the summer. Dean and Mitchell were Magruder's principal contacts on the cover-up. Dean was not merely one of the architects of the cover-up plan. He was also its most active participant. Magruder correctly concluded that Dean 'was involved in all aspects of this cover-up,' and this is from the Magruder testimony.

"It was Dean who suggested to Haldeman that the F.B.I. was concerned that it might run into a C.I.A. operation." This is from Mr. Haldeman. If you wish to comment I hope you will.

A. Yes. As you recall, when I testified I had been asked by Mr. Ehrlichman to stay abreast of what was happening in the Department of Justice. In my meeting with Mr. Gray, which I believe was on the 21st, Mr. Gray told me of the fact that they had uncovered banking transactions in Mr. Barker's account and were at that time looking for the Dahlberg check and the Mexican money and, indeed, I did report this back as the reporting channels had been developed to my superiors.

Q. Were you truly concerned—

SENATOR ERVIN: Suppose you name the superiors you reported to?

A. Mr. Haldeman and Mr. Ehrlichman.

SENATOR INOUYE: Were you truly concerned that the C.I.A. was in fact involved?

A. I had no idea that the C.I.A. was involved at that point in time.

Q. Why did you suggest that the C.I.A. might be involved?

A. This, as I believe I testified, was not at this point in time but that was at a later date when I went over to Mr. Gray's again and he told me his theories of the case. I explained these to Mr. Haldeman and Mr. Ehrlichman that one of these theories was the C.I.A. was involved. I had no idea that Mr. Haldeman and Mr. Ehrlichman were going to meet with Mr. Helms, and General Walters, this was unknown to me until I subsequently was so informed by Mr. Ehrlichman but not as to the substance of the meeting they had held.

Q. "It was Dean who suggested to General Walters on Jan. 26 that C.I.A. pay the Watergate defendants while in jail," and this is from the Walters memo for record June 28, 1972.

A. I believe I have explained that, Senator, in that I reported also at one point in time to Mr. Mitchell and Mr. Mardian about the Gray theory. That theory prompted Mr. Mardian, as I recall, to suggest that the C.I.A. might be of some assistance in providing us support and he also raised the question that the C.I.A. might have a very proper reason to do so because of the fact that these were former C.I.A. operatives.

Mr. Mitchell asked me to go back and explore this to Mr. Haldeman and Ehrlichman knowing very well that this isn't the sort of thing I could go to the C.I.A. with.

I didn't talk to Mr. Haldeman about this, rather I talked to Mr. Ehrlichman about it and he told me indeed I should explore it. In fact, I said I didn't know anybody at the C.I.A.

He told me—I told him I didn't know Mr. Helms. He told me not to call Helms but to call General Walters, General Walters is a friend of the White House and, at that time alluded to the fact that he had already met with General Walters.

Q. Did you, in fact, discuss this matter with General Walters?

A. Yes, I did and I have so testified.

Q. "It was Dean purportedly acting on behalf of Mitchell who came to Ehrlichman several weeks after the break-in to obtain approval for fund raising by Kalmbach for the arrested persons," and this is from Mr. Ehrlichman.

A. It is correct that Mr.—after the fact that there could be no assistance from the C.I.A. came out, and Haldeman and Ehrlichman agreed that they couldn't and I reported that back to Mr. Mitchell and Mr. Mardian, that the demands apparently had reached the point where they felt they had to do something to get some money and they had none themselves.

I was asked again by Mr. Mitchell to go back and raise this with Mr. Haldeman and Ehrlichman. Mr. Mitchell told me that he believed that Mr. Ehrlichman particularly would have an interest in making sure that these men were taken care of, and it did not take me any persuading at all in this conversation with Mr. Haldeman and Ehrlichman to initiate Mr. Kalmbach, and obviously Mr. Kalmbach would not have acted on my instructions at all.

Q. "It was Dean who reviewed the papers found in Hunt's safe and declared that they were 'politically sensitive' and should be given special treatment."

A. I don't think there was any doubt about the political sensitivity. Mr. Ehrlichman, as you recall, on the 19th, there was a meeting in Mr. Ehrlichman's office late that evening, Mr. Colson is the one who had expressed anxiety over what might be in Mr. Hunt's safe. As I have also testified at a subsequent time I learned that apparently Mr. Colson and Mr. Hunt had talked about the fact that there were things in his safe that somebody at the White House should take possession of.

It was during this meeting in Mr. Ehrlichman's office on the 19th that Mr. Ehrlichman said that I should report back to him the contents of the safe after he had directed Mr. Kehrli to have the safe opened.

Q. What do you think Mr. Ehrlichman meant by should be given special treatment?

A. Well, I don't know what Mr. Ehrlichman means by it. I know that Mr. Ehrlichman, when I described the documents to him, realized their political sensitivity, and that they—he had originally told me when I reported what the documents were to shred them and it was subsequently he told me to "deep six" the briefcase and shred the documents and it was only after I had reached the conclusion in my own mind that I wasn't going to do that and I persuaded him that too many people had seen them, that that might be what he refers to as special treatment, they be given directly to Mr. Gray.

Q. If I may resume reading from the memo. "It was Dean who sought successfully to have the others omit his name from the list of those who attended meetings on the Liddy plans." This is from the Magruder testimony.

A. I would like to comment on that. The meeting in which this was discussed was called by Mr. Mitchell. I was departing a meeting in his office and he asked me if he could talk to me about these matters. He called Mr. Magruder into the same meeting. They asked me to review my recollection of the meetings. I told him what my recollection was and as I testified, Mr. Magruder asked me, how do I handle this before the grand jury?

I said, "Well, I don't know what occurred at the second meeting. I know there was some brief reference in the first meeting to the election laws and that would seem to me a way to explain presence at the meetings."

Q. "It was Dean who urged Hunt to leave the country two days after the burglary."

A. I believe I testified to that. That occurred before the meeting commenced in Mr. Ehrlichman's office on the evening of the 19th, when Mr. Ehrlichman asked me where Hunt was. I said I had no idea. Mr. Colson was present also. He asked Mr. Colson a similar question and got a similar response.

At that point, Mr. Ehrlichman told me to call Liddy and tell Hunt to get out of the country, which I did.

After a subsequent discussion, I called back, after reraising the matter, thinking it was not something that the White House should be doing, and spoke again with Mr. Liddy and told him that my earlier conversation should be retracted.

Q. Then it is your testimony that it was Mr. Ehrlichman who—

A. That is correct.

Q.—Proposed the idea? A. That is correct.

Q. "It was Dean and Mitchell who prepared Magruder for his perjurious grand jury testimony."

A. I can't speak about Mr. Mitchell's involvement. I know that Mr. Magruder came to my office shortly before he was to appear before the grand jury. As you will recall from my testimony, there were a series of events that preceded that relating to the fact that I had recommended that Magruder be removed or resign from the re-election committee because I thought he was going to have problems.

Simultaneously to that, there was a discussion developing which Mr. Ehrlichman was well aware of, that there was an effort to hold the case at Mr. Liddy.

Q. Did you in fact counsel Mr. Magruder to commit perjury?

A. I did. I did in this regard: I helped him prepare a statement that I knew was false.

Q. "It was Dean who said of a memorandum Colson had prepared on August 29 stating the facts as he knew them, 'For God's sake, destroy the memo. It impeaches Magruder.' "

A. I think the facts speak for themselves on that. I did not destroy the memorandum. In fact, I turned a copy over to this committee. I think I have also explained in my testimony why I did not turn it over to the prosecutors.

Q. "It was Dean who suggested that Sloan take the Fifth Amendment, though Sloan was innocent."

A. It is correct, I did call Mr. Sloan's attorney before he was to appear in Florida before an unrelated matter down there. There had been a number of discussions within the White House about the fact that Mr. Sloan was going to testify about money that had come to the White House. He had sought meetings with a number of people in the White House. I was the only one who would talk with them. Technically, under the law, it appeared that he did have difficulties with some of the disbursements that had been made that occurred after April 7, which was the effective date of the new law. And I did call him and ask his attorney if he was prepared to take the Fifth Amendment and in doing that, suggesting that he might want to pursue that course. Because to me, the Fifth Amendment doesn't indicate innocence or guilt.

Q. "It was Dean who was the agent in some of the money dealings with the arrested persons."

A. Would you repeat that, please, Senator?

Q. "It was Dean who was the agent in some of the money dealngs with the arrested persons."

A. I never had any direct dealing with any of the arrested persons. I conveyed messages back of the pressure that was being placed, not only on the re-election committee but ultimately on the White House, particularly the one that came to my attention where a threat had been delivered directly to me of concern to Mr. Ehrlichman. I think I testified that Mr. Ehrlichman raised that immediately with Mr. Mitchell when Mr. Mitchell did attend a meeting in Mr. Ehrlichman's presence.

Q. Did you have any dealings with arrested persons?

A. Direct dealings? I had a telephone conversation, the telephone conversations I have discussed with Mr. Liddy, the meeting I had with Mr. Liddy. I have never met Mr. Hunt other than the one occasion I referred to, when he was in Mr. Colson's outer office in August of 1971, which is roughly the time I recall meeting him, after having seen him in there on a number of occasions. I have never met any other individuals.

Q. Did you in fact discuss money with Mr. Liddy?

A. Mr. Liddy at the time I called him—this was in January, I believe it was January 5 of the year. He had been trying to reach Mr. Krogh. He had received a letter from the Senate Commerce Committee investigators and they were seeking responses from Mr. Liddy regarding Mr. Krogh. Liddy called Krogh. Krogh did not take the call. That is one of the documents that was not submitted, which I have submitted to the committee, the gist of the call that was returned to Liddy.

I had a report subsequently that Mr. Liddy was rather miffed and a little outraged at the fact that he couldn't get hold of who he thought was a good and loyal friend, Mr. Krogh. Mr. Krogh asked me if I would personally do something about that.

That Saturday, I called Mr. Liddy just to tell, to convey to him the reasons that Mr. Krogh did not wish to speak with him, because he wanted to testify before the Senate Commerce Committee in connection with his confirmation hearing that he had not talked with Mr. Liddy.

So, I explained this to Mr. Liddy and during the course of that conversation, Mr. Liddy told me, he said he hoped that somebody would take care of the attorney's fees. I reported to Mr. Liddy that I would pass that message along.

Q. "It was Dean who told Colson not to make a transcript of Colson's taped conversation with Hunt and said that he, Dean, would handle the matter."

This is a report from the Federal prosecutors, reported in The New York Times.

A. That is not correct. To the contrary, I made a transcript of Mr. Colson's telephone conversation on a cassette tape shortly after Mr. Colson brought me his I.B.M. tape of the conversation. I took a copy of that and played it for Mr. Haldeman and Mr. Ehrlichman at Camp David on Nov. 15. Later that afternoon, after getting instructions that I should raise this with Mr. Mitchell, that he should take care of the problem for Mr. Haldeman and Mr. Ehrlichman, I took it to New York with me and played it for Mr. Mitchell as well. I got no instructions at that point in time from Mr. Mitchell.

Q. "Throughout all of this, Dean was perfectly situated to mastermind and to carry out a cover-up since, as Counsel to the President and the man in charge for the White House, he had full access to what was happening in the investigation. He sat in in on F.B.I. interviews with White House witnesses and received investigative reports. Dean and Ehrlichman met with Attorney General Kleindienst late in July. The Attorney General described the investigation and said that 'It did not appear that any White House people or any high-ranking committee people were involved in the preparation or planning or discussion of the break-in.' "

This is from Mr. Ehrlichman.

A. I never discussed with Mr. Kleindienst the cover-up that was going on at the White House and the investigation I am sure he is referring to there was his own conclusion.

Q. "History fails to record that at that moment, Dean corrected the Attorney General's erroneous impression by pointing out that Mitchell, Magruder and Dean had all been involved in planning of operations of which Watergate was an obvious derivative or that Strachan had knowledge of the fruits of this kind of operation, or that all of them were suborning perjury and otherwise seeking to conceal the facts."

A. Senator, I would just like to make a general statement. This document has obviously been prepared by somebody who was not at the White House at the time this was all occurring. It sounds like they are putting it back together through newspaper accounts.

Q. This is from the office of your successor, sir.

A. I understand. And I don't believe my successor was there and didn't spend the nearly three years in the White House that I did.

Q. "Dean's activity in the cover-up also made him, perhaps unwittingly, the principal author of the political and constitutional crisis that Watergate now epitomizes. It would have been embarrassing for the President if the true facts had become known shortly after June 17, but it is the kind of embarrassment that an immensely popular President could easily have weathered. The political problem has been magnified one thousandfold because the truth is coming to light so belatedly, because of insinuations that the White House was a party to the cover-up, and above all, because the White House was led to say things about Watergate that have since been found untrue. These added consequences were John Dean's doing."

A. Well, Senator, I think that my testimony answers in great detail my dealings with Mr. Haldeman, Mr. Ehrlichman, and the President, and based on what I know, and knowing the position I held in the White House staff, there is no way conceivable that I could have done and conceived and implemented the plan that they are trying to suggest I did.

Q. "Dean was responsible within the White House for becoming apprised of what had happened. From June 17 on, Dean had periodic conversations with Ehrlichman 'about virtually every aspect of this case.' " This is from Mr. Ehrlichman.

"Dean reported also to Haldeman and to Ziegler, to whom he gave repeated assurances that he had made an 'intensive investigation' and had found no White House involvement." This is from Mr. Ziegler.

"Dean was 'the foundation of the proposition that the White House was not involved' " and this is from Ehrlichman.

Spring 1973. "With the election past and public interest in Watergate on the wane, Dean may have thought that this cover-up had been a success, although he purported to continue an on-going investigation."

A. Senator, if I might interject, I don't know how quickly they are jumping from winter to spring, but I would draw to the attention of the committee and the Senator the La Costa meeting and the events that transpired there, which I believe are documented by materials prepared by Mr. Haldeman and Mr. Higby, his assistant, as well as subsequent materials that were prepared for the President, and I think these speak for themselves.

Q. "At the same time, Dean was affecting a failing memory and talking to Magruder as if Dean did not recall the pre-Watergate planning meetings in which he had participated." This is from Magruder's testimony.

A. We reviewed that earlier, and as I said, I did, when I was talking to Magruder, I was telling him I did not understand what had happened between Feb. 4 and June 17 that resulted in that even occurring, that I never had hard evidence, I never knew for sure what the facts were, I didn't know how the plan had been approved; I didn't know how much White House pressure had been put on him; I didn't know for a fact if Mitchell had or had not approved it; I had never talked with Mr. Mitchell about it. I think that is what Mr. Magruder is referring to, or, as I said earlier, he may have confused later meetings when I came back from Camp David and I did indeed give him the impression that I could not remember what had happened, because I didn't want to get into any discussions about what had happened at that time.

Q. Were you surprised when you heard of the June 17 break-in?

A. Was I surprised?

Q. Yes.

A. As I told you, my immediate reaction was, after hearing the facts, that it was something that Mr. Colson had been involved in. I was more appalled than surprised.

Q. You had anticipated something like this?

A. I hadn't anticipated anything like this, no. I can't say I anticipated it, but I can't say I was surprised to hear of it because I was aware of the fact that there had been a past effort to accomplish a burglary on the Brookings Institute [Institution] and I had also heard of the Ellsberg psychiatrist break-in by that time.

Q. You were not surprised because you were an author of the plan?

A. No sir, that was not my immediate reaction. I didn't think the plan had been approved.

Q. "In February, however with the Ervin committee beginning its work, the President was again concerned that all of the available facts be made known. In the middle of February, 1973, Dean and Richard Moore met with Ehrlichman and Haldeman at San Clemente. Dean was assigned to reduce 'to written form all of the detailed facts as they related both to the committee to re-elect and the White House.' " This is from Mr. Ehrlichman.

A. I received no such instruction when I was at La Costa to prepare any written report and have no knowledge of ever being given such an instruction.

Q. This is also substantiated by Mr. Moore.

A. I have no knowledge of that. There was, as I say, an earlier effort in December to prepare such a report and I have submitted that document to the committee. If there were discussions of preparing a written report, it was of the ilk of a report that was prepared in the December period, which I, for lack of a better term, call a fairy tale.

Q. "Dean was pressed continually for that statement, particularly, by Haldeman, but never produced it."

A. Well, as I say, I recall, the only time I recall Mr. Haldeman and Mr. Ehrlichman pushing me and pressing me for a statement is when I was up at Camp David and not in that time frame.

Q. "At this point, the Gray confirmation hearings were imminent and the Ervin hearings were on the horizon. The President, who had barely known Dean, determined that Counsel to the President was the appropriate person with whom to work in formulating the President's position on executive-privilege and similar legal issues in that these hearings in news conferences on March 2 and 15, at which they would arise, would be present. Between Feb. 27 and April 16 the President met with Dean and usually others, 21 or 22 times and there were 14 telephone conversations between March 10 and April 22."

A. Senator. I will stand on my testimony with regard to those last few paragraphs you have read.

Q. "It is probable that Dean helped induce the views on attorney-client privilege and on separation of powers that would have immunized Dean himself from having to testify under oath."

A. I will comment on that to the effect that—or the President and I when we discussed the Dean appearance. I told him that if I go up there I am going to testify. There is no way to go up. We had had countless occasions when the executive privilege issue had come up before, there was a parallel developing between the Gray hearings and I.T.T. hearings where Mr. Flanigan made an appearance before the Senate Judiciary Committee. This was quite evident. In my discussions with the President he made it clear to me he did not want Mr. Ehrlichman or Haldeman to appear and I told him the strongest case for executive privilege would rest on the counsel to the President and we did discuss that.

Q. "During this period Dean was developing other problems. On March 10 there were press reports it was Dean who had recommended Liddy to the Committee to Re-elect the President. On March 22, Pat Gray testified that Dean had lied to him during the course of the F.B.I. investigation of Watergate. On March 28 McCord's letter to Judge Sirica was made public. The cover-up was coming uncovered.

"During this period the point was frequently raised by various people, including primarily the President, that the 'whole story of the Watergate should be made public.' Dean's answer always was, 'We cannot do it while the investigation is continuing. There are conflicting versions of events and the rights of defendants might be prejudiced by the statement.' "

And this is from Mr. Haldeman.

A. I think that relates back to a conversaton that I had with Mr. Haldeman shortly after the election and before I prepared the, was requested to prepare, a written version of the Dean report when he asked me for what the facts would entail. At that time I told him that I thought that the grand jury would be reconvened and I thought that they would undoubtedly get into obstruction of justice and I thought that those—that that investigation would come directly to the White House and that Haldeman, Ehrlichman and Dean could be indicted, and he said to me, "I do not believe that is a very viable option."

Q. "On March 20 the President indicated that he still did not have all the facts."

A. What date was that, Senator?

Q. March 20.

A. The President did not state to me, on the 20th when I received a call from the President I told him at that time that I would like to meet with him the next morning and I would like to tell him what I thought the implication of the situation was, what had really prompted me at that time was the new demand from Mr. Hunt that indeed, this thing was getting far out of hand, that the White House was now being directly subject to blackmail and I did not know how to handle it.

Q. Is it your testimony that on March 20 the President did in fact have all the facts? A. I did not hear you, again, Senator, I am sorry.

Q. Is it your testimony that on March 20 the President did not have all the facts?

A. I do not know what the President knew on March 20. We had had conversations before that. We had conversations that I was personally engaged in on Sept. 15 of the preceding year. We had had conversations in early February or late February in which I tried to start telling him some of my own involvement. We had also had a discussion on March 13 about the money demands that were being made. At that time he discussed the fact that a million dollars is no problem. He repeated it several times.

I can very vividly recall that the way he sort of rolled his chair back from his desk and leaned over to Mr. Haldeman and said, "a million dollars is no problem," and then he came back and asked "well, who is making these demands," and I said they are principally coming from Mr. Hunt and he got into the fact that Hunt had been given clemency and his conversation about his annoyance that he had also talked to Colson about this in addition to Ehrlichman, and the money matter was left very much hanging at that meeting. Nothing was resolved.

Q. As the President's counsel did you, in a very legal fashion, advise him of your meetings in February in the Attorney General's office?

A. My channel of reporting was through Mr. Haldeman or Mr. Ehrlichman. At the completion of the second meeting I sought out an appointment with Haldeman. I recall—

Q. In the subsequent meetings with the President did you clearly advise him of the break-in, your involvement and the cover-up, and your involvement?

A. I certainly did on the 21st and I had attempted to do it

earlier in February but he was not interested in it when I raised it, and the conversation got cut short. I told him I thought I had an obstruction of justice problem and gave him, started to give him the highlights. He did not want to pursue it further.

Q. "In the preceding week Dean had begun to express to Richard Moore concern about Dean's own involvement. Referring to the meetings in Mitchell's office, the plumbers operation and the Ellsberg break-in and the demands by Hunt possibly on March 16 for more money."

A. I did discuss with Mr. Moore the fact that, but that was not the first time I had discussed it with Mr. Moore. Mr. Moore and I had talked about this on many occasions, that I thought that the cover-up was harmful, bad, it had to stop at some point. We were searching for answers as to how to end it. We could not find an answer, and finally, at one point when I was having direct access to the President I thought, and discussed with Moore that I can do something to end it now and I will go in and tell the President what this is going to mean if it continues.

Q. "After the two of them met with the President on March 20, Moore told Dean 'I do not think the President has any idea of the kind of things that you have told me about.' When Dean agreed that the President did not, Moore told Dean that it was his obligation to advise the President and lectured Dean on this subject."

A. Well, Richard Moore to me is a wonderful man, and I often went to him for counsel. He is an older man, and I respected his judgment very much.

I believe I raised these things with Mr. Moore, I had raised them before and I told him what prompted my conversation that afternoon with Mr. Moore were the demands from Hunt and I wanted—by this time he was aware himself of the money demands because this had come up at La Costa when Mr. Ehrlichman had instructed Mr. Moore to go to New York and get Mr. Mitchell to take care of these problems. So for that reason I had never told Dick Moore everything I knew but I had given him enough knowledge so that he could see the breadth of the problem.

Q. As the trusted aide and Counsel to the President of the United States, did you feel that it was your obligation and duty to as soon as possible advise him of the involvement in the Watergate break-in and the ensuing cover-up?

A. Well, Senator, I think I have expressed before, to walk into the President's door is not the easiest thing to do. My channel of reporting was through Mr. Haldeman or Mr. Ehrlichman, principally through Mr. Haldeman.

Q. Did the enormity of the problem compel you to walk into the President's office?

A. Well, I can only assume that everything I told Mr. Haldeman and Ehrlichman would be going to the President also. As I have testified, on some occasions Mr. Haldeman would take notes about things I was telling him. He would take these notes shortly before he would go into meetings with the President. I can also recall occasions when we were meeting when a call would come from Mr. Haldeman to come to the President's office or once in Florida to come over to his residence and he would wait until I completed reporting. I assumed that everything I was telling Mr. Haldeman was going to the President.

Q. When did you begin to distrust Mr. Haldeman?

A. I think that the first signal I got that Mr. Haldeman had decided that, you might say, I was off the reservation was when I came back from Camp David.

Q. What was the date, sir?

A. That was the 28th. I think that was prompted by my attitude in a meeting with the President on the afternoon of the 21st when there was more discussion of different essentially cover-up techniques without getting into great detail because I cannot recall in great detail, everything they were saying.

The President was asking me, do I agree and I was saying no, and finally, at one point in that meeting I said that, right in front of the President that, I felt that Dean, Haldeman and Ehrlichman could be indicted for obstruction of justice and this has to be recognized. And I think as a result of that meeting they saw that I had begun to change my attitude about any further involvement in a cover-up.

Q. "On March 21 Dean gave the President a more complete, but still laundered version of the facts and so surprised the President that according to press accounts of what Dean is saying 'the President came out of his chair.' "

A. I do not know where that press account came from, the President did not come out of his chair. I have never seen the President come out of his chair other than very easily and slowly at the time that he got up on April 15 to walk around to the corner of the E.O.B. [Executive Office Building] Office and then raise something with me. The President of the United States does not come flying out of his chair.

Q. "At this meeting Dean indicated that Magruder was involved but that he did not know about Mitchell."

A. That is correct. As I have said before this committee I have never had a direct conversation with John Mitchell to ask him what his involvement was. On the 28th when I came down from Camp David after there was this discussion about whether I would be willing to perpetuate the story that there had been one meeting in Mitchell's office, there had been a discussion of the election laws and that that was the reason for my presence and it was to introduce Mr. Liddy, at the end of that discussion I said to Mr. Mitchell, "I have never asked you of your involvement but I want to hypothesize what I see to be the situation" and I then gave them my hypothesis of the situation and, as a result of that hypothesis, Mr. Mitchell said "that is not far from accurate, but we thought it would be two or three times removed."

Q. If you did not know about Mitchell why did you advise the President that Mr. Mitchell could be indicted?

A. Because based on the information Mr. Magruder had given me, which was inferential and my general assumption of the fact, I was aware of the fact that he had received the information from the electronic surveillance.

Q. Did you so advise the President?

A. Did I so advise the President? I do not recall that I got into a detailed discussion. I was giving the President what I would say was a general overview and letting him come back and ask any specific questions he might wish to ask.

Q. Do you not feel it was important enough to advise the President of the U.S. that his former Attorney General was involved and implicated?

A. Well, I told him I thought he could be indicted but I told him I did not have the facts for certainty myself that he was indictable.

Q. "He mentioned the Ellsberg break-in and possibly a second story job at the Brookings Institute [Institution]. He told about the attempt by Hunt to blackmail Ehrlichman over the Ellsberg break-in. He suggested that Haldeman, Ehrlichman and Dean might all have some problem about the financial transactions with the defendants but that he thought they were more technical and political than legal."

A. I do recall saying that I thought that some of the obstruction problems were technical. I said some of them are more serious than others. As far as discussion of the Ellsberg burglary, Senator, I don't recall raising that at that point in time with the President as the reason for Mr. Hunt's threat. In fact I was—when I raised it with Mr. Ehrlichman as to what these seamy things were Mr. Ehrlichman said, "Well, you know I just have no idea what he could be talking about."

And subsequently on the 28th or 29th when I talked to Mr. Krogh I was very curious myself to find out what it was, and that is when I asked Mr. Krogh if, in fact, Mr. Ehrlichman had authorized the burglary of the doctor's office and he had told me that he didn't think Mr. Ehrlichman knew in advance.

Q. Didn't you believe that the offer of money for silence was a criminal offense? A. Yes, I did.

Q. Why did you say that these problems were more technical and political than legal?

A. That isn't the way I believe I cast it. When I said they were indictable I meant despite the degree of technicality as an indictment, I can't say I was a criminal lawyer but I did recognize an obstruction of justice.

Q. "He gave no hint, however, of his orchestration of perjured testimony by Magruder and others. Ehrlichman suggested that everyone be made to appear before the grand jury and waive executive privilege."

A. I have no recollection of that at all. To the contrary, when we met subsequently I kept shaking my head and saying, no, Ehrlichman, Dean and Haldeman are indictable and the tone of the conversation was not going to come forward but rather to continue the cover-up and I think the subsequent meetings on the 22d with Mr. Mitchell, if the President indeed had received the message I was trying to give, certainly wouldn't have engaged in the conversation with Mr. Mitchell that afternoon which would leisurely discuss the status of this committee and the like.

Certainly nothing of any significance occurred at all after that 21st [of March] meeting.

Q. "Dean thought this would be a good idea but only if the persons who appeared before the grand jury were given immunity."

A. I don't recall that at all. I do recall general discussions that I thought that one of the best ways to get the truth out would be if people could receive immunity because I knew a lot of people would be unwilling to talk or that their stories would be less than forthcoming if they felt they were going to incriminate themselves.

Q. "At another meeting that day Ehrlichman strongly opposed immunity."

A. I never heard that.

Q. This did not happen? A. Not to my knowledge.

Q. "On March 23 Dean was sent to Camp David in order to complete the long-promised report. Dean was at Camp David for six days but came down on the night of the 28th and delivered nothing."

A. That is correct, I delivered nothing because I had, as I have testified, had earlier conversation about my testimony. Every time I revealed the slightest inch of my knowledge, recollections began to change, characterizations began to change. I was asked to handle testimony in different ways. When I came down from Camp David there was no doubt in my mind that I wasn't going to play the cover-up game and I wasn't going to give them any further information with which they could play the cover-up game.

Q. Were you in fact, Mr. Dean, preparing your own testimony?

A. I was going through and recalling everything I could remember about the incidents. I had been asked to do that, and if the President had called and asked me for that report—

Q. Did you spend the six days preparing testimony for your own use?

A. Let me complete, Senator. If the President called me and asked me for that report, I would have sent it to the President of the United States. There is no doubt about that. That isn't who was calling and asking me for it. It was Mr. Ehrlichman who was calling me from California. He wanted any part I had of it, and based on the earlier conversations I had had I wasn't about to give it to Mr. Ehrlichman. So I can't say I was preparing my own testimony because I wasn't preparing my own testimony. I was trying to reconstruct, as I had been asked to do, what I remembered as to what had occurred.

Q. "The failure of Dean's muse while he was on the mountain is understandable since by this time it would have been impossible to write a believable report that would not have been self-indicting. While he was at Camp David, Dean told Ehrlichman's assistant that he was not getting the statement done but was planning his own defense." And this is from Mr. Ehrlichman.

A. That is not true, Senator.

Q. "Haldeman talked with him several times and felt that 'Dean was not having much progress in writing his report but it became clear that he was worrying more about himself.'" This is from Haldeman.

A. Well, as I say when I came down from Camp David, I don't think it was a question of worrying about myself as what I was witnessing was Mr. Haldeman and then subsequently Mr. Ehrlichman becoming very concerned about themselves.

Q. "On the 25th the President suggested it be announced that Dean would appear before the grand jury."

A. On what date?

Q. The 25th of March.

A. On the 25th of March I was at Camp David. The President was in Florida. That was a Sunday, as I recall, and I recall no conversation with the President. I have no knowledge of that at all. That is a new one to me.

Q. "On the 26th Dean agreed but said he would do so only if given immunity."

A. No, sir, I had no conversations with anybody. They were in Florida at that time. The discussion that morning, if you will recall, was that the President came out with a statement that he warmly endorsed me, he expressed new confidence or renewed confidence in me, that he had allegedly spoken directly with me, and had no concern at all about my prior knowledge of this matter and I do not recall any statement about going before the grand jury being issued when he was giving me this very warm embrace.

Q. "On March 30, the President relieved Dean of any further responsibility for the Watergate investigation. He called Ehrlichman in, told him that it was evident to the President that 'Dean was in the thing up to his eyebrows,' and asked Ehrlichman to look into Watergate."
This is from Mr. Ehrlichman.

"The President indicated to Ehrlichman that his conversations with Dean throughout the preceding month had given him 'a growing awareness of Dean's personal involvement in this.' Relieved of his Watergate duties by the President and aware that"—

A. Senator, I might just note at this point and call it to the attention of the record, that Mr. Ehrlichman also resigned from the White House on the same day that my resignation was requested, and Mr. Haldeman as well.

Q. "Relieved of his Watergate duties by the President and aware that his own complicity had become obvious, Dean decided to strike out on his own to hunt for immunity for the long list of wrongs he had committed. According to the press, it was April 2 when he first established contact with the prosecutors and attempted to bargain for immunity. While he carried on these negotiations, Ehrlichman completed his report and advised the President on April 14 that Mitchell, Magruder and Dean were all involved."

A. I would like to comment on that. As I have testified, Mr. Ehrlichman told me after he had returned from San Clemente back to Washington, I met with him on the afternoon, late afternoon of the 8th and had periodic meetings with him during the week of the 8th to the 14th. It was on the 4th that he told me that he had talked with Kleindienst and that the grand jury was doing nothing. He was particularly asking me when I was likely to appear before the grand jury. I was already, per the instructions of my own counsel limiting conversations with Mr. Haldeman and Mr. Ehrlichman about testimonial areas.

But it was that day that I drew up the list which I wanted to get the message very clear to Mr. Haldeman and Mr. Ehrlichman that they had very serious problems. It was on the, as a result of that list that the Attorney General suddenly received a call, because I informed him that my counsel had been in direct communication with the prosecutors and the prosecutors had indicated that indeed, Mr. Haldeman and Mr. Ehrlichman were potential targets of the grand jury. At 1 o'clock that night, I realized that they had gotten the Attorney General late at night to get a briefing from the prosecutors, and that is when things really started moving. That is when the activities began to occur.

Q. "On the 16th, Dean was asked by the President to resign, but refused to do so. On the 30th, he was dismissed. His increasingly shrill efforts since that date to save himself by striking out recklessly at others are too familiar and too painful to require mention."

This ends the memorandum.

A. I would only add to that, Senator, that I think that if anyone has been on the receiving end of adverse publicity, it has been this witness and not any of the other witnesses and I have not dealt in personalities, nor will I deal in personalities at any time during these hearings.

Q. Mr. Chairman, that ends the memorandum. I have several questions which were submitted by the office of the counsel for the President, with a closing statement. Knowing the lateness of the time, may I request that I be permitted to continue the interrogation tomorrow, sir?

SENATOR ERVIN: Yes.

June 28, 1973

SENATOR INOUYE: Mr. Chairman, before proceeding I would like to advise the committee that we have had a bit of confusion here. Statements attributed to the press office of the White House office indicated last evening that the memo which I presented to the committee might not have been an official document of the White House. However, about 15 minutes ago I had a personal chat with Mr. Fred Buzhardt, and he indicated to me that these questions were in fact prepared by his office. Mr. Dean, we have been advised that these questions have appeared in The New York Times. Have you seen those questions? A. No, I have not.

Q. Mr. Dean, you quote the President as saying on Feb. 27 that Haldeman and Ehrlichman were principals in the Watergate matter and that therefore you could be more objective. What did you understand by this?

A. Frankly, Senator, I never understood what the President was saying when he said that they were principals. Before he said that, he told me that the involvement of their time in dealing with Watergate matters was taking them away from their other duties, and then he also added to me that they were principals in this matter and, therefore, that he thought I could be very objective in it; and that was what subsequently prompted me the next day later to make sure he understood that I felt I was also a principal.

Q. Mr. Dean, did you have any evidence then or now that Mr. Erhlichman had prior knowledge of the break-in? A. No, I did not nor I do not now.

Q. The second question: Mr. Dean, if the President was referring to the post-June 17 events, were you not equally a "principal" as you claim to have indicated to the President on Sept. 15?

A. Well, as I just mentioned in answering the last question, when the President raised this, it stuck in my mind, and I returned the next day and after thinking about what he had said, and told him that I also felt I was a principal and that he should understand that.

And I then began to explain to him why I felt I was involved in obstruction of justice and he said, "You don't have any legal problem in this matter," and the discussion was terminated.

Q. Your 245-page statement is remarkable for the detail with which it recounts events and conversations occurring over a period of many months. It is particularly remarkable in view of the fact that you indicated that it was prepared without benefit of note or daily diary. Would you describe what documents were available to you in addition tlo those which have been identified as exhibits.

A. What I did in preparing this statement, I had kept a news-

paper clipping file from roughly June 17 up until about the time
these hearings started when I stopped doing any clipping with any
regularity. It was by going through every single newspaper article
outlining what had happened and then placing myself in what I
had done in a given sequence of time, I was aware of all of
the principal activities I had been involved in, the dealings I had
had with others in relationship to these activities.

Many times things were in response to press activities or press
stories that would result in further activities. I had a good
memory of most of the highlights of things that had occurred,
and it was through this process, and being extremely careful in
my recollection, particularly of the meetings with the President.

Before I did leave the White House, well I was ultimately
denied access to the logs; I called the man who was in charge of
keeping the logs and asked him if he could give me a list of
all my meetings with the President. He did so on an informal
basis before he realized that—when I sent a formal memorandum
asking for more information and a formal confirmation that then
they denied me that information when I sent the formal memorandum.

Q. In addition to your press clipping, the logs, what other
sources did you use in the process of reconstruction?

A. Well, Senator, I think I have a good memory. I think that
anyone who recalls my student years knew that I was very fast
at recalling information, retaining information. I was the type of
student who didn't have to work very hard in school because I
do have a memory that I think is good. I might also add this:
That I did have an opportunity to go through my daily chrono
files which was another part of the process, plus while I was at
Camp David I had sent for some files in preparation of the
report I was writing up there, so I did have some documentary
materials many of which have been submitted to the committee,
some of the exhibits that the committee has, and from these I
was very easily able to put in time sequence various specifics.

Q. The next question; have you always had a facility for
recalling the details of conversations which took place many
months ago?

A. Well, I would like to start with the President of the United
States. It was not a regular activity for me to go in and
visit with the President. For most Americans it is not a regular
activity to go in and visit with the President. For most of the
members of the White House staff it is not a daily activity.
When you meet with the President of the United States, it is a
very momentous occasion, and you tend to remember what the
President of the United States says when you have a conversation
with him.

With regard to others, some of the things, for example, the
"deep six" conversation and shredding of documents was so vivid
in my memory because of the circumstance that had occurred,
that it was very indelibly put in my mind. Going back even while

I was at the Justice Department to seeking the information on Mary Jo Kopechne, that is the sort of thing that would stick in a person's mind because of the nature of the sensitivity of the information being sought. So I would say I have an ability to recall, not specific words necessarily, but certainly the tenor of a conversation and the gist of a conversation.

I would like to give another example. I remember I referred at one point in one of the meetings I had with the President after he had, after Mr. Gray had, made the statement about, that he had jolly well proceeded with the investigation at the White House despite the fact that Mr. Dean had been sitting in on the investigations. I remember vividly when the President mimicked Mr. Gray in saying this and saying it was absurd. That sort of thing is very easy to remember, and it sticks very clearly in one's mind.

Q. Then why is it Mr. Dean, that you were not able to recall precisely the account of the meeting of Sept. 15, very likely the most important meeting in the year 1972?

A. Well, I think I have recalled that meeting.

Q. If I recall, in your colloquy with Mr. Gurney, with Senator Gurney, your response was, "I had an impression."

A. Well, we were talking about the one line out of the first part of the meeting. I would recall to the Senator that after I had had the conversation, I sat down, and the President told me that "Bob had said that you had done a good job," and I turned on the fact of—I said that I could not take responsibility for this alone myself; I remember a sequence of events in the conversation ending up with something when we were discussing a book I was reading, and I remember very vividly the book I was reading at the time we discussed it.

Q. Is it your testimony that you cannot recall precisely what the President said to you?

A. I cannot repeat the very words he used, no, sir. As I explained to Senator Gurney, my mind is not a tape recorder, but it certainly receives the message that is being given.

Q. Did you take any notes of this meeting?

A. No, sir, and I did not take notes of the other meetings for very specific reason. I recall at one time Mr. Moore saying to me, John, you are having a lot of meetings with the President; you ought to be recording these. Some of the things that were being discussed in these meetings I did not want to make records of, Senator.

Q. Why, sir?

A. I thought they were very incriminating to the President of the U.S.

Q. Mr. Chairman, this is not part of the questioning, but could you advise this committee what sort of information you received?

A. Well, I have recalled most of it in my testimony regarding the conversation on clemency for Mr. Hunt, the million-dollar conversation, when the President told me that it would be no problem to raise a million dollars on the 13th. I did not think documents should be around the White House, because the White House had a similar problem as far as information getting out.

Q. You have indicated in your testimony that you were certain after the Sept. 15 meeting that the President was fully aware of the cover-up, did you not? A. Yes, sir.

Q. If that was the case, why did you feel it necessary on Feb. 27 to tell the President that you had been participating in a cover-up and, therefore, might be chargeable with obstruction of justice?

A. Because, on the preceding day, he had indicated to me that Mr. Haldeman and Mr. Ehrlichman were principals, and I was wrestling with what he meant by that. I wanted him to know that I felt also that I was a principal. So I wanted him to be able to assess whether I could be objective in reporting directly to him on the matter.

Q. If the President was aware on Sept. 15 of the cover-up, was he not aware that you were implicated also?

A. I would think so, but I did not understand his remark at the time.

Q. Then, why was it necessary on Feb. 27 to advise him that you were guilty of obstruction of justice?

A. Because, as I said, Senator, when he mentioned the fact that Ehrlichman and Mr. Haldeman were principals, I did not understand what he meant. I wanted to make it clear to him that I felt I also had legal problems and I had been involved in obstruction of justice. Any time I was in the Oval Office, I did not want to withhold anything from the President at any time and felt that any information that he was seeking or came out as a result of the conversation, that I should give it to him.

Q. If you were not clear as to whether the President clearly understood, are you suggesting that on Sept. 15, he did not clearly understand what was happening?

A. I have testified that one of the reasons I sought the meeting on the 21st is because I did not think the President fully understood the implications of the cover-up, the fact that people had been involved in obstruction of justice, and I wanted to make it very clear to him that this was my interpretation of the situation. At that time, I did have access to the President. When he did call me the night before, I did raise it and felt that I should go in and tell him the implications of this entire matter.

Q. If you felt that the President of the U.S. did not fully understand the implications on Feb. 27, how did you expect the President to understand the implications on Sept. 15 of the prior year?

A. When I went in on the prior year, as I say, this was sort of a congratulations, good job, John, Bob's told me what you have been doing. At the time, we went on to discuss other aspects of the efforts to prevent the entire matter from coming out before the election. He talked about when the civil suit would proceed, we talked about when the criminal suit would be tried. The discussion at that time was very, the President was asking most of the questions and I was giving very short answers.

Q. Did you and your counsel develop a strategy for obtaining immunity from prosecution? And what were the elements of that strategy?

A. Well, I recall the chairman starting to raise that question yesterday. First of all, I do not know what is meant by a strategy for immunity. What happened is my counsel went down and began discussing, first of all, how the prosecutors could hear my testimony to make their own determination as prosecutors as to what they wanted to do with me—whether I was to be a witness, whether I was to be a defendant, and the like.

I went to counsel because I had made my determination that I was going to go to the prosecutors and tell them what I knew about the case. But there is an old saying that all lawyers know that the lawyer who represents himself is a fool. I did not feel that I could be objective about my situation. I sought out a man whose judgment I would respect in regard to the criminal law and he said, John, if I am going to represent you, you have to take my counsel, otherwise, you do not need a lawyer if you just want to walk down there. I said, well, I think I will take counsel. I am a lawyer myself and I think to follow counsel is a good idea.

Q. I'll return to the White House questions. Didn't your strategy include deliberate leaks of information to the media on what you had told investigators and what you might be prepared to testify about in the future?

A. Senator, in any testimonial areas, I dealt directly with the appropriate investigative forum. I conceived of no strategy to leak my testimony or anything of that nature. In fact, any comments I have had with the press, I believe, were a matter of public record and I think that most of the press know that I have refused on countless occasions to give what I consider testimonial areas.

Q. The next question, Mr. Dean, is rather lengthy.

Mr. Dean, one point of distinction you drew in your testimony puzzles me. You have testified that you had received and placed in your safe the sum of $15,200 which you never turned over to anyone because you didn't want funds you had physically handled to be used for payments to the Watergate defendants. You also testified that you called Mr. Stans and asked him for $22,000 to make the $350,000 fund whole and that you had your deputy, Mr. Fielding, go to Mr. Stans' office, pick up the money, and later deliver it directly to Mr. Strachan, knowing that $22,000 would probably be used for payments to the Watergate defendants.

Now, do you mean to imply that you think there is some moral basis for the distinction, or were you just being cautious

to protect yourself technically from committing the criminal offense
of obstructing justice at the expense of implicating your deputy?

A. Well, if you will recall my testimony on that when I spoke
with Mr. Stans, I told him Mr. Fielding would be over to pick
up the package. I also informed Mr. Stans that Mr. Fielding would
not know what he was picking up.

I was quite surprised and, I must say, annoyed when Mr.
Fielding came back and told me he had realized that he had
received cash. I did not have any desire to involve Mr. Fielding in
this, because he had not been involved in it before that. I assumed
when he was making the trip that he would be no more than
an innocent agent in the matter and he would be unknowing
as to what he was doing.

I still think to this day he didn't know what the full purpose
of that money was and I told him at the time, I said, "Well,
don't worry about it. It is nothing for you to be concerned
about."

Q. Mr. Dean, you have testified as to your close working relationship to your deputy, Mr. Fielding. It was he who you sent
to pick up the $22,000 from Mr. Stans, he who helped you to
sort the documents from Mr. Hunt's safe and he who sent to
England to retrieve Mr. Young's secretary. Did Mr. Fielding
know that you were involved in a conspiracy to obstruct justice,
perjure testimony and pay defendants for their silence?

A. I have no idea what Mr. Fielding knew. I didn't discuss
these things with him. To the best of my knowledge, his involvement merely was dealing with, going through the material in Mr.
Hunt's safe with me and then dealing with Miss Chenow and
going to England to get her and brief her. He also assisted in
briefing Mr. Krogh and he also accompanied me when Mr.
Ehrlichman requested that he join me in preparing himself for
his interview before the F.B.I. because it related to matters
with the plumbers unit.

Mr. Fielding had become familiar with some of the problems
of the plumbers unit as a result of dealing with Miss Chenow,
and he had also talked to David Young, who was in the
plumbers unit. So, he was more knowledgeable than I was. That
is my knowledge of Mr. Fielding's knowledge.

Q. Mr. Dean, if your deputy, Mr. Fielding, who worked so
closely with you and who carried out some of your missions
connected with the conspiracy, had absolutely no knowledge of
the cover-up conspiracy, how do you so blithely assume that others on the White House staff, and even the President, did know
of your conspiracy?

A. Well, I wouldn't classify it as my conspiracy. I would say
that I was involved with others in a cover-up operation. I recall,
on countless occasions, Mr. Fielding complaining to me that I
was leaving him out, I wasn't explaining to him what I was doing.
We had had a very close working relationship. I think today,
Mr. Fielding is very happy that I did not tell him what I was

doing or involve him any more than the degree he was involved in the entire matter. In fact, he has subsequently thanked me for not involving him.

Q. The question was, if I may repeat it again, if your deputy Mr. Fielding, who worked so closely with you and who carried out some of your missions connected with the conspiracy, had absolutely no knowledge of the cover-up conspiracy, how do you so blithely assume that others on the White House staff and even the President did know of the conspiracy?

A. Well, as I say, I don't know how many other people on the White House staff knew of the conspiracy, not my conspiracy but the general cover-up conspiracy. I certainly know that I was getting instructions from Mr. Haldeman and Ehrlichman and I know of my conversation with the President. I know that there were other people on the staff who were quite aware of the fact that the White House was not baring its soul on this matter. There were, as I said, parallel cover-up situations with regard to Mr. Segretti, where people who were not involved in other aspects become involved in that.

There was the Patman hearing, where it was quite evident that the White House did not want to have the Patman hearings. There were a series of various phases to the cover-up, and various people in the White House knew.

Q. Mr. Dean, beginning in late May and early June there were a series of newspaper stories reporting with what you had told various investigators as quoted sources close to you as to what he had said. A number of these news reports, for example, the page 1 story in The Washington Post of June 3, alleged that you began your private meetings with the President either early in the year or, as in the case of this particular story, beginning on Jan.1.

According to your testimony, your first private meeting with the President in 1973 was not until Feb. 27. Did you or did you not tell investigators and/or friends that you began meetings with the President firstly, either the first of the year or beginning Jan. 1, and were these stories an attempt to exaggerate the length of time which you had been dealing directly with the President and by implication imparting to him knowledge of the Watergate?

A. Senator, where the source of that story came from I do not have any idea. It certainly was not from me. I always, in dealing with any of the investigators from either this committee or from the prosecutor's office, told them exactly what I knew. I do not know of any exaggeration at any time, any place, regarding my knowledge of this matter. So I cannot—it is obviously a loaded question, and I do not know how to answer it other than to say what I just said.

Q. Is it your testimony that the first private meeting you had with the President of the United States in the year 1973 was on Feb. 27? A. That is correct.

Q. Mr. Dean, the number of source stories containing allegations against the President attributed directly or indirectly to you over the last four or five weeks—

A. Excuse me, Senator, I do recall—was that, did you say, private meetings? In other words, after the Inauguration there was a Church service meeting as I recall, where I had a brief encounter with the President where he actually stopped me in the reception line as a result of an incident that had occurred during the Inauguration. It may be relevant. I had not planned to discuss this, but if the committee wishes me to show my recollection of dealings with the President, this may be very well relevant. Right after the Inauguration or during the Inauguration apparently there was a demonstrator who ran through the police lines and toward the President's car.

The next Sunday morning when I was going through the reception line the President pulled me aside and said to me, "I want something done about that man, that fellow that charged the car." I had looked into the case. The best this man could be charged with was a collateral offense for breaking police lines.

I had occasion to request the Secret Service to make a full investigation of the matter. They said they, after examining the man, had released him.

I also talked to Mr. Petersen at the Justice Department, and Mr. Silbert at the Justice Department, and they told me there is no case here. They had talked to the Secret Service.

Meanwhile, I was receiving further reports from Mr. Haldeman, saying "What are you going to do with the man? We want a case made against him." That is one where I just quietly let it go away because there was no case.

Q. Mr. Dean, the number of source stories containing allegations against the President attributed directly or indirectly to you over the last four or five weeks have been most numerous. Do you deny that these stories were planted in a calculated attempt to influence Federal prosecutors to believe you had such important testimony that they should give you transactional immunity from the crimes which you have committed in return for your testimony against others?

A. I gave my testimony directly to the prosecutors. I planted no stories at all to do that, and the prosecutors certainly would not make any decision based on what they are reading in the newspaper. They would want to hear it directly from me, and I was dealing directly with the prosecutors. As likewise with Mr. Dash when he began to interview me to find out what the scope of my knowledge was, to make a decision for this committee as to whether they wished to grant me immunity.

Q. Mr. Dean, the May 14, 1973 edition of Newsweek carried a long article about you and your prospective testimony. In this article you are quoted a number of times and instances. The quotes in that article were word-by-word identical to the testimony you have given this week. Indeed, for the most part this Newsweek article was a very accurate preview summary of the lengthy statement which you detailed before this committee.

There are, however, several very noticeable differences. One difference is an omission from the testimony you gave here. You told this committee that when the President discussed the matter of your investigation of Watergate, you did not tell him you made no investigation.

The Newsweek article, however, reports that in your meeting with the President of March 21, and I quote "Dean also bore down hard, he said, on the fact that there had never been any study clearing White House staffers. Mr. Nixon replied that he had had verbal reports of Dean's work, but the counsel insisted 'Nobody asked me for reports, Mr. President,' he said.

"He said, 'I did not go around asking people questions in their offices. There was no report.'

"At this point sources quoted Dean as saying 'The President came out of his chair into a half crouch of astonishment and shock.' "

If the Newsweek account is correct, Mr. Dean, the President's reaction was most inconsistent with that to which you have testified before this committtee. Did you or did you not tell the President that you had never conducted an investigation, and have you made the statement previously that "the President came out of his chair into a half crouch of astonishment and shock"?

A. Well, I have testified here already that I have never seen the President come out of his chair in that manner. I recall the interview that you are talking about, and the ground rules for that interview my wife was present with me, and she will recall that well; Mr. McCandless was with me, and the rules were set that I would enter into no, what I considered testimonial areas at all of a substantive nature regarding my direct dealings with the President. I was asked if I had prepared an investigation or done an investigation into that, I merely just said, no.

As I say, the interview that was given, and that story does not meet with what I told the reporter, because I said anything I say I want it for attribution, I am not giving you any anything on background or the like and I will not enter into testimonial areas and it was very clearly understood that I would not. I would recall to the Senator again that at this time I was coming under increasing character assassination attacks.

People said, "John, you just cannot sit down and take that, you have got to come out and say at least a few words that you are living and breathing and a real human being," and that is the reason I held that interview.

Q. Mr. Dean, if I recall correctly, you testified to this committee that it was not your idea for Magruder's diary to be altered, nor were you aware before Mr. Magruder testified before the grand jury last September that Mr. Magruder would testify that the first meeting appearing in his diary had been canceled, and the second meeting had been to discuss election laws.

On both of these points, your testimony is in direct conflict with the sworn testimony of Mr. Magruder. Are we to believe that Mr. Magruder lied as to these details concerning you and, if that is your position, what could be Mr. Magruder's motive for lying about the details of the manner in which Mr. Magruder's perjury was conceived?

A. Well, Senator, I will stand on my testimony and not on the conclusions drawn in the question that has been propounded by you at the request of the White House.

Q. Mr. Dean, Mr. Magruder also testified that Mr. Liddy told him that you, among others, had indicated to him that he would have a million dollars for his plans, which he had been working on before he even came to the committee. You testified, on the other hand, that you were surprised when Mr. Liddy briefed his million-dollar intelligence plan to Mr. Mitchell in your presence. To what motive do you attribute Mr. Liddy's report to Mr. Magruder that you knew about his extensive plans before you saw them in Mr. Mitchell's office?

A. Well, if the Senator will check the exhibits, there is one of the exhibits in there where I had an interview or a discussion with Mr. Mitchell. At that time Mr. Mitchell reported to me that Magruder had made this statement to him.

My response at that time to Mr. Mitchell was that I had no recollection at all of ever making such a statement to Mr. Liddy, and I can't conceive of the statement being made for this reason: I was quite aware of the fact that a far different plan, Operation Sandwedge, that had a half-million-dollar budget suggestion, had been deemed to be far more than necessary for anything to deal with even the security problems that were going to confront the campaign.

Q. Mr. Dean, just prior to taking Mr. Liddy to meet Mr. Magruder in early December, 1971 did you and Mr. Liddy not have a meeting with Mr. Egil Krogh and did you not at that time have one million dollars for intelligence gathering at the committee?

A. I recall a meeting with Mr. Krogh and Mr. Liddy when I described the job, and I don't recall specifying a dollar amount as to what the intelligence for dealing with demonstrators would be. I have no recollection of that, Senator, no sir.

Q. Mr. Dean, Mr. Magruder testified that in March, 1972, Mr. Liddy had threatened to kill Mr. Magruder and that Mr. Magruder made a decision to terminate Mr. Liddy's employment. In this connection, Mr. Magruder testified that he received a call from you encouraging him not to become personally concerned about Mr. Liddy and not to let personal animosity get in the way of Mr. Liddy's project. Did you in March intercede with Mr. Magruder on Mr. Liddy's behalf and, if so, since you have said you assumed Mr. Liddy's intelligence project died after your meeting in February, what was the project of Mr. Liddy that you urged Mr. Magruder to give priority over his personal animosities?

A. I did not intercede for Mr. Liddy, in answer to that question, and I think I have described yesterday, I believe it was yesterday, yes, that what happened is I was aware of the fact of a strained relationship between Liddy and Magruder.

Mr. Strachan at one point called me and told me that there were serious difficulties between Liddy and Magruder and Liddy —Magruder wanted to fire Liddy. I said, well, that is a personnel problem for the re-election committee, they need a lawyer over there, that I suggested Mr. Mardian deal with the problem because I didn't think it was something worth taking to Mr. Mitchell.

Q. Mr. Dean, Mr. Magruder testified under oath that prior to his Aug. 16 grand jury appearance at a meeting in your office you told him that if the worst happened "everything would be taken care of, even executive clemency." Did you make such a promise of executive clemency to Mr. Magruder as he testified and, if so, did you have authority from anyone else to make such an offer or was it on your own initiative.

A. Well, I can recall on numerous occasions that Mr. Magruder was very worried, he was very shaky at some stages. As I alluded earlier, or discussed earlier, the fact that the strategy that had been developed, that Mr. Haldeman, Mr. Ehrlichman were quite aware of was that, stop the case with Liddy. That is why apparently they made the decision to keep Mr. Magruder on at the re-election committee, contrary to my recommendation that he be removed. There were a number of occasions that they asked me how was he doing and the like, and I would say, you know, he is either calm today or upset today or the like.

I do recall his having a conversation with me, "What happens if this whole thing comes tumbling down, will I get executive clemency and will my family be taken care of?" And in a manner of not serious import or serious discussion I said something to the effect, "I am sure you will."

But I wouldn't call that what I would consider a firm offer of executive clemency, and it was not in that context at all. He didn't specifically ask "will I get executive clemency." He was just saying he wanted assurances.

Q. Then your testimony, your answer to the question, did you have authority from anyone else to make such an offer is, no.
A. That is correct.

Q. And was it on your own initiative, the answer is yes? A. Yes.

Q. Mr. Dean, did I understand you to testify earlier that you had led Mr. Caulfield to believe you were assisting him in obtaining approval and funding for what he called Operation Sandwedge, but that in fact you let Operation Sandwedge die a natural death?

A. I wasn't encouraging Mr. Caulfield. Mr. Caufield was anxious for my assistance. I told him that I would talk to Mr. Mitchell about it, which I did. Mr. Mitchell virtually rejected it out of hand. In an effort to save a man's feelings who had spent a great deal of time, he had involved a number of other good friends of his own who had major positions and had taken time off to work on the project, rather than come back and bluntly say, "You have been shot out of the water" and it had been dis-approved, I realized that through a period of time he would realize the plan was going nowhere, and it did die a natural death.

Q. I call your attention to Exhibit No. 11, which is a memo-randum for the Attorney General from John Dean, dated Jan. 12, 1972, and I call your attention to the first sentence of the second paragraph, which says:

"Operation Sandwedge will be in need of refunding at the end of this month, so the time is quite appropriate for such a re-view."

Mr. Dean, if you let Operation Sandwedge die a natural death, why did you state to Mr. Mitchell that it would be in need of refunding at the end of January?

A. Well, as I testified to this committee, after the Nov. 24 meeting that Mr. Caulfield had had with Mr. Mitchell, he contin-ued to do various investigative assignments. He was doing an in-vestigative assignment with Mr. McCloskey; Mr. Mitchell was in-terested in that. He continued to call what had formerly been just his relationship with Mr. Ulasewicz, Operation Sandwedge.

Mr. Ehrlichman had raised with me the fact that he thought Mr. Ulasewicz could be of assistance, he would like to keep him around, and that Mr. Mitchell and Mr. Caulfield should decide what Mr. Ulasewicz's future should be. This is the result of the label that Mitchell understood all of Caulfield's operations and I think he has a mis-impression that, dating back to some-where in 1969, I think Mr. Mitchell assumed that everything had been called Operation Sandwedge.

At least in my conversations with him, that is the way he referred to it. So rather than go into a lengthy explanation when I was communicating with him on this matter, I merely called it Operation Sandwedge.

Q. Mr. Dean, you have depicted all others in the White House as excessively preoccupied with political intelligence, use of covert methods and security, and yourself as a restraining in-fluence on these preoccupations. Yet, your background of respon-sibilities at the Justice Department seems to suggest that your experience in these very types of activities might have contrib-uted to your being invited to join the White House staff. What, precisely, were your duties in connection with demonstrations while you were at the Justice Department?

A. I do believe I was a restraining influence at the White House to many wild and crazy schemes. I have testified to some of them; some of them I have not testified to. Many of the memo-randums that came into my office became a joke, in fact, some of the things that were being suggested.

I think if you talk to some of the other members of my staff or if your investigators would like to talk to them, they would tell you some of the things that we would automatically just file—just like the "political enemies" project. Many of these just went right into the file and never anything further, until extreme pressure was put on me to do something, did I ever do anything. So I do feel I had some restraining influence. I did not have a disposition or a like for this type of activity.

Now, let me go to my responsibilities for the Department of Justice. And I will speak specifically with the area of demonstrators. When the demonstration situation was first developing, it was quite obvious that somebody was going to have to talk to the demonstration leaders. I can recall that the first time that I had any knowledge of being involved in this was when I was on my way, doing my normal Congressional relations work, coming up here to Congress on some project.

I had a call just as I was leaving the department, down at the gate of the 10th Street entrance. I was on my way out and they said, the Deputy Attorney General wants to see you right away, would you go up to his office?

I went into his office and here was a large gathering in his conference room, many members of the military, representatives of all the different departments and agencies, the metropolitan police, and the like. At that time, the Deputy Attorney General said, John, you are going to be the negotiator for the Government with the demonstrators to determine who will have permits and what the parameters of those permits will be.

At that time, when I started discussing permits with demonstration leaders, I was offered F.B.I. information on all the demonstration leaders that I was negotiating with.

I said I do not want to have that information, I want to deal as one man looking in another man's eye and know that man for the reaction I get from him just dealing across the table; I do not want to know what he has been doing all his life or the like. I said, that is for others to judge rather than me. I just merely want to tell you the results of my negotiations.

So I was not involved in intelligence from the outset. Now, as I testified, I did become aware from time to time of requests from the White House, because of my proximity to the decision-making processes, for various intelligence that would relate to political figures in their associations with the demonstrations and also, I was hearing complaints that the White House staff was unhappy about the quality of this intelligence.

But my role was merely a conduit from the demonstration leaders back to a major committee that would make decisions and talk about what I would report.

Q. Immediately after you were appointed Counsel to the President, did you not take over the responsibilities of Mr. Tom Huston in connection with intelligence activities?

A. I think that you would have to know Tom Huston and my relationship with Tom Huston to know that there was no way I would take over anything regarding Mr. Tom Huston.

He is a very brilliant, independent man. I did not even know what he was doing half the time. In fact, it was some months after he had joined my staff that I learned he had some sort of scrambler phone locked in a safe beside him, and he made a lot of calls.

Mr. Huston did an awful lot of things that I have no idea what he was doing in the intelligence field. The only thing I know is that at that point, he was the liaison for the receipt of F.B.I. information regarding radical groups and he would be the distributor throughout the White House and he put me on a distribution list. Most of this material was not, even to me, worth reading, because I was not particularly interested unless it was a very current demonstration.

So I inherited Mr. Huston. Mr. Huston and I worked with a friendly relationship. As I say, he is a very independent man, and he and I think a little differently and handle memoranda a little differently.

Q. You did testify, did you not, Mr. Dean that political intelligence was routed to you in the White House?

A. Political intelligence? I had requests for political activities to embarrass people. I think I have turned over in Exhibits 5, 6, 7 and 8 a fair sampling of the sort of things. If the committee would like to go through those at some point, I would like to explain that most of those ended up in my file with no action.

Q. Mr. Dean, I believe that you were the author of the memorandum to the Attorney General which led to the establishment of the Intelligence Evaluation Committee. Did you hold the first meeting of that committee in your office? A. Yes, I believe that is correct.

Q. Were you not the one on the White House staff who levied requirements on and received the reports from the Intelligence Evaluation Committee?

A. That is correct—well, I didn't—I asked them to suggest areas they would like to go into. This would get into a couple of areas that they wanted to get into that directly relate to national security under the rulings of the chair, so we will have to defer from those. But they would often suggest areas that they would like to be into, and I would have to check them with others on the White House staff, particularly the foreign areas, which I didn't think was appropriate for this group, but they had domestic implications. I went to Mr. Haig and he in turn checked with Mr. Kissinger and he would decide there was nothing to be done in this area. We would receive regular calendars from them of events.

I would have a man on my staff, initially Mr. Caulfield and subsequently Mr. David Wilson, who would decide if there was a demonstration coming based on these regular calendars they would send to us, was this a demonstration that we would need intelligence on. And I would, in turn, either summarize or

send a direct report to Mr. Haldeman or any other member of
the staff that the I.E.C. report would relate to.

Q. In interagency meetings to plan for handling demonstrations, were you not the White House representative?

A. From the time I went to the White House, I was, yes,
with some exceptions. There were some types of demonstrations
that I did not go to the Justice Department on or I went with
others, because they were of a particular nature that I had no
expertise in the problem area. I am thinking particularly of the
Wounded Knee situation. I did go over to the meeting on how
to deal with Wounded Knee, but I really was not personally
aware of the Indians' grievance problems, so Mr. Garment took
over and dealt with that.

When there was a demonstration to occur in Washington like
the May Day demonstrations, I did participate with the Attorney
General in those in finding out what the Government was going
to do, because I was asked and expected to report in my summaries that the President had a great interest in as to what was
going to be the Government's response in dealing with such
situations.

Q. In the St. Louis Post Dispatch of May 14, 1973, there is a
report that you attempted to recruit a Department of Interior
employe, Mr. Kenneth Tapman, for undercover work at the
Democratic convention. Did you attempt to recruit Mr. Tapman
or any other for undercover work and what prior experience
did you have in recruiting for undercover work?

A. Mr. Tapman had been with the Department of the Interior
for a number of years. He and I had worked very closely with
the demonstrators. He was with me during most of the negotiations we had on the major demonstrations.

Mr. Tapman wears his hair far longer than I do; he developed an excellent rapport with many of these people. He also
had rapport with the police officials, the metropolitan police and
the like. When I was having no relationships at this point in time
as we went down toward the planning for the convention with
what the re-election committee was going to do, but I knew that
there was going to be a need for the White House to be well informed, I suggested that Mr. Tapman might like to do this.

I thought Mr. Tapman would serve as an excellent source of
information for me and I told him that I wanted him, asked
him if he was interested in going down there. I said, you can't
be on the White House payroll to do this, quite obviously.

Q. Then your answer to this question, did you attempt to
recruit Mr. Tapman—A. Is yes.

Q. This is another very lengthy question: Mr. Dean, you have
testified concerning your conversations on three different occasions with Gen. Vernon Walters, the deputy director of the C.I.A.,
beginning on the 26th of June. General Walters prepared a memorandum for the record of each of these conversations with you.

In General Walter's memorandum record for your meeting with

him on 26 June, you are reported to have asked General Walters whether there was not some way that the Central Intelligence Agency could pay bail for the Watergate defendants and if the men went to prison, could C.I.A. find some way to pay their salaries while they were in jail out of covert action funds.

In your testimony, you made no mention of asking General Walters whether the C.I.A. could pay the Watergate defendants bail or salaries while they were in prison. Was this an intended omission on your part in the interest of saving them or do you deny that you made these specific requests of General Walters?

A. I recall I did make those requests and as I say, the omission was not intentional. I have never really read in full General Walter's depositions. So the answer is that, in fact, I recall that, that was discussed.

Q. Mr. Dean, I believe you testified that on March 26, while you were at Camp David, you called Mr. Maroulis, the attorney for Mr. Liddy, and asked for a statement by Mr. Liddy that you had no prior knowledge of the Watergate break-in. Is that correct?

A. That is correct, and I have so testified.

Q. Now, you also testified, did you not, that it was on March 28 that Mr. Haldeman called you to meet with Mr. Mitchell and Mr. Magruder and that it was at that time you became convinced you would have to look out for yourself. Isn't that correct?

A. That isn't my interpretation. I had decided while I was at Camp David, in fact before I went to Camp David, that I didn't have to watch out for myself, but I saw what others were doing and I realized that I ought to, well, as I say, I retained counsel up there initially and told him because of the L. A. Times story, I retained him.

At that point in time, I told him I would like to talk to him when I got back and suggested to him that he begin to think about a criminal lawyer.

Q. If on March 26, after you, according to your testimony, had admitted to making payments to Watergate defendants to obstruct justice, offering clemency to defendants to obstruct justice and suborning perjury, you were still actively trying to build your defense against having prior knowledge of the break-in of March 26, doesn't this demonstrate that throughout this affair, your motivation was to protect yourself against the criminal charge of authorizing and directing the Watergate break-in?

A. The reason I sought the statement from Mr. Liddy is, you willl recall, I testified that on the 25th, I learned there was going to be a story published in the L. A. Times that I had prior knowledge. I felt that was libelous. I was trying to build what I thought would be a good defense or a good case if I decided I wanted to bring a libel action. In fact, I had mentioned that in my conversation with Mr. Maroulis also.

Q. Mr. Dean, you stated that Mr. Maroulis called you back on the 29th of March and told you he could not get you the statement you wanted from Mr. Liddy. Did you record either of these telephone conversations you had with Mr. Maroulis?

A. Yes. The first telephone conversation was recorded. It is almost inaudible, and I don't know if it is because of the form I recorded it in. I would be happy to turn it over to the committee, and if the committee can get off the tape what is on there, fine. I have been unable to.

Q. Mr. Chairman, that was the last question from the White House. However, the White House has also submitted a short statement, I presume this is the closing statement, sir. "A central credibility question is what prompted Dean's tactics in March and April, 1973—the desire to have the truth told or the effort to achieve immunity from prosecution?

"Dean's admitted personal connection with the offer of clemency to McCord in January (Dean to Caulfield to McCord via Ulasewicz). Dean's admitted personal connection with Hunt's demand for more money on March 19 (Hunt to O'Brien to Dean).

"Dean's meeting with the President on March 21-22. On any version of this meeting it was an effort to get the President to take action on what was becoming a personal problem for Dean.

"McCord's letter to Judge Sirica on March 23."

A. May I just comment there?

Q. Please do, sir.

A. I, in the [March] 21st meeting, had hoped that would be the true punctuation point that ended the cover-up.

It was after that, that morning meeting when I saw that it was not going to end, that the period had not been placed in the story, that my whole thinking began to change and I began to think of how can I now proceed while others are unwilling to proceed, particularly Mr. Haldeman and Mr. Ehrlichman, and at that point in time I certainly wanted to try to still get the President out in front of this entire matter.

Q. "McCord's letter to Judge Sirica on March 23. This was the crucial break in the cover-up. Dean learned via a call from O'Brien. On March 25 press comments directly linked Dean with knowledge of the Watergate break-in. He called Liddy's attorney, Maroulis, on March 27 to get a statement that he did not have prior knowledge of break-in. Maroulis called back on March 29 with word that he couldn't give him a statement. This statement might have been taped. On March 28 and March 29 he solicited names of criminal counsel. On March 30, he decided to retain Mr. Shaffer.

"Time had run out; the cover-up had come apart; Dean was centrally involved. He sent his lawyers to the U.S. attorney on Monday, April 2, and commenced his negotiations for immunity." Mr. Chairman, this ends the statement.

SENATOR ERVIN: When did you transfer from the Justice Department to the White House?

A. July of 1970.

Q. Was he [Tom Huston] at the White House when you arrived there? A. Yes, he was there.

Q. Do you know anything about a meeting having been held in the office of the President on or about the 5th of June, 1970, at which the President and Mr. Huston and others discussed laying plans for gathering domestic intelligence?

A. I have hearsay knowledge of that, Mr. Chairman, that such a meeting did occur.

Q. Now, you were informed in substance that the President assigned to Tom Charles Huston White House staff responsibility for domestic intelligence and internal security affairs? A. That is correct.

Q. Does that not constitute a recommendation from Tom Charles Huston concerning domestic intelligence, the part you have there? Now that document, does not that document, in short, make these recommendations as to the manner or rather the technique that should be followed, in Mr. Huston's view, in gathering domestic intelligence and matters affecting internal security?

Now, as a result of this meeting there was a review by the heads of the C.I.A., the F.B.I., the N.S.A. and the D.I.A. of the techniques used by these information or intelligence gathering organizations to gather intelligence both domestic and foreign, was there not?

A. That was my general understanding, on hearsay again.

Q. Now, I will ask you to look at the exhibit entitled "Recommendations, Top Secret, Handle via Comint Channels Only, Operational Restraints on Intelligence Collection," that you have there.

What I asked was the first recommendation, was techniques for removing limitations on electronic surveillance and penetration. Then the next, the second recommendation was for the use of the mail coverage. The third recommendation was a recommendation of a technique designated as surreptitious entry. A. That is correct.

Q. Now does not the exhibit show that surreptitious entry, does it not state that, this third technique is described by Mr. Huston in that document as follows: "Use of this technique is clearly illegal. It amounts to burglary. It is also highly risky and could result in great embarrassment if exposed. However, it is also the most fruitful tool and can produce the type of intelligence which cannot be obtained in any other fashion."

A. That isn't on the document I have before me, but I do recall something to that effect in the larger report that we are referring to.

Q. Yes, the fourth technique was development of campus sources of information concerning violence prone student groups or campus groups, wasn't it? And the fifth technique recommended by this statement is the use of undercover military agents? A. That is correct.

Q. Now, did not the original document point out in several occasions that Mr. Hoover, the Director of the F.B.I., was wholly opposed to the use of any of these techniques for domestic surveillance? A. Yes, sir, it did.

Q. And I will ask you if the only, the Americans who were to be the subject of these information or intelligence gathering activities were designated by such terms as subversive elements without further definition?

A. It was very broad, that is correct.

Q. And second, selected targets of internal security interests.

A. Yes, sir, again that was a very broad description.

Q. Now, was there anything in the document that told who was going to do the selecting? These selected targets of internal security interests? And that was left up, by the document, to the imagination or interpretation of anybody engaged in the intelligence work? A. That is correct.

Q. And I will ask you, as a lawyer, if you do not think that surreptitious entry or burglary and the electronic surveillance and penetration constituted a violation of the Fourth Amendment? A. Yes, sir, I do.

Q. Hasn't it always been a violation of the Fourth Amendment under the decisions of the court to resort to burglary for the purpose of getting information? And hasn't the Supreme Court recently held by unanimous opinion that the use of electronic surveillance and penetration to obtain information concerning persons allegedly guilty of subversive—of domestic subversive activities—is also a violation of the Fourth Amendment? A. That is correct, Mr. Chairman.

Q. Now, I call your attention to what I designate as Document No. 3 and ask if you will read this document to the committee.

A. This is a memorandum for Mr. Huston, subject, Domestic Intelligence Review: I might add here it is from Mr. Haldeman to Mr. Huston—"The recommendations you have proposed as a result of the review have been approved by the President. He does not, however, want to follow the procedure you have outlined on page 4 of your memorandum regarding implementation.

"He would prefer that the thing simply be put into motion on the basis of this approval. The formal official memorandum should, of course, be prepared than should be the device by which to carry it out.

"I realize this is contrary to your feeling as to the best way to get this done. I feel very strongly that this procedure won't work and you had better let me know and we will take another stab at it. Otherwise let's go ahead."

Q. Now, that letter can only be construed as a statement on the part of Mr. H. R. Haldeman to Mr. Tom Charles Huston, the aide in charge of domestic intelligence, to the effect that the President of the U.S. had approved his recommendations about removing the limitations on surreptitious, or rather, on electronic surveillance and penetration, surreptitious entry or burglary, the use of mail coverage, and of sources of information on the campuses and the military undercover agents for the purposes of gathering information upon the objectives of that. A. That is correct, Mr. Chairman.

Q. Now, do you know that this plan was put into effect—was, rather, approved for use by the President without the prior knowledge of Mr. Mitchell?

A. I do not know that for a fact, no, sir. When I talked to Mr. Mitchell about it, it had reached the state that they wanted to do something. Mr. Mitchell and I talked about it and we decided that the best thing to do was to create the I.E.C.

Q. Now, the I.E.C., in effect, was a proposal to set up a group representing or representatives from the F.B.I., C.I.A., N.S.A., D.I.A., and the counter-intelligence units of the Army, the Navy and the Air Force to furnish information about the activities of all of these agencies to the White House? A. I believe that is correct.

Q. Now, as a lawyer, you are aware of the fact that the Section 403(d) of Title 50 of the U.S. Code provides that the C.I.A. "shall have no police, subpoena, law enforcement powers, or internal security functions."

A. Yes, I was entirely aware of that.

Q. Yet, despite the fact that the statute forbade the C.I.A. exercising any internal security functions, here was a coordination of activities of the C.I.A. in the domestic intelligence field, was there not? And notwithstanding the fact that the statute gave them no internal security functions, they were called upon to evaluate domestic intelligence gathering by other agencies? A. That is correct.

Q. Did you ever receive any instruction from anybody to the effect that the President had rescinded these plans recommended by Mr. Huston?

A. No. To the contrary, as this document indicates, on Sept. 18, I was asked to see what I could do to get the first step started on the document.

Q. Isn't it true to say that among some of the officials in the Committee to Re-elect the President and the White House, there was a great complement of fear during 1970 and '71?

A. I would say there was a great concern about demonstrators.

Q. Now, was not there a feeling there among some White House officials such as Mr. Colson, and perhaps among some in the Committee to Re-elect the President, that every person who was not backing their efforts to re-elect the President or who dissented from the program of the President was an enemy? And that was applied to a great list of people, including some of the most distinguished commentators of the news media on the national scene, was it not? A. Yes sir.

Q. Didn't those in the White House interested in President Nixon's re-election and then the re-election committee classify among their enemies people who dissented from President Nixon's programs?

A. As I say, those who were able to command audience were singled out.

Q. So we have here plans to violate the Fourth Amendment, which were approved by the President, according to Mr. Haldeman; we have people being branded enemies whose mere offense is that they believed in enforcing the First Amendment as proclaimed by the Supreme Court of the United States just about a week ago.

I would like to invite your attention to this very short statement [from Mr. Buzhardt's statement]:

"In February, however, with the Ervin committee beginning its work, the President was concerned that all the available facts be made known."

Do you know any action that the President took subsequent to the establishment of this committee and prior to the time this committee started to function, which showed his concern that all the available facts with respect to the Watergate be made known?

A. Mr. Chairman, I must testify to the contrary.

Q. Now, isn't it true that a short time after the break-in, the news media carried information to the effect that five burglars had been caught in the Democratic national headquarters in the Watergate, and that four of the burglars had money in their pockets which came from the Committee to Re-elect the President? And notwithstanding that fact, was it not revealed shortly thereafter that this money had been paid to Mr. Liddy by Mr. Sloan at the instigation of Mr. Magruder and with the consent of Mr. Stans and Mr. Mitchell? A. I believe that is correct.

Q. Do you not agree with me that these facts indicated that there were footsteps which went from the Watergate right into the office rather, right into the Committee to Re-elect the President. A. There is no doubt of that.

Q. Yet nobody in the committee except Mr. Liddy and Mr. Hunt were indicted. And so this meeting in which the President said that Bob Haldeman had told him about your activities was held in the office of the President right after it had been announced that the indictments had stopped with Mr. Liddy and Mr. Hunt and Mr. McCord?

A. That is correct, and there had been discussion within the White House of this very strategy of stopping them at, or stopping the case at Mr. Liddy and there was an awareness of the fact that Mr. Magruder was going to have to perjure himself to have that accomplished.

Q. Now returning to Mr. Buzhardt's assertion that the President was desirous, beginning in September, to have all of the facts revealed after the establishment of this committee, will you tell us again what meetings were had in the White House with respect to this committee, and who was present?

A. Well, it was when the President was in San Clemente, and I arrived on the, left on the 9th, was out there on the 10th and

11th for meetings, I recall that—of [in] February of this year, I recall that Mr. Haldeman departed the meeting once or twice and he finally told the President what we were meeting on while we were out there.

We left there and went down to La Costa where the meetings proceeded and there we had the remainder of the two days of discussions about how to deal with this committee. During the course of the meetings at one point in time, as I had mentioned earlier, there was an assessment made by Mr. Ehrlichman, there had been disappointment that they had not been able to influence the selection of the committee, there had been disappointment they had not been able to amend successfully your resolution to have equal representation between Republican and Democrats; that the floor amendments that had been offered had been defeated.

Q. Was that one of the times you said that there was, the consensus was there should be an effort to show, to claim open cooperation with the committee but an effort to impede it from discovering the truth?

A. I would call the chairman's attention to the exhibit regarding the meeting with the Attorney General where there was great concern that the committee might uncover additional criminal activity.

Q. You spoke of some meeting that the President attended in which he wondered if the committee was going to swallow the bait he had put out in the press conference about a court decision?

A. That was on St. Patrick's Day.

Q. And this was about a month after Mr. Buzhardt says that the President was anxious for all the facts to be revealed. So you know something about those facts? A. No, sir, I do not.

Q. I believe you discussed at that time the assertion that I made I was not willing to accept written statements because you cannot cross-examine a written statement.

A. Yes, and I had discussion with the President about that very statement.

Q. Just one other matter. Article II of the Constitution says, in defining the power of the President, Section 3 of Article II, "He"—that is the President—"shall take care that the laws be faithfully executed."

Do you know anything that the President did or said at any time between June 17 and the present moment to perform his duty to see that the laws are faithfully executed in respect to what is called the Watergate affair?

A. Mr. Chairman, I have given the facts as I know them and I don't—I would rather be excused from drawing my own conclusion on that at this point in time.

Q. I will ask you as a lawyer if the experience of the English-speaking race, both in its legislative bodies and in its courts, has not demonstrated that the only reliable way in which the credibility of a witness can be tested is for that witness to be interrogated upon oath and have his credibility determined not only by what he says but by his conduct and demeanor while he is saying it and also by whether his testimony is corroborated or not corroborated by other witnesses? A. That is correct.

SENATOR BAKER: Some of the specific allegations that you make in your testimony are at least prima facie extraordinarily important. The net sum of your testimony is fairly mind-boggling.

As I said just a moment ago, it is not my purpose now to try to test your testimony.

It is not my purpose to try to impeach your testimony, to corroborate your testimony, to elaborate or extend particular aspects of it but rather to try to structure your testimony so that we have a coherent presentation against which we can measure the testimony of other witnesses heretofore given, and the testimony of other witnesses later to appear. The central question is simply put: what did the President know and when did he know it?

In trying to structure your testimony I would ask that you give attention to three categories of information: That information that you can impart to the committee that you know of your own personal knowledge: That type of information that we lawyers refer to as circumstantial evidence, which would include evidence given based on your opinion or on inferences you draw from circumstances in the situation and, third, that type of evidence that ordinarily would not be admitted in a court of law but is admitted here for whatever purpose it may serve, that is hearsay evidence or evidence about which you have only second-hand information.

Under the heading of what did the President know and when did he know it fall several subdivisions. The first one is the break-in at the Democratic National Committee headquarters of the Watergate complex on the morning of June 17, 1972. Do you have any information that he [the President] did know of it?

A. I only know that I learned upon my return to the office that events had occurred that indicated that calls had come from Key Biscayne to Washington to Mr. Strachan to destroy incriminating documents in the possession of Mr. Haldeman.

I can only testify as to the fact that anything that came to Mr. Haldeman's attention of any importance was generally passed to the President by Mr. Haldeman, and if Mr. Haldeman had advance knowledge or had received advance indications it would be my assumption that that had been passed along, but I do not know for a fact.

Q. The cover-up is a second heading. What did the President know and when did he know it, about the cover-up?

A. I would have to start back from personal knowledge, and that would be when I had a meeting on Sept. 15 when we discussed what was very clear to me in terms of cover-up. We discussed in terms of delaying lawsuits, compliments to me on my efforts to that point. Discussed timing and trials, because we didn't want them to occur before the election. That was direct conversation that I testified to.

Now, going back to the June 17 time, I believe I have testified to countless occasions in which I reported information to Mr. Haldeman and Mr. Ehrlichman, made recommendations to them regarding Mr. Magruder, I was aware of the fact that often Mr. Haldeman took notes. I know that Mr. Haldeman met daily with the President, I was quite aware of the fact that this was one of the most important and virtually the only issue that was really developing at all, and given the normal reporting channels I worked through it was my assumption, without questioning, that this was going in to the President.

Q. Go ahead, Mr. Dean, on the Sept. 15 meeting.

A. As I tried to describe in my statement, the reception was very warm and very cordial. There was some preliminary pleasantries, and then the next thing that I recall the President very clearly saying to me is that he had been told by Mr. Haldeman that he had been kept posted or made aware of my handling of the various aspects of the Watergate case and the fact that the case, you know, the indictments had now been handed down, no one in the White House had been indicted, they had stopped at Liddy.

Q. Stop, stop, stop just for one second. Let's examine those particular words just for a second. That no one in the White House had been indicted. Is that as near as the exact language —I don't know so I am not laying a trap for you, I just want to know.

A. Yes, there was a reference to the fact the indictments had been handed down and it was quite obvious that no one in the White House had been indicted . . .

Q. Did he say that, though?

A. Did he say that no one in the White House had been handed down? I can't recall it. I can recall a reference to the fact that the indictments were now handed down and he was aware of that and the status of the indictments and expressed what to me·was a pleasure to the fact that it had stopped at Mr. Liddy.

Q. Tell me what he said.

A. Well, as I say, he told me I had done a good job—

Q. No, let's talk about the pleasure. He expressed pleasure the indictments had stopped at Mr. Liddy.

Can you just for the purposes of our information tell me the language that he used?

A. Senator, let me make it very clear the pleasure that it had stopped there is an inference of mine based on, as I told Senator Gurney yesterday, the impression I had as a result of the, of his, complimenting me.

Q. Can you give us any information, can you give us any further insight into what the President said?

A. Yes, I can recall he told me that he appreciated how difficult a job it had been for me.

Q. Is that close to the exact language?

A. Yes, that is close to the exact language. That stuck very clearly in my mind because I recall my response to that was that I didn't feel that I could take credit. I thought that others had done much more difficult things and by that I was referring to the fact that Mr. Magruder had perjured himself.

Q. All right. Now, tell us about the status of the case.

A. When we talked about the fact that the indictments had been handed down, at some point, and after the compliment I told him at that point that we had managed, you know, that the matter had been contained, it had not come in to the White House, I didn't say that, I said it had been contained.

Q. What was the President's or Mr. Haldeman's reaction to that word because that is a rather significant word, I think.

A. Everyone seemed to understand what I was talking about. It didn't evoke any questions and I was going on to say that I didn't think it could be contained indefinitely. I said that this is, you know, there are a lot of hurdles that have to be leaped down the road before it will definitely remain contained and I was trying to tell the President at that time that I was not sure the cover-up even then would last indefinitely.

Q. What was his reaction to this?

A. As I say, I don't recall any particular reaction.

Q. Was there any statement by him or by Mr. Haldeman at that point on this statement?

A. No, not to my recollection. Then, the conversation turned to the press coverage that had been following the Watergate incident, and during this discussion he told me that I should keep a good list of people who were giving us trouble in the press because we would give them trouble after the election.

Q. This was stated by the President? A. That is correct.

Q. What was, what else was said by him or by Mr. Haldeman or by you in that context?

A. Well, this evolved into a, immediately into a conversation about the Internal Revenue Service and using the Internal Revenue Service to audit returns of people.

I went on to tell the President that we did not seem to have the clout at the White House to get this done.

Q. Did you in fact initiate I.R.S. inquiries or audits as a result of suggestions from the White House staff or the President?

A. Well, the President at this time—told me to keep a good list, so that these could be—you know, we would take care of these people after the election, and we went into—I told him that I.R.S. was a Democratically oriented bureaucracy and to do something like that was a virtual impossibility. And then the conversation moved to the fact that he was going to make some dramatic changes in all of the agencies and, at this point in time, I can remember Mr. Haldeman opened up his pad and started making notes as to what the President was describing as to his post-election intentions.

Q. As you know, Mr. Haldeman will be a witness before this committee. The only other person present was the President. I am not prepared to say at this point how we may be able to gain access to the President's knowledge and perception of that meeting. But in a three-way meeting, I think it is important to this committee that we have all the information we can get.

SENATOR WEICKER: I think, Mr. Chairman, that the American people should know that the author of the White House memorandum read by Senator Inouye yesterday makes statements of facts concerning John Mitchell which, in effect, assume that he took part in a conspiracy to break and enter, that he took part in obstructing justice and suborning perjury, and all this without an admission or conviction of John Mitchell. And this, Mr. Chairman, done in the document sent by the White House to this committee.

I don't believe that in anything that the committee has done to date we have overstepped our bounds to this extent and I think it important to note, not only in the case of Mr. Dean, who sits before us, but also in the case of Mr. Mitchell, who is to come before us.

Now, Mr. Chairman, I would like to go ahead and repeat now as to exactly what acts have been testified to, have actually been proven or admitted in the illegal area, acts committed by various members of the executive branch of Government—conspiracy to obstruct justice, conspiracy to intercept wire or oral communications, subornation of perjury, conspiracy to obstruct a criminal investigation, conspiracy to destroy evidence, conspiracy to file false sworn statements, conspiracy to commit breaking and entering, conspiracy to commit burglary, misprision of a felony, filing of false sworn statements, perjury, breaking and entering, burglary, interception of wire and oral communications, obstruction of criminal investigation, attempted interference with administration of the internal revenue laws and attempted unauthorized use of internal revenue information.

These are illegal matters proven or admitted that have been accomplished by the executive branch of this Government.

As to those matters that are unconstitutional attempts to infringe upon people's First Amendment rights of free speech, and the press, the enemy list which we have seen, First Amendment rights to peaceable assembly, Fourth Amendment rights to be secure in our houses and papers and effects, and Fourth Amendment rights, denial of rights to fair trial, right to due process of law. That is what we have heard has been done in the way of unconstitutional acts by the executive branch of the Government.

June 29, 1973

SENATOR MONTOYA: Mr. Dean, I presume while you were counsel at the White House that you probably provided input to some legal opinions with respect to the possibility that the President might be subpoenaed before any Congressional committee. A. No sir I do not.

Q. Did anyone else?

A. Not while I was present at the White House do I recall that subject being researched by my office, certainly.

Q. Did you have any discussions pursuant to this?

A. It was the President who told me that rather than refer to the matter as executive privilege that Mr. Ziegler should start referring to it as separation of powers.

Now, when we were looking into the problems of executive privilege, there were reviews but not as far as the President vis-à-vis an appearance was ever researched as opposed to staff appearances.

Q. Now, referring to the President's news conference on Aug. 29, 1972, and I will quote from that. Answer. "The President. The F.B.I. is conducting a full field investigation. The Department of Justice, of course, is in charge of the prosecution and presenting the matter to the grand jury. The Senate Banking and Currency Committee"—I presume he meant the House—"is conducting an investigation. The General Accounting Office, an independent agency, is conducting an investigation. Now with all these investigations that are being conducted, I don't believe that adding another special prosecutor would serve any useful purpose."

Now, you stated before that there was a move at the White House to try to stop the House Banking and Currency investigation.

And that was about the time that he was making this statement to the press?

A. That is correct. There was an ever-increasing effort of the White House to deal with the Patman committee hearings as I have so testified.

Q. Was it before Aug. 29 when he made the statement at the press conference or after?

A. It was after, Sept. 15.

SENATOR GURNEY: I would like to go back to the Kalmbach meeting again, when you and he first discussed this cover-up money.

A. On the 29th, Senator? He was staying at the Mayflower Hotel.

Q. Was there anyone else at the meeting? A. No, sir, there was not.

Q. And my recollection is that you had a short meeting in the coffee shop, is that right?

A. I was to meet him in the coffee shop and I recall we sat down in the booth and it did not appear very private in the booth, so we decided to go to his room to discuss the matter.

Q. And that was there in the Mayflower Hotel? A. That is correct.

Q. Well, the committee has subpoenaed the records of the hotel. I have a letter here from the Mayflower, and also one from the Statler Hilton. The letter is from the Mayflower Hotel.

"Dear Senator Gurney, the records do not reflect a Mr. Herbert B. Kalmbach as being a registered guest during the period June 1, 1972, through July 1; 1972.

Then the other letter from the Statler Hilton, again addressed to me. "Mr. Herbert W. Kalmbach was registered in our hotel from June 29-30, 1972."

Now, you have testified three times that you met with Mr. Kalmbach in the coffee shop of the Mayflower Hotel. A. Absolutely. That is correct.

Q. And then retired to his room in the Mayflower. How do you account for these records here?

A. The only thing I can suggest is that Mr. Kalmbach may have been registered under another name.

Mr. Kalmbach often discussed matters in a code name. For example, after our discussion, he began referring to Mr. Hunt as "the Writer." He began referring to Mr. Haldeman as "the Brush." He began referring to Mr. Mitchell as "the Pipe."

Q. If he was coming into the city under an assumed name so that no one would know he was here why in the world would he register under his own name at a nearby hotel, the Hilton, and then engage another room over in the Mayflower to meet with you? It just does not add up.

A. I see what you are saying. I have testified the Mayflower and I am never sure which is the the Mayflower and which is the Statler Hilton. The hotel I recall is the one that is in 16th Street up from the White House. [The location of the Statler Hilton.]

Q. How long have you lived in Washington?

A. I have been here about 10 years.

Q. And you don't know the difference between the Hilton and the Mayflower hotel?

A. I continually get them confused.

Q. Well, I must say I am reminded of your colloquy with the chairman yesterday, Mr. Dean, when you said what an excellent memory you had right from school days.

A. I might go back over one point. The name of the coffee shop at the Statler Hilton is the Mayflower.

Q. Is that what your attorney just told you? A. Yes, he did.

Q. I am interested in this meeting of March 21 with the President. I was going over that yesterday, and that there was one part of that that I must say totally confused me.

You mentioned that you talked to the President about perjury being committed, you talked about the cover-up, if it was going to continue it would require more perjury and more money and you said it was the time for the surgery on the cancer itself.

But then, you also made this statement, "After I finished I realized that I had not really made the President understand because after he asked me a few questions he suggested it would be an excellent idea if I gave some sort of briefing to the Cabinet."

I must say I overlooked that totally when the testimony was first given, and I must say it does not seem to make any sense to me at all.

If the President was not fully acknowledgeable about this whole cover-up business, and a part of it, as I think you have indicated before the committee here, why in the world would he want the Cabinet briefed?

A. Well the conversation had tapered down and we were into a light question and answer session about some of the areas that I had gone into, and I must say that I had a similar reaction, and I said to the President, "Mr. President, I do not think this is the sort of thing that I could give a briefing on even a tailored-down briefing on," but he felt it might be important that I explained some of the parameters of the problem and the like.

I might add I never did give a briefing to the Cabinet and that was dropped immediately in the conversation. I added that because it stuck in my mind that as one of the points that I really did not feel that I had made the full implications of this thing clear.

Q. Well, now, you went before the grand jury last week, did you not? A. That is correct.

Q. Did you tell them the whole story?

A. I decided to exercise my constitutional rights.

Q. What do you mean by that? A. I invoked the Fifth Amendment.

MR. SHAFFER [attorney for Mr. Dean]: I hate to interrupt, Senator—I would like to defend my client's constitutional rights and by so doing I would like to call to the attention of the Chair the fact that in 1959 our Supreme Court decided the case of United States versus Gruenwald and in that case the Supreme Court said that it is not proper cross-examination and it is not inconsistent for a witness on one occasion to take his Fifth Amendment right and on another occasion testify.

SENATOR GURNEY: I might state to the counsel that just about all of the testimony that has been presented here before this committee, whether by this witness or any other witness, would never be admissible in a court of law, a good bit of it.

SENATOR ERVIN: The rule of law, as I understand it where

you have evidence tending to show two or more people conspired either to do an unlawful act or to do a lawful act by unlawful means, then any action or statement made by one of the parties to the conspiracy in furtherance of the objective of the conspiracy is admissible in evidence, and in my judgment as a lawyer, while we have some hearsay and we have had some questions asked that were not admissible in a court of law, I think the great bulk of the testimony that has been produced here would be admissible in a court of law.

SENATOR GURNEY: No question has been posed that I know of to the witness at this moment that interferes with his constitutional rights. I simply asked him if he had gone before the grand jury, he said he had and said he had taken the Fifth Amendment.

SENATOR ERVIN: I would just like to make the observation that Felix Frankfurter wrote a very interesting article at the time about the Teapot Dome and he laid great stress on the wisdom of the fact that Congressional committees should not be bound by technical rules of evidence. However I had read several articles by commentators who are not lawyers and who were criticizing the committee on the ground that it had received hearsay testimony. I am not concerned much about criticism, because I have been criticized very much over the years but I think it is well for the general public to know that under the rules governing the admissibility of declarations of co-conspirators, the great bulk of the hearsay testimony that has been received in this case would have been admissible in a court of law for an indictment charging a conspiracy to obstruct justice.

SENATOR INOUYE: Your exhibits have listed, I would say, a couple of hundred names of very distinguished Americans, most of them, and other exhibits have suggested that extra-legal activities had been carried out in connection with these names.

Mr. Colson has gone on the air suggesting that the lists you submitted were a social list, that this was a list used by the White House so that they would not invite the names listed there for the White House dinners.

Did you know if anything ever happened to these 20 on the top hit parade?

A. I cannot answer that, because I think it was realized that my office had less than enthusiasm for dealing with things like this.

Q. Are you aware of any person or any agency or any official using these lists to do harm or injury or to assist?

A. They were principally used by Mr. Colson and Mr. Haldeman and I don't know what they did with them. On one occasion, I had a call regarding the fact that some of the President's friends—and these are in exhibits and I just think it would be inappropriate right now to mention the individuals' names—were having tax problems and I was to look into those. I had Mr. Caulfield, who had, who was the person on my staff who was the only one I knew who had a relationship with the Internal Revenue Service—because I could only deal with the director.

At any rate, as I was saying, I was told that I was to do something about these audits that were being performed on two friends of the President's. They felt that they were being harassed and the like.

There is a third instance where this occurred also. When I got around to checking on it, Mr. Caulfield sent me some information, Mr. Higby sent it in to Mr. Haldeman and Mr. Haldeman wrote a note on the bottom, "This has already been taken care of." So obviously, things were happening that I had no idea on.

Now, I would again like to defer from using names in this instance, but there was a request of an audit that was commencing on somebody who was close to the President and several people got involved in this. They said, John, you have got to do something about this, because the President is just going to hit the roof when he finds out about it.

Well, I went to the Justice Department because it had already gone from Internal Revenue to the Criminal Division of the Justice Department. I spoke with Mr. Erickson about it. He said, this man is just up to his teeth in the problem.

I reported back to the people who were asking me. I said, just do not touch this, there is just no way; this man is in trouble and he has got to be told he is in trouble.

Q. Do you know from your personal knowledge, Mr. Dean, if any member of the U.S. Congress was ever subjected to an Internal Revenue Service audit or surveillance by the F.B.I.?

A. I do know that there was extensive surveillance on Senator Kennedy, which I have testified to.

Q. Was this for political purposes? A. Yes sir, it was.

Q. Was the F.B.I. aware that this surveillance was for political purposes?

A. The F.B.I. did not perform this. This was performed directly by the White House.

Q. Then, your testimony is that with the exception of this columnist [Robert Green of Newsday] and this television commentator [Daniel Schorr of C.B.S.] and Mr. Chet Huntley and Senator Kennedy, you are not aware of how these lists were ever used?

A. No, sir. I am also aware, and I would have to again be able to look through my files on this, there were a number of requests from various members of the White House staff to see if tax exemptions and alternation of the tax status could be removed from various charitable foundations and the like, that were producing material that was felt hostile to the Administration, or their leaders were taking positions that were hostile to the Administration, and on occasions I checked this out and their activities were deemed to be perfectly proper within the provisions of the Internal Revenue Code and nothing was done on these.

Q. I refer to an article which appeared in The Charlotte Observer, dated May 17, 1973, and it reads as follows: "High officials in the North Carolina Republican party confirmed Wednesday that H. R. (Bob) Haldeman, at the time President Nixon's chief of staff, made two attempts to get local party officials to 'dig up something to discredit Ervin and blast him with it.' "

Are you aware if this activity did in fact occur?

A. The only recollection I have of any effort to get any information on the chairman came to me—Mr. Baroody told me he was meeting with some people from North Carolina and they thought they may have some interesting information on the Senator.

SENATOR ERVIN: The committee will come to order. Was George Wallace of Alabama on the list of enemies?

A. Senator, I never really have gone through the list of enemies so I cannot name that. The only thing I know about Mr. Wallace in the relationship at all is that, the fact that, I understand that during Mr. Wallace's, Governor Wallace's last gubernatorial campaign, that a substantial amount of money was provided by Mr. Kalmbach to Mr. Wallace's opponent. That was told me by Mr. Kalmbach, who apparently made the arrangements.

Q. Mr. Dean would you tell me of your conversation with the President on the 15th [of April]?

A. I was rattled by the fact that I had not been to the President to tell him that I had been to the prosecutors when I went in. To be rather specific, he realized I was rattled and I had had enough rapport with him by this time that I was comfortable in dealing with him. I had thought on the way in, I wonder if I'm being set up by the President. Now, this was an awful thought to run through my own mind, because I knew that Haldeman and Ehrlichman knew that anything the President asked me, I would answer and I would answer truthfully. You do not lie to the President of the United States.

Q. Move on to the conversation.

A. Right. Well, I am telling you that—all right, the conversation. So the President offered me a cup of coffee.

Q. First of all, where was the meeting?

A. This was in the Executive Office Building. I told the President that I had been to the prosecutors. I told him I did not believe this was an act of disloyalty, I felt I had to go and do it. I said I thought in the end that it would be considered an act of loyalty and I felt that and I felt that when I made my decision to go, that was the way I felt.

I told him that in my discussion with the prosecutors, I

had discussed my own involvement and the involvement of others.

I told him that I had not discussed any conversations I had with him with the prosecutors, and I had not had any dealings with the prosecutors vis-à-vis myself and the President.

At one point in the conversation, I recall the President asking me about whether I had reported to him on the fact that Mr. Haldeman had been told by me after the second meeting with Mr. Mitchell on Feb. 4 of 1972, about what occurred in that meeting. I said, yes, I had.

Then, the President raised the fact that this had come up in a discussion he had had with Henry Petersen and Petersen had raised with him why had not Haldeman done something to stop it.

Then, the President went on to tell me, well, now, John, you testify to that when asked. Now, I want you to testify to that when asked, that you told Mr. Haldeman.

Q. Was there anything else?

A. The question came up as to whether I had immunity from the Government as a result of my dealings with the prosecutors. I told the President that my lawyers had discussed this with the Government, but I assured him that I had no deal with the Government at all.

The President at that point said, and I remember this very clearly, he said, John, I will do nothing, I assure you, to interfere in any way with your negotiations with the Government. And that would be fairly close to the words I believe he used.

As I was leaving the office, he said to me, say hello to your pretty wife and some things of this nature, which I came home and conveyed to her, because she always liked to hear those things.

Then also, as I was standing by the door, I remember I had the door open and I turned to the President, who was standing not 10 feet away from me, and told the President that I certainly hoped that the fact that I was going to come forward and tell the truth did not result in impeachment of the President. And I told him that I hoped the thing would be handled right, and he assured me that it would be handled right.

And the meeting ended on that note.

Testimony by John N. Mitchell

July 10   *Says he concealed Watergate from Nixon to prevent election damage; charges Magruder lied and disputes Dean; denies he authorized any plan that led to break-in.*

July 11   *Says Ehrlichman and Haldeman participated in cover-up to shield Nixon and defends President.*

July 12   *Defends credibility as to conflicts in testimony.*

July 10, 1973

MR. DASH: During 1971, were you aware of an intelligence operation that had been set up in the White House under Mr. Ehrlichman and Mr. Krogh which has become known as the "plumbers" operation?

MR. MITCHELL: No, sir.

Q. Did you—was there a time that you did become aware of that operaton? A. Yes, sir, I did.

Q. When was that?

A. After June 17, 1972

Q. Now also, Mr. Mitchell, in 1971 were you aware of the so-called Sandwedge plan proposed by Mr. Caulfield for political intelligence operations?

A. I was aware of the concept that Mr. Caulfield was proposing and, of course, I opposed that and it never came to fruition.

Q. Did you ever have a copy of the so-called Sandwedge proposal or plan in your possession?

A. Not to the best of my knowledge, my knowledge of it came in discussions with John Dean.

Q. Were you aware that that plan also included a so-called covert operation and the use of bugging or electronic surveillance?

A. No, I have seen that in one of Mr. Dean's exhibits but that was not the understanding that I had of the so-called Sandwedge proposal.

Q. Did you know that the budget included actual funds to purchase electronic surveillance equipment?

A. No, sir, I had never got that far with the subject matter.

Q. Now, in any event, did you, after the recommendation of

Mr. Caulfield for the so-called Sandwedge plan, did you hire Mr. Caulfield for any operation or any particular assignment?

A. There has been shown to me by this committee a memorandum that had to do with an investigation that apparently was made under Mr. Caulfield's aegis having to do with the so-called McCloskey campaign up in New Hampshire. I do not know who hired him or who paid him. I have seen the memorandum.

Aside from that, I would go to the point that Mr. Caulfield, who I saw on the 24th day of November 1971, wherein Mr. Dean brought him over to discuss the concept of his working for me in the campaign if and when I joined the campaign, Mr. Caulfield did come to work for the committee as what was purported to be an aide-de-camp at sometime in March and within two weeks or so, he was gone, had left the committee.

Q. Now, Mr. Mitchell, what role did you play in the setting up of the Committee for the Re-election of the President?

A. Well, the basic role, I believe, was the discussion with the President to the point that he still had to get nominated in his second term and there was a committee needed to undertake that function and that there should be one established. Also, with respect to the people who originally organized the committee, we discussed those, and of course, the personnel that originally came to the Committee for the Re-election of the President were also discussed.

Q. Now, I think you have indicated that Mr. Haldeman also played a role in both the creation of the Committee to Re-elect the President and the selection of personnel. What was the relationship between you and Mr. Haldeman in the operation of the committee?

A. Well, it was one of liaison, I would think, at the highest level, in which he, of course, would be representing the President and the interest of the President in connection with the campaign, and that most major decisions were discussed with Mr. Haldeman and/or the President, and I say very major decisions.

Q. And did you have fairly frequent conversations or meetings with Mr. Haldeman on this subject?

A. I would think that the meetings were not that frequent. Undoubtedly, we had numerous telephone conversations about various subject matters.

Q. Now, in the fall of 1971, Mr. Mitchell, when Mr. Caulfield's Sandwedge plan was not accepted, were you aware of a continuing concern on the part of Mr. Haldeman and the White House or Mr. Magruder's part for an intelligence capacity for the Committee to Re-elect the President to deal with the problems of demonstrations and the possible violence during the campaign?

A. Yes, that first came up, of course, in that, or at least, occurred in my recollection, it first came up in that Nov. 24 meeting, when Dean brought Liddy over into my office to discuss the general counsel for the Committee for the Re-election of the President.

Q. Was that one of the reasons that Mr. Liddy was being introduced to you, to take over fact and intelligence gathering?

A. No, I don't believe that is one of the reasons he was introduced to me. They were looking for a general counsel. What I am pointing out to you is that in one of the exhibts that Mr. Dean has provided you with, in what you might call a prospectus dealing with Mr. Liddy's job, there is a one-line short sentence in which it refers to intelligence gathering.

Q. Was that discussed at all during that meeting with you?

A. No. The meeting was a very, very short one and the contents of the prospectus was not discussed.

Q. Did you understand that a portion of Mr. Liddy's time would be spent in fact gathering or intelligence gathering for the committee?

A. I don't believe I focused on it at the time, but later on I came to understand that Mr. Liddy was expending his time or portions of his time in gathering information of this sort.

Q. I think you said Mr. Dean brought Mr. Liddy over. A. That is correct.

Q. Was that the first time you had met Mr. Liddy?

A. To the best of my recollection, that is the first time I ever met him.

Q. Well, did you know that Mr. Liddy also worked for Mr. Krogh as one of the plumbers?

A. No, I had not been advised of those activities as of that time.

Q. Now, after Mr. Liddy was hired and did become counsel to the committee, there came a time when there was a meeting in your office Mr. Mitchell, on Jan. 27, 1972, at the Department of Justice, attended by Mr. Dean, Mr. Magruder, Mr. Liddy and of course, yourself.

Now the committee has heard, Mr. Mitchell, considerable testimony about this particular meeting, at least from the other side of your desk. What, to your best recollection, was the intelligence plan that Mr. Liddy presented to you as Attorney General or in your role as adviser to the Committee for the Re-election of the President?

A. I think it can be best described as a complete horror story that involved a mishmash of code names and lines of authority, electronic surveillance, the ability to intercept aircraft communications, the call girl bit and all the rest of it.

Q. Do you recall the use of charts in the show and tell operation?

A. I recall the use of charts because this is where the lines were all crossing with the authority, et cetera, et cetera.

Q. Do you recall any of the code names that were used, Mr. Mitchell?

A. No, I can't, Mr. Dash. The matter was of such striking content and concept that it was just beyond the pale.

Q. When Liddy completed his presentation what was your reaction?

A. Well, I think it was very simple. As I recall, I told him to go burn the charts and that this was not what we were interested in. What we were interested in was a matter of information gathering and protection against the demonstrators.

Q. Mr. Mitchell, if this was the kind of plan that you have described and, as has been described this way by other witnesses before this committee, and since you were the Attorney General of the United States, why didn't you throw Mr. Liddy out of your office?

A. Well, I think, Mr. Dash, in hindsight I not only should have thrown him out of the office, I should have thrown him out of the window.

Q. Well, since you did neither—why didn't you at least recommend that Mr. Liddy be fired from his responsible position at the committee since obviously he was presenting to you an irresponsible program?

A. Well, in hindsight I probably should have done that, too. About the belief I had at the time in turning the matter over we would get back to the purpose that was originally intended, and that he was qualified to pursue that particular segment that we had been talking about.

Q. Well, it's been testified that although you didn't take an affirmative action, you did not approve the plan that was presented by any means, that Mr. Liddy at least went away from your office with the idea that he could come back with a scaled-down version and a version of a plan for intelligence gathering that would have a lower price tag. By the way, what was the price tag? Do you recall the price tag?

A. Oh, just a million dollars.

Q. Now, just carrying on from what my previous observation was as to what Mr. Liddy may have come away from the meeting, obviously Mr. Magruder and Mr. Liddy would not get the impression that you completely disapproved of the program because they did set up only eight days later a meeting in your office on Feb. 4 with the same participants in which they presented a half million dollar program, I understand, which included electronic surveillance.

A. Well, Mr. Dash, I would disagree with the testimony to which you refer insofar as Mr. Magruder or Mr. Liddy either one of them was invited back under the basis of the same concept with respect to the presentation of a plan, and I think Mr. Dean, if I recall his testimony, agrees a little bit more with what my recollection was and it was to the point of this was not what we were interested in. What we were interested in was the gathering of information and the security and protection against the demonstrations.

Q. But nevertheless, Mr. Magruder and Mr. Liddy did come back and Mr. Dean attended that meeting with you, on Feb. 4, and did present a scaled-down version but this version did include electronic surveillance and break-ins, did it not?

A. It did that but there again there are faulty recollections with what was discussed at that meeting, what the concept of it was. I violently disagree with Mr. Magruder's testimony to the point that the Democratic National Committee was discussed as a target for electronic surveillance for the reasons that he gave, number one with respect to the Democratic kickback story. We are talking now about the 4th of February.

Q. Yes, I know, Mr. O'Brien's, the reason for centering in on Mr. O'Brien, I believe—

A. That is correct, and, of course, the newspaperman did not have his column that Magruder referred to until the 23d of February. He said we were focusing on the Democrats and Mr. O'Brien because Mr. O'Brien's vocal activities in connection with the I.T.T. case, and Mr. Anderson did not publish his column until the 29th of February, and so that what I am pointing out is that this meeting was a relatively short meeting and it was rejected again because of the fact that it had these factors involved. But these targets were not discussed.

Q. Were any targets discussed, Mr. Mitchell? A. To the best of my recollection, there were none.

Q. Do you also disagree with Mr. Magruder's testimony that you actually volunteered a particular target, which was Hank Greenspun's office in Las Vegas for the purpose of obtaining some documents that might involve a political candidate?

A. Mr. Dash, you gave me a great opportunity to correct the record on this. You know, Mr. Magruder said that it could have been Mitchell or Dean and then when you picked up the questioning you said Mitchell, so we are now correcting that record. To the best of my recollection, there was no such discussion of any——

Q. However, your recollection is there was no discussion of it? A. No discussion whatsoever.

Q. Do you recall Mr. Dean's reaction at that meeting?

A. I recall both of our reactions to it. Although it has been given, Mr. Dean's reaction has been given a different connotation and, of course, it depends on who is telling the story and under what circumstances to who looks like the White Knight and who looks like the Black Knight, of course.

The fact of the matter is that Dean, just like myself, was again aghast that we would have this type of presentation, John Dean, as I recall, not only was aghast at the fact that the program had come back again with electronic surveillance, perhaps a necessary entry in connection with it, I am not sure that entries were always discussed with electronic surveillance because they are not necessarily synonymous, but Mr. Dean was quite strong to the point that these things could not be discussed in the Attorney General's office, I have a clear recollection of that and that was one of the bases upon which the meeting was broken up.

Q. What specifically did you say?

A. I cannot tell you specifically any more than I can tell you specifically what Mr. Dean said but my observation was to the point that this was not going to be accepted. It was entirely out of the concept of what we needed and what we needed was again an information-gathering operation along with, of course, the program to get information on and to be able to have security against the demonstrators that we knew were coming.

As you recall, Mr. Dash, at this particular time they had already started to form in substantial numbers in San Diego in connection with the proposed convention, even though that convention was not to happen until August of that year.

Q. Well, since this reappearance, and repression of the so-called Liddy plan to you which included these obviously objectionable portions to you as you testified, and you did not take any violent action on the preceding meeting did you take any action against Mr. Liddy as a result of his coming back again on Feb. 4 and re-presenting it?

A. Other than to cut off the proposals, no.

Q. Why not? Here is a man talking to you as Attorney General about illegal wiretapping and perhaps break-ins, why not at least, if you do not have him ordered arrested for trying to conspire to do things like this, why not have him fired?

A. In hindsight I would think that would have been a very viable thing to do. And probably should have been done. Liddy was still an employe of the campaign and I presumed that he would go back to the duties that he was performing without engaging in such activities.

Q. Well, you had to be aware at least at that time, Mr. Mitchell, that Liddy could become a very embarrassing employe of the campaign.

A. Not necessarily, unless he violated directions under which he was operating to that point there was no such, there was no such evidence that he was violating.

Q. Certainly, from your point of view, he did not exercise or did not demonstrate any responsibility?

A. He did not exercise any responsiveness to my desire in the matter, if that is your question, no.

Q. Did you report to anybody the Jan. 27 meeting or the Feb. 4 meeting? A. To the best of my recollection, no, Mr. Dash.

Q. Did you ever take it up with Mr. Haldeman or anybody in the White House? A. No, sir.

Q. Were you aware that Mr. Liddy left the Feb. 4 meeting believing that his plan was not objectionable in itself but only that the price tag was too high and that he reported that to Mr. McCord and Mr. Hunt?

A. I cannot conceive of anybody leaving that meeting with such an understanding.

Q. Were you aware, by the way, that Mr. McCord and Mr. Hunt were involved in the planning operation?

A. In no way. I have never met Mr. Hunt. I do not know Mr. Hunt and, of course, Mr. McCord was the security officer of the Committee for the Re-election of the President and one of the last people I would have believed would have been involved in such activity.

Q. Now, after the Feb. 4th meeting, did you receive any urging or pressures from anybody in the White House with regard to approving the Liddy plan? A. No, sir.

Q. Well, now, once again, Mr. Mitchell, and for a third time, on March 30, 1972, and this time in Key Biscayne, Mr. Magruder himself, not Mr. Liddy, presented a decision paper on the so-called Liddy wiretapping political intelligence plan scaled down now to a price tag of $250,000.

Do you recall the meeting with Mr. Magruder and yourself down at Key Biscayne on March 30?

A. Yes, I do, Mr. Dash. I was on a vacation and it gave an opportunity to catch up on some of the things that were happening in the Committee for the Re-election of the President that I was to be associated with shortly, there were two days of meetings. Mr. Magruder was down there in connection with the operational program, programatic side of the campaign.

Mr. LaRue had come down with us and was living in the house with us and he sat in on all of these meetings that we had while we were down there.

Q. Now, I understand Mr. Magruder came down not only with this so-called Liddy plan proposal but he had a number of other items on the agenda.

A. Yes, he had a substantial number of items on the agenda because I had been otherwise engaged and had for weeks I had not had an opportunity to meet with these people. I was about to become officially associated with the campaign and he came down with a big stack of documents that were to be considered immediately.

Q. Would it be fair to say, Mr. Mitchell, that the so-called quarter million dollar Liddy plan for wiretapping and break-in was actually different in degree and kind than any other agenda item that he was presenting to you?

A. Mr. Dash, you can rest assured of this. There were no other such plans in the documents that were submitted.

Q. What would have given Mr. Magruder the idea that you would even consider this proposal again if you had indeed, as you stated, rejected it so categorically twice before?

A. Well, I would have presumed that you would ask Mr. Magruder that question when he was here, Mr. Dash, but in hindsight I presume there were other people interested in the implementation of some type of activity in this area. Because I believe that Mr. Magruder was very clearly aware of the position that I had taken in connection with it.

Q. So that it is at least your present feeling that he was acting under some pressure for somebody to represent this plan to you?

A. This has been continued to be my feeling but I have no basis for knowing that.

Q. Do you know who might be involved? A. No, I do not.

Q. Now, what is your recollection of what decision you made in Key Biscayne on the so-called Liddy plan?

A. Well, it was very simple. This, again, "We don't need this. I am tired of hearing it. Out. Let's not discuss it any further. This sort of a concept."

Q. Then how do you explain, Mr. Mitchell, Mr. Magruder's sworn testimony that you, however reluctantly, approved the quarter million dollar Liddy plan at Key Biscayne?

A. Mr. Dash, I can't explain anybody's testimony up here but my own.

Q. Now, Mr. Mitchell, were you aware that on or about May 27, 1972, there was in fact a break-in of the Democratic National Committee headquarters at the Watergate? A. No, sir.

Q. And did you know of the code name, "Gemstone" or any of the wiretap proofs that came from that break-in?

A. Not until a great deal later down the road, Mr. Dash.

Q. When you say that, how far down the road? Before June 17 or after June 17?

A. Oh, much after June 17.

Q. Were you aware that Mr. Magruder kept a so-called Mitchell Gemstone file as well as a Haldeman Gemstone file, prior to June 17?

A. I have heard testimony here, Mr. Dash, that I believe it was Mr. Reisner, that they kept a Mitchell file, in which documents would be placed for Mr. Magruder to come up and discuss them with me.

Q. Yes, I believe Mr. Magruder has also testified about that.

A. Yes, about a file that would have documents, memorandums, et cetera. I am not aware of anybody testifying to the fact that there was a special Mitchell Gemstone file.

Q. Well, the Mitchell file did include, on that testimony, you will recall, that it included Gemstone—

A. I recall Reisner stating that he had put the documents in there, yes.

Q. But do you recall Mr. Magruder testifying that he had taken these documents and showed them to you?

A. I recall it very vividly because it happens to be a palpable, damnable lie.

Q. What is the lie, Mr. Mitchell?

A. Well, let me lay out the scenario for you, because my answer will come in the scenario. I paid particular attention to this because of the fact that Mr. Magruder said that at his regular 8:30 morning meeting, sometime within a week or a week and a half from the time of the initial break-in, that he brought certain documents to my office at the regular 8:30 meeting to display them to me and that I was dissatisfied with them and that I called Gordon Liddy up to my office and raised holy hell with him about the fact that they were not the type of information that was wanted.

Now, let me go back and pick up the facts with respect to the meeting. First of all, I had an 8:15 meeting every day over at the White House in connection with activities that were governmental, but I sat in on.

Secondly, if you have my logs, that are very, very accurate and correct, you will note that there was no meeting in any morning during that period when Mr. Magruder and I were alone during that meeting.

Thirdly, I have never seen or talked to Mr. Liddy from the 4th day of February, 1972, until the 15th day of June, 1972, either in person or on the telephone.

I would like to point out that Mr. Dean's testimony is that when he first debriefed Mr. Liddy on the 19th day of June, Mr. Liddy told Mr. Dean that Magruder was the one that had pushed him concerning the second entry on the 17th day of June and I cannot conceive of anybody, if they had Mitchell as a scapegoat, why they would get down to Magruder and use him as the one that had pushed him.

So I am using that dialogue to point out the reasons why this meeting could not and did not take place.

Q. Just taking that dialogue, you were aware that there was no love lost between Mr. Liddy and Mr. Magruder and he might well have wanted to, since we are speculating, put the blame on Mr. Magruder.

A. As I am stating, Mr. Dash, I never saw Mr. Liddy from the 4th of February until the 15th of June and I cannot tell you whether there was love lost or not. I think there is testimony that if they had a controversy, it should be kept away from me and settled at lower echelons.

Q. Well, if Mr. Liddy did not see you, did Mr. Magruder show you the Gemstone file, as he indicated he did?

A. No, he did not and I just got through denying that fact that he did and I am pointing out the reasons why he did not because of the circumstances and time in which he is talking about the meetings that are referred to in those logs.

Q. You do not recall then, any statement by Mr. Liddy to you indicating that the O'Brien microphone was not working and he would have to fix it?

A. Mr. Dash, the only statement that I have had with Mr. Liddy and the only conversation from the 4th of February until this very day was one single meeting that shows in my log on June 15, 1972, where Mr. Liddy was brought into my office by Mr. Van Shumway, the public information officer, to discuss with me a letter that Mr. Liddy had written on Mr. Stans's request to The Washington Post having to do with some charges that had been made by the General Accounting Office dealing with the Corrupt Practices Act and Mr. Shumway did not want that letter to go to The Post without my approval.

I looked at the letter and gave it the approval and that was the end of it. That was the only conversation I had with Mr. Liddy so it could not possibly be as you were inferring.

Q. All right, now, Mr. Mitchell, where and when did you first learn of the break-in of the Democratic National Committee headquarters that took place on June 17, 1972?

A. Well, I was in California for the weekend on an extensive round of activities and, to the best of my recollection, Mr. Dash, it was on Saturday morning, I am not sure who the individual was who told me. We were, I was, moving with Governor Reagan from a hotel to a place where there was a series of political meetings, to the best of my recollection, when I arrived there I was advised of it. There was considerable concern about the matter because I was holding a press conference out there, and we did not know what the circumstances were. I believe that by that time that they had—Mr. McCord, his name had surfaced or Mrs. McCord had called somebody at the committee about it, and obviously, there was an involvement in the Committee for the Re-election of the President.

Q. What, if anything, did you do, while still in California?

A. While in California? I did a number of things. First of all, I continued to carry out the schedule that I had there which was quite extensive for two days. I asked the people, particularly Mr. Mardian who was there, to get as much information about it as he could. I put out a statement to the effect that, I do not know whether it went out there or after we came back, to the effect that we did not understand this, that Mr. McCord was one of our employes, he also had a separate consulting firm, that it was basically an attempt to carry on the extensive schedule that I had which, of course, is in the book that you are well aware about and, at the same time, trying to get information as to what had happened back in the District of Columbia.

Q. At that time, out in California, did it ever cross your mind when you read about this that perhaps the Liddy plan had been put in operation?

A. Well, that had crossed my mind but the players were different and, of course, there was a lot of discussion about C.I.A. and because of the Cuban Americans who were involved in it. It wasn't until actually later on that it struck home to me that this could have been the same operation that had a genesis back in the earlier conversation.

Q. When and how were you briefed as to what actually happened in this matter?

A. [It] was after Mr. Mardian and Mr. LaRue had met with Mr. Liddy and Mr. Liddy provided them with quite an extensive story on Mr. Liddy's activities.

It included the fact that he was involved with other individuals in the Watergate activity, that he had also made surveillance of McGovern headquarters, I believe it was, and that he had previously, as part of what has since become known as the "plumbers" group, acted extensively in certain areas while he was at the White House in connection with the Ellsberg matter, in the Dita Beard matter and a few of the other little gems.

Q. And when you refer to the Dita Beard matter what specifically did you learn through Mr. LaRue and Mr. Mardian?

A. Well, if my recollection is correct he was assisting in spiriting her out of wherever they spirited her out of, either New York or Washington.

Q. Was there a meeting in your apartment on the evening that you arrived in Washington on June 19, attended by Mr. LaRue, Mr. Mardian, Mr. Dean, Mr. Magruder?

A. Magruder and myself, that is correct.

Q. Do you recall the purpose of that meeting, the discussion that took place there?

A. I recall that we had been traveling all day and, of course, we had very little information about what the current status was of the entry of the Democratic National Committee, and we met at the apartment to discuss it. They were, of course, clamoring for a response from the committee because of Mr. McCord's involvement and we had quite a general discussion of the subject matter.

Q. Do you recall any discussion of the so-called either Gemstone files or wiretapping files that you had in your possession?

A. No, I had not heard of the Gemstone files as of that meeting and, as of that date, I had not heard that anybody there at that particular meeting knew of the wiretapping aspects of that or had any connection with it.

Q. Did either you or anybody in your presence at that meeting discuss Mr. Liddy having a good fire at his house?

A. Not in my recollection was there any discussion of destruction of documents at that meeting.

Q. You are aware of the testimony of Mr. Magruder that he did get the idea to destroy the documents and he did in fact burn the Gemstone documents?

A. I am aware of his testimony and I think his testimony was one of these general things, "It was decided that" or something to that effect but, to my recollection, there was no such discussion of it.

Q. Well, you did become aware during June and July of Mr. Magruder's involvement in the break-in of the Democratic National Committee headquarters?

A. We had people such as Mr. Liddy and so forth say yes, that Magruder was involved, Magruder was saying no at one time and maybe yes the other time and so forth, but we were aware of the fact that certainly Mr. Magruder had provided the money if nothing else and that during the latter part of June and the early part of July seemed to be what all the focus was as to how much money Mr. Magruder had provided to Mr. Liddy.

Q. There came a time when you were aware that Mr. Magruder himself was, had admitted to certain persons, whether Mr. Mardian or Mr. Parkinson, that he had been involved but was going to give a false story about what he had done.

A. Well, I don't want to get Mr. Parkinson in there and I don't know about Mr. Mardian because Mr. Magruder told them two or three different stories, and Mr. Parkinson, and Mr. O'Brien obviously went ahead on the story that they thought was to be the facts.

As I understand the sequence of events when this thrashing around was involved, occurred, involving everybody from the President of the United States and the chairman of this committee and everybody on down the line as anybody they could think of to name, Mr. Parkinson.

SENATOR ERVIN: Just a minute, did they accuse this chairman?

A. No sir, this committee, I was going to use some other committee, I think we had better use some other committe. The fact of the matter is that to the best of my recollection that Mr. Parkinson got Mr. Magruder and Mr. Porter down to his office and put them in a room and said now "I want you to write down what your statement is on this subject matter because it probably is going to be used as a deposition before the grand jury or certainly for submission to the Justice Department," so I want to make sure that Mr. O'Brien—that Mr. Parkinson is not involved in this. It got to the point where I had a very, very strong suspicion as to what the involvement was, yes.

MR. DASH: With that you also had the suspicion, if that is the word you want to use, that Mr. Magruder's story that he was writing down and he was going to give in a deposition to the grand jury was not a true story.

A. Well, this came out later. I didn't know what he was writing down July 15 or whatever it was, it came later.

Q. There came a time when it did become a fact. A. That is right.

Q. When was that?

A. I would say it was sometime before he want to the grand jury, sometime.

Q. You did become aware by the time he testified on the grand jury that Mr. Magruder was, in fact, testifying to a false story.

A. I became aware or had a belief that it was a false story.

Q. I think the calendar would show there were quite a number of meetings in which you met—

A. There were a lot of meetings, with a lot of matters being discussed at that time.

Q. Also was it true that Mr. Dean began to serve as sort of a liaison between this group that you were meeting with and Mr. Haldeman and Mr. Ehrlichman?

A. Well, Mr. Dean was serving as a liaison between the Committee for the Re-election of the President and the White House and I am sure that would have meant Mr. Haldeman and Mr. Ehrlichman.

Q. And then, to the best of your recollection and knowledge, were you aware that Mr. Haldeman and Mr. Ehrlichman were being kept informed on the question of the strategy to conceal Mr. Magruder's actual—

A. I had no specific knowledge of that.

Q. Did you ever discuss that with Mr. Ehrlichman or Haldeman?

A. No, sir, I never did. You are talking about the Magruder testimony?

Q. Yes.

A. To the best of my recollection I have never discussed it with them.

Q. You don't recall that at all?

A. I don't recall that, no. I can only say that Mr. Dean was the conduit, was the party who acted between the two committees and came back and forth and discussed things with us so that whether—

Q. Did you have any communication with Mr. Haldeman or Mr. Ehrlichman yourself during this period of time?

A. Oh, I am sure I had numerous communications but it probably had to do with the running of the campaign, with other such matters rather than what Mr. Magruder might be testifying to.

Q. Did it have anything to do with the so-called White House horror stories or the scandals you learned about from Mr. Mardian, Mr. LaRue based on Mr. Liddy's statement, to back them up?

A. Before Magruder's testimony before the grand jury, I would believe that during that period of time there were some discussions of the so-called White House stories, yes.

Q. Was there a concern expressed by you to Mr. Haldeman or Mr. Ehrlichman concerning whether stories would be revealed during this campaign.

A. I think that we all had an innate fear that during the campaign that they might be revealed. I do not recall discussing it specifically in that area but I am sure we must have had a mutual concern about the subject matter.

Q. Well, did you yourself form a personal position as to what should be done about revealing of this material?

A. I formed the opinion and a position that I did not believe that it was fair to the President to have these stories come out during his political campaign.

Q. Were you aware that there was a program actually going on so as to actually prevent these stories from coming out?

A. Now, which program are you talking about, Mr. Dash, so I can be sure to answer your question properly?

Q. Well, a program on the part of yourself, Mr. Dean, Mr. Haldeman, Mr. Ehrlichman, and perhaps Mr. LaRue and Mr. Mardian to see to it that the information that got to the prosecutor or to the grand jury or to the civil suits did not in any way include this information concerning the so-called White House horrors, as you described them?

A. Well, Mr. Dash, that is a very broad question and covers a lot of areas. I may answer it, perhaps, by saying that we sure in hell were not volunteering anything. In addition to that, we were involved in a very difficult series of civil litigation, as you know, that involved discovery and all the rest of it. So we were not volunteering anything.

Q. But you say you did come to know that, prior to Mr. Magruder's testimony, that he was going to testify falsely?

A. I think I can put it on the basis that I had a pretty strong feeling that his testimony was not going to be entirely accurate.

Q. Right, and this discussion, I think you have already testified, was part of the discussion of some of the meetings with Mr. LaRue, Mardian, Dean and Magruder.

A. That is correct. I think the best way to put it is that Mr. Magruder would seek an audience to review his story that he was going to tell, rather than somebody was trying to induce him to do so. I think Mr. Magruder has testified that nobody coerced him to do this, that he made up the story, that he did it of his own free will. So it was more of a basis of Mr. Magruder recounting to these assembled groups what he was going to testify to.

Q. Would you say that whatever cover-up was taking place to this point, concealment and not volunteering information, had to do with actually preventing the so-called White House horror stories rather than Watergate break-in?

A. This was certainly my belief and rationale and I would believe the people in the White House, certainly some of them, might well be involved and certainly would have similar interests.

Q. Did you believe, Mr. Mitchell and I use the term belief at this point—have any belief as to whether the President was aware of the events either prior to or after the break-in of the Democratic National Committee headquarters? When I say events, I mean the actual bugging or the cover-up which took place thereafter?

A. I am not aware of it and I have every reason to believe, because of my discussions and encounters with him up through the 22d of March, I have very strong opinions that he was not.

Q. How do you arrive at that conclusion? Was it by particular conversations with the President that he talked to you about this subject, or did you talk to him about this subject?

A. No, it is primarily—I do not want to say not to exclude it, and I will explain the natures of the conversations, if you so desire. As a matter of fact, you may go through that list and I will get a chance to do them one by one. What I am saying is that I think I know the individual, I know his reactions to things, and I have a very strong feeling that during the period of time in which I was in association with him and did talk to him on the telephone, that I just do not believe that he had that information or had that knowledge; otherwise, I think the type of conversations we had would have brought it out.

Q. Generally, is it fair to say that much of your opinion that you express is based on your faith in the President and your knowledge of the man, rather than any specific statement the President made to you or that you made to the President?

A. Well, I subscribe to the first two. I do have faith in the President and I do think I have knowledge of the man and I do think there were enough discussions in the area, in the general area, to the point where I think the general subject matter would have come out if the President had had knowledge.

Q. Well, now, Mr. Mitchell, you did become aware, as you indicated, somewhere around June 21 or 22, when you were briefed or debriefed by Mr. LaRue and Mr. Mardian about the so-called, as you described it, the White House horrors, the Liddy operation and the break-in. Did you, yourself, as the President's adviser and counselor, tell the President what you knew or what you learned? A. No, sir, I did not.

Q. Why did you not?

A. Because I did not believe that it was appropriate for him to have that type of knowledge, because I knew the actions that he would take and it would be most detrimental to his political campaign.

Q. Could it have been actually helpful or healthy, do you think?

A. That was not my opinion at the particular time. He was not involved; it wasn't a question of deceiving the public as far as Richard Nixon was concerned, and it was the other people that were involved in connection with these activities, both in the White House horrors and the Watergate. I believed at that particular time, and maybe in retrospect, I was wrong, but it occurred to me that the best thing to do was just to keep the lid on through the election.

Q. Then it is your testimony that you in fact did not say anything to the President at that time. A. No, sir, I did not.

Q. So whether the President had any knowledge of it, it certainly couldn't have come from, his lack of knowledge or knowledge, from any statement that you made to him? A. That is correct, Mr. Dash.

Q. Now, were you aware of the fact that actually prior to Mr. Magruder's testimony, Mr. Dean rehearsed Mr. Magruder for his testimony before the grand jury?

A. I do not recall that, Mr. Dash, if you are talking about the testimony that took place on the—

Q. In August.

A. In August, the second appearance.

Q. The second appearance.

A. I am not aware of that.

Q. Then prior to Magruder's third appearance, which dealt with the diaries and the meetings in your office, were you aware or do you recall the meeting between you, Magruder and Dean, in which a discussion was had concerning how to handle that testimony and how he was to testify in some of those meetings?

A. Well, it wasn't a question so much of how to handle the testimony; it was a question of what the recollection was. That, as I recall, Magruder's testimony had to do with the destruction of diaries that were already in the possession of the grand jury. But I think Mr. Dean's testimony is a lot closer to the recollection that I have of the meeting. It was a question of what was the purpose of it, who was there, and what could be said about it to limit the impact of the whole . . .

Q. And did Mr. Magruder indicate that he was going to not testify concerning any intelligence plans, but would testify that he was there to discuss the election laws.

A. Well, the election laws were discussed and I think the result was that he would limit it to the election laws.

Q. And you were aware, then, in December that he would testify not completely, if not falsely, concerning the meetings on Jan. 27 and Feb. 4?

A. Well, that is generally correct. As I say again, this is something that Dean and I were listening to, as to his story as to how he was going to present it.

Q. Well, wasn't it the result of your effort or program to keep the lid on? You were interested in the grand jury not getting the full story. Isn't that true?

A. Maybe we can get the record straight so you won't have to ask me after each of these questions: Yes, we wanted to keep the lid on. We were not volunteering anything.

Q. As a matter of fact, would it not be fair to say, Mr. Mitchell, that the most consuming issue that occupied you and some of those you were meeting with at this time was exactly the question of keeping the lid on during the—

A. No, I wouldn't say that was correct, Mr. Dash. There were many other political activities that took place and, of course, we probably spent more time in connection with the civil litigation than we did in connection with this particular aspect of it.

Q. Well, did you become aware at this time—in July or August —that payments were being made to defendants and support for the family?

A. I became aware in the fall sometime, and I can't tell you when it was. Probably it was a time in which one individual stopped making the payments and the other individual took it up, whatever time reference that was.

Q. And did you know that Mr. Kalmbach had been involved in that at all? A. I had learned that, yes.

Q. Did you also learn that in September he had decided not to be involved any more and that Mr. LaRue took up the responsibility of landing the funds, making pay-offs? A. Yes, sir.

Q. Now, when did you leave your position as the director of the campaign?

A. On the 1st of July, 1972.

Q. And when you did leave, you were aware, were you not, that Mr. Magruder was staying on as deputy director of the campaign.

A. Yes, he stayed on as Mr. MacGregor's deputy.

Q. And were you not aware when you were leaving that Mr. Magruder at least faced some serious problem of being indicted on the break-in of the Democratic National Committee headquarters as of July 1?

A. As of July 1? I think that was a potential, yes.

Q. Now, you did meet with the President on June 30, 1972, just before you left. As I understand, you had lunch with the President. A. That is correct, sir.

Q. Did you think it your duty to tell the President at that lunch before you left that the man who was playing such a key role in his campaign, Magruder, had such a problem that he might be indicted for the break-in of the Democratic National Committee headquarters?

A. Mr. Dash, I think you and I have gone over to the point where we have established that the White House horror stories had come out in connection with the problem at that particular time and there wasn't the question of lifting of the tent slightly in order to get with respect to one individual or another; it was a keeping the lid on and no information volunteered.

Q. Even if the lid had been kept on on the so-called White House horrors, wouldn't it be very embarrassing to the President of the United States in his effort to be re-elected if his deputy campaign director was indicted in the break-in of the Democratic National Committee headquarters?

A. I don't think as far as the Watergate was concerned, there was a hell of a lot of difference between the deputy campaign director and the counsel for the finance committee and the security officer. Quite frankly, as far as the Watergate was concerned, that was already a public issue. It was the parties that were involved.

Q. There came a time, did there not, Mr. Mitchell, that the pressures for money by the defendants or by Mr. Hunt increased. Would you tell us what you know about that?

A. Well, I am not sure, Mr. Dash, that I can tell you very much about them other than the fact that somewhere along in the fall,

Mr. Hunt had a telephone conversation with Mr. Colson, which, I think, and then later on, as I recall, covered the subject matter Mr. Dean has got in the record a letter from Mr. Hunt to Mr. Colson, which I think is quite suggestive of the fact that he was being abandoned.

Then I heard later in, in March of this year, there were oral communications from either Hunt or his attorney relating to requests for legal fees and so forth, which were communicated to the White House.

Q. How did you hear about that request, the March request?

A. The March request? I think I probably heard about it through Mr. LaRue, if my memory serves me right.

Q. Do you know about how much money was actually being requested at that time?

A. I can't really tell you about the monies across this period of time. It seems to me that the March request had some amount in the area of $75,000 which Mr. LaRue described to me, that was being requested by counsel for their legal fees in connection with the representation of Mr. Hunt.

Q. Did Mr. LaRue ask you what your opinion was or whether he should pay that amount of money to Mr. Hunt or his counsel?

A. Mr. LaRue, to the best of my recollection, put it in this context: I have got this request, I have talked to John Dean over at the White House, they are not in the money business any more, what would you do if you were in my shoes and knowing that he had made prior payments? I said, if I were you, I would continue and I would make the payment.

Q. You are aware that there was a sum of money available for that at the White House, were you not?

A. I was aware that there had been one at one time, but I didn't know how far Liddy had gotten into that particular fund.

Q. Did you ever make any suggestions that the money that should be used for that purpose was the $350,000?

A. No, to the best of my recollection, I had a conversation with Mr. LaRue, I am sure at his instance, not mine, in which he pointed out that the funds, whatever source they were, that he had for the support of and the payment of lawyers' fees of these individuals, had run out, did I know whether there was any other money? And I suggested that maybe you ought to call over to the White House and see if the $350,000 that had been sitting over there since April was available for the purpose. I understand that he did so.

Q. Do you recall attending a meeting in January with Mr. Kalmbach and Mr. Dean in which you asked Mr. Kalmbach to help raise money for these legal fees and support of families? That occurred in January, '73.

A. In January, '73. Since our conversation of yesterday, Mr. Dash, I have continued to rack my brain and I have no recollection of that.

Q. Now, did you become also aware of Mr. McCord's demands and were you in touch with Mr. Dean concerning Mr. Caulfield's approach to Mr. McCord?

A. Somewhere through the middle of it, because I was in Florida from sometime, I think the 20th of December through the 8th or 9th of January, while a lot of this was occurring—

Q. What role did you play? What did you learn?

A. I learned that Mr. Dean had Mr. Caulfield contacting Mr. McCord and talking to Mr. McCord.

Q. About what? Do you know about what?

A. About what Mr. McCord's attitude was concerning the predicament that he was in and what he was going to do.

Q. At that time, did you hear that Mr. Caulfield had been authorized to promise some form of executive clemency to Mr. McCord?

A. I don't believe so. I think the only conversations that I had heard about executive clemency had to do with Mr. Colson and Mr. Hunt.

Q. Well, what was that, to the best of your recollection?

A. To the best of my recollection, it was that somewhere along the line, and I gather that that would be in 1973, early 1973, there were discussions of whether or not Mr. Hunt—well, I gather he had approached Colson or through his lawyer had approached Colson on the subject matter. The essence of it was that Mr. Colson's word was the only word that Mr. Hunt would take with respect to executive clemency, whatever that meant. That is the subject and substance of my overhearing of discussions on executive clemency.

Q. Now, Mr. Mitchell, did it become aware to you, apparently, that after the election and after the questions concerning the funds that were being used by Mr. Hunt and Mr. McCord's concern, that whatever you discussed as keeping the lid on might become uncovered? Did that, sometime around December or January, did that occur to you?

A. Well, it always occurred to me, the possibility that the so-called lid would become uncovered. Of course, I always hoped that it didn't, for the very simple reason that there was no necessity of scarring the President, who was not involved, through his White House activities or the activities in the White House.

Q. But the real possibility of it becoming uncovered, and now that the election was over, so it would not affect his election.

A. No. It would not affect his election but it would affect his Presidency, Mr. Dash.

Q. But you were aware, and I think from your own statement, that the President was unaware, and you had personal knowledge or knowledge or knowledge of, that you had received from others of certain activities, that if they did become known publicly could either injure or destroy the President's second Administration, after the election did it occur to you to tell the President then?

A. Well, I am sure it occurred to me and probably on hindsight I probably should have. I do not think there is any doubt about it.

Q. Did you not think it was the President's prerogative to know what to do about these matters?

A. The decision had to be made, and it is a tough one, whether or not he is not involved in it but he does not know about them, will this go away. I knew they were going to change the personnel in the White House and hopefully they would be gone and he would not have to deal with it and he could go on to his second term, the second Presidency, without this problem.

Q. Were you personally aware of Mr. Dean's meetings with the President in March and April that he testified to before this committee?

A. Only the meeting of March 22 at which, of course, I was present.

Q. At that meeting was there any discussion by the President, by you or by Mr. Dean, concerning the Watergate, either cover-up or who may be involved in an indictment or anything like that on the 22d?

A. None whatsoever. The total discussion had to do with the White House's response to this committee, and I think it was prompted, or at least that was my understanding at the time, it was prompted by the fact that the President was getting a pretty good knocking around in the press on the question of executive privilege. I believe it arose with respect to the Gray hearings but it certainly was to be applicable to this committee's hearings.

Q. Well, just a couple of last questions, Mr. Mitchell: I think you testified already, and quite frequently, that you did not personally inform the President of any of these so-called White House horrors or the efforts to keep the lid on and the "plumbers" activities, that is correct? A. Yes.

Q. Are you personally aware of anybody else having any conversation with the President concerning these activities?

A. Not in my presence. I am not aware of anybody ever having reported to me that they have had.

Q. Likewise it is your testimony that the President did not discuss these events of the cover-up with you or, to your knowledge, with anyone else?

A. He has not discussed them with me, to my knowledge, the answer is correct.

Q. To your knowledge. Therefore, then, Mr. Mitchell, I am briefing your testimony at this time before the committee, is it not fair to say or is it not true that, according to your testimony, you are not in a position to state to this committee of your own knowledge whether the President in fact knew or did not know of the break-in or the bugging of the Watergate or the cover-up efforts that took place after June 17, 1972?

A. The only thing that I can state to my own knowledge, Mr. Dash, is that so far as I know he does not know of either of those circumstances.

Q. That statement you have just made is not based on anything the President told you specifically, anything anybody told you that he had told the President?

A. I understand the thrust of your question. That is correct. It is based solely on my association with the President and not conversations on the affirmative side of the subject matter.

MR. THOMPSON: You never saw any Gemstone documents that you remember?

A. No, sir.

Q. In retrospect, would there be any materials that were a product of electronic surveillance without knowing that they were?

A. No, I would believe that electronic surveillance, after my experience in the Justice Department—I do not know in what forms they are; I have not seen them to this date. But after my experience in the Justice Department, I think I would have a pretty good idea of what the source of it might have been, unless it was totally disguised.

Q. At the time that the break-in occurred, what was your professional political judgment as to how the President stood with regard to his chances for re-election?

A. Well, we go back to the middle of June and, of course, he had improved substantially from his previous lows vis-à-vis the then front-runner, Senator Muskie. That looked like he was on the ascendancy.

Q. Had not some polls indicated that at one time or another, Mr. Muskie was ahead of Mr. Nixon?

A. Yes, but I believe, if my recollection is correct, that this was somewhat earlier than in June.

Q. You didn't consider him in trouble at that time?

A. When you are running a campaign, you consider anybody who is likely to get the nomination against your candidate, you may have a substantial amount of trouble with them.

Q. The extent of the problems you might visualize might have something to do with the measures you might take to confront it, would it not?

A. I don't believe that anybody thought the election was locked up, certainly with respect to the time element of June 17, with the potentials of the people that might become the Democrat candidate at the convention that was taking place in July. There were a great deal of uncertainties as to who the candidate might be and as to what the circumstances might be vis-à-vis the incumbent who was seeking re-election.

Q. Let me refer to June 19 or 20, I am not quite sure when it was, Mr. Mitchell. As I understand it, Mardian and LaRue debriefed Liddy and found out what he knew about the break-in, his involvement, and the involvement of others.

And at that time, he related to them some of the White House horror stories, I believe you characterized them as, the plumbers activities and so forth. I will go back to that in a minute, but as

I understand your testimony this morning, this is really the reason, the knowledge you got from that debriefing was really the reason why you, in effect, stood by while Mr. Magruder was preparing a story which, according to what you knew from Liddy, was going to be a false story to present to the grand jury.

A. Along, Mr. Thompson, with some of the other stories that Mr. Dean brought forward to him, the Diem papers and the suspected extra-curricular wiretapping, and a few of the others.

Q. Okay. That caused you to take that position with regard to Magruder. And also, I assume that those factors were the reasons why you, in effect, acquiesced, anyway, in the payments to the families of support money and lawyers' fees and that sort of thing, which I am sure you realize could have been pretty embarrasing, to say the least, if not illegal, at that time. Would that be correct as far as your motivations are concerned?

A. That is a correct summary of my motivation and rationale for the actions that I did take.

Q. Do you recall the date that you became aware of any money that was being paid to any of the defendants or families or attorneys?

A. No, I do not recall the date but it was well after the matter was in progress and in operation. There is testimony by Mr. Dean that there was a meeting.

Q. June 23 or 24, I believe.

A. On June 28.

Q. And 28th.

A. June 28. You see, Mr. Dean had testified that they had been playing games with the C.I.A. up to the 28th. Then, Mr. Dean testified that there was a meeting in my office with Mardian, La-Ruc and Mitchell and I do not know who all else including Mr. Dean in the afternoon of the 28th in which it was decided, naturally Mitchell was always deciding these things, according to Dean, that the White House, somebody in the White House, John Ehrlichman should call Kalmbach and ask him to fly back from California that night of the 28th, which led to their meetings on the 29th. The only problem with all of that was that I was in New York and could not have been at such a meeting, and I was not aware of it.

Q. I believe your logs reflect that, Mr. Mitchell. It reflects that according to your logs that you were in New York on the 28th. And that you arrived in D. C. at 5:30. A. Yes, sir.

Q. There is no indication of any meeting after 5:30.

A. That is correct. The passenger that I had with me coming back from New York was not about to allow me to go to any more meetings on that particular day.

Q. Without getting into a great deal more detail, Mr. Mitchell, can you answer any further point of verification that Mr. Dean gave you concerning this matter we mentioned, the Ellsberg psychiatrist, the Dita Beard situation, any of those matters?

A. Well, of course, there was the purported fire bombing of the

Brookings Institute [Institution] which had been discussed and so forth, I have already—

Q. Did Dean tell you that was seriously proposed at one time?

A. Yes, I believe that I took it as a very serious proposal because of the fact that he flew across the country in order to get it turned off.

Q. Dean testified that during the first week of December you called Dean and said that you would have to use some of the $350,000 at the White House to take care of the demands that were being made by Hunt and that others—for money and that you asked him to get Haldeman's approval for that. Is that a correct statement?

A. No, that is absolutely untrue as far as I am concerned. I had no official capacity, I had no control over the money and there would be no reason why I should call Dean or anybody else with respect to it and I did not so call Dean.

Q. Dean testified that shortly before the trial when the demands for money were reaching the crescendo point again you called Dean and once again asked him to ask Haldeman to make the necessary funds available and that after Dean talked to Haldeman the decision was made to send the entire $350,000.

A. Well, I would respond to that the same way I did to your last question.

Q. Dean testified that on Jan. 10 he received a call from O'Brien and you indicating that since Hunt had been given assurances of clemency and that those assurances were being passed to Hunt and others that Caulfield should give the same assurances as to McCord who was becoming an increasing problem and again Dean was told that McCord's lawyer was having problems with him. Is that true?

A. I think that Mr. Dean if he will go back and check his logs will find that I was out of town in Florida when he started the McCord dialogue, and that there would be no reason in the world for me to direct Mr. Dean to do anything vis-à-vis Caulfield or McCord or anybody else.

Q. Let me ask you about one more piece of testimony, the meeting on March 22 which you had with Mr. Haldeman, Ehrlichman and Dean, I understand you met with them and that afternoon you met with the President. A. Yes, sir.

Q. I believe that Dean testified that Ehrlichman turned to you and said, asked if Hunt had been taken care of or his money situation had been taken care of and you assured him that he had been taken care of, is that correct?

A. It is absolutely false as far as I am concerned because I have never, to my knowledge, discussed any of these payments with John Ehrlichman and any of the specifics of that nature with respect to any individual, and I wouldn't have known on the 2d of March whether Mr. Hunt had been taken care of or hadn't been taken care of.

SENATOR TALMADGE: Mr. Mitchell, in your testimony, you have repeatedly referred to "White House horrors." What do you mean by that phrase?

A. Well, as we have discussed them here, Senator, they certainly involved the break-in of Dr. Ellsberg's doctor, I think we had better put it instead of the other phrase that is used; the Dita Beard matter, both with respect to, apparently, the removal of her from the scene as well as visits or attempted visits. We are talking about the Diem cables: we are talking about the alleged extra-curricular activities in the bugging area, the bombing of the Brookings Institute [Institution], and a lot of miscellaneous matters with respect to Chappaquiddick and this, that and the next thing. Those are the areas of which I am talking.

Q. Did you play an active supervisory role in the campaign before you resigned as Attorney General?

A. What I did was succumb to the President's request to keep an eye on what was going on over there and I had frequent meetings with individuals dealing with matters of policy; also with individuals who would bring other individuals over to introduce them to me and discuss their talents and their qualities with respect to filling certain jobs in that particular area. Yes sir, I did.

Q. You would consider, then, that you did play an active supervisory role before you resigned as Attorney General?

A. If you would change "supervisory" to "consulting," I think I would be much happier.

Q. Did it get beyond the consulting capacity?

A. Well, it might have been in areas where I let them know my opinion quite forcefully and strongly, but I think that would still fit under the role of consultant.

Q. Didn't you testify to the contrary before the Judiciary Committee on March 14, 1972?

A. Senator, I am glad you asked me that, I was waiting for somebody to. May I read the dialogue?

Q. Yes.

A. I was hoping that would come up.

Q. I am glad to accommodate you, sir.

A. Thank you. Because this subject matter has been bandied about and I think quite unfairly. This is a question by Senator Kennedy: "Do you remember what party responsibilities you had prior to March 1?

"Mitchell. Party responsibilities?

"Kennedy: Yes. Republican party.

"Mitchell. I do not have and did not have any responsibilities. I have no party responsibilities now, Senator."

Now, it seems to me that this committee has spent about six weeks trying to make a distinction between the different parties and the committees for the re-election of the President, and I look upon it the same way.

Q. Let's read a little further, Mr. Mitchell.

A. This is the only quote I have. Do you have something more on that?

Q. Yes. Let me read it for you.

Next question: "Senator Kennedy: No re-election campaign responsibilities?

"Mr. Mitchell: Not as yet. I hope to. I am going to make the application to the chairman of the committee if I ever get through with these hearings."

A. I can't believe that The Washington Post could be so mistaken.

Q. May I send it to you for the refreshment of your memory, sir?

A. I would like to see it.

Q. I will ask a member of the staff to show Mr. Mitchell page 633 of the hearings of Mr. Richard G. Kleindienst, resumed, on March 14, 1972.

A. Senator, I still think that relates, that phrase that you read that isn't in The Washington Post, relates back to the same subject matter.

Q. You testified a moment ago in response to a question that I have asked you that you did have campaign responsibilities prior to the time you resigned as Attorney General. And yet, on March 14, before the Judiciary committee, I quote again: "Senator Kennedy: No re-election campaign responsibilities?" That is a question.

"Mr. Mitchell. Not as yet." Isn't that negative?

A. That is negative. It relates back to the Republican party, Senator, in the way I read the context and this one was so intended.

Q. "No re-election campaign responsibilities?" I ask you who was running? Mr. Nixon? And is he a Republican?

A. I think the answer to both those questions is yes.

Q. I would concur with that. I still don't get the thrust of your testimony when you testified a moment ago that you had no, that you did have election responsibilities and yet before the Judiciary Committee of the United States Senate on March 14, 1972, you testified exactly the opposite.

A. Senator, I got back to the statement that I made before, that this refers to the Republican party and this is the reason that I raised the question and responded to it and it was my intention to do so in that context.

Q. Mr. Chairman, I desire to send to Mr. Mitchell a number of documents here wherein he was exercising his responsibility as director of the campaign, one dated June 22, 1971, one dated as far back as Jan. 14, 1972, all marked "confidential," memorandum to the attorney general, one involving the Republican National Committee budget, the other a telephone plan for the Florida primary.

A. Senator, I have no recollection of the first one relating to the Republican National Committee budget. I have a vague recollection of this one in January, having to do with the telephone plan for the Florida primary, and I am quite sure that the writing at the bottom here in connection with the comment which says, "hold for November pending standing in the polls"—"hold for now," I guess it is, not November—"pending standing in polls" is not my writing. But—

Q. Mr. Mitchell, you testified under oath in response to a question of mine a moment ago that at the request of the White House you were actively involved in the campaign. If I can read the English language correctly, on March 14 of last year, you testified to the opposite before the Judiciary Committee. One or the other of your statements is in error. I am inserting them in the record only so the public can draw their own conclusions as to which was in error.

A. I dispute your statement with respect to the discussion before the Judiciary Committee and I would like to go back to my statement and stand on that answer.

Q. That is part of the record and that is the reason, Mr. Mitchell, that I inserted both of them in the record so the American people can draw their own conclusion as to which is correct. I am not arguing with your testimony, but if I can read the English language in two different places, they are the opposite of each other. You state that they aren't. If I understand English, and I learned it in a small country school, in Telfair County—

A. So did I, Senator, a very small one.

Q. We both studied the same English, I assume.

A. That is why I am surprised you don't agree with my interpretation.

SENATOR ERVIN: Could I ask for his interpretation so I can understand it? It is your position that working for a Republican candidate for President gave you no responsibilities in respect to the Republican party?

A. That is it entirely, Mr. Chairman. That is the question that I asked of Senator Kennedy.

Q. Thank you.

SENATOR TALMADGE: One thing I can't understand, Mr. Mitchell. As I understand it, you have been probably closer associated with the President than probably any man. You were his law partner, probably his most trusted confidant and adviser. You had immediate access to the White House at any time, to the President's office, including a direct line. Is that a fair statement?

A. It is extremely complimentary.

Q. Now, you have been in public office, in positions of high responsibility in government. I have had that privilege also as Governor of my state and now for 16½ years in the United States Senate. To my mind, the first requirement of a subordinate and adviser and confidant in any capacity is absolute and implicit trust. If they see anything going wrong involving their superior that needs immediate corrective action, they report it instantly. When you found out all these crimes and conspiracies and cover-ups were being committed, why on earth didn't you walk into the President's office and tell him the truth?

A. It wasn't a question of telling him the truth. It was a question of not involving him at all so that he could go through his campaign without being involved in this type of activity, and I am talking about the White House horrors particularly. As I have testified this morning, I was sure that, knowing Richard Nixon, the President, as I do, he would just lower the boom on all of this matter and it would come back to hurt him and it would affect him in his re-election. And that is the basis upon which I made the decision. And apparently, others concurred with it.

Now, I am not speaking for them. It may very well be that I was wrong, that it was a bad matter of judgment.

Q. Am I to understand from your response that you placed the expediency of the next election above your responsibilities as an intimate to advise the President of the peril that surrounded him? Here was the deputy campaign director involved, here were his two closest associates in his office involved, all around him were people involved in crime, perjury, accessory after the fact, and you deliberately refused to tell him that.

Would you state that the expediency of the election was more important than that?

A. Senator, I think you have put it exactly correct. In my mind, the re-election of Richard Nixon, compared with what was available on the other side, was so much more important that I put it in just that context.

July 11, 1973

SENATOR INOUYE: Mr. Mitchell, if the re-election of President Nixon was so important that you were willing to engage in activities which have been well described as being irregular to insure his re-election, I think a question lies in many minds at this time. To what length are you now willing to go to deceive in an effort to avoid further implication of the President in the activities under investigation by this panel? More specifically, are you willing to lie to protect the President?

A. Senator, there is one great thing about the answer that I can give to that question to you. I do not have to make that choice, because to my knowledge, the President was not knowledgeable, certainly about the Watergate or certainly knowledgeable about anything that had to do with the cover-up, if that is the phrase that we are using. So I do not have to make that choice.

Q. In your testimony, Mr. Mitchell, you have suggested that it would not be fair—that is the word you have used—fair to the President if the facts relating to Watergate and the White House horrors had been brought to his attention and to the attention of the American people during the election campaign. Have you ever considered whether it was fair to the members of the opposition party or fair to the American people to conspire to keep them from the true facts of this matter?

A. Yes, I am sure that that subject matter has crossed my mind many, many times. But I do not believe now, I did not believe then that the President should be charged with the transgressions of others. And it is just as simple as that.

Q. I am reminded that as Attorney General, like all public officials, you were required to take an oath of office to uphold the Constitution of the United States and I am reminded by telegrams that I have been receiving that this is a government of laws and not of men. Did you feel that the President was above the laws of the land?

A. The President is never above the laws of the land to my knowledge, he has faithfully executed the laws of the land.

Q. You have said on several occasions that if the President had been notified he would have lowered the boom and would have taken drastic steps, and you have also suggested that you know the man very well. What would the President have done if you had notified him of the Watergate and the cover-up?

A. I would say that the President would have brought in the appropriate governmental officials from the investigative side and from those who were the prosecutors and laid it all out to them and said, "Here it is, take it in the proper process of law."

Q. What would the President have done if he found out that his choice for the directorship [of the F.B.I.] had destroyed evidence?

A. Well, I am sure he would have done what he has done since and that is, made sure he was replaced very rapidly by somebody who was not so involved.

SENATOR BAKER: We must move forward to June 22, when you received your briefing from those involved on what happened at the Watergate. A. That is right.

Q. At that moment, in retrospect, aren't you certain now that the country would have been better served and the President would have been better served by calling to account every single person in the Administration who even allegedly had anything to do with it and to express to the President personally what happened?

A. Now, you are talking about not only the Watergate but these other activities that we have just gotten through with?

Q. I am speaking of everything that occurred from Jan. 20, 1969, to June 22, 1972.

A. Senator, if I could have been assured at that time that the President would have been re-elected, I would agree with you wholeheartedly.

Q. You understand, I am sure, what an enormous premium, then, you put on success? I suppose all politicians put a great premium on success. But do you care to weigh that any further and tell me that the concealment from the President of facts such as you have described as the Watergate horrors, the break-in—

A. No, the White House.

Q. The White House horrors and the break-in to the Watergate on June 17, that all of those things were inferior in importance to the ultimate re-election of the President.

A. I had no doubt about it at that time and I have no doubt about it now.

Q. What would the President have to have done before his re-election was not as important as the event? Or what would someone have had to have done other than the President?

A. Well, Senator, I am sure you are well aware that the President was not knowledgeable of the or involved in that and this would have been a derivative rub-off on many of something that was, would have been absolutely unfair and unjustified.

Q. Isn't it unfair that he is now undergoing the hostility and the suspicion of a nation in this respect with the allegations of cover-up, with the lingering suspicion about what he knew? Isn't that greatly, isn't that far more unfair?

A. That is a statement that I am not prepared to accept, Senator. I do not believe the nation feels that way and I do not believe that anybody has come to the point where they have one shred of evidence that he was knowledgeable of the break-in or the cover-up.

Q. I think you and I are talking about two different things.

A. Obviously, because we generally get along fine.

Q. Well, we still do get along fine and I am delighted that I have this opportunity to probe into the great mentality of a great man.

And I think one thing that I might say in that respect that may shed some light on that situation is a remark you made in Gatlinburg, Tenn., when you spoke to the Tennessee Bar Association at my request; you graciously accepted that invitation.

I introduced you at the reception to some of my friends who are attorneys in Tennessee. I said, Mr. Mitchell, as you know, was once President Nixon's law partner, and our distinguished witness said, no, Mr. Nixon was my law partner.

Now, Mr. Mitchell, I have no quarrel with you. I welcome this opportunity to find out where the threshold is, where the crossover point is on the importance of an event versus the responsibility to tell the President.

Now, what I spoke of a moment ago was not evidence of the President's involvement. I have imposed on myself a discipline that I will not comment on the importance, the relevance, or the competence of the testimony of any witness until all of the testimony is taken. And I am not going to do that with respect to the President, either. But what I am talking about is suspicion. What I asked you is whether or not the decision to expose all of this to the President for a Presidential decision, would not it have been infinitely better than to undergo the suspicion, the blemish, the uncertainty in the minds of the American people that does exist—not proof; I think the American people are remarkably forebearing in this respect—but the suspicion. Would not it have been infinitely better to do that in June of 1972?

A. In the Monday morning quarterback field in what has developed into the circumstances that exist today, I don't doubt for a moment that you are probably absolutely correct, and I believe so.

Q. We have no defendants. We are not trying to establish the guilt or innocence of anyone. We are trying to prevent this in the future by legislative relief. So that statement by you is most helpful. That is, in hindsight, you are certain, are you not, that it would have been better to permit a President to make a Presidential grade decision in June of 1972?

A. I don't think there is any question about that based upon what has developed out of this, Senator, and how it has developed to the point we are today is another question that has to be examined.

Q. Entirely different, separate and aside. It has to do with guilt and innocence, it has to do with circumstances, it has to do with involvement or noninvolvement. But for our purposes, as a senatorial committee, our future is to find the ways to avoid this in the future—I mean our responsibility is to find ways to avoid this in the future and that is why I keep pressing for your hindsight, whether or not you are convinced, and I am happy you are convinced.

A. Well, there is no question about the developments that have taken place since the weeks of June of 1972 to July of 1973. I don't think there is any question about it at all, that it might even have been better, Senator, as you say, take them out on the White House lawn; it would have been simpler to have shot them all and that would have been less of a problem than has developed in the meantime.

SENATOR MONTOYA: Did you, during your visits to the White House, engage in any conversations with Mr. Ehrlichman or Mr. Haldeman about the course of the investigation as it was being conducted by the lawyers for the C.R.P. and others with respect to Watergate?

A. Oh, I am sure that somewhere, sometime along the way, that these discussions were held. I can't pinpoint any particular meeting. We were more heavily engaged in the matters of the campaign than we were discussing the particular aspects of the Watergate investigation.

Q. Did you discuss the testimony before the grand jury on the part of Mr. Magruder or the testimony that might, that was going to be presented by Mr. Dean with anyone at the White House?

A. The testimony that was going to be presented by Mr. Dean?

Q. Yes, before the prosecutors and the testimony that was going to be presented by Mr. Magruder before the grand jury?

A. No, to the best of my recollection, Senator, those discussions were not held with anybody at the White House. They were held with Mr. Dean and the lawyers and other people at the committee and not the White House.

Q. Can you tell this committee whether or not Mr. Haldeman or Mr. Ehrlichman knew anything about the so-called activities trying to cover up the White House involvement with respect to the Watergate?

A. Well, the White House involvement in what respect, Senator? White House involvement in connection with the Watergate?

Q. Yes.

A. Well, I do not know as there has been any testimony to the effect that the people in the White House were involved in the Watergate.

Q. Well, with respect to the cover-up?

A. Well, eventually along the road, there was discussion in connection with the fact that there was no volunteering or coming forward and that there was a design not to have the stories come out that had to do with the White House horror activities. There is no question about that.

Q. Your concern being that you did not want to trigger off any action that might impair the President's re-election, and that is why you did not advise him before the election, did it not occur to you that your desire to insulate the President against disclosure by you of the exact details of Watergate was not exclusive because there were others close to the President who might have done the same thing?

A. I am sure there were others who were close to the President that might have had the same thoughts and the same opportunities. I do not know what their subjective thoughts were.

Q. What I am suggesting is that the possibility existed at that time that if you did not tell the President, that Mr. Ehrlichman, Mr. Haldeman or Mr. Dean might do this, did you insure against that thing happening?

A. No sir. We had no discussion along the lines that you are inferring with respect to the subject matter.

Q. Well, if your interest was so profound in trying to trigger off any Presidential action that might endanger his chances of re-election, why did you not go to people close to the President to make sure that they would not tell the President about the details involving Watergate?

A. I believe that they are capable of making their decisions on their own. I obviously made mine and I presume that they made theirs independently.

Q. We have a situation here before the committee and I will close with this, Mr. Mitchell, we have a situation of whether or not the Liddy plan was approved. Was any part of the plan approved by you? A. No sir, none whatsoever.

Q. Did you disapprove of the Liddy plan at Key Biscayne? A. Yes sir, I did.

Q. Completely, did you disapprove it all three times? A. Yes, sir.

SENATOR ERVIN: Mr. Mitchell, on yesterday, when Senator Talmadge asked you concerning your political activities in respect to the Committee to Re-elect the President while you were still serving as Attorney General you pointed out that it was not illegal for you to do that. A. Yes sir, that is correct, Mr. Chairman.

Q. Yes. Now I think we might meditate just a minute on what St. Paul said. He said, "All things are lawful unto me but some things are not expedient."

Don't you think it is rather inexpedient for the chief law enforcement officer of the United States to be engaging in, directly or indirectly, in managing political activities? A. I do, Senator.

Q. Yes. I was in hopes that was what you were going to do because when you appeared before the Judiciary Committee on your nomination back on Jan. 14, 1969, you and I had this little colloquy.

A. I remember it very well, Senator.

Q. Yes. "Senator Ervin: Mr. Mitchell, until comparatively recent years it has been customary for Presidents to appoint the Postmaster General his chief political adviser and agitator. Unfortunately, during recent years this role has been largely taken away from the Postmaster General and given to and exercised by the Attorney General. To my mind there is something incompatible with marrying the function of the chief political adviser and chief agitator with that of prosecutor of crimes against the Government.

"Now, I would just like to know whether you think that the primary function and objective of the Attorney General should be giving political advice or doing political agitating before Congressional committees or enforcing Federal law and acting as an adviser to the President in his Cabinet in legal matters rather than political.

"A. Senator, I would hope that my activities in a political nature and of a political nature have ended with the campaign.

"I might say that this was my first entry into a political campaign, and I trust it will be my last. From the termination of the campaign and henceforward my duties and functions will be related to the Justice Department, and as the legal and not the political adviser of the President.

"Q. Thank you, sir. I commend your answer."

I am very sorry that you didn't carry out the purpose you announced on that occasion.

A. Mr. Chairman, that would have been my fondest wish. Unfortunately, it is very, very difficult to turn down a request by the President of the United States.

Q. Now, don't you think that what we have been investigating here indicates the desirability of the Congress giving serious consideration to divorcing the Department of Justice from political matters?

A. I would perhaps even go further and suggest that you divorce all of the departments from political matters. I think it would be a very constructive move.

Q. Now here we had a criminal prosecution in which the prosecutors held office at the pleasure of the President, and the tracks from the burglary in the Watergate led directly into the Committee to Re-elect the President, and it turns out that the lawyers who are defending the seven men indicted in the criminal action were paid, either directly or indirectly, by the Committee to Re-elect the President or Presidential aides in the White House, and that is a condition which is not calculated to accomplish justice, in my opinion. Of course, you were out of the Department of Justice at that time.

Now, twice while you were still Attorney General of the United States and the chief law enforcement officer of the United States, and the chief legal adviser to the President of the United States, meetings were held in your office in the Department of Justice in which such matters were discussed as proposals to bug the opposition political party and to burglarize the headquarters of the opposition party and to employ prostitutes to induce members of the opposition party to disclose secrets, weren't they?

A. They were so discussed and, of course, disapproved.

Q. But the burglary and the bugging was discussed in the second? A. That is correct.

Q. Then on the third occasion, namely on the 30th of March, Mr. Magruder, who was your deputy director of the committee, visited Key Biscayne where you were and discussed these matters, at least the bugging and the break-in, a third time with you, didn't he?

A. I wouldn't use the term "discussed." They were presented—

Q. And you declined to do that on three occasions. A. That is correct, sir.

Q. Can you explain to me why it was, after you declined on the first occasion, that you had a second discussion on the matter and after you declined on the second occasion, that you had a third discussion of the matter or presentation of the matter?

A. I cannot for the life of me understand as to why this matter was constantly brought back, except for the point that somebody obviously was very interested in the subject matter.

Q. Wouldn't the evidence justify the inference that you did not communicate your disapproval in such an emphatic enough matter to prevent the bugging and the break-in?

A. No, I think the testimony of Mr. Dean and my testimony of yesterday and today is quite to the contrary. In fact, this was not the type of concept that was envisioned. It was quite different.

Q. And the man who was in charge of your committee when

you were absent was Mr. Magruder, wasn't he? A. That is correct.

Q. And didn't you shortly after, didn't you find out shortly after the 17th day of June that Magruder had financed the burglaries?

A. Yes, sir, that was in the week following the break-in.

Q. In other words, it appeared very shortly that five burglars had been caught in the Watergate and that one of them was Mr. McCord, an employe of your committee? A. That is correct, sir.

Q. And it also appeared that four of the burglars at that very time had in their pockets money which came from your committee.

A. That was eventually established, yes, sir.

Q. Now, very shortly after you found out the things I inquired of you about, you also found that Liddy, who had been general counsel to the committee, the Finance Committee to Re-elect the President, and another employe of your committee, E. Howard Hunt, had been arrested for complicity in the break-in.

A. Senator, may I point out that to the best of my knowledge, Mr. Hunt was never an employe of either one of the committees. Mr. McCord—

Q. Mr. Hunt was employed in the White House, was he not?

A. I have learned that since, yes.

Q. Well, you found out sometime in the summer, did you not, that Mr. Hunt had been sent over to the committee by Mr. Colson? A. Yes, sir.

Q. And you found about the same time that Mr. Hunt had been implicated in the burglary of the office of the psychiatrist of Ellsberg? A. Yes, sir.

Q. And you found out, therefore, that Hunt, a burglar, had been retained on the White House payroll from September, 1971, 'til the break-in.

A. Well, I was not aware of the periods, but I did learn that he had been a consultant to the White House.

Q. And then, after you came back from California, you talked to Mr. Robert Mardian and Mr. Fred LaRue and Mr. Dean and Mr. Magruder about these matters. A. That is correct, sir.

Q. And from your conversation with these men, you realized that Dean and Magruder participated—that Magruder had participated in the break-in and that he and Dean were engaged in what has been called the cover-up?

A. If I can answer just slightly different, Mr. Chairman, we did learn that Magruder had obviously been providing the funds that were used in connection with the activities of the group that did break in.

Q. And did you not find out that Dean and Magruder were trying to conceal these events?

A. Well this came a bit later down the pipe but we did obviously learn that this was the case.

Q. About how long afterwards?

A. I would believe that it would probably have been the middle of July or some time thereafter.

Q. And you also found that money which had been contributed for the re-election of President Nixon had found its way into the bank account of Barker, one of the burglars at the Watergate?

A. Yes, sir, that came forward quite early.

Q. And then Magruder told you that, in effect—well, first, you talked to LaRue and Mardian and they both knew about these events. You could tell that from the conversations they had with you, did you not?

A. They told me, repeated what Mr. Liddy had told them, yes, sir.

Q. And that was that he had participated, had instigated this burglary at the instance of Magruder?

A. That is the basis of their representation to me as to what Liddy had said.

Q. Yes, and from that, your conversation with Robert Mardian and Fred LaRue, you learned that they had been apprised of that fact? A. That is correct.

Q. You also were informed by Magruder that he, Magruder, was prepared to commit perjury when it went before the grand jury in August rather than to reveal what he knew about these matters? A. That was correct, sir.

Q. Now, did you agree that that was the proper course of action to take?

A. It was a very expedient one, Senator. At that time in the campaign so close to the election, we certainly were not volunteering any information.

Q. Well, did you advise Mr. Magruder that perjury was a felony and he ought not to commit perjury when he proposed to you that he commit perjury?

A. I am sure Mr. Magruder was well aware of it.

Q. Yes. Well, did Mr. Mardian and Mr. LaRue ever talk to you about the Magruder proposal to commit perjury?

A. They were present on an occasion or more in which Mr. Magruder stated what he was going to testify to.

Q. Did you ever have any conversation with Mr. Haldeman about these matters?

A. Not until much later on, Senator.

Q. How much later on?

A. This year.

Q. You mean you never had any conversation with Mr. Haldeman until 1973?

A. About the subject matter that you are referring to with respect to—

Q. Well, what about Mr. Ehrlichman?

A. I had no such conversations with Mr. Ehrlichman.

Q. Did you have any information at the time of these other White House horrors, as you call them, about Mr. Ehrlichman trying to enlist the aid of the C.I.A. to suppress investigation of the Mexican checks by the F.B.I.?

A. No, sir, I did not learn of that until a more recent date here, when it has been made public.

Q. You knew about all these other things, however, before the indictments were returned in September against the seven original defendants?

A. When you say all of the other things, you mean the items that we have just discussed here?

Q. Yes. A. Yes, sir, I did.

Q. And you were aware of the fact that sometime about early September or late August that the President made a statement to the American people to the effect that nobody involved, nobody presently employed in the White House had anything to do with any of these matters?

A. As I recall the statement, Senator, and I am not sure that I can recall it specifically, I believe the statement was to the effect that there was nobody in the White House that was involved in the breaking and entering of the Watergate.

Q. Then the President didn't make, his statement as you construed it didn't indicate that the President was saying that nobody in the White House knew anything about it, about the cover-up?

A. Well, I believe the statement referred to involvement. I could be wrong, because I don't remember the contents of it, but I believe that was the case.

Q. Well, I think you stated that Mr. Strachan was liaison between Haldeman in the White House and the Committee to Re-elect the President?

A. I think you can broaden that, Senator, to the fact that he was liaison between the White House and the Committee to Re-elect the President.

Q. Yes. And did you not learn that he had been advised by Mr. Dean and Mr. Magruder as to what was going on in the Committee to Re-elect the President at these times?

A. Well, Mr. Strachan was constantly being advised as to what was going on in connection with the matters at the Committee for the Re-election of the President. In fact, he attended meetings from time to time of the committee.

Q. And he attended there for the purpose of advising the people at the White House as to what the committee was doing, didn't he?

A. I presume that was his purpose.

Q. That was his sole function, was not it?

A. I don't know what he did at the White House, but it was the sole function of his relationship with the committee.

Q. Now, as I understand your testimony, you talked to the President twice about Watergate, the first time in June, 1972, and the second time on the 22d of March, 1973.

A. When we talked about Watergate, Senator, those were two

occasions upon which they were discussed. I also testified yesterday that in some of the political meetings that were had, the general subject matter was discussed as to how the President should approach it with respect to a type of Warren commission or special prosecutors and other such items. These were in large groups.

Q. Well, you had a conversation with the President about Watergate in June, 1972, didn't you? I believe it was June 20.

A. The 20th of June, a short telephone conversation, that is correct.

Q. And you apologized to the President for Watergate?

A. I apologized to the President for not keeping track of the personnel in the committee to the extent that the Watergate matter could have happened.

Now, this is the 20th of June before I had learned of a lot of other circumstances.

Q. Well, you had learned enough by the 20th of June to feel that the Committee to Re-elect the President, or at least some officials of it, were implicated in the Watergate break-in, didn't you?

A. With respect to McCord, yes, and this is the basis for my apology.

Q. Well, didn't the President ask you what you meant by your apologizing?

A. I think I made it quite clear to him that I hadn't exercised sufficient control over the activities of all of the people in the committee.

Q. Didn't the President ask you then what you knew about Watergate and why you were apologizing?

A. I think I told him what I knew about Watergate at that particular time, which was very, very little.

Q. Now, as I recall, you testified you—after you had moved to New York that you came down to Washington and were here on the 22d of March and had attended a meeting where the President and Dean and perhaps Ehrlichman and Haldeman were present. A. Yes sir, that is correct.

Q. And you discussed this committee? A. Yes sir.

Q. And the President was adhering at that time to the notion that he could invoke executive privilege and keep any of his present or former White House aides from testifying before the committee, isn't that so?

A. I believe that the fact that that impression had been put out from the White House was one of the reasons for the meeting. Obviously, of course, the President could waive it any time he wanted to and that was one of the subject matters that was discussed at the meeting of March 22.

Q. Didn't you advise him not to invoke any such claim of executive privilege?

A. I had told the President, and I presume it was by way of

advice, if he thought it was appropriate to accept it, and this is, of course, in the time frame of the Gray hearings, where this subject matter became very lively, in which I suggested that I thought that his only problem, his only public problem, with respect to these matters was the fact that he was indicating that he would invoke executive privilege with respect to the staff and the White House and I thought this was something he should not do because it was putting him in a very poor light.

Q. Don't you agree with me that any person, whether it is the President or a Senator or a hod carrier or anybody else, who gives the impression to the public that he is withholding information within his power is putting himself in a bad light?

A. Well, Mr. Chairman, if we will leave out the President, I will certainly agree with you whole-heartedly. I think the President has a separate question with respect to the separation of powers.

Q. I was discussing psychology. From a psychological standpoint, don't you think that the President who withholds information or papers about a matter that is being investigated runs the risk of having many Americans draw an inference that the reason he withholds them is because he realizes they would be unfavorable to him.

A. I think they may, but I am sure that there is not always that simple question or other factors involved that have to be weighed and you have, frequently you have, two risks that have to be weighed and certainly it is the case in this area.

Q. Do you accept the concept that executive privilege is— entitles the President to deny a court or a Congressional committee the testimony of his former or present aides about everything?

A. It depends entirely upon the area, Mr. Chairman. And, of course, if they are conversations or direct communications with the President and particularly with respect to certain subject matters, I think that he has that power.

Q. Well, let me state my concept of executive privilege and see if we agree or disagree. I think a President is entitled to have kept secret confidential communications had between him and an aide or had among his aides which were had for the purpose of assisting the President to perform in a lawful manner one of his constitutional or legal duties.

A. Senator, I agree with that concept.

Q. Yes. And I think also that is the full scope and effect of executive privilege. Since the President, there is nothing in the Constitution requiring the President to run for re-election. I don't think that executive privilege covers any political activities whatsoever. They are not official and have no relation to his office. Do you take the position that the President is entitled to keep political secrets from the Congress or political activities under executive privilege?

A. Not under the outline that you have provided.

Q. I also take the position that executive privilege does not entitle a President to have kept secret information concerning criminal activities of his aides or anybody else because there is nothing in the Constitution that authorizes or makes it the official duty of a President to have anything to do with criminal activities.

A. I would agree.

Q. Yes. So, I cannot see, if the President has any—if any aide has any information about criminal activities or if any papers in the White House that constitute reports from—to any White House official about criminal activities, that they are privileged in any way whatsoever.

A. I would have to qualify that with respect to certain areas that might involve national security, and if we will leave that out I will agree with you.

Q. Well, national security is defined in the executive order as comprising only two fields: first, is national defense and the other is our relations with foreign countries. I don't think there is anything else that falls in the field of national security, according to the definition in the executive order which was signed by President Nixon, and I think that is also clear that the acts of Congress make it very clear what national defense is.

A. I made the exception and you have very properly, I think, defined it.

Q. Now, in his campaign in 1968 Nixon appealed to voters for their support in these words:

"America is in trouble today not because her people have failed but because her leaders have failed. Let us begin by committing ourselves to the truth, to see it like it is, and to tell it like it is, to find the truth, to speak the truth, and to live the truth."

Now, do you have any reason to think that between that time and 1972 that President Nixon has changed his position, his fidelity to the truth?

A. I have no doubt whatsoever that his fidelity to the truth is the same as it was in 1968.

Q. And yet, he said that the way to save America in 1968 was "to find the truth, to speak the truth, and to live the truth." And yet, when 1972 came and these White House horrors became known to you, you did not take the advice that President Nixon gave us all in 1968, did you?

A. Not under that particular guideline, I assure you.

Q. In other words, not only was it true in your case, but it was true in the case of Mr. Mardian, Mr. LaRue, Mr. Magruder, Mr. Dean and Mr. Ehrlichman, was it not?

A. Well, I cannot characterize those gentlemen and their activities.

Q. Did the President at any time ask you what you knew about Watergate?

A. Not after that first discussion that we had on the telephone, I believe it was on June 20.

Q. Well, if the cat hadn't any more curiosity than that it would still be enjoying its nine lives, all of them.

A. Well, I hope the President enjoys eight more of them.

Q. Now, on Sept. 5, 1972, in the deposition in the case of Lawrence O'Brien versus James McCord, when you were asked the following question by Edward Bennett Williams, you were asked, "Was there any discussion at which you were present or about which you heard when you were campaign director concerning having any form of surveillance on the Democratic National Committee Headquarters," and your answer at that time on Sept. 5, 1972, was "No, sir, I can't imagine a less productive activity than that."

A. That is correct, and I stand on the answer that I gave this morning that refers to the activities of the security group the question was asked with respect to.

Q. All right. Let's start at the beginning here, if we can, in going over the testimony that has been presented by you, and do some probing. I must confess, Mr. Mitchell, that as I have sat here and listened to your testimony the only difficulty I find with it is that it sometimes is difficult to realize that we have sitting before the committee not some administrative assistant to some deputy campaign director but we have the campaign director sitting before this committee, and indeed we don't have some deputy assistant Attorney General sitting before the committee, we have the Attorney General of the United States sitting before the committee.

Now, on the 27th of January, 1972, Gordon Liddy presented a plan in your office, in the office of the Attorney General of the United States, and that plan, complete with visual aids, included elaborate charts of electronic surveillance and breaking and entering and prostitution and kidnapping and mugging. Now you have indicated that in hindsight you probably should have thrown him out of the office.

A. Out of the window.

Q. Maybe even out of the window, in hindsight. The life of every American is or to a great degree, his liberty, protection of all of his rights, sits in the hands of the Attorney General of the United States, and do you mean to tell me that you sat there through that meeting and, in fact, actually had the same man come back into your office for a second meeting without in any way alerting appropriate authorities in this particular case, the President of the United States?

A. That is exactly what happened, Senator. And, as I say, in hindsight it was a grievous error.

Q. You mean after listening to what we would both agree are outlandish plans, that you were neither moved to great anger in your capacity as Attorney General of the United States, which certainly everything that he proposed runs contrary to what you were supposed to stand for at that moment?

A. I was moved to considerable anger. That is the reason that the plans were turned down and he was to go and burn them and forget about such things.

Q. Well, obviously you didn't make much of a point to the man since he was back in your office on Feb. 4, isn't that correct?

A. He should have understood, got the message.

Q. Well, the fact is, forget for one minute politics, let's just talk about your position as Attorney General of the United States. I find it inconceivable, unless there seems to be at least some willingness to share a portion of the mentality that you didn't go ahead and have the fellow arrested for even suggesting this to the Attorney General of the United States.

A. Senator, I doubt if you can get people arrested for suggesting such things, but, as I said—

Q. For suggesting illegal acts to the Attorney General of the United States, I think that is probably grounds for arrest.

A. I would have some doubts. I don't know what part of Title 18 would cover that but that is not the point that I am sure you are trying to get at. The point is that I think I made it eminently clear that those acts were not in accord with the concept that we had for the purpose of gathering information of intelligence and to secure the campaign against harmful demonstrators. That was the concept of the plan that was discussed, and if you recognize Mr. Dean's testimony it was so stated at one of those meetings that that was the concept in which we were interested.

Q. Now, since your sensibilities as Attorney General were not overtly offended in this matter, what about your sensibilities as the shortly-to-be-appointed director of the President's campaign effort? Here is a man who is standing before you as the chief counsel of his re-election effort, I mean it didn't occur to you to call up the President and say, "I have got some pinwheel in my office here that is going to be the counsel to your re-election campaign and I think I ought to warn you, I think I ought to warn you you have got a lot of trouble on your hands."

In other words, in a political sense, it didn't occur to you to go ahead and warn anybody to get this fellow off the boat, if you will.

A. Senator, it never occurred to me that anybody would carry out such activities particularly without any authorization to do so.

Q. Well, in any event, he still had sufficient standing before the Attorney General and the to-be-director of the campaign so that he was back in your office on Feb. 4, with, admittedly a scaled-down plan. But let us get back to the 27th of January, 1972. At 11:15 in the morning, you go through this presentation, which both of us would describe as incredible. At 2:30 that afternoon, at 2:30 that afternoon, you talked to the President of the United States, and no mention is made at all of what had transpired in the office of the Attorney General that morning?

A. Absolutely, Senator. I do not know how often you get to talk to the President of the United States, but he is the one that normally initiates the conversation and the subject matters that are discussed.

Q. Now, Mr. LaRue states that on March 30, 1972, when Mr. Magruder presented the Liddy plan to you in Mr. LaRue's presence, that rather than rejecting it, you merely told Mr. Magruder that it did not have to be decided at that time. Is there any way that you can relate to Mr. LaRue's testimony as to what occurred at that moment in time?

A. No, my recollection is very distinctly as to what I testified on yesterday, that the matter was rejected and it was rejected on the basis that I was tired of hearing of these things and did not want to hear about them again.

Q. All right. Now, let's move to your meeting with Mr. Liddy on June 15, 1972, two days before the break-in. What time of day did you usually leave the office when you were Attorney General or campaign director?

A. It ranged all the way from 6 to 9.

Q. Well, in the first five months of 1972, your logs show no appointments after 6 P.M. Does that seem to correspond with your recollection?

A. No, it—after 6 P.M.?

Q. That is right.

A. Well, I haven't been through them to ascertain that, but it was not unusual for me to work on until 7 or 8 o'clock, sometimes 9 o'clock at night.

Q. Well, there is no record of it, certainly that I have in my possession, and the pattern of ending at 6 o'clock or before continued into June, with one exception. On the 15th of June, you had a 6:40 P.M. appointment, an appointment with a man who, as it turns out, it would been well not to have been seen coming to and from your office, G. Gordon Liddy. This after hours appointment happened only once in all the time, at least as to the logs we had, that you were Attorney General or campaign director in '72 prior to June 17.

A. Senator, are you aware of the purpose and contents of that meeting?

Q. I am going to get—my question is simply do you maintain that this meeting was not arranged because you were aware you were meeting with a man whose association could embarrass you?

A. That is not the case at all, Senator. Do you want the facts as to how the meeting was structured?

Q. Yes, I would like to have the fact as to how the meeting was structured and the contents—

A. It is very simple, Mr. Liddy had written a letter to The Washington Post, which was subsequently published, at the request of Mr. Stans responding to some charges that were made by somebody on the staff of the General Accounting Office about the failure of the finance committee, the failure of the finance committee to comply with certain provisions of the Corrupt

Practices Act. The letter was brought to Mr. Shumway, who was in charge of public information at the Committee for the Re-election of the President. Mr. Shumway said that he did not want that letter published without my approval, so Mr. Shumway brought Mr. Liddy into my office.

Q. Was there not a far greater threat that Hunt and Liddy would expose these activities than the President of the United States?

A. That was always a possibility but the fond hope was that they would, of course, not because they were involved in them.

Q. What did you do to prevent it?

A. I did not do anything to prevent it.

Q. In other words, you took care of the Presidential situation by not telling him? A. That is correct.

Q. And you took care of the Hunt and Liddy situation by just letting it run its course?

A. Senator, the fact of the matter is that the rationale is that Hunt and Liddy were involved in those other activites and there was every indication or belief that they were not about to go and incriminate themselves in those particular areas.

Q. Didn't anybody discuss the fact, Mr. Mitchell, that the reason why you should leave as the head of the Committee to Re-elect the President was because it might be considered that in that capacity, you were subject to the daily confrontations with the press, which press might go ahead and continue to ask you questions relative to Watergate? Was this ever discussed?

A. If it was, it was not discussed with me, no. The determination, Senator, for my leaving the campaign was made entirely on the basis of that luncheon conversation that I had with the President.

Q. July 1. Saturday, 9:40, you met with LaRue and Moore and Magruder. 12:08, LaRue and Magruder. 12:20, Kleindienst by telephone and then from 5:13 to 5:36, it does not appear on your logs, you have a phone conversation with the President from San Clemente?

A. Yes, I had a phone conversation from San Clemente which I have described to this committee. And obviously, the phone call came to my apartment, since the log here shows that I left the office at 2 o'clock.

Q. Did the President call you the next day, July 2? A. That is also correct.

Q. On July 11, you meet with Fred LaRue at 11 o'clock in the morning. Then at 12:48, you had a conversation with the President, which again does not appear on your log.

A. The July 11 conversation, to the best of my recollection, as I testified yesterday, had to do with the discussion of the President's determination to keep Vice President Agnew on the ticket, or to recommend him to the convention, that he be kept on the ticket.

Q. Now, on March 22, you have stated that you spoke with the

President, along with Dean and Haldeman and Ehrlichman and that the sole subjects were executive privilege and developing a liaison with the select committee, am I correct? And that nothing else concerning Watergate was discussed.

A. I said that those were the main topics of the meeting. There was also the discussion, as I said, of having somebody provide liaison with the committee up here. Dean was discussed and apparently rejected. And then Ehrlichman, and as I think the record will show, and I think I can bear out Mr. Dean's recollection of it, the President called Mr. Ehrlichman on the subject matter while we were there.

Q. Everybody seems to be very much in tune with the conversations of that particular meeting. And yet, in the President's remarks of April 17, 1973, he states that on March 21, "as a result of serious charges which came to my attention, some of which were publicly reported, I began intensive new inquiries into this whole matter."

That is by the President's own statement. "On March 21, as a result of serious charges which came to my attention some of which were publicly reported, I began intensive new inquiries into this whole matter."

And on March 22, on March 22, you and Mr. Dean, Mr. Haldeman, Mr. Ehrlichman all met with the President and the subject matter of Watergate never comes up. Is that correct?

A. Now, what part of—you are talking about Watergate. We are talking about this committee up here whose purpose was to investigate Watergate. As I understand it. So obviously, the subject matter of Watergate came up in connection with this committee, being the committee to investigate Watergate. But if you are talking about did the meeting have any conversations that went back and reviewed the bidding as to who did what to whom under what circumstances, the answer is no, it did not.

Q. But we knew from the President's own statement that on the day before, new inquiries were made into the whole matter. And here he had standing before him the following day the head of the Committee to Re-elect the President. Were any inquiries made at all of the former head of the Committee to Re-elect the President?

A. No, sir, the conversations were just as I have reported them.

Q. So in effect, no inquiry, even though the President stated that new inquiries were being made, no inquiry was being made of you by this particular group of gentlemen, either the President or Mr. Haldeman or Mr. Ehrlichman or Mr. Dean, in that room at that time?

A. There was no discussion, Senator.

Q. Do you find that surprising, in light of the March 21 statement?

A. I find it surprising in light of what Mr. Dean said about the March 21 conversation that he purportedly had with the President.

Q. I am not talking about Mr. Dean, I am talking about what is reported as said by the President.

A. What is the date of that statement, Senator?

Q. It is the statement of April 17, 1973, and the statement says: "My second announcement concerns the Watergate case directly. On March 21, as a result of serious charges which came to my attention, some of which were publicly reported, I began intensive new inquiries into this whole matter. Last Sunday afternoon, the Attorney General, Assistant Attorney General Petersen and I met at length in my E.O.B. [Executive Office Building] office to review the facts which had come to me in my investigation and also to review the progress of the Department of Justice investigation. I can report today that there have been many .developments in the case concerning which it would be improper to be more specific now except to say that real progress has been made in finding the truth."

That is the President speaking relative to what he did on March 21.

A. Now, what question would you like me to answer?

Q. My question to you is, do you find it surprising when you appear on the scene on March 22, and sweeping new investigations are being made that nobody goes ahead and raises the Watergate insofar as any participation of those in the room? Do you find this rather surprising? A. I do not.

Q. Do you think one of the reasons it was not, no reason to be discussed, with anybody in the room was because nobody was gaining that knowledge because they already had that knowledge?

A. No, I had not thought of it in those concepts but I don't believe it was the case. When you meet with the President, you meet with the President for a specific purpose and the purpose was, the purposes were, as I have stated them here.

Q. Dean gave the President his theory of what had happened. He still said no prior June 17 White House knowledge, Magruder probably knew, Ehrlichman probably knew, Haldeman has possibly seen the fruits of the wiretaps from Strachan, et cetera. Your name came up in the conversation, it had been bandied about.

A. This is still a Dean allegation. Well, Senator—

Q. This is the White House version, this is the White House version, Mr. Mitchell, of the meeting with John Dean.

A. I understand that but it is still John Dean who is being the one who is being quoted.

Q. Well, why—do you find it unusual that the President didn't ask you on March 22 to comment upon Mr. Dean's conversations with him as they related to you?

A. I don't find it at all unusual because the basis of the meeting and the purpose of the meeting was a different one or different ones, as I have stated.

Q. Is this your definition, by the way, this kind of testimony, of, what is the expression, "of stonewalling it."

A. I don't know that term. Is that a Yankee term from Connecticut?

Q. Is there anything in this country, aside from the President of the United States that puts you in awe, Mr. Mitchell?

A. To put me where?

Q. That puts you in awe?

A. There are very, very many things.

Q. Do the courts put you in awe? A. Very much so.

Q. Does your oath as attorney, does that put you into awe?

A. Very much so.

Q. Do you feel as an officer of the court you did the right thing?

A. In connection with the Ellsberg matter?

Q. Why did you not notify the prosecution or did you not notify rather Judge Byrne of the information you had in your possession?

A. I think in retrospect, it probably would have been the right thing to do.

Q. I have no further questions at this time.

A. It is a great trial being conducted up here, isn't it?

July 12, 1973

SENATOR INOUYE: Mr. Mitchell, I have just one question and the question relates to "lowering the boom." I believe on March 21, the President had a meeting with John Wesley Dean 3d, at which time Mr. Dean has testified that he notified the President as to his involvement in all of the irregular activities.

On the following day we have testimony to indicate that the President met with high officials, staff members of the White House, including Mr. Dean. Now, according to what you have said, we would expect the President to have lowered the boom on John Wesley Dean 3d. But on the 22d of March, instead of lowering the boom, testimony indicates that the President designated Mr. Dean to serve as his liaison with this committee. Is this your concept of lowering the boom?

A. No. Senator, it most assuredly is not. I believe that the facts were that there was a discussion of Mr. Dean being the liaison with the committee to get certain areas straightened out. What actually the President was doing in other areas to "lower the boom," I am not quite sure but as we all know, things started to happen from thence forward in the area where I do believe that steps were taken to the point here you could call it lowering the boom.

Q. For the record could you tell us where the President has really lowered the boom?

A. I think he has done so by his appointment of a special prosecutor, removing the people from the White House who were involved in the activities that were covered up.

Q. Was not the appointment of the special prosecutor brought about because of intensive pressure initiated by the Congress of the United States? Does not the record indicate that the White House and the President resisted this?

A. It was the President's determination. He was the one who made that determination. What were the causes of it, I think we can all have different opinions upon but it was his action that did provide for the special prosecutor.

Q. And in the case of so-called removals of staff members, the record seems to indicate that Mr. Haldeman and Mr. Ehrlichman submitted letters of resignation and the President most reluctantly accepted this and said publicly that these were the two finest men he has ever known. Is this lowering the boom, sir?

A. No, but it shows the streak in the President of warmth and kindness that most people have not attributed to him before. I think it could be considered in that light.

Q. I believe your lowering the boom statement is an important one and that is why I am pursuing this. You have indicated that you did not advise the President of the United States as to your knowledge of the facts involved in this matter before us, because you were concerned that the President would lower the boom and thereby lift the lid off the scandal. I am trying to find out where the President has, since learning of these activities, lowered the boom.

A. It is my opinion, Senator, that particularly during the month of April and the succeeding intervening period of time, he has done exactly what he should have done in lowering the boom by removing the people from the White House and by providing for the special prosecutor within our system of government. That is what the chief executive should do.

Q. With the exception of Mr. Dean, when he advised the President that he is going to do some talking here he, I presume, was removed, but was anyone else removed? A. Well, Mr. Haldeman and Mr. Ehrlichman were.

Q. They were not removed, sir.

A. They were not removed from the White House?

Q. If you read the public statement, they submitted their resignations and the President reluctantly accepted this, and in so accepting the resignations praised them to the highest.

A. Senator, I have an entirely different interpretation of that.

Q. Besides Mr. Haldeman and Mr. Ehrlichman, did anyone else suffer from the lowering of the boom?

A. Yes, I believe that Mr. Magruder was removed from his job, Mr. Krogh was. I don't know whether other people that don't come to mind at the moment but these who had been participants through the information of the President were removed and the boom was lowered and the judicial process is going on under an independent special prosecutor.

Q. This may be a matter of disagreement, but I have done whatever research I could do last evening to find evidence of the lowering of this boom, and I regret very much, sir, that I just could not see much evidence of this boom being lowered on any alleged participant in this tragedy.

A. I believe that the matters that I have discussed, and we have discussed and I have recounted here this morning is a lowering of the boom in the area of the prerogative of the executive.

Q. And do you believe that with this soft lowering of the boom the lid would have blown off?

A. It has, and I don't think it was necessarily soft.

Q. But the lid wasn't blown off by the so-called removal of Mr. Haldeman and Mr. Ehrlichman. The lid was blown off, I believe, by two men in The Washington Post.

A. Well, it depends on what areas you are talking about, Senator. If you go back to our White House horror stories, I think they came out from other sources and at other times.

MR. DASH: Now, Mr. Mitchell, your log shows from June 17 all the way to Aug. 29 certainly and thereafter, but certainly to Aug. 29, you had almost daily meetings with John Dean and sometimes twice or three times a day, and you knew, I think, from your testimony before this committee, what Mr. Dean was doing during this time, that he was serving as a liaison between you and Mr. Haldeman or Ehrlichman, White House people, and that he was not making any investigation of the Watergate case for the President.

Yet, on Aug. 29, the President did make an announcement that Mr. Dean had made an investigation to give him a report. What was your reaction to that announcement knowing, having been meeting with Mr. Dean almost on a daily basis during that whole period of time?

A. Well, Mr. Dash, I think your question provides an assumption that I am not willing to accept. It is perfectly conceivable in my mind so far as the involvement of personnel in the White House were concerned, that Mr. Dean was making such an investigation as to the involvement of people in the White House, and I think that was the context of the statement of August, whatever date it was.

Q. Well, as a matter of fact, didn't Mr. Dean discuss with you what he was doing? You said he met with you regularly, he was at your meetings, and if he were making such an investigation, would you not know about it?

A. I think Mr. Dean was making an investigation with respect to the involvement or potential involvement of individuals in the White House in the knowledge of the Watergate break-in or participation.

Q. His testimony was that rather than make an investigation he was engaging in a cover-up.

A. Well, I don't doubt that for a moment, and I have so stated here, that there was that aspect of it. Now, the cover-up is an entirely different thing, and the statement made by the President with respect to the involvement of individuals in the Watergate affair and prior to the June 17 or at the June 17 activities, and I think that was the thrust of the statement.

Q. Well, you know from what Mr. Dean I think has testified or may have indicated to you is that he indicated to Mr. Strachan and certainly as recently as the June 17 break-in, June 19 that Mr. Strachan had admitted to him that he had destroyed certain intellligence papers. Did Mr. Dean tell you about that?

A. Yes, he did eventually.

Q. Eventually. When did he tell you this?

A. I am not quite certain.

Q. Was it before Aug. 29?

A. I can't say that for sure, Mr. Dash, but he did somewhere along the way.

Q. Well, if he did, you would have been somewhat surprised that Mr. Dean had said nobody in the White House—

A. I think I would have been quite surprised if that had come out.

Q. Did Mr. Dean tell you personally that he made a report to the President? A. No, Mr. Dean did not so tell me.

Q. Did you ever ask him after the President's statement came out whether he made such a report?

A. Yes, I discussed—I am not sure that I put it quite in the form of that type of a question. We did have discussions of it, and he told me that he, of course, had been discussing the matters with Haldeman and Ehrlichman, but that he had not specifically made a direct report to the President. That whatever information he was providing was going through Haldeman and Ehrlichman, one or the other, I forget which.

Q. From that testimony or from the information you got from Mr. Dean that he was reporting to Mr. Haldeman and Mr. Ehrlichman was it your impression that the President was being misled by that group just as you were misleading the President after your knowledge from June 21 to June 22?

A. I would believe that would certainly be what—the impression that I would have, because Mr. Dean was not talking directly to the President.

Q. You have told Senator Talmadge, and I don't want to re-state it too dramatically but I think you did make a dramatic statement in terms of what you thought was necessary to get the President to assure the re-election of President Nixon, I think you did state kind of dramatically to Senator Baker that you would pretty much not want to allow anything to stand in the way of re-election and I know you, of course, drew certain exceptions to that. Would you have included, and I am now talking about the time prior to the election, perjury as an activity that would stand in your way in getting the President re-elected?

A. I would think that that would be a subject matter, Mr. Dash, that I would have to give very long and very hard thought to.

Q. All right, now, you have told us repeatedly during your testimony on Tuesday, Wednesday and today that Mr. Mardian told you of his conversation with Mr. Liddy and I think the date on which he debriefed you was, according to your testimony, around February—excuse me, June 21 or 22, and that it was that debriefing that gave you all the information of Liddy's operation, which included the so-called White House horrors and break-in.

Now, have you ever denied at any time that Mr. Mardian told you about his conversation with Mr. Liddy? A. I have no recollection of having done so, Mr. Dash.

Q. Let me—did you give a deposition on Sept. 5 in the civil case that the Democratic National Committee brought, civil action 1233? A. Yes sir, I did.

Q. Let me read you, Mr. Mitchell, and I can send it to you if you wish to look at it yourself or counsel wishes to look at it from page 45 of that deposition. Question put to you, "Did you know whether or not Mr. LaRue had a discussion with Mr. Gordon Liddy about Mr. Liddy's involvement in the Watergate episode?" Answer by you, "I don't really know. I believe that according to my best recollection it was that Liddy—I mean LaRue and Mardian, one or the other or maybe both, talked to Liddy when Liddy decided he was not going to cooperate with the F.B.I. I am not sure which one of them. It was either one or the other, it may have been both of them."

Question put to you, "You were not present at this conversation?" And by you. "No, I have not seen Mr. Liddy since the middle of June, I have not seen Mr. Liddy or talked to him."

Question put to you, "Did either Mr. Mardian or Mr. LaRue report to you on their conversation with Liddy?" Your answer, "No, only to the extent that his services had been terminated in whatever way it was."

Now that was your testimony as of Sept. 5, 1972 in the deposition.

A. Mr. Dash, that relates to the basis of the termination of Mr. Liddy.

Q. No, the question put to you was, "Did either Mr. Mardian or Mr. LaRue report to you on their conversation with Liddy."

A. If you go back to the basis of it it had to do with the subject matter of the termination of Mr. Liddy.

Q. Let me ask you again the question that was put to you, and I will reread it and you may look at this on page 45, "Did you know whether or not Mr. LaRue had a discussion with Mr. Gordon Liddy about Mr. Liddy's involvement in the Watergate episode?"

And then you said, "I don't really know."—But your answer was that Mr. Mardian and Mr. LaRue did and the question was,

"Did either Mr. Mardian or Mr. LaRue report to you on the conversation with Mr. Liddy," and your answer, "No," and it was your limitation "only to the extent his service had been terminated in whatever way it was."

A. Well, the answer speaks to the termination of the services. My response with respect to the other subject matter was equivocal because of my recollection at the particular time.

Q. Well, it certainly was equivocal because you have testified three days here that the important part of that conversation that Mr. Mardian was talking to you about was the White House horrors and the Watergate break-in and since this was Sept. 5, 1972, before the election, didn't you answer no in that case as part of your willingness to keep the lid on so that if you had answered yes and had to tell about that conversation you would have been opening the lid?

A. Mr. Dash, I have spent many, many hours reconstructing the events in connection with what happened during this period of time, in preparation for the testimony of this committee, and that is one of the reasons why that I have more specific knowledge or better recollect with what had gone on than at that particular time in September.

Q. This was Sept. 5? A. Sept. 5.

Q. Which was closer to the June meeting?

A. Was closer to the particular time when there were two subject matters contained in that discussion there, one of which had to do, of course, with his termination and the other had to do with the other subject matter.

Q. Well, Mr. Mitchell, your answer, no, that Mr. Mardian did not tell you anything about his conversation with Liddy with regard to Liddy's involvement in the Watergate episode is actually quite contrary to your testimony under oath before this committee.

A. Mr. Dash, I would point out that there are two subject matters there, and one is in relation to the termination aspect of it, and the other answer is as I say.

Q. Mr. Mitchell, I don't want to argue with you but you put the limitation on. The question put to you was dealing with the questioning of Mr. Liddy concerning his involvement in the Watergate episode and you said that Mr. Mardian did not tell you about that conversation and all you said was except about his termination.

Now, all I am asking you is whether or not that answer no, that he did not, Mr. Mardian did not tell you about the conversation with Liddy concerning his Watergate involvement is directly contrary to the testimony you have given here.

A. I still disagree with the interpretation that you have put on it, Mr. Dash.

Q. Now, it seems to me that—

A. Let me also point out that in addition to the hours that have been put in reconstructing these events of course there have been other matters presented to us that relate to the subject matters which have refreshed my recollection, including testimony before this committee.

Q. Well, is your testimony at the time you said, "No" there that you actually had no recollection that Mardian had told you about the White House horrors, that Liddy had told them. Could you have forgotten that?

A. No, that is not the subject matter of that question.

Q. That is the subject matter of the question.

A. The White House horrors?

Q. Liddy's involvement in the Watergate episode.

A. Those are not the White House horrors, Mr. Dash.

Q. Well, did you also forget about Liddy's involvement in the break-in of the Democratic National Committee headquarters?

A. I go back and stand on the statement, the answer that I gave you, I think there are two subject matters there and there are two answers.

Q. This statement was made under oath, was it not, Mr. Mitchell? A. It was made under oath, that is correct.

Q. Now Mr. Mitchell, you told, you have testified seveal times to the committee as to the circumstances under which Mr. Liddy was hired as counsel to the Committee for the Re-election of the President, involving Mr. Dean's introduction, your interview with him on Nov. 24, and your hiring of Mr. Liddy, is that not correct?

A. Well, I think my testimony and my recollection as to how it happened is after Mr. Dean had brought Mr. Liddy over to meet with me on Nov. 24, 1971, and discussed the areas in which he would be working, we met, this is Liddy, Dean and myself, we discussed it, and then, as I understand it, the suggestion was that since Mr. Magruder was then overrunning the committee that Mr. Liddy be put in touch with Mr. Dean—Mr. Magruder by Mr. Dean and that the hiring of him took place over there.

Q. But you were aware of the circumstances under which he was hired.

A. I was aware of the circumstances, Mr. Dean having brought Mr. Liddy over to meet with me, and I having said that it looked to me like he could be perfectly competent.

Q. And you have approved his being hired?

A. As counsel for that committee?

Q. Right, and Mr. Magruder hired him on your approval, is that not true?

A. I would presume that that had followed.

Q. Now, have you ever denied to anybody that you were aware of these circumstances of Mr. Liddy's employment with the committee?

A. There was one occasion in which my recollection failed with respect to who actually hired Mr. Liddy. It is still my opinion that Mr. Magruder hired Liddy, and not John Mitchell.

Q. Without the question of who actually hired him, the circumstances under which he became employed, which would include at least your interviewing of him and your having some role, I mean have you ever denied knowing any of those circumstances? A. I don't recall, Mr. Dash.

Q. Under the same testimony of Mr. Mitchell on Sept. 5, 1972, the question was put to you on page 18 of the transcript: "Mr. Mitchell, do you have any information as to the circumstances under which Mr. Liddy was hired," with reference to the Committee for the Re-election of the President.

The answer: "No sir, I do not."

Question: "Have you ever made inquiry to find out how it came that he was hired?

"Have I made inquiry?"

Question: "Yes."

Now, that testimony was under oath. Could you have been actually able to answer no to that question?

A. Very easily, because I was not aware of how Mr. Magruder ultimately hired Mr. Liddy.

Q. Well, the question was not really that, was it, Mr. Mitchell?

A. In the context as you have read it and as I understood it at that particular time, the answer is yes.

Q. You were asked, do you have any information as to the circumstances under which Mr. Liddy was hired? Would not the truthful answer to that be, I may have not hired him myself, it may have been Magruder, but I interviewed him when Mr. Dean brought him over. I approved. Maybe I didn't hire him, Mr. Magruder did. Would not that have been a more factual answer than no, I have no information?

A. It gets to a point of degree, Mr. Dash, and the question was as to the hiring and the hiring was done by Mr. Magruder in the following month and I have no knowledge of those aspects of Mr. Magruder hiring him.

Q. Did you remember at that time of the interview of Mr. Dean when you were asked that question? A. No, I had no recollection of the interview at that time.

Q. And you had no recollection of your approving Mr. Liddy at that time?

A. You are using the word "approving." It was not that extent. It was the basis of the conversation that yes, I think he would be perfectly all right for counsel for the committee and the ultimate decision was to be made by Magruder.

Q. Mr. Mitchell, you know an agenda was prepared for that interview and you know that if you didn't approve Mr. Liddy, Mr. Magruder would never have hired him. You know that.

A. That could have been the case, or it might have been otherwise, because Mr. Magruder might have gotten approval.

Q. Did you have any information—

A. I might have had information on that meeting. That was my recollection.

Q. Isn't it so, Mr. Mitchell, that you answered no in this context, because at that time on Sept. 5, Mr. Liddy had been identified as being involved and that you did not want to have any relationship with Mr. Liddy's involvement or hiring by the committee?

A. I think that would have been the magnitude or consequence. Obviously Mr. Liddy was known to me, attended meetings in the Justice Department on different subject matters including the drug abuse law enforcements and so forth, that would not have been of that magnitude.

Q. In any event, your statement that you had no information whatsoever as to any of the circumstances on Sept. 5 is quite different than your testimony before this committee, is that not so?

A. I believe that to be true, and I believe the rechecking of the records, and the committee being kind enough to furnish me a copy of the agenda that Mr. Dean provided, and further reflection so it has brought the subject matter very much into focus.

Q. Mr. Mitchell, you enjoy the distinction, and you have made it from time to time, that it was your purpose to not volunteer anything. Is there a distinction between your not volunteering anything and lying?

If you do not volunteer an answer to a direct question, you might say you do not volunteer anything, but actually, you are lying.

A. I think we would have to find out what the specifics are, what the particular occasion and—

Q. Well, the information received from Mardian about Liddy is that Magruder pushed him into it. Now, nobody in the newspapers had ever mentioned that Magruder had anything to do with it.

A. I am not talking about it being in the newspapers. It was still an open question whether it had happened or had not happened. We still had Magruder telling us to the contrary and advising the lawyers to the contrary.

Q. In any event, it seems to me that there are two instances where your testimony on Sept. 5 in the civil deposition was diametrically opposed to your testimony before this committee. What I have to say to you on that, Mr. Mitchell, is that since you may have given false testimony under oath on prior occasions, is there really any reason for this committee to believe your testimony before this committee, especially to the issue of whether you did or did not give final approval at the Key Biscayne meeting to the Liddy plan, whether or not you had any knowledge about the President's knowledge of the cover-up or participation in the cover-up, or whether you took any active part in the payoffs or cover-up, the Watergate case or any other part of the White House horrors?

A. Mr. Dash, I disagree, of course, with your interpretation of the matters that you have just read. As far as the determina-

tions of this committee, I think they can judge their testimony—
my testimony—and make their own conclusions after my appearance here for four days, three and a half days, whatever it is.

Q. I think that is true, Mr. Mitchell.

A. And anything else I would say would be self-serving.

Q. I think that is true, and actually, if one were to take your
testimony to the various parts, which would include what you
have had to say about the Key Biscayne meeting and what you
have had to say about the raising of funds to pay off the defendants and some other parts, that in order to believe your testimony,
you would have to disbelieve Mr. Magruder, Mr. Sloan, Mr. Mc-
Cord, Mr. Reisner, Mr. Stans and in some respects, Mr. Dean.

A. I disagree vehemently on the list of the people that you
have talked about. I would suggest that you wait until the rest of
the witnesses that you are going to have appear and they will be
testifying on these same subject matters and Senator Weicker yesterday pointed out something unbeknownst to me about Mr. La-
Rue's statement as to what transpired at the March 30 meeting
down in Key Biscayne.

Q. You didn't have any recollection that Mr. LaRue, in fact,
had that recollection of that meeting, did you?

A. I didn't have any recollection that he had that recollection?

Q. Your testimony is that Mr. LaRue would have agreed or
agree with your testimony that when Mr. Magruder presented the
proposal to you in Key Biscayne that you just dismissed it out
of hand at that point. And I think Senator Weicker said to you
that Mr. LaRue's testimony would probably be the fact that you
stated it didn't have to be decided at that time.

A. This, Mr. Dash, is an affirmation of the fact that it wasn't
approved at Key Biscayne. I say it wasn't approved subsequently
and it is certainly contrary to Magruder's testimony that it was
approved in Key Biscayne on March 30.

Q. Not approved in Key Biscayne in that room at that minute.
I don't know whether you may have taken either walks with Mr.
Magruder or whether you spoke to Mr. Magruder outside of Mr.
LaRue's presence. But I think we will have Mr. LaRue's testimony.

Testimony of Richard A. Moore

July 12 *Contradicts Dean's assertions that Nixon knew of cover-up.*

July 13 *Says Nixon was troubled at not knowing of cover-up earlier.*

July 12, 1973

MR. MOORE: My name is Richard A. Moore. I am special counsel to the President, a position to which I was appointed on April 26, 1971. But I speak today only for myself.

For the 10 years following my graduation from Yale University Law School in 1939, I practiced law in New York, with four years out for Army service in World War II. After the war I migrated to California, where I was a lawyer and later an executive in the television industry. To save the committee's time, I will not recite biographical details now, but I refer you to the résumé attached to this statement.

In California, I became a friend and supporter of Richard Nixon, and advised on the television aspects of his 1962 campaign. In 1968 I accompanied him on his campaign tours. I was then invited to join the Administration.

For a year beginning in April, 1970, I served as a special assistant to Attorney General Mitchell. I assisted him primarily in the preparation of speeches, statements and position papers on current public issues within the department's responsibilities. In April, 1971, I was appointed a special counsel to the President.

My principal role has been to assist the President and his staff in communicating their positions in the most convincing manner to the general public. Since convincing communications depend on having a convincing position to communicate, my job necessarily involves me in the substance of particular issues in the public eye. But I do not have a line responsibility either on the communications or on the substantive side. I serve primarily as an extra hand—as a source of white-haired advice and experience—whenever the President or the younger men with line responsibility seek my help.

I shall be glad, of course, to answer any questions concerning any aspect of these hearings, but I believe that the most significant testimony I can give to this committee relates to a limited time frame—that is basically the period from Feb. 6, 1973, the day Senator Ervin introduced his resolution creating this select committee, to March 21, 1973. March 21 is the date when

President Nixon, as he later announced to the nation, learned of "serious charges" which caused him to begin "intensive new inquiries into this whole matter." This was the day when Mr. Dean, at my urging, went into the President's office and, as he has testified, told him "everything."

In December, 1971, and January, 1972, I was primarily involved with inaugural matters and can recall no direct meetings or consultations with regard to the Watergate or related matters until Feb. 6. On that day I attended a meeting in Mr. Ehrlichman's office to discuss our legislative position with respect to the proposed resolution creating this select committee. Except for the discussion at this meeting, I knew of no other planning or preparation that had been going on with regard to these hearings. Within the White House, I was a critic of this lack of preparation.

This may explain why I was called to the meetings in California on February 10-11. I had been home with intestinal flu for two days and had been planning to take the weekend off and had reservations for my wife and family at the Greenbrier for the long weekend of Feb. 9 to 12. But late on the afternoon of Feb. 9, Mr. Dean called me at home to say that we were both asked by Mr. Ehrlichman to meet with Mr. Haldeman and himself in San Clemente on Feb. 10 to discuss the forthcoming Senate hearings. I therefore took my family and baggage to the Far West instead of heading South.

Mr. Dean and I met on Saturday, Feb. 10, 1973, at San Clemente with Messrs. Haldeman and Ehrlichman in Ehrlichman's office from 10:30 or 11:00 in the morning until 3 or 4 in the afternoon. On Sunday, we went to Mr. Haldeman's cottage at La Costa.

All four of us were present for the majority of the time. One or more of us would leave the group on occasion to make or take a telephone call or to perform some other function.

At the outset, Mr. Ehrlichman or Mr. Haldeman asked Mr. Dean and me what we had been doing to prepare for the hearings. The answer was nothing. The focus of these hearings, they said, would be the activities of the Committee to Re-elect the President, and it would be the committee that would have to take the primary responsibility for the defense.

Had we had any discussion or, as they put it, any input, from John Mitchell? The answer was no. Either Mr. Haldeman or Mr. Ehrlichman then said that in that case, Dick Moore ought to sit down with John Mitchell as soon as he could and fill him in on the things that we discuss here and get Mr. Mitchell actively interested—he is the only one who could give real leadership to the people at the committee.

Either Haldeman or Ehrlichman then suggested that Mr. Dean be the White House coordinator for the hearing, and that I hold myself available to advise him. I suggested that the White House have a writer-spokesman who could issue statements or go on television, if necessary, to reply quickly to testimony or commentary that was wrong or slanted. Mr. Dean, I believe, suggested that Pat Buchanan be this spokesman.

Early in the discussions, Mr. Ehrlichman made it clear that the President wanted our position in the hearings to be one of full cooperation, subject only to the doctrine of separation of powers. It was agreed it would be important to work out a statement on executive privilege (the President had recently promised the press he would do so) that would enable us to cooperate and supply the information that the committee wanted. It is my recollection that at this time the question whether Presidential advisors would be permitted to appear was still unresolved, although the consensus was that appearances should be permitted where the subject matter did not relate to their official duties for the President.

There was, as I have said, no prepared sequence to our discussions, and I cannot recall all the other subjects we discussed. I do recall a discussion about putting out a White House statement in advance of the hearings setting forth all the known facts about the Watergate episode. It was also agreed that more manpower would be needed by the Committee to Re-elect the President— possibly in the form of young lawyers and researchers to review each day's testimony and prepare rebuttals. This was among the items I agreed to discuss with Mr. Mitchell.

Mr. Dean, of course, has testified about a discussion of money. His recollection differs from mine. The brief mention of money made at this meeting may have had a very different significance to a person with Mr. Dean's knowledge of the circumstances than it had to a person with my lack of knowledge. My recollection on that subject is as follows:

The subject came up, I believe, on the second day at the hotel. In the context of a discussion of the litigation in which the committee was then involved, John Dean, in a sort of by-the-way reference, said he had been told by the lawyers that they may be needing some more money, and did we have any ideas? Someone said, isn't that something that John Mitchell might handle with his rich New York friends. It was suggested that since I would be meeting with Mr. Mitchell I should mention this when I saw him and I said I would.

As I look back now, of course, with the knowledge I subsequently began acquiring in the latter part of March, Mr. Dean's reference to a need for money might well have stimulated some further inquiries on my part at La Costa. But I did not have that knowledge on Feb. 11—at that point I knew nothing about any prior payments to any defendants or their counsel—and no one else at the meeting went into any details. Moreover, I had served for a year as special assistant to Mr. Mitchell at the Department of Justice, and I know him well. I was certain that he wasn't about to be programed into becoming a fund raiser by Mr. Haldeman and Mr. Ehrlichman, and I anticipated that Mitchell's answer would be no, as it turned out to be.

Mr. Dean has testified that we left the meeting together and that he had a conversation with me at which time he cautioned me against conveying this fund-raising request when I saw Mr. Mitchell. I have absolutely no recollection of any such conversation and I am convinced it never took place.

I returned to my office in Washington on Feb. 13, and telephoned Mr. Mitchell to inquire whether he had any immediate plans to be in Washington. He said he did not, and I said I needed two or three hours with him to tell him about the meetings in California. He suggested that I come to New York and we could take as much time as we needed. On Feb. 15, I took a morning shuttle to New York, went to Mr. Mitchell's office, visited briefly before lunch, and after lunch we had a discussion about the California meetings and the upcoming hearings.

Knowing Mr. Mitchell as I do, I felt there were several points where he would resist being "programed" by the White House staff, as I mentioned earlier, and I elected to get those out of the way at the start. At the beginning of our discussion I said something like this, "Well, you will be glad to know that the group in San Clemente thinks you should be taking a more active interest in the Ervin hearings." I had a somewhat blunt reply, such as, thank them very much, I am indeed interested and, as you know, I may be a star witness.

I told him it was suggested that it would be most helpful if he could spend part of each week in his law firm's Washington office. He made a chilly reply that he would come to Washington whenever he felt it necessary. Then I said to him that I didn't know what it was all about but that it had been suggested that the committee lawyers might be needing more money and that his White House friends had nominated him for the honor of being a fund raiser. I don't remember his exact words, but I believe he said something like, "Tell them to get lost."

Thereafter I began my report of the meetings. We had a wide-ranging discussion and a pleasant visit that lasted most of the afternoon. I left his office at about 4 or 5 o'clock and took the shuttle home.

From mid-February to early March, I was not asked to participate in any follow-up to the La Costa-San Clemente discussions about preparing for these hearings, except for my continuing participation in the preparation of the statement on executive privilege. By the beginning of March, the Gray nomination hearings had become a major preoccupation for me and for Mr. Dean. During those hearings, Mr. Dean's role in the Watergate investigation became a subject of headline news.

The Judiciary Committee's invitation to Mr. Dean to testify before it brought the question of executive privilege into critical focus. A Presidential press conference was scheduled for March 15, and Mr. Dean and I prepared, for the President's "briefing book" a list of more than 20 possible questions on the subject. Although it was not the President's usual practice to hold face-to-face briefing sessions before a press conference, he chose to do so on this occasion. And so began a series of meetings about which Mr. Dean has testified and which marked the first occasion I had to discuss with the President any subject related to Watergate.

The first meeting on March 14 was in progress when I was called to the President's office. Messrs. Ziegler and Dean were already there. We went over the questions and answers with considerable discussion on each. The meeting recessed temporarily while the President kept another appointment and had lunch. It reconvened after lunch for several hours.

At no time during this meeting, or during succeeding meetings on March 15, 19 and 20—all of which were attended only by the President, Mr. Dean and myself—did anyone say anything in my presence which related to or suggested the existence of any cover-up, or any knowledge of involvement by anyone in the White House, then or now, in the Watergate affair.

On March 19, I was called to meet with the President and Mr. Dean in the President's Executive Office Building office. The President reiterated his desire to get out a general statement in advance of the hearings. He asked us to be thinking about ways that this could be done. This would include issuing a full statement or "white paper." He was also interested in our thoughts about ways to present our story to the Senate in terms of possible depositions, affidavits, or possible conferences or meetings which would not cut across the separation of powers. He asked Dean and me to consider ways to do this.

On March 19 or possibly on March 20—before we met later that day with the President—Mr. Dean told me that Howard Hunt was demanding that a large sum of money be given to him before his sentencing on March 23, and that he wanted the money by the 21st. If the payment were not made, Dean said, Hunt had threatened to say things that would be very serious for the White House. I replied that this was pure blackmail, and that Dean should turn it off and have nothing to do with it. I could not imagine, I said, that anything that Hunt could say would be as bad as paying blackmail. I don't recall Mr. Dean's exact words, but he expressed agreement.

This revelation was the culmination of several other guarded comments Mr. Dean had made to me in the immediately preceding days. He had said that he had been present at two meetings attended by Messrs. Mitchell, Magruder and Liddy before the bugging arrests, during which Liddy had proposed wild schemes that had been turned down—specifically, espionage, electronic surveillance and even kidnapping.

He said that the Watergate location had not been mentioned, and that he had "turned off the wild schemes." I believed then and believe today that Mr. Dean had no advance knowledge of the Watergate bugging and break-in. In addition, he had said that if he ever had to testify before the grand jury, his testimony would conflict with Mr. Magruder's, and that he had heard that if Magruder faced a perjury charge, he would take others with him.

Mr. Dean had also mentioned to me that earlier activities of Messrs. Hunt and Liddy—not directly related to Watergate —could be seriously embarrassing to the Administration if they ever came to light. He had also implied to me that he knew of payments being made to the defendants for litigation expenses, and Hunt's explicit blackmail demand raised serious questions in my mind as to the purpose of these payments.

This brings me to the afternoon of March 20, when Mr. Dean and I met with the President in the Oval Office. The meeting lasted about half an hour. The President again stated his hope that we could put out a full statement in advance of the hearings, and again he expressed his desire that we be forthcoming, as he put it. He made some comparisons as to our attitude and the attitude of previous Administrations, and he wanted us to make sure that we were the most forthcoming of all.

As I sat through the meeting of March 20 with the President and Mr. Dean in the Oval Office, I came to the conclusion in my own mind that the President could not be aware of the things that Dean was worried about or had been hinting at to me, let alone Howard Hunt's blackmail demand. Indeed, as the President talked about getting the whole story out—as he had done repeatedly in the recent meetings—it seemed crystal clear to me that he knew of nothing that was inconsistent with the previously stated conclusion that the White House was uninvolved in the Watergate affair, before or after the event.

As we closed the door of the Oval Office and turned into the hall, I decided to raise the issue directly with Mr. Dean. I said that I had the feeling that the President had no knowledge of the things that were worrying Dean. I asked Dean whether he had ever told the President about them. Dean replied that he had not, and I asked whether anyone else had. Dean said he didn't think so.

I said, "Then the President isn't being served, he is reaching a point where he is going to have to make critical decisions and he simply has to know all the facts. I think you should go in and tell him what you know, you will feel better, it will be right for him and it will be good for the country."

I do not recall whether he told me he would take action or not, but certainly have the impression that he was receptive. In any event, the question was resolved that very evening when I received a call at home sometime after dinner and it was Mr. Dean who said that the President had just phoned him and that he had decided that this was the moment to speak up. He said that he told the President that things had been going on that the President should know about and it was important that Dean see him alone and tell him. Dean said that the President readily agreed and told Dean to come in the following morning. I congratulated Mr. Dean and wished him well.

The next day, March 21, Mr. Dean told me that he had indeed met with the President at 10 o'clock and had talked with him for two hours and had "let it all out." I said, "Did you tell him about the Howard Hunt business?" Dean replied that he had told the President everything. I asked if the President had been surprised and he said yes.

Following this critical meeting on March 21, I had several subsequent meetings and telephone conversations with Mr. Dean alone, as well as several meetings with the President which Mr. Dean did not attend. I do not dispute Mr. Dean's account of the meetings between us as to any substantive point, and I have no direct knowledge of what transpired in Mr. Dean's subsequent meetings with the President. But nothing said in my meetings with Mr. Dean or my meetings with the President suggests in any way that before March 21 the President had known—or that Mr. Dean believed he had known—of any involvement of White House personnel in the bugging or the cover-up.

I have given you the most complete account I can as to my knowledge of the events being examined by this committee. It is my deep conviction—as one who has known the President over the years and has had many private conversations with him—that the critical facts about the Watergate did not reach the President until the events that began when John Dean met with him on March 21, 1973.

MR. LENZNER: Mr. Moore, I want to go back briefly to some dates prior to your testimony from your statement.

First, I would like to ask you whether you had a meeting on Feb. 10, 1972, with Mr. Kleindienst and Mr. Mitchell at Mr. Mitchell's office at the Committee to Re-elect the President. Do you recall that meeting? A. I don't recall.

Q. You don't recall meeting with Mr. Mitchell or Mr. Kleindienst?

A. I don't recall any such meeting. It could well have happened.

Q. Approximately 12:30 on the mid-day.

A. That is '72? 1972?

Q. Yes, sir.

A. In Mitchell's office?

Q. At 1701 Pennsylvania Avenue, at the Committee to Re-elect offices. Do you have any recollection of that? A. No, I don't.

Q. Do you have a recollection of a meeting on March 14, 1972, at 8:30 in the morning, also attended by Mr. Kleindienst and Mr. Mitchell? A. At what, I am sorry.

Q. That date was Feb. 14, 1972.

A. It would help if I knew Mr. Kleindienst's nomination was presented or when the issue arose.—

Q. Let me help you, since you don't have—do you recall when Mr. Lackritz and myself interviewed you at June 7 in Mr. Miller's office?

Do you recall our discussing this with you in Mr. Miller's office on June 7?

A. I don't recall this conversation.

Q. Well, the results of our notes indicate that you said those meetings were related to Mr. Kleindienst's confirmation hearings.

A. They could well have. That is why I asked about the dates.

Q. Does that refresh your recollection as to what those meetings were about? A. Yes.

Q. Do you recall the meetings now?

A. Well, I don't have an independent recollection of the meeting, but if that is in the time frame of the Judiciary Committee hearings on Mr. Kleindienst's nomination, that is most likely what they were about.

Q. Do you recall a meeting with Mr. Kleindienst, Mr. Mitchell, and Mr. Mardian on March 10, 1972, beginning at approximately 10:30 A.M., in the morning?

A. Not independently but—no, sir.

Q. Do you recall telling us on June 7 that you did recall that meeting and it referred to the upcoming Kleindienst confirmation hearings?

A. Well, I don't recall saying it that firmly. Obviously, that is what could have been, and—

Q. On June 7, when Mr. Lackritz and myself interviewed you, do you recall telling us that you did remember that meeting and it referred to the Kleindienst confirmation hearings?

A. I don't think we are quite on the same frequency when you say remember the hearings. I remember that during the hearing or the pendency of the Kleindienst nomination, I met frequently with Mr. Mitchell, sometimes Mr. Kleindienst, and others—Mr. Mardian, who was the assistant Attorney General then—to discuss the hearing and the steps which should be taken to help support the confirmation of the nomination of Mr. Kleindienst. But I don't know the day or that I was at a meeting on March 10, 1972. I could check them, of course, but that is what these meetings would have been about.

Q. Well, Mr. Moore, let me ask you this: Those hearings involved the issue of I.T.T., is that correct? A. Yes, sir.

Q. And did you have any involvement in the question of I.T.T. as it affected Mr. Kleindienst's confirmation?

A. Yes, I was a White House liaison or adviser, helping the department to support and present the case in favor of the confirmation of the nomination of Mr. Kleindienst.

Q. Let me first ask, Mr. Moore, you have no independent recollection now of a White House investigation involving I.T.T. Is that correct, without—and I will then ask you a question which I hope will refresh your recollection.

A. Well, it is so general, you mentioned a White House memorandum.

Q. No, no, I am speaking of any information you obtained involving a White House investigation with regard to I.T.T. Let me ask you this. Did you meet with Mr. Colson during that period of time? A. Yes.

Q. Did you have discussions with Mr. Colson involving the I.T.T. matter?

A. Was this—I am not being difficult but I just cannot recall, was this the investigation where a young man tried to prove that Mr. Jack Anderson's secretary was a friend of Miss Dita Beard, is that the investigation?

Q. Yes, that is correct.

A. Yes, I do remember that. But this—

Q. Was that an individual who was an employe of the Internal Security Division of the Department of Justice named John Martin?

A. It could have been. I do not remember his name.

Q. Did you attend a meeting at which he was present at when he was asked to conduct that investigation? A. Yes.

Q. Who else was present?

A. I cannot recall exactly.

Q. Well, do you recall telling us on June 7 that it was a meeting when Mr. Colson, Mr. Mardian, Mr. Wally Johnson and yourself and Mr. John Martin came in and was requested to interview people about a relationship between Dita Beard and Jack Anderson's secretary? A. That is correct.

Q. You recall that?

A. Yes, as my counsel says, I have been concentrating on other matters and this has been—yes, that sounds like it.

Q. Do you recall telling Mr. Lackritz and myself that on June 7 in Mr. Miller's office. You do so—

A. I do not recall it independently but I will not quarrel with your report of it.

Q. O.K. You will accept my version? A. Yes, no problem.

Q. But you do not remember telling us that, you do not now remember telling us?

A. I remember this discussion, Mr. Lenzner, but I did not remember what five names I mentioned but I accept that, that is fine.

Q. O.K. Do you recall whether you ever saw the results of that investigation in writing or heard them orally?

A. I recall hearing a result, whether it was oral or writing, I do not know.

Q. Do you know who, you do not recall whether it was in writing or who gave it to you, gave you information orally, sir?

A. No, I do not.

Q. Do you recall if it was orally who was the person who spoke to you? A. No, I do not recall.

Q. Now, do you recall that you received information as to

how the Dita Beard memorandum was furnished to Mr. Colson
as part of your participation in preparation for the I.T.T. hearings?

A. I think I might have said but I do not remember, you
know, the conversation, that I learned it in the newspapers, that
the memorandum went from the F.B.I. to Justice to the White
House, someone in the White House, I should say, and then
was given an independent examination by a commercial firm specializing in identifying typewriters. Something like that, I do not
recall.

Q. Do you have any information on that besides what you
read in the newspaper, information received directly from either
White House or government employes? A. I simply do not remember.

July 13, 1973

MR. THOMPSON: Let me ask you about the meetings that you
and Mr. Dean had with the President, and I will start with
March 14. Would you tell us the purpose of the meeting, what
was discussed and what was resolved, if anything?

A. The purpose of the meeting was to go over with the President the possible questions that might be asked in the next day's,
the next morning's press conference on the general subject of
executive privilege and these hearings, the Gray hearings were
still also going on, and in that sense, the Watergate. Now, Dean
and I—the way that worked was Mr. Buchanan, who usually
coordinates the President's briefing book, had sent us a list of at
least 20 questions that could be asked, more were handed, and
for two or three days before that we divided them up, we suggested answers or gave background answers so that the President
could consider them, and they were then edited by Mr. Buchanan
and put in the briefing book.

The President now wished to discuss those answers with us.

Q. What about March 15?

A. March 15 was a very pleasant and relaxed meeting at the
end of the day in the Oval Office where the President kind of
wanted to chat about the press conference. He wanted to know
how we thought it went, and Mr. Dean correctly testified that
the President said, "You know, the very first thing that I said,
I made an announcement that I thought was quite historic, first
representative to the People's Republic of China, and I was
nominating a most important man as our first representative,
David E. K. Bruce. I made the announcement and what do you
think the first question was? Dean's testimony at the hearings
and it shows where their minds are."

And then we talked a little bit about the press conference
and then he got into this discussion where he had been thinking
more and more where we had been using the wrong, the more
narrow phrase. That what was involved here was the separation of

powers and the President's responsibilities to preserve that separation.

And then he got talking about how he wanted us to be outgoing and he recalled the days when he was a Congressman, when he could not get a report, an F.B.I. report, not raw files but an F.B.I. report, in the Hiss matter, and he said, "But we are going to tell this committee, give them anything that they want in terms of information. Now we may do it," he said, "that is where you fellows come in," he said, "it should be depositions or private meetings and this kind of things." We got back into that, and that was that meeting.

Q. What about the meeting on the 19th?

A. The meeting of the 19th was again a comment, he said that —I think that, whether we came in together or whether Dean was already there I am not sure. It may be—but in any event he turned to me and said, "John is going to have to sort of take the lead in these matters of executive privilege and the hearings and I asked you to join the meeting because I know you have been working with him."

And he said, "I want you to go about how to get our story out," and that kind of thing.

In this period of March where I had five personal meetings with the President, in every single one of those meetings I think, he emphasized, "Why don't we get the story out ourselves."

At the meetings in San Clemente and La Costa Mr. Ehrlichman had made that point, and I believe he indicated that he was echoing the President's desire.

On March 16, Mr. Ehrlichman again relayed that desire to me. So that this white paper, depositions, forthcoming was the word the President kept using, be forthcoming, was also—and, of course, that is one of the reasons I was convinced that the President had no permanent idea of what we knew is going on or he would not be pressing to get it out.

[At a March 20, 1973 meeting with President Nixon] we had been asked for ideas where we could take the initiative, and in that meeting at one point, Mr. Dean said to the President, you know, one way for us to take the initiative. He said, I have worked on the Hill. He said, I do not know, I know of few political campaigns where someone, with or without the knowledge of the candidate, has not gotten involved in something that was improper, at least, if not illegal. He said, I think it might be a good idea if someone responsible would invite or suggest that the committee that was about to investigate campaign practices voluntarily offered to submit each of his most recent senatorial campaigns to a full field investigation by the F.B.I.

Q. He suggested this to the President in your presence? A. He did. Yes.

Q. What was the President's reaction?

A. First, he gave him what I regarded as a puzzled look. And he said, what would that do? Why that? And I think he used the words "I don't understand."

Dean then said, well, sir, people who live in glass houses shouldn't throw stones. Then he repeated that he had been here on the Hill and he knew politics and knew campaigning.

And the President sat there shaking his head. Then the President said, well, let us think about that.

I took that as a complete dismissal of the suggestion, and of course, nothing was done about it, it was never heard of again.

Q. Was there any discussion about comparing the use of the F.B.I. by this Administration and other Administrations?

A. Yes, sir. Mr. Dean said that he had, it had come to his attention that at least one preceding Administration, perhaps two, that this previous President or Presidents had used or attempted to use the F.B.I. for personal or political purposes in ways that the President, in ways that were quite inappropriate and whereas the President, President Nixon, had made it a policy personally to avoid that kind of thing, particularly through his friendship with Mr. Hoover, that this would make a good contrast, because Dean had been, in effect, accused of using the F.B.I. by getting reports or sitting in on interviews, and that that information would be quite harsh. And the President simply reacted by saying, well, if you develop anything, let me know. And nothing came of that.

Q. During this period of time, did you really wonder in your own mind as to whether or not the President did know these things?

A. I suppose I did. I am trying to recall my state of mind. I had not thought of his—I will put it this way. I knew in my heart, if you will, I was totally convinced that the President knew, believed that no one in the White House had been involved, and believed right up till he learned differently. I guess March 21.

But until I heard of the Howard Hunt matter, I did not connect it in my mind with—the point about the Hunt matter was that Mr. Hunt was demanding money or the White House would be embarrassed. That was something of a difference of degree, a quantum and quality difference, in the kind of guarded things which Dean had been suggesting. And that resolved the doubts.

And let me say right here in front of anybody who is watching, I certainly wish that the minute I began to get suspicious, I had gone to the President. One does not go to him lightly, one does not go to him and say, I think something may be wrong. Maybe there are times when one should. I came to that conclusion, and all I know is that before the phone rang on the night of March 20, Mr. Dean's happy and committed call that the President had called him and was going to see him in the morning, I think maybe I would have gone in the next day.

Q. Did you talk to him after he said he called the President?

A. Yes, and I saw him, I cannot place that conversation,

whether it was his office or mine or it could have been that I ran into him, this was a short conversation, in the hall but I said, "Well, John," you know, "did you see him?" and he said, "I sure did for two hours, I had two hours with him." And I said, "Well, did you tell him everything" and he said, I think his phrase was, I cannot remember, "I let it all out," and I said, "Did you tell him about the Hunt matter," because that was the one I thought was the serious thing and he said, "I told him everything."

I asked him was the President surprised, and he replied he was or he sure was; or perhaps he volunteered. But in any event, that there was a final touch to that conversation which, where he either concurred or volunteered that the President had been surprised by the things he told him.

Q. Tell us about the conversation you had with the President on April 19.

A. Well, when I came in to see him, he had issued his April 17 statement that serious new charges had come to his attention, and so on. So when I came in I paid him a compliment about the statement in terms of what the reactions I had heard and I said: "I note that March 21 date. John Dean must have been the source of those charges," and he said something to the effect: "Oh, did you know about that?" And I said "Yes." I said: "After we met with you the day before John and I talked about it," and I said: "I urged him to go in and tell you." I said: "Now the thing that got me committed was that blackmail business with Hunt, did he tell you about that." He said "Yes, yes he mentioned that," and he said "imagine"—and again no quotation marks please, I have to give you my recollection—and he said, I think, "imagine or just think of that," he said, "I told him it was not only wrong but stupid. That you can't do that. First of all the demands never stop," and he said: "Dean said this could go on," and the word "to a million dollars." The President said: "That isn't the point. Money is not the point. You could raise money, money is not the point, it's wrong, we could not, shouldn't consider it and it's stupid because the truth comes out anyway."

Q. To go on as succinctly as we can, let's explore for other meetings briefly that you had with the President after that.

A. I had a brief meeting with him the next day, April 20. I said, "Yes, sir. You are going down for that Easter weekend and it is a good time to contemplate," and I think I made a reference about, "Maybe this is the sort of a resurrection of the whole thing we are talking about."

At least I gave him a little, just that comment. Then I said. "The reason I wanted to see you, sir, is I have been thinking about this whole thing. You now have facts," and I said, "you know and I know and I am convinced the country will accept that you did not know about the cover-up."

I said, "but you do now," and I said, "if you don't take action and get the facts quickly then it will be—you will be accused of a cover-up, and that, sir, will come into this Oval Office and affect you. Now, you are involved," and I said, "and my other message I wanted to see you, I just hope that as you assess the facts you will get the benefit of outside counsel because everybody in this building has his own relationships, his own bias and perhaps his own involvement and when you are assessing the legal and factual issues please get someone, wiser head from outside," and that was it.

He thanked me, and went out and got in the chopper.

I don't know what came of it. All I know is that the suggestion that he—it was a short time after that, that the April 30 speech resulted, and all I know is that outside, that outside counsel did talk to him. All I know is he went to Key Biscayne. I don't know, I know no more than that.

Q. Did you see the President after April 20?

A. Yes, sir. I saw him on May 8.

And he said at that point—let me just recall—he said, well, now, I am only wondering now, or I wonder now, about—and he had said this once before, but he said it with greater conviction, he said, I have racked my brain, I have searched my mind. Were there any clues I should have seen that should have tipped me off? He said, maybe there were. He said, I know how it is when you have a lot on your mind, and I did, but he said, I still wonder. And he said, what do you think?

I said, Mr. President, I did not have that much on my mind and I did not see any clues. If that is all that is worrying you, you can get back to business as far as your role is concerned, and I think that was that.

SENATOR ERVIN: Mr. Moore, you have testified that you believe that the President knew nothing about the critical facts relating to Watergate at any time between the 17th day of June, 1972, and the 21st day of March, 1973? A. Yes, sir.

Q. That is purely a conjecture on your part, is it not?

A. Well, he told me he did not, sir, and I have no evidence to the contrary. So it is a conclusion.

Q. Well, it is a conclusion, it is a surmise. A. That is right.

Q. Yes. Now, I would ask you this question. Do you not agree with me that of all the inhabitants of this earth, the one best qualified to testify as to the knowledge the President had concerning the Watergate affair or anything else at any time between the 17th day of June 1972 and the 21st day of March 1973, is President Nixon? A. I could agree with that.

Q. Yes. Now, you found out on the morning of June 17, 1972, or shortly thereafter, by reading the press and watching television, that five men had been caught red-handed in an act of burglary in the Democratic National headquarters?

A. Yes, I found out the morning of June 18.

Q. Now, I will ask you if you did not state on page 20 of

your records that "in one of my talks with the President, the President kept asking himself whether there had been any sign or clue which should have led him to discover the true facts earlier" —that is, earlier than March 21, 1973. A. Yes, sir.

Q. I will ask you, during the approximately two months after the burglary at the Watergate was discovered if the news media —that is, the newspapers, and TV and radio—did not contain statements—did not contain statements, many statements concerning the Watergate matter? A. That the newspapers when, sir?

Q. During the two months starting with the morning of June 17, 1972, during those following two months? A. Yes, they did.

Q. I will ask you if this first fact did not appear in the news media.

First, I ask you, can we safely assume that Mr. Haldeman, Mr. Ehrlichman, Mr. Chapin, Mr. Colson, Mr. Strachan, Mr. Ziegler, Mr. Dean, Mr. Mitchell, and Mr. Stans, Mr. Magruder, Mr. Sloan, and Mr. Porter, and the President, read the newspapers?

A. I am not an eye witness to that, sir, but I would make that assumption.

Q. Well, you certainly do not know that Mr. Dean did anything to keep those parties from reading the newspapers and watching television and radio? A. No, sir.

Q. You were interested in his campaign. You were interested in his welfare, did you not keep up with what the newspapers were saying about the Watergate affair and what the radio was broadcasting and what the TV was disclosing? A. I agree, sir.

Q. I will ask you if the same news media did not proclaim within the same time period that shortly after the burglary was discovered, G. Gordon Liddy, the chief legal adviser of the Stans committee, and E. Howard Hunt, a White House consultant, who had an office in the Executive Office Building, were arrested upon the charge of masterminding and procuring the commission of the burglary?

A. They certainly were arrested, I do not know about master— yes, sir, they were arrested.

Q. Well, I invite your attention—you take The Washington Post, do you not?

A. Yes, sir. You know something, I take two copies.

Q. Yes. And you read one, did you not read one or the other of those two copies? A. Yes, sir.

Q. Well, The Washington Post for Jan. 15, 1973, a copy of which I believe that you read—. A. Yes, sir.

Q. —stated that "sources close to the Watergate case have said that at least four of the five men arrested last June in the Watergate are still being paid, The New York Times reported in its early editions today."

A. Mr. Chairman, that is what is called a double whammy.

Q. Mr. Moore, now I have recounted a great many things, all of which except one, I think you admit, were made known by the news media within two months after the Watergate burglaries were discovered. Can you imagine any better way on which a person interested in the President's campaign and people who read the Washington papers and The New York Times and watched the radio and listened to television could have had more reason to suspect that something was rotten in the committees to re-elect the President than were divulged by these news media?

Everybody in Washington, D. C. had an opportunity to learn about this except the President, didn't he?

A. Well, Mr. Chairman, in all fairness, I think that everybody in Washington, D. C., had a different, the people have their own viewpoints and we have a lot of people here who are making a lot of charges.

Q. And don't you know that the tracks led right straight from the Watergate into the offices of the Committee to Re-elect the President, just as straight as a marten going to its home? A. Yes, sir.

Q. When did you first start suspecting that something was rotten in the committees to secure the re-election of the President?

A. Well, I would say the morning I got a phone call that said, what do you think of that caper—that burglary, on Sunday morning, and I picked it up and read it. I said something like, sure is. This was not Sunday. It was when I learned that McCord and Liddy were involved, within that week, that obviously, something was rotten. I thought that the rotten had been exposed and there was the cancer and there it was. That is what I thought.

Q. You do not have any information that anybody, any aide of the President, kept either Mr. Haldeman or Mr. Ehrlichman or the President from reading the newspapers or listening to the radio or watching television during this time?

A. I have heard it alleged, sir, but it is not true. The President reads newspapers and—of course.

Q. And even Mr. Dean could not keep him, or anybody up there, from reading the newspapers or listening to the radio.

A. The grand jury was also reading the same newspapers and —no.

Testimony by Alexander P. Butterfield

July 16, 1973

Discloses Nixon had listening devices in White House that taped all conversations.

MR. DASH: Mr. Chairman, at a staff interview with Mr. Butterfield on Friday, some very significant information was elicited and was attended by the majority members of the staff and the minority members. The information was elicited by a minority staff member. Therefore, I would like to change the usual routine of the questioning and ask minority counsel to begin the questioning of Mr. Butterfield.

MR. THOMPSON: I thank you, Mr. Dash. During what period of time were you employed at the White House, Mr. Butterfield?

MR. BUTTERFIELD: I was at the White House as a deputy assistant to the President from the first day of the Nixon Administration, Jan. 21, 1969, until noon of March 14, 1973.

Q. And what were your duties at the White House?

A. My duties were many and varied. I was in charge of administration—that is to say that the staff secretary, who is the day-to-day administrator at the White House, reported directly to me. And, of course I reported to Mr. Haldeman, as did every one.

In addition to administration, I was responsible for the management and ultimate supervision of the Office of Presidential Papers and the Office of Special Files. Both of those offices pertained to the collection of documents which will eventually go to the Nixon library.

Thirdly, I was in charge of security at the White House insofar as liaison with the Secret Service and the Executive Protective Service is concerned and insofar as F.B.I. background investigations for prospective Presidential appointees is concerned.

A fourth duty was that I was the Secretary to the Cabinet.

I was additionally the liaison between the President and the Office of the President and all of the various support units. By that I mean the Office of the Military Assistant to the President and the Office of White House Visitors, again the Secret Service, the Executive Protective Service, the residence staff, Mrs. Nixon's staff—I served as sort of a conduit between all those elements and the Office of the President.

Finally, I was in charge of the smooth running of the President's official day, both in Washington, D. C., and at the Western White House in San Clemente.

Q. Mr. Butterfield, are you aware of the installation of any listening devices in the Oval Office of the President?

A. I was aware of listening devices, yes sir.

Q. When were those devices placed in the Oval Office?

A. Approximately the summer of 1970.

Q. Are you aware of any devices that were installed in the Executive Office Building Office of the President?

A. Yes sir, at that time.

Q. Were they installed at the same time?

A. They were installed at the same time.

Q. Would you tell us a little bit about how those devices worked, how they were activated, for example?

A. They were installed, of course, for historical purposes, to record the President's business and they were installed in his two offices, the Oval Office and the E.O.B. [Executive Office Building] Office. Within the West Wing of the White House, there are several, at least three, perhaps four—the three that I know of—boxes called Presidential locator boxes. These are square boxes approximately 10 by 10 inches, and on them are several locations, about seven locations, which would tell where the President might be at any time, locations such as the residence—that is one of them; the South Grounds is another; Oval Office is another: E.O.B. Office is still another; West Wing, meaning West Wing of the White House, is another; and out, I think, is the last one. When the President moves—East Wing is still another and I think that covers all the locations indicated on the box.

When the President moves from his Oval Office, for instance, to his Executive Office Building Office and he departs the West Wing and crosses the street, it is my understanding that the Secret Service agents, members of the Executive Protective Division who cover him—it is my understanding there are four, five, six of them—when he moves across the street, one of them covers the central location.

It says the President is leaving the West Wing and going to the E.O.B. Office. And the little light moves from the Oval Office to E.O.B. Office. It doesn't actually move to the E.O.B. Office until the President actually enters the E.O.B. Office. As that light moves, there is a tie-in audio signal so that if one is preoccupied, as I might be, I realize that the locator box is indicating a change in the President's location and that kind of information was important to me.

Mr. Steve Bull, who at that time worked on the other side of the President, on the East side of the Oval Office, had one of these locator boxes, and Mr. Haldeman had a third. I believe there was a fourth in Mr. Chapin's office—in fact, I am sure there was a fourth in Mr. Chapin's office. We were probably the four who would be the most immediately concerned with the President's whereabouts and the fact that he was changing locations.

In that the Oval Office and the Executive Office Building Office were indicated on this locator box, the installation was installed in such a way that when the light was on "Oval Office," the taping device was at least triggered. It was not operating, but it was triggered—it was spring-loaded, if you will, it was voice-actuated. So when the light was on "Oval Office," in the Oval Office and in the Oval Office only, the taping device was spring-loaded to a voice-actuating situation.

Q. Was there a taping device in the Cabinet Room?

A. Yes, sir, there was.

Q. Was it activated in the same way?

A. No, sir. In the Cabinet Room a manual installation was made.

Q There were buttons on the desk in the Cabinet Room that activated that device?

A. There were two buttons. To my knowledge, the President never did pay any attention to the buttons at the Cabinet table. It was activated, the button on my telephone, by me.

Q. So far as the Oval Office and the E.O.B. Office is concerned, would it be your testimony that the device would pick up any and all conversations no matter where the conversations took place in the room and no matter how soft the conversations might have been? A. Yes, sir.

Q. Was it a little more difficult to pick up in the Cabinet Room?

A. Yes, sir, it was a great deal more difficult to pick up in the Cabinet Room.

Q. All right. We talked about the rooms now and if we could move on to telephones. Are you aware of the installation of any devices on any of the telephones, first of all, the Oval Office?

A. Yes, sir.

Q. What about the Executive Office Building Office of the President?

A. Yes, sir. The President's business telephone at his desk in the Executive Office Building.

Q. What about the Lincoln Room?

A. Yes, sir, the telephone in the Lincoln sitting room in the residence.

Q. What about Aspen Cabin at Camp David?

A. Only in, on the telephone at the President's desk in his study in the Aspen Cabin, his personal cabin.

Q. It is my understanding this cabin was sometimes used by foreign dignitaries. Was the device still present during those periods of time?

A. No, sir, the device was removed prior to occupancy by chiefs of state, heads of government and other foreign dignitaries.

Q. All right. Would you state who installed these devices.

A. The Secret Service. The Technical Security Division of the Secret Service.

Q. Would you state why, as far as your understanding is concerned, these devices were installed in these rooms?

A. There was no doubt in my mind they were installed to record things for posterity, for the Nixon library. The President was very conscious of that kind of thing. We had quite an elaborate set-up at the White House for the collection and preservation of documents, and of things which transpired in the way of business of state.

Q. On whose authority were they installed?

A. On the President's authority by way of Mr. Haldeman and Mr. Higby. Mr. Haldeman instructed Mr. Higby to tell me and I was the liaison with the Secret Service.

Q. Who else knew about the presence of these recording devices?

A. The President, Mr. Haldeman, Mr. Higby and I, plus the Secret Service people.

My secretary knew also although she was not informed early on. She was informed much later because there were a number of occasions on which I just could not be there to press this button and I briefed her and asked her to do it for me but she does not, did not, have any idea of the extent of this. I think she was only aware of the Cabinet Room. Perhaps she was aware of the Oval Office. When I departed I was authorized to brief Steve Bull, who now occupies that office, and now has many of the responsibilities that I had.

General Haig, who is sitting at Mr. Haldeman's desk now, and I believe that is all, sir.

Q. As far as you know, did Mr. Ehrlichman or Mr. Dean know about the existence of the presence of those devices?

A. It would be very unlikely. My guess is they definitely did not know.

Q. Where were the tapes of these conversations kept, maintained?

A. I cannot say where. I am quite sure in the Executive Office Building in some closets or cupboards or files which are maintained by the Technical Security division of the United States Secret Service.

Q. Were these tapes checked periodically?

A. Yes, they were checked at least daily. Some were used more frequently than others. Of course the Secret Service knew this; they made sure that they were checked periodically and sufficiently.

It was my duty to insure that the equipment was working properly. I checked the Oval Office, E.O.B. Office, Cabinet Room tapes several times and it was always working properly in the Oval Office and E.O.B. Office. It was very, very difficult to pick up conversation in the Cabinet Room and I never did check any of the telephones.

Q. Were any of these tapes ever transcribed as far as you know? A. To my recollection, no.

Q. Mr. Butterfield, as far as you know from your own personal knowledge, from 1970 then until the present time all of the President's conversations in the offices mentioned and on the telephones mentioned, were recorded as far as you know? A. That is correct.

Q. And as far as you know, those tapes are still available?

A. As far as I know, but I have been away for four months, sir.

MR. DASH: Now was your understanding that this operated on an on-going basis daily? A. Yes sir.

Q. To your knowledge, did the President ever ask while he

In front from left, minority counsel Fred Thompson, Senator Baker, Senator Ervin, majority counsel Sam Dash and assistant counsel James Hamilton. In rear from left, Senator Gurney, assistant counsel Bill Shure, Senator Montoya and deputy counsel Rufus Edmisten (rear).

The Watergate Hearings

A Pictorial Documentation

Photo Research by
Renato E. Perez

President Nixon
at his desk in the
Oval Office; from left,
H. R. Haldeman,
Dwight Chapin and
John Ehrlichman.

Official White House Photograph

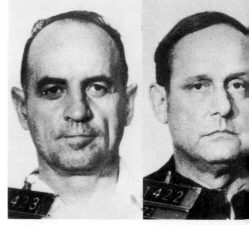

Men arrested while burglarizing the Democratic Headquarters, June 17, 1972: from left, James McCord, Bernard Barker, Eugenio Martinez, Frank Sturgis and Virgilio Gonzalez.

The Watergate complex

DNC OFFICES

HOWARD JOHNSON'S

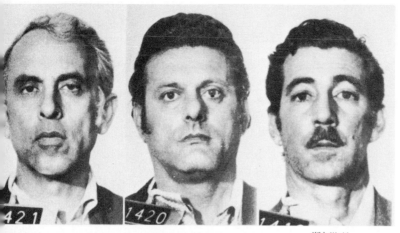

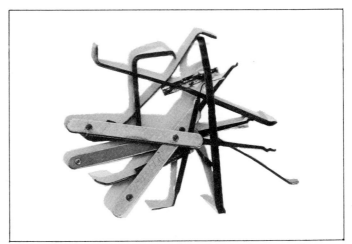

Items found on the Watergate defendants at the time of arrest: telephone bugging device, camera equipment and the lock picks.

Bills and rubber gloves were also found on the arrested men. Below, Frank Wills, who discovered and reported the break-in.

Mr. and Mrs.
Daniel Ellsberg
in the audience at
the hearings.

Visitors wait in line to get into the hearings.

Robert Odle, an early witness at public hearings.

Sally Harmony, former secretary to Gordon Liddy.

James McCord, testifying with telephone and bug.

The Committee and staff listen to Jeb Magruder's testimony.

John W. Dean being sworn in before the Committee.

Mrs. Dean pours a glass of water for her husband.

Senator Sam Ervin, chairman of the Committee.

John N. Mitchell, former Attorney General and chairman of the CRP.

Senator Herman E. Talmadge listening to a witness.

Richard A. Moore

Alexander Butterfield

Herbert W. Kalmbach

Frederick C. LaRue

Tony Ulasewicz
testifies about his
activities as a
bagman. Below,
Senator Inouye, with
Senator Montoya
on his left,
breaks up.

Senator Lowell P. Weicker listens to witness's testimony.

Views of John Ehrlichman as he occupied the witness's chair.

H. R. Haldeman,
right, with his
attorney,
John J. Wilson.

John J. Wilson argues a point before the Committee members.

Senator Inouye, whom Wilson called " **that** little Jap," listens.

Senator Edward J. Gurney

Richard Helms

L. Patrick Gray

Richard G. Kleindienst

Henry E. Petersen

Senators Baker and
Ervin vote to
subpoena
White House tapes.

Wide World

President Nixon speaking to the nation on August 15, 1973.

was in the Oval Office to have the system not operate, the locator light not show in the office so as to trigger the device?

A. No, sir. As a matter of fact, the President seemed to be totally, really oblivious, or certainly uninhibited by this fact.

Q. The tapes you mentioned were stored, are they stored by a particular date? A. Yes sir, they are.

Q. And so that if either Mr. Dean, Mr. Haldeman, Mr. Ehrlichman or Mr. Colson had particular meetings in the Oval Office with the President on any particular dates that have been testified before this committee, there would be a tape recording with the President of that full conversation, would there not? A. Yes sir.

Q. Just one last question. If one were therefore to reconstruct the conversations at any particular date, what would be the best way to reconstruct those conversations, Mr. Butterfield, in the President's Oval Office?

A. Well, in the obvious manner, Mr. Dash—to obtain the tape and play it.

SENATOR TALMADGE: I shall be quite brief, Mr. Chairman. Mr. Butterfield, I understood you to say that all calls to the White House of whatever nature and character would be taped. Is that an accurate statement?

A. Into those telephones, to and from those telephones I mentioned, yes, sir, that is an accurate statement.

Q. If a Senator or Congressman or Governor called, it was taped?

A. Yes, the tape would not discriminate.

Q. Was there any warning signal to let them know the conversation would be taped?

A. I am told that when devices are on telephones, there is oftentimes a clicking sound. But other than that, I would guess that no one would be aware, sir.

Q. No one verbally undertook to say, Governor, your conversation will be taped? A. No, sir.

Q. Or Mr. Senator, or Congressman, or Mr. Private Citizen, whatever the case might be? A. No, sir.

Q. Were the visitors who went into the White House warned that their conversations with the President would be taped? A. No, sir.

Q. None of them had knowledge that their conversations were being taped?

A. No, sir, although I say one thing, which I think perhaps should be said at this point. When people go to visit the President, almost always I know of very, very few exceptions, a staff member sits in on the conversation, often takes notes. That is standard procedure in order to record commitments made by the President, at least the thread or the substance of the business discussed.

Q. Do you know whether or not the Attorney General of

would stop recording. It was only for the President's business. That again, supports my earlier guess that it was purely for historical purposes.

Q. Now, in the interview which you had with the staff of this committee, on July 13, 1973, at 2:15 P.M. the interview, as reported by this staff, concludes with: "Butterfield stated this is all something I know the President did not want revealed, but you asked me and I feel it is something you ought to know about in your investigations. I was told no one was to know about the information I have told you."

Is that a correct quotation?

A. I could not say that it was correct, but there was some reluctance on my part to reveal information which I felt could have a number of serious repercussions with regard to foreign governments. It is very obvious that this could be embarrassing to our Government.

Q. Did anybody indicate to you that you should not reveal it? A. No, sir.

SENATOR GURNEY: Do you know of your own knowledge whether anyone has ever sought to get any of these tapes or has gotten any of these tapes, other than yourself in the testimony that you have just given this committee?

A. No, sir, If Mr. Haldeman wanted to do that, he could call the same individual, the chief of the Technical Security Division, and ask him to bring the tape over, or whatever, and not inform me. And, of course, the Secret Service agent would do that. But all of that was channeled through me. I feel certain that Mr. Haldeman would not have done that and under any normal circumstances, should anyone else do it, I would have been notified and the Secret Service would not have responded, in fact, until I had given my approval.

Q. Now, is it your testimony that if anybody had ever asked the Secret Service for these tapes, that they would have notified you? A. Yes, that is correct.

SENATOR ERVIN: The chair has received a letter from Mr. J. Fred Buzhardt, counsel for the President, dated July 16, 1973, reading as follows:

"Dear Chairman:

"This letter is to confirm the fact stated to your committee today by Mr. Alexander Butterfield that the President's meetings and conversations in the White House have been recorded since the spring of 1971. I am advised that this system, which is still in use, is similar to that employed by the last Administration, which was discontinued from 1969 until the spring of 1971. A more detailed statement concerning these procedures will be furnished to the committee shortly.

"Sincerely,"

Mr. Butterfield, on behalf of the committee, I want to commend you for the forthrightness of your testimony.

A. Thank you, sir. I will be the first to agree with Mr. Buzhardt. I only guessed at the time. That is pretty good evidence, I think, of how fuzzy one's recollections can be to be off a full year, but if they say the spring of '71, obviously, that has been checked with the Secret Service, who would have a record, and I stand corrected on that point.

Testimony by Herbert W. Kalmbach

July 16   *Describes raising and disbursing funds for seven defendants.*

July 17   *Says he provided $400,000 in cash to men he did not know.*

July 16, 1973

MR. KALMBACH: Since early 1969, I have been engaged in activities on the President's behalf in three major areas.

First, it has been the source of great pride and personal satisfaction to me and to my partners to have had the responsibility for handling personal legal matters for President Nixon and members of his immediate family for the past four years. During this period, practically all of the contacts that I had relative to these matters were handled through either John Ehrlichman or John Dean.

Second, I acted as trustee during the period from January of 1969 to early February of 1972 for certain surplus funds which had accrued principally from the primary period of the 1968 campaign. While Maurice H. Stans was the individual with whom I dealt at the time I accepted such trusteeship, I disbursed from such funds only at the express direction of H. R. Haldeman or others clearly having the authority to direct such disbursements.

Third, I agreed to solicit early pledges of financial support for the President's 1972 campaign beginning in November 1970. This- assignment was completed in the spring of 1972. The original records of this activity were turned over to the finance committee after Mr. Stans had assumed the post of finance chairman on Feb. 15, 1972. I thereupon directed my secretary to destroy my files which were wholly personal and supportive of the original files earlier transferred to the finance committee.

This action on my part was intended to insure the continued confidentiality of the contacts that I had had with various contributors with whom I had dealt during this period. Copies of what remaining records I have and such bank records as I have been able to retrieve have been supplied to the committee's staff prior to my appearance here today.

Finally, I want to take this opportunity to deny any prior knowledge of the Watergate break-in or participation in the formulation of any planned conspiracy to cover up that incident or act of campaign sabotage or unethical activity. My actions in the period immediately following the break-in which involved the raising of funds to provide for the legal defense of the Watergate defendants and for the support of their families were prompted in the belief that such was proper and necessary to discharge what I assumed to be a moral obligation that had arisen in some manner unknown to me by reason of earlier events.

The fact that I had been directed to undertake these actions by the number 2 and number 3 men on the White House staff made it absolutely incomprehensible to me that my actions in this regard could have been regarded in any way as improper or unethical.

MR. DASH: Now you played a role in campaign fund raising for the President prior to the 1972 campaign.

A. In 1968 I was associate finance chairman for that campaign.

Q. Now, what, if anything, did you do with any funds left over from the 1968 campaign?

A. Mr. Stans in mid-January of 1969 asked me to accept the trusteeship for certain surplus funds from that campaign.

Q. Who could authorize disbursements from these funds?

A. Mr. Haldeman principally, and at a later time also Mr. Ehrlichman, Mr. Mitchell and others who were, clearly would stand, in the shoes of these people.

Q. Would that include Mr. Strachan and Mr. LaRue at all?

A. Yes, sir, it would.

Q. When were you first asked to raise money for the 1972 campaign and by whom?

A. It was in November of 1970 by Mr. Haldeman.

Q. What position did you have in the '72 campaign?

A. Beginning on Feb. 15, 1972, I agreed to act as the associate finance chairman through the period ending April 7, the date that the new law became effective.

Q. Now in February, 1972, did you have funds in your possession that were raised during campaigns? A. Yes, sir.

Q. What did you do with those funds in February, 1972?

A. In the first few days of February of 1972, I closed all of the checking accounts and sent all of those checks to Mr. Sloan at the finance committee in Washington, and I also closed and emptied the several safe deposit boxes and transferred those funds to Mr. Sloan so that I zeroed out my account.

Q. Do you know approximately how much money was involved in terms of turning over the money to Mr. Sloan?

A. In February of 1972 the total was $915,000 and that total would include approximately $233,000 in cash, and approximately $670,000 in checking account balances.

Q. After you turned over this money did you destroy any records that you had? A. Yes sir, I did.

Q. Will you tell us what records and why?

A. After I turned over the monies I transferred my files on the people that I had seen, the pledges that I had received, the essentials of my records, to Mr. Stans and to the finance committee. Once I was certain in my own mind that the original records had been in fact, transferred to the finance committee then I directed my secretary to destroy those personal and supportive records for the reason of confidentiality.

Q. Now, did you give Mr. Stans an advance on his expenses in February, 1972? A. Yes, sir.

Q. How much?

A. I gave him $50,000.

Q. Why did you give him that?

A. Mr. Stans had come to me and asked me for these funds as an advance for personal expenses for the forthcoming campaign.

Q. Was a receipt given to you for that? A. No, sir.

Q. Now, are you aware of the transaction whereby $350,000 left the Committee for the Re-election of the President, the finance committee, and went over to the White House? A. I am.

Q. Can you tell us briefly of your own knowledge how that took place?

A. About the last week in March or very early in the first few days of April I was called by Mr. Higby from the White House and was asked as to how much cash would be available for transfer to the White House. I then checked with Mr. Sloan. I called Mr. Higby back and told him that I had found there was $350,000 in cash in Mr. Sloan's safe that would be available.

Q. Do you know why the request, why the $350,000 was needed? Was any information given to you?

A. I am not certain, Mr. Dash, that it was expressed to me, the purpose. But I know that it was my assumption, and it may have been expressed to me, but it was my assumption that it would be used for polling purposes.

Q. Now, did you receive a telephone call from Mr. John Dean on June 28?

A. Yes, I did. He told me that it was a matter of extreme importance that I come back to Washington, preferably by the first available flight, to undertake a very important assignment.

Q. Well, what, actually, did you and Mr. Dean discuss?

A. Well, he indicated that the reason for this call and for

my coming back to Washington was that it was necessary to talk to me about a very important assignment, namely that, he said—he used the editorial "we"—said: "We would like to have you raise funds for the legal defense of these defendants and for the support of their families.

Q. These were the seven defendants, Mr. Hunt, Mr. Liddy, Mr. McCord, Mr. Barker, Mr. Sturgis, Mr. Gonzalez—A. That is correct.

Q. Now you knew that they were for all of these defendants?

A. I just remember that he said the Watergate defendants at that time and I was not even certain at that point in time that I even knew their names.

Q. All right. Did you ask him any questions about that?

A. Yes, I did. I recall that in my conversation with him, I asked whether or not it would not be perhaps preferable to have a public committee formed to raise funds for these people and for these purposes. And also, I recall that I wondered aloud about whether or not maybe they could mortgage homes or raise funds in that way until a public committee could be established. His answer to that was that there was no time for this, that a public committee might be misinterpreted.

Q. Did he tell you how much money might be involved?

A. My recollection is that he indicated 50 to 100 thousand dollars for this assignment.

Q. Did he stress, that this had to be completely secret?

A. Yes, he made a very strong point that there was absolute secrecy required, confidentially indicating that if this became known, it might jeopardize the campaign and would cause misinterpretation as to the reasons for raising these funds and for the help of these people.

I asked him when I raised the funds, should I give them to him for distribution, and he said, no not to me. And he indicated, I think, Mr. Fred LaRue would be the person who would be giving me directions as to specific amounts and specific individuals.

Q. Did you indicate that you would accept this assignment from Mr. Dean? A. I did.

Q. And you did accept it under the basis that if Mr. Dean was asking you as the President's counsel, that he had authority to ask for that? A. Absolutely.

Q. When did you next return to Washington, after this first series of meetings, where you received this money, met with Mr. Ulasewicz, when did you next return to Washington?

A. Well, the next time that I was back in Washington involved in this assignment was, I think, on July 19.

I was asked to come back by either Mr. Dean or Mr. LaRue, and to meet with Mr. Dean and Mr. LaRue in Mr. Dean's office in the Executive Office Building.

Q. Did you receive any money from Mr. LaRue at that time?

A. Yes, sir, I did.

Q. How much was that?

A. Some $40,000.

Q. What did you do with this $40,000?

A. I went to New York late that afternoon, stayed at the Regency Hotel, and gave the funds to Mr. Ulasewicz.

Q. Now, you returned the following week, did you not, Mr. Kalmbach, to Washington?

A. Yes. About this time, I was asked by either Mr. Dean or Mr. LaRue to raise additional funds. I began to have a degree of concern about this assignment.

Q. What began to cause you to have that degree of concern?

A. I think the primary reason for my concern was the secrecy and the clandestine, covert nature of this activity.

The concern was sufficient to make me certain in my own mind that I wanted to talk to John Ehrlichman.

I wanted John Ehrlichman to confirm that John Dean did in fact have the authority to direct me to undertake this assignment.

Second, I wanted him to assure me as to the propriety of this assignment. In any event, I requested a meeting with John Ehrlichman. My records indicate that I met with him in his office at 3:30 on July 26.

Q. At this time, you were being asked to go out and to raise some additional funds on your own?

A. Yes sir, and this would be the first time, Mr. Dash, that I would be going to an outside contributor.

Q. What did you say to Mr. Ehrlichman and what did he say to you?

A. I went through it as far as the secrecy and how this secrecy was bothering me, the whole secrecy thing—the press.

Q. What do you mean, the press?

A. I mean the press coverage on the Watergate. I was beginning to have concern about this assignment. And I said, John, I want you to tell me, and you know, I can remember it very vividly because I looked at him, and I said, John, I am looking right into your eyes. I said, I know that my family and my reputation mean everything to me, and it is just absolutely necessary, John, that you tell me, first, that John Dean has the authority to direct me in this assignment, that it is a proper assignment and that I am to go forward on it.

Q. And did he look at you in the eyes? A. Yes, he did.

Q. What did he say to you?

A. He said, Herb, John Dean does have the authority. It is proper, and you are to go forward.

Now, he said, in commenting on the secrecy, he explained that as saying that but for the secrecy, this whole assignment, getting these funds to these people for this purpose could get into the press and be misinterpreted. And then I remember he used the figure of speech, he said, they would have our heads in their laps, which again would indicate to me that it would jeopardize the campaign.

The effect actually was that it washed out the concern that I had had that had built up preliminary to this meeting, and I went out of that meeting certain that it was proper for me to go back to California and approach this contributor, this first contributor that I would approach in this program.

Q. Now, how could your providing funds through either Mr. Dean's aegis or through Mr. Ehrlichman's aegis, through the committee, to burglars, wiretappers, and conspirators be misinterpreted?

A. Well, the misinterpretation would be that this was being done to silence these people.

Q. Could anybody have had any other interpretation?

A. I did.

Q. What interpretation did you have, Mr. Kalmbach?

A. I had the interpretation, that I felt that the green light had been given to these people in some manner and that someone felt that even though these people had done an illegal act, the decent thing to do is to provide them with lawyers and provide them with family support.

Q. Did you raise that additional amount of money that you were asked to raise?

A. Yes, I did. I called Mr. Thomas V. Jones sometime between, I think it was Aug. 1 and Aug. 5 and indicated that I would like to come by and see him. He had earlier indicated to me that he would have funds for me if there was any special need.

Q. Who is Mr. Jones?

A. He is chairman of the Northrop Corporation in California.

Q. And has he been a political contributor to Mr. Nixon, the President?

A. Yes, sir. He indicated immediately that he would be glad to see me. I went to his office, in Century City in West Los Angeles, and he took from his desk a package, and handed it to me. I put it in my briefcase, and left his office and went back to Newport Beach.

Q. What was in the package?

A. It was $75,000 in cash.

Q. And do you know what denomination the money was in?

A. $100 bills, as I remember it.

Q. When you spoke to Mr. Jones did you tell him why you wanted the money?

A. No, again just as with Mr. Stans, I told him that it was for a special assignment that I would not reveal the nature of, that I had been given the assignment by one in authority at the White House.

Q. Were you ever again, Mr. Kalmbach, asked to raise money for the defendants, after you broke off. A. Yes, I was.

Q. Could you tell us when you can recall that happening and who was there?

A. I remember with great particularity a meeting that occurred on the 19th of January [1973] in Washington, in Mr. Mitchell's office.

Q. Who was there with Mr. Mitchell?

A. There was Mr. Mitchell, Mr. Dean, Mr. LaRue and myself.

Q. Now, when did you decide to stop raising any money for the defendants and their attorneys?

A. Probably in mid-August, Mr. Dean and Mr. LaRue contacted me indicating they needed additional funds, and this whole degree of concern had come back on me to the level that I knew that I did not want to participate any longer in this assignment.

I don't recall that I ever discussed this with Mr. Ehrlichman after making that decision.

Q. Did you tell John Dean anything?

A. Well, I just simply told him that I would do no more, and I advised Mr. LaRue too, that I could do no more.

I think it was Mr. Dean that led the conversation and immediately I could see that the purpose of this meeting was to ask me to raise additional funds for lawyers and for family support. I knew I wanted to withdraw as soon as possible, and I excused myself, within, I think, 10 minutes at the most, 10 or 15 minutes.

July 17, 1973

SENATOR MONTOYA: It was then [June 28, 1972] that you met Mr. Dean at the Hay-Adams Hotel? A. Yes sir.

Q. And after a little conference there you proceeded to Lafayette Park. A. Yes, sir.

Q. And Mr. Dean testified as follows and I quote from his testimony. It appears on page 3174 of the transcript:

"Mr. Dean: Well, I told him everything that I knew about the case at that time. I told him that I was very concerned that this could lead right to the President. I did not have any hard facts. I hoped that I was incorrect. I explained to him in full the seriousness of the matter. I relayed to him the fact that some records had been destroyed. I told him virtually everything I knew at that time and I think there was no doubt in his mind about the sensitivity of the situation."

Would you say this is a correct statement on the part of Mr. Dean?

A. Senator, my recollection of that conversation was simply that he indicated that he wished me—he used the word "we"—that I was being asked to raise funds for the legal defense of these people and for the support of the families.

Q. Well, did he mention possible involvement of the White House? He had already indicated to you that the President might be hurt by this. A. No, sir.

Q. He did not. Now, it has been reported that the sum of $450,000 was expended with respect to the Watergate defendants, including their defense and also the cover-up, and I believe that you have testified that you were responsible only for approximately $205,000.

A. Senator, my memory is that approximately $220,000 was the amount that was my distribution to Mr. Ulasewicz.

Q. Do you know who raised the rest of the money? A. No sir, I do not.

Q. Now, as you look back in retrospect, Mr. Kalmbach, and in view of the secrecy that was imposed upon you and what you had to go through in order to develop a line of communication in carrying out your mission, do you feel that you proceeded correctly?

A. In retrospect, Senator, I feel that I, it was something I should not have been involved in.

SENATOR WEICKER: What factors prompted you to believe that your conduct was proper and necessary? Did you assume that there was a moral obligation?

A. That was my own assumption, Senator, just based on this assignment and the request that had been given to me by Mr. Dean that there must have been some feeling that there was a moral obligation here to be discharged.

Q. Did you feel that maybe somebody owed somebody something here, is that another way of phrasing it?

A. I had the feeling that someone in some manner expressly had directed these people to go forward on this assignment, and the assignment was, as I say, stupid and illegal, idiotic, but there was a feeling that as long as they had been directed to undertake this, that there was at least a moral obligation to provide for lawyers for them and for the support of their families.

Q. Now, as an attorney, are you telling me that you would commence activities that in effect might risk your entire career on a belief that such activities were proper and necessary to discharge a moral obligation that had arisen in some manner unknown to you?

A. Yes sir. It was a matter of absolute trust in Mr. Dean, and later in Mr. Ehrlichman. It is incomprehensible to me, and was at that time, I just didn't think about it, that these men would ask me to do an illegal act.

Q. If these activities were believed by you to be proper why was it necessary to obtain the services of Anthony Ulasewicz to distribute the money to the defendants and their attorneys?

A. Again this was the procedure that I was directed to follow.

SENATOR GURNEY: Did you receive word from Dean or LaRue to give X amount to Mrs. Hunt?

A. Yes, sir, I remember that, I was told from time to time to give X amount to Mrs. Hunt.

Q. Do you remember what those amounts were and when?

A. No sir. But in reconstructing this history in trying to develop what the amounts were and to whom these funds went, my memory is that approximately $150,000 or thereabouts went to Mrs. Hunt out of which certain of the attorneys were paid and various of the defendants.

Beyond that $150,000 there was $30,000 that was given to Mr. LaRue in the final disbursal. Twenty-five thousand dollars was given to Mr. Bittman, I think $8,000 was given to Mr. Liddy, as I remember it, $1,000 to Mr. Ulasewicz, and $1,000 which I retained and delivered to Mr. Strachan. Now that total is approximately $220,000.

Q. If these activities were believed by you to be proper why was Mr. Ulasewicz given a code name, Mr. Rivers, and why were Mr. and Mrs. Hunt given the code name of the Writer and the Writer's wife, and Mr. Haldeman the code name of the Brush?

A. Senator, again this was just an abundance of caution in the carrying out of the assignment, the confidentiality and the secrecy of the assignment all of which gave me this on-going concern.

Q. If these activities were believed by you to be proper then why did Mr. Ulasewicz at your instructions distribute the monies to the defendants and their attorneys in luggage lockers at National Airport and telephone booths and counters in restaurants and in trash cans?

A. Senator, again this was in the carrying out of this assignment. I spoke to Mr. Ulasewicz and he indicated to me that the manner in which these distributions would be made was something that he would take care of and it would be better that if I didn't even know about it.

Q. I just have a few more questions. During the course of this testimony, Mr. Mitchell has testified that he wished he had known of the $1,110,000 surplus left over from the 1968 campaign. A. Yes sir.

Q. Now, I would like your comments about that statement. Do you have any evidence that Mr. Mitchell might have known or did know about the fact that there was a surplus in the 1968 campaign?

A. Senator, I believe that I had advised Mr. Mitchell at various times that I did have funds under my control.

Q. And this would possibly account for the fact that his law partner, Mr. Evans, is one of the co-trustees of a portion of that money?

A. Well, Mr. Evans was a signatory on the accounts and on the safe deposit boxes—certainly the accounts.

Q. And to the best of your recollection, there were times when you indicated to Mr. Mitchell that there were such surplus funds from the '68 campaign? A. Yes sir.

SENATOR INOUYE: Mr. Kalmbach, you are a senior member of a most prestigious law firm and among your clients, you number some of the nation's corporate giants—Marriott Corporation, United Airlines, Travelers Insurance, M.C.A., Atlantic-Richfield, Dart Industries, Great Southwest Corporation. Then you have the University of Southern California, the Nixon Foundation, the

Stans Foundation. I would gather from your success that you must be a great lawyer. Therefore, like Senator Weicker, I find it extremely difficult to believe that you are not aware that illegal activities were being carried out.

If a client came to you and related the exact story that is now being related here, and he said, Mr. Kalmbach, should I raise these funds, what would you have advised this client?

A. If the client had come to me in this situation, which is wholly separate from any situation that I could believe anyone would be faced with, I would have asked him to exercise caution and make inquiries. But in my situation, Senator, I was dealing with the counsel to the President of the United States. It was a matter of absolute trust in the man's integrity and honesty.

Q. You were in charge of the surplus 1968 funds? A. Yes, sir.

Q. These were cash funds?

A. Sir, there were one million nine in cash and $570,000 in a checking account.

Q. Isn't it strange that when the campaign closed, the campaign committee for the President indicated that they had a debt? Why wasn't this surplus used to pay the debt?

A. Senator, I was spoken to by Mr. Stans in mid-January of 1969 and was advised that these funds were surplus and he characterized the funds as primarily from the primary campaign.

Q. But you were aware that the Nixon campaign committee of 1968 had declared that they were in debt?

A. I don't recall that that was the case, Senator. It would be my recollection that there was, that we finished that campaign in the black.

Q. In retrospect are you now convinced that you were involved in a criminal activity?

A. In retrospect now, in this testimony, realizing from what Mr. Dean has testified that this was improper, an illegal act. It is just as if I had been kicked in the stomach.

SENATOR GURNEY: I understand from your testimony that you disbursed certain amounts of money to Mr. Segretti. This was done on the orders of whom?

A. It was done on the orders of Mr. Chapin, Senator.

Q. And what did he tell you in his instructions to you?

A. This was in either late August or early September of 1971, Mr. Chapin asked me to meet with then Captain Segretti who was in the Army, asked me to meet with him to come to an agreement with him as to a compensation level and reach that agreement and begin disbursing funds to him for activities that he would be performing for the White House.

Q. In this connection was it your understanding that you were disbursing these funds which were in your control at that time pursuant to the instructions of Mr. Haldeman or under his jurisdiction?

A. Yes, sir, it was. Mr. Chapin, as I remember our conversation, did not mention Mr. Haldeman but Mr. Chapin was standing, clearly standing, in the shoes of Mr. Haldeman as one of Mr. Haldeman's senior deputies.

Q. Did you ever have any discussion with Mr. Haldeman about this?

A. About the disbursal of funds?

Q. To Segretti.

A. I do not recall that I ever did, Senator. My recollection is clear as to my meeting with Mr. Chapin and my understanding was clear that he was speaking on behalf of Mr. Haldeman, but I do not recall that Mr. Haldeman's name was mentioned.

Q. Just one final question, Mr. Kalmbach. Did you have discussions following the break-in of Watergate down to now with the President? A. No sir.

SENATOR TALMADGE: Mr. Kalmbach, I want to get into an area that you have not testified on, that we have had reports in the press about it. Are you familiar with funds going into the state of Alabama during the 1970 election?

A. Senator, I am familiar with funds that I disbursed in 1970 under instructions. At that time, I had no knowledge as to where the ultimate distributees would be.

Q. Will you tell us about that fund, please?

A. Yes sir. During the 1970 period I was raising funds towards the, in the senatorial races, and also I was directed by Mr. Higby on three different occasions to disburse funds out of trust funds that I had under my control. I recall that there was a call that Mr. Higby made to me, in I think it was in late March of 1970 directing that I disburse $100,000 to someone there in New York.

I took these funds from the box, safe deposit box, at the Chase Manhattan Bank in New York and delivered them to an individual at the Sherry-Netherlands Hotel in New York.

Q. Who was the individual?

A. I did not know his name, and do not know him.

Q. How did you know you gave the $100,000 to the right man?

A. I was advised at a later date that I had given the funds to the right person.

Q. Who gave you the instructions as to whom to meet and where?

A. I talked to Mr. Higby, and he instructed me, and I said that I would deliver the funds at the Sherry-Netherlands hotel, and an individual then came up to me and the identification was proper, and I—

Q. Was there a password?

A. No, sir, I don't recall the procedure now but it was definite that it was the man—.

Q. You didn't walk into the lobby and give the first hundred thousand, give the hundred thousand to the first man you saw, did you? A. No, sir.

Q. What was the arrangement whereby you could make the proper contact?

A. I don't recall the specific arrangements, Senator. It was simply that he—I was in the lobby, and I think I was in a particular colored suit and he came up to me and identified himself as being from someplace and I don't recall where it was.

Q. Did he have a Southern drawl? A. I don't remember it, no, sir.

Q. You didn't hear his voice?

A. I heard his voice but it was not distinctive.

Q. What was the signal as to how he could identify himself to you to receive the $100,000?

A. Well, I think the signal was that he asked me if I was, I forget whether I was, from some state, and I replied yes, or something, and that was sufficient but I don't recall the exact procedure.

Q. Do you know what the purpose of that money was for?

A. I did not.

Q. Did you have any suspicions? A. No, sir, I did not.

Q. You didn't think they were going to take it somewhere and burn it up, did you? A. No, sir.

Q. Now, tell us about the next contribution that you made and the circumstances thereof. That was the first one hundred thousand? A. Yes, sir.

Q. Was that left-over money from the 1968 campaign? A. Yes, sir.

Q. Proceed, please.

A. Then I think within a month, Senator, I was again asked to disburse $200,000 following the same procedure.

Q. Did Mr. Higby also request you the second time?

A. That is correct. My recollection is that I asked one of the signatories on the box, Mr. France 'Raine to take the funds to the, again to the, Sherry-Netherlands Hotel, and disburse to an individual which he did.

Q. You didn't deliver the second hundred thousand? A. No, sir, I did not.

Q. All right, that is three hundred thousand. Now, tell us about the next amount.

A. Then finally there was a third communication again, I think it was from Mr. Higby directing that another hundred thousand be disbursed in the same manner, although at this time I was asked to disburse to an individual in Los Angeles in the lobby of the Bank of California Building on Flower and Sixth Street.

Q. You delivered two hundred thousand and an agent delivered the other two hundred thousand? A. That is correct.

Q. And your directions or instructions to deliver the money came from Higby twice and who the third time?

A. From Mr. Higby the third time.

Q. Did you have any suspicion as to where that money was going?

A. No, sir, I did not. I made the assumption without knowing that it was going into campaigns but I did not know which campaign.

Q. Was that not, in fact, money that was used to try to defeat Governor Wallace in Alabama in 1970?

A. Senator, I have never known this to be a fact. I think subsequent to the disbursals I heard comments to the effect that part or all of those funds did, in fact, go to that campaign but I did not know at the time and the only evidence or indication that I have had subsequent was just various comments.

Q. A man of your intelligence and ability and background certainly would not be in the business of just walking up to strangers in hotels and giving them $400,000 for nothing, would you? A. No, sir.

Q. You suspected that it was going to stop Governor Wallace in Alabama, did you not?

A. I did not at that time.

Q. But you subsequently suspected that? A. Yes, sir.

Q. Do you know that of your own knowledge?

A. I do not know it as a fact, Senator.

Q. It is common knowledge in the circles that raised the money and dispensed it, is it not?

A. Well, I think there is a belief that part or all of it did go to that campaign but again, Senator, I would not have the certainty that that is true.

Q. You stated yesterday that you believe that this payment plan was so important because it came from Mr. Dean, the President's personal counsel. Did you, because of that, suspect that the President himself might have approved it? A. No, sir.

Q. You just took it at face value because the President's counsel himself indicated that to you?

A. Well, again, Senator, here was a man that I had been dealing with for a year and a half, or two years, at that time, a man in whom I had absolute and complete trust. He was standing, really, in the shoes of the President, on the President's legal work that a partner and I would be talking to him about. It was again without—because my own nature is that I trust my friends and trust my partners, and I had absolute trust in this man. And when he made this request of me, I did not hesitate.

Q. Did the President ever speak to you after the press had released an account of the stories involving you with Mr. Segretti in September of last year to ask you what had occurred? A. No, sir.

Q. Did the President call you after the election in November, 1972? A. Yes, sir, he did.

Q. That was after you had raised funds for payment to these defendants and other purposes, was it not?

A. It was, and it was after the election and after I had raised a substantial amount of money for the re-election campaign beginning back in November of 1970, Senator.

Q. What was discussed in that conversation relating to Watergate?

A. Nothing.

Q. You didn't think you were performing a service for Mr. Dean, did you? You thought you were performing a service for the President of the United States, didn't you?

A. Senator, I thought I was performing a service for the people that Mr. Dean referred to as "we."

Q. Who did you think were "we"?

A. I thought probably he was talking about the senior people at the Committee to Re-elect and possibly some of the people at the White House.

Q. You would not go all over the country, giving away hundreds of thousands of dollars in cash and engaging in surreptitious activities, for some clerk in the White House, would you? A. No sir.

SENATOR BAKER: Did the thought occur to you that there might be something odd or strange about a· White House involvement or the involvement of a principal staff person, in this case Mr. Dean, in this fund-raising effort for defendants who had received prominent publicity at that time and obviously were going to be charged with a serious offense, did that raise any ripples of concern?

A. Again, Senator, it did not. I knew that Mr. Dean had been very involved in matters involving the Committee to Re-elect, and he was probably wearing several hats but I know that he had had that association with the Committee to Re-elect, and I felt that here was a man who I had this trust in asking me to take on this assignment, and I did not question it. It would have been inconceivable, as I have said, Senator, for me to have believed that this man would ask me to do something illegal.

Q. That gets us to the point I would really like to inquire about, Mr. Kalmbach. You may or may not know but with other witnesses on occasion I have asked for their perception of the arrangement in a situation or even the institution of the Presidency that would cause them to act or fail to act in a particular way. Can you visualize, in that vein, any other person or situation in the whole wide world for whom you would have done this other than a representative of the White House?

A. Senator, I feel, as I look back on it, that almost certainly Mr. Dean had been asked to talk to me because the people knew of the relationship I had with this man and the relationship of trust.

Q. You see what I am striving for once again is what is there about the nature of the White House or the Presidency or of the aura that surrounds it? A. Yes sir.

Q. That would cause you to act without question, without concern, as apparently you did, placing great reliance on the propriety of the request because of its origins, is that—

A. Total reliance on the trust.

Q. Yes. You base that on your reverence for the institution of the Presidency or on your personal friendship with him or long acquaintance with either the President or Mr. Dean or was it a composite of several things?

A. I think it was a composite of all those factors.

Q. Did it ever occur to you—I know you testified that you spoke to Mr. Ehrlichman about the matter to verify Mr. Dean's authority, did it ever occur to you to speak to the President about it to find out whether he knew what was going on or did not know what was going on?

A. No, sir. I felt that in talking to Mr. Ehrlichman, I was talking to someone who would give me the assurance that I required and I did not think to talk to the President.

Q. Mr. Kalmbach, you have already testified that you have not spoken to the President about Watergate, although I believe you did talk to him the night of the election.

A. No sir, it was several days after the election.

Q. I see. Well, sometime shortly after the election? A. Yes sir.

Q. Did it ever occur to you to talk to the President about this and find out what the situation was or how this situation might relate to him?

A. No, Senator. All during this period from the August-September, when I discontinued and withdrew, on through until the time that Mr. Ehrlichman left the White House I had the feeling always that these men were, Mr. Dean, Mr. Ehrlichman had the absolute trust of the President, and all I had was this concern. I had no certainty at all, Senator, that there was an impropriety. The level of concern that I had was simply it was, it bothered me to the point that I would not be involved in it but I did not know that it was, in fact, what it is, and it—all through this period, I just had that level of concern, and here was Mr. Ehrlichman, Mr. Dean continuing at the White House, and I was certain with these people there that my concern probably really was not based on anything at all, but it was sufficient for me, Senator, at that early time to desist.

Q. Now, if you didn't want to be involved any longer at that point, did the thought occur to you that if your concern was that great that there was some obligation or at least an opportunity to take this matter up with the President and see if he was aware of all these circumstances?

A. No, sir, it did not. Again, I had been advised by Mr. Dean, and then Mr. Ehrlichman, that this was proper and to go forward, and frankly, my concern was based on the secrecy and these procedures, and I felt it would be presumptuous, frankly, with just rumor and just a sixth sense, to have gone to the President.

Now, I again, I have not met with the President more than four or five times other than in social gatherings over these entire —throughout this period.

Q. Were you still his personal attorney at that time? You see, I am still a little perplexed. Here we have a man who had known the President for a long time, who was his personal counsel, who accepted a job, in effect, on faith, who became concerned about it, concerned to the point that he sought out a verification of the authority of Mr. Dean to give you this assignment, and later became so concerned that you disengaged from it.

Now surely the body, the substance, of your concern, at some point must have flickered a warning light that there is trouble here, at least trouble, potentially trouble, for you, and did it never flicker the light that there might be trouble for the President in that respect?

A. It didn't flicker the light, as you put it, that there was trouble in that sense. There was—it bothered me, the secrecy, that was the primary thing, it was distasteful to me, this back and forth in the telephone booth. The press, the accumulation, as you put it, Senator, the composite of several factors, but it never reached the point in my mind where I felt that I should go to the President. I had been assured first by this man in whom the President had complete trust, Mr. Ehrlichman, and earlier by Mr. Dean to go forward in this, and I thought frankly it would be presumptuous of me to take it beyond my own decision to desist.

SENATOR ERVIN: Now didn't you suspect that when you raised this money and distributed it in this surreptitious manner to the lawyers and families of the parties that had been indicted in the Watergate that you were aiding the Nixon campaign for re-election?

A. I was carrying out an assignment, Mr. Chairman.

Q. Well, didn't you suspect that you were asked to do this because it would aid the campaign of the President for re-election?

A. No sir. I was doing this for the purpose that I stated, that it was an assignment. I thought a moral obligation had in some manner been created and I was raising funds for the purposes stated.

Q. You didn't have the remotest idea that you were doing anything to assist the re-election of the President? A. No sir.

Q. And you didn't even suspect, you didn't even have any idea of that kind in your mind when you applied to Mr. Jones for a contribution for the President's campaign funds? A. No, sir.

Q. No, unfortunately, people, you know—I do not know whether in California, you have lightning bugs, but we have them in North Carolina, sometimes, I wish that people were not like lightning bugs. Lightning bugs carry their illumination behind them.

I would like to ask you if in retrospect, and with your illumination behind you instead of in front of you if you do not think that people could reasonably conclude that this money was paid to these defendants and their families to induce them to keep silent?

A. Yes, sir. I do, now again, in hindsight.

SENATOR INOUYE: In your testimony you indicated that someone pressed the "green button" thereby putting into motion the Watergate burglary, something that you describe as being idiotic and I agree with you it was idiotic and monumentally stupid.

However idiotic, I gather from your testimony that you assumed that this burglary was carried out to benefit the re-election campaign of the President of the United States. Is my assumption correct, sir? A. Yes, sir, I would agree with that.

Q. But, however, you did not know as to the identity of the person who pressed the green button? A. No sir.

Q. Now, then, Mr. Dean directed you to raise these funds for humanitarian purposes, and was later assured by Mr. Ehrlichman that Mr. Dean was authorized to ask you to risk your career and carry out this covert fund raising, you must have assumed that these men either participated in pressing the button or knew who pressed the button is that assumption correct, sir? A. Yes.

Q. And without question, you obeyed the direction of Mr. Dean and Mr. Ehrlichman? A. Without question.

Q. Because you were certain that, as you said, they were trusted implicitly by the President of the United States?

A. And, sir, trusted by me.

Q. And everything in that was done in the President's best interest?

A. Everything that was done, I know was done in the President's best interest and in the best interest of the campaign.

Q. I do not suppose you listened to Mr. Dean because you were convinced he was the button pusher or the mastermind?

A. I did not understand that he was the button pusher. I think Mr. Dean was—had received the assignment to approach me, knowing whoever gave him the directions, Senator, knowing that I would trust Mr. Dean.

Q. Now, in the hierarchy of influence and authority in the committee and in the White House above Mr. Dean you will find Mr. Ehrlichman, is that not correct, sir? A. Yes, sir.

Q. And above Mr. Ehrlichman, Mr. Haldeman? A. Yes, sir.

Q. And above Mr. Haldeman?

A. Yes, sir, the President.

Q. The President. I do not suppose you considered Mr. LaRue to be the mastermind?

A. No, sir, I think Mr. LaRue again was doing what had been requested of him.

Q. I do not suppose you considered Mr. Ehrlichman to be the button pusher? A. I did not know, Senator. I just did not.

Q. What did you think when Mr. Ehrlichman told you that Mr. Dean had authority? From whom?

A. I was not certain, Senator. I did not know whether it was someone in authority at the Committee to Re-elect or someone in authority at the White House, I just did not know.

Q. Was it possible that someone in the Committee to Re-elect would have ordered Mr. Ehrlichman to do something? Was there anyone greater in influence or authority in the committee?

A. No, Senator, no one could have ordered Mr. Ehrlichman to do anything but Mr. Ehrlichman—

Q. It would have to be Ehrlichman, the button pusher, Mr. Haldeman the button pusher or someone higher than Mr. Haldeman.

A. Well, Senator, I think it could be someone in authority in the committee to re-elect, and Mr. Ehrlichman was advised of this, and Mr. Ehrlichman agreed that this was the proper thing to do. I don't know what went through his mind. I know when I spoke to Mr. Ehrlichman he told me that "it was proper and to go forward, Herb," and without more and that was good enough for me. But I do not know, Senator, I do not know whether Mr. Ehrlichman knew that it was someone in authority at the Committee to Re-elect or someone else.

Q. In listening to your testimony, would I be correct to contend that it is your suggestion to the committee that your candidate for the button pusher is Mr. Ehrlichman?

A. No, sir. I don't have a candidate for, as the button pusher. I had the feeling, and I think I have expressed, Senator, that it was someone in authority at the committee to re-elect but I don't know.

SENATOR WEICKER: Do you know Mr. James Knapp? A. Yes, sir.

Q. Do you consider him to be a confidant, a friend of yours? A. A very close friend of mine.

Q. Have you ever told Mr. Knapp anything in the way of a relationship between you and Mr. Haldeman, the fact that possibly you might be being used by Mr. Haldeman? Did you ever converse with Mr. Knapp on this subject?

A. I think I have been, in recent times, I think that I have indicated that I feel that I was used.

Q. That you were used? A. Yes, sir.

Q. Used by whom? A. Used by the people who knew the true purpose of this assignment without my knowledge.

Q. Now, I think we really have come past the point and again, I want to commend you. I do not want to give any other impression but the fact that it is obviously a difficult situation for you and I think you are honestly trying to respond to the questions of the committee. But the term "we" is wearing a little thin and I refer specifically now to the conversation that you had with Mr. Knapp. Do you feel that you have been used by Mr. Haldeman in this matter? A. Yes, sir.

Q. You do? Do you feel you have been used by Mr. Ehrlichman?

A. If they, Senator, if they had knowledge of the true, what has been alleged to be the true purpose of this and did not advise me, then I think I was used.

Q. Do you feel you have been used by Mr. Mitchell?
A. In that same context, yes, sir.
Q. Do you feel you have been used by Mr. Dean.
A. Again, the same.

Testimony by Anthony T. Ulasewicz

July 18, 1973

Gives details of intrigue and undercover techniques in channeling funds to conspirators.

MR. LENZNER: In June of 1969 did you meet Mr. Herbert Kalmbach here in the District of Columbia?

MR. ULASEWICZ: That is correct. Mr. Kalmbach advised me that he had a very important assignment, and he went at least three times over the statement saying that it was a situation that developed that he was asked to do something and needed my help in doing it. He said that it was legal, that it was to provide funds for persons in difficulty for payment of their counsels, and for payment to assist their families during some troublesome period. He repeated the statement several times. He was very ill at ease, very nervous and we got to the point where I said, "Well, Mr. Kalmbach, just what is this now" and he says, "You have probably guessed it's the Watergate situation."

And he said:

"Let me assure you I would not in any way or fashion ask anyone to do anything that I would not engage my own services in. It is an assignment for me and I am asking you to do this. It will necessitate confidential methods possibly."

Mr. Kalmbach suggested whenever he might call me in relation to this matter he would use the name Novak. He said that if another name would probably be necessary it would be Rivers.

Q. Who was supposed to use that name?
A. He anticipated that I might use that name in contact with distributing this money to the people. At a point in the conversation he said that he had the money with him, and it was $75,100 which he gave me. It was in hundred-dollar bills.
Q. What did you put it in?
A. I went to the closet of the room and took a laundry bag and put the money in a laundry bag.
Q. Where was the next place that you received money from Mr. Kalmbach?
A. At the Regency Hotel in New York City.
Q. Approximately how much?
A. $40,000.
Q. Where was the next delivery?

A. At the Hilton here in Washington, $28,900. And then my recollection is the final amount was $75,000 at the Airporter Inn in Los Angeles opposite the Orange County Airport.

Q. Did you hear from Mr. Kalmbach again? A. I did.

Q. And what instructions, if any, did he give you?

A. He told me to call a Mr. Caddy.

He instructed me to use I believe it was John Rivers when I called Mr. Caddy and I at this occasion was to say the purpose of my call to Mr. Caddy was that I was asking the cost of a script, of a play plus the salaries of the players, which I did.

I contacted Mr. Caddy, and he was—and he responded and said he would meet me in a restaurant sometime in the afternoon here in Washington, D. C.

Q. Now, did you go to that restaurant in Georgetown? A. Yes, I did.

Q. What happened there?

A. I waited for Mr. Caddy's arrival. However, a phone call came in, I was paged by the bartender, Mr. Caddy got on the phone and said that he couldn't meet me, after speaking to somebody in his office, in the attorney's office, that he could not meet me, would I be able to come and see him. I told him I would get in touch with him. My instructions originally with Mr. Kalmbach was that I enter no negotiations at any time that he would not enter negotiations. In this case I reported Mr. Caddy's message and Mr. Kalmbach said, "Well, give me the number you are at," that is at a phone booth here in Washington. "I will get back to you."

Q. You had the money with you on that date? A. Oh, yes.

Q. How did you carry it on that date?

A. I carried it in a brown bag with, you know, the ordinary type, with a little string around it. You know, sometimes carrying what is most obvious doesn't raise any suspicion, carrying an armored box would ask for trouble.

Q. You were just carrying your lunch?

A. Carrying my lunch.

Q. At some point, did Mr. Kalmbach tell you to drop the whole Caddy business? A. Yes.

Q. I take it you were having these conversations phone booth to phone booth between yourself and Mr. Kalmbach? A. That is correct.

Q. Were you loaded down with change, Mr. Ulasewicz? A. Oh, yes, indeed.

Q. How did you carry that change?

A. When I started out, I started with a kind of little box deal. When I finished up, I had a bus guy's, one of these things that the bus drivers have.

Q. After you got back to New York, did you again receive instructions from Mr. Kalmbach?

A. Yes. Just about the time it ended with Caddy, which we got nowhere, and I still had the $75,100, I was asked to call Mr. O'Brien, using the name of John Rivers.

Q. Did you call him?

A. I called Mr. O'Brien, received a very tart kind of brush-off response, and that was the end of that conversation. It was one phone call. He showed no interest in any script, players, or any type of message that I would give.

Q. You were given the same instructions by Mr. Kalmbach to talk about a script, a scenario, the players? A. Yes.

Q. Did you call Mr. Kalmbach again, telephone booth to telephone booth? A. I did.

Q. Did he come back again with other instructions?

A. He came back, gave me a telephone number this time, no name involved. And I may have called from the city of New York at that time, because running around with $75,100, trying to get rid of it was becoming a problem.

I then was instructed to call Mr. Bittman in Washington, who I understood was an attorney.

Q. What instructions did you have to talk to him?

A. The same thing, the cost of the script, the writer, get what the attorney fees—not the attorney fees at this point. The cost of the script, the players, et cetera.

Q. You were using the same name, Mr. Rivers? A. I believe so, yes.

Q. Did you call Mr. Bittman. A. I did.

Q. Did you speak to him?

A. I spoke to Mr. Bittman and I recall that in the first conversation, Mr. Bittman said, well, this is very unusual. He said something like, I do not know if you are an attorney, but an attorney does not anticipate fees and costs in this manner.

I said, well, I am instructed not to negotiate in any manner. I understood that you would have a figure and I told him that I am prepared at this time if we can get down to this, because at this point, I still wanted to get rid of all those cookies, $75,100.

Something was not according to the way he liked. I so reported to Kalmbach, received my call back from Mr. Kalmbach. He told me again to call and contact Mr. Bittman.

Now, this is some period of time passes by. Mr. Bittman said, all right, his initial fee would be $25,000.

Q. What period of time, Mr. Ulasewicz, are we talking about?

A. This would be around July 8 to the 10th, in that period of time.

Q. And did you call Mr. Kalmbach and tell him Mr. Bittman had indicated he wanted an initial fee of $25,000? A. I did.

Q. What was Mr. Kalmbach's response?

A. He said to deliver it to Mr. Bittman in any manner I saw fit.

Q. Did he give you any instructions about not being seen by Mr. Bittman?

A. Oh, yes, those came in after the Caddy call, that somehow conversations were arranged that I would not now be seen by anybody, to do the money without being observed, in a confidential manner.

Q. That was Mr. Kalmbach's instructions to you? A. Right.

Q. Now, you expressed some concern about carrying this amount of money around with you. How were you traveling during this period of time?

A. By airplane, Eastern Airlines shuttle, usually.

Q. Did you ever change your mode of travel? Did you have a problem on the plane?

A. Well, there was a period of time, of course, with the hijacks and all, they started a searching system on the airlines and that was a little problem. I got in line one time to come back; when I had the problem it would be only $50,000 at this time. A fellow in front of me, two or three persons in front of me stopped and had to produce—I think four packs of cigarettes or something, set off the alarm. So I went into a coughing fit and I went down to the Pennsylvania Railroad and took the train home.

Q. And how did you arrange to deliver that money?

A. I contacted Mr. Bittman right from the lobby of his office there. I spoke with him and I told him that I had the cash. Prior to that, I went out to a drugstore in the area, bought a couple of envelopes and some Scotch tape, and I had to count out $25 from that $75,100—$25,000 from the $75,100 original, which I did, and I put it into a plain Kraft brown envelope.

I called Mr. Bittman from the lobby of his building and told him that I had the delivery and that would he come right down and that it would be on the ledge at the telephone booth.

I told him it would be a brown sack and that the money would be lying right there, would he come right down, if he walked right through and pick it up and go back to the elevator, I would be satisfied.

Q. Did you have a conversation with Mrs. Hunt where you arranged to furnish her with some funds? A. Yes, I did.

Q. Would you just describe what you told her, how she could pick up her money?

A. I told Mrs. Hunt that at a certain time in a day, and I picked an hour, to come into the lounge for the American Airlines, there was opposite, and about 25 feet away, across from Northwest Orient Airlines, there is a series of telephone booths. I spent some time observing the telephone booths and for some reason, people didn't use the very end one.

So five minutes prior to the time I would tell her to come, I would go into this telephone booth and underneath where the coin drop is, I would Scotch tape the key to the locker where I made my drop.

Her directions were, don't hesitate, go right into the booth, remove the key, go to the locker.

Q. Now, I believe on May 19 of this year, when we went out to that phone booth with you, there was some Scotch tape underneath that telephone box? A. That is correct.

Q. Now did there come a time when you were asked to deliver money to Mr. Fred LaRue by Mr. Kalmbach? A. Yes.

Q. Was that in September of 1972? A. That is correct.

Q. And approximately how much was that?
A. $29,900.

Q. What arrangements did you make with Mr. LaRue to deliver that, those funds?

A. There is a garage opposite where Mr. LaRue lived in the Watergate.

I placed the key, I called Mr. LaRue, and asked him to come down, I had a package, he was waiting the call 6 P.M. exactly, he was awaiting the call and he says fine, he would be right down. I had never met Mr. LaRue. I asked him to put two magazines under his arm, come across the street, come into the motel entrance and the money would be on the ledge in the motel.

When he came out, it is a wide street, I watched him through the motel window here, and he had the two magazines. He stopped at the island because of the heavy traffic, when he stepped off the island he was now approaching, I laid the money on the ledge in the envelope and I proceeded through a door back to the cigarette machines and I could see him come in, pick up the money, hesitate a moment, go right out and go back, back to his apartment.

Q. Could you describe the conversations that you had with Mrs. Hunt? I take it, Mr. Ulasewicz, you had a series of phone conversations during July of 1972 with Mrs. Hunt? Can you tell the committee the substance of what those conversations concerned.

A. I would inform her that I am not to negotiate, I was simply in a position to deliver whatever was necessary. However, she injected herself continually feeling that I would pass a message on. She started with herself, the fact that she had lost her own job due to this and that should be taken into consideration, and that with that there are certain things with the job that, for instance, hospitalization, and whatever benefits might be there, that had been lost, and that she thought that perhaps $10,000 or $15,000 might.

Subsequently, she would mention that Mrs. Liddy was undergoing some psychiatric treatment or might be undergoing, and that she was a schoolteacher and that she probably would not be able to work as a result of this and that should be another amount of money.

When she spoke of costs to Mr. Hunt, her husband, Mr. McCord, Mr. Liddy, she gave figures of approximately $3,000 a month would be satisfactory, and she had hoped that that might be done in some multiples so we would not go through this thing monthly.

When she got into Barker she explained Mr. Barker had some peculiar problem in this matter, he was dealing with the people down South, there were some bail problems down South. Then she mentioned Sturgis, Gonzalez, Martinez, and when she had mentioned Barker she mentioned a sum of $10,000 for under the table.

Q. With reference to Mr. Barker she was seeking a specific sum of money?

A. She was asking a sum of money which wound up to $23,000.

Q. Did there come a time when you totaled up the amounts of money that Mrs. Hunt was seeking?

A. Well, it was, yes, it was in the vicinity of four hundred to four hundred and fifty thousand dollars.

Q. And did you have a conversation with Mr. Kalmbach concerning that figure and Mrs. Hunt's demands?

A. Yes, that was in August, and it was the last pick-up from Mr. Kalmbach, and shall I go through it?

Q. Yes.

A. When he picked me up in his car in Orange County airport and we sat in the car, and just prior to this, I had already suggested to Mr. Kalmbach that this thing has definitely gone a different direction than originally anticipated.

Mr. Kalmbach was as upset about it as I was as I related it to him. He certainly didn't like it in any fashion as no more than I did. When we met in the automobile, I got in the car and Mr. Kalmbach said, "Tony, what's your opinion of all this?" and I said, well, I am going to try to recall some exact words because the first statement I made to him, I said "Well, Mr. Kalmbach, I will tell you something here is not kosher." We are into negotiations, we started with 75 and now we are into a sum which we have raised, we have now got something like 220,000 coming in or 219 was the exact figure and we are only approaching half and I know that the next conversation I have that figure has go to up from all inferences and all."

I said, "Mr. Kalmbach, I know your feelings in the matter, I know how we started, what you said, it was legal but it was not leading up to a point and I feel I must tell you," and he understood that was my last and I recommended very strongly to Mr. Kalmbach that he likewise desist and he said that he would.

Q. Now, after that meeting in California, did you receive a call from him in September of 1972 asking you to deliver money to Mrs. Hunt and Mr. LaRue? A. Yes.

Q. Would you just tell us what he said to you about delivery and what you said to him?

A. In that call, it was a little unusual, because the inflection in his voice indicated irritation or something unusual as compared to any other time that I spoke with him. I didn't ask him why but he was very anxious that I make the deliveries on the same day.

I explained to him there is an airplane problem. I mentioned to him that the laundry was in the icebox.

Q. What was his response to that?

A. Well, kind of a long pause and I said, "Well, you know the money is in the vault in New York." I did get an early flight out and I got into Washington and I managed to make the arrangements as previously described of delivery to Mrs. Hunt in the same manner, and then to Mr. LaRue.

Q. And you delivered $53,500 to Mrs. Hunt on that date?

A. Correct, and $29,900 to Mr. LaRue.

Q. Approximately when you delivered those funds?

A. Sept. 19.

SENATOR BAKER: Did you ever work with Mr. Ehrlichman?

A. I had no assignments with Mr. Ehrlichman.

Q. Mr. Haldeman? A. No sir.

Q. Anybody else at the White House or the C.R.P.?

A. The only one in the White House who relayed or gave me an assignment was Mr. Caulfield.

Q. I have a copy of the transcript of your previous testimony, page 702, which we will supply you. It indicates that it was your thought that it was Mr. Ehrlichman who was originally responsible for your being hired?

A. Yes, he interviewed me for the position, right. Mr. Caulfield was not in a position to hire me or pay my salary. Subsequently, a meeting was arranged where I would be interviewed about the job by Mr. Ehrlichman.

Q. Did Ehrlichman describe to you the type of your problable assignments if you were in fact hired?

A. Confidential investigations that might come from time to time of any type.

Q. Surely he described to you what he meant by confidential investigations.

A. Yes sir. He mentioned that there would be some, some would be political figures of Republican or any other party, Democratic party. There would be backgrounds on persons who may be sought for positions in the Government, types of investigations that they might not want a public, say an agent or a bureau or the Secret Service or somebody of that type, because a record would be made.

Q. Was it also your impression that Mr. Ehrlichman was the one who set and directed your assignment responsibilities and that Mr. Caulfield simply carried out those instructions, or that Mr. Caulfield chose your assignments and responsibility?

A. I would say both, that Mr. Ehrlichman would give some assignments, and possibly other people in the White House, to Mr. Caulfield and probably to me.

Q. Both Ehrlichman and Caulfield gave you assignments from time to time. You are under the impression that Ehrlichman was the final authority in that respect and you went forward with those projects? A. Yes sir, except Mr. Ehrlichman never gave me an assignment personally.

SENATOR WEICKER: Now I would like to get into the general nature of the other investigations, which you conducted. Is it a fact that some of these investigations were background checks on individuals intended to develop questionable facets of the personal lives of these individuals. A. That is correct, sir.

Q. Now, when we are talking about questionable facets would this include sexual habits?

A. These were allegations and that might be included in the category, I guess.

Q. Drinking habits? A. Yes, sir.

Q. Personal social activities? A. Yes, sir.

Q. Is there any other type of activity which was investigated relative to any corporation or individual?

A. It would depend on the allegation. There wasn't a complete investigation on any one person with all those titles involved. Sometimes it was an allegation of drinking and I might just keep my investigation to that particular category.

Q. Now, can we categorize in a general way those individuals or corporations that were investigated by you? Were political opponents of the President so investigated? A. Yes, sir.

Q. Were other political figures, aside from potential political opponents of the President investigated? A. Probably, yes, sir.

Q. And were the individuals in this category, were they entirely background checks prior to employment or was it for some other reason?

A. Some would be prior to employment and some would be as a result of an allegation in a newspaper or something of that type.

Q. Did you ever file your investigations in a written form? A. No, sir.

Q. Why not?

A. When I took the assignment it was set up that I would report directly and verbally. I was to keep no files.

Q. Did you at any time, did you at any time conduct any electronic surveillance on any individual, either in the form of the bug or the tap? A. No, sir.

Q. How was it possible to get into the matters of domestic problems, drinking habits, social activity and sexual activity, just from a matter of public record?

A. If it was a drinking allegation I would then develop that lead by going into the area in the most discreet manner that I would know how. A very high percentage of these allegations were false. But I would develop my leads by interviewing bartenders, patrons—if it were a hotel, hotel employes, waiters. Those kind of people are the most talkative.

Q. What other types of individuals did you investigate?

A. They might be members, might be members of a political

family. It might be a son or nephew or something of that type, perhaps an allegation of some possible misconduct.

Q. Would it be fair to say that you dealt in dirt at the direction of the White House?

A. Allegations of it, yes sir.

Q. How would you categorize the information which you turned over to Mr. Caulfield? Was it of a national security nature? A. No sir.

Q. Domestic security nature? A. No sir.

Q. Dirt?

A. It would be of a political nature.

Q. Political dirt? A. All right, sir.

Testimony by Frederick C. LaRue

July 18   *Says he believed break-in and payments had high-level sanction.*

July 19   *Says he assumes Mitchell knew money was for cover-up.*

July 18, 1973

MR. DASH: Mr. LaRue, I understand that you do have a brief statement to make.

MR. LARUE: I learned that the Democratic National Committee headquarters had been broken into on June 17, 1972, shortly after the occurrence.

Prior to that time, I did know of the existence of a proposal to conduct political espionage by electronic surveillance. I learned of this plan at a meeting I attended in late March, 1972. At that meeting I recommended against the plan. It was not approved in my presence, and I have no personal knowledge of its approval by anyone.

I later sat in on meetings with Mr. Magruder and others at which the protective story he had evolved was discussed, and I joined in that cover-up, at least by acquiescence.

I am fully aware now that what I did then was wrong, both ethically and legally, and I have faced up to that fact and I am prepared to accept the consequences.

Q. What brought you to Key Biscayne at the end of March?

A. I accompanied the Mitchells on a vacation.

Q. Did Mr. Jeb Magruder, come down to Key Biscayne around that time? A. Yes, sir.

Q. Do you know what the purpose of Mr. Magruder's visit to Key Biscayne was about?

A. Yes, sir, I do. Mr. Magruder came down to Key Biscayne

to discuss with Mr. Mitchell several activities that needed decisions made relating to the campaign.

Q. Was any particular one of interest to you?

A. I ran across a paper which outlined a plan of electronic surveillance.

Q. Did you know it was Mr. Liddy's plan?

A. There was no reference to Mr. Liddy.

Q. Once that plan was being presented, what did Mr. Mitchell say, what did you say, what did Mr. Magruder say?

A. Mr. Magruder handed this paper to Mr. Mitchell. Mr. Mitchell read it. He asked me what I thought of it and I told him I did not think it was worth the risk.

Q. What did Mr. Mitchell say to that?

A. Mr. Mitchell to the best of my recollection, said something to the effect that, "Well, this is not something that will have to be decided at this meeting."

Q. To your recollection then, Mr. Mitchell did not reject the plan out of hand at that time? A. Not to my recollection, no sir.

Q. Now, during the time that they were in the house together and with you during the meeting, were you in the room at all times?

A. I could not state definitely that I was in the room at all times.

Q. Now, Mr. LaRue, when and where did you actually first hear about the June 17 break-in?

A. At the Beverly Hills Hotel in Los Angeles. We were having breakfast. Mr. Magruder was paged, went to the telephone. He came back to the table and he said Mr. Liddy indicated that there was a problem he wanted to discuss and Mr. Magruder, in an aside to me, said that, you know, I think maybe last night was the night they were going into the Democratic National Committee.

He called Mr. Liddy back and then came back and told me that Liddy had told him that there had been a break-in at the Democratic National Committee; I think five people had been caught inside, and that one of the people was Mr. McCord, who was our security man at the re-election committee.

Q. Now, was that relayed to Mr. Mitchell, that information?

A. Yes, I personally relayed that to Mr. Mitchell.

Q. What was Mr. Mitchell's reaction?

A. He was very surprised. I think he made the statement, "That is incredible."

Q. All right. On that [following] Monday in the evening, did you attend a meeting in Mr. Mitchell's Washington apartment at the Watergate? A. Yes, sir.

Q. Who was at this meeting?

A. Mr. Mitchell was. I was at the meeting, Mr. Mardian, Mr. Dean and Mr. Magruder.

The only specific incident that I recall was a discussion by Magruder of some sensitive files which he had, and that he was seeking advice about what to do about those files. There was a response from Mr. Mitchell that it might be good if Mr. Magruder had a fire.

Q. Do you recall in any discussion of the politically sensitive files that the information was that they involved electronic surveillance?

A. As I recall, there was a reference to files pertaining to electronic surveillance, yes sir.

Q. When did you first learn that Mr. Magruder was going to be involved and what role you were going to have with regard to his activities?

A. I received a phone call from Mr. Kalmbach to meet him at the Statler-Hilton Hotel, the latter part of June.

I met with Mr. Kalmbach. Our discussion centered on a way that contact could be made with the defendants and in which the amount of money could be discussed or be determined.

During this meeting [we] determined that we would use a code name, Mr. Rivers, for this person.

Q. Did you provide any special instructions concerning how much money was to be given to which person?

A. No sir, Mr. Dash. I would have had no way to have any knowledge of this, and I think Mr. Kalmbach has testified that I furnished this information. I think Mr. Kalmbach is just mistaken in this. I had no way to have this information. I have never discussed, never talked to any of the defendants and don't know any of them other than Liddy.

Q. Did you and Mr. Kalmbach meet again in Mr. Dean's office on Sept. 19, 1972?

A. Yes, sir. Mr. Kalmbach indicated that he wished to get out of it, his role concerning the payment to defendants, and he gave an accounting of the payments to the defendants at that time.

Q. What happened to the records of his accounting?

A. Those records were burned.

Q. Were they burned right there in the office?

A. Yes, sir, he had records, as I recall, a very small sheet of paper and they were put in an ash tray and burned.

Q. Did you then take on the responsibility of carrying out the transfer of funds for legal defense of the defendants and support of the families?

A. As the events occurred, I did.

Q. When was your last payment to Mr. Bittman, counsel for Mr. Hunt?

A. It would be in March.

Q. Of 1973? A. Yes sir.

Q. Can you tell us how much was involved in that payment?

A. $75,000. I got a phone call from Mr. Dean. Mr. Dean stated that he had a conversation with Mr. O'Brien, in which Mr. O'Brien had told him that there was a need for $75,000 asserted that by Mr. Bittman for attorneys' fees. I asked Mr. Dean if I should indeed make a delivery of this money. He said that he was out of the money business. I told Mr. Dean I would not make the delivery without somebody else's O.K. Mr. Dean suggested I call Mr. Mitchell. I asked Mr. Mitchell whether I should make this delivery or not.

Q. What did he say?

A. He asked me the purpose of it. I told him my understanding was that it was for attorneys' fees. He told me he felt I ought to pay it.

MR. THOMPSON: By the latter part of June you had in effect two stories. You had Liddy saying that Magruder had pushed him into it, and not saying anything about Mr. Mitchell, and you have Mr. Magruder saying that Mitchell approved the plan. Did you go to Mr. Mitchell with this apparent conflict?

A. No, sir, I never discussed that with Mr. Mitchell.

Q. Could you tell us why?

A. I don't know of any particular reason why. I just never discussed with Mr. Mitchell the question of whether or not he approved this plan, never discussed it with him.

SENATOR GURNEY: Let us go to these monies that were paid to Mr. Bittman, Hunt's attorney. How much did you pay to him altogether?

A. Excuse me just one second, Senator. Let me add some figures.

Q. Was it $210,000? A. $210,000 correct.

Q. That was my calculation, too. I added them rather hurriedly here. Now upon whose instructions was that money paid to Mr. Bittman?

A. Except for the last payment, Senator, of $75,000, this money, the payments of this money was discussed with Mr. Dean.

Q. And what about the last $75,000?

A. This came from Mr. Mitchell.

Q. Now, then, what was your understanding Mr. Bittman was doing with all this? Is that not a rather large sum of money to pay a lawyer who represents a client who finally pleaded guilty?

A. Senator, my understanding is that not all of this money was for his attorney's fees but represented some money that was also going to Mr. Hunt.

Q. How did you know that monies were going to Mr. Hunt?

A. In the conversations that Mr. O'Brien or Mr. Parkinson had with Mr. Bittman, I think there were indications that part of it was for attorneys' fees and part of it was necessarily necessary for maintenance of families.

July 19, 1973

SENATOR INOUYE: How did you get involved in this cover-up scheme?

A. Early 1972 I joined the re-election committee in 1972 with the title eventually of Special Assistant to the Campaign Director.

Q. You have testified on several occasions that you discussed the matter of $75,000 with Mr. Mitchell. [The $75,000 was the final bundle of bills, totaling $230,000 distributed by Mr. LaRue, of which $210,000 went to William O. Bittman.] A. That is correct.

Q. Why did you call upon Mr. Mitchell? Mr. Mitchell was no longer Attorney General of the United States nor was he chairman of the Committee to Re-elect the President.

A. Senator, I think I stated in my testimony yesterday that I had a phone call from Mr. Dean regarding this $75,000. He would not authorize or instruct me to make this payment, and he suggested that I call Mr. Mitchell.

Q. Why did Mr. Dean tell you to call Mr. Mitchell?

A. Mr. Dean indicated to me that he was not going to become involved any further in the distribution of funds, and that if I were to get any authorization on this it would have to come from someone else and he suggested that I call Mr. Mitchell.

Q. Am I correct to assume that Mr. Dean was aware that the $75,000 was part of the grand scheme, the grand cover-up scheme?

A. I think that would be a safe assumption, yes, sir.

Q. Am I correct to assume that you were aware that this was part of the grand cover-up scheme? A. Yes, sir.

Q. Am I correct to assume that Mr. Mitchell was aware that this was part of the grand cover-up scheme? A. I would say, Senator, that that is a correct assumption.

Q. Then, when Mr. Mitchell suggested to the committee that he was not aware of these cover-up activities he was not absolutely correct, was he?

A. Senator, I did not gather from Mr. Mitchell's testimony that he stated he was not aware of the cover-up activities.

SENATOR BAKER: Yesterday, you said that Mr. Magruder indicated after the telephone call [on June 18] from Washington to California, "Last night was the night he [G. Gordon Liddy] was going into the Democratic National Committee headquarters."

A. I think, Senator, that that is substantially correct. I think I said that he told me he thought last night may be the night that they were going to go into the Democratic National Committee headquarters, yes, sir.

Q. It sounds like Mr. Magruder was stating a fact that he already knew, that last night was the night that they may have been going into the Democratic National Committee headquarters. Is that your impression, Mr. LaRue? A. Yes, sir.

Q. So you are under the impression from that statement by Mr. Magruder, that he did in fact know that there was a planned entry into the Democratic National Committee headquarters the early morning hours of June 17, 1972? A. That would be my assumption, yes, sir.

Q. Did you, Mr. LaRue, know that they were going to break into the Watergate? A. No, sir, I did not.

Q. Who else was present when Magruder made that statement?

A. Well, Senator, we [Mr. Mitchell, Mr. LaRue, Herbert D. Porter and Robert C. Mardian] were at breakfast. I am sure several people were present at breakfast, but he made the statement to me in an aside, where no one else heard it.

Q. Did you convey that information to anyone else? A. No, sir, I didn't.

SENATOR WEICKER: Do you know from whom or from what office the payoff money that you distributed came from?

A. $81,000 that I received in early July [came] from Mr. Stans and Mr. Sloan, $30,000 in September from Mr. Ulasewicz, $50,000 in December from Mr. Strachan, $14,000 in January from Mr. Babcock, a former Governor of Montana.

Q. In what capacity was he [Mr. Babcock] delivering the money?

A. My understanding, Senator, is that this was a pledge made during the campaign and there was a delivery just happened to be made after the campaign. And then in January $280,000 from Mr. Strachan.

SENATOR ERVIN: The proposal of G. Gordon Liddy to commit burglary and bugging on the Democratic national headquarters was discussed by and between John Mitchell, the director of the Committee to Re-elect the President, and his deputy director, Jeb Magruder, in your presence at the meeting in Key Biscayne [on March 20, 1972]. A. This is correct.

Q. Now, you also know that John Mitchell did not disapprove of the project at that meeting, in your presence? A. That is my recollection, Senator, yes, sir.

Q. He said that that was a matter that did not have to be determined or decided at that meeting. A. That is to the best of my recollection, yes, sir.

Q. And you are not able to either affirm or disaffirm that John Mitchell subsequently by word or wink or nod conducted himself in such a way as to give Magruder the impression that Mitchell had approved it?

A. I can only state that he did not conduct himself in such a way in my presence, Senator.

Q. Now, you and Mardian and Mitchell were in Los Angeles when the news broke that the five men, including the security chief for the Committee to Re-elect the President, had been caught redhanded in the act of burglary in the Watergate, Democratic national headquarters. A. Yes, that is correct.

Q. And naturally you became concerned with the possibility that the persons charged with enforcing the criminal law might undertake to trace this money [in the pockets of four apprehended] and trace criminality from the Watergate into the Committee to Re-elect the President? A. Yes, sir, that is correct.

Q. And after you and Mr. Mitchell and Mr. Mardian and Mr.

Magruder had returned to Washington you all had—and Mr. Dean —had almost daily conversations among yourselves with respect to the dilemma which had been posed by this tragic event? A. That is correct, Senator.

Q. And you all were concerned with the re-election of President Nixon, and you felt, and so agreed among yourselves that it would be—it might have tragic repercussions if the responsibility for this burglary was traced by the press or prosecuting attorneys into the Committee to Re-elect the President?

A. Senator, I can't recall any meetings or discussions with these individuals in which that was discussed. I can only say that certainly I had this concern, and this is what motivated my actions.

Q. Well, don't you know from your conversations with Mr. Mitchell, Mr. Mardian, Mr. Dean and Mr. Magruder that they also shared that concern?

A. I would assume they did, sir.

Q. Yes, and so it was either expressly or implicitly agreed among you all, that is Mr. Mitchell, Mr. Mardian, Mr. Magruder, Mr. Dean and yourself, that you would do everything in your power to keep any information about any connection between the burglary and the Committee to Re-elect the President a secret.

A. Senator, that, as I say, is what motivated my actions and that certainly was my impression of what I was doing. As far as the other individuals, I just can't speak for them.

Q. Well, you had conversations with them, you say, about this matter almost daily. I am just asking you if you do not know, if you do not infer in your own mind and know in your own mind from conversations with the others whom I have mentioned that they shared your desire to keep from the public and keep from the press and keep from prosecuting attorneys knowledge of the events that had happened in connection with this matter in the Committee to Re-elect the President?

A. That would be my inference, Senator, yes, sir.

Q. Now, did you not apprehend that there was danger that some of the five burglars and that there was danger that Mr. Liddy and Mr. Hunt after they were arrested, might, in the common parlance, spill the beans about this matter? A. Yes, sir.

Q. And so, thereupon, you joined other persons connected with the Committee to Re-elect the President in an effort to finance these people pending their trials and finance legal defense?

A. Senator, yes, I engaged in such activity as I have testified here previously.

Q. And you know that some $400,000 was furnished directly or indirectly at the instance of members of the Committee to Re-elect the President, if not at the instance of aides in the White House, to the families and counsel for these seven Watergate defendants? A. That is correct, Senator, yes.

Q. And how much of this money did you yourself pay or deliver to any of these defendants or their counsel?

A. I come up with a figure of $242,000.

Q. Now, was that additional to money that was delivered to them through the arrangements with Kalmbach and Ulasewicz? A. Yes, sir.

Q. And as a result of this we had a situation which arose which is calculated as to pollute justice, that is, we had the prosecution of these seven men [which] was in the hands of men who held offices at the pleasure of the President, and the Committee to Re-elect the President was furnishing the money to pay the lawyers who were supposed to defend these men, is that not true? A. Yes, sir, that is true.

Q. And that kind of situation is enough to make justice weep, is it not?

A. I agree with that, Senator.

Q. I can't resist the temptation to philosophize just a little bit about the Watergate.

The evidence thus far introduced or presented before this committee tends to show that men upon whom fortune had smiled benevolently and who possessed great financial power, great political power and great governmental power undertook to nullify the laws of man and the laws of God for the purpose of gaining what history will call a very temporary political advantage.

The evidence also indicates that it might possibly, the efforts to nullify the laws of man might have succeeded if it had not been for a courageous Federal judge. Judge Sirica, and a very untiring set of investigative reporters. But I come from a state like the state of Mississippi [Mr. LaRue's home state], where they have great faith in the fact that the laws of God are embodied in the King James Version of the Bible, and I think that those who participated in this effort to nullify the laws of man and the laws of God overlooked one of the laws of God which is set forth in the seventh verse of the sixth chapter of Galatians: "Be not deceived. God is not mocked; for whatsoever a man soweth, that shall he also reap."

Testimony by Robert C. Mardian

July 19 *Says Liddy gave impression that Nixon had authorized burglary of Ellsberg's psychiatrist's office.*

July 20 *Says Nixon told him to transfer logs of telephone taps from F.B.I. to White House, and that Nixon probably feared misuse of records by J. Edgar Hoover.*

July 19, 1973

MR. HAMILTON: Mr. Mardian, did you, prior to June 17, 1972, have knowledge of any covert intelligence plans or operations that had as their purpose the gathering of information for political purposes?

MR. MARDIAN: None whatsoever, and I have been involved in numerous campaigns and it's the first time I have ever heard of this type of activity in a campaign. It may have gone on but I never was aware of it.

Q. When did you first learn of the break-in at the Democratic headquarters?

A. On the morning of June 17. I was at the Airporter Hotel in Englewood, Calif. We were on the way to the hotel, from one hotel to the other, we were following a limousine in which Mr. Mitchell and Governor Reagan were riding and present with me were the National Committeeman from California, Mr. Magruder and Mr. LaRue, and Mr. Magruder told me in the car on the way to the Airporter that he had a slight problem he wished to discuss with me.

At the hotel he told me that he had this call from Mr. Liddy and he had been informed that Mr. McCord, who was the security officer for the committee, along with five Cuban Americans, maybe four, I am not sure, had been arrested in a break-in of the Democratic National Committee headquarters.

He told me that the people arrested all, all had fake ID cards, which Mr. Hunt had procured for them from the C.I.A., and that although they were incarcerated the identities of the accused were not known.

He told me that, I guess in response to my question of how and why, he told me that Mr. Liddy was some kind of nut, he should have suspected that something like this would happen. He regretted that he had not insisted on firing him when he attempted to some weeks or months before.

He also told me, I believe, that this was not the first break-in of the Democratic national headquarters.

Q. Now, did there come a time later that afternoon when you had a further discussion on the events surrounding the break-in with Mr. Mitchell and Magruder and LaRue? Was there a discussion that afternoon about a budget that had been approved for dirty tricks and black advance. A. Yes.

Q. Did Mr. Magruder inform you who had approved the budget for dirty tricks and black advance? A. Yes.

Q. Whom did he say?

A. He told me that the budget had been approved by Mr. Mitchell.

Q. Did Mr. Mitchell later that afternoon confirm that he had approved such a budget?

A. I would like to put it this way: It is my best recollection that I think the subject was discussed and he didn't deny it. And again, it may have come up when Mr. Mitchell wasn't in the room. I want to be fair on that point.

Q. Mr. Mardian, when we broke for lunch we were discussing the meeting in Mr. Mitchell's apartment on the evening of June 19 [present also were Magruder, LaRue and Dean]. Now, at this meeting was there any discussion as to burning or otherwise destroying a Gemstone file or any other sensitive file?

A. Not in my presence. I never heard the word Gemstone until this investigation this year came out.

Q. Mr. Mardian, I would like to read portions of Mr. Magruder's testimony to you and Mr. LaRue's testimony to you of yesterday, and receive your comments. First from Mr. Magruder's testimony at page 1913 and 1914:

"Mr. Dash: Did you have a meeting on that evening, the evening of June 19, when you came back to Washington in Mr. Mitchell's apartment?

"Mr. Magruder: Yes. Mr. Mitchell flew back that Monday with Mr. LaRue and Mr. Mardian. We met in his apartment with Mr. Dean, Mr. Mardian and myself and the general discussion again was what we were going to do about the problem. It was again we had very little information. We did not, of course, know what type of investigation would then be had and we talked about times of alternative solutions. One solution was recommended in which I was to, of course, destroy the Gemstone file so I called my office and—

"Mr. Dash: That solution came up as a result of the meeting?"

"Mr. Magruder: Well, I think, yes. It was generally concluded that that file should be immediately destroyed."

Now reading from Mr. LaRue's testimony of yesterday at pages 4589 and 4590:

"Mr. Dash: You said Mr. Magruder asked what he should do about these sensitive files?

"Mr. LaRue: Yes sir.

"Mr. Dash: Did he get a response to that?

"Mr. LaRue: As I remember, there was a response from Mr. Mitchell that it might be a good idea if Mr. Magruder had a fire."

Now, previous to that testimony, Mr. LaRue had testified that you were at that meeting. Do these portions that I have read of the testimony refresh your recollection as to what was discussed?

A. I heard the testimony and I just read Mr. Dean's testimony —or Mr. Magruder's testimony, I am sorry. No such discussion took place in my presence.

Q. Mr. Mardian, did you in the several days following June 19 have an occasion to interview Mr. Liddy? A. Yes.

Q. And who else was present in this interview?

A. Mr. Fred LaRue. Mr. Liddy was reluctant to come to my office. He wanted to meet some place else, and we met in Mr. LaRue's apartment.

Q. Mr. Mardian, tell us what information Mr. Liddy imparted to you.

A. Mr. Liddy came into the room. The first thing he asked Mr. LaRue was whether or not he had a radio. Mr. LaRue indicated a radio which was in the corner of the living room. Mr. Liddy went over and turned the radio on and asked me to sit by the radio in a chair, and he sat in a couch, as I recall, that was next to an end table that the radio was on.

He apologized to me by saying something to the effect that it is not that I do not trust you, but his conversation cannot be recorded. My inference from that was he thought I had some kind of a device on me, possibly something in the room, I do not know.

He said that he wanted to hire me as his lawyer, as his personal attorney. I told him that I was acting as attorney for the committee and that I could not relieve myself of that responsibility to represent him. He then said it was imperative that he be able to talk to me in confidence and that under no circumstances could I disclose what he told me.

One of the things that he told me was that he had a message from Mr. Hunt, that Mr. Hunt felt that it was the committee's obligation to provide bail money to get his men out of jail.

About the arrest of the five people, Mr. McCord and the others, their plight, he indicated to me that there was nothing to fear, because the only person that could identify Mr. Liddy was Mr. McCord and Mr. McCord would not divulge his identity, that the Cuban-Americans were old soldiers who had worked in the C.I.A. with Mr. Hunt since the Bay of Pigs, and that they would never under any circumstances disclose Mr. Hunt's identity, and that the committee had nothing to fear in that regard.

I tried to convince him he would be identified, that his best bet was to give himself up rather than try to wait for them to arrest him.

He discounted this completely by saying that this group had been operating together for some considerable period of time, that they were all real pros, that they had engaged in numerous jobs. And when I asked him what kind of jobs, he said, we pulled two right under your nose.

I inquired as to what he meant by that, and he said that they had invaded the office of the psychiatrist of Dr. Ellsberg and that they were the ones who got Dita Beard out of town.

I expressed my strong displeasure with respect to—I pointed out that the worst thing that had happened in the hearings was that Dita Beard disappeared.

I asked him because of the Ellsberg break-in what, if anything, they had obtained? He told me that they had obtained nothing, that they had searched all the files and couldn't find his record.

I asked him on whose authority he was operating, and I wish to be very careful here, because I don't know that he used the name of the President, but the words he did use were clearly meant to imply that he was acting on the express authority of the President of the United States, with the assistance of the Central Intelligence Agency.

Q. Did Mr. Liddy also say to you that the operations that he had been involved in such as the Ellsberg burglary and the Dita Beard incident had the approval of the President and the C.I.A.? Is that a correct paraphrase, and if not, please correct me.

A. As I told you before, the staff, I don't recall, I can't say that he said the President of the United States, but the words he used or the word he used were meant to imply that, and that is the impression he left with me.

Q. Now, did Mr. Liddy mention to you that he had shredded any documents?

A. Yes. In trying to demonstrate to me that there was no way of tracing him he told me he had shredded every bit of evidence that would have linked him to this operation as well as all the other operations. He told me he had even gone home—he has a habit, he told me, or a hobby, I should say, of collecting soap from the various hotels—he had taken the soap wrappers off and shredded all the soap wrappers.

He also told me that during this process he had shredded all of the $100 bills that he had in his possession that were new and serialized.

He did make the statement that the committee could be assured that he would never talk and if they doubted that, as Mr. LaRue testified, if we would tell him what corner to stand on he was ready to be assassinated.

I told Mr. Liddy that I did not think Mr. Mitchell would approve the use of committee funds to bail out the defendants and he should so advise Mr. Hunt, and that it seemed to me that if Mr. Hunt had such good connections in the Miami [Cuban] community that they should look to that community for the bail money.

Q. When you spoke to Mr. Mitchell did you transmit this request for bail money to Mr. Mitchell?

A. Mr. Mitchell told me that under no circumstances would bail money be forthcoming and for me to call Mr. Liddy and tell him. And I did so.

Q. Mr. Mardian, I would like to read you a portion of Mr. Dean's testimony and ask you to comment on this, please. Mr. Dean was responding to a statement found in what has been, what is now known as the Buzhardt memo which reads like this:

"It was Dean who suggested to General Walters on January 6 [1973], that C.I.A. pay the Watergate defendants while in jail," and Mr. Dean in commenting on this particular passage said this:

"I believe I have explained that, Senator, in that I reported also at one point in time to Mr. Mitchell and Mr. Mardian about the Gray theory. That theory [that the C.I.A. was involved in Watergate] prompted Mr. Mardian, as I recall, to suggest that the C.I.A. might be of some assistance in providing us support, and he also raised the question that the C.I.A. might have a very proper reason to do so because of the fact that these were former C.I.A. operatives."

Mr. Mardian, do you remember a conversation of this sort?

A. I do not recall that conversation. I do recall a discussion and there may have been discussions concerning C.I.A. involvement, and I can tell you that whatever point in time that was that it was my opinion that the C.I.A. was involved for a number of reasons, and I do not recall any money demand as such, but the only ones I recall are bail, bail the defendants out, and I may have said, "C.I.A. ought to take care of its own people," or it is "a C.I.A. problem and not a committee problem." That is, would be, my best recollection.

July 20, 1973

SENATOR TALMADGE: Did you ask Mr. LaRue if he had known about the break-in ahead of time?

A. I cannot recall any specific time I said, Fred, did you know about it ahead of time, until after these hearings started. He called me and told me that he was going to the U.S. attorney's office and I asked him on that occasion, Fred, did you know about it ahead of time? And he said, yes.

Pardon me. The question that I asked him was not specifically about the break-in itself. Did he know about the activities? And he said, yes.

Q. Did you ask him if John knew?

A. My next question, as I recall it at that time, was did John know about it ahead of time? He said, yes.

Q. And you were referring to John Mitchell?

A. Yes. I then said what does John say? He says John says no. Now, subsequently, after my appearance before, I believe, the grand jury, I talked to Fred. He called me and asked me about what had transpired with reference to him. I related what I just told you; and Fred said, My God, you did not say that, did you? I said yes. And he said, Bob, I do not think I said that.

Now, I could be mistaken, but I am giving you my best recollection, and disclosing everything I knew, I felt that my oath as an attorney prevented me from doing that.

Q. Now, I believe you and Mr. Magruder and Mr. Mitchell were all together and there was something said about $40,000.

A. The date, I believe, was the 23d or [2]4th. I asked Mr. Magruder in the presence of Mr. Mitchell how much money he had given to Mr. Liddy. He said he had given Mr. Liddy $40,000. I must have registered surprise and said, $40,000? And Mr. Mitchell did much the same. And he turned to Mr. Mitchell and he said, well, that is not much out of the total budget of $250,000.

Mr. Mitchell's answer was, but the campaign has not even started yet.

Q. You understood that declaration on the part of Mr. Mitchell to mean that he had approved the $250,000 operation, these espionage activities?

A. Based on the conversation I heard, I would assume that Mr. Mitchell, not having denied that statement, acquiesced in it. His response was not I did not authorize 250, his response was, the campaign has not started yet.

SENATOR WEICKER: Now, as I recall, you talked to Mr. MacGregor at the Miami convention?

A. Yes, sir. I suggested to him that there was a serious exposure with respect to certain employees of the committee, he should be made aware of it, and hopefully, to prevent him from making further statements that might put him in a bad light subsequently.

Q. And he turned you down?

A. He told me—he was in a hurry; he wanted to leave before I got in the room—that he had been assured before he took the job that no one employed in the committee at that time had been involved, he accepted that, and he didn't want to hear any more about it, or words to that effect.

Q. You were indicating to him that such assurances just weren't fact? A. Yes, sir.

Q. At any subsequent time, did you try to make contact with Mr. MacGregor?

A. Sir, I tried on numerous occasions prior to that time, and I think that was the last attempt.

Q. As I understand it you were contacted by Mr. William Sullivan, on the matter that he had these tapes [of wiretaps ordered on National Security staff] and he wanted to hand them over to somebody?

A. He told me that [the tapes] were not in the ordinary channels of the bureau, they were in his office safe, that his opinion was that he was going to be terminated pretty soon. He was concerned about what would happen to them if they fell into the possession of his successor.

Q. Upon his initial communication with you, did you then go to the Attorney General? A. Yes.

Q. Why do you think Mr. Sullivan came to you? Do you feel it was because of his dislike of the Director that he didn't turn to his immediate superior, the Director of the F.B.I.?

A. Based upon what he told me, he was concerned about the motives of the Director.

Q. And what were those motives as he described them to you?

A. My best recollection is that he thought that the Director might use these logs to maintain his position as director.

Q. In your meeting at San Clemente you met with the President on this matter specifically? A. Yes, sir.

Q. What did the President order done?

A. He instructed me to obtain the materials from Mr. Sullivan, deliver them to Mr. Ehrlichman.

Q. What you are telling this committee is you returned to Mr. Sullivan and ordered him to turn over those materials in his possession relative to the Kissinger tapes?

A. I didn't order him. I told him what my instructions were and he—

Q. On the authority of the President, is that correct?

A. I told him that is where my instructions came from. I may have said the Attorney General, I am not sure.

Q. Obviously this was a matter of some urgency if in fact you had been put aboard a courier plane to fly out to California and given orders personally by the President. This is not something that is just left hanging. It was obviously a matter of considerable urgency to the President, wasn't it?

A. I did not obtain any expressions of urgency. The only urgency was on the part of Mr. Sullivan.

Q. Did you think it rather strange that he should go the route of you to Mr. Ehrlichman rather than to have these materials handed over to the Director of the F.B.I.?

A. The purpose was to take them out of the custody of his office because of the concern he expressed with respect to the Director of the F.B.I.

Testimony by Gordon C. Strachan

July 20   *Says Haldeman knew about political intelligence gathering system two months before Watergate break-in.*

July 23   *Says he is sure Haldeman wanted files on Liddy's intelligence operation destroyed.*

July 20, 1973

MR. STRACHAN: Turning to my duties and reporting activities with the Committee to Re-elect the President, I found myself in an unusual and not entirely comfortable situation. I was the White House conduit for reporting the activities of 1701 [the Committee to Re-elect the President], including the activities of Mr. Magruder—the man who shortly before had been my boss at the White House.

Mr. Magruder's reporting practices were marked by two features. First, he considered it a burden to report through me. My role—as Mr. Haldeman intended it—was somewhat of a constraint upon Mr. Magruder's ability to have free rein at the committee, independent of the scrutiny of the White House. As a result, Mr. Magruder frequently tried to avoid the reporting system. When Mr. Magruder did report, he reported as much as possible on successful developments that reflected favorably on his campaign leadership and as little as possible on projects that were not going well.

On projects that went smoothly or portrayed him in a good light, Mr. Magruder would often give a full report directly to Mr. Higby or Mr. Haldeman. On ineffective or failing projects he would seldom do more than make brief mention to me on the general subject matter—just enough to protect himself from later criticism that he had withheld information from the White House in case the project went totally sour.

Second, he considered it a serious impairment of his status to report to me rather than to someone more senior, especially since he had previously been my boss at the White House. He asked that I deal with Mr. Reisner, his administrative assistant, whose position on Mr. Magruder's staff corresponded more to my position on Mr. Haldeman's staff. I did increase my contacts with Mr. Reisner and other campaign aides, but continued to insist on dealing directly with Mr. Magruder on many projects.

With respect to the particular subject of political intelligence, Mr. Magruder has testified in very general, carefully hedged and characteristically vague terms that he assumes he either automatically sent me materials about or called me and gave me a general description of intelligence plans. Had anyone ever heard the details of prostitution, goon squads, kidnapping and wiretaps, he would be unlikely to forget it. I certainly would not forget it. Mr. Magruder never gave me that information and certainly not those details, because if he had, I would immediately have passed it on to Mr. Haldeman, I would remember it and I would be here today testifying about it.

By any standard the meeting at which the Liddy plans were presented were classic examples of poor staff work by the committee and a waste of time. The testimony has been virtually unanimous that Mr. Mitchell and Mr. Dean were shocked by Liddy's plan; Mr. Magruder's staff man, Gordon Liddy, was apparently quite humiliated; and nothing was approved. In other words, if those meetings were routinely reported to Mr. Haldeman, as evidence of Mr. Magruder's administrative ability and judgment, the meetings would not very likely inspire the confidence of Mr. Haldeman or the President.

Yet Mr. Magruder testified that "as he recalled" he returned to his office after both these embarrassing meetings and routinely called Mr. Haldeman's staff assistant, me, and told me about his blunder, presumably so that I could inform Mr. Haldeman. That testimony is difficult to reconcile with good sense. Presumably, Mr. Magruder knew that Mr. Dean would report on the meetings to Mr. Haldeman—as Mr. Dean has testified he did—why would Mr. Magruder want two people reporting the same disaster to Mr. Haldeman?

It is true, however, that Mr. Magruder called me after he returned from the March 30, 1972, meeting at Key Biscayne with Mr. Mitchell and Mr. LaRue and reported on about 30 major campaign decisions. Each of these decisions was briefly described in that rather short phone conversation. During this call, he told me, and I am repeating his words rather precisely: "A sophisticated political intelligence gathering system has been approved with a budget of 300." Unfortunately, he neither gave me, nor did I ask for any further details about the subject.

Soon, thereafter, I wrote one of my regular "political matters" memos for Mr. Haldeman. This particular memo for early April was 8 to 10 pages long with more than a dozen tabs or attachments, but it contained only one three-line paragraph on political intelligence. That paragraph read almost verbatim as Mr. Magruder reports that 1701 now has a sophisticated political intelligence gathering system with a budget of 300. A sample of the type of information they are developing is attached at tab "H."

At tab "H," I enclosed a political intelligence report which had been sent to me from the committee. It was entitled Sedan Chair II. This report and two others somewhat like it that I had received began with a statement such as "a confidential source reveals" or "a reliable source confidentially reports." This was followed by a summary of some political information.

In April, 1972, I was mainly interested in reporting to Mr. Haldeman on those 30 campaign decisions and other relevant political items. I did not give much thought to what Mr. Magruder meant by "sophisticated political intelligence gathering system." Nor did I give much thought to the real identity of Sedan Chair II, but I remember that the information dealt with Senator Humphrey's Pennsylvania organization.

However, on June 17, 1972, and afterward, as the news began unfolding about the break-in at the Democratic National Committee, I certainly began to wonder who else but people from 1701 could have been involved. I suspected that maybe the Watergate break-in was part of the "sophisticated political intelligence operation" Mr. Magruder had mentioned to me on the phone in early April.

And worse, I feared that Sedan Chair II's so-called confidential source might really have been a wiretap, or might in some way have been connected with the Watergate break-in. I immediately tried to call Mr. Magruder. I was not able to reach him until around noon on Sunday, when I again called him in California.

When I finally reached him and began to ask him what he knew about the Watergate break-in, he cut me off and said that he had been on the phone with Mr. Haldeman that morning and the matter was being taken care of.

I doubted that Mr. Magruder had actually spoken with Mr. Haldeman so I called Mr. Higby who clears most calls to Mr. Haldeman. Mr. Higby told me that Mr. Magruder had talked to Mr. Haldeman and that Mr. Ehrlichman was handling the entire matter.

I met with Mr. Haldeman on June 19 or 20 and showed him the April political matters memo that mentioned the intelligence gathering system. After speaking to him, I destroyed that memo and Sedan Chair II, as well as several other documents I have told this committee and the prosecutors about. I also told Mr. Dean that I had destroyed a political matters memo to Mr. Haldeman showing a $300,000 intelligence budget at the committee and three confidential source memos which I said could possibly have been wiretap reports with the sources carefully camouflaged. I did not tell Mr. Dean that I had, in fact, destroyed wiretap logs, because I was not then sure what they were, I only had suspicions.

I also told the prosecutors in April of this year what specific items I destroyed, and I told them I still suspected Sedan Chair II might have been a wiretap summary. It was not until Mr. Reisner and Mr. Porter testified before this committee in June that I learned Sedan Chair II was not an illegal wiretap, but was instead an informer planted in the Humphrey camp.

In fact, you will recall that Mr. Magruder's testimony has established that I never received his wiretap data, nor could I have passed it on to others or shredded a wiretap transcript. He says he made only one copy of the Watergate wiretap log, testified that it was so sensitive that he would not let it out of his office.

Turning to matters after the election, I have told the committee that I returned approximately $350,000 in cash to Fred LaRue. I was not told by anyone, nor did I know what use was being made of this money. I had received the money from the campaign committee on Mr. Haldeman's instructions and, at that time, returning it to Mr. LaRue seemed appropriate since he was the top official left at the committee. I took it to him in December, 1972, or January, 1973, after I had left the White House staff. This money was the fund I had picked up in April, 1972, for the purpose of conducting White House polling. It had not been used to pay polling expenses as originally planned and after the election I had been asking Mr. Haldeman, Mr. Dean and Mr. Higby what to do with the money.

The delivery to Mr. LaRue was made in two parts, on two occasions, in December or January, after talking to Mr. Dean, I took approximately $40,000 in two envelopes to Mr. LaRue at his apartment at the Watergate. I lived two blocks away and the delivery was made on my way home from work.

Later, I was asked to return the remainder of the money. I again called Mr. LaRue, who again asked if I could deliver it to his apartment. On this occasion, before picking up the money, Mr. LaRue donned a pair of gloves and then said, "I never saw you." I had been instructed by Mr. Dean to ask for a receipt, so I did, but Mr. LaRue refused, saying you will have to talk to John Dean about it.

At that point I became more than a little suspicious. Frankly, after Mr. LaRue put on the gloves, I did not know what to say —so I said nothing. Nor did I know what to do—so I left. The next day I told Mr. Dean that Mr. LaRue would not give me a receipt for the money. Mr. Dean said he would speak to Mr. LaRue about it. I don't know if he ever got the receipt, but I imagine he tried to follow up on it because I have since learned from Mr. Dean's testimony that it was Mr. Haldeman who asked that a receipt be given.

At no time did Mr. Dean or Mr. LaRue advise me what was being done with the money or that payments were being made to the defendants. Neither of them ever asked me to do or say anything that I can interpret as being part of a cover-up.

In fact, there was only one occasion when I was expressly asked to do something that I knew was improper and which I could see was aimed at a cover-up. That related to my upcoming grand jury testimony of April 11, 1973, and I refused to do it.

July 23, 1973

MR. DASH: What was Mr. Haldeman's role with regard to the campaign itself?

A. Well, Mr. Haldeman was obviously quite interested in the

campaign. He would express his views as to the way certain things would be done. In particular, he insisted upon clearing, that is personally approving by initial every piece of advertising, be it radio, TV, bumper strip, whatever that went out from the committee.

Q. And would it be fair to say that on many important issues the committee that these issues would be communicated to Mr. Haldeman for his approval, actions of the committee?

A. No, not all matters would be communicated for action. He had very little interest, for example, in what the field organization would be doing. I would advise him on an FYI [For Your Information] basis of who had been selected to head the campaigns in the various states but he showed very little interest in that.

Q. When you made your reports to Mr. Haldeman, especially those reports that came from the committee, could you briefly tell us but in some detail what kind of reports did you make, how did you report to Mr. Haldeman?

A. Well, usually once a week or once every two weeks, memoranda entitled, "political matters memos."

These memoranda would summarize the information that I had accumulated from the politically active people on the White House staff, Mr. Colson, Mr. Dent, information I had accumulated from 1701 [Pennsylvania Avenue, C.R.P. headquarters] from the various state organizations, he had quite an interest.

He had quite an interest in California so I would talk with the California people, and then I would write a memorandum usually quite long, 8, 9, 10 pages, with several attachments as back-up. The main purpose of attaching the tabs would be that I would refer in the paragraphs to information that I thought he should read in the original form, and would attach it as a tab.

Q. All right, now, when he received from you a political matter memorandum with the various items indicated, and the tabs, how would he respond to you concerning those items that were brought to his attention by you?

A. Well, he would always read with a pen and he would write his comments beside them or check the item as he read each particular paragraph.

Q. In instances, I take it, you would be given or at least indications from him as to what he wanted to do to follow up on various matters?

A. Well, usually, his comments on the side would be cryptic and humorous. If he had a disagreement as to the way things were being done at the committee, he would send a memorandum to John Mitchell or on occasion to Jeb Magruder, or make a note to me that I should contact a particular individual about something.

Q. Now, when he wanted to have a meeting with somebody, would you prepare any particular paper with regard to that meeting?

A. Yes. I would prepare what would be characterized as a talking paper.

Q. Now, do you recall whether Mr. Magruder gave you any information concerning an intelligence plan prior to March 30, 1972? A. No, he did not.

Q. Mr. Magruder did testify that certainly after the Feb. 4, 1972, meeting, he communicated to you about the meeting, about the contents of the meeting, and in fact, sent you copies of the notes or memoranda of the so-called Liddy plan that had been presented to Mr. Mitchell in Mr. Mitchell's office where Mr. Dean, Mr. Magruder, Mr. Liddy met with Mr. Mitchell. Did Mr. Magruder do that?

A. No, he did not. Mr. Magruder relies on the fact that, automatically, materials would have come over to me. The Federal Bureau of Investigation has established that that is not true. Materials do not automatically come over to me.

Q. How did the Federal Bureau of Investigation establish that that is not true?

A. They interviewed several of his secretaries and people in his office and they indicated that matters were not always sent to Mr. Strachan or to the White House, that they would be held back at the express direction of Mr. Magruder.

Q. Would it be true that important matters, matters of significance, would be sent over to you, and would you not agree that a plan such as the so-called Liddy plan to engage in electronic surveillance for political intelligence was a significant matter?

A. Obviously, that is a significant matter, but I think Mr. Magruder probably relied upon the fact that John Dean was present at the meeting to report to the appropriate people at the White House.

Q. Could you tell us at this point about that separate relationship? What was Mr. Dean's relationship with Mr. Haldeman as apart from your relationship?

A. Well, Mr. Dean had line responsibility as distinguished from mine of staff responsibility. He would have a certain amount of independent authority and would function on projects of his own and report to Mr. Haldeman and Mr. Ehrlichman on matters on which he needed guidance.

Q. All right, now. If Mr. Dean attended an important meeting as the one we have already had ample testimony about, the Feb. 4 meeting in Mr. Mitchell's office, the Jan. 27 meeting in the first instance and the Feb. 4 meeting, 1972, in the second instance, would it be likely or actually, would you expect that Mr. Dean would, in fact, report that meeting to Mr. Haldeman?

A. Yes, I would think so, because Mr. Dean was aware of the interest over the six months previous, interest in political intelligence, and Mr. Dean has testified he reported to Mr. Haldeman about that meeting.

Q. Well, what was Mr. Haldeman's interest in political intelligence in the past?

A. Well, it was a subject that I was expected to raise in talking papers and to periodically follow up with John Dean to see that certain individual projects were on track.

Q. Were you aware of a particular interest Mr. Haldeman had in political matters, intelligence matters?

A. Well, he was particularly interested in the area of political intelligence and information about Senator Kennedy.

Q. Now, you say that Mr. Dean would, to your expectation, report this meeting—in fact, did report this meeting. Could you give us a little more description, to your knowledge, of Mr. Dean's relationship to you and to other members of the staff? How did he carry out his responsibilities in making reports and giving factual information to various members of the White House?

A. Well, as I say, he had line responsibility, a certain number of staff people under him. He handled conflict of interest matters, would usually have an opinion as to what stand the President should take on legislation, and so forth. My role on Mr. Haldeman's personal staff was to follow up with John Dean on certain matters that he was working with for him. The best example is when John Dean was working on the President's estate plan. He would prepare memoranda addressed to Mr. Haldeman and to Mr. Ehrlichman, and I would have a chance to look over those memoranda, but they would go in their original state.

Q. But would Mr. Dean share generally with you the information that he would give to other members of the White House staff, Mr. Haldeman or Mr. Ehrlichman or others?

A. No, not necessarily. Mr. Dean had a remarkable facility, almost that of a litigator, to remember facts and to keep track of which facts which staff members knew or should be informed about.

Q. Would you say that, over what period of time that you experienced this remarkable quality of Mr. Dean to recollect and also to separate out who was to receive what facts?

A. Well, I observed that the whole time I was on the White House staff. Whatever the particular subject would be on the President's estate plan, he could keep track of who was handling which tax returns, which people should have access to which parts of which tax returns, very tough questions of fact and internal politics. But most particularly, during the summer of 1972, for example, when he interviewed me regarding Segretti, he had interviewed both me and Chapin, both of us knew something about the subject, yet John Dean was able to keep which of us knew what perfectly straight.

Q. Well, you also said that you believe he probably told Mr. Haldeman (about the Jan. 27 and Feb. 4 meetings) because he has testified that he told Mr. Haldeman. Is that based on your opinion or knowledge of Mr. Dean when he makes a statement, whether that is a true statement?

A. Well, I have confidence in John Dean's ability to state the facts as he recalls them.

Q. And your knowledge of John Dean's relationship with Mr. Haldeman would lead you to what conclusion concerning his giving Mr. Haldeman all the facts that he had at any one time that he felt Mr. Haldeman ought to have?

A. My opinion would be that John Dean would disclose the facts to Mr. Haldeman.

Q. Now, you are also familiar with Mr. Magruder's testimony that after the Feb. 4 meeting and when there was an installation of wiretap equipment in the Watergate or Democratic National Committee headquarters, that he showed you at a particular time the so-called Gemstone material. Did he in fact show you such Gemstone material? A. No, he did not.

Q. Now, did you ever hear, prior to June 17, the term, the code term "Gemstone?" A. No, I did not.

Q. Why would Mr. Magruder keep from you this very sensitive material? I think his testimony here was that he thought it was so sensitive that he did not, as he would usually, send you the materials, he asked you to come over to the office to see them. Would it not be natural that Mr. Magruder would ask you to come see these materials?

A. Well, his testimony that it was too sensitive to send over is inconsistent with his testimony that he sent automatically the budgets [for intelligence activities] over to me. If the budgets contain bugging and wiretapping, that would strike me as far more sensitive a matter to send through normal messenger channels than some file which other witnesses have indicated was not patently illegal on its face.

Q. In other words, what you are saying is that you never did see the Gemstone file, Mr. Magruder never invited you over to see it, and that prior to March 30, you had no knowledge of any so-called Liddy intelligence plan? A. That is correct.

Q. Now, did that change, at least after March 30?

A. Yes, I was aware that Mr. Magruder would be going down to Key Biscayne to review several campaign decisions that had accumulated during John Mitchell's working on the I.T.T. problem. He called me up in an apparently fairly brief telephone conversation and reviewed the 30 or so pending campaign decisions. I took notes on that telephone conversation and prepared shortly thereafter a political matters memorandum for Mr. Haldeman, summarizing that telephone conversation as well as other information.

Q. And what did that include? I mean did it include a Liddy intelligence plan?

A. Yes, Mr. Magruder told that a sophisticated political intelligence gathering system had been approved and I reported that to Mr. Haldeman.

Q. Were you aware that that was one of these items for decision that went down to Key Biscayne with Mr. Magruder? A. No, I was not.

Q. So that it was after he came back that he reported that to you? A. That is correct.

Q. Can you recall approximately when he made that report to you?

A. Well, it was shortly thereafter. I would guess either Friday,

March 31, maybe Saturday. My secretary recalls having typed the memorandum on Friday.

Q. And it is clear in your mind that Mr. Magruder reported that Mr. Mitchell had in fact approved a sophisticated intelligence plan?

A. Well, I concluded that Mr. Mitchell had approved it. I believe that when Mr. Magruder was going through the decisions and the way I would usually report it to Mr. Haldeman would be that Mr. Magruder reports that Mr. Mitchell has approved the following matters, and I would put a colon, and then I would list the items.

Q. But did you do it with regard to this plan?

A. Yes, that was one of the 30 items that was listed.

Q. I think in your statement you referred to a sophisticated intelligence system with a budget of 300—300 what?

A. Well, it is $300,000 on almost all of the memoranda that I wrote to Mr. Haldeman, I would leave off the last three zeroes, because usually the figures that we were dealing with were very, very large.

Q. Now, you say that you then prepared a political action memorandum—a political matters memorandum for Mr. Haldeman, and you included this approved sophisticated intelligence plan, that $300,000 budget, in that political matters memorandum. Do you recall the number of that memorandum?

A. Yes, it was political matters memorandum No. 8.

Q. And how many political matters memoranda did you write after that, can you recall approximately?

A. Well, through the campaign and towards the end of the campaign, they got a little further apart, but I wrote 28.

Q. Did you receive any information or indication that Mr. Haldeman, in fact, read the political matters memorandum No. 18 with specific reference to the sophisticated intelligence plan with a budget of $300,000?

A. Yes, it was Mr. Haldeman's practice when he would read such a memorandum to make notes and check off those paragraphs which he had indicated and then he would write it up in the upper right hand corner, "to Strachan," in this case indicating the memorandum should be returned directly to me, and I would go through his memoranda after he had read them, and this particular one I reread, and noted his checking off of all the paragraphs that I had prepared for him.

Q. Was there any other comment besides that particular one?

A. Besides the paragraph that you are concerned about there was simply a blank check.

Q. Now, did there come a time shortly afterwards when you were asked to do anything about that particular matter? Did that just stay in your file or did Mr. Haldeman take any further action on it, to your knowledge?

A. Well, after the memorandum came back out Mr. Haldeman was going to meet with Mr. Mitchell on April 4.

Q. How did you learn about that?

A. Mr. Haldeman had a system on his telephones where he could push a button and have one of his personal aides monitor the telephone conversation.

Q. Would this be similar to an extension phone where somebody would be asked to get on an extension phone and just listen in?

A. Well, it would be different from an extension phone because you could not detect the fact that it was picked up, and there was no way that the person listening on the phone could make any noise either by talking or by a secretary typing to indicate that there was someone else on the phone.

Q. How were you notified or how was it indicated to you that you were to pick up the line?

A. Well, there was a button on the call director phone that I had which would buzz when I was to pick that line up, and I pushed down the button and began listening to the conversation usually at that time which was already in progress.

Q. All right. In this particular case now with a call, I take it, to Mr. Mitchell, could you tell us, having picked up the line, what did you hear?

A. Well, Mr. Mitchell indicated that he was either going to return or had returned from Florida, and Mr. Haldeman jokingly said, "Well, that is clearly a mistake. You ought to stay down there and vacation some more," and Mr. Mitchell indicated that, "Well, we had better get together and talk about some matters." Haldeman asked him if 3 o'clock that day would be convenient.

Q. And that day was when?

A. April 4 [1972].

Q. And was there, in fact, a meeting on April 4, 1972, between Mr. Haldeman and Mr. Mitchell?

A. Well, I did not attend the meeting so I could not testify that there was in fact but I prepared a talking paper for the meeting and we would prepare a folder which would include the talking paper, and the talking paper went into his office and came back out afterwards.

Q. Now, in this talking paper, did you include the item of the sophisticated intelligence plan with a budget of $300,000?

A. Yes. In most talking papers I would frequently pose the question, is the intelligence system adequate? Is the proposal on track, just to get the conversation going on the subject, and in this particular one I did include that paragraph.

Q. Now, at that time, prior to that meeting and when you were preparing that talking paper, was there any other political intelligence plan operative or being considered, to your knowledge? A. No, not to my knowledge.

Q. All right, now. Did you receive back that talking paper after you had given it to Mr. Haldeman? A. Yes, I did.

Q. And to your knowledge, was there any indication as to whether all the items on the talking paper had been discussed?

A. Well, usually if a matter had not been discussed he would indicate that it should be raised again. In this case it was not raised again, indicating that he would have covered the subject.

Q. What did you do with that talking paper then when you received it back?

A. I put it back in the file with the political matters memo 18 files.

Q. And there was no indication from Mr. Haldeman that he had either not discussed it or it needed any further action on your part? A. That is correct.

Q. Now did there come a time after that meeting between Mr. Mitchell and Mr. Haldeman, and also in the same month of April, that Mr. Haldeman asked you to give some communication to Mr. Gordon Liddy?

A. Yes. Mr. Haldeman called me up into his office. I carried a clip board and he told me to contact Mr. Liddy and tell him to transfer whatever capability he had from Muskie to McGovern with particular interest in discovering what the connection between McGovern and Senator Kennedy was.

Q. Was that the limit of the instruction that you had? A. Yes, sir.

Q. What did you do with that instruction? Did you make a record of it?

A. Well, I had taken notes as he had dictated that to me. I walked down to my office, called Gordon Liddy, had him cleared into the White House, had him come over to my office, and literally read the statement to him.

Q. When he came into your office could you describe what Mr. Liddy did, if anything?

A. Yes. Mr. Liddy reached over and turned on the radio.

Q. Do you know why he did that?

A. Well, I have heard descriptions later that is what you do if you want to drown out and prevent a bug from picking up the conversation.

Q. Did you in fact have any bug in the room at that time?

A. I have no way of knowing.

Q. At least to your knowledge that you hadn't installed one yourself? A. No, not that I installed.

Q. Now he turned on the radio and how did you communicate the Haldeman message to Mr. Liddy?

A. I said that Mr. Haldeman had asked me to give him this message, and read it to him.

Q. In other words, read it, that is you read it almost word for word as you got it from Mr. Haldeman?

A. Yes, I opened my clipboard and just read it.

Q. And you didn't give any further explanation as to what you meant by transfer his capabilities from Mr. Muskie to Mr. McGovern. What capabilities? A. No.

Q. Did you know what capabilities he was referring to?

A. No, I didn't except I suspected that there were plants in

Muskie's campaign. It was fairly common knowledge that Muskie's driver was either in the pay of the C.R.P. or supplying information to us. I presumed that these employes would be transferred over to Senator McGovern.

Q. We know already from the testimony, even from Mr. Mitchell, that the so-called March 30 Liddy plan included fairly sophisticated electronic surveillance plans and, as you have indicated, it was that plan that Mr. Magruder said was approved by Mr. Mitchell which you submitted to Mr. Haldeman. With that kind of knowledge would you also now assume that those capabilities could also have included electronic surveillance?

A. Well, it's quite an assumption but I think you would have to make it.

Q. Did Mr. Liddy ask you any questions of what did you mean or did he seem to understand what the message meant?

A. Oh, he seemed to understand and didn't spend very much time and left.

Q. Did you learn anything afterwards as to what he did or did not do? A. No, I did not.

Q. Was any further report made through you to Mr. Haldeman concerning whether he carried out that mission? A. No, not through me.

Q. Now, if Mr. Haldeman actually wanted Mr. Liddy to have that instruction and asked you to communicate that to Mr. Liddy, I take it Mr. Haldeman would be interested in seeing that instructions of his were carried out. A. That is correct.

Q. I think you have indicated that Mr. Haldeman was very well organized and wanted to have all the facts.

Would you be the only one, the only avenue or conduit through which a communication back as to whether Mr. Liddy has followed that instruction would get back to Mr. Haldeman?

A. No. The information could have come back through a variety of channels.

Q. Would you assume that Mr. Haldeman would have pursued that and that a communication would have gotten back to Mr. Haldeman?

A. Well, Mr. Haldeman would normally follow up on particular matters. Frequently he just assumed something was going to be done, and that he would not have to follow up on it.

Q. If he gave orders for something to be done and they weren't done, what was Mr. Haldeman's usual reaction?

A. Well, to his personal aides he would explain his dissatisfaction in no uncertain terms.

Q. Now, when was the first time that you heard about or learned of the break-in of the Democratic National Committee headquarters of the Watergate on June 17, 1972.

A. I was sitting in my car outside Waterman's drug store, my wife was out shopping and I heard it on the radio.

Q. What passed through your mind when you heard that news?

A. Shock, disbelief, surprise.

Q. What did you do?

A. Well, I drove to the White House to get a telephone number for Mr. Magruder in California, to call him and find out if he knew anything about it.

Q. Did you reach Mr. Magruder? A. No, I did not.

Q. Did you later learn from Mr. Magruder anything about this event?

A. Well, I called him that afternoon and then tried to call him again that evening, and did not reach him. Placed a third call on Sunday about noon, Washington time, and asked him if he knew anything about this since I had rather expected a phone call from Mr. Haldeman, and he said, "Don't worry about it, I have been on the phone this morning with Bob," and you needn't know anything on it.

Q. What did you do after that?

A. I called Mr. Higby, because I didn't really believe that Magruder had talked to Mr. Haldeman. Haldeman was down in Key Biscayne. Mr. Higby told me yes, in fact Magruder had talked with Mr. Haldeman and Mr. Ehrlichman was handling the entire matter.

Q. At that point having learned that Mr. Haldeman now had spoken to Mr. Magruder and was informed did a concern come into your mind?

A. Yes, I expected over the entire weekend Mr. Haldeman to call me and ask me that I knew, if I knew anything why I had not reported to him, the usual very tough questions he would ask.

Q. Did you begin at that time to suspect any problem that Mr. Haldeman may have with regard to this?

A. Well, you have to draw one of three conclusions: Either he knew about it ahead of time; either he didn't expect me to report to him, or he had received a report and had calmed down.

Q. Did you arrive at any one conclusion?

A. It was either one of the latter [sic] two, either he knew or he didn't expect me to report to him.

Q. What did you do after you now learned that he had heard about it, what did you do yourself?

A. I didn't do anything. The White House logs indicate that I was in the White House for a minute Sunday, I don't know what that was for. The next day, Monday—

Q. Monday was June 19, 1972?

A. I began going through my files, Mr. Haldeman's files, to see if there were any indications of any information that would be in any way related to this act.

Q. Well, did you come to any conclusion as to whether there was anything in the files that would be in any way related?

A. Yes, I pulled out several documents, most particularly political matters memorandum No. 18.

Q. And that was the one that referred to the sophisticated intelligence plan? A. That is correct.

Q. Did you also pull out that memorandum or these little notes that you had taken concerning the communication that you had from Mr. Haldeman to contact Mr. Liddy about his capabilities being switched from Muskie to McGovern?

A. Well, I pulled that document out but I did not take that up to Mr. Haldeman.

Q. Now, what did you believe at that time when you took the document out? Did you believe that a break-in at the Democratic National Committee headquarters was in fact related to this plan?

A. I didn't know for sure but I had pretty strong suspicions.

Q. Did you meet with Mr. Haldeman shortly after you did that, after you pulled that file out? A. Yes, I did.

Q. Could you tell us when?

A. I believe it was the morning of June 20. He had returned from Florida, I had given a note to Mr. Higby that I thought I should see Mr. Haldeman. Mr. Haldeman summoned me to his office, and I walked in with the political matters memorandum.

Q. I think you had indicated that you were somewhat concerned about Mr. Haldeman's reaction to you about not being informed. Were you still concerned when you met with Mr. Haldeman on June 20?

A. Yes, I was scared to death. I thought I would be fired at that point for not having figured that out.

Q. Were you fired or did he berate you?

A. No, he did not berate me. He said almost jokingly, well, what do we know about the events over the weekend? And I was quite nervous and retreated to sort of legal protective terms and I said, well, sir, this is what can be imputed to you through me, your agent, and opened the political matters memorandum to the paragraph on intelligence, showed it to him. He acknowledged his check and that he had read that, and said that he had not read the tab, which had been attached, turned, began reading it, said, maybe I should have been reading these, these are quite interesting, and read the tab.

Q. What tab was that?

A. That was Sedan Chair II.

Q. Then what, if anything, did you tell him or did he tell you after he had gone through this memorandum again?

A. He told me, well, make sure our files are clean.

Q. What did that mean to you?

A. Well, I went down and shredded that document and others related.

Q. Now, did you do that on your own initiative as such, or did you feel that you were making sure that you were following Mr. Haldeman's instruction that you should make sure the files are clean?

A. No, I believed I was following his orders.

Q. And you shredded all of that, all of No. 18, the political matters memorandum No. 18? A. That is correct.

Q. What about the memorandum that you had made on the communication with regard to Mr. Liddy?

A. Yes, I shredded that also.

Q. Were there any other documents that you shredded?

A. Yes, I did go through and make sure our files were clean. I shredded the talking paper between Mr. Haldeman and Mr. Mitchell on April 4, I shredded a reference to Mr. Segretti, I shredded Mr. Segretti's telephone number.

Q. What reference was that to Mr. Segretti?

A. Well, that had been a dispute between whether or not Mr. Segretti should continue out in the field functioning somehwat independent. Mr. Magruder wrote a memorandum to Mr. Mitchell entitled, "Matter of Potential Embarrassment," in which he described this individual in the field and how that individual should be under the direction of Mr. Liddy. Mr. Mitchell had a copy of that and Mr. Haldeman had a copy of that. And Mr. Haldeman had told me to call up Mr. Segretti and to tell him to expect a call and his directions from Mr. Liddy. I shredded that memorandum also.

Q. Now, after you shredded these papers on the 20th of June, 1972, did you inform anybody that you had done this?

A. Yes, I went over to John Dean's office and gave him a list orally of the documents that I had shredded and told him that those had been Mr. Haldeman's instructions.

Q. Why did you inform John Dean?

A. Well, John Dean was, as you know, the Counsel to the President and the man who would presumably be handling this problem.

Q. Did you inform anybody else? A. No.

Testimony by John D. Ehrlichman

July 24 *Denies illegal conduct on his part, says Dean misled White House, defends Ellsberg break-in.*

July 25 *Denies role in cover-up, says Nixon rejected clemency idea, disputes testimony of Dean, Mitchell, Gray.*

July 26 *Says national security made secrecy vital to intelligence work.*

July 27 *Says he briefed Nixon April 14, 1973, on Watergate and that it was President's first thorough briefing. Disputes Dean and suggests cover-up was intended to disguise involvement of Mitchell.*

July 30 *Reaffirms innocence, defends President and proclaims loyalty to him.*

July 24, 1973

MR. EHRLICHMAN: I welcome this opportunity to lay out the facts and publicly set the record straight on a number of questions. Some of these questions have been legitimately raised. Others are created by leaks to the press, falsehoods and misunderstandings.

I am here to refute every charge of illegal conduct on my part which has been made during the course of these hearings, including material leaked to the news media. What I say here will not be new but it may be different from what you have been reading in the papers.

It has been repeatedly said that this is not a trial; that the committee will recommend legislation, not assess guilt or innocence. At the same time, the soundness and integrity of the President, his staff and many close associates have been impugned and directly put in issue here. Many important questions about the White House, the Presidency, and its staff system have also been asked here, but not answered. I hope and believe I can contribute a few of those answers and also perhaps some measure of perspective.

Mr. Dean began his statement with a somewhat superficial but gallery-pleasing repetition of the old story about fear and paranoia in the Nixon White House. Why, Mr. Dean wondered, was there all that overplayed concern about hippies coming to Washington to march peacefully down Pennsylvania Avenue? Mr. Dean's explanation is simply that we were all suffering from some advanced forms of neurosis, and nothing else—some strange White House madness. He suggests he was the only sane one in the bunch.

Since he began his statement there, let me take up that subject briefly. I submit that on his general subject there are some realities of governmental life to be weighed in your deliberations.

From its first days, the Nixon Administration sought a stable peace abroad and a return of our P.O.W.'s from Southeast Asia; to get these results required the President to undertake foreign policy moves and initiatives which were completely inter-related and extremely delicate. In pursuit of this result we necessarily gave earnest attention to the staffing of critical Government positions with people loyal to the President's objectives. And the problems of leaks, demonstrations, bombings and terrorism, public opinion and Congressional support were understandably on the President's mind.

Today, the Presidency is the only place in the nation where all the conflicting considerations of domestic and international politics, economics and society merge; it is there that street violence and civil rights and relations with Russia and their effect on China and the Cambodian military situation and a thousand other factors and events are brought together on the surface of one desk and must be resolved.

Some of these events in 1969 and 1970 included hundreds of bombings of public buildings in this country, a highly organized attempt to shut down the Federal Government, which you will all remember, intensive harassment of political candidates and violent street demonstrations which endangered life and property.

Taken as isolated incidents these events were serious. Taken as part of an apparent campaign to force upon the President a foreign policy favorable to the North Vietnamese and their allies, these demonstrations were more than just a garden variety exercise of the First Amendment.

Just as, and because, they affected the President's ability to conduct foreign policy, they required the President's attention and concern. Had he and his staff been ignorant of the significance of such a campaign, or merely indifferent, they, that is the President and his staff, would have been subject to the proper criticism of all citizens interested in securing a stable peace in Southeast Asia and the return of our P.O.W.'s.

But the President did understand these events to be important in the over-all foreign policy picture and they received balanced attention along with other events and factors.

In 1969, when he first came into office, the President took this nation into a new international era in which the stakes were extremely high. From close observation I can testify that the President is not paranoid, weird, psychotic on the subject of demonstrators or hypersensitive to criticism. He is an able, tough, international politician, practical, complex, able to integrate many diverse elements and to see the interrelationships of minute and apparently disassociated particles of information and events.

Why didn't everyone know all about Watergate?

It has been my experience that, in the trial of a long lawsuit with a great number of witnesses, it becomes hard for the lawyers, witnesses, judge and jury to remember that anything else ever happened in the community back at the time of the disputed event except that event itself. I sense some of that shrinkage of perspective in some of the questions here, and in some of the comments of the network people on the television.

Here is what appears to be this great big thing, a burglary, a "cover-up," "horrors," all going on, and witness after witness goes over the exquisite details of a few meetings, phone calls, memos, and conversations, day after day here. One begins to think, surely all of this could not possibly have passed unseen by anyone of even average awareness. How, then, could people on the White House staff have failed to know all of these so-obvious and often repeated and significant details, and failed to blow the whistle on the wrongdoings long before the ninth month?

John Dean said one thing in his testimony falser than all the other falsehoods there, when he said,

"[The Watergate] was probably the major thing that was occurring at this point in time," meaning in the context of Senator Baker's question, in the White House between June 17 and Sept. 15, 1972.

I do not suggest that we were all just too busy to have noticed. We did notice and we kept informed through John Dean and other sources on the assumption that he was giving us complete and accurate information.

But it is important to know that in today's White House, there must be, and there is, a heavy delegation of responsibility and duties.

This narrative goes to the question: How could all of this have been avoided?

And it goes to the important point that a chain of delegation is only as strong as its weakest link.

Because I once was counsel to the President and I know what the President has delegated to the one who holds that post, specifically, in this case, John Dean.

Aside from being the President's liaison to the departments and agencies concerned with legal matters, the Counsel to the President is supposed to be the "conscience of the White House." It is his job to keep a sharp eye out for wrongdoing, such as potential conflicts of interest, to insure that Presidential appointees cannot put personal interest ahead of the interest of the public in governmental matter. He reviews the F.B.I. checks of all potential appointees for such problems. He keeps abreast of legal and other questions which are before the executive branch, to be able to answer questions when asked by the President or his staff. He reviews documents before they go to the President for signing.

In addition, he is a conduit for all kinds of miscellaneous information relating to Federal law and regulatory agencies, logistical technicalities and legislation. It is his job to keep the White House informed of a whole raft of subjects within these general areas. And, perhaps most important, he must be a self-starter. He must take the initiative because in the Nixon White House there is no one else who is going to have the time to supervise, make assignments, decide what should be looked into. Everyone else is fully occupied with his own area of responsibility.

Thus, the counsel is a vital link in a chain of delegation. In my view one in that position must bring to the job sufficient training and experience to know what to do and when to do it.

The counsel also has had political duties. The President is the nation's chief executive. But he is also, by longstanding tradition, his political party's leader. Any President has a political role to play, whether he is going to run for re-election or not. But if he is a candidate, then he is both an executive and a practicing politician. Every such politician wants information. And the President, in his politician role is no different from the others. He needs and wants information about issues, supporters, opponents and every other political subject known to man.

For the year 1969, to 1970, when I left the post of counsel, I attempted to gather some purely political information for the President, as I was expected to do. Out of real concern for the proprieties, I attempted to use only conventional nongovernmental sources of information. As one might hire political aides in a political campaign, Tony Ulasewicz was hired to do this chore of information gathering. He was paid from existing Nixon political money, by check, under an appropriate employer's tax number. Among other assignments, he scouted the potential opposition for vulnerability. So far as I am aware, during my tenure as counsel, Mr. Ulasewicz conducted his assignments legally and properly in all respects.

As liaison [after becoming assistant for domestic affairs in early 1970] to the domestic operating departments and agencies I frequently carried to them the President's expressions of criticism and suggestions for change. To the uninformed this undoubtedly would appear to create tensions between a Cabinet Secretary and me. But, actually, I think I maintained a good and frequent contact and good relations with our domestic secretaries, including the several Attorneys General, over my three years in this position. I confess I did not always bring them good news, but then that was not my job. They and I share a mutual objective, I think, and that was to do all we could to help the President accomplish his stated goals.

As many here know, not everyone in the executive branch in the first term shared these goals. There were a number of holdovers in the executive branch who actively opposed the President's policies, especially his foreign policy, but also in the area of domestic affairs I can assure you.

These people conducted a kind of internal guerrilla warfare against the President during the first term, trying to frustrate his goals by unauthorized leaks of part of the facts of a story, or of military and other aspects, or by just plain falsehood. The object was to create hostility in the Congress and abroad and to affect public opinion.

Henry Kissinger, Secretary Rogers and others were seriously concerned that this kind of internal sabotage of Administration policy could actually ruin our chances to negotiate a strategic arms limitation treaty and terminate the Vietnam situation on a stable basis, for example. A similar threat to a good result in Vietnam was posed by the combination of street demonstrations, terriorism-violence and their effect on public and Congressional support for the President's policy.

In his 1960 campaign, Mr. Nixon was involved in every minute detail. In 1968 when he invited me to work in the 1968 campaign to manage the campaign. I agreed to manage the campaign tour only after securing his promise that he would completely delegate detailed control of the advance work, logistics and schedule. And his participation in those details was minimal in 1968.

In 1972 with the foreign situation as it was, the President decided quite early that he simply could not and would not involve himself in the day-to-day details of the Presidential primaries, the convention and the campaign. He made a very deliberate effort to detach himself from the day-to-day strategic and tactical problems. And so the regular work of the White House relating to Government and the nation's problems continued unabated. If anything, we on the domestic side were busier with the President on governmental business than in other years.

In 1972, the President had to delegate most of his political role and it went to people not otherwise burdened with governmental duties. As a result, I personally saw very little of the campaign activity during the spring and early summer of 1972. The President asked me to be sure that the campaign organization and the national committee said or did nothing inconsistent with Administration policy. And so I had a few meetings, with the C.R.P. people to explain existing domestic policy, that is, on campaign issues.

I began to spend more time with Ron Ziegler, press secretary at the White House, in the late spring of 1972, helping him to understand the campaign issues, reviewing the research with him, etc. It became more important than ever for me to keep ahead of developments and in this connection I asked Mr. Dean to inform me as early as possible of significant changes, or new events in the Watergate case, so Ron Ziegler and I could deal with new issues which would be arising in the press. It was for this purpose that I talked to Dean about Watergate in most instances. As my log will show I spent considerable time every week with the press, attempting to explain and outline for the media the President's domestic goals and programs.

From June to September, 1972, my staff and I put in long days, the convention platform having imposed additional burdens on some of us. After the convention, the speeches, position papers and political statements and releases kept the pressure on us. It was a very busy time.

John Dean, on the other hand, never found things so quiet and he planned the most expensive honeymoon in the history of the White House staff right along this period.

The committee has had the log of how I spent my office time over the years. As it shows, the vast percentage of my time was devoted to domestic policy issues.

Nor was I anyone's Siamese twin during these years. Listening to the star witness [Mr. Dean] "hyphenate" me for five days, I began to know a little of how a caboose feels. Mr. Dean repeatedly and facilely would testify "and so I informed Haldeman-and-Ehrlichman of so-and-so" as if it were possible to do with one phone call or drop-by. It could not really happen and in virtually every case to which he referred in testimony it did not happen.

And how much time did I actually spend with Mr. Dean learning about the break-in or keeping abreast of developments to assist Ron Ziegler on the issues, or with Mr. Dean on any other subject for that matter in the weeks following Watergate?

We invariably met either in my office, or more rarely in Mr. Haldeman's (with the exception of just three or four meetings most of which were held out of town).

The logs for these two offices, Mr. Haldeman's and mine, demonstrate clearly the frequency of my meetings with Mr. Dean.

Remember: Dean testified that keeping Watergate covered up was a tremendous drain of my time and told of all the conferences and meetings I have, having with him about it. Let's be clear: I did not cover up anything to do with Watergate. Nor were Mr. Dean and I keeping steady company during all these weeks.

I have compiled our meetings in two-week periods from June 17 through the election, the critical period, presumably, for a total of 22

Of the total 22 contacts, two related to Presidential papers and testamentary planning, one related to convention planning. one related to grain sales, two on general campaign planning, one regarding the President's financial statement to be released, one regarding settlement of the Common Cause lawsuit. Of the remainder not all were devoted to talk about aspects of Watergate, I am certain.

Now, again, on this Siamese twin business, Mr. Haldeman and I had vastly different duties, areas and methods of operation.

I had a number of talks with Mr. Dean about Watergate, largely to keep posted on the campaign issues which I never had occasion to mention to Mr. Haldeman, but about which I talked to others, Mr. Ziegler, for example.

I simply want to make the point without overdrawing it, that Mr. Haldeman and I lived very separate lives and careers in and out of the office, Mr. Dean to the contrary notwithstanding.

The vast percentage of my working time was spent on substantive issues and domestic policy. About one-half of 1 per cent was spent on politics, the campaign and the events with which you have been concerning yourself as a committee. That is the context in which I hope you will receive this testimony.

Similarly, you must measure the President's role in all of this in true perspective. The 1972 campaign, the Watergate and its investigation competed for his attention with the claims of hundreds of members of Congress, economists, diplomats, educators, scientists, labor leaders, businessmen and countless other citizens, and with the demands of the problems of the nation in their manifold and compound complexities, with the daily mail and the endless meetings, the speeches and other communication with the public, with the need for management, leadership, inspiration and the need and desire for the time to study and think. I see redeeming aspects in this process.

I have faith that good can result from this committee's efforts. In the future, participants in political campaigns will surely be aware of the history of this time. And the standards which they will wish to impose upon themselves will be the product of the lessons of that history, whatever it may turn out to be. I have great optimism that the lessons of the history of this era will bring only good for this country.

MR. DASH: Were you aware of the fact that by the summer of 1970 Mr. Haldeman and the President had felt a need for an improved intelligence system with regard to domestic dissent or internal security?

A. Well, I was aware of the feeling of the need and I shared it. I was aware of a proposal which eventually, I believe, was put into effect to establish a small office in the Justice Department to collate and coordinate and bring together in one place what the various law enforcement agencies, both in and out of the Federal Government, knew about these terrorism bombings and the street violence and these other activites that were going on around the country because it looked then like there really was a pattern, and that it was a coordinated, planned and executed thing.

These things went in waves from one part of the country to the other and it appeared that if what the police knew, for instance, in the city of New York could be shared with the police in other parts of the country, that you would get a whole lot better response to this kind of lawbreaking.

So under Mr. Mardian's aegis this effort was made to bring together the things that were known to all of the law enforcement people around the country.

Q. All right. Now did you know about the Huston plan [for internal security, approved by the President in 1970 and canceled a few days later]?

A. I did not know about the Huston plan until I was invited

to attend a meeting that I think has been previously referred to here in the President's office, attended by Admiral Gayler and J. Edgar Hoover and the heads of the various intelligence agencies, where this proposal was announced.

Q. What was the stage of that proposal at this point announced as a proposal that would go forward?

A. I gathered it was an accomplished fact.

Q. Yes. Did you know what the proposal was about?

A. Just from what I heard at that meeting. I had not seen that write-up.

Q. Did you know that the proposal included removal of certain restrictions on break-ins, surreptitious entry or wiretapping?

A. No, I do not believe that was discussed at the meeting.

Q. It never came to your attention that was in the plan? A. No it did not.

Q. Mr. Haldeman, who played an important role in working on the plan and having it recommended to the President, never discussed those aspects of the plan with you?

A. No, nobody discussed any aspects of the plan with me.

Q. Why were you called to the meeting?

A. Well, I do not know that. There were quite a few spare characters at the meeting from the White House staff and I was simply there to get information.

Q. Were you asked to express an opinion? A. No.

Q. So far as you know, the plan was approved?

A. That was the tenor of the meeting.

Q. Did you ever hear of anything else about the plan?

A. Yes, I heard that the Director of the F.B.I. in effect, scuttled it by his objection to it, with the support of the Attorney General.

Q. Do you know why he objected to it?

A. I do not think I ever knew with any particularity why. It was pretty obvious that he was losing a good deal of sovereignty and the bureau was going to be asked to enter into intelligence gathering activities that the director did not want it in and I assumed that that was the basis for his objection.

Q. In other words, your assumption was that Mr. Hoover objected to the plan because it invaded his territory rather than because it had any parts to it that dealt with more surreptitious entry or wiretapping?

A. I am not your best witness on this Mr. Dash. It was purely an assumption on my part and I do not think anybody ever told me.

Q. You never sought to inquire why a plan that you saw at a meeting was being approved and would go forward was being ditched because of Mr. Hoover's objection? You never sought to inquire as to why?

A. It was so far out of my bailiwick at that time that I just had no occasion.

Q. Was it out of your bailiwick to be interested in the gathering of political intelligence?

A. At that time, yes.

Q. Now did there come a time when it did not be outside your bailiwick?

A. Well, it had been my bailiwick when I was counsel. As assistant for domestic affairs, I had very little occasion to be involved in questions of political intelligence or political anything, for that matter.

Q. Well, after the Huston plan did not go forward, were you assigned a role to create in the White House a capability for intelligence gathering at any time?

A. I do not know quite what you are getting at. It you are getting at the special unit and the problems of leaks—

Q. I do not know why you have to find out what I am getting at, if you just answer my question as I ask it.

A. It is an obscure question.

Q. It is a simple question. If the answer is no, say no. If the answer is yes, say yes. Did there come a time when you were asked to develop a capability in the White House for intelligence gathering? A. Intelligence gathering, the answer would be no.

Q. Now, you were trying to see what I was getting at. Were you ever asked to set up a special unit in the White House for the purpose of determining whether certain leaks had occurred in major national security areas?

A. In point of fact I was—and strictly in terms of your question. I was not asked to set it up. Mr. Krogh was asked to set it up.

Egil Krogh Jr. was a member of the Domestic Council staff, and he was asked by the President to form this special unit. I was designated as one to whom Mr. Krogh could come with problems in connection with it, and the President said also that he could come to him with problems.

Q. Were you in at the beginning of the setting up of this plan? A. Yes.

Q. And you knew what the unit was to do? A. Yes.

Q. What was the unit to do?

A. The unit as originally conceived was to stimulate the various departments and agencies to do a better job of controlling leaks and the theft or other exposure of national security secrets from within their departments. It was a group which was to bring to account, so to speak, the various security offices of the Departments of Defense and State and Justice and C.I.A., to get them to do a better job.

Q. And, therefore, this unit was to gather facts, if there was a leak or to act as a deterrent, I take it, to prevent leaks.

A. No, there would have been no need to gather facts under the concept, except to know that there had been an occurrence but to require vigorous and very active effort on the part of the responsible people in the departments and agencies to find out who was responsible and how it happened and to make sure it couldn't happen again.

Q. Isn't that getting facts. Would you say some people who go to seek facts in an investigative way can also say they seek intelligence?

A. Well, but you see what I am trying to say to you in as originally set up and conceived this was not an investigative unit in the sense that your question implies. It was far more a group that was established for the purpose of getting the security people in the departments and agencies to do a better job of their job.

Q. Did it ever—was it ever called or was it ever referred to as an investigative unit?

A. Subsequently it was because it became an investigative unit subsequently.

Q. So there came a time when you were administering an investigative unit?

A. Yes. In a literal sense, that is true.

Q. Literal sense? A. Yes, sir.

Q. Not in an actual sense?

A. Well, here I am dueling with a professor.

Q. I am not dueling with you. I am just trying—

A. Professor, if you say actual, it is actual.

Q. I don't want you to take my questions, and I don't want to put words in your mouth.

A. Sure, I am trying to give you—

Q. I really want to have you answer to the best of your recollection.

A. Sure, I am trying to give you the real essence of this as we go along and I don't mean to be fencing over words.

Q. Could you please tell us in as clear a way as you can what the responsibilities of this particular unit were both in the beginning and how it developed, and as it developed later?

A. At a point in time in connection with the Pentagon Papers theft, a whole series of events took place. One of the first of them was that the Pentagon Papers which were marked secret and top secret and which were largely Defense Department documents, were turned over to the Russian Embassy.

I knew this because I had a call from Mr. Mardian, the assistant Attorney General, advising me that the Justice Department had this firm fact. The Attorney General came over and reported to the President that this theft had evidently been perpetrated by a number of people, a conspiracy, and that some of the people were identified by the Department of Justice as having had previous ties to domestic Communist activities.

The Attorney General then reported in response to an inquiry, and maybe I had better tell you how the inquiry came up. Mr. Krogh came to me and said, "I am having real trouble getting the F.B.I. to move on this." And so I said "well" and this was basically my function was to do downfield blocking for Mr. Krogh when he had problems in the department. I said, "O.K., I will contact the Attorney General and see what I can do," which I did. The Attorney General called me back and he said, "We have a very tough problem here. It appears that a top man in the F.B.I. put in a routine request that Mr. Ellsberg's father-in-law be interviewed. The Director has given notice that the interview and interviews of that family are not to take place."

Now this was the area in which Mr. Krogh and the special unit were pressing for the Department of Justice to bring information together as was their job to do. The Attorney General said, "I am going to reverse this decision on the part of the Director to transfer this man and demote him," but he said, "We have a very touchy situation with the Director. Mr. Sullivan in the bureau is extremely upset and concerned and disagrees strongly with the Director in this matter. I don't know but what Mr. Sullivan may quit as a result of this whole episode. It's very touchy within the bureau." I said, "What are our chances of getting the bureau to move ahead on this right away?" and he said "very slim or none."

So it was this set of facts, and the real strong feeling of the President that there was a legitimate and vital national security aspect to this that it was decided, first on Mr. Krogh's recommendation, with my concurrence, that the two men in this special unit who had had considerable investigative experience, be assigned to follow up on the then leads and rather general leads which were in the file.

Q. Who were those two men?

A. Hunt and Liddy.

Q. Now, you did become aware at some point in time of the activities of staff members of the special investigations unit, Mr. Hunt and Mr. Liddy, with regard to the office of Mr. Ellsberg's psychiatrist?

A. Yes, it was around Labor Day of 1971.

Q. And I take it that was a fact-gathering project?

A. That was the fact-gathering project that I mentioned before in relation to the theft of the secrets and the turn over to the Russians and the dilemma we had of the bureau (F.B.I.) not moving on this.

Q. Now, when did you Mr. Ehrlichman, learn for the first time of the break-in of the Democratic National Committee headquarters?

A. It was the following day when I received a telephone call.

Q. And what, if anything did you do?

A. I made a couple of phone calls in response.

Q. How soon thereafter did you learn that Mr. Hunt was involved?

A. His name was mentioned in the original phone call.

Q. And who made that phone call to you?

A. Mr. Boggs of the Secret Service.

Q. And then, shortly after did Mr. Dean make a report to you about what he had learned about the break-in?

A. That would have been the afternoon of the 19th, the following Monday.

Q. What did he tell you?

A. He just gave me a run-down of the identity of the individuals. He told me that he had talked to Liddy. That Liddy had told him that it was his operation, in effect, that he, Liddy, was involved but that nobody at the White House was involved.

Q. So at least by the 19th of June, which is two days after the break-in, one, on the basis of a call from a Secret Service man, and the other from Mr. Dean, that the two men who had been involved in the so-called Ellsberg break-in were involved in the break-in of the Democratic National Committee headquarters? A. That is correct.

Q. These two men, at least one of them specifically, Mr. Liddy had a position of some responsibility with the Committee to Re-elect the President of the United States.

A. Well, I obviously learned that he was working at the committee. I do not know about the responsibility part.

Q. Did you know he was counsel for the Finance Committee of, for the Re-election of the President? A. I am not sure that I did.

Q. Now, having learned that persons who had the prior history that you knew about were working in a close relationship to the campaign for the re-election of the President you were so dedicated, honestly dedicated to see that he was re-elected, did this produce any concern on your part with regard to the campaign itself?

A. Yes, I was concerned about it.

Q. Would it also be a, even more of a serious campaign issue if it developed or was revealed that Mr. Hunt and Mr. Liddy had broken into the office of Mr. Ellsberg's psychiatrist, the same two people?

A. No, I would not think so. They were certainly identified as former White House people in the media, and that was, that connection was, known. This connection was established.

Q. What connection was established?

A. Their connection with the White House.

Q. Yes, but it had not been established, is it not true, that Mr. Hunt and Mr. Liddy had broken in the psychiatrist's office of Mr. Ellsberg, at that point it had not been publicly known? A. No, it was not publicly known.

Q. Are you telling the committee that that additional information that these former White House staffers working under your direction had broken into Mr. Ellsberg's psychiatrist's office, would not have created an even more serious embarrassing situation for the campaign?

A. I would not think so, Mr. Dash, for several reasons. Number one that episode was a part of a very intensive national security investigation which had been impressed with a very high security classification. The likelihood of that being disclosed was very slight.

Number two, those people were operating, at least I believe they were operating, under express authorization.

Q. Express authorization to break in?

A. Yes, sir. Under a national security situation, under a situation of considerable moment to the nation in the theft of top secret documents, and their apparent delivery to the Soviet Embassy. It never was my view that Hunt and Liddy, as individuals, had done something that was completely irrational in that break-in. In other words, they were operating in a national security setting and pursuant to either instructions or authorization and, that being the case, that had never been a subject which I considered to be seriously embarrassing.

Q. Let us first take the first point you made, which was that it would be unlikely that it would be revealed. A. Right.

Q. And I take it, it would be unlikely to be revealed was because neither Mr. Hunt or Mr. Liddy would talk about it?

A. Neither would they talk about it nor would a prosecutor talk about it if they told him, nor any employe of the Federal Government aware of the national security characteristic of it be talking about it.

Q. How would you be assured of the fact that Mr. Hunt and Liddy would not talk about it?

A. Well, the only assurance that one could have, I suppose you have a couple of individuals here with long training and experience as law enforcement or intelligence people in the Government, Hunt for what, 20 years, and Liddy for 7 or something of this kind, and it never occurred to me to be a serious likelihood at that time.

Q. Now, I think you have heard the testimony of Mr. Mitchell that he first became aware of the so-called Liddy operations, which included the Ellsberg break-in, on the 21st of June [1972] and Mr. Mardian, Mr. LaRue debriefed him after speaking to Mr. Liddy and that he characterized this kind of operation, plus some others as White House horrors. It was his view as presented to the committee that the potential for embarrassment to the re-election of the President was such, that he withheld this information from the President because he thought it might cause the failure of the President for being re-elected. You disagree with his evaluation.

A. Well, I certainly disagreed with it at the time. In other words, trying to reconstruct my frame of mind at the time, I considered the special unit's activities to be well within the President's inherent constitutional powers, and this particular episode, the break-in in California, likewise to have been within the President's inherent constitutional powers as spelled out in 18 U.S. Code 2511

Q. Once the information did become public, and the press dealing with it, and the reaction generally by the public to the break-in, would you say that this was treated as a normal function of Government to authorize Mr. Hunt and Liddy to break into Mr. Ellsberg's psychiatrist's office. By the public, not as you saw it, but how the public reacted when they heard about it?

A. I think if it is clearly understood that the President has the constitutional power to prevent the betrayal of national security secrets, as I understood he does, and that is well understood by the American people, and an episode like that is seen in that context, there shouldn't be any problem.

Q. Well, then, you would not have had the same concern that Mr. Mitchell expressed, that if he had told the President about it, one, the President would have lowered the boom and, in lowering the boom, he would have probably caused his own defeat for President of the United States?

A. In point of fact, on the first occasion when I did discuss this with the President, which was in March of this year, he expressed essentially the view that I have just stated, that this was an important, a vital national security inquiry, and that he considered it to be well within the constitutional, both obligation and function of the Presidency.

Q. Mr. Ehrlichman, prior to the luncheon recess you stated that in your opinion, the entry into the Ellsberg psychiatrist's office was legal because of national security reasons. I think that was your testimony. A. Yes.

Q. Have you always maintained that position?

A. Well, I do not know——

Q. Well, do you recall when we had our first interview in my office, and we discussed this issue you expressed shock that such a thing had occurred, and indicated that you had informed Mr. Young or Mr. Krogh to see that this thing should not happen again but you did not take any action such as ordering the firing these people because of the general sensitive issues that were involved. Do you recall that?

A. Well, that is not on the ground of illegality, Mr. Dash. I do not think you asked me at that time whether—what my legal opinion was, for whatever it is worth. What you were asking me was what I did, and that is what I did.

Q. Well, if it was legal you would ordinarily have approved it would you not?

A. Well, no, the thing that troubled me about it was that it was totally unanticipated. Unauthorized by me.

Q. Who was it authorized by?

A. Well, I am under the impression that it was authorized by Mr. Krogh, but it is not based on any personal knowledge.

Q. Well, now, as a matter of fact, Mr. Ehrlichman, did you not personally approve in advance a covert entry into the Ellsberg psychiatrist office for the purpose of gaining access to the psychoanalysts's reports?

A. I approved a covert investigation. Now, if a covert entry means a breaking and entering the answer to your question is, no.

Q. Well, let me read to you a memorandum dated Aug. 11, 1971, and it is a memorandum to you from Bud Krogh and David

Young, "Subject: Pentagon Papers Project—Status Report as of Aug. 11, 1971."

I think the relevant information is in paragraph 2 rather than the progress report of 1. Let me just read paragraph 2. "We have received the C.I.A. preliminary psychological study (copy attached at Tab A) which I must say I am disappointed in and consider very superficial. We will meet tomorrow with the head psychiatrist, Mr. Bernard Malloy, to impress upon him the detail and depth that we expect. We will also make available to him here some of the other information we have received from the F.B.I. on Ellsberg."

Now, more significant. "In this connection we would recommend that a covert operation be undertaken to examine all the medical files still held by Ellsberg's psychoanalyst covering the two-year period in which he was undergoing analysis."

And there is a provision here for approve, disapprove. There is an "E," which I take it you would recognize as your "E." and in handwriting which I would ask if it is your handwriting, the approve, and the handwriting is, "if done under your assurance that it is not traceable." A. That is correct.

Q. Now, how would you interpret in this connection your assistance recommended to you in this connection.

A. Well, no interpretation is necessary, Mr. Dash. This was in the setting of a previous conversation in which it was contemplated that these two men would go to the Coast to do this investigation as the President's statement of May 22 says.

The effort here was to find out everything that could be found out about the people and the circumstances surrounding Ellsberg in all respects.

Now, whether a psychiatric profile, as such, helps an investigation or in that situation, is something that the experts would have to tell you. It is something that I certainly cannot second-guess about. But the point here is that the investigation was already authorized and was going to go forward. Now covert, in its literal meaning, and in its everyday meaning, is simply that it is a covered operation, that is to say you do not identify yourself as being an investigator from the separate committee.

My concern, and the reason that I certainly acquiesced in the use of the term "covert" here was that I was not keen on the concept of the White House having investigators in the field and known to be in the field, and I just don't think from a public standpoint, from a public relations standpoint, from a public policy standpoint, that that is a desirable situation.

Now, if you are asking me whether this means that I had in my contemplation that there was going to be a breaking and entering, I certainly did not. I heard a remark by a member of the committee to the effect that there are only two ways that one can see a medical file and that is either to get the doctor to violate his oath or to break or enter. Well, I know that is not so and I imagine those of you who have been in private practice will recognize there are a lot of perfectly legal ways that medical information is leaked, if you please, and when I saw this that is the thing that occurred to me. That that by one way or another this information could be adduced by an investigator who was trained and who knew what he was looking for.

Q. Now, would your understanding of covert operation be, not a breaking and entering, but being let in by impersonating themselves to be somebody else into the building. Isn't that a covert operation?

A. I suppose that phrase could include that. It could include a lot of things.

Q. Yes and, therefore, I don't think we have to quarrel about whether you approved a break-in, an entering or even what you might consider to be a common-law burglary, what I am now saying is that the language here is not covert investigation, but a covert operation being undertaken to examine all medical files.

A. Again I don't mean to quibble with you. The words here are not my words. They are the words of the writers of the memo. The thing that was imparted to me by the word "covert" was that these people would not identify themselves as investigators of the White House or anything of this kind, and that their identities would not be known to the people that they were interrogating.

Q. So they would not identify themselves as representatives of the White House but through some identification they might get access to the building.

A. Not necessarily. They might have gotten access through another doctor, through a nurse. There are all kinds of ways that one could get this information.

Q. But it would include getting access to the building, would it not?

A. Not inevitably.

Q. I didn't say inevitably, it would include it.

A. As one of a number of possibilities.

Q. And also access, say by some covert activity, not identify themselves as a member of the White House staff, getting access to the office. Would it not include that as one of the alternatives that they could take?

A. Well you are asking me to define phrases in somebody else's memo.

Q. Well, you approved this memo. You didn't put any other conditions on it did you?

A. No, I am trying to tell you what I thought I was approving.

Q. Well, those who read it undertook to also interpret what you thought you were approving. Did Mr. Young and Mr. Krogh call you while you were in Cape Cod after Mr. Hunt and Mr. Liddy came back, and tell you that they had established that it was feasible that they could get access and that you said, "O.K., go ahead and let them do it."

Do you recall that call that Mr. Krogh and Mr. Young made to you in Cape Cod?

A. I don't recall any business calls while I was up there at all.

Q. Would you be surprised if I told you that Mr. Young would so testify? A. Yes, I would.

SENATOR ERVIN: Mr. Ehrlichman, do I understand that you are testifying that the Committee to Re-elect the President and those associated with them constituted an eleemosynary institution that gave $50,000 to some burglars and their lawyers merely because they felt sorry for them?

A. I am afraid I am not your best witness on that, Mr. Chairman. I do not know what their motives were. I think those will appear in the course of the proceeding.

Q. You stated this was a defense fund just like that given to Angela Davis and to Daniel Ellsberg, did you not?

A. I stated that was my understanding of it.

Q. Yes, well, Daniel Ellsberg and the Angela Davis defense funds were raised in public meetings and the newspapers carried news items about it, did they not?

A. I am not sure that we know who the donors to those funds were. I dare say there are many people in this country who contributed to those funds who would not want it known.

Q. Yes. But do you not think most of the people contributed their funds because they believed in the causes they stood for?

A. I assume that.

Q. Well, certainly, the Committee to Re-elect the President and the White House aides like yourself did not believe in the cause of burglars or wiretappers, did you? A. No.

Q. Can you—

A. I didn't contribute a nickel, Mr. Chairman.

Q. Yes. You authorized somebody else to contribute?

A. No, I would like to set that straight, if I might, Mr. Chairman.

The only reason that anybody ever came to me about Mr. Kalmbach raising money was because of this arrangement that we had entered into that we would protect Mr. Kalmbach if he wished to be protected from requests to raise money.

Now that is—it was a situation where obviously he didn't wish to be protected. He made the judgment, he made it independent of me, and whether I conceded to it or not obviously didn't make any difference.

Q. Did he ever talk to you about that?

A. Not until after the fact.

Q. I will ask you if he didn't come to you and not only talk about having known you a long time and you having known his family but didn't he ask you whether it was a proper or legal operation?

A. Mr. Chairman, the testimony is that that meeting, according to Mr. Kalmbach, was the 26th of July when he was long into this, and as I have already testified.

Q. He testified he had become dubious about the propriety of it and he went to you for reassurance? And he also testified when he got to you, you told him it was all right and to see that the money was delivered in secret because if he didn't deliver it in secret their heads would be in their laps. Didn't that occur?

A. No. I would be terribly slow to reassure Herb Kalmbach whom I consider a good and close friend of the propriety of any such undertaking, of any such undertaking without checking it first, if he had asked me, and I am testifying to you, Mr. Chairman, that he did not ask me.

Q. My question is didn't he have a conversation in which you told him to do it in secret because otherwise "if it gets out, our heads will be in their laps." You can answer that yes or no. I have just 20 minutes at this time and I want to ask my questions.

A. I had a conversation with Mr. Kalmbach, Mr. Chairman, and I have no doubt that we, if he says so, that we discussed the question of secrecy because I do recall his saying that Mr. Ulasewicz was carrying money back and forth.

Now, I had in my mind at that time the realization that this, what I considered to be a legitimate undertaking, could be terribly misconstrued if someone were to impute the efforts of the President's lawyer to this defense fund for Watergate burglars. I mean there is room for misunderstanding, I think you have stated the misunderstanding very eloquently in your opening question.

Q. So that was the reason that you made arrangements by which a gentleman who resided in California would deliver the money in cash and sometimes in laundry bags to an ex-policeman in New York, and allow the ex-policeman to come down and deliver the money under orders that he wasn't going to permit the people he delivered it to to see him.

A. Well, Mr. Chairman, as you know, I had nothing to do with those details at all.

Q. Well, I have always thought that if a political institution or committee enacted the role of an eleemosynary institution it would, like the Pharisee, brag about it on all opportunities, and so you agreed with me that a Doubting Thomas might think that this money was routed in this clandestine way not only to keep it secret but also to keep these people that were receiving the money.

A. No, I don't agree with that because I don't know that.

Q. Didn't you have a phone conversation with Mr. Kalmbach just before he came to Washington to testify before the grand jury about this matter?

A. I believe he was in Washington with his attorneys at the time.

Q. Yes, And didn't you bug his telephone conversation with you? A. No, sir.

Q. Didn't you record it then?

A. Yes, sir. I think the result is about the same as having your secretary listen in on the other line and take it down in shorthand.

Q. Yes, but you didn't tell Mr. Kalmbach that you were recording his conversation did you?

A. Sir. No more did he tell me that he had two lawyers in the room with him.

Q. Well, you see no difference between a man who is going before a grand jury having two lawyers and a man having a recording or bugging instrument annexed to his telephone. Now on this recording Mr. Kalmbach said, "You know, when you and I talked and it was after John had given me the word and I came to ask you, 'John, is this an assignment I have to take on?'

"You said. 'Yes, it is, period, and move forward.' Then that was all that I needed to be assured that I wasn't putting my family in jeopardy."

Now, didn't Kalmbach make that statement to you in the telephone conversation the day before that he came to testify before the grand jury and was recorded on this view annexed to your telephone? And your answer is, "Sure."

A. Well, I have to disagree with you, Mr. Chairman. I suppose what we have to do is take the whole context of what Mr. Kalmbach said in order to understand its meaning.

Q. Yes. Now, you denied a while ago that you gave Kalmbach any such assurance, did you not?

A. No, sir, what I denied was this very vivid and dramatic moment when we looked deep into each other's eyes and I said with solemn assurance that this was both legal and proper. And I made no such solemn assurance and, as a matter of fact, in what you read here the word "period" stands out graphically because "period" means that was the end of the conversation and you will notice that there is nothing in there about my assuring Mr. Kalmbach that this was either proper or legal.

Q. But you told him that this was an assignment he had to take on.

A. Well, obviously, Mr. Chairman, he is not my employe, he is not my vassal. I hold no sway over him. It was very much a situation where Mr. Kalmbach undertook this, and you will recall he undertook it some six weeks before we had this conversation.

Q. Well, let us go on to something else. You said something about the burglarizing of the office of the psychiatrist of Ellsberg was justified power under the Constitution, did you not? A. Yes.

Q. And you referred to a certain statute.

A. I referred to a statute in which the Congress in 1968 made a recognition of that inherent power.

Q. Is that 18 U.S. Code 2511? A. Yes.

Q. This statute has nothing to do with burglary.

A. It has to do with the United States Constitution, Mr. Chairman.

Q. No, sir. That is not the purpose of the statute. The Constitution takes care of itself even there. This has to do with the interception or disclosure of wire or oral communications prohibited.

A. No, sir, it also has to do with the Congress's recognition of what the Constitution provides with relation to the powers of the President.

Q. Is there a single thing in there that says that the President can authorize burglaries?

A. Well, let us read it, Mr. Chairman.

Q. I can ask about it without reading. It says here that this statute, which makes it unlawful to intercept and disclose wire or other communications, says that this shall not interfere with the constitutional power of the President to—

A. To do anything.

Q. —To do anything necessary to protect the country against five things. The first says actual or potential attacks or other hostile acts of a foreign power. You do not claim that burglarizing Dr. Ellsberg's psychiatrist's office to get his opinion, his recorded opinion, of intellectual or psychological state of his patient is an attack by a foreign power, do you?

MR. WILSON [attorney for Mr. Ehrlichman]: May I get into this, may I get into this legal debate?

SENATOR ERVIN: Well, yes. You claim that, Mr. Wilson, do you?

MR. WILSON: Then, you read into that sentence which says or to protect national security information against foreign intelligence activities.

SENATOR ERVIN: Against foreign intelligence activities. The foreign intelligence activities had nothing to do with the opinion of Ellsberg's psychiatrist about his intellectual or emotional or psychological state.

MR. WILSON: How do you know that, Mr. Chairman?

SENATOR ERVIN: Because I can understand the English language. It is my mother tongue.

MR. WILSON: Mr. Chairman, may I answer that? The C.I.A. must have thought that it had some foreign relationship because they had done an ineffective profile on Ellsberg.

SENATOR ERVIN: Well, the C.I.A. had no business doing that because the law prohibits them from having anything to do with internal security.

MR. WILSON: Sir, you would not consider that foreign intelligence activity is a—

SENATOR ERVIN: No, it was a domestic intelligence activity. These people were from the plumbers, from the White House doing this.

MR. WILSON: We had a man passing secrets to the Soviet Government.

SENATOR ERVIN: Well, Ellsberg's psychiatrist wasn't doing that.

A. Of course, that is just the point, Mr. Chairman.

MR. WILSON: Of course. Why did the C.I.A. want to do a profile?

SENATOR ERVIN: Because the C.I.A. in my book has nothing to do with the bugging the psychiatrist's office in the United States to find out what the emotional or psychological or intellectual state of an American is.

A. I think that basically you have to take this in context. We had here an unknown quantity in terms of a conspiracy. We had an overt act in the turning over of these secret documents to the Russian Embassy, and moreover we have a technique here in the development of a psychiatric profile which apparently, in the opinion of the experts, is so valuable that the C.I.A maintains an entire psychiatric section for that purpose.

Now, putting those all together, I submit that certainly there is in 2511 ample constitutional recognition of the President's inherent constitutional powers to form a foundation for what I said to this committee.

Q. Well, Mr. Ehrlichman, the Constitution specifies the President's powers to me in the Fourth Amendment. It says: "The right of the people to be secure in their persons, houses, papers, and effects, against unreasonable searches and seizures, shall not be violated, and no warrant shall issue, but upon probable abuse, supported by oath or affirmation, and particularly describing the place to be searched and the person or things to be seized."

Nowhere in this does it say the President has the right to suspend the Fourth Amendment.

A. No, I think the Supreme Court has said the search or seizure or whatever it is has to be reasonable and they have said that national security undertaking can be reasonable and can very nicely comply with the Fourth Amendment.

But, Mr. Chairman, the Congress in 1968 has said this: "Nothing contained in this chapter or in Section 605 of the Communications Act" and so forth, "shall limit the constitutional power of the President to take such measures as he deems necessary to protect the nation against," and then it goes on, "to protect national security information against foreign intelligence activities."

Now, that is precisely what the President was undertaking. He was not undertaking under this statute. He was undertaking it under that constitutional power which you gentlemen and the other members of the Congress recognized in this section.

Q. Yes, I have studied that statute. I have committed that statute. And there is not a syllable in there that says the President can suspend the Fourth Amendment or authorize burglary. It has no reference to burglary. It has reference only or interception and disclosure of—interception of wire or oral communications.

Now, Mr. Ehrlichman, when did you learn about the fact that two people employed by the White House, Liddy and Hunt, had burglarized the office of Ellsberg's psychiatrist?

A. I believe that it was either the day after or two days after I returned from a vacation at Cape Cod which would have put it or two days after Labor Day of 1971.

Q. 1971? A. Yes.

Q. And so Liddy and Hunt, who were accessories to the fact of a felony before the burglary were kept on the White House payroll and given an office in the Executive Office Building, to your knowledge until after the break-in of the Watergate?

A. Well Mr. Chairman, I can't adopt the various assumptions of your question with regard to the criminality of the act and so forth. My advice at the time was that both Hunt and Liddy had acted pursuant to an authorization, and taking into account the—

Q. An authorization from whom?

A. Well, I assumed from Mr. Krogh.

Q. Well, Mr. Krogh, I believe, got his authorization from you, didn't he? A. No sir. Not as far as I know he didn't.

Q. Well, he was under your supervision.

A. He was generally under my supervision on the Domestic Council staff as a routine proposition.

Q. Mr. Ehrlichman you are a lawyer and you know that a psychiatrist is forbidden to divulge the information about his patient, don't you, without his patient's consent?

A. Well, I think we are going to split hairs.

Q. That is not splitting hairs. That is a Hippocratic oath which started back in ancient Greece and has been going ever since.

A. I am not sure psychiatrists in every case are M.D.'s, but let's assume that for the sake of argument. The fact is that as I have stated earlier, my assumption is that it is possible to get special medical and other kinds of confidential information through a trained investigator if he knows what he is looking for without a violation of law.

Q. Mr. Ehrlichman, you are a lawyer and you know that a psychiatrist is forbidden by law to divulge the confidential information he gets from his client, his patient, on examination of the patient to make a diagnosis without his client's consent. Now, don't you know that?

A. I didn't know that was a matter of law. I know there is a privilege that exists as a matter of law, but I don't know that it's a criminal violation. It may well be I just didn't know.

Q. Don't you know there's a statute to that effect in every state in this union and the only statutes that make an exception to that is a judge in a court can require the physician or the psychiatrist to testify about his patient if he finds it's in the interest of justice? A. No, I didn't know that, Mr. Chairman.

Q. And yet you were adviser to the President of the United States?

A. Well, I dare say there are a lot of things I don't know, Mr. Chairman.

Q. Well, if you had known the law, I would submit that in all probability, you would also have known that the only way you could get the opinion of the psychiatrist, Ellsberg's psychiatrist, was by some surreptitious manner in some surreptitious fashion.

A. I don't know what you mean by surreptitious, Mr. Chairman. I do know this from experience, that information of this kind is obtainable. Insurance adjusters obtain it, investigators obtain it, attorneys obtain it, and they obtain it through nurses, through nurses' aides, through all kinds of sources. And we would be kidding ourselves if we didn't admit that.

Q. You don't know what the word "surreptitious" means?

A. Well, I don't know what you meant by it in that question, Mr. Chairman.

Q. Well, can't you answer? Don't you know really?

A. I did know the word. You were using it in a pejorative sense, Mr. Chairman, and I was not sure just how.

Q. Some people do things in illegal fashion, obtain information in illegal fashion. But I would assert as a lawyer that when you go to getting the record of a patient, of a doctor's opinion of his patient, his recorded opinion that you cannot get it legally without consent of the patient or without an order of a judge. The only other way you can get it is in an illegal or unethical way.

July 25, 1973

SENATOR TALMADGE: Now, if the President could authorize a covert break-in [of Dr. Ellsberg's psychiatrist's office] and you do not know exactly what that power would be limited, you do not think it could include murder or other crimes beyond covert break-ins, do you?

A. I do not know where the line is, Senator.

Q. Where is the check on the chief executive's inherent power as to where that power begins and ends, that is what I am trying to determine. Do you remember when we were in law school we studied a famous principle of law that came from England and also is well known in this country, that no matter how humble a man's cottage is that even the King of England cannot enter without his consent.

A. I am afraid that has been considerably eroded over the years, has it not?

Q. Down in my country we still think it is a pretty legitimate principle of law. Now, you authorized this in the name of national security I believe.

A. We believe that we had a serious national security problem at that time, yes, sir.

Q. If you had thought that the psychiatrist's profile had been in a lock box in a bank in Washington you would not authorize the entry would you, Mr. Ehrlichman?

A. Mr. Chairman, I wonder if we could perhaps escalate this to the level of seriousness that it was viewed in the Government at the time. This was not simply an effort to pick up gossip. This was an effort to crack what was at that moment the largest raid on top secret documents that had ever been made in the history of this Government. I think it would be much more.

Q. I agree with your statement [in] that I thought it was a very reprehensible act but does one reprehensible act authorize another? Now, did the President authorize that break-in? A. Not in express terms, no sir. At least not to my knowledge.

Q. As a matter of fact, in a subsequent statement he expressly denied it, didn't he?

A. I read his statement, and I have heard testimony here. I would not be totally responsive to your question, however, if I did not add one thing, Senator. On the 24th of July [1971], I sat in a meeting where the President gave Mr. Krogh his charter, his instructions. I must say that the President put it to Mr. Krogh very strong that he wanted Mr. Krogh and the people in this unit to take such steps as were necessary and I can recall in that conversation specific reference to the use of polygraphs and summary procedure for the discharging of Federal employes who might have been involved in this episode.

Q. Let me read the President's own language to you taken from the Congressional Record of May 23, 1973. "Consequently, as President, I must and do assume responsibility for such acts despite the fact that I, at no time, approved or had knowledge of them." And he was talking about the break-in of [Dr. Lewis] Fielding's office. [i.e., the office of Daniel Ellsberg's psychiatrist.]

A. Senator, I think it's important in that same connection, however, to read the previous two paragraphs which say "At about the time the unit was created Daniel Ellsberg was identified as the person who had given the Pentagon Papers to The New York Times. I told Mr. Krogh—'this is the President speaking'—that as a matter of first priority the unit should find out all it could about Mr. Ellsberg's associates, and his motives. Because of the extreme gravity of the situation and not then knowing what additional national secrets Mr. Ellsberg might disclose, I did impress upon Mr. Krogh the vital importance to the national security of his assignment. I did not authorize and had no knowledge of any illegal means to be used to achieve this goal. However, because of the emphasis I put on the crucial importance of protecting the national security I can understand how highly motivated individuals could have felt justified in engaging in specific activities that I would have disapproved had they been brought to my attention."

Now that refers to this July 24 conversation between the President and Mr. Krogh, and I must say that I think that is a fair characterization of the urgency which the President expressed to Mr. Krogh and undoubtedly a recognition of the fact that one in Mr. Krogh's situation might well believe that he had been charged with taking extraordinary measures to meet what the President described in very graphic terms.

Q. Mr. Ehrlichman, isn't it a fact, assuming for the sake of argument that your theory is correct, that the President could authorize such a break-in, isn't it a fact that the President himself and not Mr. Ehrlichman would have to authorize that break-in?

A. Sir, I did not ever authorize a wiretap or any other extraordinary measure on my own.

Q. Isn't it a fact that the break-in occurred more than 60 days after publication of those papers in The New York Times?

A. Oh, I think two things have to be said here: One, the investigation was not to prevent the newspapers from publishing the Pentagon Papers because that was, of course, an accomplished fact. The investigation here was to find out who had stolen top secret documents, and disseminated them, not only to the newspapers but, and we had at the time strong reason to believe that the documents delivered to the Soviet Embassy were not the same documents as were printed in The New York Times.

Q. Why didn't the F.B.I. handle the job?

A. Well, I have explained that yesterday. The situation was a unique one, which the Attorney General described to us, in which the Director simply refused to permit his top people, Mr. Brennan, particularly, to conduct interviews of some of Mr. Ellsberg's family and it was a situation where the case was not being treated as a primary case by the bureau, and Mr. Krogh came to us and said, "I can't move the bureau on this with the kind of cooperation that the case deserves."

Q. You are not saying that the President of the United States was helpless in trying to get the cooperation of the F.B.I. are you?

A. I am saying that the Attorney General reported to the President an extremely difficult situation with the Director which he felt could lead to the resignation of some of the top people in the bureau. That while the Attorney General felt that he could reverse the Director's decision with regard to the suspension of Mr. Brennan he did not think that at the time he could force the Director to an acceleration of the bureau effort on this subject without a total rupture with the Director.

Q. You don't mean to intimate in any way, shape, fashion or form, do you, Mr. Ehrlichman, that J. Edgar Hoover was in any way soft on Communism or national security, do you?

A. J. Edgar Hoover clearly was not that. At the same time it appears that Dr. Ellsberg's father-in-law was a very close friend of his and I think everyone who knew of the Director knew of his loyalty to his close friends.

SENATOR GURNEY: Now, as you recall, Mr. Dean testified before this committee and was very positive in his testimony that as a result of this meeting on Jan. 3 [1973] Ehrlichman checked with Nixon and told Colson to give Bittman [attorney for E. Howard Hunt] assurance clemency would be offered. Would you comment on that?

A. Yes, sir. That is a story that had an out-of-town try-out like many of Mr. Dean's episodes. Now, what we would see is that a story would appear in one of the news magazines or a newspaper in a certain version and when Mr. Dean got here to testify, he had a slightly different version, but the differences were extremely material. This was one of them. The version which got the try-out was that I had jumped up from the meeting, run out—presumably to the President's office—come back and said, fine, fellows, it is all set, you have got it. And that had its problems, because, of course, the meeting to which he was referring did not take place until 7 o'clock in the evening and the President's log makes very clear the fact that I had no meetings with the President that day. So factually, the printed story in the media would not wash.

Now, when Mr. Dean testified, his story was, well, we had this meeting and this was discussed, and then I heard a day or two later that Mr. Ehrlichman had given assurances to Mr. Colson that he had checked this and that it was O.K.

Now, that likewise is not going to wash, because the only meeting that I had with the President, as shown by the President's log and by my log, was a meeting which involved other people at half past—no, at 3:02 on the 4th of January. Mr. Haldeman was in the meeting the entire time, Dr. Kissinger was in the meeting a substantial portion of time, and I can assure you, Senator, that executive clemency was not discussed at any time.

Q. You never took up this matter with President Nixon at any time?

A. I did not have to.

Q. Except in July?

A. I knew what the marching orders were from July, and I particularly knew because it was my strong feeling, that he [Mr. Nixon] ratified and adopted, that this was a closed subject and we must never get near it, and that it would be the surest way of having the actions of these burglars imputed to the President.

Q. To put it bluntly, your testimony is that John Dean told an untruth?

A. Yes, sir, twice. Once in the out-of-town try-out, once here.

Q. Let us go to another area which involved you and Mr. Dean and that is the papers that were taken from Hunt's safe after it was opened by Dean's people. Some of these papers, as you know, were very sensitive. Some were contained in a briefcase of Mr. Hunt's. The testimony, of course, here is that Dean had a conversation with you about this and you made some suggestions about disposing of the papers that were in the briefcase. My recollection is that you advised Mr. Dean to "deep six" these papers. Would you care to tell us about this meeting?

A. That was a meeting, if I heard the testimony correctly, which was also attended by other people and should be susceptible of determination from independent witnesses. To correct an assumption in your question, Senator, I did not know the contents of Mr. Hunt's safe except in the most general terms. I was told, and I can't say who told me—probably Mr. Dean—that there was a pistol and a tape recorder and a number of documents, some of which had nothing to do with Watergate but were very politically sensitive. Now, that was the general description. I had no occasion to look at them, I never saw them except as a few of them were sealed in an envelope and handed to Pat Gray.

We had had a meeting for two purposes on the 19th [June, 1972], which included Mr. Colson, Mr. Kehrli, staff secretary, and Ken Clawson on the White House staff. The meeting was for, as I say, two purposes—one, to try to determine what the facts were about Howard Hunt's employment status, which was very murky at that point in time, because of some lack of documents or some confusion of documents.

The other purpose was to talk about what to do about this safe which had been found on the premises, and apparently had things in it that related to Howard Hunt, who was then, if not arrested, at least a prime suspect.

The instructions which we agreed upon at that meeting were that a number of people should be present at the opening of that safe. We knew we had to have something from the G.S.A. because they had to open the safe. But in addition to that, I specified to Mr. Kehrli, being present, that Mr. Dean be present and take custody. Then I think Mr. Kehrli suggested that a Secret Service agent be present under the circumstances, because we were breaking into a safe in the White House. And that was the arrangement that was agreed upon when we broke up on the 19th.

My purpose in doing that was twofold. One, this was a kind of extraordinary procedure and I thought there ought to be people who could, one, later on tell what had happened, two, I was concerned about the custody of these documents, the chain of evidence, the perfectibility of proof if the time came and there were documents in there that bore on Mr. Hunt's liability.

So that was done, and it was done, I believe, that same day or that evening.

Q. Yes.

A. Now, it seems to me that it would have been folly for me at some later time, then, to suggest that the briefcase be thrown into the flood tide of the Potomac.

Now, there was in this story also the suggestion of shredding. I don't think in my life that I have suggested to anybody that a document be shredded, shredding is just not something that I have ever resorted to under any circumstances, nor proposed to anybody under any circumstances. As I said, we have a great disposal system at the White House. If you really want to get rid of a document, you put it in a burn bag and you seal it up and it's never opened again, and it goes into a furnace and that is the end of it.

Q. But to get back to this second meeting when John Dean comes to you and tells you, we have got some pretty sensitive papers here, and, as he alleges, you say, "Well, deep six this briefcase." What's your testimony on that?

A. I did not. I have no recollection of that kind of a conversation.

Q. Did you make any other suggestion to him that he dispose of these papers in any other way?

A. We discussed what to do about some papers which he told me about in the safe which really should not be leaked. Again, we have to come back to our F.B.I. problem. And he was genuinely concerned and when he explained it to me, I shared his concern, that if these documents were simply wholesaled to the Washington field office, the F.B.I., we would be reading about it in Time magazine in very short order.

Q. Now you are talking about the ones that were turned over to Gray?

A. And so Mr. Dean came up with this idea, turning them over to Pat Gray personally. And I certainly concurred in it. I thought that was an ideal solution to the problem.

Q. Did that come up in this meething when supposedly the deep six conversation came up?

A. Well, I gathered that that meeting was supposed to have been the meeting when Mr. Kehrli and the others were there. It would have necessarily been at that meeting, because the die was cast thereafter. You know the 20 bishops had witnessed the opening of the safe at this point. So it had to be that meeting.

Q. What happened to those papers?

A. He [Mr. Dean] agonized for several days about what to do with this situation [and then] said he thought he had an idea as to how to solve this problem and that would be to deliver these documents in two parcels—one parcel to the [F.B.I.] field office and the other parcel to Pat Gray. I certainly concurred in that suggestion. It seemed to me like a good way of making sure that the documents did not leak as long as Mr. Gray held on to them.

Q. And then what happened?

A. I think what I said to him was Mr. Gray was coming over that day for another appointment and why didn't he just bring them over when Pat Gray was there and deliver them to him so two of us could say that the delivery had been made and we would put an end to this evidentiary chain, so to speak.

Q. I understand that he did come over and he did bring the documents and Gray and he and you were there. Then, what happened?

A. We were there. He said, Pat, I would like to give you these. The sense of it was that these contents of Hunt's safe that were politically sensitive and that we just could not stand to have them leaked. I do not know whether he had talked to Gray before or not, because Gray seemed to understand the setting and the premise, so to speak. And he turned the documents over to him and John Dean then left.

Q. I seem to recall there was some testimony about, to Gray by someone, either Dean or you, that these documents should never see the light of day. Do you recall that?

A. I don't think—well, I don't know whether there was testimony about that. That is not a phrase that I have ever testified to. I don't recall that phrase being used.

Q. Your recollection then is that it was just made known to Gray that these were very sensitive documents, and he ought to make sure they were kept very sensitive and no one saw them. Is that the gist of it?

A. No, I think the word "politically" was in it. I think it was very clear they had political overtones rather than saying sensitive from a national security standpoint or something of that kind.

Q. Was there any discussion at that meeting that would give Gray the thought that he ought to destroy them? A. No, sir.

Q. You are positive on that score?

A. And the reason that I am positive, Senator, is that when I heard that he had in fact destroyed them I was just nonplussed. There was just nothing in the contemplation of the people in that room at the time of the delivery that would have led to that kind of a conclusion.

SENATOR INOUYE: Mr. Ehrlichman, your record indicates that you are a fine lawyer, you served for a time as the President's most trusted legal aide, so I would assume that like most of us here, you are aware of the code of ethics written and unwritten about the profession. A. Yes, sir.

Q. Now, in April, 1973, the so called U.S. v. Russo-Ellsberg case was in full bloom. The papers were covering this almost daily. It was a matter of grave interest and concern, not just for the press but for, I think, members of the Congress, and the people of the United States. Now, in April of 1973 you called the presiding judge, Judge W. Matthew Byrne, did you not, and invited him to visit you at San Clemente? A. Yes.

Q. And it was to discuss a possible appointment of Judge Byrne as the Director of the F.B.I.

A. Well generally speaking, yes, not precisely but generally.

Q. And you involved the President of the United States, who is also a lawyer, in the discussions. A. No sir, I did not.

Q. Did the President also meet Judge Byrne?

A. Yes, but I cannot say that I involved him. As Judge Byrne and I were talking the President came out of his office and came over and greeted Judge Byrne.

Q. What was the nature of your conversation with Judge Byrne?

A. It was evident that the Gray nomination was not going to be sustained, and at the President's instruction I contacted Judge Byrne. Before I talked to Judge Byrne I talked with the Attorney General [Kleindienst] and told him of the President's instruction to me and of the fact that that Judge Byrne was going to be coming to San Clemente for a meeting.

The Attorney General expressed his wholehearted approval of that meeting. He was a very enthusiastic advocate of Judge Byrne to be nominated it Mr. Gray could not be.

The conversation which I had with Judge Byrne on the telephone was substantially this: I said, Judge, I have been asked by the President to call you. I have been asked to discuss with you a Federal appointment which is not judicial in character. I do not know whether this is an appropriate time for us to have a conversation like this because I do not know what the present situation in your trial is. The impression I had from the newspapers was that the case was in its last stages, they were either in surrebuttal or had completed surrebuttal, and I did not know at that point what the posture of the case really was.

Q. Were you aware at that point the judge had not rendered his decision?

A. Well, it was a jury case, and I was aware it had not gone to the jury yet.

Q. Had not given instructions to the jury?

A. So I said to the judge, "This is not a conversation which is urgent. We need not have it now but at some point in time I would like to have this conversation." The judge responded, "I see no reason why we couldn't talk right away."

So I said, "Well, if that is the case, what is convenient for you?" This was a Friday, I believe.

He said, "Well, I could come down this afternoon." So I said "Fine," and that is what happened. We set an appointment for four o'clock in the afternoon and he came down to my office.

When he came into my office I said again, "I am sensitive to the fact that you are trying an important lawsuit. I propose that we take a walk out toward the bluff from the office. If at any point a subject arises that you feel in any way impinges upon your ability to fairly try the case you just turn around and walk away from me and, as said before, this is not something that needs to be discussed right now. We can talk about it later without prejudice."

He said, "Fine, let's proceed on that basis." So we did.

We walked out to the bluff and back and it was a conversation of perhaps five minutes total. The gist of the conversation was that I advised him it was the President's conclusion that he was going to have to resubmit a nomination for Director of the F.B.I., that he was interested in knowing whether or not Judge Byrne had an interest in the position.

The judge indicated a very strong interest. He told me a number of his experiences with the F.B.I., that is to say he had been a U.S. attorney, he had had a number of experiences with the bureau, he had some ideas about how the bureau was falling short, some ideas about how it might be improved.

As we walked back, as I say, the President came out of his office, didn't know the judge apparently, was introduced to him. They chatted just very briefly, not about the case obviously but about just pleasantries. Their conversation lasted perhaps 30 seconds, and the President went back in his office. We returned to my office, where I said, "Well, I think the way we have to leave this is that I now know you have an interest and obviously the President has to reserve his options completely as to whether there is an offer to you or not."

So that was the end of that conversation.

The next afternoon about mid-afternoon which would have been Friday, my secretary interrupted a conversation I was having to say that the judge was on the telephone. He said, "I have been giving a lot of thought to our conversation of yesterday, and I would like to talk with you again."

I said, "Fine, I am planning to be in Santa Monica on Saturday. Would you like to meet me there?"

And he said, "Sure, I am glad to work it out."

I said, "My mother lives a block from Palisades Park in Santa Monica. Why don't we meet there and have another walk," so he said, "Fine."

We had a short walk during which he again evidenced very strong interest. He did not press me for an offer. When we got finished with the conversation, which again took about 5, no more than 10 minutes, he got in his car and left. Again no offers had been made, no acceptances.

Q. This all occurred at a time when Judge Matthew Byrne was the presiding judge in the case of United States v. Russo, Ellsberg and others, and I think it would be an understatement to say that your interest and the President's interest in the outcome of the case was more than casual.

This was a case of major importance as far as the Justice Department was concerned. You wanted the outcome to be in favor of the Government and under all those circumstances you still felt it was proper to call upon the presiding judge to make this offer. Didn't you think it was highly improper, unethical?

A. I can assure you that there was no such motive in my thoughts at the time of this meeting, and I am sure that is also true of the Attorney General, and I am sure it is true of the President. We were trying to get the best man that we could to be Director of the F.B.I., and that was the sole and singular motive.

Q. You were not aware that this would present an impression of impropriety? A. I was not.

Q. Then, I gather you were much surprised and shocked at the reaction of the public and the reaction of the legal profession when this was known?

A. In candor, I have been surprised, yes, sir, and I think it was in part because it has not been fully explained. I am grateful for this opportunity to tell exactly what happened.

Q. Did you at any time advise the judge of your knowledge of the break-in into Dr. Fielding's office? A. No.

Q. Why did you not advise him of that, sir?

A. Well, I think that would have been extraordinarily improper from two standpoints.

Q. I would like to know them.

A. The first one, of course, was that I was under a strict

injunction from the President as to that entire national security subject matter.

But secondly, for a member of the executive branch to talk to a sitting judge about a matter affecting a trial before him at that time without going through the counsel of the President or the Attorney General or the trial lawyers involved in the case, it seems to me, would have been, if what I did was improper, that would have been impropriety squared.

Q. I have been sent this note from the chief counsel on the Canon of Ethics. "The attorney is under duty not to impair the confidence of the public and the integrity of the judiciary."

A. Well, I am afraid that is a great catchall.

Q. Is that not rather clear? Did it give the impression to the public that an attempt was made to compromise Judge Byrne?

A. Well, if it were given, it was certainly a false impression.

SENATOR WEICKER: Mr. Ehrlichman, this morning, I believe you discussed the justification for the plumbers group—that you were not getting cooperation from the F.B.I. and had the opposition of the Director, Mr. Hoover.

A. No. The special unit itself was created in response to a strong feeling by the President that the White House had to more closely supervise the departments, to do their own job in plugging leaks, finding out who were disseminating these documents, and so forth. So the origin of that unit and the original reason for that being was for that purpose. It was not originally set up as a police organization or an investigatory organization or anything of that kind.

But then, what Mr. Krogh ran into this hard place in getting information, it was a last resort to use these two people who were in the unit to do this one particular [Ellsberg] investigatory job.

Q. Because, in fact the information could not be obtained by the F.B.I., is that correct?

A. Would not, yes.

Q. Would not.

I would like to read to you a letter dated Aug. 3, 1971, to Mr. Krogh from the director, J. Edgar Hoover.

"Dear Mr. Krogh:

"By letter dated July 29, 1971, the President advised me that he had directed that you examine in depth the circumstances of the many recent disclosures of top secret and other sensitive material to the public. He asked that I forward to you all information acquired to date, including individual reports for interviews, with respect to 17 persons who were named in an attachment to his letter. One of these was Daniel Ellsberg, principal suspect in the disclosure of the 'McNamara Study' to various newspapers. He asked that a comprehensive background paper on Ellsberg be sent to you.

"Enclosed are 17 memoranda containing the information mentioned by the President. We have interviewed five of the individuals involved in connection with our investigation in the Ellsberg case. We also endeavored to interview a sixth one, Mr. Charles M. Cooke, but he declined to submit to interview by the F.B.I. without the specific clearance of Deputy Attorney General Richard G. Kleindienst.

"If you concur, we will proceed with interviews of all of the remaining individuals except Daniel Ellsberg."

Would you say this is fairly clear evidence that the F.B.I. was perfectly willing to perform its functions insofar as the Ellsberg matter was concerned?

A. I think all of us who have had experience with Mr. Hoover recognize that letters of this kind were a method that he had frequently of justifying short-fall in performance by the bureau. I don't know whether this was window dressing or what this was.

Q. Do you feel, in other words, Mr. Hoover is lying in this letter?

A. No, I think Mr. Hoover is resorting to a well-known bureaucratic device of papering the file and particularly a device that is familiar to those who have seen the President shake up somebody in one of the departments or agencies. You immediately get an enormous column of justification back and when you thumb through it you see most of it is stale bread.

SENATOR ERVIN: The Senate is going to have several more votes, and there will be very little interrogation of the witness until the morning but I do want to take this occasion to amplify the legal discussion and I want to mention a little, I want to mention a little of the Bible, a little of history and a little of law.

The concept embodied in the phrase every man's home is his castle represents the realization of one of the most ancient and universal hungers of the human heart. One of the prophets said, described the mountain of the Lord as being a place where every man might dwell under his own vine and fig tree with none to make him afraid.

And then this morning, Senator Talmadge talked about one of the greatest statements ever made by any statesman, that was William Pitt the Elder, and before this country revolted against the King of England, he said this:

"The poorest man in his cottage may bid defiance to all the forces of the crown. It may be frail, its roof may shake, the wind may blow through it, the storm may enter, the rain may enter, but the King of England cannot enter. All his force dares not cross the threshold of the ruined tenements."

And yet we are told here today, and yesterday, that what the King of England can't do, the President of the United States can.

The greatest decision that the Supreme Court of the United States has ever handed down in my opinion is that of Ex Parte Millikin which is reported in 4 Wallace 2, and the things I want to mention appear on page 121 of that opinion.

In that case, President Lincoln, or rather some of his supporters, raised a claim that since the Civil War was in progress that the military forces in Indiana had a right to try for treason a man who—they called copperheads in those days, that were sympathetic towards the South—a civilian who had no connection with the military forces, so they set up a military commission and they tried this man, a civilian, in a military court, and sentenced him to death.

One of the greatest lawyers this nation ever produced, Jeremiah Black, brought the battle to the Supreme Court and he told in his argument, which is one of the greatest arguments of all time, how the Constitution of the United States came into being. He said that the people who drafted and ratified that Constitution were determined that not one drop of the blood which had been shed throughout the ages to wrest power from arbitrary authority should be lost. So they went through all of the great documents of the English law from Magna Carta on down, and whatever they found there they incorporated in the Constitution, to preserve the liberties of the people.

Now the argument was made by the Government in that case that although the Constitution gave a civilian the right to trial in civilian courts, and the right to be indicted before a grand jury before he could be put on trial and then a right to be tried before a petit jury, the Government argued that the President had the inherent power to suspend those constitutional principles because of the great emergency which existed at that time, when the country was torn apart in the civil strife.

The Supreme Court of the United States rejected the argument that the President had any inherent power to ignore or suspend any of the guarantees of the Constitution, and Judge David Davis said, in effect, "The good and wise men who drafted and ratified the Constitution foresaw that troublous times would arise, when rulers and people would become restive under restraint and seek by sharp and decisive measures to accomplish ends deemed just and proper, and that the principles of constitutional liberty would be put in peril unless established by irrepealable law."

Then he proceeded to say, "And for these reasons, these good and wise men drafted and ratified the Constitution as a law for rulers and people alike, at all times and under all circumstances."

Then he laid down this great statement, "No doctrine involving more pernicious consequences was ever invented by the wit of man than that any of its provisions can be suspended during any of the great exigencies of government."

And notwithstanding that we have it argued here in this year of our Lord 1973 that the President of the United States has a right to suspend the Fourth Amendment and to have burglary committed just because he claims, or somebody acting for him claims, that the records of a psychiatrist about the emotional or mental state of his patient, Ellsberg, had some relation to national security.

Now, President Nixon himself defined the national security

in one of his directives as including only two things: national defense, and relations with foreign countries. However, in the world opinions of a psychiatrist about the mental state or the emotional state or the psychological state of his patient, even if his patient was Ellsberg, could have any relation to national defense or relations to a foreign country is something which eludes the imagination of this country lawyer.

Now, I would like to ask you one question: Why, if the President has this much power, would he not have had the inherent power to have sent somebody out there with a pistol and had it pointed at the psychiatrist and said, "I am not going to commit burglary, I am just going to rob you of those records and give me the records," would he not have had that right under your theory?

A. Are you asking me, Mr. Chairman?

Q. Yes.

A. I think that is the same question Senator Talmadge approached and undoubtedly in a situation such as I put, for instance, where you knew there was going to be an atomic attack tomorrow, undoubtedly a measure of that kind might be necessary.

July 26, 1973

SENATOR WEICKER: You stated yesterday, Mr. Ehrlichman, that the F.B.I., through its leadership of Mr. Hoover, was not pushing the Ellsberg investigation, allegedly because of a relationship Mr. Hoover had with Mr. Ellsberg's father-in-law, Mr. Louis Marx, and that it was not until after Sept. 20, 1971, that the F.B.I. "was clicking on all eight cylinders." Would that be correct?

A. The reason that I picked that date is that on or about that date there was a meeting which the Attorney General [John N. Mitchell] had with the President where he gave the President a progress report on this matter.

Q. But in any event, one of the difficulties apparently on the F.B.I. investigation was the relationship [the friendship] between Mr. Hoover and Mr. Marx, is that correct?

A. That is what the Attorney General reported to me.

Q. Are you aware of the fact that Mr. Louis Marx was interviewed by the F.B.I. in June, 1971, before Mr. Krogh's memorandum to you of Aug. 11, which memorandum has been referred to here this morning, and before the Sept. 3, 1971, break-in by Hunt and Liddy, part of the covert operation you approved? Did you know that Mr. Marx had been interviewed in June?

A. By the F.B.I., Senator?

Q. That is correct.

A. I do not recall that fact.

Q. Well, then, how could you ascribe the reason of Louis Marx for the failure of the F.B.I. to get information from Louis Marx as the reason for setting up this unit and for having the unit investigate Ellsberg as they did?

A. Well, what I attempted to testify to was the report that I had had from two people who were intimately familiar with the progress of this case. One was Mr. Krogh and the other was the Attorney General, Mr. Mitchell. They both reported to me what I have testified to here.

Now, it may be that the explanation is that that interview was either unsatisfactory or perfunctory or did not deduce the information that was desired.

Q. Isn't it fair to say Mr. Krogh's Aug. 11 memorandum asks for Mr. Marx's interview because both you and he already knew that he had been interviewed. A. Yes.

Q. The memorandum to you says the F.B.I. have placed the Ellsberg case on special F.B.I. status.

I am going to very definitely pin down one fact here today and that is that you based the push on the F.B.I. on the fact that there was some relationship between the Director and Louis Marx which made it necessary for you to go outside of normal law enforcement channels, and we have already established the fact that Mr. Marx was interviewed in June of 1971.

Did you ever ask any member of the F.B.I. if Mr. Marx had been interviewed in June of 1971?

A. Well, if I could explain: what I attempted to testify here to the committee was the total setting in which Mr. Krogh came to me and, in turn, the representation was made to the President that the special unit inaugurate investigation of Mr. Ellsberg and his associates. It was a general problem with regard to the F.B.I.'s approach to this whole [Ellsberg] case.

And so then the recommendation was made that these two men Krogh was working with [Liddy and Hunt] be designated as investigators to go and [investigate Dr. Ellsberg]. This was very reluctantly entered into. It was not something, Senator, that the White House wanted to do or at least that I personally wanted to see the White House do, unless we had to in order to move this thing along. The President frankly was really keeping the pressure on to get results and that was the setting.

Q. Did the Attorney General know you were going to get into the covert number business?

A. The Attorney General knew. And the Director of the F.B.I. knew that the White House was going to send investigators out, yes, sir.

Q. Were you aware on July 20, 1971, that the F.B.I. had attempted to interview Dr. Fielding [Dr. Ellsberg's psychiatrist]?

A. I was aware of it at some time but I don't remember when, Senator, but I do recall the fact that they unsuccessfully attempted to interview the doctor.

Q. And this was before you decided to get into his records by covert action, is that correct?

A. I am not sure I knew that before.

Q. Now, in light of all these events, all of which transpired prior to the break-in into Dr. Fielding's office, do you maintain that this was for any other purpose, other than to smear Dr. Ellsberg?

A. I certainly do, Senator. The point is that all through this period of time on the one hand the President of the United States is pressing for results. On the other hand, Mr. Krogh is reporting to us from within the White House that he can't get the F.B.I. moving and the Attorney General is corroborating to us directly what Mr. Krogh is reporting. Now, interestingly enough, it took three months for the F.B.I. to get around to putting that special case on priority or Class A designation on this case, whatever it was, and I think the fact that some 60, 90 days passed before the bureau would put that designation on the biggest raid in top secret documents in the history of the country has to indicate a certain amount of lassitude on the part of the F.B.I. up to that point.

Q. You have seen the memorandum of Aug. 26 [1971] from Dave Young to you. [With Egil Krogh in charge of White House unit.] Do you have that memorandum with you? A. Yes, sir.

Q. Let's go to page 5. "In connection with issue 9, it is important to point out that with the recent article on Ellsberg's lawyer, Boudin, we have already started on a negative press image for Ellsberg. If the present Hunt/Liddy project No. 1 is successful, it will be absolutely essential to have an over-all game plan developed for its use in conjunction with the Congressional investigation. In this connection, I believe that the point of Buchanan's memorandum on attacking Ellsberg through the press should be borne in mind; namely, that the situation being attacked is too big to be undermined by planted leaks among the friendly press."

So you knew there was a press purpose to this break-in?

A. Well, I don't have a recollection of the memo itself. If you are asking me what I know about an express purpose of the investigation of Daniel Ellsberg, the object here was not to prosecute Mr. Ellsberg and, as far as I am concerned, not to persecute Mr. Ellsberg. The object here was to find out how it [the leak of the Pentagon papers] happened and to make sure within the Government that it did not happen again.

Now, with regard to the public relations aspects of this Ellsberg case. I do know that there was in the White House a desire to air this whole thing once the facts were known and it was hoped that a committee of the Congress would pick it up and would call witnesses and would expose how such a thing could happen in our governmental system today where the treachery was within the Government, if it was, or the treachery was in the think-tank apparatus [Rand Corporation] if there was, and I am not suggesting there was, but whether there was, and who the individuals involved were, what their motivations were, and why this thing happened.

So I don't question for a minute that there was under active consideration the possibility of fostering a Congressional inquiry into this, and I have to say it would have been a healthy thing if we could have had such a thing. But as far as the management of that particular effort is concerned I am not your man.

Q. Do you acknowledge having received it [the Aug. 26 memo]?

A. I see an "E" on it that is certainly very much my "E."

Q. And one of the questions raised in the memorandum says, "How quickly do we advance to bring about a change in Ellsberg's image?"

A. That is footnoted to the material that you just read.

SENATOR MONTOYA: On July 21 you were quoted in an article in The New York Times as being in favor of releasing the tapes which are in controversy. Did you make that kind of a statement?

A. Well, I have had a lot of trouble with quotations in The New York Times, Senator, and that is one of them.

What happened there was that I gave a television interview to a fellow, you know they come out and sit on my lawn and as I come out in the morning it is pretty well unavoidable, and this fellow said something to the effect, "Do you have anything to worry about if these tapes get out?"

And I said, "No, I don't think I have anything to worry about. I didn't know I was being taped, but I don't think I said anything there that would, that I would be ashamed of."

And he said, "Well, then, you think the President ought to release these?"

And I said, "Well, you know you have got to look at this from two standpoints, certainly from my standpoint I have no problem, but he has a much larger picture to look at."

Well, the word "certainly" is what carried on the wire, and the rest of the sentence didn't get carried, and so I saw the wire story and it said, "Ehrlichman today in response to a question should the President release these tapes, said 'certainly.'"

Well, what I said was in effect, "Certainly I don't have anything to worry about but the President has got a lot more worries than I have about the country and the separation of powers and his relationship with the Congress and so on."

Now, having just said that sentence, I will bet you The New York Times tomorrow says, "Ehrlichman says the President has a lot more to worry about than he does."

SENATOR ERVIN: You spoke of the Kerner Commission and the Warren Commission. Both of these commissions were appointed by the President in office at the time of their appointment and both of them worked in public, did they not? A. Yes, sir.

Q. And in that respect they were unlike the plumbers who were appointed in secret and whose identity was kept secret from the American people.

A. Well, Mr. Chairman, first of all, their identity was not kept secret. It was the subject of newspaper stories.

Secondly, the reason that I cited you to the reports of those commissions was because they both discussed, or so my information is, they both discussed the use of psychiatric profiles with relation to United States citizens and, of course, one of them brought me to the realization that the Secret Service does conduct such an activity with relation to United States citizens in aid of its protection of the President and the Vice President and others in trying to determine in advance who might be threats to assassination attempts.

So it goes to the point that you raised yesterday that such a technique would be illegal with regard to United States citizens.

Q. Well, was not the existence of the plumbers kept secret from the F.B.I., C.I.A. and other investigative agencies of the Government? A. No.

Q. Did you tell Mr. Hoover about them?

A. Yes, sir, and we also told the Attorney General.

Q. But anyway, you spoke in derogatory terms of Mr. Hoover.

A. No, I do not intend any derogation of Mr. Hoover.

Q. Well, you said he should have quit the office, that he did not know enough about surveillance, although he had spent his lifetime in it.

A. I did not say that and I would not intend to say that, Mr. Chairman.

Q. Well, you said he had different ideas about surveillance from what the White House had. A. No.

Q. Well, you said he would not cooperate with the White House.

A. What I said was that in a specific instance he had very fixed ideas about the degree to which the bureau should cooperate in this [Ellsberg] investigation.

Q. Yes. He had very fixed ideas when the President appointed Tom Charles Huston to devise him a method of having American citizens spied on, Mr. Hoover had the fixed idea that they ought not to resort to burglary, that they ought not to resort to the use of undercover military agents, that they ought not to resort to virtually unlimited surveillance, and they ought not to resort to mail cover, and that was stated by Tom Charles Huston in documents put in evidence here about 15 times before the President approved those documents. So he did not cooperate.

I am going to say, to speak for his defense beyond the grave since he is not here. I call attention to the fact that Tom Charles Huston told the White House 12 or 15 times in documents recommending burglary, recommending the use of undercover military agents, recommending mail coverage, recommending virtually unlimited surveillance. Twelve or 15 times he [Mr. Hoover] protested against the use of those things and yet the President approved them. And here in the very letter that he wrote to the man who had charge of the surveillance or the effort to get the record of the psychiatrist, here on Aug. 3, a month before the break-in, he said that if he, Egil Krogh, "if you concur we will proceed with interviews of all of the remaining individuals except Daniel Ellsberg."

And knowing Mr. Hoover's ideas, I think he made the exception because he did not make it a practice to interview people who were under indictment.

So there he was willing to cooperate and another thing, along about this time, as a member of the United States Senate, I was fighting the efforts of the Administration to get no-knock laws enacted, to get the detention laws enacted, to expand by executive fiat the powers of the Subversive Activity Control Board, and I was fighting against the proposition of being defender of the Department of Justice that it was all right to use undercover military agents to spy on civilians exercising their First Amendment rights.

And about at that time I got a letter from J. Edgar Hoover, "You have indeed been one of the guardians of our liberties and protectors of our freedoms. All Americans owe you a debt of gratitude."

I don't offer that as any praise of myself but I offer that as evidence of Mr. Hoover's devotion to the basic rights of American citizens, the rights not to be burglarized, and I think that since he can't speak for himself that his documents ought to be able to convey his attitude. I can understand, having heard this testimony, about the Ellsberg matter, why you say that Mr. Hoover would not cooperate with the White House, and he was on the side of liberty.

Now, you testified that the plumbers attempted to get the records of the psychiatrist in order that someone of the C.I.A. or somebody else, might develop a psychiatric profile to enable President Nixon to determine for himself whether Ellsberg was some kind of a kook or was some kind of a foreign intelligence agent. Is that what you told us?

A. Well I don't think it's a question of the President determining for himself, Mr. Chairman. I think this was an effort on the part of the special unit to do as they had done in other cases subsequently, to determine where there were holes in either in the Federal Government itself or in the Rand Corporation or these outside units that would permit a person like Ellsberg and his co-conspirators if there were any, to steal massive quantities of top secret documents and turn them over to the Russians.

Q. Well, I believe Congress set up the F.B.I. to determine what was going on in this country, didn't it?

A. Among other things, Mr. Chairman.

Q. Yes. It set up the C.I.A to determine what was going on in respect to foreign intelligence, didn't it.

A. Yes, sir. Among other agencies.

Q. It set up the National Security Agency, didn't it? A. And the Defense Intelligence Agency.

Q. And the Defense Intelligence Agency.

A. And a number of others.

Q. But it didn't set up the plumbers, did it?

A. Of course the Congress doesn't do everything, Mr. Chairman.

Q. No, But Congress is the only one [that] has got legislative power and I don't know any law that gives the President [power] to set up what some people have called the secret police, namely, the plumbers.

A. The fact is that the President is granted constitutional powers to make sure these departments of the executive branch work properly and when you have a mistake or when you have a short-fall or when you have a grievous raid on secret papers like this one, the President would be very remiss in his obligation if he didn't move forward on it.

Q. In other words, the way to cope with this thing is to set up a burglar to catch a burglar.

Now, let me ask you one other question. Didn't you know very early after the June 17 break-in that $114,000 of the President's money had been deposited, at least temporarily, in a bank account [of one] among the burglars, Bernard L. Barker.

A. I don't know that the President's money ever showed up in this.

Q. It was the proceeds of campaign funds that had been given to help elect the President, re-elect the President, don't you know that?

A. You mean campaign contributions?

Q. Yes.

A. I see. Your term was not clear.

Q. Well, I will call it Nixon's campaign funds and maybe we can agree on that. Didn't you find out very soon after the break-in that $114,000 of the President's campaign funds had found their way into the deposit account of Bernard L. Barker, one of the burglars caught in the Watergate?

A. Yes, sir. Without agreeing with the amount because I don't know the amount.

Q. Well, as a matter of fact, didn't you testify in a deposition in a civil case that on the 23d day of June, pursuant to the President's direction, that you discussed this matter of these funds being routed coming out of Mexico with General Walters?

A. Yes, sir.

Q. Yes, and the President had talked to you about it. He asked you to do that, didn't he?

A. No, he sent word to me through Mr. Haldeman.

Q. Did Mr. Haldeman bring you word and tell you it came from the President that the President wanted you to find out something about this, these Mexican checks?

A. No, sir, the thing that Mr. Haldeman said to me was that the President had asked that he and I meet with Mr. Helms and General Walters to discuss the question of whether a full all-out vigorous F.B.I. investigation might somehow turn up and compromise some on-going C.I.A. activity.

Q. Wasn't it the activity directed to the Mexican checks.

A. Not specifically. I also answered in that deposition that that subject arose at the meeting and was not a part of the instructions that came to me through Mr. Haldeman.

Q. Well, anyway, you had a meeting with General Walters on the 23d day of June. Just six days after the break-in. A. Yes.

Q. In which it became known that $114,000 of the Nixon campaign funds had been routed, rather had to come into Mr. Stans's office in the form of three Mexican checks, or four Mexican checks, and that the proceeds of those checks had been deposited in the bank accounts of a burglar in Miami.

A. I am sure that those kind of elaborate details were not discussed.

Q. Well do you know of any other campaign funds of the President, or campaign contributions that were routed into Mexico? A. Not of my own knowledge, no sir.

Q. The President was afraid that if the F.B.I. vigorously investigated these checks, it might interfere with the C.I.A.?

A. The President was concerned, he told me later, that the all-out F.B.I. investigation might compromise some C.I.A. activity in Mexico. And the way the F.B.I. was leaking that would be the surest way for that C.I.A. activity then to appear in the nation's press.

Q. And it might also explain how come $114,000 of the proceeds of a campaign contribution to him was found in the bank account of a burglar if they pursued that in investigation?

A. Well, Mr. Chairman, your inference is very unfair. Because in point of fact the President's instructions to the F.B.I were to conduct a totally unlimited all-out full-scale investigation of that and every other aspect of this Watergate matter and that Mr. Gray and Mr. Gray alone was to determine the scope. That the President would not limit that scope at all.

July 27, 1973

SENATOR GURNEY: I think Dean talked to the President on Feb. 27 and in that conversation with the President, the President assigned the investigation of Watergate, at least that current phase of it, to Dean. As I recall, he said that he wanted Dean to report directly to him. He also said that it was taking up too much of your time and also Haldeman's time.

A. Yes, Senator, except chief investigator, I think, is slightly off the track. The preoccupation at that time, as far as the President was concerned, was not in an investigation of the facts as nearly as it was to get some one person in the White House who was going to look after a number of existing problems with relation to this whole subject matter and they were primarily the problems of executive privilege and separation of powers as he saw it then, not a question of who done it.

Q. Was there ever any suspicion in your mind that the President appointed Dean to sort of be in charge of Watergate on Feb. 27 because he might have had some suspicion that maybe you were involved or Haldeman was involved or somebody else in the White House involved.

A. Well, what the President explained to me was that the central question here was one of executive privilege and the availability of Presidential assistants to testify before the Congress.

And through my notes of meetings with the President, there are three or four references to the President's strong concern that Haldeman and I were test cases, so to speak, of the availability of Presidential assistants to testify before the Congress, and I know there were some questions about his reference to us as principals. I think you have to take it in that setting. We were principals on the question of the availability of assistants to testify.

Q. Let's go to this meeting between you and Mr. Haldeman and Mr. Dean following the March 21 meeting of Dean with the President. That is when the roof sort of started to cave in, and I am curious to know what transpired in that meeting between the three. After the meeting between Dean and the President when presumably, according to Dean's testimony, Dean told the President everything he knew about Watergate.

A. There was a meeting at 3:45 on the 21st. And then that meeting moved to the President's office after about an hour.

Q. Now, could you describe to us what happened in your office?

A. The conversation, largely involved the question of testimonial availability of White House staff people. Mr. Dean did not report in my hearing what he had told the President that day.

Now, Mr. Dean and I got into a difference of opinion at that time about the question of immunity, and how that should be handled. His theory was that the President should negotiate blanket immunity for the White House staff with the Attorney General so that the entire White House staff, lock, stock and barrel could testify freely before the grand jury as to any and all facts and clear the air and everybody would be immune from prosecution. That just didn't make any sense to me from either a practical standpoint or a public appearance standpoint, and we got into a difference of opinion on that.

Q. Well now, why did he say that?

A. Well, he was looking for formula, he had come up with a concept that there ought to be some kind of a commission, an independent commission that would be set up.

Q. But when somebody talks about immunity, obviously they are afraid of ending up in the pokey. Did he say, "Now we are all going to jail so we had better get some immunity here."

A. No, he said he was concerned that people would not talk freely. Now, Mr. Dean is an immunity expert, Mr. Dean told us early in the game that he was the author of the statute which the Congress eventually adopted granting immunity to people in certain criminal situations so that they would testify against higher-ups or co-conspirators or what not, and so he gave us quite an accounting of the difference between use immunity and transactional immunity and the various technicalities of this and he explained that immunity was sort of the lubricant that was needed in this thing to get people to come forward and to fully tell their stories.

Q. Did he mention to you in this discussion who would need immunity in the White House? A. No, he did not.

Q. Who did you think might, because you had some discussion on this?

A. I don't think that I thought who might at that point. Bear in mind I had been totally out of touch with this situation for some period of time. My reaction to his proposal was to simply say to him that that was out of the question, that we simply could not expect anybody to grant immunity either on a blanket basis or on an individual basis to anybody in the White House.

Q. What was Mr. Haldeman's reaction?

A. He didn't express a reaction that I can recall to that. He was concerned, as I recall, with the general subject of executive privilege because he had been hearing from Mr. Mitchell strongly about executive privilege, and he conveyed to us Mr. Mitchell's strong feeling that the executive privilege position that the Administration was taking was untenable.

Q. Did you know at that time about who may have been knowledgeable about the break-in.

A. That developed as a result of phone calls that Bob Haldeman was getting while we were in San Clemente. I left about five or six days later for California. While we were out there, we began realizing there was a strong conflict between Dean and Mitchell on this whole question of people going to the grand jury or the committee and so on, and could not get a feel of it because I didn't know what was behind it and I began trying to find out what was behind it, and then I talked to Mr. O'Brien and that is the first time that I knew about these four meetings back in November and December [1971], January and February [1972], where these plans were laid.

Then I began inquiring through Mr. Moore and others as to what Mr. Mitchell testified to that was worrying him, and why he didn't think Dean ought to go near the U.S. attorney or the grand jury and what his concerns were.

Q. What transpired in the President's office when you moved the meeting over there?

A. There was virtually a replay of this difference of opinion between Dean and me on the question of immunity for the White House staff. The President was advancing a premise at that meeting [that] everybody goes to the grand jury, nobody goes to the Senate committee and we go to the grand jury right away, and the White House staff marches down there in platoons, if necessary, and we get it all cleaned up, and if there is any problem, why, the problems are smoked out.

Q. Was that the decision when the meeting ended?

A. No, no, as I say it was advanced as sort of a premise for argument and Mr. Dean said, "Well, that is what I have been saying, we ought to do that. We ought to do it under a blanket immunity and in that way all the truth will come out," and I was saying, I just think that is wrong, number one, I do not think anybody in the White House is entitled to immunity if they have done something wrong, and then they ought to take the penalty. More than that, I think it would be just terribly misunderstood by the American people.

Q. Well, now what did the President say to this difference of opinion between you and Dean on immunity?

A. He said that he would like to have us have a meeting with John Mitchell, and sit down and talk with him not only about that, about the basic question of whether staff should appear here or at the grand jury or both, but also recasting the Administration approach to the question of executive privilege because he knew Mr. Mitchell had very strong views on that.

Q. The next day you did have such a meeting, did you not? With the three of you and Mr. Mitchell?

A. Right, and then that meeting, likewise went over to the President's office in the afternoon. I was only in a part of the first meeting held in Mr. Haldeman's office. While I was there there was largely a discussion of executive privilege, and Mr. Mitchell's views that the Administration position had been too restrictive, and that it was untenable both from a legal standpoint and also from a political standpoint.

Q. Now, again in this meeting in the President's office, there was no discussion of gory details of Watergate.

A. There was none, there was none. When the four of us went to the President's office again, it was largely how to get the whole story out, the question again of the grand jury, of immunity, in John Mitchell's presence with the President trying these various things out on John Mitchell and it finally ended up with the President assigning to Mr. Dean that he wanted Mr. Dean to sit down and write out a statement as completely as possible of the facts of this whole subject matter.

Q. This is why he went to Camp David some time later, a few days later?

A. Apparently. That is what I was told, that he found it impossible to do this job with the Gray hearings going on and the distractions and Mr. Gray making accusations against him and so on.

Q. Now, this really puzzled me. Did not the President say at any of these meetings, "Now, listen fellows, here I have heard all about this from John Dean, what gives here, what are we going to do now, what plans do you have, who is going to get this out? We have got to do it." No discussion of that?

A. Senator, I have great difficulty in believing that the President was told what Mr. Dean says he was told because of the President's approach to this, which I saw in these two meetings.

Now, I do not know what Mr. Dean told him. I guess Mr. Haldeman was in one of those meetings or part of it and maybe he is in a position to tell you.

Q. He never told you anything about what transpired in the meeting between the President, Haldeman and Dean?

A. Well, he told me what Mr. Dean has testified to is not true. I am forced to the assumption by the President's conduct afterward that one of two things was taking place. Either he still confidently believed that the White House was without blame, and that Mr. Mitchell was without blame and was acting accordingly, or he was involved in setting a few snares on the trail and was playing it cool, because he did not get into any of the January, February, March planning meeting business or the involvement of January, of John Mitchell of any of those kinds of subjects which presumably Mr. Dean had laid all out for him, if you are to believe Mr. Dean.

Q. Well now, did the President lift the phone up at any time and say "John, I want you to come over to the office area and talk about Watergate, what you know about it."

A. No sir, not until way late in the game. He lifted up the phone one day and called me down and said, "I am satisfied that John Dean is in this so deeply that he simply cannot any longer have anything to do with it."

Q. That is when he transferred the assignment to you? A. Yes, sir.

Q. What date was that?

A. March 30.

Q. Would you tell the committee what you found and what you reported to the President.

A. The first thing that I did in another conversation with the Attorney General was to arrange to have someone in the Department of Justice prepare for me a thorough brief of the laws of attorney-client privilege, executive privilege, obstruction of justice and all of these objects that we seem to be encountering in this.

With Mr. O'Brien's arrival [at San Clemente], however, that was my first interview, and it brought me a whole new picture of this whole matter. A lot of information in what Mr. O'Brien gave me that I had never heard before—about money, about the involvements of people who had various funds of money and carried money around and who got money and how Liddy got money and this kind of thing which was all a brand new subject to me at that point.

Q. Did he give you any information on the planning of the break-in?

A. Yes, and [about] those four meetings [on intelligence gathering] and that whole business.

I had only one other substantive interview while we were at San Clemente in the remaining three or four days and that was with Mr. Kalmbach, but I became aware through Mr. Haldeman, who was reporting to me, conflicting conversations that he was having with Mitchell and Dean on this whole subject of should Dean go to the grand jury or should Dean go to the prosecutor, and we began trying to understand what lay behind this.

Well, I had the background of Mr. O'Brien's interview, and we zeroed in on the fact that it had to do with these four meetings or three meetings or whatever there were, and whether or not Mr. Mitchell might have some exposure for perjury on account of having testified that the meetings were canceled or not.

Q. Yes.

A. And so I had Bob Haldeman trying to get a straight answer out of Mr. Mitchell and he said he could not, so I called Dick Moore and asked him if he would talk to John Mitchell because I knew they had a close relationship.

Mr. Moore reported back that Mr. Mitchell was confident that he had not in any way violated any perjury statute, and that he just did not think it was a good idea for the President's lawyer to be going out and testifying, in other words, it was an attorney-client privilege kind of position that he was contending for. It did not satisfy me.

Q. Mitchell now talking about Dean should not testify?

A. That is correct.

In any event, on the way back we called and asked John Dean to meet us in my office when we returned to Washington that night, and he did so [on April 8].

We had a two-hour meeting, Bob Haldeman, John Dean and I, to try and understand what this hang-up was between Mitchell and Dean. We still did not have a feel for it. Then, for the first time, Mr. Dean talked to us about the four meetings or the three meetings back in January and February and explained some of the nuances of the cover-up story with regard to Mr. Magruder and the meeting which he, Dean, Magruder and Mitchell had had in Mr. Mitchell's law office at a time when they were gathered with the attorneys in the case to discuss grand jury testimony where the three of them had retired to Mr. Mitchell's partners' office away from the attorneys and had discussed how to reconcile their respective recollection of the events of the early 1972 period. So that was the first time that I had from Mr. Dean directly this subject matter.

Q. Did he talk to you at that time about his orchestration of the perjury of Magruder?

A. He did, but he did it in very delicate terms. He did not in any way admit to me flatly that he had, in fact orchestrated it to perjury. He indicated that he had had a part in the preparation of the testimony, that there were, well, I have forgotten how, it was a very careful explanation which did not really implicate Mr. Dean in suborning to perjury by any means, but he indicated that he was well familiar with the problems between Magruder and Mitchell, on the one hand.

He felt that Mr. Mitchell had problems which were causing Mr. Mitchell to say that Mr. Dean should not go and talk to the prosecutor or the grand jury and so this was very thoroughly discussed during that meeting.

Q. These problems between Dean and Magruder, specifically,

did they involve who was responsible for the break-in, in giving the green light to it, is that what you mean?

A. I gathered not. I think they involved disputes in their recollection as to what took place at these Liddy meetings, so-called, back in the early part of 1972.

Q. Did he go in at that meeting to any detail about his own involvement from June on [in the] cover-up?

A. No, not in evidentiary terms at all. We talked about the President's desire—the President on the flight back, as I recall, we had a meeting on the flight back of about, nearly two hours about this and the President decided he wanted Mr. Dean to go to the grand jury, so we conveyed that to Mr. Dean at that time.

Q. What was his reaction to that?

A. He was still very much interested in the question of immunity. He had some information, as I recall, about how the prosecutors felt about the White House, and so he imparted that to us, that he did not feel that anybody in the White House was a target of the prosecutors, that they were after some people who had obstructed justice, like Mardian and LaRue and people at the committee, but that he, Dean, felt that something like an estoppel or functional immunity or something could be worked out with the prosecutors if he went to testify and he seemed generally in agreement with the idea that he go and testify.

Q. Was there any discussion at that meeting about your role in Watergate or Haldeman's role in Watergate?

A. That did not come until this meeting of the 13th of April. On the 13th, after 2:30 or 3 o'clock in the afternoon I had a conversation with Dean which was apparently as a result of further contacts which he had had with the prosecutor. He told me that Liddy had talked with the prosecutors off the record very completely and that they might get him to talk on the record. That his attorney was going to try to get Mr. Mitchell to support his view that Liddy ought to talk on the record. And it turned out that that was incorrect apparently, but that was at least what he told me, and I suspect what was happening here was that the prosecutors were telling him this trying to get him to move to come forward and make a disclosure.

Apparently, the prosecutors were playing this kind of a game with a lot of these people at this time, saying, "So and so has talked so you better had come and talk," and passing this word along.

He told me that Hunt was back testifying before the grand jury at that time but lying. That that grand jury was also taking testimony, or the prosecutors, at least, were taking testimony from Strachan and McCord, that there would be no indictment of anyone in the White House, that at all costs he felt a special prosecutor should be avoided in this case, because of the involvement, he said, of Caulfield and Krogh. I did not get the significance of that at the time but presumably that referred to some of Caulfield's intelligence gathering activities and Krogh's involvement with the plumbers. He said, "They won't subpoena me but it is better if I cooperate."

Now, he went back into the meetings in Mitchell's office about money. I was inquiring of him now about cover-up money. He said that "the way I got involved" was that Mitchell "requested me to help."

He said, "LaRue and Mr. O'Brien would urge that money be made available. Mitchell would postpone making a decision until the last minute and the way he would get this thing off his desk would be by calling me—Dean." He said, "the U.S. attorney does not want to cause the White House problems. They tell Dean that Magruder, Mitchell are involved in the pre-Watergate matter and that LaRue, Mitchell and Mardian are involved in the post-Watergate matter."

He said, "I don't think Jeb can crack a deal," meaning a deal with the prosecutors, "for immunity."

Then I have a little symbol on these notes [on meeting with Dean] which summarizes the exposure which he thought that Bob Haldeman and I had in this matter, mine being my connection with Herb Kalmbach in the provision of money for the defendants, and I have the number 350 which relates to the $350,000 fund which presumably involves Bob Haldeman.

He said, "neither one of these are indictable but they are going to be awkward to explain. I don't think either of them are a problem for you in an ultimate sense."

Q. Were these notes made at the time of the meeting?

A. Yes, sir, as we talked. You will recall he testified about five different ways about looks of anguish, disbelief, scorn, whatnot, on my face at the time he said I was indictable. In point of fact at the time he said I was not indictable but that the Kalmbach thing might be a problem for me as being misunderstood. I said, "Well, I just don't see how it could, John," and then we discussed just that, the assumptions which he had made that there was nothing improper about it and so on.

Q. At one of these meetings, and I can't remember which one it was now because there were several, but Dean testified that there was a discussion between you and him, and I think Haldeman, that the best way to settle Watergate would have Mitchell come forward. Do you recall anything on that?

A. Yes. During that meeting and during subsequent meetings between Mr. Haldeman and me and meetings between Haldeman, Dean and me on the two occasions, I think we had, subsequent to that, there was a lot of speculation about John Mitchell and his place in all of this. And of course he was not saying anything to anybody at that point in time, and none of us really had a feel for this. I can recall at one of these meetings Bob Haldeman saying, "I wonder if we are taking all this anguish just to protect John Mitchell."

It was a question, it was not an assertion, but I think we all shared at various times that question in our minds as to whether the beating everybody was taking on the subject of Watergate was because he was not continuing forward.

That was one of the reasons that the President asked me to meet with Mr. Mitchell on the afternoon of, Saturday the 14th of April, to say to him for the President that if Mr. Mitchell thought his silence was now serving the Presidency that was a misapprehension, that the President didn't want him to sit silent if he knew something unless Mr. Mitchell felt from his own personal point that was an exercise of his own rights, in which case that was up to him. And I delivered that message to him at that time, but that was a continuing question all the way through this period of time.

July 30, 1973

MR. DASH: Mr. Ehrlichman, I will just ask a couple of questions to get back to the Ellsberg [psychiatrist] break-in, [on] the sincerity of your statement that you felt it was legal.

Is it not a fact, that this is the first time you have asserted publicly before any investigating body the claim that the break-in of Dr. Fielding's office was legal for national security?

A. Well, I think unlike the other investigative bodies this one goes far beyond mere fact and gets into these associated questions.

Q. But you have spoken publicly on this subject, have you not, on this so-called Ellsberg break-in?

A. Well, I do not know what you call speaking publicly. I have talked to the press.

Q. And you also appeared on Mike Wallace's program "Sixty Minutes?" A. Yes, I did.

Q. Do you recall in that interview your statement that there was no way to condone that action? Now, if in fact you believed that, at that time, that it was legal, would you be saying there was no way to condone it?

A. Well, I think you will remember my testifying here, Mr. Dash, that at the time it was reported to me, I did not condone it. It was simply beyond my contemplation that there would be a resort to the break-in in order to do this job that they were assigned to do, this investigation.

Q. But you have testified and spent quite a bit of your time testifying that the break-in was actually a legal act in the interest of national security.

A. I believe that is a sound position.

Q. When did you first get that view? You said based on the advice of eminent counsel? Is it not true that you have recently been advised by counsel based on the statutes provided for you that this was a legal act?

A. Well, certainly. I had no occasion to brief it until I left the White House, Mr. Dash.

Q. Then you never really believed at the time or had any view-point when the break-in took place that this was legal?

A. Well, I certainly had a viewpoint, and I certainly had a strong feeling of the propriety of the President's actions in attempting to plug these leaks.

Q. That is not my question. A. Yes, it is.

Q. Mr. Ehrlichman, that is not the question, the question is the break-in.

A. Mr. Dash, are you going to interrupt my answers?

Q. No, and you have used the questioning for making speeches throughout the hearing.

A. Let me give my answer and if you do not feel it is responsive why don't you point out where it is not?

Q. I hope you will give a responsive answer.

A. I will do my very best. I understand your question to be whether or not I had a belief or impression that the thing that the President had assigned here in creating this special unit was legal and proper, and my answer to you is that I had a continuing impression that the charge given to Mr. Krogh on the 24th of July was in all respects within the President's constitutional pre-rogatives. I had then a present impression at that time that this was well within the President's national security powers, and that has continued to be my impression forward.

Now, since I left the White House and have retained counsel, obviously they have done some intensive briefing on the subject and you have seen the fruits of that in the colloquy between the chairman and Mr. Wilson. It is a much more refined and precise and substantiated position on the law than I had any occasion to make prior to this time.

Q. Is it also true that you were totally ignorant, Mr. Ehrlichman, of the fact that actually the President and Mr. Haldeman had been informed that surreptitious entries, or break-ins for national security purposes were clearly illegal and constitute the crime of burglary prior to the break-in? Were you ever aware of that?

A. Well, if you are speaking of the Huston, the Tom Huston memos [of 1970 on an intelligence operation], of course, the subject there was an entirely different subject, and that was domestic intelligence, domestic security. Here you are dealing in the area of foreign intelligence and national security and it is quite another subject.

Q. Have you reviewed that document, Mr. Ehrlichman? A. No.

Q. Well, Mr. Ehrlichman, the document deals both with national security and with internal security and when that document was presented by this committee here in testimony the chairman, with the support of the committee, excised out those areas of national security. But it dealt with a total plan of dealing with intelligence gathering both involving foreign countries and national security as well as internal security, and let me read to you— . . .

I asked whether or not you were aware whether the President and Mr. Haldeman had been ever informed prior to this break-in that such break-ins for national security were in fact clearly illegal and constitute the crime of burglary? A. I was not.

Q. But you did testify, Mr. Ehrlichman, that in March of this year you spoke to the President and discussed this particular entry [into Dr. Ellsberg's psychiatrist's office] and he said that he knew that it was legal and justified for national security. Did he mention to you that he had received any kind of a contrary advice at any other time?

A. Well now, that question makes an assumption not in evidence, Mr. Dash, that the President said he knew it was legal. I don't believe I have ever testified to that. Maybe some other witness had, but I don't know where you got that idea. I could not answer the question with that assumption in it.

Q. I thought that was your testimony. I asked you the question earlier whether or not in March you talked to the President and the President said that he believed it was legal and justified for national security and I thought you answered in the affirmative.

A. Well, I certainly would not want to give you the impression that the President had given me a legal opinion on this at that time. But what the President said was that he felt that it was important, and it was necessary, that in the context of the massive thefts, the turnover to the Russian Embassy [of the Pentagon Papers] and all the context of that operation that he certainly could not criticize the men who had undertaken this in good faith believing that they were responding to the urgency of the circumstances.

Q. All right. The testimony you do leave with the committee, is that your own personal evaluation as to its legality was a recent one after advice of counsel?

A. Well, I certainly would not want to leave that impression either, Mr. Dash, and I would simply stand on my actual answers.

Q. Well, the record will so show.

MR. EHRLICHMAN: I think under the rules I am entitled to make a brief closing statement and I would like to avail myself of that privilege.

SENATOR BAKER: You are indeed and you may proceed.

MR. EHRLICHMAN: Mr. Vice Chairman and members of the committee, I prepared for this hearing with just two objectives: first to state the truth as nearly as recollection and research could enable me to do and thereby to establish the falsity of the charges made against me by your star witness. For nearly five days I have submitted to your cross-examination to permit a test of the truth of my testimony. In my opening statement I listed a number of questions which I asked you to inquire about because I believe they are central to this matter and because I have some information about them.

My secondary objective here was to be prepared to raise a voice for the President, who is unrepresented here. As your questions developed, I had no opportunity to do so as his advocate, I only shed some light on facts which disproved a few of the false allegations which have been advanced against him here. I do not apologize for my loyalty to the President any more than I apologize for my love of this country. I only hope that my testimony here has somehow served them both.

I could not close without commenting on Gordon Strachan's answer of the other day to the question, "Do you have any advice for the young Americans who are expressing their disenchantment with government and the political process?" Gordon said, "stay away." And your gallery laughed. But I don't think many other Americans laughed at that answer, I certainly didn't, nor do I agree with Gordon's advice.

Our political system and our real governmental institutions are not just the buildings and the laws and the traditions that one sees here in the city of Washington. Our Government and our politics are only as idealistic as the people in those buildings who administer the laws and run the campaigns and fulfill the traditions. If some young Americans know that their ideals or ideas or motives are sounder or purer than those of the people now in politics or government, then I think Gordon should have said to them, "Come and do better. Don't stay away.

"If you come here, come with your eyes wide open. If you go to work for the President and the executive branch there are very few in the Congress or the media that are going to throw rosebuds at you. If you favor change in what our Government is and what it does in our society you will have to fight for it. No such thing has been won here by default, at least not recently, and be prepared to defend your sense of values when you come here, too.

"You will encounter a local culture which scoffs at patriotism and family life and morality just as it adulates the opposite, and you will find some people who have fallen for that line. But you will also find in politics and government many great people who know that a pearl of great price is not had for the asking and who feel that this country and its heritage are worth the work, the abuse, the struggle, and the sacrifices. Don't stay away. Come and join them and do it better."

Mr. Vice Chairman, this select committee has an awesome responsibility to find the truth. Such a search cannot be made by one whose eyes are clouded by preconception or partisanship, it can only be found by those with open minds, free of bias and unfairness. I am confident that the truth is there to be seen. It only needs the see-ers.

Testimony by H. R. Haldeman

July 30　*Says he and Nixon had no knowledge of Watergate break-in, that Dean misled them; says he recently heard some of the White House tapes.*

July 31　*Recounts taped discussions between Nixon and Dean; denies role in cover-up.*

Aug. 1　*Describes his proposal to link 1972 protests to McGovern.*

July 30, 1973

MR. HALDEMAN: Mr. Chairman, my statement and testimony before this committee will be based on my best recollection after a careful review of logs, notes, et cetera, to try to reconstruct the facts as best I can.

I am severely limited in this effort because, despite the intense focus of attention today on each minute event of last year, at the time they happened most of these things were not of great importance and were not recorded in any detail, if at all. This is especially true for the period prior to March, 1973. From then on my Presidential notes regarding the Watergate case are much more voluminous because the President was then directing a great deal of his attention to the Watergate matter, whereas he had not done so earlier.

I have had access, under the supervision of a Secret Service agent, to my handwritten notes regarding conversations with the President which are in the President's files. I have not been permitted to make copies of them or to take notes from them. I have been under exactly the same restrictions as Gordon Strachan described. My files are in the same room as his. I kept no records of my own; all my records are in the President's file.

Turning to the question of security problems, it has been alleged that there was an atmosphere of fear at the White House regarding security matters. I can state categorically that there was no climate of fear at all. There was, however, a healthy and valid concern for a number of matters in the general area of national security and for a number of other matters in the general area of domestic security. This was a rational concern, and it was of sufficient import to require that considerable thought be given to steps to combat the actual problems and potential dangers that existed.

With regard to leaks of information, especially in the national security area, it became evident in 1969 that leaks of secret information were taking place that seriously jeopardized a number of highly sensitive foreign policy initiatives that had been undertaken by the Administration, including the ending of the war in Vietnam, the Middle East crisis, nuclear arms limitation, and the establishment of new relationships among the great powers. These initiatives were closely interrelated; leaks about any one of them could seriously endanger all of them; and such leaks were taking place.

In order to deal with these leaks, a program of wiretaps were instituted in 1969 and continued into early 1971. The President has stated that each of these taps were undertaken in accordance with procedures that were legal at the time and in accord with long-standing practice in this area. This program was authorized by the President of the United States and the wiretaps were determined by coordination between the Director of the F.B.I., the President's assistant for national security affairs and the Attorney General of the United States.

In 1970, the domestic security problem reached critical proportions as a wave of bombings and explosions, rioting and violence, demonstrations, arson, gun battles and other disruptive activities took place across the country—on college campuses primarily—but also in other areas.

In order to deal with this problem, the President set up an interagency committee consisting of the directors of the F.B.I., the C.I.A., the Defense Intelligence Agency and the National Security Agency. This committee was instructed to prepare recommendations for the President—which they did. The report they submitted included specific options for expanded intelligence operations and Mr. Huston, the White House staff man for this project, was notified by a memorandum from me of the approval of the President.

As has been reported, Director Hoover expressed opposition to parts of this program and as a result, the agencies were subsequently notified that the approval had been rescinded. This approval was withdrawn before the plan was implemented so the net result was that it never went into effect.

Instead of this program, an Intelligence Evaluation Committee was created in December of 1970 that included representatives of the White House, C.I.A., F.B.I., N.S.A. and the departments of Justice, Treasury and Defense and the Secret Service. The mission of this committee was to improve coordination among the intelligence community and to prepare evaluations and estimates of domestic intelligence.

In mid-1971, The New York Times started publication of the so-called Pentagon Papers which had been stolen from the sensitive files of the Departments of State and Defense and the C.I.A. and which covered military and diplomatic moves in a war that was still going on. The implications of this security leak were enormous, and it posed a threat so grave as to require, in the judgment of the President and his senior advisors, extraordinary action. As a result, the President approved creation of the special investigations unit within the White House which later became known as the plumbers. John Ehrlichman was responsible for supervision of this group, Mr. Krogh and Mr. Young of the Domestic Council and National Security Council staffs were the two principal staff members. While I was aware of the existence and general purpose of this unit, I was not familiar with any of its specific activities or assignments.

Also, in mid-1971, to deal with the general problem of leaks throughout Government departments and agencies, the President directed me to set up a program of spotting these leaks and reporting them to the department head involved. He announced this in a Cabinet meeting and unfortunately dubbed me with the dubious honor of Lord High Executioner—that was his phrase, not mine. The purpose of this program was to make department heads throughout the Government conscious of the leak problem and aware of their responsibility to deal with it in their departments. This involved no investigations on the part of the White House.

Turning to the surplus campaign funds, during the interim period between the 1968 elections and the start of the 1972 campaign, Herbert Kalmbach was custodian of a large cash fund which I understand was a surplus from the 1968 primary elections. In addition, he undertook to raise funds from supporters of the President to aid Congressional and senatorial candidates in the 1970 elections. Also, in 1971 Mr. Kalmbach raised a substantial fund as the "start up" for the 1972 campaign.

I requested or approved use of these funds for such purposes as the continuing polling that we did during that period; for campaign support to a candidate for Governor in Alabama; and for funding Donald Segretti. It is my understanding that these funds were also used for other purposes such as the funding of Mr. Ulasewicz; operations with which I was not familiar.

The Alabama campaign funds were in support of the candidate for the Democratic nomination for Governor who was opposing former Governor George Wallace. It was the belief of some of the President's friends and advisers on the Southern political scene that Mr. Wallace might very well become a third-party candidate in 1972 and thus raise again the potential problem of an indecisive election that might be turned to the House of Representatives. They felt that the best way to avoid this eventuality was to defeat Governor Wallace in his bid for the gubernatorial nomination in Alabama. This was the reason for providing campaign financial support to his opponent.

Turning on the Segretti matter. Early in the pre-campaign period I agreed with an idea that was suggested to set up a man functioning independently of the White House, the Committee to Reelect and the National Committee, for the purpose of generating for our side the same kind of campaign activities that were so ably carried out over the years for the Democratic candidates and in 1972 for Senator McGovern by Dick Tuck, a man who has been widely praised by political writers as a political prankster, whose basic stock in trade is embarrassing Republican candidates by activities that have been regarded as clever and acceptable parts of our political tradition.

The repertoire of the political prankster includes such activities as printing up embarrassing signs for the opponent, posing in trainman's clothes and waving the campaign train out of the station, placing an agent on the opponent's compaign train to produce witty newsletters mocking the candidate, distributing opposition signs at rallies for use by members of the crowd, encouraging band leaders to play rival songs at rallies and so forth.

The activities we had in mind, and for which we drew careful boundaries, specifically excluded anything remotely connected with the Watergate type of activity.

Moreover, the pranksterism that was envisioned would have specifically excluded such acts as the following: violent demonstrations and disruption, heckling or shouting down speakers, burning or bombing campaign headquarters, physical damage or thrashing of headquarters and other buildings, harassment of candidates' wives and families by obscenities, disruption of the national convention by splattering dinner guests with eggs and tomatoes, indecent exposure, rock throwing, assaults on delegates, slashing bus tires, smashing windows, setting trash fires under the gas tank of a bus, knocking policemen from their motorcycles.

I know that this committee and most Americans would agree that such activities cannot be tolerated in a political campaign. But unfortunately, the activities I had described are all activities which took place in 1972—against the campaign of the President of the United States by his opponents. Some of them took place with the clear knowledge and consent of agents of the opposing candidate in the last election; others were acts of people who were clearly unsympathetic to the President but may not have had direct orders from the opposing camp.

There is no question that the 1972 campaign was not a classic in decorum—for either side. In any event, having agreed to the suggestion of a "Dick Tuck for our side," I was told by Dwight Chapin and Gordon Strachan that they had a former college friend they felt would be a good man for this project. They may have told me that his name was Don Segretti, but it would have meant nothing to me. I have never met or had any personal communication with Mr. Segretti.

I agreed that if this man wanted to take on this activity, Herbert Kalmbach should arrange for his compensation and expenses from the 1968 campaign fund surplus.

It was my clear understanding that Segretti would act independently and on his own initiative within the broad guidelines outlined above. It was also my clear understanding that he was to engage in no illegal acts. Mr. Strachan has told me that he was so advised and that he understood that. I had no specific knowledge of Segretti's activities or the details of how or with whom he worked. I do not believe that there was anything wrong with the Segretti activity as it was conceived. I have only limited knowledge, and that acquired only lately, as to how it was actually carried out.

If, as alleged, he or those under his direction were responsible for the letter which falsely defamed Senators Muskie and Humphrey, then, on behalf of everyone associated with the Nixon campaign, I would like to and do apologize to both of those men. That act was clearly outside the bounds within which he was to work.

The President and all of us at the White House were determined that the campaign organization and operation should be set up outside of and independent of the White House and this was the reason for the development of the Committee to Re-elect the President. The committee operated autonomously under the direction of John Mitchell and later Clark MacGregor but, of course, with close liaison and communication with the White House at many levels.

The President looked to me as his basic contact with the campaign organization, and I maintained communication with John Mitchell in this regard until July, 1972, and then with Clark Mac-Gregor.

I did not function as the White House liaison with the Committee to Re-elect the President. This function was handled by various people at various levels with regard to specific areas or projects. For example, John Dean on legal matters, John Ehrlichman and his staff on substantive domestic policy, Chuck Colson on group support, etc. I had no official relationship with or position on the Committee to Re-elect the President or the Finance Committee.

Gordon Strachan on my staff handled the day-to-day liaison with the committee for me, and virtually all my contact with the committee, except for that with Mitchell or MacGregor, was through Strachan. He received copies of committee materials and memoranda, sat in on many of their meetings and stayed in touch with key people. I met with Strachan only about once every week or two during the campaign.

Strachan periodically sent me general information on campaign planning, organization and activities. He sent me from time to time, the over-all budget and various campaign materials. This was primarily for information purposes and it usually took the form of a summary memorandum, backed up by a huge amount of supporting material which I rarely read.

In the specific case of advertising and promotional materials the standard procedure required a final sign-off by me before the ads or materials were considered approved. Thus, in this particular area I did, in effect, exercise approval authority but even here I did not have control over either the personnel or the policies involved in developing the material. I only had a final sign-off on the end product.

I also had a particular interest in polls and in scheduling and paid more detailed attention to these areas.

I do not believe I had control over any funds at the committee nor did I exercise any authority or directions as to the utilization of funds, except in a general sense. I never signed a campaign check.

I was, to some degree, involved in the decision process regarding funds to be used for advertising and polling. The committee also allocated funds to pay for expenses incurred by the President or the White House that were clearly campaign expenses as contrasted to Government expenses. This would include such things as cost of campaign travel, advance men, et cetera.

Also, I had very few meetings with any members of the staff of the Committee to Re-elect the President, except those with John Mitchell, which were on a frequency of about once a week during the time he was campaign director. In addition to that, I did sit in the semiweekly campaign review meetings held in John Erlichman's office and, of course, as has been indicated, Mr. Mitchell and Mr. MacGregor sat in the regular morning White House staff meeting so that there could be full coordination between the White House and the committee on over-all strategy.

My contact with the campaign, in other words, was through fairly infrequent meetings with Mr. Mitchell and fairly infrequent meetings with Gordon Strachan of my staff; but I kept in general touch with campaign activities through Strachan's summary memoranda and the meetings described above.

Turning to the $350,000, prior to the April 7 date on which the new campaign spending legislation took effect it was agreed by Mitchell, Stans, I believe Mr. Kalmbach and me that $350,000 of the 1968 surplus cash funds should be set aside to cover possible needs for special private polling by the White House apart from the regular polls conducted by the committee. This was in anticipation of a close election.

I understand from Gordon Strachan that he received the cash from Hugh Sloan on April 6. He, in turn, arranged to have this cash held in a safe deposit box or safe by another individual outside the Government. It is my understanding from Strachan that this transfer was made immediately and the entire $350,000 was placed in safe keeping outside the White House.

I did not feel we should keep such a large amount of cash at the White House, nor did I feel it was a good idea for it to be in the physical custody of a member of the White House staff, which was why these arrangements were made. I never at any time saw or handled the currency, and I must rely on Strachan's reports to me as to how it was handled.

I have been informed by Strachan that there was one withdrawal in April or May of 1972 of $22,000 to pay for some advertising not directly related to the election campaign. This was at the request of Dick Howard of Chuck Colson's office. I think Strachan said the money was delivered directly to the advertising agency.

The balance of $328,000 was not used. I instructed Strachan after the election in November to turn over the unused funds to the committee since the White House had no further need for them. I told him to work out with John Dean the means of doing this. Strachan has informed me that the funds were turned over in January, 1973, although he incurred some difficulty in doing so after he took possession of the funds on Nov. 28, 1972.

In December I became aware, probably via Dean, that there was some difficulty in turning over the cash to the committee, presumably because it posed reporting problems.

At a later time, Dean mentioned to me the committee's need for funds for legal and family support for the Watergate defendants. I suggested to Dean that he try to work out a way of solving both the problems of our desire to deliver funds to the committee and the committee's need for funds.

Dean later told me that he had worked this out and that part of the cash, I believe $40,000, could be delivered immediately to the committee via Fred LaRue. He had Strachan do this, I am told, and several days thereafter, Dean had Strachan deliver the balance to LaRue.

To sum up, after my original instruction to Strachan to transfer the money to the committee, my involvement in the transfer of funds was entirely through John Dean. He told me of the problem in transferring the $350,000 to the committee. He told me he had worked out the problem. He told Strachan how, when and to whom to make the transfer. He told me the transfer had been made.

He did not, at any time in this sequence, advise me or imply that the transfer itself or the purpose of the transfer was to buy the Watergate defendants' silence or that it was in any way illegal or improper.

It is my understanding that all this took place in the period of November to January, but I am not sure of the timing.

I have no recollection of any knowledge of the reported transaction on November 28 when Dean had Fred Fielding of his office pick up $22,000 in cash from Mr. Stans, ostensibly for the purpose of replacing the $22,000 that had been expended from the $350,000 in April.

I do recall that one of Dean's problems in the process of transferring the $350,000 to the committee was the fact that $22,000 had been disbursed. So it is quite possible that he did have it replenished prior to having the cash turned over to LaRue, but I do not believe that he ever reported this fact to me.

Turning to Watergate itself.

I had no knowledge of, or involvement in, the planning or execution of the break-in or bugging of the Democratic National Committee headquarters.

To the best of my knowledge I did not see any material produced by the bugging of the Democratic headquarters.

After the June 17 break-in, I asked Gordon Strachan whether

he had had any knowledge of such an operation. He said he had not; but that he realized in thinking back that there had been three "intelligence reports" received by him identified by the code name Sedan Chair that said something to the effect that "confidential sources report that . . ." He said he did not at the time know the identity of the confidential sources. He realized after the June 17 break-in, thinking back, that these reports could have been based on the Watergate or some other wiretap source.

I have absolutely no recollection of seeing any such report and it is quite likely that I did not see it even if it was included in a Strachan transmission to me since I rarely, if ever, read through or even looked at all of the materials that he sent in to me in these reports.

I do not recall ever seeing any material identified by the name Gemstone [from tapes on the Democratic National Committee].

I have no recollection of giving Mr. Strachan instruction to destroy any materials, nor do I recall a later report from Strachan that he had done so or that the files were clean.

I should point out that on two occasions in April, 1973—once to me before his grand jury appearance and the other to John Ehrlichman—Strachan listed the areas of what he considered to be tough questions or trouble spots. On neither of these occasions did he mention to either of us that he had been instructed to destroy any materials or make sure files were clean.

I think the effort to bring in my April 4 meeting with John Mitchell as in some way significant with regard to intelligence is a little far-fetched. By his testimony, Strachan doesn't know what was discussed at that meeting—all he says is that, in routine fashion, he put an item on the talking paper regarding the adequacy of intelligence. As a matter of fact, the meeting with Mr. Mitchell that day was in connection with a meeting of Mitchell and me with the President. My notes taken at the meeting with the President indicate the discussion covered the I.T.T.-Kleindienst hearings and a review of Mitchell's plans for assigning regional campaign responsibilities to specific individuals. They indicate no discussion of intelligence.

Turning to the Dean investigation, John Dean, in his Camp David report says that when he arrived in Washington on Sunday afternoon, June 18, he realized that the President would have to know everything that he could find out. He realized at that point that he would be asked to assemble all of the facts so that the White House could be fully informed as to what had transpired and how it would affect the President, but having been on an airplane for approximately 25 hours he did nothing further that evening.

The next morning, after reading all of the news accounts of the Watergate incident, he spoke with John Ehrlichman, who instructed him to get the facts together and report to him. He then called the Attorney General to get what facts he knew. He called Gordon Liddy and met with him. Dean asked Liddy if anyone at the White House was involved and he told him no.

During the days and weeks that followed, Dean discussed the incident with everyone who he thought might have any knowledge or involvement.

The source of these facts is John Dean's report, or the start of it, which he wrote at Camp David in March of this year.

There is absolutely no question in my mind, or, I'm sure, in the minds of anyone at the White House, or at the Justice Department, that John Dean was in fact conducting an investigation for the White House regarding the Watergate as it might involve the White House. It is inconceivable to me that there could be any doubt in Dean's mind.

Dean moved in immediately after the incident as sort of the Watergate project officer in the White House. This was in keeping with our usual procedure; the responsibility was his and he had the authority to proceed. Dean kept Ehrlichman and me posted from time to time on developments and, through us, the President. He apparently did not keep us fully posted and it now appears he did not keep us accurately posted.

The President, Ehrlichman and I were very much involved in many other vital matters through this entire period and we made no attempt to get into the details of, or in any way take over, the Watergate case.

The view of all three of us through the whole period was that the truth must be told, and quickly; although we did not know what the truth was. Every time we pushed for action in this direction we were told by Dean that it could not be done. His concern, as I understood it, was that the case was complex, it involved rights of defendants and other legal complexities, the facts were not clear, and that nothing should be done publicly.

As long as we were confident that the facts he told us were correct, we had to agree with this, since there was no proof of any involvement of higher-ups at the committee, and any premature speculation regarding any involvement would have been unfair and damaging, especially since the top officials at the committee had denied any involvement.

Thus, as it now appears, we were badly misled by one or more of the principals and even more so by our own man, for reasons which are still not completely clear.

At no time did I give Dean any instructions to cover up anything in this case. I did, however, occasionally receive his verbal reports of the facts and his intended actions and relayed these to the President. None of these reports concerned a cover-up.

I had no personal motivation to cover up anything because I had no personal involvement and I knew the President had no involvement. I understood and believed that no one else in the White House was involved in the Watergate planning and break-in, and I still understand and believe that. It was obvious that some people at the committee were involved, but I had no

idea who, or how far up, and I still don't—because I don't know
now whom to believe. I may add that until the recent period
both John Mitchell and Jeb Magruder denied any Watergate involvement.

The President raised questions as to the facts of Watergate
from time to time during the period of June through the election.
His interest consistently was to get the facts and get them out.
He had some concern, especially in the early stages, regarding
the possibility of compromising national security and an interest,
therefore, in seeing that the investigation was thorough with regard to Watergate, but that it was limited to Watergate and not
extended into earlier unrelated national security activities of some
of the people involved.

Throughout this period, Dean assured us that there was absolutely no evidence that anyone in the White House had been
involved in Watergate in any way. He was sitting in on F.B.I.
interviews; reviewing F.B.I. reports; he was in constant communication with officials of the Justice Department and the re-
election committee; and was clearly staying closely in touch
with all facets of the investigation and related matters.

On or about Aug. 27 the President instructed me to ask Mr.
Ehrlichman to give to Pat Buchanan the information that
Buchanan would need for preparing the President's briefing book
for an upcoming press conference on any questions that might
arise regarding Watergate. I passed this request on to Ehrlichman
and assumed that he carried it out. On Aug. 29 the President had
a press conference at which he stated the Dean investigation
indicated that no one in the White House or in the Administration presently employed had been involved in Watergate. I was
not at all surprised to hear the President say this at the press
conference since it was thoroughly consistent with everything
that Dean had told me and I, therefore, find it hard to understand
why Mr. Dean now professes to have had such great surprise
when he heard this statement.

In these hearings and in the general discussion of Watergate,
the word "cover-up" has come to have a broad and very ill-
defined meaning. As John Dean said, the cover-up had a broad
range. Anything that might cause a problem came within the
cover-up.

Definition by usage has now come to connote illegal or improper activities—although some steps were taken to contain
the Watergate case in several perfectly legal and proper aspects.

One, as the President has stated, was to avoid the Watergate
investigation possibly going beyond the facts of the Watergate
affair itself and into national security activities totally unrelated
to Watergate.

Another was to avoid or at least reduce adverse political and
publicity fall-out from false charges, hearsay, and so on, arising
from various activities in connection with Watergate, such as

the Justice Department investigation, the Democratic National Committee suit, the Common Cause suit, the Patman hearings and the Ervin committee hearings.

A third was concern for distortion or fabrication of facts in the heat of a political campaign that would unjustly condemn the innocent or prevent discovery of the guilty.

The containment effort, as I would use the term, did not contemplate or involve any acts in obstruction of justice. To the contrary, while hoping to contain the Watergate inquiry to the facts of Watergate, there was a concurrent effort to try to get the true facts of Watergate and get them out to the public. The President frequently cautioned against any cover-up of Watergate or even the appearance of a cover-up.

On the basis of testimony now before this committee, it appears that there also was an effort to cover up, as well as to contain. This cover-up appears to have involved illegal and improper activities, such as perjury, payments to defendants for their silence, promises of executive clemency, destruction of evidence and other acts in an effort to conceal the truth regarding the planning and commission of crimes at the Watergate.

The critical question then becomes the determination of who committed these acts, who directed them, who was aware of them.

I committed no such acts and directed no such acts and I was aware of no such acts until March of this year, when the President intensified his personal investigation into the facts of the Watergate. I am convinced that the President had no awareness of any such acts until March of this year.

The question is asked: "How could the President not have known?" Very easily. Reverse the question. How could the President have known?

Only if he were directly involved himself or if he were told by someone who was either directly involved or had knowledge. The fact is that the President was not directly involved himself and he was not told by anyone until March, when he intensified his own investigation. Even then, he was given conflicting and unverified reports that made it impossible to determine the precise truth regarding Watergate or the cover-up and, at the outset at least, he was relying primarily on one man, John Dean, who had admitted that he was a major participant in the illegal and improper cover-up, a fact unknown to the President until March, 1973.

Any attempt on my part at this time to try to identify those who participated in, directed, or knew of the illegal cover-up would of necessity be based totally on hearsay.

There was a concern at the White House that activities which had been in no way related to Watergate or to the 1972 political campaign, and which were in the area of national security, would be compromised in the process of the Watergate investigation and the attendant publicity and political furor. The recent public disclosure of the F.B.I. wiretaps on press and N.S.C. personnel, the details of the plumbers operations, and so on, fully justifies that concern.

As a result of this concern and the F.B.I.'s request through Pat Gray to John Dean for guidance regarding some aspects of the Watergate investigation, because of the possibility of C.I.A. involvement, the President directed John Ehrlichman and me to meet with the Director [Richard Helms] and Deputy Director of the C.I.A. [General Vernon Walters] on June 23.

We did so and ascertained from them that there had not been any C.I.A. involvement in the Watergate affair and that there was no concern on the part of Director Helms as to the fact that some of the Watergate participants had been involved in the Bay of Pigs operations of the C.I.A.

We discussed the White House concern regarding possible disclosure of non-Watergate-related covert C.I.A. operations or other nonrelated national security activities that had been undertaken previously by some of the Watergate participants, and we requested Deputy Director Walters to meet with Director Gray of the F.B.I. to express these concerns and to coordinate with the F.B.I. so that the F.B.I.'s area of investigation of the Watergate participants not be expanded into unrelated matters which could lead to disclosures of earlier national security or C.I.A. activities.

Walters agreed to meet with Gray as requested. I do not recall having any other communication or meeting with Walters, Helms or Gray on this subject. I did not, at this meeting, or at any other time, ask the C.I.A. to participate in any Watergate cover-up, nor did I ever suggest that the C.I.A. take any responsibility for the Watergate break-in. I believe that the action I took with the C.I.A. was proper, according to the President's instructions and clearly in the national interest.

There were a number of newspaper stories and allegations raised during the period following the Watergate break-in that posed news questions regarding the facts of Watergate or related matters. Whenever any such questions arise, the President would again ask that the facts be ascertained and made known publicly as completely and quickly as possible, but there always seemed to be some reason why this could not be done.

There was no effort on my part to direct my personal attention or take any personal action on these matters because the F.B.I. and the Justice Department were responsible for and were conducting an extremely extensive investigation and because Mr. Dean was responsible for White House liaison with all aspects of the investigation. I knew John Dean to be an extremely capable, thorough, hardworking and intelligent man and I had full confidence, as did the President at that time, that Mr. Dean was in fact carrying out this responsibility diligently and thoroughly.

I was told several times, starting in the summer of 1972, by John Dean and possibly also by John Mitchell that there was a need by the committee for funds to help take care of the legal fees and family support of the Watergate defendants. The committee apparently felt obliged to do this.

In March, 1973, Dean told me that at some point in 1972 he, at Mitchell's suggestion, had asked me if it would be O.K. for him to contact Herb Kalmbach to ask him to raise some such defense funds. He says I agreed. He also says that he checked Ehrlichman on the same point. I do not recall such a request. I should also point out that at some time Dean has said that he checked with both Ehrlichman and me on this point and at other times he has said only that he checked with Ehrlichman.

Later in March, 1973, Dean raised the point that there was a potential problem with relation to the funds for defendants. He described this as a possible political embarrassment, and indicated that it might even become a legal problem. The problem would arise if it was determined that these funds had been used to induce the defendants to refuse to testify.

I emphasized my clear understanding that the purpose of the funds, as described to me by Dean, was for legal fees and family support; and that I had understood from Dean that both Mitchell and Dean felt this was a proper and important obligation to the defendants.

Since all information regarding the defense funds was given to me by John Dean, the counsel to the President, and possibly by John Mitchell, and since the arrangements for Kalmbach's collecting funds and for transferring the $50,000 cash fund were made by John Dean, and since John Dean never stated at the time that the funds would be used for any other than legal and proper purposes, I had no reason to question the propriety or legality of the process of delivering the $350,000 to the committee via LaRue or of having Kalmbach raise funds.

I have no personal knowledge of what was done with the funds raised by Kalmbach or with the $350,000 that was delivered by Strachan to LaRue.

It would appear that, at the White House at least, John Dean was the only one who knew that the funds were for "hush money," if, in fact, that is what they were for. The rest of us relied on Dean and all thought that what was being done was legal and proper. No one, to my knowledge, was aware that these funds involved either blackmail or "hush money" until this suggestion was raised in March of 1973.

To the best of my recollection, I had no meetings or discussions with Jeb Magruder regarding Watergate after our phone call of June 18, 1972, which has already been reported, until Feb. 14, 1973. A review of my log confirms that I had no meetings at all with Magruder in 1973 until Feb. 14.

We did meet on Feb. 14 for about an hour and a quarter at Mr. Magruder's request in my office. The purpose of the meeting was to discuss his plans for the future.

I met with Magruder again on March 2 (I believe again at his request) at my office, with John Dean also present, for about an hour. At this meeting we reviewed the same general subjects we had discussed on Feb. 14, and I gave him a list of jobs in the Government that had been developed by the personnel office. He expressed interest in one of the jobs on the list, a post at the Department of Commerce, and he subsequently did take that post.

I do not recall any discussion of any of the particulars of the Watergate matter or the so-called cover-up—other than what I have already indicated regarding his feeling that the matter was now behind him.

Mr. Magruder has stated that he met with me in early January of 1973, before the Inaugural, although he was unable to specify a date.

Mr. Dean, on the other hand, has indicated in his testimony that I met with Mr. Magruder in late January.

I do have a vague feeling that I talked with Magruder or at least knew about his plans prior to his trip to California, which I believe was in early February. I cannot recall any specific conversation or meeting.

Magruder's recollection of the substance of the alleged January conversation is in many respects very much along the lines of my recollection of our conversation on Feb. 14, and I have the feeling that we are dealing here with a simple error in recollection of specific dates, which is certainly understandable.

At no meeting with Magruder did he raise with me a monologue as he has described laying out the "true facts" or claiming that he had committed or was going to commit perjury or that there had been any other illegal cover-up activities undertaken in connection with the Watergate investigation.

On April 14, 1973, I phoned Magruder at the President's request and asked him to meet with Ehrlichman that day. I have turned over to the committee a tape recording of his conversation. At the time we talked, Magruder had already decided to tell the full truth, and in fact, I believe, had done so in a meeting with the U.S. attorneys. During the phone conversation, Magruder said that his testimony had not implicated me. He also said that one of the problems he was facing was that he had committed perjury when he testified before the grand jury and the trial. I responded that I did not know anything about that, and he replied that even if I didn't, he did. He did not contradict me, thus showing that, at that point in time at least, I did not know he had perjured himself.

Turning to the Sept. 15 [1972] meeting, I was in meetings with the President all afternoon on Sept. 15, 1972. At the end of the afternoon, the President had John Dean come in. This was the day that the indictments had been brought down in the Watergate case, and the President knew John Dean had been concentrating for a three-month period on the investigation for the White House. I am sure therefore that the President thought it would be a good time to give Dean a pat on the back.

There was no mood of exuberance or excitement on the President's part at the time the indictments were brought down. He does not take joy from the misfortunes of other people, and I don't think he found it very pleasant that the people had been indicted. Naturally, however, it was good news as far as the White House and the Administration were concerned that when the indictments were brought down, after a thorough investigation, it had been established there was not any involvement by anyone in the White House. This confirmed what Mr. Dean had been telling us, and we had been reporting to the President over the period of the past three months.

As was the case with all meetings in the Oval Office when the President was there, this meeting with Mr. Dean was recorded. At the President's request, I recently reviewed the recording of that meeting (at which I was present throughout) in order to report on its contents to the President. I should interject here that I also reviewed the recording of the March 21 (1973) meeting of the President, Mr. Dean and myself for the same purpose, and I have made reports to the President on both of those meetings. I have not at any time listened to any other recordings of the meetings in the President's office or of the President's phone calls.

The President did not open the meeting of Sept. 15 with the statement that "Bob has kept me posted on your handling of the Watergate" or anything even remotely resembling that. He said, "Hi, this is quite a day, you've got Watergate on the way" or something to that effect. Dean responded that it had been quite a three months and then reported to the President on how the press was handling the indictments and, apparently, a Clark MacGregor press conference.

The discussion then covered the matter of the new bug that had recently been discovered in the Democratic National Committee and the question of whether it had been planted by the D.N.C. and the matter of Mr. Nixon's campaign being bugged in 1968 and some discussion of whether to try to get out evidence of that. There was some discussion about Judge Charles R. J. Richey hearing the civil case and a comment that he would keep Roemer McPhee abreast of what was happening. I don't recall any comment about the judge trying to accommodate Dean's hopes of slowing down the suit, but there was some discussion about the problem of the civil case depositions interfering with the criminal prosecution—apparently as a result of a conversation between Judge Richey and Assistant U.S. Attorney Earl J. Silbert.

Dean indicated that the indictments meant the end of the investigation by the grand jury and now there would be the G.A.O. [General Accounting Office] audit and some congressional inquiries, such as the Patman committee. But he assured the President that nothing would come out to surprise us. In other words, there was apparently no information that would be harmful that had not been uncovered already.

The President did at that point commend Dean for his handling of the whole Watergate matter, which was a perfectly natural thing for him to do. Dean reported that he was keeping a close eye on possible campaign law violations by the opposition; said there were some problems of bitterness at the re-election committee between the Finance Committee and the political group; and said he was trying to keep notes on people who were emerging out of all this that were clearly not our friends.

There was, as Mr. Dean has indicated, quite a lengthy discussion of the Patman hearings and the various factors involved in that. There was some discussion of the reluctance of the I.R.S. [Internal Revenue Service] to follow up on complaints of possible violations against people who were supporting our opponents because there are so many Democrats in the I.R.S. bureaucracy that they won't take any action.

There was a discussion of cleaning house after the election, moving quickly to replace people at all levels of the Government. The meeting closed, as I recall, with a fairly long philosophical discussion.

I totally disagree with the conclusion [by Mr. Dean] that the President was aware of any type of cover-up and certainly Mr. Dean did not advise him of it at the Sept. 15 meeting.

On Feb. 7, 1973, the Watergate case moved into a new phase with the establishment of the Senate Select Committee. The announcement of the plans for the Senate probe was the reason for holding a weekend meeting, February 10 and 11 in Southern California [at La Costa] with Mr. Ehrlichman, Mr. Dean, Mr. Moore and myself. These meetings have been thoroughly reported and I would concur in Mr. [Richard] Moore's description of them as sort of brainstorming sessions regarding the whole range of questions of strategy regarding the Senate hearings, a review of possible problems and general discussion of how to deal with a number of new factors.

I feel that Mr. Dean in his statement to the committee has, in a number of instances, substantially misinterpreted the intent or implications of things that might have been said at the meeting.

Also I believe he has overlooked one of the principal purposes of the meeting, which was a discussion at great length of how to develop some way to learn the entire Watergate story—including the other activities that were by then bunched together as Watergate—and get it out in its totality and accurately. This was considered as one of the best ways to counteract the potential of adverse publicity from a drawn-out public hearing. The feeling was that putting all of the facts out, in one place, at one time, would give the American people a more accurate picture of the truth than would the drawn-out process of hearing one witness at a time over an extended period.

Another objective, which was the President's objective, was to try to work out ways and means by which the facts of Watergate or any testimony that could be provided by anybody in the White House who had any knowledge which would be of interest to this committee could be provided in the most complete form but without getting into the problem of the separation of powers and executive privilege.

I don't recall any discussion of the question of raising money, but I am sure that if there were any, it was in the form that Mr. Moore described; that is, a very incidental item occupying only a few minutes in a series of meetings that lasted for many hours. It was not a principal point of discussion. There was no discussion of a cover-up of Watergate during these meetings.

Dean put into evidence as Exhibit 32 an agenda he says was requested by me for a meeting with the President as a follow-up to La Costa on February 19 or 20. He seems to feel that this is a very significant document that is self-explanatory as evidence of a continuing cover-up. I completely fail to see it that way.

There were five items on the agenda. First, a meeting of Senator Baker with the President which, it was my understanding, Senator Baker had requested, and which seems to me to be perfectly natural as one step to be taken in working out the various problems regarding White House staff appearances at the Senate committee hearings, etc.

Second, the question of submitting Maurice Stans's name for confirmation to the Senate for a post requiring such confirmation. This was a step designed to deal with two questions, first to give Mr. Stans the opportunity to re-enter Government at a suitably high level and, secondly, to provide him with the opportunity in a very short period of time to appear publicly and under questioning, to clear up all charges regarding his role in the Watergate, if any, and to give him a chance to, as he requested of this committee, get back his good name.

Third, a question of whether Magruder could have a White House job.

Fourth, the question of [Patrick] Buchanan sitting in on the hearings as a watchdog of the press—an idea that Dean says I suggested, although it is my recollection he suggested it at the La Costa meeting. In any event, this was certainly not a cover-up move, but exactly the opposite.

Fifth, the question of the Attorney General [Kleindienst] meeting with the President. That, too, was a logical step because we were into the matters of executive privilege and the question of White House staff members going to the hearings was important for the President to discuss with the Attorney General. As it concurrently or shortly thereafter developed, Senator Baker requested that Mr. Kleindienst be his contact with the Administration.

In the latter part of February, as the questions of executive privilege and other matters dealing with the Senate Watergate inquiry intensified, the President saw that this was involving a substantial amount of time of a number of people in the White House and particularly seemed to be involving Ehrlichman and me in more expenditure of time than the President felt was productive. Consequently, he met with John Dean at the end of February regarding the matters of executive privilege, the Senate hearings and so forth, and he gave instructions to me and I am sure to others, that all Watergate matters were to be handled by Dean at the White House and by Kleindienst at the Justice Department and that no one else was to devote time to the subject and that no one else was to get into the matter with the President.

This decision of the President's led to the series of meetings that he had with Mr. Dean starting Feb. 27 and running through March 21, meetings that were primarily concerned, at the outset, I believe, with executive privilege matters. That continued to be a major point, but as that three-week period went on, the President's concern did grow regarding conflicting Watergate stories and from what he indicated to me, he was intensifying pressure on Dean to find out a way to get the full story out.

Dean at this time point was clearly in charge of any matters relating to the Watergate. He was meeting frequently with the President and he still indicated that he was positive there was no White House involvement. During this time, the [L. Patrick] Gray [confirmation] hearings also became a matter of focus and the executive privilege question arose in connection with them, too. I have the feeling that during this period the President was gradually getting more of a feel of the possibility that there might be some problems involved in the Watergate matter that he had not even dreamed of and that led to the meeting of March 21, in which John Dean was going to give the President the full story.

I should point out one question that Mr. Dean raised regarding a comment made by the President in his meeting of Feb. 27. He said the President told him he wanted Dean to handle the Watergate matter as it was taking too much of Ehrlichman and Haldeman's time and they were principals in it. Dean indicates that he did not understand what it was that the President meant by the statement that Haldeman and Ehrlichman were principals.

If this statement was made, I think it is quite clear in the context in which that meeting was held. At that time the major issue was whether the President would permit his principal aides to be called up to the Senate committee to testify. At that time the President considered it inconceivable that anyone would think that the White House Counsel would be called to testify and, therefore, was not even considering the possibility of Mr. Dean going before the Senate hearings.

He was concerned about the question of Haldeman and Ehrlichman being called. In that sense, I was a principal in the matter of executive privelege. It is significant that the President, according to Dean's report, also emphasized that he would never let Ehrlichman and Haldeman go to the Hill, and I think it is in that connection that he would look at us as principals.

The March 13 meeting Mr. Dean had with the President shows on the President's log as having run from 11:42 to 2:00, an 80-minute meeting, approximately. The President's log also shows that I was in that meeting for 12 minutes from 12:43 to 12:55.

Mr. Dean has testified that this was a long meeting, mainly regarding the Gray hearings and Dean's invitation to appear there. He says that toward the end of the conversation they got into a discussion of Watergate matters and the question of money demands being made by the defendants. He says that it was during this conversation that Haldeman came into the office for a brief interruption but that Haldeman then stayed on.

It was then, Dean says, that he told the President there was no money to pay the individuals. The President asked how much it would cost; Dean estimated a million dollars. The President said that was no problem and looked over at Haldeman and repeated that statement. Dean then goes on to describe a conversation regarding executive clemency and then back to the question of money, ending with a laugh from me at Dean's comment that next time he would be more knowledgeable.

The log, however, shows that I was in for 12 minutes at the beginning of the meeting and not at the end.

I have no notes on the March 13 meeting and I have no recollection of that meeting at all. I do not recall going into the President's office and interrupting the meeting with John Dean, but I am sure that I did if the log so indicates. However, I seriously doubt that the conversation John Dean has described actually took place on March 13. I doubt it because of the difference in timing as shown in the President's log, but I also doubt it because a discussion of some of those matters actually occurred during a meeting on March 21.

There is also a timing problem regarding the meeting of March 21 since Dean has stated that I was only in that meeting for the last five minutes or so when the President called me in to suggest that a meeting be set up with John Mitchell. My log indicates that I was in a meeting with the President from 11:15 to 11:55 on the morning of March 21. I do recall that meeting and I recall being in it for substantially more than the five minutes that Mr. Dean remembers.

I was not present for the first hour of the meeting, but I did listen to the tape of the entire meeting—including that portion before I came in.

While I am free to testify to everything which I can recall happening during the time I was present, the President has directed that I not testify as to any facts which I learned solely by listening to the tape of the meeting.

My counsel will present a letter in this respect and I shall obey the decision of the committee as to its ruling thereon. Depending on that decision, I shall issue an appropriate addendum to this statement concerning the March 21 meeting.

Addendum: March 21st Meeting

I was present for the final 40 minutes of the President's meeting with John Dean on the morning of March 21. While I was not present for the first hour of the meeting, I did listen to the tape of the entire meeting. Following is the substance of that meeting to the best of my recollection.

Dean reported some facts regarding the planning and the break-in of the D.N.C. [Democratic National Committee] and said again there were no White House personnel involved. He felt Magruder was fully aware of the operation, but he was not sure about Mitchell. He said that Liddy had given him a full rundown right after Watergate and that no one in the White House was involved. He said that his only concerns regarding the White House were in relation to the Colson phone call to Magruder which might indicate White House pressure and the possibility that Haldeman got some of the "fruits" of the bugging via Strachan since he had been told the "fruits" had been supplied to Strachan.

He outlined his role in the January planning meetings and recounted a report he said he made to me regarding the second of those meetings.

Regarding the post-June 17 situation, he indicated concern about two problems, money and clemency. He said that Colson had said something to Hunt about clemency. He did not report any other offers of clemency although he felt the defendants expected it. The President confirmed that he could not offer clemency and Dean agreed.

Regarding money, Dean said he and Haldeman were involved. There was a bad appearance which could be developed into a circumstantial chain of evidence regarding obstruction of justice. He said that Kalmbach had raised money for the defendants; that Haldeman had O.K.'d the return of the $350,000 to the committee, and that Dean had handled the dealings between the parties in doing this. He said that the money was for lawyers' fees.

He also reported on a current Hunt blackmail threat. He said Hunt was demanding $120,000 or else he would tell about the seamy things he had done for Ehrlichman. The President pursued this in considerable detail, obviously trying to smoke out what was really going on. He led Dean on regarding the process and what he would recommend doing. He asked such things as—well, this is the thing you would recommend? We ought to do this? Is that right? And he asked where the money would come from? How it would be delivered? And so on.

He asked how much money would be involved over the

years and Dean said probably a million dollars—but the problem
is that it is hard to raise. The President said there is no problem
in raising a million dollars, we can do that, but it would be
wrong. I have the clear impression that he was trying to find
out what it was Dean was saying and what Dean was recommending. He was trying to get Dean's view and he was asking
him leading questions in order to do that. This is the method
the President often used when he was moving toward a determination.

Dean also mentioned his concern about other activities getting
out, such as the "Ellsberg" break-in, something regarding Brookings, the other Hunt activities for Colson on Chappaquiddick,
the Segretti matter, use of Kalmbach funds, etc.

When I entered the meeting, there was another discussion
regarding the Hunt threat and the President again explored in
considerable depth the various options and tried to draw Dean
out on his recommendation.

The meeting then turned to the question of how to deal with
the situation and the President mentioned Ehrlichman's recommendation that everybody should go to the grand jury. The
President told Dean to explore all of this with Haldeman, Ehrlichman and Mitchell.

There was no discussion while I was in the room, nor do I
recall any discussion on the tape on the question of clemency
in the context of the President saying that he had discussed this
with Ehrlichman and with Colson. The only mention of clemency
was Dean's report that Colson discussed clemency with Hunt and
the President's statement that he could not offer clemency and
Dean's agreement—plus a comment that Dean thought the others
expected it.

Dean mentioned several times during this meeting his awareness
that he was telling the President things the President had known
nothing about.

I have to surmise that there is a genuine confusion in Mr.
Dean's mind as to what happened on March 13 vs. what happened on March 21, because some of what he describes in quite
vivid detail as happening on March 13 did, in fact, happen on
March 21. The point about my laughing at his being more
knowledgeable next time, and the question that he says he raised
on March 13 regarding the million dollars are so accurately
described, up to a point, as to what really happened on March
21 that I believe he is confused between the two dates.

Mr. Dean's recollection that the President had told him on
March 13 that Ehrlichman had discussed an offer of clemency
to Hunt with him and he had also discussed Hunt's clemency
with Colson is at total variance with everything that I have ever
heard from the President, Ehrlichman or Colson. I don't recall
such a discussion in either the March 13 or the March 21
meeting.

Now, to the question of impression. Mr. Dean drew the erroneous conclusion that the President was fully knowledgeable of a cover-up at the time of the March 13 meeting in the sense (1) of being aware that money had been paid for silence and that (2) the money demands could reach a million dollars and that the President said that was no problem. He drew his conclusion from a hypothetical discussion of questions since the President told me later that he had no intention to do anything whatever about money and had no knowledge of the so-called cover-up.

I had no difficulty accepting the President's version, based on years of very close association with President Nixon and on hundreds of hours of meetings with him. Having observed the President all those years, in many different situations, it was very clear to me on March 21 that the President was exploring and probing; that he was surprised; that he was trying to find out what in the world was going on; he didn't understand how this all fit together and he was trying to find out. He was pushing hard for that kind of information about Mr. Dean.

The President further was concerned about how this ought to be dealt with and he was interested in getting views from Ehrlichman, Dean, Haldeman and Mitchell because he felt that those views might be enlightening as to what the true situation was. For that reason he asked that a meeting be held with the four of us in the immediate future and such a meeting was scheduled for the next day.

July 31, 1973

MR. DASH: As chief of staff, Mr. Haldeman, could you tell us how tight a ship you ran in the White House?

A. Well, it has been amply reported here as being a tight ship, and I tried to run a tight ship, and I think successfully most of the time.

Q. And would it be fair to say that you were a hard taskmaster and often cracked the whip?

A. I don't know. I didn't feel I was a hard taskmaster. I felt I was a just taskmaster, but I guess some who didn't rise to the task felt that the whip was cracked sometimes. We operated of necessity on a basis of very extensive delegation of authority and of expecting people to get done what they were told to get done, to handle the responsibilities that they were understood to be handling and to do them without making any mistakes. We did throughout the White House operation operate on what is known in some views as a zero defect system. We attempted to do everything right.

Q. How close to zero did you get? A. I am not sure. That is hard to evaluate.

Q. Well, therefore, would it not be also true that in your job especially in making recommendations to the President or being able to make decisions that you certainly wanted to be on top of the important facts you needed to make those decisions?

A. I didn't have to make decisions for the President.

Q. I said, in making recommendations or in any decisions that you had to make in the White House. . . .

Could you tell us how the Committee for the Re-election of the President got started for the 1972 campaign.

A. The concept of the committee was a result of a desire on the part of the President and the rest of us that the campaign for re-election be handled outside of the White House and by people not on the White House staff but assigned to general White House duties.

We looked to the Committee to Re-elect to handle the mechanics and operations of the political campaign. We had close liaison with the committee, at a lot of levels—in the White House, from the White House to the committee and from the departments in the Government to the committee and Government appointees.

Q. Why was it necessary to set up this separate entity, when there was a national Republican committee and a political entity in the Republican party for the campaign of 1972?

A. Well, very simply because the national committee is the official body of the Republican party. It has the responsibility for mobilizing the Republican vote and turning out the Republican vote, for developing and supporting candidates, Republican candidates for office at all levels, state and Federal, and the campaign for the President required beyond the Republican party the effort to reach out to independent voters and to Democratic voters to make an appeal to them for support as well as to mobilize the Republican troops that the national committee had the responsibility for. So there was quite naturally a need for an organization beyond the Republican National Committee.

As you know, after the convention there was a further organization set up of Democrats for Nixon which was directly involved in an effort to develop Democratic support specifically.

Q. Did not this committee really constitute a form of alter ego to the White House and the Administration? In other words, the political branch?

A. Well, no, I do not believe so. I think it was set up so that the White House would not be totally involved in the business of preparing for a political campaign.

Q. Now, were you consulted in any way at times on budgets, or matters involving the financing of the committee?

A. Only on a very general basis. I reviewed the advertising budgets primarily with relation to the question of timing, of intensity of advertising, and to some degree regional concentration. I did not get into the details of the budgets.

Q. I would like to show you, Mr. Haldeman, a memorandum of Feb. 3, 1972, from Mr. Bruce Kehrli to you concerning Committee for re-election support which discusses general budget items.

Do you recall that this particular memorandum, which has "administratively confidential" on it, deals with the question of the Presidential and first family travel budget and then it has items for preconvention, convention and postnomination budget, and then on the second page there is some reference to staff and also there is a reference to Mr. Colson and a statement $900,000 for the Colson office consists of $600,000 for mailing and information retrieval, $150,000 to expand his mailing list, and about $90,000 for "black" projects, black in quotes.

Do you recall those items and why they were being presented to you in a memorandum?

A. This over-all memorandum is for financial support for the White House from the Committee for the Re-election of the President. As I think I indicated, the committee provided financial support for activities that were not deemed to be governmental activities but that were conducted by the White House, the principal of these being, of course, the travel of the President when he was on a purely political trip. This same would apply to other activities that were carried out by other staff members.

The Colson office question appears to be primarily for mailings and Mr. Colson's office was the point of contact with groups and organizations, business organizations, veterans' organizations, other particular interest groups, and I am sure that at his instance there were a number of mailings designed for these specific groups, and that this was to cover support for those mailings.

Q. Do you know what the reference to "black projects" means? A. I am not sure.

Q. We have had testimony before on black advance projects, do you know what that means?

A. I have heard that testimony. I would not think that this would relate to black advance projects as such because Mr. Colson was not concerned with advance work or campaign travel at all that I am aware of.

Q. Well, then there is one item that says, "This budget does not include White House polling expense which I understand will be handled in another way." Is that a reference to what later did happen, the transmittal of $350,000 from the committee to the White House for polling purposes? A. I think that probably is, yes.

Q. Well, at least to this extent, would this cover this area of general budget?

A. No, not at all. This is what I would call campaign support for White House budget. I also saw from time to time or at all times the over-all campaign budget, the big spread sheets that spread out the planned expenditures on a month by month basis for the various campaign activities.

Q. Now, what was your relationship with Mr. Mitchell in the Committee for the Re-election of the President?

A. It was one of very close communication and cooperation, not on a very frequent basis but he kept me posted on what was going on and what problems he had, if any, in the campaign, and he had problems from time to time with the White House in cooperation and he was seeking for information that he would raise with me, and I passed on to him complaints and information and suggestions from the White House, other people in the White House, and from the President.

Q. In the summer or the fall of 1970, were you not concerned about the existing program of intelligence gathering with regard to either domestic dissent or security.

A. 1970 was the time of the concern on domestic security. The problem was the wave of violence, bombings, arson, trashing and other sorts of activities of damaging property, some of them killing people, that were sweeping across the country at that time.

Q. And this led to what we have now been referring to as the Huston plan, did it not? A. Yes, it did.

Q. And I take it you were aware of all of the facets of the Huston plan, what the recommendations were that were being made and as it finally went up to the President?

A. Not in any detail. The inception of the so-called Huston plan was a meeting that the President called. First, Mr. Huston, as a staff man, had done some preliminary work on analysis of the problem, and of the shortcomings that appeared to be in existence at that time with relation to the problem and the efforts to deal with it, as a result of which, the President called a meeting of the heads of the various security agencies, the F.B.I., the N.S.A., the C.I.A. and the D.I.A.

I sat in that meeting, as did Mr. Huston. The President discussed with these agency heads the nature of the problem: the shortcomings of domestic intelligence, the concern that some of these activities that were under way or being threatened during that period of time were possibly at least, and I think demonstrably, connected with foreign activities.

Q. How did you receive specific evidence of these events? You didn't know, you say, who was doing, but obviously you were concerned that the events occurred, what evidence occurred as to who might be involved?

A. There was evidence in terms of the people who were carrying some of them out. There was some intelligence, there was some F.B.I. intelligence, in this area, there was some Secret Service intelligence in this area as it related to Presidential threats and security. And there was some investigative reporting by the press going on as to background of some of these activities, and all of these I think would add together to be the sources at that time of what we did have.

Q. But is it your statement that you were not fully aware of the specifics of the Huston plan?

A. I was not—let me get into how that was set up. In the meeting with the President and the heads of the security agencies, the President made it very clear that he expected some cooperation—which did not exist at that time between these agencies —in getting better information, evaluating the information more effectively, and disseminating it so that action could be taken if there was action indicated.

The group assembled in his office at that time was designated by the President as a task force to prepare recommendations for him as to what ought to be done, what steps should be taken to meet the problem and carry out the request that the President made of this group.

It is my understanding that such a task force under the chairmanship of Director Hoover which prepared an extensive set of recommendations. Mr. Huston worked with them and those recommendations were submitted to the President. They were submitted, through Mr. Huston, to me and through me to the President.

Q. Mr. Huston actually reported to you.

A. He reported through me in this particular area.

Q. You saw all of the papers that were being reviewed, did you not?

A. Not all the working papers of the committee. I saw the recommendations that went to the President.

Q. Did you read the recommendations that went to the President?

A. I am not sure I did or not. If I did it was not in any detail. I had an idea it was a proposal for an expanded intelligence activity.

Q. Were you aware in that proposal there was a recommendation for both national and internal security, that there be an increased use of wiretapping and surreptitious entry or break-in?

A. I am not sure whether I was or not. I may very well have been.

Q. Were you aware that Mr. Hoover, Director of the F.B.I., opposed, at least entered his opposition to most of the recommendations in that plan?

A. He had indicated in the various recommendations his disagreement with some of them in spite of the fact that they were the committee recommendations. [As chairman] he was transmitting them as the committee recommendation with his dissent.

Q. Well, now, did Mr. Huston seek to get your assistance in overriding Mr. Hoover's objections? A. I think he did.

Q. And did he send a series of memorandums to you with regard to that?

A. I have seen the memoranda that have been put into exhibit and reprinted in the papers and they would indicate that he did, yes.

Q. Well, did you just see them as they were reprinted in the papers or do you actually recall receiving those memoranda and reading them?

A. I have a general recollection. I do know that there was a definite concern on Mr. Huston's part and on the President's part that there was a problem. One of the reasons for bringing this group together was the fact that communication between the F.B.I. and other intelligence agencies was at best minimal.

Q. Do you know why Mr. Hoover opposed the plan? A. I am not sure.

Q. Now, are you aware that this plan was in fact approved by the President? A. Yes.

Q. After that approval, was the plan implemented?

A. No, it was not. As I understand it, the approval was rescinded, I believe it was five days later.

Q. Why was it rescinded?

A. Again, as I understand it, because of Director Hoover's objection to a number of parts of the plan.

Q. Did you know that Mr. Mitchell opposed his plan, the Attorney General? A. I am not sure that I knew that he did or that he did not.

Q. Well, he has testified here before this committee that he was not in on the original planning of the plan but when he first learned about it, he went to see you and the President and strongly opposed it and then the plan was not implemented and he assumed that it was partly on the basis of his objection. Do you recall that?

A. I do not, but I certainly would not deny that, if Mr. Mitchell does feel that is the case.

Q. Did you become aware of an in-house White House effort for that special investigative unit?

After the Huston plan was rescinded? [This was the Intelligence Evaluation Committee.]

A. It was not an in-house White House group, although there was a White House representative. Its purpose was coordination between the various intelligence agencies and an attempt to share and evaluate intelligence.

Q. And who was supervising this?

A. I am not sure. I believe John Dean was the White House representative on it and I am not sure how it was structured.

Q. Would it be true that it was Mr. John Dean's role to be liaison for the White House on intelligence programs like this?

A. Yes. It would be.

Q. Now, did there come a time when there was an in-house White House special investigative unit?

A. The question relates, I assume, to this special investigations unit that was set up in 1971.

Q. Yes.

A. I was aware that such a unit was set up at the President's request.

Q. And did you know who was put in charge of that?

A. I think that David Young of the National Security Council staff and Bud Krogh of the Domestic Council staff were the principal men assigned to that work.

Q. Did you know that Mr. Hunt and Liddy took a part in the role of the so-called plumbers?

A. I guess so. It is hard now knowing it so thoroughly through testimony here to know whether I specifically knew they were at that time or not.

Q. Well, is it your testimony, Mr. Haldeman, that with your role as chief of staff, that an operation of this kind, a special investigative unit would not, one, come to your attention, so you would know who was involved, who the staff people would be, who would be working, who would be on its payroll?

A. No. I would know that such a unit existed but this unit was set up as an internal unit using as the two principal staff people, people that were already on staff. This wasn't an addition to staff. This was a reassignment of people, one on Dr. Kissinger's staff and one on Mr. Ehrlichman's staff, to a special project. That was done very frequently and probably most of the time without my knowledge because these were assignments that would come and go.

Q. Well, if new people were brought on staff like Mr. Hunt or Mr. Liddy, wouldn't you have to know about that as the staff director?

A. Not necessarily by name.

Q. You know the reason why this separate investigating unit was set up, do you not?

A. Yes, I knew the approximate cause was the Pentagon Papers leak and that it was set up for the purpose of looking into that and other national security leaks at that time.

Q. You were concerned about such leaks, were you not?

A. I was personally concerned about, them, yes.

Q. Did you discuss with Mr. Ehrlichman, at any time, the work of the special investigating unit?

A. No, I do not think so, other than the fact there was such a unit and they were working on this.

Q. Did this come up in the senior staff meetings?

A. It may have. I do not recall any specific reference to it. The subject of leaks came up often, of course.

Q. As a matter of fact, I think in your own statement, at one point the President dubbed you the Lord High Executioner— A. Yes, sir.

Q. —for leaks.

A. That, however, was on a broad basis but specifically related to any individual leak, or to the area of national security or domestic security.

Q. Now, did you learn in discussion with Mr. Ehrlichman or at your senior staff meetings about the focusing in on Mr. Ellsberg not only as a suspect but as an effort to get more information about him?

A. I do not think so; not through those means.

Q. Did you know there was an effort to get a psychiatric profile on Mr. Ellsberg? A. No.

Q. Did you know that a group had been sent out to California to seek through covert activity access to Dr. Fielding's records? A. No.

Q. Mr. Ehrlichman at no time would be discussing this with you? A. He did not discuss it with me.

Q. Now, I take it you were also aware of hte Sandwedge plan which Mr. Caulfield presented? A. Yes.

Q. And that also was a proposed intelligence plan, was it not? A. Yes.

Q. Are you aware of what occurred on that?

A. It was dropped.

Q. Did you have any role in seeing to it that it was dropped?

A. I do not believe I did. I think that it sort of dropped of its own weight.

Q. Did you know Mr. Tony Ulasewicz? A. No.

Q. Never met him? A. No.

Q. Did you know that he was working for certain White House projects?

A. I knew there was a man employed outside on certain White House projects. I at some point knew his name but at that point did not know how to pronounce it.

Q. Did not Mr. Magruder talk to you directly or by memoranda concerning the need for the committee to have its own in-house capabilities for intelligence with regard to the campaign? A. He may have.

Q. Did you become aware that Mr. Gordon Liddy was employed by the Committee for the Re-election of the President? A. At some point I did.

Q. Were you aware prior to the June 17 break-in?

A. That Mr. Liddy was at the committee, yes.

Q. Did his name come by your desk for approval?

A. His name came by my desk at some point in connection with his salary.

Q. Did you learn at a point in time of a meeting in Mr. Mitchell's office, one on Jan. 27, 1972, and then another meeting on Feb. 4, 1972, attended not only by Mr. Mitchell but by Mr. Dean, Mr. Liddy and Mr. Magruder?

A. Yes, I learned of it in recent months and probably also in the summer of 1972 by way of Mr. Dean recounting to me that there had been these two meetings. That there had been presented an intelligence plan that was totally inconceivable and absurd. That Mitchell had concurred with him in turning this plan off, that he felt that there should be no further discussions of this kind of an intelligence program, and he intended to participate in no such discussions, and that he recommended the White House not participate, if there were any such further discussions, and that there should not be any and that I agreed with him.

Q. Now, this discussion you had with Mr. Dean, is that after the June 17 break-in that this took place? A. Yes.

Q. Now, you say in that discussion you had with Mr. Dean, Mr. Dean told you that right after the Feb. 4 meeting in 1972. He came to you and said the White House should not be involved and you agreed. Do you recall his doing that?

A. I do not recall it with any clear recollection but I was willing to accept Mr. Dean's very specific and very positive recounting to me of what had happened.

Q. Well, then, leaving aside any report that Mr. Dean made to you of these meetings, were you not informed by Mr. Strachan through a political matters memorandum of a sophisticated intelligence system that the Committee for the Re-election of the President had developed for the approval of Mr. Mitchell shortly after March 30.

A. I don't recall Dean so informed [me] but I don't recall any of the other 30 or 29 decision items that were apparently also covered in that memorandum and it is not surprising that I wouldn't.

Q. Would a political matters memorandum dealing with a sophisticated intelligence plan for the committee at a budget of $300,000 strike your attention?

A. As Mr. Strachan has described it, a three-line item in a rather thick political matters memorandum would not strike my attention, no.

Q. Well, do you recall having Mr. Strachan prepare a talking paper [for a meeting with Mr. Mitchell on April 14] that covered a number of these items and including the intelligence plan? A. No.

Q. [Mr. Strachan's] testimony is that this particular political matters memorandum was numbered No. 18 and if you wanted to find out what was included in political matters memorandum No. 18 to refresh your recollection right now, where would you go?

A. I would go to Mr. Strachan.

Q. Mr. Strachan doesn't have the document, I take it. Would the document be at the White House?

A. Well, I understand from Mr. Strachan's testimony that he destroyed the document, so I presume it wouldn't be.

Q. It is not at the White House. A. I don't know whether it is or not, Mr. Dash.

Q. Have you gone to the White House in preparation for your testimony? A. Yes.

Q. Have you looked at any of the political matters memorandum? A. No.

Q. You heard Mr. Strachan's testimony prior to your testimony here. Did you go to the White House to see if there was a political matters memorandum No. 18 at the White House? A. No.

Q. Now, Mr. Strachan has testified that he did present to you shortly after the break-in when you returned to Washington this particular political matters memorandum No. 18 which included the reference to the sophisticated intelligence plan at $300,000 and the talking paper and I think some other matters, and that you said, and this is his testimony, you said that the file should be clean after he had indicated that this particular file might link you by some way to the break-in or the activity of the break-in. Do you recall that conversation with Mr. Strachan?

A. I don't recall the coversation. I don't recall my giving Mr. Strachan such an instruction.

Q. You didn't use that expression. A. I don't remember using it.

Q. Do you have any explanation as to why after that meeting Mr. Strachan would go out and shred that political matters memorandum No. 18?

A. Well, by Mr. Strachan's statement indicates that he destroyed what he considered to be politically embarrassing material and as I recall under direct questioning he quite specifically said that he did not think he was destroying anything that contained any evidence of illegal activities.

Q. Do you recall telling Mr. Strachan in April, sometime shortly after the meeting with Mr. Mitchell, that he should contact Mr. Liddy and tell Mr. Liddy to transfer his capabilities from Mr. Muskie to Mr. McGovern with special emphasis on the relationship to Senator Kennedy? A. No, I don't.

Q. Do you have any idea why Mr. Strachan would testify under oath here that he received that instruction from you?

A. Mr. Dash, I think that my attempt to determine why someone else does something is something that I should not get into.

Q. Well, you say that Mr. Strachan worked for you from 1970 on. A. That is correct.

Q. Did you during that period of time develop an opinion concerning his loyalty, concerning his character for veracity?

A. Yes. I had a very high opinion of both his loyalty and his thoroughness and his veracity.

Q. Now, were you aware, that during this period after the break-in, during the latter part of June through July and in August, there actually were daily meetings between Mr. Dean, Mr. Mitchell, Mr. Mardian, Mr. LaRue and frequently Mr. Magruder and at such meetings the discussion of Mr. Magruder's involvement came up and a plan developed for Mr. Magruder to tell a false story before the grand jury. Did that ever come to your attention? A. No.

Q. Mr. Dean has testified he was serving merely as a liaison. The reason he was over at these meetings over at the committee was that he was there to report back to you and Mr. Ehrlichman what was going on, and that in fact did report back and inform you explicitly about Mr. Magruder's problem, that Mr. Magruder was involved and that it would be a serious question as to whether he could get through the grand jury. Do you recall Mr. Dean making reports to you?

A. He did not so inform me.

Q. Did you ever have any information that led you to be concerned about Mr. Magruder's involvement in the break-in of the Democratic National Committee headquarters at the Watergate?

A. At that time? I do not believe so.

Q. Mr. Mitchell has testified before this committee that he learned for the first time on June 2 after being debriefed by Mr. Mardian and Mr. LaRue when they spoke to Mr. Liddy, that he learned for the first time about Liddy's operation, which not only included the break-in at the Democratic National Committee headquarters but his plumbers operation which included the Ellsberg break-in, the forged Diem cables and some other things and Mr. Mitchell characterized these things as White House horrors and he testified that shortly after learning of these things, he reported them to you and to Mr. Ehrlichman for the purpose of discussing the need to keep the lid on these things, that they should not get revealed to the public.

Do you recall Mr. Mitchell reporting what he learned from Mr. Mardian and Mr. LaRue in these areas?

A. No. The reason I say that is that I do not know of any of the items that I can recall reading of in the newspaper or hearing Mr. Mitchell testify to under the category of White House horrors, at this time last year. I learned of some of them in March and April of this year and others of them in the course of these hearings, but I did not know of the items which he catalogued as White House horrors.

Q. I will give you some examples. He spoke of the Ellsberg break-in.

A. I did not know of that.

Q. The Diem cable.

A. I did not know of that.

Q. The spiriting-out of Miss Dita Beard from town.

A. I did not know of that.

Q. And certain wiretaps that had been taking place for certain security purposes.

A. I did not know of security wiretaps.

Q. Now, when did it come to your attention, Mr. Halderman, that certain funds were being raised to pay for the legal fees of the defendants?

A. Sometime in the period shortly after the Watergate break-in and I am not sure again of any specific date or occasion on which I became aware of that, but I was told at some time in that period and I was told at other times subsequently—I am sure by John Dean and I think possibly also by John Mitchell—that there was an effort by the committee to raise funds to pay for the legal fees and for family support of the defendants who had been arrested in the Watergate burglary.

Q. Now, there came a time, and I think we referred to this briefly when you looked at that memorandum, that you learned that a large sum of money, $350,000, had come from the Committee to Re-elect the President to the White House.

A. Well I did not learn that it had come from them. I caused it to come.

Q. You asked for it? A. Yes.

Q. And I think your statement indicates that you wanted it for polling purposes. A. Yes.

Q. As a matter of fact, it was not used for polling purposes, was it? A. That is correct, it was not.

Q. Then you learned [that the money] went back to the committee. A. That is correct.

Q. And is it your statement that you saw or knew of no connection between that money going back and the need for more funds to pay legal defense fees and family support fees of these Watergate defendants?

A. I was asked by Mr. Strachan after the election what should be done with the cash fund that he had been custodian of. I told him that it should be turned over to the Committee to Re-elect and that he should work out the means of doing that with John Dean.

Subsequently, I was told that there was a problem in doing that. Subsequently to that I was told by John Dean again as I had been told earlier, that there was a continuing need for legal funds, legal fees, for the Watergate defendants. And at that time, following this sequence of events I then said we have a desire to deliver funds to the committee. The committee apparently has a desire for funds, and I suggested that Dean try to carry out both of those two objectives, which he subsequently did.

Q. All right. Now you knew, at least that this $350,000 represented campaign funds, did you not?

A. No, they did not in my understanding represent campaign funds. The $350,000 came from, as I indicated in my statement the 1968 primary surplus fund.

Q. I think your testimony [yesterday] was that you did review these tapes [of a meeting with the President and Mr. Dean on Sept. 15, 1972] and that you had access to these tapes actually in this very month of July, is that true? Could you tell us who initiated the request for your listening to that tape?

A. I am not sure whether I did or whether the President did in a message to me, but it was one way or the other, on the basis that it ended up being that I should listen to it and give him a report as to its content.

Q. Do you know when you actually received that tape, when in July?

A. This was after I moved to California, and I came back to Washington for a several-day period that I believe was July 9, 10 and 11, and it would have been during that trip.

Q. Was it prior to Mr. Butterfield's testimony to this committee concerning the tapes? A. Oh yes.

Q. In what form was the tape?

A. It is a reel.

Q. And you say you listened to this in your home here in Washington? A. That is correct.

Q. Was it delivered to you or did you go and obtain it?

A. It was delivered to me at the E.O.B. [Executive Office Building] in a guest office that I was using. The reason I was back here was to spend some time reviewing notes in the files that I can't take out, and those are in the E.O.B. up in the attic and I was over there. And they had provided me with an office to work in when I wasn't up in the file, and the tape was delivered to me at that office.

Q. Why did you select at this time this particular tape?

A. Well, let's see, I am not sure. I had already heard, as I indicated, the March 21 tape. The President as he has said, had already listened to some of the other tapes. This was a tape that he had not listened to and a tape that I had not listened to, and it was obviously of a meeting of considerable importance, and testimony [of Mr. Dean] regarding which was contradictory to both my recollection and the President's

Q. At that point did you ask or request to listen to any other tapes beside the Sept. 15 one?

A. I am not sure whether I asked or whether there was a suggestion of listening to some other tapes also, but I did not do it.

Q. Why?

A. Because they were [of] meetings in which I was not present at all, and I made the decision myself that it would not be appropriate for me to be in the position of listening to tapes of meetings at this point in time at least, of listening to tapes of meetings at which I had not been present.

Q. But in late April you listened to a tape of March 21 when Mr. Dean and the President, when you were not present at that meeting.

A. I was present at a substantial portion of it.

Q. Substantial portion of it but you did listen to the full tape? A. That is right.

Q. I take it if you had asked for it you could have had access to all of the relevant tapes that were testified to by Mr. Dean.

A. I don't know that as the case. Had the President asked me to review others I would have had access to them to review them, yes. I would not have had access on my own authority to any tape.

Q. Did you make notes? A. Yes.

Q. Did you retain those notes?

A. I retained them at that time and then turned them over to the President later.

Q. And you kept no copy of it? A. No.

Q. Did you show those notes to your counsel? A. No.

Q. Did you meet with the President after listening to that tape and make a report to him? A. No.

Q. Did you make any written report to him?

A. Only by turning the notes over to him.

Q. Now, this committee has a subpoena which was a continuing subpoena to you to turn over such things as tapes, notes or things of that matter. Why did you not turn your notes over or the tapes to this committee which was in your possession?

A. I did not consider it to be in my custody. It was handed to me to listen to the President and report back.

SENATOR WEICKER: The fact is no other witness has had access to these tapes, and very frankly, and I don't cite any great privilege theory and I am not a great constitutional lawyer, but I think I understand the concept of fairness in the American way, and to me it is grossly unfair to any witness who is before this committee and testifies on the basis of something which has been given to him and to him alone, and I raise this as a point of order that I intend to raise not only as on the March 21 meeting but also as to the Sept. 15 meeting, that this committee should not hear from this particular witness information which has been solely accorded to him and which has been denied to anyone else in the United States of America.

SENATOR ERVIN: Well, I ruled yesterday that executive privilege didn't apply. This is, I think, a little planned action in which the White House allows Mr. Haldeman to use the tape which the White House denies to this committee and lets Mr. Haldeman make the interpretation for this committee and then sends down through the counsel a three-paragraph letter protesting in a feeble way the coverage of executive privilege.

I share the feeling about the Senator from Connecticut about the President of the United States denying this committee the tape, the original tape, and if this was a court of law this would never have been admitted in evidence because the ruling is that only the best evidence can be received and this evidence really, with all due respect to it, is, since the original tape is up in the White House in the exclusive possession of the President, and this is just some kind of a post facsimile of it I think it is counter to evidence but I am going to admit it because it is the best we can get.

Q. Now, the President consented for you to put in—your interpretation of these tapes in your statement.

A. The President authorized me to testify as to my recollection of meetings in which I was present.

Q. Did the President give you consent to put your interpretation of these two tapes in your statement? That is my question.

A. No sir, he specifically authorized me to give my recollection, obviously aided by having listened to the tapes.

Q. Wasn't there a little bit of collaboration between you and attorneys for the White House in the preparation of this statement?

A. I don't know what you mean, Mr. Chairman.

Q. Collaboration. Don't you know what the word collaboration means? Didn't the attorneys for the President know what was in your statement? A. No.

Q. Well, will you please tell me why they put this third paragraph in this letter of July 30, 1973, that, "If asked to testify as to facts which he learned about meetings or portions of meetings which he did not attend, but of which he learned solely by listening to a tape recording of such meeting, the President has requested that you inform the committee that Mr. Haldeman has been instructed by the President to decline to testify to such matters, and that the President, in so instructing Mr. Haldeman, is doing so pursuant to the constitutional doctrine of separation of powers."

MR. WILSON [attorney for Mr. Haldeman]: Mr. Chairman—

Q. Wait a minute. I am asking your witness a question, Mr. Wilson. This is no question of law. I am asking you how the attorneys for the President, why they wrote such a letter as this and gave it to your lawyer instead of this committee.

A. I don't know how they knew it. I represented to my attorneys my concern that in preparing my statement I was obviously of necessity dealing with matters that covered events the knowledge of which I had as a result of listening to the tapes, and I asked my attorneys to ascertain for me what requirements I would be under in terms of separation of powers restrictions as to my testimony in that regard.

Q. Isn't the inference irresistible that the attorneys for the White House knew that you had in your statement references to your interpretation of these tapes?

A. At the time I raised the question I did not have them in my statement, Mr. Chairman. I was trying to determine what to put in my statement and on the other hand what not to put in.

Q. Do you mean to tell me, Mr. Haldeman, that you had no communication in any fashion with attorneys for the White House about what you had put in your statement or contemplated putting in your statement?

A. I had no specific discussion.

Q. I am not asking about specific. Any kind.

A. No. No. I haven't discussed with them what I was putting in my statement. I have discussed with them the knowledge on my part that this was an area in which I would have to testify.

Q. You have told me just exactly what I have been asking you. You do say that you informed the attorneys for the White House of the area you were going to have to testify and that included the tapes.

A. No, sir. I am sorry. If I gave that impression I didn't mean to. I informed via any attorneys.

Q. Do you know if your attorneys consulted with the White House attorneys? A. I understand they did, yes, sir.

Q. So instead of sending the letter to the White House attorneys about what they objected to from the committee they gave it to your lawyer to communicate to the committee.

A. What is wrong with that, Mr. Chairman?

Q. I am not saying anything wrong. It just shows there has been a little what we call in North Carolina "canoodling together."

The White House has stated [that] the tapes "have been under my sole personal control and will remain so," [that] none has been transcribed or made public and none will be, and yet despite that fact, here a witness appears and makes them public just a few days after that and it raises this inference in my mind, Mr. Haldeman—we infer that the private word of the White House becomes inoperative a few days after it is given.

A. No, sir. I think that it is quite clear that, because the President had made that statement, I was faced with a question as to what I was to do with knowledge that I had when I appear here with the requirement and the desire to transmit all of the knowledge that I have as best I can, and I faced with that dilemma, asked my attorneys how to deal with it in the terms of what I was permitted to testify to and what I was restricted from testifying to, and in that regard, it would appear to me that the White House's response was that they obviously could not restrict me from testifying as to knowledge I had as a result of my having been in attendance at a meeting, but they did place upon me the restriction that I must not testify to information which I had gained solely from the process of listening to the tape.

Q. When did the White House lawyers learn that you contemplated using this, your interpretation of the tape, these tapes?

MR. WILSON: May I answer that?

Q. Yes.

MR. WILSON: Last weekend.

Q. Now, when the privilege of executive privilege belongs to the White House, and it ought to have been asserted by the White House lawyers, why did they have your lawyer call the matter to the attention of this committee and ask for a ruling?

So I would say that the clear indication is that the White House's counsel wanted Mr. Haldeman to reveal his interpretation of the tapes to the public.

A. If I could simply say that anything that I have discussed regarding information I gained solely from the tapes I have so spoken here after the chair overruled the objection of the White House to my doing so.

Q. Yes, this was what I would call a powder-puff objection. If they had really meant the objection to be sustained they would have been right here raising Cain about it themselves.

SENATOR BAKER: One statement in your addendum seems to be of extraordinary importance and I want to test the accuracy of your recollection and the quality of your note-taking from those tapes, and I am referring to the third from the last sentence on page 2, "The President said there is no problem in raising a million dollars [for the Watergate convicted]. We can do that but it would be wrong."

Now if the period were to follow after "we can do that," it would be a most damning statement. If, in fact, the tapes clearly show he said "but it would be wrong," it is an entirely different context. Now, how sure are you, Mr. Haldeman, that those tapes, in fact say that?

A. I am absolutely positive.

Q. Was there any distortion in the quality of the tapes in that respect? A. No, I do not believe so.

SENATOR TALMADGE: Mr. Haldeman, why were you and you alone, to the exclusion of every other witness who has been before this committee, permitted to listen to the tapes?

A. I was not permitted to listen in my capacity as a witness before this committee. I was asked to listen in my capacity or former capacity as a staff assistant to the President and as the assistant to the President who knew of the existence of the tapes.

Q. Mr. Ehrlichman was not permitted to listen to them?

A. Mr. Ehrlichman, I do not believe, was aware of the existence of them.

Q. Now, you listened, I believe, once in April, that was before you left the White House.

A. That is correct. I listened to one of the tapes at that time.

Q. And subsequent thereto in July after you became a private citizen? A. That is correct.

Q. Why would a private citizen be more entitled to listen to those tapes than a Senate committee of the Congress of the United States?

A. That is a question that I cannot answer, Senator, except that I did it as a means of reporting to the President.

Q. You are aware that the President has stated that he himself has listened to the tapes, and that he is satisfied that they sustain his point of view, although he stated that someone else might get a different interpretation. Now, you have listened to the tapes. In your judgment, is there any way you could get a different interpretation other than what the President of the United States said about it?

A. It would be [my opinion] that any reasonable person who listened to the tape, as I did, would come up with the same conclusion that I have and that the President has on an over-all basis.

Aug. 1, 1973

SENATOR TALMADGE: Did you or anyone within the White House ever request the White House to make a political, an audit of any taxpayer?

MR. HALDEMAN: In the sense of referring information that

had come to our attention or information that appeared to indicate a reason for an audit, it is quite possible that that was done. I recall no specific such request.

Q. Now would they be foes of Administration or friends of the Administration?

A. These would be inquiries or information that would come in from friends of the Administration regarding foes of the Administration.

Q. Do you remember a particular effort to "get" Clark Clifford. A. No, I don't.

Q. You don't recall that.

A. I know that there was considerable—now wait a minute, Clark Clifford.

Q. He is a prominent Washington attorney, as you know.

A. I am sorry, I was thinking of a different person.

Q. Do you recall any effort to quash an audit of any friendly taxpayer? A. No.

Q. I am the second ranking member of the Senate Finance Committee and our jurisdiction is the Internal Revenue Service among others. And we have tried our dead level best to keep that totally nonpolitical and nonpartisan, totally objective, without favor, without fear to any taxpayer in the United States, and I certainly hope we can continue to keep it that way.

A. I am sure, sir, that you have attempted to do so and I hope that you have been successful.

SENATOR INOUYE: On Page 30 of your opening statement, the last paragraph says: "If, as alleged, he [Donald H. Segretti] or those under his direction were responsible for the letter which falsely defamed Senators Muskie and Humphrey, then on behalf of everyone associated with the Nixon campaign, I would like to and do apologize to both of these men."

Did you have any purpose in leaving out Senator Jackson?

A. Absolutely not. If Senator Jackson was also defamed in that letter, I would very much want to correct my omission, as being unintentional and to extend my apology very definitely to include Senator Jackson.

Q. Would I be correct in assuming that at the end of the year 1972 you were aware that the campaign committee had a surplus of over $3 million?

A. I was aware by the end of '72 that there was a very substantial surplus.

Q. Now, if you considered the raising of funds for the Watergate defendants to be legal, moral, an obligation proper, humanitarian, why didn't you use these campaign funds? You had surplus of over $3 million.

A. First of all, Senator, I didn't consider it either to be any of those things or the opposite of any of those things. I did not weigh it in its context of legality, morality or necessity. I simply accepted what I was told, which was that these funds were being raised for the purpose of legal fees for the defendants.

As to the question of why I didn't use those funds, I didn't have the control of those funds or the position to use those funds.

Q. You were the President's representative, the chief of staff of the White House. Couldn't you have suggested this? A. I could have suggested this, yes.

Q. But you decided not to.

A. It didn't occur to me to.

Q. Was this special fund raising necessary because the using of the money was illegal? A. Not to my knowledge.

SENATOR WEICKER: I want to submit to you a document on White House stationery, memorandum for Mr. H. R. Haldeman from Ronald H. Walker.

At the same time I would like to submit for your inspection and your counsel's inspection a document dated Feb. 10, 1973, memorandum for John Dean from H. R. Haldeman.

All right now, let's discuss the first memorandum which I presented to you.

"The White House, Washington, Oct. 14, 1971, 5 P.M.

"Memorandum for: Mr. H. R. Haldeman.

"From: Ronald H. Walker

"Re: Charlotte, North Carolina—Demonstrations

"1. The most recent intelligence that has been received from the advance man Bill Henkel and the United States Secret Service is that we will have demonstrators in Charlotte tomorrow. The number is running between 100 and 200; the advance man's gut reaction is between 150 and 200. They will be violent"—with a penciled underlining of "violent"—"they will have extremely obscene signs" —underlining "obscene." And next to the word "obscene," penciled in writing, which to me and you will have to confirm this— seems to be the same as the writing below your initial, appears to be yours, saying, "Good."

Is that your writing there where it says "Good?" A. I believe it is.

Q. "As has been indicated by their handbills. It will not only be directed toward the President, but also toward Billy Graham." Underlining "Also Toward Billy Graham," where you penciled in "Great."

"According to Henkel and the U.S.S.S. [United States Secret Service] and it is also indicated on the handbills being distributed by the demonstrators, the Charlotte Police Department is extremely tough and will probably use force to prevent any possible disruption of the motorcade or the President's movements."

And again the penciling, "Good" next to that.

Then No. 3, I had better read the whole exhibit:

"My instructions to Henkel are to control the demonstrators outside the Coliseum as much as he can with the help of the

U.S.S.S. and the Police Department, from the city of Charlotte. He is to set up as fine a screening system as possible. There are 8,000 seats in the Coliseum and we have printed up 25,000 tickets. It is a known fact that there are demonstrators who have tickets. Therefore it will be necessary for us to set up a screening system to eliminate anyone that has a false or fake ticket. We will set up our normal checkpoints, using 25 Veterans of Foreign Wars and between 50 and 60 ushers that are being provided by the local Republican party. There will also be a volunteer lawyer corps to handle any legal questions that might arise, as far as denying entrance on the grounds of a phony ticket.

"The thing that bothers me is that we are for the most part paralleling the system that we had designed for the Wright-Patterson Air Force Museum dedication in Dayton, Ohio. Realizing the attention that was drawn to and the concern that has since been expressed by Ziegler, Warren, and most vehemently by Pat Buchanan, the feeling is that the [White House] press corps, especially the liberals, are very much aware of how the demonstrators are being handled, and although the White House has not been identified with these processes, we are very much suspect.

"Buchanan maintains that they will be on the lookout for demonstrators and how they are being handled, and it is his feeling that this could be extremely damaging even if the White House is only indirectly involved. The Billy Graham people have been of great help but they've got their own problems with citizens' organizations sponsoring the Billy Graham Day, and have pretty well backed off from any of the arrangements with the exception of crowd building. Therefore, we have got very little support in handling demonstrators in the hall.

"Question: Should we continue with our plan to prevent demonstrators from entering the Coliseum?"

Under "Yes," the initial "H," and the pencil notation, "As long as it is local police and local volunteers doing it, not our people."

My question specifically relates to what mentality it is in the White House that goes ahead and indicates, "Good," when the word "violence" is mentioned, when "obscene" is mentioned, which violence and which obscenity is to be directed against the President of the United States. How in any way can that be good?

A. Senator, I can explain that I think very easily.

The problems that we had during the campaign of violence, of demonstrations, of obscene signs, of efforts to heckle and shout down the President when he was delivering a speech were very great.

They were not recognized as being very great and there was an attempt made in the coverage of many of these events to present this as a totally off-the-cuff reaction of certain people in the audience who were just there and disagreed with what the President said and were expressing their disagreement in a proper exercise of their right to do so as contrasted to planned organizations that were put together for the purpose of creating violence.

The reason for reacting to the indication that they would be violent, obscene and directed toward Billy Graham as, "Good," was that if, in fact, they were going to do this in this way, it would be seen that they were doing so clearly. Sometimes they weren't that ineffective. They did a better job of disguising their true intents and their true method of operation, and the reaction of, "Good," to those indications was very much in that sense.

SENATOR MONTOYA: Are you acquainted with the project which was launched in the White House to develop an enemies list?

A. I am aware of the existence of enemy lists or opponents lists.

I know that from time to time we received from within the White House and from outside the White House, from supporters of the Administration, both in the Congress and from the general public, complaints that people in and out of Government who were expressing vocal opposition [to Administration policies, particularly on Vietnam] were at the same time being extended extraordinary courtesies by the White House in the form of invitations to social events and other functions at the White House, appointments to honorary boards and commissions, inclusion on delegations to events, and that sort of thing.

Q. I am talking about enemies, not friends.

A. No, sir, that is what I am talking about, people, I am talking about complaints by friends that people who were opponents and were vocally expressing their opposition were being, in the view of our friends, treated like friends in the sense of receiving these special courtesies from the White House.

Q. And you were compiling a list of these people?

A. And as a result of the concern by our friends that we were in their view unwisely extending these courtesies to the people who were opposing Administration policies, and on some occasions people who, after receiving an invitation to the White House and being at the White House used that as a platform for getting extraordinary publicity for their expression of opposition, that as a result of these complaints there was a program of drawing up a list of those who in prominent public positions were believed to be expressing opposition to Administration policies, and who, therefore, should not be receiving these courtesies.

This was in the same context as a list of those who were supporting such policies and who should be extended such courtesies and who many times were not.

Q. I will read you some names [on two "enemies" lists submitted by Mr. Dean]. What did these people have to do with the Vietnam War?:

Eugene Carson Blake, Leonard Bernstein, Arthur Fisher, Ed

Guttman, Maxwell Cain, Charles Dyson, Howard Stein, Al Lowenstein, Morton Halperin, Leonard Woodcock, Dan Schorr, Mary McGrory, Lloyd Cutler, Thomas Watson, Tom Wicker, Clark Clifford. That is the list.

A. I would think that the public record of the time would indicate that a number of those people were, in fact, quite vocally and publicly opposing Administration positions on the war.

Q. Why did you label them as enemies, then? Did they not have a right to comment on the war?

A. Why, certainly, they did, but they did not have a right to be extended the courtesy of the President's hospitality in order to express their opposition.

Q. Well, are you in effect telling me that this enemies list was compiled so that it would serve as a exclusion list for the White House? A. In effect, yes.

Q. Why was so much time wasted in the White House with memos and communications between staff members in trying to compile this list, then?

A. First of all, I don't believe a great deal of time was wasted in doing so. The time that was expended in doing it was for the purpose that I have indicated.

Q. Well, if your objective was as you have stated it, why was it an effort to involve I.R.S. in auditing [the tax returns of] some of these people and why were there orders from the White House to the F.B.I. to check on some of these people?

A. I would like to know what these orders were and perhaps I can respond to them.

Q. All right. Mr. Higby, who was your administrative assistant, has given information to this committee that while he was in the Grand Tetons with the President and you, he was asked by you to call Mr. Hoover and get a complete background on Daniel Schorr, and Mr. Higby did this, and he has submitted testimony to this committee in secret to that effect. Now, would you deny that?

A. I requested a background report on Mr. Schorr, or asked Mr. Hibgy to request one, not in connection with the enemies list, and I am not sure in what connection it was, but I am sure there was something that arose at the time that this request was made and I don't know in what context, but there had been, as has been indicated here in earlier testimony, concern from time to time about statements that were made and the reasons for them in terms of national security questions, and I don't know that this was in such a context because I simply don't recall what the reason was for it.

Q. Why would you order a check in that context? Was Mr. Schorr being considered for an appointment? A. No, he was not.

Q. Why would you check on him, then?

A. I don't know why, but the check was made.

Q. You ordered it?

A. The request for the check was in connection with something apparently—I assume—that arose at that time that generated a request for the background report on Mr. Schorr. The request, I would like to emphasize, Senator, was not a request for an investigation of Mr. Schorr, and at the time that the request was made it was for the background file which the F.B.I. has on individuals, that is, a summary report on their activities and background.

Q. Wouldn't you call that "investigate," when the F.B.I. goes out to try to get the background on an individual?

A. When they go out to do it I would, but the request was not that they go out to do it. The request was for the file, what happened.

Q. What file? Do you have a file in the White House on Mr. Schorr?

A. No, sir. The F.B.I. did, or may have.

Q. How did you know they have?

A. They have a file on most people who are known publicly, and the request was for whatever file they have.

Q. You mean the F.B.I. has a file on every American that is known publicly?

A. I think they probably do. I have not been through their files so I can't verify that.

Q. Now I will give you an instance where you ordered F.B.I. checks on eight other individuals. The testimony of Mr. Butterfield is [that] Haldeman and occasionally Ehrlichman had requested an F.B.I. check on nonappointees. To Butterfield's recollection there may have been eight such requests. Among them were Frank Sinatra, Daniel Schorr, Helen Hayes.

Now, what do you have to say to that? Was Helen Hayes being considered for an appointment?

A. Quite possibly so. Helen Hayes held Presidential appointments and commissions at a number of times and that is quite possible.

Q. Was Frank Sinatra being considered for an appointment?

A. No, sir. Frank Sinatra was being considered as an entertainer at the White House and was an entertainer at the White House.

Q. And was Daniel Schorr being considered for entertainments at the White House?

A. No. I would simply like to say in the case of any entertainer at the White House and for that matter I believe any guest at the White House there is automatically a check made of his F.B.I. file to determine whether he poses any security threat or any potential embarrassment in any other sense, and it is unfortunate that those particular names have been raised and singled out in this forum because I would not like the record to imply that there was an allegation of wrongdoing on the part of any of those three people, and of the other five that were apparently on the list of eight that have not been named or any of the others of hundreds of people who have been so checked.

And since this question has come up, I would also like to say that it has become popularly referred to here as the enemies list and

I would like to plead guilty to a certain indelicacy, if that is what it was referred to in our Administration, because in reading one of the books by one of the learned scholars who served in the Johnson Administration, I saw that at their time, this list was referred to as the anathema list and I must say that is a much more delicate term for it.

Q. Did you or did you not in June of 1972 arrange directly or through John Dean or anyone else for a 24-hour surveilliance of Senator Kennedy?

A. I don't recall making such an arrangement. I know that it has been testified that such a request was made and was not carried out and I am not familiar with the specifics of the reason for the request but there were times when there was a very definite interest in the activities of Senator Kennedy, some political and some not political at all, but in relation to trips that he made with regard to early release of P.O.W.'s and matters dealing with the North Vietnamese and the peace settlement efforts that were under way.

Q. What I am trying to develop is whether or not you authorized such surveillance or observation or investigation of Senator Kennedy.

A. I do not recall ordering any surveillance of Senator Kennedy but I do want to emphasize that there were questions raised about Senator Kennedy's activities in various regards from time to time, and such a question could have come up.

Q. Do you recall or do you have any knowledge of any surveillance of Senator Kennedy relating to Mr. Caulfield in 1970 or 1971?

A. No, I do not recall that but I was not familiar with Mr. Caulfield's activities.

Q. Do you recall any surveillance of Senator Kennedy in 1969 in which Mr. Ulasewicz may have been involved? A. No.

Q. Do you have any information about Mr. Ulasewicz's observation, investigation or surveilliance of Senator Kennedy at any time, Mr. Haldeman?

A. I have no familiarity at all with Mr. Ulasewicz's operations with regard to any individual. I was not familiar with what he was doing or with what his objectives were or what his results were.

SENATOR ERVIN: Mr. Haldeman, it appears from your answers to my previous questions that prior to Sept. 15, five burglars were caught in the Democratic national headquarters, with campaign funds belonging to the Nixon committee in their pockets. A short time thereafter a former White House consultant, Hunt, and G. Gordon Liddy, the chief legal officer of the Stans committee, were also arrested, charged with procuring these five burglars to do the burglarizing.

Now, certainly, President Nixon had some control over his committee. Did he at any time, to your knowledge, summon John

Mitchell, the director of the Committee to Re-elect, to procure his re-election, or Jeb Stuart Magruder, the deputy director of that committee, or Maurice Stans, the head of the Finance Committee for his re-election, or Hugh W. Sloan Jr., the treasurer of that committee, or Robert Mardian or any other person, into the White House and demand of them how it happened that burglars were caught in the headquarters of the opposition political party with funds donated for his re-election, in their pockets?

A. He did not call any of those people in and demand that. I believe Mr. Mitchell said he had met with the President shortly after the Watergate and had talked with him about it at that time.

Q. But Mr. Mitchell testified with the most absolute positiveness that he never told the President about any of these things and that the President at no time asked him about it, notwithstanding the fact that he met with the President on many occasions in reference to the campaign.

A. But, Mr. Chairman, we are dealing with two different things here. One is the fact of the Watergate burglary, and that, as I understand it, Mr. Mitchell did talk with the President about shortly after the burglary.

Q. He called him up and told him he was sorry that matters had got out of hand, and he had not exercised as much supervision but he also testified the President did not ask him any questions about what he was talking about, as I recall the testimony.

A. Well, at that point I believe the President had been told what the facts were as they were known at that time. I do not believe he had anything to question him about other than what Mr. Mitchell talked with him about. The things that developed from that time on, the President was not aware were developing.

Q. Mr. Haldeman, we have not got a particle of testimony so far that the President himself personally took any active interest in any time between June 17, 1972, and March [21], 1973, except to make inquiries allegedly through Dean as to how this all happened.

A. Through Dean, through Ehrlichman and through me. He made inquiries at various times, as John Ehrlichman has testified and as I have and as John Dean has.

Q. What did you and Ehrlichman do about it?

A. We referred them to John Dean who was the man responsible for dealing with them.

Q. Oh, John Dean was the only man in the White House who was asked to take any concern of finding out how it was that these burglars were caught in the Watergate with the President's campaign funds in their pockets?

A. This is absolutely correct, Mr. Chairman, he was the only man in the White House asked to do that because there were hundreds of people outside of the White House in the executive branch doing precisely that.

SENATOR GURNEY: In these conversations which you had with the President and Mr. Mitchell prior to his resignation, was there any discussion that he ought to resign because he had knowledge of the Watergate break-in. A. No.

Q. And because, after that he participated in the cover-up? A. Absolutely not.

Q. Around about this March 21 meeting was there any discussion about having John Mitchell step forward, I think that term was used, [and] take the rap for Watergate?

A. I do not think at that time, there was in the second week in April a developing view on both John Dean's and John Ehrlichman's part, as they were getting additional information from various people, that there was a real possibility, at least, growing in their mind that John Mitchell had been aware of the Watergate break-in, and so forth, and that if that would be a major step in opening up the problems of what really had happened in the Watergate case.

It was not discussed in terms of scapegoatism or someone taking the rap, and it was not discussed in terms of putting the pressure on Mr. Mitchell to do this. It was discussed in the terms if this were the case and if it happened that would certainly be a major step in the direction of trying to unravel this whole thing. And that unfortunately now as it gets talked about gets misplayed.

Q. In any of your meetings with Mitchell or in any phone calls that you had with him in this time-frame, say, now, look, John, didn't you really know about this break-in and weren't you deeply involved in this cover-up and don't you think it is time to take the lead and unravel all this?

A. I did not. That was, I believe, the essence of John Ehrlichman's meeting with Mr. Mitchell on April 14.

SENATOR WEICKER: Now, Mr. Haldeman, I had presented to you two documents. You briefly went over the first. Now, let me read it [the second]. Dated, Feb. 10, 1973.

"Memorandum for: John Dean

"From: H. R. Haldeman:

"We need to get our people to put out the story on the foreign or Communist money that was used in support of demonstrations against the President in 1972. We should tie all 1972 demonstrations to McGovern and, thus, to the Democrats as part of the peace movement.

"The investigation should be brought to include the peace movement which leads directly to McGovern and Teddy Kennedy. This is a good counteroffensive to be developed. In this connection we need to itemize all the disruptions such as the Century Plaza, San Francisco, Statute of Liberty, and so on.

"You should definitely order Gray to go ahead on the F.B.I. investigation against those who tapped Nixon and Agnew in 1968.

"We need to develop the plan on to what extent the Democrats were responsible for the demonstrations that led to violence or disruption.

"There's also the question of whether we should let out the Fort Wayne story now—that we ran a clean campaign compared to theirs, libel and slander such as against Rebozo, et cetera.

"We could let Evans and Novak put it out and then be asked about it to make the point that we knew and the President said it was not to be used under any circumstances.

"In any event, we have to play a very hard game on this whole thing and get our investigations going as a countermove."

Is that a memorandum that you prepared?

A. I will accept responsibility for the memorandum, although because of some bad English and other problems in it, I would point out that it is not initialed by me, which it would have been had I written the memorandum and sent it. I believe that this was a memorandum prepared from notes or from telephonic instructions to a staff member who then wrote it up and sent it out over my name. Having said that, I am disclaiming responsibility for the English and typos, and accepting over-all responsibility for the memorandum.

Q. Well, I guess the first thing to ask here is I would like to get your version as to what this first paragraph means, "We need to get our people to put out the story on the foreign or Communist money that was used in support of demonstrations against the President in '72. We should tie all 1972 demonstrations to McGovern and, thus, to the Democrats as part of the peace movement."

A. I think there was, or I know that there was, some information, I don't know how good it was, that there was foreign money used to support the financing of demonstrations. The point here was to develop the facts on it.

In other words, this was to determine the facts and get out the story with the objective of tying, where the facts did so, tying those demonstrations to those who were responsible for them.

Q. What are you tying the Democratic party to? Let's be specific. Are you trying to tie the Democratic party to Communist money or foreign money?

A. I am trying to tie the demonstrations that were instigated by McGovern or McGovern campaign people to those people. I am trying to get out the story of what the facts were in regard to the instigation of and financing of demonstrations.

Q. I had my impression of your opening statement in trying to tie the Democratic party and George McGovern to the image of being soft on Communism and being soft on law and order and all of a sudden this memorandum appears and here you are suggesting as a counteroffensive that these entities, this individual, and this party be tied in with foreign and Communist money and that it be tied into the demonstrations. Is this what you believed during the course of the campaign of 1972? Was this to be the thrust of the attack?

A. Let me—I don't understand your references to soft on Communism and soft on law and order. Is there something that I have said that leads to that?

Q. Well, I think that you're definitely trying to make a link-up here. I just have your own memorandum before me on that point.

A. My own memorandum makes no reference to McGovern being soft on Communism.

Q. Do you mean to tell me that as a man closest to the President of the United States, you issued a directive linking the Democratic party, and the Democratic candidate to Communist money, to demonstrations because you thought that was the case, that you are willing to go ahead and do that as the man closest to the President of the United States, you were willing to throw that party and that name around in that fashion?

A. Only if it is the case, Senator.

Q. Isn't it your job before you issue a memorandum to make sure that it either is or is not the case? Isn't that what this country is about?

A. That is why the memorandum was directed to the Counsel to the President who had the facts, as I understood it, on this case.

Q. "We need to get our people to put out the story." This is not a request for an investigation. If it were a request for an investigation, wouldn't this be the type of thing which certainly we should put into the hands of our law enforcement branches here in the United States, either the F.B.I., C.I.A., the national security group or any valid law enforcement branch? This isn't a request for an investigation of these facts. This is to put out the story.

A. It was my understanding that there were facts that let to these points.

Q. What are the facts? A. I don't know.

MR. DASH: Now besides the particular Sept. 15, 1972, tape [that Mr. Haldeman took home] you mentioned that you had other tapes. Would you tell us what dates those tapes referred to?

A. I am not sure. I was asked that this morning and I am not sure what dates they were. They were dates within that sequence of meetings in the period from Feb. 27 through April.

Q. You testified that you listened only to the Sept. 15 tape but you did not listen to the others, and I think— A. That is correct.

Q. I think you indicated you were not a party to those conversations. A. That is correct.

Q. You had listened to the March 21 tapes that part of it which you were not a party when Mr. Dean was with the President. Why when you had the tapes over a period of time now we know, overnight, and had time to do so, actually what prevented you, why did you not listen to the tapes?

A. I simply decided not to because I had not attended the meetings and I didn't feel comfortable listening to those tapes.

Q. But you were under no instruction not to, were you not? There was no instruction you shouldn't listen to the tapes.

A. That is correct. This was not conveyed to me.

Q. Because you were actually given those tapes.

A. The tapes were given to me.

Q. And for the purpose of, I take it, to hear. A. That is correct.

Q. And you made your own decision then not to listen to them.

A. That is correct.

SENATOR BAKER: How many were there?

A. I think there were three.

Q. Three rolls of tape.

A. Three dates which would be three reels.

MR. DASH: Now, I would like to show you an exhibit memorandum, Mr. Haldeman of March 30, 1972, from Mr. Colson to you, subject, I.T.T. I am going to refer to a particular part of it but if you would like to read the entire memorandum first, please take the time to do so.

A. I guess I had better. I have not seen this.

Q. Yes. I should ask you do you recall the memorandum?

A. Not so far. Let me look at it. Yes, I have not tried to read it comprehensively because it is long and general. I have a general feel of it.

Q. It deals obviously with Mr. Colson's concerns about matters that might be coming before the hearing [on the] confirmation of Mr. Kleindienst as Attorney General and I am just going to refer actually to two paragraphs.

On page 3 of the first part of the memorandum, the last paragraph says, "Neither Kleindienst, Mitchell nor Mardian know of the potential dangers. I have deliberately not told Kleindienst or Mitchell, since both may be recalled as witnesses and Mardian does not understand the problem. Only Fred Fielding, myself and Ehrlichman have fully examined all the documents and/or information that could yet come out. A summary of some of these is attached."

Now, I am referring now to the attached summary. Could you look at the very next page and paragraph 2 at the bottom.

"There is a Klein to Haldeman memo dated June 30, 1971, which, of course, precedes the date of the I.T.T. settlement setting forth the $400,000 arrangement with I.T.T. Copies were addressed to Magruder, Mitchell and Timmons. This memo puts the Attorney General on constructive notice at least of the I.T.T. commitment at that time and before the settlement, facts which he has denied under oath. We do not know whether we have recovered all the copies. If known, this would be considerably more damaging than Reineke's [Lieutenant Governor of California] statement [that I.T.T. had pledged $400,000 for the convention]. Magruder believes it is possible the A.G. [Attorney General] transmitted his copy to Magruder. Magruder does not have the copy he received; this memo could be lying around anywhere at 1701"—1701 being the Committee for the Re-election of the President.

Now, that, I take it, was kind of explosive information to come into your possession on March 30, 1972, five days before you met with the President and which you said your notes showed that the discussion was I.T.T. and the Kleindienst confirmation. Did you bring that matter to the attention of the President?

A. I do not know. I do not think so. I do not believe that I received or read this memorandum. It is not familiar to me. Certainly, the attachment is not. There was discussion of the problems of the Kleindienst nomination and as he has spelled out here, apparently there had been a meeting that morning with Clark MacGregor and Wally Johnson, who were the Congressional liaison people at that time and Colson felt that there were matters that they disagreed with me on the analysis of the Kleindienst nomination. I do not know what that was.

Q. The question is whether or not you recall the memorandum and ever receiving that information.

A. I do not recall—I recall a lot of problems and a lot of information that conflicted on the problems of the nomination and the maneuvering that was going on to block the nomination. I was not, again as in almost any of these cases, was not a principal as this memo really indicates in the effort to work out the problems of the nomination and I do not recall reading the information in the back-up memorandum. I do not recall any of it.

Q. And if you had in fact received this memorandum, which would have given you information that the Attorney General may have committed perjury in the Kleindienst confirmation hearings, would this not be a matter that you would have taken up with the President?

A. I would have either taken it up with the President or taken it up with someone who had direct knowledge of the situation to take it up with the President.

Testimony by Richard M. Helms

Aug. 2, 1973

Tells of White House pressures on C.I.A.; challenges Haldeman testimony.

MR. DORSEN: Did you have a conversation with General Cushman concerning Howard Hunt in the summer of 1971?

MR. HELMS: Yes, I recall that General Cushman informed me that he had authorized giving to Howard Hunt a tape recorder and a camera, and I asked for what purpose and he said he wanted to conduct a one-time interview and that he had been properly authenticated by the White House and that he was working at their behest.

Q. Now you have indicated that in your conversation with General Cushman that you indicated to General Cushman that John Ehrlichman should be called. Why was it that John Ehrlichman was to be called?

A. Because it was my distinct impression that he was one who had arranged with General Cushman to have Hunt get these pieces of equipment.

Q. Mr. Helms, I would like to move then to June 23, 1972, and ask you if you recall attending the meeting with Mr. Ehrlichman, Mr. Haldeman and General Walters. A. I do recall attending that meeting.

Q. Where was that meeting held?

A. That meeting was held in Mr. Ehrlichman's office on the second floor.

Q. Could you please describe to us in substance what happened at that meeting.

A. General Walters and I arrived first and waited for a few minutes. Then Mr. Haldeman and Mr. Ehrlichman came into the room. As best I can recall what was said, and Mr. Haldeman did most of the talking, so—and whatever Mr. Ehrlichman contributed in the course of this was either to nod his head or smile or to agree with what Mr. Haldeman said. I just simply want to introduce it this way because it is a little easier for me to describe.

Mr. Haldeman said that there was a lot of flak about the Watergate burglary, that the opposition was capitalizing on it, that it was going to—it was apparently causing some sort of trouble, and he wanted to know whether the agency had anything to do with it. He then said that the five men who had been found in the Democratic National Committee headquarters had been arrested and that that seemed to be adequate under the circumstances, that the F.B.I. was investigating what this was all about, and that they, unified, were concerned about some F.B.I. investigations in Mexico.

He also at that time made some, what to me was an incoherent reference to an investigation in Mexico, or an F.B.I. investigation, running into the Bay of Pigs. I do not know what the reference was alleged to be, but in any event, I assured him that I had no interest in the Bay of Pigs that many years later, that everything in connection with that had been dealt with and liquidated as far as I was aware and I did not care what they ran into in connection with that.

At some juncture in this conversation Mr. Haldeman then said something to the effect that it has been decided that General Walters will go and talk to Acting Director Gray of the F.B.I. and indicate to him that these operations—these investigations of the F.B.I. might run into C.I.A. operations in Mexico and that it was desirable that this not happen and that the investigation, therefore, should be either tapered off or reduced or something, but there was no language saying stopped, as far as I recall.

At this point, the references to Mexico were quite unclear to me. I had to recognize that if the White House, the President, Mr. Haldeman, somebody in high authority, had information about something in Mexico which I did not have information about, which is quite possible—the White House constantly has information which others do not have—that it would be a prudent thing for me to find out if there was any possibility that some C.I.A. operation was being—was going to be affected and, therefore, I wanted the necessary time to do this.

I say this in explanation of the fact that there seems—that since I had consistently pointed out that no C.I.A. operations had been violated by an investigation up to then, that we had had nothing to do with the Watergate burglary, the fact of the matter was that if an investigation continued to go on it might run into something we were doing in Mexico. This possibility always had to exist. Nobody knows everything about everything.

So at this point I think it was repeated a second time that General Walters was to go and see Acting Director Gray with this charge. It was then indicated that Acting Director Gray would probably be expecting the call, that he was looking for some kind of guidance in this matter, and that this should take place as soon as possible. I believe Mr. Ehrlichman at that point made his sole contribution to the conversation, which was that he should get down and see Gray just as fast as he could.

We left this meeting, General Walters and I, and went downstairs to the automobile and I spoke to General Walters along the following lines. I said when you go to see Acting Director Gray, I think you should confine yourself to reminding him that the agency and the F.B.I. have a delimitation agreement, an understanding for many years that if the agency runs into any F.B.I. agents or operations, the F.B.I. shall be immediately notified and if the F.B.I. runs into any agents or operations, it shall be immediately notified.

I was not sure whether Acting Director Gray was familiar with this because he had not been acting director of the F.B.I. for very long. I wanted General Walters to understand about this because he had been with the agency, I think, only about six weeks at that time, had been having briefings, and I was not sure whether this had ever come to his attention.

In other words, I was asking him to make a legitimate request of the Acting Director of the F.B.I. that if they ran into any C.I.A. operations in Mexico or any place else they were to notify us immediately and I thought General Walters should restrict his conversation with Acting Director Gray to that point. Precisely whether he did or not, well, you will have an opportunity to ask him.

Q. To your knowledge, did General Walters have a meeting with Patrick Gray?

A. Yes, he had one very shortly after this meeting in the

White House because he reported to me later in the day about his meeting with Gray, that he had been to see him, that the general purport of what they had discussed, and then the first time I learned that Acting Director Gray had told General Walters at this meeting about some money having been sent to Mexico. I was unaware of any money having been sent there at the time, and even that explanation did not say what the money was for.

But also floating around in this at the time was the name of a Mexican lawyer that we had been asked to check out by the F.B.I. to find out if this man was in any way connected with the C.I.A. His name was Ogarrio, I believe, and we had been running traces, going through the record to find out and check with our people in Mexico to see if they knew him, and so forth, and it was some day subsequent that we got the information back that he was indeed a lawyer in Mexico but we had never had any connection with him and I so notified the F.B.I.

Q. Could you briefly summarize, of course, Ambassador, what General Walters told you with respect to the meeting of the 27th and the meeting of the 28th?

A. It is my recollection that it was at the meeting of the 27th, which was Tuesday, I believe, that the issue first came up of whether or not the C.I.A. out of its covert funds was prepared to provide bail money for the defendants in the Watergate burglary. Not only did this issue come up, but I also believe that the additional point was made would it be possible for the C.I.A. to pay the salaries of these individuals while they served their jail sentences.

General Walters and I have told you about the conversation I had with General Walters the day before about how he was to guide himself in this matter, pointed out to Mr. Dean that the agency could not possibly do anything like that.

MR. THOMPSON: I would like to refer to your testimony before the Committee on Armed Services, Thursday, May 17, 1973.

Mr. Helms, were Mr. Walters and yourself being questioned at the same time on this occasion? Were you in the same room together?

A. On that occasion General Walters was sitting on my right and General Cushman was sitting on my left and we were in the room together the whole time.

Q. All right. Let me read, if I might.

"Ambassador Helms: Were you"—first of all, "Mr. Woolsey: Let us go back to the meeting itself for a moment. When Mr. Haldeman said that it had been decided that the general should call on Mr. Gray, did he say or intimate in any way who had decided upon that course of action?

"Ambassador Helms: Well, you can make an intimation of that but I would rather not draw out the intimation, if the chairman will relieve me of that. Here was Mr. Haldeman, Mr. Ehrlichman, the two most senior officials in the White House next to the President himself, giving this instruction. And I really feel like now, as I did then, that it would have been presumptuous to have pressed them any harder as to how they had come up with this, or where they had gotten the idea, or who was behind it.

"Mr. Woolsey: You said Mr. Haldeman mentioned the Bay of Pigs. Did he mention the Watergate case itself in the course of the conversation?

"Ambassador Helms: No.

"Mr. Woolsey: He did not?

"Ambassador Helms: No.

"Senator Symington: General Walters, you confirm that, do you?

"General Walters: Yes, sir. He did not mention the Watergate.

"He did in the introduction when he said this case had stirred up a lot of things and the opposition is attempting to exploit it. That was the reference I testified to previously. I believe as he came in he said, the Watergate has stirred up a lot of things. And the opposition is attempting to exploit it"—this is General Walters talking—"and it has been decided that you will go. That was the inevitable lead into the whole reference.

"Senator Jackson: He decided that you will go?

"General Walters: To Mr. Gray, tell him that if he pursues the Mexican part of the financing of this business it will uncover C.I.A. assets or schemes for moving money.

"Mr. Woolsey: I should perhaps read into the record here a few sentences from General Walters's affidavit: 'As I recall it, Mr. Haldeman said that the Watergate incident was causing trouble and was being exploited by the opposition. It had been decided at the White House that I would go to Acting F.B.I. Director Gray and tell him that now that the five suspects were arrested, further inquiries into the Mexican aspect of the matters might jeopardize the C.I.A.'s activities in this area.'

"Was there any discussion in the meeting at all of Watergate?

"Ambassador Helms: Not to the best of my recollection. And I frankly was hard put at the time to understand what Mexico was involved with. This was only a week after the break-in. I did not know why Mexico was being mentioned, and it never occurred to me that it had anything to do with the Watergate burglary.

"Senator Symington: General Walters, do you agree with that?

"General Walters: To me the whole question was connected by virtue of the beginning of the thing when he said the Watergate could be opened as a preliminary, as a lead-in, as to why he wanted me to go. It was obviously a lead-in to this, but he did not go into any discussion of the Watergate other than what I said in the beginning."

Then you go to other matters, Mr. Helms.

Let me see if I summarized this correctly. The question was

put directly to you first, as to whether or not there was any Watergate discussion and you said there was not.

A. That was the way I recalled it, Mr. Thompson, at the time. Since then I have seen General Walters' memorandum for the record. I have talked with him about this and we went over again what had occurred and I frankly at that point had forgotten this lead-in to the conversation. After all, I had been away for some time.

Q. Well, I am certainly not accusing you or any other witness of anything but I do want to clear it up. Let me make sure I have my chronology right. I am reading from page 21-A of the transcript. The question was posed to you, you said no. He said did you know? you said no.

"General Walters, do you confirm that," and General Walters said, "Yes, sir, he did not mention the Watergate." Then Mr. Woolsey said this is something we should get cleared up and he refers to General Walters's affidavit at that time which he had previously submitted in which he mentioned these things.

A. Mr. Thompson, what I am referring to and what I saw subsequently was a memorandum for the record which I believe is in the custody of the committee which was written several days after this 23 June conversation.

Q. Mr. Helms, are you basing your testimony now on your own memory or on Mr. Walters's memory? I mean, you recounted your faith in his memory which I am sure is probably well placed, but I would think that this would be a rather significant matter.

If Haldeman and Ehrlichman, as has been widely reported from the basis of this memorandum which I just referred to, I suppose, came in and said, five people have been arrested and that ought to be enough, and if that is the lead into as how the C.I.A. or F.B.I. should conduct its investigation and the basis of C.I.A. contact with F.B.I., I would think that this was something that you would remember.

So, I am really trying to determine whether your testimony is based upon your own independent recollection or just after having read this memorandum and your faith in General Walter's recollection.

A. Well, it is a combination of the two, Mr. Thompson, because when he jogged my memory and we went back over the meeting together then I did recall these other remarks having been made.

SENATOR ERVIN: You did know that Mr. Ehrlichman was a very important aide in the White House and also you knew that C.I.A. put an end to the—when C.I.A. put an end to giving help to Mr. Hunt, that Mr. Ehrlichman was notified that Mr. Hunt had become a pain in the neck.

So, didn't it strike you when you learned of these things, didn't it strike you as strange that the White House would engage in undercover work on its own initiative rather than resort to the use of the F.B.I.?

A. Well, you know, Senator Ervin, at that time there was no intimation that this was even undercover work. What I understood Mr. Hunt had told General Cushman was that he wanted to conduct an interview and there was no intimation that this was undercover work.

Q. I would just like to say this, Mr. Helms, from the observation of the work you did as Director of the C.I.A. and from the contacts I had with you, I think you did a magnificent job in that capacity.

A. Thank you, Mr. Chairman.

Testimony by General Robert E. Cushman Jr.

Aug. 2, 1973

Disputes Ehrlichman on assistance to Hunt.

MR. HAMILTON: Did there come a time on or about July 7, 1971, when you received a call from the White House requesting C.I.A. assistance in regard to a White House project?

GENERAL CUSHMAN: Yes, sir, I received a call on the 7th of July, 1971, from Mr. Ehrlichman who said that Howard Hunt had been hired as a consultant to the White House on security matters, that he would be coming to see me, and could I lend him a hand or words to that effect.

Q. Did you subsequently meet with Mr. Hunt in your office on July 22, 1971? A. Yes, I did.

Q. Was the conversation of that meeting taped? A. Yes, sir.

Q. Why did you tape this conversation?

A. I taped it so that I would have a recollection of it since Mr. Hunt did not want anyone else in the room. When he arrived he asked that it just be the two of us. Consequently I recorded the conversation so I wouldn't have to take notes.

Q. Now, is this transcript that I have given you an accurate partial recording of the meeting between you and Mr. Hunt on that date? A. I think it is, yes, sir.

Q. Now, referring you to page 3 of the transcript, General, does it show that you affirmed to Mr. Hunt on that date that Mr. Ehrlichman had called you regarding assistance to Mr. Hunt?

A. It seems to, in that Mr. Hunt used the word "Ehrlichman" in starting a sentence, and I said "Yes, he called me."

Q. And did you make a similar statement that it was Mr. Ehrlichman who had called you in a July 8, 1971, meeting between senior agency officials that is recorded in the official minutes of that meeting? A. Yes, sir, I did.

Q. Did Mr. Hunt request that he be given a New York address and phone services in New York?

A. Yes, sir. And this was when we decided that these requests were clearly escalating into improper requests, in that they would involve C.I.A. people. He wanted an office, and he wanted the telephone to be monitored, as an answering service would, when he was not there, and this, so to speak, was just too much, and I called up Mr. Ehrlichman and told him we could not accede to these types of requests, that I thought he was, he, Mr. Hunt, was not exercising proper judgment, and that, therefore, I passed the word on.

Q. What was Mr. Ehrlichman's comment at that time?

A. He said "O.K.," which I took to mean that we did not have to accede to Hunt's request, and said that he would restrain Mr. Hunt.

Q. Do these memoranda contain a summary of your experience with Mr. Hunt that you have just given us in testimony?

A. Yes, sir, they do.

Q. Would you give us the circumstances that surrounded the preparation of these memoranda in your own words, please, sir?

A. Yes, sir.

I believe the date was the 13th of December, 1972, I was Commandant of the Marine Corps at the time, and Mr. Colby came to see me, he was then the number three man in the C.I.A., he came to see me and stated that the agency had been directed to prepare a summation of their contacts with Howard Hunt. This had been directed, I gathered by the Department of Justice, the prosecutors in the case.

I then prepared the first memo which is dated on the 8th of January—wait, I have to go back a little bit. Apparently, these papers were the subject later of conversation between Mr. Colby and the prosecutor and, I gather, Mr. Ehrlichman, I do not know. The next thing that happened, to my own knowledge was along about the 7th or 8th of January this year. Mr. Colby called and said that Mr. Ehrlichman disputed the phone call incident, and would I prepare a memorandum stating to the best of my recollection, what had happened. So I prepared the first memorandum, which I said Ehrlichman, Mr. Colson or perhaps Mr. Dean. I simply cannot recall at this later date which one it is, of my own knowledge.

I then got a call, as I remember it, from John Ehrlichman saying, "Look, I can't recall prior to the 22d of July and, in fact, my records show I was out of town for a considerable length of time."

Well, this shook up my recollection even worse, and so I offered, without being asked, I offered to take names out of it since I did not think it would be fair when I could not swear to it.

Q. General Cushman, so the record will be clear I would like to read the relevant portions from these two memoranda, a sentence or two from each.

The Jan. 8 memorandum states:

"I received a call over the White House line from either Mr. Ehrlichman, Mr. Colson, or perhaps Mr. Dean (I simply cannot recall at this late date just which one it was) stating that Mr. Hunt would call on me to ask for some support and that he was working on a matter for the person calling."

Now, in the Jan. 10 memorandum this sentence appears:

"I cannot recall at this late date who placed the call but it was someone with whom I was acquainted as opposed to a stranger," and the names of Mr. Ehrlichman, Mr. Colson and Mr. Dean appear nowhere in the memorandum.

A. Right.

Q. Is it your testimony that Mr. Ehrlichman put no pressure at all on you to have his name removed? A. No, sir.

Q. You keep referring to a partial transcript. Why is it partial?

A. I don't know, sir. Just what they gave me.

Q. Is it partial in that not all—in that it cuts off at some point in the conversation or is it partial because there are excerpts from it where the tape cannot be—

A. I don't know whether the tape is unreadable or whether it was just simply chit-chat. There are portions of the tape that are unreadable, I have been told, because of airplane noises and the like.

SENATOR INOUYE: General Cushman, we have spent much time discussing the break-in into the office of Dr. Ellsberg's psychiatrist. I believe we have testimony telling us how it was done and who were the participants and when it was done. I believe the most important question is why was it done or the justification for this break-in.

A few days ago Mr. John Ehrlichman said that the justification was national security and that these Pentagon Papers had been given to some official in the Soviet Embassy.

The New York Times on June 16 began its publication of the Pentagon Papers. As deputy director of the Central Intelligence Agency at that time, were you aware or did you have information indicating that copies of the Pentagon Papers had been transmitted to the—some official in the Soviet Union prior to June 16, 1971?

A. Yes, sir. I do not know of my own knowledge, but it was so stated at one of our morning staff conferences, I believe.

Q. Are you aware of who was responsible for this? A. No, sir.

Q. Articles have appeared quoting "reliable sources" from the F.B.I. suggesting that they are not aware of any transmittal of copies of the Pentagon Papers to the Soviet Embassy. Was this matter discussed with the F.B.I.?

A. I do not know, sir, I was not involved in that. We had quite a session with a small group of people, not including me, who read all the volumes to see what—as they were printed, of course, in The New York Times—everyone would be reading them, so they were read from the point of view of what intelligence sources, methods, and so on, were going to be compromised and given away.

As I recall—well, I do not know. These people reported to Mr. Helms. They did not report to me and I do not know just when it stopped, when they finished reading them, what they did with their conclusions, except that I imagine some kind of action may have had to have been taken concerning certain intelligence sources and methods, perhaps, to stop using them if they had been compromised.

Q. It says—the activities of the Soviet Union, I presume, come within your jurisdiction. Did you make any effort to investigate whether these Pentagon Papers did in fact get into the hands of the Soviets?

A. No, sir. That was not part of my job.

Q. Was it not considered important enough for an investigation?

A. Well, this was up to the Director, sir—Mr. Helms.

Q. Do you know whether the Director made an effort toward this end?

A. Only that he put together this group of people, an ad hoc committee, if you will, to read the entire Pentagon Papers, all the volumes, [to] see if there had been any compromise.

Testimony by General Vernon A. Walters

Aug. 3, 1973

Says White House ordered C.I.A. to object to F.B.I. investigation of Watergate break-in.

MR. DASH: Did you shortly actually after you became Deputy Director of the Central Intelligence Agency, did you attend a meeting at the White House with Mr. Haldeman, Mr. Ehrlichman and Director Helms on June 23, 1972?

GENERAL WALTERS: Yes, I did.

Q. All right, now, would you relate to the committee what Mr. Haldeman said and what you or Mr. Helms said?

A. Mr. Haldeman said that the bugging of the Watergate was creating a lot of noise, that the opposition was attempting to maximize this, that the F.B.I. was investigating this and the leads might uncover some C.I.A. people, and he then asked Mr. Helms what the agency connection was. Mr. Helms replied quite emphatically that there was no agency connection and Mr. Haldeman said that nevertheless, the pursuit of the F.B.I. investigation in Mexico might lead to some important activities or assets.

Mr. Helms said that he had told Mr. Gray on the previous day, the Acting Director of the F.B.I., that there was no agency involvement, that none of the investigations being carried out by the F.B.I. were in any way jeopardizing any agency activity. Mr. Haldeman then said, "Nevertheless, there is concern that this investigation in Mexico may expose some covert activity of the C.I.A., and it has been decided that General Walters will go to Director Gray, Acting Director Gray, and tell him that the further pursuit of this investigation in Mexico," and I wish to emphasize that the only question of investigation involved was Mexico, "the investigation in Mexico, could jeopardize some assets of the Central Intelligence Agency."

Again Mr. Helms said he was not aware of any activity of the agency that could be jeopardized by this. Mr. Haldeman repeated, "Nevertheless, there is concern that the further pursuit of this investigation will uncover some activity or assets of the C.I.A. in Mexico and it has been decided that you will go and tell this," addressed to me, "You will tell this to Acting Director Gray."

Q. But, Mr. Walters, could it have been that Mr. Haldeman asked you or Mr. Helms to go to Mr. Gray and—to first inquire at the C.I.A. whether or not there might be some problem at the C.I.A. if there was an investigation in Mexico rather than saying it was decided that you should go?

A. I do not recall it being put in a question form. It was put in a directive form.

Q. In other words, you understood that to be a direction.

A. I understood that to be a direction and since Mr. Haldeman was very close to the top of the governmental structure of the United States, and as Mr. Helms testified yesterday, the White House has a great deal of information that other people do not have, I had been with the agency approximately six weeks at the time of this meeting, I found it quite conceivable that Mr. Haldeman might have some information that was not available to me.

Q. Now, would you briefly relate to your best recollection what conversation you had with Mr. Gray at that time? This was on June 23, 1972?

A. I said to Mr. Gray that I had just come from the White House where I had talked to some senior staff members and I was to tell him that the pursuit of the F.B.I. investigation in Mexico, the continuation of the F.B.I. investigation in Mexico, could—might uncover some covert activities of the Central Intelligence Agency. I then repeated to him what Mr. Helms had told me about the agreement between the F.B.I. and C.I.A. and he said he was quite aware of this and intended to observe it scrupulously.

Q. All right. Will you relate to the committee the conversation you had with Mr. Dean at that time, on June 26, 1972?

A. Mr. Dean said that he was handling this whole matter of the Watergate, that it was causing a lot of trouble, that it was very embarrassing. The F.B.I. was investigating it. The leads had led to some important people. It might lead to some more important people.

The F.B.I. was proceeding on three hypotheses, namely, that this break-in had been organized by the Republican National Committee, by the Central [Intelligence] Agency or by someone else, whereupon I said I do not know who else organized it but I knew that the Central Intelligence Agency did not organize it. I said furthermore, I have—I related to my conversation with Mr. Dean—Mr. Haldeman and Mr. Ehrlichman on the previous Friday and told him I had checked within the agency and found there was nothing in any of the ongoing F.B.I. investigations that could jeopardize C.I.A. activities or sources or compromise them in any way in Mexico.

He then said, well, could this not have happened without your knowledge? Well, I said, originally perhaps, but I have inquired. I have talked to Mr. Helms and I am sure that we had no part in this operation against the Democratic National Committee.

He kept pressing this. There must have been. These people all used to work for the C.I.A., and all this thing. I said maybe they used to but they were not when they did it and he pressed and pressed on this and asked if there was not some way I could help him, and it seemed to me he was exploring perhaps the option of seeing whether he could put some of the blame on us.

There was not any specific thing he said but the general tenor was in this way and I said to him—I did not have an opportunity to consult with anybody—I simply said, Mr. Dean, any attempt to involve the agency in the stifling of this affair would be a disaster. It would destroy the credibility of the agency with the Congress, with the nation. It would be a grave disservice to the President. I will not be a party to it and I am quite prepared to resign before I do anything that will implicate the agency in this matter.

This seemed to shock him somewhat. I said that anything that would involve any of these Government agencies like the C.I.A. and F.B.I. in anything improper in this way would be a disaster for the nation. Somewhat reluctantly he seemed to accept this line of argument and I left.

Q. I think you mentioned earlier that you did again meet with Mr. Dean.

A. On the following morning, the 27th of June, I received another telephone call from Mr. Dean summoning me down to his office. I went down to Mr. Dean's office.

Mr. Dean said that the investigation was continuing, that some of the suspects were wobbling and might talk and I said, well, that is just too bad but it has nothing to do with us because nothing that they can say can implicate the agency. So he again said, have you not discovered something about agency involvement in this matter and I said no, I have not discovered anything about agency involvement in this matter.

He said is there not something the agency can do to help? I said I do not see how we can be helpful. Then he said, well, would there be any way in which you could go bail or pay the salaries of these defendants while they are in jail? And I said, no way. To do so would implicate the agency in something in which it is not implicated. I will have no part in this.

I further told Mr. Dean that when we expended funds, covert funds within the United States, we were required to report this to our Congressional oversight committees and this seemed to cool his enthusiasm considerably. We had a few more discussions and again he asked me whether there was any way we could be helpful and I said, no, we could not be.

Q. All right now, the meeting on the 28th it appears was a fairly significant meeting because it was a follow-up again of a third meeting that you had with Mr. Dean. Do you have a copy of that memorandum [of conversation]?

A. "On 28 June at 11:30 John Dean asked me to see him at his office in the Executive Office Building. I saw him alone.

"He said that the director's meeting," that is Director Helm's meeting, "with Patrick Gray, F.B.I. Director, was canceled and that John Ehrlichman had suggested that Gray deal with me instead.

"The problem was how to stop the F.B.I. investigation beyond the five suspects. Leads led to two other people—Ken Dahlberg and a Mexican named Guena. Dean said that the $89,000 was unrelated to the bugging case and Dahlberg was refusing to answer questions. Dean then asked hopefully whether I could do anything or had any suggestions.

"I repeated that as Deputy Director, I had no independent authority. I was not in the channel of command and had no authority other than that given me by the Director. The idea that I could act independently was a delusion and had no basis in fact.

"Dean then asked what might be done and I said that I realized he had a tough problem, but if there were agency involvement, it could be only at Presidential directive and the political risks that were concomitant appeared to me to be unacceptable. At present there was a high-explosive bomb but intervention such as he had suggested would transform it into a megaton hydrogen bomb. The present caper was awkward and unpleasant. Directed intervention by the agency could be electorally mortal if it became known and the chances of keeping it secret until the election were almost nil. I noted that scandals had a short life in Washington and other newer, spicier ones soon replaced them. I urged him not to become unduly agitated by this one.

"He then asked if I had any ideas and I said that this affair already had a strong Cuban flavor and everyone knew the

Cubans were conspiratorial and anxious to know what the policies of both parties would be towards Castro. They, therefore, had a plausible motive for attempting this amateurish job which any skilled technician would deplore. This might be costly but it would be plausible.

"Dean said he agreed that this was the best tack to take but it might cost half a million dollars. He also agreed (for the second time) that the risks of agency involvement were unacceptable. After a moment's thought he said that he felt that Gray's cancellation of his appointment with Director Helms might well be reversed in the next few hours.

"Dean thanked me and I left."

Q. Now, did you receive, General Walters, a call from Mr. Gray on July 5? Could you tell us briefly what that call was about?

A. I believe that Mr. Gray said to me at this point that the pressures were mounting to continue the investigation and that unless he received a written letter from Mr. Helms or from me to the effect that the further pursuit of this investigation in Mexico would uncover C.I.A. assets or activities he would have to go ahead with the investigation. I did not wish to discuss this with Mr. Gray over the telephone. I told him I would come down and see him the first thing the next morning.

Q. Would you briefly tell the committee what the nature of your conversation was with Mr. Gray at that time [the next morning]?

A. I told Mr. Gray right at the outset that I could not tell him and even less could I give him a letter saying that the pursuit of the F.B.I.'s investigation would in any way jeopardize C.I.A. activities in Mexico. I told him I had to be quite frank with him. I told him that I had seen Mr. Dean on three occasions, that I had told Mr. Gray what Mr. Dean had told me. Mr. Gray seemed quite disturbed by this, and we both agreed that we could not allow our agencies to be used in a way that would be detrimental to their integrity.

I think basically this was it, I said I could not give him a letter to this effect. I could not tell him this and I could not give him a letter to the effect that further investigation would compromise assets of the C.I.A. He said he understood this. He himself had told Ehrlichman and Haldeman that he could not possibly suppress the investigation in the matter, even within the F.B.I. there were leaks.

He had called in the components of his field office and chewed them out for these leaks. I said the only basis on which he and I could deal was absolute frankness and I wished to recount my involvement in the case. I told him of a meeting at the White House with Mr. Helms. I did not mention Haldeman or Ehrlichman's name. I told him that I had been directed to tell him that the investigation of this case further in Mexico could compromise some C.I.A. activities.

Subsequently, I had seen Mr. Dean, the White House counsel, and told him that whatever the current unpleasant implications of the Watergate were that to implicate the agency would not serve the President, would enormously increase the risk to the President. I had a long association with the President, and was desirous as anyone of protecting him. I did not believe that a letter from the agency asking the F.B.I. to lay off this investigation on the spurious grounds that it would uncover covert operations would serve the President.

Such a letter in the current atmosphere of Washington would become known and could be frankly electorally mortal. I said quite frankly, I would write such a letter only on direction from the President and only after explaining to him how dangerous I thought his action would be to him, and if I were really pushed on this matter I would be prepared to resign.

Mr. Gray thanked me for my frankness. He said he could not suppress this investigation within the F.B.I. He had told Mr. Kleindienst this, he had told Mr. Ehrlichman and Mr. Haldeman that he would prefer to resign, but that his resignation would raise many questions. It would be detrimental to the President's interest.

He did not see why he or I should jeopardize the integrity of our organization to protect some middle level White House figure who had acted imprudently. He was prepared to let this go to Ehrlichman, to Haldeman or to Mitchell. He felt it was important that the President should be protected from his would-be protectors. He had explained to Dean as well as to Haldeman and Ehrlichman, he had explained this.

Finally, I said that if I were directed to write a letter to him saying the future investigation of this case would jeopardize the security of the United States in covert operations of the agency I would ask to see the President and explain to him the disservice I thought this would do to his interest. The potential danger to the President of such a course far outweighed any protective aspects it might have for other figures in the White House and I was quite prepared to resign on this issue. Mr. Gray said this was a very awkward matter for this to come up at the outset of our tenure. He looked forward to good relations between our two agencies. Thanked me for my frankness and that was it.

Q. Now, General Walters, did there come a time shortly after, several days after that you met with Mr. Gray again, Acting Director Patrick Gray?

A. It was on the 12th of July, Mr. Dash. In the meantime, the C.I.A. had been cooperating fully with the F.B.I. investigation, passing them all the material we had on these former employees of ours and any other matters that were of interest to them.

Q. Now, during this meeting with Mr. Gray, did Mr. Gray tell you that he had received a call from the President? A. Yes, he did.

Q. Could you read that part of your memorandum where he discussed that call?

A. He had received a phone call from the President—"The President had called up to congratulate him on the F.B.I. action which had frustrated the airplane hijacking in San Francisco.

"Toward the end of the conversation the President asked him if he had talked to me about the case. Gray replied that he had. The President then asked him what his recommendation was in this case. Gray had replied that the case could not be covered up and it would lead quite high and he felt the President should get rid of the people that were involved. Any attempt to involve the F.B.I. or the C.I.A. in this case would almost prove a mortal wound."

Then I put in brackets: "He used my words" because these were the words I had used in talking with Mr. Gray.

"The President then said, 'Then, I should get rid of the people that were involved no matter how high?' Gray replied that was his recommendation. The President then asked what I thought and Gray said my views were the same as his. The President took it well and thanked Gray."

In all fairness I must say that Mr. Gray did tell me—I did not put it in here that the President had told him to go ahead with his investigation.

Testimony by L. Patrick Gray 3d

Aug. 3   *Changes his story, saying he examined Hunt papers before burning them.*

Aug. 6   *Says Nixon paid little attention to his warning about aides.*

Aug. 3, 1973

MR. GRAY: I returned to Washington on the evening of June 20 and received a phone call from John Ehrlichman the next morning. Mr. Ehrlichman informed me that John Dean would be handling an inquiry into Watergate for the White House, that I should deal directly with John Dean concerning the investigation and that Mr. Dean was expecting a call from me. Mr. Ehrlichman and I then discussed the matter of procedural safeguards against leaks and I told him that we were handling this case as a major special with all of our normal procedures in effect. I also indicated to him that we were going to conduct an aggressive and vigorous investigation and would probably be interviewing people at the White House.

I called Mr. Dean upon my return to my own office at 10 A.M. and arranged to meet with him at 11:30 A.M. in my office on June 21, 1972. At our meeting he discussed with me the sensitivity of the investigation and the need to avoid leaks in a political year. He also informed me that he had the responsibility to handle this inquiry for the White House and would sit in on any interviews of White House staff personnel. Mr. Dean stated that he would be there in his official capacity as Counsel to the President.

I asked Mr. Dean if he would be reporting directly to the President or through Mr. Haldeman or Mr. Ehrlichman. He informed me that he would be reporting directly to the President.

I met with General Walters at 2:34 P.M. on Friday, June 23, 1972. He informed me that we were likely to uncover some C.I.A. assets or sources if we continued our investigation into the Mexican money chain. I understood his statement to mean that if the F.B.I. persisted we would uncover C.I.A. covert operations and that the C.I.A. had an interest in Messrs. Ogarrio and Dahlberg and in the $114,000 involved. He also discussed with me the agency agreement under which the F.B.I. and C.I.A. have agreed not to uncover and expose each other's sources. I had not read this agreement and still have not, but it was logical to me at the time and I did not question General Walters.

On Tuesday morning, June 27, 1972, I met with Mr. Bates and Mr. Mark Felt, acting associate director, to receive a briefing on the latest developments. While they were in the office Mr. Dean called. The call involved establishing the chain of custody for the contents of Howard Hunt's safe and his providing us with photographs of certain White House staff members to aid us in identifying an individual who had been with Mr. Hunt at the Miami Playboy Club in December of 1971.

In this conversation I also told Mr. Dean that if Mr. Dahlberg continued to evade us he would be called before the grand jury. Although I cannot pinpoint the exact telephone conversation I believe that by this date Mr. Dean had requested that Mr. Dahlberg not be interviewed because of alleged C.I.A. interest in him.

In this same conversation, I also told Mr. Dean that it was extremely important that the F.B.I. continue its aggressiveness until we determine the motive, reasons and identity of all persons involved. I said that I might be called upon at a later date to testify before Congressional committees and we could not have the F.B.I. accused of not pursuing the case to the end.

Following the briefing by Mr. Felt and Mr. Bates and as an outgrowth of it, I telephoned Director Helms of the C.I.A. and asked him to tell me specifically if the C.I.A. had any interest in Mr. Ogarrio that would prevent us from interviewing him and also asked that he and General Walters meet the following day at 2:30 P.M. in my office with me, Mr. Felt and Mr. Bates to review our respective positions in this investigation. Director Helms told me that he would have to check to determine whether the C.I.A. had any interest in Mr. Ogarrio and would call me later. Director

Helms called me back later that afternoon, told me the C.I.A. had no interest in Mr. Ogarrio and confirmed our meeting for the next day.

Just seven minutes after Director Helms's call to me, Mr. Dean called me (3:45 P.M.) and although I cannot be absolutely certain, I believe that was a call again requesting me to hold off interviewing Mr. Ogarrio and Mr. Dahlberg because of C.I.A. interest in these men. I cannot recall if I told him that I had just talked to Director Helms who informed me that C.I.A. had no interest in Mr. Ogarrio and that I was going to order that Mr. Ogarrio be interviewed. I seem to remember that Mr. Dean said to me that these men have absolutely nothing to do with Watergate, but I cannot remember whether he said this to me in this conversation or in earlier conversations.

On Wednesday, June 28, 1972, at 10:25 A.M., Mr. Dean telephoned me and talked about rumors of leaks from the F.B.I., the material from Hunt's safe previously delivered to the F.B.I., rumors of a slow-down in the F.B.I., and leaks from the F.B.I. concerning the tracing of the $114,000.

At 10:55 A.M. on this same day Mr. Ehrlichman called me. I was not available, but I returned his call at 11:17 A.M. His first words, issued abruptly, were, "Cancel your meeting with Helms and Walters today. It is not necessary." I asked him for his reasons and he simply said that such a meeting is not necessary. I then asked him point blank who was going to make the decisions as to who is to be interviewed. He responded, "You do."

I met with Mr. Felt and Mr. Bates in my office at 2:30 P.M. on this Wednesday afternoon, June 28, to review the C.I.A. situation. Mr. Bates pointed out that under no circumstances should we back off any investigation at the request of C.I.A. without forcing them to reveal completely their interest in this matter. We all agreed that the F.B.I.'s reputation was at stake and I assured them that I would not hold back the F.B.I. in this investigation at anyone's request, including the President of the United States, in the absence of overriding and valid considerations. I told them that if I were ordered to do so without valid reasons, I would resign.

It was in this meeting that I believe I gave Mr. Felt and Mr. Bates instructions to go ahead with the interview of Mr. Ogarrio and to continue our efforts to locate and interview Mr. Dahlberg.

In San Diego, on Friday, June 30, I received a call from Mr. Felt. He informed me that Assistant United States Attorney Silbert wanted the F.B.I. to interview Mr. David Young, Mr. Ogarrio and Miss Chenow and that our Washington field office recommended interviews of Mr. Mitchell, Mr. Young and Miss Chenow. I instructed Mr. Felt to tell Mr. Dean that we were going to interview Mr. Mitchell, Mr. Young, Miss Chenow and any others that we must interview, and I also told him to give to Mr. Dean the message from Assistant United States Attorney Silbert just as we received it.

I recall that General Walters indicated a feeling of irritation and resentment at the extent to which White House aides had involved themselves in the question of C.I.A. interest but I do not recall his giving me any details and I have absolutely no recollection of his disclosing to me that he had been instructed to bring a false report to me. I asked for no details.

I, too, was concerned and disturbed at the contradictory reports I had been receiving from Director Helms, Mr. Dean and General Walters with respect to C.I.A. interest and at the abrupt cancellation by Mr. Ehrlichman of the meeting I had scheduled with Director Helms and General Walters on June 28. I undoubtedly so expressed myself to General Walters.

My recollection is that he and I then engaged in a general discussion of the credibility and position of our respective institutions in our society and of the need to ensure that this was maintained.

Toward the end of the conversation, I recall most vividly that General Walters leaned back in the red overstuffed leather chair in which he was sitting, put his hands behind his head and said that he had come into an inheritance and was not concerned about his pension, and was not going to let "these kids" kick him around any more.

We stood up together as he prepared to leave. I cannot recall which one of us suggested that we ought to call the President to tell him of this confusion and uncertainty that had been encountered in determining C.I.A. interest or no C.I.A. interest. I believe it was General Walters who suggested it first, because I can firmly recall saying to him, "Dick, you should call the President, you know him better than I." I believe he said, "No, I think you should because these are persons the F.B.I. wishes to interview." We did not settle on who, if anyone, would make such a call and General Walters left.

At this point I would like to comment on some aspects of General Walters' memorandum of our meeting of July 6.

A) With respect to General Walters' assertion in paragraph 1 that, "In all honesty I [Walters] could not tell him to cease future investigations on the grounds that it would compromise the security interest of the United States even less so could I write him a letter to this effect."

We did not at any time discuss a curtailment of the entire investigation. In our July 6 meeting I most definitely recall General Walters saying that he could not write a letter stating that our investigation of Ogarrio and Dahlberg would jeopardize national security. I distinctly remember that his inability to write such a letter to the F.B.I. was the strong central theme of his comments throughout the meeting.

B) With respect to General Walters' assertion in paragraph 1 that "he [Gray] himself had told Ehrlichman and Haldeman that he could not possibly suppress the investigation of this matter. . . ."

I did not discuss the Watergate investigation with Mr. Haldeman at any time except that during my confirmation hearings in 1973 at the request of Senator Kennedy I telephoned Mr. Haldeman to ask whether Mr. Dean had shown Haldeman copies of the F.B.I. reports of interviews.

At no time did anyone ever order or request me to suppress this investigation. As I have testified, I was obviously aware of the "hot potato" aspect of the investigation, sensitive to any implication that the F.B.I. would not do a thorough job and undoubtedly told any number of people, perhaps including Mr. Ehrlichman and certainly including Mr. Dean, that the F.B.I. would follow its leads wherever they led.

C) With respect to General Walters' assertion in paragraph 2 concerning his alleged report to me of his White House conversations.

I have no recollection of being told by General Walters that he and Director Helms had met with White House staff assistants and that General Walters had been directed to tell me that pursuit of the investigation would uncover C.I.A. covert operations. I have absolutely no recollection of any kind of being told by General Walters that he had been instructed by White House aides to bring a false tale to me concerning C.I.A. interest and that he had in fact done so on June 23.

As I have already indicated, I do remember that he repeatedly stated his inability to write a letter indicating that the C.I.A. had an interest in Messrs. Ogarrio and Dahlberg and that he would resign if directed to do so. I am quite certain that he spoke of such a course as dangerous to the President and, although I do not recall his use of the phrase "mortal wound," I know that I used it in my subsequent conversation with the President and it seems to me quite likely that I picked up the phrase from General Walters.

D) With respect to General Walters' assertion in paragraph 3 that I informed him that I had told Attorney General Kleindienst that I could not suppress the investigation.

Never did I have any occasion to say to the Attorney General that I could not suppress the investigation within the F.B.I. And I certainly do not believe I said this to General Walters. I had no reason to do so. Again I believe that General Walters may be confusing my possible references to my public remarks and my thoughts that to control an investigation of the F.B.I., one would have to control everyone involved from the Attorney General down to the case agent. In fact, at the outset of the investigation I had a telephone conversation with Mr. Kleindienst in which we explicitly agreed that this should be a vigorous investigation. I may very well have mentioned this to General Walters.

E) With respect to General Walter's assertion that "he [Gray] had told Ehrlichman and Haldeman that he would prefer to resign, but his resignation would raise many questions that would be detrimental to the President's interests."

I have no recollection whatever of having made this statement to General Walters. I certainly never made such a statement to either Mr. Ehrlichman or Mr. Haldeman. I had so expressed myself to my people within the F.B.I. in the context of our discussions of our determination to proceed to interview Messrs. Ogarrio and Dahlberg unless we received a written statement of C.I.A. interest.

After General Walters left the office I sat at my desk quietly and mulled over our conversation. I was confused, uncertain and uneasy. I was concerned enough to believe that the President should be informed.

I decided to call Clark MacGregor to request that he inform the President of what I would tell him. I decided on Mr. MacGregor because I knew he was close to the President and had his confidence.

At 10:51 A.M., Thursday, July 6, 1972, I spoke to Mr. MacGregor at San Clemente, Calif., via the White House switchboard and I told him that Dick Walters and I were uneasy and concerned about the confusion that existed over the past two weeks in determining with certainty whether there was or was not C.I.A. interest in people that the F.B.I. wished to interview in connection with the Watergate investigation. These of course are not my exact words but they do express the thoughts that I conveyed to him.

Again, although these are not the exact words, I also conveyed to him the thought that I felt that people on the White House staff were careless and indifferent in their use of the C.I.A. and the F.B.I. I also expressed the thought that this activity was injurious to the C.I.A. and the F.B.I., and that these White House staff people were wounding the President.

I asked if he would please inform the President and it is my best recollection that he said he would handle it.

Thirty-seven minutes later, at 11:28 A.M. on Thursday, July 6, 1972, the President called me. He expressed his congratulations to the F.B.I. and asked that I express his congratulations to the agents in San Francisco who successfully terminated a hijacking there the previous day. I thanked the President and then said to him, and to the very best of my recollection these are the words:

"Mr. President, there is something I want to speak to you about.

"Dick Walters and I feel that people on your staff are trying to mortally wound you by using the C.I.A. and F.B.I. and by confusing the question of C.I.A. interest in, or not in, people the F.B.I. wishes to interview.

"I have just talked to Clark MacGregor and asked him to speak to you about this."

There was a slight pause and the President said, "Pat, you just continue to conduct your aggressive and thorough investigation."

General Walters came to my office again on July 12, 1972. At his meeting he apparently gave me a memorandum which, I am now informed, contained information to the effect that the C.I.A. furnished certain aliases to Liddy and Hunt and certain paraphernalia to Hunt. Until I briefly saw a copy of this memorandum this spring in the offices of the United States Attorney for the District of Columbia containing a notation of its receipt in my handwriting, I had no recollection of this memorandum.

I still do not recall noting its contents at the time. I am told that the original of this memorandum was found in my safe after I left the F.B.I. I probably gave it to my secretary to put in the safe after General Walters left my office. It is also possible that I may have routed it to Messrs. Felt and Bates as I know I did with the July 6, 1972, memorandum that General Walters brought to me.

At this point I would like to comment on General Walters' memorandum of July 13 with respect to his meeting with me on July 12.

With respect to my report to General Walters of my phone call with the President, including the statements attributed to me, that the President asked if I had talked to General Walters about the case, that the President asked for my recommendation in the case, that I told the President it could not be covered up, would lead quite high, and that the President should get rid of the people that were involved.

I have already testified as to my entire recollection of my telephone call with the President.

With regard to General Walters' version of my conversation with the President, I have to say that it does not square with my memory of what I said to the President or what I said to General Walters about the call from the President. At this July 12, 1972, meeting with General Walters it is my best recollection that I merely said to him that I had spoken to the President last week on the subject we discussed when the President called to congratulate us on a hijacking. I certainly do not remember discussing the conversation other than to tell him just what I had said to the President.

I am quite positive that I did not say to the President that the case could not be covered up, and I have no recollection whatever of telling him that it would lead quite high, and that I felt the President should get rid of the people who were involved. And I am just as positive that I did not make such remarks to General Walters.

I probably did tell General Walters that on several occasions I had told John Dean that this investigation would have to expose whoever is involved no matter how high it reached, that Mr. Dean had responded, "No matter how high?" and that I said, "Yes, no matter how high." Perhaps General Walters has confused my conversation with Mr. Dean with my conversation with the President.

The only response by the President I now recall or have ever recalled to my remarks was that we should continue our thorough and aggressive investigation.

There has been hearsay testimony before this committee to the effect that I was furnished material from the C.I.A. containing photographs of Gordon Liddy standing in front of Dr. Ellsberg's psychiatrist's office. This statement records my entire recollection of receipt of information concerning Hunt or Liddy. I never at any time was in possession of such photographs or knew of their existence. I also had and have no information related to any discussions between the White House, Department of Justice and C.I.A. on the subject of retrieval by the C.I.A. of C.I.A. information furnished to the Department of Justice.

Prior to a meeting I had with Mr. Dean and Mr. Ehrlichman in Mr. Ehrlichman's office on the evening of June 28, 1972, I had no knowledge from any source whatever of the existence of these particular files or of the information I was to receive that evening.

I arrived at Mr. Ehrlichman's office at about 6:30 P.M. that evening for the purpose of discussing with him the many rumors and allegations concerning leaks of information from the F.B.I. regarding the Watergate investigation. One of his secretaries told me to go right on into his private office. Mr. Dean was in the office talking with Mr. Ehrlichman. I remember being surprised at Mr. Dean's presence because I had not known that he would be at the meeting.

After the usual greetings were exchanged, Mr. Ehrlichman said something very close to, "John has something that he wants to turn over to you." I then noticed that Mr. Dean had in his hands two white manila legal size file folders. It is my recollection that these folders were not in envelopes at this time.

Mr. Dean then told me that these files contained copies of sensitive and classified papers of a political nature that Howard Hunt had been working on. He said they have national security implications or overtones, have absolutely nothing to do with Watergate and have no bearing on the Watergate investigation whatsoever. Either Mr. Dean or Mr. Ehrlichman said that these files should not be allowed to confuse or muddy the issues in the Watergate case.

I asked whether these files should become a part of our F.B.I. Watergate file. Mr. Dean said these should not become a part of our F.B.I. Watergate file, but that he wanted to be able to say, if called upon later, that he had turned all of Howard Hunt's files over to the F.B.I.

I distinctly recall Mr. Dean saying that these files were "political dynamite," and "clearly should not see the light of day."

It is true that neither Mr. Ehrlichman nor Mr. Dean expressly instructed me to destroy the files. But there was, and is, no doubt in my mind that destruction was intended. Neither Mr. Dean nor Mr. Ehrlichman said or implied that I was being given the documents personally merely to safeguard against leaks.

As I believe each of them has testified before this committee the White House regarded the F.B.I. as a source of leaks. The clear implication of the substance and tone of their remarks was that these two files were to be destroyed and I interpreted this to be an order from the Counsel to the President of the United States issued in the presence of one of the two top assistants to the President of the United States.

It is my recollection that I asked for large brown envelopes in which to place the files. I believe that Mr. Dean stepped briefly into the outer office to obtain the envelopes and placed each file in a separate brown envelope in Mr. Ehrlichman's inner office and handed them to me.

Although my memory is not perfectly clear on this, I believe Mr. Dean then left Mr. Ehrlichman's office and I stayed for 5 or 10 minutes to discuss the rumors and allegations of leaks from the F.B.I. These were the same rumors that had been rampant in the first week of the investigation. I believe that I told Mr. Ehrlichman that I had spoken to all of the agents assigned to the case and was quite confident that these leaks had not come from the F.B.I.

I then left Mr. Ehrlichman's office with the two manila envelopes containing the files, went to my car, placed the files in my briefcase and proceeded to my apartment. I placed the files on a closet shelf under my shirts. After two or three weeks I took them into the office and placed them in my personal safe.

To the best of my recollection I removed the files to my home in Stonington, Conn., in late September or early October, 1972, and placed them in a chest of drawers in the area just outside my bedroom. I intended to burn them but I did not get around to doing so until after my illness, hospitalization and convalescence in the latter half of November and December.

I distinctly recall that I burned them during Christmas week with the Christmas and household paper trash that had accumulated immediately following Christmas. To this point I had not read or examined the files. But immediately before putting them in the fire I opened one of the files. It contained what appeared to be copies of "top secret" State Department cablegrams. I read the first cable. I do not recall the exact language but the text of the cable implicated officials of the Kennedy Administration in the assassination of President Diem of South Vietnam.

I had no reason then to doubt the authenticity of the "cable" and was shaken at what I read. I thumbed through the other "cables" in this file. They appeared to be duplicates of the first "cable." I merely thumbed through the second of the two files and noted that it contained onionskin copies of correspondence. I did not absorb the subject matter of the correspondence and do not today, of my own knowledge, know what it was.

Mr. Dean has described in testimony before this committee a conversation with me at a Department of Justice luncheon which he placed during or shortly after January of this year at which I allegedly told him to "hang tight" on not disclosing my receipt of the documents and informed him that I had destroyed them. I recall no such meeting or conversation with Mr. Dean at a Department of Justice luncheon, and my records do not indicate any such luncheon meeting.

I shall now set forth for the committee my recollection of all conversations I have had with Messrs. Dean, Ehrlichman and others about the June 28 meeting and its aftermath.

I believe that Mr. Dean called me at my home in Connecticut in late October or early November. As I recall it, he asked me on that occasion if I still had the two files he gave to me. I said I did and that they were in a safe place in my home at Stonington. I believe Mr. Dean asked if I had read them and I told him, truthfully, that I had not.

The sequence of the next discussions I had about these files is somewhat hazy in my mind. My best recollection now is that over a span of several days during my confirmation hearings in early March of this year I had discussions on the subject with Assistant Attorney General Petersen, John Dean and John Ehrlichman in that order.

I believe that Mr. Petersen called me and told me that Dean had stepped out of an interview being conducted by assistant United States attorneys in Mr. Petersen's presence to inform Mr. Petersen that he had turned two files from Hunt's safe, having nothing to do with Watergate, over to me. Mr. Petersen told me that he informed Dean to take it up with me and asked me if Dean had done so. I told Mr. Petersen truthfully, that Dean had not.

I certainly did not acknowledge to Mr. Petersen that Mr. Dean had turned over any such files to me but I do not recall Mr. Petersen asking me that question on this occasion. I must acknowledge the possibility, however, that Mr. Petersen may have asked me if Dean had turned over such files to me. If he did ask, I am certain that I would have denied receipt of such files because of the instructions I received from Messrs. Ehrlichman and Dean on June 28, the information I have been given about their national security implications and the injunction that they "should never see the light of day."

I recall calling John Dean shortly thereafter and asking him whether he had told Henry Petersen about the two files. He told me that he had. I then asked him, in effect, if he told Mr. Petersen the whole story, namely that the files were given to me in John Ehrlichman's presence with the assurance that they had nothing to do with Watergate, were sensitive and classified with national security overtones, should not be part of the F.B.I. files, were political dynamite and clearly should not see the light of day.

He said he had not told Mr. Petersen all of this. I told Mr. Dean that if, as I had been assured, these files were of the character he described and had nothing to do with Watergate he ought not be discussing them at all but that, if he did, he should at least tell Mr. Petersen the full story of their significance and the instructions to me.

Within a few days after this call, perhaps the next day, I called John Ehrlichman. This is the conversation which, unknown to me, John Ehrlichman tape recorded. I believe this committee has a transcript of that tape. I believe this call to be a call reflected in my logs as made on March 6, 1973, at 6:34 P.M.

I come to this conclusion in substantial part because at the outset of the conversation the transcript reports me as informing Ehrlichman that during my confirmation hearings "this morning" members of the Judiciary Committee received copies of a letter from the American Civil Liberties Union objecting to my offer that members of the Judiciary Committee could examine the entire F.B.I. Watergate file. The transcript of my confirmation hearings reveals that such a letter was received by the committee on the morning of March 6.

The transcript of this conversation with Mr. Ehrlichman also reveals that I state to Mr. Ehrlichman that "I am being pushed awfully hard in certain areas and I am not giving an inch and you know those areas." The assumption appears to have been made by Mr. Ehrlichman and by various members of this committee in their questioning of Mr. Ehrlichman that the "certain areas" in which I was being pushed was the receipt by the F.B.I. of the contents of Hunt's safe.

In fact the subject of the contents of Hunt's safe did not arise in my confirmation hearings until the next day, March 7.

I was being "pushed" however with respect to my turning over F.B.I. reports to Mr. Dean and it was clear to me that my relationship with Mr. Dean was coming under increasing criticism by members of the Judiciary Committee. There is no doubt that I was concerned that the committee would, as it subsequently did, inquire into the circumstances of the turnover to the F.B.I. of the contents of Hunt's safe.

Because of the instructions I had received from Messrs. Dean and Ehrlichman when the two files were given to me and my absolute conviction that these files, tinged with political and national security implications, had nothing whatsoever to do with Watergate, I had no intention of volunteering to the committee my receipt and destruction of these files and did not do so. I would not and did not make any false statements under oath but I acknowledge that I purposely did not volunteer this information to the committee.

I justified my reticence not only because I then believed in the rectitude of the Administration whose nominee I was and in the integrity of the men who gave me the files and instructions, but because my brief look at the file of State Department "cables" had confirmed for me what I thought were overwhelming considerations of national security.

I had no way of knowing then, of course, that the "cables" were fabricated nor, I might add, did I know then what I have since learned—that I was being left, in Mr. Ehrlichman's elegant phrase, to "hang there" and "twist slowly in the wind."

It was in this context, and knowing that Mr. Dean had already told Mr. Petersen about the files, that I had my conversation with Mr. Ehrlichman on March 6. There is no doubt that the message I intended to give to Mr. Ehrlichman was that he should tell Mr. Dean that he should not disclose the delivery to me of those two files.

At about 10:30 P.M. on the evening of April 15, 1973, I received a call from Mr. Ehrlichman. His remarks were very short, terse and to the point. He simply told me that Dean had been talking to the prosecutors for some time and "we" think you ought to know about it. It was obvious from his tone and the manner in which he spoke that no questions were invited and none were asked. I merely said thanks as he was hanging up the phone.

I may have said, "Good evening, John" or "Hello, John" when I picked up the phone and it is my firm recollection that he started talking right away and made no response.

At shortly after 11 P.M., Ehrlichman called me again. This time his remarks were just as short, terse and to the point. He said, "Dean has been talking about the files he gave you and you better check your hole card." I said, "John, those papers were destroyed long ago." Again it was plain and obvious from his tone and the manner in which he spoke that no questions were invited and none were asked.

Both of these calls were of extremely short duration, less than 15 seconds each. His manner was fast talking and he seemed tense.

I know that Mr. Ehrlichman has testified that in these conversations I told him I would deny receiving the files and asked him to support me in that denial. I have absolutely no recollection of such an exchange and believe that both conversations were substantially as I have described them. I realize that the conversations may have been recorded without my knowledge.

On Monday, April 16, 1973, at 10:54 A.M., Assistant Attorney General Petersen came to see me. He said that Mr. Dean told the prosecutors he had turned over two of Hunt's files to me. I denied that I had received them. Mr. Petersen went on to say that Mr. Dean had said these two files had nothing to do with Watergate. He also said that Mr. Dean told the prosecutors that Mr. Ehrlichman had said to him, "Dean, you drive across the bridge each day, throw them in the river."

I was extremely troubled at my denial to Mr. Petersen. I slept little, if any, that night.

On Tuesday, April 17, 1973, at approximately 9 A.M., I placed a call to Mr. Petersen on my private line. He was not in and I left word. He called me back and, at my request, we met in my office later in the morning. I started our meeting by admitting that Dean had given me two white manila files in Ehrlichman's office.

He asked if I had them and I told him I had burned them. He

asked if I knew what was in them. I told him I had not read the files. He said the assistant United States attorneys will want you before the Federal grand jury. I told him I would go willingly and "tell it to them straight."

On Wednesday, April 25, 1973, I telephoned Senator Weicker asking to meet with him. For a week I had thought about this matter and of Senator Weicker's staunch and valiant support of me and his warm friendship. I had a duty to tell him of these two files, yet my shame was so deep that it was hard to pick up the phone and call.

Senator Weicker and I met twice that day in my office and again the next day. I told him the manner in which I had received the files, that I had not read them, and that I had torn them in half and thrown them in my burn wastebaskets under my desk in my office on July 3, 1972, after returning from a visit to the San Diego and Phoenix field divisions.

We discussed this subject at great length and he questioned me intensively on the entire matter. I persisted in my assertions to him that I had not read them, and that I had thrown them in my burn wastebasket in my office on July 3, 1972.

I really cannot explain why I failed to tell Senator Weicker all the facts at this time and made the misstatements to him concerning the date I destroyed the files and my knowledge of what one of them contained. A sense of shame is all I can remember.

I suppose I felt, in some irrational way, that I would look better in his eyes if I had destroyed them promptly and never looked at them. I have subsequently revealed all the facts of the matter to Senator Weicker, the staff of this committee, the prosecutors and the grand jury.

At the time I accepted the two files from Dean and Ehrlichman, at the time I destroyed them, and on the several occasions, prior to my denial to Henry Petersen on April 16, in which I resisted disclosure of the fact that I had received and destroyed the documents, I believed that I was acting faithfully, loyally, properly and legally pursuant to instructions given me by top assistants to the President of the United States. I have come to believe, however, what I should have realized then, that my acceptance of the documents in the first place, and my keeping them out of the normal F.B.I. files, was a grievous misjudgment.

My destroying them and resistance of disclosure only compounded the error. That the documents were not in fact Watergate evidence, while legally significant, does not lessen my present belief that I permitted myself to be used to perform a mere political chore. I shall carry the burden of that act with me always.

Aug. 6, 1973

Mr. EDMISTEN: Did you meet with Mr. John Dean in an area around your apartment on one of the first two Sundays in July? I think maybe in one of your interviews you thought it was the first Sunday. Did you have that meeting?

A. Yes, sir.

Mr. Dean called me, as I recollect, called me on the telephone on a Sunday morning and said that he wanted to meet with me and wanted to talk with me and I said, "well, fine, we can meet in my office in the department," and he stated that this would not be practical because of the fact that there are not too many people present at the department on Sunday and that it would be easily noticed that he would be coming into the Department of Justice and there would be another leak and I suggested, all right, we can meet over here. My apartment is very small, we cannot meet in the apartment but we can meet over here, and we agreed to meet over at the apartment and I met him outside the apartment and we walked around the apartment building and sat down and chatted on a bench overlooking the channel there. This is in southwest Washington in Harbour Square Apartments.

Q. At this meeting with Mr. Dean did he discuss with you his desire that you turn over any F.B.I. documents relating to the Watergate investigation to him?

A. I cannot be absolutely certain. I know that one of the first remarks he made was that this was a heck of a note when the Acting Director of the F.B.I. and the Counsel to the President have to meet on a park bench in order to avoid leaks. We could have discussed on that particular Sunday afternoon the various theories of the case that the F.B.I. had been considering and that he and I had already discussed.

We could have discussed the leaks that were rampant in that first two-week period and it is entirely possible that he could have raised with me the question of making available to him the F.B.I. materials available to me for his use in the conduct of his inquiry. I cannot state it with that kind of certainty but I can say that it is entirely possible. My recollection is and my remembrance is that that subject was raised in a telephone call with Mr. Dean following that Sunday meeting.

Q. So that the first, then, the first occasion when Mr. Dean, when you turned over any kind of F.B.I. documents to Mr. Dean was when, the first occasion, any documents?

A. To the best of my recollection, following this meeting, on the bench there at the Harbour Square Apartments, a phone call ensued following that during the week and it was in that phone call that Mr. Dean raised the question of making available to him the materials, F.B.I. file materials that were available to me.

Q. Is that around July 9 or something like that?

A. I would say that I believe it to be in the week of July 9.

Q. Now, the first thing then, that you turned over to Mr. Dean were F.B.I. teletypes, is that true?

A. That is correct. He asked me if I would make available to him F.B.I. file materials that I had available to me.

Q. Mr. Gray, I know you mentioned this memorandum a moment ago but I want to read certain portions of it and first of all, you had this memorandum written, did you not, Mr. Gray?

A. Yes. I asked that this memorandum be prepared.

Q. And your desire to be informed "on the legal basis for dissemination by the F.B.I. to the White House of information concerning a criminal case being investigated, more specifically a case being investigated as a criminal case for prosecution, involving violation of Title 18, U.S.C., and which does or may implicate Federal employes or subjects"—now, we are talking about the Watergate case, are we not?

A. That is correct, and I do not think there was any doubt in anybody's mind that that is what we were talking.

Q. Now, Mr. Gray, did you consult with Mr. Petersen and Mr. Kleindienst about the advisability of giving the F.B.I. data to Mr. Dean? A. No, sir, I did not.

Q. Why did you not?

A. I didn't do it because I thought I was the Acting Director of the Federal Bureau of Investigation and when I have a request from the Counsel to the President of the United States I don't have to go run around to the Attorney General and to the Assistant Attorney General in charge of the Criminal Division and ask them to hold my hand and help me respond in making a decision. I did not do that and I would not do that.

Q. I don't mean to quibble with you but you had 26 years of military experience and you know things about the chain of command. You didn't work for Mr. Dean, did you? Your direct supervisor and your boss, so to speak, was Mr. Kleindienst, wasn't it?

A. That is correct. And also the President of the United States is my boss and when the Counsel to the President levies a request upon me, I am going to comply with that request and I did comply with it.

Q. Well, if every person in departments and agencies were to follow that rule, then I can see having to call off the Federal Government—various counsels to the President were called up by the Government agencies and countermand, in other words, step into the internal operations of every agency.

A. I don't think that that would occur. I think the F.B.I. occupies a peculiar position with reference to the President of the United States and that the President of the United States looks to the Federal Bureau of Investigation in a little different manner than he does the other departments of government.

Q. You did understand, Mr. Gray, that Mr. Dean was speaking for the President of the United States. He said that to you, I believe. A. No question about it.

Q. I am going to move on to that date which has had a great effect on your life, I am sure, the 28th of June, 1972, when you met with Mr. Ehrlichman early that morning and you told him that you would like to see him that afternoon and you finally did go to the White House and you met in Mr. Ehrlichman's office with Mr. Dean. Why did you want to see Mr. Ehrlichman that day?

A. On June 28, that was the day of the telephone call from Mr. Ehrlichman in which I believe that either we set up the appointment to meet that evening with regard to the heat that I was taking concerning the leaks that were alleged to be coming from the F.B.I. or that was an appointment set up by his secretary dealing indirectly with my secretary but it was in a telephone call, Mr. Edmisten, at 11:17 A.M. that morning. That was the call in which he cancelled my meeting with Director Helms and Deputy Director Walters of the C.I.A.

Q. In your statement you made reference to the fact that when you arrived at the White House and you walked into Mr. Ehrlichman's office, you were very surprised to see Mr. Dean. That surprises me that you were surprised. You had met with him or spoken with him—you had spoken with him, I think 16 times since the 21st and you had met with him at least once. Why were you surprised to see John Dean in the meeting in Mr. Ehrlichman's office?

A. Because I had been led to believe—it was my understanding that I was going to meet with Mr. Ehrlichman. I was not told that anyone else was going to be there.

Q. Can you reconstruct that meeting a little better than you did in your answer. Were Mr. Dean and Mr. Ehrlichman acting strangely?

A. I didn't think that they were acting strangely at all, no, I didn't notice anything strange about the meeting. I was surprised to see John Dean there and Mr. Ehrlichman's first remarks to me were, as I remember, as closely as I can remember it, John Dean has something to turn over to you.

Q. Now Mr. Dean said that the files had national security implications, they were political dynamite, they were absolutely not connected with the Watergate; and I know you have asked yourself this question probably dozens of times—why didn't you tell Mr. Dean and Mr. Ehrlichman to take their own files and destroy them?

A. I don't think that the thought ever entered my mind to do that. These men were telling me that these are sensitive, they were classified, they had national security implications with political overtones, had absolutely nothing to do with Watergate; as I recall, it was either Mr. Ehrlichman or Mr. Dean who said they should not be allowed to muddy the issues in the Watergate case, and then it was in conclusion that Mr. Dean emphasized the national security implications and the fact that they were political dynamite and clearly should not see the light of day. I was receiving orders from the Counsel to the President and one of two top assistants to the President and I was not about to question those.

Q. Did you ever think that after you took the files out yourself, might these not involve Watergate, why shouldn't I turn them over to Mr. Walters, I have had a great relationship with him?

A. I didn't know whether they involved C.I.A., didn't know what they involved in that point of time. In point of fact going back to that period, those files were not of that moment to me because of assurances that I had received that they had absolutely nothing to do with Watergate and were not connected with Watergate in any way.

Q. You held those files for approximately six months, and I am not going to ask questions about the different versions of where you got them or whether you looked at them or didn't, but your final testimony is that you took them to Connecticut and you burned them with the Christmas trash. I just want to know what kind of state of mind were you in to hold those so-called explosive files for that amount of time and never look at them.

A. I didn't believe they were explosive files in the first place. I was told they had absolutely nothing to do with Watergate and had no connection with Watergate and on the basis of all my background, training and experience, I had no need to know and I wasn't concerned about looking. I didn't have the natural curiosity of the cat or of the female. In hindsight, granted, God knows, I should have looked at those files. I should have looked at them that evening in the office and said if I had looked at them that evening in the office I would have said give these to the State Department.

When I did look at them just before burning them I saw they were State Department cables, what I believed to be bona fide State Department cables, but they weren't of that moment to me so that the burning was on my mind every single day.

Q. When you had that little brief glimpse of these cables at that time with your Christmas burning trash, you saw that they involved State Department, did it occur to you at that moment, "I can give these to the State Department now, I know they are not in my bailiwick and I haven't been the recipient of withholding something from my own agency." Why didn't you give them to the State Department at that time?

A. No, I didn't think in those terms at all and I must honestly say that to you, I wish I had. I wish I had brought them back. I wished a hundred thousand times I had been a blackmailer or a leverage man or an edge man to hold those things, you know, and have them and be able to produce them in front of this committee today, but the facts are otherwise. I carried out my orders and I destroyed them. In fact I was ashamed of what I read in that dispatch to believe that my Government would be involved in that kind of an effort to assassinate the President of another nation.

Q. Who, in your mind, when you were burning the papers, did you think wanted them burned, the President, John Ehrlichman, John Dean, somebody else?

A. I really can't be sure of that. I felt that I was taking orders from the Counsel to the President and the assistant to the President but I have got to say in all honesty and fairness and decency if I had looked at those files that evening and saw what they were and said to those two men I want a written order from the President before I am going to take these files, I don't think I would have gotten that order.

SENATOR WEICKER: I would like to read to you, if I might, Mr. Gray, a portion of the President's statement of April 30, 1973, specifically that portion which states, "Until March of this year I remained convinced that the denials were true and that the charges of involvement by members of the White House staff were false. The comments I made during this period and the comments made by my press secretary in my behalf were based on the information provided to us at the time we made those comments. However, new information then came to me which persuaded me that there was a real possibility that some of these charges were true, and suggesting further that there had been an effort to conceal the facts both from the public, from you, and from me. As a result, on March 21 I personally assumed the responsibility for coordinating intensive new inquiries into the matter and I personally ordered those conducting the investigations to get all the facts and to report them directly to me right here in this office."

My first question to you, in light of the President's statement of April 30, where he states that on March 21 he personally assumed the responsibility for new inquiries and personally ordered those conducting the investigations to "get all the facts and report them directly to me right here in this office," my first question to you is did you ever receive after March 21 or from March 21 on a directive from the President of the United States relative to these Watergate matters, which directive inquired of you as to what your investigations were producing, sir?

A. No, sir. The President did telephone me on March 23 and this was the typical buck-up type of call.

Q. Then, at any point, I repeat, between March 21 and April the 27th, which marked the date of your resignation, at any time during that period did you or were you requested by the President of the United States to give to him information, facts, et cetera, relative to the Watergate situation?

A. I was not given any orders by the President of the United States or anyone to give them any facts about the Watergate situation until Mr. Petersen came to me on April 16, and I have already testified to that in my statement. This is when they asked me whether John Dean had given me two of Howard Hunt's files.

SENATOR TALMADGE: Let's read some more of General Walters' statement now and see where the conflict is between you and he. I am quoting further General Walters and he is reporting your telephone conversation to the President. "Any attempt to involve the F.B.I. or the C.I.A. in this case would only prove a mortal wound. He used my words. And would achieve nothing." Did you tell the President that?

A. I told the President that Dick Walters and I feel that people on your staff are trying to mortally wound you by using the F.B.I. and the C.I.A. and by confusing the question of whether or not there is C.I.A. interest in or not in the people that the F.B.I. wishes to interview.

Q. Who did you have reference to when you mentioned members of his staff?

A. Had the President asked me I would have mentioned Mr. Dean and Mr. Ehrlichman because I was still smarting a little bit under the cancellation of the June 28 meeting.

Q. Let me read further now, still quoting General Walters. The President said then, and I quote, "Then I should get rid of whoever is involved no matter how high, Gray replied. That was his recommendation." Did that conversation take place?

A. Senator Talmadge, I have no, absolutely no memory of that, and my recollection of my conversation with the President is as I have testified to. And I have also submitted to this committee some exhibits, some response with regard to General Walters' statements. I don't believe we are that far apart but I believe that he is talking over things that we talked about at that time and put them in there in improper context, not direct context.

Q. Let me ask you something that I think is very important. The only evidence that this committee has had to date implicating the President of the United States is that of John Dean and you and General Walters. Did you think that your conversation with the President on July 6, 1972, was sufficient to adequately put him on notice that the White House staff was engaged in obstructing justice?

A. I don't know that I thought in terms of obstruction of justice but I certainly think there was, it was adequate to put him on the notice that the members of the White House staff were using the F.B.I. and the C.I.A.

Q. Do you think an adequate, do you think a reasonable and prudent man on the basis of the warning that you gave him at that time, would have been alerted to the fact that his staff was engaged in something improper, unlawful and illegal?

A. I do because I frankly expected the President to ask me some questions and for two weeks thereafter, I think it was on the 12th and again on the 28th, I asked General Walters if the President had called him and when I heard nothing, you know, I began to feel that General Walters and I were alarmists, that we had ahold of nothing here and it is true that I just say that I called Clark MacGregor with some fear and trepidation because I didn't have all of the specifics. I had General Walters' continued reiteration that if he was directed to write such a letter to me he would resign and we did discuss his resignation and I even mentioned to him I had already said this to my people.

SENATOR INOUYE: Now, on March 23 of this year you had a conversation, a telephone conversation with the President, and you have just testified that when the President said, "Pat, remember, I told you to conduct a thorough investigation," you said you had an eerie feeling. What did you mean by that?

A. Yes, I thought he was trying to put that on the record, so to speak, relating all the way back to the July 6 conversation.

Q. Are you suggesting that the President was putting this on tape?

A. You know, at the time, Senator Inouye, I didn't know that these conversations were being taped but nevertheless, I had that eerie feeling that the President is reminding me of something and why. That was my reaction. But at that time I didn't know that these were on tape.

SENATOR MONTOYA: What did Mr. Helms tell you when you called him?

A. I told Mr. Helms that I was calling to tell him of the thought that we may be poking into a C.I.A. operation in connection with the Watergate burglary, and he told me that he had been meeting with his men on this every day and that, although we know the people, we cannot figure this one out, but there is no C.I.A. involvement.

Q. All right. Then, that evening you met with Mr. Dean. A. That is correct, sir.

Q. Did you tell Dean about Helm's statement previously that there was no C.I.A. involvement?

A. I either told Mr. Dean in that evening meeting or I told him in a telephone call the following morning, yes, sir.

Q. Mr. Dean called you approximately 18 times between June the 22d and July 6 when you talked to the President. Now, most of these calls were concentrated on Mr. Dean trying to prevail on you not to go through with the inquisition of Mr. Ogarrio or Mr. Dahlberg. Didn't this indicate to you, Mr. Gray, that there was an attempted cover-up emanating from the White House?

A. No, sir, it did not because all along we in discussing our various theories had considered that there was the possibility that this was a C.I.A. covert operation, a C.I.A. money change, a political operation, a political money change, and if I had any thought at all on this thing it was zealous counsel trying to avoid political embarrassment to his President, but I did not really have any suspicion on that.

SENATOR BAKER: What was the relationship between you and General Walters, were you friendly and cordial, were you antagonistic or hostile toward each other, why did you have such varying viewpoints?

A. I thought the relationship was friendly and cordial and I have no reason to believe it is other than that today.

Q. You suspect it may be less friendly and cordial after disputing him on 27 major issues?

A. I don't think so because I told him this in the assistant U.S. attorney's office. "Dick, this isn't the way it happened and this is not my recollection or memory of it at all." And my outrage when I first saw a newspaper article commenting on his testimony was very genuine and very real.

Q. Your outrage? A. Yes, sir.

Q. Is there any one or two, are there a few examples of what caused that outrage?

A. Yes, sir, that these men had apparently had a meeting at the White House and no one called me and told me about a meeting at the White House prior to them coming over to me. That is one of the things.

SENATOR WEICKER: Now, at what point in time did your antennae alert you to the fact that somebody might be trying to interfere with the investigation?

A. I think that I had perhaps a feeling along those lines or a feeling that somebody at the White House knows a lot more than we know, beginning when my meeting with Mr. Helms was canceled, but it was a feeling then that maybe this is an activity on the part of people to put some kind of cloak on the political contribution aspects of the thing. But the suspicions really began to generate along those lines rather solidly when I had the meeting with General Walters.

Q. Now, let us continue on that phone conversation with the President. Did you in that phone conversation suggest to the President that the matter of Watergate might lead higher?

A. No, sir. To the best of my recollection, the words that I have been using consistently or the words that stick in my mind are the words that have always been in my mind and the only other things that I did say to the President was that I have just spoken to Clark MacGregor about this morning and asked him to talk with you about it, Mr. President, and there was a slight pause and then the President said to me, "Pat, you continue to conduct your thorough and aggressive investigation."

Q. Did you raise to the President the fact that you and Dick Walters were concerned or was this a question from the President to you?

A. No, sir, this was a question, really, it was a matter that I raised and I didn't really from my meeting with General Walters draw the feeling that I had to call the President and indeed and in fact that is why I called Clark MacGregor, and I was surprised that the President called me and I just blurted out to him when he finished congratulating me on the hijacking, I just blurted out to him, Mr. President, there is something that I have to speak to you about.

Q. And then what did you say?

A. I gave him the message, "Dick Walters and I feel that there are people on your staff who are trying to mortally wound you by using the F.B.I. and the C.I.A. to confuse the question of whether or not there is C.I.A. interest in or noninterest in people that the F.B.I. wishes to interview."

Q. Did you get into a discussion with him relative to your being given assurances that the C.I.A. was not involved?

A. No, sir, the President as best I can recollect it did not ask me any questions because if he had I would have suspected that he would have asked me "Who do you mean?" and I would have told him.

Q. Well, now, Mr. Gray, I want to read to you a statement made by the President of the United States on May 22, 1973:

"On July 6, 1972, I telephoned the acting director of the F.B.I., L. Patrick Gray, to congratulate him on his successful handling of the hijacking of a Pacific Southwest Airline plane the previous day. During the conversation Mr. Gray discussed with me the progress of the Watergate investigation and I asked him whether he had talked with General Walters. Mr. Gray said that he had and that General Walters had assured him the C.I.A. was not involved. In the discussion Mr. Gray suggested that the matter of Watergate might lead higher. I told him to press ahead with his investigation."

Now, you have characterized or you set your description of this conversation alongside that of General Walters and you said that you will stick with your version of the conversation. A. Yes, sir.

Q. Will you also stick with your version of the conversation set beside that version given by the President of the United States on May 22?

A. Yes, sir, because this is my memory and my best recollection and it is a memory I have had for a long, long time.

Q. When was the first time that you realized—I had it written down a certain way and I realized that could be misconstrued. I have, When was the first time you started to realize you were "swinging?" That could be interpreted both ways. When was the first time that you realized that you were hanging, twisting slowly in the wind?

A. I think perhaps, Senator Weicker, the first time that I realized this and realized I was in a situation where I was going to have to scramble to extricate himself was really either in my April 25 conversation with you, but I think more the point was really made with me on the evening of April 26 in the meeting in the Attorney General's office when I had the conversation with Assistant Attorney General Petersen.

Q. And this relates to Mr. Petersen's statement relative to you and he being expendable?

A. Yes, he said, "Pat, I am scared."

SENATOR INOUYE: When did you interview Mr. Dean and Mr. Ehrlichman?

A. Mr. Dean was never interviewed because quite frankly, Senator, I believe everyone in the F.B.I. thought he was on our side. We were working with him on a practically almost daily basis.

Q. Even if he was about to mortally wound the President you felt he was on your side?

A. We kept working with him and when the President did not respond in any way and when the concerns that I had with regard to any interference on the part of the C.I.A. were removed, I had no suspicions, and as I told you earlier, I felt that I was an alarmist and that General Walters and I were both alarmists.

Q. You have testified that on April 27 of this year Mr. Petersen said that you and he were expendable and Mr. Ehrlichman and Mr. Haldeman were not.

A. Senator Inouye, I think that was the evening of April 26 in the little office of the Attorney General's larger private office. Yes, sir, he did say that to me.

Q. Did you agree with this observation?

A. No, sir, I was sitting, I was sitting in the overstuffed chair and I remained sitting there as Mr. Petersen paced up and down and he said to me, "I am scared, Pat," and I said, "Why?" He said "Because I believe that you and I are expendable and Haldeman and Ehrlichman are not," and I still sat in the chair and I said "Do you think I should get a lawyer?" and he said, "Yes, I do," and then I did get up out of the chair.

SENATOR MONTOYA: I am going to be very brief with you. I think we have covered almost every phase of your part in the investigation. I want you to know that I have read your statement very carefully, not once, not twice, but three times trying to figure out what motivated you to say in your last sentence, "I shall carry the burden of that act with me always." Now, this moved me very much and I can appreciate your situation. And I see that throughout your statement—I see a thread of hurt which encompasses a pattern experienced by many others at the White House and at the Committee to Re-elect the President.

Now, we as human beings cannot help but have compassion and intense feeling brought about by the burning rays of Watergate. Why do you think that the tentacles of Watergate touch so many good people so adversely? Can you explain that to me?

A. Well, Senator, I would like to say in Spanish to you, if you would not be insulted, "Yo tengo mucho dolor en mi corazón ahora."

Q. I have a lot of hurt in my heart at this time. A. Sí.

Q. That is what you said.

A. Yes, sir, yes sir. I said early in the game that I thought that Watergate would prove to be a spreading stain that would tarnish everyone with whom it came in contact and I am no exception. I had a responsibility, Senator Montoya, I believe, not to permit myself to be used, not to permit myself to be deceived, and I failed in that responsibility and I have never failed in anything that I have undertaken until this point in time. And it hurts.

Testimony by Richard G. Kleindienst

Aug. 7, 1973

Recalls telling Nixon about Justice Department's findings; says Ehrlichman asked advice on clemency.

MR. DORSEN: Mr. Kleindienst, when for the first time did you learn that there was electronic surveillance of the Democratic National Committee headquarters at the Watergate?

MR. KLEINDIENST: I learned it for the first time after June 17 [1972] when the individuals who were arrested at the headquarters were arrested. I don't know whether I learned of the electronic surveillance on Saturday, June 17, or sometime in the early part of the next week.

Q. But on June 17 you were notified of the fact that there had been a break-in?

A. At approximately 8 o'clock in the morning, Assistant Attorney General Henry Petersen of the Criminal Division of the Department of Justice called me at my home and indicated to me that there had been a break-in at the Democratic National Headquarters at the Watergate Hotel. All the information that he had at that time was that there was a break-in and I believe he said to me it looks like it might have been a bombing case.

Q. Did you participate in a conversation with Mr. Henry Petersen and Mr. Dean concerning the possibility of going to the President because the circumstances and events indicated that there was more to the Watergate break-in than appeared?

A. Well, the characterization that you put at the end I don't think was relevant to our meeting. But I believe it was either Monday or certainly no later than Tuesday that Mr. Dean, Mr. Petersen and I had a conference that took place in my office. The purpose of Mr. Petersen and Mr.—and myself being with Mr. Dean was to indicate to Mr. Dean the apprehension and the grave seriousness with which we received the news of this fantastic event that had occurred at the Watergate Hotel, to inform him as counsel to the President that the Department of Justice and the F.B.I. would be compelled and would immediately launch a full-scale intensive, thorough investigation into all the facts surrounding it, that this was a felony, that in addition to being a felony, if you can think of anything worse, it also went to the very heart of our political system, and that it was an act of such a heinous nature that we were going to call forth and bring about an investigation immediately.

I think Mr. Petersen interrupted or said that either myself or

Mr. Dean should contact the President personally to indicate to him the gravity of the situation, the consequences of it, and I believe Mr. Petersen said in that remark that either Mr. Dean or I should urge the President to make a statement immediately setting forth his attitude in response to this fantastic event.

I believe that Mr. Dean volunteered at that point to the effect that, well, I am going out to San Clemente, and I will convey your suggestion, Mr. Petersen, because I will be seeing the President myself. I believe I concurred in that. I don't know how long that meeting lasted but I think that that is the substance of what transpired at that time.

Q. During the summer of 1972, were you aware that Patrick Gray was making available to John Dean F.B.I. teletypes and 302's?

A. No, sir. The first time I became aware of that was in the confirmation hearing of Mr. Gray to be the permanent Director of the F.B.I.

Q. Had Mr. Dean spoken to you about the possibility of the F.B.I. supplying to the White House such documents?

A. Mr. Dean raised a question with both myself and Mr. Petersen. Both of us were very quick to tell him that we did not—that we would not give him raw investigative data from F.B.I. files.

Q. Am I correct that on the early morning hours of April 15, 1973, you had a meeting with Mr. Petersen, United States Attorney Harold Titus and the prosecutors at your home?

A. It was just one of the prosecutors and that was the chief prosecutor, Mr. Silbert.

Q. Am I correct that this meeting dealt with the disclosure of Mr. Magruder and Mr. Dean to the prosecutors? A. Yes, sir.

Q. Following that meeting, am I correct that you made an appointment to see the President later in the day on April 15, 1973?

A. Around 1 o'clock in the afternoon, approximately, I met with the President in his office in the Executive Office Building.

Q. Now, am I correct that at least part of the meeting was devoted to briefing the President and that one of the decisions made on the afternoon of April 15 by you would be that you would in effect withdraw from the supervision of the prosecution of the Watergate case?

A. The whole meeting was devoted solely to talking about the information that I had obtained that night and the consequences that inevitably must flow from it.

SENATOR ERVIN: You stated, as I understand your testimony, that the President indicated by his conversation when you reported what you knew about the Watergate affair, to him, that——

A. What meeting are you talking about, Mr. Chairman?

Q. The 15th. A. Yes, sir.

Q. That he indicated by his reply that he did not know, that he was ignorant about the Watergate affair?

A. Well, I would say that the information, the nature that I described with him, would have come to his attention contemporaneously. If Mr. Ehrlichman is talking to Magruder all afternoon the day before I would just assume, although he didn't say, that Mr. Ehrlichman would have made a report like this to the President. But I would gather from my meeting with the President that he had no such knowledge until immediately prior to my meeting, Mr. Chairman.

SENATOR BAKER: It appears that when on June 17, 1972, you were approached on trying to get these Watergate burglars out of jail, you in fact said no, they are going to be treated like everybody else. Is that essentially correct? A. Yes, sir.

Q. And when John Dean asked for F.B.I. files, you in effect said if the President wants F.B.I. files, let the President ask, but you are not going to get them, is that right?

A. Yes, sir, or anybody else.

Q. And when John Ehrlichman called your people and complained and then called you to complain about the way certain matters were being handled, you told John Ehrlichman, don't you talk to my people any more. If you want to talk, talk to me. Is that essentially correct? A. Yes, sir.

Q. And when you received information about the Ellsberg break-in, you found it to be of extraordinary importance and you went to the President and talked to him about it. A. Yes, sir.

Q. When on April 15, 1973, the U.S. attorney's office and others came to you at the late hours of the night and laid out a detailed case of extraordinary involvement by White House officials apparently and the Committee to Re-elect officials apparently you promptly set up a meeting with the President, is that right? A. Yes, sir.

Q. And you told the President about it? A. Yes, sir.

Q. And when you told the President about it, you wrote a note on the spot virtually saying that because of my personal and professional relationship with some of the people that may be charged with crimes, mentioning John Mitchell and others, that I excuse myself and require, Petersen, that you assume these responsibilities and act as Attorney General, is that correct? A. Yes, sir.

SENATOR GURNEY: Did the President at any time during all of this period of time instruct you to go soft or slow upon this F.B.I. investigation? A. Never at any time.

Q. One thing about these affairs is that some people get brushed with tar when I don't think that is probably a fair thing. I must say as far as you are concerned, I think this is a good time to bring it out, that when you departed you were lumped with Haldeman, Ehrlichman and Dean. I thought this was most unfortunate myself because actually you were not in their class;

I guess we might put it that way, in any respect. Do you want to comment on that?

A. No, the President asked me whether I would consent to have my name mentioned that following night. I did, and I would prefer not to make any other comment about it.

Q. But in any event your resignation was your own decision and you were the one who suggested to the President that you resign? A. Yes, sir.

SENATOR MONTOYA: When Mr. Ehrlichman was testifying before this committee I asked him if the White House knew of the burglary of the Ellsberg psychiatrist's office on or about September 4, why didn't you tell the Department of Justice, and he indicated in his answer that that information had been imparted to the Department of Justice. A. That is absolutely untrue.

MR. DORSEN: Do you recall attending a luncheon with Mr. Ehrlichman and Mr. Dean between the time of the conviction of the Watergate defendants and the time of their sentence at which the subject of possible leniency for the defendants came up?

A. I did not when I talked to you or Mr. Haire yesterday. I talked to Mr. Petersen yesterday to see if he could recall anything and I now remember that at a luncheon I had there, I think we had several matters to discuss, the question came up as to the procedures of sentencing, what happens, and Mr. Ehrlichman did not have much of a knowledge of the criminal justice system and I think they were talking about what happens when somebody is convicted of a crime, how the sentence is meted out, what is the probation report, what happens when you go to jail, when are you eligible for a pardon, when do the circumstances arise for executive pardon, and it was a technical procedural discussion that I had. No individual name was mentioned at that time.

Testimony by Henry E. Petersen

Aug. 7, 1973

Describes President's reactions to news of high-level involvement.

MR. DASH: Do you recall a meeting on or about June 20, 1972, in Mr. Kleindienst's office, where Mr. Dean was and at which Mr. Dean made some statements to you, according to his testimony, that this investigation should go very high in fact it might involve the White House; in fact he testified he didn't know how far it might go.

MR. PETERSEN: I remember the circumstances, I don't remember it as Mr. Dean testified to it. I was called up to Mr. Kleindienst's office. Mr. Dean was already there. They asked for a status report and I gave them a general status report on the nature of the investigation. We had some discussion. I think commonplace discussion. My God, what has happened, who is doing this and what type of a situation is this.

And I told him that, I remember the words very distinctly, I said, "John, I don't know what I am talking about but whoever is responsible for this is a damn idiot and there is only one thing that the President of the United States can do and that is cut his losses and the way that he should do that is to instruct the Attorney General publicly to run an all-out investigation and let the devil take the hindmost. And that ought to be done immediately."

We had some discussion of that and finally Dean said, "Well, the President is out in San Clemente." I said it is well enough for somebody to go out there and Mr. Kleindienst said, "John set that up." Dean then got up to leave and we had some conversations about the investigations and I told him I had no intention of conducting a fishing expedition but we were certainly going to conduct a thorough investigation of this matter. Later on I asked him what had been decided and he said, "Yes somebody is going to go out but it has been decided it should be me."

Q. Meaning Mr. Dean?

A. Mr. Dean rather than Mr. Kleindienst, which I thought was a little awkward, but quite honestly I took it as another indication or as an indication that perhaps the Attorney General who I think most highly of was perhaps not in the best graces at the White House and that they would rather have Mr. Dean brief the President.

After that there was an all consuming silence, I never heard anything and I finally asked Dean about it and he said, "Yes, you are to run an all-out investigation" but unfortunately we never heard anything from the President.

If I can jump ahead. In my later conversations with the President on April 15, I told him this and he said, one, Dean had never come to him, and I said if it occurred again, and I certainly hoped it did not, I would be up there knocking on the door myself.

Q. Did it ever come to your attention that such raw [F.B.I.] files were being used by Mr. Dean, that he had them in his possession during any inquiry that he was making?

A. No, sir. Mr. Kleindienst called me at one stage and I recall this very vividly, it was on the telephone, and he said I have just spoken to John Dean and he has asked if he can have the F.B.I. reports and I answered him. very quickly and abruptly and said, tell him no, and I was so abrupt that he just started to laugh, his reaction was, you are a big help. And I then was a little embarrassed to think he might feel that I was inconsiderate of his relationship with the President or the White House and I said, well, hear me out. If the President calls you up and says I want those reports, you click your heels and say, yes, sir, or if they want to send out a memorandum, say, from the President and say send those reports over to X, Y, and Z, I said we can do that, but we ought not to give those reports on an oral request to any White House staffer, and he said, I think I agree with that. That is the last I heard of it.

Q. Did you ever discuss with Mr. Dean Mr. Magruder's appearance before the grand jury?

A. John Dean called me at the time of Magruder's appearance before the grand jury and asked how Magruder made out. I did not know and I called Earl Silbert and he said, "Well, you know, as you all know, he is a very articulate young man, and he described him, "He made a good witness in his own behalf, but Henry, nobody believes the story about the money." And, you know, that is—in those words are what I told Mr. Dean.

Q. Now, can you recall a time when Mr. Ehrlichman got in touch with you concerning the appearance of Mr. Stans before the grand jury. A. Yes, sir, I can.

Q. What did Mr. Ehrlichman want?

A. What did he want? I asked him that question twice and he never spelled it out except to stop harassing Mr. Stans and I said we were not harassing him and he charged that Earl Silbert was acting like a local prosecutor. Well, Mr. Silbert is a local prosecutor.

Q. Did you get the impression that Mr. Ehrlichman was perhaps asking that Mr. Stans be excused from going to the grand jury?

A. Well, that is what he was driving at. I asked him twice what he wanted and he never answered other than to say stop harassing. I asked him, I said, well, if Stans has a problem with the subpoena, why doesn't his lawyer call him, and he said it was not necessary, that Ehrlichman was calling me and we ended up telling him to tell his lawyer to call me.

Q. Well, now, did you participate in a decision not to get into the so-called "dirty tricks" activity of Donald Segretti. A. I sure did. I sure did.

Q. Can you recall, did Mr. Dean raise that question to you?

A. No, sir. Well, I don't remember whether he did or not. I don't recall him raising it. That question was raised with me by two people, one, Earl Silbert, who said, you know, in effect, we are not experts on the Corrupt Practices Act. We don't see any violation. Do you? And I said, no, not on the basis of what we have. This is around August or September. The F.B.I. in October —Charley Bowles, who was in charge of the acounting and fraud section, called me and said, "Henry, do you see a violation," and I said, "no."

You know, dirty tricks per se are not a violation to my knowledge and the only violation we have been unable to uncover in connection with these things is the failure to accurately subscribe to a political statement that is promulgated—failure to subscribe being a violation of U.S. 18, 613, and that is what the investigations have gone off on, but mere dirty tricks, oral false schedules, for example, or passing an item of information on, was not a violation to my knowledge.

Q. On the 26th [of March 1973] Mr. Gray has testified that on that day, apparently that is the day he did admit to you that he destroyed the documents [from Hunt's safe], that you said to him, that you were scared and that you and he, Mr. Gray, were expendable and Mr. Haldeman and Mr. Ehrlichman were not expendable. Did you say anything like that to him and, if so, why?

A. I am not sure you have the time right, Mr. Dash. As I recall it, that was the night before Mr. Gray resigned. It was the day on which this item that we are discussing was publicized and I received a call from the President as did Mr. Kleindienst in the evening, and the President asked me whether or not I thought Mr. Gray ought to resign and I told him that I thought Mr. Gray's position was untenable. And he said we will discuss it with the Attorney General.

He, too, had talked to the Attorney General and, of course, I did discuss it with the Attorney General and pursuant to the President's instructions we asked Pat Gray to meet us and we did meet in the back office of Mr. Kleindienst's office and we discussed the situation and in my conversations with the President I expressed some sympathy for Mr. Gray who I think most highly of. I have no hesitancy, I liked the man very much. And I told the President, "Mr. President, I think he is an innocent victim," and the President said "Yes, Henry," he said, "maybe, but there are going to be a lot of innocent victims before this is over."

So it was in that context, the context of commiseration, I did not want to be there, we were in effect, suggesting that the man resign, and when Mr. Kleindienst went out of the room to talk to the President again you know, I said Pat, we are all going to be embarrassed before this is over, I am scared we have a constitutional confrontation here, we have the Presidency of the strongest nation in the world teetering on the brink. I do not remember saying that we were expendable, Ehrlichman and Haldeman were not, but I may have, I was upset.

Q. Do you recall that sometime after the conviction of the seven Watergate defendants and the sentence having lunch with Mr. Kleindienst, Mr. Dean and Mr. Ehrlichman and a question of leniency for the defendants coming up?

A. No, no, I never had—

Q. Let me rephrase the question. Are you aware of a lunch that Mr. Kleindienst had with Mr. Dean and Mr. Ehrlichman in which a question of leniency came up concerning the defendants in the Watergate case?

A. Well, I am aware of a time when I received a telephone call from Mr. Kleindienst who said I am just now leaving the White House and I am on the way to the airport and on the way by I will stop by and you go downstairs and I will pick you up and you can ride out to the airport with me and I want to get some information from you, and I cannot fix the date except that it was a time when Mr. Kleindienst was going to Boston and he was meeting his wife at the airport.

We rode out to the airport and he said, "I just had lunch with Dean and Ehrlichman and they raised a question of whether or not leniency could be accorded these defendants." And I said "absolutely not." I said, "Indeed we are going to do just the contrary. It is not the practice in the District of Columbia to recommend specific terms, jail terms, but it certainly is the practice to recommend for jail or no jail. We intend to recommend jail time for these people and beyond that, after they are sentenced we intend to call them back and immunize them in order to compel their testimony as to whether or not other persons are involved, and if they are contumacious and refuse to testify they will be held in contempt."

We discussed more what the procedure was, the sentencing procedure, and when they would be sentenced and what have you, and he finally said, "Do me a favor, go on back and go on over to the White House and tell those crazy guys over there what you just told me before they do something they will be sorry for." And I said, "Well, O.K.," and I went back to my office and on the way back I thought I have not been over there yet and this is not the time to go, so I called John Dean on the telephone and told him, "John, there is no point in my coming over there, we are going to recommend jail time and these people are going to be immunized," and we then discussed what immunity meant, what the alternatives are and what they are is, one, you can be contumacious and go to jail almost immediately or you can lie and take your risk that the Government will be able to prove it, which may give you a little bit of time, or you can cooperate, and I spelled those out for him and that ended the conversation.

Q. Did you set up a meeting or did Mr. Kleindienst set up a meeting with the President?

A. Mr. Kleindienst agreed he would set up such a meeting with the President and as I recall, he said he was going to—there was a prayer breakfast over there and he would attempt to set it up while he was there.

I next heard Mr. Kleindienst at approximately 2 o'clock Sunday afternoon and he asked me to come down to the office and I did so, and while there, he said he was going to go and see the President again at 3 or 3:30, and maybe it would be a good idea if I would come with him, and I said O.K.

Q. Was it at that time that you and Mr. Kleindienst gave a complete briefing as to what you had learned from the prosecutors—A. Yes, sir.

Q. —To the President? A. Yes, sir.

Q. Can you tell the committee what the reaction of the President was at that time?

A. Well, I guess the reaction of the President was I guess one of concern. When I remember remarking to Mr. Kleindienst how I admired his calm. I would have been cussing and fuming. He was concerned, and you have to understand that I had seen the President only on ceremonial occasions or briefing on legislation. He didn't know me from Adam.

Q. This was your first face-to-face meeting with the President, then, wasn't it?

A. Yes, at any time in a situation where he was relying solely on my advice, and here I was there recommending that two people whom he had known and worked with for years be dismissed.

Q. Who were they?

A. Mr. Haldeman and Mr. Ehrlichman.

Q. What was his reaction to that recommendation?

A. He understood my concerns and he appreciated my candor and my concern for the Presidency, and my position was that I can't guarantee you that we have a criminal case at this point, but I can guarantee you that these people are going to be a source of vast embarrassment to the Presidency and for that reason I think that the best thing that you could do would be to get rid of them immediately.

The President's response was interesting. He said, yes, but he owed them an obligation of fairness, too, and I didn't disagree with that. If somebody came in and said about my two assistants you have got to fire them immediately, I would take time to look.

Q. Now, did you make any recommendation with regard to Mr. Dean?

A. Yes, I did. The President said, "You know, Haldeman and Ehrlichman deny this and I have to go to find this out. Dean in effect has admitted it. Should I request his resignation?" And I said, "My goodness, no. Now, here is the first man who has come in to cooperate with us and certainly we don't want to give the impression that he is being subjected to reprisal because of his cooperation. So please don't ask for his resignation at this point."

And the President agreed to hold off until I—until he heard from me further on that issue. That carried on until about the 26th or 27th of October and in a statement on the telephone I reached the conclusion after discussion with Silbert that we had reached an impasse in our negotiations with Mr. Dean.

Q. You don't mean October. You mean April.

A. Right, Senator, April, excuse me. We had reached an impasse in our discussions with Mr. Dean and that I could no longer justify the President's not asking his resignation, and—

Q. Prior to that time, Mr. Petersen, do you recall having a discussion with the President concerning immunity that might be afforded witnesses? A. Yes sir.

Q. Could you tell us briefly about that?

A. Well, I think that started—that started the preceding Wednesday. Mr. Ehrlichman had called Mr. Kleindienst and Kleindienst called me up there and said he just had a call from John Ehrlichman and Ehrlichman wants to say he didn't think any White House aides ought to be immunized and it didn't make much of an impression on me and I just made a witticism and said, "Well, tell Ehrlichman he can't count on it," and I didn't think anything more about it. Of course, when I learned at the end of the week—

Q. At this time Mr. Dean was in these conversations, in cooperation with the prosecutor.

A. That is right. At the end of the week when I learned Dean was cooperating it made more sense. The President took it up. The President—we went on with this for about two or three days. We had a difference in viewpoints, of course. One, the President's concern—I hope I accurately reflect him but it seemed to me the President's concern was that from a public relations point of view, certainly he wanted to leave the impression that he as President was not causing persons who were in the upper echelons of his Administration to be immunized and freed from liability. He wanted to make certain that in that respect no one got the impression that they were getting favored treatment.

Well, you know, I understood that to be a consideration but I also understood that if it were in the interests of the prosecution, that it might be necessary to immunize some high echelon person.

Q. Did you explain that to the President? A. I did indeed.

Q. And did you get an understanding of who would make the ultimate decision on immunity? A. Yes, I did.

Q. And who would be given that ultimate decision?

A. Me.

Q. Now, did that point in time—

A. At that point in time.

Q. On April 18, the President call you concerning the immunity question? A. Yes.

Q. Can you tell us briefly about that call?

A. The President called me—I recall it was in middle or late afternoon—and said that Dean had said he had been immunized, and I said, "Mr. President, that is not so. We are in the process of determining whether or not he should be immunized but we have made no decision and so far as normal immunity is concerned, only I can grant it. The prosecutors don't have the authority. I am certain that is not so but I will check."

I called Earl Silbert and said—and he said, of course, just what I said, and I said, "that is fine, but go on back to his counsel" and his counsel agreed. "No, we are just in a preliminary negotiation, and no immunity has been offered or accepted."

When I called the President back I told him that. He said, "Well, you know, I have it on tape if you want to hear it," and I said "No, I don't want to hear it because I don't want to get anything except what we are getting from John Dean directly."

Q. He said he had it on tape. Did he indicate it as a tape of Mr. Dean?

A. No he did not, and I didn't ask him.

Q. Is that where the matter stood? A. That is where the matter stood, yes, sir.

Q. Did [the President] indicate that he knew anything about the [Ellsberg's psychiatrist's office] break-in when you told him about it?

A. No, he did not, Mr. Dash. I have to be very careful there. I would like to rephrase the question for you, if I can. I suppose it—

Q. Please do.

A. The question probably would be, did he indicate he knew anything about it rather than anything about the break-in. And the President said when I told him, "I know about that. That is a national security matter. You stay out of that. Your mandate is to investigate Watergate."

Now, he didn't say he knew about the burglary. He said he knew about it—about the report. I think that is a vital distinction to be recognized.

Q. When were you reporting this to the President?

A. It was on April 18, sir. And he said stay out of it and after I got off the telephone, why, I called up Mr. Silbert and I called up Mr. Maroney and said, "Mr. Silbert," I said, "the President said stay out of it, Earl and that is it." I called up Mr. Maroney and said, "Just forget it." . . . Now, one of the things, you will excuse me, I have to get something off my chest. I resent the appointment of a special prosecutor. Damn it, I think it is a reflection on me and the Department of Justice. We would have broken that case wide open and we would have done it in the most difficult of circumstances. And do you know what happened? That case was snatched out from under us when we had it 90 per cent complete with a recognition of the Senate of the United States that we can't trust those guys down there, and we would have made that case and, maybe you would have made it different, but I would have made it my way and Silbert would have made it his way and we would have convicted those people and immunized them and we would have gotten a breakthrough. I am not minimizing what you have done or the press or anyone else, but the Department of Justice had that case going and it was snatched away from us and I don't think it fair to criticize us because at that point we didn't have the evidence to go forward.

SENATOR ERVIN: I am just—

A. Excuse my emotions, but I have been there too long and this has been a terrible year.

SENATOR GURNEY: One general question here. I don't know whether you can put a handle on it or not. During all of this investigation and trials and everything did you at any time suspect that there was a cover-up going on Watergate? Did you have a feeling on it?

A. A visceral reaction. The word I used to the prosecutors and Kleindienst, nobody acts innocent. You couldn't translate that. There was an overriding concern. There were no records. Things were destroyed. They didn't act like innocent people. Innocent people come in and say, "Fine, what do you want to know?" It was not like that, it was a visceral reaction. Yes, that is the reason we were so insistent to get this thing, get them tied down to sentence and immunize them.

Testimony by E. Howard Hunt

Sept. 24 *Hunt links Colson to plan that led to 1972 Watergate break-in.*

Sept. 25 *Hunt theorizes that Watergate burglars were exposed by Baldwin acting as a double agent.*

Sept. 24, 1973

Mr. DASH: In the early part of 1971, Mr. Hunt, did you discuss with Mr. Colson the possibility of your obtaining a position at the White House?

HUNT: I did.

Q. Did you have a telephone conversation with Mr. Colson, and who initiated that telephone conversation?

A. I had numerous telephone conversations with Mr. Colson, Mr. Dash. I'd appreciate your being a little more specific.

Q. Yes. On July 2, 1971—or July 1, actually—did you receive a telephone call from Mr. Colson? A. I did.

Q. Let me show you what purports to be a transcript of that conversation. Would you please look at it? A. I have examined the purported transcript, Mr. Dash.

Q. Does that purport to be or reflect the conversation you had with Mr. Colson? A. It does.

Q. Now, in that conversation with Mr. Colson, does Mr. Colson question you concerning your viewpoints and attitudes concerning the Pentagon Papers and Mr. Ellsberg? A. Yes.

Q. Would you look at page 2 and the last line? Would you read that for the committee? A. Colson's question?

Q. Yes.

A. "Let me ask you this, Howard, this question. Do you think with the right resources employed that this thing could be turned into a major public case against Ellsberg and co-conspirators?"

Q. And how did you respond to that on the top of the next page?

A. My response was as follows: "Yes I do. But you've established a qualification here that I don't know whether it can be met."

Q. Did you understand, Mr. Hunt, that from that conversation Mr. Colson was exploring the idea with you of a major effort to discredit Mr. Ellsberg in the press? A. Yes.

Q. Now, did Mr. Colson eventually offer you a position in the White House? A. He did.

Q. And I think you've indicated that he referred to specific qualifications. Can you repeat that? What did he indicate to you your qualifications led you to that particular position, what qualifications?

A. The fact that I had an investigative background of some years. And also that I had been involved in political action operations.

Q. Now, were you interviewed by anyone besides Mr. Colson? A. Yes.

Q. And who was that? A. Mr. John D. Ehrlichman.

Q. Whose direction, Mr. Hunt, did you work when you took this position—under whose direction? A. Under Mr. Colson's direction.

Q. Can you describe your initial assignment under Mr. Colson?

A. Mr. Colson instructed me to become the White House resident expert on the origins of the Vietnam war. At the same time I had a collateral responsibility for determining certain leaks of highly classified information, which included the leaks of the Pentagon Papers.

Q. Now, is it true, Mr. Hunt, that from the beginning of your employment, Mr. Colson asked you to collect what could be called derogatory information about Daniel Ellsberg? A. Yes.

Q. Now, what was to be done with this information when it was collected?

A. My assumption was that it would be made available by Mr. Colson or someone in his confidence to selected members of the media.

Q. Did you, by the way, early in your employment, collect a list of certain media representatives who might be interested in such material? A. I did.

Q. Now, how did you develop the information on Mr. Ellsberg following the assignment you received from Mr. Colson?

A. It was developed through an intensive study of reports furnished by the Federal Bureau of Investigation.

Q. Were there any other materials that you used?

A. There were certain overt materials.

Q. What do you mean by overt materials?

A. Materials published in the press.

Q. Now . . .

A. Let me—to be more responsive, Mr. Dash, I have a feeling that I have left something hanging here, which I don't want to do. The same unit—the special investigations unit—that was receiving information on a frequent basis from the Federal Bureau of Investigation also received reports from other Government agencies, such as the Department of Defense, the Department of

State, the National Security Agency, the Immigration and Naturalization Service and so on.

So that as part of my reply to your question, I would include those Government agencies as sources of information on Dr. Ellsberg.

Q. All right now, do you recall Mr. Colson asking you to interview Col. Lucien Conein? A. I do.

Q. Who is Colonel Conein? Or who was he at the time you interviewed him?

A. At the time I interviewed Colonel Conein, he had just retired from the Army, I believe, and was in the process of retiring from the Central Intelligence Agency, or had retired therefrom. He and I had trained together in the Office of Strategic Services for service in the Far East. And, in fact, we had shipped out to China together and worked in China together during World War II. I had seen him infrequently during the intervening years, but we had maintained a friendly relationship.

Q. Do you recall when this interview took place, your initial interview with Mr. Conein?

A. It was on or about the eighth of July of 1971.

Q. Do you know what the purpose of Mr. Colson's asking you to interview Colonel Conein was?

A. I would have to go back a number of years and make it a matter of record that Colonel Conein had worked for the Central Intelligence Agency in Vietnam, I would say almost uninterruptedly since 1954. Colonel Conein had a high degree of intimacy with senior officials of the several governments that had held power in South Vietnam. He was also a military officer, he spoke French, he spoke Vietnamese to some extent. He was intimately familiar too, and I believe this gets to the crux of your question, with the events leading up to the coup that resulted ultimately in the deaths of Premier Diem and his brother.

Q. And was the interview supposed to be directed toward the coup and the underlying causes of that coup, the assassination of Premier Diem? A. It was.

Q. Do you have, Mr. Hunt, a copy, a transcript of that telephone conversation which I think that committee has provided you during the executive session? A. I do.

Q. Now would it be also fair to say that one of the purposes of the conversation was to get information from Colonel Conein which might be derogatory against Dr. Ellsberg? A. One of the purposes, yes, sir.

Q. Now, if you'd turn to page 6. The transcript indicates that you were asking questions of Colonel Conein concerning certain cables—State Department cables. Could you instruct the committee as to what the purpose of your request of Colonel Conein were being led to?

A. Yes, sir. Mr. Colson and I were jointly interested in the circumstances that led up to the assassination of the President and I believe the Premier of South Vietnam. We felt that somewhere there should be an instructive record of exchanges between Washington and Saigon.

We knew also that there were several channels that could have been utilized. In addition to the normal State Department communications with its Embassy, there was the normal C.I.A. communication channel with its station in Saigon. There were also so-called back channel communications facilities for both organizations. There were communication cable facilities—

Q. At this early time of your employment at the White House, Mr. Hunt, did you have access to State Department cables covering the period of the Diem assassination? A. I did.

Q. Why did you have access to them?

A. Because I had requested such access and it had been granted me.

Q. Now, in the review of these cables did you notice any irregularity in the sequence? A. I did.

Q. And at what period did the gap in sequence occur?

A. The period immediately leading up to the assassination of the Premier of South Vietnam.

Q. Did you show the cables to Mr. Colson and offer an interpretation of them?

A. I showed him copies of those chronological cables, yes, sir.

Q. And what interpretation, if any, did you give him concerning the cables?

A. I told him that the construction I placed upon the absence of certain cables was that they had been abstracted from the files maintained by the Department of State in chronological fashion. And that while there was every reason to believe, on the basis of the accumulated evidence and the cable documentation, that the Kennedy Administration was implicitly if not explicitly responsible for the assassination of Diem and his brother-in-law, that there was no hard evidence such as a cable emanating from the White House or a reply coming from Saigon, the Saigon Embassy.

Q. What was Mr. Colson's reaction to your statement and the showing of the cables to him? Did he agree that the cables were sufficient evidence to show any relationship with the Kennedy Administration and the assassination? A. He did.

Q. Did he ask you to do anything?

A. He suggested I might be able to improve on the record.

Q. And what did you understand him to mean when he said to improve upon the record.

A. To create, to fabricate cables that could substitute for the missing chronological cables.

Q. Did you in fact fabricate cables for the purpose of indicating the relationship of the Kennedy Administration and the assassination of Diem? A. I did.

Q. And did you show these fabricated cables to Mr. Colson? A. I did.

Q. What was his response to the fabricated cables?

A. He indicated to me that he would be probably getting in touch with a member of the media, of the press, to whom he would show the cables.

Q. Now are you aware from your conversations with Mr. Colson and the use of these cables any strategy that Mr. Colson had with regard to Catholic voters? A. Yes sir.

Q. Could you describe that more fully.

A. I believe it was desired by Mr. Colson, or at least some of his colleagues, to demonstrate that a Catholic United States Administration had, in fact, conspired in the assassination of a Catholic chief of state in another country.

Q. Do you have a memorandum the committee provided you dated Aug. 27, 1971, from Mr. Ehrlichman to Charles Colson with the subject "Hunt-Liddy Special Project No. 1?"

A. I have such a memorandum.

Q. Just let me read the memorandum in brief. "Ehrlichman to Colson. On the assumption that the proposed undertaking by Hunt and Liddy would be carried out and would be successful I would appreciate receiving from you by next Wednesday a game plan as to how and when you believe the material should be used. This referring to the Hunt-Liddy Special Project No. 1."

Mr. Hunt, what from your understanding on the day of Aug. 27, 1971, would Hunt and Liddy's special project No. 1 be?

A. I would assume it to be the Fielding entry, based on the fact that Mr. Liddy and I as of that were just returned from our initial reconnaissance of Dr. Fielding's professional premises in Beverly Hills, and would have made—submitted a feasibility study.

Q. And that the reference there to Hunt and Liddy's Special Project No. 1 would refer to the proposed covert entry of Dr. Fielding's office for the psychiatric file? A. Yes.

Q. Now, in fact, you and Mr. Liddy did go to Los Angeles to observe whether a covert entry was feasible and you concluded that it was, did you not? A. Yes.

Q. And, in fact, you and Mr. Liddy and three Cuban-Americans did break into Dr. Fielding's office, over the Labor Day weekend in 1971, is that true?

A. With one limitation. Neither Mr. Liddy nor I were ever on the premises of Dr. Fielding.

Q. And no files were ever found? A. None were found, no sir.

Q. Did you take photos of the inside of Dr. Fielding's office to show the forced-open files? A. No sir.

Q. Did somebody in the room take photos? A. Yes sir.

Q. Right. Now, to whom were these photos shown?

A. They were shown within Room 16 to Messrs. Krogh and Young.

Q. Now would you say relative to Messrs. Krogh and Young, by the time this program developed which led up to the covert entry of Dr. Fielding's office you had begun to work with Mr. Krogh, Mr. Young and Mr. Liddy, was not that so? A. Yes, sir.

Q. How did that occur? You originally, I think testified that you were assigned to work with Mr. Colson. How did the transfer of relationship in the assignment take place?

A. Through a process resembling osmosis, almost. I had discovered early in my reading of the overt materials relating to the publication of the Pentagon Papers, my researches into Dr. Ellsberg's background, that considerably more documentation would be necessary for my purposes. I so advised or informed Mr. Colson and he told me that these materials—that is classified materials bearing on my researches were to be found in Room 16 and I should check with Mr. Liddy for that purpose.

I found that the holdings were—in Room 16—were quite extensive and I began as a matter of course and custom to go there every day to acquaint myself with additional information as it flowed into Room 16 from the various Government agencies who were making contributions. So it was that I spent less and less time in office 338, which had been assigned me by Mr. Colson and a great deal more time in Room 16, which became known as the plumbers unit—special investigations unit.

Q. And by the time you had filed your memorandum on neutralization of Mr. Ellsberg, you at this time were working with the so-called plumbers? A. Not entirely, yes sir.

Q. Did you attempt to show the photographs that were taken during the Fielding break-in to Mr. Colson? A. I did.

Q. And what occurred when you did? A. I told Mr. Colson I would like to try to put a date on this, Mr. Dash.

Q. You have a date, Mr. Hunt?

A. Yes, I do. On Labor Day weekend, 1971, that is to say the third of September, the entry in Dr. Fielding's offices is accomplished. The following Tuesday, that is to say the first working day after Labor Day, was the morning on which I attempted to show Mr. Colson that Polaroid photographs that had been taken by team members of the violated cabinets in Dr. Fielding's premises.

Q. And how did he react to your effort to show him the photographs?

A. He declined to look at what I had in my hand, continued striding into his office without breaking his pace and said, "I don't want to hear anything about it."

Q. Now in the last part of 1971 did you become aware of the fact that Mr. Liddy was to become counsel for the Committee for the Re-election of the President? A. I did.

Q. And did Mr. Liddy recruit you to help him develop a large-scale covert political intelligence plan for the Committee to Re-elect the President?

A. In late November, 1971, Mr. Liddy approached me, saying that the Attorney General of the United States, Mr. John Mitchell, required the establishment of a large-scale intelligence and counter-intelligence program. That he, Mr. Liddy, was about to become its chief and Mr. Liddy would like to assure himself of my cooperation.

Q. Was this the plan that came later to be known as Gemstone? A. Yes, sir.

Q. And I think—who did you understand from the conversation with Mr. Liddy, actually were directing the development of this political intelligence plan?

A. My understanding was as follows: that the plan had been proposed and/or required by the Attorney General of the United States, Mr. Mitchell. That Messrs. John W. Dean 3d, the then Counsel to the President of the United States, and Mr. Jeb Stuart Magruder, a recent White House aide, were those who were active in its formulation.

Q. Now, did you, in fact, help Mr. Liddy prepare the detailed plan and budget of this plan?

A. I did, with the exception of that portion of the plan which dealt with electronic surveillance.

Q. Now prior to the presentation of the plan—and, Mr. Hunt, the committee has already had ample testimony concerning presentation of this particular plan from former Attorney General Mitchell, Mr. Dean and Mr. Magruder by Mr. Liddy on Jan. 27, 1972 and Feb. 4, 1972.

Now prior to that presentation, however, prior to the Jan. 27 presentation, did you have a discussion with Mr. Colson concerning that you would be giving fewer hours to the White House work because of the time that you would have to spend with Mr. Liddy?

A. I told Mr. Colson that because of the increased amount of time I was spending with Mr. Liddy, that I would be able to give far less time to Mr. Colson than I had done in the past.

Q. And what, if anything, did Mr. Colson say to you about that?

A. He said that he understood this.

Q. And did he indicate by any words or statement that he understood the plan that you were working with Mr. Liddy on?

A. Yes.

Q. Could you give us a little fuller explanation of that?

A. On one occasion—and it must have been in conjunction with this particular interview—Mr. Colson told me that he had in fact supplied Mr. Mitchell with my bona fides. He further indicated that he was aware of the over-all intelligence plan and his only problem with it was that he would much prefer to see me heading it rather than Mr. Liddy.

I told him that the situation was fine as far as I was concerned, that I had cooperated with Mr. Liddy before, we got along well. I had already a full-time job with a public relations firm and was not seeking full-time employment such as Mr. Liddy had.

Q. Do you know where the conversation with Mr. Colson took place? A. Between myself and Mr. Colson?

Q. Yes. A. In Mr. Colson's office.

Q. Now, did you tell Mr. Colson at that time that you planned to recruit and use members of the same Cuban-American community that had worked with you in the Ellsberg break-in?

A. Either on that or another occasion. Mr. Dash.

Q. And Mr. Colson was aware, was he not, of the role you and Mr. Liddy played in the break-in at Dr. Fielding's office?

A. I was not so aware at the time. I have come to understand that subsequently.

Q. Now at the time that Mr. Colson was indicating to you that he was aware of an intelligence plan that Mr. Liddy was working on, was there any other intelligence plan besides the Gemstone plan that Mr. Liddy was working on? A. No.

Q. And was it your impression therefore that Mr. Colson was speaking of the so-called Gemstone plan? A. Yes.

Q. Now, Mr. Colson has submitted to this committee an affidavit. Do you have a copy? The affidavit, signed by you, dated April 5, 1973—I think it's brief enough to read, is:

"I, E. Howard Hunt, having been duly sworn do hereby depose and state as follows:

"I understand that allegations and statements have been made to the effect that Charles Colson, former counsel to the President, had prior knowledge or in some way was involved in or participated in the break-in of the Democratic National Committee headquarters at the Watergate Hotel on June 17, 1972.

"I never had any time discussed with Mr. Colson any plans with respect to this incident. I have no knowledge whatever, personal or otherwise, that Mr. Colson had any prior knowledge whatever of this knowledge. To my knowledge no one else ever discussed this matter with him prior to June 17, 1972."

Did you sign this affadavit? A. I did.

Q. What were the circumstances that led you to sign this affidavit?

A. This affidavit was passed to me in the Federal Court House by my then attorney, Mr. William O. Bittman, prior to an appearance of mine before the Federal grand jury. To the best of my recollection, Mr. Bittman indicated to me that he had received the affidavit in draft from Mr. Colson's office and wondered if there would be any problem on my part about signing it. I indicated I had no difficulty with it whatever and did, in fact, sign the affidavit.

MR. SACHS: Excuse me, Mr. Chairman, I detect a little bit of confusion. If I could have just one minute to talk to Mr. Hunt, I think it might expedite this?

I think I have a notion, Mr. Dash, as to the line of questioning you are about to pursue in order to refresh Mr. Hunt's recollection as to the testimony he recently gave in executive session. And I—it was clear to me before you undertook this last question that he didn't quite clearly understand what you were driving at. And he and I have now discussed that briefly, and I think perhaps if you will ask your first question—or perhaps I could ask it—he could quickly answer it and we could go on to something else.

I think what you were asking him is whether in the past few weeks he had added to his explanation of his conversations with Mr. Colson the fact that in January of 1972 there was a conversation between him and Mr. Colson which indicated that Mr. Colson had knowledge of the Gemstone program.

MR. DASH: Yes.

MR. SACHS: I think he can answer that quickly.

MR. DASH: Right. And the question was that I put to you is isn't this the first time you told the committee that?

A. Yes, sir.

Q. Prior to telling the committee that, have you informed any other investigative body, including the grand jury that is presently sitting, about that information? A. No, sir.

Q. Can you explain to the committee, Mr. Hunt, what appears to be contradictory testimony in the executive session and now before this committee as to Mr. Colson's prior knowledge of this general plan? A. I can attempt to, Mr. Dash.

Q. Would you please do that?

A. Yes. It derived as a result of repeated questioning by the committee staff concerning events which transpired on the occasion of my having introduced Mr. Liddy and Mr. Colson for the first time.

A theory of Mr. Colson's perceptions of the meeting was entered into and developed which brought back to my mind for the first time the prior conversation that I had held in January with Mr. Colson.

Q. Now did you ever call Mr. Colson to complain about the problems of the payment of fees [payment to the families of the convicted Watergate conspirators]? A. I did.

Q. And so you recall when you made that call?

A. On Nov. 24, last.

Q. Now do you have a transcript that Mr. Colson made of the telephone call? A. I do.

Q. During that call, what in effect were you telling Mr. Colson? Why did you make that call?

A. I made the call, Mr. Dash, because my wife had indicated to me that because she had been placed in a very false and difficult position vis-à-vis the Cubans and the other people who were or had become her "clients," she was unwilling to continue to be the go-between.

She felt also that perhaps because she was a woman her words, her urgings, her representations were receiving insufficient weight, were not being seriously enough received by whoever the sponsors were. And it was in that spirit that she asked me to communicate with Mr. Colson, which I did.

Q. Now on page 3 of that transcript, did you say the following: "All right, now we've set a deadline now for close of business on the 25th of November"—and I take it that's the deadline to receive funds—"for the resolution on the liquidation of everything that's outstanding. And they're now talking about promises from July and August. There just has been an apparent unconcern. Of course we can understand some hesitancy prior to the election, but there doesn't seem to be any of that now. Of course we're well aware of the upcoming problems of the Senate and——" Did you make that statement during that call? Does this transcript, by the way, reflect to your recollection the conversation you had with Mr. Colson? Do you recall that we showed you that transcript during the executive session?

A. I do, Mr. Dash.

Q. You've had a chance to read it? A. Yes, sir.

Q. And what is your answer to my question as to whether that statement was made? It appears in the transcript.

A. I have no specific recollection of making the statement, Mr. Dash. However, inasmuch as it appears in a transcript I accept it in good faith and will say under those circumstances that I made the statement.

Q. One further reference, on page 5, if you look at the large paragraph at the top, where you say: "Well, that's fine but we're protecting the guys who are really responsible. But now that's—and of course that's a continuing requirement. But at the same time this is a two-way street and as I said before we think that now is the time when a move should be made and surely the cheapest commodity available is money." Do you see that statement? A. Yes, sir.

Q. Would you adopt that as something you would have said during that conversation? A. Yes, sir.

MR. BAKER: Mr. Chairman, could I ask a question about it just very briefly? Mr. Hunt, were you aware that this conversation was being recorded? A. No, sir.

Q. Did you—how did you come to know of its existence?

A. I don't recall whether I learned about it through the grand jurors or through this committee.

Q. Could I ask counsel how we received it?

MR. DASH: We received this from Mr. Colson.

HUNT: I might say I felt in retrospect I was set up on this one.

MR. BAKER: I'm sorry, I didn't hear you.

A. That I was set up, as it were. I had requested an opportunity to speak with Mr. Colson and the message I got back was that if I would call him from a phone booth at a particular time on a particular day he would speak with me. Obviously, he had his recording equipment running at that time.

MR. BAKER: Do you have any reason to suspect that any part of the transcript is not correct?

A. No, sir.

MR. DASH: But isn't it true that you may have been set up, having had a chance to read this transcript, is it not true that throughout the transcript Mr. Colson repeatedly said to you whenever you wished to give him any facts that he doesn't want to hear anything about the facts? Not to tell him anything. That goes through the entire transcript.

A. It certainly does.

Q. Mr. Hunt, shortly before your sentencing on March 23, 1973, did you meet with Mr. Paul O'Brien?

A. Mr. O'Brien, I knew, was the current contact that Mr. Bittman had on the committee [for the Re-election of the President], not only for matters relating to the various civil suits that had been filed, but also and more relevantly in connection with the payment of legal fees for Mr. Bittman's services in my behalf.

I spoke to Mr. O'Brien at some length about the size and nature of the legal bills. I think at that time, they amounted to approximately $60,000. I told him at the same time that I was very much concerned about the future of my family, that I would very much like to have the equivalent of two years' subsistence available to them before I was incarcerated. And I put it to Mr. O'Brien that I had engaged, as he might or might not know, in other activities which I believe I described as seamy activities for the White House. The context of such reference was that if anyone was to receive benefits at that time in view of my long and loyal service, if not hazardous service, for the White House, that certainly I should receive priority consideration.

Q. Did you intend to create that threat, that unless that money was paid, you would make public the acts that you had engaged in on behalf of the White House? A. No, sir.

Q. How did Mr. O'Brien respond to you when you asked for this money?

A. He recognized that assurances had been given, that to some extent they had in the past been carried out, but he felt that he was becoming less and less effective as an intermediary.

Q. Did he mention Mr. Colson to you?

A. Mr. O'Brien suggested that I originate and send to Mr. Colson what he termed a strongly worded memorandum or a tough or a hard memorandum to Mr. Colson.

I asked him why he wanted me to send the memorandum to Colson and Mr. O'Brien said, to the best of my recollection, "Well, there are some of us who feel that Chuck stayed out of this too long, that it is time he got his feet wet along with the rest of us," words to that effect.

Q. What efforts did you make to follow up on Mr. O'Brien's suggestion?

A. I told Mr. Bittman that I had no intention of writing the recommended memorandum, but I thought that I should get in touch with Mr. Colson so that I could explain the situation to him, notify him of the suggestion that had been made by O'Brien. Mr. Bittman did get in touch with the law offices—by then Mr. Colson was in private practice of Colson & Shapiro, and made the representations in my behalf; i.e., that I desired a meeting with Mr. Colson. A day or so later, I was informed by Mr. Bittman that although Mr. Colson would not see me, his partner, David Shapiro, would see me. He would see me the following Friday, I believe the 16th of February, early in the afternoon.

Q. And did you tell Mr. Shapiro substantially the same thing that you told Mr. O'Brien? A. I did.

Q. Including the other activities that you engaged in on behalf of the White House?

A. I did not specify them. I referred to them. I might add that the context of our meeting was entirely different. Whereas Mr. O'Brien had approached me, I might say, almost apologetically, Mr. Shapiro approached me rather aggressively and subjected me to a lengthy monologue which I considered to be highly self-serving. My response was that I had expected actually to see Colson, although I could understand that I had met only with Shapiro rather than with Colson.

Q. Now, did you make it clear to Mr. Shapiro and Mr. O'Brien that you needed to get the money prior to the date of sentence? A. Yes.

Q. Why was that?

A. If it was to be of any assistance to me in terms of making prudent distribution of that among the members of my family, my dependents, taking care of insurance premiums and that sort of thing, it would have to be delivered to me before I was in jail. This was not only implicit but explicit as well, Mr. Dash.

Q. Now, what did Mr. Shapiro say to you when you made those representations to him?

A. He indicated to me that he would use his own discretion as regards such portions of my conversation as he chose to convey to Mr. Colson. I responded rather angrily that I felt that he should convey all of what I had to say to Mr. Colson.

Q. Despite what you consider to be an unsatisfactory reception by Mr. O'Brien and Mr. Shapiro, you in fact did receive a large sum of money prior to being sentenced, is that not true? A. Yes.

Q. How much did you receive? A. $75,000.

MR. THOMPSON: Mr. Hunt, you state in your opening statement that in your opinion the Watergate break-in was an unfortunate use of executive power. What executive power are you referring to?

A. I am referring to power delegated to the Attorney General of the United States by the President of the United States.

Q. Who involved in the Watergate break-in or the planning of the break-in had that power, in your opinion?

A. The concept, as I understood it from Mr. Liddy, and again I must be very clear that this is hearsay information, that the project, program, if you will, had been conceived, proposed, engendered by the Attorney General of the United States with the assistance of the counsel to the President, Mr. John W. Dean 3d, and with a former and very recent White House aide, Mr. Jeb Magruder. The proposal had been put to me at the time by Mr. Gordon Liddy, who was a full-time White House employe and with whom I had worked in the Fielding and other operations.

Q. Did you consider the Watergate break-in then, a legitimate Government operation?

A. In the context in which the break-in requirement was levied on me I did, yes, sir.

Q. What context was that?

A. Foreign monies were reported to have been sent or received by the Democratic National Committee.

Q. When did it first come to your attention that the Democratic National Committee headquarters were going to be broken into?

A. Not until April the following year.

Q. Was this before you were informed that foreign money was coming into the D.N.C?

A. We did not begin to formulate plans for the Watergate break-in until after reception of the report to the effect that foreign monies were being received by the Democratic National Committee.

Q. But a plan was under way which included the possibility of surrepitious entry before that time? A. Yes, sir.

Q. I wonder what was in your mind at that time as to what the Attorney General could do and could not do. Surely anything that he decided to do would not necessarily be a legitimate activity, whether or not the President went along with it. I am wondering what justification you had in your mind for subscribing to a plan which was designed toward an opposition party in an election year.

A. I can really say only this, Mr. Thompson: Having spent 21 years in the C.I.A. following orders without question and a prior five years with the armed services following orders without question, it never occurred to me to question the—if you will—the legality, the propriety, of anything that might be ordered by the Attorney General of the United States.

Q. And you took Mr. Liddy's word for that? A. I did.

Q. Who told you that foreign money was coming into the D.N.C. A. Mr. Liddy.

Q. Where did he get his information?

A. I believe that he was receiving it from a Government agency.

Q. Did he specify which agency? A. No. Sir.

Q. Did you have an opinion as to which agency?

A. Yes, sir. My opinion was that it came from the F.B.I. Mr. Liddy had on the basis of prior associations with the F.B.I. a private channel, a person or persons who would telephone or send him memoranda from time to time, providing him with information which was not distributed generally within the White House; there were really two channels of reporting from the F.B.I. into the White House.

There was the J. Edgar Hoover channel to, let us say, Mr. Ehrlichman and Mr. Krogh, who would see copies of those memoranda. There were also materials that were coming to Mr. Liddy from Mr. Mardian in the Justice Department, and I believe telephonic information that came to Mr. Liddy from close and old-time associates of his at the F.B.I. So I had every reason to believe that he was still well plugged into the bureau.

Q. Did he tell you precisely the source of these foreign monies of the country?

A. Yes, sir. Cuba.

Q. Was the plumbers unit in any way operative in April of 1972. A. Yes, indeed.

Q. Do you know whether or not they were looking into this matter? A. I am quite sure they were not.

Q. With regard to the actual scene, who was in charge of the various operations on the night of the break-in, the early morning hours of June 17, 1972?

A. The responsibilities were the same as they were during the prior break-in on May 27th, and that is to say I was in over-all charge of the entry operation. I planned it, and with Mr. McCord's help surveyed the ground work, developed the operational plan.

Mr. McCord had certain electronic responsibilities, the precise nature of which I was unaware of. My team, that is to say, the four men from Miami, were charged with photographic documents that would bear on the object of our search while Mr. McCord went about his electronic business.

Q. Was there any financial reward in any way for Mr. Barker or any of the other Cuban-Americans out of the Watergate break-in?

A. There was compensation for them for time lost from their normal businesses, yes.

Q. Was there anything additional to that? A. Not that I know of, no, sir.

Q. We have heard testimony about how the entry was carried out that night. I believe Mr. McCord first taped the locks on the door, returned, found the tape had been removed. Then there was a discussion among the people there as to whether or not entry would be made after finding that situation there. Relate to us that discussion as best you can remember.

A. Mr. McCord said that he had previously taped the locks on the entry door of the basement of the Watergate office building. He said that on returning just prior to the meeting that was then in progress he had noticed that the tape had been removed and he had retaped the door. I asked him why he had done that and he said that he had noticed a large pile of mail sacks in the vicinity and he felt that the mailman, on exiting the Watergate office building premises, had taken off the tape.

At that point, I said, let us junk it, meaning let us scratch the operation. Mr. Liddy and Mr. McCord talked between themselves and the decision was made to go. I thought that it was very foolhardy to proceed on that basis. I might add that I had argued for three days in advance ineffectively with Mr. Liddy prior to the 17th of June against the second entry of the Watergate.

Q. Why?

A. Because it had been known to me through reports Mr. McCord had made that Mr. O'Brien was no longer in residence there, that there was evidently a large-scale movement of books, files, call it what you will, from the Watergate office to the convention headquarters of the Democrats in Miami. I felt that, in effect, the bird had flown.

Q. Did you hear any of the conversation as to who made the final decision or who was for or against re-entry?

A. I think it was a mutual decision, a common decision between Mr. Liddy and Mr. McCord.

Sept. 25, 1973

SENATOR TALMADGE: You stated that you participated and were directed with Mr. Colson, counsel for the President in the White House, in a number of clandestine operations. I wanted to find out exactly what those were and I hope to enumerate them— some of them to get your assent or whether or not that's an accurate statement. Was one of them the breaking and entering of Dr. Fielding's office?

A. At the time of the break-in of Dr. Fielding's office, Senator, I was not aware of the extent of Mr. Colson's participation as I have subsequently come to understand it. Certainly my compilation of Mr. Leonard Boudin's legal history, let me put it, and providing that to Mr. Colson for the use by a member of the local press was one of the activities in which I engaged. I interviewed Mr. Clifton DeMotte of Providence, R. I., at Mr. Colson's behest. I also interviewed former retired Gen. Paul Harkins at Mr. Colson's request.

Q. The Diem cables? A. The Diem cables, yes, sir.

Q. Dita Beard?

A. Yes, sir, I visited and elicited information from Mrs. Dita Beard at his request.

Q. Did he suggest to you that you go break in Bremer's apartment after George Wallace was shot down in Maryland?

A. He suggested that I review the contents of Mr. Bremer's apartment.

Q. And you declined to do that?

A. I argued against it. I subsequently received word from him or from his secretary—I can't recall which—that this was no longer required.

Q. And did he participate in your visit to California to see the security officer for the Hughes Tool Company? A. No, sir.

Q. He did not. And did he participate in your visit to survey the newspaperman in Las Vegas with a view of breaking and entering there? A. No sir.

Q. He did not. Did he participate in organizing the efforts of spying and eavesdropping and electronic surveillance of the Democratic National Convention in Miami? A. Not to my knowledge.

Q. He did not to your knowledge. About photographing the papers of the Muskie headquarters?

A. I have no knowledge that he was aware of that.

SENATOR GURNEY: Thank you, Mr. Chairman. Mr. Hunt, let's go back to the Watergate break-in. There's been a good deal of speculation in many quarters as to whether or not this was a double-agent action in that the tapes were on the door and they seemed to be rather unnecessary and maybe even unwise. And you, yourself, testified that the second break-in didn't make a great deal of sense, and then after the tapes were discovered to have been removed you thought it was certainly foolhardy to go ahead. Do you have theories on whether there was a double agent here or not?

A. The series of events of that night taken in their totalities, Senator Gurney, have suggested to me for many months that we might have been, as it were, entrapped by information having been provided beforehand to local law enforcement authorities by a member of our unit.

Q. Who do you think that was?

A. I would have to indicate that the most likely subject would be Mr. Alfred Baldwin.

Q. And why is that?

A. First of all he had been only recently hired by Mr. McCord on the basis of a want ad placed in a magazine—"help wanted" ad. Nothing was known about . . .

Q. Do you mean to say that that actually was the method of his hiring for this very sensitive operation?

A. I believe Mr. McCord has testified, Senator, that he read in a magazine published by the ex-F.B.I. Bureau Association that a particular individual's services were available. He got in touch with that gentleman, read his resume and hired him, not for Watergate itself but rather for the personal protection of the Attorney General and/or Mrs. Martha Mitchell.

Q. Do you know whether he did any background checks on him or not?

A. I do not know. I suspect he did not.

Q. Go on with you reasoning why he might be the double agent. Or may be a double agent?

A. It further developed subsequently that Mr. Baldwin had rather intimate ties with the Democratic party in Connecticut.

Q. What were those ties?

A. Without notes I would have to suggest that he was the nephew of a judge that—a Democratic judge; that he, as least at one point in time, represented himself as being a nephew of John Bailey who had been previous—or at one time was chairman of the Democratic party of Connecticut.

SENATOR INOUYE: Assuming that Mr. Baldwin was in fact a double agent, and further assuming that Mr. Baldwin did in fact advise the local police officials in advance of the break-in, did you consider that his actions were wrong or illegal in notifying the police of the burglary?

A. I believe you're posing a legal hypothesis, Senator, which I'd like to consult counsel on, if I might.

My assumption, of course, Senator Inouye, was that the project itself was legal. Now, Mr. Baldwin's actions in disclosing the project or setting up an entrapment really is another matter. That's a subjective matter. Certainly if was a matter of the greatest disloyalty to his employer and to those of us who comprised the entry group. The courts have yet to decide the legality or nonlegality of the operation itself.

Q. It is your contention that the break-in was a legal break-in, because of national security?

A. I believed, Senator, then, and I believe now that it was a lawful activity.

SENATOR WEICKER: I'd just like to touch upon for a minute, Mr. Hunt, your comments on the double agent theory relative to Mr. Baldwin. You indicated that one of the bases for your theory would be Mr. Baldwin having an uncle who is a Democratic judge. Is that correct?

A. That was my understanding, yes, sir.

Q. Right. Is the judge Raymond Baldwin?

A. I don't know his name.

Q. Well, let me put it this way so that the record is very clear: the only relative that Mr. Baldwin has who is or has been a judge is the former Chief Justice of the Supreme, State Supreme Court in Connecticut, who would be Raymond Baldwin, who was also the Republican Senator from Connecticut, who was also the Republican Governor of Connecticut and who is generally looked upon as Mr. Republican in the state of Connecticut.

SENATOR ERVIN: When Mr. Colson asked you to go to Denver to consult Dita Beard, what did he say he wanted you to tell Dita Beard or ask Dita Beard?

A. This was a very complicated mission, Mr. Chairman. I might say that I know that the special prosecutor has in his possession an eight-page memorandum which I drew up immediately following my return from Washington. According to the best evidence rule, I would hope that that would soon be in the possession of the committee, if it is not, because it does contain my reconstruction of the events immediately following their occurrence.

However, my two basic instructions when I set out to elicit information from Mrs. Beard were to determine (a) why she had left Washington, and—in effect hidden herself out—hidden herself away, and (b) whether or not the famous or infamous memorandum concerning I.T.T. was according to the best of her knowledge fraudulent. Now there were many other items that I was charged with. Some of these were reduced to the form of an aide mémoire which I took out to Denver with me and interrogated her from.

Q. Did you disguise youself in any way when you visited Mrs. Beard? A. Yes, sir.

Q. Did you tell Mrs. Beard who you were representing when you saw her?

A. I—the question came up during the course of one of our numerous dialogues that night. I simply confirmed what she had been given to understand by her daughter that I represented high levels of the Administration who were interested in her welfare.

Q. You did actually represent the special counsel to the President, Charles W. Colson? You performed the mission at his instance, didn't you?

A. At his initial request, sir, but I was referred by him to Mr. Wallace Johnson, who was the gentleman who actually dispatched me on the mission and prepared the aide mémoire from which I talked subsequently to Mrs. Beard.

Q. And who was Mr. Johnson?

A. Mr. Johnson was at that time, I believe, in the office of Congressional relations at the White House.

Q. Now I understood you testified yesterday that you recently learned that Mr. Krogh—Egil Krogh—had received money to cover the expense of the break-in of the Fielding office from Mr. Colson. A. Yes, Mr. Chairman.

Q. Now when did you learn this and how did you learn it?

A. I learned it in connection with one of my interviews with the Office of the Special Prosecutor or in connection with testimony I was giving before the Watergate grand jury.

Q. Do you know where Mr. Colson received the money he gave to Mr. Krogh? A. Not specifically.

SENATOR TALMADGE: I am impressed with your background. You have served in the United States Navy honorably. You are a graduate of one of the better colleges in the United States of America. You served your country honorably in the Office of Strategic Services during World War II. You had an outstanding career in the C.I.A. in which you were commended twice. Why on earth after a record of that type, would you get involved in clandestine activities and commit a series of felonies?

A. I would have to answer, Senator Talmadge, in two parts: First, I became engaged because I believed that the activities that were proposed to me had the sanction of the highest authorities in our country.

Secondly, my 26-year record of service to this country pre-disposed me to accept orders and instructions without question and without debate.

Q. Let me see if I understand your reply. First, you thought the end justified the means and, second, if higher authority ordered that you thought it was your duty to obey; does that answer it?

MR. SACHS: Senator Talmadge, may I intervene and suggest that the first part of your question, in my humble opinion, was not an exact paraphrase of what he said.

Q. I certainly don't want to put words in his mouth but I understood the answer to be similar thereto

A. As a general rule, Senator Talmadge, I do not believe that the end justifies the means.

Q. You had been trained to instantly obey orders of higher authority and that was the reason you did what you did. A. Yes, sir.

SENATOR MONTOYA: Mr. Hunt, in light of what has been developed, do you feel that you were let down by people in the White House and the Committee to Re-elect the President?

A. I do.

Q. In what manner?

A. Their failure to interpose themselves between the seven of us who were initially indicted and the severe penalties of the law that have been imposed upon us, their failure to support our families, to continue to pay our legal fees, to exert every reasonable effort in our behalf.

Q. What particular individuals in authority at either the White House or the C.R.P. or both would you feel had some kind of responsibility to reciprocate to you and the other defendants?

A. I would say primarily the Attorney General, the Attorney General's successors.

Q. Is it not a fact that the only man with respect to this operation that you were in touch with at the White House level was Mr. Colson? A. And Mr. Liddy.

PRESIDENT NIXON'S STATEMENTS

News Conference, Washington, D.C. (excerpts)

June 22, 1972

Q. Mr. O'Brien has said that the people who bugged his headquarters had a direct link to the White House. Have you had any sort of investigation made to determine whether this is true?

A. Mr. Ziegler and also Mr. Mitchell, speaking for the campaign committee, have responded to questions on this in great detail. They have stated my position and have also stated the facts accurately.

This kind of activity, as Mr. Ziegler has indicated, has no place whatever in our electoral process, or in our governmental process. And, as Mr. Ziegler has stated, the White House has had no involvement whatever in this particular incident.

As far as the matter now is concerned, it is under investigation, as it should be, by the proper legal authorities, by the District of Columbia police and by the F.B.I. I will not comment on those matters, particularly since possible criminal charges are involved.

Q. Mr. Mitchell has declined to make public the source of about $10 million of contributions to your re-election fund. I know that this is in the letter of the law, but I wonder in the spirit of the law of more openness what you think about that, and might you make them public?

A. Mr. Ziegler has responded to that and Mr. Mitchell and Mr. Stans. I think it is Mr. Stans who has declined to do that. I support the position that Mr. Stans has taken.

When we talk about the spirit of the law and the letter of the law, my evaluation is that it is the responsibility of all, a high moral responsibility to obey the law and to obey it totally.

Now, if the Congress wanted this law to apply to contributions before the date in April that it said the law should take effect, it could have made it apply. The Congress did not apply it before that date and under the circumstances, Mr. Stans has said we will comply with the law as the Congress has written it and I support his decision.

News Conference, San Clemente, Calif. (excerpts)

Aug. 29, 1972

Q. Mr. President, are you personally investigating the mishandling of some of your campaign funds, and do you agree with former Secretary Connally that these charges are harmful to your re-election?

A. Well, I commented upon this on other occasions, and I will repeat my position now.

With regard to the matter of the handling of campaign funds, we have a new law here in which technical violations have occurred and are occurring, apparently, on both sides. As far as we are concerned, we have in charge, in Secretary Stans, a man who is an honest man and one who is very meticulous—as I have learned from having him as my treasurer and finance chairman in two previous campaigns—in the handling of matters of this sort.

Whatever technical violations have occurred, certainly he will correct them and will thoroughly comply with the law. He is conducting an investigation on this matter, and conducting it very, very thoroughly, because he doesn't want any evidence at all to be outstanding, indicating that we have not complied with the law.

Q. Mr. President, wouldn't it be a good idea for a special prosecutor, even from your standpoint, to be appointed to investigate the contribution situation and also the Watergate case?

A. With regard to who is investigating it now, I think it would be well to notice that the F.B.I. is conducting a full field investigation. The Department of Justice, of course, is in charge of the prosecution and presenting the matter to the grand jury. The Senate Banking and Currency Committee is conducting an investigation. The Government Accounting Office, an independent agency, is conducting an investigation of those aspects which involve the campaign spending law.

Now, with all of these investigations that are being conducted, I don't believe that adding another special prosecutor would serve any useful purpose.

The other point that I should make is that these investigations—the investigation by the G.A.O., the investigation by the F.B.I., by the Department of Justice—have, at my direction, had the total cooperation of the—not only the White House but also of all agencies of government.

In addition to that, within our own staff, under my direction, counsel to the President, Mr. Dean, has conducted a complete investigation of all leads which might involve any present members of the White House staff or anybody in the Government. I can say categorically that his investigation indicates that no one in the White House staff, no one in this Administration, presently employed, was involved in this very bizarre incident.

At the same time, the committee itself is conducting its own investigation, independent of the rest, because the committee desires to clear the air and to be sure that, as far as any people who have responsibility for this campaign are concerned, that there is nothing that hangs over them. Before Mr. Mitchell left as campaign chairman he had employed a very good law firm with investigatory experience to look into the matter. Mr. MacGregor has continued that investigation and is continuing it now.

I will say in that respect that anyone on the campaign committee, Mr. MacGregor has assured me, who does not cooperate with the investigation or anyone against whom charges are leveled where there is a prima facie case where those charges might indicate involvement, will be discharged immediately. That, also, is true of anybody in the Government. I think under these circumstances we are doing everything we can to take this incident and to investigate it and not to cover it up.

What really hurts in matters of this sort is not the fact that they occur, because overzealous people in campaigns do things that are wrong. What really hurts is if you try to cover it up. I would say that here we are, with control of the agencies of the Government and presumably with control of the investigatory agencies of the Government with the exception of G.A.O., which is independent. We have cooperated completely. We have indicated that we want all the facts brought out and that as far as any people who are guilty are concerned, they should be prosecuted.

This kind of activity, as I have often indicated, has no place whatever in our political process. We want the air cleared. We want it cleared as soon as possible.

Q. Mr. President, back to the campaign financing. You said that there had been technical violations of the law on both sides. I was just wondering what Democratic violations you had in mind?

A. I think that will come out in the balance of this week. I will let the political people talk about that, but I understand there have been on both sides.

News Conference, Washington, D. C. (excerpts)

Oct. 5, 1972

Q. Mr. President, what are you planning to do to defend yourself against the charges of corruption in your Administration?

A. Well, I have noted such charges; as a matter of fact, I have noted that this Administration has been charged with being the most corrupt in history, and I have been charged with being the most deceitful President in history.

The President of the United States has been compared in his policies with Adolf Hitler. The policies of the U.S. Government to prevent a Communist take-over by force in South Vietnam have been called the worst crime since the Nazi extermination of the Jews in Germany. And the President, who went to China and to Moscow, and who has brought 500,000 home from Vietnam, has been called the number one warmaker in the world.

Needless to say, some of my more partisan advisers feel that I should respond in kind. I shall not do so; not now; not throughout this campaign. I am not going to dignify such comments.

In view of the fact that one of the very few members of the Congress who is publicly and actively supporting the opposition ticket in this campaign has very vigorously, yesterday, criticized this kind of tactics, it seems to me it makes it not necessary for me to respond.

I think the responsible members of the Democratic party will be turned off by this kind of campaigning, and I would suggest that responsible members of the press, following the single standard to which they are deeply devoted, will also be turned off by it.

Q. Mr. President, don't you think that your Administration and the public would be served considerably and that the men under indictment would be treated better, if you people would come through and make a clean breast about what you were trying to get done at the Watergate?

A. One thing that has always puzzled me about it is why anybody would have tried to get anything out of the Watergate. Be that as it may, that decision having been made at a lower level, with which I had no knowledge, and, as I have pointed out——

Q. Surely you know now, sir.

A. I certainly feel that under the circumstances that we have to look at what has happened and to put the matter into perspective.

Now when we talk about a clean breast, let's look at what has happened. The F.B.I. has assigned 133 agents to this investigation. It followed out 1,800 leads. It conducted 1,500 interviews.

Incidentally, I conducted the investigation of the Hiss case. I know that it is a very unpopular subject to raise in some quarters, but I conducted it. It was successful. The F.B.I. did a magnificent job, but that investigation involving the security of this country was basically a Sunday School exercise compared to the amount of effort that was put into this.

I agree with the amount of effort that was put into it. I wanted every lead carried out to the end because I wanted to be sure that no member of the White House staff and no man or woman in a position of major responsibility in the Committee for Re-election had anything to do with this kind of reprehensible activity.

Now, the grand jury has handed down indictments. It has indicted, incidentally, two who were with the Committee for Re-election and one who refused to cooperate and another who was apprehended. Under these circumstances, the grand jury now having acted, it is now time to have the judicial process go forward and for the evidence to be presented.

I would say finally with regard to commenting on any of those who have been indicted, with regard to saying anything about the judicial process, I am going to follow the good advice, which I appreciate, of the members of the press corps, my constant, and I trust will always continue to be, very responsible critics.

I stepped into one on that when you recall I made inadvertently a comment in Denver about an individual who had been indicted in California, the Manson case. I was vigorously criticized for making any comment about the case, so of course, I know you would want me to follow the same single standard by not commenting on this case.

News Conference, Washington, D. C. (excerpts)

March 2, 1973

Q. Mr. President, Mr. Gray has been up before the Senate Judiciary Committee, and he has been under attack for political speeches in 1972, and there is a controversy about those that are or are not political speeches. I wonder if you have looked at those, whether you have a view on that, and it seemed to me the most vulnerable point was a memo from Patrick O'Donnell from the White House that was distributed to all the surrogates for the President that went to Pat Gray on the Cleveland situation, and it involved a setting out of how crucial Ohio was in the campaign in 1972, and I wonder if you felt that was a breach of your instructions relative to the politics of Pat Gray, and whether you had investigated this.

A. Well, Mr. Mollenhoff, that is a very proper question. I mean I would not suggest other questions are improper, but it is a very proper question because when I appointed Mr. Gray, as you remember, I said I was not going to send his name last year because I felt that we should wait until we got past the political campaign so that the Senate could consider it in a nonpolitical and nonpartisan atmosphere, and the Senate is now doing that.

As far as Mr. Gray is concerned—and not the individual, but the Director of the F.B.I.—he must be, as Mr. Hoover was before him, a nonpartisan figure. He should not be involved in making political statements and that does not mean, if we look at Mr. Hoover's record, that he will not say some things that will not sound political at times, but it means that he must not become involved in partisan politics, supporting a candidate, opposing a candidate, and Mr. Gray, on the basis of what I have seen, had no intention of doing so. If there was anything indicating that during the campaign that we were trying to enlist him in that it certainly didn't have my support and would not have it now.

I would also say, too, that the current Senate investigation or hearing, I should say, of Mr. Gray, is altogether proper. They should ask him all these questions. I want the people of this country to have confidence in the Director of the F.B.I. I had confidence in him when I nominated him.

I believe that the Senate will find, based on his record since he was nominated, that he has been fair, he has been efficient and that he will be a good, shall we say, lawman in the tradition of J. Edgar Hoover and I am sure that the Senate will overwhelmingly approve him.

Q. Mr. President, do you think it is fair and efficient for Mr. Gray and the F.B.I. not to question Mrs. Mitchell when they think there was cause to because her husband was a former Attorney General and campaign official of yours?

A. With regard to other questions on Mr. Gray, it has always been my practice, as you ladies and gentlemen know, not to comment on a hearing while it is in process. This is a matter that was brought up in the hearing.

I am sure that if the members of the Senate feel that that was an improper activity on his part, they will question him about it and he will answer it, but whether it is this hearing or any other hearing, I will not comment on a hearing while it is in process.

My answer to Mr. Mollenhoff stated a principle. Your question goes to a matter that the committee has a right to look into and the answer should come from the committee.

.　　.　　.

Q. Mr. President, now that the Watergate case is over, the trial is over, can you give us your view on the verdict and what implications you see in the verdict on public confidence in the political system?

A. No, it would not be proper for me to comment on the case when it not only is not over, but particularly when it is also on appeal.

I will simply say with regard to the Watergate case what I have said previously; that the investigation conducted by Mr. Dean, the White House counsel, in which, incidentally, he had access to the F.B.I. records on this particular matter because I directed him to conduct this investigation, indicates that no one on the White House staff, at the time he conducted the investigation—that was last July and August—was involved or had knowledge of the Watergate matter and, as far as the balance of the case is concerned, it is now under investigation by a Congressional committee and that committee should go forward, conduct its investigation in an even-handed way, going into charges made against both candidates, both political parties, and if it does, as Senator Ervin has indicated it will, we will, of course, cooperate with the committee just as we cooperated with the grand jury.

Q. Mr. President, yesterday at the Gray hearings, Senator Tunney suggested he might ask the committee to ask for John Dean to appear before that hearing to talk about the Watergate case and the F.B.I.-White House relationship. Would you object to that?

A. Of course.

Q. Why?

A. Well, because it is executive privilege. I mean you can't— I, of course—no President could ever agree to allow the Counsel to the President to go down and testify before a committee.

On the other hand, as far as any committee of the Congress is concerned, where information is requested that a member of the White House staff may have, we will make arrangements to provide that information, but members of the White House staff, in that position at least, cannot be brought before a Congressional committee in a formal hearing for testimony. I stand on the same position every President has stood on.

Q. Thank you, Mr. President.

Q. Mr. President, on that particular point, if the counsel was involved—

A. He also gets two.

Q. If the counsel was involved in an illegal or improper act and the prima facie case came to light, then would you change the rules relative to the White House counsel?

A. I do not expect that to happen and if it should happen I would have to answer that question at that point.

Let me say, too. that I know that since you are on your feet,

Clark, that you had asked about the executive privilege statement and we will have that available toward the end of next week or the first of the following week, for sure, because obviously the Ervin committee is interested in that statement and that will answer, I think, some of the questions with regard to how information can be obtained from a member of the White House staff, but consistent with executive privilege.

Q. Thank you again.

Statement (excerpts)

March 12, 1973

The doctrine of executive privilege is well established. It was first invoked by President Washington, and it has been recognized and utilized by our Presidents for almost 200 years since that time.

The doctrine is rooted in the Constitution, which vests "the executive power" solely in the President, and it is designed to protect communications within the executive branch in a variety of circumstances in time of both war and peace.

Without such protection, our military security, our relations with other countries, our law enforcement procedures and many other aspects of the national interest could be significantly damaged and the decision-making process of the executive branch could be impaired.

The general policy of this Administration regarding the use of executive privilege during the next four years will be the same as the one we have followed during the past four years: Executive privilege will not be used as a shield to prevent embarrassing information from being made available but will be exercised only in those particular instances in which disclosure would harm the public interest.

During the first four years of my Presidency, hundreds of Administration officials spent thousands of hours testifying before committees of the Congress. Secretary of Defense Laird, for instance, made 86 separate appearances before Congressional committees, engaging in over 327 hours of testimony.

By contrast, there were only three occasions during the first term of my Administration when executive privilege was invoked anywhere in the executive branch in response to a Congressional request for information. These facts speak not of a closed Administration but of one that is pledged to openness and is proud to stand on its record.

Requests for Congressional appearances by members of the President's personal staff present a different situation and raise different considerations. Such requests have been relatively infrequent through the years, and in past Administrations they have been routinely declined.

I have followed that same tradition in my Administration, and I intend to continue it during the remainder of my term.

Under the doctrine of separation of powers, the manner in which the President personally exercises his assigned executive powers is not subject to questioning by another branch of government. If the President is not subject to such questioning, it is equally inappropriate that members of his staff not be so questioned, for their roles are in effect an extension of the Presidency.

This tradition rests on more than constitutional doctrine: It is also a practical necessity to insure the effective discharge of the executive responsibility, a President must be able to place absolute confidence in the advice and assistance offered by the members of his staff. And in the performance of their duties for the President, those staff members must not be inhibited by the possibility that their advice and assistance will ever become a matter of public debate, either during their tenure in government or at a later date. Otherwise, the candor with which advice is rendered and the quality of such assistance will inevitably be compromised and weakened.

What is at stake, therefore, is not simply a question of confidentiality but the integrity of the decision-making process at the very highest levels of our government.

As I stated in my press conference on Jan. 31, the question of whether circumstances warrant the exercise of executive privilege should be determined on a case-by-case basis.

In making such decisions, I shall rely on the following guidelines:

1. In the case of a department or agency, every official shall comply with a reasonable request for an appearance before the Congress, provided that the performance of the duties of his office will not be seriously impaired thereby. If the official believes that a Congressional request for a particular document or for testimony on a particular point raises a substantial question as to the need for invoking executive privilege, he shall comply with the procedures set forth in my memorandum of March 24, 1969. Thus, executive privilege will not be invoked until the compelling need for its exercise has been clearly demonstrated and the request has been approved first by the Attorney General and then by the President.

2. A Cabinet officer or any other governmental official who also holds a position as a member of the President's personal staff shall comply with any reasonable request to testify in his non-White House capacity, provided that the performance of his duties will not be seriously impaired thereby. If the official believes that the request raises a substantial question as to the need for invoking executive privilege, he shall comply with the procedures set forth in my memorandum of March 24, 1969.

3. A member or former member of the President's personal staff normally shall follow the well-established precedent and decline a request for a formal appearance before a committee of the Congress. At the same time, it will continue to be my policy to provide all necessary and relevant information through informal contacts between my present staff and committees of the Congress in ways which preserve intact the constitutional separation of the branches.

News Conference, Washington, D. C. (excerpts)

March 15, 1973

Q. Mr. President, do you plan to stick by your decision not to allow Mr. Dean to testify before the Congress, even if it means the defeat of Mr. Gray's nomination?

A. I noted some speculation to the effect that the Senate might hold Mr. Gray as hostage to a decision on Mr. Dean. I cannot believe that such responsible members of the United States Senate would do that, because as far as I am concerned, my decision has been made.

I answered that question rather abruptly, you recall, the last time it was asked by one of the ladies of the press here. I did not mean to be abrupt. I simply mean to be firm.

Mr. Dean is counsel to the White House staff. He has, in effect, what I would call a double privilege, the lawyer-client relationship, as well as the Presidential privilege.

And in terms of privilege, I think we could put it another way. I consider it my constitutional responsibility to defend the principle of separation of powers. I recognize that many members of the Congress disagree with my interpretation of that responsibility.

But while we are talking on that subject—and I will go on at some length here because it may anticipate some of your other questions—I am very proud of the fact that in this Administration we have been more forthcoming in terms of the relationship between the executive, the White House and the Congress, than any Administration in my memory. We have not drawn a curtain down and said that there could be no information furnished by members of the White House staff because of their special relationship to the President.

All we have said is that it must be under certain circumstances, certain guidelines, that do not infringe upon or impair the separation of powers that are so essential to the survival of our system.

In that connection, I might say that I had mentioned previously that I was once on the other side of the fence, but what I am doing here in this case is cooperating with the Congress in a way that I asked the then President, Mr. Truman, to cooperate with a committee of the Congress 25 years ago and in which he refused.

I don't say that critically of him now, he had his reasons, I have mine. But what we asked for in the hearings on the Hiss case—and all of you who covered it like Bill Theis and others will remember—what we asked for was not that the head of the F.B.I. or anybody from the White House staff testify. There was very widespread information that there was a report of an investigation that had been made in the Administration about the Hiss case. We asked for that report. We asked for the F.B.I. information with regard to that report.

And Mr. Truman, the day we started our investigation, issued an executive order in which he ordered everybody in the executive department to refuse to cooperate with the committee under any circumstances. The F.B.I. refused all information. We got no report from the Department of Justice and we had to go forward and break the case ourselves.

We did and to the credit of the Administration, after we broke the case, they proceeded to conduct the prosecution and the F.B.I. went into it.

I would like to say, incidentally, that I talked to Mr. Hoover at that time. It was with reluctance that he did not turn over that information. Reluctance, because he felt that the information, the investigation they had conducted, was very pertinent to what the committee was doing.

Now, I thought that decision was wrong and so when this Administration has come in, I have always insisted that we should cooperate with the members of the Congress and with the committees of the Congress and that is why we have furnished information, but, however, I am not going to have the Counsel to the President of the United States testify in a formal session before the Congress. However, Mr. Dean will furnish information when any of it is requested, provided it is pertinent to the investigation.

Q. Mr. President, would you then be willing to have Mr. Dean sit down informally and let some of the Senators question him, as they have with Dr. Kissinger?

A. No, that is quite a different thing. In fact, Dr. Kissinger, Mr. Ehrlichman, as you know, not only informally meet with members of the Congress on matters of substance, the same is true with members of the press. As you know, Dr. Kissinger meets with you ladies and gentlemen of the press and answers questions on matters of substance.

In this case, where we have the relationship that we have with Mr. Dean and the President of the United States, his counsel, that would not be a proper way to handle it. He will, however, the important thing is, he will furnish all pertinent information. He will be completely forthcoming. Something that other Administrations have totally refused to do until we got here, and I am very proud of the fact that we are forthcoming, and I would respectfully suggest that members of the Congress might look at the record as they decided to test it.

Q. Mr. President, are you concerned, sir, that any of the confidential F.B.I. interviews that were conducted in their Watergate investigation were in any way compromised by Pat Gray's having given information to John Dean or talked about to John Ehrlichman or others?

A. No, I am not concerned about that. I would say that there is no possibility whatever that any information from the F.B.I. that may have been provided in the line of their duties to a member of the White House staff would be bandied about in the press.

I would express concern on another point. In my long-time association with Mr. Hoover, he always was hard line in dealing with the members of Congress and with Congressional committees in terms of what he called "raw files," and when I first came into this office, he showed me a "raw file." I had not seen any before.

And when I saw the gossip, the hearsay, and unsubstantiated kind of slanderous statements, libelous, in this case, because they were in writing, having been made orally and transmitted into writing. I was really shocked.

Mr. Hoover, after showing me the "raw file," gave me an appraisal by the F.B.I. of what could be believed and what could not be believed. And in the case of this particular individual—the reason I saw the file, it involved a check on an individual who I was nominating for a position and I needed to get the facts and, of course, I always have access to those files—what we found was that every charge that had been made against the individual was false.

Now, for the F.B.I., before a full committee of the Congress, to furnish "raw files" and then to have them leak out to the press, I think could do innocent people a great deal of damage. I understand why Mr. Gray did, because his hearing was involved. But I would say that should not be a precedent for the future.

The way Mr. Hoover handled it with members of the Congress was that he would show the "raw files," for example, to Mr. Eastland, the chairman of the committee, and the ranking minority member, where a judge was up for a confirmation, but nothing ever leaked from those files, and the sanctity of those files must be maintained, and I believe that the practice of the F.B.I. furnishing "raw files" to full committees must stop with this particular one.

Q. Mr. President, one of the revelations made by Mr. Gray during the course of the hearings has been that Mr. Kalmbach was involved with Mr. Chapin in the hiring of Mr. Segretti for amounts up to $40,000. Can you tell us, sir, did you know of that relationship, and did you know of that transaction, and if not, can you tell us your opinion of it now that it has been revealed by Mr. Gray?

A. This gives me an opportunity to not only answer that question, but many others that I note you have been asking Mr. Ziegler.

First—and incidentally, I am not complaining about the fact you are asking the question of me or Mr. Ziegler. It is a very proper question. A Senate committee is conducting investigations. These investigations will go on, I understand, over a period of many months. I respect the right of the Senate to conduct those investigations. We will cooperate; we will cooperate fully with the Senate, just as we did with the grand jury, as we did with the F.B.I., and as we did with the courts when they were conducting their investigations previously in what was called the Watergate matter.

As far as these investigations are concerned, there are all kinds of information, charges, et cetera, et cetera, that have been made and will be made in the future. I could comment upon them. Mr. Ziegler could in the future. I will not. He will not. And the reason that we will not is that when the committee completes its investigation, we will then have comments, if we consider it appropriate to do so. But it is the right of the committee to conduct the investigation, so that all the facts can come out.

I have confidence in all of the White House people who have been named. I will express that confidence again. But I am not going to comment on any individual matter that the committee may go into.

Let me say, with regard to the committee, too. Do not intend to raise questions about its conduct. I have been very pleased to note that Senator Ervin—at least this is the way I read what he says—has indicated that the investigation will be bipartisan; that it will look into charges that have been made against both election campaigns, and that is as it should be. He has also indicated that he, as a great constitutional lawyer, will accept no hearsay; that he will not tolerate any guilt by innuendo; he will not tolerate any guilt by association.

As long as the committee conducts its investigations with those very high guidelines—guidelines I tried to follow, incidentally, in the Hiss case; not perhaps as well as I might have, but I did what many thought was pretty well—but in any event, as long as it is conducted that way, I do not intend to make any statements with regard to matters before the committee. That is for the committee to look into.

. . .

Q. Mr. President, does your offer to cooperate with the Ervin committee include the possibility that you would allow your aides to testify before his committee, and if it does not, would you be willing to comply with a court order, if Ervin went to court to get one, that required some testimony from White House aides?

A. In answer to your first part of the question, the statement that we made yesterday answered that completely—not yesterday, the 12th I think it was, my statement on executive privilege. Members of the White House staff will not appear before a committee of Congress in any formal session.

We will furnish information under the proper circumstances. We will consider each matter on a case-by-case basis.

With regard to the second point, that is not before us. Let me say, however, that if the Senate feels at this time that this matter of separation of powers, whereas I said, this Administration has been more forthcoming than any Democratic Administration I know of, if the Senate feels that they want a court test, we would welcome it. Perhaps this is the time to have the highest court of this land make a definitive decision with regard to this matter.

I am not suggesting that we are asking for it. But I would suggest that if the members of the Senate, in this wisdom, decide that they want to test this matter in the courts, we will, of course, present our side of the case, and we think that the Supreme Court will uphold, as it always usually has, the great constitutional principle of separation of powers rather than to uphold the Senate.

Q. Mr. President isn't there an essential difference really between your investigation of the Hiss case and the request of this subcommittee to Mr. Dean to appear? In the former, foreign affairs was involved and possibly security matters, where here they only wish to question Mr. Dean about the breaking into the Watergate.

A. Yes, I would say the difference is very significant. As a matter of fact, when a committee of Congress was investigating espionage against the Government of this country, that committee should have had complete cooperation from at least the executive branch of the Government in the form that we asked. All that we asked was to get the report that we knew they had already made of their investigation.

Now, this investigation does not involve espionage against the United States. It is, as we know, espionage by one political organization against another. And I would say that as far as your question is concerned, that the argument would be that the Congress would have a far greater right and would be on much stronger ground to ask the Government to cooperate in a matter involving espionage against the Government than in a matter like this involving politics.

Q. Mr. President, you have talked about the responsibility within the White House and responsibility between Congress and the White House. Where do you feel your responsibility for the Committee to Re-elect the President begins and ends, Mr. Mitchell or any other people who were working for them?

A. Well, the responsibility there, of course, is one that will be replied to by Mr. Mitchell, Mr. Stans and all of those in due course. None of them have the privilege, none of them, of course, will refuse to testify, none has when he is asked to, and I am sure they will give very good accounts of themselves, as they have in the court matters that they have been asked to.

Statement

April 17, 1973

I have two announcements to make. Because of their technical nature, I shall read both of the announcements to the members of the press corps.

The first announcement relates to the appearance of White House people before the Senate Select Committee, better known as the Ervin committee.

For several weeks, Senator Ervin and Senator Baker and their counsel have been in contact with White House representatives John Ehrlichman and Leonard Garment. They have been talking about ground rules which would preserve the separation of powers without suppressing the fact.

I believe now an agreement has been reached which is satisfactory to both sides. The committee ground rules as adopted totally preserve the doctrine of separation of powers. They provide that the appearance by a witness may, in the first instance, be in executive session, if appropirate.

Second, executive privilege is expressly reserved and may be asserted during the course of the questioning as to any questions.

Now, much has been made of the issue as to whether the proceedings could be televised. To me, this has never been a central issue, especially if the separation of powers problem is otherwise solved, as I now think it is.

All members of the White House staff will appear voluntarily when requested by the committee. They will testify under oath and they will answer fully all proper questions.

I should point out that this arrangement is one that covers this hearing only in which wrongdoing has been charged. This kind of arrangement, of course, would not apply to other hearings: Each of them will be considered on its merits.

My second announcement concerns the Watergate case directly.

On March 21, as a result of serious charges which came to my attention, some of which were publicly reported, I began intensive new inquiries into this whole matter.

Last Sunday afternoon, the Attorney General, Assistant Attorney General Petersen and I met at length in the E.O.B. [Executive Office Building] to review the facts which had come to me in my investigation and also to review the progress of the Department of Justice investigation.

I can report today that there have been major developments in the case concerning which it would be improper to be more specific now, except to say that real progress has been made in finding the truth.

If any person in the executive branch or in the Government is indicted by the grand jury, my policy will be to immediately suspend him. If he is convicted, he will, of course, be automatically discharged.

I have expressed to the appropriate authorities my view that no individual holding, in the past or at present, a position of major importance in the Administration should be given immunity from prosecution.

The judicial process is moving ahead as it should; and I shall aid it in all appropriate ways and have so informed the appropriate authorities.

As I have said before and I have said throughout this entire matter, all Government employes and especially White House staff employes are expected fully to cooperate in this matter. I condemn any attempts to cover up in this case, no matter who is involved.

Statement by President Nixon and Letters of Resignation of Three Aides

April 29, 1973

Nixon Statement

I have today received and accepted the resignation of Richard G. Kleindienst as Attorney General of the United States. I am appointing Elliot L. Richardson to succeed him as Attorney General and will submit Mr. Richardson's name to the Senate for confirmation immediately.

Mr. Kleindienst asked to be relieved as Attorney General because he felt that he could not appropriately continue as head of the Justice Department now that it appears its investigation of the Watergate and related cases may implicate individuals with whom he has had a close personal and professional association.

In making this decision, Mr. Kleindienst has acted in accordance with the highest standards of public service and legal ethics. I am accepting his resignation with regret and with deep appreciation for his dedicated service to this Administration.

Pending Secretary Richardson's confirmation as Attorney General, I have asked him to involve himself immediately in the investigative process surrounding the Watergate matter. As Attorney General, Mr. Richardson will assume full responsibility and authority for coordinating all Federal agencies in uncovering the whole truth about this matter and recommending appropriate changes in the law to prevent future campaign abuses of the sort recently uncovered. He will have total support from me in getting this job done.

In addition, I have today accepted the resignations of two of my closest friends and most trusted assistants in the White House, H. R. Haldeman and John D. Ehrlichman.

I know that their decision to resign was difficult; my decision to accept it was difficult; but I respect and appreciate the attitude that led them to it.

I emphasize that neither the submission or the acceptance of their resignations at this time should be seen by anyone as evidence of any wrongdoing by either one. Such an assumption would be both unfair and unfounded.

Throughout our association, each of these men has demonstrated a spirit of selflessness and dedication that I have seldom seen equaled. Their contributions to the work of this Administration have been enormous. I greatly regret their departure.

Finally, I have today requested and accepted the resignation of John W. Dean 3d from his position on the staff as White House counsel.

Effective immediately, Leonard Garment, special consultant to the President, will take on additional duties as Counsel to the President, and will continue acting in this capacity until a permanent successor to Mr. Dean is named. Mr. Garment will represent the White House in all matters relating to the Watergate investigation and will report directly to me.

Resignation Letters

John D. Ehrlichman

For the past two weeks it has become increasingly evident that, regardless of the actual facts, I have been a target of public attack. The nature of my position on your staff has always demanded that my conduct be both apparently and actually beyond reproach. I have always felt that the appearance of honesty and integrity is every bit as important to such a position as the fact of one's honesty and integrity.

Unfortunately, such appearances are not always governed by facts. Realistically, they can be affected by repeated rumor, unfounded charges or implications and whatever else the media carries. For instance, this week totally unfounded stories appeared in The Los Angeles Times claiming I had asked our embassy in Lebanon to help the Vesco group in a banking deal. I not only did not do so but, in actual fact, I caused the State Department to cable the embassy that no one at the White House had any interest in the Vesco dealings.

Since I have already reported to you many of the facts in the Gray case, I need only say that at no time did I directly or indirectly suggest that Mr. Gray should do other than keep the Hunt documents, although there have been reports to the contrary. Equally without merit are the source stories about some alleged involvement in the Watergate matter.

As I analyze my situation, I have to conclude that my present usefulness to you and ability to discharge my duties have been impaired by these attacks, perhaps beyond repair.

It is not fair to you and my staff colleagues for me to try to do my job under these circumstances. Too much of my time and attention is and will be consumed in concern for and straightening our such allegations. At my request, I am going to have separate interviews this week with the District Attorney and the Senate committee counsel.

Thus, I am looking forward to an early review of the facts and evidence with the appropriate authorities, and I should spend the time necessary in relation thereto.

One of the toughest problems we have in this life is in seeing the difference between the apparent and the real, and in basing our actions only on that which is real. We all must do that more than we do. I have confidence in the ultimate prevalence of truth; I intend to do what I can to speed truth's discovery.

Therefore, Mr. President, I submit to you my resignation. There are on the Domestic Council staff so many good people of ability that I am confident a transition of my responsibilities can be affected without loss of progress. I will do all I can to assist in accomplishing the transition.

H. R. Haldeman

As you know, I had hoped and expected to have had an earlier opportunity to clear up various allegations and innuendos that have been raised in connection with matters related to the Watergate case. It now appears that this process may consume considerable time. Meanwhile, there is apparently to be no interruption in the flood of stories arising every day from all sorts of sources.

I fully agree with the importance of a complete investigation by the appropriate authorities of all the factors that may be involved; but am deeply concerned that, in the process, it has become virtually impossible under these circumstances for me to carry on my regular responsibilities in the White House.

It is imperative that the work of the Office of the President not be impeded and your staff must be in a position to focus their attention on the vital areas of domestic and international concern that face you, rather than being diverted by the daily rumors and developments in the Watergate case. For these reasons, I submit my resignation as Assistant to the President.

I intend to cooperate fully with the investigation—and will at my request be meeting this week for that purpose with the U.S. attorneys and with the counsel to the Senate Select Committee.

I am convinced that, in due course, I will have the opportunity not just to clear up any allegations or implications of impropriety but also to demonstrate that I have always met the high and exacting standards of integrity which you have so clearly and properly demanded of all who serve on the White House staff.

I have full confidence that when the truth is known the American people will be totally justified in their pride in the Office of the President and in the conduct of that office by President Nixon.

Richard O. Kleindienst

It is with deep regret and after long and searching thought that I hereby submit my resignation as Attorney General, to take effect upon the appointment and qualification of my successor.

Even though, as you know, I had previously indicated a desire to leave the Government this year for family and financial reasons, the circumstances surrounding the disclosures made to me on Sunday, April 15, 1973, by Assistant Attorney General Petersen, United States Attorney Titus, and Assistant United States Attorney Silbert, dictate this decision at this time. Those disclosures informed me, for the first time, that persons with whom I had close personal and professional associations could be involved in conduct violative of the laws of the United States. Fair and impartial enforcement of the law requires that a person who has not had such intimate relationships be the Attorney General of the United States.

It is not for me to comment now on the tragedy that has occurred. However, I will always be mindful of your charge to me from the very beginning that the entire matter be fully investigated and that the full effect of the law be administered no matter who it might involve or affect. You can be proud of the Department of Justice for the manner in which it, from the beginning, has responded to that charge.

Finally, let me express my deep personal appreciation to you for having appointed me the 68th Attorney General of the United States. It is the greatest honor I shall ever have. I shall always be humbly proud to have been a part of the Department of Justice and to have had the opportunity to serve my country as a part of your Administration.

Broadcast Address

April 30, 1973

Good evening. I want to talk to you tonight from my heart on a subject of deep concern to every American.

In recent months members of my Administration and officials of the Committee for the Re-election of the President—including some of my closest friends and most trusted aides—have been charged with involvement in what has come to be known as the Watergate affair.

These include charges of illegal activity during and preceding the 1972 Presidential election and charges that responsible officials participated in efforts to cover up that illegal activity.

The inevitable result of these charges has been to raise serious questions about the integrity of the White House itself. Tonight I wish to address those questions.

Last June 17 while I was in Florida trying to get a few days' rest after my visit to Moscow, I first learned from news reports of the Watergate break-in. I was appalled at this senseless, illegal action, and I was shocked to learn that employes of the re-election committee were apparently among those guilty. I immediately ordered an investigation by appropriate Government authorities.

On Sept. 15, as you will recall, indictments were brought against seven defendants in the case.

As the investigation went forward, I repeatedly asked those conducting the investigation whether there was any reason to believe that members of my Administration were in any way involved. I received repeated assurances that there were not. Because of these continuing reassurances, because I believed the reports I was getting, because I had faith in the persons from whom I was getting them, I discounted the stories in the press that appeared to implicate members of my Administration or other officials of the campaign committee.

Until March of this year, I remained convinced that the denials were true and that the charges of involvement by members of the White House staff were false.

The comments I made during this period, the comments made by my press secretary in my behalf, were based on the information provided to us at the time we made those comments.

However, new information then came to me which persuaded me that there was a real possibility that some of these charges were true and suggesting further that there had been an effort to conceal the facts both from the public—from you—and from me.

As a result, on March 21 I personally assumed the responsibility for coordinating intensive new inquiries into the matter and

I personally ordered those conducting the investigations to get all the facts and to report them directly to me right here in this office.

I again ordered that all persons in the Government or at the re-election committee should cooperate fully with the F.B.I., the prosecutors and the grand jury.

I also ordered that anyone who refused to cooperate in telling the truth would be asked to resign from Government service.

And with ground rules adopted that would preserve the basic constitutional separation of powers between the Congress and the Presidency, I directed that members of the White House staff should appear and testify voluntarily under oath before the Senate committee which was investigating Watergate.

I was determined that we should get to the bottom of the matter, and that the truth should be fully brought out no matter who was involved.

At the same time, I was determined not to take precipitive action and to avoid if at all possible any action that would appear to reflect on innocent people.

I wanted to be fair, but I knew that in the final analysis the integrity of this office—public faith in the integrity of this office—would have to take priority over all personal considerations.

Today, in one of the most difficult decisions of my Presidency, I accepted the resignations of two of my closest associates in the White House—Bob Haldeman, John Ehrlichman—two of the finest public servants it has been my privilege to know.

I want to stress that in accepting these resignations I mean to leave no implication whatever of personal wrongdoing on their part, and I leave no implication tonight of implication on the part of others who have been charged in this matter.

But in matters as sensitive as guarding the integrity of our democratic process, it is essential not only that rigorous legal and ethical standards be observed, but also that the public, you, have total confidence that they are both being observed and enforced by those in authority, and particularly by the President of the United States.

They agreed with me that this move was necessary in order to restore that confidence, because Attorney General Kleindienst —though a distinguished public servant, my personal friend for 20 years, with no personal involvement whatever in this matter —has been a close personal and professional associate of some of those who are involved in this case, he and I both felt that it was also necessary to name a new Attorney General.

The counsel to the President, John Dean, has also resigned.

As the new Attorney General, I have today named Elliot Richardson, a man of unimpeachable integrity and rigorously high principle. I have directed him to do everything necessary to insure that the Department of Justice has the confidence and the trust of every law-abiding person in this country. I have given him absolute authority to make all decisions bearing upon the prosecution of the Watergate case and related matters. I have instructed him that if he should consider it appropriate he has the authority to name a special supervising prosecutor for matters arising out of the case.

Whatever may appear to have been the case before, whatever improper activities may yet be discovered in connection with this whole sordid affair, I want the American people, I want you, to know beyond the shadow of a doubt that during my term as President justice will be pursued fairly, fully and impartially, no matter who is involved.

This office is a sacred trust, and I am determined to be worthy of that trust!

Looking back at the history of this case, two questions arise:

How could it have happened—who is to blame?

Political commentators have correctly observed that during my 27 years in politics, I've always previously insisted on running my own campaigns for office.

In both domestic and foreign policy, 1972 was a year of crucially important decisions, of intense negotiations, of vital new directions, particularly in working toward the goal which has been my overriding concern throughout my political career—the goal of bringing peace to America, peace to the world.

And that is why I decided as the 1972 campaign approached that the Presidency should come first and politics second. To the maximum extent possible, therefore, I sought to delegate campaign operations, to remove the day-to-day campaign decisions from the President's office and from the White House.

I also, as you recall, severely limited the number of my own campaign appearances.

Who then is to blame for what happened in this case?

For specific criminal actions by specific individuals, those who committed those actions must of course bear the liability and pay the penalty. For the fact that alleged improper actions took place within the White House or within my campaign organization, the easiest course would be for me to blame those to whom I delegated the responsibility to run the campaign. But that would be a cowardly thing to do.

I will not place the blame on subordinates, on people whose zeal exceeded their judgment and who may have done wrong in a cause they deeply believed to be right. In any organization the man at the top must bear the responsibility.

That responsibility, therefore, belongs here in this office. I accept it.

And I pledge to you tonight from this office that I will do everything in my power to insure that the guilty are brought to justice and that such abuses are purged from our political processes in the years to come long after I have left this office.

Some people, quite properly appalled at the abuses that occurred, will say that Watergate demonstrates the bankruptcy of the American political system. I believe precisely the opposite is true.

Watergate represented a series of illegal acts and bad judgments by a number of individuals. It was the system that has brought the facts to light and that will bring those guilty to justice.

A system that in this case has included a determined grand jury, honest prosecutors, a courageous judge—John Sirica—and a vigorous free press.

It is essential now that we place our faith in that system, and especially in the judicial system.

It is essential that we let the judicial process go forward, respecting those safeguards that are established to protect the innocent as well as to convict the guilty.

It is essential that in reacting to the excesses of others, we not fall into excesses ourselves.

It is also essential that we not be so distracted by events such as this that we neglect the vital work before us, before this nation, before America, at a time of critical importance to America and the world.

Since March, when I first learned that the Watergate affair might in fact be far more serious than I had been led to believe, it has claimed far too much of my time and my attention. Whatever may now transpire in the case, whatever the actions of the grand jury, whatever the outcome of any eventual trials, I must now turn my full attention—and I shall do so—once again to the larger duties of this office.

I owe it to this great office that I hold, and I owe it to you, to my country.

I know that, as Attorney General, Elliot Richardson will be both fair and he will be fearless in pursuing this case wherever it leads. I am confident that with him in charge justice will be done.

There is vital work to be done toward our goal of a lasting structure of peace in the world—work that cannot wait, work that I must do.

Tomorrow, for example, Chancellor Brandt of West Germany will visit the White House for talks that are a vital element of the Year of Europe, as 1973 has been called.

We are already preparing for the next Soviet-American summit meeting later this year.

This is also a year in which we are seeking to negotiate a mutual and balanced reduction of armed forces in Europe which will reduce our defense budget and allow us to have funds for other purposes at home so desperately needed.

It is the year when the United States and Soviet negotiators will seek to work out the second and even more important round of our talks on limiting nuclear arms, and of reducing the danger of a nuclear war that would destroy civilization as we know it.

It is a year in which we confront the difficult tasks of maintaining peace in Southeast Asia and in the potentially explosive Middle East.

There's also vital work to be done right here in America to insure prosperity—and that means a good job for everyone who wants to work; to control inflation that I know worries every housewife, everyone who tries to balance the family budget in America, to set in motion new and better ways of insuring progress toward a better life for all Americans.

When I think of this office, of what it means, I think of all the things that I want to accomplish for this nation, of all the things I want to accomplish for you.

On Christmas Eve, during my terrible personal ordeal of the renewed bombing of North Vietnam which, after 12 years of war, finally helped to bring America peace with honor, I sat down just before midnight. I wrote out some of my goals for my second term as President. Let me read them to you.

To make this country be more than ever a land of opportunity —of equal opportunity, full opportunity—for every American; to provide jobs for all who can work and generous help for those who cannot; to establish a climate of decency and civility in which each person respects the feelings and the dignity in the God-given rights of his neighbor; to make this a land in which each person can dare to dream, can live his dreams not in fear but in hope, proud of his community, proud of his country, proud of what America has meant to himself, and to the world.

These are great goals. I believe we can, we must work for them, we can achieve them.

But we cannot achieve these goals unless we dedicate ourselves to another goal. We must maintain the integrity of the White House.

And that integrity must be real, not transparent.

There can be no whitewash at the White House.

We must reform our political process, ridding it not only of the violations of the law but also of the ugly mob violence and other inexcusable campaign tactics that have been too often practiced and too readily accepted in the past, including those that may have been a response by one side to the excesses or expected excesses of the other side.

Two wrongs do not make a right.

I've been in public life for more than a quarter of a century. Like any other calling, politics has good people and bad people and let me tell you the great majority in politics, in the Congress, in the Federal Government, in the state government are good people.

I know that it can be very easy under the intensive pressures of a campaign for even well-intentioned people to fall into shady tactics, to rationalize this on the grounds that what is at stake is of such importance to the nation that the end justifies the means.

And both of our great parties have been guilty of such tactics.

In recent years, however, the campaign excesses that have occurred on all sides have provided a sobering demonstration of how far this false doctrine can take us.

The lesson is clear. America in its political campaigns must not again fall into the trap of letting the end, however great that end is, justify the means.

I urge the leaders of both political parties, I urge citizens—all of you everywhere—to join in working toward a new set of standards, new rules and procedures to insure that future elections will be as nearly free of such abuses as they possibly can be made. This is my goal. I ask you to join in making it America's goal.

When I was inaugurated for a second term this past Jan 20, I gave each member of my Cabinet and each member of my senior White House staff a special four-year calendar with each day marked to show the number of days remaining to the Administration.

In the inscription on each calendar I wrote these words:

"The Presidential term which begins today consists of 1,461 days, no more, no less. Each can be a day of strengthening and renewal for America. Each can add depth and dimension to the American experience.

"If we strive together, if we make the most of the challenge and the opportunity that these days offer us, they can stand out as great days for America and great moments in the history of the world."

I looked at my own calendar this morning up at Camp David as I was working on this speech. It showed exactly 1,361 days remaining in my term.

I want these to be the best days in America's history because I love America. I deeply believe that America is the hope of the world, and I know that in the quality and wisdom of the leadership America gives lies the only hope for millions of people all over the world that they can live their lives in peace and freedom.

We must be worthy of that hope in every sense of the word.

Tonight, I ask for your prayers to help me in everything that I do throughout the days of my Presidency to be worthy of their hopes and of yours.

God bless America. And God bless each and every one of you.

Statement

May 22, 1973

Allegations surrounding the Watergate affair have so escalated that I feel a further statement from the President is required at this time.

A climate of sensationalism has developed in which even second- or third-hand hearsay charges are headlined as fact and repeated as fact.

Important national security operations which themselves had no connection with Watergate have become entangled in the case.

As a result, some national security information has already been made public through court orders, through the subpoenaing of documents and through testimony witnesses have given in judicial and Congressional proceedings. Other sensitive documents are now threatened with disclosure; continued silence about those operations would compromise rather than protect them, and would also serve to perpetuate a grossly distorted view—which recent partial disclosures have given—of the nature and purpose of those operations.

The purpose of this statement is threefold:

—First, to set forth the facts about my own relationship to the Watergate matter.

—Second, to place in some perspective some of the more sensational—and inaccurate—of the charges that have filled the headlines in recent days, and also some of the matters that are currently being discussed in Senate testimony and elsewhere.

—Third, to draw the distinction between national security operations and the Watergate case. To put the other matters in perspective, it will be necessary to describe the national security operations first.

In citing these national security matters it is not my intention to place a national security "cover" on Watergate, but rather to separate them out from Watergate—and at the same time to explain the context in which certain actions took place that were later misconstrued or misused.

Long before the Watergate break-in, three important national security operations took place which have subsequently become entangled in the Watergate case.

—The first operation, begun in 1969, was a program of wiretaps. All were legal, under the authorities then existing. They were undertaken to find and stop serious national security leaks.

—The second operation was a reassessment, which I ordered in 1970, of the adequacy of internal security measures. This resulted in a plan and a directive to strengthen our intelligence operations. They were protested by Mr. Hoover, and as a result of his protest they were not put into effect.

—The third operation was the establishment, in 1971, of a special investigations unit in the White House. Its primary mission was to plug leaks of vital security information. I also directed this group to prepare an accurate history of certain crucial national security matters which occurred under prior Administrations, on which the Government's records were incomplete.

Here is the background of these three security operations initiated by my Administration.

By mid-1969, my Administration had begun a number of highly sensitive foreign policy initiatives. They were aimed at ending the war in Vietnam, achieving a settlement in the Middle East, limiting nuclear arms, and establishing new relationships among the great powers. These involved highly secret diplomacy. They were closely interrelated. Leaks of secret information about any one could endanger all.

Exactly that happened. News accounts appeared in 1969, which were obviously based on leaks—some of them extensive and detailed—by people having access to the most highly classified security materials.

There was no way to carry forward these diplomatic initiatives unless further leaks could be prevented. This required finding the source of the leaks.

In order to do this, a special program of wiretaps was instituted in mid-1969 and terminated in February, 1971. Fewer than 20 taps, of varying duration, were involved. They produced important leads that made it possible to tighten the security of highly sensitive materials.

I authorized this entire program. Each individual tap was undertaken in accordance with procedures legal at the time and in accord with long-standing precedent.

The persons who were subject to these wiretaps were determined through coordination among the Director of the F.B.I., my assistant for national security affairs, and the Attorney General. Those wiretapped were selected on the basis of access to the information leaked, material in security files, and evidence that developed as the inquiry proceeded.

Information thus obtained was made available to senior officials responsible for national security matters in order to curtail further leaks.

1970 Intelligence Plan

In the spring and summer of 1970, another security problem reached critical proportions. In March a wave of bombings and explosions struck college campuses and cities. There were 400 bomb threats in one 24-hour period in New York City. Rioting and violence on college campuses reached a new peak after the

Cambodian operation and the tragedies at Kent State and Jackson State. The 1969-70 school year brought nearly 1,800 campus demonstrations, and nearly 250 cases of arson on campus. Many colleges closed. Gun battles between guerrilla-style groups and police were taking place. Some of the disruptive activities were receiving foreign support.

Complicating the task of maintaining security was the fact that, in 1966, certain types of undercover F.B.I. operations that had been conducted for many years had been suspended. This also had substantially impaired our ability to collect foreign intelligence information. At the same time, the relationships between the F.B.I. and other intelligence agencies had been deteriorating. By May, 1970, F.B.I. Director Hoover shut off his agency's liaison with the C.I.A altogether.

On June 5, 1970, I met with the director of the F.B.I. (Mr. Hoover), the Director of the Central Intelligence Agency (Mr. Richard Helms), the Director of the Defense Intelligence Agency (General Donald V. Bennett) and the Director of the National Security Agency (Admiral Noel Gayler). We discussed the urgent need for better intelligence operations. I appointed Director Hoover as chairman of an interagency committee to prepare recommendations.

On June 25, the committee submitted a report which included specific options for expanded intelligence operations, and on July 23 the agencies were notified by memorandum of the options approved. After reconsideration, however, prompted by the opposition of Director Hoover, the agencies were notified five days later, on July 28, that the approval had been rescinded. The options initially approved had included resumption of certain intelligence operations which had been suspended in 1966. These in turn had included authorization for surreptitious entry—breaking and entering, in effect—on specified categories of targets in specified situations related to national security.

Because the approval was withdrawn before it had been implemented, the net result was that the plan for expanded intelligence activities never went into effect.

The documents spelling out this 1970 plan are extremely sensitive. They include—and are based upon—assessments of certain foreign intelligence capabilities and procedures, which of course must remain secret. It was this unused plan and related documents that John Dean removed from the White House and placed in a safe deposit box, giving the keys to Judge Sirica. The same plan, still unused, is being headlined today.

Coordination among our intelligence agencies continued to fall short of our national security needs. In July, 1970, having earlier discontinued the F.B.I.'s liaison with the C.I.A., Director Hoover ended the F.B.I's normal liaison with all other agencies except the White House. To help remedy this, an Intelligence Evaluation Committee was created in December, 1970. Its members included representatives of the White House, C.I.A., F.B.I., N.S.A, the Departments of Justice, Treasury, and Defense, and the Secret Service.

The Intelligence Evaluation Committee and its staff were instructed to improve coordination among the intelligence community and to prepare evaluations and estimates of domestic intelligence. I understand that its activities are now under investigation. I did not authorize nor do I have any knowledge of any illegal activity by this committee. If it went beyond its charter and did engage in any illegal activities, it was totally without my knowledge or authority.

The Special Investigations Unit

On Sunday, June 13, 1971, The New York Times published the first installment of what came to be known as "the Pentagon Papers." Not until a few hours before publication did any responsible Government official know that they had been stolen. Most officials did not know they existed. No senior official of the Government had read them or knew with certainty what they contained.

All the Government knew, at first, was that the papers comprised 47 volumes and some 7,000 pages, which had been taken from the most sensitive files of the Departments of State and Defense and the C.I.A., covering military and diplomatic moves in a war that was still going on.

Moreover, a majority of the documents published with the first three installments in The Times had not been included in the 47-volume study—raising serious questions about what and how much else might have been taken.

There was every reason to believe this was a security leak of unprecedented proportions.

It created a situation in which the ability of the Government to carry on foreign relations even in the best of circumstances could have been severely compromised. Other governments no longer knew whether they could deal with the United States in confidence. Against the background of the delicate negotiations the United States was then involved in on a number of fronts —with regard to Vietnam, China, the Middle East, nuclear arms limitations, U.S.-Soviet relations, and others—in which the utmost degree of confidentiality was vital, it posed a threat so grave as to require extraordinary actions.

Therefore during the week following the Pentagon Papers, publication, I approved the creation of a special investigations unit within the White House—which later came to be known as the "plumbers." This was a small group at the White House whose principal purpose was to stop security leaks and to investigate other sensitive security matters. I looked to John Ehrlichman for the supervision of this group.

Egil Krogh, Mr. Ehrlichman's assistant, was put in charge. David Young was added to this unit, as were E. Howard Hunt and G. Gordon Liddy.

The unit operated under extremely tight security rules. Its existence and functions were known only to a very few persons at the White House. These included Messrs. Haldeman, Ehrlichman and Dean.

At about the time the unit was created, Daniel Ellsberg was identified as the person who had given the Pentagon Papers to The New York Times. I told Mr. Krogh that as a matter of first priority, the unit should find out all it could about Mr. Ellsberg's associates and his motives. Because of the extreme gravity of the situation, and not then knowing what additional national secrets Mr. Ellsberg might disclose, I did impress upon Mr. Krogh the vital importance to the national security of his assignment. I did not authorize and had no knowledge of any illegal means to be used to achieve this goal.

However, because of the emphasis I put on the crucial importance of protecting the national security, I can understand how highly motivated individuals could have felt justified in engaging in specific activities that I would have disapproved had they been brought to my attention.

Consequently, as President, I must and do assume responsibility for such actions despite the fact that I at no time approved or had knowledge of them.

I also assigned the unit a number of other investigatory matters, dealing in part with compiling an accurate record of events related to the Vietnam war, on which the Government's records were inadequate (many previous records having been removed with the change of Administrations) and which bore directly on the negotiations then in progress. Additional assignments included tracing down other national security leaks, including one that seriously compromised the United States, negotiating position in the SALT talks.

The work of the unit tapered off around the end of 1971. The nature of its work was such that it involved matters that, from a national security standpoint, were highly sensitive then and remain so today.

These intelligence activities had no connection with the break-in of the Democratic headquarters, or the aftermath.

I considered it my responsibility to see that the Watergate investigation did not impinge adversely upon the national security area. For example, on April 18, 1973, when I learned that Mr. Hunt, a former member of the special investigations unit at the White House, was to be questioned by the U.S. attorney, I directed Assistant Attorney General Petersen to pursue every issue involving Watergate but to confine his investigation to Watergate and related matters and to stay out of national security matters. Subsequently, on April 25, 1973, Attorney General Kleindienst informed me that because the Government had clear evidence that Mr. Hunt was involved in the break-in of the office of the psychiatrist who had treated Mr. Ellsberg, he, the Attorney General, believed that, despite the fact that no evidence had been obtained from Hunt's acts, a report should nevertheless be made to the court trying the Ellsberg case. I concurred, and directed that the information be transmitted to Judge Byrne immediately.

Watergate

The burglary and bugging of the Democratic National Committee headquarters came as a complete surprise to me. I had no inkling that any such illegal activities had been planned by persons associated with my campaign; if I had known, I would not have permitted it. My immediate reaction was that those guilty should be brought to justice and, with the five burglars themselves already in custody, I assumed that they would be.

Within a few days, however, I was advised that there was a possibility of C.I.A. involvement in some way.

It did seem to me possible that, because of the involvement of former C.I.A. personnel, and because of some of their apparent associations, the investigation could lead to the uncovering of covert C.I.A. operations totally unrelated to the Watergate break-in.

In addition, by this time, the name of Mr. Hunt had surfaced in connection with Watergate, and I was alerted to the fact that he had previously been a member of the special investigations unit in the White House. Therefore, I was also concerned that the Watergate investigation might well lead to an inquiry into the activities of the special investigations unit itself.

In this area, I felt it was important to avoid disclosure of the details of the national security matters with which the group was concerned. I knew that once the existence of the group became known, it would lead inexorably to a discussion of these matters, some of which remain, even today, highly sensitive.

I wanted justice done with regard to Watergate; but in the scale of national priorities with which I had to deal—and not at that time having any idea of the extent of political abuse which Watergate reflected—I also had to be deeply concerned with insuring that neither the covert operations of the C.I.A. nor the operations of the special investigations unit should be compromised. Therefore, I instructed Mr. Haldeman and Mr. Ehrlichman to insure that the investigation of the break-in not expose either an unrelated covert operation of the C.I.A. or the activities of the White House investigations unit—and to see that this was personally coordinated between General Walters, the Deputy Director of the C.I.A., and Mr. Gray of the F.B.I. It was certainly not my intent, nor my wish, that the investigation of the Watergate break-in or of related acts be impeded in any way.

On July 6, 1972, I telephoned the acting Director of the F.B.I., L. Patrick Gray, to congratulate him on his successful handling of the hijacking of a Pacific Southwest Airlines plane the previous day. During the conversation Mr. Gray discussed with me the progress of the Watergate investigation, and I asked him whether he had talked with General Walters. Mr. Gray said that he had, and that General Walters had assured him that the C.I.A. was not involved. In the discussion, Mr. Gray suggested that the matter of Watergate might lead higher. I told him to press ahead with his investigation.

It now seems that later, through whatever complex of individual motives and possible misunderstandings, there were apparently wide-ranging efforts to limit the investigation or to conceal the possible involvement of members of the Administration and the campaign committee.

I was not aware of any such efforts at the time. Neither, until after I began my own investigation, was I aware of any fund raising for defendants convicted at the break-in at Democratic headquarters, much less authorize any such fund raising. Nor did I authorize any offer of executive clemency for any of the defendants.

In the weeks and months that followed Watergate, I asked for, and received, repeated assurances that Mr. Dean's own investigation (which included reviewing files and sitting in on F.B.I. interviews with White House personnel) had cleared everyone then employed by the White House of involvement.

In summary, then:

(1) I had no prior knowledge of the Watergate bugging operation, or of any illegal surveillance activities for political purposes.

(2) Long prior to the 1972 campaign, I did set in motion certain internal security measures, including legal wiretaps, which I felt were necessary from a national security standpoint and, in the climate then prevailing, also necessary from a domestic security standpoint.

(3) People who had been involved in the national security operations later, without my knowledge or approval, undertook illegal activities in the political campaign of 1972.

(4) Elements of the early post-Watergate reports led me to suspect, incorrectly, that the C.I.A. had been in some way involved. They also led me to surmise, correctly, that since persons originally recruited for covert national security activities had partipated in Watergate, an unrestricted investigation of Watergate might lead to and expose those covert national security operations.

(5) I sought to prevent the exposure of these covert national security activities, while encouraging those conducting the investigation to pursue their inquiry into the Watergate itself. I so instructed my staff, the Attorney General and the acting Director of the F.B.I.

(6) I also specifically instructed Mr. Haldeman and Mr. Ehr-

lichman to insure that the F.B.I. would not carry its investigation into areas that might compromise these covert national security activities or those of the C.I.A.

(7) At no time did I authorize or know about any offer of executive clemency for the Watergate defendants. Neither did I know, until the time of my own investigation, of any efforts to provide them with funds.

Conclusion

With hindsight, it is apparent that I should have given more heed to the warning signals I received along the way about a Watergate cover-up and less to the reassurances.

With hindsight, several other things also become clear:

—With respect to campaign practices, and also with respect to campaign finances, it should now be obvious that no campaign in history has ever been subjected to the kind of intensive and searching inquiry that has been focused on the campaign waged in my behalf in 1972.

It is clear that unethical, as well as illegal, activities took place in the course of that campaign.

None of these took place with my specific approval or knowledge. To the extent that I may in any way have contributed to the climate in which they took place, I did not intend to; to the extent that I failed to prevent them, I should have been more vigilant.

It was to help insure against any repetition of this in the future that last week I proposed the establishment of a top-level, bipartisan, independent commission to recommend a comprehensive reform of campaign laws and practices. Given the priority I believe it deserves, such reform should be possible before the next Congressional elections in 1974.

It now appears that there were persons who may have gone beyond my directives, and sought to expand on my efforts to protect the national security operations in order to cover up any involvement they or certain others might have had in Watergate. The extent to which this is true, and who may have participated and to what degree, are questions that it would not be proper to address here. The proper forum for settling these matters is in the courts.

To the extent that I have been able to determine what probably happened in the tangled course of this affair, on the basis of my own recollections and of the conflicting accounts and evidence that I have seen, it would appear that one factor at work was that at critical points various people, each with his own perspective and his own responsibilities, saw the same situation with different eyes and heard the same words with different ears. What might have seemed insignificant to one seemed significant to another; what one saw in terms of public responsibility, another saw in terms of political opportunity; and mixed through it all, I am sure, was a concern on the part of many that the Watergate scandal should not be allowed to get in the way of what the Administration sought to achieve.

The truth about Watergate should be brought out in an orderly way, recognizing that the safeguards of judicial procedure are designed to find the truth, not to hide the truth.

With his selection of Archibald Cox—who served both President Kennedy and President Johnson as Solicitor General—as the special supervisory prosecutor for matters related to the case, Attorney General-designate Richardson has demonstrated his own determination to see the truth brought out. In this effort he has my full support.

Considering the number of persons involved in this case whose testimony might be subject to a claim of executive privilege, I recognize that a clear definition of that claim has become central to the effort to arrive at the truth.

Accordingly, executive privilege will not be invoked as to any testimony concerning possible criminal conduct or discussions of possible criminal conduct in the matters presently under investigation, including the Watergate affair and the alleged cover-up.

I want to emphasize that this statement is limited to my own recollections of what I said and did relating to security and to the Watergate. I have specifically avoided any attempt to explain what other parties may have said and done. My own information on those other matters is fragmentary, and to some extent contradictory. Additional information may be forthcoming of which I am unaware. It is also my understanding that the information which has been conveyed to me has also become available to those prosecuting these matters. Under such circumstances, it would be prejudicial and unfair of me to render my opinions on the activities of others; those judgments must be left to the judicial process, our best hope for achieving the just result that we all seek.

As more information is developed, I have no doubt that more questions will be raised. To the extent that I am able, I shall also seek to set forth the facts as known to me with respect to those questions.

Broadcast Address

Aug. 15, 1973

Good evening.

Now that most of the major witnesses in the Watergate phase of the Senate committee hearings on campaign practices have been heard, the time has come for me to speak out about the charges made and to provide a perspective on the issue for the American people.

For over four months Watergate has dominated the news media. During the past three months the three major networks have devoted an average of over 22 hours of television time each week to this subject. The Senate committee has heard over 2 million words of testimony.

This investigation began as an effort to discover the facts about the break-in and bugging at the Democratic national headquarters and other campaign abuses.

But, as the weeks have gone by, it has become clear that both the hearings themselves and some of the commentaries on them have become increasingly absorbed in an effort to implicate the President personally in the illegal activities that took place.

Because the abuses occurred during my Administration and in the campaign for my re-election, I accept full responsibility for them. I regret that these events took place. And I do not question the right of a Senate committee to investigate charges made against the President to the extent that this is relevant to legislative duties.

However, it is my constitutional responsibility to defend the integrity of this great office against false charges. I also believe that it is important to address the overriding question of what we as a nation can learn from this experience, and what we should now do. I intend to discuss both of these subjects tonight.

The record of the Senate hearings is lengthy. The facts are complicated, the evidence conflicting. It would not be right for me to try to sort out the evidence, to rebut specific witnesses, or to pronounce my own judgments about their credibility. That is for the committee and for the courts.

I shall not attempt to deal tonight with the various charges in detail. Rather, I shall attempt to put the events in perspective from the standpoint of the Presidency.

On May 22, before the major witnesses had testified, I issued a detailed statement addressing the charges that had been made against the President.

I have today issued another written statement, which addresses the charges that have been made since then as they relate to my own conduct, and which describes the efforts that I made to discover the facts about the matter.

On May 22, I stated in very specific terms—and I state again to every one of you listening tonight—these facts: I had no prior knowledge of the Watergate break-in; I neither took part in nor knew about any of the subsequent cover-up activities; I neither authorized nor encouraged subordinates to engage in illegal or improper campaign tactics.

That was and that is the simple truth.

In all of the millions of words of testimony, there is not the slightest suggestion that I had any knowledge of the planning for the Watergate break-in. As for the cover-up, my statement has been challenged by only one of the 35 witnesses who appeared—a witness who offered no evidence beyond his own impressions, and whose testimony has been contradicted by every other witness in a position to know the facts.

Tonight, let me explain to you what I did about Watergate after the break-in occurred, so that you can better understand the fact that I also had no knowledge of the so-called cover-up.

From the time when the break-in occurred, I pressed repeatedly to know the facts, and particularly whether there was any involvement of anyone at the White House. I considered two things essential:

First, that the investigation should be thorough and aboveboard; and second, that if there were any higher involvement, we should get the facts out first. As I said at my Aug. 29 press conference last year, "What really hurts in matters of this sort is not the fact that they occur, because overzealous people in campaigns do things that are wrong. What really hurts is if you try to cover it up." I believed that then, and certainly the experience of this last year has proved that to be true.

I knew that the Justice Department and the F.B.I. were conducting intensive investigations—as I had insisted that they should. The White House counsel, John Dean, was assigned to monitor those investigations, and particularly to check into any possible White House involvement. Throughout the summer of 1972, I continued to press the question, and I continued to get the same answer: I was told again and again that there was no indication that any persons were involved other than the seven who were known to have planned and carried out the operation, and who were subsequently indicted and convicted.

On Sept. 12 at a meeting that I held with the Cabinet, the senior White House staff and a number of legislative leaders, Attorney General Kleindienst reported on the investigation. He told us it had been the most extensive investigation since the assassination of President Kennedy, and that it had established that only those seven were involved.

On Sept. 15, the day the seven were indicted, I met with John Dean, the White House counsel. He gave me no reason whatever to believe that any others were guilty; I assumed that the indictments of only the seven by the grand jury confirmed the reports he had been giving to that effect throughout the summer.

On Feb. 16, I met with Acting Director Gray prior to submitting his name to the Senate for confirmation as permanent director of the F.B.I. I stressed to him that he would be questioned closely about the F.B.I.'s conduct of the Watergate investigation. I asked him if he still had full confidence in it. He replied that he did; that he was proud of its thoroughness and that he could defend it with enthusiasm before the committee.

Because I trusted the agencies conducting the investigations, because I believed the reports I was getting, I did not believe the newspaper accounts that suggested a cover-up. I was convinced there was no cover-up, because I was convinced that no one had anything to cover up.

It was not until March 21 of this year that I received new information from the White House counsel that led me to conclude that the reports I had been getting for over nine months were not true. On that day, I launched an intensive effort of my own to get the facts and to get the facts out. Whatever the facts might be, I wanted the White House to be the first to make them public.

At first I entrusted the task of getting me the facts to Mr. Dean. When, after spending a week at Camp David, he failed to produce the written report I had asked for, I turned to John Ehrlichman and to the Attorney General—while also making independent inquiries of my own. By mid-April I had received Mr. Ehrlichman's report, and also one from the Attorney General based on new information uncovered by the Justice Department.

These reports made it clear to me that the situation was far more serious than I had imagined. It at once became evident to me that the responsibility for the investigation in the case should be given to the Criminal Division of the Justice Department. I turned over all the information I had to the head of that department, Assistant Attorney General Henry Petersen, a career Government employe with an impeccable nonpartisan record, and I instructed him to pursue the matter thoroughly. I ordered all members of the Administration to testify fully before the grand jury.

And with my concurrence, on May 18 Attorney General Richardson appointed a special prosecutor to handle the matter, and the case is now before the grand jury.

Far from trying to hide the facts, my effort throughout has been to discover the facts—and to lay those facts before the appropriate law-enforcement authorities so that justice could be done and the guilty dealt with.

I relied on the best law-enforcement agencies in the country to find and report the truth. I believed they had done so—just as they believed they had done so.

Many have urged that in order to help prove the truth of what I have said, I should turn over to the special prosecutor and the Senate committee recordings of conversations that I held in my office or on my telephone.

However, a much more important principle is involved in this question than what the tapes might prove about Watergate.

Each day a President of the United States is required to make difficult decisions on grave issues. It is absolutely necessary, if the President is to be able to do his job as the country expects, that he be able to talk openly and candidly with his advisers about issues and individuals. This kind of frank discussion is only possible when those who take part in it know that what they say is in strictest confidence.

The Presidency is not the only office that requires confidentiality. A member of Congress must be able to talk in confidence with his assistants. Judges must be able to confer in confidence with their law clerks and with each other. For very good reasons, no branch of Government has ever compelled disclosure of confidential conversations between officers of other branches of Government and their advisers about Government business.

This need for confidence is not confined to Government officials. The law has long recognized that there are kinds of conversations that are entitled to be kept confidential, even at the cost of doing without critical evidence in a legal proceeding. This rule applies, for example, to conversations between a lawyer and a client, between a priest and a penitent, and between a husband and a wife. In each case it is thought so important that the parties be able to talk freely to each other that for hundreds of years the law has said that these conversations are "privileged" and that their disclosure cannot be compelled in a court.

It is even more important that the confidentiality of conversations between a President and his advisers be protected. This is no mere luxury, to be dispensed with whenever a particular issue raises sufficient uproar. It is absolutely essential to the conduct of the Presidency, in this and in all future Administrations.

If I were to make public these tapes, containing as they do blunt and candid remarks on many different subjects, the confidentiality of the office of the President would always be suspect from now on. It would make no difference whether it was to serve the interests of a court, of a Senate committee or the President himself—the same damage would be done to the principle, and that damage would be irreparable. Persons talking with the President would never again be sure that recordings or notes of what they said would not suddenly be made public. No one would want to advance tentative ideas that might later seem unsound. No diplomat would want to speak candidly in those sensitive negotiations which could bring peace or avoid war. No Senator or Congressman would want to talk frankly about the Congressional horse-trading that might get a vital bill passed. No one would want to speak bluntly about public figures, here and abroad.

That is why I shall continue to oppose efforts which would set a precedent that would cripple all future Presidents by inhibiting conversations between them and those they look to for advice. This principle of confidentiality of Presidential conversations is at stake in the question of these tapes. I must, and I shall, oppose any efforts to destroy this principle, which is so vital to the conduct of this great office.

Turning now to the basic issues which have been raised by Watergate, I recognize that merely answering the charges that have been made against the President is not enough. The word "Watergate" has come to represent a much broader set of concerns.

To most of us, "Watergate" has come to mean not just a burglary and bugging of party headquarters, but a whole series of acts that either represent or appear to represent an abuse of trust. It has come to stand for excessive partisanship, for "enemy lists," for efforts to use the great institutions of Government for partisan political purposes.

For many Americans, the term "Watergate" also has come to include a number of national security matters that have been brought into the investigation, such as those involved in my efforts to stop massive leaks of vital diplomatic and military secrets, and to counter the wave of bombings and burnings and other violent assaults of just a few years ago.

Let me speak first of the political abuses.

I know from long experience that a political campaign is always a hard and a tough contest. A candidate for high office has an obligation to his party, to his supporters, and to the cause he represents. He must always put forth his best efforts to win. But he also has an obligation to the country to conduct that contest within the law and within the limits of decency.

No political campaign ever justifies obstructing justice, or harassing individuals, or compromising those great agencies of Government that should and must be above politics. To the extent that these things were done in the 1972 campaign, they were serious abuses. And I deplore them.

Practices of that kind do not represent what I believe Government should be, or what I believe politics should be. In a free society, the institutions of Government belong to the people. They must never be used against the people.

And in the future, my Administration will be more vigilant in insuring that such abuses do not take place, and that officials at every level understand that they are not to take place.

And I reject the cynical view that politics is inevitably or even usually a dirty business. Let us not allow what a few overzealous people did in Watergate to tar the reputation of the millions of dedicated Americans of both parties who fought hard but clean for the candidates of their choice in 1972. By their unselfish efforts, these people make our system work and they keep America free.

I pledge to you tonight that I will do all that I can to insure that one of the results of Watergate is a new level of political decency and integrity in America—in which what has been wrong in our politics no longer corrupts or demeans what is right in our politics.

Let me turn now to the difficult questions that arise in protecting the national security.

It is important to recognize that these are difficult questions and that reasonable and patriotic men and women may differ on how they should be answered.

Only last year, the Supreme Court said that implicit in the President's constitutional duty is "the power to protect our Government against those who would subvert or overthrow it by unlawful means." How to carry out this duty is often a delicate question to which there is no easy answer.

For example, every President since World War II has believed that in internal security matters the President has the power to authorize wiretaps without first obtaining a search warrant.

An act of Congress in 1968 had seemed to recognize such power. Last year the Supreme Court held to the contrary. And my Administration is of course now complying with that Supreme Court decision. But until the Supreme Court spoke, I had been acting, as did my predecessors—President Truman, President Eisenhower, President Kennedy, President Johnson—in a reasonable belief that in certain circumstances the Constitution permitted and sometimes even required such measures to protect the national security in the public interest.

Although it is the President's duty to protect the security of the country, we of course must be extremely careful in the way we go about this—for if we lose our liberties we will have little use for security. Instances have now come to light in which a zeal for security did go too far and did interfere impermissibly with individual liberty.

It is essential that such mistakes not be repeated. But it is also essential that we do not overract to particular mistakes by tying the President's hands in a way that would risk sacrificing our security, and with it all our liberties.

I shall continue to meet my constitutional responsibility to protect the security of this nation so that Americans may enjoy their freedom. But I shall and can do so by constitutional means, in ways that will not threaten that freedom.

As we look at Watergate in a longer perspective, we can see that its abuses resulted from the assumption by those involved that their cause placed them beyond the reach of those rules that apply to other persons and that hold a free society together.

That attitude can never be tolerated in our country. However, it did not suddenly develop in the year 1972. It became fashionable in the 1960s, as individuals and groups increasingly asserted the right to take the law into their own hands, insisting that their purposes represented a higher morality. Then, their attitude was praised in the press and even from some of our pulpits as evidence of a new idealism. Those of us who insisted on the old restraints, who warned of the overriding importance of operating within the law and by the rules, were accused of being reactionaries.

That same attitude brought a rising spiral of violence and fear, of riots and arson and bombings, all in the name of peace and in the name of justice. Political discussion turned into savage debate. Free speech was brutally supressed as hecklers shouted down or even physically assaulted those with whom they disagreed. Serious people raised serious questions about whether we could survive as a free democracy.

The notion that the end justifies the means proved contagious. Thus it is not surprising, even though it is deplorable, that some persons in 1972 adopted the morality that they themselves had rightly condemned and committed acts that have no place in our political system.

Those acts cannot be defended. Those who were guilty of abuses must be punished. But ultimately the answer does not lie merely in the jailing of a few overzealous persons who mistakenly thought their cause justfied their violations of the law.

Rather, it lies in a commitment by all of us to show a renewed respect for the mutual restraints that are the mark of a free and civilized society. It requires that we learn once again to work together, if not united in all of our purposes, then at least united in respect for the system by which our conflicts are peacefully resolved and our liberties maintained.

If there are laws we disagree with, let us work to change them—but let us obey them until they are changed. If we have disagreements over Government policies, let us work those out in a decent and civilized way, within the law, and with respect for our differences.

We must recognize that one excess begets another, and that the extremes of violence and discord in the 1960s contributed to the extremes of Watergate.

Both are wrong. Both should be condemned. No individual, no group and no political party has a corner on the market on morality in America.

If we learn the important lessons of Watergate, if we do what is necessary to prevent such abuses in the future—on both sides—we can emerge from this experience a better and a stronger nation.

Let me turn now to an issue that is important above all else, and that is critically affecting your life today and will affect your life and your children's in the years to come.

After 12 weeks and 2 million words of televised testimony, we have reached a point at which a continued, backward-looking obsession with Watergate is causing this nation to neglect matters of far greater importance to all of the American people.

We must not stay so mired in Watergate that we fail to respond to challenges of surpassing importance to America and the world. We cannot let an obsession with the past destroy our hopes for the future.

Legislation vital to your health and well-being sits unattended on the Congressional calendar. Confidence at home and abroad in our economy, our currency and our foreign policy is being sapped by uncertainty. Critical negotiations are taking place on strategic weapons, on troop levels in Europe that can affect the security of this nation and the peace of the world long after Watergate is forgotten. Vital events are taking place in Southeast Asia which could lead to a tragedy for the cause of peace.

These are matters that cannot wait. They cry out for action now. And either we, your elected representatives here in Washington, ought to get on with the jobs that need to be done—for you—or every one of you ought to be demanding to know why.

The time has come to turn Watergate over to the courts, where the questions of guilt or innocence belong. The time has come for the rest of us to get on with the urgent business of our nation.

Last November, the American people were given the clearest choice of this century. Your votes were a mandate, which I accepted, to complete the initiatives we began in my first term and to fulfill the promises I made for my second term.

This Administration was elected to control inflation, to reduce the power and size of Government, to cut the cost of Government so that you can cut the cost of living, to preserve and defend those fundamental values that have made America great, to keep the nation's military strength second to none, to achieve peace with honor in Southeast Asia and to bring home our prisoners of war, and to build a new prosperity, without inflation and without war, to create a structure of peace in the world that would endure long after we are gone.

These are great goals.They are worthy of a great people. And I would not be true to your trust if I let myself be turned aside from achieving those goals.

If you share my belief in these goals—if you want the mandate you gave this Administration to be carried out—then I ask for your help to insure that those who would exploit Watergate in order to keep us from doing what we were elected to do will not succeed.

I ask tonight for your understanding, so that as a nation we can learn the lessons of Watergate, and gain from that experience.

I ask for your help in reaffirming our dedication to the principles of decency, honor and respect for the institutions that have sustained our progress through these past two centuries.

And I ask for your support, in getting on once again with meeting your problems, improving your life and building your future.

With your help, with God's help, we will achieve these great goals for America.

Thank you and good evening.

Statement

Aug. 15, 1973

On May 17 the Senate Select Committee began its hearings on Watergate. Five days later, on May 22, I issued a detailed statement discussing my relationship to the matter. I stated categorically that I had no prior knowledge of the Watergate operation and that I neither knew of nor took part in any subsequent efforts to cover it up.

I also stated that I would not invoke executive privilege as to testimony by present and former members of my White House staff with respect to possible criminal acts then under investigation.

Thirty-five witnesses have testified so far. The record is more than 7,500 pages and some 2 million words long. The allegations are many, the facts are complicated, and the evidence is not only extensive but very much in conflict.

It would be neither fair nor appropriate for me to assess the evidence or comment on specific witnesses or their credibility. That is the function of the Senate committee and the courts. What I intend to do here is to cover the principal issues relating to my own conduct which have been raised since my statement of May 22, and thereby to place the testimony on those issues in perspective.

I said on May 22 that I had no prior knowledge of the Watergate operation. In all the testimony, there is not the slightest evidence to the contrary. Not a single witness has testified that I had any knowledge of the planning for the Watergate break-in.

It is also true, as I said on May 22, that I took no part in, and was not aware of, any subsequent efforts to cover up the illegal acts associated with the Watergate break-in.

In the summer of 1972 I had given orders for the Justice Department and the F.B.I. to conduct a thorough and aggressive investigation of the Watergate break-in, and I relied on their investigation to disclose the facts. My only concern about the scope of the investigation was that it might lead into C.I.A. or other national security operations of a sensitive nature. Mr. Gray, the acting Director of the F.B.I., told me by telephone on July 6 that he had met with General Walters, that General Walters had told him the C.I.A. was not involved, and that C.I.A. activities would not be compromised by the F.B.I. investigation. As a result, any problems that Mr. Gray may have had in coordinating with the C.I.A. were moot. I concluded by instructing him to press forward vigorously with his own investigation.

During the summer of 1972, I repeatedly asked for reports on the progress of the investigation. Every report I received was that no persons, other than the seven who were subsequently indicted, were involved in the Watergate operation. On Sept. 12, at a meeting attended by me, and by the Cabinet, senior members of the White House staff and a number of legislative leaders, Attorney General Kleindienst reported on the investigation. He informed us that it had been the most intensive investigation since the assassination of President Kennedy, and that it had been established that no one at the White House, and no higher-ups in the campaign committee, were involved. His report seemed to be confirmed by the action of the grand jury on Sept. 15, when it indicted only the five persons arrested at the Watergate, plus Messrs. Liddy and Hunt.

Those indictments also seemed to me to confirm the validity of the reports that Mr. Dean had been providing to me, through other members of the White House staff—and on which I had based my Aug. 29 statement that no one then employed at the White House was involved. It was in that context that I met with Mr. Dean on Sept. 15, and he gave me no reason at that meeting to believe any others were involved.

Not only was I unaware of any cover-up, but at that time, and until March 21, I was unaware that there was anything to cover up.

Then and later, I continued to have full faith in the investigations that had been conducted and in the reports I had received based on those investigations. On Feb. 16, I met with Mr. Gray prior to submitting his name to the Senate for confirmation as permanent Director of the F.B.I. I stressed to him that he would be questioned closely about the F.B.I.'s conduct of the Watergate investigation, and asked him if he still had full confidence in it. He replied that he did; that he was proud of its thoroughness, and that he could defend it with enthusiasm.

My interest in Watergate rose in February and March as the Senate committee was organized and the hearings were held on the Gray nomination. I began meeting frequently with my counsel, Mr. Dean, in connection with those matters. At that time, on a number of occasions, I urged my staff to get all the facts out, because I was confident that full disclosure of the facts would show that persons in the White House and at the Committee for the Re-election of the President were the victims of unjustified innuendoes in the press. I was searching for a way to disclose all of the facts without disturbing the confidentiality of communications with and among my personal staff, since that confidentiality is essential to the functioning of any President.

It was on March 21 that I was given new information that indicated that the reports I had been getting were not true. I was told then for the first time that the planning of the Watergate break-in went beyond those who had been tried and convicted, and that at least one, and possibly more, persons at the re-election committee were involved.

It was on that day also that I learned of some of the activities upon which charges of cover-up are now based. I was told that funds had been raised for payments to the defendants, with the knowledge and approval of persons both on the White House staff and at the re-election committee. But I was only told that the money had been used for attorneys' fees and family support, not that it had been paid to procure silence from the recipients. I was also told that a member of my staff had talked to one of the defendants about clemency, but not that offers of clemency had been made. I was told that one of the defendants was currently attempting to blackmail the White House by demanding payment of $120,000 as the price of not talking about other activities, unrelated to Watergate, in which he had engaged. These allegations were made in general terms, they were portrayed to me as being based in part on supposition, and they were largely unsupported by details or evidence.

These allegations were very troubling, and they gave a new dimension to the Watergate matter. They also reinforced my determination that the full facts must be made available to the grand jury or to the Senate committee. If anything illegal had happened, I wanted it to be dealt with appropriately according to the law. If anyone at the White House or high up in my campaign had been involved in wrongdoing of any kind, I wanted the White House to take the lead in making that known.

When I received this distressing information on March 21, I immediately began new inquiries into the case and an examination of the best means to give to the grand jury or Senate committee what we then knew and what we might later learn. On March 21, I arranged to meet the following day with Messrs. Haldeman, Ehrlichman, Dean and Mitchell to discuss the appropriate method to get the facts out. On March 23, I sent Mr. Dean to Camp David, where he was instructed to write a complete report on all that he knew of the entire Watergate matter. On March 28, I had Mr. Ehrlichman call the Attorney General to find out if he had additional information about Watergate generally or White House involvement. The Attorney General was told that I wanted to hear directly from him, and not through any staff people, if he had any information on White House involvement or if information of that kind should come to him.

The Attorney General indicated to Mr. Ehrlichman that he had no such information. When I learned on March 30 that Mr. Dean had been unable to complete his report, I instructed Mr. Ehrlichman to conduct an independent inquiry and bring all the facts to me. On April 14, Mr. Ehrlichman gave me his findings, and I directed that he report them to the Attorney General immediately. On April 15, Attorney General Kleindienst and Assistant Attorney General Petersen told me of new information that had been received by the prosecutors.

By that time the fragmentary information I had been given on March 21 had been supplemented in important ways, particularly by Mr. Ehrlichman's report to me on April 14, by the information Mr. Kleindienst and Mr. Petersen gave me on April 15, and by independent inquiries I had been making on my own. At that point, I realized that I would not be able personally to find out all of the facts and make them public, and I concluded that the matter was best handled by the Justice Department and the grand jury. On April 17, I announced that new inquiries were under way, as a result of what I had learned on March 21 and in my own investigation since that time. I instructed all Government employes to cooperate with the judicial process as it moved ahead on this matter and expressed my personal view that no immunity should be given to any individual who had held a position of major importance in this Administration.

My consistent position from the beginning has been to get out the facts about Watergate, not to cover them up.

On May 22, I said that at no time did I authorize any offer of executive clemency for the Watergate defendants, nor did I know of any such offer. I reaffirm that statement. Indeed, I made my view clear to Mr. Ehrlichman in July, 1972, that under no circumstances could executive clemency be considered for those who participated in the Watergate break-in. I maintained that position throughout.

On May 22, I said that "it was not until the time of my own investigation that I learned of the break-in at the office of Mr. Ellsberg's psychiatrist, and I specifically authorized the furnishing of this information to Judge Byrne." After a very careful review, I have determined that this statement of mine is not precisely accurate. It was on March 17 that I first learned of the break-in at the office of Dr. Fielding, and that was four days before the beginning of my own investigation on March 21. I was told then that nothing by way of evidence had been obtained in the break-in. On April 18 I learned that the Justice Department had interrogated or was going to interrogate Mr. Hunt about this break-in. I was gravely concerned that other activities of the special investigations unit might be disclosed, because I knew this could seriously injure the national security. Consequently, I directed Mr. Petersen to stick to the Watergate investigation and stay out of national security matters. On April 25 Attorney General Kleindienst came to me and urged that the fact of the break-in should be disclosed to the court, despite the fact that since no evidence had been obtained, the law did not clearly require it. I concurred and authorized him to report the break-in to Judge Byrne.

In view of the incident of Dr. Fielding's office, let me emphasize two things.

First, it was and is important that many of the matters worked on by the special investigations unit not be publicly disclosed because disclosure would unquestionably damage the national security. This is why I have exercised executive privilege on some of these matters in connection with the testimony of Mr. Ehrlichman and others. The Senate committee has learned through its investigation the general facts of some of these security matters, and has to date wisely declined to make them public or to contest in these respects my claim of executive privilege.

Second, I at no time authorized the use of illegal means by the special investigations unit, and I was not aware of the break-in of Dr. Fielding's office until March 17, 1973.

Many persons will ask why, when the facts are as I have stated them, I do not make public the tape recordings of my meetings and conversations with members of the White House staff during this period.

I am aware that such terms as "separation of powers" and "executive privilege" are lawyers' terms, and that those doctrines have been called "abstruse" and "esoteric." Let me state the common sense of the matter. Every day a President of the United States is required to make difficult decisions on grave issues. It is absolutely essential, if the President is to be able to do his job as the country expects, that he be able to talk openly and candidly with his advisers about issues and individuals and that they be able to talk in the same fashion with him. Indeed, on occasion, they must be able to "blow off steam" about important public figures. This kind of frank discussion is only possible when those who take part in it can feel assured that what they say is in the strictest confidence.

The Presidency is not the only office that requires confidentiality if it is to function effectively. A member of Congress must be able to talk in confidence with his assistants. Judges must be able to confer in confidence with their law clerks and with each other. Throughout our entire history the need for this kind of confidentiality has been recognized. No branch of government has ever compelled disclosure of confidential conversations between officers of other branches of government and their advisers about government business.

The argument is often raised that these tapes are somehow different because the conversations may bear on illegal acts, and because the commission of illegal acts is not an official duty. This misses the point entirely. Even if others, from their own standpoint, may have been thinking about how to cover up an illegal act, from my standpoint I was concerned with how to uncover the illegal acts. It is my responsibility under the Constitution to see that the laws are faithfully executed, and in pursuing the facts about Watergate I was doing precisely that. Therefore, the precedent would not be one concerning illegal actions only; it would be one that would risk exposing private Presidential conversations involving the whole range of official duties.

The need for confidence is not something confined to the Government officials. The law has long recognized that there are many relations sufficiently important that things said in that relation are entitled to be kept confidential, even at the cost of doing without what might be critical evidence in a legal proceeding. Among these are, for example, the relations between a lawyer and his client, between a priest and a penitent, and between a husband and wife. In each case it is thought to be so important that the parties be able to talk freely with each other, that they need not feel restrained in their conversation by fear that what they say may someday come out in court, that the law recognizes that these conversations are "privileged" and that their disclosure cannot be compelled.

If I were to make public these tapes, containing as they do blunt and candid remarks on many subjects that have nothing to do with Watergate, the confidentiality of the office of the President would always be suspect. Persons talking with a President would never again be sure that recordings or notes of what they said would not at some future time be made public, and they would guard their words against that possibility. No one would want to risk being known as the person who recommended a policy that ultimately did not work. No one would want to advance tentative ideas, not fully thought through, that might have possible merit but that might, on further examination, prove unsound. No one would want to speak bluntly about public figures here and abroad. I shall therefore vigorously oppose any actions which would set a precedent that would cripple all future Presidents by inhibiting conversations between them and the persons they look to for advice.

This principle of confidentiality in Presidential communications is what is at stake in the question of the tapes. I shall continue to oppose any efforts to destroy that principle, which is indispensable to the conduct of the Presidency.

I recognize that this statement does not answer many of the questions and contentions raised during the Watergate hearings. It has not been my intention to attempt any such comprehensive and detailed response, nor has it been my intention to address myself to all matters covered in my May 22 statement. With the Senate hearings and the grand jury investigations still proceeding, with much of the testimony in conflict, it would be neither possible to provide nor appropriate to attempt a definitive account of all that took place. Neither do I believe I could enter upon an endless course of explaining and rebutting a complex of point-by-point claims and charges arising out of that conflicting testimony which may engage committees and courts for months or years to come, and still be able to carry out my duties as President. While the judicial and legislative branches resolve these matters, I will continue to discharge to the best of my ability my constitutional responsibilities as President of the United States.

News Conference, San Clemente, Calif.

Aug. 22, 1973

Opening Statement

First, gentlemen, I have an announcement before going to your questions.

It is with the deep sense of not only official regret but personal regret that I announce the resignation of Secretary of State William Rogers, effective Sept. 3.

A letter which will be released to the press after this conference will indicate my appraisal of his work as Secretary of State.

I will simply say at this time that he wanted to leave at the conclusion of the first four years.

He agreed to stay on because we had some enormously important problems coming up including the negotiations which resulted in the end of the war in Vietnam, the Soviet summit, the European Security Conference as well as in other areas, Latin America and in Asia where the Secretary of State as you know has been quite busy over these past eight months.

As he returns to private life we will not only miss him in terms of his official service but I shall particularly miss him because of his having been through the years a very close personal friend and adviser. That personal friendship and advice, however, I hope still to have the benefit of and I know that I will.

As his successor I shall nominate and send to the Senate for confirmation the name of Dr. Henry Kissinger.

Dr. Kissinger will become Secretary of State, assume the duties of the office after he is confirmed by the Senate.

I trust the Senate will move expeditiously on the confirmation hearings because there are a number of matters of very great importance that are coming up. There are, for example, some matters that might even involve some foreign travel by Dr. Kissinger that will have to be delayed in the event that the Senate hearings are delayed.

Dr. Kissinger's qualifications for this post I think are well known by all of you ladies and gentlemen as well as those looking to us and listening to us on television and radio.

He will retain the position, after he becomes Secretary of State, of assistant to the President for national security affairs. In other words he will have somewhat a parallel relationship to

the White House which George Shultz has. George Shultz as you
know is Secretary of the Treasury but is also an assistant to the
President in the field of economic affairs.

The purpose of this arrangement is to have a closer coordination between the White House and the departments and in this
case between the White House and the National Security Affairs,
the N.S.C., and the State Department, which carries a major
load in this area.

And also another purpose is to get the work out in the departments where it belongs and I believe that this change in this
respect with Dr. Kissinger moving in as Secretary of State and
still retaining the position as assistant to the President for
national security affairs will serve the interest not only of coordination but also of the interests of an effective foreign policy.

I will simply say finally with regard to Secretary Rogers that
he can look back on what I think and I suppose it is a self-serving
statement, but I will say it about him rather than about myself
at the moment, one of the most successful eras of foreign policy
in any Administration in history, an era in which we ended a
war, the longest war in America's history, an era in addition
in which we began to build a structure of peace, particularly involving the two great powers, the People's Republic of China and
the Soviet Union, where before there had been nothing but ugly
and at some times very, very difficult confrontation.

We still have a long way to go. There are trouble spots in the
area of the Mideast, others, Southeast Asia which we could go into in detail. But as Secretary Rogers looks back on his years, four
and a half years of service as Secretary of State, he can be very
proud that he was one of the major architects of what I think
was a very successful foreign policy.

And now we'll go to the questions. I think, A.P.

Questions

1. Why Tapes Were Made

PRESIDENT NIXON: A.P., Miss Lewin, has the first question.

Q. On Watergate you have said that disclosure of the tapes
could jeopardize and cripple the posture of the Presidency. Question. If disclosure carries such a risk, why did you make the tapes
in the first place and what is your reaction to surveys that show
three out of four Americans believe you were wrong to make the
tapes?

A. Well, with regard to the questions as to why Americans feel
we were wrong to make the tapes, that is not particularly surprising. I think that most Americans do not like the idea of the
taping of conversations and, frankly, it is not something that
particularly appeals to me. As a matter of fact that is why when
I arrived in the White House and saw this rather complex situation set up where there was a taping capacity not only in the Presi-

dent's office, the room outside of his office, but also in the Cabinet Room and at Camp David and in other areas, that I had the entire system dismantled.

It was put into place again in June of 1970 because my advisers felt it was important in terms particularly of national security affairs to have a record for future years that would be an accurate one, but a record which would only be disclosed at the discretion of the President, or according to directives that he would set forth.

As you know, of course, this kind of capability not only existed during the Johnson Administration, it also existed in the Kennedy Administration, and I can see why both President Johnson and President Kennedy did have the capability because, not because they wanted to infringe upon the privacy of anybody but because they felt that they had some obligation particularly in the field of foreign policy and some domestic areas to have a record that would be accurate.

As far as I'm concerned, we now do not have that capability and I am just as happy that we don't. As a matter of fact, I have a practice whenever I'm not too tired of my dictating my own recollections of the day. I think that perhaps will be the more accurate record of history in the end. I think we'll go to the U.P. now and then we'll come to the television . . .

2. Why Gray Was Ignored

Q. On July 6, 1972, you were warned by Patrick Gray you were being mortally wounded by some of your top aides. Can you explain why you didn't ask who they were, and why, what was going on?

A. Well, in the telephone conversation that you refer to that has been, of course, quite widely reported in the press as well as on television, Mr. Gray said that he was concerned that as far as the investigation that he had responsibility for, that some of my top aides were not cooperating. Whether the term used was "mortally wounded" or not, I do not know. Some believe that it was. Some believe that it wasn't. That it is irrelevant. He could have said that.

The main point, however, I asked him whether or not he had discussed this matter with General Walters because I knew that there had been meetings between General Walters representing the C.I.A. to be sure that the C.I.A. did not become involved in the investigation and between the Director of the F.B.I. He said that he had. He told me that General Walters agreed that the investigation should be pursued and I told him to go forward with a full press on the investigation, to which he has so testified. It seemed to me that with that kind of directive to Mr. Gray that that was adequate for the purpose of carrying out the responsibilities. As far as the individuals were concerned, I assume that the individuals that he was referring to involved this operation with the C.I.A.

That's why I asked him the Walters question. When he cleared that up, he went forward with the investigation and he must have thought that it was a very good investigation because when I sent his name down to the Senate for confirmation the next year, I asked him about his investigation and he said he was very proud of it and he said it was the most thorough investigation that had ever taken place since the assassination of President Kennedy, that he could defend it with enthusiasm and that under the circumstances, therefore, he had carried out the directive that I had given him on July 6. So there was no question about Mr. Gray having direct orders from the President to carry out an investigation that was thorough, Mr. Jerrold.

3. Haldeman's Use of Tapes

Q. Assistant Attorney General Henry Petersen has testified that on April 15 of this year he met with you and warned you at that time there might be enough evidence to warrant indictments against three of your top aides, Messrs. Ehrlichman, Haldeman, Dean. You accepted their resignations on April 30 calling Mr. Haldeman and Mr. Ehrlichman two of the finest public servants you have known. After that you permitted Mr. Haldeman, after he had left the White House, to hear confidential tapes of conversations you had had in your office with Mr. Dean. My question is why did you permit a man who you knew might be indicted to hear those tapes which you now will not permit the American public or the Federal prosecutors handling the case to listen to?

A. The only tape that has been referred to, that Mr. Haldeman has listened to, he listened to at my request and he listened to that tape, that was the one on Sept. 15, because he had been present and was there. I asked him to listen to it in order to be sure that as far as any allegations that had been made by Mr. Dean with regard to that conversation is concerned, I wanted to be sure that we were absolutely correct in our response.

That's all he listened to. He did not listen to any tapes in which only Mr. Dean and I had participated. He listened only to the tape on Sept. 15, this is after he left office, in which he had participated in the coversation throughout.

4. Panel to Hear Tapes

Q. Mr. President, one of the lingering doubts about your denial of any involvement in, is concerning your failure to make the tapes available, either to the Senate committee or the special prosecutor. You've made it perfectly clear you don't intend to release those tapes but is there any way that you could have some group listen to tapes and give a report so that that might satisfy the public mind?

A. I don't believe first that it would satisfy the public mind, and it shouldn't. The second point is that as Mr. Wright, who argued the case, I understand, very well before Judge Sirica this morning, has indicated. To have the tapes listened to—he indicated this also in his brief—either by a prosecutor or by a judge or in camera or in any way would violate the principle of confidentiality, and I believe he is correct.

That is why we are standing firm on the proposition that we will not agree to the Senate committee's desires to have, for example, its chief investigator listen to the tapes or the special prosecutor's desire to hear the tapes, and also why we will oppose, as Mr. Wright did in his argument this morning, any compromise of the principle of confidentiality. Let me explain very carefully that the principle of confidentiality either exists or it doesn't exist. And once it is compromised, once it is known that a conversation that is held with the President can be subject to a subpoena by a Senate committee, by a grand jury, by a prosecutor, and be listened to by anyone, the principle of confidentiality is thereby irreparably damaged.

Incidentally, let me say that now that tapes are no longer being made I suppose it could be argued what difference does it make now, now that these tapes are also in the past. What is involved is not only the tapes, what is involved, as you ladies and gentlemen well know, is the request on the part of the Senate committee, and the special prosecutor as well, that we turn over Presidential papers, in other words, the record of conversations with the President made by his associates. Those papers and the tapes as well cannot be turned over without breaching the principle of confidentiality. It was President Truman that made that argument very effectively in his letter to a Senate committee for his response to a Congressional committee, a House committee, it was, in 1953 when they asked him to turn over his papers. So whether it is a paper or whether it's a tape, what we have to bear in mind is that for a President to conduct the affairs of this office and conduct effectively, he must be able to do so with the principle of confidentiality intact.

Otherwise, the individuals who come to talk to him, whether it's his advisers or whether it's a visitor in the domestic field or whether it's someone in a foreign field, will always be speaking in a eunuch-like way, rather than laying it on the line. It has to be laid on the line if you're going to have the creative kind of discussions that we have often had and have been responsible for some of our successes in the foreign policy period particularly in the past few years.

5. Magruder and MacGregor

Q. Mr. President, could you tell us who you personally talked to in directing that investigations be made both in June of '72 and after the Watergate incident and last March 21, when you got new evidence and ordered a more intensive investigation?

A. Certainly. In June I of course talked to Mr. MacGregor first of all who was the new chairman of the committee. He told me that he would conduct a thorough investigation as far as his entire committee staff was concerned. Apparently that investigation was very effective except for Mr. Magruder who stayed on. But Mr. MacGregor does not have to assume responsibility for that, I say not responsibility for it because basically what happened there was that he believed Mr. Magruder and many others had believed him, too. He proved, however, to be wrong.

In the White House, the investigation's responsibility were given to Mr. Ehrlichman at the highest level and, in turn, he delegated them to Mr. Dean, the White House counsel, something of which I was aware and of which I approved. Mr. Dean, as White House counsel, therefore sat in on the F.B.I. interrogations of the members of the White House staff because what I wanted to know was whether any member of the White House staff was in any way involved. If he was involved, he would be fired.

And when we met on Sept. 15 and again throughout our discussions in the month of March, Mr. Dean insisted there was not—and I use his words—a scintilla of evidence indicating that anyone on the White House staff was involved in the planning of the Watergate break-in.

Now in terms of after March 21, Mr. Dean first was given the responsibility to write his own report but I did not rest it there— I also had a contact made with the Attorney General himself, and Attorney General Kleindienst told him—this was on the 27th of March—to report to me directly anything that he found in this particular area, and I gave the responsibility for Mr. Ehrlichman on the 29th of March to continue the investigation that Mr. Dean was unable to conclude, having spent a week at Camp David and unable to finish the report.

Mr. Ehrlichman questioned a number of people in that period at my direction, including Mr. Mitchell, and I should also point out that as far as my own activities were concerned I was not leaving it just to them.

I met at great length with Mr. Ehrlichman, Mr. Haldeman, Mr. Dean, Mr. Mitchell on the 22d. I discussed the whole matter with them. I kept pressing for the view that I had had throughout, that we must get this story out, get the truth out, whatever and whoever it's going to hurt, and it was there that Mr. Mitchell suggested that all the individuals involved in the White House appear in an executive session before the Ervin committee.

We never got that far. But at least that was, that's an indication of the extent of my own investigation.

I think we'll go to Mr. Lisagor now.

6. Did Mitchell Lie?

Q. Mr. President, you have said repeatedly that you tried to get all facts and just now you mentioned a March 22 meeting. Yet former Attorney General John Mitchell said that if you had ever asked him at any time about the Watergate matter he would have told you the whole story chapter and verse. Was Mr. Mitchell not speaking the truth when he said that before the committee?

A. Now Mr. Lisagor, I'm not going to question Mr. Mitchell's veracity. And I will only say that throughout I had confidence in Mr. Mitchell. Mr. Mitchell, in a telephone call that I had with him immediately after it occurred, expressed great chagrin that he had not run a tight enough shop and that some of the boys, as he called them, got involved in this kind of activity, which he knew could be very, very embarrassing to—apart from its illegality—to the campaign.

Throughout I was expecting Mr. Mitchell to tell me, in the event that he was involved or that anybody else was. He did not tell me. I don't blame him for not telling me. He's given his reasons for not telling me. I regret that he did not; because he's exactly right—had he told me I would have blown my stack. Just as I did at Ziegler the other day.

7. Blame for Conditions

Q. Mr. President. How much blame, what degree of personal blame do you accept for the climate in the White House and of the reorgan— of the re-election committee for the abuses of Watergate?

A. I accept it all.

8. Pentagon Papers Case

Q. Mr. President, I want to state this question with due respect to your office but also as directly as . . .

A. That would be unusual.

Q. I'd like to think not. It concerns the events surrounding Mr. Ehrlichman's contact and on one occasion your own contact with the judge in the Pentagon Papers case, Judge Byrne. As I understand your own explanation of events in putting together your statement with Mr. Ehrlichman's testimony and what is currently said, what happened here is sometime late in March, on March 17, I believe he said, you first found out about the break-in at the psychiatrist's office of Mr. Ellsberg, that you asked to have that looked into and that you later, I think in late April, talked with Attorney General Kleindienst to inform the judge. Now, my question is this, that while the Pentagon Papers trial was going on, Mr. Ehrlichman secretly met once with the judge in that case, you secretly met another time the judge with Mr. Ehrlichman, now, you're a lawyer and given the state of the situation and what you did, could you give us some reason why the American people shouldn't believe that that was at least a subtle attempt to bribe the judge in that case and it gave at least the appearance of a lack of moral leadership.

A. Well I would say the only part of your statement that is perhaps accurate is that I'm a lawyer. Now, beyond that, Mr. Rather, let me say with regard to the secret meeting that we had with the judge that as he said, I met the judge briefly—after all, I had appointed him to the position—I met him for perhaps one minute outside my door here in full view of the whole White House staff and everybody who wanted to see.

I asked him how he liked his job. We did not discuss the case. And he went on with his meeting with Mr. Ehrlichman. Now why did the meeting with Mr. Ehrlichman take place. Because we had determined that Mr. Gray could not be confirmed, as you will recall. We were on a search for a Director of the F.B.I. Mr. Kleindienst had been here, and I asked him what he would recommend with regard to a director and I laid down certain qualifications.

I said I wanted a man preferably with F.B.I. experience and preferably with prosecutor's experience. And preferably, if possible, a Democrat, so that we would have no problem on confirmation. He said the man for the job is Byrne. He says he's the best man. I said, are you, would you recommend him? He said yes. Under those circumstances, then, Mr. Ehrlichman called Mr. Byrne. He said under no circumstances will we talk to you, he, Ehrlichman will talk to you, unless if he felt that it would in any way compromise his handling of the Ellsberg case.

Judge Byrne made the decision that he would talk to Mr. Ehrlichman, and he did talk to him privately, here. And on that occasion he talked to him privately. The case was not discussed at all. Only the question of whether or not at the conclusion of this case Mr. Byrne would like to be considered as Director of the F.B.I.

I understand, incidentally, that he told Mr. Ehrlichman that he would be interested. Of course, the way the things broke, eventually his, we found another name with somewhat the same qualifications, although in this case, not a judge, in this case, a chief of police with former F.B.I. experience.

Now, with regard to the Ellsberg break-in, let me explain that in terms of that I discussed that on the telephone with Mr. Henry Petersen on the 18th of April. It was on the 18th of April that I learned that the grand jury was going away from some of its Watergate investigation and moving into national security areas.

I told Mr. Petersen at that time about my concern about the security areas and particularly about the break-in as far as the Ellsberg case was concerned. And then he asked me a very critical question, which you as a nonlawyer will now understand, and lawyers probably will too. He said, was any evidence developed out of this investigation, out of this break-in, and I said, no, it was a dry hole. He said, good. Now what he meant by that was that in view of the fact that no evidence was developed as the result of the break-in, which is incidentally, illegal, unauthorized as far as I was concerned, and completely deplorable, but since no evidence was developed, there was no requirement that it be presented to the jury that was hearing the case.

That was why Mr. Petersen, a man of impeccable credentials in the law enforcement field, did not at that time, on the 18th, at a time that I told him about, that I had known about the Ellsberg break-in, say, "Let's present it then to the grand jury" because nothing had been accomplished, nothing had been obtained that would taint the case.

It was approximately 10 days later that Mr. Kleindienst came in and said that after a review of the situation in the prosecutor's office in Washington in which Mr. Petersen had also participated that they believe that it was best that we bend over backwards in this case and send this record of the Ellsberg break-in even though there was no evidence obtained from it that could have affected the jury one way or another, send it to the judge.

When they made that recommendation to me I directed that it be done instantly. It was done. Incidentally, the prosecutor argued this case just the way that I've argued it to you, and whether or not it had an effect on the eventual outcome, I do not know. At least as far as we know, Mr. Ellsberg went free, this being one of the factors, but that is the explanation of what happened, and obviously you in your commentary tonight can attach anything you want to it. I hope you will be just as fair and objective as I try to be in giving you the answer.

9. Confidence in Agnew

Q. Mr. President, what is the state of your confidence in your Vice President at this point in time?

A. I noted some press speculation to the effect that I have not expressed confidence in the Vice President and therefore I welcome this question, because I want to set the record straight.

I had confidence in the integrity of the Vice President when I selected him as Vice President when very few knew him, as you may recall, back in 1968, knew him nationally.

My confidence in his integrity has not been shaken, and in fact it has been strengthened by his courageous conduct and his ability even though he's controversial at times, as I am, over the past four and a half years and so I have confidence in the integrity of the Vice President and particularly in the performance of the duties that he has had as Vice President, and as a candidate for Vice President.

Now obviously the question arises as to charges that have been made about activities that occurred before he became Vice President.

He would consider it improper, I would consider it improper for me to comment on those charges and I shall not do so. But I will make a comment on another subject that I think needs to be commented upon and that is the outrageous leak in information from either the grand jury or the prosecutors or the Department of Justice or all three—and incidentally I'm not going to put the responsibility on all three till I have heard from the Attorney General who at my request is making a full investigation of this at the present time.

I'm not going to put the responsibility—but the leak of information with regard to charges that have been made against the Vice President and leaking them all in the press, convicting an individual, not only trying him but convicting him in the headlines and on television before he's had a chance to present his case in court is completely contrary to the American tradition. Even a Vice President has a right to some, shall I say consideration in this respect, let alone the ordinary individual.

And I will say this, and the Attorney General I know has taken note of this fact, any individual in the Justice Department or in the prosecutor's office who is in the employ of the United States, who has leaked information in this case, to the press or to anybody else, will be summarily dismissed from Government service. That's how strongly I feel about it and I feel that way because I would make this ruling whether it was the Vice President or any individual.

We have to remember that a hearing before a grand jury and that determination in the American process is one that is supposed to be in confidence, is supposed to be in secret, because all kinds of charges are made which will not stand up in open court, and its only when the case gets to open court that the press and the TV have a right to cover it. Well, they have a right to cover it, but I mean, have a right, it seems to me to give such broad coverage to the charges.

10. Thoughts on Resigning

Q. Mr. President, did at any time during the Watergate crisis have you ever considered resigning? Would you consider resigning if you felt that your capacity to govern had been seriously weakened? And in that connection, how much do you think your capacity to govern has been weakened?

A. The answer to the first two questions is no. The answer to the third question is that it is true that as far as the capacity to govern is concerned, that to be under a constant barrage— 12 to 15 minutes a night on each of the three major networks for four months—tends to raise some questions in the people's minds with regard to the President; and it may raise some questions with regard to the capacity to govern.

But I also know this: I was elected to do a job. Watergate is an episode that I deeply deplore; and, had I been running the campaign—other than trying to run the country, and particularly the foreign policy of this country at this time—it would never have happened. But that's water under the bridge. Let's go on now.

The point that I make now is, that we are proceeding as best we know how to get all those guilty brought to justice in Watergate. But now we must move on from Watergate to the business of the people—the business of the people is continuing with initiatives we began in the first Administration.

Q. Mr. President—

A. Just a moment. We've had 30 minutes of this press conference. I have yet to have, for example, one question on the business of the people. Which shows you are—how we're consumed with it.

I'm not criticizing the members of the press; because you naturally are very interested in this issue. But let me tell you, years from now people are going to perhaps be interested in what happened in terms of the efforts of the United States to build a structure of peace in the world. They are perhaps going to be interested in the efforts of this Administration to have a kind of prosperity that we haven't had since 1955—that is, prosperity without war and without inflation.

Because, throughout the Kennedy years and throughout the Johnson years, whatever prosperity we had was at the cost of either inflation or war, or both.

I don't say that critically of them. I'm simply saying, we've got to do better than that.

Now our goal is to move forward then—to move forward to build a structure of peace. And when you say, have I—do I consider resigning: the answer is no. I shall not resign. I have three and a half years to go, or almost three and a half years, and I'm going to use every day of those three and a half years trying to get the people of the United States to recognize that whatever mistakes we have made that in the long run this Administration, by making this world safer for their children, and this Administration, by making their lives better at home for themselves and their children, deserves high marks rather than low marks.

11. Question of Impeachment

Q. Mr. President, as long as we're on the subject of the American tradition and following up Mr. Rather's questions, what was authorized even if the burglary of Dr. Fielding's office wasn't, what was authorized was the 1970 plan which by your own description permitted illegal acts, illegal breaking and entering, mail surveillance and the like. Now, under the Constitution you swore an oath to execute the laws of the United States faithfully. If you were serving in Congress, would you not be considering impeachment proceedings and discussing impeachment possibility against an elected public official who had violated his oath of office?

A. I would if I had violated the oath of office. I would also, however, refer you to the recent decision of the Supreme Court or at least an opinion that even last year which indicates inherent power in the Presidency to protect the national security in cases like this. I should also point to you that in the three Kennedy years and the three Johnson years through 1966 when burglarizing of this type did take place, when it was authorized, on a very large scale there was no talk of impeachment and it was quite well known.

I should also like to point out that when you ladies and gentlemen indicate your great interest in wiretaps and I understand that the height of the wiretaps was when Robert Kennedy was Attorney General in 1963. I don't criticize him, however. He had over 250 in 1963 and of course the average in the Eisenhower Administration and the Nixon Administration is about 110.

But if he had had 10 more and as a result of wiretaps had been able to discover the Oswald plan it would have been worth it.

So I will go to another question.

12. Ehrlichman and Haldeman

Q. Mr. President, do you consider Haldeman and Ehrlichman two of the finest public servants you have ever known?

A. I certainly do. I look upon public servants as men who've got to be judged by their entire record—not by simply parts of it. Mr. Ehrlichman, Mr. Haldeman for four and a half years served with great distinction, with great dedication and, like everybody in this deplorable Watergate business, at great personal sacrifice and with no personal gain.

We admit the scandalous conduct. Thank God, there's been no personal gain involved. That would be going much too far, I suppose.

But the point that I make with regard to Mr. Haldeman and Mr. Ehrlichman is that I think, too, that as all the facts come out, that—and when they have an opportunity to have their case heard in court, not simply to be tried before a committee, and tried in the press and tried in television—they will be exonerated.

13. Watergate Defense Fund

Q. Mr. President, could you tell us your recollection of what you told John Dean on March 21 on the subject of raising funds for the Watergate defendants?

A. Certainly. Mr. Haldeman has testified to that, and his statement is accurate.

Basically, what Mr. Dean was concerned about on March 21 was not so much the raising of money for the defendants but the raising of money for the defendants for the purpose of keeping them still. In other words so-called hush money.

The one would be legal, in other words raising the defense funds for any group, any individual, as you know is perfectly legal and is done all the time. But you raise funds for the purpose of keeping an individual from talking, that's obstruction of justice.

Mr. Dean said also, on March 21, that there was an attempt to, as he put it, to blackmail the White House, to blackmail the White House by one of the defendants; incidentally, that defendant has denied it, but at least this is what Mr. Dean had claimed and that unless certain amounts of money were paid, I think it was $120,000 for attorneys' fees and other support, that this particular defendant would make a statement, not with regard to Watergate but with regard to some national security matters in which Mr. Ehrlichman had particular responsibility.

My reaction very briefly was this: I said as you look at this, I said isn't it quite obvious first, that if it is going to have any chance to succeed, that these individuals aren't going to sit there in jail for four years, they're going to have clemency. Isn't that correct?

He said yes.

I said we can't give clemency.

He agreed.

Then I went to another point. The second point is that isn't it also quite obvious, as far as this is concerned, that while we could raise the money, and he indicated in answer to my question that it would probably take a million dollars over four years to take care of this defendant and others on this kind of a basis, the problem was, how do you get the money to them. And also, how do you get around the problem of clemency because they're not going to stay in jail simply because their families are being taken care of.

And so that was why I concluded, as Mr. Haldeman recalls, perhaps, and did testify very effectively, 1) when I said John, it's wrong, it won't work, we can't give clemency, and we've got to get this story out. And therefore I direct you and I direct Haldeman and I direct Ehrlichman and I direct Mitchell to get together tomorrow and then meet with me as to how we get this story out.

And that's how the meeting on the 22d took place.

14. Coordinating Defense

Q. Mr. President, earlier in the news conference you said that you gave Mr. Haldeman the right to listen to one tape because you wanted to be sure "that we are correct." And I think I'm quoting you correctly. Now, you have indicated that you still feel that Mr. Haldeman and Mr. Ehrlichman are two of the finest public servants that you've ever known. You have met with their lawyer at least twice that we know of. Are you and Mr. Haldeman and Mr. Ehrlichman coordinating their and your defense and if so why?

A. No, no. As far as my defense is concerned, I make it myself. As far as their defense is concerned, their lawyer demonstrated very well before the committee that he can handle it very well without any assistance from me.

15. Should Agnew Resign?

Q. Mr. President, a follow-up question on the Agnew situation. You have said in the past that any White House official who was indicted would be suspended and that anyone convicted would be dismissed. Should Vice President Agnew be indicted, would you expected him to resign or somehow otherwise stand down temporarily until cleared?

A. Well Mr. Tivesser, a perfectly natural question and one that any good newsman as you are would ask. But as you know it's one that would be most inappropriate for me to comment upon. The Vice President has not been indicted. Charges have been thrown out by innuendo and otherwise, which he had denied to me personally and which he has denied publicly. And the talk about indictment and the talk about resignation even now. I'm not questioning your right to ask the question, understand. But for me to talk about it would be totally inappropriate and I make no comment in answer to that question.

Q. Mr. President—

A. I'll take the big man.

Q. Thank you, Mr. President.

A. I know my troubles if I don't take him—or if I do.

Q. Looking to the future on executive privilege, there are a couple of questions that come to mind.

A. I thought we just raised the point. That was a year ago.

Q. Well we speak here of the future.

A. All right.

16. Limits on President

Q. Where is the check on authoritarianism by the executive that the President is to be the sole judge of what the executive branch makes available and suppresses? And will you obey a Supreme Court order if you are asked and directed to produce the tapes or other documents for the Senate committee or for the special prosecutor? And if this is not enough, is there any limitation on the President, short of impeachment, to compel the production of evidence of a criminal nature?

A. Is there anything else?

Q. No. I think that will be enough.

A. No, I was not being facetious; but I realize it's a complicated question. The answer to the first question is that there's a limitation on the President in almost all fields like this. There's, of course, the limitation of public opinion; and, of course, Congressional and other pressures that may arise.

As far as executive privilege is concerned in the Watergate matter—and I must say the I.T.T. file, etc.—that this Administration has, I think, gone further in terms of waiving executive privilege than any Administration in my memory. Certainly a lot further than Mr. Truman was willing to go when I was on the other side, as you recall, urging that he waive executive privilege.

Now, with regard to what the Supreme Court will do, or say— the White House press secretary, assistant secretary, Mr. Warren has responded to that already. I won't go beyond that. And particularly I won't make any statement on that matter at this time, while the matter is still being considered by Judge Sirica.

I understand his decision will come down on Wednesday, and then we will make a comment. As far as the statement that Mr. Warren has made with regard to the President's position of complying with a definitive order of the Supreme Court is concerned, that statement stands.

17. Exploiters of Watergate

Q. Mr. President, sir, last week in your speech you referred to those who would exploit Watergate to keep you from doing your job. Could you specifically detail who those are?

A. I would suggest that where the shoe fits, people should wear it. I would think that some political figures, some members of the press perhaps, some members of the television, perhaps, would exploit it. I don't impute, interestingly enough, motives, however, that are improper interests, because here's what is involved.

There are a great number of people in this country that would prefer that I do resign. There are a great number of people in this country that didn't accept the mandate of 1972. After all, I know that most of the members of the press corps were not enthusiastic. And I understand that about either my election in '68 or '72. That's not unusual. Frankly, if I had always followed what the press predicted or the polls predicted, I would have never been elected President.

But what I am saying is this. People who did not accept the mandate of '72, who do not want the strong America that I want to build, who do not want the foreign policy leadership that I want to give, who do not want to cut down the size of this Government bureaucracy that burdens us so greatly and to give more of our Government back to the people, people who do not want these things naturally would exploit any issues. If it weren't Watergate, anything else in order to keep the President from doing his job.

And so I say I have no improper motives to them. I think they would prefer that I failed. On the other hand, I'm not going to fail. I'm here to do a job, and I'm going to do the best I can, and I'm sure the fair-minded members of this press corps, and that's most of you, will report when I do well, and I'm sure you'll report when I do badly.

18. Wiretaps and Oswald

Q. Mr. President, you recently suggested that if the late Robert Kennedy had initiated 10 more wiretapes, he would have been able to discover the Oswald plan, as you described it, and thereby presumably prevent the assassination of President Kennedy.

A. Let me correct you, sir. I want to be sure that the assumption is correct. I said if 10 more wiretaps could have found the conspiracy, if it was a conspiracy, or the individual, then it would have been worth it. As far as I'm concerned, I'm no more of an expert on that assassination than anybody else, but my point is that wiretaps in the national security area were very high in the Kennedy Administration for a very good reason.

Because there were many threats on the President's life, because there were national security problems, and that is why that in that period of 1961 to '63 there were wiretaps on news organizations, on news people, on civil rights leaders and on other people. And I think they were perfectly justified and I'm sure that President Kennedy and his brother, Robert Kennedy, would never have authorized them as I would never authorize them, unless he thought they were in the national interest.

Q. Do you think, then, that threats to assassinate the President merits more national security wise—

A. No, no, as far as I'm concerned, I was only suggesting that in terms of those times that to have the Oswald thing happen just seemed so unbelievable that it—with his record, with his record, that it, with everything that everybody had on him, that that fellow could have been where he was in a position to shoot the President of the United States seems to me to be, to have been a terrible breakdown in our protective security areas. I would like to say, however, that as far as protection generally is concerned, I don't like it. And my family doesn't like it. Both of my daughters would prefer to have no Secret Service. I discussed it with the Secret Service. They say they have too many threats and they have to have it. My wife doesn't want to have Secret Service. And I would prefer and I recommended this just three days ago, to cut my detail by one third because I noticed there were criticisms of how much the Secret Service is spending.

Let me say that whether, that we always are going to have

threats against the President. But I frankly think that one man, probably, is as good against a threat as a hundred, and that's my view, but my view doesn't happen to be in a majority there and it doesn't happen to agree with the Congress, so I will still have a great number of Secret Service around me, more than I want, more than my family wants.

19. Staff and Prosecutors

Q. Mr. President, during March and April you received from your staff, on several occasions, information about criminal wrongdoing and some indication that members of your staff might have been involved. The question, sir, is why didn't you turn this information over immediately to the prosecutors, instead of having your own staff continue to make these investigations?

A. Well, for the very obvious reason that in March, for example, the man that was in constant contact with the prosecutors was my counsel, Mr. Dean. Mr. Dean was talking to Mr. Petersen. I assumed that anything he was telling me, he was telling the prosecutors.

And in April, after Mr. Dean left the investigation, Mr. Ehrlichman was in charge. I would assume—and, incidentally, Mr. Ehrlichman did talk to Mr. Kleindienst—that is why it was done that way.

The President doesn't pick up the phone and call the Attorney General every time something comes up on a matter. He depends on his counsel, or whoever he'd done the job to—or, given that assignment to—to do the job. And that is what I expected in this instance.

Q. Following on that, Mr. President—

A. You've had one now, you don't—you've had three. Go ahead.

20. Cover-up on Cambodia

Q. Mr. President, in your Cambodian invasion—in your Cambodian invasion speech of April, 1970, you reported to the American people that the United States had been strictly observing the neutrality of Cambodia. I'm wondering if you, in light of what we now know, that there were 15 months of bombing of Cambodia previous to your statement, whether you owe an apology to the American people?

A. Certainly not, and certainly not to the Cambodian people. Because, as far as this area is concerned, the area of approximately 10 miles—which was bombed during this period—no Cambodians had been in it for years. It was totally occupied by the North Vietnamese Communists. They were using this area for the purpose of attacking and killing American marines and soldiers by the thousands.

The bombing was taking—took place against those North Vietnamese forces in enemy-occupied territory.

And as far as the American people are concerned, I think the American people are very thankful that the President ordered what was necessary to save the lives of their men and shorten this war—which he found when he got here, and which he ended.

Q. Thank you, Mr. President.

THE BASIC CONFLICTS
By Walter Rugaber

In 37 days of nationally televised hearings and 7,573 pages of testimony, the opening phase of the Senate's Watergate investigation produced a huge outpouring of evidence, assertion and insight.

Reduced to manageable proportions, the inquiry into last year's wiretapping at the Democratic National Committee offices and the subsequent cover-up turns on relatively few questions. But on most of them there are serious conflicts.

Witnesses hostile to the President—mainly John W. Dean 3d—have sought to show a pattern of words and actions implicating Mr. Nixon in the cover-up.

Loyalist witnesses such as H. R. Haldeman and John D. Ehrlichman have insisted on an innocent interpretation of the same words and actions, contending that the conspirators kept the truth completely hidden from the President.

Without additional evidence—the tape recordings of White House meetings withheld by Mr. Nixon, for example—any effort to resolve the conflicts must finally depend on one's perceptions of probability, of surrounding events, of men's characters.

What follows is a breakdown of the wiretapping and cover-up scandals into their main components and brief, compacted excerpts of what the most important witnesses had to say directly on each of the aspects selected.

To what extent, if any, was President Nixon aware of either the Watergate wiretapping or cover-up?

DEAN: "I cannot testify of any first-hand knowledge of that [the President's awareness in advance of the eavesdropping]. If Mr. Haldeman had advance knowledge or had received advance indications it would be my assumption that that had been passed along, but I do not know that for a fact."

HALDEMAN: "There doesn't seem to be much contention about what he knew [in advance of the Watergate arrests]. He knew [only] through the normal channels that the events had occurred. He expressed [afterward] just utter incomprehension as to how such a thing could have happened and why such a thing would have happened."

NIXON: "The burglary and bugging of the Democratic National Committee headquarters came as a complete surprise to me. I had no inkling that any such illegal activities had been planned by persons associated with my campaign; had I known I would not have permitted it." [May 22 statement.]

DEAN: "The President told me [at a meeting on Sept. 15] I had done a good job, and he appreciated how difficult a task it had been; and the President was pleased that the case had stopped with Liddy. I left the meeting with the impression that the President was well aware of what had been going on regarding the success of keeping the White House out of the Watergate scandal."

HALDEMAN: "I recently reviewed the recording of that meeting. This was the day that the indictments had been brought down, and the President knew John Dean had been concentrating for a three-month period on the investigation for the White House. Naturally it was good news [that] there was not any involvement by anyone in the White House. This confirmed what Mr. Dean had been telling us. The President did commend Dean for his handling of the whole Watergate matter, which was a perfectly natural thing for him to do. I totally disagree with the conclusion that the President was aware of any type of cover-up, and certainly Mr. Dean did not advise him of it at the Sept. 15 meeting."

DEAN: "I told the President [on March 13] about the fact that there was no money to pay [the defendants] to meet their demands. I told him that it might be as high as a million dollars or more. He told me that that was no problem, and he also looked over at Haldeman and repeated the same statement."

HALDEMAN: "I seriously doubt that the conversation John Dean has described actually took place on March 13. A discussion of some of those matters actually occurred during a meeting on March 21. I did listen to the tape of the entire meeting. The President said, 'There is no problem in raising a million dollars; we can do that, but it would be wrong.' "

NIXON: "I did not know, until the time of my own investigation, of any effort to provide the Watergate defendants with funds." [May 22 statement.]

DEAN: "The President then [March 13] referred to the fact that Hunt had been promised executive clemency. He said that he had discussed this matter with Ehrlichman and, contrary to instructions that Ehrlichman had given Colson not to talk to the President about it, that Colson had also discussed it with him later. [The President], in a nearly inaudible tone, said to me [on April 15] he was probably foolish to have discussed Hunt's clemency with Colson."

HALDEMAN: "There was no discussion while I was in the room [nor do I recall any discussion on the tape] on the question of clemency in the context of the President saying he had discussed this with Ehrlichman and with Colson. The only mention of clemency was Dean's report that Colson had discussed clemency with Hunt and the President's statement that he could not offer clemency and Dean's agreement."

EHRLICHMAN: "It was my strong feeling, that he [the President] ratified and adopted [in July, 1972] that this was a closed subject and we must never get near it, and that it would be the surest way of having the actions of these burglars imputed to the President for there to be any kind of entertainment [of clemency]. I mentioned [to Colson] that I did not think anybody ought to talk to the President about this subject—outsiders or staff people—that it is just a subject that should be closed as far as the President is concerned."

NIXON: "At no time did I authorize any offer of executive clemency for the Watergate defendants, nor did I know of any such offer."

GRAY: "I told the President [on July 6, 1972] that people on your staff are trying to mortally wound you by using the

F.B.I. and the C.I.A. and by confusing the question of whether or not there is C.I.A. interest [in Watergate]." Mr. Gray was asked: "Do you think a reasonable and prudent man, on the basis of the warning that you gave him at that time, would have been alerted to the fact that his staff was engaged in something improper, unlawful and illegal?" And he answered: "I do, because, frankly, I expected the President to ask me some questions. And when I heard nothing, you know, I began to feel that General Walters and I were alarmists, that we had a hold of nothing here."

NIXON: "On July 6, 1972, I telephoned the Acting Director of the F.B.I., L. Patrick Gray, [and] in the discussion Mr. Gray suggested that the matter of Watergate might lead higher. I told him to press ahead with his investigation."

Who approved the eavesdropping conspiracy?

MAGRUDER: "Mr. Mitchell approved the project [at a meeting in Key Biscayne, Fla., on March 30, 1972]. Mr. Mitchell simply signed off on it in the sense of saying, 'O.K., let's give him [Liddy] a quarter of a million dollars and see what he can come up with.' "

MITCHELL: "Well, it was very simple. [I said.] 'We don't need this; I am tired of hearing it; out; let's not discuss it any further'—this sort of a concept. In my opinion, it was just as clear as that. There could very well have been pressures [on Magruder] from collateral areas in which they decided that this was the thing to do. I can't speculate on who they might be."

LARUE: "Mr. Mitchell, to the best of my recollection, said something [at the March 30 meeting] to the effect that, 'Well, this is not something that will have to be decided at this meeting.' " Asked whether Mr. Mitchell had rejected the wiretapping program "out of hand," Mr. Larue said: "Not to my recollection, no, sir."

REISNER: "He [Magruder] appeared in my doorway [upon his return from Key Biscayne] and said, 'Call Liddy; tell him it is approved and that we need to get going in the next two weeks.' "

DEAN: In mid-February, 1973, eight months after the first wiretapping, Mr. Dean said, Mr. Magruder "told O'Brien that he had received his final authorization for Liddy's activities from Gordon Strachan and that Strachan had reported that Haldeman had cleared the matter with the President."

STRACHAN: "It is my opinion that that version of the facts was presented by Mr. Magruder to [force the White House into offering him an Administration job]." At no time, Mr. Strachan said, did he give final authorization for the Liddy operation.

DEAN: "I had also received information from Magruder that he had been pressured by Colson and members of Colson's staff into authorizing the adoption of Liddy's plans on several occasions."

Mr. Colson has said publicly on a number of occasions that he was unaware "Liddy's plans" involved any wiretapping or other illegal activity and that he simply wanted the Nixon organization to pursue legitimate intelligence goals.

Who received information from the wiretap?

McCORD: "He [Baldwin] was listening with headphones to the conversations that were being transmitted [in late May and early June, 1972] and would take down the substance of the conversations, the time, the date, and then ultimately would type up a summary of them and I would deliver them to Mr. Liddy."

MAGRUDER: "Approximately a week or a week and a half after the initial entry I received the first reports. I brought the materials into Mr. Mitchell in the 8:30 morning meeting I had each morning with him. He, as I recall, reviewed the documents and indicated, as I did, that there was really no substance to these documents, and he called Mr. Liddy up to his office, and Mr. Mitchell indicated his dissatisfaction with the results of his work."

MITCHELL: That "happens to be a palpable, damnable lie. First of all, I had an 8:15 meeting every day over at the White House. Secondly, there was no meeting in any morning during the period when Mr. Magruder and I were alone. Thirdly, I have never seen or talked to Mr. Liddy from the 4th day of February, 1972, until the 15th day of June, 1972."

MAGRUDER: "As I recall, because of the sensitive nature of these documents, I called Mr. Strachan and asked would he come over and look at them in my office rather than sending a copy to his office. As I recall, he did come over and look over the documents and indicate to me the lack of substance to the documents."

STRACHAN: "He [Magruder] did not show me the [wiretap reports]. His statement is couched with, 'As I recall, I called him up,' 'As I recall, he came over,' and 'As I recall, he read it.' Mr. Magruder told me that a sophisticated political intelligence gathering system had been approved [at Key Biscayne] and I repeated that to Mr. Haldeman. Unfortunately, he [Magruder] neither gave me nor did I ask for any further details about the subject."

HALDEMAN: "I had no knowledge of or involvement in the planning or execution of the break-in or bugging of the Democratic National Committee headquarters. To the best of my knowledge I did not see any material produced by the bugging of the Democratic headquarters. He [Strachan] confirmed that he had reread the contents [of political intelligence reports reaching the White House] many times and that they did not suggest any illegality or criminal activity."

Who took part in destruction of possible evidence?

STRACHAN: "I said [to Haldeman immediately after the Watergate arrests on June 17], 'Well, sir, this is what can be imputed to you through me, your agent,' and I opened the political matters memorandum to the paragraph on intelligence, showed it to him [and] he told me, 'Well, make sure our files are clean.' I went down and shredded that document and others related."

HALDEMAN: "I have no recollection of giving Mr. Strachan instructions to destroy any materials, nor do I recall a later report from Strachan that he had done so or that the files were clean."

MAGRUDER: "Mr. Mitchell flew back [from California] that Monday [June 19, 1972] with Mr. LaRue and Mr. Mardian. We met in his apartment with Mr. Dean. It was generally concluded that that file [containing the wiretap reports] should be immediately destroyed."

MITCHELL: "Not in my recollection was there any discussion of destruction of documents at that meeting."

LARUE: "I recall a discussion by Magruder of some sensitive files which he had, and that he was seeking advice about what to do about those files. As I remember there was a response from Mr. Mitchell that it might be good if Mr. Magruder had a fire."

REISNER: "I think Mr. Magruder's secretary and I looked through his own files. I think other people on the committee did similar things, and virtually anything that concerned the opposition [was destroyed]."

GRAY: "Mr. Dean then [June 28, 1972] told me that these files contained copies of sensitive and classified papers of a political nature that Howard Hunt had been working on. I distinctly recall Mr. Dean saying that these files were 'political dynamite' and 'clearly should not see the light of day.' It is true that neither Mr. Ehrlichman [present during the transaction] nor Mr. Dean expressly instructed me to destroy the files. But there was, and is, no doubt in my mind that destruction was intended. I burned them during Christmas week."

DEAN: "I remember well his [Ehrlichman's] instructions [prior to the June 28 turnover of the files to Mr. Gray]. He told me to shred the documents. I [later] suggested that they be given directly to Gray. At no time while I was present with Gray and Ehrlichman was he instructed by myself or Ehrlichman to destroy the documents."

EHRLICHMAN: "I don't think in my life that I have suggested to anybody that a document be shredded."

Who was involved in paying the Watergate conspirators, and what was their purpose?

DEAN: "On the afternoon of June 28, in a meeting in Mr. Mitchell's office—and I believe that Mr. LaRue and Mr. Mardian were also present—there was a discussion of the need for support money in exchange for the silence for the men in jail. Mitchell asked me to get the approval of Haldeman and Ehrichman to use Mr. Herbert Kalmbach to raise the necessary money. They told me to proceed to contact Mr. Kalmbach."

KALMBACH: "My actions were prompted in the belief that such was proper and necessary to discharge what I assumed to be a moral obligation. I said [in a July meeting with Ehrlichman], 'It is just absolutely necessary, John, that you tell me, first, that John Dean has the authority to direct me in this assignment, that it is a proper assignment, and that I am to go forward on it.' He said, 'Herb, John Dean does have the authority, it is proper, and you are to go forward.' "

ULASEWICZ: "I said [in August], 'Well, Mr. Kalmbach, I will tell you something here is not kosher.' He did agree with me that this was time to quit it."

LARUE: "After he [Kalmbach] got out, then I, in effect, became involved in it. My understanding of the payments of money is that this money was paid to satisfy commitments that had been made to them [the defendants]."

MITCHELL: "I became aware [of the payments] in the fall sometime. I was in New York [on June 28, when, Mr. Dean said, payments had been discussed] and could not have been at such a meeting." Mr. Mitchell acknowledged that he had "acquiesced" in payments which, in the words of one questioner, "could have been pretty embarrassing, to say the least, if not illegal."

HALDEMAN: "I was told several times, starting in the summer of 1972, by John Dean and possibly also by John Mitchell, that there was a need by the [Nixon] committee for funds to take care of the legal fees and family support of the Watergate defendants. I had understood this was an important and proper obligation. I do not think I was called upon to condone or condemn."

EHRLICHMAN: "I was aware that there was a need for a defense fund. I do not know what [the] motives were." He denied that he had vouched for the propriety of the effort in his meeting with Mr. Kalmbach.

Who was behind offers of executive clemency to the defendants?

DEAN: "He [Colson] said that he felt it was imperative that Hunt be given some assurances of executive clemency. Ehrlichman said he would have to speak with the President. On Jan. 4, I learned from Ehrlichman that he had given Colson an affirmative regarding clemency for Hunt."

EHRLICHMAN: "Clemency was obviously at the forefront of everybody's mind in this meeting as one of the things which was a potential danger, and I advised both people of a previous conversation that I had had with the President on that subject. The President wanted no one in the White House to get into this whole area of clemency with anybody involved in this case, and surely not make any assurances to anyone."

McCORD: "Political pressure from the White House was conveyed to me in January, 1973, by Jack Caulfield to remain silent [and] take executive clemency by going off to prison quietly. Caulfield stated that he was carrying the message of executive clemency to me 'from the very highest levels of the White House.' "

DEAN: "It was on Jan. 10 that I received calls from both O'Brien and Mitchell indicating that since Hunt had been given assurance of clemency Caulfield should give the same assurances to McCord."

MITCHELL: "That [Dean's testimony on Mitchell's role in the offer to McCord] is a complete fabrication because the negotiations with McCord started when I was entirely out of the way. I was down in Florida."

What was the motive for involving the Central Intelligence Agency in the Watergate investigation?

HALDEMAN: "The President directed John Ehrlichman and me to meet with the director [Helms] and Deputy Director [Walters] of the C.I.A. on June 23. We did so and ascertained from them that there had not been any C.I.A. involvement. We discussed the White House concern [nonetheless] regarding possible disclosure of non-Watergate-related covert C.I.A. operations or other nonrelated national security activities that had been undertaken previously by some of the Watergate participants, and we requested Deputy Director Walters to meet with Director Gray of the F.B.I. to express these concerns. I did not, at this meeting or at any other time, ask the C.I.A. to participate in any Watergate cover-up."

EHRLICHMAN: "If the C.I.A. were involved in the Watergate then obviously that would be embarrassing, awkward and difficult for the C.I.A. Mr. Helms and General Walters assured us that this was not the case. Then Mr. Haldeman said disclosure of C.I.A. operations disassociated from the Watergate would be awkward. It was there that we did not get the same kind of flat assurance, and so it was simply agreed that General Walters would make an early appointment with Pat Gray."

HELMS: "Mr. Haldeman said that there was a lot of flak about the Watergate burglary, that the opposition was capitalizing on it. Mr. Haldeman then said something to the effect that it has been decided that General Walters will go and talk to Acting Director Gray and indicate to him that these investigations might run into C.I.A. operations in Mexico and that it was desirable that this not happen."

WALTERS: "Mr. Haldeman said, 'It has been decided that General Walters will go to Director Gray and tell him that the further pursuit of this investigation in Mexico could jeopardize some assets of the Central Intelligence Agency.' It was put in a directive form."

GRAY: "I believed, and General Walters believed, that people on his [the President's] staff were using the F.B.I. and the C.I.A. to confuse the question of whether or not there was C.I.A. interest in or noninterest in people that we wanted to interview, and it could very well have been activity on the part of over-zealous individuals over there [the White House] to protect the President."

Who was involved in perjury during the first Watergate investigation?

MAGRUDER: "I personally felt that it was important to be sure that this story did not come out in its true form at that time. I want to make it clear that no one coerced me to do anything. I volunteered to work on the cover-up story. My primary contacts on the story were Mr. Dean and Mr. Mitchell."

PORTER: "He [Magruder] said, 'Would you corroborate a story that the money [paid to Liddy] was authorized for something a little bit more legitimate-sounding than dirty tricks?' I thought for a moment, and I said, 'Yes, I probably would do that.' It was a false statement."

DEAN: "I do not know when I first learned of Magruder's proposed testimony. I informed Haldeman and Ehrlichman of the story. We discussed it, and no one was sure it would hold up. We, of course, knew that it was a fabricated story."

HALDEMAN: "There was a reference to his [Dean's] feeling that Magruder had known about the Watergate planning and break-in ahead of it; in other words, that he was aware of what had gone on at Watergate. I don't believe there was any reference to Magruder committing perjury."

EHRLICHMAN: He said it was "not correct" that Mr. Dean had informed him of Mr. Magruder's perjury.

MITCHELL: "I became aware or had a belief [by the time Mr. Magruder testified to the grand jury] that it was a false story. To the best of my recollection I have never discussed it with them [Haldeman and Ehrlichman]."

DOCUMENTS

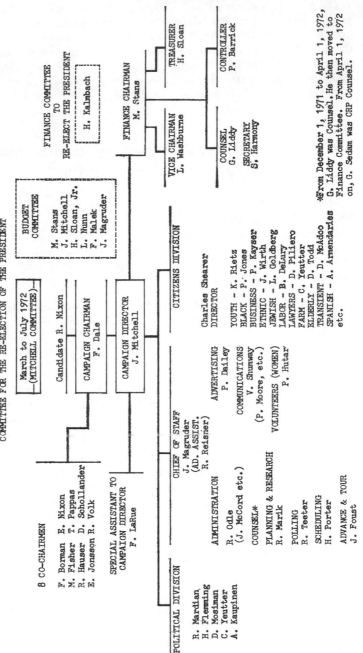

COMMITTEE FOR THE RE-ELECTION OF THE PRESIDENT

FINANCE COMMITTEE
TO
RE-ELECT THE PRESIDENT

H. Kalmbach

FINANCE CHAIRMAN
M. Stans

VICE CHAIRMAN   TREASURER
L. Washburne   H. Sloan

COUNSEL   CONTROLLER
G. Liddy   P. Barrick

SECRETARY
S. Harmony

BUDGET
COMMITTEE

M. Stans
J. Mitchell
H. Sloan, Jr.
L. Nunn
F. Malek
J. Magruder

March to July 1972
(MITCHELL COMMITTEE)

Candidate R. Nixon

CAMPAIGN CHAIRMAN
F. Dale

CAMPAIGN DIRECTOR
J. Mitchell

8 CO-CHAIRMEN

F. Borman   E. Nixon
M. Fisher   T. Pappas
R. Hauser   D. Schollander
E. Jonsson   R. Volk

SPECIAL ASSISTANT TO
CAMPAIGN DIRECTOR
F. LaRue

CHIEF OF STAFF
J. Magruder
(AD. ASSIST.
R. Reisner)

ADMINISTRATION
R. Odle
(J. McCord etc.)

COUNSEL*

PLANNING & RESEARCH
R. Marik

POLLING
R. Teeter

SCHEDULING
H. Porter

ADVANCE & TOUR
J. Foust

ADVERTISING
P. Dailey

COMMUNICATIONS
V. Shumway
(P. Moore, etc.)

VOLUNTEERS (WOMEN)
P. Hutar

CITIZENS DIVISION

Charles Shearer
DIRECTOR

YOUTH - K. Rietz
BLACK - P. Jones
BUSINESS - P. Kayser
ETHNIC - J. Wirth
JEWISH - L. Goldberg
LABOR - B. DeLury
LAWYERS - D. Piliero
FARM - C. Yeutter
ELDERLY - D. Todd
TRANSIENT - D. McAdoo
SPANISH - A. Armendaries
etc.

POLITICAL DIVISION

R. Mardian
H. Flemming
D. Mosiman
C. Yeutter
A. Kaupinen

*From December 1, 1971 to April 1, 1972,
G. Liddy was Counsel. He then moved to
Finance Committee. From April 1, 1972
on, G. Sedam was CRP Counsel.

WHITE HOUSE ORGANIZATION CHART
1971-1972, with subsequent personnel changes noted

PRESIDENT
R. Nixon

COUNSELORS
R. Finch (12-15-72)
D. Rumsfeld (2-1-73)

CONGRESSIONAL RELATIONS
C. MacGregor (7-1-72)
W. Timmons
etc.

DOMESTIC AFFAIRS
J. Ehrlichman (5-19-73)
K. Cole

DOMESTIC COUNCIL
J. Campbell (2-16-73)
E. Krogh (12-9-72) G. Liddy (12-10-71)
etc.
K. Chenow (5-19-72)
etc.

WHITE HOUSE OPERATIONS
H. Haldeman (5-19-73)

L. Higby
G. Strachan (12-3-72)

FOREIGN AFFAIRS
H. Kissinger
A. Haig (1-4-73)

NATIONAL SECURITY COUNCIL
D. Young
(Detailed to Dom. Ccl. July 1971, left staff 3-30-73)

BUSINESS & REGULATORY AGENCIES
P. Flanigan

COMMUNICATIONS
H. Klein
J. Magruder (5-1-71)
R. Odle (5-1-71)
H. Porter (4-29-71)

PRESS
R. Ziegler

ADMINISTRATION
A. Butterfield (3-14-73)
B. Kehrli

SPEECHES
R. Price
P. Buchanan
K. Khachigan

SCHEDULING
D. Chapin (2-28-73)
R. Walker (1-9-73)
H. Sloan (3-6-71)
etc.

COUNSEL TO PRESIDENT
J. Dean (5-19-73)
J. Caulfield (6-30-72)
etc.

PERSONNEL
F. Malek (7-1-72)

POLITICAL
H. Dent (12-26-72)
F. LaRue (2-15-72)

OUTSIDE ORGANIZATIONS
C. Colson (3-10-73)
R. Howard
R. Moore
etc.

CONSULTANT
E. Hunt (4-1-72)

The following three documents are the texts of (1) recommendations for increased domestic intelligence gathering made to President Nixon by an interagency Government committee; (2) an analysis of the committee's report and of strategy to be used to secure the cooperation of J. Edgar Hoover; and (3) a "decision memorandum" reflecting President Nixon's approval of the committee's recommendations. The President later rescinded his approval after the plan was opposed by Mr. Hoover.

Domestic Intelligence Gathering Plan: Recommendations

July, 1970

TOP SECRET
Handle via Comint Channels Only

Operational Restraints on Intelligence Collection

A. Interpretive Restraint on Communications Intelligence

RECOMMENDATION:
Present interpretation should be broadened to permit and program for coverage by N.S.A. [National Security Agency] of the communications of U.S. citizens using international facilities.
RATIONALE:
The F.B.I. does not have the capability to monitor international communications. N.S.A. is currently doing so on a restricted basis, and the information is particularly useful to the White House and it would be to our disadvantage to allow the F.B.I. to determine what N.S.A. should do in this area without regard to our own requirements. No appreciable risk is involved in this course of action.

B. Electronic Surveillance and Penetrations

RECOMMENDATION:
Present procedures should be changed to permit intensification of coverage of individuals and groups in the United States who pose a major threat to the internal security.
Also, present procedures should be changed to permit intensification of coverage of foreign nationals and diplomatic establishments in the United States of interest to the intelligence community.
At the present time, less than [unclear] electronic penetrations

are operative. This includes coverage of the C.P.U.S.A. [Communist Party, U.S.A.] and organized crime targets, with only a few authorized against subject of pressing internal security interest.

Mr. Hoover's statement that the F.B.I. would not oppose other agencies seeking approval for the operating electronic surveillances is gratuitous since no other agencies have the capability.

Everyone knowledgeable in the field, with the exception of Mr. Hoover, concurs that existing coverage is grossly inadequate. C.I.A. and N.S.A. note that this is particularly true of diplomatic establishments, and we have learned at the White House that it is also true of New Left groups.

C. Mail Coverage

RECOMMENDATION:
Restrictions on legal coverage should be removed.

Also, present restrictions on covert coverage should be relaxed on selected targets of priority foreign intelligence and internal security interest.

RATIONALE:
There is no valid argument against use of legal mail covers except Mr. Hoover's concern that the civil liberties people may become upset. This risk is surely an acceptable one and hardly serious enough to justify denying ourselves a valuable and legal intelligence tool.

Covert coverage is illegal and there are serious risks involved. However, the advantages to be derived from its use outweigh the risks. This technique is particularly valuable in identifying espionage agents and other contacts of foreign intelligence services.

D. Surreptitious Entry

RECOMMENDATION:
Present restrictions should be modified to permit procurement of vitally needed foreign cryptographic material.

Also, present restrictions should be modified to permit selective use of this technique against other urgent security targets.

RATIONALE:
Use of this technique is clearly illegal: it amounts to burglary. It is also highly risky and could result in great embarrassment if exposed. However, it is also the most fruitful tool and can produce the, type of intelligence which cannot be obtained in any other fashion.

The F.B.I., in Mr. Hoover's younger days, used to conduct such operations with great success and with no exposure. The information secured was invaluable.

N.S.A. has a particular interest since it is possible by this technique to secure material with which N.S.A. can break foreign cryptographic codes. We spend millions of dollars attempting to break these codes by machine. One successful surreptitious entry can do the job successfully at no dollar cost.

Surreptitious entry of facilities occupied by subversive elements can turn up information about identities, methods of operation, and other invaluable investigative information which is not otherwise obtainable. This technique would be particularly helpful if used against the Weathermen and Black Panthers.

The deployment of the executive protector force has increased the risk of surreptitious entry of diplomatic establishments. However, it is the belief of all except Mr. Hoover that the technique can still be successfully used on a selective basis.

E. Development of Campus Sources

RECOMMENDATION:
Present restrictions should be relaxed to permit expanded coverage of violence-prone campus and student-related groups.

Also, C.I.A. coverage of American students (and others) traveling or living abroad should be increased.

RATIONALE:
The F.B.I. does not currently recruit any campus sources among individuals below 21 years of age. This dramatically reduces the pool from which sources may be drawn. Mr. Hoover is afraid of a young student surfacing in the press as an F.B.I. source, although the reaction in the past to such events has been minimal. After all, everyone assumes the F.B.I. has such sources.

The campus is the battleground of the revolutionary protest movement. It is impossible to gather effective intelligence about the movement unless we have campus sources. The risk of exposure is minimal, and where exposure occurs the adverse publicity is moderate and short-lived. It is a price we must be willing to pay for effective coverage of the campus scene. The intelligence community, with the exception of Mr. Hoover, feels strongly that it is imperative the [unclear] increase the number of campus sources this fall in order to forestall widespread violence.

C.I.A. claims there are not existing restraints on its coverage of overseas activities of U.S. nationals. However, this coverage has been grossly inadequate since 1965 and an explicit directive to increase coverage is required.

F. Use of Military Undercover Agents

RECOMMENDATION:
Present restrictions should be retained.

RATIONALE:
The intelligence community is agreed that the risks of lifting these restraints are greater than the value of any possible intelligence which would be acquired by doing so.

Budget and Manpower Restrictions

RECOMMENDATION:
Each agency should submit a detailed estimate as to projected manpower needs and other costs in the event the various investigative restraints herein are lifted.

RATIONALE:
In the event that the above recommendations are concurred in, it will be necessary to modify existing budgets to provide the money and manpower necessary for their implementation. The intelligence community has been badly hit in the budget squeeze. (I suspect the foreign intelligence operations are in the same shape) and it maybe will be necessary to make some modifications. The projected figures should be reasonable, but will be subject to individual review if this recommendation is accepted.

Measures to Improve Domestic Intelligence Operations

RECOMMENDATION:
A permanent committee consisting of the F.B.I., C.I.A., N.S.A., D.I.A. [Defense Intelligence Agency] and the military counterintelligence agencies should be appointed to provide evaluations of domestic intelligence estimates, and carry out the other objectives specified in the report.

RATIONALE:
The need for increased coordination, joint estimates, and responsiveness to the White House is obvious to the intelligence community. There are a number of operational problems which need to be worked out since Mr. Hoover is fearful of any mechanism which might jeopardize his autonomy. C.I.A. would prefer an ad hoc committee to see how the system works, but other members believe that this would merely delay the establishment of effective coordination and joint operations. The value of lifting intelligence collection restraints is proportional to the availability of joint operations and evaluation, and the establishment of this interagency group is considered imperative.

Domestic Intelligence Gathering Plan: Analysis and Strategy

July, 1970

TOP SECRET

Memorandum for: H. R. Haldeman
From: Tom Charles Huston
Subject: Domestic intelligence review

1. Background

A working group consisting of the top domestic intelligence officials of the FBI, CIA, DIA, NAS, and each of the military services met regularly throughout June to discuss the problems outlined by the President and to draft the attached report. The discussions were frank and the quality of work first-rate. Cooperation was excellent, and all were delighted that an opportunity was finally at hand to address themselves jointly to the serious internal security threat which exists.

I participated in all meetings, but restricted my involvement to keeping the committee on the target the President established. My impression that the report would be more accurate and the recommendations more helpful if the agencies were allowed wide latitude in expressing their opinions and working out arrangements which they felt met the President's requirements consistent with the resources and missions of the member agencies.

2. Mr. Hoover

I went into this exercise fearful that C.I.A. would refuse to cooperate. In fact, Dick Helms [Director of Central Intelligence] was most cooperative and helpful, and the only stumbling block was Mr. Hoover. He attempted at the first meeting to divert the committee from operational problems and redirect its mandate to the preparation of another analysis of existing intelligence. I declined to acquiesce in this approach, and succeeded in getting the committee back on target.

When the working group completed its report, Mr. Hoover refused to go along with a single conclusion drawn or support a single recommendation made. His position was twofold:

(1) Current operations are perfectly satisfactory and (2) No one has any business commenting on procedures he has established for the collection of intelligence by the F.B.I. He attempted to modify the body of the report, but I successfully opposed it on the

grounds that the report was the conclusion of all the agencies, not merely the F.B.I. Mr. Hoover then entered his objections as footnotes to the report. Cumulatively, his footnotes suggest that he is perfectly satisfied with current procedures and is opposed to any changes whatsoever. As you will note from the report, his objections are generally inconsistent and frivolous—most express concern about possible embarrassment to the intelligence community (i.e., Hoover) from public disclosure of clandestine operations.

Admiral Gayler and General Bennett were greatly displeased by Mr. Hoover's attitude and his insistence on footnoting objections. They wished to raise a formal protest and sign the report only with the understanding that they opposed the footnotes. I prevailed upon them not to do so since it would only aggravate Mr. Hoover and further complicate our efforts. They graciously agreed to go along with my suggestion in order to avoid a nasty scene and jeopardize the possibility of positive action resulting from the report. I assured them that their opinion would be brought to the attention of the President.

3. Threat Assessment

The first 23 pages of the report constitute an assessment of the existing internal security threat, our current intelligence coverage of this threat, and areas where our coverage is inadequate. All agencies concurred in this assessment, and it serves to explain the importance of expanded intelligence collection efforts.

4. Restraints on Intelligence Collection

Part Two of the report discusses specific operational restraints which currently restrict the capability of the intelligence community to collect the types of information necessary to deal effectively with the internal security threat. The report explains the nature of the restraints and sets out the arguments for and against modifying them. My concern was to afford the President the strongest arguments on both sides of the question so that he could make an informed decision as to the future course of action to be followed by the intelligence community.

I might point out that of all the individuals involved in the preparation and consideration of this report, only Mr. Hoover is satisfied with existing procedures.

Those individuals within the F.B.I. who have day-to-day responsibilities for domestic intelligence operations privately disagree with Mr. Hoover and believe that it is imperative that changes in operating procedures be initiated at once.

I am attaching to this memorandum my recommendations on the decision the President should make with regard to these operational restraints. Although the report sets forth the pros and cons on each issue, it may be helpful to add my specific recommendations and the reasons therefore in the event the President has some doubts on a specific course of action.

5. Improvement in Interagency Coordination

All members of the committee and its working group, with the exception of Mr. Hoover, believe that it is imperative that a continuing mechanism be established to effectuate the coordination of domestic intelligence efforts and the evaluation of domestic intelligence data. In the past there has been no systematic effort to mobilize the full resources of the intelligence community in the internal security area and there has been no mechanism for preparing community-wide domestic intelligence estimates such as is done in the foreign intelligence area by the United States Intelligence Board. Domestic intelligence information coming into the White House has been fragmentary and unevaluated. We have not had for example, a community-wide estimate of what we might expect short- or long-term in the cities or on the campuses or within the military establishment.

Unlike most of the bureaucracy, the intelligence community welcomes direction and leadership from the White House. There appears to be agreement, with the exception of Mr. Hoover, that effective coordination within the community is possible only if there is direction from the White House. Moreover, the community is pleased that the White House is finally showing interest in their activities and an awareness of the threat which they so acutely recognize.

I believe that we will be making a major contribution to the security of the country if we can work out an arrangement which provides for institutionalized coordination within the intelligence community and effective leadership from the White House.

6. Implementation of the President's Decisions

If the President should decide to lift some of the current restrictions and if he should decide to authorize a formalized domestic intelligence structure, I would recommend the following steps:

(A) Mr. Hoover should be called in privately for a stroking session at which the President explains the decision he has made, thanks Mr. Hoover for his candid advice and past cooperation, and indicates he is counting on Edgar's cooperation in implementing the new decisions.

(B) Following this Hoover session, the same individuals who were present at the initial session in the Oval Office should be invited back to meet with the President. At that time, the President should thank them for the report, announce his decisions, indicate his desires for future activity, and present each with an autographed copy of the photo of the first meeting which Ollie took.

(C) An official memorandum setting forth the precise decisions of the President should be prepared so that there can be no misunderstanding. We should also incorporate a review procedure which will enable us to ensure that the decisions are fully implemented.

I hate to suggest a further imposition on the President's time, but think these steps will be necessary to pave over some of the obvious problems which may arise if the President decides, as I hope he will, to overrule Mr. Hoover's objections to many of the proposals made in this report. Having seen the President in action with Mr. Hoover, I am confident that he can handle this situation in such a way that we can get what we want without putting Edgar's nose out of joint. At the same time, we can capitalize on the goodwill the President has built up with the other principals and minimize the risk that they may feel they are being forced to take a back seat to Mr. Hoover.

7. Conclusion

I am delighted with the substance of this report and believe it is a first-rate job. I have great respect for the integrity, loyalty, and competence of the men who are operationally responsible for internal security matters and believe that we are on the threshold of an unexcelled opportunity to cope with a very serious problem in its germinal stages when we can avoid the necessity for harsh measures by acting swift, discreetly, and decisively to deflect the threat before it reaches alarming proportions.

I might add, in conclusion, that it is my personal opinion that Mr. Hoover will not hesitate to accede to any decision which the President makes, and the President should not, therefore, be reluctant to overrule Mr. Hoover's objections. Mr. Hoover is set in his ways and can be bull-headed as hell, but he is a loyal trooper. Twenty years ago he would never have raised the type of objections he has here, but he's getting old and worried about his legend. He makes life tough in this area, but not impossible—for he'll respond to direction by the President and that is all we need to set the domestic intelligence house in order.

Domestic Intelligence Gathering Plan: Decision Memorandum

July 15, 1970

TOP SECRET
Handle via Comint Channels Only

Subject: Domestic Intelligence

The President has carefully studied the special report of the interagency Committee on Intelligence (ad hoc) and made the following decisions:

1. Interpretive Restraint on Communications Intelligence

National Security Council Intelligence Directive Number 6 (NSCID-6) is to be interpreted to permit N.S.A. to program for coverage and communications of U.S. citizens using international facilities.

2. Electronic Surveillances and Penetrations

The intelligence community is directed to intensify coverage of individuals and groups in the United States who pose a major threat to the internal security. Also, coverage of foreign nationals and diplomatic establishments in the United States of interest to the intelligence community is to be intensified.

3. Mail Coverage

Restrictions on legal coverage are to be removed, restrictions on covert coverage are to be relaxed to permit use of this technique on selected targets of priority foreign intelligence and internal security interest.

4. Surreptitious Entry

Restraints on the use of surreptitious entry are to be removed. The technique is to be used to permit procurement of vitally needed foreign cryptographic material and against other urgent and high priority internal security targets.

5. Development of Campus Sources

Coverage of violence-prone campus and student-related groups is to be increased. All restraints which limit this coverage are to be removed. Also, C.I.A. coverage of American students (and others) traveling or living abroad is to be increased.

6. Use of Military Undercover Agents

Present restrictions are to be retained.

7. Budget and Manpower

Each agency is to submit a detailed estimate as to projected manpower needs and other costs required to implement the above decisions.

8. Domestic Intelligence Operations

A committee consisting of the directors or other appropriate representatives appointed by the directors, of the F.B.I., C.I.A., N.S.A., D.I.A., and the military counterintelligence agencies is to be constituted effective August 1, 1970, to provide evaluations of domestic intelligence, prepare periodic domestic intelligence estimates, carry out the other objectives specified in the report, and perform such other duties as the President shall, from time to time, assign. The director of the F.B.I. shall serve as chairman of the committee. Further details on the organization and operations of this committee are set forth in an attached memorandum.

The President has directed that each addressee submit a detailed report, due on September 1, 1970, on the steps taken to implement these decisions. Further such periodic reports will be requested as circumstances merit.

The President is aware that procedural problems may arise in the course of implementing these decisions. However, he is anxious that such problems be resolved with maximum speed and minimum misunderstanding. Any difficulties which may arise should be brought to my immediate attention in order that an appropriate solution may be found and the President's directives implemented in a manner consistent with his objectives.

Tom Charles Huston

Organization and Operations of the Interagency Group on Domestic Intelligence and Internal Security (IAG)

TOP SECRET
Handle via Comint Channels Only

1. Membership

The membership shall consist of representatives of the F.B.I., C.I.A., D.I.A., N.S.A., and the counterintelligence agencies of the Departments of the Army, Navy, and Air Force. To insure the high level consideration of issues and problems which the President expects to be before the group, the directors of the respective agencies should serve personally. However, if necessary and appropriate, the director of a member agency may designate another individual to serve in his place.

2. Chairman

The director of the F.B.I. shall serve as chairman. He may designate another individual from his agency to serve as the F.B.I. representative on the group.

3. Observers

The purpose of the group is to effectuate community wide coordination and secure the benefits of communty-wide analysis and estimating. When problems arise which involve areas of interest to agencies or departments not members of the group, they shall be invited, at the discretion of the group, to join the group as observers and participants in those discussions of interest to them. Such agencies and departments include the Departments of State (I & R, Passport); Treasury (I.R.S., Customs); Justice (B.N.D.D., Community Relations Service); and such other agencies which may have investigative or law enforcement responsibilities touching on domestic intelligence or internal security matters.

4. White House Liaison

The President has assigned to Tom Charles Huston staff responsibility for domestic intelligence and internal security affairs. He will participate in all activities of the group as the personal representative of the President.

5. Staffing

The group will establish such subcommittee or working groups as it deems appropriate. It will also determine and implement such staffing requirements as it may deem necessary to enable it to carry out its responsibilities, subject to the approval of the President.

6. Duties

The group will have the following duties:

(A) Define the specific requirements of member agencies of the intelligence community.

(B) Effect close, direct coordination between member agencies.

(C) Provide regular evaluations of domestic intelligence.

(D Review policies governing operations in the field of domestic intelligence and develop recommendations.

(E) Prepare periodic domestic intelligence estimates which incorporate the results of the combined efforts of the intelligence community.

(F) Perform such other duties as the President may from time to time assign.

7. Meetings

The group shall meet at the call of the chairman, a member agency, or the White House representative.

8. Security

Knowledge of the existence and purposes of the group shall be limited on a strict "need to know" basis. Operations of, and papers originating with, the group shall be classified "top secret handle via Comint channels only."

9. Other Procedures

The group shall establish such other procedures as it believes appropriate to the implementation of the duties set forth above.

Dean Memorandum to Mitchell

Sept. 18, 1970

Memorandum for the Attorney General:

Pursuant to our conversation yesterday, Sept. 17, 1970, I suggest the following procedures to commence our domestic intelligence operation as quickly as possible.

1. Interagency domestic intelligence unit. A key to the entire operation will be the creation of an interagency intelligence unit for both operational and evaluation purposes. Obviously, the selection of persons to this unit will be of vital importance to the success of the mission. Hoover has indicated a strong opposition to the creation of such a unit. I believe we agreed that it would be inappropriate to have any blanket removal of restrictions; rather, the most appropriate procedure would be to decide on the type of intelligence we need, based on an assessment of the recommendations of this unit and then to remove the restraints, as necessary.

2. Housing. We discussed the appropriate housing of this operation and, upon reflection, I believe that rather than a White House staffer looking for suitable space, that a professional intelligence person should be assigned the task of locating such space. Acordingly, I would suggest that a request be made that Mr. Hoover assign an agent to this task. In connection with the housing problem, I think serious consideration must be given to the

appropriate Justice Department cover for the domestic intelligence operation. The I.D.I.U. cover would eliminate the problem of discovering a new intelligence operation in the Department of Justice. However, I have reservations about the personnel in I.D.I.U.

3. Assistant to Attorney General. We also discussed the need for you to have a right hand man to assist in running this operation. It would seem that what is needed is a man with administrative skills, a sensitivity to the implications of the current radical and subversive movements within the United States, and preferably, some background in intelligence work. To maintain the cover, I would think it appropriate for the man to have a law degree in that he will be a part of the Department of Justice. You suggested the possibility of using a prosecutor who had had experience with demonstrations or riot type cases.

Bob Haldeman has suggested to me that if you would like him to join you in a meeting with Hoover he will be happy to do so.

White House "Enemies" List and Memorandums Relating to Those Named

The original list of 20 names of White House "enemies" was submitted with comments to John W. Dean by the office of Charles W. Colson and released by the Senate Watergate committee.

In addition there is another list submitted by Mr. Dean that he said was prepared by Mr. Colson's office that is apparently the master list of "political opponents" of the White House. No date is on that list.

Following this are two memorandums from Mr. Colson to Mr. Dean relating to such lists and a memorandum from Mr. Dean to John D. Ehrlichman and H. R. Haldeman that were all submitted to the committee by Mr. Dean.

Following these is a memo from Mr. Dean to Larry Higby, former assistant to Mr. Haldeman, giving a list of names Mr. Dean prepared.

Original List

Having studied the attached material and evaluated the recommendations for the discussed action, I believe you will find my list worthwhile for go status. It is in priority order.

1. Picker, Arnold M., United Artists Corporation, 929 Seventh Avenue, New York, N. Y.: Top Muskie fund raiser. Success here

could be both debilitating and very embarrassing to the Muskie machine. If effort looks promising, both Ruth and David Picker should be programed and then a follow-through with United Artists.

2. Barkan, Alexander E., national director of A.F.L.-C.I.O.'s Committee on Political Education, Washington, D.C.: Without a doubt the most powerful political force programed against us in 1968 ($10-million, 4.6 million votes, 115 million pamphlets, 176,000 workers—all programed by Barkan's C.O.P.E.—so says Teddy White in The Making of the President '68). We can expect the same effort this time.

3. Guthman, Ed, managing editor, L.A. Times [actually Mr. Guthman is national editor]: Guthman, former Kennedy aide, was a highly sophisticated hatchetman against us in '68. It is obvious he is the prime mover behind the current Key Biscayne effort. It is time to give him the message.

4. Dane, Maxwell, Doyle, Dane and Bernbach, New York: The top Democratic advertising firm—they destroyed Goldwater in '64. They should be hit hard starting with Dane.

5. Charles Dyson, Dyson-Kissner Corporation, New York: Dyson and Larry O'Brien were close business associates after '68. Dyson has huge business holdings and is presently deeply involved in the Businessmen's Educational Fund which bankrolls a national radio network of 5 minute programs—anti-Nixon in character.

6. Stein, Howard, Dreyfus Corporation, New York: Heaviest contributor to McCarthy in '68. If McCarthy goes, will do the same in '72. If not, Lindsay or McGovern will receive the funds.

7. Lowenstein, Allard, Long Island, New York: Guiding force behind the 18 year old "Dump Nixon" vote drive.

8. Halperin, Morton, leading executive at Common Cause: A scandal would be most helpful here.

9. Woodcock, Leonard, UAW, Detroit, Michigan: No comments necessary.

10. S. Sterling Munro Jr., Senator [Henry M.] Jackson's aide, 711 Lamberton Drive, Silver Spring, Md.: We should give him a try. Positive results would stick a pin in Jackson's white hat.

11. Feld, Bernard T., President, Council for a Livable World: Heavy far left funding. They will program an "all court press" against us in '72.

12. Davidoff, Sidney, New York City, Lindsay's top personal aide: a first class S.O.B., wheeler-dealer and suspected bagman. Positive results would really shake the Lindsay camp and Lindsay's plans to capture youth vote. Davidoff in charge.

13. Conyers, John, Congressman, Detroit: Coming on fast. Emerging as a leading black anti-Nixon spokesman. Has known weakness for white females.

14. Lambert, Samuel M., President, National Education Association: Has taken us on vis à vis Federal aid to parochial schools —a '72 issue.

15. Mott, Stewart, Rawlings, Mott Associates, New York: Nothing but big money for radic-lib candidates.

16. Dellums, Ronald, Congressman, California: Had extensive [Edward M. Kennedy] EMK-Tunney support in his election bid. Success might help in California next year.

17. Schorr, Daniel, Columbia Broadcasting System, Washington: A real media enemy.

18. S. Harrison Dogole, 2011 Walnut Street, Philadelphia, Pa.: President of Globe Security Systems—fourth largest private detective agency in U. S. Heavy Humphrey contributor. Could program his agency against us.

19. Paul Newman, California: radio-lib causes. Heavy McCarthy involvement '68. Used effectively in nation-wide T.V. commercials. '72 involvement certain.

20. McCrory, Mary, 2710 Macomb Street, Washington columnist: Daily hate Nixon articles.

"Political Opponents"

Senators—Birch Bayh, J. W. Fulbright, Fred R. Harris, Harold Hughes, Edward M. Kennedy, George McGovern, Walter Mondale, Edmund Muskie, Gaylord Nelson, William Proxmire.

Members of the House—Bella Abzug, William R. Anderson, John Brademas, Father Robert F. Drinan, Robert Kastenmeier, Wright Patman.

Black Congressmen—Shirley Chisolm, William Clay, George Collins, John Conyers, Ronald Dollums, Charles Diggs, Augustus Hawkins, Ralph Metcalf, Robert N. C. Nix, Parren Mitchell, Charles Rangel, Louis Stokes.

Miscellaneous politicos—John V. Lindsay, Mayor, New York City; Eugene McCarthy, former U. S. Senator; George Wallace, Governor, Alabama.

Organizations

Black Panthers, Hughie Newton
Brookings, Institution, Lesley Gelb and others
Business Executives Move for VN Peace—Henry Niles, Nat. Chmn, Vincent McGee, Exec. Director
Committee for an Effective Congress, Russell D. Hemmenway
Common Cause, John Gardner, Morton Halperin, Charles Goodell, Walter Hickel
COPE Alexander E. Barkan
Council for a Livable World, Bernard T. Feld, President; Prof. Physics, MIT
Farmers Union, NFO
Institute of Policy Study, Richard Barnet, Marcus Raskin
National Economic Council, Inc.
National Education Association, Sam M. Lambert, President

National Student Association, Charles Palmer, President
National Welfare Rights Organization, George Wiley
Potomac Associates, William Watts
SANE, Sanford Gottlieb
Southern Christian Leadership, Ralph Abernathy
Third National Convocation on The Challenge of Building Peace, Robert V. Roosa, Chairman
Businessmen's Educational Fund

Labor

Karl Feller, Pres. Internat. Union of United Brewery, Flour, Cereal, Soft Drink and Distillery Workers, Cincinnati
Harold J. Gibbons, International Vice Pres., Teamsters
A. F. Grospiron, Pres., Oil, Chemical & Atomic Workers International Union, Denver
Matthew Guinan, Pres., Transport Workers Union of America, New York City
Paul Jennings, Pres., International Union of Electrical, Radio & Machine Workers, D. C.
Herman D. Kenin, Vice Pres., AFL-CIO, D.C.
Lane Kirkland, Secretary-Treasurer, AFL-CIO (but we must deal with him)
Frederick O'Neal, Pres., Actors and Artists of America, New York City
William Pollock, Pres., Textile Workers Union of America, New York City
Jacob Potofsky, General Pres., Amalgamated Clothing Workers of America, New York City
Leonard Woodcock, President, United Auto Workers, Detroit
Jerry Wurf, International President, American Federal, State, County and Municipal Employees, Washington, D.C.
Nathaniel Goldfinger, AFL-CIO
I. W. Abel, Steelworkers

Media

Jack Anderson, columnist, "Washington Merry-Go-Round"
Jim Bishop, author, columnist, King Features Syndicate
Thomas Braden, columnist, Los Angeles Times Syndicate
D. J. R. Bruckner, Los Angeles Times Syndicate
Marquis Childs, chief Washington corespondent, St. Louis Post Dispatch
James Deakin, White House correspondent, St. Louis Post Dispatch
James Doyle, Washington Star
Richard Dudman, St. Louis Post Dispatch
William Eaton, Chicago Daily News
Rowland Evans, Jr., Syndicated columnist, Publishers Hall

Saul Friedmann, Knight Newspapers, syndicated columnist
Clayton Fretchey, syndicated columnist, Washington correspondent, Harpers
George Frazier, Boston Globe
Pete Hamill, New York Post
Michael Harrington, author and journalist; Member, Executive Comm. Socialist party
Sydney Harris, columnist, drama critic and writer of 'Strictly Personal,' syndicated Publishers Hall
Robert Healy, Boston Globe
William Hines, Jr., journalist; science and education, Chicago Sun Times
Stanley Karnow, foreign correspondent, Washington Post
Ted Knap, syndicated columnist, New York Daily News
Edwin Knoll, Progressive
Morton Kondracke, Chicago Sun Times
Joseph Kraft, syndicated columnist, Publishers Hall
James Laird, Philadelphia Inquirer
Max Lerner, syndicated columnist, New York Post; author, lecturer, professor.
Stanley Levey, Scripps Howard
Flora Lewis, syndicated columnist on economics
Stuart Loory, Los Angeles Times
Mary McGrory, syndicated columnist on New Left
Frank Mankiewicz, syndicated columnist, Los Angeles Times
James Millstone, St. Louis Post Dispatch
Martin Nolan, Boston Globe
Ed Guthman, L. A. Times
Thomas O'Neill, Baltimore Sun
John Pierson, Wall Street Journal
William Prochnau, Seattle Times
James Reston, New York Times
Carl Rowan, syndicated columnist, Publishers Hall
Warren Unna, Washington Post, NET
Harriet Van Horne, columnist, New York Post
Milton Viorst, reporter, author, writer
James Wechsler, New York Post
Tom Wicker, New York Times
Gary Wills, syndicated columnist, author of "Nixon-Agonistes"
The New York Times
Washington Post
St. Louis Post Dispatch
Jules Duscha, Washingtonian
Robert Manning, Editor Atlantic
John Osborne, New Republic
Richard Rovere, New Yorker
Robert Sherrill, Nation
Paul Samuelson, Newsweek
Julian Goodman, Chief Executive Officer, NBC

John Macy, Jr., Pres., Public Broadcasting Corporation; former Civil Service Comm.
Marvin Kalb, CBS
Daniel Shorr, CBS
Lem Tucker, NBC
Sander Vanocur, NBC

Celebrities

Carol Channing, actress
Bill Cosby, actor
Jane Fonda, actress
Steve McQueen, actor
Joe Namath, New York Giants [Jets]; businessman; actor
Paul Newman, actor
Gregory Peck, actor
Tony Randall, actor
Barbra Streisand, actress
Dick Gregory [comedian]

Businessmen

Charles B. Beneson, President, Beneson Realty Co.
Nelson Bengston, President, Bengston & Co.
Holmes Brown, Vice President, Public Relations, Continental Can Co.
Benjamin Buttenweiser, Limited Partner, Kuhn, Loeb & Co.
Lawrence G. Chait, Chairman, Lawrence G. Chait & Co., Inc.
Ernest R. Chanes, President, Consolidated Water Conditioning Co.
Maxwell Dane, Chairman, Exec. Committee, Doyle, Dane & Bernbach, Inc.
Charles H. Dyson, Chairman, The Dyson-Kissner Corp.
Norman Eisner, President, Lincoln Graphic Arts
Charles B. Finch, Vice President, Alleghany Power System Inc.
Frank Heineman, President, Men's Wear International
George Hillman, President, Ellery Products Manufacturing Co.
Bertram Lichtenstein, President, Delton Ltd.
William Mancaloff, President, Concord Steel Corp.
Gerald McKee, President, McKee, Berger, Mansueto
Paul Milstein, President, Circle Industries Corp.
Stewart R. Mott, Stewart R. Mott, Associates
Lawrence S. Phillips, President, Phillips-Van Heusen Corp.
David Rose, Chairman, Rose Associates
Julian Roth, Senior Partner, Emery Roth & Sons
William Ruder, President, Ruder & Finn, Inc.
Si Scharer, President, Scharer Associates, Inc.
Alfred P. Slaner, President, Kayser-Roth Corp.
Roger Sonnabend, Chairman, Sonesta International Hotels

Business Additions

Business Executives Move for Vietnam Peace and New National Priorities Cont.

Morton Sweig, President, National Cleaning Contractors

Alan V. Tishman, Exec. VP, Tishman Realty & Construction Co., Inc.

Ira D. Wallach, President, Gottesman & Co., Inc.

George Weissman, President, Philip Morris Corp.

Ralph Weller, President, Otis Elevator Company

Business

Clifford Alexander, Jr., Member, Equal Opportunity Comm.; LBJ's Spec. Assistant

Hugh Calkins, Cleveland lawyer, member, Harvard Corporation

Ramsey Clark, partner, Weiss, Goldberg, Rifkind, Wharton & Garrison; former Attorney General

Lloyd Cutler, lawyer, Wilmer, Cutler & Pickering, Washington, D. C.

Henry L. Kimelman, chief fund raiser for McGovern; Pres., Overview Group

Raymond Lapin, former Pres., FNMA; corporation executive

Hans F. Loeser, Chairman, Boston Lawyers' Vietnam Committee

Robert McNamara, President, World Bank; former Secretary of Defense

Hans Morgenthau, former U.S. Attorney in New York City [Robert Morgenthau]

Victor Palmieri, lawyer, business consultant, real estate exec., Los Angeles

Arnold Picker, Muskie's chief fund raiser; Chmn. Exec. Comm., United Artists

Robert S. Pirie, Harold Hughes' chief fund raiser; Boston lawyer —

Joseph Rosenfield, Harold Hughes' money man, retired Des Moines lawyer

Henry Rowen, Pres., Rand Corp., former Asst. Director of Budget (LBJ)

R. Sargent Shriver, Jr., former U.S. Ambassador to France; lawyer, Strasser, Spiegelberg, Fried, Frank & Kempelman, Washington, D.C.

Theodore Sorensen, lawyer, Weiss, Goldberg, Rifkind, Wharton & Garrison, New York

Ray Stark, Broadway producer

Howard Stein, President and Director, Dreyfus Corporation

Milton Semer, Chairman, Muskie Election Committee; lawyer, Semer and Jacobsen

George H. Talbot, Pres., Charlotte Liberty Mutual Insurance Co.; headed anti-VN ad

Arthur Taylor, Vice President, International Paper Company

Jack Valenti, President, Motion Picture Association

Paul Warnke, Muskie financial supporter, former Asst. Secy. of Defense

Thomas J. Watson, Jr., Muskie financial supporter; Chmn., IBM

Academics

Michael Ellis De Bakey, Chmn., Dept. Surgery, Baylor University; Surgeon-in-chief, Ben Taub General Hospital, Texas

Derek Curtis Bok, Dean, Harvard Law School

Kingman Brewster, Jr., President Yale University

McGeorge Bundy, President, Ford Foundation

Avram Noam Chomsky, Professor of Modern Languages, MIT

Daniel Ellsberg, Professor, MIT

George Drennen Fischer, Member, Executive Committee, National Education Assn.

J. Kenneth Galbraith, Professor of Economics, Harvard

Patricia Harris, educator, lawyer, former U.S. Ambassador; Chmn. Welfare Committee Urban League

Walter Heller, Regents Professor of Economics

Edwin Land, Professor of Physics, MIT

Herbert Ley, Jr., former FDA Commissioner; Professor of Epidemiology, Harvard

Matthew Stanley Meselson, Professor of Biology, Harvard

Lloyd N. Morrisett, Professor and Associate Dir., Education Program, U. of Calif.

Joseph Rhodes, Jr., Fellow, Harvard; Member, Scranton Comm. on Campus Unrest

Bayard Rustin, civil rights

First Colson Memo (June 12, 1972)

I have received a well-informed tip that there are income tax discrepancies involving the returns of Harold J. Gibbons, a vice president of the Teamsters Union in St. Louis. This has come to me on very, very good authority.

Gibbons, you should know, is an all out enemy, a McGovernite, ardently anti-Nixon. He is one of the three labor leaders who were recently invited to Hanoi.

Please see if this one can be started on at once and if there is an informer's fee, let me know. There is a good cause at which it can be donated.

Second Colson Memo (Nov. 17, 1972)

I have received from an informer some interesting information on Jack Anderson, including a report that Jack Anderson was found in a room with wiretap equipment and a private investigator in connection with the Dodd investigation. Anderson, according to my source, had the wiretap equipment supplied to him by a Washington, D.C., man.

According to the same source, Anderson and Drew Pearson were paid $100,000 in 1958 by Batista to write favorable articles about the former Cuban dictator. In 1961 Anderson wrote several very favorable articles on Fidel Castro. Fredo de la Campo, Batista's Under Secretary of State, sent Anderson a telegram saying "I hope you were paid well, as well for the Castro articles as you were for the Batista articles." My source has a copy of the telegram.

You know my personal feelings about Jack Anderson. After his incredibly sloppy and malicious reporting on Eagleton, his credibility has diminished. It now appears as if we have the opportunity to destroy it. Do you agree that we should pursue this activity?

Dean Memo

This memorandum addresses the matter of how we can maximize the fact of our incumbency in dealing with persons known to be active in their opposition to our Administration. Stated a bit more bluntly—how we can use the available Federal machinery to screw our political enemies.

After reviewing this matter with a number of persons possessed of expertise in the field, I have concluded that we do not need an elaborate mechanism or game plan, rather we need a good project coordinator and full support for the project. In brief, the system would work as follows:

—Key members of the staff (e.g., Colson, Dent, Flanigan, Buchanan) could be requested to inform us as to who they feel, we should be giving a hard time.

—The project coordinator should then determine what sorts of dealings these individuals have with the Federal Government and how we can best screw them (e.g., grant availability, Federal contracts, litigation prosecution, etc.).

—The project coordinator then should have access to and the full support of the top officials of the agency or departments in proceeding to deal with the individual.

I have learned that there have been many efforts in the past to take such actions, but they have ultimately failed—in most cases —because of lack of support at the top. Of all those I have discussed this matter with, Lyn Nofizger [President's California manager] appears the most knowledgeable and most interested. If Lyn had support he would enjoy undertaking this activity as the project coordinator. You are aware of some of Lyn's successes in the field, but he feels that he can employ limited efforts because there is a lack of support.

As a next step, I would recommend that we develop a small list of names—not more than ten—as our targets for concentration. Request that Lyn "do a job" on them and if he finds he is getting cut off by a department agency, that he inform us and we evaluate what is necessary to proceed. I feel it is important that we keep our targets limited for several reasons: (1) a low visibility of the project is imperative; (2) it will be easier to accomplish something real if we don't over expand our efforts; and (3) we can learn more about how to operate such an activity if we start small and build.

Approve—
Disapprove—
Comment—

Dean List of Names (Sept. 14, 1971)

Attached is the list of names you requested, as well as additional materials containing other names.

The list I have prepared is merely suggestive; it is based on conversations I have had with others regarding persons who have both the desire and capability of harming us.

The list is limited to less than twenty persons, as it would be most difficult to proceed with more at this time. I would hope that we would continue to feed additional names into the process every few months, but we must keep this project within reasonable bounds.

I will await the review of these names—as I feel certain there will probably be additions and deletions from the list—before I take any action. Please keep the list at twenty or less

Eugene Carson Blake (per request) [General Secretary World Council of Churches]

Leonard Bernstein (per request) [Conductor/Composer]

Arnold Picker (United Artists Corp. Top Muskie fund raiser)

Ed Guthman (managing editor L.A. Times)

Maxwell Dane (Doyle Dane & Bernbach)

Charles Dyson (associate of Larry O'Brien bankrolls anti-RN radio programs)

Howard Stein (Dreyfus Corp.—big Demo contributor)

Allard Lowenstein (pushing the dump RN [Richard Nixon] move with young people)

Morton Halperin (top executive Common Cause)

Leonard Woodcock (UAW)

Dan Schorr (CBS)

Mary McGrory

Lloyd Cutler (principal force behind Common Cause law suit against RNC, DNC, et al)

Thomas Watson (Muskie backer—IBM)

Tom Wicker (N.Y. Times)

Clark Gifford [Clifford] (former Secretary of Defense)

Two Memorandums on Internal Revenue Service

Following are two memorandums on how the White House could use the Internal Revenue Service for political advantages, submitted to the Watergate committee by John W. Dean 3d. Mr. Dean told the committee that the memos are undated; it is probable that they were written at the request of H. R. Haldeman for the Secretary of the Treasury. Since the memo is undated, it is unclear whether they were prepared for David Kennedy or John Connally (both former Treasury Secretaries). Mr. Dean said he prepared the first memo and that John Caulfield prepared the second memo.

Dean Memo

A. The Bureaucracy:

I.R.S. is a monstrous bureaucracy, which is dominated and controlled by Democrats. The I.R.S. bureaucracy has been unresponsive and insensitive to both the White House and Treasury in many areas.

In brief, the lack of key Republican bureaucrats at high levels precludes the initiation of policies which would be proper and politically advantageous. Practically every effort to proceed in sensitive areas is met with resistance, delay and the threat of derogatory exposure.

B. Administration Appointees

Randolph Thrower became a total captive of the Democratic assistant commissioners. In the end, he was actively fighting both Treasury and the White House.

Johnnie Walters has not yet exercised leadership. Unevaluated reports assert he has been either reluctant or unwilling to do so.

Walters has appointed as his deputy William Loeb, career Democrat from Georgia. Loeb has asserted his Democratic credentials in staff meetings, according to reliable sources.

Walters appears oversensitive in his concern that I.R.S. might be labeled "political" if he moves in sensitive areas (e.g. audits, tax exemptions).

During the Democrat Administrations, I.R.S. was used discreetly for political purposes, but this has been unavailable during this Administration.

Suggestions:

Walters should be told to make the changes in personnel and

policy which will give the Administration semblance of control over the hostile bureaucracy of I.R.S. Malek should supply recommendations.

Walters must be made to know that discreet political actions and investigations on behalf of the Administration are a firm requirement and responsibility on his part.

We should have direct access to Walters for action in the sensitive areas and should not have to clear them with Treasury.

Dean should have access and assurance that Walters will get the job done—properly!

Caulfield Memo

A knowledgeable source at I.R.S. was contacted and given a hypothetical situation in which the White House made a request for an I.R.S. audit of a group of specific individuals who have the same occupation. This source advised that I.R.S. procedures would require that such request be handled by Assistant Commissioner Donald Bacon.

It is known that Bacon is a liberal Democrat holdover who has been continually identified with anti-Nixon intrigues at I.R.S. within the past two years.

The source suggested that a priority target be established within the group with preference given to one residing in the New York area. He further stated such target could discreetly be made subject to I.R.S. audit without the clear hazard for a leak traceable to the White House as postured above.

A. To Accomplish:

Make I.R.S. politically responsive. Democrat Administrations have discreetly used I.R.S. most effectively. We have been unable.

B. The Problem:

Lack of guts and effort, The Republican appointees appear afraid and unwilling to do anything with I.R.S. that could be politically helpful. For example:

—We have been unable to crack down on the multitude of tax-exempt foundations that feed left-wing political causes.

—We have been unable to stimulate audits of persons who should be audited.

—We have been unable to obtain information in the possession of I.R.S. regarding our political enemies.

—We have been unsuccessful in placing R. N. [Nixon] supporters in the I. R. S. bureaucracy.

C. H.R.H. [Haldeman] Should Tell the Sec:

Walters must be more responsive, in two key areas: personnel and political actions.

First, Walters should make personnel changes to make I.R.S. responsive to the President. Walters should work with Fred Malek immediately to accomplish this goal. (Note: There will be an opening for a general counsel of I.R.S. in the near future—this should be a first test of Walters's cooperation.)

Second, Walters should be told that discreet political action and investigations are a firm requirement and responsibility on his part. John Dean should have direct access to Walters, without Treasury clearance, for purposes of the White House. Walters should understand that when a request comes to him, it is his responsibility to accomplish it—without the White House having to tell him how to do it!

Transcript of Taped Conversation Between Hunt and General Cushman

July 22, 1971

Following is the transcript, made public at the Senate Watergate committee hearings, of a taped conversation between General Robert E. Cushman Jr. and E. Howard Hunt Jr. regarding aid for a mission from the Central Intelligence Agency. Material in brackets indicates the transcriber's interpretation and comments.

HUNT: Could we make this just the two of us?

GENERAL CUSHMAN: All right, sure. We certainly can.

H. Thank you very much. I've been charged with quite a highly sensitive mission by the White House to visit and elicit information from an individual whose ideology we aren't entirely sure of, and for that purpose they asked me to come over here and see if you could get me two things: flash alias documentation, which wouldn't have to (it's—to be backstopped) and some degree of physical disguise, for a one-time op—in and out.

C. I don't see why we can't.

H. We'll keep it as closely held as possible. I don't know how you or your cover people want to work it, but what I would like would be to meet somebody in a safe house [Note: plane comes over at this point, and words are very indistinct.] physical disguise. We're planning on traveling either Saturday or Sunday. To-morrow afternoon probably would be the earliest it could be accomplished, so if somebody could do it by tomorrow aftenoon, it would be a great job.

Well, you're looking very well.

C. Well, it's a nice job.

H. I know. I saw you at the Wisner Memorial presentation that

day, you know, the plaque that's downstairs, and, if you pardon
my saying so, you seem to have lost a little weight.

C. Yes, I've taken some off. I sort of go up and down. When I
go down, it's because I go on the wagon and don't eat very much
at all, and this is hell to pay when you're being entertained and
going to embassies and dinners, but it's the only way I can lose
weight is to be miserable, relatively miserable.

H. Yes. I have the same problem. And, curiously, since I've
retired, the thing I've missed most is the gym facilities, because I
used to go down there. I'd be there about 15 minutes before the
director would arrive, so we'd kind of overlap a bit, and that really
kept my weight down, because it discouraged midafternoon snack-
ing, you know, and then I didn't feel a need to drink when I got
home because I was too tired, you know, so I do miss that facility.

C. Well, I don't use it. I ordinarily trot or jog for thirty
minutes in the morning at home. If I wait until afternoon, I'm
too tired. I'm just getting to that old-age point where, when I
get home in the afternoon, I may work in the workshop or do a
little bit of work in the yard, but I don't feel like running.

H. I know what you mean.

C. I'm amazed at the boss, because he's still doing it, you
know. It may be five-thirty or five o'clock when he gets down
there. I'm usually pooped. I don't want athletics at that point.

H. Yes, that's right. I try to do a little setting-up exercise in
the morning, but I'm not consistent about it. [Next part indistinct,
but they're still talking about exercises.]

C. Say, I can get in touch with you at the White House, can't I?
(To tell you) what address to go to, and so forth.

H. Right. So we can lay on—you think tomorrow afternoon is
ample time?

C. I'll give it a try, yes. I haven't talked to anybody yet. I suppose they can do it. I haven't been in this business before, haven't
had to.

H. Well, Ehrlichman said that you were the—

C. Yes, he called me. I mean I haven't been in the cover
business, so I don't know if they operate real fast, but I suppose
they do.

H. Well, I know they can.

C. Yes, I suppose they—

H. It's just a question of getting some—some physical disguise.

C. What do you need? That will be the first thing they'll ask.

H. Well, I'll need, let's see, what have I got here? I probably
need just a driver's license and some pocket litter.

C. Driver's license—

H. Driver's license in any state at all, I don't care; some
pocket litter of some sort—pretty standard stuff.

C. Pocket litter?

H. Yes, that's what they call it.

[Note: They both speak together at this point, and I can't make out what is said. Transcriber.]

C. You don't care in what name?

H. I would like the first name to be Edward, that's all, if it could be Edward, because I'm being introduced to this gentleman by just one name. [Note: few words indistinct] early this morning that somebody by the name of Edward would be getting in touch with him.

C. And any state for the driver's license?

H. Yes, any state, it doesn't make any difference, and I'm just going to have to check into a hotel, and I'll use this alias documentation for that.

C. Yes.

H. And I'll be talking to the same people in and out, and if it goes a little bit well, that's swell. [You can't be a . . . beggar.] I just won't exist. It's not possible this Friday.

C. OK. Let's see, you gave a number one time where I could get you.

H. Right. Chuck Colson—my office is unattended so far, but— that's a direct line to Colson's office, and my office is two floors up [and I'm only there part of the time].

C. All right, fine. Whoever is there can get a hold of you.

H Anybody can get a hold of me—

C. And I can give them the—or should I ask for you to call me back?

H. No, Joan Hall is—

C. Is the gal who answers the phone.

H. Yes, she'll answer the phone, Joan Hall, and—

C. And I can give her the time and the address.

H. Uh huh.

C. OK. I just—you know, I know so many people out here, it's just well that I'm not seen—if I'm going to put on a physical disguise, it's going to stick. I wouldn't want to be seen walking out of here. I'm sure they've got [safe] facilities downtown.

C. Yes. They sure as hell did on my last tour of duty here.

H. I remember F.E.—my private office is just a stone's throw from the Roger Smith Hotel—and it was practically an F.E. division. They had so many spooks.

C. The place I used to meet people was at an office building— right near where the Press Club is—it was the Washington Building, next door to the Press Club. There used to be a nightclub on the second floor, and we used to meet people up there. I had a gal who thought it was just lots of fun to be in this business. She used to have me meeting people out on the damn park benches and all this stuff, and I'd give her hell, if necessary. She just thought it was fun, playing a game. Well, they're keeping you busy with this new—

H. Well, they sure are, I'll tell you. But, actually, I'm delighted that they thought about me and thought to call on me and that I had the time. This gives me about a 12-hour day now.

C. Keep you from thinking you're retired.

H. I'm not going into retirement. It just [Note: Another plane comes over at this point] I'm convinced that the reason we're doing all this is for a good purpose.

C. Yes.

H. An essential purpose.

C. If you see John Ehrlichman, say hello for me.

H. I will indeed. [I expect to see him tomorrow.]

C. He's an old friend of mine from previous days. He's got a full platter too.

H. Oh, that he does.

C. How's that Domestic Council working out? You don't hear about it much in this business.

H. It's working out pretty well. Of course, two things that have really electrified the White—and I don't know why I'm telling you this because your contacts are undoubtedly much higher than mine over there but, the Pentagon Papers, of course.

C. Well, John—I think John is in charge of the security over-haul, isn't he?

H. That's right.

C. Well, I guess that's right. It's sort of a domestic problem rather than a Kissinger problem.

H. [That it is indeed.]

C. I really don't know. I only substitute for the boss, you know, at Kissinger meetings, at whatever group it is, they all have different names, but the same people sit there.

H. I find the same type of compartmentalization over there that I do here.

C. Well, let me get to work on this, and I'll get the word back to you.

H. Yes, and the less my name comes up, absolutely the better.

C. Yes.

H. If you want me to use a pseudonym with this guy—actually, I suppose the best—if he's in the room I'll get there at a specified time and I'll just go in and . . .

C. OK, Fine, I'll get the word to you on how we'll work it.

H. I hope Karl didn't resent that I asked him to—

C. Oh, no, no. I just had him in here in case there was—we needed staff [calling].

Young Memorandum to Ehrlichman on Investigation of Disclosure of Pentagon Papers

1971

MEMORANDUM FOR: John Ehrlichman
FROM: David R. Young
SUBJECT: Status of information which can be fed into Congressional investigation on Pentagon papers affair.

Initial Situation

On July 20, 1971, after a meeting with Congressmen [F. Edward] Hébert and [Leslie C.] Arends [Chairman and ranking Republican on House Armed Services Committee], [Robert C.] Mardian [Assistant Attorney-General], [William B.] Macomber [Deputy Under Secretary of State], [J. Fred] Buzhardt [General Counsel Department of Defense], reported that the Congressmen:
—Were willing to pursue the idea of an investigation;
—Would begin the investigation in a low key under a subcommittee of the House Armed Services Committee. Beginning with the questions of security clearance, classification and declassification, they would then move into the more specific case of the Pentagon study:
—agreed that Mardian, Macomber and Buzhardt would set the format, supply the substantive date and develop the scenario.

At that time it was also believed that the principal person involved in the whole publication of the Pentagon study was Ellsberg. On this basis it was estimated that it would take a little over 30 days to develop sufficient information for a Congressional investigation.

The plan then was to slowly develop a very negative picture around the whole Pentagon study affair (preparation to publication) and then to identify Ellsberg's associates and supporters on the New Left with this negative image. The end result would be to show (1) how they were intent on undermining the policy of the Government they were supposedly serving, and (2) how they have sought to put themselves above the law.

Present Situation

The above assumption that Ellsberg was the principal person responsible for the publication in The Times is no longer valid.

In fact, it appears that those in Justice and Defense most familiar with this whole enterprise believe that substantial evidence is being developed for the criminal prosecution of individuals other than Ellsberg: namely, [Leslie] Gelb, [Morton] Halperin, [Paul] Warnke and Rand executives. Buzhardt states that only the F.B.I. is disposed to thinking that Ellsberg is the sole prime mover.

In addition, the investigations have uncovered a proliferation of drafts involved in the 8, 43 and 7 volume sets and the number of copies of the sets has expanded far beyond what was initially estimated on the basis of distribution lists, etc.

It may well be that although Ellsberg is guilty of the crimes with which he is charged, he did not in fact turn the papers over to The New York Times. The Defense Department's analysis of the printed material may even show that Ellsberg did not have some of the papers which The New York Times printed.

Furthermore, the whole distribution network may be the work of still another and even larger network.

Examples of the types of problems which are presently being examined are as follows:

1) The likelihood that a good portion of the four volumes were prepared in final during the spring of 1969 while Gelb was still at Defense, and Halperin at the N.S.C. [National Security Council].

2) The curious discovery that Bill Bundy [former Assistant Secretary of State] received his 47-volume set two months before anyone else.

Status of Actions

Over 30 people (some a number of times) have been interviewed by Defense and Justice, and this week investigative teams have been dispatched to Europe and Vietnam.

Buzhardt will be interviewing Clark Clifford this Friday.

Buzhardt will interview William Kaufman shortly and this could be quite helpful in that Kaufman was one of the few people that apparently quit the project after protesting to Gelb that it was biased. Buzhardt has reason to believe that Kaufman will name names and identify those who were using the study as a brief.

An interview with [Robert S.] McNamara [former Secretary of Defense] will be conducted by Buzhardt as soon as McNamara returns from vacation in early September.

An all-out adversary interrogation of Halperin, Gelb, Warnke, Rand executives and any other prime targets developed by that time is to be undertaken by Buzhardt's team shortly.

Comment

My own impression of Buzhardt (and most of the above is based on his investigations, since Mardian's boys are concentrating on Ellsberg) is that, although he is not moving as fast as we'd like, he should get us what we want. He believes that within 14 days, when he has been able to reach some reasonably certain preliminary conclusions, we will have a good basis for setting a Congressional strategy. He is convinced that at least Gelb and the Rand executives are lying in a very grave manner, and if he can prove this I think we'll have a good idea of where we want to go and how to get there.

Recommendations

That we give Defense and Justice a little more time to develop their cases and that we set up a strategy meeting for September 9, 1971, to determine an overall game plan.

Issues to be addressed would include the following:

(1) If there is enough to bring criminal actions against Gelb, the Rand executives, etc., do we want to prosecute or do we want to bring such material out through the Congressional investigation?

(2) If criminal prosecution is decided against for all except Ellsberg, when would it be most desirable to undertake the Congressional investigation?

(3) What strategy should be followed in the actual committee investigation (A) if only Ellsberg is to be prosecuted, or (B) if all the persons are to be prosecuted?

(4) Do we want the Congressional investigation to also get into the substance of the Pentagon study? If so, a game plan must be devised for determining what, when and how information should be fed to the committee.

(5) If the decision is made to move ahead in these substantive areas careful consideration should be given to the effect of the credibility fallout on us. For this reason it might be best to stick with specific blunders such as the 1963 coup, the miscalculation on the need of forces, etc.

(Note: I am sending you a separate Hunt to Colson memorandum which attempts to select the politically damaging material involving the Democratic hierarchy. I personally believe a good deal more material could be developed along these lines. To begin with, we have [Lucien] Conein, [Edward G.] Lansdale [both former C.I.A. officers], [Gen. Paul D.] Harkins [former commander in South Vietnam] and [Frederick E.] Nolting [former Ambassador in South Vietnam] who could possibly be called upon to testify.)

(6) To what extent should we try to show the lack of objectivity and the intent of the participants in the Pentagon study to distort and mislead? (Note that exploitation of this theme undercuts points (4) and (5).)

(7) Effect of South Vietnamese election of timing of investigation.

(8) Effect of Ellsberg trial which will not come up before March of 1972 on timing of investigation.

(9) How quickly do we want to try to bring about a change in Ellsberg's image?*

*In connection with issue (9), it is important to point out that with the recent article on Ellsberg's lawyer, [Leonard B.] Boudin, we have already started on a negative press image for Ellsberg. If the present Hunt/Liddy project Number 1 is successful, it will be absolutely essential to have an overall game plan developed for its use in conjunction with the Congressional investigation. In this connection, I believe that the point of Buchanan's memorandum on attacking Ellsberg through the press should be borne in mind; namely, that the situation being attacked is too big to be undermined by planted leaks among the friendly press.

If there is to be any damaging of Ellsberg's image and those associated with him, it will therefore be necessary to fold in the press planting with the Congressional investigation. I mentioned these points to Colson earlier this week, and his reply was that we should just leave it to him and he would take care of getting the information out. I believe, however, that in order to orchestrate this whole operation we have to be aware of precisely what Colson wants to do.

Recommendation: That you sign the memorandum to Colson asking him to draw up a game plan (Tab A).

Action

That you schedule a strategy meeting on September 9th with Macomber, Mardian, Buzhardt, Krogh and Young. (I have discussed this approach with Bud and he is in agreement.)

Approve [Ehrlichman]
Disapprove
Other

C.I.A. Psychological Study of Ellsberg

August, 1971

Following is the text of the Central Intelligence Agency's first psychological study of Dr. Daniel Ellsberg. It was prepared in early August, 1971, at the request of the White House in connection with its investigation of the disclosure of the Pentagon Papers and became public on August 2, 1973. This study was found unsatisfactory and a second was prepared.

This indirect personality assessment is based primarily on background material and current impressions derived from press reports, including newspaper and magazine articles and television interviews. In addition, selected State Department and Federal Bureau of Investigation memoranda have been reviewed. As the data base is fragmentary and there has been no direct clinical evaluation of the subject, this indirect assessment should be considered highly speculative and in no way definitive.

There is nothing to suggest in the material reviewed that subject suffers from a serious mental disorder in the sense of being psychotic and out of touch with reality. There are suggestions, however that some of his long-standing personality needs were intensified by psychological pressures of the mid-life period and that this may have contributed significantly to his recent action.

An extremely intelligent and talented individual, subject apparently early made his brilliance evident. It seems likely that there were substantial pressures to succeed and that subject early had instilled in him expectations of success, that he absorbed the impression that he was special and destined for greatness. And indeed he did attain considerable academic success and seemed slated for a brilliant career.

There has been a notable zealous intensity about the subject throughout his career. Apparently finding it difficult to tolerate ambiguity and ambivalence, he was either strongly for something or strongly against it. There were suggestions of problems in achieving full success, for although his ideas glittered, he had trouble committing himself in writing.

He had a knack for drawing attention to himself and at early ages had obtained positions of considerable distinction, usually attaching himself as a "bright young man" to an older and experienced man of considerable stature who was attracted by his brilliance and flair.

But one can only sustain the role of "bright young man" so long. Most men between the ages of 35 and 45 go through a period of re-evaluation. Realizing that youth is at an end, that many of their golden dreams cannot be achieved, many men transiently drift into despair at this time.

In an attempt to escape from these feelings of despair and to regain a sense of competence and mastery, there is an increased thrust towards new activity at this time. Thus this is a time of career changes, of extramarital affairs and divorce.

It is a time when many men come to doubt their earlier commitments and are impelled to strike out in new directions.

For the individual who is particularly driven towards the heights of success and prominence, this mid-life period may be a particularly difficult time. The evidence reviewed suggests that this was so for Ellsberg, a man whose career had taken off like a rocket, but who found himself at mid-life not nearly having achieved the prominence and success he expected and desired.

Thus it may well have been an intensified need to achieve significance that impelled him to release the Pentagon Papers.

There is no suggestion that subject thought anything treasonous in his act. Rather, he seemed to be responding to what he deemed a higher order of patriotism. His exclusion of the three volumes of the papers concerned with the secret negotiations would support this.

Many of subject's own words would confirm the impression that he saw himself as having a special mission, and indeed as bearing a special responsibility. On several occasions he castigated himself for not releasing the papers earlier, observing that since he first brought them to the attention of the [Senate] Foreign Relations Committee, there had been "two invasions," more than 9,000 American lives lost, and hundreds of thousands of Vietnamese deaths.

He also on several occasions had suggested quite strongly that his action will not only alter the shape of the Vietnam war, but will materially influence the conduct of our foreign policy and the relationship between the people and the Government.

Ellsberg's reactions since emerging from seclusion have been instructive. Initially there was jubilation, an apparent enjoyment of the limelight. This was succeeded by a transient period wherein there was a sense of quiet satisfaction, of acceptance of his new-found stature, as if his personally significant actions had accomplished what he sought to achieve.

But then, embittered that Congress and the press had not whole-heartedly supported him, he turned against them. This is not surprising, for there would seem to be an insatiable quality to Ellsberg's strong need for success and recognition.

Colson Memorandum to Haldeman on Kleindienst Nomination

March 30, 1972

Following is the text of a memorandum from Charles W. Colson, to H. R. Haldeman regarding on-going hearings before the Senate Judiciary Committee on the nomination of Richard G. Kleindienst to be Attorney General. The critical issue before the committee was an allegation that Justice Department officials had decided an antitrust case involving the International Telephone and Telegraph Corporation to the advantage of the company after the company pledged $400,000 toward expenses for the Republican National Convention originally scheduled for San Diego.

Memorandum For: H. R. Haldeman March 30, 1972
From: Charles Colson
Subject: I.T.T

There are four points in the analysis you outlined to Mac-Gregor and me this morning with which MacGregor, Wally Johnson and I disagree:

[1]

Mitchell, Kleindienst or Mardian dealing with Eastland and MacGregor presumably dealing with the other members of the committtee guarantees a divided approach. One or the other has to call the shots. Kleindienst has already this morning told Mac-Gregor that he, MacGregor, should not deal with any of the other Republican Senators (Scott, Cook, etc.) but rather should deal only through Hruska. In the kind of day-to-day operation this is, that is simply an untenable arrangement.

I know you and the President are concerned that all of us are taken away from other more important matters. You should be, however, equally concerned that Mitchell in the last 30 days has done little with respect to the campaign and that may be a more serious loss than MacGregor's time and mine.

[2]

On the one hand, you have the assessment of Kleindienst, Mardian and Mitchell as to what will happen in the committee and on the floor. On the other hand, you have the legislative assessment of MacGregor, Colson and Johnson which is very different. (Johnson spent from 1968-1970 as minority counsel of this same committee and has been involved in all of the confirmation battles of this Administration either from the committee end or from the Justice Department end. He left the committee to go to Justice in 1970. MacGregor spent 10 years in Congress. I spent 5 years as a senior Senate assistant and 9 years in law practice, involving very considerable contact with the Hill. The Justice team simply has not had the same experience.)

Admittedly it is all opinion at this point, but Johnson, Mac-Gregor and I unanimously do not believe that Kleindienst can be confirmed by June 1. Johnson does not feel he can be confirmed at all and on this point I am at least doubtful. I emphasize that this is an opinion and a judgment call. Lots of things could happen. We could get a big break in the case; the media could turn around and become sympathetic to Kleindienst; the Democrats could decide that they are better having him in the job than beating him. Obviously, there are many unforeseen possibilities, but as of now that is our best assessment. I would think that whatever decision we make now should be based on the most knowledgeable—and I would add the most detached—assessment of our legislative prospects.

Wally Johnson has done a detailed analysis of the various procedural moves that are likely to be made in committee or on the floor. He is not shooting from the hip. He has analyzed it, and a Senate vote, in his judgment, cannot be achieved by June 1; the Democrats will only let it come to a vote if they have votes to reject Kleindienst, which is the least desirable outcome. Neither Johnson, MacGregor or Colson are prepared to predict whether we can hold the votes necessary to confirm him should the nomination in fact get to a vote.

[3]

Assuming MacGregor, Johnson and Colson are correct, then setting June 1 as our deadline date merely puts the hard decision off to a time when it will be considerably more volatile politically than it is today. Kleindienst's withdrawal will then be an admission of defeat but it will come two months closer to the election. In June Kleindienst will be a hot issue for the Democratic convention. Confirmation of Kleindienst's replacement will also be vastly more difficult in June than it would be now. Obviously this again is opinion.

[4]

The most serious risk for us is being ignored in the analysis you gave us this morning—there is the possibility of serious additional exposure by the continuation of this controversy. Kleindienst is not the target, the President is, but Kleindienst is the best available vehicle for the Democrats to get to the President. Make no mistake, the Democrats want to keep this case alive—whatever happens to Kleindienst—but the battle over Kleindienst elevates the visibility of the I.T.T. matter and, indeed, guarantees that the case will stay alive. It may stay alive in any event and, hence, the key question not addressed in your analysis is whether pendency for withdrawal of the Kleindienst nomination serves to increase the Democrats' desire to continue. That is the hardest call to make but for the following reasons it may be the most important point to make.

Neither Kleindienst, Mitchell nor Mardian know of the potential dangers. I have deliberately not told Kleindienst or Mitchell since both may be recalled as witnesses and Mardian does not understand the problem. Only Fred Fielding, myself and Ehrlichman have fully examined all the documents and/or information that could yet come out. A summary of some of these is attached.

[1]

Certain I.T.T. files which were not shredded have been turned over to the S.E.C., there was talk yesterday in the committee of subpoenaing these from I.T.T. These files would undermine

Griswold's testimony that he made the decision not to take the appeal to the Supreme Court. Correspondence to Connally and Petersen credits the delay in Justice's filing of the appeal to the Supreme Court in the Grinell case to direct intervention by Peterson and Connally. A memo sent to the Vice President, addressed, "Dear Ted," from Ned Gerrity tends to contradict John Mitchell's testimony because it outlines Mitchell's agreement to talk to McLaren following Mitchell's meeting with Geneen in August, 1970.

It would carry some weight in that the memo was written contemporaneous with the meeting. Both Mitchell and Geneen have testified they discussed policy only, not this case, and that Mitchell talked to no one else. The memo further states that Ehrlichman assured Geneen that the President had "instructed" the Justice Department with respect to the bigness policy. (It is, of course, appropriate for the President to instruct the Justice Department on policy, but in the context of these hearings, that revelation would lay this case on the President's doorstep.) There is another internal Ryan to Merriam memo, which is not in the hands of the S.E.C.; it follows the 1970 Agnew meeting and suggests that Kleindienst is the key man to pressure McLaren, implying that the Vice President would implement this action. We believe that all copies of this have been destroyed.

[2]

There is a Klein to Haldeman memo, date June 30, 1971, which of course precedes the date of the I.T.T. settlement, setting forth the $400,000 arrangement with I.T.T. Copies were addressed to Magruder, Mitchell and Timmons. This memo put the A.G. on constructive notice at least of the I.T.T. commitment at that time and before the settlement, facts which he has denied under oath. We don't know whether we have recovered all the copies. If known, this would be considerably more damaging than Rieneke's statement. Magruder believes it is possible, the A.G. transmitted his copy to Magruder. Magruder doesn't have the copy he received, he only has a Xerox of the copy. In short, despite a search this memo could be lying around anything at 1701.

[3]

The Justice Department has thus far resisted a request for their files, although their files were opened to Robert Hammond, one of Turner's deputies and a holdover who is now a practicing Democratic lawyer in Washington. Hammond had access to several memos that could be embarrassing. Whether he kept them or not is unknown, but it is probable that he recalls them. One is a memo of April, 1969, from Kleindienst and McLaren to Ehrlichman responding to an Ehrlichman request with respect to the rationale for bringing the case against I.T.T. in the first place. There is a subsequent April, 1970, memo from Hullin to McLaren stating that Ehrlichman had discussed his meeting with Geneen with the A.G., and suggesting to McLaren that Mitchell could give McLaren "more specified guidance."

There is another memo of September, 1970, from Ehrlichman to the A.G. referring to an "understanding" with Geneen and complaining of McLaren's actions. There is a May 5, 1971, memo from Ehrlichman to the A.G. alluding to discussions between the President and the A.G. as to the "agreed upon ends" in the resolution of the I.T.T. case and asking the A.G. whether Ehrlichman would work directly with McLaren or through Mitchell. There is also a memo to the President in the same time period. We know we have control of all the copies of this, but we don't have control of the original Ehrlichman memo to the A.G. This memo would once again contradict Mitchell's testimony and more importantly directly involve the President. We believe we have absolute security on this file within Justice, provided no copies were made within Justice and provided there are no leaks. We have no idea of the distribution that took place within Justice.

[4]

Merriam's testimony will of necessity involve direct contact with Jack Gleason. I can't believe that after Merriam's testimony. Gleason will not be called as a witness.

C.I.A. Memorandums About Watergate

Following are excerpts from nine memorandums and a note of transmittal by Lieut. Gen. Vernon A. Walters, deputy director of the Central Intelligence Agency, and a memorandum by James R. Schlesinger, Director of Central Intelligence, that were supplied in May, 1973, to a Senate Appropriations subcommittee in connection with its investigation of the Watergate case. The excerpts were transcribed by The New York Times from photocopies of the original documents. The first is a covering note apparently provided to the subcommittee prior to General Walter's testimony before the subcommittee. The excerpts appear in chronological order.

Covering Note (May 18, 1973)

The attached memoranda were never intended to be a full or verbatim account of the meetings they covered. These were notes to refresh my memory if I should need it. Originally, the only copy was held in my personal files.

Apparent inconsistency between my testimony that the President's name was not used by Haldeman in our June 23 conversation and a note that he had said that "It was the President's wish"—I wrote this note five days after the talk. When I showed it to Mr. [Richard] Helms [Director of Central Intelligence at the time], he pointed out that Haldeman had not actually used the expression, "It was the President's wish." Obviously the thought was implicit in my mind. I did not, however, correct the memo since it was for my own use only. The fact that I agreed with Helms is shown by my saying to [L. Patrick] Gray [acting director of the F.B.I.] on 5 July that it was "implicit." And in several other talks, both with Gray and [John W.] Dean [President Nixon's counsel], showing clearly that I did not believe the President knew.

In my talk with Dean on 26 June, I said "Those who were not touched by the matter would be so" if I were to do what Dean wanted.

The fifth paragraph of my memo on my talk with him on 28 June covers this also.

My whole talk with Gray on 6 July also makes this view clear.

Paragraph 5 of my memo of the July 28 conversation with Gray also reflects this view.

With regard to the reference to the Cubans in my notes on my talks with Dean on 28 June, he had expressed the view that there were three hypotheses on the bugging: 1) The Committee to Re-elect the President; 2) The C.I.A.; 3) Some other group. He never admitted any participation by the first group. I told Dean C.I.A. was not involved. He was casting about desperately for someone and pressed me for ideas. My remarks were intended only as a hypothetical assumption.

VERNON A. WALTERS

Memo (June 28, 1972)

On June 23 at 1300 [1 P.M.] on request I called with director Helms on John Ehrlichman and Robert Haldeman at Ehrlichman's office at the White House. Haldeman said that the "bugging" affair at the Democratic National Committee headquarters at the Watergate apartments had made a lot of noise and that the Democrats are trying to maximize it.

The F.B.I. had been called in and was investigating the matter. The investigation was leading to a lot of important people and this could get worse. He asked what the connection with the agency was and the director repeated that there was none.

Haldeman said the whole affair was getting embarrassing and it was the President's wish that Walters call on Acting Director L. Patrick Gray and suggest to him that, since the five suspects had been arrested, this should be sufficient and that it was not advantageous to have the inquiry pushed, especially in Mexico, etc.

Director Helms said he had talked to Gray on the previous day and made plain to him that the agency was not behind this matter and that it was not connected with it. None of the suspects was working for it nor had worked for the agency in the last two years. He had told Gray that none of his investigators was touching any covert projects of the agency, current or ongoing.

Haldeman then stated that I could tell Gray that I had talked to the White House and suggested that the investigation not be pushed further. Gray [was] receptive as he was looking for guidance in the matter.

The director repeated that the agency was not connected with the matter. I then agreed to talk to Gray, as directed. Ehrlichman implied that I should do this soon and I said that I would try to do it today.

Upon leaving the White House, I discussed the matter briefly with the director. Upon returning to the office, I called Gray [and] indicated that this was a matter of some urgency, and he agreed to see me at 1430 [2:30 P.M.] that day.

VERNON A. WALTERS
Lieutenant General,
U.S.A.

Memo (June 28, 1972)

At 1430 on 23 June I called on the acting director of the F.B.I., L. Patrick Gray, at his office in the F.B.I. building and saw him alone. I said that I had come to see him after talking to the "White House." I cited no names and he asked for none.

I added that I was aware of the director's conversation with him the previous day and while the further investigation of the Watergate affair had not touched any current or ongoing covert projects of the agency, its continuation might lead to some projects.

I recalled that the F.B.I. and the agency had an agreement in this respect and that the bureau had always scrupulously respected it. Gray said that he was aware of this and understood what it was conveying. His problem was how to low-key the matter now that it was launched.

He said that a lot of money was apparently involved and that it was a matter of a check on a Mexican bank for $89,000. He asked if the name "Dahlberg" meant anything to me and I said it did not. But that was not really significant as I had only been with the agency for a few months.

Gray then said that this was a most awkward matter to come up during an election year and he would see what he could do. I repeated that if the investigations were pushed "south of the border" it could trespass on some of our covert projects and, in view of the fact that the five men involved were under arrest, it would be best to taper off the matter there.

He replied that he understood and would have to study the matter to see how it could best be done. He would have to talk to John Dean about it. Gray said he looked forward to cooperating closely with the agency.

After some pleasantries about J. Edgar Hoover and our past military careers, I left saying that my job had been an awkward one but he had been helpful and I was grateful.

VERNON A. WALTERS

Memo *(June 28, 1972)*

June 26 at about 10 A.M. I received a phone call from Mr. Dean at the White House. He said he wished to see me about the matter that John Ehrlichman and Bob Haldeman had discussed with me on the 23d of June. I could check this out with them if I wished.

I agreed to call on him at his office in Room 106 [of the] Executive Office Building at 1145 that morning. Immediately after hanging up, I called Ehrlichman to find out if this was all right and after some difficulty I reached him and he said I could talk freely to Dean.

At 1145 I called at Dean's office and saw him alone. He said that the investigation of the Watergate "bugging" case was extremely awkward and that there were a lot of leads to important people and that the F.B.I., which was investigating the matter, was working on three theories: 1) It was organized by the Republican National Committee; 2) It was organized by the C.I.A.; 3) It was organized by some other party.

I said that I had discussed this with Director Helms and I was quite sure that the agency was not in any way involved and I knew that the director wished to distant himself and the agency from the matter.

Dean then asked whether I was sure the agency was not involved. He believed that Barker had been involved in a clandestine entry into the Chilean Embassy. I said that I was sure none of the suspects had been on the payroll for the past two years.

Dean then said that some of the accused were getting scared and "wobbling." I said that even so, they could not implicate the agency. Dean then asked whether there was not some way that the agency could pay bail for them (they'd been unable to raise bail), added that it was not just bail, but that if these men went to prison could we [the C.I.A.] find some way to pay their salaries while they were serving out their convictions?

I said that I must be quite clear. I was a deputy director and as such had only authority specifically delegated to me by the director and was not in the chain of command but that the great strength of the agency and its value to the President of the

United States lay in the fact that it was apolitical and had never gotten itself involved in political disputes. Despite the fact that I had only been with the agency a short time, I knew that the director felt strongly about this.

I then said that as big as the troubles might be with the Watergate affair, if the agency were to provide bail and pay salaries, this would become known sooner or later in the current "leaking" atmosphere of Washington and that at that point, the scandal would be 10 times greater, as such action could only be done upon direction at "the highest level" and that those who were not touched by the matter now certainly would be so.

Dean seemed at first taken aback and then very much impressed by this argument and said that it was certainly a very great risk that would have to be weighed. I repeated that the present affair would be small potatoes compared to what would happen if we did what he wanted and it leaked. He nodded gravely.

I said that, in addition, the agency would be completely discredited with the public and the Congress and would lose all value to the President and the Administration. Again he nodded gravely.

He then asked if I could think of any way we [the C.I.A.] could help. I said that I could not think of any but I would discuss the matter with the director and would be in touch with him. However, I felt that I was fully cognizant of the director's feelings in the matter. He thanked me and I left.

VERNON A. WALTERS

Memo (June 29, 1972)

On 28 June, at 1130 John Dean asked me to see him at his office in the Executive Office Building. I found him alone.

He said that the director's meeting with L. Patrick Gray, F.B.I. director, was canceled and that John Ehrlichman had suggested that Gray deal with me instead.

The problem was how to stop the F.B.I. investigation beyond the five suspects. Leads led to two other people—Ken Dahlberg, and a Mexican named Guena. Dean said that the $89,000 was only related to the bugging case and that Dahlberg was refusing to answer questions. Dean then asked hopefully whether I could do anything or had any suggestions.

I repeated that as the deputy director, I had no independent authority. I was not in the chain of command and had no authority other than that given me by the director. The idea that I act independently had no basis in fact.

Dean then asked what might be done and I said that I realized he had a tough problem, but if there were agency involvement, it could only be at Presidential directive and that the political risks that were concomitant appeared to me to be unacceptable.

At present it was a high-explosive bomb but intervention such as he suggested could transform it into a megaton hydrogen bomb. The present caper was awkward and unpleasant. Direct intervention by the agency would be electorally mortal if it became known and the chances of keeping it secret to the election were almost nil.

I noted that scandals had a short life in Washington and that other newer, spicier ones soon replaced them. I urged him to not become unduly agitated by this one.

He then asked if I had any ideas and I said that this affair already had a strong Cuban flavor and that everyone knew that the Cubans were conspiratorial and anxious to know what the policies of both parties would be toward Castro. They, therefore, had a plausible motive for attempting this amateurish job which any skilled technician would deplore. This might be costly but it would be plausible.

Dean said he agreed that this was the best tack to take, but it might cost a half million dollars. He also agreed (for the second time) that the risks of agency involvement were unacceptable.

After a moment's thought, he said that he felt that Gray's cancellation of the appointment with Director Helms might well be reversed within the next few hours.

Dean thanked me and I left.

VERNON A. WALTERS

Memo (July 5, 1972)

Memo for the Record

On July 5, '72 at 5:50 P.M., I received a phone call from the acting director of the F.B.I., L. Patrick Gray. He said that the pressures on him to continue the investigation were great. Unless he had documents from me to the effect that their (F.B.I.) investigation was endangering national security, he would have to go ahead with the investigation of Dahlberg and Daguerre. He had talked to John Dean. I said I could not give him an immediate answer but would give him one by 1000 on 6 July. He said that would be agreeable.

VERNON A. WALTERS

Memo (July 6, 1972)

At 1005 on 6 July I saw acting director L. Patrick Gray at his office. We were alone during our conversation. I handed him the memorandum which is attached and said that it covered the entire relationship between the Watergate suspects and the agency.

In all honesty I could not tell him to cease future investigations on the grounds that it would compromise the security interests of the United States. Even less so could I write him a letter to this effect. He said that he fully understood this. He himself had told

Ehrlichman and Haldeman that he could not possibly suppress the investigation of this matter.

Even within the F.B.I. there were leaks. He had called in the components of his field office in Washington and chewed them out on this case because information had leaked to the press concerning the Watergate case which only they had.

I said that the only basis on which he and I could deal was absolute frankness and I wished to recount my involvement in this case. I said that I had been called to the White House with Director Helms and had seen two senior staff assistants (I specifically did not name Haldeman and Ehrlichman).

I said that we had been told that if this case were investigated further, it would lead to some awkward places, and I had been directed (the implication being that the President directed this although it was not specifically said) to go to acting director Gray and tell him that if this investigation were pursued further, it could uncover some ongoing covert operations of the agency. I had done this.

Subsequently, I had seen Mr. Dean, the White House counsel, and told him that whatever the current and present implications of the Watergate case were, that to implicate the agency would not serve the President but would enormously increase the risks to the President.

I had a long association with the President and was as desirous as anyone of protecting him. I did not believe that a letter from the agency asking the F.B.I. to lay off this investigation on spurious grounds that it would uncover covert operations would serve the President.

Such a letter in the current atmosphere in Washington would become known prior to election. What was now a minor wound could become a mortal wound. I said quite frankly that I wouldn't write such a letter.

Gray thanked me for my frankness and said that this opened the way for fruitful cooperation between us. He would be frank with me, too. He could not suppress this investigation with the F.B.I. He had told Kleindienst this. He told Ehrlichman and Haldeman that he would prefer to resign, but his resignation would raise many questions that would be detrimental to the President's interest.

He did not see why he or I should jeopardize the integrity of our organizations to protect some mid-level White House figures who had acted imprudently. He was prepared to let this go to Ehrlichman, to Haldeman, or to Mitchell, for that matter. He felt it important that the President should be protected from his would-be protectors. He had explained this to Dean as well as to Ehrlichman and to Haldeman.

He said he was anxious not to talk to Mitchell because he was afraid that at his confirmation hearings he would be asked whether he had talked to Mitchell about the Watergate case and he wished to be in a position to reply negatively. He said that he would like to talk to the President about it but he feared that a request from him to see the President would be misinterpreted by the media.

I said that if I were directed to write a letter to him saying that the future investigation of this case would jeopardize the security of the United States and covert operations of the agency, I would ask to see the President and explain to him the disservice I thought this would do to his interest.

The potential danger to the President of such a course far outweighed any protective aspects it might have for any other figures in the White House and I was quite prepared to resign myself on this issue. Gray said he understood this fully and hoped I would stick to my guns. I assured him I would.

Gray than said though this was an awkward position, our mutual frankness had created the basis for a new and happy relationship between the two agencies. I said the memorandum I had given him described in detail the exact measure of agency involvement and noninvolvement in this case, including information on Dahlberg and Daguerre. He thanked me again for my frankness and confidence and repeated that he did not believe that he could sit on this matter and that the facts would come out eventually. He walked me to the door.

VERNON A. WALTERS

Memo (July 13, 1972)

On 12 July at 1450 I called on acting director L. Patrick Gray at his office and saw him alone.

I told him that shortly after I had seen him the last time and given him the memorandum concerning former C.I.A. association of the suspects in the Watergate case, I had since discovered one additional item concerning Howard Hunt. I gave him that memorandum concerning the assistance given to Hunt, which terminated in August, 1971, when his demands escalated to an inappropriate level. We had assisted him following a request from the White House and it was our understanding that it was for the purpose of tracking down security leaks in the Government.

He thanked me and said that this case could not be snuffed out and it would lead quite high politically. Dahlberg was in the clear. He had gotten the check from Maurice Stans and deposited it in the Mexican bank. It was undoubtedly political money.

Last Friday, the President called [Gray] to congratulate him on the F.B.I. action which had frustrated the aircraft hijacking in San Francisco. The President asked him if he had talked to me about the case. Gray replied that he had.

The President then asked him what his recommendation

was on the matter. Gray had replied that the case could not be covered up and would lead quite high and he felt that the President should get rid of the people that were involved. Any attempt to involve the F.B.I. or the C.I.A. in this case would only prove a mortal wound (he used my words) and would achieve nothing.

The President then said, "Then I should get rid of whoever is involved no matter how high?" Gray replied that was his recommendation.

The President then asked what I thought and Gray said my views were the same as his. The President took it well and thanked Gray. Later that day, Gray had talked to Dean and repeated the conversation to him. Dean had said, "O.K."

Gray had heard no more on the subject. He asked whether the President had spoken to me and I said he had on another matter but had not brought up this matter with me.

Gray then said that the U. S. Attorney had subpoenaed the financial records of the Committee to Re-elect the President. It had been suggested to him that he stop this. He had replied that he could not. Whoever wanted this done should talk to the Attorney General and see if there was any legal way to do this. He could not.

He said that he had told the President in 1968 that he should beware of his subordinates who try to wear his Commander in Chief stripes. I agreed, saying that in my view the President should be protected from the self-appointed protectors who would harm him while trying to cover their own mistakes.

Gray said that our views coincided on this matter. He would resign on this issue if necessary and I said that in maintaining the integrity of our agencies we were rendering the President the best possible service. I too, was quite prepared to resign on this issue.

He thanked me for my frankness and said that we had established a warm, personal, frank relationship at the outset of our tenure in our respective jobs.

VERNON A. WALTERS

Memo (July 28, 1972)

[1]

On Friday, July 28, 1972, at 11 A.M. I called on the acting director of the F.B.I., L. Patrick Gray, at his office in the F.B.I. building. He saw me alone. I said I had come to clarify the last memorandum I had given him in reply to inquiries from Mr. Pirham "Cleo."

[2]

I said that "Cleo" was Mr. Cleo [blank], an electronics engineer who was in contact with Mr. Hunt during August of 1971. Mr. [blank] supplied a recorder pursuant to Mr. Hunt's request and had assisted him to get it in shape for use in overt, not clandestine, recordings of meetings with agents. There was no attempt to make the recorder useful for clandestine activities.

Mr. [blank] had two additional meetings, generated by a phone call to the above number (a sterile telephone in one of our offices), to straighten out some difficulties that had arisen with respect to the microphones. We never recovered the recorder.

[3]

Aside from the above contact with respect to the recorder, there were contacts with Mr. Hunt with respect to false documents and disguises for himself and an associate. He was also loaned a clandestine camera, which he returned. We developed one roll of film for Mr. Hunt, of which we have copies showing some unidentified place, possibly the Rand Corporation. We had no contact whatsoever with Mr. Hunt subsequent to 31 August 1971.

[4]

He thanked me for this information. I added that when Hunt's requests had escalated, we terminated our assistance to him and had no further contact with him subsequent to 31 August 1971. He was grateful for this information.

[5]

Gray asked me if the President had called me on this matter and I replied that he had not. Gray then said a lot of pressure had been brought on him on this matter but he had not yielded.

[6]

I told him that we intended to terminate the 965-9598 number [the C.I.A.'s sterile phone] and he nodded. Then he said, "This is a hell of a thing to happen to us at the outset of our tenure with our respective offices." I agreed heartily.

[7]

He thanked me for coming to see him and for maintaining such a frank and forward relationship with him. I left him a short, unsigned memo embodying what I had told him.

VERNON A. WALTERS

Schlesinger Letter (Feb. 9, 1973)

Subject: Telephone Call from John Dean

This evening at 6:10 I received a telephone call from John Dean at the White House. Dean indicated that he wanted to discuss two topics.

First, he [referred] to a packet of material that had been sent to the Department of Justice in connection with the Watergate investigation. He suggested that Justice be required to return his package to the agency [the C.I.A.]

The only item that would be left at Justice would be a card in the files indicating that a package had been returned to the agency, since the material in the package was no longer needed for the purposes of the investigation. He indicated that the agency had originally provided these materials to the Department of Justice at the request of the [Assistant] Attorney General, Mr. [Henry E.] Petersen.

The second subject that he raised was the pending investigation by the Senate on the I.T.T. affair in relation to the Chilean problem. He felt that this investigation could be rather explosive. He also indicated that there might be some sensitive cables at the agency that might be requested by the Senate investigators.

I indicated to him that while I had not seen any cables, I had been briefed on the subject, and that the role of the Government appeared to be clean. He expressed his delight at hearing this assessment. I indicated that I would look into the cables for that period.

In this connection, he mentioned that there is a hot story being passed about in the press, primarily instigated by Seymour Hersh of The New York Times. The story suggests that [Frank] Sturgis, who sometimes went by the code name Federini, was the individual responsible for the burglarizing of the Chilean Embassy in Washington.

He also indicated that he expected Senator [J. W.] Fulbright to request the Justice Department to produce Sturgis for the Senate hearings.

I indicated that I would look further into the matter. He then made some rather jovial remarks about not always being the bearer of bad tidings, and I inquired what the good news might be. Further references were made to a pending appointment at the A.E.C.

Shortly thereafter, I discussed those matters with Bill Colby [then a high-ranking C.I.A. official], who indicated that Sturgis had not been on the payroll for a number of years and that whatever the allegations about the Chilean Embassy, the agency had no connection at all.

We also agreed that he would discuss the question of the package relative to the Watergate investigation with General Walters and a discussion would be made with regard to the appropriate action.

J. R. S.

JAMES R. SCHLESINGER

cc: General Walters

Memo (May 11, 1973)

Memorandum of Conversation of Feb. 21, 1973

At the request of the director, Dr. Schlesinger, I called on Mr. John Dean in his office at the White House at 1430.

I explained to him that, in connection with his request that the agency ask the Department of Justice to return a package of material that had been sent to them in connection with the Watergate investigation, it was quite impossible for us to request the return of this, as this would simply mean that a note would be left in the Department of Justice files that the material had been sent back to the agency, and we had been asked not to destroy any material in any way related to the case.

I again told him that there was no agency involvement in this case, and that any attempt to involve the agency could only be harmful to the United States. He seemed disappointed. I then left.

VERNON A. WALTERS

News Briefing "Practice Session" for Ronald Ziegler

Following is a transcript of a news briefing "practice session" for Ronald L. Ziegler, the Presidential press secretary, with members of the White House staff, which was referred to by John W. Dean 3d before the Senate Watergate committee. The transcript was provided by Mr. Dean to the committee. No date on the practice session was provided, but the transcript indicates it was in mid-October, 1972.

ZIEGLER: Dwight Chapin has already made it clear that the story was fundamentally inaccurate and one based on hearsay. Now there have been a number of stories which have appeared over the last few days—and over the last few months—that you gentlemen have asked me about. All of these stories have been based on hearsay or on sources which have not been identified. These stories have resulted in substantial confusion. All of them seem to be lumped together as the Watergate affair. The Watergate affair is one that has been thoroughly investigated and seven men have been indicted. It has been one of the most extensive investigations in history.

The other stories that have run relate to the Watergate where criminal action is involved. But still we see such stories as espionage, sabotage, spying, surveillance—all being charged to activities of the re-election campaign. But none of the charges are based upon anything more than hearsay or unidentified sources.

Now I can tell you I have nothing more to say or add on this subject beyond what Dwight Chapin said in his statement—but I will tell you this. At no time has anyone in the White House or this Administration condoned such activities as spying on individuals, or sabotaging campaigns in an illegal way. The President has said before and I will repeat it again. He does not condone this type of activity.

Now three weeks before the election there is a flurry of sensationalism. I am not going to inject the White House into these stories. I am not going to assume the responsibility from this podium and from the White House press room to answer every unfounded story based on hearsay or unidentified sources. . . . Every story based on some sensational charge during this period . . .

EHRLICHMAN: We are going to see all kinds of Presidential friends, Presidential staff, Presidential relatives, dogs, etc., pictures on the front pages of local newspapers to counteract the fact that McGovern is 2 to 1 behind. I am not going to try to cope with these unfounded stories.

CHAPIN: I am not going to dignify desperation politics.

Q. Ron, that was a self-righteous, self-serving statement. Simply, is the answer yes or no? Did Dwight Chapin, the President's appointments secretary—man who meets with the President regularly—hire Segretti and instruct him to engage in sabotage?

ZIEGLER: Gentlemen, I have nothing to add to what Mr. Chapin has already said on this and that is that the story is fundamentally inaccurate and based on hearsay.

Q. But Ron, why don't you just ask Dwight or why doesn't the President just ask him. Did or did he not hire Segretti?

ZIEGLER: Gentlemen, I have nothing to add to what Chapin has already said on the subject.

Q. Are you telling us that you won't say whether or not the President condones activities such as sabotage, espionage, surveillance?

ZIEGLER: If you would listen to what I said, you will note that I stated that the President in no way condones this type of activity and no one in the White House under any circumstances directed, encouraged, or suggested that people at any level in the campaign involve themselves in surveillance of individuals, spying on individuals, stealing documents or any illegal or repulsive steps such as have been charged in the source sensational stories that have been published.

Q. Is it true that Segretti was a close, personal friend of Chapin's?

ZIEGLER: Mr. Chapin covered that in the statement.

Q. When was the last time that Chapin saw Segretti?

A. I don't know.

Q. Why don't you ask him?

A. Gentlemen, I told you I had nothing to add.

EHRLICHMAN: We just don't take as seriously as you do these campaign pranks. Some of you for your own purposes have blown these into something that is not there.

ZIEGLER: I don't think we can take on the press.

EHRLICHMAN: Dwight Chapin is terribly offended at the treatment he got over the weekend. I approached him to the possibility of coming out here. He said he would never again speak to any member of the press and he would like your apologies.

MOORE: This refers to a statement of policy and it is clear that it is the right one. What is the right of anyone to expect an answer from this podium on a story which is based on sources you will not reveal? Good citizens are being vilified based on irresponsible, unidentified stories and stories which draw broad-sweeping conclusions. You have this right under the First Amendment—make charges on hearsay evidence.

Today you had a four-column picture in which Dwight Chapin was named as a contact in sabotage. The person who said it was not named. To take this admittedly unsupported, non-knowledge and assert it as knowledge to the point where—you may do so, but it does not give you a right to expect an answer from the President's press secretary or from the President of the United States. When and if anyone comes in here with evidence of wrongdoing you will receive an answer. Until that occurs, we will go on to the next questions or next subject. Jim Mitchell—Fund. He denied it. Bill Timmons—he denied it.

Clawson and the letter—he denied it. In none of these cases was the source for the story revealed, but these men for the rest of their lives will have to live with these charges for which they have no recourse.

Q. If you feel so strongly about this, then why don't you just deny it?

These are the rules. Mr. Chapin has asked me to make a voluntary statement. As a man who has worked in campaigns for X number of years and have seen many pranks and hoaxes, it occurred to me we should have our own Dick Tuck in this campaign. Gordon Strachan recalled that our old friend, Don Segretti, was coming out of the Army in September. We called him and he expressed interest in the assignment of being a counter-agent. On that basis I said to him that perhaps I could get an O.K. for you to be supported and take off on your own on activities as long as they are legal.

I referred him to Mr. Kalmbach, who did supply funds which would allow him to act on his own for a few months. I did this on my own without any knowledge or encouragement or authority.

I have read nothing to the contrary that Segretti has done anything illegal or inconsistent with traditional stories in politics—and the most I heard was a postcard or clipping from the newspaper.

I have noted that nothing has been said that anything was illegal or of any consequence.

Then you might read a statement from the President of the United States. . . . Dwight Chapin is one of the most able and most respected men on my staff. In my opinion, he made a mistake in encouraging pranks. However, this has occurred in my campaigns in the past and had no effect there. I am sure these pranks have had no effects here.

EHRLICHMAN: Two exceptions—the Government and the White House. Chapin is the White House and the separation—you bridge the separation when you get the President in it.

ZIEGLER: Who paid him and how was he paid?

MOORE: On Mr. Chapin's recommendation that he was going to further the cause of the campaign, Mr. Kalmbach paid him.

DEAN: If we are doing something about them, there are a host of charges here and we are looking into them and we are going to have a response for you.

MOORE: We make investigations and we check the evidence.

DEAN: It is being looked into—we are looking into it. We don't have the answers.

MOORE: Does the President have any reaction?

Yes, he is absolutely revolted and distressed that the word sabotage is connected by picture and name of a man whom he considers—based on an unsubstantiated story.

RESPONSE A:

Let's get to the question of precisely what the allegation is. With regard to the Watergate, it was quite evidently a crime—a serious crime—with regard to the other allegations, they range from allegations of political highjinks, pranks and hoaxes, all the way to more serious matters such as spying and surveillance on individuals. The President is under no obligation to comment upon these charges for the reason (a) they are unsubstantiated; (b) they are unsupported; and (c) in our judgment, both the timing, character, and the placement of these stories is political in character. The purpose is to focus attention from the central issues of the campaign. The President is under no obligation nor should he get into discussion or comment on these tactics.

RESPONSE B:

I have already made my comment that (a) Dwight Chapin did direct the hiring of Segretti, that (b) once Segretti was hired, the day-to-day activities were not Chapin's responsibility.

RESPONSE C:

The President does not comment on allegations of campaign tactics, i.e., militants at the rally in California.

Nixon Memorandum to Dean

March 12, 1973

Following is a memorandum from President Nixon to John W. Dean 3d that was submitted by Mr. Dean to the Senate Watergate committee.

March 12, 1973—(Note: this is one where you will make only one copy for my file and deliver the other copy to him—it is private.)

Memo for John Dean from the President

I noted the story in The [Washington] Post this morning (3/11/73) with regard to some college student who had been hired to get some information with regard to demonstrations which might be useful in keeping those activities from developing into violence or have other unpleasant consequences. It is difficult for me to understand why we have not done an adequate job of getting the facts out chapter and verse on the massive activities of McGovern and the so-called peace groups in funding demonstrations against me, members of the family, and others during the campaign. As you are aware, there were virtually no demonstrations whatever on our part against their meetings. This I had ordered at the beginning of the year.

On the other hand, I cannot recall a meeting in which I participated where there were not demonstrations, including the non-political type meeting like the one at the Statue of Liberty. There was hard evidence of the McGovern people supporting and inciting the violent demonstrations in San Francisco which resulted in several thousand dollars in property damage. There was also hard evidence of the McGovern headquarters inciting the demonstration in L.A. the following day. And it would be hard for me to believe that the fire-bombing of our Phoenix headquarters, with a loss of $100,000, was done by one of our own people. It would seem to me that the facts on such activities should be accumulated and that somebody—perhaps Goldwater is the only man who has the guts to do it—should blast the McGovernites for their vicious activities. Needless to say, it would be helpful if Hruska, or someone on the Ervin committee on our side, could see that at a time they are investigating our campaign activities they are also investigating the charges that have been made against their actions. I have raised this point to no avail on previous occasions. Perhaps you can now follow through and see that something is done. Give me a report at your convenience.

Ehrlichman-Kleindienst Telephone Call and Weicker Statement

Following are two texts from the remarks of Senator Lowell P. Weicker at the Senate Watergate Committee hearing on June 28, 1973. The first is the transcript of a telephone conversation on March 28, 1973, between Richard G. Kleindienst and John D. Ehrlichman. The second is the concluding statement of Senator Weicker.

Ehrlichman Call

EHRLICHMAN: The President wanted me to cover with you. Are you on an outside line?

KLEINDIENST: I'm at my parents' house.

E. Oh, fine, O.K., so it's a direct line? Number one, he wanted me to ask you those two things that I did yesterday about the grand jury and about Baker. He had me call Pat Gray and have Pat contact Lowell Weicker to ask Weicker about this second story that he put out yesterday to the effect that he had information about White House involvement. And Weicker told Gray that he was talking there about political sabotage and not about the Watergate.

K. About the Segretti case?

E. Yeah, and that he was quite vague with Pat as to what he had.

K. I called him also, you know, after I talked to the President on Monday.

E. Well, the President's feeling is that it wouldn't be too bad for you in your press conferences in the next couple of days to take a swing at that and just say we contacted the Senator because we continue to exercise diligence in this thing and we're determined to track down every lead and it turns out he doesn't have anything.

K. I would really at this delicate point question the advisability of provoking, you know, a confrontation with Weicker. He's essentially with us, and he and Baker get along good.

E. Is he?

K. Baker has had a long talk with him and told him to shut up and said that he would, and I talked with him on Sunday after he said he didn't have anything, but he's kind of an excitable kid and we just might not want to alienate him, and I think that if he finds himself in a direct word battle with the White House and me and loses face about it, I think in the long run we might need that guy's vote.

E. I see. You don't think that this is evidence of alienation to the point of no return then?

K. No. You mean by Lowell?

E. Yeah.

K. No, I don't. He's pretty disenchanged with the whole concept of it. Connecticut politician [inaudible].

E. Well, use your own judgment on it, Richard.

K. [inaudible] on TV, I guess seven or eight times this Sunday when I finished my testimony before my appropriations committee on all three networks, I referred to the letter that I sent to Sirica and I also emphasized and repeatedly said (a) the President wants this investigated, let the chips fall where they will, but secondly, that if anybody has any information, we not only want it, we expect to get it, so we can investigate it and if necessary indict these people, and that anybody who withholds information like that is obstructing justice. But I did not refer to Weicker. And my judgment right now is not to do so.

E. O.K., O.K.

K. If he gets to that point, the hell with him.

E. Well, our uneducated and uninformed impression was that he was trying to develop an attack line here on the White House or the President.

K. If that [inaudible] If we would conclude that, that is what he's up to, that he is completely alienated, then I say we've got to take him on.

E. Well, keep on that and you'll be talking to Baker and you get a feel of it.

K. O.K. Now, the President said for me to say this to you: That the best information he had and has is that neither Dean nor Haldeman nor Colson nor I nor anybody in the White House had any prior knowledge of this burglary. He said that he's counting on you to provide him with any information to the contrary if it ever turns up and you just contact him direct. Now as far as the Committee to Re-elect is concerned, he said that serious questions are being raised with regard to Mitchell, and he would likewise want you to communicate to him any evidence or inferences from evidence on that subject.

With respect to them, unless something develops with these seven people who were convicted, all those people testified under oath before a grand jury and their testimony was not contradicted and until something comes along I think this fellow McCord, if he has something beside his own testimony in addition to that to refute the sworn testimony, then you'd have to do it.

E. Take him for what he is.

K. He's facing a long jail sentence and he has all kinds of motives to say all kinds of things, but I also pointed out that most of the people, well, these people who were involved were interviewed by the F.B.I. and they testified under oath before a grand

jury to the contrary of what McCord is saying. But I understand
the President's direction.

E. He's concerned about Mitchell.

K. So am I.

E. And he would want to have a private communication from
you if you are possessed of any information that you think he
ought to have with regard to John. Now he [inaudible].

K. [Inaudible] ought to think about John [inaudible] McCord
or Liddy or Hunt or any of these seven, you know, testify under
oath specifically to their knowledge they have a basis for saying so
that Mitchell or any of these guys knew about it. We have a very
serious problem—possible perjury, possibility of going back to the
grand jury, they have a grand jury to determine whether anyone
should be indicted. When you talk about Mitchell and me, that
really creates the highest conflict of interest. And we want to give
some thought to having, in such an event, having a special prosecutor.

E. What is the procedure for that?

K. Well, I don't know. I think that the President could appoint
somebody as a special prosecutor to direct the F.B.I. to cooperate
with him, giving them an opportunity to hire some attorneys you
know, on his staff, and then just have complete authority to have
his own investigation, and if there's evidence that comes out
that there were acts of criminal behavior, have them presented
to a grand jury, then proceed with it.

E. Could you have somebody brief out how that's done? Just
to [sic] we know? And the question would be whether the
President or Sirica or you know who actually does it?

K. Well, it wouldn't be the judge. The judge has no jurisdiction. I think it would be the President.

E. O.K.

K. But it has its own problems that by doing that you in effect
say publicly well, O.K., the Department of Justice and the Attorney General, the United States Attorney, and the F.B.I. are
all corrupt. I've now found out and have got to myself a new
[inaudible].

E. Of course, we've resisted that right straight through.

K. I think that we have to do it in the event that it appears that
Mitchell himself is going to be involved in any further litigation
because all the men who are doing this, who worked for him,
have been appointed, and I think if it came down to him that
that's what I would seriously start thinking about recommending.

E. Also, this business of the grant of immunity to witnesses
before the grand jury, is that peculiarly in the province of the
court?

K. No, that's the Department of Justice.

E. That is?

K. In almost every criminal case of any consequence, when we convict somebody the next thing to do is haul them back in before a grand jury to find out what they know. You have to do it in this case [inaudible] always going to do it. Quite a limitation posed on us. John, is that [inaudible] who couldn't cut it [inaudible]. But you have two really distinct situations here. You have the Watergate inquiry by Senator Ervin, that's the political side of it. And then you have the obligation imposed upon us to investigate criminal conduct. Two separate distinct operations. They're getting all fuzzed up.

E. What progress are they making right now, have you had a reaction on it?

K. Well, the last time I talked to Henry [E. Petersen of the Justice Department] Monday because of Sirica's sentencing procedures, it got a little boxed up. Sirica is really lousing this thing up. I don't know. I'm going to talk to Petersen this morning and get I'll call you back.

E. O.K., great, that's all I had on my list.

K. Thanks, John.

E. Now, he said that there was a possibility he'd like to see you in San Clemente Saturday morning first thing. So you might just keep that in the back of your mind. Don't rearrange any of your schedules or anything, but I'll let you know if that materializes. We'd send a chopper up to L.A. for you. Thank you.

K. O.K.

Weicker Statement

Now I am going to conclude this way, Mr. Chairman, and then I am done, and I have tried to, as I say, accomplish one role that I think needed accomplishing in these hearings:

Among the rumors that are floated around, and this isn't hearsay, are on three different occasions plants to take effect that I am such a disloyal Republican and I am going to switch to the Democratic party.

Now I am going to tell you, in your memorandum, Mr. Dean, you went ahead and had me described, whether it was you or Mr. Haldeman or whoever was there, as an independent who would give the White House trouble. But I say before you and I say before the American people and this committee that I am here as a Republican and, quite frankly, I think that I express the feelings of the 42 other Republican Senators that I work with, and the Republicans of the state of Connecticut and, in fact, the Republican party, far better than these illegal, unconstitutional and gross acts which have been committed over the past several months by various individuals.

Let me make it clear because I have got to have my partisan comment: Republicans do not cover up. Republicans do not go ahead and threaten. Republicans do not go ahead and commit illegal acts. And, God knows, Republicans don't view their fellow

Americans as enemies to be harassed. But rather, I can assure you, that this Republican and those that I served with, look upon every American as human beings to be loved and won.

Ehrlichman-Kalmbach Telephone Call

April 19, 1973

Following is a transcript of a telephone conversation at 4:50 P.M. between John D. Ehrlichman and Herbert W. Kalmbach. Mr. Ehrlichman recorded the conversation and provided the transcript to the Senate Watergate committee.

EHRLICHMAN: Hi, how are you?

KALMBACH: I'm pretty good. I'm scheduled for 2 tomorrow afternoon.

E. Where—at the jury or the U.S. Attorney?

K. At the jury and I'm scheduled at 5:30 this afternoon with Silver.

E. Oh, are you?

K. Yeah. I just wanted to run through quickly several things, John, in line with our conversation. I got in here last night and there was a telephone call from O'Brien. I returned it, went over there today and he said the reason for the call is LaRue has told him to ask him to call me to say that he had to identify me in connection with this and he wanted me to know that and so on.

E. Did he tell about Dean?

K. Nope.

E. Well, Dean has totally cooperated with the U.S. attorney in the hopes of getting immunity. Now what he says or how he says nobody seems to be able to divine but he.

K. The whole enchilada?

E. He's throwing off on Bob and me heavily.

K. He is?

E. Yep.

K. He is?

E. And taking the position that he was a mere agent. Now on your episode he told me before he left, so to speak, he, Dean, told me that really my transaction with him involving you was virtually my only area of liability in this thing and I said, well, John, what in the world are you talking about? He said, well I came to you from Mitchell and I said Mitchell needs money. Could we call Herb Kalmbach and ask him to raise some? And I said, and Dean says to me, and you said yes. And I said, yep, that's right. And he said, well that does it. And I said well that's hard for me to believe, I don't understand the law but I don't think Herb entered into this with any guilty intent and I certainly didn't and so I said I just find that hard to imagine. Now since then I've retained counsel.

K. Oh, you have?

E. Very good and who agrees with me that it is the remotest kind of nonsense but the point that I think has to be clarified, that I'm going to clarify if I get a chance, is that the reason that Dean had to come to me and to Bob where you were concerned is that we had promised you that you would not be run pillar to post by Maurice Stans.

K. And also that you knew I was your friend and you knew I was the President's attorney.

E. Sure.

K. Never do anything improper, illegal, unethical or whatever.

E. Right.

K. And.

E. But the point is that rather than Mitchell calling you direct Mitchell knew darn well that you were no longer available.

K. Yep.

E. Now this was post-April 6, was it not?

K. Yep, April—.

E. So that Mitchell and Stans both knew that there wasn't any point in calling you direct because we had gotten you out of that on the pretext that you were going to do things for us.

K. That's right.

E. And so it was necessary for Dean to come to me and then in turn to Bob and plead a very urgent case without really getting into any specifics except to say you had to trust me, this is very important, and Mitchell is up his tree, or, you know, I mean is really worried, he didn't use that phrase, but is really exercised about this. And I said, well, John, if you tell me it's that important, why yes.

K. You know, when you and I talked and it was after John had given me that word, and I came in to ask you, John is this an assignment I have to take on? You said, yes it is period and move forward. Then that was all that I needed to be assured that I wasn't putting my family in jeopardy.

E. Sure.

K. And I would just understand that you and I are absolutely together on that.

E. No question about it, Herb, that I would never knowingly have put you in any kind of a spot.

K. Yeah. Well and when we talked you knew what I was about to do, you know, to go out and get the dough for this purpose; it was humanitarian.

E. It was a defense fund.

K. . . . to support the family. Now the thing that was disquieting about this thing with O'Brien was that he said that there is a massive campaign evidently under way to indict all the lawyers including you, Herb, and I was a little shocked and I guess what I need to get from you, John, is assurance that this is not true.

E. Well I don't know of any attempt to target you at all. My hunch is that they're trying to get at me, they're trying to corroborate. See what he said to Dean is that he gets no consideration from them unless they corroborate Haldeman and my liability.

K. God, if I can just make it plain that it was humanitarian and nothing else.

E. Yeah, and the point that I undoubtedly never expressed to you that I continually operated on the basis of Dean's representations to me.

K. Yep. It was not improper.

E. Right.

K. And there was nothing illegal about it.

E. See, he's the house lawyer. Yep, exactly and I just couldn't believe that you and Bob and the President, just too good friends to ever put me in the position where I'm putting my family on the line.

K. And it's just unbelievable, unthinkable. Now shall I just— I'll just if I'm asked by Silver I'll just lay it out just exactly that way.

E. Yeah, I wouldn't haul the President into it if you can help it.

K. Oh, no, I will not.

E. But I think the point that which I will make in the future if I'm given the chance that you were not under our control in any sort of a slavery sense but that we had agreed that you would not be at the beck and call of the committee.

K. And, of course, too, that I act only on orders and, you know, on direction and if this is something that you felt sufficiently important and that you were assured it was altogether proper, then I would take it on because I always do it and always have. And you and Bob and the President know that.

E. Yeah, well as far as propriety is concerned I think we both were relying entirely on Dean.

K. Yep.

E. I made no independent judgment.

K. Yep. Yep.

E. And I'm sure Bob didn't either.

K. Nope and I'm just, I just have the feeling, John, that I don't know if this is a weak reed, is it?

E. Who, Dean?

K. No, I mean are they still going to say, well Herb you should have known.

E. I don't know how you could. You didn't make any inquiries.

K. Never. And the only inquiries I made, John, was to you after I talked to John Dean.

E. And you found that I didn't know just a whole helluva lot.

K. You said this is something I have to do and . . .

E. Yeah, and the reason that I said that, as you know, was not from any personal inquiry but was on the basis of what had been represented to me.

K. Yeah, and then on—to provide the defense fund and to take care of the families of these fellas who were then . . .

E. Indigent.

K. Not then been found guilty or not guilty.

E. And the point being here without attempting to induce them to do a damn thing.

K. Absolutely not and that was never, that was exactly right.

E. O.K.

K. Now, can I get in to see you tomorrow before I go in there at 2?

E. If you want to. They'll ask you.

K. Will they?

E. Yep.

K. Well, maybe I shouldn't.

E. They'll ask you to whom you've spoken about your testimony and I would appreciate it if you would say you've talked to me in California because at that time I was investigating this thing for the President.

K. And not now?

E. Well, I wouldn't ask you to lie.

K. No, I know.

E. But the point is . . .

K. But the testimony was in California.

E. The point is. Well, no, your recollection of facts and so forth.

K. Yes, I agree.

E. See, I don't think we were ever seen together out there but at some point I'm going to have to say that I talked to O'Brien and Dean and Magruder and Mitchell and you and a whole lot of people about this case.

K. Yeah.

E. And so it would be consistent.

K. Do you feel, John, that calling it straight shot here, do you feel assured as you did when we were out there that there's no culpability here?

E. Yes.

K. And nothing to worry about?

E. And Herb, from everything I hear they're not after you.

K. Yes, sir.

E. From everything I hear.

K. Barbara, you know . . .

E. They're out to get me and they're out to get Bob [Haldeman].

K. My God. All right, well, John, it'll be absolutely clear that there was nothing looking towards any cover-up or anything. It was strictly for the humanitarian and I just want . . . when I talked to you I just wanted you to advise me that it was all right on that basis.

E. On that basis.

K. To go forward.

E. That it was necessary.

K. And that'll be precisely the way it is.

E. Yeah, O.K. Thanks, Herb. Bye.

WHO'S WHO

Alch, Gerald—attorney for James W. McCord Jr.

Andreas, Dwayne—Minnesota grain executive who made a contribution to the Nixon 1972 campaign

Babcock, Tim—former Governor of Montana

Bailey, F. Lee—Boston attorney, associate of Gerald Alch

Baker, Senator Howard H. Jr.—Tennessee Republican, member of Senate Watergate committee

Baldwin, Alfred C. 3d—former F.B.I. agent hired by McCord

Barker, Bernard L.—pleaded guilty as Watergate spy

Beard, Dita—former public relations aide with I.T.T.

Bennett, General Donald V.—Director, Defense Intelligence Agency

Bernstein, Carl—Washington Post reporter

Bittenbinder, Gary—member of District of Columbia metropolitan police department

Bittman, William O.—attorney for E. Howard Hunt Jr.

Boggs, Patrick—Secret Service agent

Boudin, Leonard B.—Daniel Ellsberg's attorney

Bowles, Charles—official, Justice Department

Boyce, Eugene—assistant chief counsel, Senate Watergate committee

Brennan, Charles D.—former assistant director, F.B.I.

Buchanan, Patrick J.—special consultant to the President

Bull, Stephen—special assistant to President Nixon

Bush, George—Republican national chairman

Butterfield, Alexander P.—F.A.A. administrator, former Presidential appointments secretary

Buzhardt, J. Fred Jr.—special counsel to the President

Byrd, Senator Robert C.—West Virginia Democrat

Byrne, W. Matthew Jr.—presiding judge at Ellsberg-Russo trial (U.S. District Court, Los Angeles)

Caddy, C. Douglas—original attorney for five men caught in Watergate

Campbell, Donald E.—U.S. attorney, a prosecutor at Watergate break-in trial

Caulfield, John J.—former employe of the Committee for the Re-election of the President

Chapin, Dwight L.—former Presidential appointments secretary

Chenow, Kathleen—former White House secretary

Clawson, Ken W.—deputy director for communications, White House

Clifford, Clark—former Secretary of Defense

Colby, William E.—Director, C.I.A.

Colson, Charles W.—former special counsel to the President

Conein, Colonel Lucien—retired C.I.A. officer

Connally, John B.—former Secretary of the Treasury; former domestic and foreign affairs adviser to President Nixon

Cook, G. Bradford—former chairman, Securities and Exchange Commission

Cox, Archibald—former Solicitor General; special Watergate prosecutor

Cushman, General Robert E. Jr.—former Marine Corps commandant; former Deputy Director, C.I.A.

Dahlberg, Kenneth H.—former treasurer, Finance Committee to Re-elect the President

Dalbey, Dwight J.—assistant director, F.B.I.

Dash, Samuel—chief counsel and staff director, Senate Watergate committee

Dean, John W. 3d—former Counsel to the President

De Diego, Felipe—allegedly took part in break-in at Daniel Ellsberg's psychiatrist's office

DeLoach, Cartha D.—former assistant director, F.B.I.

DeMotte, Clifton—former motel public relations director in Hyannisport, Mass.

Dent, Harry S.—former special counsel to the President

Dorsen, David M.—assistant chief counsel, Senate Watergate committee

Edmisten, Rufus L.—deputy chief counsel, Senate Watergate committee

Ehrlichman, John D.—former chief domestic affairs adviser to the President

Ellsberg, Dr. Daniel J.—defendant in Pentagon Papers case

Ervin, Senator Sam J. Jr.—North Carolina Democrat, Chairman of Senate Watergate committee

Evans, Rowland Jr.—syndicated Washington columnist

Felt, Mark W.—former number two man, F.B.I.

Fensterwald, Bernard W.—attorney for James W. McCord Jr.

Fielding, Fred F.—former assistant to John W. Dean 3d

Fielding, Dr. Lewis—Daniel Ellsberg's psychiatrist

Finch, Robert H.—former Secretary of Health, Education, and Welfare; former White House counsel; now practicing law in Los Angeles

Fitzgerald, A. Ernest—Defense Department cost analyst

Gagliardi, Lee P.—Judge in Vesco case (U.S. District Court, New York)

Garment, Leonard—Counsel to the President

Gayler, Admiral Noel—Director, National Security Agency

Glanzer, Seymour—U.S. attorney, a prosecutor at Watergate break-in trial

Gonzalez, Virgilio R.—pleaded guilty as Watergate spy

Gray, L. Patrick 3d—former Acting Director, F.B.I.

Greenspun, Hank—Publisher, The Las Vegas Sun

Gregory, Thomas J.—student who testified he conducted campaign espionage

Gurney, Senator Edward J.—Florida Republican, member of Senate Watergate committee

Haig, General Alexander M. Jr.—former Army vice chief of staff; interim White House chief of staff (succeeding Haldeman)

Haire, Phillip—assistant chief counsel, Senate Watergate committee

Haldeman, H. R.—former White House chief of staff

Hamilton, James—assistant chief counsel, Senate Watergate committee

Harkins, General Paul—former U.S. commander in Vietnam

Harlow, Bryce—White House liaison chief

Harmony, Sally H.—former secretary to G. Gordon Liddy

Hart, Gary—Senator George McGovern's campaign manager

Hart, Senator Philip A.—Michigan Democrat

Helms, Richard M.—former Director, C.I.A.

Herge, J. Curtis—aide, Committee for the Re-election of the President

Higby, Lawrence M.—former assistant to H. R. Haldeman

Hoover, J. Edgar—former Director, F.B.I.

Hughes, Howard R.—billionaire industrialist

Hunt, E. Howard Jr.—former C.I.A. agent and White House consultant. Pleaded guilty as spy in Watergate case.

Hunt, Dorothy—wife of E. Howard Hunt Jr. Killed in plane crash, Dec. 8, 1972

Huntley, Chet—former TV newsman

Huston, Tom Charles—White House aide who designed 1970 intelligence gathering plan

Inouye, Senator Daniel K.—Hawaii Democrat, member of Senate Watergate committee

Jackson, Senator Henry M.—Washington Democrat

Johnson, Wallace H. Jr.—former White House Congressional liaison; assistant attorney general

Jones, Thomas V.—president and chairman, Northrop Corporation; G.O.P. campaign contributor

Kalmbach, Herbert W.—the President's personal attorney

Kehrli, Bruce A.—staff secretary to the President

Kennedy, Senator Edward M.—Massachusetts Democrat

Kissinger, Henry A.—former Presidential adviser on national security; now Secretary of State

Klein, Herbert G.—former White House communications director

Kleindienst, Richard G.—former Attorney General

Kopechne, Mary Jo—former member of Senator Robert F. Kennedy's staff who drowned at Chappaquiddick Island in July, 1969

Krogh, Egil Jr.—former chief assistant to John D. Ehrlichman

Lackritz, Marc—assistant chief counsel, Senate Watergate committee

Laird, Melvin R.—former Secretary of Defense; chief domestic affairs adviser to the President (succeeding Ehrlichman)

Lambert, William G.—former investigative reporter for Life magazine

Lankler, Alexander M. Jr.—Republican chairman, Maryland

LaRue, Frederick C.—former White House aide, assistant to John N. Mitchell at the Committee for the Re-election of the President

Leeper, Sergeant Paul W.—Washington policeman who participated in the arrest of five Watergate burglars

Lenzner, Terry F.—assistant chief counsel, Senate Watergate committee

Liddy, G. Gordon—former White House aide on staff of Domestic Council; former counsel of Committee for the Re-election of the President and on staff of Finance Committee to Re-elect the President; convicted of conspiracy, burglary, and wiretapping in Watergate case

Liebengood, Howard S.—assistant minority counsel, Senate Watergate committee

Lipset, Harold K.—former chief investigator, Senate Watergate committee

Lisker, Joel—deputy to John Martin of Justice Department

MacGregor, Clark—former director of the Committee for the Re-election of the President (succeeded Mitchell)

Magruder, Jeb Stuart—former chief of staff, Committee for the Re-election of the President

Malek, Frederic V.—Deputy Director, Office of Management and Budget

Marchetti, Victor L.—author and former C.I.A. agent

Mardian, Robert C.—former deputy manager, Committee for the Re-election of the President

Maroney, Kevin T.—deputy assistant attorney general

Maroulis, Peter L.—attorney for G. Gordon Liddy

Martin, John—chief of evaluation section, Internal Security Division, Justice Department

Martinez, Eugenio R.—pleaded guilty as Watergate spy

Marx, Mr. and Mrs. Louis—parents of Mrs. Daniel J. Ellsberg

Mayton, William—assistant chief counsel, Senate Watergate committee

McCandless, Robert C.—attorney for John W. Dean 3d

McClellan, Senator John L.—Arkansas Democrat

McCloskey, Representative Paul N. Jr.—California Republican, challenged President Nixon in Republican primaries

McCord, James W. Jr.—convicted participant in Watergate break-in

Mitchell, John N.—former Attorney General; former director, Committee for the Re-election of the President

Mitchell, Martha—wife of John N. Mitchell

Mittler, Austin—attorney for E. Howard Hunt Jr.

Mollenhoff, Clark—former White House assistant, now Des Moines Register & Tribune journalist

Montoya, Senator Joseph M.—New Mexico Democrat, member of Senate Watergate committee

Moore, Richard A.—special counsel to the President

Novak, Robert D.—syndicated Washington columnist

O'Brien, Lawrence F.—Democratic national chairman at time of Watergate break-in

O'Brien, Paul L.—attorney for Committee for the Re-election of the President

Odle, Robert C. Jr.—director of administration, Committee for the Re-election of the President

Ogarrio, Manuel—Mexican lawyer

Oliver, R. Spencer—executive director, association of state democratic chairmen, Democratic National Committee

Parkinson, Kenneth W.—attorney for Committee for the Re-election of the President

Patman, Representative Wright—Texas Democrat, chairman of the House Banking and Currency Committee

Percy, Senator Charles H.—Illinois Republican

Petersen, Henry E.—assistant attorney general, headed Watergate inquiry in Justice Department

Pico, Reinaldo—Cuban exile, a member of Barker's team

Porter, Herbert L.—scheduling director, Committee for the Re-election of the President

Rebozo, Charles G.—personal friend of President Nixon

Reisner, Robert—assistant to Jeb Stuart Magruder at the Committee for the Re-election of the President

Richardson, Elliot L.—Attorney General

Richey, Charles R.—judge, U.S. District Court, Washington, D.C.

Rietz, Kenneth S.—in charge of Nixon youth campaign, 1972

Rockefeller, Nelson—Governor of New York

Rogers, William P.—former Secretary of State

Rothblatt, Henry B.—attorney for four Miami defendants who pleaded guilty in Watergate break-in case

Rotunda, Ronald—assistant chief counsel, Senate Watergate committee

Russo, Anthony J. Jr.—co-defendant with Ellsberg in Pentagon Papers trial

Safire, William—former special assistant to the President, now a New York Times columnist

Sanders, Donald G.—assistant minority counsel, Senate Watergate Committee

Schlesinger, James R.—former Director, C.I.A.; Secretary of Defense

Schorr, Daniel—C.B.S. newsman

Schultz, George P.—Secretary of the Treasury

Sedam, J. Glenn Jr.—former general counsel to Committee for the Re-election of the President

Segretti, Donald H.—former Treasury Department attorney; accused of operating a sabotage campaign against the Democrats

Shaffer, Charles N.—attorney for John W. Dean 3d

Shankman, Bernard—attorney for James W. McCord Jr.

Shapiro, David—law partner of Mr. Colson

Shoffler, Carl M.—Washington policeman who participated in the arrest of five Watergate burglars

Shumway, Devan L.—director of public affairs, Committee for the Re-election of the President

Shure, H. William—assistant minority counsel, Senate Watergate committee

Silbert, Earl J.—principal assistant U.S. attorney, was chief prosecutor at Watergate break-in trial

Silverstein, Robert—assistant minority counsel, Senate Watergate committee

Sirica, John J.—chief judge, U.S. District Court, Washington, D.C.

Sloan, Hugh W. Jr.—former treasurer, Finance Committee to Re-elect the President

Stans, Maurice H.—former Secretary of Commerce; former chairman, Finance Committee to Re-elect the President

Stone, Roger—former head, District of Columbia Young Republicans

Strachan, Gordon C.—former assistant to H. R. Haldeman

Sturgis, Frank A.—pleaded guilty as Watergate spy

Sullivan, William C.—former associate director, F.B.I.

Symington, Senator Stuart—Missouri Democrat

Talmadge, Senator Herman E.—Georgia Democrat, member of Senate Watergate committee

Tapman, Kenneth C.—employe, Department of the Interior

Thompson, Fred D.—chief minority counsel, Senate Watergate committee

Timmons, William E.—director of Congressional relations, White House

Titus, Harold H. Jr.—U.S. attorney, District of Columbia

Tolson, Clyde A.—former assistant director, F.B.I.

Treese, James T.—attorney for Hugh W. Sloan Jr.

Turner, Major General Carl C.—former Provost Marshal General of the Army

Ulasewicz, Anthony T.—former detective, New York City Police Department; former aide to John J. Caulfield

Vesco, Robert L.—New Jersey financier, secretly donated $200,-000 to Nixon campaign; indicted with Mitchell and Stans

Walker, Ronald H.—White House aide

Walters, Johnnie—former Commissioner of Internal Revenue

Walters, Lieutenant General Vernon A.—Deputy Director, C.I.A.

Warren, Gerald C.—White House deputy press secretary
Weicker, Senator Lowell P. Jr.—Connecticut Republican, member
  of Senate Watergate committee
Wilson, Jerry V.—chief of police, District of Columbia
Wilson, John J.—attorney for John D. Ehrlichman and H. R.
  Haldeman
Woodward, Robert—Washington Post reporter
Wright, Charles Alan—special White House legal consultant on
  Watergate
Young, David R. Jr.—former White House aide
Ziegler, Ronald L.—White House press secretary

PROFILES OF KEY FIGURES

Howard H. Baker Jr.

Senator Baker, the ranking Republican on the Senate Watergate committee, is 47 years old but looks 10 years younger. With a boyish face, a quick grin, a soft voice and a relaxed manner, he may be able to use the televised committee hearings to build a base of national political support.

"We couldn't have picked a better man," a fellow Republican said recently. "Howard has the best television personality in the Senate."

The Tennessee Senator was born into politics. His father was a member of the House for 13 years and his mother filled out his father's unexpired term. His sister, May, is married to Representative William C. Wampler of Virginia, and his wife, Joy, is the daughter of Everett McKinley Dirksen, the late Senate Republican leader.

He said he was assured by the Republican leadership before he accepted his position on the Watergate panel that he would not be expected to take a partisan line or take orders from the White House.

Alexander Porter Butterfield

As a flying colonel in the Air Force, as a top administrative officer in the Nixon White House, and in the last four months as head of the Federal Aviation Administration, Mr. Butterfield seems to have impressed everybody as the sort of quiet, successful professional that any mother could be proud of.

Joseph A. Califano Jr., a Pentagon "whiz kid" in the Kennedy and Johnson Administrations, remembers him as an exceptionally bright, 14-hour-a-day policy planner—"a first-class staff guy, straight, essentially apolitical," Mr. Califano said. He added, "If he disagreed with you, you knew it. I was thinking this afternoon, what if they had asked him to hold back about the tapes, but with Butterfield, nobody would have asked."

A former colleague at the White House recalled him as a model of dedication, without zealotry. It seemed typical that the morning after his wife and daughter were seriously injured in an automobile accident three years ago, Mr. Butterfield was on duty as usual at 7:30 A.M. because, as he said, he knew that the President relied on him to get the morning schedule moving.

At the F.A.A. he told his staff that safety was henceforth going to be the agency's primary mission. "He read all the accident reports himself," said an associate. "He almost took them personally."

Mr. Butterfield was born "under the noise of airplanes," his mother said, at Pensacola, Fla., on April 6, 1926. He is the elder son of Horace B. Butterfield, a Navy pilot now retired. Flying has been his career and his lifelong passion.

After failing the Naval Academy's eye test, he joined the Air Force and flew the twin-fuselage P-38's with the late General Emmett (Rosie) O'Donnell in the Pacific during World War II. According to his official résumé, he has logged approximately 5,000 hours in 34 types of fighter aircraft and a grand total of 7,800 hours—the equivalent of 10 months—in almost the entire range of flying machines.

In Vietnam he commanded a squadron of low-level reconnaissance fliers, for which he was awarded the Distinguished Flying Cross. He also holds the Legion of Merit.

On his last military assignment—as the Air Force's F-111 project officer and senior Defense Department representative in Australia—he appeared to be heading for major command.

But as H. R. Haldeman assembled a new White House staff at the end of 1968, he remembered an old friend from the University of California at Los Angeles—the man, as it happened, who had married Mrs. Haldeman's sorority roommate at U.C.L.A.—and persuaded Mr. Butterfield to take an early retirement from the Air Force.

To become the F.A.A. Administrator this year, Mr. Butterfield had to resign from the Air Force entirely, sacrificing a pension that would now be more than $10,000 a year.

Mrs. Butterfield, the former Charlotte Mary Maguire, was his sweetheart in the fifth grade in the public schools of Coronado, Calif., the seaside town across the bay from San Diego that Mr. Butterfield now calls home.

The Butterfields' son, Alexander Jr., is a premedical student at Duke University. Susan Carter Butterfield is an undergraduate at the University of Virginia, and Elizabeth Gordon Butterfield goes to Fort Hunt High School in Alexandria, Va.

John J. Caulfield

Until the summer of 1968, when Richard M. Nixon's campaign for the Presidency rolled into full swing, John J. Caulfield was an obscure, undistinguished $12,000-a-year police detective attached to the Bronx homicide squad.

Since then, during an extended leave of absence that carried him to 20-year retirement from the New York Police Department last September, Mr. Caulfield's career as a law enforcement officer and consultant has—largely behind the scenes—soared to national influence.

Mr. Caulfield, accused in Watergate testimony of having offered Presidential clemency to a conspirator, was placed on administrative leave of absence as assistant director of the Treasury Department's Bureau of Alcohol, Tobacco and Firearms.

The $31,203-a-year post as head of the bureau's 1,600 special agents across the nation was just the latest in a series of Federal staff and executive jobs that brought Mr. Caulfield close to if not into the highest circles of Government during the last five years.

The 44-year-old former police officer, who walked a beat in the Bronx for two years and spent 10 of his 13 years as an active city detective in the department's Bureau of Special Services, which protects visiting dignitaries and gathers intelligence data, began his leave of absence on June 5, 1968.

He was first an "adviser-consultant" on Mr. Nixon's campaign staff, specializing in law enforcement matters, and later was a personal guard of former Attorney General John N. Mitchell.

From April, 1969, to March, 1972, Mr. Caulfield was a member of the White House staff, serving as liaison with all Federal law enforcement agencies and reporting to John D. Ehrlichman and later to John W. Dean 3d.

In March and April, 1972, Mr. Caulfield was one of numerous White House staff members who had switched to the Committee for the Re-election of the President. As an aide to Jeb Stuart Magruder, who briefly headed the committee, he was assigned to examine and advise the committee on the Administration's programs on law enforcement.

In April, 1972, Mr. Caulfield changed jobs again, this time joining the Treasury Department as a consultant to the director of law enforcement.

On July 1, 1972, when the Bureau of Alcohol, Tobacco and Firearms came under the Treasury Department's jurisdiction (it had formerly been a division of the Internal Revenue Service), Mr. Caulfield became acting assistant to the director for law enforcement, a civil service title from which the "acting" was dropped Dec. 17, 1972.

After The Los Angeles Times reported that he had tried to put pressure on James W. McCord Jr., one of the Watergate break-in team, to keep quiet with a promise of executive clemency, Mr. Caulfield went on vacation—a status that was changed to administrative leave on orders of the bureau's director, Rex Davis.

It was during Mr. Caulfield's service with the old Bureau of Special Services, now the New York Police Department's Security Investigation Section, that he came in contact with Mr. Nixon. This was several years before the 1968 campaign, according to sources in the Police Department.

And it was at Mr. Nixon's request that he obtained a leave of absence to join the 1968 campaign. The leave was renewed on May 1, 1969, shortly after he joined the White House staff. It ended with his retirement Sept. 30, 1972, with a pension of about $7,000 after 20 years of service that included some military service time.

Mr. Caulfield, a ruggedly handsome Irishman with black curly hair, lives with his wife, Marjorie, and three teen-age sons in Fairfax, Va., a Washington suburb.

Born in New York on March 12, 1929, he attended parochial schools in the Bronx, was graduated from Rice High School in 1947 and attended Wake Forest College, the John Jay College of Criminal Justice and Fordham University, though he holds no academic degree.

After military service and a brief period working as a draftsman with the New York Telephone Company, Mr. Caulfield joined the police on June 1, 1953, became a detective in 1955 and served in the special services bureau from 1956 to 1966, when he was transferred to the Bronx homicide squad. His highest rank was second-grade detective, and police records show no special commendations or awards for his police service.

Robert Everton Cushman Jr.

At a time when the other military forces were relaxing their training and discipline in an effort to attract more recruits, General Cushman, the man named in 1971 to become Commandant of the Marine Corps, seemed likely to retain the Corps' Spartan atmosphere.

General Cushman was the natural choice for the job. He has been personally close to President Nixon since the late nineteen-fifties, when he spent the last four years of Mr. Nixon's Vice Presidency as his chief adviser on national security affairs.

In March, 1969, shortly after he became President, Mr. Nixon made General Cushman Deputy Director of the Central Intelligence Agency, a position he held when he was identified as the C.I.A. official who supplied equipment to E. Howard Hunt, one of those convicted for the Watergate break-in.

General Cushman was born in St. Paul, Minn., on Christmas Eve, 1914. He went to public schools there and then to the United States Naval Academy, where he graduated 10th in his class of 1935. Classmates at the academy remember him as a fine lacrosse player.

In South Vietnam from 1967 until he returned to Washington in 1969, he was commanding officer of 163,000 Army and Marine troops in the northernmost provinces. No other Marine officer has ever commanded so many battlefront troops.

General Cushman has the physique and demeanor of a story-book marine. He is barrel-chested and six feet tall, with closely cropped hair and ramrod posture. He wears glasses nearly all the time these days.

According to his colleagues, he is an extraordinarily articulate and forceful speaker, the kind of person who commands immediate attention when he begins to speak. He is anything but flamboyant, but a friend said it would be a mistake to describe him as colorless.

In Vietnam, General Cushman gained a reputation for independence, especially after he privately took issue with his superiors over the static defense concept employed at Khesanh, the American bastion that was besieged by the enemy for months.

General Cushman was said to have argued that the

Americans at Khesanh were sacrificing their greatest advantage, the ability to maneuver infantry and artillery rapidly by helicopter.

His opposition to the Khesanh strategy, however, did not keep him from being an effective commander. "After all," a friend who was in Vietnam at the same time remarked, "he is a Marine."

General Cushman's wife is the former Audrey Boyce of Portsmouth, Va. They live in˙McLean, Va., and have two grown children and two grandchildren.

Samuel Dash

Samuel Dash admitted that he was "a little nervous" before the Watergate committee's opening session began, and there was reason. He is a central figure in the drama, and he himself has said of his appointment as the committee's chief counsel: "Everything I've done personally led up to this job." For the 48-year-old, partly bald Mr. Dash, "everything" is a word that takes in a lot. He is now a professor of law at the Georgetown University Law Center and director of the center's Institute of Criminal Law and Procedure. He has been, among other things, a trial lawyer, a district attorney, a consultant to or member of numerous American Bar Association projects and committees, the author of a study of electronic investigation, "The Eavesdroppers," and a classmate of former Attorney General Richard G. Kleindienst at Harvard Law School.

Mr. Dash, after admitting a little preopening nervousness, "like all performers," added that "once we got going, I was relaxed because I knew I was prepared." He also made sure that the committee's members were prepared on the first day of the nationally televised hearings, by supplying them with questions ahead of time.

According to Mr. Dash's 70-year-old father, Joseph, his son told him at the age of 14 or so "that he would be a lawyer or a judge." His mother, Ida, 68, said in the course of the same telephone interview from Atlantic City, where they now live, that the second of her six children was "a perfectionist." She described him as "the most honest person in the world," which she sees as the reason for his selection for the chief counsel's post.

The elder Dashes had emigrated from the Soviet Union, where they were born, to Camden, N. J. When Samuel was about 7 years old, the family moved to Philadelphia, where he graduated from Central High School. His undergraduate career at Temple University there was interrupted by World War II. After Air Force service, he returned to receive his degree in 1947.

It was in high school that he met his future wife, but they did not really get to know each other until July, 1945, when they were both strolling on the Atlantic City Boardwalk and a mutual friend recalled the acquaintance. Later, says Sara Dash, they "bumped into" each other while swimming, and were married exactly a year later.

She confirms that the law—and history—has always been her husband's principal interest. But he is also a devotee of archeology: "If he ever retired," his wife said, "I think he'd go dig."

Another lifelong avocation has been writing poetry, an aptitude that he now confines to such special occasions as his wedding anniversary or, most recently, the 17th birthday of his younger daughter, Rachel.

The Dashes' other daughter, Judy, 21, is in her third year at Brown University. They live in Chevy Chase, a Maryland suburb, and are, according to Mrs. Dash, "to a certain degree observant" of the Jewish holidays.

Mr. Dash used to paint, too, and some of his oils are hung in their house. He still does all the household repairs, says his wife, who adds:

"One thing that impressed me when I met him was that this man was pretty good at anything he set his mind to."

As for his professional life, it began in 1950, when he received his law degree cum laude and went to Northwestern University as a teaching associate. From there, he went to the Justice Department a year later to serve as a trial lawyer; then back to Philadelphia as an assistant district attorney, becoming chief of the appeals division in 1962 and first assistant in 1954. From 1955 to 1956 he was the district attorney, having been appointed to fill a vacancy. He did not run for the post at the next election.

Instead, he became a partner in the firm of Blank, Rudenko, Klaus & Rome until 1958, when he became a partner in his own firm of Dash & Levy, specializing in criminal trial work. In 1963, he became director of the Philadelphia Council for Community Advancement, where he remained until coming to Georgetown in 1965.

He has also been the president of the National Association

of Defense Lawyers in Criminal Cases, executive director of
the District of Columbia Judicial Conference Project on
Mental Disorders, and a special consultant to the National
Association of Attorneys General and to the Ford Foundation.

He has been a member of the A.B.A.'s Commission on
Campus Government and Student Dissent and its Special Committee on Crime Prevention and Control.

He also directed the Pennsylvania Bar Association Endow-
ment's study of wiretapping and eavesdropping from 1956
to 1958, the year before his own book on the subject was
published. Mr. Dash is also a director of the International
League for the Rights of Man, a private group that has con-
sultative status with the United Nations.

John Wesley Dean 3d

Until the spring of 1973, when the base of the Watergate iceberg surfaced, John Wesley Dean 3d basked in his
own notion of success.

Inside the Nixon circle he ranked nowhere near the top
on scales of power and independence. In fact it is difficult
now to determine what impact the smiling young lawyer
made on the Administration. But he relished his imposing
title—Counsel to the President—even though he rarely counseled the President on important matters. And his trappings
advertised a man who had made it to the top.

In one of many $200 suits, he drove a maroon Porsche
911 to the White House each day from his townhouse in
Alexandria, Va., overlooking the Potomac. He and his beau-
tifully groomed blonde wife, Maureen, sailed their 20-foot
boat on the Chesapaake Bay on weekends. There were vacations in the Mediterranean and the Philippines.

Now, discharged from his position, he is locked in an epic
stuggle with the President over White House involvement in
the Watergate affair. Fighting to stay out of prison for his
role in the Watergate cover-up, Mr. Dean, who is 34 years
old, took the stand as the star witness in the hearings of
the Senate Select Committee on Watergate.

Colleagues, friends and enemies have searched for the
ingredients that distinguished John Dean in the plentiful
ranks of young lawyers in Washington and led Mr. Nixon
to appoint him Presidential counsel—a position often reserved

in previous Administrations for some of the finest minds in the country.

All agree that he is bright, but not brilliant, that he works hard, and with a certain charm. But did he claw his way up, chronically using people and turning on them—as he has turned against the Administration—for immediate advantage? Or was he, rather—as his Watergate testimony suggested—a mere ornament, a man who was used by the real powers in the Administration?

Friends say he was manipulated; foes say he was always a manipulator himself. Both may be partly right.

John Dean's roots sprouted in solid Nixon country—mid-America and society—upper middle class. His father was a middle-level executive at the Firestone Tire and Rubber Company in Akron, Ohio, when Mr. Dean was born on Oct. 14, 1938, and provided his only son with more than a few advantages.

But young Dean left no distinguished academic record behind at any of the schools he attended as he floundered in choosing his directions—not at Staunton Military Academy in Virginia (where he roomed with Barry Goldwater Jr., now a Representative from California); not at Colgate University; not at American University; not at Wooster College, where he earned a bachelor of arts degree in 1961; and not at Georgetown Law School, where he attained his law degree.

"Average" is the common term used by the professors and classmates who recall John Dean.

He did possess a boyish smile, a trim physique and gentle manner, which attracted, among others, Karla Hennings, the daughter of Senator Thomas Hennings, Republican of Missouri. Mr. Dean's marriage to Miss Hennings ended in divorce, but his association with Senator Hennings—a highly respected member of the Judiciary Committee who died in 1960—gained him entree to many of the power centers in Washington.

Thus, when he graduated from Georgetown Law School, he was hired by the law firm of Welch and Morgan because, as one member put it, "he was Tom Hennings's son-in-law." Edward P. Morgan, the senior partner who hired Mr. Dean, had been a friend of Senator Hennings.

After only six months as an associate in the law firm, Mr. Dean was dismissed. Vincent B. Welch, senior partner in the firm, which specializes in television licensing, charged Mr. Dean with "unethical conduct"—a phrase he later softened to "basic disagreement" over policy.

The problem, in any event, was that Mr. Dean, while preparing a St. Louis television application for Mr. Welch, was, at the same time, privately working on a rival application with friends.

Another Welch and Morgan lawyer says that Mr. Dean had already decided to leave the firm before he was dismissed.

"John realized his strongest talents couldn't be brought to bear" in private practice, said the lawyer. "What distinguished John was the combination of a shrewd judgment of people with a very pleasant manner. He knew it to be one of his marketable capabilities."

The market that beckoned was politics, and Mr. Dean quickly sold himself as minority counsel on the House Judiciary Committee.

"I knew what happened at Welch and Morgan," said former Representative William M. McCulloch of Ohio, who, as ranking minority member of the committee, hired Mr. Dean.

"John Dean was a handsome young man, a well-dressed person, who knew how to use the English language," Mr. McCulloch went on. "He made a good impression on me and I suppose the old school tie [Wooster College in Ohio, from which Mr. McCulloch also graduated] had a little influence on me."

During Mr. Dean's year on the committee, he impressed Mr. McCulloch as an "able, perceptive young man," but "so far as I was concrned, he was never tested."

In Mr. Dean's year on Capitol Hill he made a valuable friend, however, in Republican Representative Richard Poff, now a justice on the Virginia Supreme Court and once considered by President Nixon for appointment to the United States Supreme Court.

Mr. Poff made Mr. Dean associate director of the National Commission on the Reform of Federal Criminal Laws.

One of the projects Mr. Dean worked on during his two years on the commission was the proposal that gave birth to the provision in the Omnibus Crime Control Act of 1970 allowing prosecutors to grant "limited immunity" to witnesses.

"Use immunity," as it is also known, prevents the Watergate prosecutors from using Mr. Dean's testimony before the Senate committee against him unless they can establish the evidence independently.

Louis B. Schwartz, now a professor of law at the University of Pennsylvania, who served on the commission, said he was "unimpressed by any great principles" Mr. Dean held.

Mr. Dean, he explained, "knows there is an exception to everything." Professor Schwartz said that Mr. Dean kept an "open mind" and was "flexible" and had changed his position, for example, from approval to disapproval of capital punishment.

In his spare time, Mr. Dean worked on position papers on crime for Richard M. Nixon during the 1968 Presidential campaign.

Law and order was a major issue, and Mr. Poff knew John N. Mitchell, who was about to become Attorney General. In February, 1969, Mr. Dean was named associate deputy attorney general and designated the Justice Department's liaison with Congress.

Before the big antiwar demonstration in Washington in 1969, Mr. Dean negotiated with the protest leaders, dickering over routes and the parade permit. The Administration had predicted mass violence. And when the troubles proved minimal, Mr. Dean was given a piece of the credit.

The next summer, when John D. Ehrlichman, then the President's chief domestic adviser, looked around for someone to take his old title of counsel, Mr. Dean was one of the few possibilities.

"He got the job as counsel for two reasons," said one Justice Department official. First, "he was bright and good looking. Those are public relations people in the White House," he added. "Secondly, John Ehrlichman didn't want someone in that job who would challenge him."

In June, 1970, John Dean joined the flock of bright young men in the White House—men beholden to the President and his chief lieutenants for their authority and chance of advancement. They were not men who had known distinction before they were chosen to serve the President. They were grateful and they were diligent in return.

Mr. Dean plowed through his assignments, which included handling some personal affairs for the President and interviewing candidates for nomination to the Supreme Court. He earned the reputation of an expert on the unwritten doctrine of executive privilege.

In 1972, three years after his divorce, Mr. Dean remarried and went on a honeymoon partly financed by several thousand dollars from money entrusted to him.

The second Mrs. Dean, the former Maureen Kane, was a Los Angeles insurance woman before her marriage.

John Daniel Ehrlichman

Maybe there really are "two Ehrlichmans," as a former White House associate insists, but the Senate Watergate committee certainly saw only one of them when he testified.

The heavy-browed, frequently scowling John Daniel Ehrlichman who sat under the television lights on the committee's witness stand was a combative, cocky defender of the faith. The "relaxed, easy" fellow who was known around the White House as a "closet liberal," according to his old acquaintance, was nowhere to be seen in the crowded Caucus Room on the third floor of the Old Senate Office Building.

Not that the tanned and muscular-looking former chief domestic affairs adviser to the President didn't smile now and then. But the smiles were those of a man who enjoys a good scrap—and he came out fighting.

"It's an effective side of Ehrlichman," his former coworker mused as he watched the baldish head bob and the dark brows rise and fall expressively on television. "I've seen him under hostile pressure before. He doesn't flap, nor does he become a doormat."

Mr. Ehrlichman was a new kind of witness for the committee, a tough, unapologetic Nixon stalwart who obviously felt that a good offense was the best defense.

Most of those who had previously testified had been deferential and had at least assumed an air of cooperativeness.

Even John N. Mitchell, the former Attorney General and Presidential campaign director, presented a muted version of his usual crusty self in most of his appearances before the committee.

But from Mr. Ehrlichman's opening statement, which was reminiscent of a high school civics lecture as he detailed the duties of the President and the "drudgery" of "work that is really never done," the former domestic affairs adviser seemed to be challenging or chiding the committee.

Putting on his glasses, Mr. Ehrlichman read the 30-page statement to the seven Senators and their aides as if he were a teacher trying to get through to a particularly slow class.

Why everyone, including Mr. Nixon, didn't know, Mr. Ehrlichman insisted, was that they depended on John W. Dean 3d to keep them informed and he failed them.

Mr. Dean was dismissed last April 30. Mr. Ehrlichman and H. R. Haldeman, who had been linked by Mr. Dean to the Watergate affair, resigned the same day.

But the John Ehrlichman who sparred vigorously with the committee and its counsel did not act like an unemployed 48-year-old lawyer with a wife and five children to feed.

He was still President Nixon's man, no doubt about it— in fact and faith, if not in pay.

A graduate of the University of California, Los Angeles, and the Stanford Law School, Mr. Ehrlichman returned to his family home near Seattle, where he became a lawyer with a special interest in urban affairs and the conservation of natural resources.

Mr. Ehrlichman was born in Tacoma, Wash., March 20, 1925. His wife, Jeanne, attended U.C.L.A. with the Presidential adviser-to-be.

During his college days, he met H. R. Haldeman. In the late nineteen-fifties, Mr. Haldeman, who later managed Mr. Nixon's unsuccessful campaign for the governorship in California in 1962, asked Mr. Ehrlichman to do some advance work for Mr. Nixon, who was then Vice President. Mr. Ehrlichman was loyal and efficient. When the 1968 campaign started, Mr. Haldeman, on Mr. Nixon's behalf, asked Mr. Ehrlichman to run the 50,000-mile campaign tour.

Growing bald and a bit portly, Mr. Ehrlichman, a Christian Scientist, combines an arch sense of humor with a severe conception of duty. He can be a charming, quick-witted and informative companion. In the early days of the Nixon Administration, when he was talking to reporters, his official sense of discretion seemed constantly at war with his natural instinct for candor. But he demanded of his staff the same energy and loyalty his boss demanded of him.

Sam J. Ervin Jr.

In the running tug-of-wag between Congress and the White House in 1973, Senator Ervin seems to be holding the rope at the east end of Pennsylvania Avenue on virtually every issue. It is his bill that seeks to limit the President's power to impound funds and his committees that are looking into the questions of newsmen's right to withhold their sources of information and the President's right to withhold information and staff members from Congressional scrutiny. It is also, his colleagues emphasize, his committee that is investigating the Watergate affair.

It is not coincidental that all these tasks should fall on the ample shoulders of the Democrat from North Carolina. In 18 years in the Senate, he has sided at times with the conservatives and at times with the liberals, but he has gained the respect of virtually all of his colleagues for his unswerving principles and his dedication to the Constitution.

"Sammy is the only man we could have picked out on either side who'd have the respect of the Senate as a whole," Senator Mansfield said.

At the age of 76, Mr. Ervin is the third oldest man in the Senate (George D. Aiken of Vermont and John L. McClellan of Arkansas are older). But he was 58 when he first came to the Senate and had had a full career as a lawyer and judge. Except for three years at Harvard Law School and two years as a Representative in the nineteen-forties, he had spent his entire life in North Carolina.

Louis Patrick Gray 3d

"I came to this town with reputation and integrity and I'm going to take it away, so help me God!"

So spoke L. Patrick Gray during a particularly emotional moment in the Senate hearings in March, 1973, on his nomination to head the Federal Bureau of Investigation. He had little reason, then, to doubt that he could make good his promise, but revelations of Mr. Gray's involvement in the Watergate scandal have insured that when he finally returns home to Stonington, Conn., the reputation he carries with him will have been tarnished.

His career is not the only one damaged by Watergate, of course. But the story that Mr. Gray told in his characteristic monotone is a bit sadder than most of those the Senate Watergate committee has heard, because for him the chance to "make it" came so late and ended so abruptly.

Until he was appointed acting director of the F.B.I. at the age of 55, Pat Gray was only one of the solid, crisp, calm and efficient "number two men" who inhabit Washington— the deputies and assistants who are permitted access to the chambers of power, but only to take notes.

To have come that far was perhaps an admirable accomplishment for the eldest son of a moderately poor railroad man. The son, born in St. Louis July 18, 1916, managed to eke out an education in the midst of the Depression by dint of brains alone. He gained admission to the tuition-free Rice Institute in Houston, which accepted only honor students, then won a four-year scholarship to the United States Naval Academy.

Mr. Gray had always wanted a naval career, and the Navy was good to him. It made him a submarine commander in his mid-twenties, and he led the U.S.S. Steelhead on five combat patrols in the Pacific during World War II.

After the war, the Navy selected him over hundreds of other applicants and sent him to the George Washington University Law School here. After graduating with honors in 1949 he embarked on a new career as a naval legal officer.

His last assignment, before he retired as a captain in 1960, was as military assistant to the chairman of the Joint Chiefs of Staff and special assistant to the Secretary of Defense.

That job allowed him to attend meetings of the National Security Council and the Cabinet, and Mr. Gray was enamored of what he saw of Government policymaking. "I wanted to get in," he recalled in 1972. "Not on the electoral side; I didn't want to run for office. I wanted to get in on the managerial and administrative side of policymaking."

He would have been "in" sooner if Richard Nixon, whom he has known and admired since their first meeting at a Washington party in 1947, had won the Presidency in 1960.

The friendship between the two men, although never close, remained alive over the years, and when Mr. Gray left the Pentagon he moved to the Vice President's campaign staff, where he established himself as a solid administrator, according to one man who worked with him.

But Mr. Nixon's bid failed, and Mr. Gray moved to Connecticut, which he had become fond of during naval service there, to practice law and bide his time.

He did well financially, earning a reputed $70,000 a year, which, with his Navy pension, enabled him to move into a large new home on a hill with a striking view of Stonington harbor.

He kept his political contacts up to date, too, and when Mr. Nixon was elected President in 1968, Mr. Gray joined the new Administration as an executive assistant to Robert H. Finch, then the Secretary of Health, Education and Welfare, with whom he had worked closely in the 1960 Nixon campaign.

"Submariners are unflappable," he once said, but despite the extraordinary self-control, bordering on stoicism, that he exhibits both in public and private, those who know him well say he is compassionate and sensitive. In the year that Mr. Gray spent at Health, Education and Welfare, says a former Administration official, "A lot of liberal stuff got slipped in through him. You'd take him aside and say, 'Pat, here's a good one for the old folks.' "

Mr. Gray's self-discipline and administrative talents at the department won him a reputation that finally began to move him progressively closer to the inner circles of Government.

He was named an assistant Attorney General in December, 1970, and, little more than a year later, was nominated by Mr. Nixon to become the Deputy Attorney General, the second most important office in the Justice Department.

Three months later the string of number two jobs was broken when, on May 2, 1972, J. Edgar Hoover died in his sleep. The next day, the President named Mr. Gray to replace Mr. Hoover in an acting capacity, explaining that he would not nominate a permanent director until after the November election, to prevent the confirmation hearings from becoming a campaign issue.

Mr. Gray would have liked nothing better than to finish his career in public service at the head of the F.B.I., but Mr. Nixon had promised him only that his name would be among those considered.

Mr. Gray set out immediately to capture the nomination with all the energy and imagination he could muster. Conscious of criticism that the bureau, under Mr. Hoover, had grown archaic and insular, he tried to establish himself as an accessible, innovative administrator, making speeches, accepting reporters' telephone calls, permitting agents to wear longer hair and colored shirts, opening the bureau's ranks to women.

The speech-making and frequent travels to F.B.I. field offices were seen as a public relations campaign by some of the Hoover loyalists in the bureau's headquarters. They resented it, and some retaliated by leaking confidential F.B.I. files to the press, a warning to the White House that Mr. Gray could not control the bureau as Mr. Hoover had.

Mr. Gray, who has a well-developed sense of bureaucratic

politics, praised his predecessor in public, while he quietly dispersed many of the old Hoover men to other F.B.I. offices around the country or forced them into retirement.

But for Watergate, Mr. Gray's hopes of becoming J. Edgar Hoover's permanent successor might well have been realized. He did receive the nomination, but the confirmation hearings before the Senate Judiciary Committee proved disastrous to him.

Some Democratic Senators accused him from the outset of being a political appointee, too closely tied to the White House to head a traditionally nonpartisan agency, and as the hearings progressed they buttressed their assertion with examples of laxity in the bureau's Watergate investigation.

Mr. Gray conceded that he had sent raw F.B.I. reports on Watergate to the White House, for example, but explained that he had been acting on the belief that there should be "a presumption of regularity" about the men close to the President, and that he had simply followed their orders, which had come to him "down the chain of command." It was the old submarine captain speaking.

To demonstrate his impartiality, Mr. Gray began to drop facts about Watergate unfavorable to the Administration, such as the revelation that Herbert W. Kalmbach, Mr. Nixon's personal lawyer, had financed a Republican campaign sabotage effort last year. Incensed by the headlines he was producing, the White House ordered him to stop providing investigative data on Watergate to the committee. He obeyed, and angered the Senators even more.

By the time Mr. Gray was forced to resign from the F.B.I. in April, following the disclosure that he had destroyed papers taken from the safe of a principal suspect in the Watergate bugging case, the nomination was already dead, withdrawn by the President at Mr. Gray's request a month earlier after it had become clear that he could not be confirmed.

Mr. Gray is a thoroughly disciplined man who exercises daily and does not smoke or drink, a Roman Catholic who attends early mass every day, "a great square," as one friend called him, a principled and idealistic man who kept a copy of "Jonathan Livingston Seagull" on a coffee table in his office at the Justice Department and commended its wisdom to his top officials.

But after John W. Dean 3d told Federal prosecutors what

had happened to the papers taken from the safe of E. Howard
Hunt Jr., a Watergate conspirator, Mr. Gray did a most uncharacteristic thing. He lied. He told a high Justice Department official that he had not read the files before burning
them, when he had read some of them. He told Senator Lowell
P. Weicker Jr., the Connecticut Republican who had been one
of his most enthusiastic supporters, that he had destroyed the
papers immediately, when he had actually kept them intact
for months.

He told Senator Weicker and the other members of the
Watergate committee that he was ashamed, not of what he
had done, but of having been untruthful.

His appearance before the committee marked the first time
since March, 1973, that he had been seen in public, and the
revelations of the intervening months had taken their toll.

If he escapes indictment, he will return to his old law firm
of Suisman, Shapiro, Wool, Brennan & Gray, which has
made him a partner, and his beloved home in Stonington,
where his wife, Bea, four sons and two grandchildren are
living now.

Edward J. Gurney

In 1972, Senator Gurney acknowledged, he was the chief
defender of the Nixon Administration during the Judiciary
Committee's investigation of the International Telephone and
Telegraph Corporation.

"It was such a highly partisan investigation," he said.
"Someone had to play the role of defending the President,
and I did."

But he said that he saw the Watergate inquiry as a different
matter.

"I want to see that it is as nonpartisan as possible, but I
certainly want to bring out every last piece of information,"
he said.

Senator Gurney, a conservative, was elected in 1968 as
the first Republican Senator from Florida since Reconstruction. A native of Maine and a graduate of the Harvard Law
School, he moved to Florida and went into law practice in
1948. Now 59 years old, he served three terms in the House
before moving on to the Senate.

Mr. Gurney said he had asked to be on the Watergate

committee because "investigative work is my favorite kind of Senate work."

Harry Robbins Haldeman

One day several years ago, a subordinate received from H. R. Haldeman, then the White House chief of staff, a memorandum that the subordinate had drafted. In one corner Mr. Haldeman had written, in his precise hand, "TL². " When he was asked what what notation meant, the often curt and unbending Mr. Haldeman replied, "Too little, too late." Mr. Haldeman's friends hope that the same comment will not apply to his attempt to clear himself—and, not incidentally, the President whom he served with such fervor for more than four years—of any implication in the Watergate case and the ensuing cover-up. That attempt began when he took the stand before the Senate investigating committee on Capitol Hill.

At a time when his former colleagues were defending themselves publicly, or leaking material favorable to themselves and damaging to their onetime friends, Mr. Haldeman clung punctiliously to his insistence on saying nothing until the "proper moment" in the proper forum. The result was that he came before a public conditioned to view him as a villain.

Mr. Haldeman resigned from the White House staff on April 30, 1973, after weeks of public and private accusations. Mr. Nixon described him as one of his "closest friends and most trusted assistants." The former staff chief spent a few weeks cleaning out his desk and poring over his papers, then moved his family out of their red brick house in suburban Kenwood, Md., and back to his native California.

Unlike his boss, Mr. Haldeman watched much of the Watergate testimony on television. But he told a reporter who brazened his way past the "no admittance" sign on the narrow bridge leading to his rented house: "After all the things I've seen lobbed out of Washington which have died of their own weight or proven false, not answering the charges has usually proven wise."

In his days of power at the White House, Mr. Haldeman never had to resort to indirection. His legendary clout arose precisely from the fact that almost every piece of paper and almost every visitor that reached the President did so by way of Bob Haldeman. He was the keeper of the Nixon portal.

Among bureaucrats, Congressmen, reporters and even Cabinet members who wanted to see the President and failed, Mr. Haldeman soon won a reputation for hauteur. Not only did he say "no"; he said it without the charm or humor that most politicians use as a kind of lubricant to ease the unpleasant.

Those who worked inside the White House with Mr. Haldeman were dazzled by his efficiency, inspired by his loyalty to Mr. Nixon and relatively unconcerned about his toughness. One of them remarked recently that "Bob was a little arrogant, sure, but in the job he held down, he needed it to get through the day."

A former colleague in advertising, now working for an agency in New York, called him "a completely obnoxious man who was totally uninterested in what anyone else thought, only his own ideas."

Mr. Haldeman's reputation for brusqueness may stem from his appearance. He has the look of a Marine Corps drill instructor or perhaps a zealous scoutmaster, with shadowed eyes, the crew cut, thin lips and a muscular jaw. He seldom smiles, which emphasizes the impression of wintriness.

But he is apparently quite capable of relaxation, particularly with his family. They like listening to country music together, talking, staying at home rather than attending Washington or California parties. One of his sons, Hank, has shoulder-length hair, a fact that Mr. Haldeman has learned to accept with an equanimity that doesn't fit his public image.

Advertising and Richard Nixon have taken up most of Mr. Haldeman's adult life. Born in Los Angeles on Oct. 27, 1926, he grew up in the privileged environment of Beverly Hills, went to the University of California at Los Angeles (where he met his wife, Joanne, and his future colleague John D. Ehrlichman) and went to work for the J. Walter Thompson advertising agency. He stayed there for two decades.

All the while, he was helping Mr. Nixon—in the Vice-Presidential campaign, then in the 1960 Presidential, 1962 California gubernatorial and 1968 and 1972 Presidential efforts. For the four years of Mr. Nixon's first term, he was at the President's side almost constantly, even on trips, during which he became famous for taking home movies of the more ceremonial moments.

Richard McGarrah Helms

When Richard Helms presented his credentials as Ambassador to Iran to the Shah, the official press in neighboring and not particularly friendly Iraq described Mr. Helms as an "ugly American." To an outsider—one who had seen Mr. Helms's biography but did not know him personally—that appellation might have seemed apt. He was a professional spy for most of his adult life and the Director of Central Intelligence in the United States for the last seven years before he became an ambassador.

In fact, he was a high official in the Central Intelligence Agency in 1953 when the agency engineered the overthrow of the Communist-oriented regime then in power in Iran and the return of the Shah to the throne.

But to those who know Mr. Helms, the description of him by the press in Iraq could not have been further from the truth.

Physically, the 60-year-old envoy is slim and dark-complexioned, with graying hair that is just beginning to recede. He keeps himself in outstanding condition, and, if it were not for a slightly jutting lower lip, he would be strikingly handsome.

Personally, he is friendly, gregarious and sensitive to the feelings of others. Women, young and old, find him a charming dinner partner and a smooth dancer.

Professionally, he worked diligently to improve the public image of the C.I.A., worried about allegations that the agency was overstepping the boundaries of morality and managed to maintain a reputation as a speaker of facts, while avoiding the political fights that often emerged around them.

Throughout his long career at the C.I.A., Mr. Helms was highly regarded in Congress. And it was significant that, at the conclusion of his testimony before the Senate Foreign Relations Committee about the agency's involvement in the Watergate scandal, he was warmly praised by several of the Senators.

Richard Helms (he prefers not to use his middle name or initial) was born to a family of means in St. Davids, Pa., on March 30, 1913. His father was an Alcoa executive and his maternal grandfather, Gates McGarrah, was a leading international banker. He was reared in South Orange, N. J., and spent two high school years in Switzerland, where he learned fluent French and German, a fact that was to be a guiding factor in his career.

At Williams College, from which he graduated in 1935, Mr. Helms was clearly the outstanding member of his class— a member of Phi Beta Kappa, class president, editor of the newspaper and yearbook and president of the senior honor society.

From Williams, Mr. Helms went to Europe as a reporter for United Press and won a brief glimpse of reporter's glory when he had an exclusive interview with Hitler.

World War II ended Mr. Helms's newspaper career. Having joined the Naval Reserve, he was assigned, principally because of his linguistic talents, to the Office of Strategic Services. He stayed in intelligence after the war, with the Joint Strategic Services of the War Department, which gave way in 1946 to the Central Intelligence Agency.

From 1946 to 1966, he served as Deputy and Assistant Director of Central Intelligence, and in 1966 he became the first career official to head the C.I.A.

Mr. Helms's first marriage, to the former Julia Shields of Indianapolis, ended in divorce in 1968 after a long separation. His son by that marriage, Dennis, is a lawyer.

Mr. Helms is now married to the former Cynthia McKelvie, an English-born redhead with four grown children from a previous marriage. Both Mr. Helms and his wife are fond of tennis, playing regularly when they are in Washington.

There are many rumors, none of them confirmed as accurate, about the reasons for Mr. Helms's departure as Director of Central Intelligence at the beginning of 1973.

One is that Mr. Helms had always insisted on others retiring from the agency at age 60 and that it was thus incumbent upon him to do so. Another is that Henry A. Kissinger, then President Nixon's national security adviser, was dissatisfied with Mr. Helms's direction of intelligence operations, a rumor that Mr. Kissinger has vigorously and publicly denied.

Another possible reason has developed with disclosures that Mr. Helms refused to cooperate with H. R. Haldeman and other White House officials in various domestic operations.

When the Foreign Relations Committee asked Mr. Helms if that was why he was removed from the C.I.A. and sent to Iran, he responded, "I do not know."

Everette Howard Hunt Jr.

Everette Howard Hunt Jr. left the Central Intelligence Agency in 1970 after 21 years of clandestine operations. But after the convicted Watergate conspirator left to take a more mundane public relations job, "he couldn't get over the fact," according to a friend, "that he'd been a C.I.A. agent. You couldn't have a conversation with him for 10 minutes without him bringing it up some way or other. This was a romanticist who couldn't get over the fact that he had been a spy."

This was a role that Hunt relished, admitting that "I was an intelligence officer—a spy—for the Government of the United States," a role that also eventually led to his being hired as a White House consultant by a fellow alumnus of Brown University, Charles W. Colson.

It was a role that teamed Hunt with G. Gordon Liddy, another Watergate culprit, to organize the break-in at the office of the psychiatrist of Dr. Daniel Ellsberg because of Ellsberg's "peculiar background," and his leaking of the Pentagon Papers.

It was a role that made Hunt consider breaking into the safe of a Las Vegas newspaper publisher to get presumably damaging evidence on the then candidate for the Democratic presidential nomination, Senator Edmund S. Muskie.

And finally it was a role that contributed to Hunt's conviction for conspiring to break into the Democratic national headquarters at the Watergate complex. In the end, it was a career, that led Hunt to proclaim, "I cannot escape the feeling that the country I have served for my entire life and which directed me to carry out the Watergate entry is punishing me for doing the very thing it trained and directed me to do."

Hunt was born Oct. 9, 1918 in Hamburg, N.Y., the only son of Everette Howard Hunt and Ethel Jean Totterdale. His father, a judge, practiced law at one time in Miami Beach. While a schoolboy Hunt visited Havana. Years later, in 1960, Hunt returned to Havana on a secret visit to observe life under Fidel Castro. As a result Hunt recommended the assassination of Castro.

Hunt, known as Eduardo during his connection with the abortive Bay of Pigs invasion of Cuba, assumed a variety of aliases, including Edward Hamilton and Ed Warren, during his spy days. His many novels about spying were also written under pseudonyms like Robert Salisbury Dietrich, Gordon Davis, John Baxter and David St. John.

In speaking of these books, one friend said, "Howard tried to act out his novels and his hidden emotional drives. You know, he wanted to be a hero of intelligence work and a sexually irresistible male."

While he wrote of spying smattered with a variety of sexual activities, friends report that his real romantic life was not as flamboyant. According to Cuban friends, Hunt spent a night with a certain young lady in a Miami motel. But, she later complained, "All he did was to keep me up all night talking about his novels."

After Hunt was graduated from Brown in 1940, he volunteered for the Navy before the United States entered World War II. He was discharged after an accident at sea, subsequently worked as a movie scriptwriter and a war correspondent for Life magazine for the next two years.

In 1943 he joined the Office of Strategic Services, the forerunner of the C.I.A. He was stationed in Orlando, Fla., and Southern China until the war ended. He won a Guggenheim fellowship in 1946 and spent a year in Mexico writing and learning Spanish. Three years later he joined the C.I.A. and spent time in Paris, Vienna and Latin American, where he acquired a background that was used in his later novels.

Since Hunt was indicted in connection with the Watergate break-in, he has lost his public relations job, and his wife, Dorothy, died in a plane crash last December.

During six months of imprisonment, he has been in solitary confinement for a time, was physically attacked and has been robbed and transferred from place to place in manacles and chains. He has been "isolated" from his four children, Lisa, Kevan, Saint John and David.

Hunt, who faces a provisional sentence of 35 years, said that he was faced with "an enormous financial burden" in defending himself in various court suits.

"Beyond all this," Hunt said, "I am crushed by the failure of my Government to protect me and my family as in the past it has always done for its clandestine agents."

Tom Charles Huston

The young lawyer who drafted the White House's new domestic security plan in the summer of 1970, Tom Charles

Huston, is a fervent, scholarly conservative who wishes he had lived in the 18th century. His intellectual heroes are Cato, the Roman moralist, and Thomas Jefferson; the portrait on his office wall here was of John C. Calhoun, the Southern theorist of states' rights and nullification of Federal statues.

His explanation of the proposed counteroffensive against anti-Nixon insurgents used the language of a stern public philosopher, not a law-and-order fanatic.

"The real threat to internal security—in any society—is repression," Mr. Huston explained in a telephone interview from Indianapolis, where he has been practicing law for the last two years. "But repression is an inevitable result of disorder. Forced to choose between order and freedom, people will take order.

"A handful of people can't frontally overthrow the government," he continued, recalling the troubled mood of spring, 1970, a season of widening war in Indochina, terrorist bombing at home and civil strife at Kent State University in Ohio.

"But if they can engender enough fear, they can generate an atmosphere that will bring out of the woodwork every repressive demagogue in the country. Unless this stuff was stopped, the country was going to fall into the wrong hands."

The 1970 draft plan for domestic security included resumption of certain intelligence operations that had been suspended in 1966. These had "included authorization for surreptitious entry—breaking and entering, in effect—on specified categories of targets in specified stituations relating to national security," President Nixon said in a statement May 22, 1973.

The recommendations were never put into effect because the late J. Edgar Hoover, then Director of the Federal Bureau of Investigation, opposed the plan after reconsidering it. Mr. Hoover was chairman of an interagency intelligence committee designed to prepare recommendations, Mr. Nixon said.

Security was actually just a sideline for Mr. Huston in an intense, ultimately frustrated two-year term of service with the Nixon Administration.

Mr. Huston, who was born May 9, 1941, the son of an insurance man, in Logansport, Ind., remembers a teen-age phase as a "Stevenson Democrat." But by the time he graduated from high school, he was a conservative ideologue, a "Jeffersonian Republican," a believer in individual responsibility, small government and "what the framers of the Constitution called republican virtue."

A campus conservative at Indiana University, where he won both bachelor's (1963) and law (1966) degrees with high honors, Mr. Huston became the national chairman of Young Americans for Freedom in 1965. In 1966, as the antiwar movement grew among students, he organized the World Youth Crusade for Freedom, which sent campus leaders to tour Vietnam and tried to build support for the anti-Communist commitment there.

It was also in 1966 that he took his first political plunge. His personal endorsement of Richard M. Nixon for President was a somewhat controversial move at a moment when many young conservatives preferred Ronald Reagan; and it was early enough to attract the grateful attention of Mr. Nixon's close aides.

Accordingly, after the Nixon victory in 1968 and the end of Mr. Huston's two-year stint with Army intelligence, he was invited to join the group of speechwriters in the Executive Office Building, next door to the White House.

His experience was in many ways disenchanting. "The Administration's domestic programs were never rooted in any philosophical view of what government ought to be doing," he complained. When the liberal Daniel P. Moynihan prevailed over the conservative Arthur F. Burns in the internal White House debate over welfare reform, "it was all over for me," Mr. Huston said. Yet things got worse, he felt, when the real winners in the White House proved to be not the liberals but the "technocrats" and advertising men.

For most of a year, from the end of 1969 until the fall of 1970, Mr. Huston worked on the security program—first as a researcher and writer, later as the project officer for the White House. But by the spring of 1971 he recognized with regret that the spirit of pragmatism, not philosophical conservatism, was running the Administration, and he moved quietly back to Indianapolis.

The hardest thing about leaving Washington was moving his large collection of antique books and furniture. With his wife, the former Brenda Courtney, he has assembled a library of Presidential campaign biographies going back to 1824 and a houseful of period furniture.

He says he does not miss the capital, especially since the

Watergate scandal burst on his old associates. But he still has a profound respect for President Nixon. "The last thing I'd ever do is count Richard Nixon out," he said. "He's still the greatest living politician. If anyone can survive, he can."

Daniel K. Inouye

Senator Inouye was a protégé of two famous Texans—former President Lyndon B. Johnson and former Speaker of the House Sam Rayburn. He is now a favorite of Senator Mansfield, and many of his colleagues believe that Mr. Inouye, now an assistant Democratic whip, wants to be a majority leader himself some day.

Handsome and urbane, Mr. Inouye, 48 years old, is enormously popular in his home state, Hawaii. He was a World War II hero who lost his right arm while serving as an Army captain during the Italian campaign. After graduating from law school, he went back to Hawaii and went into politics. He has represented Hawaii in Washington since the islands became a state, as a member of the House for two terms and as a Senator since 1962. In 1968, he was re-elected with 83 per cent of the vote.

Politically, Mr. Inouye is moderate to liberal. He supported Mr. Johnson's unsuccessful Presidential campaign in 1960, even giving a seconding speech for him at the Democratic convention.

Herbert Warren Kalmbach

For five years Herbert Warren Kalmbach quietly served President Nixon as a political confidant and his personal attorney on the West Coast.

Even more quietly, he traveled back and forth across the United States and to sources of wealth in this country's embassies abroad, serving as collector of millions of dollars to finance Mr. Nixon's two election campaigns. In May, 1973, Ronald L. Ziegler, the White House press secretary, said Mr. Kalmbach was no longer handling business for Mr. Nixon.

Described by an admiring California Republican as "one of the five men closest to the President," Mr. Kalmbach is credited with personally raising more than $6 million for the President's election in 1968 and at least $9 million last year in his role as vice chairman of finance of the Committee for the Re-election of the President.

He was linked to the Watergate case as the custodian of a $350,000 secret Republican fund from which he allegedly paid out some $35,000 in unreported funds to Donald Segretti, another California lawyer, to cover the expenses of political espionage.

His name was brought into the Watergate case by the grand jury testimony of one of the Watergate burglars, James W. McCord Jr. His payment to Mr. Segretti reportedly was on instructions from the President's appointment secretary, Dwight L. Chapin.

Mr. Kalmbach's political interest grew out of his long-time friendship with Robert H. Finch, a former White House aide who is thinking of running for governor of California.

The two were classmates at the University of Southern California Law School, from which they graduated in 1951. Mr. Kalmbach's entry into politics was as Orange County chairman for Mr. Finch's successful race for lieutenant governor in 1958. In 1962, he labored on behalf of Mr. Nixon's unsuccessful bid for governor.

Mr. Kalmbach was born Oct. 19, 1921, in Port Huron, Mich. He was admitted to the California bar in 1952 and became vice president that year of the Los Angeles Security Title Insurance Company, a position he held until 1957 when he entered law practice in Newport Beach, Calif.

In 1962 he went to Phoenix as president of the Arizona Title & Trust Company but returned to Newport Beach two years later as vice president and director of the Macco Realty Company.

Since 1967 he has been a partner of the law firm of Kalmbach, DeMarco, Knapp & Chillingworth, which occupies the lushly furnished top floor of the Irvine Tower in Newport Beach, with a panoramic sweep of the Pacific Ocean and the yachts lined up along "Millionaire's Row." The firm also has offices in Los Angeles.

The law firm's practice has mushroomed since Mr. Kalmbach involved himself with Mr. Nixon's political fortunes and took over as chief strategist of the Lincoln Club of Orange County.

In Washington he maintained an office on the second floor at 1701 Pennsylvania Avenue, the address of the Committee for the Re-election of the President, and worked closely with former Presidential assistant H. R. Haldeman.

The Kalmbachs have a large home on Santiago Drive in Newport Beach. Mrs. Kalmbach is the former Barbara Helen

Forbush, whom he married June 19, 1948, while still an undergraduate at U.S.C. She says she sees very little of him even on weekends because "he's off traveling somewhere."

She declines to talk about his business because "I don't have much opportunity to discuss things with him, I see him so rarely."

The Kalmbachs have two sons, Kurt and Kenneth, and a daughter, Lauren Ann.

Richard Gordon Kleindienst

In some ways a marginal player in the drama of Watergate, Richard Kleindienst nevertheless became one of the many top officials whose lives were scarred by the break-in and the events surrounding it. As Attorney General (he had been named to succeed John N. Mitchell in 1972, when Mitchell left to head President Nixon's second campaign) he liked his $60,000-a-year job and was proud of it.

Thus, when he decided to resign as Attorney General because of his relationship to some of those linked to the Watergate case, he said, "It was the saddest realization I have ever had to make in my life." He left a job that had put him in the thick of a series of sensitive Justice Department situations, ranging from Supreme Court nominations to May Day antiwar protests to Congressional attacks on the Federal Bureau of Investigation.

He had also been in the thick of things at his confirmation hearings, when he was questioned closely about the issue of political influence in the I.T.T. merger case. As for Watergate, the department's handling of the investigation had been brought into question, and in his testimony before the Watergate committee he told of his efforts to assure an unimpeded investigation.

Mr. Kleindienst is a man not known for his caution. Even his close friends acknowledge that "Dick sometimes shoots from the hip."

By all accounts Mr. Kleindienst is both bright and outspoken. He graduated Phi Beta Kappa from Harvard in 1947 and from Harvard Law School.

Mr. Kleindienst tells with relish how his Phi Beta Kappa certificate (in Latin) was sent to his parents' home in Arizona and his father, not realizing what it was, threw it in the trash. When Richard came home, he dug it out.

Mr. Kleindienst's role in sensitive Justice Department situations plus his role as campaign director of Barry Goldwater's 1964 Presidential campaign made him a target for Congressional and other liberals. His problems in his confirmation hearings were compounded by a proclivity to be quoted making bold statements. He was said to be "profane in two languages"—English and Navajo.

Yet, on the basis of interviews, newsmen have portrayed him as a misunderstood man of social conscience and as a moderate.

Mr. Kleindienst was born in Winslow, Ariz., Aug. 5, 1923, the son of a brakeman on the Santa Fe Railroad. His mother had come west from Concord, Mass., because of her health.

He served during World War II as a navigator in the Air Force and reached the rank of first lieutenant. He returned to Arizona in 1950 after completing college and law school.

Mr. Kleindienst joined the firm of Jennings, Strouss, Salmon, Trask in Phoenix. In 1958 he left to form Shimmel, Hill, Kleindienst, Bishop. In March, 1969, after Mr. Kleindienst became Deputy Attorney General, the firm—now called Shimmel, Hill, Bishop—opened a Washington office.

From 1953 to 1954 Mr. Kleindienst was a member of the Arizona Legislature, and in 1964 he ran as the Republican candidate for governor. He worked for Senator Barry Goldwater's election and in 1968 was national director of field operations for Richard Nixon's Presidential campaign.

Mr. Kleindienst is married to the former Margaret Dunbar of Cleveland. They have four children and live in McLean, Va.

At the time he resigned he said that he could live "about 30 days" without a job. He started practicing law in Washington, but acknowledged several months later that business could be better.

Frederick Cheney LaRue

Frederick LaRue, who pleaded guilty to obstruction of justice and will help the Government prosecute the Watergate cover-up, is a Mississippi oil heir who for the last five years was an intimate friend and political lieutenant of former Attorney General John N. Mitchell.

A shy, squinting man, given to mumbling, he had a White House pass during the first Nixon term but no title and no salary. He was an elusive, anonymous, secret operator at the highest levels of the shattered Nixon power structure.

He is a man of personal mystery, too—a latter-day character, it sometimes seemed, out of a Southern Gothic novel.

His father, Ike Parsons La Rue Sr., whom Fred LaRue shot and killed in a Canadian duck-hunting accident in 1957, was a first cousin of Sid Richardson, the late Texas oil and ranching tycoon. Ike LaRue, who had gone to jail in Texas for banking violations in his first business career, started again in Mississippi, looking for oil and backed by Texas money.

In 1954, the family company—including Fred, Ike Jr. and their brother-in-law—made its first big strike in the Bolton field, 20 miles from Jackson. They worked the field themselves until 1967, when it was sold for a reported $30 million.

Some Mississippi sources say the LaRues never really controlled the fortune; others believe they lost much of it in a Las Vegas casino investment. Fred LaRue himself was quoted in 1972 as saying, "I'm no millionaire."

In any case, oil money that the LaRues reportedly "spread around" in Mississippi politics made Fred a power in his home state and permitted him to roam free as John Mitchell's surrogate in a wheeling-dealing world he came to love.

A heavy and bitterly disappointed contributor to Senator Barry Goldwater's 1964 Presidential campaign, LaRue introduced himself as a contributor to the Nixon forces in 1967. By the 1968 Republican convention, he was a close friend and ranking "Southern strategist" in Mr. Mitchell's campaign apparatus.

At the start of the 1972 re-election campaign, LaRue was a ranking member—with others such as Robert C. Mardian and Harry S. Flemming—of the "hard-core Mitchell group" at the headquarters. But he also got along well with Jeb Stuart Magruder, a representative of H. R. Haldeman's White House team who became the deputy campaign manager.

"It was a close, almost teacher-pupil relationship," Mr. Flemming remarked of the ties between the 44-year-old La-Rue and the 38-year-old Mr. Magruder. The two men were often referred to by others in the organization as a single personality: "Magrue."

As it happened, on the night of the Watergate burglary arrests, June 17, 1972, Mr. Magruder and LaRue were on a California campaign swing with Mr. Mitchell and Mr. Mardian—all staying together in the Beverly Hills Hotel.

According to Mr. Magruder's testimony before the Senate Watergate committee, the four men worked hand in glove from the next day onward to draft and preserve a cover-up story.

According to numerous reports, LaRue and Mr. Mardian were immediately assigned the job of cleaning out all incriminating documents from the Nixon re-election headquarters.

Jeb Stuart Magruder

Up the escalator and down, Jeb Stuart Magruder has seemed the classic young Nixon assistant.

A California marketing man with a tennis-court tan, he is aggressive but likable and the father of four handsome children.. He managed the details of President Nixon's landslide campaign and looked destined, before his 38th birthday (Nov. 5, 1972) for a big-league political career of his own.

His downfall was swift. In April, 1973, he muttered, "My whole life is over, I'm ruined," before giving his Watergate confession to Federal prosecutors. "The walls were coming in on him," a friend said. One Justice Department official felt that he was the likeliest of the many defendants to crack under the strain, and many people in Washington cast him for a specially tragic role in the dark Watergate drama.

Mr. Magruder was a visibly nervous witness before inquiring Senators and television cameras in the Watergate hearings. Yet friends say that for several weeks before his appearance he seemed once again the boyish go-getter, repentant but insistently upbeat about himself, prepared to go to prison but immersed, meanwhile, in new business ventures and still spouting management jargon even about the most personal aspects of his life.

In conversation he spoke clinically of suicide as "a process" and as "one solution to a problem"—but one that he never considered himself. Of the whole Watergate experience he said, "I wouldn't recommend it as a learning-curve method, but I guess I do think of it that way."

His humor has survived the ordeal. "Time magazine wrote that this is the end of my political career; now I'd say that's probably an astute comment," Mr. Magruder concurred, laughing heartily. He also reflects that though his face and name are momentarily infamous, "nine out of ten Americans couldn't remember Bobby Baker today."

Robert G. Baker, the onetime secretary to Senate Democrats, went to jail in a scandal of the mid-nineteen-sixties.

From Mr. Magruder's closest friends have come indications of moral reflection on his part. The Rev. C. Blaney Colmore, an Episcopal minister who spent hours "commiserating" with Mr. Magruder in the winter and spring of 1973, said in an interview that Mr. Magruder was "very relieved" when he admitted guilt two months ago.

"I'll tell you the honest-to-God truth," Mr. Colmore said, "I had the feeling from the first moment that he was dying to get caught. He was just miserable. Like so many guys in this Administration, Jeb's a pragmatist. But he was unhappy, and that to me is an indication of how much he wanted to believe in his own integrity, how he feared it was coming unglued."

Mr. Magruder's conversation does not dwell on guilt or excuses. He said before he testified:

"I've made peace with myself on grounds—it's corny, but we've all sinned, right? There's more rejoicing over the one lost sheep that is found, et cetera. I think I'll be able to survive and be better for it. I think I've been as down as I've ever been down, but I've never been the kind that stays down."

There was more than a little pragmatism in his decision to confess, Mr. Magruder has acknowledged. To have fought the prosecution and appealed a conviction might have taken two years and $200,000—money he does not have. "So you go the other way," he said in explanation of his agreement to plead guilty to one felony count. "You cooperate, and get the decision over with and then you move ahead."

It is a point of satisfaction, he has said, that of all the famous Watergate conspirators, he is the only one who is working, who has a business and income coming in. Lawyers are more vulnerable to scandal than businessmen, he grants, and his own recovery may yet be interrupted by a jail sentence.

Still, he hopes to move eventually from his one-man marketing consulting company, called Metropolitan Research, Inc., to a management job in a big company. And even after Watergate, he believes that his experience in the Nixon campaign will someday count in his favor.

"In spite of what's been said about poor old CREP," he said, pronouncing it "Creep," as Democrats did when they referred to the Committee for the Re-election of the President, "we did a hell of a good job. We got the message to our people, and we got them out to vote. The substantive work we did in that campaign—the work with computers, telephones and direct mail—will be used as a model in the future."

A certain cocky glibness has always marked the smooth, friendly, somehow unpretentious Magruder style.

The scion of an old Maryland family, he grew up on Staten Island in New York where his father owned a modestly successful print shop. At Williams College (in the class of 1958) he focused on political science and, as he told the Senate committee, studied ethics with the Rev. William Sloan Coffin Jr., now the chaplain at Yale.

But even as an undergraduate he was intensely interested in sales, a classmate recalls. He spent one college summer promoting Vicks cough medicines and also sold cosmetics to help pay his way.

In 1959 he married the former Gail Nicholas, a Vassar graduate, and became a father in 1961. He received a business degree at the University of Chicago in 1963 and entered a marketing career with the Jewel Tea Company and later with Broadway-Hale Stores, Inc., of Los Angeles.

By the fall of 1969, when he joined the White House staff, he was the president of two small, apparently promising cosmetic companies in Santa Monica. But his interest in politics, whetted by staff work in a variety of mostly conservative Republican campaigns, had replaced his business ambitions.

At the White House, where he was a deputy to Herbert G. Klein, the director of communications, and later at the re-election committee, Mr. Magruder was clearly marked as a protégé of H. R. Haldeman, whom he had assisted in the campaign of 1968.

Colleagues recall Mr. Magruder as an apt, competitive, unoriginal practitioner of staff politics. Another former White House aide remembers his dropping the names of his superiors to heighten his own influence saying "H [for Haldeman] wants such and such," or "The General [for former Attorney General Mitchell] told me to tell you so and so."

He was always regarded as a follower, not a self-starter. Mr. Magruder seemed to confirm some of that when he said that he had tentatively volunteered to "take the heat" for the Watergate break-in, but that others had decided, in effect, that no one would believe Magruder was powerful enough to order the raid officially or eccentric enough to order it unofficially.

The agreed-on cover-up story, for which Mr. Magruder perjured himself in the first Watergate trial, was that G. Gordon Liddy had planned the bugging on his own.

"Perhaps that was the key," said a friend, "simply that he got associated in that campaign with a lot of able, aggressive people and a situation in which each one was trying to outdo the other's zeal."

In that atmosphere, which Mr. Magruder helped to discredit further in his testimony, he was an eager competitor. Until he saw the cover-up story unraveling late in the winter of 1973, he said, it never occurred to him to tell the truth.

On Aug. 16, 1973, Mr. Magruder pleaded guilty to one count of conspiracy to obstruct justice, to defraud the United States and to unlawfully intercept wire and oral communications.

Robert Charles Mardian

A bright-eyed, muscular man who looks and growls like George C. Scott, the actor, in "Patton," Robert Mardian was one of the most aggressive conservatives in the first Nixon Administration.

He is greatly concerned with security and was a determined, if unsuccessful, advocate before the Supreme Court of the Government's freedom to tap and bug subversives.

But the evidence, even before he took the stand in the Senate Watergate hearings, was that Mr. Mardian got involved in the Watergate cover-up belatedly, unhappily and by an excess of loyalty that had made him a bitter man even before the Watergate scandal broke.

"When things are going great they ignore me," he told a friend in 1972, after being passed over for two appointments he coveted—first, to be Deputy Attorney General and then to be deputy manager of the Nixon re-election campaign. "When things get screwed up, they lean on me."

The Watergate burglary, he said before the television cameras, outraged his nuts-and-bolts tactical instincts; an intelligence raid on Democratic party headquarters, even before the Democrats had named their candidate, was "ridiculous," he said.

But it was doubly galling, he told friends, as the work of a campaign staff that had scorned his services. Mr. Mardian never concealed his contempt for Jeb Stuart Magruder, who beat him out for the deputy campaign manager's title, the same man who testified that Mr. Mardian was "to some extent involved" in the cover-up.

"I didn't know they had this intelligence operation," Mr. Mardian said of the pre-Watergate period at re-election headquarters. "My role was political organization. I know a lot of people in a lot of states." But in fact, he said, "I spent most of my time arguing with a bunch of dumb kids with demographic charts. I went through that part of my education 20 years ago."

In Nixon politics and government Mr. Mardian was conspicuously a member of the John N. Mitchell faction. In the 1968 campaign, which Mr. Mitchell managed, he coordinated the Republican effort in the Western states, where President Nixon won all but Washington. As general counsel to the Department of Health, Education and Welfare in 1969 and 1970, he was a persistent apostle of Mr. Mitchell's "Southern strategy," trying to ease the pace of school integration.

Later, as an assistant attorney general under Mr. Mitchell, in charge of the Internal Security Division, he pressed the Justice Department's fight against the antiwar left. Throughout, he was the sort of loyal, versatile confidant who got many special assignments, including the delicate transfer to the White House of wiretap logs that the late J. Edgar Hoover thought he had hidden in the Federal Bureau of Investigation.

In addition to being a Mitchell man, Mr. Mardian qualifies as a Goldwaterite on several scores. His brother Samuel Mardian Jr., a former mayor of Phoenix, is one of the three or four largest contractors in Arizona and a pillar of the conservative Republican establishment in Senator Barry Goldwater's home state.

Robert Mardian himself managed the 1964 Goldwater-for-President campaign in Western states. His closest friend is one of Senator Goldwater's closest friends, Richard G. Kleindienst, the former Attorney General.

In a more essential way, Mr. Mardian, like Senator Goldwater, embodies the latter-day rugged individualism of immigrant stock that worked hard and struck it rich in the booming Southwest.

His father, an Armenian refugee from the Turks, told his sons that reaching the freedom and opportunity of America was "like going to heaven before your time"; his political heroes were men such as Hiram Johnson, the Progressive Governor of California, and Franklin D. Roosevelt.

But the second generation of Mardians—four brothers now preside over a $25-million-a-year construction and development empire—tended to be defensive about success.

Mr. Mardian was born on Oct. 23, 1923, attended public school in Pasadena and later studied at Columbia University, North Dakota State Teachers College and the University of California at Santa Barbara. He received a law degree from the University of Southern California in 1949.

After law school, he went into private law practice to start a successful career as a corporate lawyer. But he left private practice in 1962 to become vice president and chief legal officer of a savings and loan association. He entered politics in 1956 when he was appointed a member of the Pasadena school board. He was elected the following year but resigned almost immediately to devote time to his work.

In 1946, he married Dorothy D. Denniss, whom he met while serving in the Navy. They have three sons, Robert Charles Jr., William Denniss and Blair Anthony.

At the Justice Department, where he served after his tour at the Department of Health, Education and Welfare, Mr. Mardian enthusiastically revived an atrophied security program, quickly multiplying prosecutions against draft evaders and starting a broad series of grand jury investigations into radical groups.

He had wanted to hire as his deputy Tom Charles Huston, who initiated a short-lived White House crack-down on revolutionary violence. But even Mr. Huston, whose white House plan included official burglaries and mail interception, was unnerved by Mr. Mardian's zeal.

"Mardian didn't know the difference between a kid with a beard and a kid with a bomb," Mr. Huston once remarked.

A whispered reputation for extremism apparently contributed to Mr. Mardian's political decline. In addition, the selection of Mr. Kleindienst to succeed Mr. Mitchell as Attorney General in 1972 militated against the appointment of an intimate friend and fellow Arizonan as deputy.

Mr. Mitchell took Mr. Mardian with him to the re-election committee, but H. R. Haldeman insisted on making one of his protégés, Mr. Magruder, the campaign's second-in-command.

Friends knew that Mr. Mardian was "damned upset" with the vague title of "political coordinator"; some say he thought of quitting the campaign before Watergate. But as it happened, he was with Mr. Mitchell, Mr. Magruder and

Frederick LaRue in California on the night the Watergate burglars were arrested, and he took a major part thereafter in
planning the campaign committee's response.

His defense against the charge of cover-up complicity is that
his relations with G. Gordon Liddy and other conspirators he
interviewed after the Watergate break-in were bound by the
privacy between lawyer and client. Federal District Judge John
J. Sirica dismissed that claim last May when he ordered Mr.
Mardian to tell all he knew to the Watergate grand jury.

Yet Mr. Mardian insists his conscience is clear and scorns
the possibility of indictment.

James Walter McCord Jr.

Although he is a man about whom little was and is known,
James Walter McCord Jr. has already left a permanent rec-
ord in the history books. In the words of Senator Herman
E. Talmadge, on the first day of McCord's testimony at the
Watergate hearings: "Mr. McCord, you have made some
very serious charges implicating the President of the United
States probably as an accessory after the fact, the former
Attorney General of the United States as probably an acces-
sory before the fact and perhaps guilty of a conspiracy in-
volving the Watergate bugging."

McCord, one of the men convicted of the break-in at the
Watergate, had just testified, among other things, that he had
been told that President Nixon had offered him clemency,
financial aid and a job to win his silence over the bugging.
In a near-nonotone and at times in an almost inaudible
voice, he laid out in a precise manner his story of his
involvement—and others'—in Watergate. His manner as he
hunched over the witness table was thoughtful, unhurried
and careful.

He described leaving his home to discuss things on a pay
phone, recalled the use of an alias, "Mr. Watson," and
told of meetings in out-of-the-way places. He "respectfully"
declined to tell in detail what he had done before returning
in 1970 from the Central Intelligence Agency, saying that he
did not wish to violate the National Security Act by spilling
spy secrets.

McCord was an employe of the Central Intelligence
Agency for more than 20 years. Some say he was just a
technician, a subordinate whose days were consumed as-

signing guards, guarding safes and generally securing the C.I.A. headquarters hidden in the woods at Langley, Va.

Others say he was the chief of all security for the agency. "He was the number one man," L. Fletcher Prouty, a retired Air Force colonel, asserts.

Mystery also shrouds McCord's private life. He was born somewhere in Texas—those who know will not say definitely where or when.

When he was arrested on June 16, 1972, McCord told the police he was born Oct. 9, 1918. He did not give the place. Later, bail records indicated he was born July 26, 1924. These data would make the baldish McCord, who has kept his sturdy physique, either 48 or 54 years old.

Reports have floated around Washington that he and his wife, Sarah, are both graduates of Baylor University but officials there say he never attended the school.

The first concrete bit of James McCord's biography begins with the Federal Bureau of Investigation, where he began as a clerk in 1942. He was still a clerk when, in 1946, he left; for what reason has not been determined. In 1948 he returned to the bureau as a special agent.

McCord joined the C.I.A. in 1951 and is believed to have played a role in the abortive Bay of Pigs invasion of Cuba in 1961. Little else is known of his work in either agency.

More is known about McCord's life after his retirement in 1970.

He went to his pastor, the Rev. Walter C. Smith of the Rockville United Methodist Church in suburban Maryland, and said he wanted to spend half a day each week working for the church. Mr. Smith, who said McCord attended church every Sunday with his family before he was jailed, set up a program for older members of the congregation to meet once a month for a "social fellowship."

In the spring of 1971, McCord set up his own security consulting firm in Rockville, but the following January he became director of security for the President's re-election committee.

McCord, who has a retarded daughter, Nancy, also spent many hours working to help handicapped children. He was the chairman of a group called Concerned Citizens for Exceptional Children, and he volunteered to help get a new wing for his daughter's school, the Kennedy Institute, in Washington.

"They are just a lovely family, and wonderful neighbors," according to one housewife living on the cul-de-sac in Rockville where the McCords reside in their $38,000 brick home.

The neighbors say the McCords' son, Michael, is a student at the Air Force Academy and that their other daughter, Carol Anne, attends the University of Maryland.

McCord taught at nearby Montgomery College for two semesters in 1971. The course, "Industrial and Retail Security," was described in the school catalogue as "the historical, philosophical and legal basis of government and industrial security programs in a democratic society."

Despite all the secrecy surrounding him, McCord said in June, 1973, that he had made tentative arrangements with a New York company to publish a book he is writing, titled "Watergate Sanction." But, true to his calling, he declined to reveal any details of the book.

John Newton Mitchell

As a young man John Mitchell was such a good lawyer that, while he served in the Pacific as a Navy officer during World War II, clients solicited his counsel by mail on the highly specialized subject of housing bonds. No one seeks his advice these days.

His name was stricken from the roster of the Broad Street law firm—Mudge Rose Guthrie & Alexander—where Mr. Mitchell was a rich but never, it seems, popular partner. Old associates there, refusing all calls and comment on Mr. Mitchell, seem determined to pretend that he never existed.

Few of his once powerful friends in Washington call or comment either. Richard G. Kleindienst, his alter ego and successor for a brief term in the Attorney General's office, cut off all contacts with Mr. Mitchell in spring, 1972, regretfully, he says, but fearing charges of impropriety.

Others have attacked him. Jeb Stuart Magruder, who had been the first deputy at the Nixon re-election headquarters when Mr. Mitchell was managing the campaign last summer, has accused his old boss of approving the Watergate bugging during at least one of three formal meetings early last year.

John W. Dean 3d, a political protégé who once felt like a son to Mr. Mitchell, tended to support Mr. Mitchell's contention that he tried to "turn off" the bugging scheme; but Mr. Dean also accused Mr. Mitchell of taking an active role in the perjured cover-up.

Meanwhile, Charles W. Colson, formerly a special counsel in the White House, has suggested that he and President Nixon both doubted Mr. Mitchell's competence as a campaign manager, and long ago suspected his complicity in the Watergate affair. And finally, in the closest thing yet to a Presidential accusation, an unofficial White House memo—since disavowed by Mr. Nixon through his press spokesman—charged that John Dean had masterminded the cover-up to protect himself and "his patron, Mitchell."

All through those angry denials of Watergate involvement in 1972, Mr. Mitchell now says, he always felt that "somewhere along the line," his colleagues would make him the villain. Sure enough, and with masses of what they contend is supportive detail, they have tried.

Yet despite his deep and perhaps even desperate dilemma, there is still a certain stubborn pride about John N. Mitchell.

Solidarity with President Nixon seems to represent an emotional necessity as much as it represents Mr. Mitchell's view of the facts in the case. The keenest hurts have been the persistent reports, which he vigorously denies, that the two men fell out long ago—that Mr. Mitchell's influence never recovered from his sponsorship of Judges Clement F. Haynsworth Jr. and G. Harrold Carswell for the Supreme Court; that he lost his automatic access to the President in 1971; and that he was dismissed from the campaign staff in 1972 when he was contending that his wife's threat of divorce had forced his departure on him.

Most painful of all was the official White House statement that when Mr. Mitchell was summoned to Washington as the cover-up crumbled April 14, 1973, he was allowed to meet only with an old rival for the President's ear, John D. Ehrlichman.

"I'm not going to tell you," Mr. Mitchell cautioned a visitor to the apartment, "whether I then went over to see the President."

"My husband," Mrs. Mitchell interposed, "is a very proud man."

More than anything else, friends sense, and contrary to the whole spirit of Martha Mitchell's attacks on the President, John Mitchell wants to redeem a personal relationship with Richard Nixon.

The bond between the two men is an old Washington mystery, though it was usually framed as a question of how and why Mr. Nixon came to rely so on Mr. Mitchell, not vice versa.

There were some similarities of background, and more
striking differences of personality. Mr. Mitchell, born in Detroit on Sept. 5, 1913—nine months after Mr. Nixon—was
the son of a modestly successful businessman but worked
his own way—through Fordham and the Fordham Law
School—to wealth and prominence in the law. Like Mr.
Nixon, he adopted an individualistic conservatism on the way.

Unlike the awkward young Nixon, Mr. Mitchell had been a
superb athlete—a semiprofessional hockey player in college
and no-handicap golfer until he gave up the game for government—and remained a physically commanding figure.

He knew politics but not, like Mr. Nixon, as a public advocate or a student of popular opinion. "He learned it all
in the back rooms of statehouses arranging bond issues," a
campaign associate once explained. "I remember traveling
around the country with him; he'd point to something and
say, 'see that bridge, or that hospital, or that school—I
worked on that.' "

The President met Mr. Mitchell in the Wall Street legal
fraternity in 1963—a period of depression and readjust-
ment for Mr. Nixon, the former Vice President who had been
defeated for the Presidency in 1960 and again for the governorship of California in 1962. From the beginning, it appears, he found Mr. Mitchell a thoughtful listener, a sympathetic analyst of legal and public affairs, and a solid symbol of strength.

In 1966, their law firms merged to form what was
known as Nixon Mudge Rose Guthrie Alexander & Mitchell.
By 1967 Mr. Nixon's Presidential campaign was drawing
heavily on Mr. Mitchell's counsel, and after several more
conventionally political figures dropped out as campaign man-
agers Mr. Mitchell became the unquestioned strategic and
organizational boss of the narrowly victorious 1968 campaign.

When Mr. Nixon named him Attorney General, he presented him not only as his right-hand man but also as a
sort of personal hero. "John Mitchell is more than one of
the nation's great lawyers," Mr. Nixon said. "I have learned
to know him over the past five years as a man of superb
judgment, a man who knows how to pick people and to
lead them and to inspire them with a quiet confidence and
poise and dignity."

Mr. Nixon added, a few months later: "He is my closest
adviser, as you know, on all legal matters and on many

other matters as well. I would say that I don't know of any man in the Administration whose views on the law are closer to mine than Attorney General Mitchell's."

Mr. Mitchell's motto—one of many ironies today—was "watch what we do, not what we say." But in fact his conduct of the Attorney General's office was as aggressive, particularly against political dissenters, as his law-and-order rhetoric.

He had wide authority beyond the Justice Department—as a member of the National Security Council, in the patronage field and as a political adviser to the President. Yet he also put a distinctly, and controversially, personal stamp on the Administration's efforts in law enforcement, including the beefing up of strike forces against organized crime; the advocacy of no-knock laws and preventive detention; and the reform of drug abuse laws, including the repeal of mandatory minimum sentences.

Many of his most famous efforts were failures: His suit to block publication of the Pentagon Papers in The New York Times was rejected by the Supreme Court; his prosecutions of the Chicago 7, the Harrisburg 7 and Dr. Daniel Ellsberg—all manifestations of the hated antiwar movement —produced no lasting convictions; and the Supreme Court unanimously rejected his theory that the Government had an inherent right to use electronic surveillance, without court supervision, against domestic subversives.

Yet when he left the Attorney General's office to run the Nixon re-election campaign in February, 1972, Mr. Nixon still prized his friend as a symbol of his own goals and a political asset—"the leader," President Nixon called him, "of our fight against crime and lawlessness."

Joseph M. Montoya

Mr. Montoya, a member of one of New Mexico's most prominent families, has held elective offices since he was 21 years old, serving in both houses of the state legislature, in the United States House of Representatives for four terms and in the Senate since 1964. But, at the age of 57, he is not widely known outside his home state, and even there he must campaign constantly to maintain his office. In 1970, he received barely 52 percent of the vote in his re-election campaign.

Mr. Montoya concentrates his Senate activities on tending to the needs of his constituents in New Mexico. He has a

solid liberal voting record on domestic issues and was an
early opponent of the war in Vietnam.

He became concerned last year about the Government's
use of wiretaps. He had several private meetings with Senator Ervin on the subject. He said he believed that these
meetings led to his appointment to the Watergate committee.

Richard Arthur Moore

At Yale in the nineteen-thirties, "Red" Moore was the flamboyant Irishman from Brooklyn. As editor of The Yale Daily
News, he devoted an entire issue of the paper to a spoof
about how the university was dominated by Communists.

In addition to being a member of Skull and Bones, an
exclusive senior society, he also had a reputation for mastery at frequent late night poker parties.

Mr. Moore, now 59 years old, only vaguely resembles the
youth at Yale. His shock of flaming red hair has changed to
crew-cut white. His sloppy clothes have been abandoned for a
carefully groomed appearance. His nickname is now "Dick."
The big man on campus is now one of the anonymous "special
counsels to the President"—an unknown adviser until he
became a new name in the cast of characters in the Watergate affair.

Sitting in the witness chair at the Senate Watergate hearings, he denied many allegations made by former White
House counsel John W. Dean 3d, but he sometimes faltered
in his testimony as he failed to recall details of his own
testimony before the committee staff on June 7.

As a Presidential adviser, Mr. Moore has been an idea man
more than an operations chief, spending hours with White
House "image men," such as Herbert G. Klein, Charles
W. Colson and Ronald L. Ziegler, contemplating what the
President should be doing, where he should go, how to solve
problems and how to keep the President's best foot forward.

In the 1968 campaign and again in 1972, he searched for
bits of humor and local events to add to Presidential
speeches. He was one of the men who briefed the President
on local politicians and issues.

Some say that during the campaigns, when the candidate
felt like talking informally, it was often Mr. Moore, long a
friend of the President's, who was called to the Presidental
suite.

Richard Moore began his political life as a New Deal

Democrat at Yale. After graduation from Yale in 1936 and from Yale Law School in 1939, he practiced law in New York at the firm of Cravath, Swaine & Moore. About the same time he became the executive director of the America First Committee, which opposed United States involvement in World War II.

Now he is the defender of a conservative Republican Administration and committed to a President who has opened new avenues to the Communists in China and Moscow.

Mr. Moore has not lost all his youthful personality. His humor is still so sharp that he is often called on to be toastmaster at his Yale class reunions. There is even a twist to his choice of Lloyd Cutler, whose name is on the White House "enemies" list, to be his lawyer in the Watergate case.

When Mr. Moore's relations with the President began is hazy. After serving in the Air Force in World War II, Mr. Moore returned to the Cravath law firm for a brief time before moving to California in 1949.

Like his brother, John D. J. Moore, now Ambassador to Ireland, he probably met the President in the early nineteen-fifties. His brother has said that he met Mr. Nixon on the golf course about that time.

Richard Moore was climbing his way up the executive ladder at television station KTTV in Los Angeles when he worked for the Republicans in the 1956 campaign. By 1962, he became president of the Times-Mirror Broadcasting Corporation, and many fellow Republicans believe that he did some work in Mr. Nixon's unsuccessful campaign for governor that year.

Some believe that Mr. Moore was influential in persuading Mr. Nixon to move to New York after he lost the race.

In 1970, Mr. Moore left Pasadena and brought his wife and five children to Washington to join the Administration. As a special assistant to the Attorney General, Mr. Moore is credited with altering somewhat John N. Mitchell's image of the tough law enforcer. Mr. Moore is said to have "opened Mitchell" and brought forth a softer-tongued official.

In 1971, Mr. Moore became special counsel to the President.

In addition to his official roll at the White House, Mr. Moore is the man many Presidential aides confide in. They trust him because he is an older man (born Jan. 23, 1914, in Albany, N. Y.), and because they believe in his integrity and maturity.

"If I wanted to confide in anybody in the White House," said one former staff member. "I would confide in Moore."

Henry Edward Petersen

Twenty-five years ago Henry E. Petersen was hired as a clerk at the Federal Bureau of Investigation. Gradually he climbed his way through the bureaucracy of the Justice Department, immersing himself in the battle against organized crime and winning a reputation as a "completely honest man, as tough as nails," who "doesn't get snowed easily."

After 20 years he earned a top civil service job—chief of the organized crime and racketeering section. Then John N. Mitchell became Attorney General in 1969 and promoted Mr. Petersen to jobs normally reserved as political rewards.

First Mr. Petersen was named a deputy assistant attorney general, then acting assistant attorney general and then assistant attorney general in charge of the Criminal Division.

"His tremendous advances in the department were because of Mitchell," said a former colleague.

Mr. Petersen returned his benefactor's regard, calling him "a man of high integrity and a tough prosecutor—he's such a refreshing breath of air after Ramsey Clark," the former Attorney General.

As the man initially responsible for the Justice Department's Watergate investigation, Mr. Petersen faced the possibility of deciding whether to prosecute his mentor.

It was not the first time Mr. Petersen had faced decisions on how to handle charges of scandal in the Justice Department.

His critics say he compromised himself in 1971 when the Justice Department was investigating allegations of improper conduct by the United States Attorney in San Diego, Harry D. Steward, who came under attack for quashing a subpoena for a Nixon contributor during a grand jury investigation last year.

When Mr. Petersen was drawn into the dispute at confirmation hearings for Richard G. Kleindienst as Attorney General in March, 1972, he told the committee that Mr. Steward had been wrong.

But he defended the Justice Department's decision to clear Mr. Steward because he said it was in the best interest of the department since Mr. Steward was needed in the prosecution of a major tax case in southern California.

Mr. Petersen's family had dual opinions of his personality. "The children all love him," said his wife, Jean, "but they fear him too. They know he means what he says and he lets them know, in no uncertain terms, when he's displeased."

The father is proud of his seven children, ranging in age from 25 to 2 years old, and spends most of his summer weekends with them on his 26-foot cruiser on the Chesapeake Bay.

Henry E. Petersen, a native of Philadelphia, was born on March 26, 1921.

He was a staff sergeant in the Marine Corps during World War II and served in the South Pacific.

After the war he went to Georgetown University and then put himself through law school at Catholic University by taking a job as a clerk for the F.B.I.

While pressures focused on the chief of the Watergate investigation, he tried to find a respite on the putting greens.

Robert Alan Fernon Reisner

"I imagine what happened was that Fred Malek called Bob one day and told him that if he was interested in doing something different for a while to see this guy Jeb Magruder."

That was the way a former boss speculated that Robert Reisner was put in touch with Jeb Stuart Magruder, former deputy director of the Committee for the Re-election of the President, in November, 1971, by Frederic V. Malek, then Under Secretary of the Department of Health, Education and Welfare. "This was a case of a bright young guy who took the job as an interesting aside," the former boss continued. "He probably saw it as a year and a half adding to his knowledge of the public sector."

Mr. Reisner, a witness before the Senate Watergate committee, was described by another former superior as "working harder and trying harder" than a dozen other Harvard Business School students in a 1970 Department of Health, Education and Welfare panel setting up the Environmental Protection Agency.

"In a town where people play games angling for their next job, Bob concentrated on his present job. I never got the impression he was out for his own ends," the former boss said.

Mr. Reisner (pronounced Reesner) was born in Washington but grew up in Philadelphia. He attended Germantown

Friends School, where he was a quarterback on the football team. He switched to lacrosse when he entered Yale University in the fall of 1964.

"He made up what he lacked in ability by plenty of desire," a Yale roommate said of his lacrosse play.

After graduating from Yale in 1968, Mr. Reisner was awarded a Corning Fellowship, which enabled him to travel for a year in Asia, parts of Africa and Latin America.

"He decided the best thing to do then was to get out in the real world," a friend recalled. "He also felt it would increase his chances of getting into Harvard."

He was married in June, 1969, and entered Harvard that fall. After receiving his master's degree in 1971, he worked for the Environmental Protection Agency for a short time until he joined the President's re-election committee. He is now a management associate at the Office of Management and Budget.

Mr. Reisner's father, the late Herbert W. Reisner, was vice president of an insurance company in Philadelphia. His mother, who lives in Chestnut Hill, Pa., has been active in the alumnae affairs of Bryn Mawr College.

Mr. Reisner, who was born Dec. 1, 1946, married the former Elizabeth Craig Reavis of New Orleans, a graduate of Smith College. They live in Washington and have no children.

The baby-faced, 26-year-old Mr. Reisner was described by friends as being consistently "clean cut and meticulously dressed." He was wearing a conservative, dark, pin-striped suit as he calmly answered the questions of Senators. "I doubt if he owns a double knit sport coat," one friend joked.

A former coworker said it was "a logical move" for him to go to work for the President's re-election campaign. "But he couldn't have known what was going on," another friend said. "He has an awful lot of integrity."

Reached after his testimony, Mr. Reisner described the Senators' questioning as "very fair." He refused to comment on the outcome of the hearings. "We'll just have to see what happens," he said.

Hugh W. Sloan Jr.

Hugh Sloan is well-born, well-bred, well-educated, well-paid, well-traveled, well-spoken and well-dressed—a Princeton honors graduate with a good job, a promising future in corporate management, a pretty wife, a beautiful baby, a healthy relationship with his affluent parents, and a wide circle of close friends who enjoy his company and respect his opinions.

Yet, there is about him a certain sense of sadness these days—a mantle of melancholy that lends to his voice, his eyes, his gestures and even his laughter a hint of grief. For, like a number of other bright young people who once worked for Richard Nixon and the Republican party, he has been caught up in the ever-widening swirls of the Watergate scandal and, like most of them, his life has been inexorably altered.

"I'm not really bitter," he said as he reminisced about his sunshine days at the White House, the happy challenges of two Presidential campaigns and his abrupt resignation in July, 1972, from the Finance Committee to Re-elect the President. "But I suppose it's also accurate to say that I'm not exactly happy about what happened."

He came home from the Navy and Vietnam in 1965 when he was 24 years old and began groping for a career.

His father, a vice president of St. Regis Paper Company, Inc., suggested a career in diplomacy and Mr. Sloan tentatively agreed. He moved to Washington and enrolled in the Georgetown School of Foreign Service.

In December, he quit and went to work for the Republican Congressional Campaign Committee, handling direct-mail projects, raising funds and, as he said, "enjoying the hell out of it."

He moved quickly up through the national party's structure. He went to work for the Republican National Finance Committee in late 1966 and in 1968 became the assistant finance director of the Nixon-Agnew campaign.

After the election, he served briefly as Mr. Nixon's persional aide. After the Inauguration in January, 1969, he was named to the White House staff, working directly under Dwight L. Chapin, the appointments secretary, and indirectly under H. R. Haldeman, ultimately the President's chief of staff.

"It was great," he said, remembering those days of his proximity to power.

Then, in early 1971, he left the White House and moved to Mr. Nixon's campaign organization again—once more as a finance expert. By February of the next year, he was its treasurer, responsible as a custodian for a campaign fund that would eventually reach nearly $50 million.

"That's the reason they wanted him for that job," a friend and former colleague said. "He was scrupulously honest and they had money rolling into that place right and left."

A part of the money—no one is certain yet precisely how much of it—was disbursed in cash by Mr. Sloan to some of the men now implicated in the scandal, including G. Gordon Liddy, a convicted Watergate conspirator who allegedly masterminded a burglary and electronic bugging of the Democrats' national headquarters.

Then, according to Mr. Sloan, he was approached by Jeb Stuart Magruder and Fred LaRue, two high-ranking campaign officers, and asked to come to some agreement with them on precisely how much he had paid Liddy over the months. Mr. Sloan was about to appear before a grand jury investigating the Watergate break-in.

"It was obvious to me . . . by what had been addressed to me in terms of suggestions that I tell an untrue story, a general atmosphere of suggesting a Fifth Amendment, that this was something I didn't want to be a party to," he said.

So after attempting "to get some guidance or justification for the money—to get an answer essentially to what the hell was going on," he quit the campaign.

When Mr. Sloan was a student at the Hotchkiss School in 1958, the student elections were rigged by a small clique of upper-classmen. He found out about it, gave a faculty member the details and some of those involved were punished.

"This whole thing," Mr. Sloan said quietly as he relaxed in his father's chair in his father's house, "this whole thing is tragic—for the people involved, for their families and for the country.

"I'm not going to get into recriminations and I'm not going to get into any of the details because, as you know, I'm a defendant in the Democrats' civil suit against the finance committee but I don't mind telling you how I feel.

"I feel lousy. I have a clear conscience personally, I believe I did the right things—but I feel lousy."

Nevertheless, he did talk a bit about his feelings toward the White House and its philosophy of government. "There was no independent sense of morality there," he said. "I mean if you worked for someone, he was God and whatever the orders were, you did it—and there were damned few who were able to make or willing to make independent judgments.

"It was all so narrow, so closed. Nobody listened to anybody who wasn't in a superior position. They were guys who had committed themselves economically to politics—you know, in a way in which it was not only what they were doing at the moment but what they were going to be doing all their lives, and because of that there emerged some kind of separate morality about things."

He paused briefly and glanced around his parents' home— a haven for him in the spring of 1973. A house full of oil portraits and gleaming silver and dark wood. His wife and infant daughter are still in Washington, waiting while he goes through a period of orientation before becoming assistant to the president of the Budd Company.

He met his wife while they were both working in the White House, and there is a photograph in his parents' den showing the two of them with President Nixon on the day they announced their engagement.

There are other mementos around from those days: a picture of his family with a flag that flew over the White House, a picture of his parents with the President on his mother's birthday, and a note to his father on White House stationery.

"To Dad," it reads, "with deepest appreciation on your sixtieth birthday, from your son whose one misfortune is to have shared but 28 of those years."

His father is very proud of that inscription. "He's a good kid. He's going to be O.K. now because he's still the same kid he always was. He's everything I ever wanted him to be."

His son sighed and concluded the conversation.

"I learned one thing in politics," he said. "If you go into it for a career—I mean as a matter of life's work and economics—then sooner or later you have to compromise. You either compromise or get out. It just, sooner or later, takes the edge off your values."

Maurice Hubert Stans

From the time he walked out of Shakopee, Minn., Maury Stans was an achiever, says an admirer who worked closely with Stans when he was director of the Bureau of the Budget under President Eisenhower. And that is the way Maurice Stans would almost certainly describe himself. Testifying before the Senate Select Committee investigating the Watergate affair, Mr. Stans concluded his formal statement by declaring that as chairman in 1972 of the Finance Committee to Re-elect the President, he raised "the largest amount of money ever spent in a political campaign."

Furthermore, Mr. Stans said, "I can assure the committee that I have made an honest and careful effort to abide by the spirit and intent of the election law."

No one could challenge the claim of the former Secretary of Commerce to be a political fund raiser without peer. Building on his experience as Mr. Nixon's finance chairman in 1968, he outdid himself in 1972, amassing more than $50 million.

Hundred-dollar bills poured into Mr. Stans's safe. According to some testimony, as much as $350,000 to $700,000 in cash was stashed in the safe at one time.

On May 10, 1972, a grand jury in New York charged Mr. Stans with lying to it about his role in a $200,000 campaign contribution from the financier Robert L. Vesco, who was under investigation by the Securities and Exchange Commission at the time, and then trying to obstruct justice by inducing the S.E.C. chairman, G. Bradford Cook, to strike all reference to the contribution from its complaint against Mr. Vesco.

Born in Shakopee on March 22, 1908, Mr. Stans went to Chicago when he was 17, worked as a stenographer daytimes and attended night school at Northwestern University. At 19, he went to New York to join the firm of Alexander Grant & Co. At 23 he became a certified public accountant and by 30 he was a senior partner of the firm.

Mr. Stans married Kathleen Carmody in 1933. They have four children, two sons and two daughters.

His first Government service was in 1953 when he served on a House of Representatives panel that was conducting a budget review. A year later he was consultant to Postmaster General Arthur E. Summerfield. In 1955, he was named Deputy Postmaster General. In 1957-58, he became Deputy Director of the Bureau of the Budget and then served the rest of President Eisenhower's second term as Director of the bureau.

After leaving the Government in January, 1961, he became senior partner in the investment banking company of William R. Staats, Inc., in New York and was president when it merged with Glore Forgan.

President Nixon appointed him Secretary of Commerce in 1969, and he served in that post until 1971, when he became chairman of the Finance Committee to Re-elect the President.

Judgments about Mr. Stans by those who have worked closely with him range from high praise to bitter contempt.

One associate at the budget bureau said that he had "a fine sense of humor," was "a tough trader," a man who "lived his job" and succeeded in "taking the budget out of the field of mystery and into the street, where people could understand it."

This associate said that Mr. Stans was as severe about using the perquisites of this office as he was in pruning department estimates of need. He never used the official car assigned to him except to go to the Hill or on business. He took taxis to and from his home.

However, at the Commerce Department, one high civil servant there said:

"He was very testy, very cold, insensitive to the niceties. When he left the department, he addressed a gathering of employes. Instead of saying a warm goodby and thanks, he suddenly launched into a defense of the free enterprise system. Among other things, he said that if blacks only read Horatio Alger, they wouldn't have any problems.

"His attitude always was that everything would be for the best if nobody tampered with the system."

Yet, it is generally agreed that Mr. Stans was deeply committed to improving opportunities for blacks when he set up in Commerce an office of minority business enterprise.

When a friend was asked how he accounted for Mr. Stans's present troubles, he said:

"Stans has an extraordinary, unquestioning kind of loyalty and commitment to Nixon. After Nixon's defeat by Pat Brown [in 1962], he said, 'He's not all through. We are going to help him become President of the United States, and he's going to be a great President.'

"This is the kind of feeling that gripped Maury and drove him—the feeling that what's good for Nixon is good for the country. And he said to himself, 'You're going to do everything you can.' And the thing he could do that this crowd liked was raise money."

Those familiar with Mr. Stans's methods agree that he raised the big money by going after the fat purses himself.

"Stans presses very hard," one associate said. "He would tell them what it was worth for them to assure that George McGovern not spend four years in the White House. One man made a commitment of $10,000 to me, but Stans got him up to $50,000. The next day the guy called me back and said, 'I've been thinking about what Maury told me. I'm going to make it $100,000.' "

Mr. Stans has frequently gone on safaris in Africa and prides himself on being the only American to have shot a bongo, a rare antelope.

He had a film of his 1966 safari to Chad, and in the dubbed-in narrative which Mr. Stans approved, the porters were referred to as "boys." Mr. Stans delighted in showing the film. Finally, the director of the African section of the United States Information Agency protested, calling the film "an Amos and Andy show." Mr. Stans promised not to show the film anymore.

Mr. Stans has scant regard for conservationists and environmentalists. While Secretary of Commerce, he created the National Industrial Pollution Control Council, which was composed entirely of industralists. The council's subcommittees issued pamphlets attacking existing and proposed legislation as unnecessarily severe and costly.

Mr. Stans himself had an environmental speech in which he called for weighing "economic goals against economic reality." The title of his speech was "Wait a Minute."

Gordon Creighton Strachan

Gordon Strachan's infatuation with politics started 24 years ago when he was elected president of his kindergarten class in Santa Rosa, Calif. At the University of Southern California he was introduced to a larger political environment. Mr. Strachan was considered a "nugget" pledge—a personable, bright and fairly good-looking young man who handled himself well—by the many fraternities that rushed him. He was popular; his fraternity brothers at Phi Kappa Sigma remember the big blond guy who taught his brothers the "Stomp," the latest dance craze. He received good grades. He belonged to the right organizations, such as the Trojan Knights and the Squires, two prestigious groups, described by one graduate as the "rah, rah" groups on campus.

It was through these clubs that Mr. Strachan (pronounced

Strawn) first made the acquaintance—or friendship, depending on who is telling the story—of men who would later join him on the White House staff roster and on the list of characters in the Watergate scandal.

His classmates included Ronald L. Ziegler, now the President's press secretary, and Dwight L. Chapin, the former appointments secretary for Mr. Nixon. Mr. Strachan and Mr. Chapin were the ones who picked Donald H. Segretti, a fraternity brother of Mr. Strachan, to work against the Democrats.

However, Mr. Strachan was not called before the Senate Watergate committee to talk about his old college friends, but to disclose whether H. R. Haldeman knew of the plans and cover-up of the Watergate scandal.

As an aide to Mr. Haldeman, Mr. Strachan was the liaison between the White House and the President's campaign organization.

He was responsible for keeping Mr. Haldeman informed on the over-all workings of the Committee for the Re-election of the President. His days were occupied by meetings and telephone conversations with scores of staff directors at the committee to keep up with the latest information on such things as polling data or advertising.

"He had to know where all the pieces of paper were" when Mr. Haldeman asked a question, said one former member of the committee.

Mr. Strachan told the Senate committee's investigators, through his lawyer, that he knew of the political intelligence-gathering plan that came to grief at Watergate and that he relayed the information to his superior, Mr. Haldeman. At the Senate hearings he told the story himself.

The relationship between Mr. Haldeman and his young aide, who could directly implicate him in the Watergate plot, is subject to diverse opinions among White House staffers.

Some say Mr. Strachan had great admiration for Mr. Haldeman. Others recall animosity derived from Mr. Haldeman's insistence that his aide wear a beeper so he could be reached at all times. Mr. Strachan has said he hated the way Mr. Haldeman made him feel guilty for taking a three-day vacation.

White House staffers agree that Mr. Strachan played a subservient role on the staff, calling him "Haldeman's gofer," and "respectful." His wry sense of humor was commonly re-

spected and many enjoyed teasing him by deliberately mis-
pronouncing his name.

A close friend said that Mr. Strachan "might not have been
fully outraged" when he heard about Watergate, because of
his education at the University of Southern California.

"Remember," said the friend, "U.S.C. was a big party
school. It took football success very seriously, business success very seriously and political success very seriously. Anything went on to win an election or a football game."

Mr. Strachan, who was elected class president in his junior
year, would have been in a position to learn a lot about how
some people win at politics.

"We had to hire Pinkertons" for the polling places, said
Thomas Hull, who was dean of men during that time. "There
were questionable things that seemed to always go on at
U.S.C. elections."

After graduating in 1965 with a degree in international
relations, Mr. Strachan ignored politics for a few years.

Returning to Berkeley, where he was born on July 24,
1943, he entered law school at Bolt Hall, University of
California, with his bride, Kristine, who proved to be a
better student by making the law review. They studied and
skied at Lake Tahoe and Sun Valley.

While some point to Mr. Strachan's friendship with Mr.
Chapin as his entree to the White House, others point to
another friend, Jeffrey Donfeld, a former White House
aide and an escort of Tricia Nixon before she was married.

Mr. Donfeld, who worked at the law firm of Mudge, Rose,
Guthrie & Alexander during his summers off from the Berkeley law school, said he had been the one who "suggested"
to his friend that he join the President's old law firm.

"He wasn't thinking about politics" when he went to the
New York law firm, said Mr. Donfeld, who is still Mr. Strach-
han's weekly tennis partner. Certainly one element in Mr.
Strachan's choice of law firms was that his wife had been
asked to join another prestigious Wall Street law firm.

Once settled into Mudge, Rose, Mr. Strachan began to mix
his work in estates and trusts with a taste of politics. During
the 1970 campaign he did some advance work for the
President.

In 1970 Herbert G. Klein, the former White House communications director, asked Mr. Strachan to join his staff,
but Mr. Strachan soon moved to Mr. Haldeman's staff.

In the fashion of many White House staffers whose names were linked to Watergate, Mr. Strachan left the White House. He became the general counsel at the United States Information Agency.

Since Mr. Strachan resigned from the Administration on April 30, 1973, he has been unemployed.

Herman E. Talmadge

Senator Talmadge of Georgia is one of the quiet powers in the Senate. As chairman of the Agriculture Committee and ranking Democrat on the Finance Committee, his authority is exceeded by few other Senators. But Mr. Talmadge prefers to do his work behind the scenes rather than in open committee or floor sessions.

Mr. Talmadge is 59 years old. His father, Eugene, was the colorful, tempestuous Governor of Georgia for three terms, but Herman Talmadge is no carbon copy of his father.

His colleagues regard him as one of the smartest men in the Senate, and he is respected for his deep, professional knowledge of a wide range of issues. He is studious and has few interests outside of his Senate duties.

When Senator Mansfield called and asked Senator Talmadge to be on the Watergate committee, he begged off.

"I told him I had more pressing business, but he said he wanted me. When you're asked like that by the leadership, you pretty much go along," he recalled.

Unlike some other members of the committee, Senator Talmadge said he planned to do no homework on the Watergate investigation but to depend on committee hearings for all his information.

"I see myself as a juror," he said, "and a juror doesn't background himself."

Vernon Anthony Walters

An angry, jeering mob surrounded the limousine, beating, on the roof and chanting anti-American slogans. Inside the car that hot May afternoon in Caracas, Venezuela, 15 years ago was Richard M. Nixon, Vice President of the United States, who was on a "good will" tour of Latin America. Sitting in the front seat was an American Army colonel, Dick Walters, who was serving as his interpreter. Recalling his harrowing experience four years later, Mr. Nixon wrote in his book "Six Crises": "One of the ringleaders—a typical tough thug—started to bash in the window next to me with a big iron pipe. The shatterproof glass did not break, but it splattered into the car. Walters got a mouthful, and I thought for an instant, 'There goes my interpreter.' "

Vernon Anthony Walters survived what Mr. Nixon would call the fourth of his "Six Crises" and now finds himself, as Deputy Director of the Central Intelligence Agency, playing a major role in Mr. Nixon's seventh crisis, the Watergate scandal.

Mr. Walters, now a lieutenant general, testified before the Senate Watergate committee and was asked why he had not made use of his long acquaintance with President Nixon to warn him about the attempts to involve the C.I.A. in the Watergate cover-up.

General Walters sought to minimize the relationship that John D. Ehrlichman had reportedly said made him a "good friend of the White House" within the intelligence agency.

As a linguist fluent in eight languages, General Walters has served a range of prominent political figures. He was in Paris as an aide to W. Averell Harriman in the early years of the cold war, with President Truman at his historic meeting with General of the Army Douglas MacArthur and with President Eisenhower at Geneva in 1953.

More recently, he won the respect of Democrats like Lincoln Gordon and Sargent Shriver for the grasp of local conditions that he acquired as military attaché in the Rio de Janeiro and Paris Embassies.

The career of the husky six-foot-three-inch general has been unorthodox in many ways. He is not a West Point graduate and has never had a field command. Much of his success seems based on his ability as an interpreter and as a military attaché who could cultivate extensive contacts in any country that he was assigned to.

This background has reportedly been the object of considerable criticism by C.I.A. career officials who feel that General Walters's experience as an attaché is insufficient qualification for the agency post President Nixon chose him for on March 2, 1972.

"His reputation," said one person familiar with the C.I.A., "is that of a guy who speaks in four or five languages and thinks in none."

But that assessment would be vehemently contested by his friends and supporters, who say that the 56-year-old general is an aggressively brilliant man with a sophistication and perception rare for a soldier.

These people describe him as a hard-working and dedicated officer who looks on his skills as an interpreter with mixed emotions, because they have prevented him from attaining the field command that he has always wanted.

In many ways, the course of the C.I.A. official's career was set by his childhood. Born in New York on Jan. 3, 1917, Vernon Walters was the youngest of a wealthy insurance agent's three children. After suffering a series of financial reverses, his father decided in 1923 that the family could live better in France.

The family moved there, and during vacations traveled in Europe. Vernon Walters learned Spanish and Italian as well as French.

After graduating from a French Lycée, Mr. Walters attended Stonyhurst College in England, where a cousin of his mother's, a Jesuit priest, was the rector.

General Walters enlisted in the Army as a private in 1941. Within a year he was made an offer in intelligence. By the end of the war he was a major. He decided to make the Army his career.

A bachelor, General Walters cared for his mother for many years until her death.

As military attaché in Paris, he entertained frequently. He lives more quietly now in the officers' quarters at Fort Myer, Va.

Lowell P. Weicker Jr.

When Senator Weicker told a news conference in late March, 1973, that he believed that the blame for the Watergate affair went deep inside the White House, it was not the first time the Connecticut Republican had taken a stance against President Nixon.

He has taken a liberal position on most domestic legislation—against proposals to limit busing for school desegregation, for increased Federal aid for mass transit and against building a supersonic airplane. But, after campaigning in 1970 on an antiwar platform, he defended Mr. Nixon's policies during the Cambodian invasion.

The son of a wealthy industrialist, Senator Weicker, now 41 years old, attended the Lawrenceville School, Yale University and the University of Virginia Law School. He served one term in the House before being elected to the Senate in 1970.

In explaining why he sought membership on the Watergate committee, he said:

"I'm a professional politician. Because of things like the Watergate, people have lost faith in politicians, and I want to see that changed. The only thing that will convince them to respect politicians is to bring dirty business like the Watergate out in the open."

John Johnston Wilson

By his own careful accounting, there are but three loves in John J. Wilson's well-ordered life: a woman named Alice, a dog named Vicki and the passionate practice of law. "But not necessarily in that order," the chunky, pink-faced, 71-year-old attorney harumphed in his office here. Yet, whatever may be his more constant priorities within that rather narrow triangle, it seemed reasonable to expect that after he took on his newest clients—John D. Ehrlichman and H. R. Haldeman, top aides to President Nixon—he would have to reduce the woman, his wife for nearly half a century, and the dog, a precocious but nervous Boston terrier, to clearly subordinate roles.

"I'm reluctant to admit it, but that's probably true," Mr. Wilson said with very little reluctance. "Ah, but what the hell? They've known me a long time. I think they'll understand."

So, it might be added, would almost everyone else who has been acquainted with Mr. Wilson for any length of time, either casually, socially or professionally. In law offices all over Washington his friends and enemies, colleagues and associates agree almost unanimously that the one thing to be said about him after everything else has been said is that he works harder than any other lawyer they've ever seen.

"It's almost as though he were trying to get his practice established," remarked one of the lawyers who works at Whiteford, Hart, Carmody & Wilson, the venerable firm depleted by the death of the first three partners, but that is "just as strong as ever with Mr. Wilson in the driver's seat."

Yet, Mr. Wilson's practice, enriched over a span of nearly

50 years by a variety of notable cases and hundreds that never caught the public eye, has been firmly affluent for as long as anyone can remember, providing him with quite a comfortable way of life.

"I've pointed that out to him," Mrs. Alice Adelaide Grant Wilson said, "but he still goes at it like we were both young again."

The couple was married in September, 1923, two years after he had finished law school at George Washington University, and a few months after he had passed his District of Columbia bar examinations and been admitted to the bar. The Wilsons have no children.

Mr. Wilson first entered private practice, then became an assistant United States attorney, and in 1940 he joined the firm in which he is now the senior partner.

Mr. Wilson represented a Swiss concern whose American assets had been seized by the United States Government during World War II because of its asserted relationship to the Nazi-controlled German chemical cartel of I. G. Farben—and after more than 20 years, the case was settled to his client's benefit.

He defended an assistant attorney general under President Truman against Republican charges of conflict of interest and won a directed acquittal—not long after he had represented a steel company's successful fight against Mr. Truman's attempt to take over the industry to prevent increased prices.

Later he helped Senator Barry Goldwater, Republican of Arizona, win a libel suit against Ralph Ginzburg, the magazine publisher—and through all the years and all the cases, he earned a reputation with lawyers, judges and clients as a man who always knew exactly what he was doing.

"He has an incisive intelligence," a junior member of his firm said. Mr. Wilson is "disarming, though" he added, "charming, courtly, usually smiling, quite soft-spoken, but with a steel trap for a mind and an instinct for the jugular."

Mr. Wilson is chairman and a director of the National Bank of Washington and a member of the Barristers, a lawyers' club, and the Metropolitan Club of Washington.

With no hobbies and a disciplined, almost ascetic life style, Mr. Wilson closely resembles the two men at the White House—Mr. Ehrlichman and Mr. Haldeman—who hired him to look after their interests as the Watergate scandal spread.

Like him, they have a deep commitment to an unvarnished work ethic and, like him, they lean to the starboard
side of the political ship.

One of Mr. Wilson's fellow lawyers here described his
politics as being "to the right of McKinley," the conservative
Republican President who died nearly two months after Mr.
Wilson was born here on July 25, 1901.

"Damned right I am," Mr. Wilson acknowledged. "I'm a
conservative Republican who hasn't approved of any conservative Republicans in years because most conservative
Republicans aren't conservative enough for me."

Nevertheless, he insists, over the years he has stayed out
of politics—until now, that is, for the men he represents are
at the center of the political swirls of the executive branch.

"It's funny, though, how you get your business," Mr. Wilson
remarked.

"I never met these two gentlemen and one day the phone
rang and there they were on the line and all of a sudden I
had two new clients."

How, he was asked, had that come about?

"I suppose," he said, "they wanted a good lawyer."

Index